The Sporting News
PRO FOOTBALL GUIDE

1999 EDITION

Editors/Pro Football Guide
CRAIG CARTER
DAVE SLOAN

The Sporting News

Efrem Zimbalist III, President and Chief Executive Officer, Times Mirror Magazines; **James H. Nuckols,** President, The Sporting News; **Francis X. Farrell,** Senior Vice President, Publisher; **John D. Rawlings,** Senior Vice President, Editorial Director; **John Kastberg,** Vice President, General Manager; **Kathy Kinkeade,** Vice President, Operations; **Steve Meyerhoff,** Executive Editor; **Joe Hoppel,** Senior Editor; **Brendan Roberts,** Assistant Editor; **Marilyn Kasal,** Production Director; **Bob Parajon,** Prepress Director; **Terry Shea,** Database Analyst; **Michael Behrens,** Art Director, Special Projects; **Christen Webster,** Production Artist.

A Times Mirror
Company

CONTENTS

ON THE COVER: Broncos running back Terrell Davis. (Cover design by Michael Behrens/THE SPORTING NEWS. Large photo by Albert Dickson/THE SPORTING NEWS, action photo by Cliff Grassmick for THE SPORTING NEWS.)

NFL week-by-week and postseason highlights written by Todd Fitzpatrick, Frank Reust, Steve Siegel, Dave Sloan and Jim Woodworth of THE SPORTING NEWS.

NFL statistics compiled by STATS, Inc., Lincolnwood, Ill.

1999 SEASON

NFL directory
Team information
Schedule
College draft
Expansion draft
Playoff plan

NFL DIRECTORY

COMMISSIONER'S OFFICE

Address
280 Park Avenue
New York, NY 10017
Phone
212-450-2000
212-681-7573 (FAX)
Commissioner
Paul Tagliabue
President
Neil Austrian
Exec. v.p. for labor rel./chairman NFLMC
Harold Henderson
Executive v.p. & league counsel
Jeff Pash
Exec. v.p. of league and football dev.
Roger Goodell
Chief financial officer
Tom Spock
Sr. v.p. of comm. and gov't affairs
Joe Browne
Senior v.p. of broadcasting & network television
Dennis Lewin
Sr. v.p. of football operations
George Young

Vice president of public relations
Greg Aiello
Director of international public affairs
Pete Abitante
Director of media services
Leslie Hammond
Director of corporate communications
Chris Widmaier
Vice president of programming
John Collins
Director of broadcasting research
Joe Ferreira
Director of broadcasting services
Dick Maxwell
V.p. club administration and stadium management
Joe Ellis
Senior director of security
Milt Ahlerich
Senior director of officiating
Jerry Seeman
Director of strategic development
Neil Glat
Director of game operations
Peter Hadhazy

Director of football development
Gene Washington
Vice president of special events
Jim Steeg
Director of special events operations
Don Renzulli
Director of special events planning
Sue Robichek
V.p.-law/enterprises, broadcast & finance
Frank Hawkins
Treasurer
Joe Siclare
Vice president-internal audit
Tom Sullivan
Controller
Peter Lops
V.p. of systems & info. processing
Mary Oliveti
Senior director of human resources & administration
John Buzzeo
Director of business planning
Dan Margoshes

OTHER ORGANIZATIONS

NFL MANAGEMENT COUNCIL

Address
280 Park Avenue
New York, NY 10017
Phone
212-450-2000
212-681-7590 (FAX)
Exec. v.p. for labor rel./chairman NFLMC
Harold Henderson
Sr. vice president and general counsel
Dennis Curran
Sr. vice president/labor relations
Peter Ruocco
V.p. of player & employee development
Lem Burnham
Sr. director of player personnel
Joel Bussert
Director of compliance
Mike Keenan
Director of player programs
Guy Troupe
Dir.-labor administration & information
John Jones

PRO FOOTBALL HALL OF FAME

Address
2121 George Halas Drive, N.W.
Canton, OH 44708
Phone
330-456-8207
330-456-8175 (FAX)
Executive director
John W. Bankert
V.p./communications & exhibits
Joe Horrigan
V.p./operations and marketing
Dave Motts
V.p./merchandising & licensing
Judy Kuntz

PRO FOOTBALL WRITERS OF AMERICA

President
John Clayton, ESPN Magazine
First vice president
Adam Schefter, Denver Post
Second vice president
John McClain, Houston Chronicle
Secretary/treasurer
Howard Balzer

NFL FILMS, INC.

Address
330 Fellowship Road
Mt. Laurel, NJ 08054
Phone
609-778-1600
609-722-6779 (FAX)
President
Steve Sabol

NFL PLAYERS ASSOCIATION

Address
2021 L Street, N.W.
Washington, DC 20036
Phone
202-463-2200
202-835-9775 (FAX)
Executive director
Gene Upshaw
Assistant executive director
Doug Allen
Dir. P.R. and NFLPA retired players org.
Frank Woschitz
General counsel
Richard Berthelsen
Director of communications
Carl Francis
Director of player development
Stacey Robinson

NFL PROPERTIES

Address
280 Park Avenue
New York, NY 10017
Phone
212-450-2000
212-758-4239 (FAX)
Interim chief operating officer
Sara Levinson
V.p., world wide retail licensing
Jim Connelly
V.p., development/special events
David Newman
V.p., corporate sponsorship
Jim Schwebel
V.p., marketing
Howard Handler
V.p., club marketing
Mark Holtzman
V.p., advertising and design
Bruce Burke
V.p., legal and business affairs
Gary Gertzog

NFL ALUMNI ASSOCIATION

Address
6550 N. Federal Highway
Suite 400
Ft. Lauderdale, FL 33308-1417
Phone
954-492-1220
954-492-8297 (FAX)
Executive director/CEO
Frank Krauser
Chairman of the board
Randy Minniear
Vice president/alumni relations
Martin Lerch
Director of communications
Remy Mackowski
Manager of player appearances
Amy Glanzman

ARIZONA CARDINALS
NFC EASTERN DIVISION

1999 SEASON

CLUB DIRECTORY

President
William V. Bidwill
Vice president
William Bidwill Jr.
Vice president, general counsel
Michael Bidwill
Secretary and general counsel
Thomas J. Guilfoil
Vice president
Larry Wilson
General manager
Bob Ferguson
Treasurer/chief financial officer
Charley Schlegel
Assistant to the president
Rod Graves
Vice president, sales
To be announced
Director/marketing
Joe Castor
Ticket manager
Steve Bomar
Director/community affairs
Adele Harris
Director/public relations
Paul Jensen
Media coordinator
Greg Gladysiewski
Player program/community outreach
Garth Jax
National scouting coordinator
Jerry Hardaway
Senior scout
Bo Bolinger
Scouts
Jim Carmody
Bob Mazie
Cole Proctor
Jim Stanley

Head coach
Vince Tobin

Assistant coaches
Alan Everest (special teams)
John Garrett (quarterbacks)
Joe Greene (defensive line)
David Marmie (defensive backs)
Dave McGinnis (defensive coordinator)
Glenn Pires (linebackers)
Vic Rapp (wide receivers)
Johnny Roland (running backs)
Marc Trestman (offensive coord.)
George Warhop (offensive line)

Head trainer
John Omohundro
Assistant trainers
Jim Shearer
Jeff Herndon
Orthopedist
Russell Chick
Internist
Wayne Kuhl
Equipment manager
Mark Ahlemeier
Assistant equipment manager
Steve Christensen
Video director
Benny Greenberg

SCHEDULE

Sept. 12—	at Philadelphia	1:00
Sept. 19—	at Miami	1:00
Sept. 27—	SAN FRAN. (Mon.)	6:00
Oct. 3—	at Dallas	12:00
Oct. 10—	N.Y. GIANTS	1:05
Oct. 17—	WASHINGTON	5:20
Oct. 24—	Open date	
Oct. 31—	NEW ENGLAND	2:05
Nov. 7—	at N.Y. Jets	1:00
Nov. 14—	DETROIT	2:15
Nov. 21—	DALLAS	2:15
Nov. 28—	at N.Y. Giants	1:00
Dec. 5—	PHILADELPHIA	2:05
Dec. 12—	at Washington	1:00
Dec. 19—	BUFFALO	6:20
Dec. 26—	at Atlanta	1:00
Jan. 2—	at Green Bay	12:00

All times are for home team.
All games Sunday unless noted.

DRAFT CHOICES

David Boston, WR, Ohio State (first round/eighth pick overall).
L.J. Shelton, T, Eastern Michigan (1/21).
Johnny Rutledge, LB, Florida (2/51).
Tom Burke, DE, Wisconsin (3/83).
Joel Makovicka, RB, Nebraska (4/116).
Paris Johnson, DB, Miami of Ohio (5/155).
Yusuf Scott, G, Arizona (5/168).
Jacoby Rhinehart, DB, Southern Methodist (6/190).
Melvin Bradley, LB, Arkansas (6/202).
Dennis McKinley, RB, Miss. St. (6/206).
Chris Greisen, QB, Northwest Missouri State (7/239).

1998 REVIEW

RESULTS

Sept. 6—at Dallas	L	10-38
Sept.13—at Seattle	L	14-33
Sept.20—PHILADELPHIA	W	17-3
Sept.27—at St. Louis	W	20-17
Oct. 4—OAKLAND	L	20-23
Oct. 11—CHICAGO	W	20-7
Oct. 18—at N.Y. Giants	L	7-34
Oct. 25—Open date		
Nov. 1—at Detroit	W	17-15
Nov. 8—WASHINGTON	W	29-27
Nov. 15—DALLAS	L	28-35
Nov. 22—at Washington	W	45-42
Nov. 29—at Kansas City	L	24-34
Dec. 6—N.Y. GIANTS	L	19-23
Dec. 13—at Philadelphia (OT)	W	20-17
Dec. 20—NEW ORLEANS	W	19-17
Dec. 27—SAN DIEGO	W	16-13
Jan. 2—at Dallas*	W	20-7
Jan. 10—at Minnesota†	L	21-41

*NFC wild-card game.
†NFC divisional playoff game.

RECORDS/RANKINGS

1998 regular-season record: 9-7 (2nd in NFC East); 4-4 in division; 8-4 in conference; 5-3 at home; 4-4 on road.
Team record last five years: 32-48 (.400, ranks T23rd in league in that span).
1998 team rankings:

	No.	NFC	NFL
Total offense	*319.3	6	13
Rushing offense	*101.7	11	21
Passing offense	*217.6	4	8
Scoring offense	325	7	15
Total defense	*329.1	11	21
Rushing defense	*124.3	9	20
Passing defense	*204.8	9	17
Scoring defense	378	T11	T24
Takeaways	39	2	3
Giveaways	36	15	28
Turnover differential	3	T4	T11
Sacks	39	8	T15
Sacks allowed	50	9	22

*Yards per game.

TEAM LEADERS

Scoring (kicking): Joe Nedney, 69 pts. (30/30 PATs, 13/19 FGs).
Scoring (touchdowns): Adrian Murrell, 60 pts. (8 rushing, 2 receiving).
Passing: Jake Plummer, 3,737 yds. (547 att., 324 comp., 59.2%, 17 TDs, 20 int.).
Rushing: Adrian Murrell, 1,042 yds. (274 att., 3.8 avg., 8 TDs).
Receptions: Frank Sanders, 89 (1,145 yds., 12.9 avg., 3 TDs).
Interceptions: Kwamie Lassiter, 8 (80 yds., 0 TDs).
Sacks: Simeon Rice, 10.0.
Punting: Scott Player, 41.7 avg. (81 punts, 3,378 yds., 1 blocked).
Punt returns: Eric Metcalf, 6.9 avg. (43 att., 295 yds., 0 TDs).
Kickoff returns: Eric Metcalf, 21.4 avg. (57 att., 1,218 yds., 0 TDs).

TRAINING CAMP ROSTER

ARIZONA CARDINALS

No.	QUARTERBACKS	Ht./Wt.	Born	NFL Exp.	College	How acq.	'98 Games GP/GS
17	Brown, Dave	6-5/230	2-25-70	8	Duke	FA/98	1/0
15	Greisen, Chris	6-3/223	7-2-76	R	Northwest Missouri State	D7/99	—
16	Plummer, Jake	6-2/197	12-19-74	3	Arizona State	D2/97	16/16
	RUNNING BACKS						
24	Bates, Mario	6-1/217	1-16-73	6	Arizona State	UFA/98	16/1
37	Centers, Larry (FB)	6-0/225	6-1-68	10	Stephen F. Austin State	D5/90	16/12
48	Hayes, Jarius (FB)	6-3/266	3-27-73	3	North Alabama	D7/96	16/0
34	Makovicka, Joel (FB)	5-10/247	10-6-75	R	Nebraska	D4/99	—
39	McKinley, Dennis (FB)	6-1/241	11-3-76	R	Mississippi State	D6c/99	—
29	Murrell, Adrian	5-11/214	10-16-70	7	West Virginia	T-NYJ/98	15/14
32	Pittman, Michael	6-0/214	8-14-75	2	Fresno State	D4/98	15/0
	RECEIVERS						
82	Anderson, Ronnie	6-1/189	2-27-74	2	Allegheny	W-GB/98	4/0
89	Boston, David	6-1/215	8-19-78	R	Ohio State	D1a/99	—
84	Gedney, Chris (TE)	6-5/250	8-9-70	7	Syracuse	FA/97	16/3
80	Hardy, Terry (TE)	6-4/266	5-31-76	2	Southern Mississippi	D5/98	9/0
86	Junkin, Trey (TE)	6-2/258	1-23-61	17	Louisiana Tech	W-Oak./96	16/0
87	McWilliams, Johnny (TE)	6-4/271	12-14-72	4	Southern California	D3/96	16/15
85	Moore, Rob	6-3/203	9-27-68	10	Syracuse	T-NYJ/95	16/16
81	Sanders, Frank	6-2/197	2-17-73	5	Auburn	D2/95	16/16
	OFFENSIVE LINEMEN						
79	Clark, Jon (T)	6-6/345	4-11-73	4	Temple	FA/98	6/0
65	Clement, Anthony (T)	6-7/355	4-10-76	2	Southwestern Louisiana	D2b/98	1/0
72	Daniels, Jerome	6-5/350	9-13-74	2	Northeastern	FA/97	8/5
69	DeGraffenreid, Allen	6-4/293	6-3-74	2	Vanderbilt	FA/97	5/0
62	Devlin, Mike (C)	6-2/318	11-16-69	7	Iowa	FA/96	15/3
64	Dexter, James (T)	6-7/319	3-3-73	4	South Carolina	D5/96	16/16
67	Dishman, Chris (G)	6-3/320	2-27-74	3	Nebraska	D4/97	12/11
54	Graham, Aaron (C)	6-4/293	5-22-73	4	Nebraska	D4/96	14/13
71	Holmes, Lester (G)	6-4/315	9-27-69	7	Jackson State	FA/98	16/16
73	Joyce, Matt	6-7/313	3-30-72	5	Richmond	FA/96	11/0
68	Scott, Yusuf (G)	6-2/324	11-30-76	R	Arizona	D5b/99	—
70	Shelton, L.J. (T)	6-6/341	3-21-76	R	Eastern Michigan	D1b/99	—
	DEFENSIVE LINEMEN						
60	Burke, Tom (E)	6-2/264	10-12-76	R	Wisconsin	D3/99	
76	Drake, Jerry (E)	6-5/310	7-9-69	4	Hastings (Neb.) College	FA/95	1/1
74	Moten, Mike (T)	6-5/266	3-12-74	2	Florida	FA/98	1/0
97	Rice, Simeon (E)	6-5/260	2-24-74	4	Illinois	D1/96	16/16
78	Simpson, Carl (E)	6-2/292	4-18-70	7	Florida State	FA/98	13/1
93	Smith, Mark (T)	6-4/290	8-28-74	3	Auburn	D7/97	14/13
98	Swann, Eric (T)	6-5/313	8-16-70	9	Wake Technical College (N.C.)	D1/91	7/5
91	Swinger, Rashod (T)	6-2/286	11-27-74	2	Rutgers	FA/97	16/11
90	Wadsworth, Andre (E)	6-4/278	10-19-74	2	Florida State	D1/98	16/15
94	Wilson, Bernard (T)	6-3/318	8-17-70	7	Tennessee State	W-TB/94	16/3
	LINEBACKERS						
61	Bradley, Melvin	6-1/269	8-15-76	R	Arkansas	D6b/99	
59	Fredrickson, Rob	6-4/240	5-13-71	6	Michigan State	UFA/99	*16/16
56	Irving, Terry	6-2/236	7-3-71	6	McNeese State	D4c/94	6/1
53	Maddox, Mark	6-1/233	3-23-68	9	Northern Michigan	UFA/98	14/3
50	McCombs, Tony	6-2/246	8-24-74	3	Eastern Kentucky	D6b/97	14/13
57	McKinnon, Ronald	6-0/240	9-20-73	4	North Alabama	FA/96	13/13
51	Rutledge, Johnny	6-2/245	1-4-77	R	Florida	D2/99	—
55	Sapp, Patrick	6-4/258	5-11-73	4	Clemson	T-SD/98	16/1
52	Walz, Zack	6-4/228	2-13-76	2	Dartmouth	D6/98	16/0
	DEFENSIVE BACKS						
28	Bennett, Tommy (S)	6-2/219	2-19-73	4	UCLA	FA/96	16/16
25	Chavous, Corey (S)	6-0/204	1-15-76	2	Vanderbilt	D2a/98	16/5
27	Howard, Ty (CB)	5-9/185	11-30-73	3	Ohio State	D3/97	9/0
46	Johnson, Paris (S)	6-2/213	1-18-76	R	Miami of Ohio	D5a/99	—
22	Knight, Tom (CB)	5-11/196	12-29-74	3	Iowa	D1/97	8/5
42	Lassiter, Kwamie (S)	6-0/202	12-3-69	5	Kansas	FA/95	16/6
44	McCleskey, J.J. (CB)	5-8/184	4-10-70	6	Tennessee	W-NO/96	12/0
23	Rhinehart, Coby (CB)	5-10/187	2-7-77	R	Southern Methodist	D6a/99	—
40	Tillman, Pat (S)	5-11/204	11-6-76	2	Arizona State	D7b/98	16/10
35	Williams, Aeneas (CB)	5-11/202	1-29-68	9	Southern	D3/90	16/16
	SPECIALISTS						
13	Jacke, Chris (K)	6-0/205	3-12-66	10	Texas-El Paso	FA/98	4/0
10	Player, Scott (P)	6-0/220	12-17-69	2	Florida State	FA/98	16/0

*Not with Cardinals in 1998.

Other free agents invited to camp: FB Rod Brown, WR Chad Carpenter, WR Jim Carpenter, LB Aaron Collins, DE Jomo Cousins, LB Mark Cusano, RB Joey Dozier, WR Kevin Drake, DL Dan Falcon, OL Antonio Fleming, WR Tony Hamler, LB Terry Houzah, DL Joe Kelenic, QB Graham Leigh, DB Justin Lucas, WR Andy McCullough, DE Brad Ottis, DB Nate Riles, P Jeff Roberts, DB Ricky Thompson, OL Derek West, DL Aaron Williams, RB Clarence Williams, WR Damon Williams.

Abbreviations: D1—draft pick, first round; SupD2—supplemental draft pick, second round; WV—claimed on waivers; TR—obtained in trade; PlanB—Plan B free-agent acquisition; FA—free-agent acquisition (other than Plan B); ED—expansion draft pick.

MISCELLANEOUS TEAM DATA

Stadium (capacity, surface):
Sun Devil Stadium (73,243, grass)
Business address:
P.O. Box 888
Phoenix, AZ 85001-0888
Business phone:
602-379-0101
Ticket information:
602-379-0102
Team colors:
Cardinal red, black and white
Flagship radio station:
KDUS, 1060 AM
Training site:
Northern Arizona University
Flagstaff, Ariz.
520-523-1818

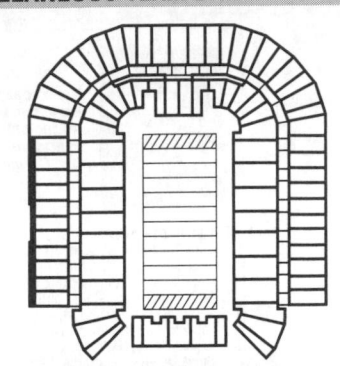

TSN REPORT CARD

Coaching staff	B +	Lingering doubts were erased with a laudable comeback after an 0-2 start. Offensive coordinator Marc Trestman was patient with a young unit, wisely trimming the playbook as the season progressed. Defensive coordinator Dave McGinnis almost needed mirrors to overcome injuries but coaxed a near-shutout of Dallas in the playoffs.
Quarterbacks	B +	Jake Plummer already has eight come-from-behind wins and he's not yet played the equivalent of two full seasons in the NFL. He has to continue to grow, and by all signs, he will. He needs to become more adept at reads and sight adjustments, and still be better in the pocket. He's at his best when creating on the run.
Running backs	B	Two years ago this was one of the most shallow spots on the team. Now there are three backs—Adrian Murrell, Michael Pittman and Mario Bates—who have significant roles. Any could start. Fullback Larry Centers remains one of the game's best third-down backs and rookie Joel Makovicka should fill the blocking back need.
Receivers	A -	Rob Moore was a Pro Bowler in 1997 and Frank Sanders came within one catch of the NFL lead last season. Rookie David Boston finally gives the Cardinals a strong third receiver, whose burning speed complements the quick underneath work of Moore and Sanders. Terry Hardy is about to bloom at tight end.
Offensive line	B -	The days of the "78 Offense" are gone. Two years ago, the line gave up a league-high 78 sacks and produced a league-low 78 yards rushing a game. Now, the line is young, deep and big. The key is young. There still is chemistry to establish without Lomas Brown.
Defensive line	B -	The grade could go lower if left tackle Eric Swann does not return healthy—or higher if he does. Lots of money has been invested in a group that has three former top-10 picks but has yet to reach its potential. Left end Andre Wadsworth is the real deal, but right end Simeon Rice has yet to establish that he is.
Linebackers	C	There are more question marks here than anywhere. The loss of Jamir Miller in free agency will hurt. This is not a big physical group, but it is quick and probably will be aligned more in space to make best use of its skills. No group would benefit more from a healthy Swann than this one, which does not have a classic run-stopper.
Secondary	B	There are more coverage players with right corner Corey Chavous and free safety Kwamie Lassiter set to start from the beginning. Aeneas Williams is without peer at left corner. The big improvement has to come from strong safety, where Tommy Bennett or Pat Tillman are good tacklers who can help the linebackers.
Special teams	B	The kicking is in good shape with either Joe Nedney or Chris Jacke. Nedney is younger and stronger but coming off an ACL tear on his kicking leg (left). Punter Scott Player must improve. Improvement also is needed in the return game, and with Boston and Pittman that should happen. The coverage teams are strong.

ATLANTA FALCONS
NFC WESTERN DIVISION

1999 SEASON

CLUB DIRECTORY

President
Taylor Smith
Special assistant to president
Jerry Rhea
Executive v.p. of administration
Jim Hay
General manager
Harold Richardson
Vice president of football operations
Ron Hill
Vice president and chief financial officer
Kevin Anthony
Administrative assistant
John O. Knox
Vice president of marketing
Rob Jackson
Vice president of corporate development
Tommy Nobis
Marketing/sales assistant
Spencer Treadwell
Marketing/sales assistants
Todd Marble   Spencer Treadwell
Director of public relations
Aaron Salkin
Assistant director of public relations
Frank Kleha
Director of community relations
Carol Breeding
Coordinator of player programs
Billy "White Shoes" Johnson
Director of ticket operations
Jack Ragsdale
Controller
Wallace Norman
Accounting
Carolyn Cathey
Dir. of player personnel/college scouting
Reed Johnson
Admin. assistant/college scouting
LaDonna Jones
National scout
Mike Hagen
Scouts
Ken Blair   Melvin Bratton
Dick Corrick   Boyd Dowler
Elbert Dubenion   Bill Groman
Bob Harrison
Director of pro personnel
Chuck Connor

**Head coach/
executive v.p.
for football
operations**
Dan Reeves

Assistant coaches
Marvin Bass (asst. to head
coach/player personnel)
Don Blackmon (linebackers)
Rich Brooks (assistant head
coach/defensive coordinator)
Jack Burns (passing game)
James Daniel (tight ends)
Steve DeBerg (quarterbacks)
Joe DeCamillis (special teams)
Tim Jorgensen (assistant strength &
conditioning)
Bill Kollar (defensive line)
Ron Meeks (secondary)
Al Miller (strength & conditioning)
George Sefcik (off. coord./RBs)
Art Shell (offensive line)
Rennie Simmons (wide receivers)
Ed West (off. quality control)
Brian Xanders (def. quality control)

Pro personnel assistant
Les Sneed
Admin. assistant/football operations
Kim Mauldin
Head trainer
Ron Medlin
Trainers
Harold King Matt Smith
Equipment manager
Brian Boigner
Sr. equip. dir./gameday op. coord.
Horace Daniel
Video director
Tom Atcheson

SCHEDULE

Sept. 12—	MINNESOTA	4:15
Sept. 20—	at Dallas (Mon.)	8:00
Sept. 26—	at St. Louis	12:00
Oct. 3—	BALTIMORE	1:00
Oct. 10—	at New Orleans	12:00
Oct. 17—	ST. LOUIS	1:00
Oct. 25—	at Pittsburgh (Mon.)	9:00
Oct. 31—	CAROLINA	1:00
Nov. 7—	JACKSONVILLE	1:00
Nov. 14—	Open date	
Nov. 21—	at Tampa Bay	1:00
Nov. 28—	at Carolina	8:20
Dec. 5—	NEW ORLEANS	1:00
Dec. 12—	at San Francisco	1:15
Dec. 19—	at Tennessee	12:00
Dec. 26—	ARIZONA	1:00
Jan. 3—	SAN FRAN. (Mon.)	9:00

All times are for home team.
All games Sunday unless noted.

DRAFT CHOICES

Patrick Kerney, DE, Virginia (first
round/30th pick overall).
Reginald Kelly, TE, Mississippi State
(2/42).
Jeff Paulk, RB, Arizona State (3/92).
Johndale Carty, DB, Utah State (4/126).
Eugene Baker, WR, Kent (5/164).
Jeff Kelly, LB, Kansas State (6/198).
Eric Thigpen, DB, Iowa (6/200).
Todd McClure, C, Louisiana State
(7/237).
Rondel Menendez, WR, Eastern
Kentucky (7/247).

1998 REVIEW

RESULTS

Sept. 6—at Carolina	W	19-14
Sept.13—PHILADELPHIA	W	17-12
Sept.20—Open date		
Sept.27—at San Francisco	L	20-31
Oct. 4—CAROLINA	W	51-23
Oct. 11—at N.Y. Giants	W	34-20
Oct. 18—NEW ORLEANS	W	31-23
Oct. 25—at N.Y. Jets	L	3-28
Nov. 1—ST. LOUIS	W	37-15
Nov. 8—at New England	W	41-10
Nov. 15—SAN FRANCISCO	W	31-19
Nov. 22—CHICAGO	W	20-13
Nov. 29—at St. Louis	W	21-10
Dec. 6—INDIANAPOLIS	W	28-21
Dec. 13—at New Orleans	W	27-17
Dec. 20—at Detroit	W	24-17
Dec. 27—MIAMI	W	38-16
Jan. 9—SAN FRANCISCO	W	20-18
Jan. 17—at Minnesota (OT)	W	30-27
Jan. 31—Denver‡	L	19-34

*NFC divisional playoff game.
†NFC championship game.
‡Super Bowl XXXIII.

RECORDS/RANKINGS

1998 regular-season record: 14-2 (1st in
NFC West); 7-1 in division; 11-1 in conference; 8-0 at home; 6-2 on road.
Team record last five years: 40-40 (.500,
ranks 11th in league in that span).
1998 team rankings:

	No.	NFC	NFL
Total offense	*342.9	4	7
Rushing offense	*131.3	3	6
Passing offense	*211.6	6	11
Scoring offense	442	3	4
Total defense	*295.9	3	8
Rushing defense	*75.2	1	2
Passing defense	*220.7	11	21
Scoring defense	289	2	4
Takeaways	44	1	1
Giveaways	24	T3	T8
Turnover differential	20	1	1
Sacks	38	T9	T18
Sacks allowed	53	T10	T23

*Yards per game.

TEAM LEADERS

Scoring (kicking): Morten Andersen, 120
pts. (51/52 PATs, 23/28 FGs).
Scoring (touchdowns): Jamal Anderson,
98 pts. (14 rushing, 2 receiving, 1 2-pt.
conv.).
Passing: Chris Chandler, 3,154 yds. (327
att., 190 comp., 58.1%, 25 TDs, 12 int.).
Rushing: Jamal Anderson, 1,846 yds.
(410 att., 4.5 avg., 14 TDs).
Receptions: Tony Martin, 66 (1,181 yds.,
17.9 avg., 6 TDs).
Interceptions: Ray Buchanan, 7 (102
yds., 0 TDs).
Sacks: Lester Archambeau, 10.0.
Punting: Dan Stryzinski, 40.0 avg. (74
punts, 2,963 yds., 0 blocked).
Punt returns: Tim Dwight, 8.5 avg. (31
att., 263 yds., 0 TDs).
Kickoff returns: Tim Dwight, 27.0 avg.
(36 att., 973 yds., 1 TD).

ATLANTA FALCONS

No.	QUARTERBACKS	Ht./Wt.	Born	NFL Exp.	College	How acq.	'98 Games GP/GS
12	Chandler, Chris	6-4/225	10-12-65	12	Washington	T-Hou./97	14/14
13	Graziani, Tony	6-2/215	12-23-73	3	Oregon	D7/97	4/1
7	Kanell, Danny	6-3/220	11-21-73	4	Florida State	FA/99	*10/10
	RUNNING BACKS						
32	Anderson, Jamal	5-11/235	9-30-72	6	Utah	D7/94	16/16
44	Christian, Bob (FB)	5-11/232	11-14-68	8	Northwestern	FA/97	14/11
45	Downs, Gary	6-1/218	6-6-72	6	North Carolina State	FA/97	16/1
24	Hanspard, Byron	5-10/200	1-23-76	3	Texas Tech	D2b/97	—
28	Oxendine, Ken	6-0/230	10-4-75	2	Virginia Tech	D7b/98	9/0
40	Paulk, Jeff (FB)	6-0/242	4-26-76	R	Arizona State	D3/99	—
	RECEIVERS						
15	Baker, Eugene	6-0/165	3-18-76	R	Kent	D5/99	—
80	Calloway, Chris	5-10/188	3-29-68	10	Michigan	FA/99	*16/16
83	Dwight, Tim	5-8/180	7-13-75	2	Iowa	D4b/98	12/0
87	German, Jammi	6-1/192	7-4-74	2	Miami	D3/98	6/0
82	Harris, Ronnie	5-11/185	6-4-70	6	Oregon	FA/98	8/0
89	Kelly, Reggie (TE)	6-3/250	2-22-77	R	Mississippi State	D2/99	—
85	Kozlowski, Brian (TE)	6-3/250	10-4-70	6	Connecticut	FA/97	16/4
81	Mathis, Terance	5-10/186	6-7-67	10	New Mexico	UFA/94	16/16
17	Menendez, Rondel	5-9/183	5-18-75	R	Eastern Kentucky	D7b/99	—
88	Santiago, O.J. (TE)	6-7/264	4-4-74	3	Kent	D3/97	16/16
	OFFENSIVE LINEMEN						
65	Bishop, Greg (G)	6-5/315	5-2-71	6	Pacific	UFA/99	*16/16
68	Collins, Calvin (C)	6-2/305	1-5-74	3	Texas A&M	D6/97	16/16
64	Hallen, Bob (C)	6-4/292	3-9-75	2	Kent	D2/98	12/0
62	McClure, Todd (C)	6-1/292	2-16-77	R	Louisiana State	D7a/99	—
76	Portilla, Jose (T)	6-6/315	9-11-72	2	Arizona	FA/98	16/0
74	Salaam, Ephraim (T)	6-7/310	6-19-76	2	San Diego State	D7a/98	16/16
67	Schreiber, Adam (C)	6-4/295	2-20-62	16	Texas	UFA/97	16/0
61	Tobeck, Robbie (C)	6-4/298	3-6-70	6	Washington State	FA/93	16/16
70	Whitfield, Bob (T)	6-5/315	10-18-71	8	Stanford	D1a/92	16/16
69	Williams, Gene (G)	6-2/320	10-14-68	9	Iowa State	T-Cle./95	16/16
	DEFENSIVE LINEMEN						
92	Archambeau, Lester (E)	6-5/275	6-27-67	10	Stanford	T-GB/93	15/15
75	Dronett, Shane (E)	6-6/298	1-12-71	8	Texas	FA/97	16/16
98	Hall, Travis (T)	6-5/298	8-3-72	5	Brigham Young	D6/95	14/13
5	Jasper, Ed (T)	6-2/305	1-18-73	3	Texas A&M	FA/99	*7/0
97	Kerney, Patrick (E)	6-5/269	12-30-76	R	Virginia	D1/99	—
99	Kuberski, Bob (T)	6-4/300	4-5-71	5	Navy	UFA/99	*16/0
77	McDaniels, Pellom (E)	6-3/295	2-21-68	7	Oregon State	UFA/99	*11/2
90	Smith, Chuck (E)	6-2/262	12-21-69	8	Tennessee	D2/92	16/16
93	Swayda, Shawn (E)	6-5/297	9-4-74	2	Arizona State	FA/98	5/0
	LINEBACKERS						
56	Brooking, Keith	6-2/242	10-30-75	2	Georgia Tech	D1/98	15/0
94	Crockett, Henri	6-2/238	10-28-74	3	Florida State	D4/97	10/10
54	Hamilton, Ruffin	6-1/235	3-2-71	4	Tulane	FA/97	16/0
51	Kelly, Jeff	5-11/256	12-13-75	R	Kansas State	D6a/99	—
52	Sauer, Craig	6-1/235	12-13-72	4	Minnesota	D6/96	16/6
59	Talley, Ben	6-3/245	7-14-72	4	Tennessee	FA/98	8/0
58	Tuggle, Jessie	5-11/230	4-4-65	13	Valdosta (Ga.) State	FA/87	16/16
	DEFENSIVE BACKS						
47	Bayne, Chris (S)	6-1/215	3-22-75	3	Fresno State	D7/97	10/0
20	Booker, Michael (CB)	6-2/200	4-27-75	3	Nebraska	D1/97	14/6
23	Bradford, Ronnie (CB)	5-10/195	10-1-70	7	Colorado	FA/97	14/10
27	Brown, Omar (S)	5-10/200	3-28-75	2	North Carolina	D4a/98	2/0
34	Buchanan, Ray (CB)	5-9/185	9-29-71	7	Louisville	UFA/97	16/16
25	Carter, Marty (S)	6-1/210	12-17-69	9	Middle Tennessee State	UFA/99	*16/16
35	Carty, Johndale (S)	6-0/203	8-27-77	R	Utah State	D4/99	—
29	Fuller, Randy (CB)	5-10/184	6-2-70	6	Tennessee State	FA/98	13/0
22	McBurrows, Gerald (S)	5-11/205	10-7-73	5	Kansas	UFA/99	*10/0
41	Robinson, Eugene (S)	6-1/200	5-28-63	15	Colgate	UFA/98	16/16
39	Thigpen, Eric (S)	6-0/199	6-19-76	R	Iowa	D6b/99	—
21	Williams, Elijah (CB)	5-10/182	8-20-75	2	Florida	D6/98	15/0
	SPECIALISTS						
5	Andersen, Morten (K)	6-2/222	8-19-60	18	Michigan State	FA/95	16/0
4	Stryzinski, Dan (P)	6-2/200	5-15-65	10	Indiana	UFA/95	16/0

*Not with Falcons In 1998.

Other free agents invited to camp: WR Corey Allen, LB Bret Ayanbadejo, WR Octavus Barnes, T Octavious Bishop, QB Shedrick Bonner, DE Emil Ekiyor, LB Schad Freeman, CB Derrick Gardner, LB Lamont Green, WR Eric Harris, RB Steve Hookfin, DT Ben Huff, FB Eric Lane, TE Rod Monroe, G Ben Nichols, T Greg Studdard, CB Keith Thibodeaux, G Kenny Watts, DE Brett Williams.

Abbreviations: D1—draft pick, first round; SupD2—supplemental draft pick, second round; WV—claimed on waivers; TR—obtained in trade; PlanB—Plan B free-agent acquisition; FA—free-agent acquisition (other than Plan B); ED—expansion draft pick.

MISCELLANEOUS TEAM DATA

Stadium (capacity, surface):
Georgia Dome
(71,228, artificial)
Business address:
Atlanta Falcons
One Falcon Place
Suwanee, Ga. 30024
Business phone:
770-945-1111
Ticket information:
404-223-8444
Team colors:
Black, red, silver and white
Flagship radio station:
WGST, 920 AM
Training site:
Atlanta Falcons
Suwanee, Ga.
770-945-1111

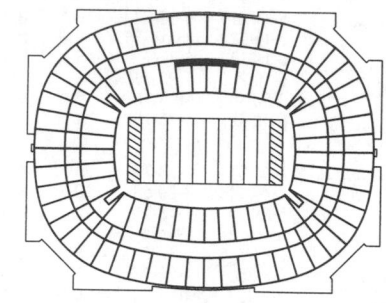

TSN REPORT CARD

Coaching staff	A -	Head coach Dan Reeves disappeared for almost a month after heart surgery and his staff held the Falcons together for a run at the championship. Reeves' solid football sense and run-first scheme is just what the franchise needed after some very poor years.
Quarterbacks	B +	Chris Chandler is in his prime, coming off a season with the league's fourth-highest quarterback rating (100.9). The addition of Danny Kanell gives the team a good backup and less worry about Chandler holding the ball too long in the pocket and taking hard sacks into the astroturf of the Georgia Dome.
Running backs	A -	Jamal Anderson is a top-shelf NFL back: he's durable, elusive, uses his blockers well and can block himself. Bob Christian is one of the top fullbacks in the league. The only reason for A- and not A is uncertainty behind Anderson with Byron Hanspard coming off surgery.
Receivers	B -	Terance Mathis and Chris Calloway find the seams and get open. But they are not deep threats, which affects their grade. It remains to be seen how good the backups are at receiver. Tight end O.J. Santiago is emerging as a very good player.
Offensive line	B +	This cohesive unit got much better in the offseason with pickup of free agent Greg Bishop. The Falcons have some depth and versatility with Robbie Tobeck, a former guard playing center, and Collins, a former center playing guard.
Defensive line	B +	The Falcons are very good against the run and able to apply pressure to the passer. They needed depth and got it in the draft with the pickup of Patrick Kerney. Travis Hall is among the top tackles in the NFL.
Linebackers	C +	Henri Crockett is a big-play linebacker and Jessie Tuggle plugs the hole in the middle. Now it's up to second-year man Keith Brooking to step in for Cornelius Bennett and fulfill some of the potential that comes with being a first-round draft pick.
Secondary	C -	The acquisition of strong safety Marty Carter is a big plus, but the Falcons are still on thin ice at the other corner if Ronnie Bradford gets hurt.
Special teams	B +	Morten Andersen may be a 17-year veteran but he can still hit the big field goals. Punter Dan Stryzinski has great hang time, and Tim Dwight is a coast-to-coast threat as a kick returner. The punt and kick coverage units usually are dependable.

BALTIMORE RAVENS
AFC CENTRAL DIVISION

1999 SEASON

CLUB DIRECTORY

Owner/chief executive officer
Arthur B. Modell
President
David O. Modell
Vice president of player personnel
Ozzie Newsome
Vice president/public relations
Kevin Byrne
Vice president of marketing and sales
David Cope
Vice president of administration
Pat Moriarty
Secretary and general counsel
Jim Bailey
Treasurer
Luis Perez
Director of operations and information
Bob Eller
Director of publications
Francine Lubera
Director of broadcasting
Lisa Bercu
Director of tickets
Roy Sommerhof
Director of pro personnel
James Harris
Director of college scouting
Phil Savage
Scouting/pro personnel
Eric DeCosta
George Kokinis
Ron Marciniak
Terry McDonough
T.J. McCreight
Ellis Rainsberger
John Wooten
Art Perkins
Facilities manager
Chuck Cusick
Head trainer
Bill Tessendorf

Head coach
Brian Billick

Assistant coaches
Matt Cavanaugh (offensive
coordinator)
Jim Colletto (offensive line)
Jack Del Rio (linebackers)
Jeff Friday (strength &
conditioning)
Wade Harman (tight ends)
Donn Henderson (assistant
defensive backs)
Milt Jackson (receivers)
Marvin Lewis (defensive
coordinator)
Chip Morton (assistant strength
& conditioning)
Russ Purnell (special teams)
Rex Ryan (defensive line)
Steve Shafer (defensive backs)
Matt Simon (running backs)
Mike Smith (defensive asst.)

Assistant trainer
Mark Smith
Team physicians
Dr. Andrew M. Tucker
Dr. Claude T. Moorman III
Dr. Andrew Pollak
Dr. Leigh Ann Curl
Equipment manager
Ed Carroll

SCHEDULE

Sept. 12—	at St. Louis	12:00
Sept. 19—	PITTSBURGH	1:00
Sept. 26—	CLEVELAND	1:00
Oct. 3—	at Atlanta	1:00
Oct. 10—	at Tennessee	3:15
Oct. 17—	Open date	
Oct. 21—	KANSAS CITY (Thur.)	8:20
Oct. 31—	BUFFALO	1:00
Nov. 7—	at Cleveland	1:00
Nov. 14—	at Jacksonville	4:05
Nov. 21—	at Cincinnati	4:05
Nov. 28—	JACKSONVILLE	1:00
Dec. 5—	TENNESSEE	1:00
Dec. 12—	at Pittsburgh	1:00
Dec. 19—	NEW ORLEANS	1:00
Dec. 26—	CINCINNATI	1:00
Jan. 2—	at New England	1:00

All times are for home team.
All games Sunday unless noted.

DRAFT CHOICES

Chris McAlister, DB, Arizona (first
round/10th pick overall).
Brandon Stokley, WR, Southwestern
Louisiana (4/105).
Edwin Mulitalo, G, Arizona (4/129).
Anthony Poindexter, DB, Virginia
(7/216).

1998 REVIEW

RESULTS

Sept. 6—	PITTSBURGH	L	13-20
Sept.13—	at N.Y. Jets	W	24-10
Sept.20—	at Jacksonville	L	10-24
Sept.27—	CINCINNATI	W	31-24
Oct. 4—	Open date		
Oct. 11—	TENNESSEE	L	8-12
Oct. 18—	at Pittsburgh	L	6-16
Oct. 25—	at Green Bay	L	10-28
Nov. 1—	JACKSONVILLE	L	19-45
Nov. 8—	OAKLAND	W	13-10
Nov. 15—	at San Diego	L	13-14
Nov. 22—	at Cincinnati	W	20-13
Nov. 29—	INDIANAPOLIS	W	38-31
Dec. 6—	at Tennessee	L	14-16
Dec. 13—	MINNESOTA	L	28-38
Dec. 20—	at Chicago	L	3-24
Dec. 27—	DETROIT	W	19-10

RECORDS/RANKINGS

1998 regular-season record: 6-10 (4th in
AFC Central); 2-6 in division; 5-7 in conference; 4-4 at home; 2-6 on road.
Team record last five years: 32-47-1
(.406, ranks T21st in league in that span).
1998 team rankings:

	No.	AFC	NFL
Total offense	*281.1	15	26
Rushing offense	*101.8	10	20
Passing offense	*179.3	13	25
Scoring offense	269	12	26
Total defense	*331.1	11	22
Rushing defense	*106.6	10	17
Passing defense	*224.5	12	24
Scoring defense	335	9	16
Takeaways	23	12	T22
Giveaways	30	9	T16
Turnover differential	-7	12	23
Sacks	39	T8	T15
Sacks allowed	41	T12	T18

*Yards per game.

TEAM LEADERS

Scoring (kicking): Matt Stover, 87 pts.
(24/24 PATs, 21/28 FGs).
Scoring (touchdowns): Jermaine Lewis,
48 pts. (6 receiving, 2 punt returns).
Passing: Jim Harbaugh, 1,839 yds. (293
att., 164 comp., 56.0%, 12 TDs, 11 int.).
Rushing: Priest Holmes, 1,008 yds. (233
att., 4.3 avg., 7 TDs).
Receptions: Jermaine Lewis, 41 (784
yds., 19.1 avg., 6 TDs).
Interceptions: Rod Woodson, 6 (108
yds., 2 TDs).
Sacks: Michael McCrary, 14.5.
Punting: Kyle Richardson, 43.9 avg. (90
punts, 3,948 yds., 2 blocked).
Punt returns: Jermaine Lewis, 12.7 avg.
(32 att., 405 yds., 2 TDs).
Kickoff returns: Corey Harris, 27.6 avg.
(35 att., 965 yds., 1 TD).

1999 SEASON
TRAINING CAMP ROSTER

No.	QUARTERBACKS	Ht./Wt.	Born	NFL Exp.	College	How acq.	'98 Games GP/GS
12	Banks, Tony	6-4/215	4-5-73	4	Michigan State	T-StL./99	*14/14
19	Mitchell, Scott	6-6/230	1-2-68	10	Utah	FA/99	*2/2
14	Richardson, Wally	6-4/225	2-11-74	3	Penn State	D7b/97	1/0
	RUNNING BACKS						
31	Broussard, Steve	5-7/201	2-22-67	10	Washington State	FA/99	*15/0
23	Cotton, Kenyon (FB)	6-0/255	2-23-74	3	Southwestern Louisiana	FA/97	12/0
29	Evans, Chuck (FB)	6-1/245	4-16-67	7	Clark Atlanta (Ga.)	UFA/99	*16/8
34	Graham, Jay	5-11/220	7-14-75	3	Tennessee	D3/97	5/2
33	Holmes, Priest	5-9/205	10-7-73	3	Texas.	FA/97	16/13
32	Rhett, Errict	5-11/210	12-11-70	6	Florida	T-TB/98	13/1
	RECEIVERS						
86	DeLong, Greg (TE)	6-4/250	4-3-73	5	North Carolina	FA/99	*15/5
87	Ismail, Qadry	6-0/195	11-8-70	7	Syracuse	FA/99	*10/1
85	Johnson, Patrick	5-10/180	8-10-76	2	Oregon	D2/98	13/0
84	Lewis, Jermaine	5-7/172	10-16-74	4	Maryland	D5/96	13/13
89	Ofodile, A.J. (TE)	6-6/260	10-9-73	3	Missouri	FA/97	5/0
80	Purnell, Lovett (TE)	6-3/245	4-7-72	4	West Virginia	T-NE/99	*16/5
83	Roe, James	6-1/187	8-23-73	4	Norfolk State	D6b/96	10/3
	Slaughter, Webster	6-1/175	10-19-64	12	San Diego State	UFA/99	*10/0
11	Stokley, Brandon	5-11/197	6-23-76	R	Southwestern Louisiana	D4a/99	—
88	Turner, Floyd	5-11/199	5-29-66	10	Northwestern (La.) State	FA/96	16/3
82	Wainright, Frank (TE)	6-3/250	10-10-67	9	Northern Colorado	UFA/99	*16/1
	OFFENSIVE LINEMEN						
74	Atkins, James	6-6/306	1-28-70	6	Southwestern Louisiana	FA/98	9/6
69	Blackshear, Jeff (G)	6-6/323	3-29-69	7	Northeast Louisiana	T-Sea./96	16/16
62	Flynn, Mike	6-3/295	6-15-74	2	Maine	FA/97	2/0
71	Folau, Spencer (T)	6-5/300	4-5-73	3	Idaho	FA/96	3/3
61	Lindsay, Everett	6-4/302	9-18-70	6	Mississippi	T-Min./99	*16/3
60	Mitchell, Jeff (C)	6-4/300	1-29-74	3	Florida	D5/97	11/10
64	Mulitalo, Edwin	6-3/328	9-1-74	R	Arizona	D4b/99	—
75	Ogden, Jonathan	6-8/318	7-31-74	4	UCLA	D1a/96	13/13
70	Swayne, Harry (T)	6-5/295	2-2-65	13	Rutgers	UFA/99	*16/16
	DEFENSIVE LINEMEN						
90	Burnett, Rob (E)	6-4/280	8-27-67	10	Syracuse	D5/90	16/16
92	Chase, Martin (T)	6-2/295	12-19-74	2	Oklahoma	D5a/98	—
91	Dalton, Lional (T)	6-1/320	2-21-75	2	Eastern Michigan	FA/98	2/1
99	McCrary, Michael (E)	6-4/270	7-7-70	7	Wake Forest	UFA/97	16/16
98	Siragusa, Tony (T)	6-3/320	5-14-67	10	Pittsburgh	FA/97	15/15
96	Smith, Fernando (E)	6-6/277	8-2-71	6	Jackson State	UFA/99	*14/0
93	Washington, Keith (E)	6-4/270	12-18-72	5	UNLV	FA/97	16/0
79	Webster, Larry	6-5/288	1-18-69	7	Maryland	FA/95	15/0
	LINEBACKERS						
58	Boulware, Peter	6-4/255	12-18-74	3	Florida State	D1/97	16/16
51	Brown, Cornell	6-0/240	3-15-75	3	Virginia Tech	D6b/97	16/1
57	Kopp, Jeff	6-3/244	7-8-71	5	Southern California	FA/98	13/0
52	Lewis, Ray	6-1/240	5-15-75	4	Miami (Fla.)	D1b/96	14/14
54	McCloud, Tyrus	6-1/250	11-23-74	3	Louisville	D4b/97	7/2
53	Peters, Tyrell	6-0/230	8-4-74	3	Oklahoma	FA/97	10/0
55	Sharper, Jamie	6-3/240	11-23-74	3	Virginia	D2a/97	16/16
	DEFENSIVE BACKS						
20	Herring, Kim (S)	5-11/210	9-10-75	3	Penn State	D2b/97	7/7
25	Jenkins, DeRon (CB)	5-11/190	11-14-73	4	Tennessee	D2/96	16/7
28	McAlister, Chris (CB)	6-1/206	6-14-77	R	Arizona	D1/99	—
27	Moore, Stevon (S)	5-11/210	2-9-67	11	Mississippi	UFA/92	16/16
43	Poindexter, Anthony (S)	6-0/210	7-28-76	R	Virginia	D7/99	—
22	Starks, Duane (CB)	5-10/170	5-23-74	2	Miami (Fla.)	D1/98	16/8
37	Thompson, Bennie (S)	6-0/214	2-10-63	10	Grambling State	FA/94	16/0
38	Trapp, James (CB)	6-0/195	12-28-69	7	Clemson	UFA/99	*16/0
21	Williams, John	5-7/180	7-26-74	2	Southern	FA/97	16/0
26	Woodson, Rod (CB)	6-0/200	3-10-65	13	Purdue	FA/98	16/16
	SPECIALISTS						
5	Richardson, Kyle (P)	6-2/190	3-2-73	3	Arkansas State	FA/98	16/0
3	Stover, Matt (K)	5-11/178	1-27-68	10	Louisiana Tech	PlanB/91	16/0

*Not with Ravens in 1998.

Other free agents invited to camp: K Scott Bentley, WR Mike Bowman, DB Cory Chamblin, S Jermaine Derricott, DE Marques Douglas, OL Brandon Dyson, DT Larry Fitzpatrick, DT Cory Francis, OL Chris Harrison, P Brad Hill, WR Ramon Huff, LB Brad Jackson, QB Jason Maas, WR Tywan Mitchell, WR Kendrick Nord, DE Charles Preston, TE Aaron Pierce, T Cleve Roberts, FB Rob Robertson, DE Kareem Robinson, OL Bob Sapp, WR Phil Savoy, RB Thomas Sieh, RB Ben Snell, RB Tony Vinson, CB Fred Wilkerson, T Sammy Williams, LB Antron Wright.

Abbreviations: D1—draft pick, first round; SupD2—supplemental draft pick, second round; WV—claimed on waivers; TR—obtained in trade; PlanB—Plan B free-agent acquisition; FA—free-agent acquisition (other than Plan B); ED—expansion draft pick.

MISCELLANEOUS TEAM DATA

Stadium (capacity, surface):
  PSINet Stadium
  (69,354, grass)
Business address:
  11001 Owings Mills Blvd.
  Owings Mills, MD 21117
Business phone:
  410-654-6200
Ticket information:
  410-261-RAVE
Team colors:
  Purple, black and metallic gold
Flagship radio stations:
  WJFK/WLIF
Training site:
  Western Maryland College
  Westminster, Md.
  401-654-6200

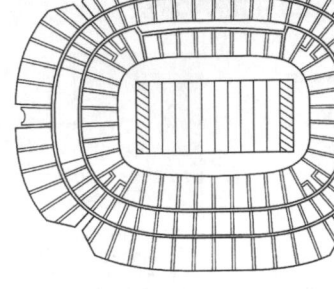

BALTIMORE RAVENS

TSN REPORT CARD

Coaching staff — B — Compared to former coach Ted Marchibroda—who had to hire his staff in a hurry back in February 1996—Brian Billick had time and seems to have hired a competent staff. Billick has been impressive thus far. He is extremely organized and understands that today's players need a motivator as well as a coach. This staff seems to have a good chemistry, a mixture of old and young, black and white. One striking characteristic is that most of the staff members have served as coordinators on either the professional or college level.

Quarterbacks — C — Both starter Scott Mitchell and backup Tony Banks are trying to resurrect their careers. Mitchell has more overall knowledge, but Banks has more athleticism and could close the gap by midseason. This situation could become interesting. But neither can carry a team alone.

Running backs — C — Priest Holmes, Errict Rhett and Jay Graham complement each other, but the team desperately lacks an every-down back. The Ravens have to be effective inside the tackles, because they can't do much damage on the perimeter. Fullback Charles Evans is the only multi-dimensional player in the backfield.

Receivers — D + — The team's top playmaker is a 5-7 smurf named Jermaine Lewis. The Ravens lack a big, go-to receiver opposite of Lewis and will have problems scoring in the red zone because of it. Look out for tight end Lovett Purnell; he could be a sleeper, especially as a pass catcher.

Offensive line — C — The Ravens have to get good interior play from the guards and center because opposing teams won't attack tackles Harry Swayne and Jonathan Ogden. The Ravens have solid depth and line coach Jim Colletto has been impressive in bringing this group together. Despite losing right tackle Orlando Brown and center/guard Wally Williams, this unit is better than it was a year ago.

Defensive line — C + — This could be an area of strength—or one decimated by injuries. Both defensive ends are strong, but also bothered by knee injuries. The team is looking for Tony Siragusa to anchor the inside, but he also is hindered by knee problems. The Ravens have some youthful talent as backups, and they might become an option.

Linebackers — B — This may be the most talented unit on the team. All three starters run extremely well and play a physical game. The major weakness among the group is that none of them play pass coverage well and teams have challenged the Ravens over the middle on short-to-intermediate passes. Because of aggressiveness, the linebackers can be fooled with play action.

Secondary — C - — The Ravens' worst unit of the past three seasons still has problems, but not as severe. Rookie Chris McAlister will provide a much-needed physical presence on the corner and veteran Rod Woodson will move to safety. The key is how much pounding Woodson can take and if fellow safety Kim Herring can fully recover from two shoulder separations last season.

Special teams — C — Lewis made the Pro Bowl as a punt returner and should challenge for the same honors again this season. Matt Stover had a quietly consistent 1998 as a field-goal kicker and Kyle Richardson could develop into one of the league's best punters. The Ravens have a number of quality choices to return kickoffs in Qadry Ismail and Steve Broussard. The potential is there for this group to have a major impact.

BUFFALO BILLS
AFC EASTERN DIVISION

1999 SEASON

CLUB DIRECTORY

President
Ralph C. Wilson Jr.
Exec. vice president/general manager
John Butler
Vice president, communications
Scott Berchtold
V.p., business dev. & marketing
Russ Brandon
Vice president/operations
Bill Munson
Corporate vice president
Linda Bogdan
Treasurer
Jeffrey C. Littmann
Director of administration/ticket sales
Jerry Foran
Director of business operations
Jim Overdorf
Controller
Frank Wojnicki
Director of marketing communications
Marc Honan
Director of merchandising
Christy Wilson Hofmann
Director of guest services
Jan Eberle
Dir. of public/community relations
Denny Lynch
Media relations coordinator
Mark Dalton
Ticket director
June Foran
Video director
Henry Kunttu
Director of stadium operations
George Koch
Director of security
Bill Bambach
Engineering and operations manager
Joe Frandina
Director of pro personnel
A.J. Smith
Director of player personnel
Dwight Adams

Head coach
Wade Phillips

Assistant coaches
Max Bowman (asst. to head coach/tight ends)
Bill Bradley (defensive backs)
Ted Cottrell (def. coordinator)
Bruce DeHaven (special teams)
Chris Dickson (off. quality control)
Bishop Harris (running backs)
Charlie Joiner (receivers)
Rusty Jones (strength & cond.)
Chuck Lester (linebackers)
John Levra (defensive line)
Carl Mauck (offensive line)
Joe Pendry (off. coordinator)
Turk Schonert (quarterbacks)

Scouts
Brad Forsyth   Tom Gibbons
Joe Haering   Doug Majeski
Buddy Nix   Bob Ryan
Chink Sengel   Bobby Williams
Dave G. Smith   Dave W. Smith
Head trainer
Bud Carpenter
Assistant trainer
Melvin Lewis
Greg McMillen
Equipment manager
Dave Hojnowski
Assistant equipment manager
Woody Ribbeck

SCHEDULE

Sept. 12—	at Indianapolis	12:00
Sept. 19—	N.Y. JETS	8:20
Sept. 26—	PHILADELPHIA	1:00
Oct. 4—	at Miami (Mon.)	9:00
Oct. 10—	PITTSBURGH	1:00
Oct. 17—	OAKLAND	1:00
Oct. 24—	at Seattle	1:15
Oct. 31—	at Baltimore	1:00
Nov. 7—	at Washington	1:00
Nov. 14—	MIAMI	1:00
Nov. 21—	at N.Y. Jets	1:00
Nov. 28—	NEW ENGLAND	1:00
Dec. 5—	Open date	
Dec. 12—	N.Y. GIANTS	1:00
Dec. 19—	at Arizona	6:20
Dec. 26—	at New England	1:00
Jan. 2—	INDIANAPOLIS	1:00

All times are for home team.
All games Sunday unless noted.

DRAFT CHOICES

Antoine Winfield, DB, Ohio State (first round/23rd pick overall).
Peerless Price, WR, Tennessee (2/53).
Shawn Bryson, RB, Tennessee (3/86).
Keith Newman, LB, North Carolina (4/119).
Bobby Collins, TE, North Alabama (4/122).
Jay Foreman, LB, Nebraska (5/156).
Armon Hatcher, DB, Oregon State (6/194).
Sheldon Jackson, TE, Nebraska (7/230).
Bryce Fisher, DE, Air Force (7/248).

1998 REVIEW

RESULTS

Sept. 6—at San Diego	L	14-16
Sept.13—at Miami	L	7-13
Sept.20—ST. LOUIS	L	33-34
Sept.27—Open date		
Oct. 4—SAN FRANCISCO	W	26-21
Oct. 11—at Indianapolis	W	31-24
Oct. 18—JACKSONVILLE	W	17-16
Oct. 25—at Carolina	W	30-14
Nov. 1—MIAMI	W	30-24
Nov. 8—at N.Y. Jets	L	12-34
Nov. 15—NEW ENGLAND	W	13-10
Nov. 22—INDIANAPOLIS	W	34-11
Nov. 29—at New England	L	21-25
Dec. 6—at Cincinnati	W	33-20
Dec. 13—OAKLAND	W	44-21
Dec. 19—N.Y. JETS	L	10-17
Dec. 27—at New Orleans	W	45-33
Jan. 2—at Miami*	L	17-24

*AFC wild-card game.

RECORDS/RANKINGS

1998 regular-season record: 10-6 (2nd in AFC East); 4-4 in division; 7-5 in conference; 6-2 at home; 4-4 on road.
Team record last five years: 43-37 (.538, ranks 10th in league in that span).

1998 team rankings:

	No.	AFC	NFL
Total offense	*346.3	3	6
Rushing offense	*135.1	2	3
Passing offense	*211.3	6	12
Scoring offense	400	3	7
Total defense	*293.2	4	6
Rushing defense	*93.3	3	5
Passing defense	*199.9	7	14
Scoring defense	333	8	15
Takeaways	31	T5	T11
Giveaways	20	T2	T3
Turnover differential	11	1	T3
Sacks	43	4	T9
Sacks allowed	41	T12	T18

*Yards per game.

TEAM LEADERS

Scoring (kicking): Steve Christie, 140 pts. (41/41 PATs, 33/41 FGs).
Scoring (touchdowns): Eric Moulds, 54 pts. (9 receiving).
Passing: Doug Flutie, 2,711 yds. (354 att., 202 comp., 57.1%, 20 TDs, 11 int.).
Rushing: Antowain Smith, 1,124 yds. (300 att., 3.7 avg., 8 TDs).
Receptions: Eric Moulds, 67 (1,368 yds., 20.4 avg., 9 TDs).
Interceptions: Kurt Schulz, 6 (48 yds., 0 TDs).
Sacks: Bruce Smith, 10.0.
Punting: Chris Mohr, 41.8 avg. (69 punts, 2,882 yds., 0 blocked).
Punt returns: Kevin Williams, 10.0 avg. (37 att., 369 yds., 0 TDs).
Kickoff returns: Kevin Williams, 22.5 avg. (47 att., 1,059 yds., 0 TDs).

BUFFALO BILLS

No.	QUARTERBACKS	Ht./Wt.	Born	NFL Exp.	College	How acq.	'98 Games GP/GS
7	Flutie, Doug	5-10/175	10-23-62	6	Boston College	FA/98	13/10
11	Johnson, Rob	6-4/214	3-18-73	5	Southern California	T-Jax./98	8/6
10	Van Pelt, Alex	6-0/220	5-1-70	5	Pittsburgh	FA/94	1/0
	RUNNING BACKS						
48	Bryson, Shawn (FB)	6-0/235	11-30-76	R	Tennessee	D3/99	—
33	Gash, Sam (FB)	6-0/235	3-7-69	8	Penn State	FA/98	16/13
35	Linton, Jonathan (FB)	6-0/248	10-7-74	2	North Carolina	D5/98	14/0
23	Smith, Antowain	6-2/224	3-14-72	4	Houston	D1/97	16/14
34	Thomas, Thurman	5-10/198	5-16-66	12	Oklahoma State	D2/88	14/3
	RECEIVERS						
84	Collins, Bobby (TE)	6-4/249	8-20-76	R	North Alabama	D4b/99	—
88	Jackson, Sheldon (TE)	6-3/237	7-24-76	R	Nebraska	D7a/99	—
89	Loud, Kamil	6-0/190	6-25-76	2	Cal Poly-SLO	D7b/98	5/0
80	Moulds, Eric	6-0/204	7-17-73	4	Mississippi State	D1/96	16/15
81	Price, Peerless	5-10/180	10-27-76	R	Tennessee	D2/99	—
83	Reed, Andre	6-2/190	1-29-64	15	Kutztown (Pa.) State	D4a/85	15/13
85	Riemersma, Jay (TE)	6-5/254	5-17-73	3	Michigan	D7b/96	16/3
82	Williams, Kevin	5-9/195	1-25-71	7	Miami (Fla.)	FA/98	16/0
	OFFENSIVE LINEMEN						
76	Albright, Ethan	6-5/283	5-1-71	6	North Carolina	FA/96	16/0
79	Brown, Ruben (G)	6-3/304	2-13-72	6	Pittsburgh	D1/95	13/13
63	Conaty, Billy	6-2/306	3-8-73	2	Virginia Tech	FA/97	15/1
70	Fina, John (T)	6-4/285	3-11-69	8	Arizona	D1/92	14/14
77	Hicks, Robert (T)	6-7/338	11-17-74	2	Mississippi State	D3/98	9/2
74	Nails, Jamie (T)	6-6/354	6-3-75	3	Florida A&M	D4/97	15/3
60	Ostroski, Jerry (G)	6-4/310	7-12-70	6	Tulsa	FA/93	16/16
72	Panos, Joe (G)	6-2/293	1-24-71	6	Wisconsin	FA/98	16/16
69	Spriggs, Marcus (T)	6-3/295	5-17-74	3	Houston	D6/97	1/0
61	Zeigler, Dusty (C)	6-5/298	9-27-73	4	Notre Dame	D6b/96	16/16
	DEFENSIVE LINEMEN						
94	Fisher, Bryce (T)	6-2/251	5-12-77	R	Air Force	D7b/99	—
90	Hansen, Phil (E)	6-5/278	5-20-68	9	North Dakota State	D2/91	15/15
98	Moran, Sean (E)	6-3/275	6-5-73	4	Colorado State	D4/96	10/2
91	Price, Shawn (E)	6-5/285	3-28-70	7	Pacific	FA/96	14/2
78	Smith, Bruce (E)	6-4/273	6-18-63	15	Virginia Tech	D1a/85	15/15
92	Washington, Ted (NT)	6-4/325	4-13-68	9	Louisville	FA/95	16/16
75	Wiley, Marcellus (E)	6-5/271	11-30-74	3	Columbia	D2/97	16/3
93	Williams, Pat (T)	6-3/270	10-24-72	2	Texas A&M	FA/97	14/0
	LINEBACKERS						
96	Brandenburg, Dan	6-2/255	2-16-73	3	Indiana State	D7a/96	16/1
56	Cowart, Sam	6-2/239	2-26-75	2	Florida State	D2/98	16/11
51	Cummings, Joe	6-2/242	6-8-74	3	Wyoming	FA/98	9/2
55	Foreman, Jay	6-1/232	2-18-76	R	Nebraska	D5/99	—
52	Holecek, John	6-2/242	5-7-72	2	Illinois	D5/95	13/13
53	Newman, Keith	6-2/243	1-19-77	R	North Carolina	D4a/99	—
99	Northern, Gabe	6-2/240	6-8-74	4	Louisiana State	D2/96	16/16
58	Perry, Marlo	6-4/250	8-25-72	5	Jackson State	D3a/94	16/1
59	Rogers, Sam	6-3/245	5-30-70	6	Colorado	D2c/94	15/15
	DEFENSIVE BACKS						
25	Greer, Donovan	5-9/178	9-11-74	2	Texas A&M	FA/98	11/2
41	Hatcher, Armon (S)	6-0/212	7-15-76	R	Oregon State	D6/99	—
27	Irvin, Ken (CB)	5-10/186	7-11-72	5	Memphis	D4a/95	16/16
20	Jones, Henry (S)	5-11/197	12-29-67	9	Illinois	D1/91	16/16
21	Martin, Manny (S)	5-11/184	7-31-69	4	Alabama State	FA/96	14/4
22	Porter, Daryl (CB)	5-9/190	1-16-74	3	Boston College	FA/98	2/0
24	Schulz, Kurt (S)	6-1/208	12-12-68	8	Eastern Washington	D7/92	12/12
40	Smedley, Eric	5-11/199	7-23-73	4	Indiana	D7c/96	16/0
28	Smith, Thomas (CB)	5-11/188	12-5-70	7	North Carolina	D1/93	14/14
26	Winfield, Antoine (CB)	5-8/180	6-24-77	R	Ohio State	D1/99	—
	SPECIALISTS						
2	Christie, Steve (K)	6-0/185	11-13-67	10	William & Mary	PlanB/92	16/0
9	Mohr, Chris (P)	6-5/215	5-11-66	10	Alabama	FA/91	16/0

Other free agents invited to camp: WR Tony Akins, WR Reginald Allen, OG Victor Allotey, S Keion Carpenter, DT Zach Carter, QB Mike Cawley, RB Kendall Cleveland, WR Jeremy Daniel, FB Brian Edwards, RB Lennox Gordon, RB Anthony Gray, LB Craig Guest, G Mercedes Hamilton, S Raion Hill, K Jaret Holmes, G Corey Hulsey, P Bill Kushner, G Andy Meyers, T David Mudge, LB Dusty Renfro, TE Jerry Ross, WR Robert Scott, TE Eric Stocz, DT Pene Talamaivo, WR A.C. Tellison.

BUFFALO BILLS

MISCELLANEOUS TEAM DATA

Stadium (capacity, surface):
Ralph Wilson Stadium (75,339, artificial)
Business address:
One Bills Drive
Orchard Park, N.Y. 14127
Business phone:
716-648-1800
Ticket information:
716-649-0015
Team colors:
Royal blue, scarlet and white
Flagship radio station:
WGRF, 96.9 FM; WEDG 103.3 FM
Training site:
Fredonia State University
Fredonia, N.Y.
716-648-1800

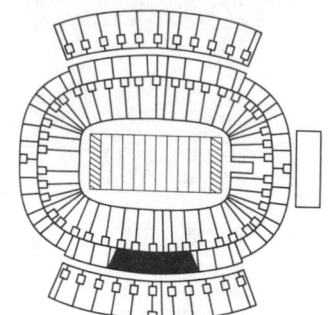

TSN REPORT CARD

Coaching staff	B +	Wade Phillips overcame an 0-3 start, turned a 6-10 team into a 10-6 team, and gained the respect of his players. Offensive coordinator Joe Pendry and defensive coordinator Ted Cottrell both showed the ability to adapt in midstream and utilize talent in the most advantageous way.
Quarterbacks	A -	Doug Flutie was one of the NFL's best stories in 1998, and he deserved all the accolades. There's no reason to think he can't excel again, but if he doesn't, talented Rob Johnson—the man who should be the Bills' quarterback of the future—is more than ready to step in.
Running backs	B +	This is a deep position and it's a good thing, because for all of Flutie's greatness the Bills still prefer to run the ball frequently. Antowain Smith could be very good, Thurman Thomas is still productive in spots and Sam Gash is one of the best blocking fullbacks in the league.
Receivers	A	If Eric Moulds can continue to progress, he could become a superstar. Andre Reed still starts and still makes plays, Peerless Price could prove to be one of the steals of the draft and tight end Jay Riemersma is an improvement over the departed Lonnie Johnson.
Offensive line	C +	They're not as physical and overpowering as they should be, but this is a hard-working group that has shown vast improvement since the start of the 1998 season. Having Flutie at quarterback will certainly help keep their sacks allowed total down.
Defensive line	B +	Bruce Smith continues to be a terror, but he has slowed down just a bit and teams can afford to occasionally single-block him. That provides the opposition with more manpower to block Ted Washington and Phil Hansen. If Smith stays at the top of his game, Hansen overcomes his knee surgery and Washington gets in shape, this can be a dominating unit.
Linebackers	B -	The inside positions are solid with John Holecek and Sam Cowart, two players who have a nose for the football. On the outside, Sam Rogers is an adequate but unspectacular player, while Gabe Northern needs to raise his level of play or he'll lose his starting job, possibly to rookie Keith Newman.
Secondary	B -	If rookie Antoine Winfield can contribute immediately, he will upgrade this area significantly because he'll be a presence in the dime defense. Strong safety Henry Jones and cornerback Thomas Smith are two very respected players, but the team needs them to make more big plays in the form of fumbles or interceptions.
Special teams	B -	Kevin Williams provided a calming effect on the punt- and kickoff-return teams because he was reliable, but he didn't have the impact that was expected in terms of long returns. The coverage teams should continue to improve and Steve Christie remains consistently good, but punter Chris Mohr has to bounce back from an off-season.

SEATTLE SEAHAWKS (9–7)

Passing

	Att	Cmp	Cmp%	Yds	Avg/a	TD	TD%	Int	Int%	Lg	Rate
Kitna	495	270	54.5	3346	6.76	23	4.6	16	3.2	51	77.7
Seahawks	525	288	54.9	3629	6.91	25	4.8	16	3.0	51	79.8
Opp.	582	320	55.0	3744	6.43	19	3.3	30	5.2	76t	64.1

Receivers

	No	Yds	Avg	Lg	TD
Mayes	62	829	13.4	43t	10
Dawkins	58	992	17.1	45t	7
Watters	40	387	9.7	25	2
Fauria	35	376	10.7	25	0
R. Brown	34	228	6.7	26	1
Pritchard	26	375	14.4	52	2
Galloway	22	335	15.2	48	1
Seahawks	288	3629	12.6	51	25
Opp.	320	3744	11.7	76t	19

Rushers

	Att	Yds	Avg	Lg	TD
Watters	325	1210	3.7	45	5
Green	26	120	4.6	21	0
Kitna	35	56	1.6	10	0
R. Brown	14	38	2.7	-9	0
Seahawks	408	1408	3.5	45	5
Opp.	484	1934	4.0	71	9

Interceptions

	No	Yds	Avg	Lg	TD
Springs	5	77	15.4	42	0
W. Williams	5	43	8.6	40t	1
D. Williams	4	41	10.3	21	0
Bellamy	4	4	1.0	7	0
Seahawks	30	336	11.2	42	2
Opp.	16	210	13.1	43	0

TDs

	TD	Run	Rec	Ret	Pts
Mayes	10	0	10	0	60
Watters	7	5	2	0	42
Dawkins	7	0	7	0	42
Pritchard	2	0	2	0	12
Bownes	1	0	1	0	6
Mili	1	0	1	0	6
Galloway	1	0	1	0	6
R. Brown	1	0	1	0	6
Seahawks	34	5	25	4	338
Opp.	30	9	19	2	298

Punt returns

	No	Fc	Yds	Avg	Lg	TD
C. Rogers	22	18	318	14.5	94t	1
Seahawks	30	24	419	14.0	94t	1
Opp.	36	18	370	10.3	81t	1

Kicking

	Ep-a	Fg-a	Lg	Pts
Peterson	32/32	34/40	51	134
Seahawks	32/34	34/40	51	134
Opp.	26/29	30/38	51	116

Kickoff returns

	No	Yds	Avg	Lg	TD
Green	36	818	22.7	54	0
C. Rogers	18	465	25.8	49	0
Seahawks	68	1547	22.8	61	0
Opp.	81	1500	18.5	39	0

Sacks — Daniels 9, Kennedy 6½, C. Brown 5½, Hanks 3, King 2, La-Bounty 2, Parker 2, Adams 1, Smith 1. **Seahawks** 38 for 252 yards, **Opp.** 38 for 232 yards.

Punters

	No	Yds	Lg	Avg	TB	Blk	No/r	R/yds	In 20	N/A
Feagles	84	3425	59	40.8	5	0	36	370	34	35.2
Opp.	81	3398	60	42.0	1	0	41	419	23	34.3

Fumbles — Kitna 14, Watters 4, C. Rogers 3, Green 2, Bloedorn 1, R. Brown 1, Dawkins 1, Fauria 1, Foley 1, May 1, Mayes 1, Mili 1. **Seahawks** 31, **Opp.** 17; **DEF. RECOVERIES** — Kitna 6-0 TD, Bellamy 1-0, Gray 1-0, Green 1-0, Jones 1-0, Walker 1-0, **Seahawks** 11-0. **Opp.** 10-0; **DEF. RECOVERIES** — Adams 1-0 TD, C. Brown 1-0, Joseph 1-0, Sinclair 1-0, Springs 1, D. Williams 1-0, **Seahawks** 6-0.

TENNESSEE TITANS (13–3)

Passing

	Att	Cmp	Cmp%	Yds	Avg/a	TD	TD%	Int	Int%	Lg	Rate
McNair	331	187	56.5	2179	6.58	12	3.6	8	2.4	65t	78.6
O'Donnell	195	116	59.5	1382	7.09	10	5.1	5	2.6	54t	87.6
Titans	527	304	57.7	3622	6.87	23	4.4	13	2.5	65t	83.1
Opp.	557	312	56.0	4000	7.18	26	4.7	16	2.9	78t	82.3

Receivers

	No	Yds	Avg	Lg	TD
Wycheck	69	641	9.3	35	2
Dyson	54	658	12.2	47t	4
E. George	47	458	9.7	54t	4
Thigpen	38	648	17.1	35	4
Harris	26	297	11.4	62t	1
Sanders	20	336	16.8	48t	1
Titans	304	3622	11.9	65t	23
Opp.	312	4000	12.8	78t	26

Rushers

	Att	Yds	Avg	Lg	TD
E. George	320	1304	4.1	40	9
McNair	72	337	4.7	38	8
Thomas	43	164	3.8	22	1
Titans	458	1811	4.0	40	19
Opp.	383	1550	4.0	72	8

Interceptions

	No	Yds	Avg	Lg	TD
Rolle	4	65	16.3	30	0
Sidney	3	12	4.0	7	0
Holmes	2	17	8.5	19	0
Titans	16	257	16.1	43	1
Opp.	13	227	17.5	47t	2

TDs

	TD	Run	Rec	Ret	Pts
E. George	13	9	4	0	78
McNair	8	8	0	0	48
Thigpen	4	0	4	0	24
Dyson	4	0	4	0	24
Hoan	3	0	3	0	18
Neal	3	1	2	0	18
Byrd	3	1	2	0	18
Wycheck	2	0	2	0	12
Titans	46	19	23	4	392
Opp.	39	8	26	5	324

Punt returns

	No	Fc	Yds	Avg	Lg	TD
Mason	26	15	225	8.7	65t	1
Titans	40	17	358	9.0	65t	1
Opp.	45	22	335	7.4	32	0

Kicking

	Ep-a	Fg-a	Lg	Pts
Del Greco	43/43	21/25	50	106
Titans	44/46	21/25	50	106
Opp.	37/39	15/22	50	78

Kickoff returns

	No	Yds	Avg	Lg	TD
Mason	41	805	19.6	41	0
Titans	61	1042	18.6	41	0
Opp.	76	1596	21.0	99t	0

Sacks — Kearse 4½, Robinson 6, Ford 5½, Thornton 4½, Fisk 4, Holmes 4, Bowden 3½, Evans 3½, Bishop 2½, Jones 1, Frederick ½, Jackson ½, Robertson ½, Wortham ½. **Titans** 54 for 305 yards, **Opp.** 26 for 143 yards.

Punters

	No	Yds	Lg	Avg	TB	Blk	No/r	R/yds	In 20	N/A
Hentrich	90	3824	78	42.5	3	0	45	335	35	38.1
Opp.	80	3435	72	42.9	5	2	40	358	25	37.2

Fumbles — E. George 5, O'Donnell 5, McNair 3, Byrd 1, Long 1, Rolle 1, Thigpen 1, **Titans** 17, **Opp.** 39; **OFF. RECOVERIES** — O'Donnell 3-0, E. George 1-0, Jackson 1-0, McNair 1-0, Olson 1-0, **Titans** 8-0, **Opp.** 14-0; **DEF. RECOVERIES** — Bowden 3-0 TD, Robinson 3-0, Wortham 3-0, Bishop 2-0, Evans 2-0, Ford 2-0, Favors 1-0, Hentrich 1-0, Jackson 1-0, Jones 1-0, Kearse 1-1, Killens 1-0, Mitchell 1-0, Rolle 1-0, Walker 1-0, Robertson 0-0, **Titans** 24-2. **Opp.** 9-1.

stats compiled by Elias Sports Bureau)

Att/Comp Own	Att/Comp Opp	Intercept Own	Intercept Opp	Fumbles lost	Penalty yards	Time of poss.
546-270	599-328	20	21	24-11	125-1010	29:24
513-290	506-269	16	12	17-11	97-789	32:12
548-300	522-312	18	17	34-14	126-1027	29:59
492-271	523-331	15	8	29-16	92-714	23:38
554-319	471-273	13	16	33-10	114-872	31:06
546-338	561-328	17	10	25-11	81-683	30:45
535-320	521-291	11	19	18-7	90-755	31:57
502-295	578-317	15	25	22-9	126-982	30:20
589-329	484-256	21	23	23-13	111-936	31:34
540-305	520-293	21	16	27-12	95-812	28:49
476-272	574-319	16	24	22-6	87-771	30:45
520-306	539-302	14	20	22-15	98-825	32:06
535-301	463-245	18	14	19-7	119-945	31:28
583-332	549-315	24	15	29-11	104-823	30:00
525-288	582-320	16	30	31-17	98-883	27:48
527-304	557-312	13	16	17-9	114-1069	31:30

RANKINGS

	Offense			Defense		
	Total	Rush	Pass	Total	Rush	Pass
Baltimore	13	10	13	2	1	5
Buffalo	4	5	10	1	3	1
Cincinnati	8	4	12	15	9	16
Cleveland	16	16	16	16	16	8
Denver	7	8	7	5	12	7
Indianapolis	1	1	1	11	11	12
Jacksonville	3	1	4	3	4	2
Kansas City	5	3	11	10	7	10
Miami	10	12	5	4	6	4
New England	9	13	2	6	13	6
N.Y. Jets	14	7	15	13	10	14
Oakland	2	2	3	8	8	9
Pittsburgh	11	6	14	7	15	3
San Diego	15	15	9	9	2	13
Seattle	12	14	8	14	14	11
Tennessee	6	9	6	12	6	15

CAROLINA PANTHERS
NFC WESTERN DIVISION

1999 SEASON

CLUB DIRECTORY

Owner & founder
Jerry Richardson
President of Carolina Panthers
Mark Richardson
Director of football administration
Marty Hurney
Director of player personnel
Jack Bushofsky
President of Carolinas Stadium Corp.
Jon Richardson
Chief financial officer
Dave Olsen
General counsel
Richard Thigpen
Dir. of marketing & sponsorships
Charles Waddell
Director of ticket sales
Phil Youtsey
Director of communications
Charlie Dayton
Director of player relations
Donnie Shell
Director of facilities
Tom Fellows
Pro scout
Hal Hunter
Mark Koncz
Area scouts
Hal Athon
Joe Bushofsky
Jason Licht
Jeff Morrow
Tony Softli
Head groundskeeper
Billy Ball
Equipment manager
Jackie Miles
Video director
Mark Hobbs

Head coach
George Seifert

Assistant coaches
Don Breaux (tight ends)
Jacob Burney (defensive line)
Chick Harris (running backs)
Gil Haskell (offensive coordinator)
John Marshall (def. coordinator)
Sam Mills (linebackers)
Bill Musgrave (quarterbacks)
Scott O'Brien (special teams)
Alvin Reynolds (def. qual. control)
Greg Roman (off. quality control)
Darrin Simmons (asst. strength
& conditioning/special teams
quality control)
Jerry Simmons (strength &
conditioning)
Bob Valesente (defensive backs)
Richard Williamson (wide
receivers)
Tony Wise (offensive line)

Head trainer
John Kasik
Assistant trainers
Dan Ruiz
Al Shuford
Orthopedist
Dr. Don D'Alessandro

SCHEDULE

Sept. 12—	at New Orleans	12:00
Sept. 19—	JACKSONVILLE	1:00
Sept. 26—	CINCINNATI	1:00
Oct. 3—	at Washington	4:05
Oct. 10—	Open date	
Oct. 17—	at San Francisco	1:15
Oct. 24—	DETROIT	1:00
Oct. 31—	at Atlanta	1:00
Nov. 7—	PHILADELPHIA	1:00
Nov. 14—	at St. Louis	12:00
Nov. 21—	at Cleveland	1:00
Nov. 28—	ATLANTA	8:20
Dec. 5—	ST. LOUIS	1:00
Dec. 12—	at Green Bay	12:00
Dec. 18—	SAN FRAN. (Sat.)	4:15
Dec. 26—	at Pittsburgh	1:00
Jan. 2—	NEW ORLEANS	1:00

All times are for home team.
All games Sunday unless noted.

DRAFT CHOICES

Chris Terry, T, Georgia (second
round/34th pick overall).
Mike Rucker, DE, Nebraska (2/38).
Hannibal Navies, LB, Colorado (4/100).
Robert Daniel, DE, Northwestern (La.)
State (6/175).
Tony Booth, DB, James Madison (7/211).

1998 REVIEW

RESULTS

Sept. 6—ATLANTA	L	14-19
Sept.13—at New Orleans	L	14-19
Sept.20—Open date		
Sept.27—GREEN BAY	L	30-37
Oct. 4—at Atlanta	L	23-51
Oct. 11—at Dallas	L	20-27
Oct. 18—at Tampa Bay	L	13-16
Oct. 25—BUFFALO	L	14-30
Nov. 1—NEW ORLEANS	W	31-17
Nov. 8—at San Francisco	L	23-25
Nov. 15—MIAMI	L	9-13
Nov. 22—at St. Louis	W	24-20
Nov. 29—at N.Y. Jets	L	21-48
Dec. 6—SAN FRANCISCO (OT)	L	28-31
Dec. 13—WASHINGTON	L	25-28
Dec. 20—ST. LOUIS	W	20-13
Dec. 27—at Indianapolis	W	27-19

RECORDS/RANKINGS

1998 regular-season record: 4-12 (4th in
NFC West); 3-5 in division; 3-9 in conference; 2-6 at home; 2-6 on road.
Team record last five years: 30-34
(.469).
1998 team rankings:

	No.	NFC	NFL
Total offense	*298.8	9	20
Rushing offense	*91.1	13	28
Passing offense	*207.6	8	14
Scoring offense	336	6	12
Total defense	*365.1	15	30
Rushing defense	*133.3	13	26
Passing defense	*231.8	13	28
Scoring defense	413	14	27
Takeaways	33	T4	T7
Giveaways	35	14	27
Turnover differential	-2	8	T17
Sacks	37	T11	T21
Sacks allowed	54	12	26

*Yards per game.

TEAM LEADERS

Scoring (kicking): John Kasay, 92 pts.
(35/37 PATs, 19/26 FGs).
Scoring (touchdowns): Raghib Ismail, 48
pts. (8 receiving).
Passing: Steve Beuerlein, 2,613 yds.
(343 att., 216 comp., 63.0%, 17 TDs, 12
int.).
Rushing: Fred Lane, 717 yds. (205 att.,
3.5 avg., 5 TDs).
Receptions: Raghib Ismail, 69 (1,024
yds., 14.8 avg., 8 TDs).
Interceptions: Eric Davis, 5 (81 yds., 2
TDs).
Sacks: Kevin Greene, 15.0.
Punting: Ken Walter, 40.7 avg. (77
punts, 3,131 yds., 0 blocked).
Punt returns: Winslow Oliver, 10.5 avg.
(44 att., 464 yds., 0 TDs).
Kickoff returns: Michael Bates, 25.1 avg.
(59 att., 1,480 yds., 1 TD).

CAROLINA PANTHERS

No.	QUARTERBACKS	Ht./Wt.	Born	NFL Exp.	College	How acq.	'98 Games GP/GS
7	Beuerlein, Steve	6-3/220	3-7-65	13	Notre Dame	UFA/96	12/12
12	Bono, Steve	6-4/212	5-11-62	15	UCLA	UFA/99	*6/2
	Lewis, Jeff	6-2/211	4-17-73	4	Northern Arizona	T-Den./99	0/0
	RUNNING BACKS						
21	Biakabutuka, Tshimanga	6-0/215	1-24-74	4	Michigan	D1/96	11/3
34	Dulaney, Mike (FB)	6-0/245	9-9-70	4	North Carolina	FA/98	8/0
40	Floyd, William (FB)	6-1/242	2-17-72	6	Florida State	UFA/98	16/13
44	Hetherington, Chris (FB)	6-3/249	11-27-72	4	Yale	FA/99	*14/1
23	Johnson, Anthony	6-0/225	10-25-67	10	Notre Dame	W-Chi./95	16/2
32	Lane, Fred	5-10/205	9-6-75	3	Lane (Tenn.)	FA/97	14/11
20	Oliver, Winslow	5-7/180	3-3-73	4	New Mexico	D3a/96	16/0
	RECEIVERS						
82	Bates, Michael	5-10/189	12-19-69	7	Arizona	FA/96	14/0
84	Broughton, Luther (TE)	6-2/248	11-30-74	3	Furman	FA/97	16/4
89	Carruth, Rae	5-11/195	1-20-74	3	Colorado	D1/97	2/1
81	Hayes, Donald	6-4/208	7-13-75	2	Wisconsin	D4/98	8/0
83	Jeffers, Patrick	6-3/218	2-2-73	4	Virginia	FA/99	*8/1
86	Kinchen, Brian (TE)	6-2/240	8-6-65	12	Louisiana State	UFA/99	*16/5
80	Kinchen, Todd	5-11/187	1-7-69	8	Louisiana State	UFA/99	*11/0
86	Mangum, Kris (TE)	6-4/249	8-15-73	2	Mississippi	D7/97	6/0
87	Muhammad, Muhsin	6-2/217	5-5-73	4	Michigan State	D2/98	16/16
19	Uwaezuoke, Iheanyi	6-2/198	7-24-73	4	California	FA/99	*11/0
85	Walls, Wesley (TE)	6-5/250	2-26-66	11	Mississippi	UFA/96	14/14
	OFFENSIVE LINEMEN						
79	Bohlinger, Rob	6-9/310	6-14-75	2	Wyoming	FA/98	13/1
66	Campbell, Matt (G)	6-4/300	7-14-72	5	South Carolina	FA/95	10/10
76	Davidds-Garrido, Norberto (T)	6-5/315	10-4-72	4	Southern California	D4a/96	16/16
65	Garcia, Frank (C)	6-2/302	1-28-72	5	Washington	D4/95	14/14
74	Janus, Paul	6-4/294	3-17-75	1	Northwestern	FA/98	5/1
75	Jones, Clarence (T)	6-6/300	5-6-68	9	Maryland	UFA/99	*14/14
64	Lacina, Corbin (G)	6-4/308	11-2-70	6	Augustana (S.D.)	FA/98	10/10
61	Redmon, Anthony (G)	6-5/308	4-9-71	6	Auburn	FA/98	10/4
67	Stoltenberg, Bryan (C)	6-1/300	8-25-72	4	Colorado	FA/98	14/10
70	Terry, Chris (T)	6-5/295	8-8-75	R	Georgia	D2a/99	—
	DEFENSIVE LINEMEN						
72	Daniel, Robert (E)	6-6/275	10-19-75	R	Northwestern State	D6/99	—
96	Edwards, Antonio (E)	6-3/271	3-10-70	7	Valdosta (Ga.) State	UFA/99	*15/0
94	Gilbert, Sean (E)	6-5/318	4-10-70	7	Pittsburgh	FA/98	16/16
90	Morabito, Tim (NT)	6-3/296	10-12-73	4	Boston College	W-Cin./97	8/8
97	Peter, Jason (E)	6-4/295	9-13-74	2	Nebraska	D1/98	14/11
93	Rucker, Mike (E)	6-5/258	2-28-75	R	Nebraska	D2b/99	—
71	Terry, Rick (E)	6-4/300	4-5-74	3	North Carolina	W-NYJ/98	7/3
	LINEBACKERS						
56	Barrow, Micheal	6-2/236	4-19-70	7	Miami, Fla	UFA/97	16/16
57	Conley, Steven	6-5/240	1-18-72	3	Arkansas	FA/99	*3/1
91	Greene, Kevin	6-3/247	7-31-62	15	Auburn	FA/98	15/15
53	Jensen, Jerry	6-0/235	2-26-75	2	Washington	D5/98	10/0
52	Jones, Donta	6-2/235	8-27-72	5	Nebraska	UFA/99	*16/4
59	Jones, Ernest	6-2/255	4-1-71	6	Oregon	W-NO/98	8/0
58	Navies, Hannibal	6-2/240	7-19-77	R	Colorado	D4/99	—
54	Reid, Spencer	6-1/247	2-8-76	2	Brigham Young	FA/98	16/0
50	Tatum, Kinnon	6-0/222	7-19-75	3	Notre Dame	D3/97	15/0
55	Tovar, Steve	6-3/244	4-25-70	7	Ohio State	UFA/99	*16/2
95	Wells, Dean	6-3/248	7-20-70	7	Kentucky	UFA/99	*9/8
	DEFENSIVE BACKS						
46	Alexander, Brent (S)	5-11/196	7-10-71	6	Tennessee State	UFA/98	16/16
31	Booth, Tony	6-1/195	8-3-75	R	James Madison	D7/99	—
25	Davis, Eric (CB)	5-11/185	1-26-68	10	Jacksonville (Ala.) State	FA/96	16/16
33	Evans, Doug (CB)	6-1/190	5-13-70	7	Louisiana Tech	UFA/98	9/7
29	Lofton, Steve (CB)	5-9/177	11-26-68	8	Texas A&M	W-NE/98	16/7
30	Minter, Mike (S)	5-10/188	1-15-74	3	Nebraska	D2/97	6/4
28	Mullen, Roderick	6-1/204	12-5-72	5	Grambling State	UFA/99	
39	Richardson, Damien (S)	6-1/210	4-3-76	2	Arizona State	D6/98	14/7
38	Scurlock, Mike (S)	5-10/200	2-26-72	5	Arizona	UFA/99	*16/0
35	Sutter, Ryan (S)	6-1/203	9-14-74	R	Colorado	D5/98	1/0
37	Wheeler, Leonard (CB)	6-0/196	1-15-69	8	Troy (Ala.) State	FA/98	16/0

No.	SPECIALISTS	Ht./Wt.	Born	NFL Exp.	College	How acq.	'98 Games GP/GS
4	Kasay, John (K)	5-10/198	10-27-69	9	Georgia	UFA/95	16/0
13	Walter, Ken (P)	6-1/195	8-15-72	3	Kent	FA/97	16/0
11	Wilmsmeyer, Klaus (P)	6-2/205	12-4-67	7	Louisville	FA/99	*16/0

*Not with Panthers in 1998.

Other free agents invited to camp: T Dan Best, DE Vernon Broughton, WR John Burden, LB Horace Cook Jr., QB Dameyune Craig, K Paul Cramer, DT Harry Deligianis, LB Chike Egbuniwe, DT Eric England, T Jeffrey Flowe, WR Daryl Heidelburg, G Michael Lies, S LaMar Lyons, QB Matt Lytte, LB Sam Manuel, DL Mitch Marrow, C Jamar Nesbit, DL Andre Slappey, FB Matt Snider, CB Michael Swift, WR Jim Turner, DL Chuck Wiley, G/T Jamie Wilson.

Abbreviations: D1—draft pick, first round; SupD2—supplemental draft pick, second round; WV—claimed on waivers; TR—obtained in trade; PlanB—Plan B free-agent acquisition; FA—free-agent acquisition (other than Plan B); ED—expansion draft pick.

MISCELLANEOUS TEAM DATA

Stadium (capacity, surface):
Ericsson Stadium
(73,248, grass)
Business address:
800 S. Mint St.
Charlotte, NC 28202-1502
Business phone:
704-358-7000
Ticket information:
704-358-7800
Team colors:
Blue, black and silver
Flagship radio station:
WBT-1110 AM
Training site:
Wofford College
Spartanburg, S.C.
704-358-7000

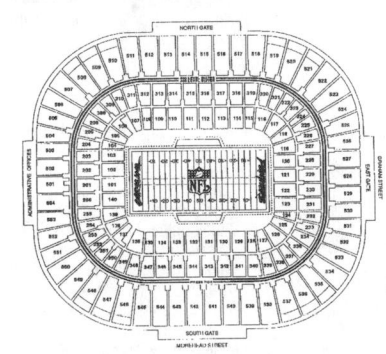

TSN REPORT CARD

Coaching staff	B	Not only was it wise to replace Dom Capers with a high-profile guy like George Seifert, but Seifert was then able to attract an all-star staff of assistants to town. John Marshall is a proven defensive coordinator, and additions like Tony Wise (offensive line), Jacob Burney (defensive line) and Bob Valesente (defensive secondary) will help.
Quarterbacks	C	It seems only a matter of time until Jeff Lewis supplants Steve Beuerlein as the starter, unless Lewis just isn't good enough. Beuerlein gets high marks for leadership but is limited in what he can do physically; at 34 he is what he is: an average NFL quarterback. Lewis' potential is intriguing.
Running backs	C -	Tshimanga Biakabutuka enters the season as the featured back after showing late last season that he might finally be reaching the potential once projected for him. But he and his backup, Fred Lane, haven't yet proven they can consistently make a difference in a game.
Receivers	C	This could emerge as a surprisingly strong group if Rae Carruth and Muhsin Muhammad stay healthy, and if Patrick Jeffers has a breakthrough year as the No. 3 receiver. That's a lot of ifs. It also could be a disaster if one or more of the above gets hurt.
Offensive line	D	Based on what transpired last year, it seems more could have been done in the offseason to address this problem area. Blake Brockermeyer was lost via free agency, so-so tackle Clarence Jones was signed and Chris Terry, who played offensive line only two years in college, was made the team's top draft pick. It may not be enough.
Defensive line	C -	For Sean Gilbert and Jason Peter, who moaned about the virtues of the 4-3 over the 3-4 they were forced to play in a year ago, it's time to produce or admit they just aren't nearly as good as originally advertised. Quality depth remains a problem at both tackle and end.
Linebackers	C	Micheal Barrow has developed into one of the game's better playmakers, but Kevin Greene is too old (37) to effectively man the outside linebacker position in the new defense. The rest of the linebackers are basically a mish-mash of talent that was cast aside elsewhere for various reasons.
Secondary	B	This is a solid group led by cornerbacks Eric Davis and Doug Evans, who are out to prove they can play better than last year. The safeties can hit and there might even be depth both there and at corner, which was lacking last season.
Special teams	B	Led once again by kick returner Michael Bates and kicker John Kasay, this unit should be decent. Scott O'Brien replaced Brad Seely as special teams coach, with the goal of improving the punting and all kick-coverage components.

CHICAGO BEARS
NFC CENTRAL DIVISION

1999 SEASON

CLUB DIRECTORY

Chairman emeritus
Edward W. McCaskey
Chairman of the board
Michael B. McCaskey
President/chief executive officer
Ted Phillips
Vice president
Timothy E. McCaskey
Secretary
Virginia H. McCaskey
Director/administration
Bill McGrane
Dir./marketing and communications
Ken Valdiserri
Mgr. of promotions and special events
John Bostrom
Manager of sales
Jack Trompeter
Director/public relations
Bryan Harlan
Assistant directors/public relations
Scott Hagel
Phil Handler
Ticket manager
George McCaskey
Vice president, player personnel
Mark Hatley
Director/pro scouting
Rick Spielman
Pro scout
George Paton
Director/college scouting
Bill Rees
Regional scouts
Marty Barrett   Phil Emery
Shemy Schembechler   Jeff Shiver
John Paul Young
Head trainer
Tim Bream
Assistant trainer
Eric Sugerman
Physical development coordinator
Russ Riederer

Head coach
Dick Jauron

Assistant coaches
Keith Armstrong (special teams)
Vance Bedford (defensive backs)
Greg Blache (defensive coord.)
Jim Bollman (tight ends)
Mike Borich (wide receivers)
Chuck Bullough (quality control assistant, defense)
Gary Crowton (offensive coord.)
Dale Lindsey (linebackers)
Steve Little (assistant strength & conditioning)
Earle Mosley (running backs)
Rex Norris (defensive line)
Russ Riederer (strength & cond.)
John Shoop (quarterbacks)
Eric Studesville (quality control assistant, offense)
Bob Wylie (offensive line)

Asst. physical development coordinator
Steve Little
Equipment manager
Tony Medlin
Assistant equipment manager
Carl Piekarski
Director of video services
Dean Pope
Assistant video director
Dave Hendrickson

SCHEDULE

Sept. 12—	KANSAS CITY	12:00
Sept. 19—	SEATTLE	12:00
Sept. 26—	at Oakland	1:15
Oct. 3—	NEW ORLEANS	12:00
Oct. 10—	at Minnesota	12:00
Oct. 17—	PHILADELPHIA	12:00
Oct. 24—	at Tampa Bay	1:00
Oct. 31—	at Washington	1:00
Nov. 7—	at Green Bay	12:00
Nov. 14—	MINNESOTA	12:00
Nov. 21—	at San Diego	1:15
Nov. 25—	at Detroit (Thanks.)	12:40
Dec. 5—	GREEN BAY	12:00
Dec. 12—	Open date	
Dec. 19—	DETROIT	12:00
Dec. 26—	at St. Louis	12:00
Jan. 2—	TAMPA BAY	12:00

All times are for home team.
All games Sunday unless noted.

DRAFT CHOICES

Cade McNown, QB, UCLA (first round/12th pick overall).
Russell Davis, DT, North Carolina (2/48).
Rex Turner, G, Texas A&M (3/66).
D'Wayne Bates, WR, Northwestern (3/71).
Marty Booker, WR, NE Louisiana (3/78).
Warrick Holdman, LB, Tex. A&M (4/106).
Rosevelt Colvin, DE, Purdue (4/111).
Jerry Wisne, G, Notre Dame (5/143).
Khari Samuel, LB, Mass. (5/144).
Jerry Azumah, RB, N. Hampshire (5/147).
Rashard Cook, DB, S. California (6/184).
Sulecio Sanford, WR, Middle Tennessee State (7/221).
Jim Finn, RB, Pennsylvania (7/253).

1998 REVIEW

RESULTS

Sept. 6—JACKSONVILLE	L	23-24
Sept.13—at Pittsburgh	L	12-17
Sept.20—at Tampa Bay	L	15-27
Sept.27—MINNESOTA	L	28-31
Oct. 4—DETROIT	W	31-27
Oct. 11—at Arizona	L	7-20
Oct. 18—DALLAS	W	13-12
Oct. 25—at Tennessee	W	23-20
Nov. 1—Open date		
Nov. 8—ST. LOUIS	L	12-20
Nov. 15—at Detroit	L	3-26
Nov. 22—at Atlanta	L	13-20
Nov. 29—TAMPA BAY	L	17-31
Dec. 6—at Minnesota	L	22-48
Dec. 13—at Green Bay	L	20-26
Dec. 20—BALTIMORE	W	24-3
Dec. 27—GREEN BAY	L	13-16

RECORDS/RANKINGS

1998 regular-season record: 4-12 (5th in NFC Central); 1-7 in division; 2-10 in conference; 3-5 at home; 1-7 on road.
Team record last five years: 33-47 (.413, ranks T19th in league in that span).

1998 team rankings:

	No.	NFC	NFL
Total offense	*297.9	10	21
Rushing offense	*107.1	9	17
Passing offense	*190.8	12	23
Scoring offense	276	14	25
Total defense	*318.9	6	14
Rushing defense	*117.2	8	19
Passing defense	*201.8	8	15
Scoring defense	368	10	23
Takeaways	28	7	17
Giveaways	34	T12	T24
Turnover differential	-6	11	22
Sacks	28	15	T29
Sacks allowed	31	4	8

*Yards per game.

TEAM LEADERS

Scoring (kicking): Jeff Jaeger, 90 pts. (27/28 PATs, 21/26 FGs).
Scoring (touchdowns): Bobby Engram, 30 pts. (5 receiving).
Passing: Erik Kramer, 1,823 yds. (250 att., 151 comp., 60.4%, 9 TDs, 7 int.).
Rushing: Edgar Bennett, 611 yds. (173 att., 3.5 avg., 2 TDs).
Receptions: Bobby Engram, 64 (987 yds., 15.4 avg., 5 TDs).
Interceptions: Walt Harris, 4 (41 yds., 1 TD).
Sacks: Jim Flanigan, 8.5.
Punting: Mike Horan, 41.3 avg. (64 punts, 2,643 yds., 0 blocked).
Punt returns: Glyn Milburn, 11.6 avg. (25 att., 291 yds., 1 TD).
Kickoff returns: Glyn Milburn, 25.0 avg. (62 att., 1,550 yds., 2 TDs).

CHICAGO BEARS

No.	QUARTERBACKS	Ht./Wt.	Born	NFL Exp.	College	How acq.	'98 Games GP/GS
12	Kramer, Erik	6-1/204	11-6-64	10	North Carolina State	FA/94	8/8
8	McNown, Cade	6-1/213	1-12-77	R	UCLA	D1/99	—
4	Moreno, Moses	6-1/205	9-5-75	2	Colorado State	D7b/98	2/1
	RUNNING BACKS						
20	Allen, James	5-10/215	3-28-75	2	Oklahoma	FA/97	6/2
32	Bennett, Edgar	6-0/218	2-15-69	8	Florida State	UFA/98	16/13
38	Chancey, Robert (FB)	6-0/250	9-7-72	3	None.	FA/98	16/1
44	Enis, Curtis	6-0/242	6-15-76	2	Penn State	D1/98	9/1
39	Finn, Jim	5-10/238	12-9-76	R	Pennsylvania	D7b/99	—
49	Hallock, Ty (FB)	6-2/256	4-30-71	7	Michigan State	UFA/98	16/12
24	Milburn, Glyn	5-8/174	2-19-71	7	Stanford	T-GB/98	16/0
	RECEIVERS						
84	Allred, John (TE)	6-4/249	9-9-74	2	Southern California	D2/97	3/0
19	Bates, D'Wayne	6-2/215	12-4-75	R	Northwestern	D3b/99	—
14	Booker, Marty	5-11/218	7-31-76	R	Northeastern Louisiana	D3c/99	—
82	Bownes, Fabien	5-11/190	2-29-72	3	Western Illinois	FA/95	16/0
80	Conway, Curtis	6-0/194	3-13-71	7	Southern California	D1/93	15/15
81	Engram, Bobby	5-10/192	1-7-73	4	Penn State	D2/96	16/16
85	Mayes, Alonzo (TE)	6-4/259	6-4-75	2	Oklahoma State	D4/98	16/16
86	Penn, Chris	6-0/198	4-20-71	6	Tulsa	T-KC/97	14/1
88	Robinson, Marcus	6-3/215	2-27-75	2	South Carolina	D4b/97	3/0
17	Sanford, Sulecio	5-10/190	3-23-76	R	Middle Tennessee	D7a/99	—
89	Wetnight, Ryan (TE)	6-2/236	11-5-70	7	Stanford	FA/93	15/3
	OFFENSIVE LINEMEN						
78	Brockermeyer, Blake (T)	6-4/305	4-11-73	5	Texas	UFA/99	*14/14
74	Herndon, Jimmy (T)	6-8/318	8-30-73	4	Houston	T-Jax./97	9/2
67	Huntington, Greg (G)	6-3/308	9-22-70	7	Penn State	FA/97	3/0
57	Kreutz, Olin (C)	6-2/300	6-9-77	2	Washington	D3/98	9/0
65	Mannelly, Patrick (T)	6-5/285	4-18-75	2	Duke	D6b/98	16/0
75	Perry, Todd (G)	6-5/308	11-28-70	7	Kentucky	D4a/93	16/16
63	Tucker, Rex	6-5/285	12-20-76	R	Texas A&M	D3a/99	—
58	Villarrial, Chris (C)	6-4/310	6-9-73	4	Indiana (Pa.)	D5/96	16/16
60	Wiegmann, Casey (C)	6-3/295	7-20-73	4	Iowa	FA/97	16/16
71	Williams, James (T)	6-7/340	3-29-68	9	Cheyney State (Pa.)	FA/91	16/16
68	Wisne, Jerry (G)	6-6/306	7-28-76	R	Notre Dame	D5a/99	—
	DEFENSIVE LINEMEN						
68	Colvin, Rosevelt (E)	6-3/252	9-5-77	R	Purdue	D4b/99	—
79	Davis, Russell	6-4/300	3-28-75	R	North Carolina	D2/99	—
90	Duff, Jamal (E)	6-7/285	3-11-72	5	San Diego State	UFA/99	*13/3
99	Flanigan, Jim (T)	6-2/288	8-27-71	6	Notre Dame	D3/94	16/16
93	Grasmanis, Paul (T)	6-2/298	8-2-74	4	Notre Dame	D4/96	15/0
98	Robinson, Bryan	6-4/283	6-22-74	3	Fresno State	W-StL/98	10/5
96	Simmons, Clyde (E)	6-5/287	8-4-64	14	Western Carolina	UFA/99	*16/16
97	Wells, Mike (T)	6-3/310	1-6-71	7	Iowa	UFA/98	16/16
	LINEBACKERS						
94	Burns, Keith	6-2/245	5-16-72	6	Oklahoma State	UFA/99	*16/0
52	Collins, Andre	6-1/240	5-4-68	10	Penn State	UFA/98	16/2
91	Draft, Chris	5-11/222	2-26-76	1	Stanford	D6/98	1/0
53	Hall, Lemanski	6-0/235	11-24-70	5	Alabama	T-Ten./98	15/0
55	Harris, Sean	6-3/248	2-25-72	5	Arizona	D3/95	16/14
65	Holdman, Warrick	6-1/233	11-22-75	R	Texas A&M	D4a/99	—
54	McDonald, Ricardo	6-2/248	11-8-69	8	Pittsburgh	UFA/98	15/14
92	Minter, Barry	6-2/242	1-28-70	7	Tulsa	T-Dal/93	16/16
62	Samuel, Khari	6-2/242	10-14-76	R	Massachusetts	D5b/99	—
59	Schwantz, Jim	6-2/240	1-23-70	6	Purdue	FA/98	16/0
	DEFENSIVE BACKS						
36	Austin, Ray (S)	5-11/198	12-21-74	3	Tennessee	W-NYJ/98	12/0
46	Azumah, Jerry	5-10/195	9-1-77	R	New Hampshire	D5c/99	—
30	Bell, Ricky (CB)	5-10/194	10-2-74	3	North Carolina State	FA/97	14/0
25	Carter, Tom (CB)	6-0/189	9-5-72	7	Notre Dame	FA/97	4/4
35	Cook, Rashard (S)	5-11/197	4-18-77	R	Southern California	D6/99	—
21	Cousin, Terry (CB)	5-9/182	4-11-75	3	South Carolina	FA/97	16/12
27	Harris, Walt (CB)	5-11/195	8-10-74	4	Mississippi State	D1/96	14/14
47	Hudson, Chris (S)	5-10/199	10-6-71	5	Colorado	UFA/99	*13/13
37	Parrish, Tony (S)	5-10/205	11-23-75	2	Washington	D2/98	16/16
29	Smith, Frankie (CB)	5-9/182	10-8-68	7	Baylor	UFA/98	15/0

No.	SPECIALISTS	Ht./Wt.	Born	NFL Exp.	College	How acq.	'98 Games GP/GS
1	Jaeger, Jeff (K)	5-11/190	11-26-64	13	Washington	FA/96	16/0
16	Sauerbrun, Todd (P)	5-10/209	1-4-73	5	West Virginia	D2/95	3/0

*Not with Bears in 1998.

Other free agents invited to camp: FB Tremayne Allen, S Curtis Anderson, DE Dunstan Anderson, DT Ken Anderson, LB Shawn Banks, WR Macey Brooks, DB Jim Cantelupe, TE Marlon Chambers, DB Quincy Coleman, P Chris Dolan, CB Nick Ferguson, G Michael Early, DT Joe Fleming, G Adam Hernandez, HB Love Jefferson, QB Shane Matthews, QB Jim Miller, R Derrell Mitchell, CB Heron O'Neal, T Chad Overhauser, G Dan Palmer, DT Emile Palmer, TE Derrick Spiller, RB Aaron Stecker, G Aaron Taylor, RB Damon Washington, DB Greg Williams.

Abbreviations: D1—draft pick, first round; SupD2—supplemental draft pick, second round; WV—claimed on waivers; TR—obtained in trade; PlanB—Plan B free-agent acquisition; FA—free-agent acquisition (other than Plan B); ED—expansion draft pick.

MISCELLANEOUS TEAM DATA

Stadium (capacity, surface):
Soldier Field (66,944, grass)
Business address:
Halas Hall at Conway Park
1000 Football Drive
Lake Forest, IL 60045
Business phone:
847-295-6600
Ticket information:
847-615-2327
Team colors:
Navy blue, orange and white
Flagship radio station:
WMAQ, 670 AM
Training site:
University of Wisconsin-Platteville
Platteville, Wis.
608-342-1201

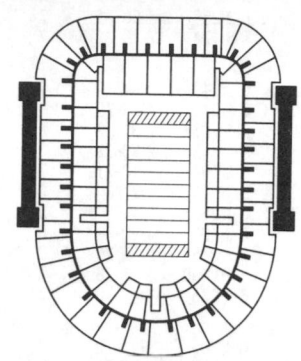

TSN REPORT CARD

Coaching staff	B	This is difficult to assess until games are played, but the mood change has been positive with Dick Jauron and his assistants. Offensive coordinator Gary Crowton's attack mode has players excited, while Jauron and defensive coordinator Greg Blache have earned high praise.
Quarterbacks	C +	Whether Erik Kramer can stay healthy for a whole season is key. He rarely has. Cade McNown may be the future but he's still a rookie until he wins the job and shows he can do the job. Both quarterbacks are untested in the new schemes, but someone must take control of a team that has lacked a clear leader.
Running backs	C -	Curtis Enis showed promise but not always consistency as a rookie last season, and he's coming off a torn ACL. How he holds up is a key to the offense. Depth is adequate but no better than that unless James Allen proves to be a breakaway change-of-pace back.
Receivers	C -	Curtis Conway is an above-average receiver when he has some continuity at quarterback. He can be a centerpiece of the offense with his deep speed. Bobby Engram is a solid threat at No. 2 but there is little after that. Chris Penn is the No. 3 for now, but the Bears drafted two receivers in the third round.
Offensive line	C +	The offense sorely needs more dominant play from the tackles and for guards Todd Perry and Chris Villarrial to regain some of the physical pop they had in '96-97. Olin Kreutz is an athletic center but has only one career start, so he has some proving to do.
Defensive line	D +	Tackles Jim Flanigan and Mike Wells are a team strength but end has been a disaster position the last two years. Bryan Robinson could be a force at left end but he needs to take the next step in his development. Russell Davis was drafted in the second round and free-agent signee Jamal Duff has to prove he can stay healthy.
Linebackers	D +	Weakside linebacker Barry Minter is the best of a below-average group. Rico McDonald is adequate but needs to be turned loose to do some quarterback pressuring. Middle linebacker is a big weakness until either Sean Harris or Keith Burns shows the ability to control the middle.
Secondary	B	Corners Tom Carter and Walt Harris have good size and speed but are not good tacklers. They are way overdue for some help from the pass rush. Tony Parrish's move to strong safety upgrades the speed there and Chris Hudson is a solid vet at free.
Special teams	A -	Punter Todd Sauerbrun was off to his best NFL start before suffering a torn ACL, and kicker Jeff Jaeger is one of the best kickers in club history. Glyn Milburn is a threat on any return and the coverage units improved dramatically last year.

CINCINNATI BENGALS
AFC CENTRAL DIVISION

1999 SEASON

CLUB DIRECTORY

President
Michael Brown
Vice president
Pete Brown
Executive vice president
Katherine Blackburn
Vice president
Paul H. Brown
Vice president
John Sawyer
Chairman of the board
Austin E. Knowlton
Administration assistant
Jan Sutton
Director of stadium development
Troy Blackburn
Stadium project manager
Mark Horton
Stadium construction manager
Eric J. Brown
Director of community affairs
Jeff Berding
Business manager
Bill Connelly
Business manager's assistant
Terri Stewart
Chief financial officer
Bill Scanlon
Controller
Johanna Kappner
Receptionist
Teri Moratschek
Dir. of corporate sales and marketing
Vince Cicero
Public relations director
Jack Brennan
Assistant public relations director
Patrick J. Combs
Public relations assistant
Inky Studley
Ticket manager
Paul Kelly
Director of pro/college personnel
Jim Lippincott

Head coach
Bruce Coslet

Assistant coaches
Paul Alexander (offensive line)
Jim Anderson (running backs)
Ken Anderson (offensive coord.)
Louie Cioffi (def. staff assistant)
Mark Duffner (linebackers)
Ray Horton (defensive backs)
Tim Krumrie (defensive line)
Dick LeBeau (assistant head
   coach/defensive coordinator)
Steve Mooshagian(wide rec.)
Al Roberts (special teams)
Frank Verducci (tight ends)
Kim Wood (strength & cond.)

Scouting
Duke Tobin
Equipment manager
Tom Gray
Athletic trainer
Paul Sparling
Assistant athletic trainer
Billy Brooks
Asst. athletic trainer/asst. equip. mgr.
Rob Recker
Video director
Travis Brammer
Assistant video director
Andy Fineberg

SCHEDULE

Sept. 12—	at Tennessee	12:00
Sept. 19—	SAN DIEGO	1:00
Sept. 26—	at Carolina	1:00
Oct. 3—	ST. LOUIS	1:00
Oct. 10—	at Cleveland	1:00
Oct. 17—	PITTSBURGH	1:00
Oct. 24—	at Indianapolis	12:00
Oct. 31—	JACKSONVILLE	1:00
Nov. 7—	at Seattle	1:15
Nov. 14—	TENNESSEE	1:00
Nov. 21—	BALTIMORE	4:05
Nov. 28—	at Pittsburgh	1:00
Dec. 5—	SAN FRANCISCO	1:00
Dec. 12—	CLEVELAND	1:00
Dec. 19—	Open date	
Dec. 26—	at Baltimore	1:00
Jan. 2—	at Jacksonville	1:00

All times are for home team.
All games Sunday unless noted.

DRAFT CHOICES

Akili Smith, QB, Oregon (first round/third
   pick overall).
Charles Fisher, DB, West Virginia (2/33).
Cory Hall, DB, Fresno State (3/65).
Craig Yeast, WR, Kentucky (4/98).
Nick Williams, RB, Miami, Fla. (5/135).
Kelly Gregg, DT, Oklahoma (6/173).
Tony Coats, G, Washington (7/209).
Scott Covington, QB, Miami, Fla. (7/245).
Donald Broomfield, DT, Clemson
   (7/249).

1998 REVIEW

RESULTS

Sept. 6—TENNESSEE	L	14-23
Sept.13—at Detroit (OT)	W	34-28
Sept.20—GREEN BAY	L	6-13
Sept.27—at Baltimore	L	24-31
Oct. 4—Open date		
Oct. 11—PITTSBURGH	W	25-20
Oct. 18—at Tennessee	L	14-44
Oct. 25—at Oakland	L	10-27
Nov. 1—DENVER	L	26-33
Nov. 8—at Jacksonville	L	11-24
Nov. 15—at Minnesota	L	3-24
Nov. 22—BALTIMORE	L	13-20
Nov. 29—JACKSONVILLE	L	17-34
Dec. 6—BUFFALO	L	20-33
Dec. 13—at Indianapolis	L	26-39
Dec. 20—at Pittsburgh	W	25-24
Dec. 27—TAMPA BAY	L	0-35

RECORDS/RANKINGS

1998 regular-season record: 3-13 (5th in
AFC Central); 2-6 in division; 2-10 in conference; 1-7 at home; 2-6 on road.
Team record last five years: 28-52 (.350,
ranks 27th in league in that span).

1998 team rankings:	No.	AFC	NFL
Total offense	*301.5	9	17
Rushing offense	*102.4	9	17
Passing offense	*199.1	9	17
Scoring offense	268	13	27
Total defense	*360.2	14	28
Rushing defense	*163.3	15	30
Passing defense	*196.9	6	12
Scoring defense	452	15	30
Takeaways	20	13	27
Giveaways	22	5	7
Turnover differential	-2	10	T17
Sacks	28	15	T29
Sacks allowed	53	14	T23
*Yards per game.			

TEAM LEADERS

Scoring (kicking): Doug Pelfrey, 78 pts.
(21/21 PATs, 19/27 FGs).
Scoring (touchdowns): Darnay Scott, 42
pts. (7 receiving).
Passing: Neil O'Donnell, 2,216 yds. (343
att., 212 comp., 61.8%, 15 TDs, 4 int.).
Rushing: Corey Dillon, 1,130 yds. (262
att., 4.3 avg., 4 TDs).
Receptions: Carl Pickens, 82 (1,023
yds., 12.5 avg., 5 TDs).
Interceptions: Sam Shade, 3 (33 yds., 0
TDs); Artrell Hawkins, 3 (21 yds., 0 TDs).
Sacks: Reinard Wilson, 6.0.
Punting: Lee Johnson, 44.7 avg. (69
punts, 3,083 yds., 1 blocked).
Punt returns: Damon Gibson, 8.1 avg.
(27 att., 218 yds., 1 TD).
Kickoff returns: Tremain Mack, 25.9 avg.
(45 att., 1,165 yds., 1 TD).

1999 SEASON
TRAINING CAMP ROSTER

No.	QUARTERBACKS	Ht./Wt.	Born	NFL Exp.	College	How acq.	'98 Games GP/GS
8	Blake, Jeff	6-0/210	12-4-70	8	East Carolina	W-NYJ/94	9/2
4	Covington, Scott	6-2/217	1-17-76	R	Miami	D7b/99	—
15	Kresser, Eric	6-2/223	2-6-73	1	Marshall (W.Va.)	FA/97	2/0
11	Smith, Akili	6-3/220	8-21-75	R	Oregon	D1/99	—
	RUNNING BACKS						
32	Carter, Ki-Jana	5-10/222	9-12-73	5	Penn State	D1/95	1/0
28	Dillon, Corey	6-1/225	10-24-75	3	Washington	D2/97	15/15
46	Groce, Clif (FB)	5-11/245	7-30-72	3	Texas A&M	W-NE/98	—
44	Milne, Brian (FB)	6-3/254	1-7-73	4	Penn State	W-Ind./96	14/14
30	Williams, Nick	6-1/267	3-30-77	R	Miami (Fla.)	D5/99	—
	RECEIVERS						
89	Battaglia, Marco (TE)	6-3/252	1-25-73	4	Rutgers	D2/96	16/0
19	Boyd, Tommie	6-0/195	12-21-71	3	Toledo	FA/99	*9/0
88	Bush, Steve (TE)	6-3/258	7-4-74	3	Arizona State	FA/97	12/2
85	Hundon, James	6-1/173	4-9-71	3	Portland State	FA/96	9/3
80	Jackson, Willie	6-1/212	8-16-71	6	Florida	FA/98	8/0
82	McGee, Tony (TE)	6-3/250	4-21-71	7	Michigan	D2/93	16/16
81	Pickens, Carl	6-2/206	3-23-70	8	Tennessee	D2/92	16/16
86	Scott, Darnay	6-1/205	7-7-72	6	San Diego State	D2/94	13/13
87	Williams, Stepfret	6-0/170	6-14-73	4	Northeast Louisiana	W-Dal./98	5/0
84	Yeast, Craig	5-7/160	11-20-76	R	Kentucky	D4/99	—
	OFFENSIVE LINEMEN						
71	Anderson, Willie (T)	6-5/340	7-11-75	4	Auburn	D1/96	16/16
66	Blackman, Ken (G)	6-6/320	11-8-72	4	Illinois	D3/96	8/8
74	Braham, Rich (G)	6-4/305	11-6-70	6	West Virginia	W-Ari./94	12/12
61	Coats, Tony (G)	6-6/305	10-5-75	R	Washington	D7a/99	—
73	DeMarco, Brian (G)	6-7/323	4-9-72	5	Michigan State	UFA/99	*16/9
63	Goff, Mike (G)	6-5/316	1-6-76	2	Iowa	D3b/98	10/5
62	Gutierrez, Brock (G)	6-3/304	9-25-73	3	Central Michigan	FA/98	1/0
60	Jones, Rod (T)	6-4/325	1-11-74	4	Kansas	D7/96	7/2
64	Payne, Rod (C)	6-4/305	6-14-74	3	Michigan	D3/97	5/0
77	Sargent, Kevin (T)	6-6/300	3-31-69	8	Eastern Washington	FA/92	16/16
68	Shaw, Scott (G)	6-3/303	6-2-74	2	Michigan State	FA/98	1/0
59	Truitt, Greg (C)	6-0/235	12-8-65	6	Penn State	FA/94	11/0
	DEFENSIVE LINEMEN						
90	Bankston, Michael (E)	6-5/285	3-12-70	8	Sam Houston State	FA/98	16/16
96	Broomfield, Donald (E)	6-3/295	6-10-76	R	Clemson	D7c/99	—
92	Copeland, John (E)	6-3/280	9-20-70	7	Alabama	D1/93	5/0
99	Gibson, Oliver (T)	6-2/290	3-15-72	5	Notre Dame	UFA/99	*16/0
93	Gregg, Kelly (T)	6-0/285	11-1-76	R	Oklahoma.	D6/99	—
94	Langford, Jevon (E)	6-3/290	2-16-74	4	Oklahoma State	D4/96	14/1
97	Purvis, Andre (E)	6-4/310	7-14-73	3	North Carolina	D5/97	9/0
70	Steele, Glen (E)	6-4/295	10-4-74	2	Michigan	D4/98	10/0
67	von Oelhoffen, Kimo (NT)	6-4/305	1-30-71	6	Boise State	D6/94	16/16
	LINEBACKERS						
98	Curtis, Canute	6-2/256	8-4-74	3	West Virginia	FA/97	5/0
95	Foley, Steve	6-3/260	9-9-75	2	Northeast Louisiana	D3a/98	10/1
50	Francis, James	6-5/257	8-4-68	10	Baylor	D1/90	14/14
91	Granville, Billy	6-3/252	3-11-74	3	Duke	FA/97	16/0
57	Ross, Adrian	6-2/244	2-19-75	2	Colorado State	FA/98	14/1
56	Simmons, Brian	6-3/233	6-21-75	2	North Carolina	D1b/98	14/12
51	Spikes, Takeo	6-2/230	12-17-76	2	Auburn	D1a/98	16/16
52	Sprotte, Jimmy	6-3/235	10-2-74	2	Arizona	FA/98	5/0
53	Tumulty, Tom	6-3/247	2-11-73	4	Pittsburgh	D6/96	4/4
55	Wilson, Reinard	6-2/261	12-17-73	3	Florida State	D1/97	16/15
	DEFENSIVE BACKS						
40	Bell, Myron (S)	5-11/203	9-15-71	6	Michigan State	UFA/98	16/2
37	Blackmon, Roosevelt (CB)	6-1/185	9-10-74	2	Morris Brown College (Ga.)	W-GB/98	15/0
25	Fisher, Charles (CB)	6-0/186	2-2-76	R	West Virginia	D2/99	—
26	Hall, Cory (S)	6-0/205	12-5-76	R	Fresno State	D3/99	—
27	Hawkins, Artrell (CB)	5-10/190	11-24-75	2	Cincinnati	D2/98	16/16
34	Mack, Tremain (S)	6-0/193	11-21-74	3	Miami (Fla.)	D4/97	12/0
24	Mathias, Ric (CB)	5-10/180	12-10-75	2	Wisconsin-LaCrosse	FA/98	3/0
29	Moore, Kelvin (S)	6-0/203	3-7-75	1	Morgan State	FA/98	4/0
31	Myers, Greg (S)	6-1/202	9-30-72	4	Colorado State	D5/96	16/16
20	Randolph, Thomas (CB)	5-9/185	10-5-70	6	Kansas State	FA/98	16/1
23	Sawyer, Corey (CB)	5-11/177	10-4-71	6	Florida State	D4/94	3/0

No.	SPECIALISTS	Ht./Wt.	Born	NFL Exp.	College	How acq.	'98 Games GP/GS
6	Costello, Brad (P).........................	6-1/230	12-12-74	1	Boston University	FA/98	3/0
9	Pelfrey, Doug (K)...........................	5-11/185	9-25-70	7	Kentucky	D8/93	16/0

*Not with Bengals in 1998.

Other free agents invited to camp: WR Greg Ainsworth, HB Michael Basnight, FB Anthony Cleary, WR Nikko Cooper, T Mike Doughty, NT Marcus Dow, T Brian Hanley, CB Rodney Heath, WR Quincy Jackson, TE John Jennings, G Greg Krause, WR Terry Murphy, WR Geoff Noisy, CB Marcus Parks, NT Chad Pegues, LB Ben Peterson, K Derek Schorejs, WR Jason Shelley, LB Tim Terry, C Brian Uhl, TE Damian Vaughn, SS Lawrence Wright.

Abbreviations: D1—draft pick, first round; SupD2—supplemental draft pick, second round; WV—claimed on waivers; TR—obtained in trade; PlanB—Plan B free-agent acquisition; FA—free-agent acquisition (other than Plan B); ED—expansion draft pick.

MISCELLANEOUS TEAM DATA

Stadium (capacity, surface):
Cinergy Field
(60,389, artificial)
Business address:
One Bengals Drive
Cincinnati, OH 45204
Business phone:
513-621-3550
Ticket information:
513-621-3550
Team colors:
Black, orange and white
Flagship radio stations:
WBOB 1160 AM; WUBE 105.1 FM
Training site:
Georgetown College
Georgetown, Ky.
502-863-7088

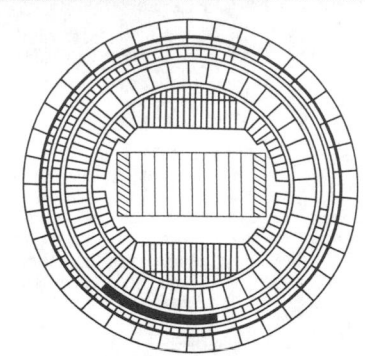

TSN REPORT CARD

Coaching staff — C
Bruce Coslet is a hard worker with a great offensive mind, but doesn't have as much say in shaping the roster as he'd like. Nevertheless, he has plenty of input. The decision two years ago to go with a youth movement made for a turbulent transition. Now's the time to get tough and show signs of a turnaround. Or else.

Quarterbacks — B
Jeff Blake and Akili Smith have the ingredients necessary to excel in the NFL. They're strong-armed and mobile, with terrific leadership skills. Blake has always looked good throwing touchdown passes, but his legacy is that he hasn't won consistently. Smith's goal as quarterback of the future is to change all that.

Running backs — B +
Corey Dillon is a tough power runner who wants to be the league's best. He'll take his "ugly 4 yards"—and anything else is gravy. Complementing him is Ki-Jana Carter, who thrives on speed and quickness. Brandon Bennett, who had been counted on to supply depth at the position, suffered a torn ACL in late May and will be out for the year.

Receivers — B -
The offense isn't designed to focus on one player, but if there's a go-to guy, he's Darnay Scott, who stretches the field with blazing speed. The other starting candidates (Willie Jackson, James Hundon and Stepfret Williams) are decent. The depth and competition will raise everyone's game.

Offensive line — C +
There's some fine individual talent here and some decent depth, but 1998 center and captain Darrick Brilz wasn't invited back. With injuries bound to crop up, chemistry becomes an issue. Run blockers are everywhere, but the quality of pass blocking needs to improve, especially with more rollouts on the agenda.

Defensive line — D
The line was too soft last season, and if it doesn't toughen up, it'll get trampled again. Ends John Copeland and Michael Bankston need to come on strong and Oliver Gibson has to assert himself as a run-stuffer at nose tackle. The switch to a "one-gap" system should help. The simpler the scheme, the better.

Linebackers — A
The 3-4 defense is a linebacker-driven scheme and this position, chock full of first-round picks, is loaded with enough pass-rushing, run-stopping talent to help clean up the line's mess. Steve Foley and Reinard Wilson have a knack for rushing the quarterback, and the inside tandem of Takeo Spikes and Brian Simmons have only scratched the surface of their enormous potential.

Secondary — D
Faced with the possibility of having to start two guys (Artrell Hawkins and Charles Fisher) with a combined total of one year of NFL experience, the Bengals re-signed Corey Sawyer, who missed most of last season with a knee injury. Sawyer isn't great, but he has made a dozen starts over five NFL seasons. Hawkins will start on the right side, with Fisher backing up Sawyer.

Special teams — C
Kicker Doug Pelfrey has been shaky the last two seasons and punter Brad Costello has only three NFL games under his belt. Consistency is the key for both. Kickoff returner Tremain Mack has breathtaking speed, but off-the-field problems make him a question mark. Fourth-round pick Craig Yeast could be the next Jermaine Lewis, but he's only a rookie.

CLEVELAND BROWNS
AFC CENTRAL DIVISION

1999 SEASON

CLUB DIRECTORY

Owner
Al Lerner
President and chief executive officer
Carmen Policy
V.p., director of football operations
Dwight Clark
V.p., chief administrative officer
Kofi Bonner
V.p. of finance and treasurer
Doug Jacobs
V.p., director of communications and public affairs
Alex Martins
V.p., director of stadium operations and security
Lew Merletti
Asst. dir. of football operations and general counsel
Lal Heneghan
Director of player personnel
Joe Collins
Director of college scouting
Phil Neri
Pro personnel coordinator
Keith Kidd
Business manager
Bill Hampton
Executive director of marketing
Bruce Popko
Director of ticket sales
Mike Jennings
Stadium operations manager
Bill Squires
Director, Cleveland Browns Foundation
Judge George White
Director of publicity/media relations
Todd Stewart
Director of publications/Internet
Dan Arthur
Coordinator of publicity/media relations
Ken Mather

Head coach
Chris Palmer

Assistant coaches
Clarence Brooks (defensive line)
Jerry Butler (wide receivers)
Kevin Butler (linebackers)
Billy Davis (def. quality control)
Jerry Holmes (def. backfield)
John Hufnagel (quarterbacks)
Tim Jorgensen (strength)
Mark Michaels (special teams quality control)
Bob Palcic (offensive line)
Ray Perkins (tight ends)
Dick Portee (running backs)
Bob Slowik (def. coordinator)
Aril Smith (assistant strength)
Tony Sparano (offensive quality control)
Ken Whisenhunt (special teams)

Facilities manager
Greg Hipp
Head athletic trainer
Mike Colello
Equipment manager
Bobby Monica
Video director
Pat Dolan
Head groundskeeper
Chris Powell

SCHEDULE

Sept. 12—	PITTSBURGH	8:20
Sept. 19—	at Tennessee	3:15
Sept. 26—	at Baltimore	1:00
Oct. 3—	NEW ENGLAND	1:00
Oct. 10—	CINCINNATI	1:00
Oct. 17—	at Jacksonville	1:00
Oct. 24—	at St. Louis	12:00
Oct. 31—	at New Orleans	12:00
Nov. 7—	BALTIMORE	1:00
Nov. 14—	at Pittsburgh	1:00
Nov. 21—	CAROLINA	1:00
Nov. 28—	TENNESSEE	1:00
Dec. 5—	at San Diego	1:15
Dec. 12—	at Cincinnati	1:00
Dec. 19—	JACKSONVILLE	1:00
Dec. 26—	INDIANAPOLIS	1:00
Jan. 2—	Open date	

All times are for home team.
All games Sunday unless noted.

DRAFT CHOICES

Tim Couch, QB, Kentucky (first round/first pick overall).
Kevin Johnson, WR, Syracuse (2/32).
Rahim Abdullah, LB, Clemson (2/45).
Daylon McCutcheon, DB, Southern California (3/62).
Marquis Smith, DB, California (3/76).
Wali Rainer, LB, Virginia (4/124).
Darrin Chiaverini, WR, Colorado (5/148).
Marcus Spriggs, DT, Troy State (6/174).
Kendall Ogle, LB, Maryland (6/187).
James Dearth, TE, Tarleton State (6/191).
Madre Hill, RB, Arkansas (7/207).

See page 107 for list of Cleveland Browns 1999 Expansion Draft picks.

CLEVELAND BROWNS

No.	QUARTERBACKS	Ht./Wt.	Born	NFL Exp.	College	How acq.	'98 Games GP/GS
2	Couch, Tim	6-4/227	7-31-77	R	Kentucky	D1/99	—
11	Detmer, Ty	6-0/194	10-30-67	8	Brigham Young	T-SF/99	*16/1
	RUNNING BACKS						
27	Blair, Michael	5-11/245	11-26-74	2	Ball State	ED/99(GB)	*13/0
40	Edwards, Marc (FB)	6-0/229	11-17-74	3	Notre Dame	T-SF/99	*16/11
34	Hill, Madre	5-11/199	1-2-76	R	Arkansas	D7/99	—
42	Kirby, Terry	6-1/213	1-20-70	7	Virginia	UFA/99	*9/0
21	McPhail, Jerris	5-11/198	6-26-72	4	East Carolina	ED/99(Det.)	*3/0
20	Moore, Ron	5-10/220	1-26-70	7	Pittsburg (Kan.) State	ED/99(Mia.)	*1/1
25	Shaw, Sedrick	6-0/214	11-16-73	3	Iowa	T-NE/99	*13/1
39	Williams, Pooh Bear (FB)	6-1/286	1-20-75	2	Florida State	ED/99(Buf.)	*2/0
	RECEIVERS						
18	Chiaverini, Darrin	6-1/205	10-12-77	R	Colorado	D5/99	—
81	Gibson, Damon	5-9/184	2-25-75	2	Iowa	ED/99(Cin.)	*16/0
12	Johnson, Kevin	5-10/188	7-15-75	R	Syracuse	D2a/99	—
6	Shepherd, Leslie	5-11/186	11-3-69	6	Temple	UFA/99	*16/16
	OFFENSIVE LINEMEN						
74	Bobo, Orlando (G)	6-3/299	2-9-74	3	Northeast Louisiana	ED/99(Min.)	*4/0
75	Brown, Lomas (T)	6-4/290	3-30-63	15	Florida	UFA/99	*16/16
77	Brown, Orlando (T)	6-7/350	12-20-70	7	South Carolina State	UFA/99	*13/13
70	Buckey, Jeff (T)	6-5/305	8-7-74	4	Stanford	ED/99(Mia.)	*7/0
63	Cavil, Ben (G)	6-2/310	1-31-72	3	Oklahoma	ED/99(Bal.)	*16/6
48	Dearth, James (T)	6-3/269	1-22-76	R	Tarleton State	D6c/99	—
61	Gordon, Steve (C)	6-3/288	4-15-69	2	California	ED/99(SF)	*13/1
71	Pyne, Jim (C)	6-2/297	11-23-71	6	Virginia Tech	ED/99(Det.)	*16/16
79	Rehberg, Scott (T)	6-8/330	11-17-73	3	Central Michigan	ED/99(NE)	*2/0
47	Smith, Ed (T)	6-4/253	6-5-69	1	None.	W-Atl./99	*15/0
82	Smith, Irv (T)	6-3/262	10-13-71	7	Notre Dame	T-SF/99	*16/8
69	Wiggins, Paul (T)	6-3/305	8-17-73	3	Oregon	ED/99(Was.)	*1/0
64	Wohlabaugh, Dave (C)	6-3/292	4-13-72	5	Syracuse	UFA/99	*16/16
	DEFENSIVE LINEMEN						
94	Alexander, Derrick (E)	6-4/286	11-13-73	5	Florida State	UFA/99	*16/16
	Ball, Jerry (T)	6-1/320	12-15-64	13	Southern Methodist	UFA/99	*16/16
92	Barker, Roy (E)	6-5/290	2-24-69	8	North Carolina	T-SF/99	*16/16
66	Holland, Darius (T)	6-5/320	11-10-73	5	Colorado	UFA/99	*16/4
67	Jurkovic, John (T)	6-2/301	8-18-67	9	Eastern Illinois	UFA/99	*16/16
96	Manuel, Rod (E)	6-5/295	10-8-74	3	Oklahoma	ED/99(Pit.)	*2/0
99	McCormack, Hurvin (T)	6-5/275	4-6-72	6	Indiana	ED/99(Dal.)	*16/1
60	Spriggs, Marcus (T)	6-4/314	7-26-76	R	Troy State	D6a/99	—
93	Thompson, Mike (T)	6-4/295	12-22-71	3	Wisconsin	ED/99(Cin.)	*9/0
	LINEBACKERS						
55	Abdullah, Rahim	6-5/233	3-22-76	R	Clemson	D2b/99	—
51	Jones, Lenoy	6-1/235	9-25-74	4	Texas Christian	ED/99(Ten.)	*9/0
57	Kyle, Jason	6-3/242	5-12-72	5	Arizona State	ED/99(Sea.)	*16/0
95	Miller, Jamir	6-5/266	11-19-73	6	UCLA	UFA/99	*16/16
59	Ogle, Kendell	6-0/231	11-25-75	R	Maryland	D6b/99	—
49	Rainer, Wali	6-2/235	4-19-77	R	Virginia	D4/99	—
50	Saleh, Tarek	6-0/240	11-7-74	3	Wisconsin	ED/99(Car.)	*11/1
54	Spielman, Chris	6-0/247	10-11-65	11	Ohio State	T-Buf./99	—
53	Thierry, John	6-4/265	9-4-71	6	Alcorn State	UFA/99	*16/9
90	Williams, James	6-0/246	10-10-68	9	Mississippi State	ED/99(SF)	*15/0
	DEFENSIVE BACKS						
28	Blackwell, Kory	5-11/185	8-3-72	2	Massachusetts	ED/99(NYG)	*5/0
30	Butler, Duane	6-1/203	11-29-73	3	Illinois State	ED/99(Min.)	*14/0
26	Devine, Kevin	5-9/179	12-11-74	3	California	ED/99(Jax.)	*5/0
47	Forbes, Marlon	6-1/215	12-25-71	4	Penn State	ED/99(Chi.)	*16/2
24	Fuller, Corey	5-10/217	5-1-71	5	Florida State	UFA/99	*16/16
31	Jackson, Raymond	5-10/189	2-17-73	4	Colorado State	ED/99(Buf.)	*14/0
38	Langham, Antonio	6-0/184	7-31-72	6	Alabama	ED/99(SF)	*11/6
33	McCutcheon, Daylon (CB)	5-8/180	12-9-76	R	Southern California	D3a/99	—
22	McTyer, Tim	5-11/181	12-14-75	3	Brigham Young	ED/99(Phi.)	*16/1
23	Pope, Marquez	5-11/193	10-29-70	8	Fresno State	UFA/99	*6/3
34	Sanders, Brandon	5-9/185	6-10-73	4	Arizona	ED/99(NYG)	*13/0
21	Smith, Marquis (S)	6-2/213	1-13-75	R	California	D3b/99	—

No.	DEFENSIVE BACKS	Ht./Wt.	Born	NFL Exp.	College	How acq.	'98 Games GP/GS
37	Stokes, Eric	5-11/200	12-18-73	3	Nebraska	ED/99(Sea.)	*4/0
36	Williams, Gerome	6-2/210	7-9-73	3	Houston	ED/99(SD)	*16/0
	SPECIALISTS						
17	Gardocki, Chris (P)......................	6-1/200	2-7-70	9	Clemson	UFA/99	*16/0

*Not with Browns in 1998.

Other free agents invited to camp: DB Tim Beauchamp, WR Corey Bridges, G Jim Bundren, T Mark Campbell, T Ryan Collins, T Kris Comstock, QB Mike Cook, K Phil Dawson, DT Bill Duff, QB John Dutton, WR Sylvain Girard, P Chris Hanson, WR Corey Hill, K Danny Kight, DT Ryan Kuehl, TE Aaron Laing, WR Curtis Marsh, DT Chris Maumalanga, CB Central McClellion, LB David Menard, DE Arnold Miller, WR Joseph Natasi, WR Ronnie Powell, FB Dawud Rasheed, DT Albert Reese, DE Tyrone Rogers, WR Jermaine Ross, LB Jerry Rudzinski, WR Mark Seay, T Pete Swanson, DB Hurley Tarver, LB Ryan Taylor, RB Malcolm Thomas.

Abbreviations: D1—draft pick, first round; SupD2—supplemental draft pick, second round; WV—claimed on waivers; TR—obtained in trade; PlanB—Plan B free-agent acquisition; FA—free-agent acquisition (other than Plan B); ED—expansion draft pick.

MISCELLANEOUS TEAM DATA

Stadium (capacity, surface):
Cleveland Browns Stadium
(72,000, grass)
Business address:
76 Lou Groza Boulevard
Berea, Ohio 44017
Business phone:
440-891-5000
Ticket information:
440-891-5000
Team colors:
Brown, orange and white
Flagship radio stations:
WMJI, 105.7 FM
Training site:
76 Lou Groza Boulevard
Berea, Ohio
440-891-5000

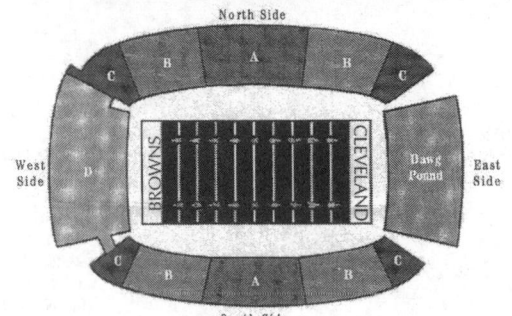

TSN REPORT CARD

Coaching staff	C	Chris Palmer was a good hire, but he's still a rookie NFL head coach who must grow and learn with an expansion team. His decision to double as offensive coordinator makes the situation even tougher. Overall, Palmer's staff is an interesting mix of college-type teachers and former players with little NFL coaching experience.
Quarterbacks	C	Ty Detmer is a career backup. Tim Couch is a 21-year-old rookie who is learning an NFL playbook that is more than 300 pages and three inches thick. Don't expect a whole lot this season as the tough, but under-sized, Detmer battles to hold off the young, but overwhelmed, franchise quarterback. If the offensive line meshes, Couch could win the job early. Eventually, Couch and Detmer will make an outstanding duo.
Running backs	C	Feature back Terry Kirby is one of the league's best pass receivers out of the backfield, but he's 29 and has never carried the ball more than 134 times in a season. Backup Sedrick Shaw is big and fast, but he's also a guy the running back-starved Patriots gave up on. Rookie Madre Hill could surprise people if he stays healthy. Unfortunately, he's had both knees reconstructed since 1996. Fullback Marc Edwards was one of the team's better acquisitions, coming from San Francisco for a fourth-round draft pick. There is little depth behind him, though.
Receivers	C -	Leslie Shepherd is a cocky 29-year-old who is focused on a contract year. Rookie Kevin Johnson is one of the fastest players in the league. Overall, it's not a deeply talented or proven group.
Offensive line	B	Left tackle Lomas Brown and right tackle Orlando Brown give the Browns one of the best tackle combos in the league. Lomas is 36, but he shows no signs of not being able to fulfill his three-year contract. Orlando brings 350 pounds of violence to the team's running game.
Defensive line	C	Roy Barker and Derrick Alexander are two of the better ends in the league. They combined for 19.5 sacks last year and their careers are still on the upswing. The starting tackles are John Jurkovic and Jerry Ball, two over-30 veterans who aren't in the best shape.
Linebackers	D	Any unit with Chris Spielman in the middle is bound to produce. But for now, this is the team's biggest question mark. The weakside spot is up for grabs among expansion draftees Lenoy Jones and Elijah Alexander. The strongside is occupied by John Thierry, who is trying to prove himself after five disappointing seasons as an end in Chicago.
Secondary	D	The Browns lack a proven cover corner that can shut down the league's top receivers one-on-one. Rookie Daylon McCutcheon could become that player, but at 5-8 he'll have trouble handling big receivers. Left cornerback Corey Fuller is a team leader and a strength at his position. Right cornerback Antonio Langham is coming off a horrible season and could lose his job to McCutcheon if he has a slow start..
Special teams	C -	The Browns have several quality athletes who can handle the non-skilled roles on special teams. However, the one glaring weakness is the lack of an experienced placekicker. Phil Dawson, a second-year pro who spent all of last season on New England's practice squad, has the early lead. The team is strong at punter with Chris Gardocki. Johnson was one of the nation's best kick returners last season at Syracuse. He might return punts as well, but that job could be handled by second-year pro Damon Gibson.

DALLAS COWBOYS
NFC EASTERN DIVISION

1999 SEASON

CLUB DIRECTORY

President/general manager
Jerry Jones
Vice presidents
Charlotte Anderson
George Hays
Jerry Jones Jr.
Stephen Jones
Treasurer
Robert Nunez
Director of public relations
Rich Dalrymple
Assistant director of public relations
Brett Daniels
Ticket manager
Carol Padgett
Director of college and pro scouting
Larry Lacewell
Scouts
Tom Ciskowski
Jim Garrett
Tommy Hart
Jim Hess
Walter Juliff
Henry Sroka
Walt Yowarsky
Head trainer
Jim Maurer
Assistant trainers
Britt Brown
Bob Haas
Physicians
Robert Vandermeer
J.R. Zamorano
Equipment/practice fields manager
Mike McCord

Head coach
Chan Gailey

Assistant coaches
Joe Avezzano (special teams)
Bill Bates (special teams/
defensive assistant)
Jim Bates (asst. head coach/
defensive line)
Dave Campo (def. coordinator)
George Edwards (linebackers)
Buddy Geis (quarterbacks)
Steve Hoffman (kickers/quality
control)
Hudson Houck (offensive line)
Jim Jeffcoat (asst. defensive line)
Joe Juraszek (strength & cond.)
Les Miles (tight ends)
Dwain Painter (wide receivers)
Clancy Pendergrast (defensive
assistant/quality control)
Tommie Robinson (off. assistant)
Clarence Shelmon (running backs)
Mike Zimmer (defensive backs)

Video director
Robert Blackwell
Director of operations
Bruce Mays

SCHEDULE

Sept. 12—	at Washington	1:00
Sept. 20—	ATLANTA (Mon.)	8:00
Sept. 26—	Open date	
Oct. 3—	ARIZONA	12:00
Oct. 10—	at Philadelphia	1:00
Oct. 18—	at N.Y. Giants (Mon.)	9:00
Oct. 24—	WASHINGTON	12:00
Oct. 31—	at Indianapolis	1:00
Nov. 8—	at Minnesota (Mon.)	8:00
Nov. 14—	GREEN BAY	3:15
Nov. 21—	at Arizona	2:15
Nov. 25—	MIAMI (Thanks.)	3:15
Dec. 5—	at New England	8:20
Dec. 12—	PHILADELPHIA	12:00
Dec. 19—	N.Y. JETS	3:15
Dec. 24—	at New Orleans (Fri.)	2:05
Jan. 2—	N.Y. GIANTS	3:05

All times are for home team.
All games Sunday unless noted.

DRAFT CHOICES

Ebenezer Ekuban, DE, North Carolina
(first round/20th pick overall).
Solomon Page, T, West Virginia (2/55).
Dat Nguyen, LB, Texas A&M (3/85).
Wane McGarity, WR, Texas (4/118).
Peppi Zellner, DE, Fort Valley State
(4/132).
Mar Tay Jenkins, WR, Nebraska-Omaha
(6/193).
Mike Lucky, TE, Arizona (7/229).
Kelvin Garmon, G, Baylor (7/243).

1998 REVIEW

RESULTS

Sept. 6—ARIZONA	W	38-10
Sept.13—at Denver	L	23-42
Sept.21—at N.Y. Giants	W	31-7
Sept.27—OAKLAND	L	12-13
Oct. 4—at Washington	W	31-10
Oct. 11—CAROLINA	W	27-20
Oct. 18—at Chicago	L	12-13
Oct. 25—Open date		
Nov. 2—at Philadelphia	W	34-0
Nov. 8—N.Y. GIANTS	W	16-6
Nov. 15—at Arizona	W	35-28
Nov. 22—SEATTLE	W	30-22
Nov. 26—MINNESOTA	L	36-46
Dec. 6—at New Orleans	L	3-22
Dec. 13—at Kansas City	L	17-20
Dec. 20—PHILADELPHIA	W	13-9
Dec. 27—WASHINGTON	W	23-7
Jan. 2—ARIZONA*	L	7-20

*NFC wild-card game.

RECORDS/RANKINGS

1998 regular-season record: 10-6 (1st in
NFC East); 8-0 in division; 9-3 in conference; 6-2 at home; 4-4 on road.
Team record last five years: 50-30 (.625,
ranks 7th in league in that span).

1998 team rankings:	No.	NFC	NFL
Total offense	*340.6	5	8
Rushing offense	*125.9	4	8
Passing offense	*214.8	5	9
Scoring offense	381	5	9
Total defense	*322.8	9	18
Rushing defense	*101.2	6	12
Passing defense	*221.6	12	22
Scoring defense	275	1	3
Takeaways	26	T8	T19
Giveaways	15	1	1
Turnover differential	11	3	T3
Sacks	34	13	25
Sacks allowed	19	1	1

*Yards per game.

TEAM LEADERS

Scoring (kicking): Richie Cunningham,
127 pts. (40/40 PATs, 29/35 FGs).
Scoring (touchdowns): Emmitt Smith, 90
pts. (13 rushing, 2 receiving).
Passing: Troy Aikman, 2,330 yds. (315
att., 187 comp., 59.4%, 12 TDs, 5 int.).
Rushing: Emmitt Smith, 1,332 yds. (319
att., 4.2 avg., 13 TDs).
Receptions: Michael Irvin, 74 (1,057
yds., 14.3 avg., 1 TD).
Interceptions: Deion Sanders, 5 (153
yds., 1 TD).
Sacks: Kavika Pittman, 6.0.
Punting: Toby Gowin, 43.4 avg. (77
punts, 3,342 yds., 1 blocked).
Punt returns: Deion Sanders, 15.6 avg.
(24 att., 375 yds., 2 TDs).
Kickoff returns: Kevin Mathis, 24.8 avg.
(25 att., 621 yds., 0 TDs).

TRAINING CAMP ROSTER

DALLAS COWBOYS

No.	QUARTERBACKS	Ht./Wt.	Born	NFL Exp.	College	How acq.	'98 Games GP/GS
8	Aikman, Troy	6-4/226	11-21-66	11	UCLA	D1/89	11/11
17	Garrett, Jason	6-2/195	3-28-66	7	Princeton	FA/93	8/5
11	Quinn, Mike	6-4/217	4-15-74	3	Stephen F. Austin	W-Ind./98	3/0
	RUNNING BACKS						
48	Johnston, Daryl (FB)	6-2/242	2-10-66	11	Syracuse	D2/89	16/13
22	Smith, Emmitt	5-9/214	5-15-69	10	Florida	D1/90	16/16
45	Sualua, Nicky (FB)	5-11/260	4-15-75	3	Ohio State	D4c/97	16/0
42	Warren, Chris	6-2/236	1-24-68	9	Ferrum (Va.)	FA/98	9/0
	RECEIVERS						
86	Bjornson, Eric (TE)	6-4/236	12-15-71	6	Washington	D4a/95	16/4
83	Clay, Hayward (TE)	6-3/260	7-5-73	3	Texas	W-Chi./98	3/2
88	Irvin, Michael	6-2/207	3-5-66	12	Miami (Fla.)	D1/88	16/15
81	Ismail, Rocket	5-11/176	11-18-69	7	Notre Dame	UFA/99	*16/15
16	Jenkins, Mar Tay	5-11/203	2-28-75	R	Nebraska-Omaha	D6/99	—
89	LaFleur, David	6-7/272	1-29-74	3	Louisiana State	D1/97	13/13
84	Lucky, Mike (TE)	6-6/273	11-23-75	R	Arizona	D7a/99	—
18	McGarity, Wane	5-8/191	9-30-76	R	Texas	D4a/99	—
80	Mills, Ernie	5-11/196	10-28-68	9	Florida	FA/98	11/1
82	Ogden, Jeff	6-0/190	2-2-75	2	Eastern Washington	FA/98	16/0
	OFFENSIVE LINEMEN						
76	Adams, Flozell (G)	6-7/335	5-10-75	2	Michigan State	D2/98	16/12
73	Allen, Larry (G)	6-3/326	11-27-71	6	Sonoma State (Calif.)	D2/94	16/16
68	Garmon, Kelvin (G)	6-2/329	10-26-76	R	Baylor	D7b/99	—
66	Hutson, Tony (G)	6-3/306	3-13-74	3	Northeastern Oklahoma State	FA/97	9/1
63	Kiselak, Mike (C)	6-3/295	3-9-67	2	Maryland	FA/98	16/7
67	McIver, Everett (G)	6-5/330	8-5-70	5	Elizabeth (N.C.) City State	FA/98	6/6
77	Page, Solomon (T)	6-4/306	2-27-76	R	West Virginia	D2/99	—
71	Ross, Oliver (T)	6-4/300	9-27-74	2	Iowa State	D5b/98	2/0
50	Shiver, Clay (C)	6-2/283	12-7-72	4	Florida State	D3a/96	13/9
53	Stepnoski, Mark (C)	6-2/265	1-20-67	11	Pittsburgh	UFA/99	*13/13
79	Williams, Erik (T)	6-6/328	9-7-68	9	Central State (Ohio)	D3c/91	15/15
	DEFENSIVE LINEMEN						
96	Ekuban, Ebenezer (E)	6-3/281	5-29-76	R	North Carolina	D1/99	—
98	Ellis, Greg (E)	6-6/286	8-14-75	2	North Carolina	D1/98	16/16
95	Hennings, Chad (T)	6-6/291	10-20-65	8	Air Force	D11/88	16/16
78	Lett, Leon (T)	6-6/290	10-12-68	9	Emporia (Kan.) State	D7/91	16/15
94	Myers, Michael	6-2/275	1-20-76	2	Alabama	D4/98	16/1
97	Pittman, Kavika (E)	6-6/267	10-9-74	4	McNeese State	D2a/96	15/15
93	Zellner, Peppi (E)	6-5/251	3-14-75	R	Fort Valley State	D4b/99	—
	LINEBACKERS						
52	Coakley, Dexter	5-10/228	10-20-72	3	Appalachian State	D3a/97	16/16
55	Coryatt, Quentin	6-3/250	8-1-70	7	Texas A&M	FA/99	—
56	Godfrey, Randall	6-2/245	4-6-73	4	Georgia	D2b/96	16/16
54	Hambrick, Darren	6-2/227	8-30-75	2	South Carolina	D5a/98	14/0
58	Hemsley, Nate	6-0/228	5-15-74	2	Syracuse	FA/97	3/0
90	Nguyen, Dat	5-11/231	9-25-76	R	Texas A&M	D3/99	—
57	Smith, Myron	6-1/225	3-28-75	1	Louisiana Tech	FA/98	1/0
59	Thomas, Robert	6-1/260	12-1-74	2	Henderson State	FA/98	16/0
	DEFENSIVE BACKS						
29	Billups, Terry (CB)	5-9/179	2-9-75	1	North Carolina	FA/98	1/0
23	Mathis, Kevin (CB)	5-9/179	4-9-74	3	East Texas State	FA/97	13/4
27	Mobley, Singor (S)	5-11/195	10-12-72	3	Washington State	FA/97	16/0
43	Reese, Izell (S)	6-2/196	5-7-74	2	Alabama-Birmingham	D6/98	16/0
21	Sanders, Deion (CB)	6-1/195	8-9-67	11	Florida State	FA/95	11/11
26	Smith, Kevin (CB)	5-11/190	4-7-70	8	Texas A&M	D1a/92	14/14
24	Stoutmire, Omar (S)	5-11/201	7-9-74	3	Fresno State	D7/97	16/12
31	Teague, George (S)	6-1/206	2-18-71	7	Alabama	FA/98	16/5
30	Wheaton, Kenny (S)	5-10/195	3-8-75	3	Oregon	D3c/97	15/1
25	Williams, Charlie	6-0/207	2-2-72	5	Bowling Green State	D3/95	15/3
28	Woodson, Darren (S)	6-1/219	4-25-69	8	Arizona State	D2b/92	16/15
	SPECIALISTS						
3	Cunningham, Richie (K)	5-10/167	8-18-70	3	Southwestern Louisiana	FA/97	16/0
4	Gowin, Toby (P)	5-10/167	3-30-75	3	North Texas	FA/97	16/0

*Not with Cowboys in 1998.

Other free agents invited to camp: DT Darren Benson, C/G Chris Brymer, G Freddie Childress, DT Nathan Davis, C Dennis Fortney, S Billy Gustin, CB Duane Hawthorne, WR Zebbie Lethbridge, RB Dennis Manns, CB LaDouphyous McCalla, FB David McCann, DE Chance

McCarty, RB Beau Morgan, TE Ryan Neufeld, DT Robert Newkirk, DT Brandon Noble, DB Zac Painter, S Grant Pearsall, LB Joe Phillips, WR Billy Powell, RB Alan Ricard, G/C Earl Scott, DE Sam Simmons, RB Tarik Smith, LB Brandon Tolbert, WR Jason Tucker, FB Brian Waters, DT Greg Wilkins, OL Brad Winn.

Abbreviations: D1—draft pick, first round; SupD2—supplemental draft pick, second round; WV—claimed on waivers; TR—obtained in trade; PlanB—Plan B free-agent acquisition; FA—free-agent acquisition (other than Plan B); ED—expansion draft pick.

MISCELLANEOUS TEAM DATA

Stadium (capacity, surface):
Texas Stadium
(65,675, artificial)
Business address:
One Cowboys Parkway
Irving, TX 75063
Business phone:
972-556-9900
Ticket information:
972-579-5000
Team colors:
Blue, metallic silver blue and white
Flagship radio station:
KVIL, 103.7 FM
Training site:
Midwestern State University
Wichita Falls, Tex.
214-556-9900

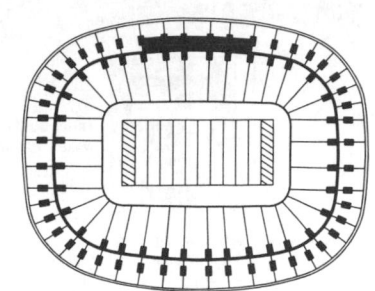

TSN REPORT CARD

Coaching staff	B	Chan Gailey showed a nice touch handling the team in his first season, as well as finding a way to repair a struggling offense while doubling as the coordinator. Defensive coordinator Dave Campo has become a master at disguising weaknesses. No telling how good he might be if all the pieces are in place.
Quarterbacks	A -	Having a Troy Aikman on board is a huge plus, and he showed midway through last season he still has what it takes to get a team to the Super Bowl. And Gailey's gamble with Jason Garrett as the backup nearly worked to perfection: Garrett went 3-2 in his five starts, losing two 13-12 games.
Running backs	B	This is a pretty solid group. The 1-2 punch of Emmitt Smith and Chris Warren can produce at a winning level, and the addition of Tarik Smith and possibly Beau Morgan adds versatility. And while Daryl Johnston might not be overpowering anymore, his experience is invaluable.
Receivers	B	The effectiveness of Rocket Ismail will determine how productive Michael Irvin and Ernie Mills will be. Irvin still has it, but he needs help. Ismail's speed must be that help. If not, this could be a long season for a group that struggled without a healthy Mills and Deion Sanders the final month last year.
Offensive line	B +	This could become one of the team's real strengths after a two-year struggle. Mark Stepnoski's return to Dallas automatically makes the line better, and if the move of Flozell Adams to left tackle (thus kicking Larry Allen to guard), works, and Everett McIver successfully returns from knee surgery, watch out for the running game.
Defensive line	C	One of the team's great unknowns, much caused by the excessive amount of inexperience and the offseason uncertainly of defensive tackle Leon Lett. An increased pass rush from Greg Ellis, Kavika Pittman and Ebenezer Ekuban makes a group struggling to be average at least good.
Linebackers	B	The addition of Quentin Coryatt brings back the speed of old to this unit. His addition allows strongside backer Randall Godfrey to play the middle, where he becomes a sideline-to-sideline defender, which can only help the speedy, but undersized, Dexter Coakley on the weakside. Backups Dat Nguyen, Darren Hambrick and Nate Hemsley add even more speed.
Secondary	B -	A healthy Deion Sanders makes an average group good by taking care of his side of the field, and allowing the safeties to help out on the other side and in the running game. Finding a suitable free safety, and a comeback by Kevin Smith, are necessities for a winning package here.
Special teams	A	A top-notch group, if last year's performance is any indication. No change in the kickers, and the return game with Sanders and Mathis should be explosive. And experience can only help last year's top newcomers, Reese and Hambrick. Watch out for Nguyen and Morgan.

DENVER BRONCOS
AFC WESTERN DIVISION

1999 SEASON

CLUB DIRECTORY

President/chief executive officer
Pat Bowlen
General manager
John Beake
Vice president of administration
Allen Fears
Vice president of business operations
Joe Ellis
Chief financial officer
Allen Fears
Dir. of ticket operations/business dev.
Rick Nichols
Stadium operations manager
Gail Stuckey
Director of operations
Bill Harpole
Senior director of media relations
Jim Saccomano
Director of special services
Fred Fleming
Director of player relations
Bill Thompson
Community relations coordinator
Steve Sewell
Director of pro personnel
Jack Elway
Director of college scouting
Ted Sundquist
Scouts
Bob Beers
Scott DiStefano
Jim Goodman
Cornell Green
Dan Rambo
Dale Strahm
Head trainer
Steve Antonopulos
Assistant trainers
Jim Keller
Corey Oshikoya

Head coach
Mike Shanahan

Assistant coaches
Frank Bush (linebackers)
Barney Chavous (defensive
assistant)
Rick Dennison (special teams)
Ed Donatell (defensive backs)
George Dyer (defensive line)
Alex Gibbs (assistant head coach/
offensive line)
Mike Heimerdinger (wide receivers)
Gary Kubiak (offensive coordinator/
quarterbacks)
Brian Pariani (tight ends)
Ricky Porter (offense assistant)
Greg Robinson (defensive
coordinator)
Greg Saporta (assistant strength &
conditioning)
Rick Smith (defensive assistant)
John Teerlinck (pass rush specialist)
Terry Tumey (defensive assistant)
Bobby Turner (running backs)
Rich Tuten (strength & cond.)

Physician
Richard Hawkins
Equipment manager
Doug West
Director/video operations
Kent Erickson

SCHEDULE

Sept. 13— MIAMI (Mon.)	7:00
Sept. 19— at Kansas City	3:15
Sept. 26— at Tampa Bay	1:00
Oct. 3— N.Y. JETS	2:15
Oct. 10— at Oakland	1:15
Oct. 17— GREEN BAY	2:15
Oct. 24— at New England	1:00
Oct. 31— MINNESOTA	2:15
Nov. 7— at San Diego	1:15
Nov. 14— at Seattle	5:20
Nov. 22— OAKLAND (Mon.)	7:00
Nov. 28— Open date	
Dec. 5— KANSAS CITY	2:15
Dec. 13— at Jacksonville (Mon.)	9:00
Dec. 19— SEATTLE	2:15
Dec. 25— at Detroit (Sat.)	4:15
Jan. 2— SAN DIEGO	2:15

All times are for home team.
All games Sunday unless noted.

DRAFT CHOICES

Al Wilson, LB, Tennessee (first round/
31st pick overall).
Montae Reagor, DE, Texas Tech (2/58).
Lennie Friedman, G, Duke (2/61).
Chris Watson, DB, Eastern Illinois (3/67).
Travis McGriff, WR, Florida (3/93).
Olandis Gary, RB, Georgia (4/127).
David Bowens, DE, Western Ill. (5/158).
Darwin Brown, DB, Texas Tech (5/167).
Desmond Clark, TE, Wake Forest (6/179).
Chad Plummer, WR, Cincinnati (6/204).
Billy Miller, WR, S. California (7/218).
Justin Swift, TE, Kansas State (7/238).

1998 REVIEW

RESULTS

Sept. 7—NEW ENGLAND	W	27-21
Sept.13—DALLAS	W	42-23
Sept.20—at Oakland	W	34-17
Sept.27—at Washington	W	38-16
Oct. 4—PHILADELPHIA	W	41-16
Oct. 11—at Seattle	W	21-16
Oct. 18—Open date		
Oct. 25—JACKSONVILLE	W	37-24
Nov. 1—at Cincinnati	W	33-26
Nov. 8—SAN DIEGO	W	27-10
Nov. 16—at Kansas City	W	30-7
Nov. 22—OAKLAND	W	40-14
Nov. 29—at San Diego	W	31-16
Dec. 6—KANSAS CITY	W	35-31
Dec. 13—at N.Y. Giants	L	16-20
Dec. 21—at Miami	L	21-31
Dec. 27—SEATTLE	W	28-21
Jan. 9—MIAMI*	W	38-3
Jan. 17—N.Y. JETS†	W	23-10
Jan. 31—Atlanta‡	W	34-19

*AFC divisional playoff game.
†AFC championship game.
‡Super Bowl XXXIII.

RECORDS/RANKINGS

1998 regular-season record: 14-2 (1st in
AFC West); 8-0 in division; 11-1 in conference; 8-0 at home; 6-2 on road.
Team record last five years: 54-26 (.675,
ranks 3rd in league in that span).

1998 team rankings:	No.	AFC	NFL
Total offense	*380.8	1	3
Rushing offense	*154.3	1	2
Passing offense	*226.5	4	7
Scoring offense	501	1	2
Total defense	*308.4	7	11
Rushing defense	*80.4	2	3
Passing defense	*228.0	14	26
Scoring defense	309	4	T8
Takeaways	30	T7	T13
Giveaways	20	T2	T3
Turnover differential	10	T2	T5
Sacks	47	2	T6
Sacks allowed	25	T3	T4

*Yards per game.

TEAM LEADERS

Scoring (kicking): Jason Elam, 127 pts.
(58/58 PATs, 23/27 FGs).
Scoring (touchdowns): Terrell Davis, 138
pts. (21 rushing, 2 receiving).
Passing: John Elway, 2,806 yds. (356
att., 210 comp., 59.0%, 22 TDs, 10 int.).
Rushing: Terrell Davis, 2,008 yds. (392
att., 5.1 avg., 21 TDs).
Receptions: Rod Smith, 86 (1,222 yds.,
14.2 avg., 6 TDs).
Interceptions: Darrien Gordon, 4 (125
yds., 1 TD).
Sacks: Maa Tanuvasa, 8.5; Trevor Pryce,
8.5.
Punting: Tom Rouen, 46.9 avg. (66
punts, 3,097 yds., 1 blocked).
Punt returns: Darrien Gordon, 11.1 avg.
(34 att., 379 yds., 0 TDs).
Kickoff returns: Vaughn Hebron, 26.4
avg. (46 att., 1,216 yds., 1 TD).

TRAINING CAMP ROSTER

DENVER BRONCOS

No.	QUARTERBACKS	Ht./Wt.	Born	NFL Exp.	College	How acq.	'98 Games GP/GS
6	Brister, Bubby	6-3/205	8-15-62	13	Northeast Louisiana	FA/97	7/4
14	Griese, Brian	6-3/215	3-18-75	2	Michigan	D3/98	1/0
12	Miller, Chris	6-2/212	8-9-65	10	Oregon	FA/99	—
	RUNNING BACKS						
30	Davis, Terrell	5-11/210	10-28-72	5	Georgia	D6b/95	16/16
24	Gary, Olandis	5-11/218	5-18-75	R	Georgia	D4/99	—
29	Griffith, Howard (FB)	6-0/230	11-17-67	7	Illinois	UFA/97	14/13
31	Loville, Derek	5-10/210	7-4-68	9	Oregon	FA/97	16/0
37	Lynn, Anthony (FB)	6-3/230	12-21-68	6	Texas Tech	FA/97	16/0
42	Smith, Detron (FB)	5-9/230	2-25-74	4	Texas A&M	D3a/96	15/2
	RECEIVERS						
89	Carswell, Dwayne (TE)	6-3/260	1-18-72	6	Liberty (Va.)	CFA/94	16/1
86	Chamberlain, Byron (TE)	6-1/242	10-17-71	5	Wayne (Neb.) State	D7b/95	16/0
88	Clark, Desmond (TE)	6-3/255	4-20-77	R	Wake Forest	D6a/99	—
87	McCaffrey, Ed	6-5/215	8-17-68	9	Stanford	UFA/95	15/15
83	McGriff, Travis	5-8/182	6-24-76	R	Florida	D3b/99	—
10	Miller, Billy	6-3/215	4-24-77	R	Southern California	D7a/99	—
82	Nash, Marcus	6-3/195	2-1-76	2	Tennessee	D1/98	8/0
13	Plummer, Chad	6-3/223	11-30-75	R	Cincinnati	D6b/99	—
84	Sharpe, Shannon (TE)	6-2/230	6-26-68	10	Savannah (Ga.) State	D7/90	16/16
80	Smith, Rod	6-0/200	5-15-70	5	Missouri Southern	FA/94	16/16
85	Swift, Justin (TE)	6-4/264	8-14-75	R	Kansas State	D7b/99	—
	OFFENSIVE LINEMEN						
79	Banks, Chris (G)	6-1/300	4-4-73	2	Kansas	D7/96	4/0
75	Berti, Tony (T)	6-6/300	6-21-72	5	Colorado	UFA/99	—
63	Diaz-Infante, David (G)	6-3/296	3-31-64	5	San Jose State	FA/96	10/0
64	Friedman, Lennie (G)	6-3/300	10-13-76	R	Duke	D2b/99	—
77	Jones, Tony (T)	6-5/291	5-24-66	12	Western Carolina	T-Bal./97	16/16
78	Lepsis, Matt (T)	6-4/290	1-13-74	3	Colorado	FA/97	16/0
66	Nalen, Tom (C)	6-2/286	5-13-71	6	Boston College	D7c/94	16/16
62	Neil, Dan (G)	6-2/281	10-21-73	3	Texas	D3/97	16/16
69	Schlereth, Mark (G)	6-3/287	1-25-66	11	Idaho	FA/95	16/16
	DEFENSIVE LINEMEN						
73	Brown, Cyron (E)	6-5/265	6-28-75	2	Western Illinois	FA/98	4/0
96	Hasselbach, Harald (E)	6-6/285	9-22-67	6	Washington	FA/94	16/3
97	Lodish, Mike (T)	6-3/270	8-11-67	10	UCLA	UFA/95	15/1
93	Pryce, Trevor (T)	6-5/295	8-3-75	3	Clemson	D1/97	16/15
99	Reagor, Montae (E)	6-2/256	6-29-77	R	Texas Tech	D2a/99	—
68	Reeves, Carl (E)	6-4/270	12-17-71	5	North Carolina State	UFA/99	*11/0
90	Smith, Neil (E)	6-4/270	4-10-66	12	Nebraska	UFA/97	14/14
98	Tanuvasa, Maa (T)	6-2/270	11-6-70	6	Hawaii	FA/95	16/16
92	Thomas, Marvin (E)	6-5/264	10-19-73	1	Memphis	FA/98	4/0
94	Traylor, Keith (T)	6-2/304	9-3-69	8	Central Oklahoma	FA/97	15/14
91	Williams, Alfred (E)	6-6/265	11-6-68	9	Colorado	FA/96	10/0
	LINEBACKERS						
47	Bowens, David	6-2/255	7-3-77	R	Western Illinois	D5a/99	—
59	Cadrez, Glenn	6-3/240	1-2-70	8	Houston	FA/95	16/15
51	Mobley, John	6-1/236	10-10-73	4	Kutztown (Pa.) University	D1/96	16/15
53	Romanowski, Bill	6-4/245	4-2-66	12	Boston College	FA/96	16/16
54	Wayne, Nate	6-0/230	1-12-75	2	Mississippi	D7b/98	1/0
56	Wilson, Al	6-0/240	6-21-77	R	Tennessee	D1/99	—
	DEFENSIVE BACKS						
34	Braxton, Tyrone (S)	5-11/190	12-17-64	13	North Dakota State	FA/95	16/6
26	Brown, Eric (S)	6-0/210	3-20-75	2	Mississippi State	D2/98	11/10
41	Brown, Darwin (CB)	5-10/170	7-6-77	R	Texas Tech	D5b/99	—
40	Carter, Dale (CB)	6-1/188	11-28-69	8	Tennessee	UFA/99	*11/9
48	Coghill, George (S)	6-0/210	3-30-70	3	Wake Forest	FA/97	9/0
39	Crockett, Ray (CB)	5-10/184	1-5-67	11	Baylor	UFA/94	16/16
20	James, Tory (CB)	6-1/195	5-18-73	4	Louisiana State	D2/96	16/0
25	Johnson, Darrius (CB)	5-9/185	9-17-72	4	Oklahoma	D4b/96	16/2
28	Paul, Tito (CB)	6-0/195	12-7-71	5	Ohio State	FA/98	16/0
21	Watson, Chris (CB)	6-1/192	6-30-77	R	Eastern Illinois	D3a/99	—
	SPECIALISTS						
1	Elam, Jason (K)	5-11/200	3-8-70	7	Hawaii	D3b/93	16/0
16	Rouen, Tom (P)	6-3/225	6-9-68	7	Colorado	FA/93	16/0

*Not with Broncos in 1998.

Other free agents invited to camp: RB Curtis Alexander, P/K Jeff Baker, QB Jeff Brohm, FB Ryan Christopherson, QB Chuck Clements, DE Herb Coleman, WR Andre Cooper, DE Ben Crosland, WR Chris Doering, LB Troy Dumas, OL Matt Elliott, G Dan Finn, LB Chris Gizzi,

WR Taj Johnson, C K.C. Jones, T Tim Kohn, DT Viliami Maumau, RB Leeland McElroy, CB Jason Moore, S Tori Noel, LB Steve Russ, CB Jason Suttle, T Trey Teague, LB Dave Thomas, DB Brad Trout, WR Shawn Turner, T Melvin Tuten, LB Artie Ulmer, LB Ronnie Ward.

Abbreviations: D1—draft pick, first round; SupD2—supplemental draft pick, second round; WV—claimed on waivers; TR—obtained in trade; PlanB—Plan B free-agent acquisition; FA—free-agent acquisition (other than Plan B); ED—expansion draft pick.

MISCELLANEOUS TEAM DATA

DENVER BRONCOS

Stadium (capacity, surface):
Mile High Stadium
(76,078, grass)
Business address:
13655 Broncos Parkway
Englewood, CO 80112
Business phone:
303-649-9000
Ticket information:
303-433-7466
Team colors:
Orange, navy blue and white
Flagship radio station:
KOA, 850 AM
Training site:
University of Northern Colorado
Greeley, Colo.
303-623-5212

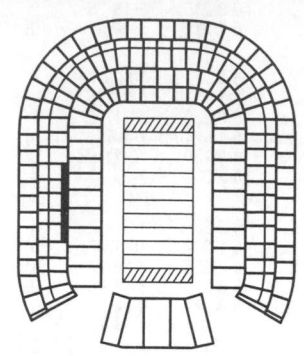

TSN REPORT CARD

Coaching staff	A	Head coach Mike Shanahan has proved he's not only a master game-planner, he's also a wonderful personnel man. Just look at his offseason acquisition of Dale Carter. Offensive coordinator Gary Kubiak is a future head coach and offensive line coach Alex Gibbs may be the best teacher in the business. No staff in the NFL outworks this one. Shanahan sees to that.
Quarterbacks	B -	With John Elway gone after 16 years, it's Bubby Brister's big chance. He'll have to prove himself to his teammates. If Brister goes down, the Broncos are in trouble. Second-year quarterback Brian Griese is not ready to lead a Super Bowl team; that's why the Broncos brought in Chris Miller. The position is a major question mark.
Running backs	A	Fresh off his 2,008-yard season, Terrell Davis worked out harder than ever during the offseason. With Elway gone, look for Davis to carry a bull's-eye on his jersey. He'll still be great, but the yards will be tougher to come by. Expect fullback Howard Griffith to keep plugging along and blowing open holes. Rookie Olandis Gary, out of Georgia, is an intriguing prospect.
Receivers	B	Ed McCaffrey made the Pro Bowl last season, and Rod Smith deserved to. Add tight end Shannon Sharpe and the trio gives Denver one of the best receiving corps in the business. Lack of depth, however, is a problem. Denver needs Marcus Nash, last year's first-round pick, to make a quantum leap. If not him, then one of the rookies better come through.
Offensive line	A -	All eyes will be on Matt Lepsis at right tackle. He replaces free agent Harry Swayne, who left for big bucks in Baltimore. If Lepsis can step up—and the coaches think he will—Denver will once again have one of the smallest, but most effective, lines in the NFL. But bear one thing in mind: the league's new rule outlawing chop-blocking near the line of scrimmage could hurt the Broncos.
Defensive line	B -	With tackles Keith Traylor and Trevor Pryce plugging up the middle, Denver was great against the run last year. The Broncos could still use a dominant pass rusher, but will have to make due with a variety of blitzes and schemes. It's time for Alfred Williams to perform well at defensive end. If he doesn't, rookie Montae Reagor will be on the field a lot.
Linebackers	A -	Bill Romanowski is 33, but looks and plays like he's 28. Expect another big year from him. John Mobley slumped a bit in 1998, but he's a wonderful athlete with big-play capability. Glenn Cadrez surprised some people with his steady play in the middle last season. Expect the same this season. If rookie Al Wilson comes through, depth won't be a problem.
Secondary	C +	The acquisition of Carter, who will team with Ray Crockett, gives the Broncos one of the best cornerback tandems in the league. Safety, however, could be the Broncos' Achilles heel. Second-year player Eric Brown is supposed to fill the huge shoes of the departed Steve Atwater at free safety, and the Broncos are still searching for a solution at strong safety. Will it be converted cornerback Darrius Johnson, or wily veteran Tyrone Braxton? The Broncos would have loved to draft a big-hitting safety, but there were none available this year.
Special teams	B	Jason Elam is one of the best placekickers in the business. Punter Tom Rouen has his moments, as well as his lapses. The kick coverage must improve (remember the 94-yard TD by the Falcons' Tim Dwight in the Super Bowl?). Most of all, the Broncos must find someone to return punts and kicks. Darrien Gordon is gone, as is Vaughn Hebron. Denver might have to turn to rookie Travis McGriff.

DETROIT LIONS
NFC CENTRAL DIVISION

1999 SEASON

CLUB DIRECTORY

Chairman and president
William Clay Ford
Vice chairman
William Clay Ford Jr.
Exec. v.p. and chief operating officer
Chuck Schmidt
Vice president of player personnel
Ron Hughes
V.p. of communications, sales and mktg.
Bill Keenist
V.p. of football administration
Larry Lee
V.p. of finance and chief financial officer
Tom Lesnau
V.p. of stadium dev. and salary cap
Tom Lewand
Secretary
David Hempstead
Director of pro scouting
Kevin Colbert
College and pro scouts
Charlie Sanders   Sheldon White
Area scouts
Russ Bollinger   Scott McEwen
Jim Owens   Chad Henry
Head athletic trainer
Kent Falb
Physicians
Keith Burch   David Collon
Terry Lock
Equipment manager
Dan Jaroshewich
Video director
Steve Hermans
Groundskeeper
Charlie Coffin
Director of security
Allen Hughes
Director of broadcast services
Bryan Bender
Human resources director
Cheryl Carrier
Director of box office operations
Mark Graham

Head coach
Bobby Ross

Assistant coaches
Brian Baker (defensive line)
Don Clemons (defensive assistant)
Sylvester Croom (off. coordinator)
Frank Falks (running backs)
Rob Graf (assistant strength and
    conditioning)
Jack Henry (offensive line)
Bert Hill (strength & condit.)
Stan Kwan (offense and special
    teams assistant)
John Misciagna (quality control-
    offense/administrative asst.)
Gary Moeller (linebackers)
Denny Murphy (quality control-
    defense)
Larry Peccatiello (def. coordinator)
Chuck Priefer (special teams)
Dick Selcer (defensive backs)
Danny Smith (tight ends)
Jerry Sullivan (wide receivers)
Jim Zorn (quarterbacks)

Executive director of marketing
Steve Harms
Dir. of ticket sales and customer service
Jennifer Manzo
Director of media relations
Mike Murray
Director of community relations and
Detroit Lions' charities
Tim Pendell

SCHEDULE

Sept. 12—	at Seattle	1:15
Sept. 19—	GREEN BAY	1:00
Sept. 26—	at Kansas City	12:00
Oct. 3—	Open date	
Oct. 10—	SAN DIEGO	1:00
Oct. 17—	MINNESOTA	1:00
Oct. 24—	at Carolina	1:00
Oct. 31—	TAMPA BAY	8:20
Nov. 7—	ST. LOUIS	1:00
Nov. 14—	at Arizona	2:15
Nov. 21—	at Green Bay	12:00
Nov. 25—	CHICAGO (Thanks.)	12:40
Dec. 5—	WASHINGTON	1:00
Dec. 12—	at Tampa Bay	1:00
Dec. 19—	at Chicago	12:00
Dec. 25—	DENVER (Sat.)	4:15
Jan. 2—	at Minnesota	12:00

All times are for home team.
All games Sunday unless noted.

DRAFT CHOICES

Chris Claiborne, LB, Southern California
(first round/ninth pick overall).
Aaron Gibson, T, Wisconsin (1/27).
Jared DeVries, DE, Iowa (3/70).
Sedrick Irvin, RB, Michigan State
(4/103).
Ty Talton, DB, Northern Iowa (5/137).
Clint Kriewaldt, LB, Wisconsin-Stevens
Point (6/177).
Mike Pringley, DT, North Carolina
(7/215).

1998 REVIEW

RESULTS

Sept. 6—at Green Bay	L	19-38
Sept.13—CINCINNATI (OT)	L	28-34
Sept.20—at Minnesota	L	6-29
Sept.28—TAMPA BAY	W	27-6
Oct. 4—at Chicago	L	27-31
Oct. 11—Open date		
Oct. 15—GREEN BAY	W	27-20
Oct. 25—MINNESOTA	L	13-34
Nov. 1—ARIZONA	L	15-17
Nov. 8—at Philadelphia	L	9-10
Nov. 15—CHICAGO	W	26-3
Nov. 22—at Tampa Bay	W	28-25
Nov. 26—PITTSBURGH (OT)	W	19-16
Dec. 6—at Jacksonville	L	22-37
Dec. 14—at San Francisco	L	13-35
Dec. 20—ATLANTA	L	17-24
Dec. 27—at Baltimore	L	10-19

RECORDS/RANKINGS

1998 regular-season record: 5-11 (4th in
NFC Central); 4-4 in division; 4-8 in conference; 4-4 at home; 1-7 on road.
Team record last five years: 38-42 (.475,
ranks 13th in league in that span).

1998 team rankings:

	No.	NFC	NFL
Total offense	*317.8	7	14
Rushing offense	*122.2	5	10
Passing offense	*195.6	10	19
Scoring offense	306	10	20
Total defense	*319.8	7	15
Rushing defense	*131.4	12	25
Passing defense	*188.4	5	8
Scoring defense	378	T11	T24
Takeaways	21	T13	T25
Giveaways	25	5	12
Turnover differential	-4	9	20
Sacks	43	6	T9
Sacks allowed	45	7	20
*Yards per game.			

TEAM LEADERS

Scoring (kicking): Jason Hanson, 114
pts. (27/29 PATs, 29/33 FGs).
Scoring (touchdowns): Tommy Vardell,
42 pts. (6 rushing, 1 receiving).
Passing: Charlie Batch, 2,178 yds. (303
att., 173 comp., 57.1%, 11 TDs, 6 int.).
Rushing: Barry Sanders, 1,491 yds. (343
att., 4.3 avg., 4 TDs).
Receptions: Johnnie Morton, 69 (1,028
yds., 14.9 avg., 2 TDs).
Interceptions: Bryant Westbrook, 3 (49
yds., 1 TD); Mark Carrier, 3 (33 yds., 0
TDs); Ron Rice, 3 (25 yds., 0 TDs).
Sacks: Robert Porcher, 11.5.
Punting: John Jett, 43.8 avg. (66 punts,
2,892 yds., 0 blocked).
Punt returns: Terry Fair, 6.3 avg. (30 att.,
189 yds., 0 TDs).
Kickoff returns: Terry Fair, 28.0 avg. (51
att., 1,428 yds., 2 TDs).

1999 SEASON

TRAINING CAMP ROSTER

No.	QUARTERBACKS	Ht./Wt.	Born	NFL Exp.	College	How acq.	'98 Games GP/GS
10	Batch, Charlie	6-2/216	12-5-74	2	Eastern Michigan	D2b/98	12/12
12	Frerotte, Gus	6-3/240	8-3-71	6	Tulsa	FA/99	*3/2
	RUNNING BACKS						
33	Irvin, Sedrick	5-11/217	3-30-78	R	Michigan State	D4/99	—
26	Olivo, Brock (FB)	6-0/226	6-24-76	2	Missouri	FA/98	1/0
36	Reece, Travis (FB)	6-3/252	4-3-75	2	Michigan State	FA/98	3/0
34	Rivers, Ron	5-8/205	11-13-71	5	Fresno State	FA/94	15/0
20	Sanders, Barry	5-8/200	7-16-68	11	Oklahoma State	D1/89	16/16
30	Schlesinger, Cory (FB)	6-0/240	6-23-72	5	Nebraska	D6b/95	15/2
	RECEIVERS						
81	Chryplewicz, Pete (TE)	6-5/253	4-27-74	3	Notre Dame	D5a/97	16/2
82	Crowell, Germane	6-3/213	9-13-76	2	Virginia	D2a/98	14/2
84	Moore, Herman	6-4/210	10-20-69	9	Virginia	D1/91	15/15
87	Morton, Johnnie	6-0/190	10-7-71	6	Southern California	D1/94	16/16
89	Rasby, Walter (TE)	6-3/247	9-7-72	6	Wake Forest	FA/98	16/16
80	Scott, Freddie	5-10/189	8-26-74	3	Penn State	FA/99	*1/0
86	Sloan, David (TE)	6-6/254	6-8-72	5	New Mexico	D3/95	10/2
83	Stablein, Brian	6-1/193	4-14-70	6	Ohio State	FA/98	10/0
15	Thomas, Corey	6-0/174	6-6-75	1	Duke	FA/98	1/0
	OFFENSIVE LINEMEN						
79	Beverly, Eric (C)	6-3/279	3-28-74	2	Miami of Ohio	FA/97	16/0
76	Brooks, Barrett (T)	6-4/320	5-5-72	5	Kansas State	UFA/99	*16/1
77	Compton, Mike (G)	6-6/297	9-18-70	7	West Virginia	D3b/93	16/16
71	Gibson, Aaron (T)	6-4/375	9-27-77	R	Wisconsin	D1b/99	—
64	Hartings, Jeff (G)	6-3/283	9-7-72	4	Penn State	D1b/96	13/13
70	Johnson, Andre (T)	6-5/314	8-25-73	4	Penn State	FA/97	3/0
75	Ramirez, Tony (T)	6-6/296	1-26-73	3	Northern Colorado	D6/97	16/7
72	Roberts, Ray (T)	6-6/308	6-3-69	8	Virginia	FA/96	16/16
74	Roque, Juan (T)	6-8/333	2-6-74	3	Arizona State	D2a/97	—
62	Semple, Tony (G)	6-5/305	12-20-70	6	Memphis State	D5/94	16/3
	DEFENSIVE LINEMEN						
95	DeVries, Jared (E)	6-4/280	6-11-76	R	Iowa	D3/99	—
94	Elliss, Luther (T)	6-5/315	3-22-73	5	Utah	D1/95	16/16
98	Jones, James (T)	6-2/290	2-6-69	9	Northern Iowa	UFA/99	*16/16
90	Owens, Dan (T)	6-3/290	3-16-67	10	Southern California	FA/98	11/11
91	Porcher, Robert (E)	6-3/270	7-30-69	8	South Carolina State	D1/92	16/16
92	Pringley, Mike (E)	6-4/270	5-22-76	R	North Carolina	D7/99	—
93	Pritchett, Kelvin (T)	6-3/301	10-24-69	9	Mississippi	UFA/99	*15/9
97	Scroggins, Tracy (E)	6-2/255	9-11-69	8	Tulsa	D2a/92	11/3
96	Taylor, Henry (T)	6-2/295	11-29-75	2	South Carolina	FA/98	1/0
	LINEBACKERS						
55	Aldridge, Allen	6-1/255	5-30-72	6	Houston	FA/98	16/15
57	Boyd, Stephen	6-0/247	8-22-72	5	Boston College	D5a/95	13/13
50	Claiborne, Chris	6-3/250	7-26-78	R	Southern California	D1a/99	—
99	Jordan, Richard	6-1/245	12-1-74	3	Missouri Southern	D7c/97	16/3
52	Kowalkowski, Scott	6-2/228	8-23-68	9	Notre Dame	FA/94	15/0
58	Kriewaldt, Clint	6-1/235	3-16-76	R	Wisconsin-Stevens Point	D6/99	—
59	O'Neill, Kevin	6-2/239	4-14-75	2	Bowling Green	FA/98	11/0
54	Russell, Matt	6-2/245	7-5-73	3	Colorado	D4/97	—
	DEFENSIVE BACKS						
24	Abrams, Kevin (CB)	5-8/175	2-28-74	3	Syracuse	D2b/97	16/7
35	Bailey, Robert (CB)	5-9/174	9-3-68	9	Miami (Fla.)	FA/97	16/0
39	Campbell, Lamar (CB)	5-11/182	8-29-76	2	Wisconsin	FA/98	12/0
27	Carrier, Mark (S)	6-1/192	4-28-68	10	Southern California	FA/97	13/13
23	Fair, Terry (CB)	5-9/185	7-20-76	2	Tennessee	D1/98	14/10
42	Stewart, Ryan (S)	6-1/207	9-30-73	4	Georgia Tech	FA/97	16/0
29	Supernaw, Kywin (S)	6-1/206	6-2-75	2	Indiana	FA/98	2/0
25	Talton, Ty (S)	5-11/200	5-10-76	R	Northern Iowa	D5/99	—
32	Westbrook, Bryant (CB)	6-0/199	12-19-74	3	Texas	D1/97	16/16
	SPECIALISTS						
4	Hanson, Jason (K)	5-11/183	6-17-70	8	Washington State	D2b/92	16/0
18	Jett, John (P)	6-0/199	11-11-68	7	East Carolina	FA/97	14/0

*Not with Lions in 1998.

Other free agents invited to camp: G Kerlin Blaise, S Nikia Codia, WR Darryl Daniel, DT Charles Dorsey, WR Henry Douglas, CB Kevin Franklin, K Brian Gowins, WR Jay Hall, LB Joey Hall, WR Donnie Hart, CB Demetrius Johnson, S Sorie Kanu, DT Travis Kirschke, G Dwayne Morgan, CB Phil Nash, C Jeremy Offutt, RB Pepe Pearson, P Daniel Pope, QB Ron Powlus, T Marek Rubin, QB Cory Sauter, DE Paul Spicer, TE Kerry Taylor, T Deron Thorpe, LB Joe Tuipala, WR Undre Williams.

MISCELLANEOUS TEAM DATA

DETROIT LIONS

Stadium (capacity, surface):
Pontiac Silverdome
(80,311, artificial)
Business address:
1200 Featherstone Road
Pontiac, MI 48342
Business phone:
248-335-4131
Ticket information:
248-335-4151
Team colors:
Honolulu blue and silver
Flagship radio station:
WXYT, 1270 AM
Training site:
Saginaw Valley State University
Saginaw, Mich.
248-972-3700

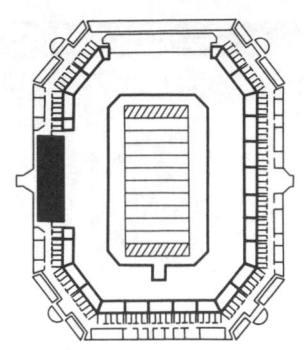

TSN REPORT CARD

Coaching staff	C +	After a miserable 1998 season, Bobby Ross has done a good job of getting the players back in his camp and buying into his program. The best thing he's done is stick with his system, but time is growing short for him to prove that it works.
Quarterbacks	C -	Charlie Batch will get a longer leash than Scott Mitchell had, but not much more. Batch has the ability and temperment to be a winner, but he has to prove he can get it done. If he doesn't produce early backup Gus Frerotte will get the call.
Running backs	B +	Barry Sanders remains a game-breaking threat and, over the course of a season, he's going to do a great deal of damage. With Tommy Vardell gone, though, there's a question of whether new fullback Cory Schlesinger can get the tough yards when the Lions need them.
Receivers	A -	Herman Moore is as unstoppable as any receiver in the league in crucial situations and Johnnie Morton and Germane Crowell have the speed to provide big plays. From top to bottom, this is Detroit's best receiving corps in decades.
Offensive line	C -	With the addition of rookie right tackle Aaron Gibson and some shuffling in the line, the Lions got bigger and better at three positions. A change in blocking philosophy also will play to their strengths, but there's still a question of chemistry and unity.
Defensive line	B	This unit is finally strong across the entire front and the depth is good. Robert Porcher is a playmaking left end and tackle Luther Elliss—with the addition of free-agent tackle James Jones—should see fewer double teams and have more opportunities to penetrate and disrupt plays.
Linebackers	B	Traditionally weak against the pass, this group is no longer vulnerable. First-round pick Chris Claiborne can cover man-to-man and Stephen Boyd is excellent in pass drops. Allen Aldridge was switched to the strong side to take advantage of his physical game.
Defensive backs	C -	The secondary is loaded with raw young talent that must begin to show some results. They're still giving up too many big plays, not just for touchdowns, but on those back-breaking third-and-longs. If they reach their potential, they'll be awesome; if they don't, the Lions are in trouble.
Special teams	C	The Lions feature some of the league's top talent at a couple of positions—kicker Jason Hanson and kick-off returner Terry Fair—but there are still too many costly inconsistencies from game to game. Until those are ironed out, these units are a 50-50 proposition.

GREEN BAY PACKERS
NFC CENTRAL DIVISION

1999 SEASON

CLUB DIRECTORY

President/chief executive officer
Robert E. Harlan
Executive v.p./general manager
Ron Wolf
Executive assistant to the president
Phil Pionek
Senior v.p. of administration
John Jones
Vice president/general counsel
Lance Lopes
Corporate security officer
Jerry Parins
Director of administrative affairs
Mark Schiefelbein
Executive director/public relations
Lee Remmel
Associate director/public relations
Jeff Blumb
Asst. director of p.r./travel coordinator
Aaron Popkey
Director/marketing
Jeff Cieply
Executive director of player programs & community affairs
Gill Byrd
Director of family programs
Sherry Schuldes
Ticket director
Mark Wagner
Vice president of personnel
Ken Herock
Director of player personnel
Ted Thompson
Dir. of player finance/football ops.
Andrew Brandt
Pro personnel director
Reggie McKenzie
Scouting coordinator
Danny Mock
Scouts
John 'Red' Cochran   Lee Gissendaner
Brian Gutekunst   Shaun Herock
Alonzo Highsmith   Scot McCloughan
Sam Seale
Video director
Al Treml

Head coach
Ray Rhodes

Assistant coaches
Charlie Baggett (wide receivers)
Larry Beightol (offensive line)
Johnny Holland (linebackers)
Jeff Jagodzinski (tight ends)
Chuck Knox Jr. (defensive asst./ quality control)
Sherman Lewis (offensive coord.)
Mike McCarthy (quarterbacks)
Steve Ortmayer (special teams)
Barry Rubin (strength & condit.)
Harry Sydney (running backs)
Emmitt Thomas (def. coord.)
Mike Trgovac (defensive line)
Joe Vitt (defensive backs)
Lionel Washington (assistant defensive backs)
Ken Zampese (offensive asst./ quality control)

Equipment manager
Gordon 'Red' Batty
Assistant equipment manager
Tom Bakken   Brian Nehring
Head trainer
Pepper Burruss
Assistant trainers
Bryan Engel   Kurt Fielding
Building supervisor
Ted Eisenreich
Fields supervisor
Allen Johnson

SCHEDULE

Sept. 12— OAKLAND	12:00
Sept. 19— at Detroit	1:00
Sept. 26— MINNESOTA	3:15
Oct. 3— Open date	
Oct. 10— TAMPA BAY	7:20
Oct. 17— at Denver	2:15
Oct. 24— at San Diego	1:05
Nov. 1— SEATTLE (Mon.)	8:00
Nov. 7— CHICAGO	12:00
Nov. 14— at Dallas	3:15
Nov. 21— DETROIT	12:00
Nov. 29— at San Fran. (Mon.)	6:00
Dec. 5— at Chicago	12:00
Dec. 12— CAROLINA	12:00
Dec. 20— at Minnesota (Mon.)	8:00
Dec. 26— at Tampa Bay	4:15
Jan. 2— ARIZONA	12:00

All times are for home team.
All games Sunday unless noted.

DRAFT CHOICES

Antuan Edwards, DB, Clemson (first round/25th pick overall).
Fred Vinson, DB, Vanderbilt (2/47).
Mike McKenzie, DB, Memphis (3/87).
Cletidus Hunt, DT, Kentucky State (3/94).
Aaron Brooks, QB, Virginia (4/131).
Josh Bidwell, P, Oregon (4/133).
DeMonn Parker, RB, Oklahoma (5/159).
Craig Heimburger, C, Missouri (5/163).
Dee Miller, WR, Ohio State (6/196).
Scott Curry, T, Montana (6/203).
Chris Akins, DB, Arkansas-Pine Bluff (7/212).
Donald Driver, WR, Alcorn State (7/213).

1998 REVIEW

RESULTS

Sept. 6—DETROIT	W	38-19
Sept.13—TAMPA BAY	W	23-15
Sept.20—at Cincinnati	W	13-6
Sept.27—at Carolina	W	37-30
Oct. 5—MINNESOTA	L	24-37
Oct. 11—Open date		
Oct. 15—at Detroit	L	20-27
Oct. 25—BALTIMORE	W	28-10
Nov. 1—SAN FRANCISCO	W	36-22
Nov. 9—at Pittsburgh	L	20-27
Nov. 15—at N.Y. Giants	W	37-3
Nov. 22—at Minnesota	L	14-28
Nov. 29—PHILADELPHIA	W	24-16
Dec. 7—at Tampa Bay	L	22-24
Dec. 13—CHICAGO	W	26-20
Dec. 20—TENNESSEE	W	30-22
Dec. 27—at Chicago	W	16-13
Jan. 3—at San Francisco*	L	27-30

*NFC wild-card game.

RECORDS/RANKINGS

1998 regular-season record: 11-5 (2nd in NFC Central); 4-4 in division; 8-4 in conference; 7-1 at home; 4-4 on road.
Team record last five years: 57-23 (.713, ranks 2nd in league in that span).
1998 team rankings:

	No.	NFC	NFL
Total offense	*352.3	3	5
Rushing offense	*95.4	12	25
Passing offense	*256.9	3	3
Scoring offense	408	4	6
Total defense	*281.7	2	4
Rushing defense	*90.1	2	4
Passing defense	*191.6	6	10
Scoring defense	319	6	11
Takeaways	23	T11	T22
Giveaways	34	T12	T24
Turnover differential	-11	15	28
Sacks	50	T3	T4
Sacks allowed	39	6	T15

*Yards per game.

TEAM LEADERS

Scoring (kicking): Ryan Longwell, 128 pts. (41/43 PATs, 29/33 FGs).
Scoring (touchdowns): Antonio Freeman, 86 pts. (14 receiving, 1 2-pt. conv.).
Passing: Brett Favre, 4,212 yds. (551 att., 347 comp., 63.0%, 31 TDs, 23 int.).
Rushing: Darick Holmes, 386 yds. (93 att., 4.2 avg., 1 TD).
Receptions: Antonio Freeman, 84 (1,424 yds., 17.0 avg., 14 TDs).
Interceptions: Tyrone Williams, 5 (40 yds., 0 TDs).
Sacks: Reggie White, 16.0.
Punting: Sean Landeta, 42.9 avg. (65 punts, 2,788 yds., 0 blocked).
Punt returns: Roell Preston, 9.0 avg. (44 att., 398 yds., 1 TD).
Kickoff returns: Roell Preston, 26.3 avg. (57 att., 1,497 yds., 2 TDs).

TRAINING CAMP ROSTER

GREEN BAY PACKERS

No.	QUARTERBACKS	Ht./Wt.	Born	NFL Exp.	College	How acq.	'98 Games GP/GS
2	Brooks, Aaron	6-4/203	3-24-76	R	Virginia	D4a/99	—
4	Favre, Brett	6-2/230	10-10-69	9	Southern Mississippi	T-Atl./92	16/16
12	Mirer, Rick	6-3/212	3-19-70	7	Notre Dame	FA/98	—

No.	RUNNING BACKS	Ht./Wt.	Born	NFL Exp.	College	How acq.	'98 Games GP/GS
33	Henderson, William (FB)	6-1/245	2-19-71	5	North Carolina	D3b/95	16/10
48	Kitts, Jim (FB)	6-1/245	12-28-72	3	Ferrum (Va.)	FA/98	5/0
25	Levens, Dorsey	6-1/228	5-21-70	6	Georgia Tech	D5b/94	7/4
30	Parker, DeMonn	5-10/189	12-24-76	R	Oklahoma	D5a/99	—

No.	RECEIVERS	Ht./Wt.	Born	NFL Exp.	College	How acq.	'98 Games GP/GS
88	Arnold, Jahine	6-0/180	6-19-73	4	Fresno State	T-Pit./99	*2/0
85	Bradford, Corey	6-1/197	12-8-75	2	Jackson State	D5/98	8/0
87	Brooks, Robert	6-0/180	6-23-70	8	South Carolina	D3/92	12/12
89	Chmura, Mark (TE)	6-5/255	2-22-69	8	Boston College	D6/92	15/14
81	Davis, Tyrone (TE)	6-4/252	6-30-72	4	Virginia	FA/97	13/1
13	Driver, Donald	6-0/174	2-2-75	R	Alcorn State	D7b/99	—
86	Freeman, Antonio	6-1/198	5-27-72	5	Virginia Tech	D3d/95	15/15
82	Manning, Brian	5-11/186	4-22-75	2	Stanford	FA/98	3/0
80	Mayes, Derrick	6-0/205	1-28-74	4	Notre Dame	D2/96	10/6
19	Miller, Dee	6-0/194	12-4-75	R	Ohio State	D6a/99	—
84	Schroeder, Bill	6-3/200	1-9-71	4	Wisconsin-La Crosse	FA/96	13/3
83	Thomason, Jeff (TE)	6-5/255	12-30-69	7	Oregon	W-Cin./94	16/2

No.	OFFENSIVE LINEMEN	Ht./Wt.	Born	NFL Exp.	College	How acq.	'98 Games GP/GS
70	Andruzzi, Joe (G)	6-3/310	8-23-75	3	Southern Connecticut	FA/97	15/1
61	Curry, Scott (T)	6-5/294	12-25-75	R	Montana	D6b/99	—
60	Davis, Rob (C)	6-3/290	12-10-68	4	Shippensburg (Pa.)	FA/97	16/0
72	Dotson, Earl (T)	6-4/315	12-17-70	7	Texas A&I	D3/93	16/16
58	Flanagan, Mike (C)	6-5/290	11-10-73	4	UCLA	D3a/96	2/0
75	Heimburger, Craig (G)	6-2/314	2-3-77	R	Missouri	D5b/99	—
63	McKenzie, Raleigh (G)	6-2/285	2-8-63	15	Tennessee	UFA/99	*16/16
77	Michels, John (T)	6-7/304	3-19-73	4	Southern California	D1/96	0/0
62	Rivera, Marco (G)	6-4/305	4-26-72	4	Penn State	D6/96	15/15
78	Verba, Ross (T)	6-4/302	10-31-73	3	Iowa	D1/97	16/16
68	Wahle, Mike (T)	6-6/306	3-29-77	2	Navy	SupD2/98	1/0
52	Winters, Frank (C)	6-3/300	1-23-64	13	Western Illinois	UFA/92	13/13

No.	DEFENSIVE LINEMEN	Ht./Wt.	Born	NFL Exp.	College	How acq.	'98 Games GP/GS
96	Booker, Vaughn (E)	6-5/300	2-24-68	6	Cincinnati	T-KC/98	16/4
93	Brown, Gilbert (T)	6-2/350	2-22-71	7	Kansas	W-Mln./93	16/16
91	Brown, Jonathon (E)	6-4/265	11-28-75	2	Tennessee	D3/98	4/
71	Dotson, Santana (T)	6-5/286	12-19-69	8	Baylor	FA/96	16/16
90	Holliday, Vonnie (E)	6-5/296	12-11-75	2	North Carolina	D1/98	12/12
97	Hunt, Cletidus (T)	6-4/300	1-2-76	R	Kentucky State	D3b/99	—
98	Lyon, Billy (T)	6-5/295	12-10-73	2	Marshall	FA/97	4/0
95	McKenzie, Keith (E)	6-3/264	10-17-73	4	Ball State	D7b/96	16/0

No.	LINEBACKERS	Ht./Wt.	Born	NFL Exp.	College	How acq.	'98 Games GP/GS
55	Harris, Bernardo	6-2/248	10-15-71	5	North Carolina	FA/95	16/16
53	Koonce, George	6-1/245	10-15-68	8	East Carolina	FA/92	14/14
56	Morton, Mike	6-4/235	3-28-72	5	North Carolina	UFA/99	*16/0
54	Waddy, Jude	6-2/220	9-12-75	2	William and Mary	FA/98	13/0
51	Williams, Brian	6-1/245	12-17-72	5	Southern California	D3c/95	16/15

No.	DEFENSIVE BACKS	Ht./Wt.	Born	NFL Exp.	College	How acq.	'98 Games GP/GS
29	Akins, Chris (S)	5-11/194	11-29-76	R	Arkansas-Pine Bluff	D7a/99	—
36	Butler, LeRoy (S)	6-0/198	7-19-68	10	Florida State	D2/90	16/16
45	Cooks, Kerry (S)	5-11/202	3-28-74	2	Iowa	W-Min./98	9/0
24	Edwards, Antuan (CB)	6-1/208	5-26-77	R	Clemson	D1/99	—
43	McGarrahan, Scott (S)	6-1/197	2-12-74	2	New Mexico	D6a/98	15/0
34	McKenzie, Mike (CB)	6-1/193	4-26-76	R	Memphis	D3a/99	—
21	Newsome, Craig (CB)	6-0/190	8-10-71	5	Arizona State	D1/95	13/13
42	Sharper, Darren (S)	6-2/210	11-3-75	3	William & Mary	D2/97	16/16
31	Vinson, Fred (CB)	5-11/177	4-2-77	R	Vanderbilt	D2/99	—
37	Williams, Tyrone (CB)	5-11/192	5-31-73	4	Nebraska	D3b/96	16/16

No.	SPECIALISTS	Ht./Wt.	Born	NFL Exp.	College	How acq.	'98 Games GP/GS
9	Bidwell, Josh (P)	6-3/228	3-13-76	R	Oregon	D4b/99	—
8	Longwell, Ryan (K)	6-0/192	8-16-74	3	California	W-SF/97	16/0

*Not with Packers in 1998.

Other free agents invited to camp: S Rodney Artmore, P Will Brice, DT Howard Burns, LB Daryl Carter, TE Alphonso Collins, WR Zola Davis, CB Andre Dixon, WR Tyrone Goodson, QB Matt Hasselbeck, LB Deon Humphrey, DE Pat Ivey, TE Rod Lewis, QB Ronnie McAda, LB Kevin McCullar, RB Basil Mitchell, CB Denorse Mosley, FB Jim Nelson, C Mike Newell, WR Pat Palmer, DE Chris Reed, DT Jermaine Smith, WR Michael Vaughn, RB Edwin Watson, CB Keith Williams.

GREEN BAY PACKERS

MISCELLANEOUS TEAM DATA

Stadium (capacity, surface):
Lambeau Field
(60,790, grass)
Business address:
P.O. Box 10628
Green Bay, WI 54307-0628
Business phone:
920-496-5700
Ticket information:
920-496-5719
Team colors:
Dark green, gold and white
Flagship radio station:
WTMJ, 620 AM
Training site:
St. Norbert College
West De Pere, Wis.
920-496-5700

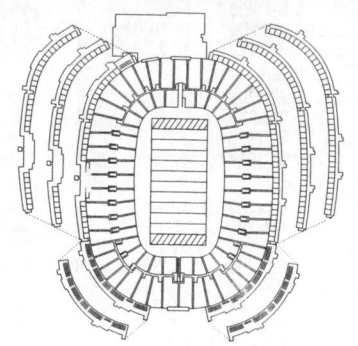

TSN REPORT CARD

Coaching	B	The Packers should respond well to Ray Rhodes' enthusiastic style and aggressive nature. The staff Rhodes assembled is solid, led by coordinators Sherman Lewis and Emmitt Thomas, both of whom are among the best in the business.
Quarterbacks	A -	Though interceptions got the best of him last season, Brett Favre still has his best years ahead of him. He should blossom now that he's free from the tight control of former coach Mike Holmgren. An injury would spell disaster, however, because of the lack of backup help.
Running backs	B	Coming off a major leg injury, Dorsey Levens has to prove he is back to Pro Bowl form. There isn't any experienced help behind him, so speedy rookie DeMonn Parker will be counted on to contribute right away. Fullback William Henderson must have a better year than he did in '98.
Receivers	C	Even with the dynamic talents of Antonio Freeman, this is a troubled position. Robert Brooks isn't the same player he once was and Derrick Mayes has been a disappointment. Management did next to nothing to improve the position in the offseason and could wind up paying for it.
Offensive line	C +	There still aren't any road graders up front, but this is a group the club can win with. It will be imperative that center Frank Winters come back at full strength because he's the glue that holds the unit together. It is time for tackles Ross Verba and Earl Dotson to prove they can play with the best in the NFC.
Defensive line	B	Reggie White's retirement hurts, even if he wasn't dominant on every play last year. Luckily for the Packers, they hit the jackpot with Vonnie Holliday, who will assume White's spot at left end. Nose tackle Gilbert Brown must prove early that he still has the legs to be a force in the middle.
Linebackers	B	In the past, the trio of Brian Williams, Bernardo Harris and George Koonce hasn't been as productive as it should have been. But under a new scheme in which the linebackers will have more freedom to roam the field the three should flourish. If Williams can overcome a chronic knee problem, he could have a big year.
Secondary	C	Too many question marks plague this unit. Can rookie Antuan Edwards overcome a turf toe injury? Can Craig Newsome return to form after a disappointing season? Can Tyrone Williams gain the consistency that has kept him from becoming a top-flight player? Can Darren Sharper handle being in charge of the defense?
Special teams	C -	The biggest concern is whether rookie Josh Bidwell can handle the punting duties. He has a strong leg, but most of his kicks will be aimed at landing the ball inside the 20. The return game doesn't appear to be anything special and the coverage units lost two great players in Lamont Hollinquest and Travis Jervey.

INDIANAPOLIS COLTS
AFC EASTERN DIVISION

1999 SEASON

CLUB DIRECTORY

Owner and CEO
James Irsay
President
Bill Polian
Vice chairman and COO
Michael G. Chernoff
Senior vice president
Bob Terpening
Sr. vice president of administration
Pete Ward
Vice president of finance
Kurt Humphrey
Controller
Herm Stonitsch
Vice president of public relations
Craig Kelley
Assistant director of public relations
Ryan Robinson
Director of ticket operations
Larry Hall
Director of football operations
Dom Anile
Director of college scouting
George Boone
Director of player development
Steve Champlin
Director of pro scouting
Chris Polian
Director of pro player personnel
Clyde Powers
College scouts
Mike Butler
Ralph Hawkins
David Caldwell
Tom Gamble
Bo Guarani
Paul Roell
Tom Telesco
Todd Vasvari
Head trainer
Hunter Smith

Head coach
Jim Mora

Assistant coaches
Bruce Arians (quarterbacks)
George Catavolos (asst. head
coach/defensive backs)
Vic Fangio (def. coordinator)
Todd Grantham (defensive line)
Gene Huey (running backs)
Tony Marciano (tight ends)
Tom Moore (off. coordinator)
Howard Mudd (offensive line)
Mike Murphy (linebackers)
Jay Norvell (wide receivers)
John Pagano (def. assistant)
Kevin Spencer (special teams)
Jon Torine (conditioning)
Tom Zupancic (strength)

Assistant trainers
Dave Hammer
Dave Walston
Orthopedic surgeon
Arthur C. Rettig, M.D.
Physician
Doug Robertson, M.D.
Video director
Marty Heckscher
Equipment manager
Jon Scott
Assistant equipment manager
Mike Mays

SCHEDULE

Sept. 12—	BUFFALO	12:00
Sept. 19—	at New England	1:00
Sept. 26—	at San Diego	1:05
Oct. 3—	Open date	
Oct. 10—	MIAMI	3:15
Oct. 17—	at N.Y. Jets	1:00
Oct. 24—	CINCINNATI	12:00
Oct. 31—	DALLAS	1:00
Nov. 7—	KANSAS CITY	1:00
Nov. 14—	at N.Y. Giants	1:00
Nov. 21—	at Philadelphia	1:00
Nov. 28—	N.Y. JETS	4:15
Dec. 5—	at Miami	1:00
Dec. 12—	NEW ENGLAND	1:00
Dec. 19—	WASHINGTON	1:00
Dec. 26—	at Cleveland	1:00
Jan. 2—	at Buffalo	1:00

All times are for home team.
All games Sunday unless noted.

DRAFT CHOICES

Edgerrin James, RB, Miami, Fla. (first
round/fourth pick overall).
Mike Peterson, LB, Florida (2/36).
Brandon Burlsworth, G, Arkansas (3/63).
Paul Miranda, DB, Central Florida (4/96).
Brad Scioli, DE, Penn State (5/138).
Hunter Smith, P, Notre Dame (7/210).
Corey Terry, LB, Tennessee (7/250).

1998 REVIEW

RESULTS

Sept. 6—MIAMI	L	15-24
Sept.13—at New England	L	6-29
Sept.20—at N.Y. Jets	L	6-44
Sept.27—NEW ORLEANS (OT)	L	13-19
Oct. 4—SAN DIEGO	W	17-12
Oct. 11—BUFFALO	L	24-31
Oct. 18—at San Francisco	L	31-34
Oct. 25—Open date		
Nov. 1—NEW ENGLAND	L	16-21
Nov. 8—at Miami	L	14-27
Nov. 15—N.Y. JETS	W	24-23
Nov. 22—at Buffalo	L	11-34
Nov. 29—at Baltimore	L	31-38
Dec. 6—at Atlanta	L	21-28
Dec. 13—CINCINNATI	W	39-26
Dec. 20—at Seattle	L	23-27
Dec. 27—CAROLINA	L	19-27

RECORDS/RANKINGS

1998 regular-season record: 3-13 (5th in
AFC East); 1-7 in division; 3-9 in conference; 3-5 at home; 0-8 on road.
Team record last five years: 32-48 (.400,
ranks T23rd in league in that span).

1998 team rankings:	No.	AFC	NFL
Total offense	*319.8	7	12
Rushing offense	*92.9	14	26
Passing offense	*226.9	3	6
Scoring offense	310	10	19
Total defense	*364.8	15	29
Rushing defense	*160.6	14	29
Passing defense	*204.1	8	16
Scoring defense	444	14	29
Takeaways	19	T14	T28
Giveaways	33	12	T21
Turnover differential	-14	14	29
Sacks	38	10	T18
Sacks allowed	22	1	2

*Yards per game.

TEAM LEADERS

Scoring (kicking): Mike Vanderjagt, 104
pts. (23/23 PATs, 27/31 FGs).
Scoring (touchdowns): Marshall Faulk,
60 pts. (6 rushing, 4 receiving).
Passing: Peyton Manning, 3,739 yds.
(575 att., 326 comp., 56.7%, 26 TDs, 28
int.).
Rushing: Marshall Faulk, 1,319 yds. (324
att., 4.1 avg., 6 TDs).
Receptions: Marshall Faulk, 86 (908
yds., 10.6 avg., 4 TDs).
Interceptions: Eight players with one
each.
Sacks: Ellis Johnson, 8.0.
Punting: Chris Gardocki, 45.4 avg. (79
punts, 3,583 yds., 0 blocked).
Punt returns: Aaron Bailey, 9.3 avg. (19
att., 176 yds., 0 TDs).
Kickoff returns: Aaron Bailey, 22.3 avg.
(34 att., 759 yds., 0 TDs).

INDIANAPOLIS COLTS

No.	QUARTERBACKS	Ht./Wt.	Born	NFL Exp.	College	How acq.	'98 Games GP/GS
15	Case, Stoney	6-3/201	7-7-72	5	New Mexico	UFA/99	*1/0
13	Holcomb, Kelly	6-2/212	7-9-73	3	Middle Tennessee State	FA/96	—
18	Manning, Peyton	6-5/230	3-24-76	2	Tennessee	D1/98	16/16
	RUNNING BACKS						
23	Elias, Keith	5-9/203	2-3-72	4	Princeton	FA/98	13/0
43	Greene, Scott	5-11/230	6-1-72	4	Michigan State	FA/98	5/0
44	Holmes, Darick	6-0/226	7-1-71	5	Portland State	UFA/99	*14/4
32	James, Edgerrin	6-0/216	8-1-78	R	Miami (Fla.)	D1/99	—
	RECEIVERS						
83	Banta, Brad (TE)	6-6/260	12-14-70	6	Southern California	D4/94	16/0
	Dawson, Lake	6-1/200	2-2-72	5	Notre Dame	FA/99	0/0
85	Dilger, Ken (TE)	6-5/259	2-2-71	5	Illinois	D2/95	16/16
84	Green, E.G.	5-11/187	6-28-75	2	Florida State	D3/98	12/0
88	Harrison, Marvin	6-0/181	8-25-72	4	Syracuse	D1/96	12/12
11	McGuire, Kaipo	5-10/174	1-16-74	3	Brigham Young	FA/98	1/0
86	Pathon, Jerome	6-0/187	12-16-75	2	Washington	D2/98	16/15
81	Pollard, Marcus (TE)	6-4/257	2-8-72	5	Bradley	FA/95	16/11
	OFFENSIVE LINEMEN						
78	Glenn, Tarik (T)	6-5/335	5-25-76	3	California	D1/97	16/16
74	Jackson, Waverly (T)	6-2/310	12-19-72	2	Virginia Tech	FA/98	7/2
60	Johnson, Jason (C)	6-3/290	2-6-74	2	Kansas State.	FA/98	14/0
58	Leeuwenburg, Jay (C)	6-3/290	6-18-69	8	Colorado	FA/96	16/16
79	Mandarich, Tony (G)	6-5/324	9-23-66	7	Michigan State	FA/96	10/10
76	McKinney, Steve (G)	6-4/297	10-15-75	2	Texas A&M	D4/98	16/16
73	Meadows, Adam (T)	6-5/299	1-25-74	3	Georgia	D2/97	14/14
72	Moore, Larry (G)	6-3/301	6-1-75	2	Brigham Young	FA/98	6/5
67	Myslinski, Tom	6-3/293	12-7-68	7	Tennessee	FA/98	4/1
	DEFENSIVE LINEMEN						
92	Bratzke, Chad (E)	6-4/275	9-15-71	6	Eastern Kentucky	UFA/99	*16/16
64	Chester, Larry (T)	6-2/305	10-17-75	2	Temple	FA/98	14/2
62	Johnson, Ellis (T)	6-2/292	10-30-73	5	Florida	D1/95	16/16
96	King, Shawn (E)	6-3/278	6-24-72	5	Northeast Louisiana	UFA/99	—
61	McCoy, Tony (T)	6-0/282	6-10-69	8	Florida	D4b/92	14/13
99	Scioli, Brad (E)	6-3/277	9-6-76	R	Penn State	D5/99	—
90	Thomas, Mark (E)	6-5/272	5-6-69	8	North Carolina State	W-Chi./98	14/5
98	Tuinei, Van	6-3/290	2-16-71	3	Arizona	FA/98	12/0
95	Whittington, Bernard (E)	6-6/280	8-20-71	6	Indiana	FA/94	15/11
	LINEBACKERS						
53	Barber, Michael	6-0/246	11-9-71	5	Clemson	W-Sea./98	12/6
97	Bennett, Cornelius	6-2/240	8-25-65	13	Alabama	FA/99	*16/16
57	Berry, Bert	6-2/248	8-15-75	3	Notre Dame	D3/97	16/12
93	Chorak, Jason	6-4/253	9-23-74	2	Washington	FA/98	8/0
91	Jordan, Antony	6-2/234	12-19-74	2	Vanderbilt	D5b/99	16/3
52	Peterson, Mike	6-2/229	6-17-76	R	Florida	D2/99	—
56	Royal, Andre	6-1/220	12-1-72	5	Alabama	T-NO/98	13/9
50	Terry, Corey	6-3/258	3-6-76	R	Tennessee	D7b/99	—
	Thomas, Ratcliff	6-1/238	1-2-74			FA/98	5/0
	DEFENSIVE BACKS						
47	Austin, Billy	5-10/195	3-8-75	1	New Mexico	FA/98	1/0
29	Belser, Jason	5-9/196	5-28-70	8	Oklahoma	D8a/92	16/16
26	Blevins, Tony	6-0/165	1-29-75	2	Kansas	W-SF/98	5/0
20	Burris, Jeff	6-0/190	6-7-72	6	Notre Dame	FA/98	14/14
27	Clark, Rico	5-10/181	6-6-74	3	Louisville	FA/97	16/0
37	Cota, Chad	6-1/198	8-8-71	5	Oregon	UFA/99	*16/16
40	McElroy, Ray (CB)	5-11/207	7-31-72	5	Eastern Illinois	D4/95	16/0
21	Miranda, Paul	5-10/184	5-2-76	R	Central Florida	D4/99	—
34	Montgomery, Monty	5-11/197	12-8-73	3	Houston	D4/97	16/5
38	Poole, Tyrone	5-8/188	2-3-72	5	Fort Valley (Ga.) State	T-Car./98	15/15
	SPECIALISTS						
17	Smith, Hunter (P)	6-2/212	8-9-77	R	Notre Dame	D7a/99	—
12	Vanderjagt, Mike (P)	6-5/210	3-24-70	2	West Virginia	FA/98	14/0

*Not with Colts in 1998.

Other free agents invited to camp: OL Jon Blackman, P Lonny Calicchio, DE Mark Campbell, WR Wes Caswell, OL Joel Davis, WR John Fassel, RB Chris Gall, DL Nate Hobgood-Chittick, OL Sale Isaia, WR Isaac Jones, RB Charles Kirby, QB Jim Kubiak, TE Joe Kuykendall, DB Craig Miller, DB Steve Muhammad, DE Chuckie Nwokorie, K Eric Olsen, TE Melvin Pearsall, KR Kevin Prentiss, DB Nakia Reddick, OL Tim Ridder, QB Roderick Robinson, LB Ron Rogers, WR Kio Sanford, T Trey Sartin, C Jeff Saturday, RB Paul Shields, DB Kirby Smart, T Paul Snellings, DB Scott Thomas, KR Terrence Wilkins.

Abbreviations: D1—draft pick, first round; SupD2—supplemental draft pick, second round; WV—claimed on waivers; TR—obtained in trade; PlanB—Plan B free-agent acquisition; FA—free-agent acquisition (other than Plan B); ED—expansion draft pick.

MISCELLANEOUS TEAM DATA

Stadium (capacity, surface):
RCA Dome (56,500, artificial)
Business address:
P.O. Box 535000
Indianapolis, IN 46253
Business phone:
317-297-2658
Ticket information:
317-297-7000
Team colors:
Royal blue and white
Flagship radio stations:
WNDE, 1260 AM
WFBQ, 94.5 FM
Training site:
Rose Hulman Technical Institute
Terre Haute, Ind.
317-297-2658

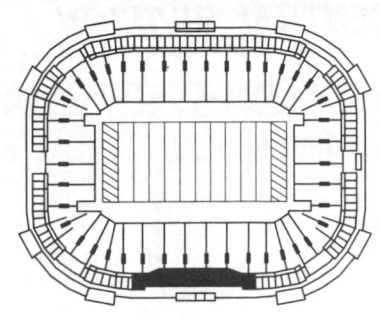

TSN REPORT CARD

Coaching staff	B	Jim Mora is a no-nonsense guy who has earned the respect of his players in a short period of time. The addition of offensive coordinator Tom Moore and offensive line coach Howard Mudd paid huge dividends a year ago. Rusty Tillman's one-year reign as defensive coordinator was a flop, but Mora admitted the mistake and remedied it by bringing in an old friend, Vic Fangio. The staff is one of the best this team has had in years.
Quarterbacks	B	Peyton Manning's rookie season was no fluke. By the end of it he was playing at a high level (10 touchdowns, five interceptions in final five games). Anyone waiting for him to suffer a sophomore jinx will have a long wait. Trouble looms, though, if Manning goes down with an injury. The potential backups are Stoney Case and Kelly Holcomb. Neither took an offensive snap in 1998.
Running backs	C	All the team is asking of rookie Edgerrin James is to replace three-time Pro Bowler Marshall Faulk. He could, but the pressure will be there until he does. James will be the focal point of a brand, spanking new group. How new? The team's top returning rusher is Manning, who had 62 yards on 15 carries. A player to keep an eye on is Darick Holmes. He was signed up to beef up short-yardage efficiency and relieve James occasionally.
Receivers	B	Marvin Harrison is one of the AFC's best-kept secrets. All that's missing is a Pro Bowl invitation. He'll once again be supported by two up-and-comers—Jerome Pathon and E.G. Green. Pathon is coming off a 50-catch rookie season while Green is eager to make up for an injury-plagued rookie year. A key to the group's success will be whether Lake Dawson can compensate for the free-agent defection of Torrance Small.
Offensive line	B	The unit was young and effective a year ago, allowing Manning to be sacked just 22 times and suffer few major hits despite throwing a franchise-record 575 passes. A year of experience should translate into improved play. Four of the five spots are solid with 23-year-old Tarik Glenn at left tackle, 23-year-old Steve McKinney at left guard, 25-year-old Adam Meadows at right tackle and Jay Leeuwenburg, the old man of the group at 30, at center. Training-camp competition will determine whether right guard is manned by Tony Mandarich or Larry Moore.
Defensive line	C	The jury is out, but evidence points to a greatly improved unit. The tackle rotation is deep with starters Ellis Johnson and Tony McCoy and backups Bernard Whittington and Larry Chester. The key to productivity hinges on how quickly free-agent acquisitions Chad Bratzke and Shawn King find their comfort zone. They should be a presence on the perimeter that was sorely missing a year ago. Pocket pressure in nickel situations should come from defensive end Mark Thomas.
Linebackers	D	Cornelius Bennett was a significant offseason free-agent acquisition and Mike Peterson a key draft pick. Both could be the starting outside 'backers come September. The rest of the group is unproven. Andre Royal is an athletic option at weakside while Michael Barber is an untapped talent who will get a long look inside. Both battled injuries a year ago.
Secondary	D +	This is a grade that had better improve as the season progresses. Cornerbacks Tyrone Poole and Jeff Burris struggled a year ago, but their play should be elevated if the front seven is as capable as it appears to be. Jason Belser will settle in at free safety and needs to rebound from a mediocre year while Chad Cota will add bite to the bunch at strong safety. If Monty Montgomery doesn't show signs of improvement, rookie Paul Miranda could see extensive playing time in nickel situations.
Special teams	D	Another area of concern. Mike Vanderjagt returns after a solid debut as the team's kicker (27-of-31 FGs), but Chris Gardocki will do his punting in Cleveland, leaving a huge void that must be filled either by rookie Hunter Smith or free agent Lonny Calicchio. The return and coverage units should be better, but that's because they can't be much worse. The release of Aaron Bailey leaves both return spots wide open.

JACKSONVILLE JAGUARS
AFC CENTRAL DIVISION

1999 SEASON

CLUB DIRECTORY

Chairman & CEO
Wayne Weaver
Senior vice president/football operations
Michael Huyghue
Senior v.p./marketing
Dan Connell
Chief financial officer/vice president
Bill Prescott
General counsel/vice president, admin.
Paul Vance
Exec. director of communications
Dan Edwards
Director of player personnel
Rick Reiprish
Director of pro scouting
Fran Foley
Director of college scouting
Rick Mueller
Director of finance
Kim Dodson
Director of facilities
Jeff Cannon
Director of football administration
Skip Richardson
Director of information technology
Bruce Swindell
Director of corporate sponsorship
Macky Weaver
Director of special events
Roddy White
Director of player programs
Quentin Williams
Director of broadcasting
Jennifer Kumik
Head athletic trainer
Mike Ryan

Head coach
Tom Coughlin

Assistant coaches
John Bonamego (assistant
   special teams)
Dom Capers (def. coordinator)
Pete Carmichael (wide receivers)
Perry Fewell (secondary)
Greg Finnegan (asst. strength &
   conditioning)
Fred Hoaglin (tight ends)
Jerald Ingram (running backs)
Mike Maser (offensive line)
Jerry Palmieri (strength &
   conditioning)
Larry Pasquale (special teams
   coordinator)
John Pease (defensive line)
John Petrino (quarterbacks)
Lucious Selmon (outside line-
   backers)
Steve Szabo (inside linebackers)

Video director
Mike Perkins
Equipment manager
Drew Hampton

SCHEDULE

Sept. 12—	SAN FRANCISCO	4:15
Sept. 19—	at Carolina	1:00
Sept. 26—	TENNESSEE	4:05
Oct. 3—	at Pittsburgh	1:00
Oct. 11—	at N.Y. Jets (Mon.)	9:00
Oct. 17—	CLEVELAND	1:00
Oct. 24—	Open date	
Oct. 31—	at Cincinnati	1:00
Nov. 7—	at Atlanta	1:00
Nov. 14—	BALTIMORE	4:05
Nov. 21—	NEW ORLEANS	8:20
Nov. 28—	at Baltimore	1:00
Dec. 2—	PITTSBURGH (Thur.)	8:20
Dec. 13—	DENVER (Mon.)	9:00
Dec. 19—	at Cleveland	1:00
Dec. 26—	at Tennessee	12:00
Jan. 2—	CINCINNATI	1:00

All times are for home team.
All games Sunday unless noted.

DRAFT CHOICES

Fernando Bryant, DB, Alabama (first
   round/26th pick overall).
Larry Smith, DT, Florida State (2/56).
Anthony Cesario, G, Colorado State
   (3/88).
Kevin Landolt, DT, West Virginia (4/121).
Jason Craft, DB, Colorado State (5/160).
Emarlos Leroy, DT, Georgia (6/182).
Dee Moronkola, DB, Washington State
   (7/242).
Chris White, DE, Southern University
   (7/246).

1998 REVIEW

RESULTS

Sept. 6—at Chicago	W	24-23
Sept.13—KANSAS CITY	W	21-16
Sept.20—BALTIMORE	W	24-10
Sept.27—at Tennessee	W	27-22
Oct. 4—Open date		
Oct. 12—MIAMI	W	28-21
Oct. 18—at Buffalo	L	16-17
Oct. 25—at Denver	L	24-37
Nov. 1—at Baltimore	W	45-19
Nov. 8—CINCINNATI	W	24-11
Nov. 15—TAMPA BAY	W	29-24
Nov. 22—at Pittsburgh	L	15-30
Nov. 29—at Cincinnati	W	34-17
Dec. 6—DETROIT	W	37-22
Dec. 13—TENNESSEE	L	13-16
Dec. 20—at Minnesota	L	10-50
Dec. 28—PITTSBURGH	W	21-3
Jan. 3—NEW ENGLAND*	W	25-10
Jan. 10—at N.Y. Jets†	L	24-34

*AFC wild-card game.
†AFC divisional playoff game.

RECORDS/RANKINGS

1998 regular-season record: 11-5 (1st in
AFC Central); 6-2 in division; 8-4 in conference; 7-1 at home; 4-4 on road.
Team record last five years: 35-29 (.547).
1998 team rankings:

	No.	AFC	NFL
Total offense	*325.9	5	10
Rushing offense	*131.4	3	5
Passing offense	*194.5	10	20
Scoring offense	392	4	8
Total defense	*347.4	12	25
Rushing defense	*125.0	13	22
Passing defense	*222.4	11	23
Scoring defense	338	10	17
Takeaways	30	T7	T13
Giveaways	20	T2	T3
Turnover differential	10	T2	T5
Sacks	30	T13	T27
Sacks allowed	39	10	T15

*Yards per game.

TEAM LEADERS

Scoring (kicking): Mike Hollis, 108 pts.
(45/45 PATs, 21/26 FGs).
Scoring (touchdowns): Fred Taylor, 102
pts. (14 rushing, 3 receiving).
Passing: Mark Brunell, 2,601 yds. (354
att., 208 comp., 58.8%, 20 TDs, 9 int.).
Rushing: Fred Taylor, 1,223 yds. (264
att., 4.6 avg., 14 TDs).
Receptions: Jimmy Smith, 78 (1,182
yds., 15.2 avg., 8 TDs).
Interceptions: Aaron Beasley, 3 (35 yds.,
0 TDs); Chris Hudson, 3 (10 yds., 0 TDs).
Sacks: Joel Smeenge, 7.5.
Punting: Bryan Barker, 45.0 avg. (85
punts, 3,824 yds., 0 blocked).
Punt returns: Reggie Barlow, 12.9 avg.
(43 att., 555 yds., 1 TD).
Kickoff returns: Reggie Barlow, 24.9 avg.
(30 att., 747 yds., 0 TDs).

JACKSONVILLE JAGUARS

No.	QUARTERBACKS	Ht./Wt.	Born	NFL Exp.	College	How acq.	'98 Games GP/GS
8	Brunell, Mark	6-1/211	9-17-70	7	Washington	T-GB/95	13/13
11	Fiedler, Jay	6-2/224	12-29-71	4	Dartmouth	FA/99	*5/0
12	Quinn, Jonathon	6-5/245	2-27-75	2	Middle Tennessee State	D3/98	4/2
	RUNNING BACKS						
22	Banks, Tavian	5-10/194	2-17-74	2	Iowa	D4a/98	6/1
24	Howard, Chris	5-10/223	5-5-75	2	Michigan	FA/98	8/0
43	Jones, George	5-9/212	12-31-73	3	San Diego State	FA/98	12/0
31	Shelton, Daimon (FB)	6-0/251	9-15-72	3	Cal State Sacramento	D6/97	14/8
33	Stewart, James	6-1/224	12-27-71	5	Tennessee	D1b/95	3/3
28	Taylor, Fred	6-0/226	6-27-76	2	Florida	D1a/98	15/12
	RECEIVERS						
84	Barlow, Reggie	6-0/191	1-22-73	4	Alabama State	D4/96	16/2
80	Brady, Kyle (TE)	6-6/268	1-14-72	5	Penn State	TFA/99	*16/16
85	Griffith, Rich (TE)	6-5/261	7-31-69	6	Arizona	FA/95	7/0
88	Jones, Damon (TE)	6-5/265	9-18-74	3	Southern Illinois	D5/97	16/7
87	McCardell, Keenan	6-1/184	1-6-70	8	UNLV	FA/96	15/15
81	Moore, Will	6-1/186	2-21-70	4	Texas Southern	FA/97	16/0
82	Smith, Jimmy	6-1/207	2-9-69	7	Jackson State	FA/95	16/15
86	Whitted, Alvis	5-11/179	9-4-74	2	North Carolina State	D7a/98	16/0
	OFFENSIVE LINEMEN						
71	Boselli, Tony (T)	6-7/324	4-17-72	5	Southern California	D1a/95	15/15
79	Cesario, Anthony (G)	6-6/312	7-19-76	R	Colorado State	D3/99	—
62	Coleman, Ben (G)	6-5/327	5-18-71	7	Wake Forest	W-Ari./95	16/16
78	Fordham, Todd (G)	6-5/308	10-9-73	3	Florida State	FA/97	11/1
65	Neujahr, Quentin (C)	6-4/297	1-30-71	5	Kansas State	FA/98	16/16
72	Searcy, Leon (T)	6-4/322	12-21-69	8	Miami (Fla.)	FA/96	15/15
76	Tylski, Rich (G)	6-5/306	2-27-71	4	Utah State	W-NE/95	11/8
66	Wade, John (C)	6-5/293	1-25-75	2	Marshall	D5/98	4/0
72	Wiegert, Zach (T)	6-4/310	8-16-72	4	Nebraska	FA/99	*13/13
	DEFENSIVE LINEMEN						
90	Brackens, Tony (E)	6-4/260	12-26-74	4	Texas	D2a/96	12/8
75	Curry, Eric (E)	6-6/269	2-3-70	7	Alabama	FA/98	11/0
77	Landolt, Kevin (T)	6-5/300	10-25-75	R	West Virginia	D4/99	—
61	Leroy, Emarlos (T)	6-2/298	7-31-75	R	Georgia	D6/99	—
91	Payne, Seth (T)	6-4/292	2-12-75	3	Cornell	D4/97	6/1
99	Smeenge, Joel (F)	6-6/270	4-1-68	10	Western Michigan	UFA/95	16/14
94	Smith, Larry (T)	6-4/290	12-4-74	R	Florida State	D2/99	—
98	Threats, Jabbar (E)	6-5/256	4-26-75	3	Michigan State	FA/97	2/0
96	Walker, Gary (T)	6-2/295	2-28-73	5	Auburn	UFA/99	*16/16
74	White, Chris (E)	6-3/280	9-28-76	R	Southern	D7b/99	—
92	Williams, Lamanzer (E)	6-4/267	11-17-74	2	Minnesota	D6a/98	1/0
97	Wynn, Renaldo (T)	6-3/290	9-3-74	3	Notre Dame	D1/97	15/15
	LINEBACKERS						
52	Boyer, Brant	6-1/232	6-27-71	6	Arizona	ED/95	11/0
54	Hamilton, James	6-5/245	4-17-74	3	North Carolina	D3/97	7/0
51	Hardy, Kevin	6-4/250	7-24-73	4	Illinois	D1/96	16/16
57	Lowe, Reggie	6-2/240	6-14-75	1	Troy State	FA/98	4/0
53	Mason, Eddie	6-0/223	1-9-72	3	North Carolina	FA/98	4/0
55	McManus, Tom	6-2/255	7-30-70	5	Boston College	FA/95	16/4
95	Paup, Bryce	6-5/247	2-29-68	10	Northern Iowa	UFA/98	16/16
58	Schwartz, Bryan	6-4/256	12-5-71	5	Augustana (S.D.)	D2b/95	13/12
	Southward, Brandon	6-4/241	12-3-76	1	Colorado	FA/99	—
50	Storz, Erik	6-2/234	6-24-75	1	Boston College	FA/98	1/0
	DEFENSIVE BACKS						
21	Beasley, Aaron (CB)	6-0/202	7-7-73	4	West Virginia	D3/96	16/15
25	Bryant, Fernando (CB)	5-10/180	3-26-77	R	Alabama	D1/99	—
29	Craft, Jason (CB)	5-9/175	2-13-76	R	Colorado State	D5/99	—
20	Darius, Donovin (S)	6-1/213	8-12-75	2	Syracuse	D1b/98	14/14
27	Figures, Deon (CB)	6-0/192	1-20-70	7	Colorado	FA/97	16/4
37	Lake, Carnell (S)	6-1/210	7-15-67	11	UCLA	UFA/99	*16/16
32	Logan, Mike (S)	6-0/206	9-15-74	3	West Virginia	D2/97	15/0
38	McElmurry, Blaine (S)	6-0/193	10-23-73	1	Montana	FA/97	2/0
26	Moronkola, Dee (CB)	5-9/203	7-1-77	R	Washington State	D7a/99	—
23	Taylor, Cordell (CB)	5-11/187	12-22-73	2	Hampton (Va.)	D2/98	10/0
41	Thomas, Dave (CB)	6-3/213	8-25-68	7	Tennessee	ED/95	14/13
	SPECIALISTS						
4	Barker, Bryan (P)	6-2/201	6-28-64	10	Santa Clara	UFA/95	16/0
1	Hollis, Mike (K)	5-7/175	5-22-72	5	Idaho	FA/95	16/0

Other free agents invited to camp: FB Trevor Bollers, FB Matt Calhoun, DT James Clyburn, T Rome Douglas, WR Damon Dunn, QB Will Furrer, G Steve Ingram, WR Lenzie Jackson, WR Nakia Jenkins, DE Ed Kehl, C David Kempfert, PK Steve Lindsey, RB Stacey Mack, S Anthony Mitchell, DT Dary Myricks, LB Jason Nevadomsky, T Jarvis Reado, WR Tory Taylor, TE Mark Thomas.

Abbreviations: D1—draft pick, first round; SupD2—supplemental draft pick, second round; WV—claimed on waivers; TR—obtained in trade; PlanB—Plan B free-agent acquisition; FA—free-agent acquisition (other than Plan B); ED—expansion draft pick.

MISCELLANEOUS TEAM DATA

Stadium (capacity, surface):
ALLTEL Stadium (73,000, grass)
Business address:
One ALLTEL Stadium Place
Jacksonville, FL 32202
Business phone:
904-633-6000
Ticket information:
904-633-2000
Team colors:
Teal, black and gold
Flagship radio station:
WOKV, 690 AM
Training site:
ALLTEL Stadium
Jacksonville, Fla.
904-633-6000

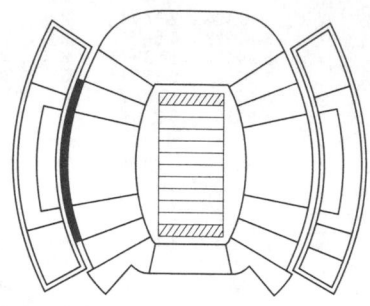

TSN REPORT CARD

Coaching staff	B -	Tom Coughlin has proved to be a very good coach, although his strict ways can be wearing on his players. Coughlin needs to improve on his clock management. It will be interesting to see how he does taking over as the offensive play-caller. Dom Capers will be a solid addition as the defensive coordinator, putting in an aggressive style of play.
Quarterbacks	B	Mark Brunell is on the verge of becoming an elite NFL quarterback, but he needs to be more consistent as a pocket passer. His legs aren't what they used to be, which will put more emphasis on him to make plays in the pocket. Second-year player Jonathan Quinn is a question as a backup, although he has big-time skills.
Running backs	A	As a rookie Fred Taylor looked like he will become the NFL's next great running back. He has power and speed, which could make him a 2,000-yard back someday. Backups James Stewart and Tavian Banks are more than capable of giving him a good rest. Fullback Daimon Shelton is a solid lead blocker, but not much as a runner or receiver.
Receivers	B -	Jimmy Smith is one of the best in the AFC, although he needs to handle double-teams better. Keenan McCardell is a very good route runner, someone who is tough for young defensive backs to handle. A third option needs to emerge. Tight end Kyle Brady will be a big-time threat in the middle of the field in this offense. Look for a 50-catch season from him.
Offensive line	B	The tackle duo of Leon Searcy and Tony Boselli is the best in the NFL. Boselli is dominant on the left side, while Searcy doesn't get the credit he deserves. He can be overpowering in the run game. Inside is a different story. The team needs better play from those three positions to get to the Super Bowl.
Defensive line	C	The key here will be how well end Tony Brackens plays. If he can become a disruptive force outside, the line should be OK. Inside, Gary Walker and second-round pick Larry Smith should add muscle to an interior that needs it. The return of Seth Payne from injuries will help.
Linebackers	B -	Kevin Hardy has emerged as one of the best in the AFC and should be even better under Capers. On the other side, Bryce Paup also should benefit from playing under Capers, although his age (31) could be a factor. Whoever starts in the middle (Bryan Schwartz or Tom McManus) may be considered the weak link of the defense.
Secondary	B	The addition of Carnell Lake should stabilize this young unit. Lake's age (32) is a concern, but he and Donovin Darius form a solid safety tandem. The cornerbacks remain an area of worry, but first-round pick Fernando Bryant may alleviate some of that concern.
Special teams	A	This has always been a strong point for the Jaguars. Punter Bryan Barker and kicker Mike Hollis both ranked near the top of the AFC last year. Returner Reggie Barlow has emerged as a big-play threat as a returner on both punts and kickoffs. The coverage teams are solid.

KANSAS CITY CHIEFS
AFC WESTERN DIVISION

1999 SEASON

CLUB DIRECTORY

Founder
Lamar Hunt
Chairman of the board
Jack Steadman
President/g.m./chief executive officer
Carl Peterson
Senior vice president
Dennis Watley
Executive vice president/assistant g.m.
Dennis Thum
Secretary/legal
Jim Seigfreid
Treasurer and director/finance
Dale Young
Vice president/sales and marketing
Wallace Bennett
Director/operations
Steve Schneider
Director/development
Ken Blume
Director/corporate sponsorship sales
Anita Bailey
Director/advance sales & hospitality
Gary Spani
Director/public relations
Bob Moore
Assistant directors/public relations
Jim Carr   Peter Moris
Director of player personnel
Terry Bradway
Director of pro personnel
John Schneider
Director of college scouting
Chuck Cook
Scouts
Frank Acevedo   Bill Baker Jr.
Scott Campbell   Jeff Ireland
Quintin Smith
Trainer
Dave Kendall
Assistant trainer
Bud Epps

Head coach
Gunther
Cunningham

Assistant coaches
Dave Adolph (assistant head
    coach/linebackers)
Frank Cignetti Jr. (offensive
    assistant/quality control)
Jeff Fish (assistant strength &
    conditioning)
Jeff Hurd (strength & cond.)
Bob Karmelowicz (defensive line)
Al Lavan (running backs)
Richard Mann (receivers)
Jimmy Raye (off. coordinator)
Tom Rossley (quarterbacks)
Keith Rowen (tight ends)
Kurt Schottenheimer (def. coord.)
Mike Solari (offensive line)
Mike Stock (special teams)
Darvin Wallis (special
    assistant/quality control)
Ron Zook (defensive backs)

Physicians
Cris Barnthouse
Joseph Brewer
Jon Browne
Mike Monaco
Equipment manager
Mike Davidson

SCHEDULE

Sept. 12—	at Chicago	12:00
Sept. 19—	DENVER	3:15
Sept. 26—	DETROIT	12:00
Oct. 3—	at San Diego	1:15
Oct. 10—	NEW ENGLAND	12:00
Oct. 17—	Open date	
Oct. 21—	at Baltimore (Thur.)	8:20
Oct. 31—	SAN DIEGO	12:00
Nov. 7—	at Indianapolis	1:00
Nov. 14—	at Tampa Bay	1:00
Nov. 21—	SEATTLE	12:00
Nov. 28—	at Oakland	1:15
Dec. 5—	at Denver	2:15
Dec. 12—	MINNESOTA	7:20
Dec. 18—	PITTSBURGH (Sat.)	11:40
Dec. 26—	at Seattle	1:05
Jan. 2—	OAKLAND	12:00

All times are for home team.
All games Sunday unless noted.

DRAFT CHOICES

John Tait, T, Brigham Young (first
    round/14th pick overall).
Mike Cloud, RB, Boston College (2/54).
Gary Stills, LB, West Virginia (3/75).
Larry Atkins, S, UCLA (3/84).
Larry Parker, WR, Southern California
    (4/108).
Eric King, G, Richmond (7/220).

1998 REVIEW

RESULTS

Sept. 6—OAKLAND	W	28-8
Sept.13—at Jacksonville	L	16-21
Sept.20—SAN DIEGO	W	23-7
Sept.27—at Philadelphia	W	24-21
Oct. 4—SEATTLE	W	17-6
Oct. 11—at New England	L	10-40
Oct. 18—Open date		
Oct. 26—PITTSBURGH	L	13-20
Nov. 1—N.Y. JETS	L	17-20
Nov. 8—at Seattle	L	12-24
Nov. 16—DENVER	L	7-30
Nov. 22—at San Diego	L	37-38
Nov. 29—ARIZONA	W	34-24
Dec. 6—at Denver	L	31-35
Dec. 13—DALLAS	W	20-17
Dec. 20—at N.Y. Giants	L	7-28
Dec. 26—at Oakland	W	31-24

RECORDS/RANKINGS

1998 regular-season record: 7-9 (4th in
AFC West); 4-4 in division; 4-8 in conference; 5-3 at home; 2-6 on road.
Team record last five years: 51-29 (.638,
ranks T4th in league in that span).

1998 team rankings:	No.	AFC	NFL
Total offense	*300.5	11	19
Rushing offense	*96.8	12	23
Passing offense	*203.8	8	16
Scoring offense	327	8	14
Total defense	*303.4	6	9
Rushing defense	*116.8	11	18
Passing defense	*186.6	3	7
Scoring defense	363	13	22
Takeaways	33	4	T7
Giveaways	32	T10	T19
Turnover differential	1	8	14
Sacks	40	7	14
Sacks allowed	36	8	13

*Yards per game.

TEAM LEADERS

Scoring (kicking): Pete Stoyanovich, 115
pts. (34/34 PATs, 27/32 FGs).
Scoring (touchdowns): Bam Morris, 48
pts. (8 rushing).
Passing: Rich Gannon, 2,305 yds. (354
att., 206 comp., 58.2%, 10 TDs, 6 int.).
Rushing: Donnell Bennett, 527 yds. (148
att., 3.6 avg., 5 TDs).
Receptions: Derrick Alexander, 54 (992
yds., 18.4 avg., 4 TDs).
Interceptions: James Hasty, 4 (42 yds.,
0 TDs).
Sacks: Derrick Thomas, 12.0.
Punting: Louie Aguiar, 43.0 avg. (75
punts, 3,226 yds., 1 blocked).
Punt returns: Tamarick Vanover, 9.8 avg.
(27 att., 264 yds., 0 TDs).
Kickoff returns: Tamarick Vanover, 23.3
avg. (41 att., 956 yds., 0 TDs).

KANSAS CITY CHIEFS

No.	QUARTERBACKS	Ht./Wt.	Born	NFL Exp.	College	How acq.	'98 Games GP/GS
18	Grbac, Elvis	6-5/232	8-13-70	7	Michigan	UFA/97	8/6
1	Moon, Warren	6-3/213	11-18-56	16	Washington	FA/99	*10/10
	RUNNING BACKS						
38	Anders, Kimble (FB)	5-11/225	9-10-66	9	Houston	FA/91	16/15
30	Bennett, Donnell	6-0/235	9-14-72	6	Miami (Fla.)	D2/94	16/10
34	Cloud, Mike	5-10/204	7-1-75	R	Boston College	D2/99	—
39	Morris, Bam	6-0/248	1-13-72	6	Texas Tech	T-Chi./98	12/5
49	Richardson, Tony (FB)	6-1/230	12-17-71	5	Auburn	FA/95	14/1
22	Shehee, Rashaan	5-10/205	6-20-75	2	Washington	D3/98	16/0
	RECEIVERS						
82	Alexander, Derrick	6-2/198	11-6-71	6	Michigan	FA/98	15/14
41	Crawford, Keith	6-2/195	11-21-70	6	Howard Payne (Texas)	FA/98	8/0
11	Dar Dar, Kirby	5-9/192	3-27-72	3	Syracuse	FA/99	*2/0
88	Gonzalez, Tony (TE)	6-4/250	2-27-76	3	California	D1/97	16/16
84	Horn, Joe	6-1/199	1-16-72	4	None.	D5/96	16/1
83	Johnson, Lonnie (TE)	6-3/240	2-14-71	6	Florida State	UFA/99	*16/16
81	Lockett, Kevin	6-0/188	9-8-74	3	Kansas State	D2/97	13/3
80	Parker, Larry	6-1/200	7-14-76	R	Southern California	D4/99	—
48	Popson, Ted (TE)	6-4/245	9-10-66	6	Portland State	FA/97	12/1
89	Rison, Andre	6-1/195	3-18-67	11	Michigan State	FA/97	14/13
85	Roche, Brian (TE)	6-5/255	5-5-73	4	San Jose State	FA/98	4/1
87	Vanover, Tamarick	5-11/220	2-25-74	5	Florida State	D3a/95	12/0
	OFFENSIVE LINEMEN						
69	Criswell, Jeff (T)	6-7/294	3-7-64	13	Graceland College (Iowa)	FA/95	14/14
61	Grunhard, Tim (C)	6-2/307	5-17-68	10	Notre Dame	D2/90	16/16
52	King, Eric (G)	6-4/290	7-27-75	R	Richmond	D7/99	—
62	Parker, Glenn (G)	6-5/305	4-22-66	10	Arizona	FA/97	15/15
66	Riley, Victor (T)	6-5/321	11-4-74	2	Auburn	D1/98	16/15
68	Shields, Will (G)	6-3/310	9-15-71	7	Nebraska	D3/93	16/16
65	Smith, Jeff (C)	6-3/322	5-25-73	4	Tennessee	D7b/96	11/3
70	Spears, Marcus (T)	6-4/320	9-28-71	6	Northwestern (La.) State	FA/97	12/0
79	Szott, Dave (G)	6-4/293	12-12-67	10	Penn State	D7/90	1/1
76	Tait, John (T)	6-6/311	1-26-75	R	Brigham Young	D1/99	—
	DEFENSIVE LINEMEN						
71	Barndt, Tom (T)	6-3/301	3-14-72	4	Pittsburgh	D6b/95	16/16
93	Browning, John (E)	6-4/295	9-30-73	4	West Virginia	D3/96	8/8
90	Dixon, Ronnie (T)	6-3/310	5-10-71	6	Cincinnati	FA/98	4/0
98	Hicks, Eric (E)	6-6/261	6-17-76	2	Maryland	FA/98	3/0
75	McGlockton, Chester (T)	6-4/320	9-16-69	8	Clemson	FA/98	10/9
91	O'Neal, Leslie (E)	6-4/275	5-7-64	14	Oklahoma State	FA/98	16/13
97	Parten, Ty (T)	6-5/295	10-13-69	5	Arizona	FA/97	16/6
95	Ransom, Derrick (T)	6-3/291	9-13-76	2	Cincinnati	D6/98	7/0
77	Smith, Artie (T)	6-5/305	5-15-70	6	Louisiana Tech	UFA/99	*16/0
92	Williams, Dan (E)	6-4/290	12-15-69	6	Toledo	D1/93	—
	LINEBACKERS						
52	Dixon, Ernest	6-1/240	10-17-71	6	South Carolina	FA/98	4/0
59	Edwards, Donnie	6-2/236	4-6-73	4	UCLA	D4/96	15/15
54	Favors, Gregory	6-1/236	9-30-74	2	Mississippi State	D4/98	16/4
55	George, Ron	6-2/241	3-20-70	7	Stanford	FA/98	16/0
56	Hollinquest, Lamont	6-3/250	10-24-70	6	Southern California	UFA/99	*14/2
51	Manusky, Greg	6-1/234	8-12-66	12	Colgate	FA/94	16/1
53	Patton, Marvcus	6-2/236	5-1-67	10	UCLA	UFA/99	*16/16
57	Stills, Gary	6-2/238	7-11-74	R	West Virginia	D3a/99	—
58	Thomas, Derrick	6-3/247	1-1-67	11	Alabama	D1/89	15/10
	DEFENSIVE BACKS						
26	Adams, Vashone (S)	5-10/201	9-12-73	4	Eastern Michigan	FA/98	—
35	Atkins, Larry (S)	6-3/215	7-21-75	R	UCLA	D3b/99	—
43	Bolden, Juran (CB)	6-2/201	6-27-74	4	Mississippi Delta C.C.	FA/99	*12/0
	Dishman, Cris (CB)	6-0/195	8-13-65	12	Purdue	FA/99	*16/16
23	Gray, Carlton (CB)	6-0/200	6-26-71	7	UCLA	FA/99	*14/3
40	Hasty, James (CB)	6-0/208	5-23-65	12	Washington State	UFA/95	16/14
24	Kaiser, Jason (S)	6-0/190	11-9-73	1	Culver-Stockton College (Mo.)	FA/98	1/0
25	Tongue, Reggie (S)	6-0/205	4-11-73	4	Oregon State	D2/96	15/15
27	Walker, Bracey (S)	6-0/204	6-11-70	6	North Carolina	FA/98	8/0
44	Warfield, Eric (CB)	6-0/192	3-3-76	2	Nebraska	D7a/98	12/0
29	Williams, Robert (CB)	5-10/177	5-29-77	2	North Carolina	D5/98	16/1
21	Woods, Jerome (S)	6-2/207	3-17-73	4	Memphis	D1/96	16/16

No.	SPECIALISTS	Ht./Wt.	Born	NFL Exp.	College	How acq.	'98 Games GP/GS
5	Aguiar, Louie (P)	6-2/218	6-30-66	9	Utah State	FA/94	16/0
10	Stoyanovich, Pete (K)..................	5-11/191	4-28-67	11	Indiana	T-Mia./96	16/0

*Not with Chiefs in 1998.

Other free agents invited to camp: DE Duane Ashman, C Eugene Chung, QB Todd Collins, TE Brandon Condie, P/K Sean Fleming, CB Ken Haslip, RB Jesse Haynes, DT Jim Hoffman, WR Reggie Jones, S Carl Kidd, G Brad Kubik, TE Sean Manuel, LB Mike Maslowski, WR Shawn McWashington, T Nate Parks, T James Parrish, G Fred Pollack, LB Terry Rice-Locket, TE Bob Rosentiel, RB Brian Shay, WR Burt Thornton, QB Ted White, CB Sean Williams, G Donald Willis, DE Mark Word.

Abbreviations: D1—draft pick, first round; SupD2—supplemental draft pick, second round; WV—claimed on waivers; TR—obtained in trade; PlanB—Plan B free-agent acquisition; FA—free-agent acquisition (other than Plan B); ED—expansion draft pick.

MISCELLANEOUS TEAM DATA

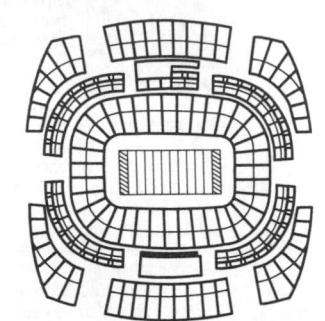

Stadium (capacity, surface):
Arrowhead Stadium
(79,451, grass)
Business address:
One Arrowhead Drive
Kansas City, MO 64129
Business phone:
816-920-9300
Ticket information:
816-920-9400
Team colors:
Red, gold and white
Flagship radio station:
KCFX, 101.1 FM
Training site:
U. of Wisconsin-River Falls
River Falls, Wis.
715-425-4580

TSN REPORT CARD

Coaching staff	C	The coaching staff—which went through an overhaul this winter—should have three goals: instill better discipline and team unity; improve run defense and run offense; and give Elvic Grbac a safe, but competitive atmosphere in which to excel. Anything short of that won't fix the problems from a year ago.
Quarterbacks	C	How many times will Grbac have to go into a season trying to prove he is NFL quarterback material? He will as long as he is coming off an injury-plagued year. Warren Moon provides the necessary incentive to make 1999 the year Grbac finishes a 16-game schedule and finishes it strongly.
Running backs	C	This group should be considered average until someone (read: Bam Morris) exploits a strong offensive line to enliven the running game. The team is overloaded with bigger runners—Morris, Donnell Bennett, Kimble Anders and Tony Richardson. They aren't short on speed, but their two quick backs are a rookie and a second-year player.
Receivers	B	Led by Derrick Alexander and Andre Rison, the Chiefs have an experienced, productive duo that can do a lot to help Grbac look good. But Rison is coming off an up-and-down year and they can't be sure what they'll get from top backup Kevin Lockett.
Offensive line	A -	The only real questions: How quickly will rookie LT John Tait be able to step into the starting lineup? And will RT Victor Riley stay in shape? The interior of center Tim Grunhard, right guard Will Shields and left guard Dave Szott is consistently one of the best in the NFL when healthy.
Defensive line	B	Chester McGlockton and Dan Williams should form a powerful pass-rush threat from the inside if they can return to their respective form from 1997. The Chiefs could be shaky at defensive end with 14-year veteran Leslie O'Neal coming back and fourth-year player John Browning trying to stay healthy after dealing with injuries all last season.
Linebackers	B +	This is probably the strongest group on defense, with speed, tenacity, experience, a few up-and-comers and depth. But you won't see how strong until weakside linebacker Donnie Edwards and strongside linebacker Derrick Thomas adjust to changing positions and newcomer Marvcus Patton establishes himself in the middle.
Secondary	B	The good news: James Hasty will anchor one corner. He joins a great, young safety duo in strong safety Reggie Tongue and free safety Jerome Woods to set an aggressive tone. The bad news: Dale Carter is gone. Carlton Gray, untested in the Chiefs' bump-and-run style, could start in his place.
Special teams	C	Only kicker Pete Stoyanovich had a strong season in 1998. And even he struggled with short kickoffs. The Chiefs cannot afford for punter Louie Aguiar and return man Tamarick Vanover to have below-average performances in 1999. Vanover is needed for his explosiveness and ability to single-handedly turn the tide in games.

MIAMI DOLPHINS
AFC EASTERN DIVISION

1999 SEASON

CLUB DIRECTORY

Owner/chairman of the board
H. Wayne Huizenga
President/chief operating officer
Eddie J. Jones
Vice president/administration
Bryan Wiedmeier
Vice president/finance
Jill R. Strafaci
Director of football operations
Bob Ackles
Director of pro personnel
Tom Heckert
Director of college scouting
Tom Braatz
Vice president/media relations
Harvey Greene
Media relations coordinator
Neal Gulkis
Vice president/sales and marketing
Bob Reif
Senior director/marketing
David Evans
Director of publications
Scott Stone
Community relations director
Fudge Browne
Vice president/ticket sales
Bill Galante
Scouts
Mike Cartwright
Tom Heckert, Jr.
Ron Labadie
Jeff Smith
Jere Stripling
Head trainer
Kevin O'Neill
Trainers
Troy Maurer
Ryan Vermillion
Physician
Daniel Kanell
John Uribe

**General manager/
head coach**
Jimmy Johnson

Assistant coaches
Doug Blevins (kicking)
Paul Boudreau (offensive line)
Kippy Brown (off. coordinator)
Joel Collier (running backs)
Robert Ford (wide receivers)
John Gamble (strength &
conditioning)
Cary Godette (defensive line)
George Hill (defensive coordinator/
linebackers)
Pat Jones (tight ends)
Bill Lewis (defensive nickel package)
Rich McGeorge (assistant
offensive line)
Mel Phillips (secondary)
Brad Roll (assistant strength and
conditioning)
Larry Seiple (quarterbacks)
Randy Shannon (def. assistant)
Dave Wannstedt (assistant head
coach)
Mike Westhoff (special teams)

Equipment manager
Tony Egues
Video director
Dave Hack

SCHEDULE

Sept. 13—	at Denver (Mon.)	7:00
Sept. 19—	ARIZONA	1:00
Sept. 26—	Open date	
Oct. 4—	BUFFALO (Mon.)	9:00
Oct. 10—	at Indianapolis	3:15
Oct. 17—	at New England	1:00
Oct. 24—	PHILADELPHIA	1:00
Oct. 31—	at Oakland	1:05
Nov. 7—	TENNESSEE	8:20
Nov. 14—	at Buffalo	1:00
Nov. 21—	NEW ENGLAND	1:00
Nov. 25—	at Dallas (Thanks.)	3:15
Dec. 5—	INDIANAPOLIS	1:00
Dec. 12—	at N.Y. Jets	4:05
Dec. 19—	SAN DIEGO	1:00
Dec. 27—	N.Y. JETS (Mon.)	9:00
Jan. 2—	at Washington	4:15

All times are for home team.
All games Sunday unless noted.

DRAFT CHOICES

James Johnson, RB, Mississippi State
(second round/39th pick overall).
Rob Konrad, RB, Syracuse (2/43).
Grey Ruegamer, C, Arizona State (3/72).
Cecil Collins, RB, McNeese State
(5/134).
Bryan Jones, LB, Oregon State (5/142).
Brent Bartholomew, P, Ohio State
(6/192).
Jermaine Haley, DT, Butte J.C. (7/232).
Joe Wong, T, Brigham Young (7/244).

1998 REVIEW

RESULTS

Sept. 6—at Indianapolis	W	24-15
Sept.13—BUFFALO	W	13-7
Sept.20—PITTSBURGH	W	21-0
Sept.27—Open date		
Oct. 4—at N.Y. Jets	L	9-20
Oct. 12—at Jacksonville	L	21-28
Oct. 18—ST. LOUIS	W	14-0
Oct. 25—NEW ENGLAND (OT)	W	12-9
Nov. 1—at Buffalo	L	24-30
Nov. 8—INDIANAPOLIS	W	27-14
Nov. 15—at Carolina	W	13-9
Nov. 23—at New England	L	23-26
Nov. 29—NEW ORLEANS	W	30-10
Dec. 6—at Oakland	W	27-17
Dec. 13—N.Y. Jets	L	16-21
Dec. 21—DENVER	W	31-21
Dec. 27—at Atlanta	L	16-38
Jan. 2—BUFFALO*	W	24-17
Jan. 9—at Denver†	L	3-38

*AFC wild-card game.
†AFC divisional playoff game.

RECORDS/RANKINGS

1998 regular-season record: 10-6 (2nd
in AFC East); 4-4 in division; 7-1 in conference; 7-1 at home; 3-5 on road.
Team record last five years: 46-34 (.575,
ranks T8th in league in that span).
1998 team rankings:

	No.	AFC	NFL
Total offense	*308.1	8	16
Rushing offense	*95.9	13	24
Passing offense	*212.2	5	10
Scoring offense	321	9	16
Total defense	*277.2	2	3
Rushing defense	*94.4	4	6
Passing defense	*182.8	2	6
Scoring defense	265	1	1
Takeaways	36	2	4
Giveaways	28	8	14
Turnover differential	8	T4	T7
Sacks	45	3	8
Sacks allowed	24	2	3

*Yards per game.

TEAM LEADERS

Scoring (kicking): Olindo Mare, 99 pts.
(33/34 PATs, 22/27 FGs).
Scoring (touchdowns): O.J. McDuffie, 42
pts. (7 receiving); Oronde Gadsden, 42
pts. (7 receiving).
Passing: Dan Marino, 3,497 yds. (537
att., 310 comp., 57.7%, 23 TDs, 15 int.).
Rushing: Karim Abdul-Jabbar, 960 yds.
(270 att., 3.6 avg., 6 TDs).
Receptions: O.J. McDuffie, 90 (1,050
yds., 11.7 avg., 7 TDs).
Interceptions: Terrell Buckley, 8 (157 yds.,
1 TD); Sam Madison, 8 (114 yds., 0 TDs).
Sacks: Trace Armstrong, 10.5.
Punting: Klaus Wilmsmeyer, 42.5 avg.
(93 punts, 3,949 yds., 1 blocked).
Punt returns: Terrell Buckley, 12.2 avg.
(29 att., 354 yds., 0 TDs).
Kickoff returns: John Avery, 25.2 avg.
(43 att., 1,085 yds., 0 TDs).

MIAMI DOLPHINS

No.	QUARTERBACKS	Ht./Wt.	Born	NFL Exp.	College	How acq.	'98 Games GP/GS
7	Erickson, Craig	6-2/215	5-17-69	8	Miami, Fla	FA/96	—
11	Huard, Damon	6-3/215	7-9-73	3	Washington	FA/97	2/0
13	Marino, Dan	6-4/228	9-15-61	17	Pittsburgh	D1/83	16/16

	RUNNING BACKS						
33	Abdul-Jabbar, Karim	5-10/205	6-28-74	4	UCLA	D3b/96	15/15
20	Avery, John	5-9/190	1-11-76	2	Mississippi	D1/98	16/0
34	Collins, Cecil	5-10/209	11-19-76	R	McNeese State	D5a/99	—
35	Johnson, James	6-1/235	4-20-74	R	Mississippi State	D2a/99	—
44	Konrad, Rob (FB)	6-3/260	11-12-76	R	Syracuse	D2b/99	—
30	Parmalee, Bernie	5-11/210	9-16-67	8	Ball State	FA/92	15/0
40	Potts, Roosevelt (FB)	6-0/250	1-8-71	6	Northeast Louisiana	UFA/99	*16/15
36	Pritchett, Stanley (FB)	6-1/242	12-12-73	4	South Carolina	D4b/96	16/12
42	Wheatley, Tyrone	6-0/235	1-19-72	5	Michigan	T-NYG/99	*5/0

	RECEIVERS						
17	Doxzon, Todd	6-0/186	3-28-75	2	Iowa State	FA/98	9/0
84	Drayton, Troy (TE)	6-3/270	6-29-70	7	Penn State	T-Stl./96	15/15
86	Gadsden, Oronde	6-2/218	8-20-71	2	Winston-Salem	FA/98	16/12
83	Goodwin, Hunter (TE)	6-5/275	10-10-72	4	Texas A&M	FA/99	*15/0
82	Green, Willie	6-4/191	4-2-66	10	Mississippi	FA/99	*15/1
87	Green, Yatil	6-2/205	11-25-73	3	Miami (Fla.)	D1/97	—
88	Jacquet, Nate	6-0/173	9-2-75	3	San Diego State	W-Ind./98	15/0
80	Martin, Tony	6-1/181	9-5-65	10	Mesa College (Colo.)	FA/99	*16/16
81	McDuffie, O.J.	5-10/195	12-2-69	7	Penn State	D1/93	16/16
89	Perry, Ed (TE)	6-4/255	9-1-74	3	James Madison	D6d/97	14/5
85	Thomas, Lamar	6-1/175	2-12-70	7	Miami (Fla.)	FA/96	16/2

	OFFENSIVE LINEMEN						
60	Bock, John (G)	6-3/298	2-11-71	5	Indiana State	FA/96	16/6
76	Brown, James (T)	6-6/330	11-30-70	7	Virginia State	T-NYJ/96	16/16
63	Dixon, Mark (G)	6-4/300	11-6-70	2	Virginia	FA/98	11/10
65	Donnalley, Kevin (G)	6-5/305	6-10-68	9	North Carolina	FA/98	14/14
66	Gogan, Kevin (G)	6-7/330	11-2-64	13	Washington	T-SF/99	*16/16
61	Ruddy, Tim (C)	6-3/300	4-27-72	6	Notre Dame	D2b/94	16/16
62	Ruegamer, Grey (C)	6-5/304	6-1-76	R	Arizona State	D3/99	—
68	Sheldon, Mike (T)	6-4/305	6-8-73	3	Grand Valley State	FA/96	9/2
74	Smith, Brent (G)	6-5/315	11-21-73	3	Mississippi State	D3d/97	8/7
67	Stokes, Barry (T)	6-4/315	12-20-73	2	Eastern Michigan	FA/97	3/0
78	Webb, Richmond (T)	6-6/320	1-11-67	10	Texas A&M	D1/90	9/9
71	Wong, Joe (T)	6-6/313	2-24-76	R	Brigham Young	D7b/99	—

	DEFENSIVE LINEMEN						
93	Armstrong, Trace (E)	6-4/270	10-5-65	11	Florida	T-Chi./95	16/0
95	Bowens, Tim (T)	6-4/315	2-7-73	6	Mississippi	D1/94	16/16
91	Bromell, Lorenzo (E)	6-6/266	9-23-75	2	Clemson	D4/98	14/0
75	Burton, Shane (T)	6-6/305	1-18-74	4	Tennessee	D5b/96	15/0
92	Gardener, Daryl (T)	6-6/315	2-25-73	4	Baylor	D1/96	16/16
	Haley, Jermaine (T)	6-4/270	2-3-73	R		D7a/99	16/
79	Mixon, Kenny (E)	6-4/273	5-31-75	2	Louisiana State	D2b/98	16/16
96	Owens, Rich (E)	6-6/281	5-22-72	5	Lehigh	UFA/99	—
72	Tanner, Barron (T)	6-3/312	9-14-73	3	Oklahoma	D5a/97	13/0
99	Taylor, Jason (E)	6-6/260	9-1-74	3	Akron	D3a/97	16/15

	LINEBACKERS						
57	Brigance, O.J.	6-0/236	9-29-69	4	Rice	FA/96	16/0
51	Harris, Anthony	6-1/240	1-25-73	4	Auburn	FA/96	5/0
50	Hollier, Dwight	6-2/242	4-21-69	8	North Carolina	D4/92	16/0
53	Izzo, Larry	5-10/228	9-26-74	4	Rice	FA/96	13/0
55	Jones, Bryan	6-4/217	12-21-75	R	Oregon State	D5b/99	—
52	Jones, Robert	6-3/250	9-27-69	8	East Carolina	FA/96	16/16
59	Rodgers, Derrick	6-1/227	10-14-71	3	Arizona State	D3b/97	16/16
54	Thomas, Zach	5-11/235	9-1-73	4	Texas Tech	D5c/96	16/16

	DEFENSIVE BACKS						
27	Buckley, Terrell (CB)	5-10/180	6-7-71	8	Florida State	T-GB/95	16/16
28	Hill, Ray (CB)	6-0/182	8-7-75	2	Michigan State	W-Buf./98	6/0
38	Jackson, Calvin (S)	5-9/195	10-28-72	5	Auburn	FA/94	16/15
25	Jeffries, Greg (CB)	5-9/185	10-16-71	7	Virginia	UFA/99	*15/3
29	Madison, Sam (CB)	5-11/185	4-23-74	3	Louisville	D2/97	16/16
31	Marion, Brock (S)	5-11/205	6-11-70	7	Nevada	FA/98	16/16
21	Stewart, Rayna (S)	5-10/200	6-18-73	4	Northern Arizona	FA/98	14/0
23	Surtain, Patrick (CB)	5-11/197	6-19-76	2	Southern Mississippi	D2a/98	16/0
45	Walker, Brian (S)	6-1/198	5-31-72	4	Washington State	FA/97	16/0

No.	DEFENSIVE BACKS	Ht./Wt.	Born	NFL Exp.	College	How acq.	'98 Games GP/GS
24	Wilson, Jerry (CB)	5-10/187	7-17-73	5	Southern (La.)	FA/96	16/0
22	Wooden, Shawn (S)	5-11/205	10-23-73	4	Notre Dame	D6/96	2/1
	SPECIALISTS						
6	Bartholomew, Brent (P)	6-2/210	10-22-76	R	Ohio State	D6/99	—
8	Gallery, Nick (P)	6-4/245	2-15-75	1	Iowa	FA/99	*1/0
10	Mare, Olindo (K)	5-10/190	6-6-73	3	Syracuse	FA/97	16/0

*Not with Dolphins in 1998.

Other free agents invited to camp: FB Kantroy Barber, TE Rickey Brady, WR Siaha Burley, LB Sammie Burroughs, DT Travis Darden, DE Eric Davis, G Justin Glasgow, QB Dan Gonzalez, RB Juan Johnson, TE Frank Leatherwood, CB Emmanuel McDaniel, S Jackie Mitchell, G O'Lester Pope, T Thomas Rayam, FB Jamie Reader, WR Larry Shannon, DT Antoine Simpson, WR Derrick Steagall, LB Derik Stevenson, S Marcus Wimberly.

Abbreviations: D1—draft pick, first round; SupD2—supplemental draft pick, second round; WV—claimed on waivers; TR—obtained in trade; PlanB—Plan B free-agent acquisition; FA—free-agent acquisition (other than Plan B); ED—expansion draft pick.

MISCELLANEOUS TEAM DATA

Stadium (capacity, surface):
Pro Player Stadium
(75,192, grass)
Business address:
7500 S.W. 30th St.
Davie, FL 33314
Business phone:
954-452-7000
Ticket information:
305-620-2578
Team colors:
Aqua, coral, blue and white
Flagship radio station:
WQAM, 560 AM
Training site:
Nova Southeastern University
Davie, Fla.
954-452-7000

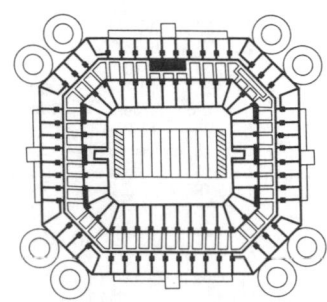

TSN REPORT CARD

Coaching staff	A -	Questions will run rampant about whether this is Jimmy Johnson's last season, and some of those questions will come from the players. However, Johnson continues to put together a team that will be good to excellent for many years. The addition of Dave Wannstedt should help Johnson stay calm, if nothing else.
Quarterbacks	B +	Dan Marino is in the twilight of his career, but he has shown the ability to adapt to a new offensive system that features less throwing. In addition, he hasn't missed a game in the past two years, so his durability seems to be there. The backup situation is reasonable with Damon Huard improving and Craig Erickson back from elbow surgery.
Running backs	C +	Seven tailbacks and five fullbacks will compete for probably six jobs, so this could be a wonderful study in survival of the fittest. If the Dolphins find the right guy, they should improve drastically. If Cecil Collins turns his talent into the superstar ability he has shown glimpses of in the past, the Dolphins will be serious contenders.
Receivers	C +	If Tony Martin can survive his bevy of legal problems, the Dolphins will have the deep threat they have lacked for years. If Yatil Green comes back from two years of knee injuries, the Dolphins will have depth. If Troy Drayton continues to progress as a receiving tight end, the Dolphins will have a big threat in the middle. That's a lot of ifs.
Offensive line	B -	The addition of Pro Bowl guard Kevin Gogan and the return to health of guard Mark Dixon should give the Dolphins great depth. That was what they lacked last season after losing three of the original five starters along the line. If nothing else, the Dolphins should have a more intense group up front, something they have been trying to get since the end of 1997.
Defensive line	A	This is the deepest, most talented position on the team, with the likes of Jason Taylor, Tim Bowens, Daryl Gardener, Kenny Mixon, Trace Armstrong and Lorenzo Bromell. Johnson has put together a group he loves. The goal this year is to get a couple of those guys to take the next step on the road to superstar status.
Linebackers	A -	With Zach Thomas and Robert Jones, the Dolphins have the perfect group of linebackers for a Johnson defense. Both are tackle machines, having each gotten at least 100 tackles last season. Thomas, who has averaged 163 tackles in his first three seasons, has the instincts to make big plays. Derrick Rodgers is solid on the weakside and the depth is very good.
Secondary	B +	The top three cornerbacks—starters Sam Madison and Terrell Buckley and nickel back Patrick Surtain—are probably the best overall trio in the NFL. The Dolphins had a league-high 29 interceptions, including a combined 16 by Madison and Buckley. The safety positions need work, with the strong safety spot to be decided and free safety Brock Marion needing to show improvement.
Special teams	B +	Kicker Olindo Mare and returners John Avery (kickoffs) and Terrell Buckley (punts) are all solid and have the potential to be very good. The punting situation needs to be decided with rookie Brent Bartholomew holding an early edge over Nick Gallery. The coverage teams are consistently among the best in the NFL.

MINNESOTA VIKINGS
NFC CENTRAL DIVISION

1999 SEASON

CLUB DIRECTORY

Owner
Red McCombs
President
Gary Woods
General manager
Tim Connolly
Vice president, player personnel
Frank Gilliam
Asssistant g.m., college scouting
Jerry Reichow
Assistant g.m., pro personnel
Paul Wiggin
Director of finance
Nick Valentine
Director of research and development
Mike Eayrs
Director of corporate sales
Kernal Buhler
Public relations director
Bob Hagan
Director of marketing
Paula Beadle
Director of marketing and sales
Terri Huml
Director of ticket sales
Phil Huebner
Director of football administration
Rob Brzezinski
Player personnel coordinator
Scott Studwell
Head scout
Don Deisch
Assistant head scout
Conrad Cardano
Regional scout
Roger Jackson
Area scout
John Fitzpatrick
Director of team operations
Breck Spinner

Head coach
Dennis Green

Assistant coaches
Hubbard Alexander (receivers)
Dave Atkins (tight ends)
Dean Dalton (quality control)
Foge Fazio (defensive coordinator)
Carl Hargrave (running backs)
John Kasper (assistant strength
& conditioning)
Tom Olivadotti (inside linebackers)
Andre Patterson (defensive line)
Ray Sherman (offensive coord.)
Richard Solomon (secondary)
Mike Tice (offensive line)
Trent Walters (outside linebackers)
Steve Wetzel (strength &
conditioning)
Alex Wood (quarterbacks)
Gary Zauner (special teams)

Equipment manager
Dennis Ryan
Medical director
Dr. David Fischer
Trainer
Fred Zamberletti
Assistant trainer
Chuck Barta

SCHEDULE

Sept. 12—	at Atlanta	4:15
Sept. 19—	OAKLAND	12:00
Sept. 26—	at Green Bay	3:15
Oct. 3—	TAMPA BAY	12:00
Oct. 10—	CHICAGO	12:00
Oct. 17—	at Detroit	1:00
Oct. 24—	SAN FRANCISCO	12:00
Oct. 31—	at Denver	2:15
Nov. 8—	DALLAS (Mon.)	8:00
Nov. 14—	at Chicago	12:00
Nov. 21—	Open date	
Nov. 28—	SAN DIEGO	12:00
Dec. 6—	at Tampa Bay (Mon.)	9:00
Dec. 12—	at Kansas City	7:20
Dec. 20—	GREEN BAY (Mon.)	8:00
Dec. 26—	at N.Y. Giants	1:00
Jan. 2—	DETROIT	12:00

All times are for home team.
All games Sunday unless noted.

DRAFT CHOICES

Daunte Culpepper, QB, Central Florida
(first round/11th pick overall).
Dimitrius Underwood, DE, Michigan
State (1/29).
Jim Kleinsasser, TE, North Dakota
(2/44).
Kenny Wright, DB, Northwestern (La.)
State (4/120).
Jay Humphrey, T, Texas (4/125).
Chris Jones, LB, Clemson (5/169).
Talance Sawyer, DE, UNLV (6/185).
Antico Dalton, LB, Hampton (6/199).
Noel Scarlett, DT, Langston (7/236).

1998 REVIEW

RESULTS

Sept. 6—TAMPA BAY	W	31-7
Sept.13—at St. Louis	W	38-31
Sept.20—DETROIT	W	29-6
Sept.27—at Chicago	W	31-28
Oct. 5—at Green Bay	W	37-24
Oct. 11—Open date		
Oct. 18—WASHINGTON	W	41-7
Oct. 25—at Detroit	W	34-13
Nov. 1—at Tampa Bay	L	24-27
Nov. 8—NEW ORLEANS	W	31-24
Nov. 15—CINCINNATI	W	24-3
Nov. 22—GREEN BAY	W	28-14
Nov. 26—at Dallas	W	46-36
Dec. 6—CHICAGO	W	48-22
Dec. 13—at Baltimore	W	38-28
Dec. 20—JACKSONVILLE	W	50-10
Dec. 26—at Tennessee	W	26-16
Jan. 10—ARIZONA*	W	41-21
Jan. 17—ATLANTA† (OT)	L	27-30

*NFC divisional playoff game.
†NFC championship game.

RECORDS/RANKINGS

1998 regular-season record: 15-1 (1st in NFC Central); 7-1 in division; 11-1 in conference; 8-0 at home; 7-1 on road.
Team record last five years: 51-29 (.638, ranks T4th in league in that span).
1998 team rankings:

	No.	NFC	NFL
Total offense	*391.5	2	2
Rushing offense	*121.0	6	11
Passing offense	*270.5	1	1
Scoring offense	556	1	1
Total defense	*316.6	5	13
Rushing defense	*100.9	5	11
Passing defense	*215.8	10	19
Scoring defense	296	4	6
Takeaways	34	3	6
Giveaways	20	2	T3
Turnover differential	14	2	2
Sacks	38	T9	T18
Sacks allowed	25	2	T4

*Yards per game.

TEAM LEADERS

Scoring (kicking): Gary Anderson, 164 pts. (59/59 PATs, 35/35 FGs).
Scoring (touchdowns): Randy Moss, 106 pts. (17 receiving, 2 2-pt. conv.).
Passing: Randall Cunningham, 3,704 yds. (425 att., 259 comp., 60.9%, 34 TDs, 10 int.).
Rushing: Robert Smith, 1,187 yds. (249 att., 4.8 avg., 6 TDs).
Receptions: Randy Moss, 69 (1,313 yds., 19.0 avg., 17 TDs).
Interceptions: Jimmy Hitchcock, 7 (242 yds., 3 TDs).
Sacks: John Randle, 10.5.
Punting: Mitch Berger, 44.7 avg. (55 punts, 2,458 yds., 0 blocked).
Punt returns: David Palmer, 10.3 avg. (28 att., 289 yds., 0 TDs).
Kickoff returns: David Palmer, 23.5 avg. (50 att., 1,176 yds., 1 TD).

– 53 –

1999 SEASON
TRAINING CAMP ROSTER

No.	QUARTERBACKS	Ht./Wt.	Born	NFL Exp.	College	How acq.	'98 Games GP/GS
12	Culpepper, Daunte	6-4/255	1-28-77	R	Central Florida	D1a/99	—
7	Cunningham, Randall	6-4/215	3-27-63	14	UNLV	FA/97	15/14
3	George, Jeff	6-4/215	12-8-67	10	Illinois	UFA/99	*8/7
	RUNNING BACKS						
49	Ayanbadejo, Obafemi (FB)	6-2/235	3-5-75	2	San Diego State	FA/98	1/0
44	Hoard, Leroy	5-11/224	5-15-68	10	Michigan	FA/96	16/1
33	Morrow, Harold (FB)	5-11/217	2-24-73	4	Auburn	W-Dal./96	11/0
22	Palmer, David	5-8/173	11-19-72	6	Alabama	D2a/94	16/0
26	Smith, Robert	6-2/212	3-4-72	7	Ohio State	D1/93	14/14
21	Williams, Moe	6-1/200	7-26-74	4	Kentucky	D3/96	12/1
	RECEIVERS						
18	Bland, Tony	6-3/213	12-12-72	2	Florida A&M	FA/99	*1/0
80	Carter, Cris	6-3/214	11-25-65	13	Ohio State	W-Phi./90	16/16
87	Crumpler, Carlester (TE)	6-6/260	9-5-71	6	East Carolina	UFA/99	*11/1
82	Glover, Andrew (TE)	6-6/252	8-12-67	9	Grambling State	FA/97	16/12
89	Hatchette, Matthew	6-2/198	5-1-74	3	Langston	D7b/97	5/0
85	Kleinsasser, Jimmy (TE)	6-3/272	1-31-77	R	North Dakota	D2/99	—
87	Mills, John Henry (TE)	6-0/235	10-31-69	7	Wake Forest	FA/99	*5/0
84	Moss, Randy	6-4/202	2-13-77	2	Marshall (W.Va.)	D1/98	16/11
86	Reed, Jake	6-3/216	9-28-67	9	Grambling State	D3/91	11/11
83	Tate, Robert	5-10/186	10-19-73	3	Cincinnati	D6/97	15/1
81	Walsh, Chris	6-1/199	12-12-68	7	Stanford	FA/94	15/0
	OFFENSIVE LINEMEN						
75	Birk, Matt (T)	6-4/310	7-23-76	2	Harvard	D6/98	7/0
62	Christy, Jeff (C)	6-3/285	2-3-69	7	Pittsburgh	FA/93	16/16
71	Dixon, David (G)	6-5/352	1-5-69	6	Arizona State	FA/94	16/16
67	Humphrey, Jay (T)	6-6/322	6-20-76	R	Texas	D4b/99	—
76	Liwienski, Chris	6-5/308	8-2-75	2	Indiana	D7/98	1/0
64	McDaniel, Randall (G)	6-3/287	12-19-64	12	Arizona State	D1/88	16/16
68	Morris, Mike (C)	6-5/272	2-22-61	13	Northeast Missouri State	FA/91	16/0
73	Steussie, Todd (T)	6-6/316	12-1-70	6	California	D1b/94	15/15
77	Stringer, Korey (T)	6-4/335	5-8-74	5	Ohio State	D1/95	14/14
	DEFENSIVE LINEMEN						
91	Burrough, John (E)	6-5/275	5-17-72	5	Wyoming	UFA/99	*16/3
92	Clemons, Duane (E)	6-5/272	5-23-74	4	California	D1/96	16/4
99	Colinet, Stalin (E)	6-6/284	7-19-74	3	Boston College	D3/97	11/3
93	Randle, John (T)	6-1/283	12-12-67	10	Texas A&I	FA/90	16/16
97	Sawyer, Talance (E)	6-2/252	6-14-76	R	UNLV	D6a/99	—
90	Scarlett, Noel (NT)	6-3/320	1-21-74	R	Langston	D7/99	—
66	Underwood, Dimitrius (E)	6-6/276	3-29-77	R	Michigan State	D1b/99	—
98	Williams, Ben (E)	6-2/287	5-28-70	2	Minnesota	FA/98	1/0
94	Williams, Tony (T)	6-1/285	7-9-75	3	Memphis	D5/97	14/9
	LINEBACKERS						
56	Bercich, Pete	6-1/239	12-23-71	5	Notre Dame	D7/94	15/1
50	Dalton, Antico	6-1/242		R	Hampton	D6b/99	—
51	Jones, Chris	5-10/229	9-30-76	R	Clemson	D5/99	—
53	Mays, Kivuusama	6-3/250	1-7-75	2	North Carolina	D4/98	16/0
58	McDaniel, Ed	5-11/230	2-23-69	8	Clemson	D5/92	16/16
54	Miller, Corey	6-2/252	10-25-68	9	South Carolina	FA/99	—
57	Rudd, Dwayne	6-2/238	2-3-76	3	Alabama	D1/97	15/15
52	Wong, Kailee	6-2/257	5-23-76	2	Stanford	D2/98	15/0
	DEFENSIVE BACKS						
30	Banks, Antonio (CB)	5-10/195	3-12-73	2	Virginia Tech	D4/97	4/0
32	Bass, Anthony	6-1/203	3-26-75	2	Bethune-Cookman	FA/98	3/0
23	Gray, Torrian (S)	6-0/200	3-18-74	3	Virginia Tech	D2/97	9/1
24	Griffith, Robert (S)	5-11/195	11-30-70	6	San Diego State	FA/94	16/16
37	Hitchcock, Jimmy (CB)	5-10/187	11-9-71	5	North Carolina	T-NE/98	16/16
34	McDonald, Ramos (CB)	5-11/194	4-30-76	2	New Mexico	D3/98	15/0
42	Thomas, Orlando (S)	6-1/214	10-21-72	5	Southwestern Louisiana	D2/95	16/16
20	Wright, Kenny (CB)	6-1/200	9-14-77	R	Northwestern State	D4a/99	—
	SPECIALISTS						
1	Anderson, Gary (K)	5-11/179	7-16-59	18	Syracuse	UFA/98	16/0
17	Berger, Mitch (P)	6-2/217	6-24-72	4	Colorado	FA/96	16/0

*Not with Vikings in 1998.

Other free agents invited to camp: T Chad Abernathy, QB Todd Bouman, TE Matt Cercone, WR Kevin Cooper, CB Tony Darden, CB Robert Davis, T Travis Hardin, DE Martin Harrison, P/K Ken Hinsley, RB Carl McCullough, FB Cory Moore, S Don Morgan, OL Eric Moss, CB Jami Oats, CB Chris Rogers, S James Souder, DT Devin Wyman.

MISCELLANEOUS TEAM DATA

Stadium (capacity, surface):
Metrodome (64,121, artificial)
Business address:
9520 Viking Drive
Eden Prairie, MN 55344
Business phone:
612-828-6500
Ticket information:
612-333-8828
Team colors:
Purple, gold and white
Flagship radio station:
WCCO, 830 AM
Training site:
Minnesota State University-Mankato
Mankato, Minn.
612-828-6500

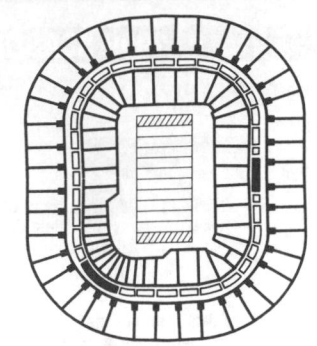

MINNESOTA VIKINGS

TSN REPORT CARD

Coaching staff	A -	Dennis Green gets consistently high marks for building a roster and creating chemistry in the locker room. He is less talented in terms of game management, as he tends to tighten up in pressure situations (see NFC title game). Offensive coordinator Ray Sherman will be under the gun in his new role. Defensive coordinator Foge Fazio gets the most out of his unit.
Quarterbacks	A	It's hard to find any fault in Randall Cunningham right now. He makes big plays, little plays and shows the poise and patience in the pocket he was not known for in Philly. Jeff George should excel with the Vikings' many offensive weapons. With Daunte Culpepper as the future, the future looks bright.
Running backs	B +	Robert Smith appears to have shook his injury label and ranks high in the second tier of NFL runners. Leroy Hoard has proven to be a very useful change-of-pace back with a nose for the end zone. David Palmer can make plays on third downs. The fullback role is being changed into an H-back slot with almost exclusively blocking assignments.
Receivers	A +	If there's a deeper position for any team in the NFL, it's not apparent. Randy Moss, Cris Carter and Jake Reed are the NFL's premier threesome, and the emerging Matthew Hatchette might push Reed for the third spot. Tight end Andrew Glover makes plays down the middle of the field and rookie Jimmy Kleinsasser is a dual threat as a blocker/receiver.
Offensive line	A	The starting five is the NFL's finest, with three Pro Bowl starters in center Jeff Christy, left guard Randall McDaniel and left tackle Todd Steussie. Right tackle Korey Stringer is no slouch, either, and right guard David Dixon has developed into a steady player. Depth is the only concern.
Defensive line	C +	The Vikings have spent mightily in the draft over the years, without much to show for it. If two among the group of Duane Clemons, Dimitrius Underwood, Stalin Colinet and John Burrough emerge as every-down ends, the line could be very solid. If not, it's back to a John Randle-and-the-other-guys routine.
Linebackers	B	Middle linebacker Ed McDaniel and weakside starter Dwayne Rudd give the Vikings two playmakers who are always around the ball. The problem has been the strongside, where the youthful Kailee Wong and the veteran Corey Miller will vie for the starting role. The Vikings must get more production from that spot.
Secondary	B -	The pass defense has fluctuated from No. 9 to No. 29 to No. 19 the past three seasons. Jimmy Hitchcock was a nice surprise last year, but loss of Corey Fuller could give opponents a target to shoot for at left corner. Safeties Robert Griffith and Orlando Thomas are good enough to win with, with Torrian Gray returning from knee surgery.
Special teams	A	Kicker Gary Anderson and punter/kickoff specialist Mitch Berger did their jobs last season as well or better than anybody on the team. Return specialist Palmer remains a threat every time he touches the ball. Long snapper Mike Morris continues to roll on.

NEW ENGLAND PATRIOTS
AFC EASTERN DIVISION

1999 SEASON

CLUB DIRECTORY

President and chief executive officer
Robert K. Kraft
Vice president/owner's representative
Jonathan A. Kraft
Vice president, business operations
Andrew Wasynczuk
Vice president, player personnel
Bobby Grier
Vice president, finance
James Hausmann
V.p., player dev. and com. relations
Donald Lowery
Director of pro scouting
Dave Uyrus
Director of media relations
Stacey James
Dir. of marketing and special events
Lou Imbriano
Director of football operations
Ken Deininger
Controller
Jim Nolan
Director of ticketing
Mike Nichols
Corporate sales executive
Jon Levy
General manager of Foxboro Stadium
Dan Murphy
Building services superintendent
Bernie Reinhart
Head trainer
Ron O'Neil
Equipment manager
Don Brocher

Head coach
Pete Carroll

Assistant coaches
Jeff Davidson (asst. off. line)
Ivan Fears (wide receivers)
Ray Hamilton (defensive line)
Ron Lynn (defensive backs)
Johnny Parker (strength & conditioning)
Bo Pelini (linebackers)
Jack Reilly (quarterbacks)
Dante Scarnecchia (off. line)
Brad Seely (special teams)
Steve Sidwell (defensive coord.)
Carl Smith (tight ends)
DeWayne Walker (defensive assistant/defensive backs)
Kirby Wilson (running backs)
Ernie Zampese (offensive coord.)

SCHEDULE

Sept. 12—	at N.Y. Jets	1:00
Sept. 19—	INDIANAPOLIS	1:00
Sept. 26—	N.Y. GIANTS	8:20
Oct. 3—	at Cleveland	1:00
Oct. 10—	at Kansas City	12:00
Oct. 17—	MIAMI	1:00
Oct. 24—	DENVER	1:00
Oct. 31—	at Arizona	2:05
Nov. 7—	Open date	
Nov. 15—	N.Y. JETS (Mon.)	9:00
Nov. 21—	at Miami	1:00
Nov. 28—	at Buffalo	1:00
Dec. 5—	DALLAS	8:20
Dec. 12—	at Indianapolis	1:00
Dec. 19—	at Philadelphia	1:00
Dec. 26—	BUFFALO	1:00
Jan. 2—	BALTIMORE	1:00

All times are for home team.
All games Sunday unless noted.

DRAFT CHOICES

Damien Woody, C, Boston College (first round/17th pick overall).
Andy Katzenmoyer, LB, Ohio State (1/28).
Kevin Faulk, RB, Louisiana State (2/46).
Tony George, S, Florida (3/91).
Derrick Fletcher, G, Baylor (5/154).
Marcus Washington, DB, Colorado (6/180).
Michael Bishop, QB, Kansas State (7/227).
Sean Morey, WR, Brown (7/241).

1998 REVIEW

RESULTS

Sept. 7—at Denver	L	21-27
Sept.13—INDIANAPOLIS	W	29-6
Sept.20—TENNESSEE	W	27-16
Sept.27—Open date		
Oct. 4—at New Orleans	W	30-27
Oct. 11—KANSAS CITY	W	40-10
Oct. 19—N.Y. JETS	L	14-24
Oct. 25—at Miami (OT)	L	9-12
Nov. 1—at Indianapolis	W	21-16
Nov. 8—ATLANTA	L	10-41
Nov. 15—at Buffalo	L	10-13
Nov. 23—MIAMI	W	26-23
Nov. 29—BUFFALO	W	25-21
Dec. 6—at Pittsburgh	W	23-9
Dec. 13—at St. Louis	L	18-32
Dec. 20—SAN FRANCISCO	W	24-21
Dec. 27—at N.Y. Jets	L	10-31
Jan. 3—at Jacksonville*	L	10-25

*AFC wild-card game.

RECORDS/RANKINGS

1998 regular-season record: 9-7 (4th in AFC East); 4-4 in division; 7-5 in conference; 6-2 at home; 3-5 on road.
Team record last five years: 46-34 (.575), ranks T8th in league in that span).

1998 team rankings:

	No.	AFC	NFL
Total offense	*321.3	6	11
Rushing offense	*92.5	15	27
Passing offense	*228.8	2	5
Scoring offense	337	6	11
Total defense	*323.9	10	20
Rushing defense	*96.7	5	7
Passing defense	*227.2	13	25
Scoring defense	329	7	14
Takeaways	31	T5	T11
Giveaways	24	T6	T8
Turnover differential	7	6	9
Sacks	36	T11	T23
Sacks allowed	40	11	17

*Yards per game.

TEAM LEADERS

Scoring (kicking): Adam Vinatieri, 125 pts. (32/32 PATs, 31/39 FGs).
Scoring (touchdowns): Robert Edwards, 72 pts. (9 rushing, 3 receiving).
Passing: Drew Bledsoe, 3,633 yds. (481 att., 263 comp., 54.7%, 20 TDs, 14 int.).
Rushing: Robert Edwards, 1,115 yds. (291 att., 3.8 avg., 9 TDs).
Receptions: Terry Glenn, 50 (792 yds., 15.8 avg., 3 TDs).
Interceptions: Ty Law, 9 (133 yds., 1 TD).
Sacks: Henry Thomas, 6.5.
Punting: Tom Tupa, 44.5 avg. (74 punts, 3,294 yds., 0 blocked).
Punt returns: Troy Brown, 13.2 avg. (17 att., 225 yds., 0 TDs).
Kickoff returns: Derrick Cullors, 24.1 avg. (45 att., 1,085 yds., 0 TDs).

NEW ENGLAND PATRIOTS

No.	QUARTERBACKS	Ht./Wt.	Born	NFL Exp.	College	How acq.	'98 Games GP/GS
7	Bishop, Michael	6-0/195	5-15-76	R	Kansas State	D7a/99	—
11	Bledsoe, Drew	6-5/233	2-14-72	7	Washington State	D1/93	14/14
17	Friesz, John	6-4/223	6-19-67	10	Idaho	UFA/99	*6/1

No.	RUNNING BACKS	Ht./Wt.	Born	NFL Exp.	College	How acq.	'98 Games GP/GS
30	Carter, Tony (FB)	6-0/230	8-23-72	6	Minnesota	UFA/98	11/7
29	Cullors, Derrick	6-0/195	12-26-72	3	Murray State	FA/96	16/0
47	Edwards, Robert	5-11/218	10-2-74	2	Georgia	D1a/98	16/15
33	Faulk, Kevin	5-8/197	6-15-76	R	Louisiana State	D2/99	—
37	Floyd, Chris (FB)	6-0/231	6-23-75	2	Michigan	D3a/98	16/2
44	Shaw, Harold	6-0/228	9-3-74	2	Southern Mississippi	D6/98	11/0
27	Warren, Lamont	5-11/202	1-4-73	6	Colorado	FA/99	*12/2

No.	RECEIVERS	Ht./Wt.	Born	NFL Exp.	College	How acq.	'98 Games GP/GS
86	Bartrum, Mike (TE)	6-5/245	6-23-70	6	Marshall	T-GB/96	16/0
82	Brisby, Vincent	6-3/193	1-25-71	7	Northeast Louisiana	D2c/93	6/1
80	Brown, Troy	5-10/190	7-2-71	7	Marshall	D8/93	10/0
87	Coates, Ben (TE)	6-5/245	8-16-69	9	Livingstone College, N.C.	D5/91	14/14
88	Glenn, Terry	5-11/185	7-23-74	4	Ohio State	D1/96	10/9
84	Jefferson, Shawn	5-11/180	2-22-69	9	Central Florida	FA/96	16/16
18	Ladd, Anthony	6-1/193	12-23-73	2	Cincinnati	FA/97	3/0
19	Morey, Sean	5-11/190	2-26-76	R	Brown	D7b/99	—
83	Rutledge, Rod (TE)	6-5/262	8-12-75	2	Alabama	D2b/98	16/4
81	Simmons, Tony	6-1/206	12-8-74	2	Wisconsin	D2a/98	11/6

No.	OFFENSIVE LINEMEN	Ht./Wt.	Born	NFL Exp.	College	How acq.	'98 Games GP/GS
78	Armstrong, Bruce (T)	6-4/295	9-7-65	13	Louisville	D1/87	16/16
61	Denson, Damon (G)	6-4/305	2-8-75	3	Michigan	D4/97	11/4
66	Ellis, Ed (T)	6-7/340	10-13-75	3	Buffalo	D4/97	7/0
64	Fletcher, Derrick	6-6/348	9-9-75	R	Baylor	D5/99	—
63	Irwin, Heath (G)	6-4/300	6-27-73	4	Colorado	D4a/96	13/3
68	Lane, Max (G)	6-6/305	2-22-71	6	Navy	D6/94	16/11
77	Moss, Zefross (T)	6-6/325	8-17-66	11	Alabama State	UFA/97	14/14
71	Rucci, Todd (G)	6-5/296	7-14-70	7	Penn State	D2b/93	16/16
65	Woody, Damien (C)	6-3/319	11-3-77	R	Boston College	D1a/99	—

No.	DEFENSIVE LINEMEN	Ht./Wt.	Born	NFL Exp.	College	How acq.	'98 Games GP/GS
90	Eaton, Chad (T)	6-5/300	4-4-72	3	Washington State	D7/95	15/14
55	McGinest, Willie (E)	6-5/255	12-11-71	6	Southern California	D1/94	9/8
98	Mitchell, Brandon (T)	6-3/289	6-19-75	3	Texas A&M	D2/97	7/1
75	Rheams, Leonta (T)	6-2/280	8-1-76	2	Houston	D4/98	6/0
94	Spires, Greg (E)	6-1/260	8-12-74	2	Florida State	D3b/98	15/1
74	Sullivan, Chris (E)	6-4/279	3-14-73	4	Boston College	D4b/96	15/10
95	Thomas, Henry	6-2/277	1-12-65	13	Louisiana Tech	FA/97	16/15

No.	LINEBACKERS	Ht./Wt.	Born	NFL Exp.	College	How acq.	'98 Games GP/GS
54	Bruschi, Tedy	6-1/245	6-9-73	4	Arizona	D3/96	16/7
45	Cottrell, Dana	6-3/244	1-11-74	1	Syracuse	UFA/97	2/0
99	Crawford, Vernon	6-4/245	6-25-74	3	Florida State	D5/97	16/1
52	Johnson, Ted	6-3/240	12-4-72	5	Colorado	D2/95	13/13
59	Katzenmoyer, Andy	6-3/264	12-2-77	R	Ohio State	D1b/99	—
58	Moore, Marty	6-1/244	3-19-71	6	Kentucky	D7/94	14/2
51	Russ, Bernard	6-1/238	11-4-73	2	West Virginia	FA/97	1/0
53	Slade, Chris	6-5/245	1-30-71	7	Virginia	D2/93	15/15
93	Stuckey, Shawn	6-0/229	10-22-75	1	Troy State	FA/98	6/0

No.	DEFENSIVE BACKS	Ht./Wt.	Born	NFL Exp.	College	How acq.	'98 Games GP/GS
26	Canty, Chris (CB)	5-9/185	3-30-76	3	Kansas State	D1/97	16/9
42	Carter, Chris (S)	6-1/201	9-27-74	3	Texas	D3b/97	16/0
32	Clay, Willie (S)	5-10/200	9-5-70	8	Georgia Tech	UFA/96	16/16
41	George, Tony (S)	5-11/200	8-10-75	R	Florida	D3/99	—
21	Israel, Steve (CB)	5-11/194	3-16-69	8	Pittsburgh	UFA/97	11/7
34	Jones, Tebucky (CB)	6-2/216	10-6-74	2	Syracuse	D1b/98	16/0
24	Law, Ty (CB)	5-11/200	2-10-74	5	Michigan	D1/95	16/16
36	Milloy, Lawyer (S)	6-0/208	11-14-73	4	Washington	D2/96	16/16
39	Washington, Marcus	6-1/217	2-26-75	R	Colorado	D6/99	—
25	Whigham, Larry (S)	6-2/205	6-23-72	5	Northeast Louisiana	FA/94	16/0

No.	SPECIALISTS	Ht./Wt.	Born	NFL Exp.	College	How acq.	'98 Games GP/GS
10	Johnson, Lee (P)	6-2/200	11-27-61	14	Brigham Young	FA/99	*13/0
4	Vinatieri, Adam (K)	6-0/200	12-28-72	4	South Dakota State	FA/96	16/0

*Not with Patriots in 1998.

Other free agents invited to camp: C Jason Anderson, CB Jason Bray, DE Willie Cohens, G Daniel Collins, G Tarren Crawford, S Cory Gilliard, DT James Grier, S Kadar Hamilton, DT Garrett Johnson, WR Nafie Karim, TE John Lumpkin, T Kendall Mack, WR Chad Mackey, DT James Manley, DE Tim Martin, DT Jonathan McCall, LB Ron Merkerson, QB Jim Murphy, T Matt Reem, CB Kato Serwanga, DT Derrick Shepard, TE Devon Smith, OL Brent Warren.

NEW ENGLAND PATRIOTS

MISCELLANEOUS TEAM DATA

Stadium (capacity, surface):
Foxboro Stadium
(60,292, grass)
Business address:
60 Washington St.
Foxboro, MA 02035
Business phone:
508-543-8200
Ticket information:
508-543-1776
Team colors:
Silver, red, white and blue
Flagship radio station:
WBCN, 104.1 FM
Training site:
Bryant College
Smithfield, R.I.
508-543-8200

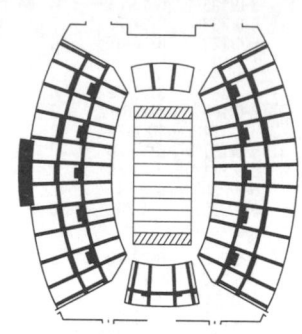

TSN REPORT CARD

Coaching staff	C	The positional and coordinator spots appear to be in good hands. The question remains with the man at the top. Does Pete Carroll have the toughness in him to carry this team through the tough times? His defenders say that he did just that the last two years, when the team was hit with an inordinate amount of injuries. The detractors point out that it was the veteran leadership and carryover from the Bill Parcells era that got the team through.
Quarterbacks	A	Drew Bledsoe passed all the tests a year ago. There are no more doubters among the fans or players after his gritty performance with a broken index finger. Despite the injury he hung in and directed the team to victories over Miami and Buffalo, the springboard to the team's making the playoffs for the third straight year. The addition of John Friesz in place of Scott Zolak upgrades the backup position.
Running backs	C +	This is an area of uncertainty. Derrick Cullors is a solid third-down back and Harold Shaw has promise on short yardage. The question is at the feature back spot where rookie Kevin Faulk and untested veteran Lamont Warren will be competing against each other. Faulk seems to be a solid fit because of his quickness to the hole and the durability he showed last year.
Receivers	B -	If Terry Glenn stays healthy and performs like he has his first three seasons, this could be jumped a full grade level. But with him playing a part-time role, the Patriots don't have a dependable big-play threat. Shawn Jefferson has the speed. Tony Simmons has the hands but hasn't shown that he's picked up the art of running routes in the NFL. Tight end Ben Coates will continue to be the lead receiver.
Offensive line	C -	The center is gone, the guards are inconsistent and unimpressive on running plays and the tackles are getting up there in the age and injury department. This team will continue to do a good job protecting Bledsoe but has to show improvement on run blocking under their third coach in four years.
Defensive line	C	With Willie McGinest in the lineup, the performance level is raised appreciably, but even with him in the game, the Patriots aren't a strong pass-rushing team. The continued development of Brandon Mitchell on the opposite side will help but the departures of Ferric Collons, Mark Wheeler and Devin Wyman leaves the team lacking depth.
Linebackers	B -	The addition of Andy Katzenmoyer to replace Todd Collins at weakside linebacker is a big plus, taking the pressure off the already overworked Tedy Bruschi. Katzenmoyer's addition to Ted Johnson and Chris Slade gives the team a solid starting group but there isn't much depth. Johnson (shoulder and biceps) and Slade (ankle and knee) were bothered by injuries last year but both are expected to be 100 percent by the start of the season.
Secondary	B +	The presence of Pro Bowl players Ty Law and Lawyer Milloy gives the Patriots strong leadership and big-play people in the defensive backfield. Steve Israel's performance after rebounding from offseason knee surgery was encouraging as well. The key will be the development of nickle and dime defenders Tebucky Jones and Chris Canty.
Special teams	B	Good coverage and quality kicking should make the special teams strong again. Lee Johnson replaces Tom Tupa as the punter and he'll also handle the kickoffs, which is an upgrade from Adam Vinatieri in that area. The coverage teams have historically been strong and the re-signing of Vinatieri gives the team a dependable clutch field goal kicker.

NEW ORLEANS SAINTS
NFC WESTERN DIVISION

1999 SEASON

CLUB DIRECTORY

Owner
Tom Benson
President/g.m./COO
Bill Kuharich
Sr. v.p. of marketing and admin.
Greg Suit
Asst. g.m./v.p. of football operations
Charles Bailey
Treasurers
Bruce Broussard
Dennis Lauscha
Comptroller
Charleen Sharpe
NFL salary cap consultant
Terry O'Neil
Director of corporate sales
Greg Seeling
Director of ticket sales
Jasen Feyerherm
Director of media and public relations
Greg Bensel
Assistant director of media and public relations/publications coordinator
Robert Gunn
Director travel/entertainment/special projects
Barra Birrcher
Director of player programs
Maurice Hurst
Director of college scouting
Bruce Lemmerman
Scouts
Matt Boockmeier   Hokie Gajan
Cornell Gowdy   Tim Heffelfinger
Tom Marino   Grant Neill
Head athletic trainer
Dean Kleinschmidt
Asst. athletic trainer/dir. of rehab.
Kevin Mangum
Assistant athletic trainer
Aaron Miller
Physicians
Dr. Charles L. Brown Jr.
Dr. Terry Habig
Dr. Timothy Finney
Facilities manager
Terry Ashburn
Assistant facilities manager
Lester Vallet

Head coach
Mike Ditka

Assistant coaches
Danny Abramowicz (off. coord.)
Bobby April (special teams)
Tom Clements (quarterbacks)
Walt Corey (defensive line)
Judd Garrett (offensive assistant)
Rodney Holman (offensive assistant/tight ends)
Harold Jackson (wide receivers)
Rickey Jackson (defensive assistant/pass rush)
Ned James (defensive assistant/linebackers)
Lary Kuharich (running backs)
Carlos Mainord (secondary)
Bill Meyers (offensive line)
Dan Neal (tight ends/offensive line assistant)
Markus Paul (assistant strength & conditioning)
Rick Venturi (asst. head coach/linebackers)
Mike Woicik (strength & cond.)
Zaven Yaralian (def. coordinator)

Equipment manager
Dan Simmons
Assistant equipment manager
Glennon "Silky" Powell
Video director
Joe Malota
Assistant video director
Bob Lee

SCHEDULE

Sept. 12—	CAROLINA	12:00
Sept. 19—	at San Francisco	1:05
Sept. 26—	Open date	
Oct. 3—	at Chicago	12:00
Oct. 10—	ATLANTA	12:00
Oct. 17—	TENNESSEE	12:00
Oct. 24—	at N.Y. Giants	1:00
Oct. 31—	CLEVELAND	12:00
Nov. 7—	TAMPA BAY	3:05
Nov. 14—	SAN FRANCISCO	12:00
Nov. 21—	at Jacksonville	8:20
Nov. 28—	at St. Louis	12:00
Dec. 5—	at Atlanta	1:00
Dec. 12—	ST. LOUIS	12:00
Dec. 19—	at Baltimore	1:00
Dec. 24—	DALLAS (Fri.)	2:05
Jan. 2—	at Carolina	1:00

All times are for home team.
All games Sunday unless noted.

DRAFT CHOICES

Ricky Williams, RB, Texas (first round/fifth pick overall).

1998 REVIEW

RESULTS

Sept. 6—at St. Louis	W	24-17
Sept.13—CAROLINA	W	19-14
Sept.20—Open date		
Sept.27—at Indianapolis (OT)	W	19-13
Oct. 4—NEW ENGLAND	L	27-30
Oct. 11—SAN FRANCISCO	L	0-31
Oct. 18—at Atlanta	L	23-31
Oct. 25—TAMPA BAY	W	9-3
Nov. 1—at Carolina	L	17-31
Nov. 8—at Minnesota	L	24-31
Nov. 15—ST. LOUIS	W	24-3
Nov. 22—at San Francisco	L	20-31
Nov. 29—at Miami	L	10-30
Dec. 6—DALLAS	W	22-3
Dec. 13—ATLANTA	L	17-27
Dec. 20—at Arizona	L	17-19
Dec. 27—BUFFALO	L	33-45

RECORDS/RANKINGS

1998 regular-season record: 6-10 (3rd in NFC West); 3-5 in division; 5-7 in conference; 4-4 at home; 2-6 on road.
Team record last five years: 29-51 (.363), ranks 26th in league in that span).

1998 team rankings:	No.	NFC	NFL
Total offense	*278.9	13	28
Rushing offense	*82.8	15	30
Passing offense	*196.1	9	18
Scoring offense	305	11	21
Total defense	*354.3	14	26
Rushing defense	*106.3	7	16
Passing defense	*248.0	15	30
Scoring defense	359	9	21
Takeaways	32	6	10
Giveaways	33	T10	T21
Turnover differential	-1	7	16
Sacks	47	5	T6
Sacks allowed	57	14	28

*Yards per game.

TEAM LEADERS

Scoring (kicking): Doug Brien, 91 pts. (31/31 PATs, 20/22 FGs).
Scoring (touchdowns): Cam Cleeland, 36 pts. (6 receiving).
Passing: Billy Joe Tolliver, 1,427 yds. (199 att., 110 comp., 55.3%, 8 TDs, 4 int.).
Rushing: Lamar Smith, 457 yds. (138 att., 3.3 avg., 1 TD).
Receptions: Sean Dawkins, 53 (823 yds., 15.5 avg., 1 TD).
Interceptions: Sammy Knight, 6 (171 yds., 2 TDs).
Sacks: La'Roi Glover, 10.0.
Punting: Mark Royals, 45.6 avg. (88 punts, 4,017 yds., 0 blocked).
Punt returns: Andre Hastings, 14.0 avg. (22 att., 307 yds., 0 TDs).
Kickoff returns: Qadry Ismail, 21.1 avg. (28 att., 590 yds., 0 TDs).

NEW ORLEANS SAINTS

No.	QUARTERBACKS	Ht./Wt.	Born	NFL Exp.	College	How acq.	'98 Games GP/GS
12	Hobert, Billy Joe	6-3/230	1-8-71	7	Washington	FA/97	1/1
11	Tolliver, Billy Joe	6-1/217	2-7-66	9	Texas Tech	FA/98	7/4
7	Wuerffel, Danny	6-1/208	5-27-74	3	Florida	D4a/97	5/4
	RUNNING BACKS						
32	Craver, Aaron (FB)	6-0/232	12-18-68	9	Fresno State	UFA/98	16/10
28	Davis, Troy	5-7/191	9-14-75	3	Iowa State	D3/97	14/2
33	Perry, Wilmont	6-1/235	2-24-75	2	Livingstone (N.C.)	D5/98	6/2
26	Smith, Lamar	5-11/225	11-29-70	6	Houston	UFA/98	14/9
47	Wilcox, Josh (FB)	6-3/255	6-5-74	2	Oregon	FA/98	3/1
34	Williams, Ricky	5-10/236	5-21-77	R	Texas	D1/99	—
	RECEIVERS						
89	Bech, Brett	6-1/201	8-20-71	3	Louisiana State	FA/96	16/0
85	Cleeland, Cam (TE)	6-4/272	4-15-75	2	Washington	D2/98	16/16
87	Farquhar, John (TE)	6-6/278	3-22-72	4	Duke	FA/97	5/0
88	Hastings, Andre	6-1/190	11-7-70	7	Georgia	UFA/97	16/12
86	Hughes, Danan	6-2/211	12-11-70	7	Iowa	FA/99	*16/0
80	Johnson, Tony (TE)	6-5/255	2-5-72	4	Alabama	FA/96	11/0
19	Johnson, Alonzo	5-11/186	4-18-73	2	Central State (Ohio)	W-NYJ/98	1/0
82	Kennison, Eddie	6-0/195	1-20-73	4	Louisiana State	T-StL/99	*16/13
83	Poole, Keith	6-0/193	6-18-74	3	Arizona State	D4b/97	15/4
84	Slutzker, Scott (TE)	6-4/240	12-20-72	4	Iowa	T-Ind./96	3/0
	OFFENSIVE LINEMEN						
69	Ackerman, Tom (C)	6-3/296	9-6-72	4	Eastern Washington	D5b/96	15/10
62	Fontenot, Jerry (C)	6-3/300	11-21-66	11	Texas A&M	UFA/97	4/4
60	Gammon, Kendall (C)	6-4/265	10-23-68	8	Pittsburg (Kan.) State	FA/96	16/0
76	Hills, Keno (G)	6-6/305	6-13-73	4	Southwestern Louisiana	D6a/96	12/1
65	Naeole, Chris (G)	6-3/313	12-25-74	3	Colorado	D1/97	16/16
77	Roaf, Willie (T)	6-5/312	4-18-70	7	Louisiana Tech	D1/93	15/15
	Scifres, Steve (T)	6-4/300	1-22-72	3	Wyoming	FA/99	*1/0
68	Turley, Kyle (T)	6-5/300	9-24-75	2	San Diego State	D1/98	15/15
63	Williams, Wally (G)	6-2/321	2-19-71	7	Florida A&M	UFA/99	*13/13
	DEFENSIVE LINEMEN						
97	Glover, La'Roi (T)	6-2/285	7-4-74	4	San Diego State	W-Oak./97	16/15
94	Johnson, Joe (E)	6-4/270	7-11-72	6	Louisville	D1/94	16/16
93	Martin, Wayne (T)	6-5/275	10-26-65	11	Arkansas	D1/89	16/16
75	Pittman, Julian (T)	6-4/294	4-22-75	2	Florida State	D4b/98	2/0
95	Robbins, Austin (T)	6-6/290	3-1-71	6	North Carolina	T-Oak./96	16/1
99	Sagapolutele, Pio (T)	6-6/302	11-28-69	9	San Diego State	FA/97	—
91	Smith, Brady (E)	6-5/260	6-5-73	4	Colorado State	D3/96	14/5
90	Tomich, Jared (E)	6-2/272	4-24-74	3	Nebraska	D2b/97	16/11
92	Wilson, Troy (E)	6-4/257	11-22-70	4	Pittsburg (Kan.) State	W-SF/98	15/0
	LINEBACKERS						
54	Aleaga, Ink	6-1/251	4-4-73	3	Washington	FA/97	15/3
58	Bordano, Chris	6-1/248	12-30-74	2	Southern Methodist	D6/98	16/6
55	Fields, Mark	6-2/244	11-9-72	5	Washington State	D1/95	15/15
59	Mitchell, Keith	6-2/245	7-24-74	3	Texas A&M	FA/97	16/15
50	Mitchell, Kevin	6-1/250	1-1-71	6	Syracuse	UFA/98	8/8
52	Smith, Vinson	6-2/247	7-3-65	12	East Carolina	UFA/98	15/0
98	Warner, Ron	6-2/252	9-26-75	1	Kansas	D7b/98	1/0
	DEFENSIVE BACKS						
30	Cherry, Je'Rod	6-1/208	5-30-73	4	California	D2/96	14/0
22	Drakeford, Tyronne (CB)	5-11/185	6-21-71	6	Virginia Tech	UFA/98	16/15
23	Hewitt, Chris (S)	6-0/210	7-22-74	3	Cincinnati	FA/97	16/2
44	Kelly, Rob (S)	6-0/199	6-21-74	3	Ohio State	D2a/97	16/3
29	Knight, Sammy (S)	6-0/205	9-10-75	3	Southern California	FA/97	14/13
21	Little, Earl	6-0/191	3-10-73	2	Miami (Fla.)	FA/97	16/0
25	Molden, Alex (CB)	5-10/190	8-4-73	4	Oregon	D1/96	16/15
24	Weary, Fred (CB)	5-10/181	4-12-74	2	Florida	D4a/98	14/1
	SPECIALISTS						
10	Brien, Doug (K)	6-0/180	11-24-70	6	California	FA/95	16/0
3	Royals, Mark (P)	6-5/220	6-22-64	10	Appalachian State	FA/97	16/0

*Not with Saints in 1998.

Other free agents invited to camp: TE Cuncho Brown, C Justin Burroughs, CB Anthony Cobbs, G Joe Cocozzo, CB Chris Cummings, QB Jake Delhomme, DT Justin Emast, WR Malcolm Floyd, WR P.J. Franklin, S Scott Gumina, T Mike Halapin, DE Uhuru Hamiter, CB Carlos Jones, S Gene Joseph, FB Ron Leshinski, LB Marc Lillibridge, DE Rob Lurtsema, CB Tony Maranto, G Rick Nord, RB Dino Philyaw, FB Marvin Powell, DT Troy Ridgley, C Thomas Schau, LB Donnie Spragan, WR L.C. Stevens, T Daryl Terrell, WR Gunnard Twyner, LB William Whitehead, LB Armon Williams, T Tashe Williams.

MISCELLANEOUS TEAM DATA

Stadium (capacity, surface):
Louisiana Superdome
(70,200, artificial)
Business address:
5800 Airline Drive
Metairie, LA 70003
Business phone:
504-733-0255
Ticket information:
504-731-1700
Team colors:
Old gold, black and white
Flagship radio station:
WWL, 870 AM
Training site:
University of Wisconsin-La Crosse
La Crosse, Wis.
608-789-4550

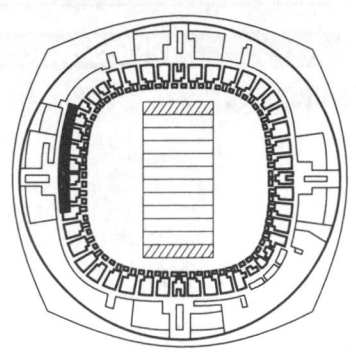

NEW ORLEANS SAINTS

TSN REPORT CARD

Coaching staff	B	Coach Mike Ditka and his staff continue to earn high marks for getting their players to play hard every week. Ditka remains the pied piper. This season Danny Abramowicz proves whether he is cut out to be an offensive coordinator in the NFL.
Quarterbacks	C	Most observers still can't believe Ditka is serious about going with Billy Joe Hobert as his starting quarterback. Believe it. Hobert may be a poor man's version of Jim McMahon, but he clearly is Ditka's kind of quarterback: tough, gritty and a leader with just enough athleticism to get the job done.
Running backs	A	More than 10 years have passed since Ditka coached a player the caliber of Ricky Williams. Does the name Walter Payton ring a bell? It did with Ditka, who repeatedly has compared college football's career rushing leader to pro football's career rushing leader. Can Williams help Ditka climb the mountain one more time?
Receivers	C +	The jury is still out on the trade for Eddie Kennison, although all of the early returns have been positive. Ditka and team officials believe Kennison wasn't used properly by the Rams the past two seasons. Barring an upset, second-year tight end Cam Cleeland appears headed for superstar status.
Offensive line	C +	Considering the talent available, the potential is there for this group to rank as the strongest position on the team. Willie Roaf and Kyle Turley represent a pair of bookend tackles comparable to any other tandem in the league. Key will be the play of right guard Chris Naeole.
Defensive line	B	Right end Joe Johnson and nose tackle La'Roi Glover make this the strongest position on the team. Johnson earned his first Pro Bowl berth last season and Glover should have. Left tackle Wayne Martin's decreased production is a legitimate cause for concern, although team officials are blaming it on knee and shoulder injuries.
Linebackers	C	Armed with a five-year, $25 million contract extension, Mark Fields now needs to play like one of the best linebackers in the league. Look for Fields to bust loose this season, particularly as a pass rusher. The remaining young players in this unit remain unproven commodities.
Secondary	D	Things can't get any worse for this group, which ranked last in pass defense last season. Or can it? Cornerbacks Alex Molden and Tyronne Drakeford and their ability to perform at a high level in man coverage are the key. Veteran Chad Cota, lost in free agency to the Colts, will be replaced by Rob Kelly or Je'Rod Cherry.
Special teams	B	Finding an adequate kickoff returner is the No. 1 priority before the season opens. Kicker Doug Brien, punter Mark Royals and deep snapper Kendall Gammon rate among the league's finest at their position. But none of them return kickoffs. Kennison should fill the bill returning punts.

NEW YORK GIANTS
NFC EASTERN DIVISION

1999 SEASON

CLUB DIRECTORY

President/co-CEO
Wellington T. Mara
Chairman/co-CEO
Preston Robert Tisch
Exec. v.p./general counsel
John K. Mara
Vice president/general manager
Ernie Accorsi
Treasurer
Jonathan Tisch
Assistant general manager
Rick Donohue
Assistant to the general manager
Harry Hulmes
V.P. and chief financial officer
John Pasquali
Controller
Christine Procops
Vice president/player personnel
Tom Boisture
Director/player personnel
Marv Sunderland
Director of administration
Jim Phelan
Vice president, marketing
Rusty Hawley
Director/promotion
Francis X. Mara
Ticket manager
John Gorman
Director/pro personnel
Dave Gettleman
Director/research and development
Raymond J. Walsh Jr.
Director/college scouting
Jerry Shay
Vice president of communications
Pat Hanlon
Assistant director/marketing
Bill Smith
Head trainer
Ronnie Barnes
Assistant trainers
Byron Hansen   Steve Kennelly

Head coach
Jim Fassel

Assistant coaches
Dave Brazil (def. quality control)
John Dunn (strength & cond.)
John Fox (defensive coordinator)
Mike Gillhamer (offensive assistant)
Mike Haluchak (linebackers)
Johnnie Lynn (defensive backs)
Larry Mac Duff (special teams)
Denny Marcin (defensive line)
Jim McNally (offensive line)
Sean Payton (quarterbacks)
Dick Rehbein (tight ends/asst.
  offensive line)
Jimmy Robinson (wide receivers)
Jim Skipper (offensive coord./RBs)
Craig Stoddard (assistant strength
  & conditioning)

Director of player development
Greg Gabriel
Scouts
Rosey Brown   John Crea
Jeremiah Davis   Ken Kavanaugh
Jerry Reese   Steve Verderosa
Team physician
Russell Warren
Locker room manager
Ed Wagner
Equipment manager
Ed Wagner Jr.
Video director
John Mancuso

SCHEDULE

Sept. 12—	at Tampa Bay	4:15
Sept. 19—	WASHINGTON	1:00
Sept. 26—	at New England	8:20
Oct. 3—	PHILADELPHIA	1:00
Oct. 10—	at Arizona	1:05
Oct. 18—	DALLAS (Mon.)	9:00
Oct. 24—	NEW ORLEANS	1:00
Oct. 31—	at Philadelphia	1:00
Nov. 7—	Open date	
Nov. 14—	INDIANAPOLIS	1:00
Nov. 21—	at Washington	4:15
Nov. 28—	ARIZONA	1:00
Dec. 5—	N.Y. JETS	1:00
Dec. 12—	at Buffalo	1:00
Dec. 19—	at St. Louis	12:00
Dec. 26—	MINNESOTA	1:00
Jan. 2—	at Dallas	3:05

All times are for home team.
All games Sunday unless noted.

DRAFT CHOICES

Luke Petitgout, T, Notre Dame (first
  round/19th pick overall).
Joe Montgomery, RB, Ohio State (2/49).
Dan Campbell, TE, Texas A&M (3/79).
Sean Bennett, RB, Northwestern (4/112).
Mike Rosenthal, T, Notre Dame (5/149).
Lyle West, DB, San Jose State (6/189).
Andre Weathers, DB, Michigan (6/205).
Ryan Hale, DT, Arkansas (7/225).
O.J. Childress, LB, Clemson (7/231).

1998 REVIEW

RESULTS

Sept. 6—	WASHINGTON	W	31-24
Sept.13—	at Oakland	L	17-20
Sept.21—	DALLAS	L	7-31
Sept.27—	at San Diego	W	34-16
Oct. 4—	at Tampa Bay	L	3-20
Oct. 11—	ATLANTA	L	20-34
Oct. 18—	ARIZONA	W	34-7
Oct. 25—	Open date		
Nov. 1—	at Washington	L	14-21
Nov. 8—	at Dallas	L	6-16
Nov. 15—	GREEN BAY	L	3-37
Nov. 22—	PHILADELPHIA	W	20-0
Nov. 30—	at San Francisco	L	7-31
Dec. 6—	at Arizona	W	23-19
Dec. 13—	DENVER	W	20-16
Dec. 20—	KANSAS CITY	W	28-7
Dec. 27—	at Philadelphia	W	20-10

RECORDS/RANKINGS

1998 regular-season record: 8-8 (3rd in
NFC East); 5-3 in division; 5-7 in conference; 5-3 at home; 3-5 on road.
Team record last five years: 38-41-1
(.481, ranks 12th in league in that span).
1998 team rankings:

	No.	NFC	NFL
Total offense	*278.4	14	29
Rushing offense	*118.1	7	12
Passing offense	*160.4	14	28
Scoring offense	287	12	23
Total defense	*323.2	10	19
Rushing defense	*125.3	10	23
Passing defense	*197.9	7	13
Scoring defense	309	5	T8
Takeaways	26	T8	T19
Giveaways	24	T3	T8
Turnover differential	2	6	13
Sacks	54	1	1
Sacks allowed	35	5	T10

*Yards per game.

TEAM LEADERS

Scoring (kicking): Brad Daluiso, 95 pts.
(32/32 PATs, 21/27 FGs).
Scoring (touchdowns): Chris Calloway,
36 pts. (6 receiving).
Passing: Danny Kanell, 1,603 yds. (299
att., 160 comp., 53.5%, 11 TDs, 10 int.).
Rushing: Gary Brown, 1,063 yds. (247
att., 4.3 avg., 5 TDs).
Receptions: Chris Calloway, 62 (812
yds., 13.1 avg., 6 TDs).
Interceptions: Percy Ellsworth, 5 (92
yds., 2 TDs).
Sacks: Michael Strahan, 15.0.
Punting: Brad Maynard, 45.2 avg. (101
punts, 4,566 yds., 0 blocked).
Punt returns: Amani Toomer, 7.2 avg.
(35 att., 252 yds., 0 TDs).
Kickoff returns: David Patten, 21.6 avg.
(43 att., 928 yds., 1 TD).

NEW YORK GIANTS

No.	QUARTERBACKS	Ht./Wt.	Born	NFL Exp.	College	How acq.	'98 Games GP/GS
18	Cherry, Mike	6-3/225	12-15-73	3	Murray State	D6/97	1/0
5	Collins, Kerry	6-5/240	12-30-72	6	Penn State	UFA/99	*11/11
10	Graham, Kent	6-5/240	11-1-68	8	Ohio State	UFA/98	11/6
	RUNNING BACKS						
21	Barber, Tiki	5-10/205	4-7-75	3	Virginia	D2/97	16/4
44	Bennett, Sean	6-1/222	11-9-75	R	Northwestern	D4/99	—
33	Brown, Gary	5-11/230	7-1-69	8	Penn State	UFA/98	16/11
34	Comella, Greg (FB)	6-1/240	7-29-75	2	Stanford	FA/98	16/0
23	Johnson, LeShon	6-0/207	1-15-71	6	Northern Illinois	FA/98	0/0
25	Montgomery, Joe	5-10/228	6-8-76	R	Ohio State	D2/99	—
30	Way, Charles (FB)	6-0/250	12-27-72	5	Virginia	D6b/95	16/15
	RECEIVERS						
80	Alford, Brian	6-1/190	6-7-75	2	Purdue	D3/98	2/0
86	Campbell, Dan (TE)	6-5/264	4-13-76	R	Texas A&M	D3/99	—
87	Cross, Howard (TE)	6-5/275	8-8-67	11	Alabama	D6/89	16/16
89	Haase, Andy (TE)	6-4/260	7-10-74	2	Northern Colorado	FA/98	7/1
88	Hilliard, Ike	5-11/195	4-5-76	3	Florida	D1/97	16/16
84	Jurevicius, Joe	6-5/231	12-23-74	2	Penn State	D2/98	14/1
83	Mitchell, Pete (TE)	6-2/240	10-9-71	5	Boston College	FA/99	*16/16
85	Patten, David	5-9/180	8-19-74	3	Western Carolina	FA/97	12/0
81	Toomer, Amani	6-3/202	9-8-74	4	Michigan	D2/96	16/0
	OFFENSIVE LINEMEN						
69	Engler, Derek (C)	6-5/300	7-11-74	3	Wisconsin	FA/97	11/0
74	Gragg, Scott (T)	6-8/325	2-28-72	5	Montana	D2/95	16/16
72	Oben, Roman (T)	6-4/310	10-9-72	4	Louisville	D3/96	16/16
77	Petitgout, Luke (G)	6-6/315	6-16-76	R	Notre Dame	D1/99	—
78	Rosenthal, Mike (T)	6-7/310	6-10-77	R	Notre Dame	D5/99	—
70	Scott, Lance (C)	6-3/285	2-15-72	5	Utah	D5/95	16/16
65	Stone, Ron (G)	6-5/325	7-20-71	7	Boston College	FA/96	14/14
62	Whittle, Jason (G)	6-6/300	3-7-75	2	Southwest Missouri State	FA/98	1/0
59	Williams, Brian (C)	6-5/315	6-8-66	11	Minnesota	FA/99	0/0
	DEFENSIVE LINEMEN						
93	Hale, Ryan (T)	6-4/298	6-10-75	R	Arkansas	D7a/99	—
75	Hamilton, Keith (T)	6-6/300	5-25-71	8	Pittsburgh	D4/92	16/16
97	Harris, Robert (T)	6-4/300	6-13-69	8	Southern (La.)	FA/95	10/10
79	Holsey, Bernard (E)	6-2/295	12-10-73	4	Duke	FA/96	16/0
94	Jones, Cedric (E)	6-4/275	4-30-74	4	Oklahoma	D1/96	16/1
99	Peter, Christian (T)	6-3/300	10-5-72	3	Nebraska	FA/97	16/6
92	Strahan, Michael (E)	6-4/280	11-21-71	7	Texas Southern	D2/93	16/15
96	Williams, George (T)	6-3/295	12-8-75	2	North Carolina State	FA/98	2/0
	LINEBACKERS						
98	Armstead, Jessie	6-1/240	10-26-70	7	Miami (Fla.)	D8/93	16/16
55	Buckley, Marcus	6-3/240	2-3-71	7	Texas A&M	D3/93	14/12
57	Childress, O.J.	6-1/244	12-6-76	R	Clemson	D7b/99	—
58	Colman, Doug	6-2/250	6-4-73	4	Nebraska	D6a/96	16/0
52	Galyon, Scott	6-2/245	3-23-74	4	Tennessee	D6b/96	10/1
51	Monty, Pete	6-2/250	7-13-74	3	Wisconsin	D4/97	11/0
91	Phillips, Ryan	6-4/252	2-7-74	3	Idaho	D3a/97	16/3
90	Widmer, Corey	6-3/255	12-25-68	8	Montana State	D7/92	16/15
	DEFENSIVE BACKS						
28	Buckley, Curtis (S)	6-0/182	9-25-70	7	East Texas State	W-SF/98	14/0
43	Ellsworth, Percy (S)	6-2/225	10-19-74	4	Virginia	FA/96	16/9
20	Garnes, Sam (S)	6-3/225	7-12-74	3	Cincinnati	D5/97	11/11
41	Hamilton, Conrad (CB)	5-10/195	11-5-74	4	Eastern New Mexico	D7/96	16/15
31	Sehorn, Jason (CB)	6-2/210	4-15-71	5	Southern California	D2b/94	—
22	Sparks, Phillippi (CB)	5-11/195	4-15-69	8	Arizona State	D2/92	13/13
35	Weathers, Andre (CB)	6-0/189	8-6-76	R	Michigan	D6b/99	—
37	West, Lyle (S)	6-0/210	12-20-76	R	San Jose State	D6a/99	—
36	Williams, Shaun (S)	6-2/215	10-10-76	2	UCLA	D1/98	13/0
29	Wooten, Tito (S)	6-0/195	12-12-71	6	Northeast Louisiana	SupD4/94	14/13
	SPECIALISTS						
3	Daluiso, Brad (K)	6-2/215	12-31-67	9	UCLA	FA/93	16/0
9	Maynard, Brad (P)	6-1/190	2-9-74	3	Ball State	D3b/97	16/0

*Not with Giants in 1998.

Other free agents invited to camp: S Ty Ardoin, QB Steve Buck, WR Kenny Cheatham, DT Keith Council, WR Ray Curry, C Greg Davis, DE Greg Derrick, TE Scott Dragos, DE Charles Estes, DE Frank Ferrara, RB LeShon Johnson, G Scott Kiernan, DT Steve Konopka, T Dan Launta, CB Bashit Levingston, T Nate Miller, T Toby Myles, WR Chris Ortiz, TE Todd Pollack, C Bryan Pukenas, LB Kenny Sanders, DE Rasheed Simmons, CB Cedric Stephens, CB Reggie Stephens, CB Kelvin Stuggs, LB Jesse Tarplin, C Brian Williams.

Abbreviations: D1—draft pick, first round; SupD2—supplemental draft pick, second round; WV—claimed on waivers; TR—obtained in trade; PlanB—Plan B free-agent acquisition; FA—free-agent acquisition (other than Plan B); ED—expansion draft pick.

MISCELLANEOUS TEAM DATA

Stadium (capacity, surface):
Giants Stadium
(79,593, artificial)
Business address:
East Rutherford, NJ 07073
Business phone:
201-935-8111
Ticket information:
201-935-8222
Team colors:
Blue, white and red
Flagship radio station:
WNEW, 102.7 FM
Training site:
University at Albany
Albany, N.Y.
201-935-8111

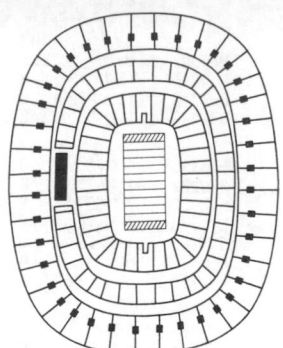

TSN REPORT CARD

Coaching staff	B	A staff that could do no wrong in 1997 endured a rocky '98. This is the rubber year, and the key will be head coach Jim Fassel's ability to repair a consistently weak offense. The big addition is offensive line coach Jim McNally, who will try to light a fire under a lackluster unit. Defensive coordinator John Fox is a rising star.
Quarterbacks	C +	What the Giants lack in quality they make up for in quantity. Kent Graham proved he could play last season (a 5-1 finish, including an upset of the Broncos), but many doubt if he can do it for the long haul. If not, Plan B is free-agent pickup Kerry Collins, who has talent but has had a rocky two years. Plan C is Mike Cherry, whose arm, some think, will make him a future starter.
Running backs	B -	Again, there are plenty of options. Gary Brown enjoyed a solid year in 1998, but now must prove he can take the step to elite status. Behind him are Tiki Barber, LeShon Johnson and rookies Joe Montgomery and Sean Bennett. If two of the five have big years, the Giants will be in good shape, because fullback Charles Way is one of the best in the league at that spot.
Receivers	B -	The grade is based mostly on potential, because the team has decided to cast its lot with young receivers Ike Hilliard, Joe Jurevicius, Amani Toomer and Brian Alford after cutting Chris Calloway. If two of the four become stars, that will be two more receiving stars than this team usually has. New tight end Pete Mitchell should help the passing game immeasurably.
Offensive line	C -	The line rallied late last season, but still needed improvement, and the team hopes it has gotten that with first-round draft pick Luke Petitgout and the return of center Brian Williams from a two-year layoff because of an eye injury. Left tackle Roman Oben could become one of the best in the league at his position. Right tackle Scott Gragg must become more consistent.
Defensive line	B +	These guys were an A+ in 1997, but injuries to the tackles took their toll last season, and now right end Chad Bratzke has left via free agency. The key is Cedric Jones' ability to step in for Bratzke, and for the tackles to stay healthy. Left end Michael Strahan is a given; he is the best end in the league and just entering what should be the prime of his career.
Linebackers	B -	Jessie Armstead is a two-time Pro Bowl pick, making it last year despite an ankle injury that nearly ruined his season. Corey Widmer is a run-stuffer and the defensive quarterback in the middle. The question mark is on the strong side, where Marcus Buckley was pushed around vs. the run in 1998. The team has to shore up that spot, a problem area for several seasons.
Secondary	A -	The strength and stability of the unit depends on how well Jason Sehorn bounces back from a season-ending knee injury he suffered last August. He says he's fine, and if so, he will join Phillippi Sparks and Conrad Hamilton to form a very solid cornerback trio. The key in the secondary is whether second-year man Shaun Williams is ready to start at free safety.
Special teams	C	The placekicker (Brad Daluiso) and punter (Brad Maynard) are fine; the coverage and return units are awful. The Giants must improve on kick returns and plan to try as many candidates as it takes to get it right. The shaky offense has to get better field position from special teams than it has in recent years. Overall team speed is a glaring weakness that shows up most on special teams.

NEW YORK JETS
AFC EASTERN DIVISION

1999 SEASON

CLUB DIRECTORY

President
Steve Gutman
Treasurer & chief financial officer
Mike Gerstle
Controller
Mike Minarczyk
Director/public relations
Frank Ramos
Assistant director/public relations
Doug Miller
Public relations assistants
Berj Najarian
Sharon Czark
Danny Ferrauiola
Coordinator of special projects
Ken Ilchuk
Exec. director of business operations
Bob Parente
Director of marketing
Marc Riccio
Senior marketing manager
Beth Conroy
Director of ticket operations
John Buschhorn
Director/operations
Mike Kensil
Travel coordinator
Kevin Coyle
Director/player personnel
Dick Haley
Director/pro personnel
Scott Pioli
Director/player contract negotiations
Mike Tannenbaum
Scouts
Trent Baake   Joey Clinkscales
Jim Cochran   Michael Davis
Sid Hall   Jesse Kay
Bob Schmitz   Gary Smith
Lionel Vital

**Head coach/
chief football
operations
officer**
Bill Parcells

Assistant coaches
Bill Belichick (assistant head
coach/secondary)
Maurice Carthon (running backs)
Romeo Crennel (defensive line)
Al Groh (linebackers)
Todd Haley (wide receivers)
Dan Henning (quarterbacks)
Pat Hodgson (tight ends)
John Lott (strength & conditioning)
Eric Mangini (defensive assistant/
quality control)
Bill Muir (offensive line)
Mike Sweatman (special teams)
Charlie Weis (off. coordinator/
fullbacks)

Head trainer
David Price
Assistant trainer
John Mellody
Equipment manager
Bill Hampton
Equipment director
Clay Hampton
Groundskeeper
Bob Hansen
Video director
John Seiter

SCHEDULE

Sept. 12—	NEW ENGLAND	1:00
Sept. 19—	at Buffalo	8:20
Sept. 26—	WASHINGTON	1:00
Oct. 3—	at Denver	2:15
Oct. 11—	JACKSONVILLE (Mon.)	9:00
Oct. 17—	INDIANAPOLIS	1:00
Oct. 24—	at Oakland	1:15
Oct. 31—	Open date	
Nov. 7—	ARIZONA	1:00
Nov. 15—	at New England (Mon.)	9:00
Nov. 21—	BUFFALO	1:00
Nov. 28—	at Indianapolis	4:15
Dec. 5—	at N.Y. Giants	1:00
Dec. 12—	MIAMI	4:05
Dec. 19—	at Dallas	3:15
Dec. 27—	at Miami (Mon.)	9:00
Jan. 2—	SEATTLE	1:00

All times are for home team.
All games Sunday unless noted.

DRAFT CHOICES

Randy Thomas, G, Mississippi State
(second round/57th pick overall).
David Loverne, T, San Jose State (3/90).
Jason Wiltz, DT, Nebraska (4/123).
Jermaine Jones, DB, Northwestern (La.)
State (5/162).
Marc Megna, LB, Richmond (6/183).
J.P. Machado, G, Illinois (6/197).
Ryan Young, T, Kansas State (7/223).
J.J. Syvrud, DE, Jamestown (7/235).

1998 REVIEW

RESULTS

Sept. 6—at San Francisco (OT)	L	30-36
Sept.13—BALTIMORE	L	10-24
Sept.20—INDIANAPOLIS	W	44-6
Sept.27—Open date		
Oct. 4—MIAMI	W	20-9
Oct. 11—at St. Louis	L	10-30
Oct. 19—at New England	W	24-14
Oct. 25—ATLANTA	W	28-3
Nov. 1—at Kansas City	W	20-17
Nov. 8—BUFFALO	W	34-12
Nov. 15—at Indianapolis	L	23-24
Nov. 22—at Tennessee	W	24-3
Nov. 29—CAROLINA	W	48-21
Dec. 6—SEATTLE	W	32-31
Dec. 13—at Miami	W	21-16
Dec. 19—at Buffalo	W	17-10
Dec. 27—NEW ENGLAND	W	31-10
Jan. 10—JACKSONVILLE*	W	34-24
Jan. 17—At Denver†	L	10-23

*AFC divisional playoff game.
†AFC championship game.

RECORDS/RANKINGS

1998 regular-season record: 12-4 (1st in
AFC East); 7-1 in division; 10-2 in conference; 7-1 at home; 5-3 on road.
Team record last five years: 31-49 (.388,
ranks 25th in league in that span).
1998 team rankings:

	No.	AFC	NFL
Total offense	*357.2	2	4
Rushing offense	*117.4	6	13
Passing offense	*239.8	1	4
Scoring offense	416	2	5
Total defense	*293.7	5	7
Rushing defense	*103.7	8	14
Passing defense	*190.0	4	9
Scoring defense	266	2	2
Takeaways	30	T7	T13
Giveaways	24	T6	T8
Turnover differential	6	7	10
Sacks	36	T11	T23
Sacks allowed	25	T3	T4

*Yards per game.

TEAM LEADERS

Scoring (kicking): John Hall, 120 pts.
(45/46 PATs, 25/35 FGs).
Scoring (touchdowns): Keyshawn John-
son, 66 pts. (1 rushing, 10 receiving).
Passing: Vinny Testaverde, 3,256 yds.
(421 att., 259 comp., 61.5%, 29 TDs, 7
int.).
Rushing: Curtis Martin, 1,287 yds. (369
att., 3.5 avg., 8 TDs).
Receptions: Keyshawn Johnson, 83
(1,131 yds., 13.6 avg., 10 TDs).
Interceptions: Aaron Glenn, 6 (23 yds., 0
TDs).
Sacks: Mo Lewis, 7.0.
Punting: John Kidd, 41.6 avg. (28 punts,
1,166 yds., 0 blocked).
Punt returns: Leon Johnson, 7.0 avg.
(29 att., 203 yds., 0 TDs).
Kickoff returns: Aaron Glenn, 24.4 avg.
(24 att., 585 yds., 0 TDs).

NEW YORK JETS

No.	QUARTERBACKS	Ht./Wt.	Born	NFL Exp.	College	How acq.	'98 Games GP/GS
6	Lucas, Ray	6-3/214	8-6-72	3	Rutgers	W-NE/97	15/0
16	Testaverde, Vinny	6-5/238	11-13-63	13	Miami (Fla.)	FA/98	14/13
11	Zolak, Scott	6-5/230	12-13-67	9	Maryland	UFA/99	*6/2
	RUNNING BACKS						
20	Anderson, Richie	6-2/230	9-13-71	7	Penn State	D6/93	8/2
32	Johnson, Leon	6-0/215	7-13-74	3	North Carolina	D4b/97	12/2
28	Martin, Curtis	5-11/210	5-1-73	5	Pittsburgh	FA/98	15/15
33	Sowell, Jerald (FB)	6-0/248	1-21-74	3	Tulane	W-GB/97	16/2
	RECEIVERS						
84	Baxter, Fred (TE)	6-3/265	6-14-71	7	Auburn	D5a/93	14/1
80	Chrebet, Wayne	5-10/185	8-14-73	5	Hofstra	FA/95	16/15
86	Green, Eric (TE)	6-5/285	6-22-67	10	Liberty (Va.)	UFA/99	*12/12
19	Johnson, Keyshawn	6-3/212	7-22-72	4	Southern California	D1/96	16/16
82	Spence, Blake (TE)	6-4/249	6-20-75	2	Oregon	D5c/98	5/0
89	Ward, Dedric	5-9/184	9-29-74	3	Northern Iowa	D3/97	16/2
	OFFENSIVE LINEMEN						
76	Elliott, Jumbo (T)	6-7/308	4-1-65	12	Michigan	UFA/96	16/16
69	Fabini, Jason (T)	6-7/312	8-25-74	2	Cincinnati	D4/98	16/16
67	Gisler, Mike (C)	6-4/295	8-26-69	7	Houston	UFA/98	16/0
65	Hudson, John (C)	6-2/270	1-29-68	10	Auburn	UFA/96	16/0
71	Jenkins, Kerry (T)	6-5/310	9-6-73	2	Troy State	FA/97	16/0
79	Loverne, David (G)	6-3/299	5-22-76	R	San Jose State	D3/99	—
63	Machado, J.P. (G)	6-4/295	1-6-76	R	Illinois	D6b/99	—
68	Mawae, Kevin (C)	6-4/305	1-23-71	6	Louisiana State	UFA/98	16/16
64	Norgard, Erik (G)	6-1/290	11-4-65	11	Colorado	FA/99	*1/1
77	Thomas, Randy (G)	6-4/301	1-19-76	R	Mississippi State	D2/99	—
74	Young, Ryan (T)	6-5/337	6-28-76	R	Kansas State	D7a/99	—
	DEFENSIVE LINEMEN						
97	Boose, Dorian (E)	6-5/292	1-29-74	2	Washington State	D2/98	12/0
72	Ferguson, Jason (T)	6-3/305	11-28-74	3	Georgia	D7b/97	16/16
94	Frederick, Mike (E)	6-5/280	8-6-72	5	Virginia	UFA/99	*10/0
92	Hamilton, Bobby (E)	6-5/280	1-7-71	4	Southern Mississippi	FA/96	16/1
75	Hansen, Carl (T)	6-5/280	1-25-76	2	Stanford	FA/98	5/0
93	Logan, Ernie	6-3/290	5-18-68	8	East Carolina	UFA/97	16/12
95	Lyle, Rick	6-5/290	2-26-71	6	Missouri	UFA/97	16/16
99	Ogbogu, Eric (E)	6-4/280	7-18-75	2	Maryland	D6a/98	12/0
98	Pleasant, Anthony (E)	6-5/280	1-27-68	10	Tennessee State	FA/98	16/15
91	Wiltz, Jason (T)	6-4/308	11-23-76	R	Nebraska	D4/99	—
	LINEBACKERS						
53	Cascadden, Chad	6-1/240	5-14-72	5	Wisconsin	FA/95	13/4
51	Cox, Bryan	6-4/250	2-17-68	9	Western Illinois	FA/98	16/10
58	Farrior, James	6-2/242	1-6-75	3	Virginia	D1/97	12/2
54	Gordon, Dwayne	6-1/240	11-2-69	7	New Hampshire	FA/97	16/4
50	Holmberg, Rob	6-3/230	5-6-71	6	Penn State	FA/98	12/0
55	Jones, Marvin	6-2/250	6-28-72	7	Florida State	D1/93	—
57	Lewis, Mo	6-3/258	10-21-69	9	Georgia	D3/91	16/16
52	Megna, Marc	6-2/250	7-30-76	R	Richmond	D6a/99	—
56	Phifer, Roman	6-2/240	3-5-68	9	UCLA	UFA/99	*13/13
46	Syvrud, J.J.	6-3/265	5-10-77	R	Jamestown	D7b/99	—
	DEFENSIVE BACKS						
27	Atwater, Steve (S)	6-3/217	10-28-66	11	Arkansas	FA/99	*16/16
44	Brown, Corwin (S)	6-1/205	4-25-70	7	Michigan	FA/97	16/1
42	Coleman, Marcus (CB)	6-2/210	5-24-74	4	Texas Tech	D5/96	14/0
47	Frost, Scott (S)	6-3/219	1-4-75	2	Nebraska	D3a/98	13/0
31	Glenn, Aaron (CB)	5-9/185	7-16-72	6	Texas A&M	D1/94	13/13
21	Green, Victor (S)	5-11/205	12-8-69	7	Akron	FA/93	16/16
30	Hayes, Chris (S)	6-0/206	5-7-72	3	Washington State	T-GB/96	15/0
22	Jones, Jermaine (CB)	5-8/173	7-25-76	R	Northwestern State	D5/99	—
24	Mickens, Ray (CB)	5-8/184	1-4-73	4	Texas A&M	D3/96	16/3
45	Smith, Otis (CB)	5-11/195	10-22-65	10	Missouri	UFA/98	16/16
23	Williams, Kevin (S)	6-0/190	8-4-75	2	Oklahoma State	D3b/98	15/6
	SPECIALISTS						
9	Hall, John (K)	6-3/223	3-17-74	3	Wisconsin	FA/97	16/0
7	Tupa, Tom (P)	6-4/220	2-6-66	11	Ohio State	UFA/99	*16/0

*Not with Jets in 1998.

Other free agents invited to camp: WR James Adderley, DT Geno Bell, G Alex Bernstein, WR Chris Brazzell, FB Odell Collins, WR Eddie Conti, LB Casey Dailey, DE Terry Day, RB Robert Farmer, WR Shawn Foreman, TE Lawrence Hart, P Dirk Johnson, LB Olrick Johnson, G/T Doug Karczewski, LB Courtney Ledyard, CB Delphrine Lee, T Greg Lotyez, T Jason Mills, TE Johnny Mitchell, WR/KR Brian Musso, S Jason Poles, TE Jermaine Wiggins.

MISCELLANEOUS TEAM DATA

Stadium (capacity, surface):
Giants Stadium
(79,466, artificial)
Business address:
1000 Fulton Avenue
Hempstead, NY 11550
Business phone:
516-560-8100
Ticket information:
516-560-8200
Team colors:
Green and white
Flagship radio station:
WFAN, 660 AM
Training site:
Hofstra University
Hempstead, N.Y.
516-560-8100

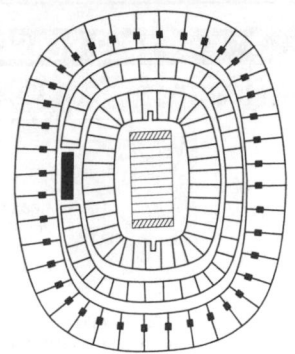

NEW YORK JETS

TSN REPORT CARD

Coaching staff	A	What can you say? Three years ago, the Jets were the dregs of the NFL. Now they're talking Super Bowl. Bill Parcells & Co. have done a masterful job. Opposing coaches say the Jets are among the toughest teams to prepare for. That's quite a compliment.
Quarterbacks	A -	Vinny Testaverde was sensational last season, but go back even further. In the last three years, he has a 2-to-1 touchdown-interception ratio. And at 35, he's still very durable. Good thing, because backup Scott Zolak doesn't remind anyone of Earl Morrall.
Running backs	B	Curtis Martin is a workmanlike back who can be penciled in for at least 1,200 yards if he stays healthy. But for $6 million a year, you'd like to see a few more big runs. Leon Johnson is a capable backup/third-down back. Jerald Sowell can contribute if he holds on to the ball.
Receivers	B +	Keyshawn Johnson, Wayne Chrebet and Dedric Ward form a nice trio of wideouts. Johnson and Chrebet are capable of dominating games. A few years back, Eric Green and Johnny Mitchell were rising stars at tight end. Now they each carry question marks, especially Mitchell.
Offensive line	C +	Center Kevin Mawae is among the best in the league, and tackles Jumbo Elliott and Jason Fabini are above average. How 'bout the guards? Welcome to the most unsettled area on the team, with five inexperienced players competing for two spots. Dial 911.
Defensive line	C -	This is an all-guts, no-glory group that does a blue-collar job in stopping the run. Nose tackle Jason Ferguson is the best of the bunch. The remainder of the unit is comprised of hold-the-fort types and unproven young players. Don't expect many sacks.
Linebackers	A -	Lots of talent and depth. Mo Lewis is an All-Pro, Bryan Cox is the spiritual leader of the defense and newcomer Roman Phifer is another toy for defensive coordinator Bill Belichick. A healthy Marvin Jones, returning from knee surgery, would mean so much.
Secondary	B -	It's not going to win any track meets, not with new free safety Steve Atwater (32) and cornerback Otis Smith (33), but this group has plenty of experience. The Atwater-Victor Green safety tandem should ring a few bells, and Pro Bowl cornerback Aaron Glenn will stick like glue to receivers.
Special teams	B -	New punter Tom Tupa upgrades a major weakness. The return units need a spark, and the coverage units need more attitude. Kicker John Hall has a powerful leg, but he's still a little too inconsistent.

OAKLAND RAIDERS
AFC WESTERN DIVISION

1999 SEASON

CLUB DIRECTORY

Owner
Al Davis
Executive assistant
Al LoCasale
Chief executive
Amy Trask
Senior assistant
Bruce Allen
Personnel executive
Mike Lombardi
Senior administrator
Morris Bradshaw
Public relations director
Mike Taylor
Administrative assistants
Craig Long
Billy Zagger
Finance
Tom Blanda
Marc Badain
Jennifer Levy
General counsel
Jeff Birren
Ticket manager
Peter Eiges
Admin. asst. to the head coach
Mark Arteaga
Head trainer
Rod Martin
Trainers
Mark Mayer
Scott Touchet
Strength and conditioning
Garrett Giemont
Player personnel
Angelo Coia
Ken Herock
Bruce Kebric
Jon Kingdon
Mike Lombardi
Mickey Marvin
David McCloughan
Kent McCloughan

Head coach
Jon Gruden

Assistant coaches
Fred Biletnikoff (wide receivers)
Chuck Bresnahan (def. backs)
Willie Brown (squad development)
Bill Callahan (offensive
  coordinator/offensive line)
Jim Erkenbeck (tight ends)
Frank Gansz Jr. (special teams)
Garrett Giemont (strength &
  conditioning)
Woodrow Lowe (def. assistant)
Don Martin (quality control-def.)
John Morton (offensive assistant)
Skip Peete (running backs)
Robin Ross (linebackers)
David Shaw (quality control-off.)
Willie Shaw (def. coordinator)
Gary Stevens (quarterbacks)
Mike Waufle (defensive line)

Building and grounds
Ken Irons
Equipment manager
Bob Romanski
Equipment assistant
Richard Romanski
Video coordinators
Dave Nash
John Otten
Jim Otten

SCHEDULE

Sept. 12—	at Green Bay	12:00
Sept. 19—	at Minnesota	12:00
Sept. 26—	CHICAGO	1:15
Oct. 3—	at Seattle	5:20
Oct. 10—	DENVER	1:15
Oct. 17—	at Buffalo	1:00
Oct. 24—	N.Y. JETS	1:15
Oct. 31—	MIAMI	1:05
Nov. 7—	Open date	
Nov. 14—	SAN DIEGO	1:05
Nov. 22—	at Denver (Mon.)	7:00
Nov. 28—	KANSAS CITY	1:15
Dec. 5—	SEATTLE	1:15
Dec. 9—	at Tennessee (Thur.)	7:20
Dec. 19—	TAMPA BAY	1:05
Dec. 26—	at San Diego	1:05
Jan. 2—	at Kansas City	12:00

All times are for home team.
All games Sunday unless noted.

DRAFT CHOICES

Matt Stinchcomb, T, Georgia (first
  round/18th pick overall).
Tony Bryant, DE, Florida State (2/40).
Dameane Douglas, WR, California
  (4/102).
Eric Barton, LB, Maryland (5/146).
Roderick Coleman, LB, East Carolina
  (5/153).
Daren Yancey, DT, Brigham Young
  (6/188).
JoJuan Armour, LB, Miami of Ohio
  (7/224).

1998 REVIEW

RESULTS

Sept. 6	—at Kansas City	L	8-28
Sept.13	—N.Y. GIANTS	W	20-17
Sept.20	—DENVER	L	17-34
Sept.27	—at Dallas	W	13-12
Oct. 4	—at Arizona	W	23-20
Oct. 11	—SAN DIEGO	W	7-6
Oct. 18	—Open date		
Oct. 25	—CINCINNATI	W	27-10
Nov. 1	—at Seattle	W	31-18
Nov. 8	—at Baltimore	L	10-13
Nov. 15	—SEATTLE	W	20-17
Nov. 22	—at Denver	L	14-40
Nov. 29	—WASHINGTON	L	19-29
Dec. 6	—MIAMI	L	17-27
Dec. 13	—at Buffalo	L	21-44
Dec. 20	—at San Diego	W	17-10
Dec. 26	—KANSAS CITY	L	24-31

RECORDS/RANKINGS

1998 regular-season record: 8-8 (2nd in
AFC West); 4-4 in division; 5-7 in conference; 4-4 at home; 4-4 on road.
Team record last five years: 36-44 (.450,
ranks 18th in league in that span).
1998 team rankings:

	No.	AFC	NFL
Total offense	*300.9	10	18
Rushing offense	*107.9	8	16
Passing offense	*193.0	11	21
Scoring offense	288	11	22
Total defense	*284.4	3	5
Rushing defense	*104.6	9	15
Passing defense	*179.8	1	4
Scoring defense	356	12	20
Takeaways	35	3	5
Giveaways	43	14	29
Turnover differential	-8	13	T24
Sacks	41	T5	T12
Sacks allowed	67	15	30

*Yards per game.

TEAM LEADERS

Scoring (kicking): Greg Davis, 82 pts.
(31/31 PATs, 17/27 FGs).
Scoring (touchdowns): Tim Brown, 54
pts. (9 receiving).
Passing: Donald Hollas, 1,754 yds. (260
att., 135 comp., 51.9%, 10 TDs, 16 int.).
Rushing: Napoleon Kaufman, 921 yds.
(217 att., 4.2 avg., 2 TDs).
Receptions: Tim Brown, 81 (1,012 yds.,
12.5 avg., 9 TDs).
Interceptions: Charles Woodson, 5 (118
yds., 1 TD); Eric Allen, 5 (59 yds., 0
TDs).
Sacks: Lance Johnstone, 11.0.
Punting: Leo Araguz, 43.4 avg. (98
punts, 4,256 yds., 0 blocked).
Punt returns: Desmond Howard, 12.0
avg. (45 att., 541 yds., 2 TDs).
Kickoff returns: Desmond Howard, 21.2
avg. (49 att., 1,040 yds., 0 TDs).

TRAINING CAMP ROSTER

No.	QUARTERBACKS	Ht./Wt.	Born	NFL Exp.	College	How acq.	'98 Games GP/GS
12	Gannon, Rich	6-3/210	12-20-65	11	Delaware	UFA/99	*12/10
5	Shuler, Heath	6-2/216	12-31-71	6	Tennessee	FA/99	—
16	Wilson, Wade	6-3/210	2-1-59	19	East Texas State	FA/98	5/3

	RUNNING BACKS						
27	Branch, Calvin	5-11/195	5-8-74	3	Colorado State	D6/97	16/0
34	Crockett, Zack	6-2/246	12-2-72	5	Florida State	UFA/99	*12/2
28	Jordan, Randy	5-10/215	6-6-70	6	North Carolina	UFA/98	16/0
26	Kaufman, Napoleon	5-9/185	6-7-73	5	Washington	D1/95	13/13
40	Ritchie, Jon	6-1/250	9-4-74	2	Stanford	D3/98	15/10
	Salaam, Rashaan	6-1/224	10-8-74	5	Colorado	FA/99	0/0
22	Williams, Harvey	6-2/220	4-22-67	9	Louisiana State	FA/94	16/3
34	Williams, Jermaine	6-0/228	7-3-72	2	Houston	FA/98	10/0

	RECEIVERS						
87	Brigham, Jeremy (TE)	6-6/255	3-22-75	2	Washington	D5a/98	2/0
81	Brown, Tim	6-0/195	7-22-66	12	Notre Dame	D1/88	16/16
	Douglas, Dameane	6-0/187	3-15-76	R	California	D4/99	—
83	Dudley, Rickey (TE)	6-6/250	7-15-72	4	Ohio State	D1/96	16/15
80	Howard, Desmond	5-10/185	5-15-70	8	Michigan	UFA/97	15/1
82	Jett, James	5-10/165	12-28-70	7	West Virginia	FA/93	16/16
85	Mickens, Terry	6-0/201	2-21-71	6	Florida A&M	UFA/98	16/2
84	Shedd, Kenny	5-10/164	2-14-71	5	Northern Iowa	FA/96	15/0
89	Williams, Rodney	6-0/185	8-15-73	2	Arizona	FA/98	1/0

	OFFENSIVE LINEMEN						
73	Ashmore, Darryl (T)	6-7/310	11-1-69	8	Northwestern	FA/98	15/4
79	Collins, Mo (T)	6-4/325	9-22-76	2	Florida	D1b/98	16/11
68	Cunningham, Rick (T)	6-7/305	1-4-67	9	Texas A&M	UFA/96	12/0
77	Harlow, Pat (T)	6-6/295	3-16-69	9	Southern California	T-NE/96	5/5
72	Kennedy, Lincoln (G)	6-6/335	2-12-71	7	Washington	T-Atl./96	16/16
63	Robbins, Barret (C)	6-3/315	8-26-73	5	Texas Christian	D2/95	16/16
75	Skrepenak, Greg (G)	6-7/316	1-31-70	6	Michigan	FA/99	0/0
	Stinchcomb, Matt (T)	6-5/297	6-3-77	R	Georgia	D1/99	—
62	Treu, Adam (T)	6-5/300	6-24-74	3	Nebraska	D3/97	16/0
76	Wisniewski, Steve (G)	6-4/305	4-7-67	11	Penn State	D2/89	16/16

	DEFENSIVE LINEMEN						
92	Amey, Vince (E)	6-2/289	2-9-75	2	Arizona State	D7b/98	4/1
	Bryant, Tony (E)	6-3/268	9-3-76	R	Florida State	D2/99	—
93	Harris, James (E)	6-6/280	5-13-68	6	Temple	FA/98	16/16
90	Jackson, Grady (E)	6-2/320	1-21-73	3	Knoxville	D6b/97	15/1
51	Johnstone, Lance (E)	6-4/250	6-11-73	4	Temple	D2/96	16/15
67	Maryland, Russell (T)	6-1/295	3-22-69	9	Miami (Fla.)	UFA/96	15/15
98	Osborne, Chuck (T)	6-2/290	11-2-73	4	Arizona	FA/98	6/0
96	Russell, Darrell (T)	6-5/320	5-27-76	3	Southern California	D1/97	16/16
97	Shello, Kendel (T)	6-3/301	11-24-73	3	Southern	FA/99	*6/1
	Taves, Josh (E)	6-7/260	5-13-72	1	Northeastern	FA/99	—
	Yancey, Daren (T)	6-5/305	12-21-73	R	Brigham Young	D6/99	—

	LINEBACKERS						
	Armour, Jo Juan	5-11/219	7-10-76	R	Miami of Ohio	D7/99	—
	Barton, Eric	6-2/229	9-29-77	R	Maryland	D5a/99	—
52	Bellisari, Greg	6-0/236	6-21-75	2	Ohio State	FA/99	*2/0
54	Biekert, Greg	6-2/245	3-14-69	7	Colorado	D7/93	16/16
	Coleman, Roderick	6-1/255	8-16-76	R	East Carolina	D5b/99	—
55	Folston, James	6-3/240	8-14-71	6	Northeast Louisiana	D2/94	16/5
52	Harvey, Richard	6-1/235	9-11-66	10	Tulane	FA/98	16/16
53	Smith, Travian	6-4/238	8-26-75	1	Oklahoma	D5b/98	2/0

	DEFENSIVE BACKS						
21	Allen, Eric	5-10/190	11-22-65	12	Arizona State	T-NO/98	10/10
33	Brooks, Bucky	6-0/192	1-22-71	5	North Carolina	FA/98	12/0
20	Carter, Perry	6-0/185	8-5-71	3	Southern Mississippi	FA/96	6/0
29	Lewis, Albert	6-2/205	10-6-60	17	Grambling State	UFA/94	15/12
22	Mincy, Charles	6-0/195	12-16-69	9	Washington	FA/99	*16/16
30	Newman, Anthony	6-0/215	11-21-65	12	Oregon	UFA/98	11/11
42	Turner, Eric	6-1/215	9-20-68	9	UCLA	FA/97	6/6
38	Walker, Marquis	5-10/175	7-6-72	4	Southeast Missouri State	FA/98	16/7
24	Woodson, Charles	6-0/200	10-7-76	2	Michigan	D1a/98	16/16

	SPECIALISTS						
2	Araguz, Leo (P)	5-11/190	1-18-70	3	Stephen F. Austin	FA/96	16/0
5	Husted, Michael (K)	6-0/190	6-16-70	7	Virginia	FA/99	*16/0

*Not with Raiders in 1998.
   Other free agents invited to camp: RB Marlon Barnes, QB Pat Barnes, G Isaac Davis, G Gennaro DiNapoli, DT Ta'ase Faumui, DT Dayroni Harris, TE Marcus Hinton, WR Chris T. Jones, T Siupeli Malamala, QB Mike McQueary, WR Isiah Mustafa, DB Marcus Ray, RB Reynard Rutherford, WR Creig Spann, CB Eric Sutton, LB Sam Sword, TE Derrick Walker, QB Andre Ware, T Scott Whittaker, LB K.D. Williams.

Abbreviations: D1—draft pick, first round; SupD2—supplemental draft pick, second round; WV—claimed on waivers; TR—obtained in trade; PlanB—Plan B free-agent acquisition; FA—free-agent acquisition (other than Plan B); ED—expansion draft pick.

MISCELLANEOUS TEAM DATA

Stadium (capacity, surface):
Oakland-Alameda County Coliseum
(63,026, grass)
Business address:
1220 Harbor Bay Parkway
Alameda, CA 94502
Business phone:
510-864-5000
Ticket information:
800-949-2626
Team colors:
Silver and black
Flagship radio station:
The Ticket, 1050 AM
Training site:
Napa, Calif.
707-256-1000

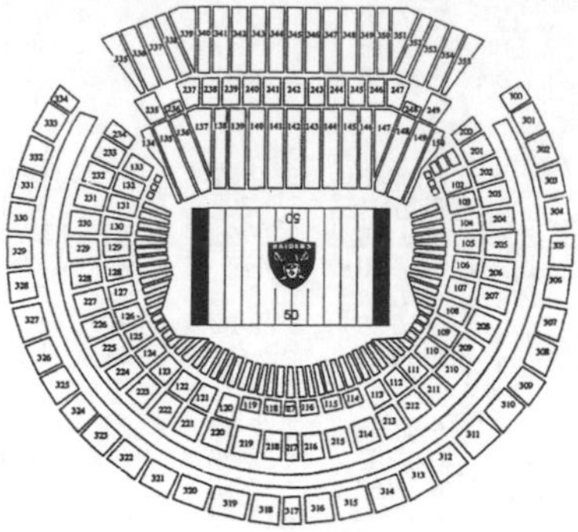

TSN REPORT CARD

Coaching staff	B -	Jon Gruden did what many thought was impossible last year by uniting a fractured football team. That showed by the lack of finger-pointing when the season turned sour. Now, the big test for Gruden is getting the offense to perform with some semblance of consistency. The main challenge for defensive coordinator Willie Shaw is proving that last year's defensive revival was no fluke.
Quarterbacks	C	The Raiders gave up the raw talent of Jeff George for Rich Gannon, a competent quarterback but nothing special. What Gannon brings is the ability to escape the pass rush, which is a necessity when playing behind the Raiders' offensive line. Gruden also feels that Gannon is a better fit for the offense.
Running backs	C	The Raiders still have not addressed their need for a power running back. Napoleon Kaufman is the type of runner who can score from any spot on the field, but when it's time to control the ball on the ground in the fourth quarter, he isn't the guy. Jon Ritchie and Zack Crockett will be asked to handle the short-yardage situations. The running backs will continue their trend of being hit-and-miss.
Receivers	D +	Unless rookie Dameane Douglas makes an immediate impact, this unit is nothing more than Tim Brown and a bunch of warm bodies. Brown, despite the anticipated double coverage, should put together another solid year. But as it has been the past few seasons, he shouldn't expect much help from his position-mates. If a definitive role can be found for tight end Rickey Dudley, things might loosen up for Brown.
Offensive line	D-	With the exception of right guard, this will be the same cast of characters who allowed a league-high 67 sacks last year. And it's also a unit that was unable to get enough push forward to convert in short-yardage situations. This remains one of the team's weakest links.
Defensive line	B +	Tackle Darrell Russell is a budding superstar and the centerpiece of the defense. With better-than-adequate depth at the tackle position and the development of end Lance Johnstone into one of the game's top pass rushers, the front line can be a dominant unit. And the addition of rookie Tony Bryant adds another pass rushing end with speed.
Linebackers	B	There is still a need for a playmaking outside linebacker, as the players currently manning that position (James Folston and Richard Harvey) are steady, not spectacular. Middle linebacker Greg Biekert is solid against the run but not as effective in pass coverage. The success here will depend on how well the defensive front does.
Secondary	A -	If Eric Allen can make it all the way back from his knee injury, this is arguably one of the best units in the league. By excelling in man-to-man coverage, cornerbacks Charles Woodson and Allen will allow safeties Anthony Newman, Eric Turner and newly acquired Charles Mincy to be more aggressive in run support.
Special teams	D-	There should be an improvement in the kicking game with the signing of free agent Michael Husted. The biggest problems last year were that the kickoff and punt coverage teams were so horrible that opponents usually started drives in favorable field position. Maybe more of Oakland's frontline players should be used on special teams.

PHILADELPHIA EAGLES
NFC EASTERN DIVISION

1999 SEASON

CLUB DIRECTORY

Owner/chief executive officer
Jeffrey Lurie
Executive vice president
Joe Banner
Director of football operations
Tom Modrak
Senior vice president-special projects
Mimi Box
Senior v.p., marketing and administration
Len Komoroski
Chief financial officer
Don Smolenski
Vice president, sales
Scott O'Neil
Vice president, corporate sales
Dave Rowan
Executive dir. of Eagles Youth Partnership
Sarah Helfman
Pro scouting coordinator
Mike McCartney
College scouting coordinator
Bryan Broaddus
Director of administration
Vicki Chatley
Director of public relations
Ron Howard
Assistant director of public relations
Derek Boyko
Public relations assistant
Rich Burg
Dir. of player and community relations
Harold Carmichael
Ticket manager
Leo Carlin
Director of sales
Jason Gonella
Director of corporate sales
Ron Skotarczak
Director of facility development
Dan McGregor
Director of merchandising
Steve Strawbridge
Director of advertising and promotions
Kim Babiak
Office manager/travel coordinator
Tracey Bucher

Head coach
Andy Reid

Assistant coaches
Tommy Brasher (defensive line)
Juan Castillo (offensive line)
Brad Childress (quarterbacks)
Dave Culley (wide receivers)
Rod Dowhower (off. coordinator)
Leslie Frazier (defensive backs)
John Harbaugh (special teams)
Jim Johnson (def. coordinator)
Tom Melvin (offensive assistant/
quality control)
Ron Rivera (linebackers)
Pat Shurmur (tight ends/
assistant offensive line)
Steve Spagnuolo (defensive
assistant/quality control)
Ted Williams (running backs)
Mike Wolf (strength & cond.)

Director of security
Anthony Buchanico
Director of penthouse operations
Christiana Noyalas
Director of broadcasting
Rob Alberino
Head athletic trainer
Rick Burkholder
Assistant trainers
Scottie Patton   Chris Peduzzi
Video director
Mike Dougherty
Equipment manager
Angelo Ortiz

SCHEDULE

Sept. 12— ARIZONA	1:00
Sept. 19— TAMPA BAY	1:00
Sept. 26— at Buffalo	1:00
Oct. 3— at N.Y. Giants	1:00
Oct. 10— DALLAS	1:00
Oct. 17— at Chicago	12:00
Oct. 24— at Miami	1:00
Oct. 31— N.Y. GIANTS	1:00
Nov. 7— at Carolina	1:00
Nov. 14— WASHINGTON	1:00
Nov. 21— INDIANAPOLIS	1:00
Nov. 28— at Washington	1:00
Dec. 5— at Arizona	2:05
Dec. 12— at Dallas	12:00
Dec. 19— NEW ENGLAND	1:00
Dec. 26— Open date	
Jan. 2— ST. LOUIS	1:00

All times are for home team.
All games Sunday unless noted.

DRAFT CHOICES

Donovan McNabb, QB, Syracuse (first
round/second pick overall).
Barry Gardner, LB, Northwestern (2/35).
Doug Brzezinski, G, Boston College
(3/64).
John Welbourn, T, California (4/97).
Damon Moore, DB, Ohio State (4/128).
Na Brown, WR, North Carolina (4/130).
Cecil Martin, RB, Wisconsin (6/172).
Troy Smith, WR, East Carolina (6/201).
Jed Weaver, TE, Oregon (7/208).
Pernell Davis, DT, Alabama-Birmingham
(7/251).

1998 REVIEW

RESULTS

Sept. 6—SEATTLE	L	0-38
Sept.13—at Atlanta	L	12-17
Sept.20—at Arizona	L	3-17
Sept.27—KANSAS CITY	L	21-24
Oct. 4—at Denver	L	16-41
Oct. 11—WASHINGTON	W	17-12
Oct. 18—at San Diego	L	10-13
Oct. 25—Open date		
Nov. 2—DALLAS	L	0-34
Nov. 8—DETROIT	W	10-9
Nov. 15—at Washington	L	3-28
Nov. 22—at N.Y. Giants	L	0-20
Nov. 29—at Green Bay	L	16-24
Dec. 3—ST. LOUIS	W	17-14
Dec. 13—ARIZONA (OT)	L	17-20
Dec. 20—at Dallas	L	9-13
Dec. 27—N.Y. GIANTS	L	10-20

RECORDS/RANKINGS

1998 regular-season record: 3-13 (5th in
NFC East); 1-7 in division; 3-9 in conference; 3-5 at home; 0-8 on road.
Team record last five years: 36-43-1
(.456, ranks 17th in league in that span).

1998 team rankings:

	No.	NFC	NFL
Total offense	*261.8	15	30
Rushing offense	*110.9	8	14
Passing offense	*150.8	15	30
Scoring offense	161	15	30
Total defense	*321.0	8	17
Rushing defense	*151.0	14	27
Passing defense	*170.0	1	1
Scoring defense	344	8	19
Takeaways	17	15	30
Giveaways	26	6	13
Turnover differential	-9	13	26
Sacks	42	7	11
Sacks allowed	56	13	27
*Yards per game.			

TEAM LEADERS

Scoring (kicking): Chris Boniol, 57 pts.
(15/17 PATs, 14/21 FGs).
Scoring (touchdowns): Duce Staley, 36
pts. (5 rushing, 1 receiving).
Passing: Koy Detmer, 1,011 yds. (181
att., 97 comp., 53.6%, 5 TDs, 5 int.).
Rushing: Duce Staley, 1,065 yds. (258
att., 4.1 avg., 5 TDs).
Receptions: Jeff Graham, 47 (600 yds.,
12.8 avg., 2 TDs).
Interceptions: Brian Dawkins, 2 (39 yds.,
0 TDs); Troy Vincent, 2 (29 yds., 0 TDs);
Michael Zordich, 2 (18 yds., 0 TDs).
Sacks: Hugh Douglas, 12.5.
Punting: Tom Hutton, 41.7 avg. (104
punts, 4,339 yds., 0 blocked).
Punt returns: Allen Rossum, 8.5 avg. (22
att., 187 yds., 0 TDs).
Kickoff returns: Allen Rossum, 24.5 avg.
(44 att., 1,080 yds., 0 TDs).

PHILADELPHIA EAGLES

No.	QUARTERBACKS	Ht./Wt.	Born	NFL Exp.	College	How acq.	'98 Games GP/GS
10	Detmer, Koy	6-1/195	7-5-73	3	Colorado	D7a/97	8/5
7	Hoying, Bobby	6-3/221	9-20-72	4	Ohio State	D3/96	8/7
5	McNabb, Donovan	6-2/226	11-25-76	R	Syracuse	D1/99	—
14	Pederson, Doug	6-3/216	1-31-68	7	Northeast Louisiana	UFA/99	*12/0
	RUNNING BACKS						
33	Bieniemy, Eric	5-9/205	8-15-69	9	Colorado	UFA/99	*16/0
27	Bostic, James	5-11/225	3-13-72	3	Auburn	FA/98	2/0
24	Hayden, Aaron	6-0/216	4-13-73	5	Tennessee	W-GB/98	1/0
38	Martin, Cecil (FB)	6-0/235	7-8-75	R	Wisconsin	D6a/99	—
39	Reed, Mike (FB)	6-0/215	1-6-75	2	Washington	FA/98	4/0
22	Staley, Duce	5-11/220	2-27-75	3	South Carolina	D3/97	16/13
34	Turner, Kevin (FB)	6-1/231	6-12-69	8	Alabama	FA/95	16/15
29	Walker, Corey	5-10/188	6-4-73	3	Arkansas State	FA/97	14/0
	RECEIVERS						
86	Asher, Jamie (TE)	6-3/245	10-31-72	5	Louisville	UFA/99	*9/7
12	Brown, Na	6-0/187	2-22-77	R	North Carolina	D4c/99	—
87	Dunn, Jason (TE)	6-4/257	11-15-73	4	Eastern Kentucky	D2a/96	10/10
85	Fontenot, Chris (TE)	6-3/250	7-11-74	2	McNeese State	FA/98	5/3
82	Hankton, Karl	6-2/202	7-24-70	2	Trinity (Ill.)	FA/98	10/0
83	Jells, Dietrich	5-10/185	4-11-72	4	Pittsburgh	T-NE/98	9/0
81	Johnson, Charles	6-0/200	1-3-72	6	Colorado	UFA/99	*16/16
88	Jordan, Andrew (TE)	6-4/254	6-21-72	5	Western Carolina	FA/98	3/0
89	Sinceno, Kaseem (TE)	6-4/259	3-26-76	2	Syracuse	FA/98	10/0
80	Small, Torrance	6-3/209	9-4-70	8	Alcorn State	UFA/99	*16/4
8	Smith, Troy	6-2/193	7-30-77	R	East Carolina	D6b/99	—
46	Weaver, Jed (TE)	6-4/246	8-11-76	R	Oregon	D7a/99	—
	OFFENSIVE LINEMEN						
74	Brzezinski, Doug (G)	6-4/305	3-11-76	R	Boston College	D3/99	—
66	Crafts, Jerry (T)	6-5/334	1-6-68	6	Louisville	FA/97	1/0
61	Everitt, Steve (C)	6-5/310	8-21-70	7	Michigan	UFA/97	13/13
69	Hegamin, George (T)	6-7/331	2-14-73	6	North Carolina State	UFA/98	16/6
71	Mayberry, Jermane (G)	6-4/325	8-29-73	4	Texas A&M-Kingsville	D1/96	15/10
65	Miller, Bubba (C)	6-1/305	1-24-73	4	Tennessee	FA/96	15/4
72	Thomas, Tra (T)	6-7/349	11-20-74	2	Florida State	D1/98	16/16
68	Unutoa, Morris (C)	6-1/284	3-10-71	4	Brigham Young	FA/96	16/0
76	Welbourn, John (T)	6-5/318	3-30-76	R	California	D4a/99	—
	DEFENSIVE LINEMEN						
93	Davis, Pernell (T)	6-2/320	5-19-76	R	Alabama-Birmingham	D7b/99	—
90	Harris, Jon (E)	6-7/300	6-9-74	3	Virginia	D1/97	16/4
79	Jefferson, Greg (E)	6-3/280	8-31-71	5	Central Florida	D3a/95	15/14
94	Johnson, Bill (T)	6-4/305	12-9-68	8	Michigan State	UFA/98	13/13
73	Martin, Steve (T)	6-4/303	5-31-74	4	Missouri	W-Ind./98	13/3
95	Slay, Henry (T)	6-2/290	4-28-75	1	West Virginia	FA/98	3/0
78	Thomas, Hollis (T)	6-0/306	1-10-74	4	Northern Illinois	FA/96	12/12
96	Wallace, Al (E)	6-5/258	3-25-74	2	Maryland	FA/97	15/0
91	Wheeler, Mark (T)	6-3/285	4-1-70	8	Texas A&M	UFA/99	*10/2
98	Whiting, Brandon (T)	6-3/278	7-30-76	2	California	D4a/98	16/5
	LINEBACKERS						
55	Alexander, Patrise	6-1/244	10-23-72	4	Southwestern Louisiana	FA/99	*1/0
56	Caldwell, Mike	6-2/237	8-31-71	7	Middle Tennessee State	FA/98	16/8
57	Darling, James	6-0/250	12-29-74	3	Washington State	D2/97	12/8
53	Douglas, Hugh	6-2/280	8-23-71	5	Central State (Ohio)	T-NYJ/98	15/13
49	Gardner, Barry	6-0/248	12-13-76	R	Northwestern	D2/99	—
59	Mamula, Mike	6-4/252	8-14-73	5	Boston College	D1/95	—
58	Reese, Ike	6-2/222	10-16-73	2	Michigan State	D5/98	16/0
51	Thomas, William	6-2/223	8-13-68	9	Texas A&M	D4/91	16/16
54	Trotter, Jeremiah	6-0/261	1-20-77	2	Stephen F. Austin	D3a/98	8/0
50	Willis, James	6-2/237	9-2-72	7	Auburn	FA/95	16/16
	DEFENSIVE BACKS						
20	Dawkins, Brian (S)	5-11/200	10-13-73	4	Clemson	D2b/96	14/14
31	Harris, Al (CB)	6-0/185	12-7-74	2	Texas A&M-Kingsville	W-TB/98	16/7
45	Hauck, Tim (S)	5-10/187	12-20-66	10	Montana	UFA/99	*16/7
28	Love, Clarence (CB)	5-10/181	6-16-76	2	Toledo	D4b/98	6/0
43	Moore, Damon (S)	5-11/215	9-15-76	R	Ohio State	D4b/99	—
25	Rossum, Allen (CB)	5-8/178	10-22-75	2	Notre Dame	D3/98	15/2
21	Taylor, Bobby (CB)	6-3/216	12-28-73	5	Notre Dame	D2a/95	11/10
23	Vincent, Troy (CB)	6-0/194	6-8-70	8	Wisconsin	FA/96	13/13

No.	SPECIALISTS	Ht./Wt.	Born	NFL Exp.	College	How acq.	'98 Games GP/GS
2	Akers, David (K)	5-10/180	12-9-74	1	Louisville	FA/99	*1/0
18	Boniol, Chris (K)	5-11/167	12-9-71	6	Louisiana Tech	FA/97	16/0
6	Landeta, Sean (P)	6-0/200	1-6-62	15	Towson State	UFA/99	*16/0

*Not with Eagles in 1998.
Other free agents invited to camp: T Chris Akins, CB Jason Bostic, P Barry Cantrell, WR Fred Coleman, G Brian Cook, WR Kotto Cotton, CB Eric Edwards, G Wendell Gaines, S Kenny Harris, T Matt Hogg, LB Dana Howard, FB Mark Kacmarynski, CB Deshone Mallard, P Tony Martino, WR Kevin McKenzie, WR Harvey Middleton, G Glenn Rountree, G Ryan Schau, WR Eric Smith, FB Jamie Spencer, G Melvin Thomas, WR Gerald Williams, S Sean Woodson.
Abbreviations: D1—draft pick, first round; SupD2—supplemental draft pick, second round; WV—claimed on waivers; TR—obtained in trade; PlanB—Plan B free-agent acquisition; FA—free-agent acquisition (other than Plan B); ED—expansion draft pick.

MISCELLANEOUS TEAM DATA

Stadium (capacity, surface):
Veterans Stadium
(65,352, artificial)
Business address:
3501 South Broad Street
Philadelphia, PA 19148
Business phone:
215-463-2500
Ticket information:
215-463-5500
Team colors:
Midnight green, silver and white
Flagship radio station:
WYSP, 94.1 FM
Training site:
Lehigh University
Bethlehem, Pa.
610-758-6868

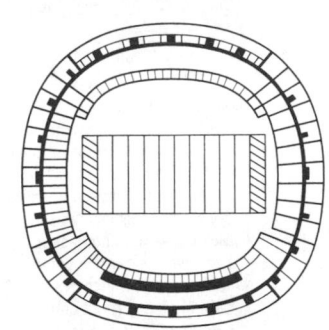

TSN REPORT CARD

Coaching staff	C	Head coach Andy Reid is making a huge jump from being a quarterbacks coach and is going to need time to grow into the position. Coordinators Rod Dowhower (offense) and Jim Johnson (defense) have experience, but not a lot of success. Surprisingly, four leftovers were kept from Ray Rhodes' staff.
Quarterbacks	C -	Until Donovan McNabb is ready to take over, the Eagles will struggle. And then there will be McNabb's learning period to deal with as well. Starter Doug Pederson, a free agent from Green Bay, is a 31-year-old career backup who has thrown all of 32 NFL passes.
Running backs	B	Duce Staley gained 1,065 yards rushing and caught 57 passes last season despite sharing time the first half of the season and playing with a hernia in the second half. Fullback Kevin Turner is not as bad as he played in '98, but he's not as good as some people in the organization think.
Receivers	C -	Free-agent signings Charles Johnson, Torrance Small and tight end Jamie Asher are all major upgrades over the people sent out on pass patterns last year, but there is still a major lack of speed and absolutely no depth. Rookie Na Brown might make a difference.
Offensive line	C	This unit could surprise if the pieces fall into place. Tra Thomas has to continue to improve at left tackle, and Steve Everett must play well at center. Then Jermane Mayberry has to be able to play right tackle, and rookie Doug Brzezinski must step right in at left guard.
Defensive line	C -	Little was done to help a unit that had just one pass rusher, Hugh Douglas, and was run against at will last season. The only addition was journeyman Mark Wheeler, who will rotate inside with Hollis Thomas and Bill Johnson. Former first-round picks Mike Mamula and Jon Harris are backups.
Linebackers	C -	For the third straight year the team drafted a middle linebacker early. Maybe this time the Eagles got it right with Barry Gardner. Former high picks James Darling and Jeremiah Trotter could see time outside along with veterans William Thomas and Mike Caldwell.
Secondary	B	Bobby Taylor is the best cornerback who hasn't intercepted a pass in two years. On the other side, Troy Vincent gets respect everywhere except Philadelphia. Free safety Brian Dawkins might be the team's best playmaker. Rookie Damon Moore is going to have to start at strong safety.
Special teams	C +	Coach John Harbaugh did a great job last year as everything else around the team fell apart. Now, he has to continue the progress. Kicker Chris Boniol has to bounce back, punter Sean Landeta has to keep going, and return man Allen Rossum needs a bigger comeback than Boniol.

PITTSBURGH STEELERS
AFC CENTRAL DIVISION

1999 SEASON

CLUB DIRECTORY

President
Daniel M. Rooney
Vice presidents
John R. McGinley
Arthur J. Rooney Jr.
Vice president/general counsel
Arthur J. Rooney II
Administration advisor
Charles H. Noll
Director of business
Mark Hart
Business coordinator
Dan Ferens
Accounts coordinator
Jim Ellenberger
Ticket sales manager
Geraldine Glenn
Director of football operations
Tom Donahoe
Player relations
Anthony Griggs
Communications coordinator
Ron Wahl
Public relations/media manager
Dave Lockett
Director of pro personnel
Max McCartney
College scouting coordinator
Charles Bailey
College scouts
Mark Gorscak
Phil Kriedler
Bob Lane
Max McCartney
Marketing coordinator
Mark Fuhrman
Trainers
John Norwig
Ryan Grove

Head coach
Bill Cowher

Assistant coaches
Mike Archer (linebackers)
Bob Bratkowski (wide receivers)
Kevin Gilbride (off. coordinator)
Jim Haslett (defensive coordinator)
Jay Hayes (special teams)
Dick Hoak (running backs)
Tim Lewis (defensive backs)
John Mitchell (defensive line)
Mike Mularkey (tight ends)
Kent Stephenson (offensive line)

Physicians
James P. Bradley
Richard Rydze
Abraham J. Twerski
Anthony P. Yates
Equipment manager
Rodgers Freyvogel
Field manager
Rich Baker
Video director
Bob McCartney
Video assistant
Andy Lizanich
Photographer
Mike Fabus

SCHEDULE

Sept. 12—	at Cleveland	8:20
Sept. 19—	at Baltimore	1:00
Sept. 26—	SEATTLE	1:00
Oct. 3—	JACKSONVILLE	1:00
Oct. 10—	at Buffalo	1:00
Oct. 17—	at Cincinnati	1:00
Oct. 25—	ATLANTA (Mon.)	9:00
Oct. 31—	Open date	
Nov. 7—	at San Francisco	1:15
Nov. 14—	CLEVELAND	1:00
Nov. 21—	at Tennessee	12:00
Nov. 28—	CINCINNATI	1:00
Dec. 2—	at Jacksonville (Thur.)	8:20
Dec. 12—	BALTIMORE	1:00
Dec. 18—	at Kansas City (Sat.)	11:40
Dec. 26—	CAROLINA	1:00
Jan. 2—	TENNESSEE	4:15

All times are for home team.
All games Sunday unless noted.

DRAFT CHOICES

Troy Edwards, WR, Louisiana Tech (first round/13th pick overall).
Scott Shields, DB, Weber State (2/59).
Joey Porter, LB, Colorado State (3/73).
Kris Farris, T, UCLA (3/74).
Amos Zereoue, RB, West Virginia (3/95).
Aaron Smith, DE, Northern Colorado (4/109).
Jerame Tuman, TE, Michigan (5/136).
Malcolm Johnson, WR, Notre Dame (5/166).
Antonio Dingle, DT, Virginia (7/214).
Chad Kelsay, LB, Nebraska (7/219).
Kris Brown, K, Nebraska (7/228).

1998 REVIEW

RESULTS

Sept. 6—	at Baltimore	W	20-13
Sept. 13—	CHICAGO	W	17-12
Sept. 20—	at Miami	L	0-21
Sept. 27—	SEATTLE	W	13-10
Oct. 4—	Open date		
Oct. 11—	at Cincinnati	L	20-25
Oct. 18—	BALTIMORE	W	16-6
Oct. 26—	at Kansas City	W	20-13
Nov. 1—	TENNESSEE	L	31-41
Nov. 9—	GREEN BAY	W	27-20
Nov. 15—	at Tennessee	L	14-23
Nov. 22—	JACKSONVILLE	W	30-15
Nov. 26—	at Detroit (OT)	L	16-19
Dec. 6—	NEW ENGLAND	L	9-23
Dec. 13—	at Tampa Bay	L	3-16
Dec. 20—	CINCINNATI	L	24-25
Dec. 28—	at Jacksonville	L	3-21

RECORDS/RANKINGS

1998 regular-season record: 7-9 (3rd in AFC Central); 3-5 in division; 5-7 in conference; 5-3 at home; 2-6 on road.
Team record last five years: 51-29 (.638, ranks T4th in league in that span).

1998 team rankings:	No.	AFC	NFL
Total offense	*286.6	14	25
Rushing offense	*127.1	4	7
Passing offense	*159.5	15	29
Scoring offense	263	14	28
Total defense	*310.2	8	12
Rushing defense	*102.6	7	13
Passing defense	*207.6	9	18
Scoring defense	303	3	7
Takeaways	29	10	16
Giveaways	32	T10	T19
Turnover differential	-3	11	19
Sacks	41	T5	T12
Sacks allowed	35	T6	T10

*Yards per game.

TEAM LEADERS

Scoring (kicking): Norm Johnson, 99 pts. (21/21 PATs, 26/31 FGs).
Scoring (touchdowns): Charles Johnson, 46 pts. (7 receiving, 2 2-pt. conv.).
Passing: Kordell Stewart, 2,560 yds. (458 att., 252 comp., 55.0%, 11 TDs, 18 int.).
Rushing: Jerome Bettis, 1,185 yds. (316 att., 3.8 avg., 3 TDs).
Receptions: Charles Johnson, 65 (815 yds., 12.5 avg., 7 TDs).
Interceptions: Dewayne Washington, 5 (178 yds., 2 TDs).
Sacks: Jason Gildon, 11.0.
Punting: Josh Miller, 43.6 avg. (81 punts, 3,530 yds., 0 blocked).
Punt returns: Courtney Hawkins, 11.7 avg. (15 att., 175 yds., 0 TDs).
Kickoff returns: David Dunn, 25.0 avg. (21 att., 525 yds., 0 TDs).

TRAINING CAMP ROSTER

No.	QUARTERBACKS	Ht./Wt.	Born	NFL Exp.	College	How acq.	'98 Games GP/GS
10	Stewart, Kordell	6-1/211	10-16-72	5	Colorado	D2/95	16/16
18	Tomczak, Mike	6-1/210	10-23-62	15	Ohio State	UFA/93	16/0
	RUNNING BACKS						
36	Bettis, Jerome	5-11/250	2-16-72	7	Notre Dame	T-StL/96	15/15
45	Fuamatu-Ma'afala, Chris	5-11/252	3-4-77	2	Utah	D6a/98	12/0
33	Huntley, Richard	5-11/225	9-18-72	3	Winston-Salem (N.C.) State	FA/98	16/1
35	King, Carlos (FB)	6-0/230	11-27-73	2	North Carolina State	D4b/98	1/0
38	Witman, Jon (FB)	6-1/240	6-1-72	4	Penn State	D3b/96	16/8
21	Zereoue, Amos	5-8/202	10-8-76	R	West Virginia	D3c/99	—
	RECEIVERS						
80	Bishop, Harold (TE)	6-5/250	4-8-70	5	Louisiana State	FA/98	6/1
89	Blackwell, Will	6-0/190	7-6-75	3	San Diego State	D2/97	16/2
87	Bruener, Mark (TE)	6-4/261	9-16-72	5	Washington	D1/95	16/16
83	Dunn, David	6-2/220	6-10-72	5	Fresno State	FA/98	11/0
81	Edwards, Troy	5-9/192	4-7-77	R	Louisiana Tech	D1/99	—
88	Hawkins, Courtney	5-9/190	12-12-69	8	Michigan State	UFA/97	15/14
16	Johnson, Malcolm	6-5/215	8-27-77	R	Notre Dame	D5b/99	—
85	Lyons, Mitch (TE)	6-5/268	5-13-70	7	Michigan State	UFA/97	15/0
15	Shaw, Bobby	6-0/186	4-23-75	2	California	FA/98	1/1
46	Tuman, Jerame (TE)	6-3/250	3-24-76	R	Michigan	D5a/99	—
84	Van Dyke, Alex	6-0/205	7-24-74	3	Nevada	T-NYJ/99	*16/0
86	Ward, Hines	6-0/197	3-8-76	2	Georgia	D3b/98	16/0
	OFFENSIVE LINEMEN						
60	Brown, Anthony (T)	6-5/315	11-6-72	5	Utah	UFA/99	*16/5
78	Conrad, Chris (T)	6-6/310	5-27-75	2	Fresno State	D3a/98	6/1
63	Dawson, Dermontti (C)	6-2/292	6-17-65	12	Kentucky	D2/88	16/16
62	Duffy, Roger (G)	6-3/299	7-16-67	10	Penn State	UFA/98	15/4
65	Faneca, Alan (G)	6-4/315	12-7-76	2	Louisiana State	D1/98	16/12
77	Farris, Kris (T)	6-8/322	3-26-77	R	UCLA	D3b/99	—
72	Gandy, Wayne (T)	6-5/310	2-10-71	6	Auburn	UFA/99	*16/16
68	Stai, Brenden (G)	6-4/310	3-30-72	5	Nebraska	D3/95	16/16
67	Stephens, Jamain (T)	6-6/330	1-9-74	4	North Carolina A&T	D1/96	11/10
73	Strzelczyk, Justin (G)	6-6/309	8-18-68	10	Maine	D11/90	7/7
66	Sweeney, Jim (C)	6-4/297	8-8-62	16	Pittsburgh	FA/96	8/1
	DEFENSIVE LINEMEN						
96	Dingle, Antonio (NT)	6-2/315	10-7-76	R	Virginia	D7a/99	—
74	Harrison, Nolan (E)	6-5/291	1-25-69	9	Indiana	FA/97	9/7
76	Henry, Kevin (E)	6-4/285	10-23-68	7	Mississippi State	D4/93	16/16
71	Roye, Orpheus (E)	6-4/288	1-21-74	4	Florida State	D6a/96	16/9
91	Smith, Aaron (E)	6-5/281	4-9-76	R	Northern Colorado	D4/99	—
94	Staat, Jeremy (E)	6-5/300	10-10-76	2	Arizona State	D2/98	5/0
93	Steed, Joel (NT)	6-2/308	2-17-69	8	Colorado	D3/92	16/16
	LINEBACKERS						
51	Emmons, Carlos	6-5/250	9-3-73	4	Arkansas State	D7/96	15/13
57	Fiala, John	6-2/235	11-25-73	3	Washington	FA/98	16/0
92	Gildon, Jason	6-3/255	7-31-72	6	Oklahoma State	D3a/94	16/16
50	Holmes, Earl	6-2/250	4-28-73	4	Florida A&M	D4a/96	14/14
97	Kelsay, Chad	6-2/252	4-9-77	R	Nebraska	D7b/99	—
99	Kirkland, Levon	6-1/270	2-17-69	8	Clemson	D2/92	16/16
95	Porter, Joey	6-2/240	3-22-77	R	Colorado State	D3a/99	—
56	Vrabel, Mike	6-4/250	8-14-75	3	Ohio State	D3b/97	11/0
	DEFENSIVE BACKS						
29	Brown, Lance	6-2/203	2-2-72	3	Indiana	FA/98	16/0
27	Davis, Travis (S)	6-0/209	1-10-73	4	Notre Dame	UFA/99	*16/5
41	Flowers, Lee (S)	6-0/211	1-14-73	5	Georgia Tech	D5a/95	16/16
24	Oldham, Chris (S)	5-9/200	10-26-68	9	Oregon	UFA/95	16/1
30	Scott, Chad	6-1/192	9-6-74	3	Maryland	D1/97	—
47	Shields, Scott (S)	6-4/228	3-29-76	R	Weber State	D2/99	—
23	Simmons, Jason (CB)	5-8/186	3-30-76	2	Arizona State	D5/98	6/0
26	Townsend, Deshea (CB)	5-10/175	9-8-75	2	Alabama	D4a/98	12/0
20	Washington, Dewayne (CB)	6-0/193	12-27-72	6	North Carolina State	UFA/98	16/16
	SPECIALISTS						
3	Brown, Kris (K)	5-10/204	12-23-76	R	Nebraska	D7c/99	—
4	Miller, Josh (P)	6-3/219	7-14-70	4	Arizona	FA/96	16/0

*Not with Steelers in 1998.

Other free agents invited to camp: DL Ernie Brown, FB Kevin Carroll, LB Bobbie Cotton, TE Matt Cushing, LB Tony D'Amato, K Matt Davenport, CB Stephen Fisher, WR John George, QB Pete Gonzalez, DE Matt Harper, LB Kevin Homer, OG Marcus Jenkins, DB Terrance Joseph, OL Todd Kollar, RB Greg Lomax, LB Ryan Olson, G Tony Orlandini, WR Shawn Scales, S Mike Schneck, S Homer Torrance, OL T.J. Washington, QB Anthony Wright.

PITTSBURGH STEELERS

Abbreviations: D I—draft pick, first round; SupD2—supplemental draft pick, second round; WV—claimed on waivers; TR—obtained in trade; PlanB—Plan B free-agent acquisition; FA—free-agent acquisition (other than Plan B); ED—expansion draft pick.

MISCELLANEOUS TEAM DATA

Stadium (capacity, surface):
Three Rivers Stadium
(59,600, artificial)
Business address:
300 Stadium Circle
Pittsburgh, PA 15212
Business phone:
412-323-0300
Ticket information:
412-323-1200
Team colors:
Black and gold
Flagship radio station:
WDVE, 102.7 FM
Training site:
St. Vincent College
Latrobe, Pa.
412-539-8515

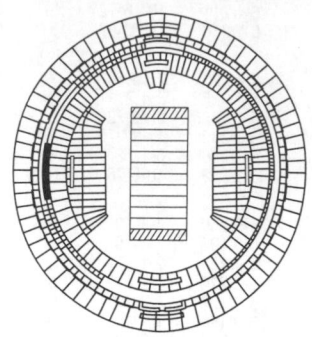

TSN REPORT CARD

Coaching staff	B +	For the first time since he took over in 1992, Bill Cowher missed the playoffs last season. What's more, his offense was just that—offensive. The addition of Kevin Gilbride as offensive coordinator was a plus; allowing him to re-tool the passing game was a must. Another good move was bringing in Bob Bratkowski as receivers coach. He was the offensive coordinator with the Seahawks. That's a lot of offensive expertise for a team that needs it.
Quarterbacks	B -	Kordell Stewart is unchallenged as the starter, despite a dramatic drop in production last season. The team is hoping the addition of Gilbride will have a positive effect on Stewart, who needs to regain his confidence after a horrendous 1998 season. Mike Tomczak will be the backup, probably for just one more season, but he will play only in an emergency.
Running backs	B	Jerome Bettis ran better late in the season when his knee was better and his weight was down. He wants to play lighter this season, and he should—it helps his agility when opposing defenses stack eight players in the box. There is plenty of depth, and rookie Amos Zereoue was a steal in the third round.
Receivers	C	Even with the drafting of Troy Edwards, there are some big holes. The loss of Yancey Thigpen last season, and Charles Johnson this season, will take its toll on the passing game. Courtney Hawkins is a good No. 3 guy, but he's not a game-breaker. And there is still not enough speed on the flanks to play the way Gilbride desires.
Offensive line	B -	More change again. Left tackle Will Wolford retired, but the good news is that the team signed Wayne Gandy to fill the void. It looks as though Justin Strzelczyk will miss the entire 1999 season, but the team took steps by signing free agent Anthony Brown and drafting Kris Farris. The potential is there to have a good line by the second half of the season, particularly if Farris gets stronger.
Defensive line	D	They are coming off a disappointing season, all the way around. And the loss of backup nose tackle Oliver Gibson, who was a good pass rusher, does not help. The best player last season was Orpheus Roye, who deserves to be on the field more despite the feelings of some members of the coaching staff.
Linebackers	B	This is the strength of the defense. However, Levon Kirkland did not have—for him—a great season. He needs to be more dominating and regain his quickness on the inside. Carlos Emmons needs to be pushed by Mike Vrabel, who could generate more pass rush and be more valuable than Emmons on the right side. This position has declined drastically since the departure of Greg Lloyd.
Secondary	B -	Turnover again, for the second year in a row. This time, it could be for the better. Chad Scott, a No. 1 draft pick in 1997, returns to left corner, which makes up for the loss of Carnell Lake. Dewayne Washington is entrenched on the right side. And Lethon Flowers made big strides in his first year as a starter.
Special teams	C	The team's reluctance to re-sign kicker Norm Johnson has brought a lot of uncertainty to the kicking game, particularly with rookie Kris Brown inheriting the job. Johnson was deadly accurate inside 40 yards, even if his leg had lost a little of its thunder. Edwards could be a great addition as a punt returner, an area the team needs to improve.

ST. LOUIS RAMS
NFC WESTERN DIVISION

1999 SEASON

CLUB DIRECTORY

Chairman
Georgia Frontiere
Vice chairman
Stan Kroenke
President
John Shaw
Executive vice president
Jay Zygmunt
Sr. v.p./administration, gen. counsel
Bob Wallace
V.p./media and community relations
Marshall Klein
Vice president/player personnel
Charley Armey
Vice president/player programs
Kevin Warren
Vice president/football operations
Lynn Stiles
Director of college scouting
John Becker
Vice president/finance
Adrian Barr
Treasurer
Jeff Brewer
Director of operations
John Oswald
Vice president/sales
Brian Ulione
Vice president/marketing
Phil Thomas
Director of ticket operations
Mike Naughton
Director of public relations
Rick Smith
Assistant director of public relations
Duane Lewis
Pro scout
Ted Plumb
Scouts
Billy Campfield   Kevin McCabe
Lawrence McCutcheon   David Razzano
Pete Russell   Harley Sewell
Howard Tippett
Head trainer
Jim Anderson
Assistant trainers
Ron DuBuque
Dake Walden

Head coach
Dick Vermeil

Assistant coaches
Steve Brown (secondary)
John Bunting (linebackers/co-def. coordinator)
Chris Clausen (strength & cond.)
Dana DeLuc (strength & cond.)
Frank Gansz (special teams)
Peter Giunta (asst. head coach/ co-defensive coordinator)
Carl Hairston (defensive line)
Jim Hanifan (offensive line)
Todd Howard (defensive assistant)
Mike Martz (offensive coordinator)
John Matsko (offensive line)
Wilbert Montgomery (run. backs)
John Ramsdell (quarterbacks/ quality control)
Al Saunders (wide receivers)
Lynn Stiles (tight ends)
Mike White (assistant head coach/quarterbacks)

Physicians
Dr. Bernard Garfinkel   Dr. James Loomis
Dr. Robert Shively   Dr. Rick Wright
Equipment manager
Todd Hewitt
Assistant equipment manager
Jim Lake
Video director
Larry Clerico
Assistant video director
Scott Nyberg

SCHEDULE

Sept. 12—	BALTIMORE	12:00
Sept. 19—	Open date	
Sept. 26—	ATLANTA	12:00
Oct. 3—	at Cincinnati	1:00
Oct. 10—	SAN FRANCISCO	12:00
Oct. 17—	at Atlanta	1:00
Oct. 24—	CLEVELAND	12:00
Oct. 31—	at Tennessee	12:00
Nov. 7—	at Detroit	1:00
Nov. 14—	CAROLINA	12:00
Nov. 21—	at San Francisco	1:15
Nov. 28—	NEW ORLEANS	12:00
Dec. 5—	at Carolina	1:00
Dec. 12—	at New Orleans	12:00
Dec. 19—	N.Y. GIANTS	12:00
Dec. 26—	CHICAGO	12:00
Jan. 2—	at Philadelphia	1:00

All times are for home team.
All games Sunday unless noted.

DRAFT CHOICES

Torry Holt, WR, North Carolina State (first round/sixth pick overall).
Dre' Bly, DB, North Carolina (2/41).
Rich Coady, DB, Texas A&M (3/68).
Joe Germaine, QB, Ohio State (4/101).
Cameron Spikes, G, Texas A&M (5/145).
Lionel Barnes, DE, Northeast Louisiana (6/176).
Rodney Williams, P, Georgia Tech (7/252).

1998 REVIEW

RESULTS

Sept. 6—	NEW ORLEANS	L	17-24
Sept.13—	MINNESOTA	L	31-38
Sept.20—	at Buffalo	W	34-33
Sept.27—	ARIZONA	L	17-20
Oct. 4—	Open date		
Oct. 11—	N.Y. JETS	W	30-10
Oct. 18—	at Miami	L	0-14
Oct. 25—	SAN FRANCISCO	L	10-28
Nov. 1—	at Atlanta	L	15-37
Nov. 8—	at Chicago	W	20-12
Nov. 15—	at New Orleans	L	3-24
Nov. 22—	CAROLINA	L	20-24
Nov. 29—	ATLANTA	L	10-21
Dec. 3—	at Philadelphia	L	14-17
Dec. 13—	NEW ENGLAND	W	32-18
Dec. 20—	at Carolina	L	13-20
Dec. 27—	at San Francisco	L	19-38

RECORDS/RANKINGS

1998 regular-season record: 4-12 (4th in NFC West); 0-8 in division; 1-11 in conference; 2-6 at home; 2-6 on road.
Team record last five years: 26-54 (.325, ranks 28th in league in that span).
1998 team rankings:

	No.	NFC	NFL
Total offense	*279.5	12	27
Rushing offense	*86.6	14	29
Passing offense	*192.9	11	22
Scoring offense	285	13	24
Total defense	*305.0	4	10
Rushing defense	*128.1	11	24
Passing defense	*176.9	3	3
Scoring defense	378	T11	T24
Takeaways	23	T11	T22
Giveaways	33	T10	T21
Turnover differential	-10	14	27
Sacks	50	T3	T4
Sacks allowed	47	8	21

*Yards per game.

TEAM LEADERS

Scoring (kicking): Jeff Wilkins, 85 pts. (25/26 PATs, 20/26 FGs).
Scoring (touchdowns): Amp Lee, 26 pts. (2 rushing, 2 receiving, 1 2-pt. conv.).
Passing: Tony Banks, 2,535 yds. (408 att., 241 comp., 59.1%, 7 TDs, 14 int.).
Rushing: June Henley, 313 yds. (88 att., 3.6 avg., 3 TDs).
Receptions: Ricky Proehl, 60 (771 yds., 12.9 avg., 3 TDs).
Interceptions: Todd Lyght, 3 (30 yds., 0 TDs); Keith Lyle, 3 (20 yds., 0 TDs).
Sacks: Kevin Carter, 12.0.
Punting: Rick Tuten, 44.2 avg. (95 punts, 4,202 yds., 0 blocked).
Punt returns: Eddie Kennison, 10.4 avg. (40 att., 415 yds., 1 TD).
Kickoff returns: Tony Horne, 23.3 avg. (56 att., 1,306 yds., 1 TD).

1999 SEASON
TRAINING CAMP ROSTER

No.	QUARTERBACKS	Ht./Wt.	Born	NFL Exp.	College	How acq.	'98 Games GP/GS
9	Germaine, Joe	6-0/203	8-11-75	R	Ohio State	D4/99	—
10	Green, Trent	6-3/215	7-9-70	6	Indiana	UFA/99	*15/14
13	Warner, Kurt	6-2/220	6-22-71	2	Northern Iowa	FA/98	1/0
	RUNNING BACKS						
28	Faulk, Marshall	5-10/211	2-26-73	6	San Diego State	T-Ind./99	*16/15
33	Harris, Derrick	6-0/252	9-18-72	4	Miami (Fla.)	D6a/96	16/14
26	Henley, June	5-10/226	9-4-75	2	Kansas	FA/97	11/3
27	Hill, Greg	5-11/212	2-23-72	6	Texas A&M	UFA/98	2/2
25	Holcombe, Robert	5-11/220	12-11-75	2	Illinois	D2/98	13/7
31	Lee, Amp	5-11/200	10-1-71	8	Florida State	UFA/97	14/1
30	Thompson, David	5-8/200	1-13-75	3	Oklahoma State	FA/97	1/0
	RECEIVERS						
80	Bruce, Isaac	6-0/188	11-10-72	6	Memphis State	D2/94	5/5
84	Conwell, Ernie (TE)	6-1/265	8-17-72	4	Washington	D2b/96	7/7
81	Hakim, Az-zahir	5-10/178	6-3-77	2	San Diego State	D4a/98	9/4
88	Holt, Torry	6-0/190	6-5-76	R	North Carolina State	D1/99	—
82	Horne, Tony	5-9/173	3-21-76	2	Clemson	FA/98	16/0
89	Jacoby, Mitch (TE)	6-4/260	12-8-73	3	Northern Illinois	FA/97	5/0
89	Lewis, Chad (TE)	6-6/252	10-5-71	2	Brigham Young	FA/98	2/0
87	Proehl, Ricky	6-0/190	3-7-68	10	Wake Forest	UFA/98	16/10
86	Williams, Roland (TE)	6-5/269	4-27-75	2	Syracuse	D4b/98	13/9
	OFFENSIVE LINEMEN						
77	Brooks, Ethan (T)	6-6/300	4-27-72	3	Williams (Conn.)	FA/97	15/0
63	Flannery, John (C)	6-4/295	1-13-69	9	Syracuse	FA/98	16/15
60	Gruttadauria, Mike (C)	6-3/297	12-6-72	4	Central Florida	FA/96	12/3
64	McCollum, Andy (G)	6-4/295	6-2-70	6	Toledo	UFA/99	*16/5
73	Miller, Fred (T)	6-7/315	2-6-73	4	Baylor	D5/96	15/15
61	Nutten, Tom (G)	6-5/300	6-8-71	3	Western Michigan	FA/98	4/2
76	Pace, Orlando (T)	6-7/320	11-4-75	3	Ohio State	D1/97	16/16
71	Spikes, Cameron (G)	6-2/310	11-6-76	R	Texas A&M	D5/99	—
63	Timmerman, Adam (C)	6-4/300	8-14-71	5	South Dakota State	UFA/99	*16/16
50	Tucker, Ryan (C)	6-5/305	6-12-75	3	Texas Christian	D4/97	4/0
	DEFENSIVE LINEMEN						
99	Agnew, Ray (T)	6-3/285	12-9-67	10	North Carolina State	UFA/98	16/12
92	Barnes, Lionel	6-4/264	4-19-76	R	Northeast Louisiana	D6/99	—
93	Carter, Kevin (E)	6-5/280	9-21-73	5	Florida	D1/95	16/16
75	Farr, D'Marco (T)	6-1/280	6-9-71	6	Washington	FA/94	16/16
94	Robinson, Jeff (E)	6-4/275	2-20-70	7	Idaho	UFA/97	16/0
95	Sears, Corey (T)	6-2/293	4-15-73	3	Mississippi State	FA/98	4/0
96	Williams, Jay (T)	6-3/280	10-13-71	4	Wake Forest	FA/94	16/1
98	Wistrom, Grant (E)	6-4/267	7-3-76	2	Nebraska	D1/98	13/0
90	Zgonina, Jeff (T)	6-2/300	5-24-70	6	Purdue	UFA/99	*2/0
	LINEBACKERS						
56	Clemons, Charlie	6-2/255	7-4-72	3	Georgia	FA/97	16/0
54	Collins, Todd	6-2/248	5-27-70	7	Carson-Newman (Tenn.)	UFA/98	*12/10
59	Fletcher, London	6-0/241	5-19-75	2	John Carroll	FA/98	16/1
53	Hesse, Jon	6-3/247	6-6-73	1	Nebraska	FA/98	5/0
52	Jones, Mike	6-1/240	4-15-69	9	Missouri	UFA/97	16/16
51	Styles, Lorenzo	6-1/245	1-31-74	4	Ohio State	FA/97	7/3
55	Ward, Phillip	6-3/235	11-11-74	1	UCLA	FA/98	2/0
	DEFENSIVE BACKS						
20	Allen, Taje (CB)	5-10/185	11-6-73	3	Texas	D5/97	16/0
29	Bly, Dre' (CB)	5-9/197	5-22-77	R	North Carolina	D2/99	—
23	Bush, Devin (S)	5-11/210	7-3-73	5	Florida State	UFA/99	*13/0
26	Carpenter, Ron (S)	6-1/188	1-20-70	3	Miami of Ohio	FA/98	6/0
38	Coady, Rich (S)	6-0/203	1-26-76	R	Texas A&M	D3/99	—
22	Jenkins, Billy (S)	5-10/205	7-8-74	3	Howard	FA/97	16/13
41	Lyght, Todd (CB)	6-0/190	2-9-69	9	Notre Dame	D1/91	16/16
35	Lyle, Keith (S)	6-2/210	4-17-72	6	Virginia	D3/94	16/16
21	McCleon, Dexter (CB)	5-10/195	10-9-73	3	Clemson	D2/97	15/6
32	Wright, Toby (S)	5-11/212	11-19-70	6	Nebraska	D2b/94	3/3
	SPECIALISTS						
11	Tuten, Rick (P)	6-2/221	1-5-65	11	Florida State	UFA/98	16/0
14	Wilkins, Jeff (K)	6-2/205	4-19-72	6	Youngstown State	FA/97	16/0
2	Williams, Rodney (P)	6-0/189	4-25-77	R	Georgia Tech	D7/99	—

*Not with Rams in 1998.

Other free agents invited to camp: S Jamaal Alexander, T Roger Chanoine, LB Matt Chatham, WR Mac Cody, WR Jermaine Copeland, CB Clifton Crosby, T Todd Frohbieter, LB Jon Hesse, S Van Hiles, RB James Hodgins, DT John Jacobs, WR Daniel Jones, T Willie Jones,

WR Kevin Knox, RB Chad Levitt, TE Derek Lewis, CB Marvin Love, G Jeremy McKinney, LB John Munch, CB Gerald Neasman, WR Mike Ogas, QB Gus Ornstein, LB Troy Pelshak, CB Joe Rowe, WR Donald Sellers, G Bobby Singh, WR Tony Small, LB Robert Smith, G Corry Spann, CB Damon Troy, G Mike Verstegen, DT Alton Weaver, RB Marvin Welch, RB Steve Wofford, DE Glenn Young.

Abbreviations: D1—draft pick, first round; SupD2—supplemental draft pick, second round; WV—claimed on waivers; TR—obtained in trade; PlanB—Plan B free-agent acquisition; FA—free-agent acquisition (other than Plan B); ED—expansion draft pick.

MISCELLANEOUS TEAM DATA

Stadium (capacity, surface):
Trans World Dome (66,000, artificial)
Business address:
1 Rams Way
St. Louis, MO 63045
Business phone:
314-982-7267
Ticket information:
314-425-8830
Team colors:
Royal blue, gold and white
Flagship radio station:
KFNS, 590 AM
Training site:
Western Illinois University
Macomb, Ill.
314-982-7267

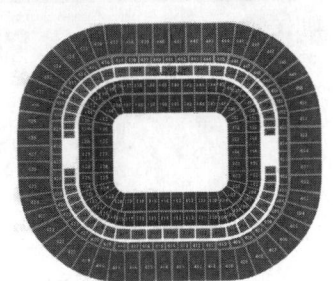

TSN REPORT CARD

Coaching staff	C -	This was not a well-coached team in '98, but the addition of offensive coordinator Mike Martz and wide receivers coach Al Saunders will help. Dick Vermeil needs to put his faith in Martz—for better or worse. On defense, some players feel the club's complex schemes need to be streamlined.
Quarterbacks	C -	The Rams signed Trent Green in free agency in the hopes they would get efficient game management and minimal mistakes. It's a gamble given Green's limited NFL experience. If he's injured there's only Kurt Warner, who's played in one NFL game, and rookie Joe Germaine.
Running backs	B +	Thanks to the Marshall Faulk trade, here's the safest best in pro sports for '99: The Rams' rushing leader will finish with more than 313 yards, which was the case last year with June Henley. Faulk, backed up by speedy Greg Hill, will keep opposing defenses honest.
Receivers	B	A healthy Isaac Bruce coupled with rookie Torry Holt would make this one of the league's better receiving corps. Green at quarterback should make for a better Ricky Proehl, and the early signs are that Az-Zahir Hakim will be much improved. Trading Eddie Kennison was addition by subtraction.
Offensive line	C -	Even with the addition of free agent Adam Timmerman, there are too many question marks to presume this unit will be markedly improved. Not that they were great, but two starters from a year ago are gone—right tackle Wayne Gandy and right guard Zach Wiegert. The key is Fred Miller at right tackle.
Defensive line	B -	Missing are a 300-pound-plus run-stuffing tackle and a reliable third end to spell Grant Wistrom. Otherwise, this has the making of a pretty good unit, especially when it comes to rushing the passer. Left end Kevin Carter and tackle Ray Agnew are both underrated.
Linebackers	C -	The losses of Roman Phifer and Eric Hill notwithstanding, the level of play may not drop off much here. It's time to see if young veteran Lorenzo Styles or youngster London Fletcher can play middle linebacker, and Todd Collins should be an adqueate replacement for Phifer outside.
Secondary	D +	There is nothing but unproven talent behind cornerback Todd Lyght and free safety Keith Lyle. New starters Devin Bush (strong safety) and Dexter McCleon (cornerback) are on the spot. If draft pick Dre' Bly doesn't improve on his collegiate play last season at North Carolina, the Rams will be desperate for a nickel back.
Special teams	C +	There are above-average legs in kicker Jeff Wilkins and punter Rick Tuten, but the coverage units still need to improve, as does the return game. Az-Zahir Hakim is untested as a punt returner, replacing the traded Kennison. With Faulk around, why not try Greg Hill on kickoff returns?

SAN DIEGO CHARGERS
AFC WESTERN DIVISION

1999 SEASON

CLUB DIRECTORY

Chairman of the board
Alex G. Spanos
President/vice chairman
Dean A. Spanos
Executive vice president
Michael A. Spanos
General manager
Bobby Beathard
Vice president/finance
Jeremiah T. Murphy
Chief financial & administrative officer
Jeanne Bonk
Director/player personnel
Billy Devaney
Director/pro personnel
Greg Gaines
Coordinator/football operations
Ed McGuire
Business manager
John Hinek
Director/ticket operations
Fred Otto
Director/public relations
Bill Johnston
Director/sales and marketing
Lynn Abramson
Director/security
Dick Lewis
Trainer
James Collins
Equipment manager
Sid Brooks
Director/video operations
Brian Duddy

Head coach
Mike Riley

Assistant coaches
DelVaughn Alexander (offensive assistant)
Mark Banker (defensive coverage)
Joe Bugel (offensive line)
Geep Chryst (quarterbacks coach/offensive coordinator)
Paul Chryst (tight ends)
John Hastings (strength & conditioning)
Kevin Lempa (def. assistant)
Wayne Nunnely (defensive line)
Joe Pascale (defensive coordinator)
Rod Perry (defensive backs)
Bruce Read (special teams)
Mike Sanford (wide receivers)
Mike Schleelein (strength & conditioning assistant)
Johnny Thomas (special teams assistant)
Jim Vechiarella (linebackers)
Ollie Wilson (running backs)

SCHEDULE

Sept. 12—	Open date	
Sept. 19—	at Cincinnati	1:00
Sept. 26—	INDIANAPOLIS	1:05
Oct. 3—	KANSAS CITY	1:15
Oct. 10—	at Detroit	1:00
Oct. 17—	SEATTLE	1:05
Oct. 24—	GREEN BAY	1:05
Oct. 31—	at Kansas City	12:00
Nov. 7—	DENVER	1:15
Nov. 14—	at Oakland	1:05
Nov. 21—	CHICAGO	1:15
Nov. 28—	at Minnesota	12:00
Dec. 5—	CLEVELAND	1:15
Dec. 12—	at Seattle	1:05
Dec. 19—	at Miami	1:00
Dec. 26—	OAKLAND	1:05
Jan. 2—	at Denver	2:15

All times are for home team.
All games Sunday unless noted.

DRAFT CHOICES

Jermaine Fazande, RB, Oklahoma (second round/60th pick overall).
Steve Heiden, TE, South Dakota State (3/69).
Jason Perry, DB, North Carolina State (4/104).
Adrian Dingle, DE, Clemson (5/139).
Reggie Nelson, G, McNeese State (5/141).
Tyrone Bell, DB, North Alabama (6/178).

1998 REVIEW

RESULTS

Sept. 6—BUFFALO	W	16-14
Sept.13—at Tennessee	W	13-7
Sept.20—at Kansas City	L	7-23
Sept.27—N.Y. GIANTS	L	16-34
Oct. 4—at Indianapolis	L	12-17
Oct. 11—at Oakland	L	6-7
Oct. 18—PHILADELPHIA	W	13-10
Oct. 25—SEATTLE	L	20-27
Nov. 1—Open date		
Nov. 8—at Denver	L	10-27
Nov. 15—BALTIMORE	W	14-13
Nov. 22—KANSAS CITY	W	38-37
Nov. 29—DENVER	L	16-31
Dec. 6—at Washington	L	20-24
Dec. 13—at Seattle	L	17-38
Dec. 20—OAKLAND	L	10-17
Dec. 27—at Arizona	L	13-16

RECORDS/RANKINGS

1998 regular-season record: 5-11 (5th in AFC West); 1-7 in division; 4-8 in conference; 4-4 at home; 1-7 on road.
Team record last five years: 37-43 (.463, ranks T14th in league in that span).

1998 team rankings:

	No.	AFC	NFL
Total offense	*287.0	13	24
Rushing offense	*108.0	7	15
Passing offense	*179.0	14	26
Scoring offense	241	15	29
Total defense	*263.0	1	1
Rushing defense	*71.3	1	1
Passing defense	*191.8	5	11
Scoring defense	342	11	18
Takeaways	27	11	18
Giveaways	51	15	30
Turnover differential	-24	15	30
Sacks	39	T8	T15
Sacks allowed	37	9	14

*Yards per game.

TEAM LEADERS

Scoring (kicking): John Carney, 97 pts. (19/19 PATs, 26/30 FGs).
Scoring (touchdowns): Natrone Means, 30 pts. (5 rushing); Terrell Fletcher, 30 pts. (5 rushing).
Passing: Craig Whelihan, 1,803 yds. (320 att., 149 comp., 46.6%, 8 TDs, 19 int.).
Rushing: Natrone Means, 883 yds. (212 att., 4.2 avg., 5 TDs).
Receptions: Charlie Jones, 46 (699 yds., 15.2 avg., 3 TDs).
Interceptions: Greg Jackson, 6 (50 yds., 0 TDs).
Sacks: Norman Hand, 6.0.
Punting: Darren Bennett, 43.9 avg. (95 punts, 4,174 yds., 0 blocked).
Punt returns: Latorio Rachal, 12.1 avg. (32 att., 387 yds., 0 TDs).
Kickoff returns: Terrell Fletcher, 23.7 avg. (3 att., 71 yds., 0 TDs).

SAN DIEGO CHARGERS

No.	QUARTERBACKS	Ht./Wt.	Born	NFL Exp.	College	How acq.	'98 Games GP/GS
4	Harbaugh, Jim	6-3/215	12-23-63	13	Michigan	T-Bal./99	*14/12
16	Leaf, Ryan	6-5/235	5-15-76	2	Washington State	D1/98	10/9
5	Whelihan, Craig	6-5/220	4-15-71	5	Pacific	D6c/95	11/7
	RUNNING BACKS						
43	Bynum, Kenny	5-11/191	5-29-74	3	South Carolina State	D5a/97	10/0
35	Fazande, Jermaine (FB)	6-2/262	1-14-75	R	Oklahoma	D2/99	—
41	Fletcher, Terrell	5-8/196	9-14-73	5	Wisconsin	D2b/95	12/5
20	Means, Natrone	5-10/245	4-26-72	7	North Carolina	UFA/98	10/10
34	Stephens, Tremayne	5-11/206	4-16-76	2	North Carolina State	FA/98	13/1
	RECEIVERS						
83	Burke, John (TE)	6-3/248	9-7-71	6	Virginia Tech	FA/98	10/6
89	Davis, Wendell (TE)	6-2/246	10-24-75	2	Temple	FA/98	11/7
85	Gaiter, Tony	5-8/170	7-15-74	3	Miami (Fla.)	FA/98	5/0
81	Graham, Jeff	6-2/206	2-14-69	9	Ohio State	FA/99	*15/15
19	Heiden, Steve (TE)	6-4/256	9-21-76	R	South Dakota State	D3/99	—
82	Jones, Charlie	5-8/175	12-1-72	4	Fresno State	D4/96	16/11
88	Jones, Freddie (TE)	6-5/270	9-16-74	3	North Carolina	D2/97	16/16
49	Pupunu, Al (TE)	6-2/260	10-17-69	8	Weber State	UFA/99	*9/0
86	Ricks, Mikhael	6-5/237	11-14-74	2	Stephen F. Austin	D2/98	16/9
80	Still, Bryan	5-11/174	6-3-74	4	Virginia Tech	D2a/96	14/9
87	Thelwell, Ryan	6-2/188	4-6-73	2	Minnesota	FA/98	6/3
	OFFENSIVE LINEMEN						
50	Binn, David (C)	6-3/245	2-6-72	6	California	FA/94	15/0
67	Fortin, Roman (C)	6-5/297	2-26-67	10	San Diego State	FA/98	16/16
65	Jackson, John (T)	6-6/297	1-4-65	12	Eastern Kentucky	UFA/98	16/16
64	Jacox, Kendyl (G)	6-2/330	6-10-75	2	Kansas State	FA/98	16/6
66	Nelson, Reggie (G)	6-4/310	6-23-76	R	McNeese State	D5b/99	—
70	Parker, Vaughn (T)	6-3/300	6-5-71	6	UCLA	D2b/94	6/6
79	Price, Marcus (G)	6-6/321	3-3-72	3	Louisiana State	FA/97	10/0
74	Roundtree, Raleigh (T)	6-4/295	8-31-75	3	South Carolina State	D4/97	15/5
73	Taylor, Aaron (G)	6-4/305	11-14-72	6	Notre Dame	UFA/98	15/15
	DEFENSIVE LINEMEN						
78	Dingle, Adrian (E)	6-3/272	6-25-77	R	Clemson	D5a/99	—
	Fontenot, Al (E)	6-4/287	9-17-70	7	Baylor	FA/99	*7/5
96	Hand, Norman (T)	6-3/313	9-4-72	5	Mississippi	W-Mia./97	16/16
99	Johnson, Raylee (E)	6-3/272	6-1-70	7	Arkansas	D4a/93	16/3
94	Mims, Chris (T)	6-5/300	9-29-70	8	Tennessee	FA/98	6/0
98	Mohring, Michael (T)	6-5/295	3-22-74	3	Pittsburgh	FA/97	10/0
97	Parrella, John (T)	6-3/300	11-22-69	7	Nebraska	FA/94	16/16
93	Sienkiewicz, Troy (T)	6-5/300	5-27-72	5	New Mexico State	D6a/95	7/0
76	Williams, Jamal (T)	6-3/305	4-28-76	2	Oklahoma State	SD-2/98	9/0
	LINEBACKERS						
58	Bush, Lew	6-2/245	12-2-69	7	Washington State	D4b/93	10/10
51	Dixon, Gerald	6-3/250	6-20-69	7	South Carolina	UFA/98	16/6
53	Hamilton, Michael	6-2/245	12-3-73	3	North Carolina A&T	D3/97	13/0
	Haskins, Jon	6-2/245	10-6-75	R	Stanford	FA/99	*2/0
54	Hill, Eric	6-2/265	11-14-66	11	Louisiana State	FA/99	*15/13
55	Seau, Junior	6-3/250	1-19-69	10	Southern California	D1/90	16/16
	DEFENSIVE BACKS						
45	Bell, Tyrone (CB)	6-2/210	10-20-74	R	North Alabama	D6/99	—
27	Dimry, Charles (CB)	6-0/176	1-31-66	12	UNLV	UFA/98	16/15
38	Dumas, Mike (S)	6-0/202	3-18-69	8	Indiana	FA/97	3/3
28	Harper, Dwayne (CB)	5-11/175	3-29-66	12	South Carolina State	UFA/94	1/1
37	Harrison, Rodney (S)	6-1/207	12-15-72	6	Western Illinois	D5b/94	16/16
25	Johnson, Melvin (S)	6-0/205	4-15-72	5	Kentucky	FA/99	*7/1
36	Lee, Lloyd (S)	6-2/215	8-8-76	2	Dartmouth	FA/98	8/0
39	Perry, Darren (S)	5-11/199	12-29-68	8	Penn State	UFA/99	*14/14
31	Perry, Jason (S)	6-0/200	8-1-76	R	North Carolina State	D4/99	—
29	Shaw, Terrance (CB)	5-11/190	11-11-73	5	Stephen F. Austin State	D2a/95	13/13
22	Spencer, Jimmy (CB)	5-10/185	3-29-69	8	Florida	FA/98	15/4
21	Turner, Scott (CB)	5-10/180	2-26-72	5	Illinois	W-Was./98	16/1
	SPECIALISTS						
2	Bennett, Darren (P)	6-5/235	1-9-65	5	None	FA/94	16/0
3	Carney, John (K)	5-11/170	4-20-64	11	Notre Dame	FA/90	16/0

*Not with Chargers in 1998.

Other free agents invited to camp: WR Rod Alexander, G Rick Austin, QB Jeff Baker, G/T Ben Bordelon, CB Paul Bradford, CB Fakhir Brown, TE Larry Brown, G Wilbert Brown, LB John Bryant, RB Brett Chappell, LB Brian Clark, WR Ray Ethridge, T Matt Gartung, T DeMingo Graham, DE Cedric Harden, LB Richard Hogans, DE Israel Ifeanylchukwu, CB Clifford Ivory, CB Tommy Jones, DE Dwight

Kelth, T Chris Knipper, WR Thomas Lewis, FB Fred McCrary, DE Bronzell Miller, WR Deon Mitchell, G Craig Moore, WR Sirr Parker, CB Corey Raymond, WR Robert Reed, LB John Reeves, WR Anthony Rodgers, LB Orlando Ruff, CB Reggie Rusk, LB Tracy Simien, WR Tyrone Taylor, DT Bruce Walker.

Abbreviations: D1—draft pick, first round; SupD2—supplemental draft pick, second round; WV—claimed on waivers; TR—obtained in trade; PlanB—Plan B free-agent acquisition; FA—free-agent acquisition (other than Plan B); ED—expansion draft pick.

MISCELLANEOUS TEAM DATA

Stadium (capacity, surface):
Qualcomm Stadium
(71,000, grass)
Business address:
P.O. Box 609609
San Diego, CA 92160-9609
Business phone:
619-874-4500
Ticket information:
619-280-2121
Team colors:
Navy blue, white and gold
Flagship radio station:
KFMB, 760 AM/STAR 100.7 FM
Training site:
UC San Diego
La Jolla, Calif.
619-455-1976

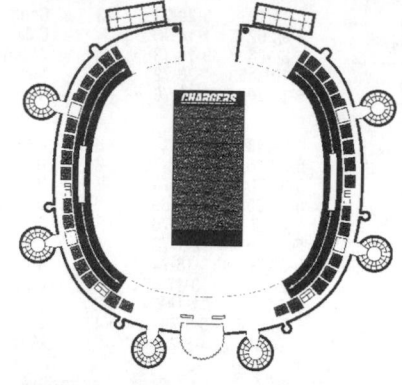

TSN REPORT CARD

Coaching staff	C	Mike Riley will get his feet wet in a hurry in the same division as Mike Shanahan and Mike Holmgren. Riley has received high marks at stops in the CFL and Pac-10, but he still must prove his worth in the NFL. Good move by Chargers in retaining defensive coordinator Joe Pascale, whose unit was No. 1 in the league last year.
Quarterbacks	C	Jim Harbaugh delivers a dose of sanity to this position, which displayed little last year. Ryan Leaf begins Year 2 where he should have started Year 1—on the bench. Maybe Harbaugh's gritty demeanor can propel an offense which was No. 26 in passing last year. And maybe Leaf—after eating helpings of humble pie—will be more mature and reliable after an embarrassing rookie year.
Running backs	B	Natrone Means continues to be among the league's most punishing running backs. But he can't deliver the goods if he's standing on the sidelines. Means must prove he can still survive a season without getting hurt. Fullback Jermaine Fazande will be a plus as a blocker, while Terrell Fletcher is a solid third-down back as a rusher and receiver.
Receivers	C	Jeff Graham was brought in to give fans someone they've actually heard of. Mikhael Ricks has promise, but must deliver consistency, too. Charlie Jones is a dynamo, but at 5-8, 175, the team has to be cautious not to overuse him. Bryan Still? A question mark with few answers.
Offensive line	B	A mostly veteran group will work in third-year pro Raleigh Roundtree at right guard. This unit has leadership—John Jackson and Aaron Taylor—and a streak of being nasty, which bodes the Chargers well.
Defensive line	D	The middle, manned by Norman Hand and John Parrella, was one of the NFL's best last year. The situation at ends though, is among the team's biggest worries.
Linebackers	B	Junior Seau remains one of the NFL's biggest impact players. He can still take over a game, playing the run or pestering quarterbacks. Eric Hill is an improvement over Kurt Gouveia in the middle, and Lew Bush does the job at the outside position.
Secondary	B -	The safeties are downright special in Pro Bowler Rodney Harrison and cagey veteran Darren Perry. But Terrance Shaw and Dwayne Harper must stay healthy—and avoid surrendering the big play.
Special teams	C	The legs—John Carney and Darren Bennett—are fine. But the coverage units need to rebound and better field position must come from the return game.

SAN FRANCISCO 49ERS
NFC WESTERN DIVISION

1999 SEASON

CLUB DIRECTORY

Owners
Edward J. DeBartolo Jr.
Denise DeBartolo-York
V.p./general manager
Bill Walsh
V.p./director of football administration
John McVay
V.p./business operations and CFO
Keith Lenhart
V.p./director of 49ers Foundation
Lisa DeBartolo
Director of player personnel
Terry Donahue
Pro personnel director
Bill McPherson
Controller
Melrene Frear
Dir. of communications & marketing
Rodney Knox
Manager of public relations
Kirk Reynolds
Public relations assistants
Tom Hastings
Darla Maeda
Demetra Marcus
Kimberly McIntyre
Chad Steele
Scouts
Jim Abrams   John Brunner
Brian Gardner   Jeremy Green
Jim Gruden   Oscar Lofton
Head trainer
Lindsy McLean
Assistant trainers
Todd Lazenby
Jasen Powell
Physicians
Michael Dillingham, M.D.
James Klint, M.D.
Stadium operations director
Murlan "Mo" Fowell
Equipment manager
Kevin "Tique" Lartigue

Head coach
Steve Mariucci

Assistant coaches
Jerry Attaway (physical
  development coordinator)
Mike Barnes (strength development
  coordinator)
Tom Batta (tight ends)
Chris Beake (def. quality control)
Dwaine Board (defensive line)
Greg Brown (defensive backs)
Larry Kirksey (wide receivers)
Greg Knapp (quarterbacks)
Brett Maxie (defensive assistant/
  secondary)
Bobb McKittrick (offensive line)
Jim Mora Jr. (def. coordinator)
Marty Mornhinweg (offensive
  coordinator)
Patrick Morris (offensive line)
Tom Rathman (running backs)
Richard Smith (linebackers)
George Stewart (special teams
  coordinator)
Andy Sugarman (offensive quality
  control)

Equipment assistants
Mike McBride
Steve Urbaniak
Robert Yanagi

SCHEDULE

Sept. 12—	at Jacksonville	4:15
Sept. 19—	NEW ORLEANS	1:05
Sept. 27—	at Arizona (Mon.)	6:00
Oct. 3—	TENNESSEE	1:15
Oct. 10—	at St. Louis	12:00
Oct. 17—	CAROLINA	1:15
Oct. 24—	at Minnesota	12:00
Oct. 31—	Open date	
Nov. 7—	PITTSBURGH	1:15
Nov. 14—	at New Orleans	12:00
Nov. 21—	ST. LOUIS	1:15
Nov. 29—	GREEN BAY (Mon.)	6:00
Dec. 5—	at Cincinnati	1:00
Dec. 12—	ATLANTA	1:15
Dec. 18—	at Carolina (Sat.)	4:15
Dec. 26—	WASHINGTON	5:20
Jan. 3—	at Atlanta (Mon.)	9:00

All times are for home team.
All games Sunday unless noted.

DRAFT CHOICES

Reggie McGrew, DT, Florida (first
  round/24th pick overall).
Chike Okeafor, DE, Purdue (3/89).
Anthony Parker, DB, Weber State (4/99).
Pierson Prioleau, DB, Virginia Tech
  (4/110).
Terry Jackson, RB, Florida (5/157).
Tyrone Hopson, T, Eastern Kentucky
  (5/161).
Tai Streets, WR, Michigan (6/171).
Kory Minor, LB, Notre Dame (7/234).

1998 REVIEW

RESULTS

Sept. 6—N.Y. JETS (OT)	W	36-30
Sept.14—at Washington	W	45-10
Sept.20—Open date		
Sept.27—ATLANTA	W	31-20
Oct. 4—at Buffalo	L	21-26
Oct. 11—at New Orleans	W	31-0
Oct. 18—INDIANAPOLIS	W	34-31
Oct. 25—at St. Louis	W	28-10
Nov. 1—at Green Bay	L	22-36
Nov. 8—CAROLINA	W	25-23
Nov. 15—at Atlanta	L	19-31
Nov. 22—NEW ORLEANS	W	31-20
Nov. 30—N.Y. GIANTS	W	31-7
Dec. 6—at Carolina (OT)	W	31-28
Dec. 14—DETROIT	W	35-13
Dec. 20—at New England	L	21-24
Dec. 27—ST. LOUIS	W	38-19
Jan. 3—GREEN BAY*	W	30-27
Jan. 9—at Atlanta†	L	18-20

*NFC wild-card game.
†NFC divisional playoff game.

RECORDS/RANKINGS

1998 regular-season record: 12-4 (2nd
in NFC West); 7-1 in division; 10-2 in conference; 8-0 at home; 4-4 on road.
Team record last five years: 61-19 (.763,
ranks 1st in league in that span).
1998 team rankings:

	No.	NFC	NFL
Total offense	*425.0	1	1
Rushing offense	*159.0	1	1
Passing offense	*266.0	2	2
Scoring offense	479	2	3
Total defense	*333.9	12	23
Rushing defense	*100.6	4	T9
Passing defense	*233.3	14	29
Scoring defense	328	7	13
Takeaways	33	T4	T7
Giveaways	30	8	T16
Turnover differential	3	T4	T11
Sacks	51	2	3
Sacks allowed	53	T10	T23

*Yards per game.

TEAM LEADERS

Scoring (kicking): Wade Richey, 103 pts.
(49/51 PATs, 18/27 FGs).
Scoring (TDs): Terrell Owens, 92 pts. (1
rushing, 14 receiving, 1 2-pt. conv.).
Passing: Steve Young, 4,170 yds. (517
att., 322 comp., 62.3%, 36 TDs, 12 int.).
Rushing: Garrison Hearst, 1,570 yds.
(310 att., 5.1 avg., 7 TDs).
Receptions: Jerry Rice, 82 (1,157 yds.,
14.1 avg., 9 TDs).
Interceptions: Darnell Walker, 4 (78 yds.,
0 TDs); Merton Hanks, 4 (37 yds., 0
TDs); Zack Bronson, 4 (34 yds., 0 TDs);
Tim McDonald, 4 (22 yds., 0 TDs).
Sacks: Chris Doleman, 15.0.
Punting: Reggie Roby, 41.9 avg. (60
punts, 2,511 yds., 0 blocked).
Punt returns: R.W. McQuarters, 8.6 avg.
(47 att., 406 yds., 1 TD).
Kickoff returns: Chuck Levy, 17.4 avg.
(22 att., 383 yds., 0 TDs).

1999 SEASON
TRAINING CAMP ROSTER

No. QUARTERBACKS	Ht./Wt.	Born	NFL Exp.	College	How acq.	'98 Games GP/GS
14 Druckenmiller, Jim	6-4/241	9-19-72	3	Virginia Tech	D1/97	2/0
5 Garcia, Jeff	6-1/195	2-24-70	1	San Jose State	FA/99	—
8 Young, Steve	6-2/205	10-11-61	15	Brigham Young	T-TB/87	15/15
RUNNING BACKS						
40 Beasley, Fred	6-0/220	9-18-74	2	Auburn	D6/98	16/0
20 Hearst, Garrison	5-11/219	1-4-71	7	Georgia	FA/97	16/16
22 Jackson, Terry	6-0/218	1-10-76	R	Florida	D5a/99	—
27 Jervey, Travis	6-0/222	5-5-72	5	The Citadel	UFA/99	*8/5
32 Levy, Chuck	6-0/206	1-7-72	4	Arizona	FA/96	12/0
44 Vardell, Tommy (FB)	6-2/234	2-20-69	8	Stanford	UFA/99	*14/9
RECEIVERS						
85 Clark, Greg (TE)	6-4/251	4-7-72	3	Stanford	D3/97	13/8
86 Fann, Chad (TE)	6-3/256	6-7-70	6	Florida A&M	FA/97	12/0
88 Harris, Mark	6-4/201	4-28-70	3	Stanford	FA/97	10/0
81 Owens, Terrell	6-3/217	12-7-73	4	Tennessee-Chattanooga	D3/96	16/8
80 Rice, Jerry	6-2/196	10-13-62	15	Mississippi Valley State	D1/85	16/16
83 Stokes, J.J.	6-4/223	10-6-72	5	UCLA	D1/95	16/13
19 Streets, Tai	6-1/193	4-20-77	R	Michigan	D6/99	
OFFENSIVE LINEMEN						
79 Barton, Harris (T)	6-4/292	4-19-64	13	North Carolina	D1/87	—
65 Brown, Ray (G)	6-5/318	12-12-62	14	Arkansas State	FA/96	16/16
67 Dalman, Chris (C)	6-3/297	3-15-70	7	Stanford	D6/93	15/15
63 Deese, Derrick (T)	6-3/289	5-17-70	8	Southern California	FA/92	16/16
74 Fiore, Dave (T)	6-4/288	8-10-74	4	Hofstra	FA/97	9/3
66 Hopson, Tyrone (T)	6-2/305	5-28-76	R	Eastern Kentucky	D5b/99	—
71 Ruhman, Chris (T)	6-5/321	12-19-74	2	Texas A&M	D3/98	6/0
DEFENSIVE LINEMEN						
78 Bonham, Shane (T)	6-2/286	10-18-70	6	Tennessee	FA/98	8/0
90 Bryant, Junior (T)	6-4/278	1-16-71	5	Notre Dame	FA/93	16/16
99 Buckner, Brentson (E)	6-2/305	9-30-71	6	Clemson	UFA/98	13/0
92 McGrew, Reggie (T)	6-1/301	12-16-76	R	Florida	D1/99	—
52 Okeafor, Chike (E)	6-4/248	3-27-76	R	Purdue	D3/99	—
96 Posey, Jeff (E)	6-4/240	8-14-75	2	Southern Mississippi	FA/98	16/0
93 Richie, David (T)	6-4/280	9-26-73	3	Washington	T-Den./98	8/0
95 Washington, Marvin (E)	6-6/285	10-22-65	11	Idaho	UFA/99	*16/0
98 Wilkins, Gabe (E)	6-5/315	9-1-71	6	Gardner-Webb (N.C.)	D4/94	8/4
97 Young, Bryant (T)	6-3/291	1-27-72	6	Notre Dame	D1/94	12/12
LINEBACKERS						
59 Givens, Reggie	6-0/234	10-3-71	2	Penn State	FA/98	16/0
53 Minor, Kory	6-0/247	12-14-76	R	Notre Dame	D7/99	—
51 Norton, Ken	6-2/254	9-29-66	12	UCLA	FA/94	16/16
50 Peterson, Anthony	6-1/232	1-23-72	7	Notre Dame	T-Chi./98	16/1
55 Tubbs, Winfred	6-4/260	9-24-70	6	Texas	D3/94	16/16
54 Woodall, Lee	6-1/224	10-31-69	6	West Chester (Pa.)	D6/94	15/15
DEFENSIVE BACKS						
31 Bronson, Zack (S)	6-1/191	1-28-74	3	McNeese State	FA/97	11/0
36 Hanks, Merton (S)	6-2/181	3-12-68	9	Iowa	D5/91	16/16
46 McDonald, Tim (S)	6-2/219	1-6-65	13	Southern California	FA/93	16/16
21 McQuarters, R.W. (CB)	5-9/198	12-21-76	2	Oklahoma State	D1/98	16/7
26 Parker, Anthony (CB)	6-1/200	12-4-75	R	Weber State	D4a/99	—
23 Prioleau, Pierson (CB)	5-10/191	8-6-77	R	Virginia Tech	D4b/99	—
30 Schulters, Lance (S)	6-2/195	5-27-75	2	Hofstra	D4/98	15/0
38 Walker, Darnell (CB)	5-8/168	1-17-70	7	Oklahoma	FA/97	16/16
SPECIALISTS						
7 Richey, Wade (K)	6-4/200	5-19-76	2	Louisiana State	FA/98	16/0

*Not with 49ers in 1998.

Other free agents invited to camp: WR Morris Anderson, WR Mike Bastianelli, TE Shonn Bell, DT Tim Croff, T Dan Dercher, DB James Dumas, DT Curtis Eason, P Shayne Edge, LB Chris Freeman, QB Mark Garcia, TE Mike Grieb, WR Damon Griffin, LB Tito Hannah, CB Kelly Herndon, S Corey Hill, S Toya Jones, T Anthony Kapp, DT Matt Keneley, RB Jamie Kimbrough, T Josh Kopdish, T Dwayne Ledford, WR Karl Lerum, CB Kelly Malveaux, DT Mark Matock, WR Jim McElroy, C Jeremy Newberry, G Phil Ostrowski, DT Dennis O'Sullivan, DE Patterson Owens, DE James Roscoe, DT Angel Rubio, K Chris Sailer, FB Ed Scissum, CB Wasswa Serwanga, LB Brian Smith, P Chad Stanley, LB Vernon Strickland, DT Jason Tenner, FB Craig Walendy, LB Joe Wesley, T Geoff Wilson, CB Sam Wilson, C/LS Joe Zelenka.

Abbreviations: D1—draft pick, first round; SupD2—supplemental draft pick, second round; WV—claimed on waivers; TR—obtained in trade; PlanB—Plan B free-agent acquisition; FA—free-agent acquisition (other than Plan B); ED—expansion draft pick.

MISCELLANEOUS TEAM DATA

Stadium (capacity, surface):
3Com Park at Candlestick Point
(70,270, grass)
Business address:
4949 Centennial Blvd.
Santa Clara, CA 95054-1229
Business phone:
408-562-4949
Ticket information:
415-656-4900
Team colors:
Forty Niners gold and cardinal
Flagship radio station:
KGO, 810 AM
Training site:
University of Pacific
Stockton, Calif.
209-932-4949

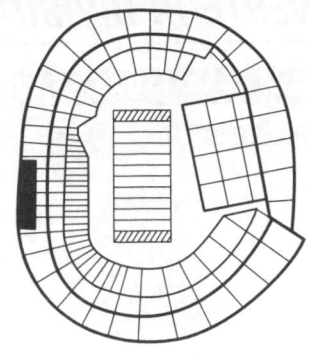

TSN REPORT CARD

Coaching staff	B	Steve Mariucci's gift is his endless reservoir of optimism and energy, not to mention an acute mind that scripted the 49ers to record highs on offense last season. Some new faces are in high-profile positions, including Jim Mora Jr., who was promoted from secondary coach to defensive coordinator, and Greg Brown, a former Tennessee assistant who is the new defensive backs coach.
Quarterbacks	B +	There's no reason why Steve Young shouldn't be a Pro Bowl quarterback again in 1999. But it could be a season of crossing fingers every time Young gets sacked. Behind him there is little or no experience. Jeff Garcia, a fine quarterback in the CFL the last five years, is an unproven NFL commodity, no matter how much Bill Walsh talks him up. Jim Druckenmiller, the team's top pick in 1997, is not in Walsh's long-term plans.
Running backs	B +	Garrison Hearst has emerged from Buddy Ryan's doghouse in Arizona and a platoon situation in Cincinnati to become the top-level NFL back he was expected to be. The 49ers will need another 1,500-yard season from Hearst to keep pace both in conference and in the NFC West. And that only happens if he stays healthy.
Receivers	A -	Only Minnesota can boast of having such a gifted trio. Jerry Rice will command double-teams until the day he hangs 'em up. Terrell Owens is a star in the making and he knows it. J.J. Stokes is as good a No. 3 receiver as there is in the league. They all have size, strength and want the ball. Hey, there are worse problems a team can have.
Offensive line	C +	If Chris Ruhman can anchor the right side, this unit could actually be pretty darn good. Offenses don't set team records in yards (as the 49ers did in 1998) without some big-time dust-busting on the line. But the bulk of that line—right tackle Kirk Scrafford and right guard Kevin Gogan—is gone, and some drop-off in level of play along the right side—Steve Young's blindside—could be inevitable.
Defensive line	C	The 49ers addressed their needs in the draft, taking linemen with their top two picks. But that won't help Bryant Young's right leg heal any faster. Charles Haley, who is expected to sign before training camp, adds a pass-rushing specialist, but the 49ers' problems will be up the middle against a run-happy division that boasts Jamal Anderson, Marshall Faulk and Ricky Williams.
Linebackers	B -	Entering the 1999 season, this is the strength of the 49ers defense. However, the unit was hurting on the big-play front in 1998 as Winfred Tubbs, Ken Norton Jr. and Lee Woodall combined to force just three fumbles all season. Tubbs, who had trouble adjusting to his new role as an inside linebacker, should be more comfortable in his second season with the team.
Secondary	C -	It was exposed early and often in 1998. The 49ers tried to fill some holes through the draft, but the depth is still young and untested. Rookie cornerback Anthony Parker might have to contribute on the 49ers' dime package immediately. Cornerbacks Darnell Walker and R.W. McQuarters will have to play over their heads—literally and figuratively. Not easy at 5-8 and 5-9, respectively.
Special teams	B -	With three game-winning field goals a year ago, unknown placekicker Wade Richey enters the season with confidence. This season the 49ers hope for a similar scenario with punter Shayne Edge, who has bounced around NFL training camps the last few years. Return man McQuarters has the ability to go the distance at any time.

SEATTLE SEAHAWKS
AFC WESTERN DIVISION

1999 SEASON

CLUB DIRECTORY

Owner
Paul Allen
Vice chairman
Bert Kolde
President
Bob Whitsitt
Senior vice president
Mike Reinfeldt
Vice president/football operations
Randy Mueller
V.p./ticket sales & services
Duane McLean
V.p./communications
Gary Wright
Public relations director
Dave Pearson
Community outreach director
Sandy Gregory
Player relations director
Nesby Glasgow
Assistant to the general manager
Gary Reynolds
Admin. assistant/football operations
Bill Nayes
Director of player personnel
John Dorsey
College scouting director
Don Deisch
Pro scouting director
Will Lewis
Eastern supervisor
Bill Baker
Western supervisor
Mike Faulkiner
Scouts
Derrick Jensen
Pat Mondock
John Peterson
Rick Thompson
Doug Whaley
Head trainer
Paul Federici

Executive v.p. of football ops. /g.m. and head coach
Mike Holmgren

Assistant coaches
Larry Brooks (defensive line)
Jerry Colquitt (off. qual. control)
Nolan Cromwell (wide receivers)
Ken Flajole (defensive backs)
Kent Johnston (head strength and conditioning)
Jim Lind (defensive coordinator)
Clayton Lopez (def. qual. control)
Tom Lovat (offensive line)
Stump Mitchell (running backs)
Dick Roach (defensive assistant)
Pete Rodriguez (special teams coordinator)
Mike Sheppard (quarterbacks)
Mike Sherman (off. coordinator)
Fritz Shurmur (def. coordinator)
Rod Springer (assistant strength and conditioning)

Assistant trainers
James Oglesby Jr.
Sam Ramsden
Ken Smith
Equipment manager
Erik Kennedy
Assistant equipment managers
Keith Graham
Brad Melland
Video director
Thom Fermstad

SCHEDULE

Sept. 12—	DETROIT	1:15
Sept. 19—	at Chicago	12:00
Sept. 26—	at Pittsburgh	1:00
Oct. 3—	OAKLAND	5:20
Oct. 10—	Open date	
Oct. 17—	at San Diego	1:05
Oct. 24—	BUFFALO	1:15
Nov. 1—	at Green Bay (Mon.)	8:00
Nov. 7—	CINCINNATI	1:15
Nov. 14—	DENVER	5:20
Nov. 21—	at Kansas City	12:00
Nov. 28—	TAMPA BAY	1:05
Dec. 5—	at Oakland	1:15
Dec. 12—	SAN DIEGO	1:05
Dec. 19—	at Denver	2:15
Dec. 26—	KANSAS CITY	1:05
Jan. 2—	at N.Y. Jets	1:00

All times are for home team.
All games Sunday unless noted.

DRAFT CHOICES

Lamar King, DE, Saginaw Valley State (first round/22nd pick overall).
Brock Huard, QB, Washington (3/77).
Karsten Bailey, WR, Auburn (3/82).
Antonio Cochran, DE, Georgia (4/115).
Floyd Wedderburn, T, Penn State (5/140).
Charlie Rogers, WR, Georgia Tech (5/152).
Steve Johnson, DB, Tennessee (6/170).

1998 REVIEW

RESULTS

Sept. 6—at Philadelphia	W	38-0
Sept.13—ARIZONA	W	33-14
Sept.20—WASHINGTON	W	24-14
Sept.27—at Pittsburgh	L	10-13
Oct. 4—at Kansas City	L	6-17
Oct. 11—DENVER	L	16-21
Oct. 18—Open date		
Oct. 25—at San Diego	W	27-20
Nov. 1—OAKLAND	L	18-31
Nov. 8—KANSAS CITY	W	24-12
Nov. 15—at Oakland	L	17-20
Nov. 22—at Dallas	L	22-30
Nov. 29—TENNESSEE	W	20-18
Dec. 6—at N.Y. Jets	L	31-32
Dec. 13—SAN DIEGO	W	38-17
Dec. 20—INDIANAPOLIS	W	27-23
Dec. 27—at Denver	L	21-28

RECORDS/RANKINGS

1998 regular-season record: 8-8 (2nd in AFC West); 3-5 in division; 5-7 in conference; 6-2 at home; 2-6 on road.
Team record last five years: 37-43 (.463, ranks T14th in league in that span).
1998 team rankings:

	No.	AFC	NFL
Total offense	*289.1	12	23
Rushing offense	*101.6	11	22
Passing offense	*187.5	12	24
Scoring offense	372	5	10
Total defense	*355.6	13	27
Rushing defense	*124.9	12	21
Passing defense	*230.6	15	27
Scoring defense	310	5	10
Takeaways	42	1	2
Giveaways	34	13	T24
Turnover differential	8	T4	T7
Sacks	53	1	2
Sacks allowed	34	5	9

*Yards per game.

TEAM LEADERS

Scoring (kicking): Todd Peterson, 98 pts. (41/41 PATs, 19/24 FGs).
Scoring (touchdowns): Joey Galloway, 72 pts. (10 receiving, 2 punt returns).
Passing: Warren Moon, 1,632 yds. (258 att., 145 comp., 56.2%, 11 TDs, 8 int.).
Rushing: Ricky Watters, 1,239 yds. (319 att., 3.9 avg., 9 TDs).
Receptions: Joey Galloway, 65 (1,047 yds., 16.1 avg., 10 TDs).
Interceptions: Shawn Springs, 7 (142 yds., 2 TDs).
Sacks: Michael Sinclair, 16.5.
Punting: Jeff Feagles, 44.0 avg. (81 punts, 3,568 yds., 0 blocked).
Punt returns: Joey Galloway, 10.0 avg. (25 att., 251 yds., 2 TDs).
Kickoff returns: Steve Broussard, 26.9 avg. (29 att., 781 yds., 1 TD).

TRAINING CAMP ROSTER

SEATTLE SEAHAWKS

No.	QUARTERBACKS	Ht./Wt.	Born	NFL Exp.	College	How acq.	'98 Games GP/GS
13	Foley, Glenn	6-2/220	10-10-70	6	Boston College	T-NYJ/99	*5/3
5	Huard, Brock	6-5/228	4-15-76	R	Washington	D3a/99	—
7	Kitna, Jon	6-2/217	9-21-72	3	Central Washington	FA/96	6/5

No.	RUNNING BACKS	Ht./Wt.	Born	NFL Exp.	College	How acq.	'98 Games GP/GS
34	Brown, Reggie (FB)	6-0/244	6-26-73	4	Fresno State	D3b/96	15/1
30	Green, Ahman	6-0/213	2-16-77	2	Nebraska	D3/98	16/0
38	Strong, Mack (FB)	6-0/235	9-11-71	6	Georgia	FA/93	16/5
32	Watters, Ricky	6-1/217	4-7-69	9	Notre Dame	UFA/98	16/16

No.	RECEIVERS	Ht./Wt.	Born	NFL Exp.	College	How acq.	'98 Games GP/GS
87	Bailey, Karsten	5-10/201	4-26-77	R	Auburn	D3b/99	—
81	Dawkins, Sean	6-4/218	2-3-71	7	California	UFA/99	*15/15
86	Fauria, Christian (TE)	6-4/245	9-22-71	5	Colorado	D2/95	16/15
84	Galloway, Joey	5-11/188	11-20-71	5	Ohio State	D1/95	16/16
	Jordan, Charles	5-11/185	10-9-69	7	Long Beach City College	UFA/99	*3/0
88	May, Deems (TE)	6-4/263	3-6-69	8	North Carolina	UFA/97	16/1
82	McKnight, James	6-1/198	6-17-72	5	Liberty (Va.)	FA/94	14/2
49	Mili, Itula (TE)	6-4/265	4-20-73	3	Brigham Young	D6/97	7/0
85	Pritchard, Mike	5-10/193	10-26-69	9	Colorado	FA/96	16/16
31	Rogers, Charlie	5-9/179	6-19-76	R	Georgia Tech	D5b/99	—
83	Wilson, Robert	5-11/176	6-23-74	3	Florida A&M	FA/97	16/0

No.	OFFENSIVE LINEMEN	Ht./Wt.	Born	NFL Exp.	College	How acq.	'98 Games GP/GS
75	Ballard, Howard (T)	6-6/325	11-3-63	12	Alabama A&M	UFA/94	16/16
63	Beede, Frank (G)	6-4/296	5-1-73	4	Panhandle State (Okla.)	FA/96	—
53	Glover, Kevin (C)	6-2/282	6-17-63	15	Maryland	UFA/98	8/8
62	Gray, Chris (G)	6-4/305	6-19-70	7	Auburn	UFA/98	15/8
68	Habib, Brian (G)	6-7/299	12-2-64	12	Washington	UFA/98	16/16
71	Jones, Walter (T)	6-5/300	1-19-74	3	Florida State	D1b/97	16/16
66	Kendall, Pete (G)	6-5/292	7-9-73	4	Boston College	D1/96	16/16
52	McEndoo, Jason (C)	6-5/315	2-25-75	R	Washington State	D7/98	1/0
60	Wedderburn, Floyd (T)	6-5/333	5-5-76	R	Penn State	D5a/99	—
74	Weiner, Todd (T)	6-4/300	9-16-75	2	Kansas State	D2/98	6/0
79	Williams, Grant (T)	6-7/323	5-10-74	4	Louisiana Tech	FA/96	16/0

No.	DEFENSIVE LINEMEN	Ht./Wt.	Born	NFL Exp.	College	How acq.	'98 Games GP/GS
98	Adams, Sam (T)	6-3/300	6-13-73	6	Texas A&M	D1/94	16/11
90	Cochran, Antonio (E)	6-4/297	6-21-76	R	Georgia	D4/99	—
93	Daniels, Phillip (E)	6-5/263	3-4-73	4	Georgia	D4a/96	16/15
96	Kennedy, Cortez (T)	6-3/306	8-23-68	10	Miami (Fla.)	D1a/90	15/15
92	King, Lamar (E)	6-3/294	8-10-75	R	Saginaw Valley State	D1/99	—
99	LaBounty, Matt (E)	6-4/271	1-3-69	7	Oregon	T-GB/96	16/1
97	Parker, Riddick (T)	6-3/274	11-20-72	3	North Carolina	FA/96	8/0
70	Sinclair, Michael (E)	6-4/267	1-31-68	9	Eastern New Mexico	D6/91	16/16

No.	LINEBACKERS	Ht./Wt.	Born	NFL Exp.	College	How acq.	'98 Games GP/GS
94	Brown, Chad	6-2/240	7-12-70	7	Colorado	FA/97	16/16
55	Butler, Hillary	6 2/244	1-5-71	2	Washington	FA/98	7/0
56	Logan, James	6-2/225	12-6-72	5	Memphis	W-Cin./95	4/1
50	Myles, DeShone	6-2/235	10-31-74	2	Nevada	D4/98	12/7
51	Simmons, Anthony	6-0/230	6-20-76	2	Clemson	D1/98	12/4
59	Smith, Darrin	6-1/230	4-15-70	7	Miami, Fla	UFA/98	13/12

No.	DEFENSIVE BACKS	Ht./Wt.	Born	NFL Exp.	College	How acq.	'98 Games GP/GS
20	Bellamy, Jay (S)	5-11/199	7-8-72	5	Rutgers	FA/94	16/16
25	Collins, Mark (S)	5-10/196	1-16-64	14	Cal State Fullerton	FA/98	9/0
43	Eloms, Joey (CB)	5-10/183	4-4-76	2	Indiana	FA/98	1/0
21	Johnson, Steve (CB)	5-10/178	3-24-76	R	Tennessee	D6/99	—
28	Joseph, Kerry (S)	6-2/205	10-4-73	3	McNeese State	FA/98	16/0
22	McGill, Lenny (CB)	6-1/202	5-31-71	6	Arizona State	UFA/99	*10/0
24	Springs, Shawn (CB)	6-0/195	3-11-75	3	Ohio State	D1a/97	16/16
22	Thomas, Fred (CB)	5-9/172	9-11-73	4	Tennessee-Martin	D2/96	15/2
33	Williams, Darryl (S)	6-0/202	1-8-70	8	Miami (Fla.)	FA/96	16/16
27	Williams, Willie (CB)	5-9/180	12-26-70	7	Western Carolina	UFA/97	14/14

No.	SPECIALISTS	Ht./Wt.	Born	NFL Exp.	College	How acq.	'98 Games GP/GS
10	Feagles, Jeff (P)	6-1/207	8-7-66	12	Miami (Fla.)	UFA/98	16/0
2	Peterson, Todd (K)	5-10/171	2-4-70	5	Georgia	FA/95	16/0

*Not with Seahawks in 1998.

Other free agents invited to camp: LB Josh Amundson, RB Michael Black, C Greg Bloedorn, CB DeAuntae Brown, G Mondell Corbett, TE Rufus French, DT T.J. Frier, RB Brian Goolsby, FB Oscar Gray, DB Matt Hickl, TE James Hill, RB Jay Hinton, DT Gary Holmes, WR Chris Jackson, WR Michael Jenkins, K Jamie Kohl, QB Kevin Kremhagen, FS Tod McBride, QB Mike McCoy, P Brian Moorman, DE Jonathan Nance, LB Brian Rogers, LB Derek Strey, DT Kevin Thomas.

Abbreviations: D1—draft pick, first round; SupD2—supplemental draft pick, second round; WV—claimed on waivers; TR—obtained in trade; PlanB—Plan B free-agent acquisition; FA—free-agent acquisition (other than Plan B); ED—expansion draft pick.

MISCELLANEOUS TEAM DATA

Stadium (capacity, surface):
Kingdome (66,400, artificial)
Business address:
11220 N.E. 53rd Street
Kirkland, WA 98033
Business phone:
425-827-9777
Ticket information:
206-682-2800
Team colors:
Blue, green and silver
Flagship radio station:
KIRO, 710 AM
Training site:
Eastern Washington University
Cheney, Wash.
206-827-9777

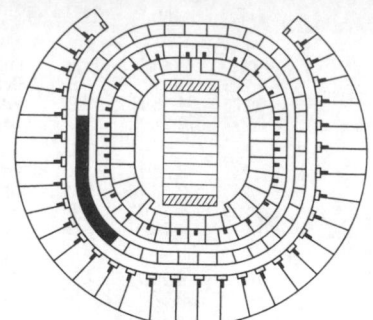

TSN REPORT CARD

Coaching staff	B +	Mike Holmgren produced six straight playoff teams in Green Bay, including a Super Bowl champion. Before that, he was an innovative offensive coordinator and quarterbacks coach with the 49ers. He has surrounded himself with assistant coaches who believe in and can teach his proven system.
Quarterbacks	C +	Jon Kitna completes the next huge step in his made-for-TV career by stepping in as a full-time starter. He has worked behind Warren Moon and John Friesz since arriving as an undrafted free agent in 1996. It is time to show what he has learned.
Running backs	B -	Ricky Watters flourished in the West Coast offense with the 49ers and was a workhorse in a variation of that attack with the Eagles. Now he slides back into that comfort zone, and should get more help than he wants from Ahman Green.
Receivers	B	Sean Dawkins should be the best thing that has happened to Joey Galloway in his productive NFL career. And vice versa. Their diverse talents are a perfect fit for Holmgren's offense, and a perfect complement to each other.
Offensive line	B	For the first time since 1988, the Seahawks are not shuffling their starting unit. They return the same blend of youth (left tackle Walter Jones and left guard Pete Kendall) and experience (center Kevin Glover, right guard Brian Habib and right tackle Howard Ballard). The new member is coach Tom Lovat, which is a definite plus.
Defensive line	B	The Seahawks already had NFL sack leader and three-time Pro Bowl defensive end Michael Sinclair and the imposing defensive tackle tandem of Cortez Kennedy and Sam Adams. The draft delivered needed depth and talent in Lamar King and Antonio Cochran to supplement an already stout unit.
Linebackers	A	In Chad Brown, Darrin Smith, DeShone Myles and Anthony Simmons, the Seahawks have never had so much talent, depth and versatility at linebacker. Brown was All-Pro last season, Smith made big play after big play (when healthy) and Myles and Simmons each made an impact in their rookie seasons.
Secondary	C +	This is the most puzzling unit on the team, as the whole has yet to be as good as the parts. Cornerback Shawn Springs was voted to the Pro Bowl last year, and Darryl Williams went the year before as a free safety. Cornerback Willie Williams is small but tenacious, and strong safety Jay Bellamy, who will flop roles with Darryl Williams this season, is solid.
Special teams	B	After having the worst special teams in the NFL in 1997, the Seahawks hired Pete Rodriguez to turn things around. He did. Seattle vaulted to No. 5 last year, but still need more consistency in all phases of the kicking game.

TAMPA BAY BUCCANEERS
NFC CENTRAL DIVISION

1999 SEASON

CLUB DIRECTORY

Owner
Malcolm Glazer
Executive vice president
Bryan Glazer
Executive vice president
Joel Glazer
Executive vice president
Edward Glazer
General manager
Rich McKay
Director of player personnel
Jerry Angelo
Director of college scouting
Tim Ruskell
Director of football administration
John Idzik
V.p. of luxury services and guest rel.
Veronica (Roni) Costello
Director of communications
Reggie Roberts
Director of marketing
George Woods
Director of special events
Meredith Chimerine
Director of premium seating
Jim Overton
Director of community relations
Stephanie Waller
Dir. of ticketing and customer relations
Mike Newquist
Director of player programs
Kevin Winston
Controller
Larry Ackerly
Luxury suite managers
Cheryll Pritcher   Hillary Frank Webber
Group sales
Bill Butler
College scouts
Mike Ackerley   Joe DiMarzo Jr.
Dennis Hickey   Ruston Webster
Mike Yowarsky
Pro personnel assistants
Mark Dominik   Lloyd Richards

Head coach
Tony Dungy

Assistant coaches
Mark Asanovich (strength & conditioning)
Wendell Avery (off. assistant)
Clyde Christensen (tight ends)
Herman Edwards (assistant head coach/defensive backs)
Chris Foerster (offensive line)
Monte Kiffin (def. coordinator)
Joe Marciano (special teams)
Rod Marinelli (defensive line)
Tony Nathan (running backs)
Kevin O'Dea (defensive assistant)
Mike Shula (off. coordinator)
Lovie Smith (linebackers)
Ricky Thomas (off. assistant)
Charlie Williams (wide receivers)

Communications managers
Scott Smith   Nelson Luis
Trainer
Todd Toriscelli
Assistant trainers
Mark Shermansky   Keith Abrams
Video director
Dave Levy
Assistant video director
Pat Brazil
Equipment manager
Darin Kerns
Assistant equipment manager
Mark Meschede

SCHEDULE

Sept. 12—	N.Y. GIANTS	4:15
Sept. 19—	at Philadelphia	1:00
Sept. 26—	DENVER	1:00
Oct. 3—	at Minnesota	12:00
Oct. 10—	at Green Bay	7:20
Oct. 17—	Open date	
Oct. 24—	CHICAGO	1:00
Oct. 31—	at Detroit	8:20
Nov. 7—	at New Orleans	3:05
Nov. 14—	KANSAS CITY	1:00
Nov. 21—	ATLANTA	1:00
Nov. 28—	at Seattle	1:05
Dec. 6—	MINNESOTA (Mon.)	9:00
Dec. 12—	DETROIT	1:00
Dec. 19—	at Oakland	1:05
Dec. 26—	GREEN BAY	4:15
Jan. 2—	at Chicago	12:00

All times are for home team.
All games Sunday unless noted.

DRAFT CHOICES

Anthony McFarland, DT, Louisiana State (first round/15th pick overall).
Shaun King, QB, Tulane (2/50).
Martin Gramatica, K, Kansas State (3/80).
Dexter Jackson, DB, Florida State (4/113).
John McLaughlin, DE, California (5/150).
Lamarr Glenn, RB, Florida State (6/195).
Robert Hunt, G, Virginia (7/226).
Autry Denson, RB, Notre Dame (7/233).
Darnell McDonald, WR, Kansas State (7/240).

1998 REVIEW

RESULTS

Sept. 6—at Minnesota	L	7-31
Sept.13—at Green Bay	L	15-23
Sept.20—CHICAGO	W	27-15
Sept.28—at Detroit	L	6-27
Oct. 4—N.Y. GIANTS	W	20-3
Oct. 11—Open date		
Oct. 18—CAROLINA	W	16-13
Oct. 25—at New Orleans	L	3-9
Nov. 1—MINNESOTA	W	27-24
Nov. 8—TENNESSEE	L	22-31
Nov. 15—at Jacksonville	L	24-29
Nov. 22—DETROIT	L	25-28
Nov. 29—at Chicago	W	31-17
Dec. 7—GREEN BAY	W	24-22
Dec. 13—PITTSBURGH	W	16-3
Dec. 19—at Washington	L	16-20
Dec. 27—at Cincinnati	W	35-0

RECORDS/RANKINGS

1998 regular-season record: 8-8 (3rd in NFC Central); 4-4 in division; 6-6 in conference; 6-2 at home; 2-6 on road.
Team record last five years: 37-43 (.463, ranks T14th in league in that span).
1998 team rankings:

	No.	NFC	NFL
Total offense	*297.1	11	22
Rushing offense	*134.3	2	4
Passing offense	*162.9	13	27
Scoring offense	314	9	18
Total defense	*271.6	1	2
Rushing defense	*98.9	3	8
Passing defense	*172.6	2	2
Scoring defense	295	3	5
Takeaways	26	T8	T19
Giveaways	31	9	18
Turnover differential	-5	10	21
Sacks	37	T11	T21
Sacks allowed	28	3	7

*Yards per game.

TEAM LEADERS

Scoring (kicking): Michael Husted, 92 pts. (29/30 PATs, 21/28 FGs).
Scoring (touchdowns): Mike Alstott, 54 pts. (8 rushing, 1 receiving).
Passing: Trent Dilfer, 2,729 yds. (429 att., 225 comp., 52.4%, 21 TDs, 15 int.).
Rushing: Warrick Dunn, 1,026 yds. (245 att., 4.2 avg., 2 TDs).
Receptions: Reidel Anthony, 51 (708 yds., 13.9 avg., 7 TDs).
Interceptions: Charles Mincy, 4 (58 yds., 1 TD).
Sacks: Brad Culpepper, 9.0.
Punting: Tommy Barnhardt, 41.2 avg. (81 punts, 3,340 yds., 0 blocked).
Punt returns: Jacquez Green, 15.1 avg. (30 att., 453 yds., 1 TD).
Kickoff returns: Reidel Anthony, 24.3 avg. (46 att., 1,118 yds., 0 TDs).

TAMPA BAY BUCCANEERS

No.	QUARTERBACKS	Ht./Wt.	Born	NFL Exp.	College	How acq.	'98 Games GP/GS
12	Dilfer, Trent	6-4/237	3-13-72	6	Fresno State	D1/94	16/16
	King, Shaun	6-0/221	5-29-77	R	Tulane	D2/99	—
	Zeier, Eric	6-1/205	9-6-72	5	Georgia	T-Bal./99	*10/4

No.	RUNNING BACKS	Ht./Wt.	Born	NFL Exp.	College	How acq.	'98 Games GP/GS
40	Alstott, Mike (FB)	6-1/255	12-21-73	4	Purdue	D2/96	16/16
	Denson, Autry	5-10/202	12-8-76	R	Notre Dame	D7b/99	—
28	Dunn, Warrick	5-8/176	1-5-75	3	Florida State	D1/97	16/14
	Glenn, Lamarr (FB)	6-1/235	12-11-75	R	Florida State	D6/99	—

No.	RECEIVERS	Ht./Wt.	Born	NFL Exp.	College	How acq.	'98 Games GP/GS
85	Anthony, Reidel	5-11/178	10-20-76	3	Florida	D1/97	15/13
80	Davis, John (TE)	6-4/262	5-14-73	4	Emporia State	FA/97	16/0
87	Emanuel, Bert	5-10/175	10-28-70	6	Rice	FA/98	11/11
81	Green, Jacquez	5-9/172	1-15-76	2	Florida	D2a/98	12/1
82	Hape, Patrick (TE)	6-4/247	6-6-74	3	Alabama	D5/97	16/2
88	Hunter, Brice	6-2/209	4-21-74	2	Georgia	FA/96	10/0
	McDonald, Darnell	6-3/190	5-26-76	R	Kansas State	D7c/99	—
83	Moore, Dave (TE)	6-2/245	11-11-69	7	Pittsburgh	FA/92	16/16
86	Williams, Karl	5-10/179	4-10-71	4	Texas A&M-Kingsville	FA/96	13/6

No.	OFFENSIVE LINEMEN	Ht./Wt.	Born	NFL Exp.	College	How acq.	'98 Games GP/GS
64	Diaz, Jorge (G)	6-4/315	11-15-73	4	Texas A&M-Kingsville	FA/96	12/12
65	Dogins, Kevin (C)	6-1/298	12-7-72	3	Texas A&M-Kingsville	FA/96	6/4
74	Gruber, Paul (T)	6-5/292	2-24-65	12	Wisconsin	D1/88	16/16
	Hunt, Robert (G)	6-3/290	7-22-75	R	Virginia	D7a/99	—
61	Mayberry, Tony (C)	6-4/282	12-8-67	10	Wake Forest	D4b/90	16/16
73	Middleton, Frank (G)	6-3/340	10-25-74	3	Arizona	D3a/97	16/16
70	Odom, Jason (T)	6-6/308	3-31-74	4	Florida	D4a/96	15/15
69	Pierson, Pete (T)	6-5/315	2-4-71	5	Washington	D5/94	16/0
75	Washington, Todd (C)	6-3/325	7-19-76	2	Virginia Tech	D4/98	4/0
71	Wunsch, Jerry (T)	6-6/334	1-21-74	3	Wisconsin	D2/97	16/1

No.	DEFENSIVE LINEMEN	Ht./Wt.	Born	NFL Exp.	College	How acq.	'98 Games GP/GS
72	Ahanotu, Chidi (E)	6-2/285	10-11-70	7	California	D6/93	4/4
98	Cannida, James (T)	6-2/285	1-3-75	2	Nevada-Reno	D6a/98	10/0
77	Culpepper, Brad (T)	6-1/270	5-8-69	8	Florida	W-Min./94	16/16
97	Jackson, Tyoka (E)	6-2/274	11-22-71	5	Penn State	FA/96	16/12
78	Jones, Marcus (T)	6-6/286	8-15-73	4	North Carolina	D1b/96	15/0
	McFarland, Anthony (T)	6-0/292	12-18-77	R	Louisiana State	D1/99	—
	McLaughlin, John (E)	6-4/247	11-13-75	R	California	D5/99	—
99	Sapp, Warren (T)	6-2/291	12-19-72	5	Miami (Fla.)	D1/95	16/16
91	Upshaw, Regan (E)	6-4/261	8-12-75	4	California	D1a/96	16/16
94	White, Steve (E)	6-2/281	10-25-73	4	Tennessee	FA/96	16/0

No.	LINEBACKERS	Ht./Wt.	Born	NFL Exp.	College	How acq.	'98 Games GP/GS
55	Brooks, Derrick	6-0/229	4-18-73	5	Florida State	D1b/95	16/16
58	Davis, Don	6-1/240	12-17-72	4	Kansas	W-NO/98	9/0
69	Duncan, Jamie	6-0/220	7-20-75	2	Vanderbilt	D3/98	14/6
50	Gooch, Jeff	5-11/219	10-31-74	4	Austin Peay	FA/96	16/16
56	Nickerson, Hardy	6-2/225	9-1-65	13	California	FA/93	16/10
57	Palmer, Mitch	6-4/250	9-2-73	2	Colorado State	FA/98	16/0
53	Quarles, Shelton	6-1/223	9-11-71	3	Vanderbilt	FA/97	16/0
51	Singleton, Alshermond	6-2/213	8-7-75	3	Temple	D4/97	15/0

No.	DEFENSIVE BACKS	Ht./Wt.	Born	NFL Exp.	College	How acq.	'98 Games GP/GS
21	Abraham, Donnie (CB)	5-10/184	10-8-73	4	East Tennessee State	D3/96	13/13
20	Barber, Ronde (CB)	5-10/180	4-7-75	3	Virginia	D3b/97	16/9
	Jackson, Dexter (S)	6-0/189	7-28-77	R	Florida State	D4/99	—
25	Kelly, Brian (CB)	5-11/195	1-14-76	2	Southern California.	D2b/98	16/3
47	Lynch, John (S)	6-2/216	9-25-71	7	Stanford	D3b/93	15/15
24	Robinson, Damien (S)	6-2/205	12-22-73	3	Iowa	FA/97	7/0
30	Smith, Shevin (S)	5-11/195	6-17-75	2	Florida State	D6b/98	3/0
33	Vance, Eric (S)	6-2/215	7-14-75	1	Vanderbilt	FA/98	3/1
31	Young, Floyd (CB)	6-0/178	11-23-75	3	Texas A&M-Kingsville	FA/97	11/0

No.	SPECIALISTS	Ht./Wt.	Born	NFL Exp.	College	How acq.	'98 Games GP/GS
	Gramatica, Martin (K)	5-8/180	11-27-75	R	Kansas State	D3/99	—
8	Howard, Eddie (P)	6-1/203	10-6-72	1	Idaho	FA/99	*2/0

*Not with Buccaneers in 1998.

Other free agents invited to camp: RB Rabih Abdullah, CB Ronald Bailey, T DeMarcus Curry, C Eric DeGroh, WR Anthony Dicosmo, CB Cedric Donaldson, S Charles Emanuel, DT Juaquin Frazell, TE Jason Freeman, LB Stanskeene Gibbs, LB Bobbie Howard, DE Ralph Hughes, RB John Humphrey, K Danny Kight, P Aron Langley, WR Felman Malveaux, S Lamar Marshall, FB Kevin McLeod, WR Dillon Micus, DE/DT Bryant Mix, WR Shannon Myers, WR Drew O'Connor, G Scott Osler, CB Troy Saunders, G Andray Spearman, P Scott Terna, T Jamie Vanderveldt.

Abbreviations: D1—draft pick, first round; SupD2—supplemental draft pick, second round; WV—claimed on waivers; TR—obtained in trade; PlanB—Plan B free-agent acquisition; FA—free-agent acquisition (other than Plan B); ED—expansion draft pick.

MISCELLANEOUS TEAM DATA

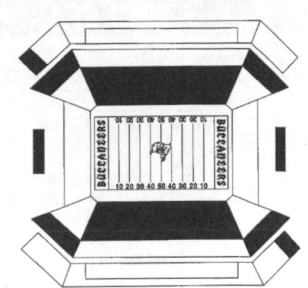

Stadium (capacity, surface):
Raymond James Stadium (65,394, grass)
Business address:
One Buccaneer Place
Tampa, FL 33607
Business phone:
813-870-2700
Ticket information:
813-879-2827
Team colors:
Buccaneer red, pewter, black and orange
Flagship radio station:
WQYK, 99.5 FM
Training site:
University of Tampa
Tampa, Fla.
813-253-6215

TAMPA BAY BUCCANEERS

TSN REPORT CARD

Coaching staff	B	Tony Dungy is one of the league's best defensive minds, but his offense has yet to become productive. Offensive coordinator Mike Shula is clearly on the hot seat and needs to improve the passing game. Clyde Christensen's move to quarterbacks coach should help, but a little more innovation also would help. Defensive coordinator Monte Kiffin will try to take a unit that ranked second in the league last year and make it even better.
Quarterbacks	C	The team's future rests on Trent Dilfer's shoulders—at least for now. Dilfer doesn't have to be spectacular, but it would be nice if opposing defenses had to at least acknowledge the threat of a passing game. Dilfer must improve on his 52 percent completion ratio of a year ago. If that doesn't happen by midseason and the team is struggling, the reins could be handed over to Eric Zeier, as Shaun King is brought along slowly.
Running backs	B +	With tailback Warrick Dunn and fullback Mike Alstott, the Bucs may have the most talented 1-2 backfield punch in the league. But there's room for improvement. Dunn scored only twice last year and that's not nearly enough for the most dangerous player on the roster. His outside running ability and skills as a receiver need to be used more. Alstott is a workhorse, but he needs to cut down on fumbles.
Receivers	C	There's more room for improvement here than any other area. But there is plenty of potential. Much of how this group fares depends on how Bert Emanuel rebounds from an ankle injury that slowed him for almost all of last season. Reidel Anthony came on strong during the second half of last year and will be even better if defenses have to worry about Emanuel. Jacquez Green had an up-and-down rookie year, but he is the team's fastest player.
Offensive line	C +	Left tackle Paul Gruber is 34 and center Tony Mayberry is 31, but they're still the heart and soul of an offensive line that can play very well at times. The run blocking is solid, but the pass blocking needs to improve. Major steps are needed from right tackle Jason Odom and guards Jorge Diaz and Frank Middleton.
Defensive line	A -	An already strong area gets even better with the drafting of Anthony McFarland and the return of Chidi Ahanotu from a shoulder injury. Mix them in with tackles Warren Sapp and Brad Culpepper and end Regan Upshaw and this may be the best front line in the league. Tyoka Jackson, who started for Ahanotu last year, can play inside or out and makes the line very deep.
Linebackers	A	Weakside linebacker Derrick Brooks has been Tampa Bay's best player the last two years. Middle linebacker Hardy Nickerson is 34 and has recovered from a heart condition that sidelined him at the end of last season. Nickerson will return to a starting role, but Jamie Duncan has established himself as a capable backup. Jeff Gooch and Alshermond Singleton will share duties on the strong side.
Secondary	B	This unit may be on the verge of great things. Cornerback Donnie Abraham and strong safety John Lynch are very solid. Ronde Barber took over as a starting cornerback early last year and made the defense even better. The only real question is at free safety, where Damien Robinson is expected to take over as the starter.
Special teams	B	Major upgrades were made in this area in the offseason. Kicker Michael Husted was inconsistent the last two seasons and has been replaced by Martin Gramatica, the best kicker in the draft. Green returned punts last year and could be bringing back kickoffs as well. The coverage units, which were young last year, should be improved. Punter remains a question mark, unless the team brings back Tommy Barnhardt, an unrestricted free agent.

TENNESSEE TITANS
AFC CENTRAL DIVISION

1999 SEASON

CLUB DIRECTORY

Owner/president
K.S. "Bud" Adams Jr.
Executive v.p./general manager
Floyd Reese
Executive assistant to president
Thomas S. Smith
Vice president/legal counsel
Steve Underwood
Vice president/finance
Jackie Curley
Exec. v.p./broadcasting and marketing
Don MacLachlan
Director of player personnel
Rich Snead
Director/sales operations
Stuart Spears
Dir. of media relations and services
Tony Wyllie
Vice president for community affairs
Bob Hyde
Director/ticket operations
Marty Collins
Director/security
Steve Berk
Director/player programs
Al Smith
Asst. dir. of media rel. and services
Robbie Bohren
Head trainer
Brad Brown
Scouts
Ray Biggs
C.O. Brocato
Dub Fesperman
Director of college scouting
Glenn Cumbee

Head coach
Jeff Fisher

Assistant coaches
Bart Andrus (offensive assistant/
quality control)
O'Neill Gilbert (linebackers)
Jerry Gray (defensive backs)
George Henshaw (offensive line/
tight ends)
Alan Lowry (special teams)
Mike Munchak (offensive line)
Jim Schwartz (def. assistant/
quality control)
Sherman Smith (running backs)
Les Steckel (offensive coordina-
tor/quarterbacks)
Steve Walters (wide receivers)
Jim Washburn (defensive line)
Steve Watterson (strength &
rehabilitation)
Gregg Williams (defensive
coordinator)

Equipment manager
Paul Noska
Videotape coordinator
Ken Sparacino
Team physicians
Elrod Burton
Craig Rutlend
John Williams

SCHEDULE

Sept. 12—	CINCINNATI	12:00
Sept. 19—	CLEVELAND	3:15
Sept. 26—	at Jacksonville	4:05
Oct. 3—	at San Francisco	1:15
Oct. 10—	BALTIMORE	3:15
Oct. 17—	at New Orleans	12:00
Oct. 24—	Open date	
Oct. 31—	ST. LOUIS	12:00
Nov. 7—	at Miami	8:20
Nov. 14—	at Cincinnati	1:00
Nov. 21—	PITTSBURGH	12:00
Nov. 28—	at Cleveland	1:00
Dec. 5—	at Baltimore	1:00
Dec. 9—	OAKLAND (Thur.)	7:20
Dec. 19—	ATLANTA	12:00
Dec. 26—	JACKSONVILLE	12:00
Jan. 2—	at Pittsburgh	4:15

All times are for home team.
All games Sunday unless noted.

DRAFT CHOICES

Jevon Kearse, LB, Florida (first
round/16th pick overall).
John Thornton, DT, West Virginia (2/52).
Zach Piller, G, Florida (3/81).
Brad Ware, DB, Auburn (4/114).
Donald Mitchell, DB, Southern Methodist
(4/117).
Kevin Daft, QB, Cal-Davis (5/151).
Darran Hall, WR, Colorado State (6/186).
Phil Glover, LB, Utah (7/222).

1998 REVIEW

RESULTS

Sept. 6—at Cincinnati	W	23-14
Sept.13—SAN DIEGO	L	7-13
Sept.20—at New England	L	16-27
Sept.27—JACKSONVILLE	L	22-27
Oct. 4—Open date		
Oct. 11—at Baltimore	W	12-8
Oct. 18—CINCINNATI	W	44-14
Oct. 25—CHICAGO	L	20-23
Nov. 1—at Pittsburgh	W	41-31
Nov. 8—at Tampa Bay	W	31-22
Nov. 15—PITTSBURGH	W	23-14
Nov. 22—N.Y. JETS	L	3-24
Nov. 29—at Seattle	L	18-20
Dec. 6—BALTIMORE	W	16-14
Dec. 13—at Jacksonville	W	16-13
Dec. 20—at Green Bay	L	22-30
Dec. 26—MINNESOTA	L	16-26

RECORDS/RANKINGS

1998 regular-season record: 8-8 (2nd in
AFC Central); 7-1 in division; 7-5 in conference; 3-5 at home; 5-3 on road.
Team record last five years: 33-47 (.413,
ranks T19th in league in that span).
1998 team rankings:

	No.	AFC	NFL
Total offense	*328.8	4	9
Rushing offense	*123.1	5	9
Passing offense	*205.7	7	15
Scoring offense	330	7	13
Total defense	*320.1	9	16
Rushing defense	*100.6	6	T9
Passing defense	*219.4	10	20
Scoring defense	320	6	12
Takeaways	19	T14	T28
Giveaways	19	1	2
Turnover differential	0	6	9
Sacks	30	T13	T27
Sacks allowed	35	T6	T10

*Yards per game.

TEAM LEADERS

Scoring (kicking): Al Del Greco, 136 pts.
(28/28 PATs, 36/39 FGs).
Scoring (touchdowns): Eddie George, 38
pts. (5 rushing, 1 receiving, 1 2-pt.
conv.).
Passing: Steve McNair, 3,228 yds. (492
att., 289 comp., 58.7%, 15 TDs, 10 int.).
Rushing: Eddie George, 1,294 yds. (348
att., 3.7 avg., 5 TDs).
Receptions: Frank Wycheck, 70 (768
yds., 11.0 avg., 2 TDs).
Interceptions: Darryll Lewis, 4 (40 yds.,
0 TDs).
Sacks: Lonnie Marts, 4.0.
Punting: Craig Hentrich, 47.2 avg. (69
punts, 3,258 yds., 0 blocked).
Punt returns: Derrick Mason, 7.4 avg.
(31 att., 228 yds., 0 TDs).
Kickoff returns: Mike Archie, 21.7 avg.
(42 att., 913 yds., 0 TDs).

TENNESSEE TITANS

No.	QUARTERBACKS	Ht./Wt.	Born	NFL Exp.	College	How acq.	'98 Games GP/GS
13	Daft, Kevin	6-1/184	11-19-75	R	California-Davis	D5/99	—
11	Matthews, Steve	6-3/228	10-13-70	4	Memphis State	W-Jax./98	1/0
9	McNair, Steve	6-2/225	2-14-73	5	Alcorn State	D1/95	16/16
	RUNNING BACKS						
22	Archie, Mike	5-8/204	10-14-72	4	Penn State	D7/96	16/0
27	George, Eddie	6-3/240	9-24-73	4	Ohio State	D1/96	16/16
26	George, Spencer	5-9/200	10-28-73	2	Rice	FA/97	5/0
41	Neal, Lorenzo (FB)	5-11/240	12-27-70	7	Fresno State	FA/99	*16/1
20	Thomas, Rodney	5-10/210	3-30-73	5	Texas A&M	D3b/95	11/0
	RECEIVERS						
83	Byrd, Isaac	6-1/188	11-16-74	3	Kansas	FA/97	4/3
67	Dyson, Kevin	6-1/201	6-23-75	2	Utah	D1/98	13/9
84	Hall, Darran	5-8/166	9-8-75	R	Colorado State	D6/99	—
88	Harris, Jackie (TE)	6-4/250	1-4-68	10	Northeast Louisiana	UFA/98	16/16
86	Kent, Joey	6-1/191	4-23-74	3	Tennessee	D2/97	10/0
85	Mason, Derrick	5-10/188	1-17-74	3	Michigan State	D4a/97	16/0
80	Roan, Michael (TE)	6-3/250	8-29-72	5	Wisconsin	D4/95	16/1
81	Sanders, Chris	6-1/188	5-8-72	5	Ohio State	D3a/95	14/1
82	Thigpen, Yancey	6-1/203	8-15-69	8	Winston-Salem (N.C.) State	FA/98	9/8
89	Wycheck, Frank (TE)	6-3/250	10-14-71	7	Maryland	W-Was./95	16/16
	OFFENSIVE LINEMEN						
72	Hopkins, Brad (T)	6-3/305	9-5-70	7	Illinois	D1/97	13/13
66	Layman, Jason (G)	6-5/310	7-29-73	4	Tennessee	D2b/96	16/15
60	Long, Kevin (C)	6-5/295	5-2-75	2	Florida State	D7b/98	16/2
76	Mathews, Jason (T)	6-5/304	2-9-71	6	Texas A&M	FA/98	3/0
74	Matthews, Bruce (G)	6-5/309	8-8-61	17	Southern California	D1/83	16/16
75	Olson, Benji (G)	6-3/315	6-5-75	2	Washington	D5/98	13/1
61	Pilgrim, Evan (G)	6-4/305	8-14-72	5	Brigham Young	FA/98	2/0
71	Piller, Zach (T)	6-5/332	5-2-76	R	Florida	D3/99	—
69	Runyan, Jon (T)	6-7/320	11-27-73	4	Michigan	D4b/96	16/16
73	Sanderson, Scott (T)	6-6/295	7-25-74	3	Washington State	D3b/97	15/3
	DEFENSIVE LINEMEN						
91	Evans, Josh (T)	6-2/288	9-6-72	5	Alabama-Birmingham	FA/95	14/11
97	Fisk, Jason (T)	6-3/295	9-4-72	5	Stanford	UFA/99	*16/0
92	Ford, Henry (T)	6-3/295	10-30-71	6	Arkansas	D1/94	13/5
99	Holmes, Kenny (E)	6-4/270	10-24-73	3	Miami (Fla.)	D1/97	14/11
96	Jones, Mike (T)	6-4/280	8-25-69	9	North Carolina State	UFA/99	*16/15
42	Kearse, Jevon (E)	6-4/260	9-3-76	R	Florida	D1/99	—
98	Lyons, Pratt (T)	6-5/295	9-17-74	3	Troy (Ala.) State	D4b/97	16/12
90	Roberson, James (E)	6-3/275	5-3-71	4	Florida State	FA/96	10/5
95	Salave'a, Joe (T)	6-3/290	3-23-75	2	Arizona	D4/98	13/0
93	Sutton, Mike (E)	6-4/265	4-21-75	1	Louisiana State	FA/98	1/0
76	Thornton, John (T)	6-2/304	10-2-76	R	West Virginia	D2/99	—
	LINEBACKERS						
58	Bowden, Joe	5-11/235	2-25-70	8	Oklahoma	D5a/92	16/16
54	Glover, Phil	5-11/239	12-17-75	R	Utah	D7/99	
50	Killens, Terry	6-1/235	3-24-74	4	Penn State	D3/96	16/1
51	Marts, Lonnie	6-2/250	11-10-68	10	Tulane	FA/97	16/15
55	Robinson, Eddie	6-1/243	4-13-70	8	Alabama State	FA/98	16/16
56	Stallings, Dennis	6-0/240	5-25-74	3	Illinois	D6/97	15/0
52	Wortham, Barron	5-11/245	11-1-69	6	Texas-El Paso	D6b/94	13/0
	DEFENSIVE BACKS						
23	Bishop, Blaine (S)	5-9/203	7-24-70	7	Ball State	D8/93	13/13
33	Dorsett, Anthony (CB)	5-11/200	9-14-73	4	Pittsburgh	D6/96	16/0
24	Jackson, Steve (CB)	5-8/188	4-8-69	9	Purdue	D3a/91	14/4
29	Lewis, Darryll (CB)	5-9/186	12-16-68	9	Arizona	D2b/91	16/15
36	McCullough, George (CB)	5-10/187	2-18-75	2	Baylor	D5/97	6/0
30	Mitchell, Donald	5-9/185	12-14-76	R	Southern Methodist	D4b/99	—
35	Phenix, Perry (S)	5-11/210	11-14-74	2	Southern Mississippi	FA/98	15/3
31	Robertson, Marcus (S)	5-11/205	10-2-69	9	Iowa State	D4b/91	12/12
21	Rolle, Samari (CB)	6-0/175	8-10-76	2	Florida State	D2/98	15/1
37	Sidney, Dainon (CB)	6-0/188	5-30-75	2	Alabama-Birmingham	D3/98	16/1
25	Walker, Denard (CB)	6-1/190	8-9-73	3	Louisiana State	D3a/97	16/16
36	Ware, Brad (S)	6-1/207	3-26-78	R	Auburn	D4a/99	—
	SPECIALISTS						
3	Del Greco, Al (K)	5-10/202	3-2-62	16	Auburn	FA/91	16/0
15	Hentrich, Craig (P)	6-3/205	5-18-71	6	Notre Dame	UFA/98	16/0

*Not with Titans (Oilers) in 1998.

Other free agents invited to camp: G Ben Adams, DT Albrey Battle, P Jason Bloom, TE Josh Bradley, TE Aaron Bryant, WR Maurice Bryant, WR Everett Burnett, DB Israel Byrd, DE Matt Caliandro, LB Delaunta Cameron, TE Tony Church, C Jason Gamble, G Lonnie Gilbert, FB Garett Gould, C Craig Page, T Ian Rafferty, S Kelvin Sigler, LB David Stroshine, DL Chris Ward.

Abbreviations: D1—draft pick, first round; SupD2—supplemental draft pick, second round; WV—claimed on waivers; TR—obtained in trade; PlanB—Plan B free-agent acquisition; FA—free-agent acquisition (other than Plan B); ED—expansion draft pick.

MISCELLANEOUS TEAM DATA

Stadium (capacity, surface):
East Bank Stadium
(67,000, grass)
Business address:
460 Great Circle Road
Nashville, TN 37228
Business phone:
615-733-3100
Ticket information:
To be announced
Team colors:
Navy, red, Titan blue and white
Flagship radio station:
WGFX, 104.5 FM
Training site:
460 Great Circle Road
Nashville, TN 37228
615-733-3100

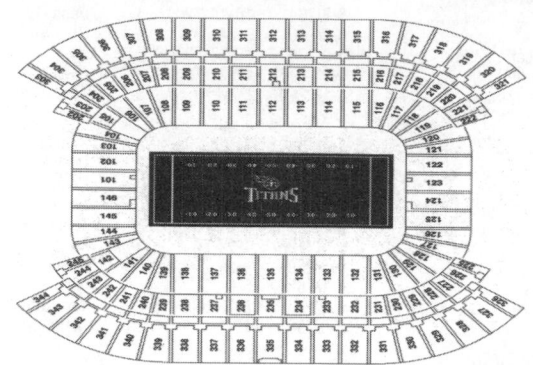

TSN REPORT CARD

Coaching staff	C	Three straight 8-8 seasons are as average as you can be. To improve the grade, the Titans have to make the postseason. But they have been unable to avoid season-killing losing streaks each year.
Quarterbacks	B	Steve McNair is the key to this offense. If he can get teams to respect the passing game, Eddie George will be that much more effective. McNair needs to be better inside the 20, but he doesn't make the kinds of mistakes that lose games. He also plays his best when the heat is on.
Running backs	B +	Eddie George is a punishing offensive weapon and adding Lorenzo Neal has the potential to be a blockbuster move if the team actually uses him. Rodney Thomas is a quality backup.
Receivers	C -	They took a lot of heat for the team's offensive struggles last season. In response, the receivers quietly said they didn't get the looks. That's partly true, but the other half of the story is their routes weren't always good enough, they dropped balls and almost never turned a bad pass into a big gain. They have to be better in '99.
Offensive line	B	This is a quality group because of Brad Hopkins, Bruce Matthews and Jon Runyan. The question marks are at guard, now that Matthews will likely move to center, but if they're answered effectively the Titans will be able to move the ball.
Defensive line	B -	If last year's group had returned intact, the grade would be a D, but the makeover is fairly complete. Three new starters are expected in the four slots. They need to hit the opposing quarterback far more than they have. If they don't, the team will miss the playoffs again.
Linebackers	B	Moving Joe Bowden back outside will help. Barron Wortham has a balky knee in the middle, but he is a productive player who is physical in the running game. Eddie Robinson is a good fit on the outside. They need to make more plays, force more turnovers.
Secondary	B +	Good quality here. Blaine Bishop is consistently one of the team's best players. If he can stay healthy, he should make another Pro Bowl. Marcus Robertson needs to stay healthy as well. Overall, they need to challenge receivers more than they have and win more of the battles.
Special teams	A	This grade is for the kickers—the return game is subpar and has been for much of the last four years. The Titans did little to fix that, but the fact they keep mistakes to a minimum means they aren't hurt too much by them.

WASHINGTON REDSKINS
NFC EASTERN DIVISION

1999 SEASON

CLUB DIRECTORY

President
John Kent Cooke
House counsel
Stuart Haney
Controller
Mark Francis
General manager
Charley Casserly
Assistant general manager
Bobby Mitchell
Director of player development
Joe Mendes
Director of college scouting
George Saimes
Scouts
Gene Bates   Larry Bryan
Scott Cohen   Mike Maccagnan
Miller McCalmon   Joel Patton
Dave Sears
Coordinator of scouting
Chuck Banker
Scouting administrator
Ray Wright
Director of public relations
Mike McCall
Director of media relations
Chris Helein
Publications/Internet director
Scott McKeen
Community relations director
Wendy Brinker
Director of administration
Barry Asimos
Vice president marketing
John Kent Cooke, Jr.
Director of marketing
John Wagner
Video director
Donnie Schoenmann
Assistant video director
Hugh McPhillips

Head coach
Norv Turner

Assistant coaches
Jason Arapoff (conditioning dir.)
Rubin Carter (co-defensive line)
Jeff Fitzgerald (defensive
  assistant/linebackers)
Russ Grimm (offensive line)
Tom Hayes (def. backs)
Bobby Jackson (running backs)
Earl Leggett (co-defensive line)
LeCharls McDaniel (special
  teams)
Mike Nolan (defensive coord.)
Rich Olson (quarterbacks)
Michael Pope (tight ends)
Dan Riley (strength)
Terry Robiskie (wide receivers)
Ed Sidwell (offensive assistant)

Ticket manager
Jeff Ritter
Vice president/stadium operations
Jeff Klein
Head trainer
Bubba Tyer
Assistant trainers
Al Bellamy, Kevin Bastin
Equipment manager
Jay Brunetti
Asst. equipment manager
Jeff Parsons

SCHEDULE

Sept. 12—	DALLAS	1:00
Sept. 19—	at N.Y. Giants	1:00
Sept. 26—	at N.Y. Jets	1:00
Oct. 3—	CAROLINA	4:05
Oct. 10—	Open date	
Oct. 17—	at Arizona	5:20
Oct. 24—	at Dallas	12:00
Oct. 31—	CHICAGO	1:00
Nov. 7—	BUFFALO	1:00
Nov. 14—	at Philadelphia	1:00
Nov. 21—	N.Y. GIANTS	4:15
Nov. 28—	PHILADELPHIA	1:00
Dec. 5—	at Detroit	1:00
Dec. 12—	ARIZONA	1:00
Dec. 19—	at Indianapolis	1:00
Dec. 26—	at San Francisco	5:20
Jan. 2—	MIAMI	4:15

All times are for home team.
All games Sunday unless noted.

DRAFT CHOICES

Champ Bailey, DB, Georgia (first
  round/seventh pick overall).
Jon Jansen, T, Michigan (2/37).
Nate Stimson, LB, Georgia Tech (4/107).
Derek Smith, T, Virginia Tech (5/165).
Jeff Hall, K, Tennessee (6/181).
Tim Alexander, WR, Oregon State
  (7/217).

1998 REVIEW

RESULTS

Sept. 6—at N.Y. Giants	L	24-31
Sept.14—SAN FRANCISCO	L	10-45
Sept.20—at Seattle	L	14-24
Sept.27—DENVER	L	16-38
Oct. 4—DALLAS	L	10-31
Oct. 11—at Philadelphia	L	12-17
Oct. 18—at Minnesota	L	7-41
Oct. 25—Open date		
Nov. 1—N.Y. GIANTS	W	21-14
Nov. 8—at Arizona	L	27-29
Nov. 15—PHILADELPHIA	W	28-3
Nov. 22—ARIZONA	L	42-45
Nov. 29—at Oakland	W	29-19
Dec. 6—SAN DIEGO	W	24-20
Dec. 13—at Carolina	W	28-25
Dec. 19—TAMPA BAY	W	20-16
Dec. 27—at Dallas	L	7-23

RECORDS/RANKINGS

1998 regular-season record: 6-10 (4th in
NFC East); 2-6 in division; 4-8 in conference; 4-4 at home; 2-6 on road.
Team record last five years: 32-47-1
(.406, ranks 21st in league in that span).
1998 team rankings:

	No.	NFC	NFL
Total offense	*313.1	8	15
Rushing offense	*105.3	10	18
Passing offense	*207.8	7	13
Scoring offense	319	8	17
Total defense	*334.6	13	24
Rushing defense	*152.3	15	28
Passing defense	*182.4	4	5
Scoring defense	421	15	28
Takeaways	21	T13	T25
Giveaways	29	7	15
Turnover differential	-8	12	T24
Sacks	33	14	26
Sacks allowed	61	15	29

*Yards per game.

TEAM LEADERS

Scoring (kicking): Cary Blanchard, 63
pts. (30/31 PATs, 11/17 FGs).
Scoring (touchdowns): Leslie Shepherd,
56 pts. (1 rushing, 8 receiving, 1 2-pt.
conv.).
Passing: Trent Green, 3,441 yds. (509
att., 278 comp., 54.6%, 23 TDs, 11 int.).
Rushing: Terry Allen, 700 yds. (148 att.,
4.7 avg., 2 TDs).
Receptions: Michael Westbrook, 44 (736
yds., 16.7 avg., 6 TDs).
Interceptions: Leomont Evans, 3 (77 yds.,
0 TDs); Darrell Green, 3 (36 yds., 0 TDs).
Sacks: Dan Wilkinson, 7.5.
Punting: Matt Turk, 44.1 avg. (93 punts,
4,103 yds., 1 blocked).
Punt returns: Brian Mitchell, 11.5 avg.
(44 att., 506 yds., 0 TDs).
Kickoff returns: Brian Mitchell, 22.7 avg.
(59 att., 1,337 yds., 1 TD).

WASHINGTON REDSKINS

No.	QUARTERBACKS	Ht./Wt.	Born	NFL Exp.	College	How acq.	'98 Games GP/GS
14	Johnson, Brad	6-5/224	9-13-68	8	Florida State	T-Min./99	*4/2
16	Peete, Rodney	6-0/225	3-16-66	11	Southern California	T-Phi./99	*5/4

RUNNING BACKS

No.	Name	Ht./Wt.	Born	NFL Exp.	College	How acq.	'98 Games GP/GS
47	Bowie, Larry (FB)	6-0/249	3-21-73	4	Georgia	FA/96	5/4
48	Davis, Stephen	6-0/234	3-1-74	4	Auburn	D4/96	16/12
20	Hicks, Skip	6-0/230	10-13-74	2	UCLA	D3/98	9/5
30	Mitchell, Brian	5-10/221	8-18-68	10	Southwestern Louisiana	D5/90	16/0
45	Sellers, Mike (FB)	6-3/260	7-21-75	2		FA/98	14/1

RECEIVERS

No.	Name	Ht./Wt.	Born	NFL Exp.	College	How acq.	'98 Games GP/GS
80	Alexander, Stephen (TE)	6-4/246	11-7-75	2	Oklahoma	D2/98	15/5
86	Alexander, Tim	6-0/186	10-14-74	R	Oregon State	D7/99	—
83	Connell, Albert	6-0/179	5-13-74	3	Texas A&M	D4/97	14/5
88	Jenkins, James (TE)	6-2/249	8-17-67	8	Rutgers	FA/91	16/4
85	Lusk, Henry (TE)	6-2/250	5-8-72	3	Utah	FA/99	*3/1
46	Sadowski, Troy (TE)	6-5/252	12-8-65	10	Georgia	UFA/99	*5/0
89	Thomas, Chris	6-2/190	7-16-71	4	Cal Poly-SLO	FA/97	14/0
87	Thrash, James	6-0/200	4-28-75	3	Missouri Southern	FA/97	10/1
82	Westbrook, Michael	6-3/220	7-7-72	5	Colorado	D1/95	11/10

OFFENSIVE LINEMEN

No.	Name	Ht./Wt.	Born	NFL Exp.	College	How acq.	'98 Games GP/GS
74	Badger, Brad (G)	6-4/298	1-11-75	3	Stanford	D5d/97	16/16
73	Brown, Jamie (T)	6-8/318	4-24-72	5	Florida A&M	FA/99	*8/5
60	Fischer, Mark (C)	6-3/293	7-29-74	2	Purdue	D5/98	6/0
76	Jansen, Jon (T)	6-6/302	1-28-76	R	Michigan	D2/99	—
77	Johnson, Tre' (G)	6-2/326	8-30-71	6	Temple	D2/94	10/10
69	Milstead, Rod (G)	6-2/290	11-10-69	8	Delaware State	FA/98	14/11
68	Patton, Joe (T)	6-5/306	1-5-72	5	Alabama A&M	D3b/94	11/10
67	Pourdanesh, Shar (T)	6-6/312	7-19-70	4	Nevada	FA/96	16/15
52	Raymer, Cory (C)	6-2/289	3-3-73	5	Wisconsin	D2/95	16/16
63	Sims, Keith (G)	6-3/318	6-17-67	10	Iowa State	FA/98	4/0
62	Smith, Derek (T)	6-6/309	4-13-76	R	Virginia Tech	D5/99	—
66	Turk, Dan (C)	6-4/290	6-25-62	15	Wisconsin	FA/97	16/0

DEFENSIVE LINEMEN

No.	Name	Ht./Wt.	Born	NFL Exp.	College	How acq.	'98 Games GP/GS
93	Boutte, Marc (T)	6-4/307	7-26-69	8	Louisiana State	FA/94	13/1
78	Brown, Doug (T)	6-7/290	9-29-74	2	Simon Fraser	FA/98	10/8
	Coleman, Marco (E)	6-3/267	12-18-69	8	Georgia Tech	UFA/99	*16/16
75	Cook, Anthony (E)	6-3/295	5-30-72	5	South Carolina State	UFA/99	*13/3
91	Hoelscher, David (T)	6-5/285	11-27-75	2	Eastern Kentucky	FA/98	1/0
72	Kalu, Ndukwe (E)	6-3/246	8-3-75	3	Rice	FA/98	13/1
97	Kinney, Kelvin (E)	6-6/264	12-31-72	4	Virginia State	D6/96	14/12
90	Lang, Kenard (E)	6-4/277	1-31-75	3	Miami (Fla.)	D1/97	16/16
94	Stubblefield, Dana (T)	6-2/315	11-14-70	7	Kansas	UFA/98	7/7
95	Wilkinson, Dan (T)	6-5/313	3-13-73	6	Ohio State	T-Cin./98	16/16

LINEBACKERS

No.	Name	Ht./Wt.	Born	NFL Exp.	College	How acq.	'98 Games GP/GS
59	Barber, Shawn	6-2/224	1-14-75	2	Richmond	D4/98	16/1
56	Burnett, Chester	5-10/238	4-15-75	2	Arizona	FA/98	5/0
58	Hamilton, Malcolm	6-1/235	12-31-72	2	Baylor	FA/98	2/0
57	Harvey, Ken	6-2/237	5-6-65	12	California	UFA/94	11/9
54	Jones, Greg	6-4/238	5-22-74	3	Colorado	D2/97	16/5
51	Ponds, Antwuane	6-2/239	6-29-75	2	Syracuse	D3/97	3/0
98	Russell, Twan	6-1/219	4-25-74	3	Miami (Fla.)	D5c/97	3/0
50	Smith, Derek	6-2/239	1-18-75	3	Arizona State	D3/97	16/15
53	Stimson, Nate	6-2/253	3-4-76	R	Georgia Tech	D4/99	—
55	Strickland, Fred	6-2/251	8-15-66	12	Purdue	FA/99	*16/15

DEFENSIVE BACKS

No.	Name	Ht./Wt.	Born	NFL Exp.	College	How acq.	'98 Games GP/GS
24	Bailey, Champ (CB)	6-1/184	6-22-78	R	Georgia	D1/99	—
41	Crutchfield, Buddy (CB)	6-0/196	3-7-76	2	North Carolina Central	FA/98	2/0
25	Denton, Tim	5-11/182	2-2-73	2	Sam Houston	FA/98	16/0
35	Evans, Leomont (S)	6-1/202	7-12-74	4	Clemson	D5/96	16/13
27	Evans, Greg (S)	6-1/208	6-28-71	3	Texas Christian	FA/97	13/0
28	Green, Darrell (CB)	5-8/184	2-15-60	17	Texas A&I	D1/83	16/16
31	Pounds, Darryl (CB)	5-10/189	7-21-72	5	Nicholls State	D3/95	16/3
35	Shade, Sam (S)	6-1/201	6-14-73	4	Alabama	UFA/99	*16/14
23	Stevens, Matt (S)	6-0/206	6-15-73	4	Appalachian State	W-Phi./98	10/1
22	Williams, Jamel (S)	5-11/205	12-22-73	3	Nebraska	D5a/97	16/0

SPECIALISTS

No.	Name	Ht./Wt.	Born	NFL Exp.	College	How acq.	'98 Games GP/GS
17	Blanchard, Cary (K)	6-1/232	11-5-68	8	Oklahoma State	FA/98	13/0
10	Conway, Brett (K)	6-2/192	3-8-75	3	Penn State	FA/98	6/0
4	Hall, Jeff (K)	5-11/190	7-30-76	R	Tennessee	D6/99	—
7	Turk, Matt (P)	6-5/237	6-16-68	5	Wisconsin-Whitewater	FA/95	16/0

*Not with Redskins in 1998.

Other free agents invited to camp: WR Kevin Alexander, CB Raphael Ball, G Lamont Burns, P Travis Colquitt, RB Leroy Collins, RB Chad Dukes, DE Derrick Ham, WR Junior Lord, RB Norman Miller, WR Kenny Mitchell, QB John Paci, S Kevin Peoples, FB Kevin Pesak, T Ozell Powell, CB Tyrone Smith, DE Rahmaan Streater, TE Robert Tardio, WR Derrius Thompson, T Kipp Vickers, DT Rod Walker, G Mike Webster, QB Casey Weldon, WR Nigel Williams.

Abbreviations: D1—draft pick, first round; SupD2—supplemental draft pick, second round; WV—claimed on waivers; TR—obtained in trade; PlanB—Plan B free-agent acquisition; FA—free-agent acquisition (other than Plan B); ED—expansion draft pick.

MISCELLANEOUS TEAM DATA

Stadium (capacity, surface):
Jack Kent Cooke
Stadium (80,116, grass)
Business address:
P.O. Box 17247
Dulles International Airport
Washington, D.C. 20041
Business phone:
703-478-8900
Ticket information:
301-276-6050
Team colors:
Burgundy and gold
Flagship radio station:
WJFK, 106.7 FM
Training site:
Frostburg State University
Frostburg, Md.
301-687-7975

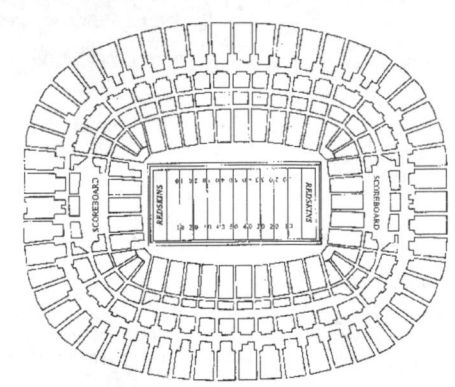

TSN REPORT CARD

Coaching staff	C	Norv Turner needs to do more than talk about the players understanding that a sense of urgency is needed—he needs to get them to perform with that sense of urgency. Coordinator Mike Nolan and his staff must design defenses that surprise and disrupt. Rubin Carter has been added to help Earl Leggett with the defensive line, and a different perspective should benefit everyone.
Quarterbacks	B	Brad Johnson is the best quarterback the Redskins have had in five years. He's smart, accurate and experienced. But he needs protection and he needs to stay healthy. Rodney Peete and Casey Weldon are adequate backups, but expecting either to step in and duplicate Trent Green's performance last season is not realistic. Johnson's blockers have to keep him upright.
Running backs	B	Skip Hicks has the jets you're looking for in a running back. He's young and should be durable. If he can run between the tackles, the Redskins will have a more than adequate replacement for Terry Allen. Hicks makes big plays, his blockers seem to have confidence in him and he has an uncanny knack for scoring touchdowns.
Receivers	D	No one in this unit has displayed consistent, season-long performances. Michael Westbrook is coming off an injury, Albert Connell is largely untested as a starter and the backups have been inconsistent. Tight end Stephen Alexander has the hands, speed and size to move into the upper echelon of the league at the position.
Offensive line	D	Rookie tackle Jon Jansen should solidify the right side of the line, but moving Shar Pourdanesh to the left side to compete with Joe Patton at tackle does not necessarily make that position stronger. Tre' Johnson's shoulders and knees make him an iffy proposition to play an entire season, and when you start with a questionable left side, you're starting with problems.
Defensive line	C	There's plenty of talent here, with three first-round draft choices starting. For whatever reason, this group underachieved last season, and that can't happen again. Dana Stubblefield and Dan Wilkinson are being paid a lot of money to stop the run and collapse the pocket, and they need to make good on that.
Linebackers	B -	What this group lacks is experience as a unit. But they're young, aggressive and fast. All three starters have shown the ability to make plays. Now, they have to do it week after week.
Secondary	B	If Darrell Green plays as he has his entire career, and if Champ Bailey is everything he's expected to be, this could be a very effective unit. Leomont Evans has to adapt quickly at free safety.
Special teams	C	Matt Turk is consistent as a punter, as is Brian Mitchell on returns. The nemesis for these units has been a lack of consistency and focus from the other players.

SCHEDULE

PRESEASON

(All times local, except Aug. 8 game in Australia, which is Eastern)

WEEK 1

SATURDAY, AUGUST 7

Indianapolis at Chicago	7:00
Oakland at St. Louis	7:00
Denver vs. San Diego at Sydney, Australia	9:00

MONDAY, AUGUST 9

Cleveland vs. Dallas at Canton, Ohio	8:00

WEEK 2

THURSDAY, AUGUST 12

Baltimore at Philadelphia	8:00
San Diego at San Francisco	5:00

FRIDAY, AUGUST 13

Carolina at Jacksonville	7:30
Chicago at Pittsburgh	7:30
Detroit at Atlanta	7:30
New Orleans at Miami	7:30
N.Y. Giants at Minnesota	7:00
Washington at New England	7:30

SATURDAY, AUGUST 14

Arizona at Denver	7:00
Buffalo at Seattle	6:00
Cincinnati at Indianapolis	7:00
Cleveland at Tampa Bay	8:00
N.Y. Jets at Green Bay	7:00

SUNDAY, AUGUST 15

Dallas at Oakland	1:00
Tennessee at Kansas City	7:30

WEEK 3

THURSDAY, AUGUST 19

Seattle at San Francisco	5:00

FRIDAY, AUGUST 20

Buffalo at Washington	8:00
Cincinnati at Detroit	7:00
Philadelphia at N.Y. Jets	7:30
Pittsburgh at Carolina	8:00
Tennessee at Arizona	7:00

SATURDAY, AUGUST 21

Baltimore at Atlanta	7:30
Dallas at New England	8:00
Indianapolis at New Orleans	7:00
Jacksonville at N.Y. Giants	7:00
Miami at San Diego	8:00
Minnesota at Cleveland	7:00

St. Louis at Chicago	7:00
Tampa Bay at Kansas City	7:30

MONDAY, AUGUST 23

Denver vs. Green Bay at Madison, Wis.	7:00

WEEK 4

THURSDAY, AUGUST 26

Kansas City at Jacksonville	8:00
Philadelphia at Minnesota	7:00

FRIDAY, AUGUST 27

Atlanta at Tennessee	7:00

SATURDAY, AUGUST 28

Arizona at Seattle	7:00
Buffalo at Cincinnati	7:30
Carolina at Baltimore	7:30
Chicago at Cleveland	8:00
Detroit at Miami	7:00
Green Bay at New Orleans	7:00
New England at Tampa Bay	8:00
N.Y. Jets at N.Y. Giants	8:00
San Diego at St. Louis	7:00
Washington at Pittsburgh	7:30

SUNDAY, AUGUST 29

Denver at Dallas	7:00

MONDAY, AUGUST 30

San Francisco at Oakland	5:00

WEEK 5

THURSDAY, SEPTEMBER 2

Cleveland at Philadelphia	7:30
St. Louis at Detroit	7:00
Jacksonville at Dallas	8:00
Miami at Green Bay	7:00
New England at Carolina	8:00
New Orleans at Tennessee	7:00
Seattle at Indianapolis	7:00

FRIDAY, SEPTEMBER 3

Atlanta at Cincinnati	7:30
Kansas City at San Diego	8:00
Minnesota at N.Y. Jets	7:30
New York Giants at Baltimore	TBA
Oakland at Arizona	7:00
San Francisco at Denver	7:00
Tampa Bay at Washington	8:00

SATURDAY, SEPTEMBER 4

Pittsburgh at Buffalo	7:30

REGULAR SEASON

(All times local)

WEEK 1

SUNDAY, SEPTEMBER 12

Arizona at Philadelphia	1:00
Baltimore at St. Louis	12:00
Buffalo at Indianapolis	12:00
Carolina at New Orleans	12:00

Cincinnati at Tennessee	12:00
Dallas at Washington	1:00
Detroit at Seattle	1:15
Kansas City at Chicago	12:00
Minnesota at Atlanta	4:15
New England at N.Y. Jets	1:00
N.Y. Giants at Tampa Bay	4:15
Oakland at Green Bay	12:00

San Francisco at Jacksonville... 4:15
Pittsburgh at Cleveland... 8:20

MONDAY, SEPTEMBER 13

Miami at Denver... 7:00
    Open date: San Diego

WEEK 2

SUNDAY, SEPTEMBER 19

Arizona at Miami... 1:00
Cleveland at Tennessee... 3:15
Denver at Kansas City.. 3:15
Green Bay at Detroit.. 1:00
Indianapolis at New England.. 1:00
Jacksonville at Carolina.. 1:00
New Orleans at San Francisco... 1:05
Oakland at Minnesota... 12:00
Pittsburgh at Baltimore... 1:00
San Diego at Cincinnati.. 1:00
Seattle at Chicago.. 12:00
Tampa Bay at Philadelphia.. 1:00
Washington at N.Y. Giants.. 1:00
N.Y. Jets at Buffalo... 8:20

MONDAY, SEPTEMBER 20

Atlanta at Dallas.. 8:00
    Open date: St. Louis

WEEK 3

SUNDAY, SEPTEMBER 26

Atlanta at St. Louis... 12:00
Chicago at Oakland.. 1:15
Cincinnati at Carolina... 1:00
Cleveland at Baltimore.. 1:00
Denver at Tampa Bay.. 1:00
Detroit at Kansas City.. 12:00
Indianapolis at San Diego... 1:05
Minnesota at Green Bay... 3:15
Philadelphia at Buffalo.. 1:00
Seattle at Pittsburgh.. 1:00
Tennessee at Jacksonville... 4:05
Washington at N.Y. Jets... 1:00
N.Y. Giants at New England... 8:20

MONDAY, SEPTEMBER 27

San Francisco at Arizona.. 6:00
    Open date: Dallas, Miami, New Orleans

WEEK 4

SUNDAY, OCTOBER 3

Arizona at Dallas... 12:00
Baltimore at Atlanta.. 1:00
Carolina at Washington.. 4:05
Jacksonville at Pittsburgh... 1:00
Kansas City at San Diego... 1:15
New England at Cleveland... 1:00
New Orleans at Chicago... 12:00
N.Y. Jets at Denver... 2:15
Philadelphia at N.Y. Giants... 1:00
St. Louis at Cincinnati.. 1:00
Tampa Bay at Minnesota... 12:00
Tennessee at San Francisco... 1:15
Oakland at Seattle.. 5:20

MONDAY, OCTOBER 4

Buffalo at Miami.. 9:00
    Open date: Detroit, Green Bay, Indianapolis

WEEK 5

SUNDAY, OCTOBER 10

Atlanta at New Orleans.. 12:00
Baltimore at Tennessee.. 3:15

Chicago at Minnesota.. 12:00
Cincinnati at Cleveland.. 1:00
Dallas at Philadelphia... 1:00
Denver at Oakland... 1:15
Miami at Indianapolis.. 3:15
New England at Kansas City... 12:00
N.Y. Giants at Arizona.. 1:05
Pittsburgh at Buffalo.. 1:00
San Diego at Detroit.. 1:00
San Francisco at St. Louis.. 12:00
Tampa Bay at Green Bay... 7:20

MONDAY, OCTOBER 11

Jacksonville at N.Y. Jets.. 9:00
    Open date: Carolina, Seattle, Washington

WEEK 6

SUNDAY, OCTOBER 17

Carolina at San Francisco... 1:15
Cleveland at Jacksonville.. 1:00
Green Bay at Denver.. 2:15
Indianapolis at N.Y. Jets.. 1:00
Miami at New England... 1:00
Minnesota at Detroit.. 1:00
Oakland at Buffalo.. 1:00
Philadelphia at Chicago... 12:00
Pittsburgh at Cincinnati... 1:00
St. Louis at Atlanta... 1:00
Seattle at San Diego.. 1:05
Tennessee at New Orleans... 12:00
Washington at Arizona... 5:20

MONDAY, OCTOBER 18

Dallas at N.Y. Giants... 9:00
    Open date: Baltimore, Kansas City, Tampa Bay

WEEK 7

THURSDAY, OCTOBER 21

Kansas City at Baltimore.. 8:20

SUNDAY, OCTOBER 24

Buffalo at Seattle... 1:15
Chicago at Tampa Bay... 1:00
Cincinnati at Indianapolis... 12:00
Cleveland at St. Louis... 12:00
Denver at New England.. 1:00
Detroit at Carolina.. 1:00
Green Bay at San Diego... 1:05
New Orleans at N.Y. Giants... 1:00
N.Y. Jets at Oakland.. 1:15
Philadelphia at Miami... 1:00
San Francisco at Minnesota... 12:00
Washington at Dallas.. 12:00

MONDAY, OCTOBER 25

Atlanta at Pittsburgh.. 9:00
    Open date: Arizona, Jacksonville, Tennessee

WEEK 8

SUNDAY, OCTOBER 31

Buffalo at Baltimore... 1:00
Carolina at Atlanta.. 1:00
Chicago at Washington... 1:00
Cleveland at New Orleans.. 12:00
Dallas at Indianapolis... 1:00
Jacksonville at Cincinnati.. 1:00
Miami at Oakland.. 1:05
Minnesota at Denver... 2:15
New England at Arizona.. 2:05
N.Y. Giants at Philadelphia.. 1:00
St. Louis at Tennessee.. 12:00
San Diego at Kansas City... 12:00
Tampa Bay at Detroit.. 8:20

MONDAY, NOVEMBER 1

Seattle at Green Bay 8:00
    Open date: N.Y. Jets, Pittsburgh, San Francisco

WEEK 9

SUNDAY, NOVEMBER 7

Arizona at N.Y. Jets	1:00
Baltimore at Cleveland	1:00
Buffalo at Washington	1:00
Chicago at Green Bay	12:00
Cincinnati at Seattle	1:15
Denver at San Diego	1:15
Jacksonville at Atlanta	1:00
Kansas City at Indianapolis	1:00
Philadelphia at Carolina	1:00
Pittsburgh at San Francisco	1:15
St. Louis at Detroit	1:00
Tampa Bay at New Orleans	3:05
Tennessee at Miami	8:20

MONDAY, NOVEMBER 8

Dallas at Minnesota 8:00
    Open date: N.Y. Giants, New England, Oakland

WEEK 10

SUNDAY, NOVEMBER 14

Baltimore at Jacksonville	4:05
Carolina at St. Louis	12:00
Cleveland at Pittsburgh	1:00
Detroit at Arizona	2:15
Green Bay at Dallas	3:15
Indianapolis at N.Y. Giants	1:00
Kansas City at Tampa Bay	1:00
Miami at Buffalo	1:00
Minnesota at Chicago	12:00
San Diego at Oakland	1:05
San Francisco at New Orleans	12:00
Tennessee at Cincinnati	1:00
Washington at Philadelphia	1:00
Denver at Seattle	5:20

MONDAY, NOVEMBER 15

N.Y. Jets at New England 9:00
    Open date: Atlanta

WEEK 11

SUNDAY, NOVEMBER 21

Atlanta at Tampa Bay	1:00
Baltimore at Cincinnati	4:05
Buffalo at N.Y. Jets	1:00
Carolina at Cleveland	1:00
Chicago at San Diego	1:15
Dallas at Arizona	2:15
Detroit at Green Bay	12:00
Indianapolis at Philadelphia	1:00
New England at Miami	1:00
N.Y. Giants at Washington	4:15
Pittsburgh at Tennessee	12:00
St. Louis at San Francisco	1:15
Seattle at Kansas City	12:00
New Orleans at Jacksonville	8:20

MONDAY, NOVEMBER 22

Oakland at Denver 7:00
    Open date: Minnesota

WEEK 12

THURSDAY, NOVEMBER 25

Chicago at Detroit	12:40
Miami at Dallas	3:15

SUNDAY, NOVEMBER 28

Arizona at N.Y. Giants	1:00
Cincinnati at Pittsburgh	1:00
Jacksonville at Baltimore	1:00
Kansas City at Oakland	1:15
New England at Buffalo	1:00
New Orleans at St. Louis	12:00
N.Y. Jets at Indianapolis	4:15
Philadelphia at Washington	1:00
San Diego at Minnesota	12:00
Tampa Bay at Seattle	1:05
Tennessee at Cleveland	1:00
Atlanta at Carolina	8:20

MONDAY, NOVEMBER 29

Green Bay at San Francisco 6:00
    Open date: Denver

WEEK 13

THURSDAY, DECEMBER 2

Pittsburgh at Jacksonville 8:20

SUNDAY, DECEMBER 5

Cleveland at San Diego	1:15
Green Bay at Chicago	12:00
Indianapolis at Miami	1:00
Kansas City at Denver	2:15
New Orleans at Atlanta	1:00
N.Y. Jets at N.Y. Giants	1:00
Philadelphia at Arizona	2:05
St. Louis at Carolina	1:00
San Francisco at Cincinnati	1:00
Seattle at Oakland	1:15
Tennessee at Baltimore	1:00
Washington at Detroit	1:00
Dallas at New England	8:20

MONDAY, DECEMBER 6

Minnesota at Tampa Bay 9:00
    Open date: Buffalo

WEEK 14

THURSDAY, DECEMBER 9

Oakland at Tennessee 7:20

SUNDAY, DECEMBER 12

Arizona at Washington	1:00
Atlanta at San Francisco	1:15
Baltimore at Pittsburgh	1:00
Carolina at Green Bay	12:00
Cleveland at Cincinnati	1:00
Detroit at Tampa Bay	1:00
Miami at N.Y. Jets	4:05
New England at Indianapolis	1:00
N.Y. Giants at Buffalo	1:00
Philadelphia at Dallas	12:00
St. Louis at New Orleans	12:00
San Diego at Seattle	1:05
Minnesota at Kansas City	7:20

MONDAY, DECEMBER 13

Denver at Jacksonville 9:00
    Open date: Chicago

WEEK 15

SATURDAY, DECEMBER 18

Pittsburgh at Kansas City	11:40
San Francisco at Carolina	4:15

SUNDAY, DECEMBER 19

Atlanta at Tennessee	12:00
Detroit at Chicago	12:00

Jacksonville at Cleveland	1:00
New England at Philadelphia	1:00
New Orleans at Baltimore	1:00
N.Y. Giants at St. Louis	12:00
N.Y. Jets at Dallas	3:15
San Diego at Miami	1:00
Seattle at Denver	2:15
Tampa Bay at Oakland	1:05
Washington at Indianapolis	1:00
Buffalo at Arizona	6:20

MONDAY, DECEMBER 20

Green Bay at Minnesota	8:00

Open date: Cincinnati

WEEK 16

FRIDAY, DECEMBER 24

Dallas at New Orleans	2:05

SATURDAY, DECEMBER 25

Denver at Detroit	4:15

SUNDAY, DECEMBER 26

Arizona at Atlanta	1:00
Buffalo at New England	1:00
Carolina at Pittsburgh	1:00
Chicago at St. Louis	12:00
Cincinnati at Baltimore	1:00
Green Bay at Tampa Bay	4:15
Indianapolis at Cleveland	1:00
Jacksonville at Tennessee	12:00

Kansas City at Seattle	1:05
Minnesota at N.Y. Giants	1:00
Oakland at San Diego	1:05
Washington at San Francisco	5:20

MONDAY, DECEMBER 27

N.Y. Jets at Miami	9:00

Open date: Philadelphia

WEEK 17

SUNDAY, JANUARY 2

Arizona at Green Bay	12:00
Baltimore at New England	1:00
Cincinnati at Jacksonville	1:00
Detroit at Minnesota	12:00
Indianapolis at Buffalo	1:00
Miami at Washington	4:15
New Orleans at Carolina	1:00
N.Y. Giants at Dallas	3:05
Oakland at Kansas City	12:00
St. Louis at Philadelphia	1:00
San Diego at Denver	2:15
Seattle at N.Y. Jets	1:00
Tampa Bay at Chicago	12:00
Tennessee at Pittsburgh	4:15

MONDAY, JANUARY 3

San Francisco at Atlanta	9:00

Open date: Cleveland

NATIONALLY TELEVISED GAMES

(All times local)

REGULAR SEASON

Sun. Sept. 12— Minnesota at Atlanta (4:15, FOX)
Pittsburgh at Cleveland (8:20, ESPN)
Mon. Sept. 13— Miami at Denver (7:00, ABC)
Sun. Sept. 19— Denver at Kansas City (3:15, CBS)
N.Y. Jets at Buffalo (8:20, ESPN)
Mon. Sept. 20— Atlanta at Dallas (8:00, ABC)
Sun. Sept. 26— Minnesota at Green Bay (3:15, FOX)
N.Y. Giants at New England (8:20, ESPN)
Mon. Sept. 27— San Francisco at Arizona (6:00, ABC)
Sun. Oct. 3— N.Y. Jets at Denver (2:15, CBS)
Oakland at Seattle (5:20, ESPN)
Mon. Oct. 4— Buffalo at Miami (9:00, ABC)
Sun. Oct. 10— Denver at Oakland (1:15, CBS)
Tampa Bay at Green Bay (7:20, ESPN)
Mon. Oct. 11— Jacksonville at New York Jets (9:00, ABC)
Sun. Oct. 17— Green Bay at Denver (2:15, FOX)
Washington at Arizona (5:20, ESPN)
Mon. Oct. 18— Dallas at N.Y. Giants (9:00, ABC)
Thur. Oct. 21— Kansas City at Baltimore (8:20, ESPN)
Sun. Oct. 24— N.Y. Jets at Oakland (1:15, CBS)
Mon. Oct. 25— Atlanta at Pittsburgh (9:00, ABC)
Sun. Oct. 31— Minnesota at Denver (2:15, FOX)
Tampa Bay at Detroit (8:20, ESPN)
Mon. Nov. 1— Seattle at Green Bay (8:00, ABC)
Sun. Nov. 7— Pittsburgh at San Francisco (1:15, CBS)
Tennessee at Miami (8:20, ESPN)
Mon. Nov. 8— Dallas at Minnesota (8:00, ABC)
Sun. Nov. 14— Green Bay at Dallas (3:15, FOX)
Denver at Seattle (5:20, ESPN)
Mon. Nov. 15— N.Y. Jets at New England (9:00, ABC)
Sun. Nov. 21— Dallas at Arizona (2:15, FOX)
New Orleans at Jacksonville (8:20, ESPN)
Mon. Nov. 22— Oakland at Denver (7:00, ABC)

Thur. Nov. 25— Chicago at Detroit (12:40, FOX)
Miami at Dallas (3:15, CBS)
Sun. Nov. 28— Kansas City at Oakland (1:15, CBS)
Atlanta at Carolina (8:20, ESPN)
Mon. Nov. 29— Green Bay at San Francisco (6:00, ABC)
Thur. Dec. 2— Pittsburgh at Jacksonville (8:20, ESPN)
Sun. Dec. 5— Kansas City at Denver (2:15, CBS)
Dallas at New England (8:20, ESPN)
Mon. Dec. 6— Minnesota at Tampa Bay (9:00, ABC)
Thur. Dec. 9— Oakland at Tennessee (7:20, ESPN)
Sun. Dec. 12— Atlanta at San Francisco (4:15, FOX)
Minnesota at Kansas City (7:20, ESPN)
Mon. Dec. 13— Denver at Jacksonville (9:00, ABC)
Sat. Dec. 18— Pittsburgh at Kansas City (11:40, CBS)
San Francisco at Carolina (4:15, FOX)
Sun. Dec. 19— N.Y. Jets at Dallas (3:15, CBS)
Buffalo at Arizona (6:20, ESPN)
Mon. Dec. 20— Green Bay at Minnesota (8:00, ABC)
Fri. Dec. 24— Dallas at New Orleans (2:05, FOX)
Sat. Dec. 25— Denver at Detroit (4:15, CBS)
Sun. Dec. 26— Green Bay at Tampa Bay (4:15, FOX)
Washington at San Francisco (5:20, ESPN)
Mon. Dec. 27— N.Y. Jets at Miami (9:00, ABC)
Sun. Jan. 2— San Diego at Denver (2:15, CBS)
Mon. Jan. 3— San Francisco at Atlanta (9:00, ABC)

POSTSEASON

Sat. Jan. 8— AFC, NFC wild-card playoffs (ABC)
Sun. Jan. 9— AFC, NFC wild-card playoffs (CBS, FOX)
Sat. Jan. 15— AFC, NFC divisional playoffs (CBS, FOX)
Sun. Jan. 16— AFC, NFC divisional playoffs (CBS, FOX)
Sun. Jan. 23— AFC, NFC championship games (CBS, FOX)
Sun. Jan. 30— Super Bowl at Georgia Dome, Atlanta (ABC)
Sun. Feb. 6— Pro Bowl at Honolulu (ABC)

INTERCONFERENCE GAMES

(All times local)

Sun.	Sept. 12—	Baltimore at St. Louis	12:00
		Detroit at Seattle	1:15
		Kansas City at Chicago	12:00
		Oakland at Green Bay	12:00
		San Francisco at Jacksonville	4:15
Sun.	Sept. 19—	Arizona at Miami	1:00
		Jacksonville at Carolina	1:00
		Oakland at Minnesota	12:00
		Seattle at Chicago	12:00
Sun.	Sept. 26—	Chicago at Oakland	1:15
		Cincinnati at Carolina	1:00
		Denver at Tampa Bay	1:00
		Detroit at Kansas City	12:00
		Philadelphia at Buffalo	1:00
		Washington at N.Y. Jets	1:00
		N.Y. Giants at New England	8:20
Sun.	Oct. 3—	Baltimore at Atlanta	1:00
		St. Louis at Cincinnati	1:00
		Tennessee at San Francisco	1:15
Sun.	Oct. 10—	San Diego at Detroit	1:00
Sun.	Oct. 17—	Green Bay at Denver	2:15
		Tennessee at New Orleans	12:00
Sun.	Oct. 24—	Cleveland at St. Louis	12:00
		Green Bay at San Diego	1:05
		Philadelphia at Miami	1:00
Mon.	Oct. 25—	Atlanta at Pittsburgh	9:00
Sun.	Oct. 31—	Cleveland at New Orleans	12:00
		Dallas at Indianapolis	1:00
		Minnesota at Denver	2:15
		New England at Arizona	2:05

		St. Louis at Tennessee	12:00
Mon.	Nov. 1—	Seattle at Green Bay	8:00
Sun.	Nov. 7—	Arizona at N.Y. Jets	1:00
		Buffalo at Washington	1:00
		Jacksonville at Atlanta	1:00
		Pittsburgh at San Francisco	1:15
Sun.	Nov. 14—	Indianapolis at N.Y. Giants	1:00
		Kansas City at Tampa Bay	1:00
Sun.	Nov. 21—	Carolina at Cleveland	1:00
		Chicago at San Diego	1:15
		Indianapolis at Philadelphia	1:00
		New Orleans at Jacksonville	8:20
Thur.	Nov. 25—	Miami at Dallas	3:15
Sun.	Nov. 28—	San Diego at Minnesota	12:00
		Tampa Bay at Seattle	1:05
Sun.	Dec. 5—	N.Y. Jets at N.Y. Giants	1:00
		San Francisco at Cincinnati	1:00
		Dallas at New England	8:20
Sun.	Dec. 12—	N.Y. Giants at Buffalo	1:00
		Minnesota at Kansas City	7:20
Sun.	Dec. 19—	Atlanta at Tennessee	12:00
		New England at Philadelphia	1:00
		New Orleans at Baltimore	1:00
		N.Y. Jets at Dallas	3:15
		Tampa Bay at Oakland	1:05
		Washington at Indianapolis	1:00
		Buffalo at Arizona	6:20
Sat.	Dec. 25—	Denver at Detroit	4:15
Sun.	Dec. 26—	Carolina at Pittsburgh	1:00
Sun.	Jan. 2—	Miami at Washington	4:15

1999 STRENGTH OF SCHEDULE

(Teams are ranked from most difficult to easiest schedules, based on 1999 opponents' combined 1998 records)

	Team	Opp. Wins	Opp. Losses	Opp. Pct.
1.	Oakland (9)	146	110	.570
2.	N.Y. Jets (T20)	138	118	.539
	Tampa Bay (T3)	138	118	.539
4.	Arizona (30)	137	119	.535
	Denver (T15)	137	119	.535
6.	New England (T11)	127	113	.529
7.	Green Bay (8)	134	122	.523
	Minnesota (10)	134	122	.523
9.	San Diego (14)	125	115	.521
10.	Detroit (T5)	133	123	.520
11.	Indianapolis (T15)	124	116	.517
12.	Dallas (T23)	132	124	.516
13.	New Orleans (T25)	123	117	.513
14.	Miami (T27)	131	125	.512
15.	Seattle (T23)	128	128	.500
16.	Kansas City (19)	127	129	.4961

	Team	Opp. Wins	Opp. Losses	Opp. Pct.
17.	Pittsburgh (1)	111	113	.4955
18.	Atlanta (22)	126	130	.4922
	San Francisco (T27)	126	130	.4922
20.	Carolina (15)	118	122	.4917
21.	Jacksonville (7)	110	114	.491
22.	Chicago (2)	125	131	.488
23.	Baltimore (T11)	108	116	.482
	Tennessee (T5)	108	116	.482
25.	Buffalo (T27)	123	133	.480
26.	N.Y. Giants (18)	123	133	.480
27.	Washington (T25)	120	136	.469
28.	Philadelphia (T11)	118	138	.461
29.	St. Louis (T20)	109	131	.454
30.	Cincinnati (T3)	100	124	.446
31.	Cleveland	101	155	.395

NOTE: Number in parentheses is 1998 rank.

COLLEGE DRAFT

ROUND-BY-ROUND SELECTIONS, APRIL 17-18, 1999

FIRST ROUND

Team	Player selected	Pos.	College	Draft pick origination
1. Cleveland	Tim Couch	QB	Kentucky	
2. Philadelphia	Donovan McNabb	QB	Syracuse	
3. Cincinnati	Akili Smith	QB	Oregon	
4. Indianapolis	Edgerrin James	RB	Miami, Fla.	
5. New Orleans	Ricky Williams	RB	Texas	From Carolina through Washington
6. St. Louis	Torry Holt	WR	North Carolina State	
7. Washington	Champ Bailey	DB	Georgia	From Chicago
8. Arizona	David Boston	WR	Ohio State	From San Diego
9. Detroit	Chris Claiborne	LB	Southern California	
10. Baltimore	Chris McAlister	DB	Arizona	
11. Minnesota	Daunte Culpepper	QB	Central Florida	From Washington
12. Chicago	Cade McNown	QB	UCLA	From New Orleans through Washington
13. Pittsburgh	Troy Edwards	WR	Louisiana Tech	
14. Kansas City	John Tait	T	Brigham Young	
15. Tampa Bay	Anthony McFarland	DT	Louisiana State	
16. Tennessee	Jevon Kearse	LB	Florida	
17. New England	Damien Woody	C	Boston College	From Seattle
18. Oakland	Matt Stinchcomb	T	Georgia	
19. N.Y. Giants	Luke Petitgout	T	Notre Dame	
20. Dallas	Ebenezer Ekuban	DE	North Carolina	From New England through Seattle
21. Arizona	L.J. Shelton	T	Eastern Michigan	
22. Seattle	Lamar King	DE	Saginaw Valley State	From Dallas
23. Buffalo	Antoine Winfield	DB	Ohio State	
24. San Francisco	Reggie McGrew	DT	Florida	From Miami
25. Green Bay	Antuan Edwards	DB	Clemson	
26. Jacksonville	Fernando Bryant	DB	Alabama	
27. Detroit	Aaron Gibson	T	Wisconsin	From San Francisco through Miami
28. New England	Andy Katzenmoyer	LB	Ohio State	From N.Y. Jets
29. Minnesota	Dimitrius Underwood	DE	Michigan State	
30. Atlanta	Patrick Kerney	DE	Virginia	
31. Denver	Al Wilson	LB	Tennessee	

SECOND ROUND

Team	Player selected	Pos.	College	Draft pick origination
32. Cleveland	Kevin Johnson	WR	Syracuse	
33. Cincinnati	Charles Fisher	DB	West Virginia	
34. Carolina	Chris Terry	T	Georgia	From Indianapolis
35. Philadelphia	Barry Gardner	LB	Northwestern	
36. Indianapolis	Mike Peterson	LB	Florida	From St. Louis
37. Washington	Jon Jansen	T	Michigan	From Chicago
38. Carolina	Mike Rucker	DE	Nebraska	
39. Miami	James Johnson	RB	Mississippi State	From Detroit
40. Oakland	Tony Bryant	DE	Florida State	From Washington through Chicago
41. St. Louis	Dre' Bly	DB	North Carolina	From New Orleans
42. Atlanta	Reginald Kelly	TE	Mississippi State	From Baltimore
43. Miami	Rob Konrad	RB	Syracuse	From Kansas City
44. Minnesota	Jim Kleinsasser	TE	North Dakota	From Pittsburgh
45. Cleveland†	Rahim Abdullah	LB	Clemson	
46. New England	Kevin Faulk	RB	Louisiana State	From Tennessee
47. Green Bay	Fred Vinson	DB	Vanderbilt	From Seattle
48. Chicago	Russell Davis	DT	North Carolina	From Oakland
49. N.Y. Giants	Joe Montgomery	RB	Ohio State	
50. Tampa Bay	Shaun King	QB	Tulane	
51. Arizona	Johnny Rutledge	LB	Florida	
52. Tennessee	John Thornton	DT	West Virginia	From New England
53. Buffalo	Peerless Price	WR	Tennessee	
54. Kansas City	Mike Cloud	RB	Boston College	From Miami
55. Dallas	Solomon Page	T	West Virginia	
56. Jacksonville	Larry Smith	DT	Florida State	
57. N.Y. Jets	Randy Thomas	G	Mississippi State	
58. Denver	Montae Reagor	DE	Texas Tech	From San Francisco
59. Pittsburgh	Scott Shields	DB	Weber State	From Minnesota
60. San Diego	Jermaine Fazande	RB	Oklahoma	From Atlanta
61. Denver	Lennie Friedman	G	Duke	

– 103 –

THIRD ROUND

Team	Player selected	Pos.	College	Draft pick origination
62. Cleveland	Daylon McCutcheon	DB	Southern California	
63. Indianapolis	Brandon Burlsworth	G	Arkansas	
64. Philadelphia	Doug Brzezinski	G	Boston College	
65. Cincinnati	Cory Hall	DB	Fresno State	
66. Chicago	Rex Turner	G	Texas A&M	
67. Denver	Chris Watson	DB	Eastern Illinois	From Carolina
68. St. Louis	Rich Coady	DB	Texas A&M	
69. San Diego	Steve Heiden	TE	South Dakota State	
70. Detroit	Jared DeVries	DE	Iowa	From Detroit through Miami
71. Chicago	D'Wayne Bates	WR	Northwestern	From New Orleans through Washington
72. Miami	Grey Ruegamer	C	Arizona State	From Baltimore through Detroit
73. Pittsburgh	Joey Porter	LB	Colorado State	From Washington through Minnesota
74. Pittsburgh	Kris Farris	T	UCLA	
75. Kansas City	Gary Stills	LB	West Virginia	
76. Cleveland†	Marquis Smith	DB	California	
77. Seattle	Brock Huard	QB	Washington	
78. Chicago	Marty Booker	WR	Northeast Louisiana	From Oakland
79. N.Y. Giants	Dan Campbell	TE	Texas A&M	
80. Tampa Bay	Martin Gramatica	K	Kansas State	
81. Tennessee	Zach Piller	G	Florida	
82. Seattle	Karsten Bailey	WR	Auburn	From New England
83. Arizona	Tom Burke	DE	Wisconsin	
84. Kansas City	Larry Atkins	S	UCLA	From Miami
85. Dallas	Dat Nguyen	LB	Texas A&M	
86. Buffalo	Shawn Bryson	RB	Tennessee	
87. Green Bay	Mike McKenzie	DB	Memphis	
88. Jacksonville	Anthony Cesario	G	Colorado State	
89. San Francisco	Chike Okeafor	DE	Purdue	
90. N.Y. Jets	David Loverne	T	San Jose State	
91. New England	Tony George	S	Florida	From Minnesota
92. Atlanta	Jeff Paulk	RB	Arizona State	
93. Denver	Travis McGriff	WR	Florida	
94. Green Bay*	Cletidus Hunt	DT	Kentucky State	
95. Pittsburgh*	Amos Zereoue	RB	West Virginia	

FOURTH ROUND

Team	Player selected	Pos.	College	Draft pick origination
96. Indianapolis	Paul Miranda	DB	Central Florida	From Cleveland through San Francisco
97. Philadelphia	John Welbourn	T	California	
98. Cincinnati	Craig Yeast	WR	Kentucky	
99. San Francisco	Anthony Parker	DB	Weber State	From Indianapolis
100. Carolina	Hannibal Navies	LB	Colorado	
101. St. Louis	Joe Germaine	QB	Ohio State	
102. Oakland	Dameane Douglas	WR	California	From Chicago
103. Detroit	Sedrick Irvin	RB	Michigan State	
104. San Diego	Jason Perry	DB	North Carolina State	
105. Baltimore	Brandon Stokley	WR	Southwestern Louisiana	
106. Chicago	Warrick Holdman	LB	Texas A&M	From Washington
107. Washington	Nate Stimson	LB	Georgia Tech	From New Orleans
108. Kansas City	Larry Parker	WR	Southern California	
109. Pittsburgh	Aaron Smith	DE	Northern Colorado	
110. San Francisco	Pierson Prioleau	DB	Virginia Tech	From Cleveland†
111. Chicago	Rosevelt Colvin	DE	Purdue	From Oakland
112. N.Y. Giants	Sean Bennett	RB	Northwestern	
113. Tampa Bay	Dexter Jackson	DB	Florida State	
114. Tennessee	Brad Ware	DB	Auburn	
115. Seattle	Antonio Cochran	DE	Georgia	
116. Arizona	Joel Makovicka	RB	Nebraska	
117. Tennessee	Donald Mitchell	DB	Southern Methodist	From New England
118. Dallas	Wane McGarity	WR	Texas	
119. Buffalo	Keith Newman	LB	North Carolina	
120. Minnesota	Kenny Wright	DB	Northwestern (La.) State	From Miami
121. Jacksonville	Kevin Landolt	DT	West Virginia	
122. Buffalo	Bobby Collins	TE	North Alabama	From Green Bay
123. N.Y. Jets	Jason Wiltz	DT	Nebraska	
124. Cleveland	Wali Rainer	LB	Virginia	From San Francisco
125. Minnesota	Jay Humphrey	T	Texas	
126. Atlanta	Johndale Carty	DB	Utah State	

Team	Player selected	Pos.	College	Draft pick origination
127. Denver	Olandis Gary	RB	Georgia	
128. Philadelphia*	Damon Moore	DB	Ohio State	
129. Baltimore*	Edwin Mulitalo	G	Arizona	
130. Philadelphia*	Na Brown	WR	North Carolina	
131. Green Bay*	Aaron Brooks	QB	Virginia	
132. Dallas*	Peppi Zellner	DE	Fort Valley State	
133. Green Bay*	Josh Bidwell	P	Oregon	

FIFTH ROUND

Team	Player selected	Pos.	College	Draft pick origination
134. Miami	Cecil Collins	RB	McNeese State	From Cleveland through San Francisco
135. Cincinnati	Nick Williams	RB	Miami, Fla.	
136. Pittsburgh	Jerame Tuman	TE	Michigan	From Indianapolis
137. Detroit	Ty Talton	DB	Northern Iowa	From Philadelphia
138. Indianapolis	Brad Scioli	DE	Penn State	From St. Louis
139. San Diego	Adrian Dingle	DE	Clemson	From Chicago
140. Seattle	Floyd Wedderburn	T	Penn State	From Carolina through Dallas
141. San Diego	Reggie Nelson	G	McNeese State	
142. Miami	Bryan Jones	LB	Oregon State	From Detroit
143. Chicago	Jerry Wisne	G	Notre Dame	From Washington
144. Chicago	Khari Samuel	LB	Massachusetts	From New Orleans through Washington
145. St. Louis	Cameron Spikes	G	Texas A&M	From Baltimore
146. Oakland	Eric Barton	LB	Maryland	From Pittsburgh
147. Chicago	Jerry Azumah	RB	New Hampshire	From Kansas City
148. Cleveland†	Darrin Chiaverini	WR	Colorado	
149. N.Y. Giants	Mike Rosenthal	T	Notre Dame	
150. Tampa Bay	John McLaughlin	DE	California	
151. Tennessee	Kevin Daft	QB	Cal-Davis	
152. Seattle	Charlie Rogers	WR	Georgia Tech	
153. Oakland	Roderick Coleman	LB	East Carolina	
154. New England	Derrick Fletcher	G	Baylor	
155. Arizona	Paris Johnson	DB	Miami of Ohio	
156. Buffalo	Jay Foreman	LB	Nebraska	
157. San Francisco	Terry Jackson	RB	Florida	From Miami
158. Denver	David Bowens	DE	Western Illinois	From Dallas
159. Green Bay	DeMonn Parker	RB	Oklahoma	
160. Jacksonville	Jason Craft	DB	Colorado State	
161. San Francisco	Tyrone Hopson	T	Eastern Kentucky	
162. N.Y. Jets	Jermaine Jones	DB	Northwestern (La.) State	
163. Green Bay	Craig Heimburger	C	Missouri	From Minnesota through Pit. and Oak.
164. Atlanta	Eugene Baker	WR	Kent	
165. Washington	Derek Smith	T	Virginia Tech	From Denver
166. Pittsburgh*	Malcolm Johnson	WR	Notre Dame	
167. Denver*	Darwin Brown	DB	Texas Tech	
168. Arizona*	Yusuf Scott	G	Arizona	
169. Minnesota*	Chris Jones	LB	Clemson	

SIXTH ROUND

Team	Player selected	Pos.	College	Draft pick origination
170. Seattle	Steve Johnson	DB	Tennessee	From Cleveland
171. San Francisco	Tai Streets	WR	Michigan	From Indianapolis
172. Philadelphia	Cecil Martin	RB	Wisconsin	
173. Cincinnati	Kelly Gregg	DT	Oklahoma	
174. Cleveland	Marcus Spriggs	DT	Troy State	From Chicago
175. Carolina	Robert Daniel	DE	Northwestern (La.) State	
176. St. Louis	Lionel Barnes	DE	Northeast Louisiana	
177. Detroit	Clint Kriewaldt	LB	Wisconsin-Stevens Point	
178. San Diego	Tyrone Bell	DB	North Alabama	
179. Denver	Desmond Clark	TE	Wake Forest	From New Orleans through Washington
180. New England	Marcus Washington	DB	Colorado	From Baltimore
181. Washington	Jeff Hall	K	Tennessee	
182. Jacksonville	Emarlos Leroy	DT	Georgia	From Kansas City through Tampa Bay
183. N.Y. Jets	Marc Megna	LB	Richmond	From Pittsburgh
184. Chicago	Rashard Cook	DB	Southern California	From Cleveland†
185. Minnesota	Talance Sawyer	DE	UNLV	From Tampa Bay through Baltimore
186. Tennessee	Darran Hall	WR	Colorado State	
187. Cleveland	Kendall Ogle	LB	Maryland	From Seattle
188. Oakland	Daren Yancey	DT	Brigham Young	From Oakland through Green Bay
189. N.Y. Giants	Lyle West	DB	San Jose State	

Team	Player selected	Pos.	College	Draft pick origination
190. Arizona	Jacoby Rhinehart	DB	Southern Methodist	
191. Cleveland	James Dearth	TE	Tarleton State	From New England through Seattle
192. Miami	Brent Bartholomew	P	Ohio State	
193. Dallas	Mar Tay Jenkins	WR	Nebraska-Omaha	
194. Buffalo	Armon Hatcher	DB	Oregon State	
195. Tampa Bay	Lamarr Glenn	RB	Florida State	From Jacksonville
196. Green Bay	Dee Miller	WR	Ohio State	
197. N.Y. Jets	J.P. Machado	G	Illinois	
198. Atlanta	Jeff Kelly	LB	Kansas State	From San Francisco
199. Minnesota	Antico Dalton	LB	Hampton	
200. Atlanta	Eric Thigpen	DB	Iowa	
201. Philadelphia	Troy Smith	WR	East Carolina	From Denver
202. Arizona*	Melvin Bradley	LB	Arkansas	
203. Green Bay*	Scott Curry	T	Montana	
204. Denver*	Chad Plummer	WR	Cincinnati	
205. N.Y. Giants*	Andre Weathers	DB	Michigan	
206. Arizona*	Dennis McKinley	RB	Mississippi State	

SEVENTH ROUND

Team	Player selected	Pos.	College	Draft pick origination
207. Cleveland	Madre Hill	RB	Arkansas	From Cleveland through Chicago
208. Philadelphia	Jed Weaver	TE	Oregon	
209. Cincinnati	Tony Coats	G	Washington	
210. Indianapolis	Hunter Smith	P	Notre Dame	
211. Carolina	Tony Booth	DB	James Madison	
212. Green Bay	Chris Akins	DB	Arkansas-Pine Bluff	From St. Louis
213. Green Bay	Donald Driver	WR	Alcorn State	From Chicago
214. Pittsburgh	Antonio Dingle	DT	Virginia	From San Diego
215. Detroit	Mike Pringley	DT	North Carolina	
216. Baltimore	Anthony Poindexter	DB	Virginia	
217. Washington	Tim Alexander	WR	Oregon State	
218. Denver	Billy Miller	WR	Southern California	From New Orleans through Washington
219. Pittsburgh	Chad Kelsay	LB	Nebraska	
220. Kansas City	Eric King	G	Richmond	
221. Chicago	Sulecio Sanford	WR	Middle Tennessee State	From Cleveland†
222. Tennessee	Phil Glover	LB	Utah	
223. N.Y. Jets	Ryan Young	T	Kansas State	From Seattle
224. Oakland	JoJuan Armour	LB	Miami of Ohio	
225. N.Y. Giants	Ryan Hale	DT	Arkansas	
226. Tampa Bay	Robert Hunt	G	Virginia	
227. New England	Michael Bishop	QB	Kansas State	
228. Pittsburgh	Kris Brown	K	Nebraska	From Arizona
229. Dallas	Mike Lucky	TE	Arizona	
230. Buffalo	Sheldon Jackson	TE	Nebraska	
231. N.Y. Giants	O.J. Childress	LB	Clemson	From Miami
232. Miami	Jermaine Haley	DT	Butte J.C.	From Green Bay through Detroit
233. Tampa Bay	Autry Denson	RB	Notre Dame	From Jacksonville
234. San Francisco	Kory Minor	LB	Notre Dame	
235. N.Y. Jets	J.J. Syvrud	DE	Jamestown	
236. Minnesota	Noel Scarlett	DT	Langston	
237. Atlanta	Todd McClure	C	Louisiana State	
238. Denver	Justin Swift	TE	Kansas State	
239. Arizona*	Chris Greisen	QB	Northwest Missouri State	
240. Tampa Bay*	Darnell McDonald	WR	Kansas State	
241. New England*	Sean Morey	WR	Brown	
242. Jacksonville*	Dee Moronkola	DB	Washington State	
243. Dallas*	Kelvin Garmon	G	Baylor	
244. Miami*	Joe Wong	T	Brigham Young	
245. Cincinnati*	Scott Covington	QB	Miami, Fla.	
246. Jacksonville*	Chris White	DE	Southern University	
247. Atlanta*	Rondel Menendez	WR	Eastern Kentucky	
248. Buffalo*	Bryce Fisher	DE	Air Force	
249. Cincinnati*	Donald Broomfield	DT	Clemson	
250. Indianapolis*	Corey Terry	LB	Tennessee	
251. Philadelphia*	Pernell Davis	DT	Alabama-Birmingham	
252. St. Louis*	Rodney Williams	P	Georgia Tech	
253. Chicago	Jim Finn	RB	Pennsylvania	From Cleveland†

*Pick awarded to team as compensation for loss of a free agent. †Supplemental pick awarded to Browns.

EXPANSION DRAFT

CLEVELAND BROWNS, FEBRUARY 9, 1999

	Player selected	Pos.	Former team		Player selected	Pos.	Former team
1.	Jim Pyne	C	Detroit	20.	Kory Blackwell	CB	N.Y. Giants
2.	Hurvin McCormack	DE	Dallas	21.	Kevin Devine	CB	Jacksonville
3.	Scott Rehberg	OT	New England	22.	Ray Jackson	CB	Buffalo
4.	Damon Gibson	WR	Cincinnati	23.	Jim Bundren	G	N.Y. Jets
5.	Steve Gordon	C	San Francisco	24.	Ben Cavil	G	Baltimore
6.	Tarek Saleh	LB	Carolina	25.	Michael Blair	RB	Green Bay
7.	Jeff Buckey	G	Miami	26.	Antonio Anderson	DT	Dallas
8.	Jason Kyle	LB	Seattle	27.	Orlando Bobo	DB	Minnesota
9.	Rod Manuel	DE	Pittsburgh	28.	James Williams	LB	San Francisco
10.	Lenoy Jones	LB	Tennessee	29.	Scott Milanovich	QB	Tampa Bay
11.	Tim McTyer	CB	Philadelphia	30.	Eric Stokes	S	Seattle
12.	Elijah Alexander	LB	Indianapolis	31.	Ronald Moore	RB	Miami
13.	Pete Swanson	OT	Kansas City	32.	Clarence Williams	RB	Buffalo
14.	Gerome Williams	S	San Diego	33.	Freddie Solomon	WR	Philadelphia
15.	Marlon Forbes	S	Chicago	34.	Brandon Sanders	S	N.Y. Giants
16.	Justin Armour	WR	Denver	35.	Mike Thompson	NT	Cincinnati
17.	Paul Wiggins	OT	Washington	36.	Jerris McPhail	RB	Detroit
18.	Duane Butler	S	Minnesota	37.	Antonio Langham	DB	San Francisco
19.	Fred Brock	WR	Arizona				

PLAYOFF PLAN

TIEBREAKING PROCEDURES

DIVISION TIES

TWO CLUBS

1. Head-to-head (best won-lost-tied percentage in games between the clubs).
2. Best won-lost-tied percentage in games played within the division.
3. Best won-lost-tied percentage in games played within the conference.
4. Best won-lost-tied percentage in common games, if applicable.
5. Best net points in division games.
6. Best net points in all games.
7. Strength of schedule.
8. Best net touchdowns in all games.
9. Coin toss.

THREE OR MORE CLUBS

(Note: If two clubs remain tied after other clubs are eliminated during any step, tie-breaker reverts to step 1 of two-club format.)
1. Head-to-head (best won-lost-tied percentage in games among the clubs).
2. Best won-lost-tied percentage in games played within the division.
3. Best won-lost-tied percentage in games played within the conference.
4. Best won-lost-tied percentage in common games.
5. Best net points in division games.
6. Best net points in all games.
7. Strength of schedule.
8. Best net touchdowns in all games.
9. Coin toss.

WILD-CARD TIES

If necessary to break ties to determine the three wild-card clubs from each conference, the following steps will be taken:
1. If all the tied clubs are from the same division, apply division tie-breaker.
2. If the tied clubs are from different divisions, apply the steps listed below.
3. When the first wild-card team has been identified, the procedure is repeated to name the second wild card (i.e., eliminate all but the highest-ranked club in each division prior to proceeding to step 2), and repeated a third time, if necessary, to identify the third wild card. In situations where three or more teams from the same division are involved in the procedure, the original seeding of the teams remains the same for subsequent applications of the tie-breaker if the top-ranked team in that division qualifies for a wild-card berth.

TWO CLUBS

1. Head-to-head, if applicable.
2. Best won-lost-tied percentage in games played within the conference.
3. Best won-lost-tied percentage in common games, minimum of four.
4. Best average net points in conference games.
5. Best net points in all games.
6. Strength of schedule.
7. Best net touchdowns in all games.
8. Coin toss.

THREE OR MORE CLUBS

(Note: If two clubs remain tied after other clubs are eliminated, tie-breaker reverts to step 1 of two-club format.)
1. Apply division tie-breaker to eliminate all but highest-ranked club in each division prior to proceeding to step 1. The original seeding within a division upon application of the division tie-breaker remains the same for all subsequent applications of the procedure that are necessary to identify the three wild-card participants.
2. Head-to-head sweep (applicable only if one club has defeated each of the others or one club has lost to each of the others).
3. Best won-lost-tied percentage in games played within the conference.
4. Best won-lost-tied percentage in common games, minimum of four.
5. Best average net points in conference games.
6. Best net points in all games.
7. Strength of schedule.
8. Best net touchdowns in all games.
9. Coin toss.

1998 REVIEW

Few great athletes leave on top, and consecutive Super Bowl wins provided Elway with the perfect exit. (Photo by Albert Dickson/THE SPORTING NEWS.)

By STEVE HARRISON

Ten or 20 years from now, the 1998 NFL season will be remembered for one thing and one thing only: John Elway scrambling for the last time.

This spring, the Denver Broncos great teased us, toying with coming back for a 17th season—and for a shot at an unprecedented third consecutive Super Bowl victory. But in the end, No. 7 was secure in his legacy, secure in his already-wondrous deeds. So he quietly walked away, joining Michael Jordan and Wayne Gretzky in retirement, leaving the National Football League with a gaping hole.

Who will follow him as an escape artist? Who will have his swagger that always seemed charming, never threatening?

It's unlikely anyone will replace him.

"I can't do it physically anymore, and that's really hard for me to say," Elway said at his farewell press conference this spring.

Of course, there were other, smaller memories and milestones from the 1998 NFL season.

Minnesota Vikings wide receiver Randy Moss gave us redemption. Atlanta Falcons cornerback Eugene Robinson gave us humiliation on, of all nights, the eve of the Super Bowl. Referees proved to be human, ushering in a return of instant replay. Big-name, big-money free agents again gave teams sticker shock—and many were lemons.

On the feel-good front, presumed washed-up quarterbacks such as Minnesota's Randall Cunningham, the New York Jets' Vinny Testaverde, and the Buffalo Bills' Doug Flutie made triumphant returns, showing that today's high-tech offenses need steady, wise hands at the controls. And, finally, Elway's Broncos made us remember Bob Griese, Mercury Morris and Manny Fernandez as they flirted with an undefeated season.

It was no surprise that Denver cruised by Atlanta, 34-19, in Super Bowl 33 in Miami. What was a surprise is that the Broncos didn't finish the season without a loss. They certainly seemed capable.

Behind running back Terrell Davis, who ran for 2,008 yards and scored 23 touchdowns, Denver won its first 13 games. Then, on a cold and windy day in East Rutherford, N.J., the New York Giants showed Denver was mortal—at least for a day. The Giants won, 20-16, as Kent Graham threw a 37-yard touchdown pass to Amani Toomer with 48 seconds remaining. The Miami Dolphins' 1972 17-0 season was safe, and members of that team began drinking champagne as they always do when the last unbeaten goes down.

The Giants' win in Week 15 denied Denver a chance at perfection, but it didn't derail coach Mike Shanahan's team. The Broncos avenged a Week 16 loss by whipping Miami in the divisional playoffs, then put away the pesky New York Jets in the AFC championship game.

In the Super Bowl, Denver won easily, returning the game to its familiar territory: blowout. The Broncos made the most of their opportunities, while Atlanta never could convert. The Falcons got the ball inside the Denver 30 six times and managed only two field goals. Meanwhile, Denver showed a knack for the big play. In the second quarter, Elway hit Rod Smith for an 80-yard touchdown. The score gave Denver a commanding 17-3 lead. The game was essentially over.

And with 50 seconds remaining, Elway jogged off the field for the last time. The Hall of Famer's career was over. Denver repeated as Super Bowl champions, joining Green Bay, Miami, Pittsburgh, San Francisco and Dallas as the only teams to do so.

NFC LEAST

The '98 season will be remembered as the year the once-dominant NFC East became a doormat. The division's five teams had a collective 16-24 record against other opponents, an embarrassing fall for a division that won seven of 10 Super Bowls from 1987 through '96.

The Giants, who lost star cornerback Jason Sehorn in preseason, stumbled early and started 3-7. But behind the running of Gary Brown, who rushed for 1,063 yards—the first Giant 1,000-yard rusher since Rodney Hampton in 1995—New York won its last four games to finish 8-8 and narrowly missed the playoffs.

The real sad sacks, however, were the Philadelphia Eagles and the Washington Redskins. They began the year with 0-5 records, then faced each other in Week 6 with both of their seasons already destroyed. Philadelphia, a playoff team as recently as 1996, started Duce Staley in the backfield and rotated Bobby Hoying, Koy Detmer and Rodney Peete at quarterback. None of the trio was the answer, and the Eagles finished the season 3-13, their first 13-loss season ever. Coach Ray Rhodes was fired and then hired by the Green Bay Packers.

The Redskins? They were a more puzzling bunch. Washington proved, once again, that signing big-name free agents can be fool's gold. The Redskins brought in big-name defensive tackles Dan Wilkinson and Dana Stubblefield—and were still 26th in the league in sacks. Norv Turner coached under a cloud all season and likely saved his job with a strong finish. Washington won four of its last five to finish 6-10.

No team benefited more from its pathetic division competition than the Dallas Cowboys. They started the year with a new coach, Chan Gailey, an offensive whiz imported from Pittsburgh. Owner Jerry Jones hoped Gailey would inject much-needed creativity in the Dallas attack. He also hoped—or perhaps prayed—Gailey would bring discipline to the organization.

For the first half of the season, Gailey was a miracle worker. Even though Troy Aikman was injured, Dallas opened the season with an 8-3 record. Emmitt Smith looked young again. The offensive line no longer resembled a still life, but a healthy, semi-fit unit that could move more than three steps without needing a breather.

The high point of Dallas' season came in Week 12, when the Cowboys won a home game against the Seattle Seahawks, 30-22. It turned out later that Seattle wasn't much. The Cowboys weren't, either.

When the season ended, Dallas hosted the Arizona Cardinals in the NFC wild-card game. The Cowboys were humiliated, 20-7.

"This team is not getting any younger," said star cornerback Deion Sanders after the loss, which was also the Cardinals' first playoff win since 1947. "It's time for some guys to step up or step out."

For years, the Cardinals had a star-laden defense, with players like Aeneas Williams and Eric Swann. But

Smith's 80-yard touchdown essentially broke the Falcons' back in Super Bowl 33. (Photo by Bob Leverone/THE SPORTING NEWS.)

in 1998, Arizona rode the young arm of Jake Plummer, a former Arizona State star. The scrambling Plummer, who reminded many of a young Joe Montana, led the Cardinals to five fourth-quarter comeback wins. Their playoff hopes, however, came down to a last-second field goal in Week 17 against the San Diego Chargers.

Arizona had allowed San Diego to tie the game at 13 with a 30-yard touchdown pass with 16 seconds left. But then Eric Metcalf returned the ensuing kickoff 46 yards, helping set up Chris Jacke's game-winning 52-yard field goal as time expired. After Jacke's field goal, fans rushed the field at Sun Devil Stadium. They had a right to: The Cardinals had just earned their first playoff birth since 1982.

A week after throttling Dallas, however, Arizona hit reality. The Cardinals were whipped by the Vikings, 41-21, in the NFC divisional playoffs.

JIMMY VS. BILL

In the AFC East, a battle of coaching egos was waged between Dolphins coach Jimmy Johnson and Jets coach Bill Parcells. Johnson, you may remember, came to Miami four years ago, expecting to play in last year's Super Bowl at Pro Player Stadium. Johnson's Miami plan moved forward, albeit at a glacial place. It ended with the team nowhere near a championship.

His principal success was with the defense, which he built into a young, fast, hungry—and, perhaps most important, cheap—unit. They played press coverage. They blitzed their linebackers. They had two behemoths on the inside of the defensive line, Tim Bowens and Daryl Gardener, who were excellent run stoppers.

Testaverde overcame his mistake-prone past to compile the best passer rating in the AFC for the surprising Jets. (Photo by Bob Leverone/THE SPORTING NEWS.)

The Dolphins' defense had seven starters under 25—and kept the anemic Miami offense afloat.

Last year, as in the previous two, the biggest question in Miami revolved around Dan Marino. Johnson wanted to take the ball out of Marino's hands, to let a rushing attack control the ball and win the game. But there was no one to carry it. Karim Abdul-Jabbar was serviceable at best. Rookie first-round pick John Avery danced around a lot and went nowhere. So the Dolphins languished in second gear, light years removed from the days of Marino and Mark Duper and Mark Clayton.

Still, Miami was a contender to win the AFC East. Then came a Sunday night showdown with the Jets in Week 15.

New York came into Pro Player Stadium and dealt Miami a humiliating 21-16 loss in Johnson's biggest game as Miami's coach. Four weeks later, Miami was out of the playoffs, drubbed by Denver, 38-3.

The days after the Denver defeat will always be remembered as some of the strangest in Miami sports history. First came word that Johnson was resigning because he wanted to spend more time with his family in the wake of his mother's death in Texas. Then owner Wayne Huizenga talked Johnson out of his decision. Johnson stayed, albeit with a new assistant head coach, Dave Wannstedt, who had been fired by Chicago.

While Johnson was debating his future, Parcells was solidifying his reputation as the league's best coach. He named journeyman Vinny Testaverde the starting quarterback in Week 7, and the Jets proceeded to win four in a row and 10 of 11. This wasn't the old Testaverde, the quarterback who tossed interceptions liberally. He was cool and confident—and he had great targets in Wayne Chrebet and Keyshawn Johnson, who finally began to fill his own shoes. The Jets were also powered by running back Curtis Martin, formerly of New England and one of the best free-agent pickups.

In the AFC playoffs, the Jets whipped Jacksonville, 34-24, before succumbing to Denver, 23-10, in the AFC championship game. The Jets stunned the Denver crowd when tight end Blake Spence blocked Tom Rouen's punt and tight end Fred Baxter recovered on the Denver 1. The Jets scored and had a 10-0 lead.

But they couldn't hold it. Martin had only 14 yards on 13 carries. Testaverde threw a pair of interceptions. The dam broke early in the second half when Elway hit wide receiver Ed McCaffrey for a 47-yard pass that set up Howard Griffith's 11-yard touchdown reception. The Broncos recovered a fumble on the ensuing kickoff, and it was over for the Jets. If Parcells had won, he would have become the first coach to lead three different teams to the Super Bowl.

The best story of the division—and perhaps the season—came from Buffalo. In Week 6, quarterback Rob Johnson was injured. Enter Flutie, a 5-10 slinger who had spent the last eight years playing in the Canadian Football League. In Week 7, the Bills trailed Jacksonville 16-10. On fourth down and goal at the Jaguars' 1, Flutie faked a handoff, turned and bootlegged toward the goal. It was a spine-tingling run, and the second coming of Doug Flutie.

He led the Bills to a 10-6 record, but the end came in Miami, in the AFC wild-card game. The Dolphins' defense led the way, 24-17.

While the New England Patriots finished a disappointing 9-7, the Indianapolis Colts were a predictable 3-13. There was a silver lining for the Colts: quarterback Peyton Manning, who had a splendid first season. At the start of the year, debate focused on who would be the best rookie: Manning or San Diego's Ryan Leaf. No contest.

By the end of the season, Manning had found a groove, throwing for 3,739 yards, with 26 touchdowns and 28 interceptions.

"Every week it has slowed down for me a little bit," Manning said. "In the offseason, I'll study this game as well as every game and hopefully learn from my mistakes."

DOMINANCE AND DISAPPOINTMENTS

In the AFC West, the main story, of course, was Denver's dominance.

But disappointment could sum up the fortunes of the division's four other teams.

The Oakland Raiders, who finished in second with an 8-8 record, once led the division but dropped five of their last six games. The lone bright spot was rookie cornerback Charles Woodson, who had a strong NFL debut after winning the Heisman Trophy.

Seattle coach Dennis Erickson lost his job after the Seahawks finished 8-8 for the third time in the last four years. Running back Ricky Watters, a free-agent pickup from Philadelphia, gave the running game a boost, but it wasn't enough. Seattle also had wicked luck. In Week 14, it lost to the Jets, 32-31, when Testaverde ran five yards for a touchdown on a quarterback sneak with 20 seconds remaining.

Problem was, replays showed Testaverde clearly didn't make it to the end zone, that he was tackled at the 1. Seattle fell to 6-7, and its playoff hopes were dashed.

"That was the most difficult loss I've ever been involved in," Erickson said.

More than any other officiating mistake, that blunder led to the return of instant replay for this season.

San Diego, which finished last in the division with a 5-11 record, pinned its hopes on rookie quarterback Leaf, chosen second overall after Manning. Though he showed promise in the preseason—even outperforming Manning in a game against the Colts—Leaf struggled mightily in his rookie campaign. His off-field behavior was suspect, and he finished the season with humbling stats: 245 attempts with 111 completions for 1,289 yards. The real kicker, though, was his knack for throwing the ball to the other team. Leaf threw 15 interceptions, compared with two touchdown passes.

But the biggest disappointment was the Kansas City Chiefs, who posted one of the worst turnarounds in NFL history. In 1997, the Chiefs finished 13-3. Last season, they were 7-9. They crippled themselves with mistakes all season and set an NFL season record with 158 penalties.

Kansas City was hindered by an underachieving defense, led by Derrick Thomas and Chester McGlockton. Thomas, long a stalwart at linebacker, was benched in running downs, and McGlockton, a pricey free-agent acquisition from Oakland, didn't live up to his salary.

At the end of the season, Chiefs coach Marty Schottenheimer shocked the organization by resigning after 10 years. He was replaced by defensive coordinator Gunther Cunningham.

Elvis Grbac's struggles mirrored those of his team: In an injury-filled season the Chiefs quarterback threw five touchdown passes and 12 interceptions. (Photo by Winslow Townson for THE SPORTING NEWS.)

JAGS ON THE RISE

In the AFC Central, the Jacksonville Jaguars proved head coach Tom Coughlin's blueprint for an expansion team is a winner. The Jaguars, behind the throwing and running of quarterback Mark Brunell, won a franchise-record 12 games (regular season and postseason combined) and captured their first division title.

Jacksonville benefited from the arrival of rookie running back Fred Taylor, who rushed for 1,223 yards and 14 touchdowns behind mammoth offensive lineman Tony Boselli, who was so popular in northern Florida that McDonald's named a burger after him.

But in the divisional playoffs, the Jaguars fell short against the Jets. Brunell played with a gimpy ankle and completed only 12-of-31 passes for 156 yards. He also threw three interceptions, and New York won, 34-24.

The most puzzling team in the division was the Pittsburgh Steelers, who closed the season by losing five consecutive games, their longest losing streak since 1988. The disastrous finish was also Pittsburgh's first losing season since 1991, Chuck Noll's last year as coach.

Much of the blame was pinned on quarterback Kordell Stewart, who wasn't the running/throwing wonder of the previous year. For the Steelers, it all came apart on December 13 at Tampa Bay, when Stewart was caught on camera arguing with coach

Few players last year were better than Moss, who had one of the most productive rookie seasons in NFL history. (Photo by THE SPORTING NEWS.)

Bill Cowher. Stewart, who was pulled by Cowher, lashed out at his coach, screaming and pointing at him, in tears.

"It was embarrassing," Stewart later said.

The same could be said for Pittsburgh's 7-9 season. Tennessee (8-8) played its last season as the Oilers and will become the Titans this season. Maybe the change will help the team's fortunes; it hasn't had a winning season since 1993, when it played in Houston.

At the bottom of the division, the story remained the same for the Baltimore Ravens (6-10) and the Cincinnati Bengals (3-13). The Ravens had five players in the Pro Bowl, but coach Ted Marchibroda still lost his job.

THE MOSS LEGEND GROWS

Throughout the season, there was little doubt the Vikings would represent the NFC in the Super Bowl. They were the second-chance team, a mix of young and old that could flat-out score. They had defensive tackle John Randle, a trash-talking terror of quarterbacks whose talent was once seen as suspect by several NFL teams. They had quarterback Randall Cunningham, who was out of football and cutting marble for kitchen counters two years ago. And they had

Moss, a rookie wide receiver who came to the NFL from Marshall University.

"We like a player to come in who feels he's got something to prove," Vikings coach Dennis Green said.

They did. After quarterback Brad Johnson was injured in Week 2, Cunningham stepped in. Running an offense that spread the field and terrorized secondaries, he threw for 3,704 yards and 34 touchdowns, and the Vikings had the league's best record at 15-1. They also scored the league's most points with 556.

The first sign of their brilliance? A 37-24 thrashing of the Green Bay Packers in Week 5 on Monday night. The second? A 46-36 whipping of Dallas on Thanksgiving, in which Cunningham threw for 359 yards and four touchdowns. Three of the touchdown passes were to the lanky Moss, who proved he could outrun and outjump anyone. He also showed he could be a model player, on and off the field.

There seemed no stopping Minnesota—or its rabid, towel-waving fans—until the Vikings ran into the "Dirty Birds." In the NFC championship game, Minnesota blew a 10-point lead and lost to Atlanta, 30-27, in overtime.

Minnesota became only the third team to go 15-1 during the regular season. The other two—the 1984 San Francisco 49ers and the 1985 Chicago Bears—both won the Super Bowl.

The two other stories in the NFC Central were the puzzling 8-8 finish of the Tampa Bay Buccaneers, a preseason Super Bowl pick, and Green Bay's slide into pro football's middle class with an 11-5 record. The Buccaneers won four of their last five but couldn't overcome a poor start. The Packers? Age—and free agency—crept up on the 1997 Super Bowl runner-ups. At the end of the season, coach Mike Holmgren fulfilled his desire to become coach and general manager and left for Seattle. The Packers plucked Rhodes, the deposed Philadelphia coach, as their new coach.

Barry Sanders wasted another 1,000-yard season with the Detroit Lions, who finished 5-11. The talentless Chicago Bears brought up the rear of the division with a 4-12 record.

THOSE DIRTY BIRDS

There was no bigger surprise than the Falcons, who won the NFC West and then rolled through the playoffs. Like the Jets, they were led by a presumed washed-up, injury-prone quarterback: Chris Chandler. But behind Chandler was the soul of the team: running back Jamal Anderson, who rushed for 1,846 yards and 14 touchdowns. As the touchdowns—and wins—piled up, Anderson and his teammates coined a dance craze: "The Dirty Bird."

But the real key to Atlanta's success was head coach Dan Reeves. In 1997, the first year under Reeves, the Falcons started 1-7. Since then, they have gone 20-4 in the regular season. In Week 16, when Atlanta clinched the NFC West title with a win over Detroit, Reeves was in the hospital recovering from quadruple heart bypass surgery.

He was back on the sidelines for the playoffs, however, leading the Falcons past San Francisco, then Minnesota in the NFC championship game.

But the real hurt for Reeves came in the Super Bowl. Atlanta's 34-19 loss to Denver wasn't just a championship loss for Reeves. It was to Elway, his former quarterback, and Shanahan, his former assistant, whom Reeves felt had worked behind his back while he was coach in Denver.

With its success, Atlanta eclipsed the San Francisco 49ers, who finished 12-4 but showed signs of age. The 49ers' 20-18 loss to Atlanta marked only the fourth time in the last 11 seasons they failed to reach the conference championship game.

But while San Francisco's season ended earlier than usual, the 49ers did provide fans with one of the most memorable catches of the season. Against the Packers in the wild-card game, San Francisco trailed 27-23 with 1:56 remaining. Quarterback Steve Young drove his team 76 yards to win the game. The deciding play: With three seconds left, Young hit Terrell Owens for a 25-yard touchdown pass.

"(Owens) made the play to win the game," said San Francisco coach Steve Mariucci. "It's one of the big catches in this organization's history."

The victory also broke a three-year run of playoff defeats to the Packers.

The rest of the division was a collection of has-beens and teams that never were. The Carolina Panthers, who were in the NFC championship game two years ago, fell to 4-12, and coach Dom Capers was fired. The Panthers' season was disappointing and horrific at the same time.

In October, after a 51-23 loss to Atlanta, quarterback Kerry Collins walked into Capers' office. What happened next is disputed: Capers said Collins asked to be benched, saying his heart wasn't in it. Collins denies quitting on his teammates. He was cut on October 13 and picked up by New Orleans.

The horror show continued for Carolina: Running back Fred Lane made an obscene gesture after scoring a touchdown against the Jets. And on December 13, linebacker Kevin Greene grabbed linebackers coach Kevin Steele by the jacket and tried to push him backward. The embarrassing episode was caught by television cameras.

The New Orleans Saints showed signs of life under coach Mike Ditka, especially on defense. But the offense was so wretched that a 6-10 finish wasn't seen as all bad. In fact, Ditka thought New Orleans was one player away from being a contender, which is why he traded his entire draft for University of Texas running back Ricky Williams, the Heisman Trophy winner and college football's all-time leading rusher.

Coach Dick Vermeil's struggles continued with the St. Louis Rams. The team, hampered by a pedestrian offense and an equally prosaic defense, finished 4-12.

FINAL STANDINGS

AMERICAN FOOTBALL CONFERENCE

EASTERN DIVISION

	W	L	T	Pct.	Pts.	Opp.	Home	Away	Vs. AFC	Vs. NFC	Vs. AFC East
N.Y. Jets*	12	4	0	.750	416	266	7-1-0	5-3-0	10-2-0	2-2-0	7-1-0
Buffalo†	10	6	0	.625	400	333	6-2-0	4-4-0	7-5-0	3-1-0	4-4-0
Miami†	10	6	0	.625	321	265	7-1-0	3-5-0	7-5-0	3-1-0	4-4-0
New England†	9	7	0	.563	337	329	6-2-0	3-5-0	7-5-0	2-2-0	4-4-0
Indianapolis	3	13	0	.188	310	444	3-5-0	0-8-0	3-9-0	0-4-0	1-7-0

CENTRAL DIVISION

	W	L	T	Pct.	Pts.	Opp.	Home	Away	Vs. AFC	Vs. NFC	Vs. AFC Central
Jacksonville*	11	5	0	.688	392	338	7-1-0	4-4-0	8-4-0	3-1-0	6-2-0
Tennessee	8	8	0	.500	330	320	3-5-0	5-3-0	7-5-0	1-3-0	7-1-0
Pittsburgh	7	9	0	.438	263	303	5-3-0	2-6-0	5-7-0	2-2-0	3-5-0
Baltimore	6	10	0	.375	269	335	4-4-0	2-6-0	5-7-0	1-3-0	2-6-0
Cincinnati	3	13	0	.188	268	452	1-7-0	2-6-0	2-10-0	1-3-0	2-6-0

WESTERN DIVISION

	W	L	T	Pct.	Pts.	Opp.	Home	Away	Vs. AFC	Vs. NFC	Vs. AFC West
Denver*	14	2	0	.875	501	309	8-0-0	6-2-0	11-1-0	3-1-0	8-0-0
Oakland	8	8	0	.500	288	356	4-4-0	4-4-0	5-7-0	3-1-0	4-4-0
Seattle	8	8	0	.500	372	310	6-2-0	2-6-0	5-7-0	3-1-0	3-5-0
Kansas City	7	9	0	.438	327	363	5-3-0	2-6-0	4-8-0	3-1-0	4-4-0
San Diego	5	11	0	.313	241	342	4-4-0	1-7-0	4-8-0	1-3-0	1-7-0

*Division champion. †Wild-card team.

NATIONAL FOOTBALL CONFERENCE

EASTERN DIVISION

	W	L	T	Pct.	Pts.	Opp.	Home	Away	Vs. AFC	Vs. NFC	Vs. NFC East
Dallas*	10	6	0	.625	381	275	6-2-0	4-4-0	1-3-0	9-3-0	8-0-0
Arizona†	9	7	0	.563	325	378	5-3-0	4-4-0	1-3-0	8-4-0	4-4-0
N.Y. Giants	8	8	0	.500	287	309	5-3-0	3-5-0	3-1-0	5-7-0	5-3-0
Washington	6	10	0	.375	319	421	4-4-0	2-6-0	2-2-0	4-8-0	2-6-0
Philadelphia	3	13	0	.188	161	344	3-5-0	0-8-0	0-4-0	3-9-0	1-7-0

CENTRAL DIVISION

	W	L	T	Pct.	Pts.	Opp.	Home	Away	Vs. AFC	Vs. NFC	Vs. NFC Central
Minnesota*	15	1	0	.938	556	296	8-0-0	7-1-0	4-0-0	11-1-0	7-1-0
Green Bay†	11	5	0	.688	408	319	7-1-0	4-4-0	3-1-0	8-4-0	4-4-0
Tampa Bay	8	8	0	.500	314	295	6-2-0	2-6-0	2-2-0	6-6-0	4-4-0
Detroit	5	11	0	.313	306	378	4-4-0	1-7-0	1-3-0	4-8-0	4-4-0
Chicago	4	12	0	.250	276	368	3-5-0	1-7-0	2-2-0	2-10-0	1-7-0

WESTERN DIVISION

	W	L	T	Pct.	Pts.	Opp.	Home	Away	Vs. AFC	Vs. NFC	Vs. NFC West
Atlanta*	14	2	0	.875	442	289	8-0-0	6-2-0	3-1-0	11-1-0	7-1-0
San Francisco†	12	4	0	.750	479	328	8-0-0	4-4-0	2-2-0	10-2-0	7-1-0
New Orleans	6	10	0	.375	305	359	4-4-0	2-6-0	1-3-0	5-7-0	3-5-0
Carolina	4	12	0	.250	336	413	2-6-0	2-6-0	1-3-0	3-9-0	3-5-0
St. Louis	4	12	0	.250	285	378	2-6-0	2-6-0	3-1-0	1-11-0	0-8-0

*Division champion. †Wild-card team.

AFC PLAYOFFS
AFC wild card: Miami 24, Buffalo 17
Jacksonville 25, New England 10
AFC semifinals: Denver 38, Miami 3
New York Jets 34, Jacksonville 24
AFC championship: Denver 23, New York Jets 10

NFC PLAYOFFS
NFC wild card: Arizona 20, Dallas 7
San Francisco 30, Green Bay 27
NFC semifinals: Atlanta 20, San Francisco 18
Minnesota 41, Arizona 21
NFC championship: Atlanta 30, Minnesota 27 (OT)

SUPER BOWL
Denver 34, Atlanta 19

WEEK 1

RESULTS

Atlanta 19, CAROLINA 14
DALLAS 38, Arizona 10
GREEN BAY 38, Detroit 19
Jacksonville 24, CHICAGO 23
KANSAS CITY 28, Oakland 8
Miami 24, INDIANAPOLIS 15
MINNESOTA 31, Tampa Bay 7
New Orleans 24, ST. LOUIS 17
N.Y. GIANTS 31, Washington 24
Pittsburgh 20, BALTIMORE 13
SAN DIEGO 16, Buffalo 14
SAN FRANCISCO 36, N.Y. Jets 30 (OT)
Seattle 38, PHILADELPHIA 0
Tennessee 23, CINCINNATI 14
DENVER 27, New England 21

Note: All caps denotes home team.

STANDINGS

AFC EAST

	W	L	T	Pct.
Miami	1	0	0	1.000
Buffalo	0	1	0	.000
Indianapolis	0	1	0	.000
New England	0	1	0	.000
N.Y. Jets	0	1	0	.000

AFC CENTRAL

	W	L	T	Pct.
Jacksonville	1	0	0	1.000
Pittsburgh	1	0	0	1.000
Tennessee	1	0	0	1.000
Baltimore	0	1	0	.000
Cincinnati	0	1	0	.000

AFC WEST

	W	L	T	Pct.
Denver	1	0	0	1.000
Kansas City	1	0	0	1.000
San Diego	1	0	0	1.000
Seattle	1	0	0	1.000
Oakland	0	1	0	.000

NFC EAST

	W	L	T	Pct.
Dallas	1	0	0	1.000
N.Y. Giants	1	0	0	1.000
Arizona	0	1	0	.000
Philadelphia	0	1	0	.000
Washington	0	1	0	.000

NFC CENTRAL

	W	L	T	Pct.
Green Bay	1	0	0	1.000
Minnesota	1	0	0	1.000
Chicago	0	1	0	.000
Detroit	0	1	0	.000
Tampa Bay	0	1	0	.000

NFC WEST

	W	L	T	Pct.
Atlanta	1	0	0	1.000
New Orleans	1	0	0	1.000
San Francisco	1	0	0	1.000
Carolina	0	1	0	.000
St. Louis	0	1	0	.000

HIGHLIGHTS

Hero of the week: Garrison Hearst, on a play the 49ers had not used since the 1990 NFC championship game, broke free for a 96-yard touchdown run in overtime as the 49ers beat the Jets, 36-30. Hearst rushed for 187 yards and two touchdowns on 20 carries.

Goat of the week: Redskins quarterback Gus Frerotte started sharp, hitting on 8-of-10 first-half passes. But he threw interceptions on consecutive passes to open the second half, enabling the Giants to blow open a game that was tied 10-10 at halftime. To add injury to insult, Frerotte later was injured and lost his starting job.

Sub of the week: Buffalo backup quarterback Doug Flutie, appearing in an NFL game for the first time in nine years after eight seasons in the CFL, replaced injured Rob Johnson and nearly led the Bills to victory against the Chargers. The Bills had 104 yards at halftime; Flutie moved them 138 yards in the third quarter alone. A missed field goal by Steve Christie as time expired ensured the Bills' defeat. Flutie completed 12-of-20 passes for 158 yards and two touchdowns.

Comeback of the week: Leading 20-17 with a first down at the Jaguars' 4-yard line late in the game, the Bears were poised to pull off an improbable upset. But the Jaguars stuffed the Bears on three consecutive plays, holding them to a field goal. Mark Brunell then completed 8-of-9 passes for 73 yards. With 29 seconds left, he connected with Jimmy Smith in the back of the end zone for the game-winning touchdown.

Blowout of the week: The Seahawks were playing without defensive tackle Cortez Kennedy, but it hardly mattered. They sacked Philadelphia quarterback Bobby Hoying nine times and harassed him into a 9-for-23 performance and a 0.4 net yards-per-pass play average. Meanwhile, the Seahawks amassed 188 yards rushing en route to beating the Eagles, 38-0.

Nail-biter of the week: With 1:26 left in regulation, the 49ers went ahead by three on J.J. Stokes' 31-yard TD reception. Glenn Foley then led the Jets on a 60-yard drive that resulted in a 31-yard field goal as time expired, sending the game into overtime. After the Jets punted, pinning the 49ers on their 4, Garrison Hearst ran off-tackle and broke free for a 96-yard game-winning touchdown. The teams combined for 1,022 yards of offense.

Hit of the week: The Kansas City defense applied the hits of the week all day long to Raiders quarterback Jeff George. The Chiefs had 10 sacks, including six by Derrick Thomas and two by Leslie O'Neal. Thomas had one sack for a safety and another that forced a fumble. Both of O'Neal's sacks forced fumbles. The Chiefs manhandled the Raiders, 28-8.

Oddity of the week: With the Jaguars leading 7-3 midway through the second quarter, the Bears' Glyn Milburn fielded a kickoff at his 12. At the Jacksonville 40, kicker Mike Hollis reached out for Milburn, who attempted to hurdle him. Milburn's right foot appeared to clip Hollis' shoulder, and Milburn fell to the ground. The Jaguars thought he was down, but Milburn got up and raced to the end zone. The officials ruled Milburn never was down, and he was credited with the 88-yard return.

Top rusher: Hearst amassed 187 yards rushing (not to mention 38 yards receiving) in leading San Francisco to its OT win.

Top passer: In a game featuring the top rusher and the top two passing performances of the week, Glenn Foley of the Jets passed for 415 yards (30-for-58) in a losing effort.

Top receiver: Joey Galloway caught six passes for 142 yards in Seattle's rout of Philadelphia.

Notes: Hearst's 96-yard run in OT was the longest in 49ers history. . . . The Eagles' 38-0 loss was their worst in 23 years, and their worst home-opener ever. It was the Seahawks' biggest rout in an opening game in their 23-year history. . . . Seattle rookie reserve Ahman Green rushed six times for 100 yards, all in the second half. . . . With 122 yards rushing, Emmitt Smith of the Cowboys passed O.J.

Simpson and John Riggins to move into ninth place on the NFL's career rushing list (11,356). . . . Detroit rookie Terry Fair returned a kickoff 101 yards for a touchdown on the last play of the third quarter. Roell Preston took the ensuing kickoff 100 yards for a score as the Packers cruised by the Lions. . . . Oilers guard Bruce Matthews started his 166th consecutive game, the league's longest active streak. . . . Chiefs quarterback Elvis Grbac left the game with Oakland after being hit by Darrell Russell on the last play of the first half. He finished the game with his right arm in a sling (in the locker room).

Quote of the week: Chargers kicker John Carney, on his 54-yard field goal that bounced off the left upright before going through and putting San Diego ahead: "Thank goodness the goal post is round and not square."

GAME SUMMARIES

STEELERS 20, RAVENS 13

Sunday, September 6

Pittsburgh	3	0	10	7—20
Baltimore	3	0	0	10—13

First Quarter
Pit.—FG, N. Johnson 27, 5:06.
Bal.—FG, Stover 41, 11:44.
Third Quarter
Pit.—FG, N. Johnson 49, 10:16.
Pit.—Stewart 1 run (N. Johnson kick), 12:54.
Fourth Quarter
Pit.—C. Johnson 20 pass from Stewart (N. Johnson kick), 5:00.
Bal.—FG, Stover 25, 8:04.
Bal.—J. Lewis 64 pass from Zeier (Stover kick), 12:12.
Attendance—68,847.

	Pittsburgh	Baltimore
First downs	14	17
Rushes-yards	30-114	28-112
Passing	157	264
Punt returns	4-21	2-28
Kickoff returns	2-8	4-52
Interception returns	0-0	2-16
Comp.-att.-int.	14-27-2	20-34-0
Sacked-yards lost	2-16	1-9
Punts	4-44	4-48
Fumbles-lost	2-1	2-0
Penalties-yards	3-25	7-50
Time of possession	29:37	30:23

INDIVIDUAL STATISTICS
RUSHING—Pittsburgh, Bettis 23-41, Stewart 5-21, Huntley 2-52. Baltimore, Rhett 16-72, Holmes 6-23, Potts 4-14, J. Lewis 1-3, K. Richardson 1-0.
PASSING—Pittsburgh, Stewart 14-27-2-173. Baltimore, Zeier 16-27-0-240, Harbaugh 4-7-0-33.
RECEIVING—Pittsburgh, C. Johnson 4-68, Hawkins 2-26, Fuamatu-Ma'afala 1-17, Coleman 1-13, Ward 1-12, Lyons 1-11, Blackwell 1-9, Bruener 1-7, Bettis 1-5, Witman 1-5. Baltimore, Jackson 6-51, Rhett 4-20, Green 3-54, J. Lewis 2-76, Johnson 2-23, Holmes 2-4, Turner 1-45.
MISSED FIELD GOAL ATTEMPTS—Baltimore, Stover 42, 42, 45.
INTERCEPTIONS—Baltimore, Staten 1-14, Starks 1-2.
KICKOFF RETURNS—Pittsburgh, Blackwell 2-8. Baltimore, Johnson 3-29, J. Lewis 1-23.
PUNT RETURNS—Pittsburgh, Coleman 4-21. Baltimore, J. Lewis 2-28.
SACKS—Pittsburgh, Emmons 0.5, Harrison 0.5. Baltimore, R. Lewis 1, McCrary 1.

CHIEFS 28, RAIDERS 8

Sunday, September 6

Oakland	0	0	8	0— 8
Kansas City	17	3	3	5—28

First Quarter
K.C.—Bennett 1 run (Stoyanovich kick), 5:21.
K.C.—Rison 30 pass from Grbac (Stoyanovich kick), 5:38.
K.C.—FG, Stoyanovich 28, 8:30.
Second Quarter
K.C.—FG, Stoyanovich 19, 2:43.
Third Quarter
K.C.—FG, Stoyanovich 48, 6:43.
Oak.—H. Williams 2 run (Dudley pass from Hollas), 14:39.
Fourth Quarter
K.C.—FG, Stoyanovich 33, 4:06.
K.C.—Safety, George sacked by Thomas in end zone, 13:02.
Attendance—78,945.

	Oakland	Kansas City
First downs	18	18
Rushes-yards	20-52	36-143
Passing	212	157
Punt returns	3-18	3-5
Kickoff returns	5-92	1-21
Interception returns	0-0	0-0
Comp.-att.-int.	19-32-0	16-35-0
Sacked-yards lost	10-58	2-12
Punts	4-47	5-46
Fumbles-lost	7-5	2-0
Penalties-yards	15-134	9-63
Time of possession	27:16	32:44

INDIVIDUAL STATISTICS
RUSHING—Oakland, Kaufman 9-27, H. Williams 9-17, George 2-8. Kansas City, Bennett 24-115, Richardson 3-7, Anders 3-6, Vanover 2-1, Shehee 2-0, Gannon 1-9, Grbac 1-5.
PASSING—Oakland, George 19-31-0-270, Hollas 0-1-0-0. Kansas City, Grbac 12-23-0-130, Gannon 4-12-0-39.
RECEIVING—Oakland, T. Brown 7-67, Kaufman 4-59, H. Williams 3-24, Ritchie 2-51, Jett 2-45, Dudley 1-24. Kansas City, Anders 5-18, Rison 4-62, Gonzalez 3-47, Lockett 2-27, Horn 2-15.
MISSED FIELD GOAL ATTEMPTS—Oakland, G. Davis 30, 42. Kansas City, Stoyanovich 47.
INTERCEPTIONS—None.
KICKOFF RETURNS—Oakland, Howard 3-70, Shedd 1-21, Branch 1-1. Kansas City, Vanover 1-21.
PUNT RETURNS—Oakland, Howard 3-18. Kansas City, Horn 1-6, Vanover 1-0, Hughes 1-(minus 1).
SACKS—Oakland, Russell 2. Kansas City, Thomas 6, O'Neal 2, Edwards 1, Barndt 1.

VIKINGS 31, BUCCANEERS 7

Sunday, September 6

Tampa Bay	0	0	7	0— 7
Minnesota	14	7	0	10—31

First Quarter
Min.—Carter 1 pass from Johnson (Anderson kick), 8:29.
Min.—R. Moss 48 pass from Johnson (Anderson kick), 13:16.
Second Quarter
Min.—R. Moss 31 pass from Johnson (Anderson kick), 8:46.
Third Quarter
T.B.—Neal 3 pass from Dilfer (Husted kick), 9:46.
Fourth Quarter
Min.—FG, Anderson 43, 0:44.
Min.—Carter 18 pass from Johnson (Anderson kick), 9:36.
Attendance—62,538.

	Tampa Bay	Minnesota
First downs	17	19
Rushes-yards	23-68	27-117
Passing	251	181
Punt returns	2-23	2-7
Kickoff returns	5-130	2-31
Interception returns	1-22	1-38
Comp.-att.-int.	23-37-1	15-25-1
Sacked-yards lost	1-9	1-8
Punts	4-41	4-43
Fumbles-lost	1-1	0-0
Penalties-yards	12-124	4-30
Time of possession	33:30	26:30

INDIVIDUAL STATISTICS

RUSHING—Tampa Bay, Dunn 12-47, Alstott 7-12, Ellison 3-6, Dilfer 1-3. Minnesota, R. Smith 18-90, Hoard 7-29, Johnson 2-(minus 2).

PASSING—Tampa Bay, Dilfer 17-25-0-207, Walsh 6-12-1-53. Minnesota, Johnson 15-25-1-189.

RECEIVING—Tampa Bay, Emanuel 7-98, Anthony 4-58, Alstott 4-29, Williams 2-24, Dunn 2-21, Hape 2-11, Moore 1-16, Neal 1-3. Minnesota, Carter 5-31, R. Moss 4-95, R. Smith 2-23, Hoard 2-23, Evans 1-14, Reed 1-3.

MISSED FIELD GOAL ATTEMPTS—Tampa Bay, Husted 41.

INTERCEPTIONS—Tampa Bay, Mincy 1-22. Minnesota, Hitchcock 1-38.

KICKOFF RETURNS—Tampa Bay, Anthony 5-130. Minnesota, Palmer 1-19, M. Williams 1-12.

PUNT RETURNS—Tampa Bay, Williams 2-23. Minnesota, Palmer 2-7.

SACKS—Tampa Bay, Parker 1. Minnesota, T. Williams 1.

49ERS 36, JETS 30

Sunday, September 6

N.Y. Jets	3	14	7	6	0—30
San Francisco	7	7	9	7	6—36

First Quarter
NYJ—FG, Hall 24, 3:26.
S.F.—Hearst 5 run (Richey kick), 11:29.

Second Quarter
NYJ—K. Johnson 41 pass from Foley (Hall kick), 4:49.
S.F.—Stokes 6 pass from S. Young (Richey kick), 12:49.
NYJ—Chrebet 6 pass from Foley (Hall kick), 14:27.

Third Quarter
S.F.—FG, Richey 22, 5:55.
NYJ—K. Johnson 21 pass from Foley (Hall kick), 7:45.
S.F.—Rice 14 pass from S. Young (kick blocked), 11:57.

Fourth Quarter
NYJ—FG, Hall 32, 11:22.
S.F.—Stokes 31 pass from S. Young (Richey kick), 13:34.
NYJ—FG, Hall 31, 15:00.

Overtime
S.F.—Hearst 96 run, 4:08.
Attendance—64,419.

	N.Y. Jets	San Francisco
First downs	26	26
Rushes-yards	24-59	24-207
Passing	406	350
Punt returns	1-9	3-38
Kickoff returns	6-105	4-91
Interception returns	1-34	1-0
Comp.-att.-int.	30-58-1	26-46-1
Sacked-yards lost	1-9	2-13
Punts	6-40	5-37
Fumbles-lost	0-0	1-0
Penalties-yards	6-33	5-56
Time of possession	34:46	29:22

INDIVIDUAL STATISTICS

RUSHING—New York, Martin 22-58, Sowell 2-1. San Francisco, Hearst 20-187, S. Young 2-14, Edwards 1-3, Levy 1-3.

PASSING—New York, Foley 30-58-1-415. San Francisco, S. Young 26-46-1-363.

RECEIVING—New York, K. Johnson 9-126, Chrebet 6-125, Ward 5-96, Martin 4-41, Sowell 2-10, Brady 2-10, Byars 1-7, L. Johnson 1-0. San Francisco, Stokes 7-111, Rice 6-86, Owens 3-60, I. Smith 3-35, Levy 3-11, Hearst 2-38, Edwards 2-22.

MISSED FIELD GOAL ATTEMPTS—New York, Hall 45. San Francisco, Richey 47.

INTERCEPTIONS—New York, Williams 1-34. San Francisco, Langham 1-0.

KICKOFF RETURNS—New York, L. Johnson 3-66, Glenn 3-39. San Francisco, Levy 4-91.

PUNT RETURNS—New York, L. Johnson 1-9. San Francisco, McQuarters 3-38.

SACKS—New York, B. Cox 2. San Francisco, Bryant 1.

DOLPHINS 24, COLTS 15

Sunday, September 6

Miami	3	14	0	7—24
Indianapolis	0	3	0	12—15

First Quarter
Mia.—FG, Mare 22, 9:19.

Second Quarter
Ind.—FG, Vanderjagt 51, 4:07.
Mia.—Gadsden 44 pass from Marino (Mare kick), 7:01.
Mia.—Abdul-Jabbar 4 run (Mare kick), 7:28.

Fourth Quarter
Ind.—FG, Vanderjagt 27, 0:47.
Ind.—FG, Vanderjagt 20, 11:07.
Mia.—Buckley 21 interception return (Mare kick), 13:41.
Ind.—Harrison 4 pass from Manning (pass failed), 15:00.
Attendance—60,587.

	Miami	Indianapolis
First downs	15	24
Rushes-yards	30-137	26-64
Passing	135	273
Punt returns	1-10	1-13
Kickoff returns	3-84	2-31
Interception returns	3-32	0-0
Comp.-att.-int.	13-24-0	21-37-3
Sacked-yards lost	0-0	4-29
Punts	5-43	3-45
Fumbles-lost	2-1	1-1
Penalties-yards	5-45	5-50
Time of possession	27:25	32:35

INDIVIDUAL STATISTICS

RUSHING—Miami, Abdul-Jabbar 23-108, Avery 5-28, Pritchett 1-1, Marino 1-0. Indianapolis, Faulk 24-56, Crockett 1-5, Pathon 1-3.

PASSING—Miami, Marino 13-24-0-135. Indianapolis, Manning 21-37-3-302.

RECEIVING—Miami, L. Thomas 2-29, McDuffie 2-14, Pritchett 2-10, Perry 2-9, Gadsden 1-44, Abdul-Jabbar 1-10, Drayton 1-9, Avery 1-5, Parmalee 1-5. Indianapolis, Harrison 5-102, Faulk 4-49, Pathon 4-44, Pollard 3-53, Dilger 3-22, Small 2-32.

MISSED FIELD GOAL ATTEMPTS—Miami, Mare 51.

INTERCEPTIONS—Miami, Buckley 2-33, Gardener 1-(minus 1).

KICKOFF RETURNS—Miami, Avery 3-84. Indianapolis, Bailey 2-31.

PUNT RETURNS—Miami, Jordan 1-10. Indianapolis, Bailey 1-13.

SACKS—Miami, Taylor 1, Rodgers 1, Armstrong 1, Jackson 1.

COWBOYS 38, CARDINALS 10

Sunday, September 6

Arizona	0	0	10	0—10
Dallas	0	14	7	17—38

Second Quarter
Dal.—Aikman 1 run (Cunningham kick), 9:12.
Dal.—E. Mills 30 pass from Aikman (Cunningham kick), 12:11.

Third Quarter
Ariz.—FG, Nedney 22, 3:21.
Dal.—Aikman 2 run (Cunningham kick), 7:51.
Ariz.—Plummer 1 run (Nedney kick), 14:31.

Fourth Quarter
Dal.—B. Davis 7 pass from Aikman (Cunningham kick), 4:08.
Dal.—FG, Cunningham 25, 14:41.
Dal.—Wheaton 15 fumble return (Cunningham kick), 14:49.
Attendance—63,602.

	Arizona	Dallas
First downs	13	30
Rushes-yards	17-45	42-183
Passing	160	256
Punt returns	4-19	5-56
Kickoff returns	3-41	1-38
Interception returns	2-34	0-0
Comp.-att.-int.	14-33-0	22-32-2
Sacked-yards lost	2-6	0-0
Punts	8-46	4-50
Fumbles-lost	2-2	2-1
Penalties-yards	7-68	11-70
Time of possession	22:35	37:25

INDIVIDUAL STATISTICS

RUSHING—Arizona, Murrell 13-35, Plummer 3-8, Centers 1-2. Dallas, E. Smith 28-122, S. Williams 6-9, Aikman 5-40, Johnston 2-11, B. Davis 1-1.

PASSING—Arizona, Plummer 14-33-0-166. Dallas, Aikman 22-32-2-256.

RECEIVING—Arizona, R. Moore 4-84, Sanders 4-33, Centers 3-21, McWilliams 1-17, Metcalf 1-7, Murrell 1-4. Dallas, Irvin 9-119, E. Mills 4-78, B. Davis 3-33, E. Smith 3-15, LaFleur 2-8, Johnston 1-3.

MISSED FIELD GOAL ATTEMPTS—None.
INTERCEPTIONS—Arizona, Bennett 1-30, McKinnon 1-4.
KICKOFF RETURNS—Arizona, Metcalf 3-41. Dallas, Mathis 1-38.
PUNT RETURNS—Arizona, Metcalf 4-19. Dallas, Sanders 5-56.
SACKS—Dallas, McCormack 1, Pittman 1.

CHARGERS 16, BILLS 14

Sunday, September 6

Buffalo	0	0	7	7—14
San Diego	3	0	10	3—16

First Quarter
S.D.—FG, Carney 48, 13:54.

Third Quarter
S.D.—Still 6 pass from Leaf (Carney kick), 1:44.
Buf.—Reed 43 pass from Flutie (Christie kick), 6:10.
S.D.—FG, Carney 47, 12:00.

Fourth Quarter
Buf.—Reed 5 pass from Flutie (Christie kick), 5:55.
S.D.—FG, Carney 54, 10:30.
Attendance—64,037.

	Buffalo	San Diego
First downs	20	14
Rushes-yards	28-90	20-67
Passing	207	187
Punt returns	2-32	2-28
Kickoff returns	4-99	3-78
Interception returns	2-0	2-12
Comp.-att.-int.	20-34-2	16-31-2
Sacked-yards lost	5-26	2-5
Punts	6-42	5-47
Fumbles-lost	1-0	1-0
Penalties-yards	7-64	8-118
Time of possession	33:08	26:52

INDIVIDUAL STATISTICS
RUSHING—Buffalo, A. Smith 20-54, Flutie 3-8, R. Johnson 2-18, Holmes 2-8, Linton 1-2. San Diego, Means 15-57, Fletcher 2-5, Leaf 2-(minus 1), Stephens 1-6.
PASSING—Buffalo, Flutie 12-20-1-158, R. Johnson 8-14-1-75. San Diego, Leaf 16-31-2-192.
RECEIVING—Buffalo, Reed 7-94, Moulds 5-68, Early 3-21, A. Smith 2-5, L. Johnson 1-27, Holmes 1-9, Gash 1-9. San Diego, Still 6-128, F. Jones 3-19, C. Jones 2-17, Fletcher 2-3, Ricks 1-14, Slaughter 1-9, Means 1-2.
MISSED FIELD GOAL ATTEMPTS—Buffalo, Christie 21, 39.
INTERCEPTIONS—Buffalo, Jones 2-0. San Diego, Harper 1-12, Shaw 1-0.
KICKOFF RETURNS—Buffalo, K. Williams 3-90, Gash 1-9. San Diego, Fletcher 2-56, Stephens 1-22.
PUNT RETURNS—Buffalo, K. Williams 2-32. San Diego, Rachal 2-28.
SACKS—Buffalo, Rogers 1, Price 1. San Diego, Harrison 3, Dixon 1, Fuller 1.

FALCONS 19, PANTHERS 14

Sunday, September 6

Atlanta	0	7	9	3—19
Carolina	0	7	7	0—14

Second Quarter
Atl.—Mathis 11 pass from Chandler (Andersen kick), 7:06.
Car.—Walls 6 pass from Collins (Kasay kick), 13:07.

Third Quarter
Atl.—Safety, Walter tackled by Bradford in end zone, 7:42.
Atl.—Dwight 44 pass from Chandler (Andersen kick), 12:53.
Car.—Ismail 56 pass from Collins (Kasay kick), 13:14.

Fourth Quarter
Atl.—FG, Andersen 43, 6:14.
Attendance—65,129.

	Atlanta	Carolina
First downs	19	16
Rushes-yards	31-93	19-54
Passing	230	263
Punt returns	2-4	3-5
Kickoff returns	3-70	4-121
Interception returns	1-1	1-0
Comp.-att.-int.	17-33-1	21-37-1
Sacked-yards lost	6-38	1-7
Punts	7-39	6-34

	Atlanta	Carolina
Fumbles-lost	1-0	2-0
Penalties-yards	11-72	6-40
Time of possession	36:18	23:42

INDIVIDUAL STATISTICS
RUSHING—Atlanta, Anderson 28-88, Green 2-4, Chandler 1-1. Carolina, Lane 14-40, Collins 3-12, Floyd 1-2, Walter 1-0.
PASSING—Atlanta, Chandler 17-33-1-268. Carolina, Collins 21-37-1-270.
RECEIVING—Atlanta, Mathis 6-74, Martin 4-92, Anderson 3-26, Dwight 1-44, Kinchen 1-19, Christian 1-9, Kozlowski 1-4. Carolina, Ismail 6-119, Carruth 4-59, Carrier 2-34, Muhammad 2-24, Walls 2-20, Floyd 2-5, Lane 1-15, Johnson 1-5, Collins 1-(minus 11).
MISSED FIELD GOAL ATTEMPTS—None.
INTERCEPTIONS—Atlanta, Buchanan 1-1. Carolina, Evans 1-0.
KICKOFF RETURNS—Atlanta, Dwight 3-70. Carolina, Bates 4-121.
PUNT RETURNS—Atlanta, Buchanan 1-4, Dwight 1-0. Carolina, Oliver 3-5.
SACKS—Atlanta, Fuller 1. Carolina, Greene 3, Brady 2, Barrow 1.

SAINTS 24, RAMS 17

Sunday, September 6

New Orleans	14	10	0	0—24
St. Louis	0	7	7	3—17

First Quarter
N.O.—J. Johnson 5 fumble return (Brien kick), 3:00.
N.O.—Hastings 20 pass from L. Smith (Brien kick), 10:47.

Second Quarter
N.O.—FG, Brien 36, 3:22.
N.O.—L. Smith 35 pass from Hobert (Brien kick), 10:15.
St.L.—J. Moore 1 run (Wilkins kick), 14:05.

Third Quarter
St.L.—Kennison 15 pass from Banks (Wilkins kick), 7:46.

Fourth Quarter
St.L.—FG, Wilkins 34, 13:34.
Attendance—56,943.

	New Orleans	St. Louis
First downs	15	22
Rushes-yards	24-37	25-56
Passing	197	267
Punt returns	4-52	5-67
Kickoff returns	1-16	5-76
Interception returns	1-8	1-6
Comp.-att.-int.	15-30-1	29-44-1
Sacked-yards lost	2-17	5-31
Punts	7-47	7-44
Fumbles-lost	2-0	5-1
Penalties-yards	6-54	10-105
Time of possession	26:01	33:59

INDIVIDUAL STATISTICS
RUSHING—New Orleans, L. Smith 16-14, Zellars 5-9, Hobert 2-13, Craver 1-1. St. Louis, J. Moore 15-31, Banks 5-17, Henley 3-5, Lee 1-3, Harris 1-0.
PASSING—New Orleans, Hobert 11-23-0-170, Wuerffel 3-6-1-24, L. Smith 1-1-0-20. St. Louis, Banks 29-44-1-298.
RECEIVING—New Orleans, Cleeland 4-82, L. Smith 3-60, Hastings 3-32, Craver 2-8, Zellars 1-12, Poole 1-12, T. Johnson 1-8. St. Louis, Bruce 10-131, Lee 8-64, Conwell 4-37, Kennison 2-27, Proehl 2-25, Henley 2-8, J. Moore 1-6.
MISSED FIELD GOAL ATTEMPTS—None.
INTERCEPTIONS—New Orleans, Knight 1-8. St. Louis, Jenkins 1-6.
KICKOFF RETURNS—New Orleans, Ismail 1-16. St. Louis, Horne 4-63, Henley 1-13.
PUNT RETURNS—New Orleans, Hastings 4-52. St. Louis, Kennison 5-67.
SACKS—New Orleans, Glover 2, Martin 2, Cota 1. St. Louis, M. A. Jones 1, Farr 1.

SEAHAWKS 38, EAGLES 0

Sunday, September 6

Seattle	14	0	17	7—38
Philadelphia	0	0	0	0— 0

First Quarter
Sea.—Springs 42 interception return (Peterson kick), 8:06.
Sea.—Galloway 25 pass from Moon (Peterson kick), 9:02.

Third Quarter
Sea.—Strong 11 pass from Moon (Peterson kick), 4:17.
Sea.—Galloway 35 pass from Moon (Peterson kick), 6:06.
Sea.—FG, Peterson 42, 14:35.

Fourth Quarter
Sea.—Green 6 run (Peterson kick), 1:35.
 Attendance—66,418.

	Seattle	Philadelphia
First downs	18	14
Rushes-yards	34-188	32-162
Passing	218	12
Punt returns	6-48	0-0
Kickoff returns	1-17	3-61
Interception returns	1-42	0-0
Comp.-att.-int.	14-22-0	9-23-1
Sacked-yards lost	0-0	9-51
Punts	4-43	9-42
Fumbles-lost	1-0	3-2
Penalties-yards	6-50	2-12
Time of possession	29:23	30:37

INDIVIDUAL STATISTICS
RUSHING—Seattle, Watters 16-67, Green 6-100, Broussard 5-4, Strong 3-14, Friesz 2-(minus 2), Moon 1-3, R. Brown 1-2. Philadelphia, Staley 20-95, Turner 8-54, Hoying 3-13, Walker 1-0.
PASSING—Seattle, Moon 13-21-0-204, Friesz 1-1-0-14. Philadelphia, Hoying 9-23-1-63.
RECEIVING—Seattle, Galloway 6-142, Strong 2-13, McKnight 1-28, Br. Blades 1-14, Pritchard 1-11, Fauria 1-9, Watters 1-2, Green 1-(minus 1). Philadelphia, Graham 3-30, Turner 3-9, Solomon 1-13, Staley 1-6, J. Johnson 1-5.
MISSED FIELD GOAL ATTEMPTS—None.
INTERCEPTIONS—Seattle, Springs 1-42.
KICKOFF RETURNS—Seattle, Broussard 1-17. Philadelphia, Hayden 1-22, Rossum 1-21, Walker 1-18.
PUNT RETURNS—Seattle, Joseph 6-48.
SACKS—Seattle, Sinclair 2.5, Smith 2, Daniels 1.5, Collins 1, Adams 1, Parker 1.

PACKERS 38, LIONS 19

Sunday, September 6

Detroit	3	3	13	0—19
Green Bay	10	7	7	14—38

First Quarter
G.B.—FG, Longwell 32, 5:41.
G.B.—Butler 32 fumble return (Longwell kick), 8:37.
Det.—FG, Hanson 47, 13:50.

Second Quarter
G.B.—Levens 4 run (Longwell kick), 5:20.
Det.—FG, Hanson 43, 14:17.

Third Quarter
Det.—Moore 25 pass from Mitchell (pass failed), 2:21.
G.B.—Freeman 6 pass from Favre (Longwell kick), 14:43.
Det.—Fair 101 kickoff return (Hanson kick), 15:00.

Fourth Quarter
G.B.—Preston 100 kickoff return (Longwell kick), 0:22.
G.B.—Freeman 84 pass from Favre (Longwell kick), 13:07.
 Attendance—60,102.

	Detroit	Green Bay
First downs	20	21
Rushes-yards	21-90	30-75
Passing	231	267
Punt returns	2-23	1-0
Kickoff returns	6-244	4-163
Interception returns	0-0	1-0
Comp.-att.-int.	23-44-1	24-32-0
Sacked-yards lost	3-17	2-10
Punts	3-47	4-46
Fumbles-lost	1-1	1-0
Penalties-yards	6-60	6-30
Time of possession	26:02	33:58

INDIVIDUAL STATISTICS
RUSHING—Detroit, Sanders 17-70, Mitchell 3-15, Rivers 1-5. Green Bay, Levens 25-59, Henderson 3-8, Jervey 2-8.
PASSING—Detroit, Mitchell 23-44-1-248. Green Bay, Favre 24-32-0-277.

RECEIVING—Detroit, Moore 9-100, Morton 9-96, Crowell 2-18, Vardell 1-21, T. Boyd 1-7, Rasby 1-6. Green Bay, Levens 7-38, Freeman 4-110, Chmura 4-51, Mayes 4-38, Schroeder 2-17, Thomason 1-13, R. Brooks 1-11, Henderson 1-(minus 1).
MISSED FIELD GOAL ATTEMPTS—None.
INTERCEPTIONS—Green Bay, Prior 1-0.
KICKOFF RETURNS—Detroit, Fair 6-244. Green Bay, Preston 4-163.
PUNT RETURNS—Detroit, Fair 2-23. Green Bay, Preston 1-0.
SACKS—Detroit, Waldroup 1, Scroggins 1. Green Bay, Holliday 1, McKenzie 1, Butler 0.5, London 0.5.

JAGUARS 24, BEARS 23

Sunday, September 6

Jacksonville	0	7	7	10—24
Chicago	3	10	0	10—23

First Quarter
Chi.—FG, Jaeger 45, 9:04.

Second Quarter
Jac.—Stewart 3 pass from Brunell (Hollis kick), 7:35.
Chi.—Milburn 88 kickoff return (Jaeger kick), 7:54.
Chi.—FG, Jaeger 35, 14:57.

Third Quarter
Jac.—Stewart 7 run (Hollis kick), 12:33.

Fourth Quarter
Jac.—FG, Hollis 23, 0:44.
Chi.—Bennett 1 run (Jaeger kick), 6:10.
Chi.—FG, Jaeger 19, 10:52.
Jac.—J. Smith 4 pass from Brunell (Hollis kick), 14:31.
 Attendance—55,614.

	Jacksonville	Chicago
First downs	21	16
Rushes-yards	33-160	34-132
Passing	207	189
Punt returns	3-24	1-4
Kickoff returns	2-34	5-197
Interception returns	0-0	2-36
Comp.-att.-int.	22-35-2	16-27-0
Sacked-yards lost	1-0	0-0
Punts	5-43	4-46
Fumbles-lost	4-1	2-2
Penalties-yards	3-26	4-26
Time of possession	29:50	30:10

INDIVIDUAL STATISTICS
RUSHING—Jacksonville, Stewart 26-115, Brunell 6-43, F. Taylor 1-2. Chicago, Bennett 13-30, Enis 12-77, Chancey 3-8, Hallock 3-6, Kramer 2-3, Conway 1-8.
PASSING—Jacksonville, Brunell 22-35-2-207. Chicago, Kramer 16-27-0-189.
RECEIVING—Jacksonville, J. Smith 9-90, McCardell 7-72, Stewart 3-22, Banks 1-10, Shelton 1-8, Mitchell 1-5. Chicago, Conway 6-91, Bennett 4-19, Engram 2-35, Wetnight 2-33, Enis 1-7, Hallock 1-4.
MISSED FIELD GOAL ATTEMPTS—Chicago, Jaeger 42.
INTERCEPTIONS—Chicago, Tom. Carter 1-19, Minter 1-17.
KICKOFF RETURNS—Jacksonville, Barlow 1-21, Mitchell 1-13. Chicago, Milburn 5-197.
PUNT RETURNS—Jacksonville, Barlow 3-24. Chicago, Milburn 1-4.
SACKS—Chicago, S. Harris 1.

GIANTS 31, REDSKINS 24

Sunday, September 6

Washington	7	3	7	7—24
N.Y. Giants	0	10	21	0—31

First Quarter
Was.—Shepherd 17 pass from Frerotte (Blanton kick), 6:16.

Second Quarter
NYG—FG, Daluiso 35, 0:09.
Was.—FG, Blanton 46, 12:03.
NYG—Calloway 5 pass from Kanell (Daluiso kick), 14:32.

Third Quarter
NYG—Way 2 run (Daluiso kick), 1:54.
NYG—Strahan 24 interception return (Daluiso kick), 2:53.
Was.—Bowie 4 pass from T. Green (Blanton kick), 11:04.
NYG—Toomer 22 pass from Kanell (Daluiso kick), 13:27.

Was.—Alexander 1 pass from T. Green (Blanton kick), 8:44.
Attendance—76,629.

	Washington	N.Y. Giants
First downs	21	15
Rushes-yards	23-73	30-82
Passing	258	153
Punt returns	3-49	2-15
Kickoff returns	4-106	5-131
Interception returns	1-4	2-41
Comp.-att.-int.	25-37-2	15-28-1
Sacked-yards lost	8-43	1-6
Punts	5-43	8-45
Fumbles-lost	2-1	0-0
Penalties-yards	9-75	6-37
Time of possession	32:10	27:50

INDIVIDUAL STATISTICS

RUSHING—Washington, Allen 18-67, Davis 2-2, Mitchell 1-5, Shepherd 1-0, Frerotte 1-(minus 1). New York, Barber 12-37, Way 10-25, Brown 7-21, Kanell 1-(minus 1).

PASSING—Washington, T. Green 17-25-0-208, Frerotte 8-12-2-93. New York, Kanell 15-28-1-159.

RECEIVING—Washington, Allen 6-42, Shepherd 4-74, Bowie 4-25, Alexander 3-25, Westbrook 2-73, Thomas 2-21, Mitchell 2-16, Thrash 1-13, Asher 1-12. New York, Toomer 3-32, Way 3-22, Calloway 3-21, Cross 3-12, Hilliard 2-50, Jurevicius 1-22.

MISSED FIELD GOAL ATTEMPTS—None.

INTERCEPTIONS—Washington, Campbell 1-4. New York, Strahan 1-24, C. Hamilton 1-17.

KICKOFF RETURNS—Washington, Thrash 2-64, Mitchell 2-42. New York, Patten 5-131.

PUNT RETURNS—Washington, Mitchell 3-49. New York, Toomer 2-15.

SACKS—Washington, Jones 1. New York, Bratzke 2, Strahan 2, K. Hamilton 2, Harris 1, Peter 1.

OILERS 23, BENGALS 14

Sunday, September 6

Tennessee	3	7	7	6—23
Cincinnati	7	0	7	0—14

First Quarter
Ten.—FG, Del Greco 38, 3:54.
Cin.—Scott 23 pass from O'Donnell (Pelfrey kick), 9:09.

Second Quarter
Ten.—Davis 8 pass from McNair (Del Greco kick), 8:53.

Third Quarter
Ten.—E. George 3 run (Del Greco kick), 8:15.
Cin.—Dillon 3 run (Pelfrey kick), 12:35.

Fourth Quarter
Ten.—FG, Del Greco 31, 0:04.
Ten.—FG, Del Greco 48, 9:31.
Attendance—55,848.

	Tennessee	Cincinnati
First downs	19	16
Rushes-yards	29-89	24-96
Passing	264	196
Punt returns	2-17	1-0
Kickoff returns	1-25	2-44
Interception returns	1-0	0-0
Comp.-att.-int.	17-34-0	24-32-1
Sacked-yards lost	0-0	1-4
Punts	4-43	5-47
Fumbles-lost	1-0	0-0

	Tennessee	Cincinnati
Penalties-yards	11-94	6-52
Time of possession	33:48	26:12

INDIVIDUAL STATISTICS

RUSHING—Tennessee, E. George 25-86, Krieg 2-(minus 1), Thomas 1-3, McNair 1-1. Cincinnati, Dillon 20-87, Carter 2-4, O'Donnell 1-5, Bieniemy 1-0.

PASSING—Tennessee, McNair 10-21-0-135, Krieg 7-13-0-129. Cincinnati, O'Donnell 24-32-1-200.

RECEIVING—Tennessee, Thigpen 4-87, Wycheck 3-34, Davis 2-46, Harris 2-27, Mason 2-24, E. George 2-15, Sanders 1-18, Kent 1-13. Cincinnati, Carter 6-25, Pickens 5-69, Bieniemy 4-24, Gibson 3-30, Scott 2-30, McGee 1-8, Battaglia 1-6, Bush 1-5, Dillon 1-3.

MISSED FIELD GOAL ATTEMPTS—Tennessee, Del Greco 47.

INTERCEPTIONS—Tennessee, Robertson 1-0.

KICKOFF RETURNS—Tennessee, Mason 1-25. Cincinnati, Mack 2-44.

PUNT RETURNS—Tennessee, Mason 2-17. Cincinnati, Gibson 1-0.

SACKS—Tennessee, Holmes 1.

BRONCOS 27, PATRIOTS 21

Monday, September 7

New England	0	7	7	7—21
Denver	10	7	3	7—27

First Quarter
Den.—FG, Elam 53, 2:29.
Den.—Sharpe 12 pass from Elway (Elam kick), 13:20.

Second Quarter
Den.—Davis 9 run (Elam kick), 5:32.
N.E.—Edwards 1 run (Vinatieri kick), 9:43.

Third Quarter
N.E.—Brown 24 pass from Bledsoe (Vinatieri kick), 2:39.
Den.—FG, Elam 42, 7:16.

Fourth Quarter
Den.—Davis 1 run (Elam kick), 4:09.
N.E.—Brisby 10 pass from Bledsoe (Vinatieri kick), 13:01.
Attendance—74,745.

	New England	Denver
First downs	17	20
Rushes-yards	24-81	30-91
Passing	258	248
Punt returns	2-8	3-53
Kickoff returns	5-170	3-52
Interception returns	0-0	0-0
Comp.-att.-int.	20-32-0	22-34-0
Sacked-yards lost	3-31	1-9
Punts	5-51	4-46
Fumbles-lost	2-0	0-0
Penalties-yards	7-49	5-30
Time of possession	26:47	33:13

INDIVIDUAL STATISTICS

RUSHING— New England, Edwards 13-50, S. Shaw 7-25, Bledsoe 3-3, Cullors 1-3. Denver, Davis 22-75, Elway 5-12, Griffith 2-2, Loville 1-2.

PASSING— New England, Bledsoe 20-32-0-289. Denver, Elway 22-34-0-257.

RECEIVING— New England, Brown 5-97, Glenn 5-71, Ton. Carter 4-25, Jefferson 2-64, Brisby 1-10, Cullors 1-9, Coates 1-9, Purnell 1-4. Denver, McCaffrey 7-97, R. Smith 6-57, Sharpe 5-51, Armour 1-23, Griffith 1-15, Davis 1-7, Chamberlain 1-7.

MISSED FIELD GOAL ATTEMPTS— New England, Vinatieri 39, 37.

INTERCEPTIONS— None.

KICKOFF RETURNS— New England, Cullors 5-170. Denver, Loville 3-52.

PUNT RETURNS— New England, Brown 2-8. Denver, Gordon 3-53.

SACKS— New England, Mitchell 1. Denver, Romanowski 2, Tanuvasa 1.

WEEK 2

RESULTS

ATLANTA 17, Philadelphia 12
Baltimore 24, N.Y. JETS 10
Cincinnati 34, DETROIT 28 (OT)
DENVER 42, Dallas 23
GREEN BAY 23, Tampa Bay 15
JACKSONVILLE 21, Kansas City 16
MIAMI 13, Buffalo 7
Minnesota 38, ST. LOUIS 31
NEW ENGLAND 29, Indianapolis 6
NEW ORLEANS 19, Carolina 14
PITTSBURGH 17, Chicago 12
OAKLAND 20, N.Y. Giants 17
San Diego 13, TENNESSEE 7
SEATTLE 33, Arizona 14
San Francisco 45, WASHINGTON 10

STANDINGS

AFC EAST

	W	L	T	Pct.
Miami	2	0	0	1.000
New England	1	1	0	.500
Buffalo	0	2	0	.000
Indianapolis	0	2	0	.000
N.Y. Jets	0	2	0	.000

AFC CENTRAL

	W	L	T	Pct.
Jacksonville	2	0	0	1.000
Pittsburgh	2	0	0	1.000
Baltimore	1	1	0	.500
Cincinnati	1	1	0	.500
Tennessee	1	1	0	.500

AFC WEST

	W	L	T	Pct.
Denver	2	0	0	1.000
San Diego	2	0	0	1.000
Seattle	2	0	0	1.000
Kansas City	1	1	0	.500
Oakland	1	1	0	.500

NFC EAST

	W	L	T	Pct.
Dallas	1	1	0	.500
N.Y. Giants	1	1	0	.500
Arizona	0	2	0	.000
Philadelphia	0	2	0	.000
Washington	0	2	0	.000

NFC CENTRAL

	W	L	T	Pct.
Green Bay	2	0	0	1.000
Minnesota	2	0	0	1.000
Chicago	0	2	0	.000
Detroit	0	2	0	.000
Tampa Bay	0	2	0	.000

NFC WEST

	W	L	T	Pct.
Atlanta	2	0	0	1.000
New Orleans	2	0	0	1.000
San Francisco	2	0	0	1.000
Carolina	0	2	0	.000
St. Louis	0	2	0	.000

HIGHLIGHTS

Hero of the week: Broncos running back Terrell Davis ran for three touchdowns and 191 yards on 23 carries (8.3-yard average) in Denver's 42-23 win over Dallas. Included were first-quarter touchdown runs of 63 and 59 yards and a 3-yard scoring run in the fourth quarter.

Goat of the week: Colts quarterback Peyton Manning, in his second NFL start, committed four turnovers—one fumble, three interceptions—that led to 20 points for the Patriots. New England routed Indianapolis, 29-6.

Sub of the week: Vikings quarterback Randall Cunningham, who replaced Brad Johnson early in the fourth quarter after Johnson suffered a sprained ankle, delivered two third-down completions on Minnesota's game-winning drive against the Rams. With the score tied, Cunningham threw a 19-yarder to Cris Carter, who twisted away from safety Keith Lyle to give the Vikings a 38-31 victory.

Comeback of the week: The Falcons overcame a 9-0 halftime deficit to beat the Eagles 17-12. Atlanta rebounded from a dismal first half by scoring on its first two possessions of the third quarter. Chris Chandler threw a 19-yard touchdown pass to Brian Kozlowski and Jamal Anderson scored on a 1-yard run. Morten Andersen hit a 23-yard field goal in the fourth quarter.

Blowout of the week: The 49ers rolled past the Redskins, 45-10, on Monday night, handing Washington its worst home loss in 51 years. San Francisco gave Redskins quarterback Trent Green a rude initiation in his first game as an NFL starter, sacking him four times and forcing three turnovers. The 49ers offense amassed 504 yards, including 303 yards passing by Steve Young and 138 yards rushing by Garrison Hearst.

Nail-biter of the week: At the end of regulation, Cincinnati and Detroit were tied 28-28, with each team having scored one touchdown in each quarter. On the fourth play of overtime, Bengals cornerback Corey Sawyer intercepted a Scott Mitchell pass intended for Johnnie Morton and returned it 53 yards for a touch-down, giving Cincinnati a 34-28 victory.

Hit of the week: Cowboys quarterback Troy Aikman was hit by Broncos defenders Neil Smith and Marvin Washington with 9:22 left in the first half and Denver ahead 28-14. Flushed from the pocket on second-and-7 from the Dallas 36, Aikman was hit as he dived a yard shy of a first down. Aikman suffered a broken collarbone, and Denver went on to beat Dallas.

Oddity of the week: Mitchell was intercepted on consecutive passes against Cincinnati. The first came in the last minute of regulation, setting up what would have been the Bengals' game-winning field goal had it not been blocked. The second pick came in overtime, and Sawyer returned it for a touchdown to give Cincinnati a 34-28 victory.

Top rusher: Terrell Davis ran for 191 yards and three touchdowns in leading Denver to a 42-23 victory over Dallas.

Top passer: San Francisco's Steve Young was 21-of-32 passes for 303 yards in the 49ers' 45-10 victory over the Redskins.

Top receiver: Muhsin Muhammad caught nine passes for 192 yards and one touchdown in Carolina's 19-14 loss to New Orleans.

Notes: The 42 points scored by Denver was the second most ever by an AFC team against the Cowboys. Cincinnati scored eight more points in a 50-24 win over Dallas in 1985. . . . Dallas running back Emmitt Smith (11,451 yards) moved into eighth place on the NFL's all-time rushing list, passing Thurman Thomas (11,405 yards). . . . The Dolphins had eight sacks against Buffalo, one short of a team record set in 1973 against the Bills. . . . La'Roi Glover's sack of Carolina quarterback Kerry Collins in the first quarter marked the 51st consecutive game the Saints had a sack, the longest current streak in the NFL and the longest this decade. . . . Kevin Greene's two sacks for the Panthers gave him 138 for his career, moving him past Richard Dent into third place all-time. . . . The Packers won their 25th consecutive home game, two shy of the Miami Dolphins' record of 27 from 1971-74. . . . Reggie White's three sacks gave him 55.5 as a Packer, surpassing Tim Harris (55) for the franchise record. . . . Reggie Barlow's 85-yard punt return for a touchdown was the first in Jaguars history and the longest punt return in team history. . . . Baltimore's Michael Jackson had 50 yards receiving, moving him past the 5,000-yard career mark (5,017). . . . Eagles kicker Chris Boniol connected on his 63rd consecutive field goal from 35 yards and closer. . . . Chris Chandler tied a Falcons record held by Steve Bartkowski and Chris Miller by throwing a TD pass in his 14th consecutive game. . . . Rams quarterback Tony Banks threw a career-high four interceptions. . . . Vikings wide receiver Cris Carter caught his 765th pass, moving him past James Lofton into sixth place on the all-time list.

Quote of the week: Bills quarterback Rob Johnson, who endured a relentless pass rush and was sacked eight times in a 13-7 loss to the Dolphins: "It's kind of like bloody water when sharks are around. . . . I'm beat up, but I wouldn't feel as bad if we had won."

GAME SUMMARIES

PATRIOTS 29, COLTS 6

Sunday, September 13

Indianapolis	0	0	0	6—	6
New England	10	6	6	7—	29

First Quarter
N.E.—FG, Vinatieri 19, 7:54.
N.E.—Law 59 interception return (Vinatieri kick), 10:47.
Second Quarter
N.E.—FG, Vinatieri 23, 9:03.
N.E.—FG, Vinatieri 52, 15:00.
Third Quarter
N.E.—Glenn 3 pass from Bledsoe (pass failed), 5:26.
Fourth Quarter
N.E.—Edwards 1 run (Vinatieri kick), 0:39.
Ind.—Small 3 pass from Manning (pass failed), 10:51.
Attendance—60,068.

	Indianapolis	New England
First downs	20	15
Rushes-yards	32-136	33-103
Passing	173	218
Punt returns	4-30	1-38
Kickoff returns	6-127	2-74
Interception returns	0-0	3-71
Comp.-att.-int.	21-33-3	15-29-0
Sacked-yards lost	2-15	0-0
Punts	6-42	5-45
Fumbles-lost	1-1	2-0
Penalties-yards	5-32	4-30
Time of possession	32:05	27:55

INDIVIDUAL STATISTICS
RUSHING—Indianapolis, Faulk 29-127, Elias 3-9. New England, Edwards 18-36, S. Shaw 5-55, Bledsoe 3-2, Zolak 3-(minus 3), Cullors 2-6, Glenn 1-7, Ton. Carter 1-0.
PASSING—Indianapolis, Manning 21-33-3-188. New England, Bledsoe 15-29-0-218.
RECEIVING—Indianapolis, Faulk 7-60, Pollard 6-53, Dilger 4-38, Harrison 2-26, Pathon 1-8, Small 1-3. New England, Edwards 3-71, Brown 3-50, Glenn 3-25, Cullors 2-6, Ton. Carter 2-6, Jefferson 1-38, Purnell 1-22.
MISSED FIELD GOAL ATTEMPTS—New England, Vinatieri 42.
INTERCEPTIONS—New England, Law 2-59, Canty 1-12.
KICKOFF RETURNS—Indianapolis, Bailey 6-127. New England, Cullors 2-74.
PUNT RETURNS—Indianapolis, Bailey 4-30. New England, Brown 1-38.
SACKS—New England, Slade 1, McGinest 1.

BENGALS 34, LIONS 28

Sunday, September 13

Cincinnati	7	7	7	7	6—	34
Detroit	7	7	7	7	0—	28

First Quarter
Cin.—Scott 70 pass from O'Donnell (Pelfrey kick), 5:44.
Det.—Vardell 1 run (Hanson kick), 8:16.
Second Quarter
Cin.—Scott 36 pass from O'Donnell (Pelfrey kick), 0:45.
Det.—Sanders 2 run (Hanson kick), 6:30.
Third Quarter
Det.—Sanders 67 run (Hanson kick), 0:55.
Cin.—Dillon 18 run (Pelfrey kick), 7:15.
Fourth Quarter
Cin.—Gibson 65 punt return (Pelfrey kick), 0:42.
Det.—Sanders 5 run (Hanson kick), 13:08.
Overtime
Cin.—Sawyer 53 interception return, 2:06.
Attendance—66,354.

	Cincinnati	Detroit
First downs	18	22
Rushes-yards	21-100	34-224
Passing	284	188
Punt returns	5-82	3-34
Kickoff returns	2-44	2-55
Interception returns	2-53	0-0
Comp.-att.-int.	25-36-0	15-31-2
Sacked-yards lost	3-19	2-16
Punts	7-48	7-47
Fumbles-lost	0-0	0-0
Penalties-yards	5-40	10-83
Time of possession	28:57	33:09

INDIVIDUAL STATISTICS
RUSHING—Cincinnati, Dillon 17-77, O'Donnell 2-15, Scott 1-8, Bieniemy 1-0. Detroit, Sanders 26-185, Vardell 4-8, Mitchell 3-20, Morton 1-11.
PASSING—Cincinnati, O'Donnell 25-36-0-303. Detroit, Mitchell 15-31-2-204.
RECEIVING—Cincinnati, Pickens 9-75, Scott 5-130, Bieniemy 5-17, McGee 2-53, Hundon 1-15, Bush 1-8, Gibson 1-6, Dillon 1-(minus 1). Detroit, Moore 7-86, Morton 5-50, Sanders 1-44, Vardell 1-12, Crowell 1-12.
MISSED FIELD GOAL ATTEMPTS—Cincinnati, Pelfrey 35, 48.
INTERCEPTIONS—Cincinnati, Sawyer 1-53, Ambrose 1-0.
KICKOFF RETURNS—Cincinnati, Mack 2-44. Detroit, Fair 2-55.
PUNT RETURNS—Cincinnati, Gibson 5-82. Detroit, Fair 3-34.
SACKS—Cincinnati, Wilson 1, Foley 1. Detroit, Aldridge 1, Scroggins 1, Porcher 0.5, Owens 0.5.

CHARGERS 13, OILERS 7

Sunday, September 13

San Diego	3	3	7	0—	13
Tennessee	0	7	0	0—	7

First Quarter
S.D.—FG, Carney 48, 12:33.
Second Quarter
S.D.—FG, Carney 23, 10:30.
Ten.—Wycheck 15 pass from McNair (Del Greco kick), 14:38.
Third Quarter
S.D.—Means 1 run (Carney kick), 11:07.
Attendance—41,089.

	San Diego	Tennessee
First downs	17	18
Rushes-yards	34-141	19-63
Passing	179	187
Punt returns	2-21	1-1
Kickoff returns	1-17	3-59
Interception returns	0-0	0-0
Comp.-att.-int.	13-24-0	21-35-0
Sacked-yards lost	0-0	3-19
Punts	3-46	6-43
Fumbles-lost	0-0	1-0
Penalties-yards	5-40	9-69
Time of possession	31:02	28:58

INDIVIDUAL STATISTICS

RUSHING—San Diego, Means 23-87, Leaf 7-31, Fletcher 3-11, Stephens 1-12. Tennessee, E. George 15-11, McNair 3-31, Thomas 1-21.

PASSING—San Diego, Leaf 13-24-0-179. Tennessee, McNair 20-34-0-193, Hentrich 1-1-0-13.

RECEIVING—San Diego, F. Jones 5-41, Still 3-59, Ricks 2-47, C. Jones 2-23, Fletcher 1-9. Tennessee, Wycheck 7-55, Thigpen 5-51, Harris 3-37, E. George 2-8, Kent 1-23, Mason 1-18, Davis 1-8, Thomas 1-6.

MISSED FIELD GOAL ATTEMPTS—San Diego, Carney 51.

INTERCEPTIONS—None.

KICKOFF RETURNS—San Diego, Stephens 1-17. Tennessee, Mason 3-59.

PUNT RETURNS—San Diego, Rachal 2-21. Tennessee, Mason 1-1.

SACKS—San Diego, Hand 1, Dumas 1, Parrella 0.5, Dixon 0.5.

SEAHAWKS 33, CARDINALS 14

Sunday, September 13

Arizona	0	0	7	7—14
Seattle	10	10	0	13—33

First Quarter
Sea.—FG, Peterson 51, 8:50.
Sea.—W. Williams 28 interception return (Peterson kick), 9:10.

Second Quarter
Sea.—Strong 4 pass from Moon (Peterson kick), 4:57.
Sea.—FG, Peterson 22, 15:00.

Third Quarter
Ariz.—Murrell 4 run (Nedney kick), 5:23.

Fourth Quarter
Sea.—Galloway 9 pass from Moon (run failed), 0:47.
Sea.—Springs 56 interception return (Peterson kick), 2:57.
Ariz.—Gedney 23 pass from Plummer (Nedney kick), 10:53.
Attendance—57,678.

	Arizona	Seattle
First downs	17	16
Rushes-yards	26-111	32-123
Passing	163	121
Punt returns	1-8	2-0
Kickoff returns	5-94	1-23
Interception returns	0-0	3-84
Comp.-att.-int.	22-36-3	14-23-0
Sacked-yards lost	7-41	3-25
Punts	6-39	4-41
Fumbles-lost	2-1	4-2
Penalties-yards	7-98	5-34
Time of possession	31:33	28:27

INDIVIDUAL STATISTICS

RUSHING—Arizona, Murrell 20-79, Plummer 3-23, Pittman 2-7, Centers 1-2. Seattle, Watters 22-105, Green 7-21, Moon 1-0, Strong 1-0, Galloway 1-(minus 3).

PASSING—Arizona, Plummer 22-36-3-204. Seattle, Moon 14-23-0-146.

RECEIVING—Arizona, Centers 7-54, Sanders 4-43, Metcalf 3-28, R. Moore 2-29, Gedney 2-25, McWilliams 2-13, Brock 1-7, Murrell 1-5. Seattle, Pritchard 3-54, Br. Blades 3-23, McKnight 2-26, Galloway 2-20, Strong 2-12, Watters 2-11.

MISSED FIELD GOAL ATTEMPTS—None.

INTERCEPTIONS—Seattle, Springs 1-56, W. Williams 1-28, Collins 1-0.

KICKOFF RETURNS—Arizona, Metcalf 5-94. Seattle, Broussard 1-23.

PUNT RETURNS—Arizona, Metcalf 1-8. Seattle, Galloway 2-0.

SACKS—Arizona, Knight 1, Miller 1, Swann 1. Seattle, Smith 2, Sinclair 2, Bellamy 1, LaBounty 1, C. Brown 0.5, Daniels 0.5.

BRONCOS 42, COWBOYS 23

Sunday, September 13

Dallas	7	10	3	3—23
Denver	21	14	0	7—42

First Quarter
Den.—Sharpe 38 pass from Elway (Elam kick), 5:37.
Dal.—E. Mills 36 pass from Aikman (Cunningham kick), 8:43.
Den.—Davis 63 run (Elam kick), 10:25.
Den.—Davis 59 run (Elam kick), 11:47.

Second Quarter
Dal.—E. Smith 4 run (Cunningham kick), 0:52.
Den.—Sharpe 23 pass from Elway (Elam kick), 4:27.
Dal.—FG, Cunningham 30, 9:34.
Den.—Elway 1 run (Elam kick), 14:35.

Third Quarter
Dal.—FG, Cunningham 54, 7:47.

Fourth Quarter
Dal.—FG, Cunningham 26, 2:06.
Den.—Davis 3 run (Elam kick), 7:27.
Attendance—75,013.

	Dallas	Denver
First downs	18	21
Rushes-yards	30-169	31-209
Passing	201	306
Punt returns	0-0	2-19
Kickoff returns	6-158	2-56
Interception returns	0-0	0-0
Comp.-att.-int.	19-31-0	17-23-0
Sacked-yards lost	1-0	0-0
Punts	2-51	2-48
Fumbles-lost	0-0	0-0
Penalties-yards	4-19	4-25
Time of possession	32:13	27:47

INDIVIDUAL STATISTICS

RUSHING—Dallas, E. Smith 20-93, S. Williams 4-33, Aikman 2-9, Garrett 2-1, Gowin 1-33, Johnston 1-0. Denver, Davis 23-191, Loville 6-15, Brister 1-2, Elway 1-1.

PASSING—Dallas, Garrett 14-19-0-113, Aikman 5-12-0-88. Denver, Elway 16-22-0-268, Brister 1-1-0-38.

RECEIVING—Dallas, Irvin 6-81, B. Davis 4-29, Johnston 3-7, E. Mills 2-42, S. Williams 2-4, Bjornson 1-31, E. Smith 1-7. Denver, Sharpe 6-97, McCaffrey 5-117, R. Smith 4-76, Chamberlain 1-12, Green 1-4.

MISSED FIELD GOAL ATTEMPTS—None.

INTERCEPTIONS—None.

KICKOFF RETURNS—Dallas, Mathis 5-146, LaFleur 1-12. Denver, Hebron 1-35, D. Smith 1-21.

PUNT RETURNS—Denver, Gordon 2-19.

SACKS—Denver, Washington 1.

STEELERS 17, BEARS 12

Sunday, September 13

Chicago	0	9	0	3—12
Pittsburgh	0	7	10	0—17

Second Quarter
Chi.—Engram 54 pass from Kramer (kick failed), 3:57.
Pit.—Bettis 1 run (N. Johnson kick), 9:54.
Chi.—FG, Jaeger 19, 15:00.

Third Quarter
Pit.—FG, N. Johnson 49, 7:04.
Pit.—Coleman 13 pass from Stewart (N. Johnson kick), 9:21.

Fourth Quarter
Chi.—FG, Jaeger 36, 2:28.
Attendance—59,084.

	Chicago	Pittsburgh
First downs	19	17
Rushes-yards	33-130	27-142
Passing	190	109
Punt returns	5-50	0-0
Kickoff returns	4-71	3-76
Interception returns	1-1	1-22
Comp.-att.-int.	18-33-1	17-30-1
Sacked-yards lost	1-4	3-28
Punts	8-50	8-51
Fumbles-lost	1-1	0-0
Penalties-yards	5-32	5-39
Time of possession	27:58	32:02

INDIVIDUAL STATISTICS

RUSHING—Chicago, Enis 22-94, Bennett 7-27, Morris 2-8, Chancey 1-2, Hallock 1-(minus 1). Pittsburgh, Bettis 21-131, Stewart 4-4, Huntley 2-7.

PASSING—Chicago, Kramer 18-33-1-194. Pittsburgh, Stewart 17-30-1-137.

RECEIVING—Chicago, Conway 5-50, Engram 4-76, Penn 2-23, Hallock 2-18, Mayes 2-12, Chancey 1-11, Bennett 1-6, Enis 1-(minus 2). Pittsburgh, C. Johnson 5-40, Bruener 3-38, Coleman 2-23, Hawkins 2-20, Witman 2-3, Blackwell 1-5, Fuamatu-Ma'afala 1-5, Lyons 1-3.

MISSED FIELD GOAL ATTEMPTS—None.

INTERCEPTIONS—Chicago, Tom. Carter 1-1. Pittsburgh, Lake 1-22.

KICKOFF RETURNS—Chicago, Milburn 4-71. Pittsburgh, Blackwell 3-76.

PUNT RETURNS—Chicago, Milburn 5-50.
SACKS—Chicago, Thomas 2, McDonald 1. Pittsburgh, Henry 0.5, Vrabel 0.5.

VIKINGS 38, RAMS 31

Sunday, September 13

Minnesota	14	10	7	7—38
St. Louis	0	10	14	7—31

First Quarter
Min.—R. Smith 24 run (Anderson kick), 4:50.
Min.—Glover 3 pass from Johnson (Anderson kick), 11:20.
Second Quarter
St.L.—G. Hill 1 run (Wilkins kick), 0:05.
Min.—FG, Anderson 24, 10:42.
St.L.—FG, Wilkins 53, 12:36.
Min.—R. Smith 74 run (Anderson kick), 13:11.
Third Quarter
St.L.—G. Hill 5 run (Wilkins kick), 9:45.
St.L.—Kennison 71 punt return (Wilkins kick), 11:23.
Min.—Hoard 1 run (Anderson kick), 14:14.
Fourth Quarter
St.L.—Bruce 80 pass from Banks (Wilkins kick), 0:10.
Min.—Carter 19 pass from Cunningham (Anderson kick), 12:51.
Attendance—56,234.

	Minnesota	St. Louis
First downs	23	22
Rushes-yards	31-194	26-139
Passing	227	271
Punt returns	2-32	3-89
Kickoff returns	4-89	5-98
Interception returns	4-39	2-0
Comp.-att.-int.	21-37-2	25-45-4
Sacked-yards lost	3-22	2-12
Punts	5-41	5-31
Fumbles-lost	1-1	0-0
Penalties-yards	10-81	9-85
Time of possession	30:18	29:42

INDIVIDUAL STATISTICS
RUSHING—Minnesota, R. Smith 23-179, Johnson 4-8, Hoard 2-4, Evans 2-3. St. Louis, G. Hill 21-82, Banks 3-28, Bruce 1-30, Lee 1-(minus 1).
PASSING—Minnesota, Johnson 18-31-2-208, Cunningham 3-6-0-41. St. Louis, Banks 25-45-4-283.
RECEIVING—Minnesota, R. Moss 6-89, Carter 4-60, Glover 3-37, R. Smith 3-7, Hoard 2-22, Reed 2-13, Walsh 1-21. St. Louis, Bruce 11-192, Conwell 5-28, Lee 5-24, J. Thomas 1-18, Kennison 1-9, G. Hill 1-6, Harris 1-6.
MISSED FIELD GOAL ATTEMPTS—None.
INTERCEPTIONS—Minnesota, Griffith 2-25, Gray 1-11, Hitchcock 1-3. St. Louis, M. A. Jones 1-0, Lyght 1-0.
KICKOFF RETURNS—Minnesota, Palmer 4-89. St. Louis, Horne 5-98.
PUNT RETURNS—Minnesota, Palmer 2-32. St. Louis, Kennison 3-89.
SACKS—Minnesota, Alexander 2. St. Louis, M. D. Jones 1, Carter 1, Farr 1.

RAVENS 24, JETS 10

Sunday, September 13

Baltimore	7	7	3	7—24
N.Y. Jets	7	0	3	0—10

First Quarter
Bal.—J. Lewis 69 punt return (Stover kick), 6:41.
NYJ—K. Johnson 4 pass from Foley (Hall kick), 14:45.
Second Quarter
Bal.—Green 20 pass from Zeier (Stover kick), 14:39.
Third Quarter
Bal.—FG, Stover 29, 4:44.
NYJ—FG, Hall 20, 8:33.
Fourth Quarter
Bal.—Woodson 60 interception return (Stover kick), 6:16.
Attendance—70,063.

	Baltimore	N.Y. Jets
First downs	16	18
Rushes-yards	34-122	23-58
Passing	209	218
Punt returns	3-88	1-7
Kickoff returns	1-22	5-79
Interception returns	3-76	0-0
Comp.-att.-int.	18-30-0	22-32-3
Sacked-yards lost	0-0	4-29
Punts	5-41	5-45
Fumbles-lost	2-1	0-0
Penalties-yards	9-109	5-30
Time of possession	31:12	28:48

INDIVIDUAL STATISTICS
RUSHING—Baltimore, Graham 13-31, Rhett 8-64, Potts 8-13, Zeier 3-4, Harbaugh 1-7, Holmes 1-3. New York, Martin 23-58.
PASSING—Baltimore, Zeier 13-20-0-173, Harbaugh 5-10-0-36. New York, Foley 22-32-3-247.
RECEIVING—Baltimore, Green 4-57, Turner 3-45, Graham 3-26, Potts 3-17, Jackson 2-50, Rhett 2-8, Yarborough 1-6. New York, Chrebet 6-91, K. Johnson 6-81, Martin 6-60, Sowell 2-4, Byars 1-7, L. Johnson 1-4.
MISSED FIELD GOAL ATTEMPTS—Baltimore, Stover 44. New York, Hall 60.
INTERCEPTIONS—Baltimore, Woodson 2-76, Jenkins 1-0.
KICKOFF RETURNS—Baltimore, Graham 1-22. New York, Glenn 3-59, L. Johnson 1-12, Baxter 1-8.
PUNT RETURNS—Baltimore, J. Lewis 3-88. New York, L. Johnson 1-7.
SACKS—Baltimore, McCrary 1.5, Burnett 1, Brady 1, Boulware 0.5.

JAGUARS 21, CHIEFS 16

Sunday, September 13

Kansas City	0	6	3	7—16
Jacksonville	7	7	7	0—21

First Quarter
Jac.—Barlow 85 punt return (Hollis kick), 4:02.
Second Quarter
Jac.—J. Smith 17 pass from Brunell (Hollis kick), 4:25.
K.C.—FG, Stoyanovich 36, 13:55.
K.C.—FG, Stoyanovich 43, 14:59.
Third Quarter
Jac.—Stewart 1 run (Hollis kick), 3:08.
K.C.—FG, Stoyanovich 29, 5:57.
Fourth Quarter
K.C.—Anders 3 run (Stoyanovich kick), 11:21.
Attendance—69,821.

	Kansas City	Jacksonville
First downs	23	18
Rushes-yards	25-111	37-149
Passing	253	107
Punt returns	1-11	3-134
Kickoff returns	4-74	4-113
Interception returns	0-0	0-0
Comp.-att.-int.	23-37-0	11-18-0
Sacked-yards lost	2-10	3-19
Punts	4-43	4-37
Fumbles-lost	3-2	0-0
Penalties-yards	5-54	6-44
Time of possession	30:16	29:44

INDIVIDUAL STATISTICS
RUSHING—Kansas City, Bennett 13-46, Anders 5-30, Gannon 4-32, Richardson 3-3. Jacksonville, Stewart 26-103, F. Taylor 6-44, Brunell 3-3, Banks 1-1, Whitted 1-(minus 2).
PASSING—Kansas City, Gannon 23-37-0-263. Jacksonville, Brunell 11-18-0-126.
RECEIVING—Kansas City, Gonzalez 7-67, Anders 5-42, Lockett 3-49, Alexander 2-41, Horn 2-29, Bennett 2-17, Popson 1-13, Shehee 1-5. Jacksonville, J. Smith 4-57, Stewart 2-22, Mitchell 2-11, Barlow 1-17, McCardell 1-14, Banks 1-5.
MISSED FIELD GOAL ATTEMPTS—Jacksonville, Hollis 37, 21.
INTERCEPTIONS—None.
KICKOFF RETURNS—Kansas City, Horn 3-66, Manusky 1-8. Jacksonville, Banks 1-65, Barlow 1-19, McCardell 1-15, Mitchell 1-14.
PUNT RETURNS—Kansas City, Hughes 1-11. Jacksonville, Barlow 3-134.
SACKS—Kansas City, Davis 1, Tongue 1, Team 1. Jacksonville, Smeenge 1, Boyer 1.

SAINTS 19, PANTHERS 14

Sunday, September 13

Carolina	0	14	0	0—14
New Orleans	7	3	3	6—19

First Quarter
N.O.—Dawkins 64 pass from Wuerffel (Brien kick), 0:59.
Second Quarter
Car.—Floyd 1 run (Kasay kick), 1:28.
N.O.—FG, Brien 46, 9:36.
Car.—Muhammad 17 pass from Collins (Kasay kick), 14:00.
Third Quarter
N.O.—FG, Brien 56, 14:34.
Fourth Quarter
N.O.—Zellars 15 run (pass failed), 5:45.
Attendance—51,915.

	Carolina	New Orleans
First downs	20	18
Rushes-yards	25-137	38-207
Passing	235	104
Punt returns	3-19	1-10
Kickoff returns	5-122	3-56
Interception returns	0-0	2-1
Comp.-att.-int.	15-35-2	13-18-0
Sacked-yards lost	3-16	6-41
Punts	4-46	6-46
Fumbles-lost	2-1	0-0
Penalties-yards	11-100	7-63
Time of possession	26:46	33:14

INDIVIDUAL STATISTICS
RUSHING—Carolina, Lane 18-100, Floyd 6-21, Collins 1-16. New Orleans, Zellars 15-83, L. Smith 12-78, Wuerffel 6-40, T. Davis 3-6, Craver 2-0.
PASSING—Carolina, Collins 15-34-1-251, Floyd 0-1-1-0. New Orleans, Wuerffel 13-18-0-145.
RECEIVING—Carolina, Muhammad 9-192, Carrier 2-32, Ismail 2-12, Walls 1-12, Lane 1-3. New Orleans, Dawkins 5-110, Craver 3-1, T. Davis 2-3, Cleeland 1-19, Hastings 1-7, Zellars 1-5.
MISSED FIELD GOAL ATTEMPTS—Carolina, Kasay 45.
INTERCEPTIONS—New Orleans, Drakeford 1-1, Cota 1-0.
KICKOFF RETURNS—Carolina, Bates 5-122. New Orleans, Ismail 3-56.
PUNT RETURNS—Carolina, Oliver 3-19. New Orleans, Hastings 1-10.
SACKS—Carolina, Gilbert 2, Greene 2, Barrow 1, Davis 1. New Orleans, Glover 2, J. Johnson 1.

DOLPHINS 13, BILLS 7

Sunday, September 13

Buffalo	0	7	0	0— 7
Miami	0	7	3	3—13

Second Quarter
Buf.—Moulds 28 pass from R. Johnson (Christie kick), 9:40.
Mia.—L. Thomas 17 pass from Marino (Mare kick), 14:01.
Third Quarter
Mia.—FG, Mare 33, 11:31.
Fourth Quarter
Mia.—FG, Mare 27, 2:31.
Attendance—73,097.

	Buffalo	Miami
First downs	12	12
Rushes-yards	28-110	27-116
Passing	77	143
Punt returns	3-9	3-35
Kickoff returns	3-59	1-41
Interception returns	0-0	1-0
Comp.-att.-int.	10-18-1	14-26-0
Sacked-yards lost	8-57	2-16
Punts	8-46	8-45
Fumbles-lost	2-0	0-0
Penalties-yards	10-70	5-42
Time of possession	30:09	29:51

INDIVIDUAL STATISTICS
RUSHING—Buffalo, A. Smith 13-34, Thomas 9-34, R. Johnson 6-42. Miami, Abdul-Jabbar 18-75, Avery 9-41.
PASSING—Buffalo, R. Johnson 10-18-1-134. Miami, Marino 14-26-0-159.
RECEIVING—Buffalo, Moulds 5-79, Reed 2-15, Early 1-24, K. Williams 1-12, Gash 1-4. Miami, McDuffie 5-60, Perry 4-26, L. Thomas 3-42, Gadsden 2-31.
MISSED FIELD GOAL ATTEMPTS—None.

INTERCEPTIONS—Miami, Surtain 1-0.
KICKOFF RETURNS—Buffalo, K. Williams 2-42, Gash 1-17. Miami, Avery 1-41.
PUNT RETURNS—Buffalo, K. Williams 3-9. Miami, Buckley 3-35.
SACKS—Buffalo, Northern 1, B. Smith 0.5, Washington 0.5. Miami, Taylor 2, Bromell 2, Armstrong 2, Z. Thomas 1, R. Jones 1.

PACKERS 23, BUCCANEERS 15

Sunday, September 13

Tampa Bay	0	0	0	15—15
Green Bay	10	6	0	7—23

First Quarter
G.B.—FG, Longwell 38, 5:00.
G.B.—T. Davis 10 pass from Favre (Longwell kick), 7:40.
Second Quarter
G.B.—FG, Longwell 27, 7:09.
G.B.—FG, Longwell 20, 15:00.
Fourth Quarter
G.B.—Freeman 38 pass from Favre (Longwell kick), 1:18.
T.B.—Green 95 punt return (Hape pass from Dilfer), 8:57.
T.B.—Moore 2 pass from Dilfer (Husted kick), 13:03.
Attendance—60,124.

	Tampa Bay	Green Bay
First downs	17	15
Rushes-yards	19-50	25-37
Passing	161	223
Punt returns	2-99	6-26
Kickoff returns	5-102	2-48
Interception returns	0-0	1-0
Comp.-att.-int.	22-40-1	22-33-0
Sacked-yards lost	6-50	4-14
Punts	7-42	6-45
Fumbles-lost	3-3	2-2
Penalties-yards	6-37	2-20
Time of possession	30:00	30:00

INDIVIDUAL STATISTICS
RUSHING—Tampa Bay, Dunn 12-36, Alstott 6-10, Dilfer 1-4. Green Bay, Levens 18-43, Favre 4-(minus 9), Blair 2-3, Henderson 1-0.
PASSING—Tampa Bay, Dilfer 20-36-0-211, Walsh 2-4-1-0. Green Bay, Favre 22-33-0-237.
RECEIVING—Tampa Bay, Dunn 7-46, Williams 6-75, Moore 3-16, Anthony 2-39, Green 2-26, Hape 1-11, Alstott 1-(minus 2). Green Bay, Levens 8-46, Freeman 5-83, Chmura 3-33, R. Brooks 2-31, Mayes 1-17, Blair 1-10, T. Davis 1-10, Henderson 1-7.
MISSED FIELD GOAL ATTEMPTS—None.
INTERCEPTIONS—Green Bay, Ty. Williams 1-0.
KICKOFF RETURNS—Tampa Bay, Green 4-81, Anthony 1-21. Green Bay, Preston 1-48, Schroeder 1-0.
PUNT RETURNS—Tampa Bay, Green 2-99. Green Bay, Preston 5-26, Prior 1-0.
SACKS—Tampa Bay, Sapp 2, Culpepper 1, Upshaw 1. Green Bay, White 3, McKenzie 2, S. Dotson 1.

FALCONS 17, EAGLES 12

Sunday, September 13

Philadelphia	6	3	0	3—12
Atlanta	0	0	14	3—17

First Quarter
Phi.—Staley 1 run (kick blocked), 7:14.
Second Quarter
Phi.—FG, Boniol 24, 14:37.
Third Quarter
Atl.—Kozlowski 19 pass from Chandler (Andersen kick), 2:22.
Atl.—Anderson 1 run (Andersen kick), 8:38.
Fourth Quarter
Phi.—FG, Boniol 42, 0:55.
Atl.—FG, Andersen 23, 7:29.
Attendance—46,456.

	Philadelphia	Atlanta
First downs	19	17
Rushes-yards	25-63	25-78
Passing	221	167
Punt returns	1-16	3-24

	Philadelphia	Atlanta
Kickoff returns	4-90	3-76
Interception returns	0-0	0-0
Comp.-att.-int.	24-35-0	14-26-0
Sacked-yards lost	2-11	3-29
Punts	5-47	6-36
Fumbles-lost	1-0	0-0
Penalties-yards	9-72	9-78
Time of possession	28:49	31:11

INDIVIDUAL STATISTICS

RUSHING—Philadelphia, Staley 18-43, Hoying 4-18, Garner 1-2, Walker 1-1, Turner 1-(minus 1). Atlanta, Anderson 20-74, Chandler 3-6, E. Williams 2-(minus 2).

PASSING—Philadelphia, Hoying 24-35-0-232. Atlanta, Chandler 14-26-0-196.

RECEIVING—Philadelphia, Staley 9-73, Fryar 5-66, Turner 3-20, Graham 2-52, Solomon 2-13, Garner 2-(minus 1), J. Johnson 1-9. Atlanta, Martin 4-88, Mathis 3-24, Santiago 2-27, Kozlowski 1-19, Christian 1-16, Anderson 1-8, Kinchen 1-8, Green 1-6.

MISSED FIELD GOAL ATTEMPTS—Philadelphia, Boniol 45.

INTERCEPTIONS—None.

KICKOFF RETURNS—Philadelphia, Rossum 4-90. Atlanta, Dwight 1-36, E. Williams 1-28, Kozlowski 1-12.

PUNT RETURNS—Philadelphia, Rossum 1-16. Atlanta, Dwight 3-24.

SACKS—Philadelphia, Wallace 1, McTyer 1, H. Thomas 0.5, B. Johnson 0.5. Atlanta, Hall 1, Burrough 1.

RAIDERS 20, GIANTS 17

Sunday, September 13

N.Y. Giants	7	0	10	0—17
Oakland	7	3	7	3—20

First Quarter
Oak.—Kaufman 80 run (G. Davis kick), 0:17.
NYG—Hilliard 10 pass from Kanell (Daluiso kick), 3:57.

Second Quarter
Oak.—FG, G. Davis 41, 15:00.

Third Quarter
NYG—Calloway 20 pass from Kanell (Daluiso kick), 3:13.
Oak.—T. Brown 22 pass from George (G. Davis kick), 6:57.
NYG—FG, Daluiso 43, 14:10.

Fourth Quarter
Oak.—FG, G. Davis 26, 13:02.
Attendance—40,545.

	N.Y. Giants	Oakland
First downs	15	21
Rushes-yards	23-71	26-162
Passing	162	252
Punt returns	3-62	1-0
Kickoff returns	4-101	1-42
Interception returns	0-0	1-14
Comp.-att.-int.	23-33-1	25-44-0
Sacked-yards lost	3-26	5-51
Punts	8-44	8-42
Fumbles-lost	1-0	4-1
Penalties-yards	15-90	16-113
Time of possession	28:50	31:10

INDIVIDUAL STATISTICS

RUSHING—New York, Barber 13-32, Way 5-28, Brown 3-0, Kanell 2-11. Oakland, Kaufman 20-139, H. Williams 4-25, George 2-(minus 2).

PASSING—New York, Kanell 23-33-1-188. Oakland, George 25-44-0-303.

RECEIVING—New York, Hilliard 8-78, Barber 5-34, Calloway 4-43, Way 3-16, Cross 2-15, Pupunu 1-2. Oakland, T. Brown 6-127, Ritchie 5-27, Jett 4-40, Mickens 3-44, Dudley 3-39, Kaufman 3-16, Howard 1-10.

MISSED FIELD GOAL ATTEMPTS—New York, Daluiso 40.

INTERCEPTIONS—Oakland, Turner 1-14.

KICKOFF RETURNS—New York, Patten 4-101. Oakland, Howard 1-42.

PUNT RETURNS—New York, Toomer 3-62. Oakland, Howard 1-0.

SACKS—New York, Bratzke 2, Strahan 2, Armstead 1. Oakland, Turner 1, Harris 1, Johnstone 1.

49ERS 45, REDSKINS 10

Monday, September 14

San Francisco	7	14	7	17—45
Washington	7	3	0	0—10

First Quarter
Was.—Shepherd 9 pass from T. Green (Blanton kick), 10:08.
S.F.—Owens 20 pass from S. Young (Richey kick), 14:57.

Second Quarter
S.F.—S. Young 3 run (Richey kick), 4:50.
Was.—FG, Blanton 37, 9:23.
S.F.—I. Smith 16 pass from S. Young (Richey kick), 11:23.

Third Quarter
S.F.—Edwards 2 pass from S. Young (Richey kick), 8:47.

Fourth Quarter
S.F.—Hearst 5 run (Richey kick), 0:41.
S.F.—FG, Richey 22, 3:05.
S.F.—Levy 21 run (Richey kick), 7:29.
Attendance—76,798.

	San Fran.	Washington
First downs	28	17
Rushes-yards	34-210	27-140
Passing	294	182
Punt returns	1-13	1-0
Kickoff returns	3-48	5-94
Interception returns	1-7	0-0
Comp.-att.-int.	21-32-0	14-25-1
Sacked-yards lost	2-9	4-19
Punts	4-35	4-50
Fumbles-lost	0-0	3-2
Penalties-yards	9-114	7-70
Time of possession	34:32	25:28

INDIVIDUAL STATISTICS

RUSHING—San Francisco, Hearst 22-138, Levy 8-44, S. Young 2-23, Edwards 2-5. Washington, Allen 18-94, Davis 4-18, T. Green 2-6, Bowie 2-3, Mitchell 1-19.

PASSING—San Francisco, S. Young 21-32-0-303. Washington, T. Green 14-25-1-201.

RECEIVING—San Francisco, Rice 4-82, Owens 4-67, Edwards 4-52, Stokes 4-52, I. Smith 3-35, Hearst 1-12, Levy 1-3. Washington, Westbrook 5-109, Mitchell 3-32, Asher 3-16, Shepherd 2-28, Thomas 1-16.

MISSED FIELD GOAL ATTEMPTS—Washington, Blanton 34, 47.

INTERCEPTIONS—San Francisco, Tubbs 1-7.

KICKOFF RETURNS—San Francisco, Levy 3-48. Washington, Mitchell 3-61, Thrash 2-33.

PUNT RETURNS—San Francisco, McQuarters 1-13. Washington, Mitchell 1-0.

SACKS—San Francisco, B. Young 2, Barker 2. Washington, Kinney 1, Wilkinson 1.

WEEK 3

ARIZONA 17, Philadelphia 3
Denver 34, OAKLAND 17
Green Bay 13, CINCINNATI 6
JACKSONVILLE 24, Baltimore 10
KANSAS CITY 23, San Diego 7
MIAMI 21, Pittsburgh 0
MINNESOTA 29, Detroit 6
NEW ENGLAND 27, Tennessee 16
N.Y. JETS 44, Indianapolis 6
St. Louis 34, BUFFALO 33
SEATTLE 24, Washington 14
TAMPA BAY 27, Chicago 15
Dallas 31, N.Y. GIANTS 7
  Open date: Atlanta, Carolina, New Orleans,
San Francisco

STANDINGS

AFC EAST

	W	L	T	Pct.
Miami	3	0	0	1.000
New England	2	1	0	.667
N.Y. Jets	1	2	0	.333
Buffalo	0	3	0	.000
Indianapolis	0	3	0	.000

AFC CENTRAL

	W	L	T	Pct.
Jacksonville	3	0	0	1.000
Pittsburgh	2	1	0	.667
Baltimore	1	2	0	.333
Cincinnati	1	2	0	.333
Tennessee	1	2	0	.333

AFC WEST

	W	L	T	Pct.
Denver	3	0	0	1.000
Seattle	3	0	0	1.000
Kansas City	2	1	0	.667
San Diego	2	1	0	.667
Oakland	1	2	0	.333

NFC EAST

	W	L	T	Pct.
Dallas	2	1	0	.667
Arizona	1	2	0	.333
N.Y. Giants	1	2	0	.333
Philadelphia	0	3	0	.000
Washington	0	3	0	.000

NFC CENTRAL

	W	L	T	Pct.
Green Bay	3	0	0	1.000
Minnesota	3	0	0	1.000
Tampa Bay	1	2	0	.333
Chicago	0	3	0	.000
Detroit	0	3	0	.000

NFC WEST

	W	L	T	Pct.
Atlanta	2	0	0	1.000
New Orleans	2	0	0	1.000
San Francisco	2	0	0	1.000
St. Louis	1	2	0	.333
Carolina	0	2	0	.000

HIGHLIGHTS

Hero of the week: Deion Sanders was a one-man gang against the Giants, breaking a scoreless tie with a 59-yard punt return for a touchdown, catching a 55-yard pass to set up a score and returning an interception 71 yards for a TD as the Cowboys beat New York 31-7. Sanders, who also had a 39-yard punt return in the third quarter, finished with 226 total yards.

Goat of the week: Rookie Ryan Leaf had one of the worst games ever by an NFL quarterback. He committed five turnovers—three fumbles, two interceptions—on the Chargers' first seven possessions and completed only one of 15 passes for 4 yards, breaking the team record for fewest completions. All but three of Kansas City's points followed turnovers as the Chiefs trounced the Chargers 23-7. Leaf's QB rating for the game was 0.0.

Sub of the week: Coming off the bench for injured James Stewart, rookie Fred Taylor had a 52-yard touchdown run and finished with 128 yards rushing to lead Jacksonville to a 24-10 victory over the Ravens. Taylor, a first-round draft pick from Florida, also had nine receptions for 85 yards.

Comeback of the week: Midway through the third quarter, St. Louis trailed Buffalo, 28-10. The Rams closed the gap and were down 33-28 when they began what turned out to be the game-winning drive at their 20-yard line with 3:57 remaining. With 11 seconds left, quarterback Tony Banks dashed into the end zone for a 2-yard touchdown and a 34-33 victory.

Blowout of the week: The Jets amassed 505 yards in a 44-6 demolition of the Colts. New York's 302 rushing yards represented the second highest total in franchise history. Curtis Martin carried 23 times for 144 yards, second-year back Leon Johnson scored three touchdowns, and quarterback Vinny Testaverde threw four TD passes.

Nail-biter of the week: With 3:57 remaining, the Rams trailed the Bills 33-28 and had the ball at their 20. Jerald Moore got a first down on third and 1 from the Rams' 29. Ricky Proehl caught a 22-yard pass over the middle on third and 15 from the Rams' 25. Completions of 34 yards to Proehl and 12 yards to

Amp Lee advanced the ball to the Buffalo 2 with 27 seconds remaining. With 11 seconds left, quarterback Tony Banks ran for a touchdown to give the Rams a 34-33 win.

Hit of the week: With 8:19 remaining and the Rams in a precarious position on their 1-yard line, Greg Hill was splattered by Bills nose tackle Ted Washington for a safety. Washington fell on top of Hill, breaking his right leg. Hill rushed for 158 yards and two touchdowns before the injury.

Oddity of the week: Deion Sanders' all-around performance in Dallas' 31-7 win over the Giants on Monday night was so unusual the NFL created a new weekly award to honor him. Sanders, who lined up at cornerback, wide receiver and as a punt returner, was named the NFC's player of the week in a special "Prime-Time" category, named for his self-proclaimed nickname. The award marked the first time the NFL had honored a player in his own category.

Top rusher: San Diego's Natrone Means ran for 160 yards and a touchdown, but Kansas City beat the Chargers, 23-7.

Top passer: Washington's Trent Green completed 27-of-54 passes for 383 yards and two touchdowns in the Redskins' 24-14 loss to the Seahawks.

Top receiver: Michael Westbrook caught seven passes for 132 yards and two touchdowns in Washington's loss at Seattle.

Notes: A crowd of 39,782 attended the Cardinals-Eagles game at Arizona's Sun Devil Stadium. It was the smallest gathering for a Cardinals home opener since the team moved to Arizona in 1988. . . . Vikings kicker Gary Anderson, with five field goals and two PATs, raised his career points total to 1,713, putting him second on the all-time list behind George Blanda's 2,002. Anderson passed Jan Stenerud (1,699) and Nick Lowery (1,711). . . . The Jets' Keith Byars tied Marcus Allen for career receptions by an NFL running back with 587. . . . Ryan Leaf's record-low one completion broke the previous Chargers mark for fewest completions, which was three, against Oakland on October 5, 1975. . . . Attendance for Buffalo's home opener was 65,199, the smallest since September 2, 1984, when 48,528 showed for a game against New England. . . . After the first three games of the season, the Eagles were averaging five points. . . . The Buccaneers played their first game in the new Raymond James Stadium. A sellout crowd of 64,328 watched Tampa Bay beat the Bears 27-15. Counting five exhibition games the Bucs had been on the road for seven consecutive games while the stadium was being completed.

Quote of the week: Broncos defensive tackle Mike Lodish, after Denver beat Oakland 34-17: "We stuffed their butts. We got (Napoleon) Kaufman good. We didn't think Jeff George could beat us, and he didn't. The only quarterback that I know of that can beat you when he's forced to throw is John (Elway), and he's on our side."

GAME SUMMARIES

CARDINALS 17, EAGLES 3

Sunday, September 20

Philadelphia	0	0	0	3— 3
Arizona	0	0	0	17—17

Fourth Quarter
Phi.—FG, Boniol 29, 0:40.
Ariz.—FG, Nedney 47, 2:45.
Ariz.—McWilliams 7 pass from Plummer (Nedney kick), 7:41.
Ariz.—Murrell 25 run (Nedney kick), 13:08.
Attendance—39,782.

	Philadelphia	Arizona
First downs	20	16
Rushes-yards	27-91	26-153
Passing	226	129
Punt returns	1-7	2-14
Kickoff returns	2-57	1-13
Interception returns	0-0	1-2
Comp.-att.-int.	26-46-1	21-35-0
Sacked-yards lost	5-40	3-8
Punts	6-37	7-36
Fumbles-lost	3-2	2-1
Penalties-yards	6-72	3-14
Time of possession	35:20	24:40

INDIVIDUAL STATISTICS
RUSHING—Philadelphia, Staley 17-67, Garner 7-6, Hoying 3-18. Arizona, Murrell 22-145, Plummer 2-5, Pittman 2-3.
PASSING—Philadelphia, Hoying 13-23-1-121, Peete 13-23-0-145. Arizona, Plummer 21-35-0-137.
RECEIVING—Philadelphia, Copeland 6-76, Fryar 5-63, Staley 5-24, Solomon 4-51, Graham 4-40, Dunn 1-7, Turner 1-5. Arizona, Centers 7-32, R. Moore 4-27, McWilliams 3-36, Metcalf 3-15, Sanders 2-14, Gedney 2-13.
MISSED FIELD GOAL ATTEMPTS—Arizona, Nedney 52.
INTERCEPTIONS—Arizona, Lassiter 1-2.
KICKOFF RETURNS—Philadelphia, Rossum 2-57. Arizona, Metcalf 1-13.
PUNT RETURNS—Philadelphia, Rossum 1-7. Arizona, Metcalf 2-14.
SACKS—Philadelphia, Douglas 1, Jefferson 1, Whiting 1. Arizona, Rice 2, McKinnon 1, M. Smith 1, Swann 1.

SEAHAWKS 24, REDSKINS 14

Sunday, September 20

Washington	7	0	0	7—14
Seattle	7	3	14	0—24

First Quarter
Sea.—Broussard 90 kickoff return (Peterson kick), 0:15.
Was.—Westbrook 36 pass from T. Green (Akers kick), 8:51.
Second Quarter
Sea.—FG, Peterson 32, 13:49.

Third Quarter
Sea.—Watters 13 run (Peterson kick), 2:22.
Sea.—Pritchard 21 pass from Moon (Peterson kick), 6:48.
Fourth Quarter
Was.—Westbrook 26 pass from T. Green (Akers kick), 14:29.
Attendance—63,336.

	Washington	Seattle
First downs	27	16
Rushes-yards	21-96	32-163
Passing	369	136
Punt returns	3-3	1-1
Kickoff returns	5-87	2-108
Interception returns	0-0	2-10
Comp.-att.-int.	27-54-2	16-33-0
Sacked-yards lost	3-14	1-5
Punts	5-43	7-46
Fumbles-lost	2-1	0-0
Penalties-yards	6-40	7-71
Time of possession	28:25	31:35

INDIVIDUAL STATISTICS
RUSHING—Washington, Allen 20-92, Bowie 1-4. Seattle, Watters 24-136, Green 6-26, Strong 1-2, Moon 1-(minus 1).
PASSING—Washington, T. Green 27-54-2-383. Seattle, Moon 16-33-0-141.
RECEIVING—Washington, Westbrook 7-132, Shepherd 5-69, Mitchell 5-40, Asher 4-74, Bowie 2-18, Connell 2-16, Thomas 1-23, Allen 1-11. Seattle, Watters 6-45, Pritchard 3-47, Fauria 3-18, McKnight 2-26, Galloway 1-5, Green 1-0.
MISSED FIELD GOAL ATTEMPTS—Washington, Akers 48, 49. Seattle, Peterson 52.
INTERCEPTIONS—Seattle, Smith 1-7, Bellamy 1-3.
KICKOFF RETURNS—Washington, Mitchell 5-87. Seattle, Broussard 2-108.
PUNT RETURNS—Washington, Mitchell 3-3. Seattle, Galloway 1-1.
SACKS—Washington, Wilkinson 0.5, Pounds 0.5. Seattle, Logan 1, Sinclair 1, C. Brown 0.5, Collins 0.5.

BRONCOS 34, RAIDERS 17

Sunday, September 20

Denver	7	10	7	10—34
Oakland	0	10	7	0—17

First Quarter
Den.—McCaffrey 1 pass from Elway (Elam kick), 7:21.
Second Quarter
Oak.—FG, G. Davis 44, 1:36.
Oak.—Turner 94 interception return (G. Davis kick), 8:26.
Den.—FG, Elam 35, 12:49.
Den.—Griffith 3 pass from Brister (Elam kick), 14:25.
Third Quarter
Den.—McCaffrey 13 pass from Brister (Elam kick), 7:52.
Oak.—Dudley 11 pass from George (G. Davis kick), 11:48.
Fourth Quarter
Den.—FG, Elam 35, 5:54.
Den.—Crockett 80 interception return (Elam kick), 10:31.
Attendance—56,578.

	Denver	Oakland
First downs	25	13
Rushes-yards	36-145	20-94
Passing	193	164
Punt returns	2-(-6)	4-42
Kickoff returns	3-62	6-98
Interception returns	3-123	1-94
Comp.-att.-int.	16-27-1	17-29-3
Sacked-yards lost	2-18	4-32
Punts	5-54	5-40
Fumbles-lost	2-1	0-0
Penalties-yards	10-91	7-80
Time of possession	34:33	25:27

INDIVIDUAL STATISTICS
RUSHING—Denver, Davis 28-104, Brister 5-38, Loville 3-3. Oakland, Kaufman 17-78, H. Williams 3-16.
PASSING—Denver, Brister 10-17-1-140, Elway 6-10-0-71. Oakland, George 16-28-3-188, Hollas 1-1-0-8.

RECEIVING—Denver, McCaffrey 5-44, R. Smith 4-67, Sharpe 3-44, Nash 1-30, Carswell 1-15, Davis 1-8, Griffith 1-3. Oakland, Jett 5-116, Kaufman 4-17, T. Brown 2-24, Dudley 2-17, Mickens 2-10, H. Williams 1-7, Ritchie 1-5.

MISSED FIELD GOAL ATTEMPTS—None.

INTERCEPTIONS—Denver, Crockett 2-105, Romanowski 1-18. Oakland, Turner 1-94.

KICKOFF RETURNS—Denver, Hebron 2-47, D. Smith 1-15. Oakland, Howard 5-87, Shedd 1-11.

PUNT RETURNS—Denver, Gordon 2-(minus 6). Oakland, Howard 4-42.

SACKS—Denver, Mobley 1, Tanuvasa 1, Pryce 1, Romanowski 0.5, Cadrez 0.5. Oakland, Johnstone 2.

JAGUARS 24, RAVENS 10

Sunday, September 20

Baltimore	3	7	0	0—10
Jacksonville	7	3	14	0—24

First Quarter

Jac.—F. Taylor 52 run (Hollis kick), 7:12.

Bal.—FG, Stover 25, 13:31.

Second Quarter

Bal.—J. Lewis 56 pass from Zeier (Stover kick), 10:53.

Jac.—FG, Hollis 34, 14:54.

Third Quarter

Jac.—J. Smith 72 pass from Brunell (Hollis kick), 1:03.

Jac.—Jones 1 pass from Brunell (Hollis kick), 10:46.

Attendance—67,069.

	Baltimore	Jacksonville
First downs	12	20
Rushes-yards	25-81	32-154
Passing	232	365
Punt returns	1-0	6-94
Kickoff returns	4-91	3-49
Interception returns	0-0	1-8
Comp.-att.-int.	17-34-1	25-34-0
Sacked-yards lost	2-16	3-11
Punts	10-49	8-38
Fumbles-lost	0-0	2-1
Penalties-yards	7-54	8-60
Time of possession	26:09	33:51

INDIVIDUAL STATISTICS

RUSHING—Baltimore, Graham 20-67, Zeier 3-7, Harbaugh 1-5, Potts 1-2. Jacksonville, F. Taylor 23-128, Banks 4-26, Brunell 4-1, Stewart 1-(minus 1).

PASSING—Baltimore, Zeier 13-25-1-189, Harbaugh 4-9-0-59. Jacksonville, Brunell 25-34-0-376.

RECEIVING—Baltimore, Potts 6-19, J. Lewis 4-117, Green 3-79, Graham 2-15, Jackson 1-15, Holmes 1-3. Jacksonville, F. Taylor 9-85, McCardell 8-108, J. Smith 2-116, Mitchell 2-47, Barlow 1-22, Jones 1-1, Banks 1-(minus 1), Stewart 1-(minus 2).

MISSED FIELD GOAL ATTEMPTS—Jacksonville, Hollis 25.

INTERCEPTIONS—Jacksonville, Hudson 1-8.

KICKOFF RETURNS—Baltimore, J. Lewis 2-65, Graham 1-15, Holmes 1-11. Jacksonville, Banks 2-33, Barlow 1-16.

PUNT RETURNS—Baltimore, J. Lewis 1-0. Jacksonville, Barlow 6-94.

SACKS—Baltimore, Boulware 2, J. Jones 1. Jacksonville, Pritchett 1, F. Smith 1.

BUCCANEERS 27, BEARS 15

Sunday, September 20

Chicago	10	5	0	0—15
Tampa Bay	0	0	13	14—27

First Quarter

Chi.—FG, Jaeger 26, 7:39.

Chi.—Milburn 93 punt return (Jaeger kick), 9:50.

Second Quarter

Chi.—Safety, Dilfer sacked by Thierry out of end zone, 13:00.

Chi.—FG, Jaeger 52, 15:00.

Third Quarter

T.B.—Anthony 13 pass from Dilfer (pass failed), 8:59.

T.B.—Moore 44 pass from Dilfer (Husted kick), 13:27.

Fourth Quarter

T.B.—Dunn 43 run (Hunter pass from Dilfer), 1:05.

T.B.—Alstott 2 run (pass failed), 9:16.

Attendance—64,328.

	Chicago	Tampa Bay
First downs	13	20
Rushes-yards	25-85	38-220
Passing	169	144
Punt returns	2-106	2-26
Kickoff returns	6-110	3-64
Interception returns	0-0	0-0
Comp.-att.-int.	19-32-0	12-18-0
Sacked-yards lost	0-0	1-3
Punts	4-46	3-49
Fumbles-lost	3-2	3-2
Penalties-yards	5-35	4-44
Time of possession	27:05	32:55

INDIVIDUAL STATISTICS

RUSHING—Chicago, Enis 15-48, Bennett 6-28, Chancey 3-9, Morris 1-0. Tampa Bay, Alstott 20-103, Dunn 10-82, Dilfer 6-3, Anthony 1-32, Neal 1-0.

PASSING—Chicago, Kramer 19-32-0-169. Tampa Bay, Dilfer 12-18-0-147.

RECEIVING—Chicago, Conway 4-77, Engram 3-29, Wetnight 3-13, Bennett 3-10, Penn 2-21, Enis 2-5, Chancey 1-9, Mayes 1-5. Tampa Bay, Anthony 5-56, Moore 2-53, Williams 2-23, Hunter 1-13, Dunn 1-4, Alstott 1-(minus 2).

MISSED FIELD GOAL ATTEMPTS—Chicago, Jaeger 29.

INTERCEPTIONS—None.

KICKOFF RETURNS—Chicago, Milburn 6-110. Tampa Bay, Anthony 3-64.

PUNT RETURNS—Chicago, Milburn 2-106. Tampa Bay, Williams 2-26.

SACKS—Chicago, Thierry 1.

JETS 44, COLTS 6

Sunday, September 20

Indianapolis	0	3	3	0— 6
N.Y. Jets	7	20	7	10—44

First Quarter

NYJ—L. Johnson 82 pass from Testaverde (Hall kick), 4:38.

Second Quarter

NYJ—Brady 1 pass from Testaverde (Hall kick), 3:46.

NYJ—Chrebet 8 pass from Testaverde (Hall kick), 8:40.

NYJ—L. Johnson 16 run (kick blocked), 11:51.

Ind.—FG, Vanderjagt 43, 14:52.

Third Quarter

NYJ—K. Johnson 11 pass from Testaverde (Hall kick), 5:11.

Ind.—FG, Vanderjagt 24, 9:45.

Fourth Quarter

NYJ—FG, Hall 36, 0:09.

NYJ—L. Johnson 1 run (Hall kick), 9:56.

Attendance—79,469.

	Indianapolis	N.Y. Jets
First downs	21	28
Rushes-yards	27-120	44-302
Passing	190	203
Punt returns	2-27	3-18
Kickoff returns	5-83	3-69
Interception returns	1-0	2-10
Comp.-att.-int.	20-44-2	12-22-1
Sacked-yards lost	1-3	0-0
Punts	6-45	3-51
Fumbles-lost	0-0	4-1
Penalties-yards	5-34	8-63
Time of possession	26:49	33:11

INDIVIDUAL STATISTICS

RUSHING—Indianapolis, Faulk 21-91, Manning 3-26, Elias 3-3. New York, Martin 23-144, Sowell 8-82, L. Johnson 8-52, Lucas 2-8, Byars 1-13, Ward 1-3, Testaverde 1-0.

PASSING—Indianapolis, Manning 20-44-2-193. New York, Testaverde 12-21-1-203, Lucas 0-1-0-0.

RECEIVING—Indianapolis, Harrison 7-77, Small 5-50, Pathon 3-24, Faulk 2-7, Pollard 1-19, Elias 1-11, Dilger 1-5. New York, Chrebet 3-25, Brady 3-17, Martin 2-30, K. Johnson 2-20, L. Johnson 1-82, Byars 1-29.

MISSED FIELD GOAL ATTEMPTS—None.

INTERCEPTIONS—Indianapolis, Burris 1-0. New York, Mickens 1-10, Glenn 1-0.

KICKOFF RETURNS—Indianapolis, Clark 3-38, Elias 2-45. New York, Glenn 2-50, L. Johnson 1-19.

VIKINGS 29, LIONS 6

Sunday, September 20

Detroit	3	3	0	0— 6
Minnesota	0	6	13	10—29

First Quarter
Det.—FG, Hanson 37, 10:59.
Second Quarter
Det.—FG, Hanson 49, 2:09.
Min.—FG, Anderson 27, 8:36.
Min.—FG, Anderson 28, 13:09.
Third Quarter
Min.—R. Moss 5 pass from Cunningham (Anderson kick), 3:19.
Min.—FG, Anderson 42, 11:24.
Min.—FG, Anderson 29, 13:58.
Fourth Quarter
Min.—Hoard 11 run (Anderson kick), 0:15.
Min.—FG, Anderson 34, 13:09.
Attendance—63,107.

	Detroit	Minnesota
First downs	19	17
Rushes-yards	31-137	24-76
Passing	142	211
Punt returns	1-1	3-60
Kickoff returns	6-123	3-62
Interception returns	0-0	2-0
Comp.-att.-int.	20-40-2	20-35-0
Sacked-yards lost	5-18	2-9
Punts	4-43	4-47
Fumbles-lost	2-2	2-0
Penalties-yards	9-69	5-45
Time of possession	34:15	25:45

INDIVIDUAL STATISTICS

RUSHING—Detroit, Sanders 22-69, Batch 8-63, Rivers 1-5. Minnesota, R. Smith 15-39, Hoard 5-16, Cunningham 3-6, Palmer 1-15.
PASSING—Detroit, Batch 20-40-2-160. Minnesota, Cunningham 20-35-0-220.
RECEIVING—Detroit, Moore 9-66, Morton 5-57, Sanders 5-29, Chryplewicz 1-8. Minnesota, R. Moss 5-37, Glover 3-50, Reed 3-44, Carter 3-27, DeLong 2-28, R. Smith 2-10, Palmer 1-18, Hoard 1-6.
MISSED FIELD GOAL ATTEMPTS—None.
INTERCEPTIONS—Minnesota, Griffith 1-0, Fuller 1-0.
KICKOFF RETURNS—Detroit, Fair 6-123. Minnesota, Palmer 2-42, Tate 1-20.
PUNT RETURNS—Detroit, Fair 1-1. Minnesota, Palmer 3-60.
SACKS—Detroit, Elliss 1, Porcher 1. Minnesota, E. McDaniel 1.5, Randle 1.5, Clemons 1, Fisk 1.

PATRIOTS 27, OILERS 16

Sunday, September 20

Tennessee	3	3	7	3—16
New England	3	3	7	14—27

First Quarter
Ten.—FG, Del Greco 34, 8:46.
N.E.—FG, Vinatieri 43, 13:47.
Second Quarter
Ten.—FG, Del Greco 26, 13:03.
N.E.—FG, Vinatieri 41, 15:00.
Third Quarter
Ten.—E. George 22 pass from McNair (Del Greco kick), 4:04.
N.E.—Edwards 7 run (Vinatieri kick), 9:19.
Fourth Quarter
Ten.—FG, Del Greco 45, 4:06.
N.E.—Glenn 51 pass from Bledsoe (Vinatieri kick), 10:35.
N.E.—Milloy 30 interception return (Vinatieri kick), 10:53.
Attendance—59,973.

	Tennessee	New England
First downs	18	13
Rushes-yards	27-110	18-94
Passing	196	228
Punt returns	4-44	1-1
Kickoff returns	3-59	4-97
Interception returns	0-0	2-48
Comp.-att.-int.	28-38-2	18-30-0
Sacked-yards lost	1-6	4-22
Punts	4-44	5-47
Fumbles-lost	0-0	0-0
Penalties-yards	6-35	5-39
Time of possession	36:30	23:30

INDIVIDUAL STATISTICS

RUSHING—Tennessee, E. George 23-100, McNair 3-6, Thomas 1-4. New England, Edwards 12-92, Bledsoe 3-1, S. Shaw 3-1.
PASSING—Tennessee, McNair 28-38-2-202. New England, Bledsoe 18-30-0-250.
RECEIVING—Tennessee, Wycheck 8-40, Harris 6-35, E. George 4-60, Davis 3-25, Thigpen 3-21, Thomas 2-9, Mason 1-8, Roan 1-4. New England, Glenn 4-102, Cullors 4-31, Brown 3-29, Brisby 2-37, Jefferson 2-32, Coates 2-15, Ton. Carter 1-4.
MISSED FIELD GOAL ATTEMPTS—None.
INTERCEPTIONS—New England, Milloy 1-30, Law 1-18.
KICKOFF RETURNS—Tennessee, Mason 3-59. New England, Cullors 2-68, S. Shaw 1-16, Eaton 1-13.
PUNT RETURNS—Tennessee, Mason 4-44. New England, Brown 1-1.
SACKS—Tennessee, Bishop 1, Marts 1, Holmes 0.5, Jackson 0.5, Lyons 0.5, G. Walker 0.5. New England, Thomas 1.

DOLPHINS 21, STEELERS 0

Sunday, September 20

Pittsburgh	0	0	0	0— 0
Miami	0	14	7	0—21

Second Quarter
Mia.—Abdul-Jabbar 3 run (Mare kick), 9:48.
Mia.—L. Thomas 8 pass from Marino (Mare kick), 12:21.
Third Quarter
Mia.—Z. Thomas 17 interception return (Mare kick), 6:54.
Attendance—73,948.

	Pittsburgh	Miami
First downs	13	11
Rushes-yards	24-122	38-110
Passing	78	109
Punt returns	6-32	2-24
Kickoff returns	2-35	1-28
Interception returns	0-0	3-38
Comp.-att.-int.	11-35-3	14-22-0
Sacked-yards lost	1-4	1-4
Punts	10-48	10-46
Fumbles-lost	0-0	2-1
Penalties-yards	5-51	10-70
Time of possession	25:14	34:46

INDIVIDUAL STATISTICS

RUSHING—Pittsburgh, Bettis 13-48, Huntley 5-26, McAfee 3-29, Stewart 2-17, Fuamatu-Ma'afala 1-2. Miami, Abdul-Jabbar 33-108, Avery 4-4, Marino 1-(minus 2).
PASSING—Pittsburgh, Stewart 11-35-3-82. Miami, Marino 14-22-0-113.
RECEIVING—Pittsburgh, Hawkins 3-4, C. Johnson 2-40, Ward 1-18, Blackwell 1-14, Fuamatu-Ma'afala 1-4, Bettis 1-2, Witman 1-2, McAfee 1-(minus 2). Miami, Gadsden 4-34, McDuffie 3-36, L. Thomas 3-20, Abdul-Jabbar 2-6, Drayton 1-9, Jordan 1-8.
MISSED FIELD GOAL ATTEMPTS—Pittsburgh, N. Johnson 47.
INTERCEPTIONS—Miami, Madison 2-21, Z. Thomas 1-17.
KICKOFF RETURNS—Pittsburgh, Blackwell 2-35. Miami, Avery 1-28.
PUNT RETURNS—Pittsburgh, Coleman 6-32. Miami, Jordan 2-24.
SACKS—Pittsburgh, Kirkland 1. Miami, Bromell 1.

CHIEFS 23, CHARGERS 7

Sunday, September 20

San Diego	0	0	7	0— 7
Kansas City	6	10	7	0—23

First Quarter
K.C.—FG, Stoyanovich 35, 4:23.
K.C.—FG, Stoyanovich 31, 12:49.

Second Quarter

K.C.—FG, Stoyanovich 33, 0:08.
K.C.—Rison 44 pass from Gannon (Stoyanovich kick), 1:23.

Third Quarter

K.C.—Richardson 1 run (Stoyanovich kick), 2:32.
S.D.—Means 72 run (Carney kick), 10:35.
    Attendance—73,730.

	San Diego	Kansas City
First downs	7	16
Rushes-yards	28-166	44-114
Passing	-19	129
Punt returns	3-36	3-44
Kickoff returns	6-87	2-28
Interception returns	0-0	2-39
Comp.-att.-int.	1-15-2	10-29-0
Sacked-yards lost	2-23	2-15
Punts	7-43	7-48
Fumbles-lost	5-4	3-1
Penalties-yards	9-93	15-129
Time of possession	20:55	39:05

INDIVIDUAL STATISTICS

RUSHING—San Diego, Means 22-160, Leaf 4-1, Fletcher 2-5. Kansas City, Bennett 30-87, Gannon 6-20, Anders 4-2, Shehee 2-12, Richardson 1-1, Horn 1-(minus 8).

PASSING—San Diego, Leaf 1-15-2-4. Kansas City, Gannon 10-29-0-144.

RECEIVING—San Diego, F. Jones 1-4. Kansas City, Gonzalez 3-24, Rison 1-44, Anders 1-17, Richardson 1-15, Bennett 1-13, Lockett 1-12, Horn 1-10, Popson 1-9.

MISSED FIELD GOAL ATTEMPTS—None.

INTERCEPTIONS—Kansas City, Carter 1-23, Hasty 1-16.

KICKOFF RETURNS—San Diego, Stephens 3-55, Rachal 2-27, Burke 1-5. Kansas City, Vanover 1-16, Manusky 1-12.

PUNT RETURNS—San Diego, Rachal 3-36. Kansas City, Vanover 3-44.

SACKS—San Diego, Fuller 1, Team 1. Kansas City, Thomas 1, Johnson 1.

PACKERS 13, BENGALS 6

Sunday, September 20

Green Bay	7	3	0	3—13
Cincinnati	3	3	0	0— 6

First Quarter

Cin.—FG, Pelfrey 37, 4:15.
G.B.—R. Brooks 16 pass from Favre (Longwell kick), 8:39.

Second Quarter

G.B.—FG, Longwell 30, 5:02.
Cin.—FG, Pelfrey 19, 15:00.

Fourth Quarter

G.B.—FG, Longwell 35, 1:19.
    Attendance—56,346.

	Green Bay	Cincinnati
First downs	22	7
Rushes-yards	30-86	17-28
Passing	242	132
Punt returns	3-20	1-(-2)
Kickoff returns	1-21	4-120
Interception returns	0-0	1-0
Comp.-att.-int.	23-35-1	16-30-0
Sacked-yards lost	3-32	3-19
Punts	3-53	8-49
Fumbles-lost	2-2	0-0
Penalties-yards	4-30	4-65
Time of possession	35:19	24:41

INDIVIDUAL STATISTICS

RUSHING—Green Bay, R. Harris 24-76, Henderson 4-11, Favre 2-(minus 1). Cincinnati, Dillon 16-28, Blake 1-0.

PASSING—Green Bay, Favre 23-35-1-274. Cincinnati, O'Donnell 16-30-0-151.

RECEIVING—Green Bay, Freeman 5-68, R. Brooks 5-67, Chmura 4-56, Mayes 4-38, R. Harris 2-10, Thomason 1-22, Henderson 1-7, T. Davis 1-6. Cincinnati, Pickens 6-58, Scott 3-58, Bieniemy 3-12, Gibson 2-5, Jackson 1-12, Milne 1-6.

MISSED FIELD GOAL ATTEMPTS—None.

INTERCEPTIONS—Cincinnati, Shade 1-0.

KICKOFF RETURNS—Green Bay, Preston 1-21. Cincinnati, Mack 4-120.

PUNT RETURNS—Green Bay, Preston 3-20. Cincinnati, Gibson 1-(minus 2).

SACKS—Green Bay, McKenzie 2, Holliday 1. Cincinnati, Tumulty 1, Bell 1, Spikes 1.

RAMS 34, BILLS 33

Sunday, September 20

St. Louis	0	10	10	14—34
Buffalo	7	7	14	5—33

First Quarter

Buf.—Gash 5 pass from R. Johnson (Christie kick), 9:06.

Second Quarter

St.L.—FG, Wilkins 27, 1:38.
St.L.—G. Hill 12 run (Wilkins kick), 10:02.
Buf.—Reed 13 pass from R. Johnson (Christie kick), 14:08.

Third Quarter

Buf.—Thomas 14 run (Christie kick), 2:54.
Buf.—Riemersma 16 pass from R. Johnson (Christie kick), 3:19.
St.L.—FG, Wilkins 25, 8:23.
St.L.—Lee 23 pass from Banks (Wilkins kick), 11:05.

Fourth Quarter

Buf.—FG, Christie 36, 0:03.
St.L.—G. Hill 1 run (Lee run), 4:28.
Buf.—Safety, Washington tackled G. Hill in end zone, 6:41.
St.L.—Banks 2 run (run failed), 14:49.
    Attendance—65,199.

	St. Louis	Buffalo
First downs	21	23
Rushes-yards	25-181	35-215
Passing	225	192
Punt returns	3-57	3-44
Kickoff returns	5-103	5-101
Interception returns	1-14	2-23
Comp.-att.-int.	13-27-2	18-30-1
Sacked-yards lost	2-10	9-39
Punts	3-54	7-46
Fumbles-lost	2-2	1-1
Penalties-yards	4-20	9-91
Time of possession	24:36	35:24

INDIVIDUAL STATISTICS

RUSHING—St. Louis, G. Hill 19-158, Banks 2-3, J. Moore 2-0, Harris 1-15, Lee 1-5. Buffalo, A. Smith 22-118, Thomas 7-32, R. Johnson 4-35, K. Williams 1-28, Gash 1-2.

PASSING—St. Louis, Banks 13-27-2-235. Buffalo, R. Johnson 18-28-1-231, Flutie 0-2-0-0.

RECEIVING—St. Louis, Lee 5-72, Proehl 4-91, J. Thomas 2-26, Kennison 1-45. Buffalo, Moulds 4-65, Reed 4-35, Thomas 3-46, Riemersma 3-44, Gash 3-31, L. Johnson 1-10.

MISSED FIELD GOAL ATTEMPTS—None.

INTERCEPTIONS—St. Louis, McCleon 1-14. Buffalo, Schulz 2-23.

KICKOFF RETURNS—St. Louis, J. Thomas 4-79, Horne 1-24. Buffalo, K. Williams 4-81, Holmes 1-20.

PUNT RETURNS—St. Louis, Kennison 3-57. Buffalo, K. Williams 3-44.

SACKS—St. Louis, Carter 2, Clemons 2, Farr 2, E. Hill 1, M. A. Jones 1, Wright 1. Buffalo, B. Smith 1, Rogers 1.

COWBOYS 31, GIANTS 7

Monday, September 21

Dallas	0	17	7	7—31
N.Y. Giants	0	7	0	0— 7

Second Quarter

Dal.—Sanders 59 punt return (Cunningham kick), 2:29.
NYG—Toomer 36 pass from Kanell (Daluiso kick), 11:06.
Dal.—B. Davis 80 pass from Garrett (Cunningham kick), 12:15.
Dal.—FG, Cunningham 40, 14:53.

Third Quarter

Dal.—S. Williams 18 run (Cunningham kick), 5:40.

Fourth Quarter

Dal.—Sanders 71 interception return (Cunningham kick), 12:35.
    Attendance—78,039.

	Dallas	N.Y. Giants
First downs	11	16
Rushes-yards	29-80	18-56

	Dallas	N.Y. Giants
Passing	222	196
Punt returns	6-98	5-41
Kickoff returns	1-16	5-57
Interception returns	3-112	0-0
Comp.-att.-int.	12-28-0	26-53-3
Sacked-yards lost	0-0	4-35
Punts	9-43	10-44
Fumbles-lost	2-0	2-1
Penalties-yards	8-67	11-92
Time of possession	29:49	30:11

INDIVIDUAL STATISTICS

RUSHING—Dallas, S. Williams 20-62, E. Smith 7-21, Quinn 2-(minus 3). New York, Way 9-26, Barber 3-11, Wheatley 3-8, Kanell 2-5, Comella 1-6.

PASSING—Dallas, Garrett 12-28-0-222. New York, Kanell 25-45-2-228, K. Graham 1-7-1-3, Toomer 0-1-0-0.

RECEIVING—Dallas, Irvin 5-67, E. Smith 3-18, B. Davis 1-80, Sanders 1-55, Johnston 1-4, S. Williams 1-(minus 2). New York, Calloway 7-77, Hilliard 5-61, Way 5-0, Barber 4-23, Toomer 2-54, Cross 1-8, Patten 1-5, Comella 1-3.

MISSED FIELD GOAL ATTEMPTS—Dallas, Cunningham 38.

INTERCEPTIONS—Dallas, Sanders 1-71, Wheaton 1-41, Mathis 1-0.

KICKOFF RETURNS—Dallas, Mathis 1-16. New York, Toomer 2-28, Wheatley 1-16, Comella 1-12, Palelei 1-1.

PUNT RETURNS—Dallas, Sanders 5-100, Mathis 1-(minus 2). New York, Toomer 5-41.

SACKS—Dallas, Godfrey 1, Stoutmire 1, Hennings 1, Lett 1.

WEEK 4

RESULTS

Arizona 20, ST. LOUIS 17
BALTIMORE 31, Cincinnati 24
Denver 38, WASHINGTON 16
Green Bay 37, CAROLINA 30
Jacksonville 27, TENNESSEE 22
Kansas City 24, PHILADELPHIA 21
Minnesota 31, CHICAGO 28
New Orleans 19, INDIANAPOLIS 13 (OT)
N.Y. Giants 34, SAN DIEGO 16
Oakland 13, DALLAS 12
PITTSBURGH 13, Seattle 10
SAN FRANCISCO 31, Atlanta 20
DETROIT 27, Tampa Bay 6
   Open date: Buffalo, Miami, New England, N.Y. Jets

STANDINGS

AFC EAST	W	L	T	Pct.
Miami	3	0	0	1.000
New England	2	1	0	.667
N.Y. Jets	1	2	0	.333
Buffalo	0	3	0	.000
Indianapolis	0	4	0	.000

AFC CENTRAL	W	L	T	Pct.
Jacksonville	4	0	0	1.000
Pittsburgh	3	1	0	.750
Baltimore	2	2	0	.500
Cincinnati	1	3	0	.250
Tennessee	1	3	0	.250

AFC WEST	W	L	T	Pct.
Denver	4	0	0	1.000
Kansas City	3	1	0	.750
Seattle	3	1	0	.750
Oakland	2	2	0	.500
San Diego	2	2	0	.500

NFC EAST	W	L	T	Pct.
Arizona	2	2	0	.500
Dallas	2	2	0	.500
N.Y. Giants	2	2	0	.500
Philadelphia	0	4	0	.000
Washington	0	4	0	.000

NFC CENTRAL	W	L	T	Pct.
Green Bay	4	0	0	1.000
Minnesota	4	0	0	1.000
Detroit	1	3	0	.250
Tampa Bay	1	3	0	.250
Chicago	0	4	0	.000

NFC WEST	W	L	T	Pct.
New Orleans	3	0	0	1.000
San Francisco	3	0	0	1.000
Atlanta	2	1	0	.667
St. Louis	1	3	0	.250
Carolina	0	3	0	.000

HIGHLIGHTS

Hero of the week: Baltimore's Jermaine Lewis caught a 73-yard touchdown pass and returned a punt 87 yards for a score in the Ravens' 31-24 victory over Cincinnati. The punt-return touchdown was his second of the season and his fifth TD in four games—all on big plays. Lewis had touchdown receptions of 64, 56, and 73 yards and punt-return scores of 69 and 87 yards.

Goat of the week: For the second consecutive week, San Diego rookie Ryan Leaf had a horrible game. He threw four interceptions before being benched in the third quarter of the Chargers' 34-16 loss to the Giants and finished the game 15-of-34 passing for 193 yards and no touchdowns.

Sub of the week: After Bengals quarterback Neil O'Donnell suffered bruised ribs in the third quarter on a sack by Baltimore's Michael McCrary, he was replaced by Jeff Blake, who led an 80-yard touchdown drive in the fourth quarter that pulled his team within four points of the Ravens. Blake, who was in the game for a little more than a quarter, finished 3-for-6 passing for 89 yards with a 67-yard touchdown pass and no interceptions.

Comeback of the week: The Jaguars rebounded from a 19-7 second-quarter deficit to beat the Oilers 27-22. Jacksonville began its rally when Mark Brunell threw a 7-yard touchdown pass to Keenan McCardell 21 seconds before halftime. Then Fred Taylor bolted 49 yards on the first snap of the second half, setting up his 1-yard touchdown run. Jacksonville added two field goals in the fourth quarter.

Blowout of the week: With John Elway on the sideline because of a hamstring injury, Bubby Brister led Denver to a 38-16 rout of Washington. Brister completed 16-of-24 passes for 180 yards and two touchdowns. Terrell Davis was the biggest weapon in Denver's ground attack, carrying the ball 21 times for 119 yards, including a 42-yard score.

Nail-biter of the week: New Orleans beat Indianapolis 19-13 in overtime thanks to two clutch passes by Danny Wuerffel. Wuerffel passed for touchdowns of 15 yards to Andre Hastings with 41 seconds left in regulation and 33 yards to Cam Cleeland at 8:50 of overtime.

Hit of the week: With the Oilers trailing Jacksonville 27-22 in the fourth quarter, backup quarterback Dave Krieg was trying to lead Tennessee to a game-winning score. But he had the ball jarred loose, and the fumble was recovered by defensive tackle Renaldo Wynn to secure the Jaguars' victory.

Oddity of the week: Mark McGwire mania was everywhere on this weekend, even at the Rams-Cardinals game. As the Rams lined up for a third-and-9 play from the Arizona 44 late in the third quarter, the roar at St. Louis' Trans World Dome was spontaneous and deafening. McGwire had just hit his 69th home run of the season a few blocks away at Busch Stadium. There was no announcement about the homer at the time, but thousands of fans brought radios with them to the Dome. With the crowd going wild, the Rams were penalized for a false start. On the next play, Tony Banks was sacked and the Rams had to punt.

Top rusher: Priest Holmes carried 27 times for 173 yards and two touchdowns in the Ravens' 31-24 victory over the Bengals.

Top passer: Brett Favre was 27-of-45 for 388 yards and five touchdowns in the Packers' 37-30 victory over the Panthers.

Top receiver: Jerry Rice caught eight passes for 162 yards and scored two touchdowns in the 49ers' 31-20 win over the Falcons.

Notes: Eagles receiver Irving Fryar had five receptions for 57 yards, pusing him past Charlie Joiner for eighth place on the NFL career list with 751 catches. . . . Fred Taylor's 49-yard run against Tennessee was the second-longest in Jaguars history. He posted the longest, 52 yards, the previous week. . . . Chris Chandler set a Falcons record by throwing a touchdown pass in his 15th straight game. . . . San Francisco's Chris Doleman moved into sixth place all-time with the first of his 2.5 sacks against Atlanta. He increased his career total to 129.5. . . . Steelers cornerback Carnell Lake had a fumble return against the Seahawks, giving him 16 for his career and tying him with Joe Greene for third on the team's all-time list. . . . Seahawks receiver Joey Galloway had 139 yards, the 10th 100-yard receiving game of his career. . . . Brett Favre's 388-yard game was the third-highest of his career. . . . John Kasay's 56-yard field goal was a Panthers record. . . . Jeff Wilkins' 57-yarder was the longest field goal in Rams history.

Quote of the week: Broncos quarterback Bubby Brister, who started in place of injured John Elway, on the efficiency of the Denver offense: "This is a machine, and I'm just glad to have the opportunity to run it. I don't know what the numbers are. I don't care. I just tried to be safe with the ball, not try to force anything. Just drive the car, don't wreck it, as (tight end) Shannon (Sharpe) says."

GAME SUMMARIES

VIKINGS 31, BEARS 28

Sunday, September 27

Minnesota	7	3	14	7—31
Chicago	7	14	0	7—28

First Quarter
Min.—R. Smith 67 pass from Cunningham (Anderson kick), 2:17.
Chi.—Engram 33 pass from Kramer (Jaeger kick), 5:56.

Second Quarter
Min.—FG, Anderson 50, 6:22.
Chi.—Penn 23 pass from Kramer (Jaeger kick), 8:48.
Chi.—Engram 4 pass from Kramer (Jaeger kick), 14:32.

Third Quarter
Min.—Glover 19 pass from Cunningham (Anderson kick), 3:36.
Min.—Carter 35 pass from Cunningham (Anderson kick), 13:16.

Fourth Quarter
Min.—R. Moss 44 pass from Cunningham (Anderson kick), 4:54.
Chi.—Wetnight 19 pass from Kramer (Jaeger kick), 13:07.
Attendance—57,783.

	Minnesota	Chicago
First downs	17	23
Rushes-yards	27-93	26-91
Passing	258	361
Punt returns	1-53	1-15
Kickoff returns	3-73	5-75
Interception returns	1-30	0-0
Comp.-att.-int.	16-25-0	25-39-1
Sacked-yards lost	3-17	1-11
Punts	5-35	6-42
Fumbles-lost	0-0	0-0
Penalties-yards	4-38	9-55
Time of possession	26:57	33:03

INDIVIDUAL STATISTICS
RUSHING—Minnesota, R. Smith 19-76, Cunningham 5-6, Hoard 2-7, R. Moss 1-4. Chicago, Enis 14-43, Bennett 11-47, Hallock 1-1.
PASSING—Minnesota, Cunningham 16-25-0-275. Chicago, Kramer 25-39-1-372.
RECEIVING—Minnesota, Carter 4-68, Reed 3-22, R. Smith 2-83, R. Moss 2-52, Glover 2-33, Palmer 1-14, Evans 1-6, Cunningham 1-(minus 3). Chicago, Engram 6-123, Penn 4-73, Hallock 4-42, Bownes 3-56, Wetnight 3-36, Mayes 2-17, Bennett 2-16, Chancey 1-9.
MISSED FIELD GOAL ATTEMPTS—None.
INTERCEPTIONS—Minnesota, Fuller 1-30.
KICKOFF RETURNS—Minnesota, Palmer 3-73. Chicago, Milburn 3-75, Chancey 1-0, Smith 1-0.
PUNT RETURNS—Minnesota, Palmer 1-53. Chicago, Milburn 1-15.
SACKS—Minnesota, Randle 1. Chicago, Minter 1, Flanigan 1, Thomas 1.

PACKERS 37, PANTHERS 30

Sunday, September 27

Green Bay	6	14	10	7—37
Carolina	10	10	0	10—30

First Quarter
Car.—FG, Kasay 42, 3:03.
Car.—Ismail 5 pass from Collins (Kasay kick), 4:43.
G.B.—Chmura 25 pass from Favre (kick failed), 13:56.

Second Quarter
G.B.—Mayes 21 pass from Favre (Longwell kick), 4:20.
Car.—Davis 16 interception return (Kasay kick), 6:02.
Car.—FG, Kasay 42, 12:33.
G.B.—T. Davis 20 pass from Favre (Longwell kick), 13:54.

Third Quarter
G.B.—Mayes 4 pass from Favre (Longwell kick), 6:52.
G.B.—FG, Longwell 41, 12:44.

Fourth Quarter
Car.—FG, Kasay 56, 1:56.
G.B.—Mayes 33 pass from Favre (Longwell kick), 4:24.
Car.—Muhammad 15 pass from Collins (Kasay kick), 10:43.
Attendance—69,723.

	Green Bay	Carolina
First downs	26	13
Rushes-yards	33-109	16-60
Passing	378	170
Punt returns	4-40	1-7
Kickoff returns	6-167	5-98
Interception returns	1-26	3-32
Comp.-att.-int.	27-45-3	20-53-1
Sacked-yards lost	2-10	4-18
Punts	4-40	8-44
Fumbles-lost	1-1	2-0
Penalties-yards	9-83	7-64
Time of possession	35:15	24:45

INDIVIDUAL STATISTICS
RUSHING—Green Bay, R. Harris 28-82, Henderson 3-5, Favre 1-17, Freeman 1-5. Carolina, Lane 14-52, Floyd 1-5, Collins 1-3.
PASSING—Green Bay, Favre 27-45-3-388. Carolina, Collins 20-53-1-188.
RECEIVING—Green Bay, Freeman 6-84, Henderson 6-53, Mayes 5-87, Chmura 5-84, R. Brooks 3-48, T. Davis 1-20, R. Harris 1-12. Carolina, Ismail 6-71, Johnson 5-31, Carrier 2-32, Muhammad 2-25, Walls 2-17, Lane 2-10, Floyd 1-2.
MISSED FIELD GOAL ATTEMPTS—None.
INTERCEPTIONS—Green Bay, Newsome 1-26. Carolina, Brady 2-16, Davis 1-16.
KICKOFF RETURNS—Green Bay, Preston 6-167. Carolina, Stone 2-55, Bates 1-28, Jensen 1-9, Saleh 1-6.
PUNT RETURNS—Green Bay, Preston 4-40. Carolina, Oliver 1-7.
SACKS—Green Bay, Holliday 2, White 2. Carolina, Greene 2. Ellis 1, Pittman 1.

CARDINALS 20, RAMS 17

Sunday, September 27

Arizona	0	17	0	3—20
St. Louis	7	3	0	7—17

First Quarter
St.L.—Holcombe 5 run (Wilkins kick), 12:26.

Second Quarter
Ariz.—FG, Nedney 22, 3:20.
Ariz.—Sanders 13 pass from Plummer (Nedney kick), 13:05.
Ariz.—Murrell 4 run (Nedney kick), 13:51.
St.L.—FG, Wilkins 57, 15:00.

Fourth Quarter
St.L.—Holcombe 4 run (Wilkins kick), 5:08.
Ariz.—FG, Nedney 29, 10:56.
Attendance—55,832.

	Arizona	St. Louis
First downs	22	17
Rushes-yards	35-78	27-120
Passing	203	144
Punt returns	4-10	2-3
Kickoff returns	3-55	4-75
Interception returns	0-0	1-0
Comp.-att.-int.	21-31-1	15-26-0
Sacked-yards lost	1-8	4-27
Punts	5-40	8-39
Fumbles-lost	0-0	1-0
Penalties-yards	5-56	10-138
Time of possession	31:48	28:12

RUSHING—Arizona, Murrell 29-68, Plummer 6-10. St. Louis, Holcombe 21-84, Banks 2-25, Proehl 1-14, Harris 1-4, Kennison 1-0, Lee 1-(minus 7).

PASSING—Arizona, Plummer 21-31-1-211. St. Louis, Banks 15-26-0-171.

RECEIVING—Arizona, Sanders 9-86, McWilliams 4-35, R. Moore 3-39, Centers 3-17, Metcalf 1-29, Murrell 1-5. St. Louis, Lee 5-53, Holcombe 3-17, Proehl 2-~~~~, ~~~~ Harris 1-8, Conwell 1-5.

MISSED F~~~~ ~~~~ns 45.

INTERCE~~~~

KICKOFF ~~~~

PUNT RE~~~~

SACKS—~~~~ ~~~~ 1.

Atlanta . . ~~~~—20
San Fran~~~~ ~~~~—31

S.F.—Ri~~~~
S.F.—Ed~~~~
Atl.—M~~~~

S.F.—S~~~~
S.F.—~~~~
S.F.—~~~~

Atl.—~~~~
Atl.—~~~~
A~~~~

	n Francisco
Firs~~~~	23
Ru~~~~	31-161
Pa~~~~	377
Pu~~~~	3-46
Ki~~~~	2-30
Ir~~~~	3-0
C~~~~	28-39-1
S~~~~	3-10
Punts ~~~~	5-46
Fumbles-lost ~~~~	2-1
Penalties-yards	7-53	5-40
Time of possession...................	27:06	32:54

INDIVIDUAL STATISTICS

RUSHING—Atlanta, Anderson 13-123, Chandler 3-13, Dwight 3-12, Oxendine 1-(minus 1). San Francisco, Hearst 18-57, S. Young 7-50, Edwards 3-41, Levy 3-13.

PASSING—Atlanta, Chandler 16-38-3-254. San Francisco, S. Young 28-39-1-387.

RECEIVING—Atlanta, Mathis 7-130, Martin 4-53, Anderson 2-43, Downs 2-20, Santiago 1-8. San Francisco, Rice 8-162, Levy 6-21, Hearst 4-105, I. Smith 4-39, Stokes 3-21, Owens 2-32, Uwaezuoke 1-7.

MISSED FIELD GOAL ATTEMPTS—San Francisco, Richey 43.

INTERCEPTIONS—Atlanta, Buchanan 1-31. San Francisco, Bronson 2-0, McDonald 1-0.

KICKOFF RETURNS—Atlanta, Dwight 6-127. San Francisco, Levy 2-30.

PUNT RETURNS—Atlanta, Dwight 3-36. San Francisco, McQuarters 3-46.

SACKS—Atlanta, Tuggle 1, Dronett 1, C. Smith 1. San Francisco, Doleman 2.5, Bryant 1.5, B. Young 1, Norton 1, McDonald 0.5, Woodall 0.5.

STEELERS 13, SEAHAWKS 10

Sunday, September 27

Seattle	0	7	3	0—10
Pittsburgh...........................	3	7	3	0—13

First Quarter
Pit.—FG, N. Johnson 33, 14:28.

Second Quarter
Sea.—Fauria 14 pass from Moon (Peterson kick), 2:21.
Pit.—Fuamatu-Ma'afala 10 run (N. Johnson kick), 10:34.

Third Quarter
Pit.—FG, N. Johnson 25, 8:36.
Sea.—FG, Peterson 47, 13:28.
   Attendance—58,413.

	Seattle	Pittsburgh
First downs	14	16
Rushes-yards	21-61	45-185
Passing	169	100
Punt returns	0-0	1-(-1)
Kickoff returns	4-65	2-42
Interception returns	0-0	1-5
Comp.-att.-int.	14-27-1	16-25-0
Sacked-yards lost	4-14	2-8
Punts	3-43	5-42
Fumbles-lost	4-3	0-0
Penalties-yards	2-5	7-57
Time of possession	21:51	38:09

INDIVIDUAL STATISTICS

RUSHING—Seattle, Watters 17-47, Strong 3-14, Moon 1-0. Pittsburgh, Bettis 28-138, Stewart 11-22, Hawkins 2-12, Huntley 2-1, Fuamatu-Ma'afala 1-10, Witman 1-2.

PASSING—Seattle, Moon 14-27-1-183. Pittsburgh, Stewart 16-25-0-108.

RECEIVING—Seattle, Galloway 7-139, Watters 3-5, Pritchard 1-15, Fauria 1-14, McKnight 1-7, Strong 1-3. Pittsburgh, Hawkins 5-42, Blackwell 3-19, C. Johnson 2-19, Bettis 2-(minus 4), Coleman 1-13, Fuamatu-Ma'afala 1-8, Witman 1-7, Bishop 1-4.

MISSED FIELD GOAL ATTEMPTS—Seattle, Peterson 52. Pittsburgh, N. Johnson 42.

INTERCEPTIONS—Pittsburgh, Washington 1-5.

KICKOFF RETURNS—Seattle, Broussard 4-65. Pittsburgh, Huntley 2-42.

PUNT RETURNS—Pittsburgh, Blackwell 1-(minus 1).

SACKS—Seattle, C. Brown 1, Sinclair 1. Pittsburgh, Gildon 2, Kirkland 1, Henry 1.

BRONCOS 38, REDSKINS 16

Sunday, September 27

Denver	7	10	14	7—38
Washington	0	7	3	6—16

First Quarter
Den.—McCaffrey 19 pass from Brister (Elam kick), 6:15.

Second Quarter
Den.—FG, Elam 37, 1:25.
Den.—Gordon 55 interception return (Elam kick), 3:40.
Was.—Allen 5 run (Blanchard kick), 7:45.

Third Quarter
Den.—Davis 42 run (Elam kick), 1:26.
Den.—Griffith 14 pass from Brister (Elam kick), 7:37.
Was.—FG, Blanchard 37, 14:01.

Fourth Quarter
Den.—Loville 1 run (Elam kick), 6:42.
Was.—Westbrook 75 pass from T. Green (pass failed), 7:04.
   Attendance—71,880.

	Denver	Washington
First downs	18	18
Rushes-yards	35-185	25-152
Passing	180	235
Punt returns	1-13	2-19
Kickoff returns	3-84	5-111
Interception returns	2-56	0-0
Comp.-att.-int.	16-24-0	19-31-2
Sacked-yards lost	0-0	3-17
Punts	5-50	4-53
Fumbles-lost	0-0	4-1
Penalties-yards	7-50	8-65
Time of possession	32:11	27:49

INDIVIDUAL STATISTICS

RUSHING—Denver, Davis 21-119, Loville 8-22, Brister 4-6, R. Smith 1-37, Hebron 1-1. Washington, Allen 16-86, T. Green 4-20, Davis 2-5, Shepherd 1-29, Mitchell 1-11, Bowie 1-1.

PASSING—Denver, Brister 16-24-0-180. Washington, T. Green 19-31-2-252.

RECEIVING—Denver, Sharpe 6-69, McCaffrey 4-74, R. Smith 2-13, Davis 2-7, Griffith 1-14, Hebron 1-3. Washington, Allen 6-26, Westbrook 3-104, Alexander 3-52, Shepherd 2-34, Bowie 1-10, Asher 1-8, Thomas 1-8, Mitchell 1-5, Davis 1-5.

MISSED FIELD GOAL ATTEMPTS—Washington, Blanchard 44.

INTERCEPTIONS—Denver, Gordon 1-55, Pryce 1-1.

Super Bowl cities

Atlanta's Georgia Dome is the site of this year's game, making Atlanta the host city for a second time.

Past hosts

City	No. of games
Miami	8
New Orleans	8
Los Angeles	7
San Diego	2
Tampa	2
Atlanta	2
Detroit	1
Houston	1
Minneapolis	1
Phoenix	1
San Francisco	1

Source: NFL

KICKOFF RETURNS—Denver, Hebron 2-66, Loville 1-18. Washington, Mitchell 5-111.

PUNT RETURNS—Denver, Gordon 1-13. Washington, Mitchell 2-19.

SACKS—Denver, Cadrez 1, Romanowski 1, N. Smith 1.

RAIDERS 13, COWBOYS 12

Sunday, September 27

Oakland	3	7	0	3—13
Dallas	0	3	0	9—12

First Quarter
Oak.—FG, G. Davis 30, 12:26.

Second Quarter
Dal.—FG, Cunningham 40, 2:36.
Oak.—Jett 75 pass from George (G. Davis kick), 13:46.

Fourth Quarter
Oak.—FG, G. Davis 38, 4:13.
Dal.—E. Smith 1 run (Cunningham kick), 9:11.
Dal.—Safety, Wheaton tackled Araguz in end zone, 14:58.
Attendance—63,544.

	Oakland	Dallas
First downs	13	16
Rushes-yards	37-129	25-68
Passing	159	207
Punt returns	2-7	4-91
Kickoff returns	2-35	5-96
Interception returns	2-24	0-0
Comp.-att.-int.	12-20-0	18-33-2
Sacked-yards lost	2-12	2-15
Punts	5-46	5-39
Fumbles-lost	1-0	1-1
Penalties-yards	4-20	4-20
Time of possession	30:45	29:15

INDIVIDUAL STATISTICS

RUSHING—Oakland, Kaufman 24-116, H. Williams 7-27, George 4-(minus 4), Ritchie 1-2, Araguz 1-(minus 12). Dallas, E. Smith 21-59, Garrett 2-5, Warren 1-4, Johnston 1-0.

PASSING—Oakland, George 12-20-0-171. Dallas, Garrett 18-33-2-222.

RECEIVING—Oakland, T. Brown 4-35, Dudley 3-53, Kaufman 3-2, Jett 1-75, Mickens 1-6. Dallas, Irvin 6-89, B. Davis 4-87, E. Mills 4-27, Warren 2-13, Johnston 2-6.

MISSED FIELD GOAL ATTEMPTS—Oakland, G. Davis 48. Dallas, Cunningham 37.

INTERCEPTIONS—Oakland, Woodson 1-24, Turner 1-0.

KICKOFF RETURNS—Oakland, Howard 2-35. Dallas, Mathis 4-91, Sanders 1-5.

PUNT RETURNS—Oakland, Howard 2-7. Dallas, Sanders 4-91.

SACKS—Oakland, Russell 1, Lewis 1. Dallas, Ellis 1, Pittman 1.

GIANTS 34, CHARGERS 16

Sunday, September 27

N.Y. Giants	14	7	7	6—34
San Diego	0	6	10	0—16

First Quarter
NYG—Brown 4 run (Daluiso kick), 10:52.
NYG—Calloway 25 pass from Kanell (Daluiso kick), 14:10.

Second Quarter
NYG—Way 1 run (Daluiso kick), 7:08.
S.D.—FG, Carney 41, 13:09.
S.D.—FG, Carney 46, 15:00.

Third Quarter
S.D.—FG, Carney 34, 5:27.
NYG—Ellsworth 20 interception return (Daluiso kick), 7:22.
S.D.—C. Jones 41 pass from Whelihan (Carney kick), 9:32.

Fourth Quarter
NYG—FG, Daluiso 32, 3:17.
NYG—FG, Daluiso 19, 10:12.
Attendance—55,672.

	N.Y. Giants	San Diego
First downs	19	17
Rushes-yards	40-105	21-89
Passing	208	266
Punt returns	3-30	3-18
Kickoff returns	3-77	2-47

	N.Y. Giants	San Diego
Interception returns	4-90	1-8
Comp.-att.-int.	17-33-1	21-49-4
Sacked-yards lost	0-0	2-24
Punts	6-48	5-47
Fumbles-lost	1-0	0-0
Penalties-yards	6-66	10-85
Time of possession	30:24	29:36

INDIVIDUAL STATISTICS

RUSHING—New York, Brown 20-66, Way 10-26, Wheatley 4-15, Barber 3-(minus 3), Kanell 2-2, K. Graham 1-(minus 1). San Diego, Means 11-56, Fletcher 6-11, Whelihan 3-13, Leaf 1-9.

PASSING—New York, Kanell 17-33-1-208. San Diego, Leaf 15-34-4-193, Whelihan 6-15-0-97.

RECEIVING—New York, Calloway 6-94, Hilliard 5-71, Way 2-15, Brown 2-12, Toomer 1-11, Barber 1-5. San Diego, Still 8-104, C. Jones 3-64, Slaughter 3-53, F. Jones 3-47, Fletcher 3-18, Burke 1-4.

MISSED FIELD GOAL ATTEMPTS—None.

INTERCEPTIONS—New York, Ellsworth 2-42, C. Gray 1-36, Sparks 1-12. San Diego, G. Jackson 1-8.

KICKOFF RETURNS—New York, Patten 3-77. San Diego, Stephens 1-36, Hartley 1-11.

PUNT RETURNS—New York, Toomer 3-30. San Diego, Rachal 3-18.

SACKS—New York, Strahan 1, Jones 1.

JAGUARS 27, OILERS 22

Sunday, September 27

Jacksonville	7	7	7	6—27
Tennessee	10	9	3	0—22

First Quarter
Ten.—FG, Del Greco 34, 5:17.
Jac.—D. Jones 5 pass from Brunell (Hollis kick), 11:35.
Ten.—Thigpen 38 pass from McNair (Del Greco kick), 13:25.

Second Quarter
Ten.—FG, Del Greco 32, 7:15.
Ten.—Thigpen 18 pass from McNair (run failed), 8:51.
Jac.—McCardell 7 pass from Brunell (Hollis kick), 14:39.

Third Quarter
Jac.—F. Taylor 1 run (Hollis kick), 3:18.
Ten.—FG, Del Greco 32, 8:53.

Fourth Quarter
Jac.—FG, Hollis 18, 5:15.
Jac.—FG, Hollis 36, 13:04.
Attendance—34,656.

	Jacksonville	Tennessee
First downs	19	15
Rushes-yards	37-148	20-40
Passing	149	179
Punt returns	2-7	1-7
Kickoff returns	2-48	5-121
Interception returns	2-34	2-18
Comp.-att.-int.	17-28-2	17-33-2
Sacked-yards lost	2-6	4-29
Punts	3-51	3-50
Fumbles-lost	1-1	3-1
Penalties-yards	10-71	9-73
Time of possession	32:54	27:06

INDIVIDUAL STATISTICS

RUSHING—Jacksonville, F. Taylor 25-116, Brunell 8-24, Banks 4-8. Tennessee, E. George 14-25, McNair 4-13, Thomas 1-2, Krieg 1-0.

PASSING—Jacksonville, Brunell 17-28-2-155. Tennessee, McNair 16-30-2-198, Krieg 1-3-0-10.

RECEIVING—Jacksonville, McCardell 6-68, Mitchell 4-35, J. Smith 3-46, F. Taylor 2-(minus 7), Shelton 1-8, D. Jones 1-5. Tennessee, Thigpen 6-102, Davis 3-45, Harris 3-17, Wycheck 2-14, Roan 1-16, E. George 1-10, Mason 1-4.

MISSED FIELD GOAL ATTEMPTS—None.

INTERCEPTIONS—Jacksonville, Davis 1-34, Hudson 1-0. Tennessee, Robinson 1-11, D. Lewis 1-7.

KICKOFF RETURNS—Jacksonville, Barlow 2-48. Tennessee, Thomas 2-53, Archie 2-44, Mason 1-24.

PUNT RETURNS—Jacksonville, Barlow 2-7. Tennessee, Mason 1-7.

SACKS—Jacksonville, Hardy 1, Paup 1, Pritchett 1, Smeenge 1. Tennessee, Robinson 1, Lyons 1.

RAVENS 31, BENGALS 24

Sunday, September 27

Cincinnati	0	10	7	7—24
Baltimore	14	7	7	3—31

First Quarter
Bal.—Holmes 3 run (Stover kick), 7:24.
Bal.—Holmes 15 run (Stover kick), 13:15.
Second Quarter
Bal.—J. Lewis 73 pass from Zeier (Stover kick), 2:33.
Cin.—FG, Pelfrey 48, 10:15.
Cin.—Pickens 1 pass from O'Donnell (Pelfrey kick), 14:43.
Third Quarter
Cin.—Mack 97 kickoff return (Pelfrey kick), 0:17.
Bal.—J. Lewis 87 punt return (Stover kick), 6:16.
Fourth Quarter
Cin.—Pickens 67 pass from Blake (Pelfrey kick), 3:42.
Bal.—FG, Stover 46, 9:45.
Attendance—68,154.

	Cincinnati	Baltimore
First downs	19	21
Rushes-yards	29-132	35-181
Passing	143	230
Punt returns	0-0	4-115
Kickoff returns	6-189	3-58
Interception returns	0-0	0-0
Comp.-att.-int.	16-25-0	15-20-0
Sacked-yards lost	5-46	3-24
Punts	5-43	3-39
Fumbles-lost	0-0	2-1
Penalties-yards	2-34	10-91
Time of possession	29:11	30:49

INDIVIDUAL STATISTICS
RUSHING—Cincinnati, Dillon 25-116, Bieniemy 2-2, Blake 1-9, O'Donnell 1-5. Baltimore, Holmes 27-173, Rhett 3-0, Graham 2-11, Zeier 2-(minus 2), J. Lewis 1-(minus 1).
PASSING—Cincinnati, O'Donnell 13-19-0-100, Blake 3-6-0-89. Baltimore, Zeier 15-20-0-254.
RECEIVING—Cincinnati, Pickens 7-120, Scott 4-46, Dillon 2-6, McGee 1-9, Milne 1-5, Gibson 1-3. Baltimore, J. Lewis 4-122, Jackson 4-80, Potts 3-23, Green 2-24, Holmes 2-5.
MISSED FIELD GOAL ATTEMPTS—None.
INTERCEPTIONS—None.
KICKOFF RETURNS—Cincinnati, Mack 6-189. Baltimore, Johnson 1-24, Holmes 1-19, Cotton 1-15.
PUNT RETURNS—Baltimore, J. Lewis 4-115.
SACKS—Cincinnati, Spikes 1, Hawkins 1, C. Simmons 1. Baltimore, McCrary 2, Sharper 1, Burnett 1, J. Jones 1.

SAINTS 19, COLTS 13

Sunday, September 27

New Orleans	0	3	3	7	6—19
Indianapolis	3	3	0	7	0—13

First Quarter
Ind.—FG, Vanderjagt 52, 7:56.
Second Quarter
Ind.—FG, Vanderjagt 19, 9:39.
N.O.—FG, Brien 22, 14:34.
Third Quarter
N.O.—FG, Brien 20, 9:23.
Fourth Quarter
Ind.—Faulk 78 pass from Manning (Vanderjagt kick), 0:11.
N.O.—Hastings 15 pass from Wuerffel (Brien kick), 14:19.
Overtime
N.O.—Cleeland 33 pass from Wuerffel, 6:10.
Attendance—48,480.

	New Orleans	Indianapolis
First downs	14	16
Rushes-yards	32-183	31-65
Passing	137	292
Punt returns	2-41	3-27
Kickoff returns	4-117	4-92
Interception returns	3-52	1-0
Comp.-att.-int.	12-28-1	19-32-3

	New Orleans	Indianapolis
Sacked-yards lost	4-16	4-17
Punts	8-51	6-46
Fumbles-lost	1-0	0-0
Penalties-yards	6-55	10-79
Time of possession	31:41	34:29

INDIVIDUAL STATISTICS
RUSHING—New Orleans, L. Smith 24-157, Zellars 7-12, Hastings 1-14. Indianapolis, Faulk 27-61, Manning 1-7, Elias 1-6, Crockett 1-0, Pathon 1-(minus 9).
PASSING—New Orleans, Wuerffel 12-27-1-153, Craver 0-1-0-0. Indianapolis, Manning 19-32-3-309.
RECEIVING—New Orleans, Hastings 4-47, Cleeland 3-49, Dawkins 2-55, Zellars 2-0, Craver 1-2. Indianapolis, Harrison 7-95, Faulk 6-128, Pathon 3-66, Green 1-17, Pollard 1-2, Crockett 1-1.
MISSED FIELD GOAL ATTEMPTS—None.
INTERCEPTIONS—New Orleans, Kelly 1-25, Drakeford 1-23, Cota 1-4. Indianapolis, Poole 1-0.
KICKOFF RETURNS—New Orleans, Ismail 4-117. Indianapolis, Elias 4-92.
PUNT RETURNS—New Orleans, Hastings 2-41. Indianapolis, Poole 3-27.
SACKS—New Orleans, Fields 2, J. Johnson 1, Robbins 1. Indianapolis, E. Johnson 1, McCoy 1, Chester 1, Tuinei 1.

CHIEFS 24, EAGLES 21

Sunday, September 27

Kansas City	0	7	0	17—24
Philadelphia	7	0	7	7—21

First Quarter
Phi.—Staley 5 run (Boniol kick), 11:43.
Second Quarter
K.C.—Bennett 1 run (Stoyanovich kick), 1:45.
Third Quarter
Phi.—Staley 3 run (Boniol kick), 7:37.
Fourth Quarter
K.C.—FG, Stoyanovich 21, 3:22.
K.C.—Bennett 7 run (Stoyanovich kick), 6:19.
K.C.—Bennett 5 run (Stoyanovich kick), 11:54.
Phi.—Staley 17 pass from Peete (Boniol kick), 13:59.
Attendance—66,675.

	Kansas City	Philadelphia
First downs	24	22
Rushes-yards	33-131	27-111
Passing	262	250
Punt returns	2-1	1-3
Kickoff returns	1-27	3-55
Interception returns	1-12	0-0
Comp.-att.-int.	17-25-0	21-36-1
Sacked-yards lost	0-0	3-10
Punts	2-43	3-39
Fumbles-lost	2-0	1-0
Penalties-yards	10-65	7-93
Time of possession	29:50	30:10

INDIVIDUAL STATISTICS
RUSHING—Kansas City, Bennett 19-87, Anders 7-36, Gannon 5-8, Richardson 1-1, Shehee 1-(minus 1). Philadelphia, Staley 16-73, Garner 9-29, Turner 1-7, Peete 1-2.
PASSING—Kansas City, Gannon 17-25-0-262. Philadelphia, Peete 21-36-1-260.
RECEIVING—Kansas City, Anders 5-63, Lockett 4-74, Gonzalez 3-31, Horn 2-68, Alexander 2-19, Popson 1-7. Philadelphia, Graham 5-79, Fryar 5-57, Turner 4-36, Copeland 2-25, Staley 2-23, Sinceno 1-28, Solomon 1-8, Garner 1-4.
MISSED FIELD GOAL ATTEMPTS—Kansas City, Stoyanovich 40.
INTERCEPTIONS—Kansas City, McMillian 1-12.
KICKOFF RETURNS—Kansas City, Vanover 1-27. Philadelphia, Rossum 3-55.
PUNT RETURNS—Kansas City, Vanover 2-1. Philadelphia, Rossum 1-3.
SACKS—Kansas City, Barndt 2, Davis 1.

LIONS 27, BUCCANEERS 6

Monday, September 28

Tampa Bay	0	3	0	3— 6
Detroit	0	6	14	7—27

Second Quarter

Det.—FG, Hanson 27, 5:26.
Det.—FG, Hanson 25, 13:04.
T.B.—FG, Husted 43, 14:47.

Third Quarter

Det.—Westbrook 34 interception return (Hanson kick), 1:49.
Det.—Batch 1 run (Hanson kick), 6:25.

Fourth Quarter

T.B.—FG, Husted 47, 4:21.
Det.—Fair 105 kickoff return (Hanson kick), 4:41.
   Attendance—74,724.

	Tampa Bay	Detroit
First downs	6	17
Rushes-yards	17-55	41-156
Passing	78	124
Punt returns	2-9	4-10
Kickoff returns	5-150	2-136
Interception returns	0-0	2-59
Comp.-att.-int.	12-32-2	15-25-0
Sacked-yards lost	4-42	1-7

	Tampa Bay	Detroit
Punts	10-39	6-34
Fumbles-lost	1-0	1-1
Penalties-yards	10-58	3-20
Time of possession	21:51	38:09

INDIVIDUAL STATISTICS

RUSHING—Tampa Bay, Dunn 8-30, Alstott 5-9, Dilfer 4-16. Detroit, Sanders 27-131, Batch 8-39, Rivers 4-(minus 11), Reich 2-(minus 3).

PASSING—Tampa Bay, Dilfer 12-30-1-120, Walsh 0-2-1-0. Detroit, Batch 14-23-0-115, Reich 1-1-0-16, Jett 0-1-0-0.

RECEIVING—Tampa Bay, Anthony 4-38, Dunn 3-35, Williams 2-18, Thomas 1-13, Hunter 1-9, Moore 1-7. Detroit, Moore 7-64, Sanders 4-23, Morton 3-36, Crowell 1-8.

MISSED FIELD GOAL ATTEMPTS—None.

INTERCEPTIONS—Detroit, Westbrook 1-34, Rice 1-25.

KICKOFF RETURNS—Tampa Bay, Anthony 5-150. Detroit, Fair 2-136.

PUNT RETURNS—Tampa Bay, Williams 2-9. Detroit, Fair 4-10.

SACKS—Tampa Bay, Culpepper 1. Detroit, Porcher 1.5, Scroggins 1, Waldroup 1, S. Boyd 0.5.

WEEK 5

RESULTS

ATLANTA 51, Carolina 23
BUFFALO 26, San Francisco 21
CHICAGO 31, Detroit 27
Dallas 31, WASHINGTON 10
DENVER 41, Philadelphia 16
INDIANAPOLIS 17, San Diego 12
KANSAS CITY 17, Seattle 6
New England 30, NEW ORLEANS 27
N.Y. JETS 20, Miami 9
Oakland 23, ARIZONA 20
TAMPA BAY 20, N.Y. Giants 3
Minnesota 37, GREEN BAY 24
    Open date: Baltimore, Cincinnati, Jacksonville,
Pittsburgh, St. Louis, Tennessee

STANDINGS

AFC EAST

	W	L	T	Pct.
Miami	3	1	0	.750
New England	3	1	0	.750
N.Y. Jets	2	2	0	.500
Buffalo	1	3	0	.250
Indianapolis	1	4	0	.200

AFC CENTRAL

	W	L	T	Pct.
Jacksonville	4	0	0	1.000
Pittsburgh	3	1	0	.750
Baltimore	2	2	0	.500
Cincinnati	1	3	0	.250
Tennessee	1	3	0	.250

AFC WEST

	W	L	T	Pct.
Denver	5	0	0	1.000
Kansas City	4	1	0	.800
Oakland	3	2	0	.600
Seattle	3	2	0	.600
San Diego	2	3	0	.400

NFC EAST

	W	L	T	Pct.
Dallas	3	2	0	.600
Arizona	2	3	0	.400
N.Y. Giants	2	3	0	.400
Philadelphia	0	5	0	.000
Washington	0	5	0	.000

NFC CENTRAL

	W	L	T	Pct.
Minnesota	5	0	0	1.000
Green Bay	4	1	0	.800
Tampa Bay	2	3	0	.400
Chicago	1	4	0	.200
Detroit	1	4	0	.200

NFC WEST

	W	L	T	Pct.
Atlanta	3	1	0	.750
New Orleans	3	1	0	.750
San Francisco	3	1	0	.750
St. Louis	1	3	0	.250
Carolina	0	4	0	.000

HIGHLIGHTS

Hero of the week: New England's Adam Vinatieri hit a 27-yard field goal in the Superdome with three seconds left to give the Patriots a 30-27 victory over the Saints, who suffered their first loss of the season. The winning kick came after New Orleans' Andre Hastings returned a punt 76 yards to set up a Doug Brien field goal with 1:29 left, tying the score.

Goat of the week: Giants quarterback Danny Kanell had a rough day, completing just 10 of 27 passes for 83 yards and three interceptions as New York lost, 20-3, to the Buccaneers in Tampa Bay. Charles Mincy returned the first interception 22 yards for a touchdown on the third play of the game to give the Bucs all the points they would need.

Sub of the week: Bubby Brister stepped in for ailing John Elway and threw four touchdown passes as the Broncos demolished the hapless Eagles, 41-16, at Mile High Stadium. The Broncos improved to 5-0 while the Eagles dropped to 0-5.

Comeback of the week: Erik Kramer passed for two touchdowns and ran for another while Edgar Bennett passed for one as the Bears scored 21 consecutive points in the fourth quarter to rally for a 31-27 victory over the Lions at Soldier Field. The Bears committed five fumbles, leading to 13 Detroit points.

Blowout of the week: The winless Panthers continued on their trail of ineptitude, allowing the Falcons to score in bunches in a 51-23 loss at the Georgia Dome. Carolina gave up a touchdown on the opening kickoff and things got worse from there. Atlanta set an NFL record by scoring three touchdowns in a span of 48 seconds in the third quarter. Bob Christian scored from the 1-yard line for the first touchdown with 6:27 remaining. After Fred Lane fumbled on the first play after the ensuing kickoff, Travis Hall recovered at the Carolina 26 and Chris Chandler connected with tight end O.J. Santiago for a touchdown with 6:01 left. Carolina fumbled on its next play from scrimmage when Muhsin Muhammad stumbled over his feet. William White picked up the ball and ran 18 yards for an Atlanta score with 5:39 to go.

Nail-biter of the week: The Arizona Cardinals, hoping for their first 3-2 start since 1991, had to set-tle for 2-3 instead as the Raiders won, 23-20, in Tempe, Ariz. Joe Nedney hit field goals of 41 and 29 yards for the Cardinals, cutting the deficit to 23-20 with 8:16 to play. But with five seconds to go, the Cardinals' attempt to pass the ball for better field goal placement failed, as the Raiders' defense pushed Eric Metcalf out of bounds as time expired.

Hit of the week: After Carolina quarterback Kerry Collins completed a quick pass over the middle to tight end Luther Broughton early in the second half, Atlanta safety William White hit Broughton and jarred the ball loose. Ronnie Bradford recovered for the Falcons at his 22, and Atlanta mounted an 78-yard touchdown drive that made the score 24-3, putting the game out of reach.

Oddity of the week: The San Francisco 49ers tied a 54-year-old NFL record and set a team mark with 22 penalties in a 26-21 loss to the previously winless Buffalo Bills. The 49ers' 178 yards in penalties also set a team mark. In all, 14 49ers were penalized. Four other San Franciso penalties were either declined or offset by the Bills, who had 12 penalties.

Top rusher: Terrell Davis ran for 168 yards and two touchdowns on 20 carries in Denver's victory over Philadelphia.

Top passer: San Francisco's Steve Young completed 23-of-38 passes for 329 yards, three touchdowns and an interception against Buffalo.

Top receiver: Johnnie Morton of Detroit gained 138 yards and scored a touchdown on just two receptions against Chicago.

Notes: The 49ers' 22 penalties tied a record set by the Brooklyn Dodgers in 1944 and tied later that season by the Chicago Bears. . . . Buffalo's Thurman Thomas moved into seventh place on the all-time NFL list with 15,656 combined yards, passing Henry Ellard. . . . Jerry Rice extended his streak of consecutive games with at least one catch to 181. . . . Tampa Bay had the third-best defensive effort in franchise history, surrendering 135 yards to the Giants. . . . Dan Marino threw his 68th touchdown pass against the Jets, his highest total against any team. . . . The Bears held Barry Sanders to 28 yards on 14 carries, his lowest output ever against Chicago. . . . Denver's Terrell

Davis gained more yards (168) on 20 carries than the entire Philadelphia team gained (157) on 58 plays. . . . Washington dropped to 0-5, tying the team's 1981 mark for worst start ever. . . . Frank Sanders of the Cardinals tied his career high with 10 catches.

Quote of the week: Chiefs coach Mary Schottenheimer, after a freak rain and lightning storm in Kansas City delayed the game against the Seahawks for 54 minutes midway through the second quarter: "My sense was that the game was going to be played if we had to stay till 2 o'clock. The officials handled it well."

GAME SUMMARIES

FALCONS 51, PANTHERS 23

Sunday, October 4

Carolina	3	0	6	14—23
Atlanta	14	3	21	13—51

First Quarter
Atl.—Dwight 93 kickoff return (Andersen kick), 0:15.
Atl.—Martin 30 pass from Chandler (Andersen kick), 6:23.
Car.—FG, Kasay 28, 13:49.

Second Quarter
Atl.—FG, Andersen 23, 13:52.

Third Quarter
Atl.—Christian 1 run (Andersen kick), 8:33.
Atl.—Santiago 26 pass from Chandler (Andersen kick), 8:59.
Atl.—White 18 fumble return (Andersen kick), 9:21.
Car.—Walls 24 pass from Collins (kick blocked), 12:20.

Fourth Quarter
Car.—Carrier 5 pass from Collins (pass failed), 1:41.
Atl.—J. Anderson 20 run (Andersen kick), 8:57.
Car.—Muhammad 72 pass from Collins (Collins run), 9:38.
Atl.—FG, Andersen 25, 11:55.
Atl.—FG, Andersen 28, 14:17.
Attendance—50,724.

	Carolina	Atlanta
First downs	16	18
Rushes-yards	17-57	42-130
Passing	289	193
Punt returns	0-0	0-0
Kickoff returns	9-200	4-169
Interception returns	2-46	2-54
Comp.-att.-int.	20-38-2	14-23-2
Sacked-yards lost	2-13	2-28
Punts	4-34	4-39
Fumbles-lost	5-4	1-0
Penalties-yards	8-47	6-53
Time of possession	22:50	37:10

INDIVIDUAL STATISTICS
RUSHING—Carolina, Lane 15-48, Collins 2-9. Atlanta, J. Anderson 31-117, Oxendine 6-12, Dwight 2-7, Christian 1-1, Chandler 1-(minus 1), Mathis 1-(minus 6).
PASSING—Carolina, Collins 20-38-2-302. Atlanta, Chandler 12-20-2-189, DeBerg 1-2-0-10, Dwight 1-1-0-22.
RECEIVING—Carolina, Muhammad 4-104, Ismail 4-82, Floyd 4-19, Carrier 3-37, Walls 2-35, Broughton 1-13, Johnson 1-8, Lane 1-4. Atlanta, Martin 4-65, Mathis 3-51, Santiago 2-38, J. Anderson 2-34, Downs 2-11, Chandler 1-22.
MISSED FIELD GOAL ATTEMPTS—Carolina, Kasay 54.
INTERCEPTIONS—Carolina, Smith 1-43, Lloyd 1-3. Atlanta, White 1-36, Buchanan 1-18.
KICKOFF RETURNS—Carolina, Bates 9-200. Atlanta, Dwight 4-169.
PUNT RETURNS—None.
SACKS—Carolina, Greene 2. Atlanta, Dronett 2.

COWBOYS 31, REDSKINS 10

Sunday, October 4

Dallas	3	14	7	7—31
Washington	7	3	0	0—10

First Quarter
Was.—Shepherd 40 pass from T. Green (Blanchard kick), 8:19.
Dal.—FG, Cunningham 42, 13:03.

Second Quarter
Dal.—E. Smith 3 run (Cunningham kick), 0:39.
Dal.—E. Mills 43 pass from Garrett (Cunningham kick), 3:26.
Was.—FG, Blanchard 31, 9:31.

Third Quarter
Dal.—Warren 6 run (Cunningham kick), 4:10.

Fourth Quarter
Dal.—Warren 6 run (Cunningham kick), 13:58.
Attendance—72,284.

	Dallas	Washington
First downs	21	14
Rushes-yards	43-224	22-92
Passing	163	164
Punt returns	2-(-4)	3-34
Kickoff returns	3-56	5-85
Interception returns	1-21	0-0
Comp.-att.-int.	14-17-0	13-29-1
Sacked-yards lost	2-6	4-29
Punts	4-48	7-44
Fumbles-lost	2-1	1-0
Penalties-yards	9-60	6-52
Time of possession	35:36	24:24

INDIVIDUAL STATISTICS
RUSHING—Dallas, E. Smith 28-120, Warren 14-104, Garrett 1-0. Washington, Allen 19-82, T. Green 3-10.
PASSING—Dallas, Garrett 14-17-0-169. Washington, T. Green 13-29-1-193.
RECEIVING—Dallas, LaFleur 4-29, E. Mills 2-72, B. Davis 2-41, Sanders 2-14, Irvin 1-14, Bjornson 1-4, Johnston 1-1, Warren 1-(minus 6). Washington, Westbrook 4-42, Asher 3-42, Shepherd 2-82, Allen 2-23, Alexander 1-3, Mitchell 1-1.
MISSED FIELD GOAL ATTEMPTS—None.
INTERCEPTIONS—Dallas, Sanders 1-21.
KICKOFF RETURNS—Dallas, Mathis 3-56. Washington, Mitchell 4-71, Sellers 1-14.
PUNT RETURNS—Dallas, Sanders 2-(minus 4). Washington, Mitchell 3-34.
SACKS—Dallas, McCormack 2, Godfrey 1, Pittman 1. Washington, M. Patton 1, Wilkinson 1.

PATRIOTS 30, SAINTS 27

Sunday, October 4

New England	3	14	10	3—30
New Orleans	0	14	3	10—27

First Quarter
N.E.—FG, Vinatieri 34, 13:39.

Second Quarter
N.O.—Kei. Mitchell 63 fumble return (Brien kick), 1:31.
N.E.—Brisby 6 pass from Bledsoe (Vinatieri kick), 9:35.
N.E.—Edwards 8 run (Vinatieri kick), 12:19.
N.O.—Cleeland 1 pass from Wuerffel (Brien kick), 15:00.

Third Quarter
N.E.—Thomas 24 interception return (Vinatieri kick), 1:41.
N.O.—FG, Brien 21, 6:34.
N.E.—FG, Vinatieri 49, 10:16.

Fourth Quarter
N.O.—L. Smith 7 pass from Wuerffel (Brien kick), 7:30.
N.O.—FG, Brien 37, 13:31.
N.E.—FG, Vinatieri 27, 14:57.
Attendance—56,172.

	New England	New Orleans
First downs	20	19
Rushes-yards	25-97	18-39
Passing	291	237
Punt returns	5-104	2-86
Kickoff returns	4-63	6-107
Interception returns	2-24	3-31
Comp.-att.-int.	21-35-3	25-47-2
Sacked-yards lost	3-26	7-41
Punts	3-52	6-39
Fumbles-lost	1-1	0-0
Penalties-yards	3-20	6-41
Time of possession	29:15	30:45

INDIVIDUAL STATISTICS

RUSHING—New England, Edwards 22-97, Ton. Carter 1-3, Bledsoe 1-(minus 1), Cullors 1-(minus 2). New Orleans, L. Smith 13-22, Wuerffel 3-13, Zellars 2-4.

PASSING—New England, Bledsoe 21-35-3-317. New Orleans, Wuerffel 25-47-2-278.

RECEIVING—New England, Coates 7-78, Glenn 4-105, Brown 3-32, Cullors 2-56, Brisby 2-33, Ton. Carter 2-9, Edwards 1-4. New Orleans, Cleeland 8-64, Hastings 6-73, L. Smith 4-44, Bech 2-52, Craver 2-6, T. Davis 1-19, Dawkins 1-11, Poole 1-9.

MISSED FIELD GOAL ATTEMPTS—None.

INTERCEPTIONS—New England, Thomas 1-24, Law 1-0. New Orleans, Drakeford 1-20, Molden 1-11, Glover 1-0.

KICKOFF RETURNS—New England, Canty 3-48, Cullors 1-15. New Orleans, Ismail 5-105, T. Davis 1-2.

PUNT RETURNS—New England, Brown 5-104. New Orleans, Hastings 2-86.

SACKS—New England, Johnson 1.5, Slade 1, Canty 1, Bruschi 1, Sullivan 1, McGinest 1, Thomas 0.5. New Orleans, Aleaga 1, J. Johnson 1, Hewitt 1.

BUCCANEERS 20, GIANTS 3

Sunday, October 4

N.Y. Giants	0	0	0	3— 3
Tampa Bay	10	0	0	10—20

First Quarter

T.B.—Mincy 22 interception return (Husted kick), 1:34.

T.B.—FG, Husted 35, 14:08.

Fourth Quarter

NYG—FG, Daluiso 22, 1:40.

T.B.—FG, Husted 26, 9:58.

T.B.—Alstott 1 run (Husted kick), 13:06.

Attendance—64,989.

	N.Y. Giants	Tampa Bay
First downs	8	16
Rushes-yards	21-64	44-171
Passing	71	59
Punt returns	2-(-1)	5-53
Kickoff returns	4-79	2-50
Interception returns	1-0	3-59
Comp.-att.-int.	10-28-3	12-20-1
Sacked-yards lost	1-12	4-26
Punts	7-46	5-45
Fumbles-lost	0-0	3-1
Penalties-yards	3-15	9-69
Time of possession	21:05	38:55

INDIVIDUAL STATISTICS

RUSHING—New York, Brown 17-67, Barber 2-(minus 2), Way 1-0, Kanell 1-(minus 1). Tampa Bay, Dunn 21-63, Alstott 17-86, Dilfer 4-0, Green 1-18, Anthony 1-4.

PASSING—New York, Kanell 10-27-3-83, Maynard 0-1-0-0. Tampa Bay, Dilfer 12-20-1-85.

RECEIVING—New York, Barber 3-10, Way 2-25, Calloway 2-23, Hilliard 1-12, Toomer 1-10, Brown 1-3. Tampa Bay, Neal 3-8, Dunn 3-4, Alstott 2-29, Williams 2-16, Moore 1-17, Davis 1-11.

MISSED FIELD GOAL ATTEMPTS—None.

INTERCEPTIONS—New York, Buckley 1-0. Tampa Bay, Upshaw 1-26, Mincy 1-22, Barber 1-11.

KICKOFF RETURNS—New York, Patten 4-79. Tampa Bay, Anthony 2-50.

PUNT RETURNS—New York, Toomer 2-(minus 1). Tampa Bay, Green 4-46, Williams 1-7.

SACKS—New York, Strahan 1, C. Gray 1, K. Hamilton 1, Wooten 1. Tampa Bay, Jackson 1.

JETS 20, DOLPHINS 9

Sunday, October 4

Miami	3	0	0	6— 9
N.Y. Jets	0	10	7	3—20

First Quarter

Mia.—FG, Mare 46, 14:21.

Second Quarter

NYJ—K. Johnson 10 pass from Testaverde (Hall kick), 5:29.

NYJ—FG, Hall 47, 14:38.

Third Quarter

NYJ—Martin 6 run (Hall kick), 11:27.

Fourth Quarter

Mia.—Drayton 2 pass from Marino (run failed), 9:18.

NYJ—FG, Hall 25, 14:12.

Attendance—75,257.

	Miami	N.Y. Jets
First downs	11	22
Rushes-yards	15-34	38-117
Passing	119	172
Punt returns	2-13	4-22
Kickoff returns	5-101	3-85
Interception returns	0-0	3-39
Comp.-att.-int.	15-34-3	19-32-0
Sacked-yards lost	3-23	2-13
Punts	7-41	5-39
Fumbles-lost	2-0	2-1
Penalties-yards	6-81	5-47
Time of possession	22:56	37:04

INDIVIDUAL STATISTICS

RUSHING—Miami, Abdul-Jabbar 9-16, Avery 4-20, Marino 1-0, Parmalee 1-(minus 2). New York, Martin 36-108, Testaverde 1-5, Ward 1-4.

PASSING—Miami, Marino 13-31-2-121, Huard 2-3-1-21. New York, Testaverde 19-32-0-185.

RECEIVING—Miami, Parmalee 3-37, Gadsden 2-30, Perry 2-18, Abdul-Jabbar 2-8, McDuffie 1-19, L. Thomas 1-11, Jordan 1-9, Pritchett 1-5, Avery 1-3, Drayton 1-2. New York, Byars 6-71, Martin 4-17, K. Johnson 3-28, Brady 2-20, Chrebet 2-18, Ward 1-16, L. Johnson 1-15.

MISSED FIELD GOAL ATTEMPTS—New York, Hall 44.

INTERCEPTIONS—New York, Green 2-7, Mickens 1-0.

KICKOFF RETURNS—Miami, Avery 3-47, Marion 2-54. New York, L. Johnson 3-85.

PUNT RETURNS—Miami, Jordan 2-13. New York, L. Johnson 3-22, Frost 1-0.

SACKS—Miami, Taylor 2. New York, Logan 1, Cascadden 1, Pleasant 1.

RAIDERS 23, CARDINALS 20

Sunday, October 4

Oakland	6	17	0	0—23
Arizona	7	7	0	6—20

First Quarter

Ariz.—McWilliams 2 pass from Plummer (Nedney kick), 6:03.

Oak.—FG, G. Davis 51, 11:53.

Oak.—FG, G. Davis 40, 14:52.

Second Quarter

Ariz.—R. Moore 13 pass from Plummer (Nedney kick), 1:20.

Oak.—FG, G. Davis 34, 4:53.

Oak.—Woodson 46 interception return (G. Davis kick), 9:46.

Oak.—Hollas 1 run (G. Davis kick), 12:42.

Fourth Quarter

Ariz.—FG, Nedney 41, 0:16.

Ariz.—FG, Nedney 29, 6:44.

Attendance—53,240.

	Oakland	Arizona
First downs	14	16
Rushes-yards	34-112	21-49
Passing	110	187
Punt returns	3-65	4-57
Kickoff returns	3-66	6-194
Interception returns	3-58	1-26
Comp.-att.-int.	16-32-1	23-39-3
Sacked-yards lost	3-10	3-21
Punts	6-46	6-44
Fumbles-lost	2-2	3-1
Penalties-yards	6-45	7-45
Time of possession	32:16	27:44

INDIVIDUAL STATISTICS

RUSHING—Oakland, Kaufman 16-58, H. Williams 13-46, Hollas 3-8, Ritchie 1-2, Dudley 1-(minus 2). Arizona, Murrell 13-28, Centers 5-7, Plummer 2-11, Pittman 1-3.

PASSING—Oakland, Hollas 12-22-0-104, George 4-10-1-16. Arizona, Plummer 23-39-3-208.

RECEIVING—Oakland, H. Williams 3-25, Jett 3-12, Dudley 2-26, Ritchie 2-15, T. Brown 2-13, Mickens 2-10, Kaufman 1-10, Shedd 1-9. Arizona, Sanders 10-118, R. Moore 4-37, Centers 4-23, McWilliams 2-12, Gedney 1-15, Metcalf 1-2, Murrell 1-1.

MISSED FIELD GOAL ATTEMPTS—None.

INTERCEPTIONS—Oakland, Woodson 1-46, Walker 1-28, Allen 1-(minus 16). Arizona, Lassiter 1-26.

KICKOFF RETURNS—Oakland, Howard 3-66. Arizona, Metcalf 6-194.

PUNT RETURNS—Oakland, Howard 3-65. Arizona, Metcalf 4-57.

SACKS—Oakland, Harvey 1, Johnstone 1, Folston 1. Arizona, Wadsworth 2, Miller 1.

BEARS 31, LIONS 27

Sunday, October 4

Detroit	10	0	17	0—27
Chicago	0	10	0	21—31

First Quarter
Det.—FG, Hanson 28, 3:34.
Det.—Morton 98 pass from Batch (Hanson kick), 13:48.

Second Quarter
Chi.—M. Robinson 20 pass from Kramer (Jaeger kick), 3:20.
Chi.—FG, Jaeger 23, 11:47.

Third Quarter
Det.—Chryplewicz 3 pass from Batch (Hanson kick), 8:04.
Det.—Vardell 1 run (Hanson kick), 10:01.
Det.—FG, Hanson 43, 12:26.

Fourth Quarter
Chi.—Penn 18 pass from Bennett (Jaeger kick), 2:08.
Chi.—Bownes 6 pass from Kramer (Jaeger kick), 10:26.
Chi.—Kramer 1 run (Jaeger kick), 13:10.
  Attendance—55,562.

	Detroit	Chicago
First downs	15	23
Rushes-yards	26-94	37-125
Passing	246	280
Punt returns	1-16	4-40
Kickoff returns	6-71	5-118
Interception returns	0-0	0-0
Comp.-att.-int.	16-31-0	27-38-0
Sacked-yards lost	4-22	2-13
Punts	8-41	4-44
Fumbles-lost	0-0	5-5
Penalties-yards	7-44	2-15
Time of possession	24:11	35:49

INDIVIDUAL STATISTICS
RUSHING—Detroit, Sanders 14-28, Batch 8-58, Vardell 2-1, Schlesinger 1-5, Rivers 1-2. Chicago, Bennett 21-88, Enis 8-18, Kramer 5-3, Chancey 2-13, Milburn 1-3.

PASSING—Detroit, Batch 16-31-0-268. Chicago, Kramer 26-37-0-275, Bennett 1-1-0-18.

RECEIVING—Detroit, Rasby 5-39, Moore 4-49, Morton 2-138, Crowell 2-22, Sanders 2-17, Chryplewicz 1-3. Chicago, Penn 6-106, Engram 4-44, Wetnight 4-5, Bennett 3-32, Chancey 3-32, M. Robinson 2-33, Mayes 2-27, Bownes 2-13, Hallock 1-1.

MISSED FIELD GOAL ATTEMPTS—Detroit, Hanson 53.

INTERCEPTIONS—None.

KICKOFF RETURNS—Detroit, McPhail 6-71. Chicago, Milburn 5-118.

PUNT RETURNS—Detroit, Abrams 1-16. Chicago, Milburn 4-40.

SACKS—Detroit, S. Boyd 1, Abrams 1. Chicago, Flanigan 3, Thomas 1.

BRONCOS 41, EAGLES 16

Sunday, October 4

Philadelphia	0	2	0	14—16
Denver	28	7	6	0—41

First Quarter
Den.—Davis 20 run (Elam kick), 2:48.
Den.—R. Smith 8 pass from Brister (Elam kick), 7:09.
Den.—Sharpe 9 pass from Brister (Elam kick), 10:47.
Den.—Davis 1 run (Elam kick), 13:49.

Second Quarter
Phi.—Safety, Rouen punt blocked out of end zone by W. Thomas, 13:26.
Den.—McCaffrey 12 pass from Brister (Elam kick), 13:44.

Third Quarter
Den.—R. Smith 31 pass from Brister (kick failed), 9:43.

Fourth Quarter
Phi.—Garner 3 run (Boniol kick), 0:05.
Phi.—Garner 3 run (Boniol kick), 5:57.
  Attendance—73,218.

	Philadelphia	Denver
First downs	12	22
Rushes-yards	19-57	39-231
Passing	100	192
Punt returns	4-21	5-54
Kickoff returns	5-79	3-48
Interception returns	2-54	1-45
Comp.-att.-int.	14-33-1	17-32-2
Sacked-yards lost	6-32	2-13
Punts	10-45	6-39
Fumbles-lost	2-1	1-0
Penalties-yards	4-28	6-50
Time of possession	24:16	35:44

INDIVIDUAL STATISTICS
RUSHING—Philadelphia, Garner 10-50, Staley 6-(minus 4), Hoying 1-6, Walker 1-3, Turner 1-2. Denver, Davis 20-168, Loville 8-25, Hebron 5-22, Griese 4-(minus 4), Brister 1-11, R. Smith 1-9.

PASSING—Philadelphia, Hoying 11-24-1-96, Detmer 3-9-0-36. Denver, Brister 16-29-1-203, Griese 1-3-1-2.

RECEIVING—Philadelphia, Dunn 3-14, Fryar 2-19, Graham 2-15, Staley 2-6, Turner 2-4, Walker 1-33, Garner 1-21, Solomon 1-20. Denver, R. Smith 7-95, Sharpe 6-46, McCaffrey 2-60, Hebron 1-2, Griffith 1-2.

MISSED FIELD GOAL ATTEMPTS—None.

INTERCEPTIONS—Philadelphia, Caldwell 1-33, W. Thomas 1-21. Denver, Johnson 1-45.

KICKOFF RETURNS—Philadelphia, Walker 3-50, Rossum 2-29. Denver, Hebron 3-48.

PUNT RETURNS—Philadelphia, Solomon 3-23, Turner 1-(minus 2). Denver, Gordon 5-54.

SACKS—Philadelphia, Douglas 1, Darling 1. Denver, Cadrez 1, N. Smith 1, Traylor 1, Hasselbach 1, Lodish 1, Pryce 1.

COLTS 17, CHARGERS 12

Sunday, October 4

San Diego	0	6	0	6—12
Indianapolis	11	0	0	6—17

First Quarter
Ind.—Faulk 19 pass from Manning (Dilger run), 6:23.
Ind.—FG, Vanderjagt 48, 10:49.

Second Quarter
S.D.—FG, Carney 50, 0:48.
S.D.—FG, Carney 25, 13:05.

Fourth Quarter
Ind.—FG, Vanderjagt 51, 8:46.
S.D.—Means 1 run (pass failed), 13:12.
Ind.—FG, Vanderjagt 40, 13:46.
  Attendance—51,988.

	San Diego	Indianapolis
First downs	18	11
Rushes-yards	34-152	29-55
Passing	143	137
Punt returns	3-86	1-6
Kickoff returns	4-85	3-85
Interception returns	1-21	1-12
Comp.-att.-int.	12-23-1	12-23-1
Sacked-yards lost	4-17	0-0
Punts	4-36	6-45
Fumbles-lost	2-2	0-0
Penalties-yards	12-95	7-62
Time of possession	32:47	27:13

INDIVIDUAL STATISTICS
RUSHING—San Diego, Means 31-130, C. Jones 1-14, Leaf 1-6, Fletcher 1-2. Indianapolis, Faulk 25-50, Heyward 2-5, Manning 2-0.

PASSING—San Diego, Leaf 12-23-1-160. Indianapolis, Manning 12-23-1-137.

RECEIVING—San Diego, Still 6-46, C. Jones 2-66, F. Jones 1-16, Means 1-13, Fletcher 1-13, Slaughter 1-6. Indianapolis, Faulk 4-44, Harrison 3-39, Small 2-33, Heyward 1-9, Dilger 1-7, Pathon 1-5.

MISSED FIELD GOAL ATTEMPTS—San Diego, Carney 47. Indianapolis, Vanderjagt 40.

INTERCEPTIONS—San Diego, Harrison 1-21. Indianapolis, Alexander 1-12.

KICKOFF RETURNS—San Diego, Stephens 2-52, Rachal 1-18, Fletcher 1-15. Indianapolis, Elias 3-71.

PUNT RETURNS—San Diego, Rachal 3-86. Indianapolis, Poole 1-6.

SACKS—Indianapolis, Blackmon 1, McCoy 1, E. Johnson 1, Berry 1.

BILLS 26, 49ERS 21

Sunday, October 4

San Francisco	0	0	0	21—21
Buffalo	10	10	3	3—26

First Quarter
Buf.—FG, Christie 24, 2:30.
Buf.—A. Smith 6 run (Christie kick), 13:33.

Second Quarter
Buf.—Early 5 pass from R. Johnson (Christie kick), 0:32.
Buf.—FG, Christie 19, 14:57.

Third Quarter
Buf.—FG, Christie 38, 12:09.

Fourth Quarter
S.F.—Edwards 47 pass from S. Young (Rice pass from S. Young), 1:44.
Buf.—FG, Christie 45, 5:56.
S.F.—I. Smith 9 pass from S. Young (pass failed), 9:27.
S.F.—Stokes 21 pass from S. Young (Richey kick), 14:03.
  Attendance—76,615.

	San Fran.	Buffalo
First downs	23	21
Rushes-yards	18-65	38-115
Passing	312	237
Punt returns	2-11	5-33
Kickoff returns	6-82	1-22
Interception returns	0-0	1-27
Comp.-att.-int.	23-38-1	19-27-0
Sacked-yards lost	5-17	3-17
Punts	5-45	5-39
Fumbles-lost	3-3	1-0
Penalties-yards	22-178	12-106
Time of possession	27:07	32:53

INDIVIDUAL STATISTICS

RUSHING—San Francisco, Hearst 12-28, S. Young 5-34, Levy 1-3. Buffalo, A. Smith 22-47, Thomas 8-42, R. Johnson 6-20, Gash 1-3, K. Williams 1-3.

PASSING—San Francisco, S. Young 23-38-1-329. Buffalo, R. Johnson 19-27-0-254.

RECEIVING—San Francisco, Hearst 5-38, Owens 4-69, Stokes 4-62, I. Smith 4-49, Rice 3-54, Edwards 2-50, Levy 1-7. Buffalo, Early 8-57, K. Williams 4-87, Moulds 3-86, Thomas 2-13, L. Johnson 1-8, Riemersma 1-3.

MISSED FIELD GOAL ATTEMPTS—San Francisco, Richey 48. Buffalo, Christie 51.

INTERCEPTIONS—Buffalo, Jackson 1-27.

KICKOFF RETURNS—San Francisco, Levy 4-47, McQuarters 1-24, Richie 1-11. Buffalo, K. Williams 1-22.

PUNT RETURNS—San Francisco, McQuarters 2-11. Buffalo, K. Williams 5-33.

SACKS—San Francisco, B. Young 1, Barkor 1, Hanks 0.5, Doleman 0.5. Buffalo, Hansen 2, B. Smith 1, Northern 1, Wiley 1.

CHIEFS 17, SEAHAWKS 6

Sunday, October 4

Seattle	3	0	3	0— 6
Kansas City	3	7	7	0—17

First Quarter
Sea.—FG, Peterson 22, 2:55.
K.C.—FG, Stoyanovich 22, 14:10.

Second Quarter
K.C.—Gannon 4 run (Stoyanovich kick), 14:47.

Third Quarter
Sea.—FG, Peterson 28, 4:59.
K.C.—Rison 80 pass from Gannon (Stoyanovich kick), 14:36.
  Attendance—66,418.

	Seattle	Kansas City
First downs	10	12
Rushes-yards	26-73	42-131
Passing	94	120
Punt returns	4-81	1-8
Kickoff returns	4-79	3-51
Interception returns	0-0	2-0
Comp.-att.-int.	11-33-2	12-19-0
Sacked-yards lost	0-0	4-22
Punts	7-44	7-41
Fumbles-lost	3-2	5-5
Penalties-yards	12-88	5-48
Time of possession	26:12	33:48

INDIVIDUAL STATISTICS

RUSHING—Seattle, Watters 22-59, Kitna 1-11, Galloway 1-2, Strong 1-2, Moon 1-(minus 1). Kansas City, Bennett 17-62, Shehee 11-28, Anders 5-17, Gannon 5-11, Richardson 4-13.

PASSING—Seattle, Friesz 8-19-1-52, Kitna 3-12-1-42, Moon 0-2-0-0. Kansas City, Gannon 12-19-0-142.

RECEIVING—Seattle, Galloway 5-50, Watters 2-(minus 6), Broussard 1-16, McKnight 1-16, Fauria 1-13, May 1-5. Kansas City, Rison 4-90, Gonzalez 3-18, Horn 1-13, Alexander 1-9, Anders 1-5, Shields 1-4, Bennett 1-3.

MISSED FIELD GOAL ATTEMPTS—Seattle, Peterson 38.

INTERCEPTIONS—Kansas City, Carter 1-0, Hasty 1-0.

KICKOFF RETURNS—Seattle, Broussard 2-40, Green 1-20, R. Brown 1-19. Kansas City, Vanover 3-51.

PUNT RETURNS—Seattle, Joseph 4-81. Kansas City, Vanover 1-8.

SACKS—Seattle, C. Brown 1, Smith 1, Team 2.

VIKINGS 37, PACKERS 24

Monday, October 5

Minnesota	3	21	3	10—37
Green Bay	0	10	0	14—24

First Quarter
Min.—FG, Anderson 33, 11:46.

Second Quarter
G.B.—FG, Longwell 40, 0:07.
Min.—Reed 56 pass from Cunningham (Anderson kick), 2:51.
G.B.—Preston 101 kickoff return (Longwell kick), 3:08.
Min.—R. Moss 52 pass from Cunningham (Anderson kick), 5:04.
Min.—R. Smith 24 pass from Cunningham (Anderson kick), 10:17.

Third Quarter
Min.—FG, Anderson 25, 3:43.

Fourth Quarter
Min.—FG, Anderson 19, 1:29.
Min.—R. Moss 44 pass from Cunningham (Anderson kick), 4:44.
G.B.—T. Davis 11 pass from Pederson (Longwell kick), 11:57.
G.B.—Schroeder 16 pass from Pederson (Longwell kick), 14:15.
  Attendance—59,849.

	Minnesota	Green Bay
First downs	22	21
Rushes-yards	34-103	20-102
Passing	442	204
Punt returns	0 0	1 0
Kickoff returns	2-55	8-256
Interception returns	3-27	0-0
Comp.-att.-int.	20-32-0	23-39-3
Sacked-yards lost	0-0	2-13
Punts	1-51	3-45
Fumbles-lost	1-1	1-0
Penalties-yards	8-76	3-20
Time of possession	34:23	25:37

INDIVIDUAL STATISTICS

RUSHING—Minnesota, R. Smith 25-78, Hoard 3-13, Palmer 2-12, Cunningham 2-(minus 1), Evans 1-2, Carter 1-(minus 1). Green Bay, Jervey 8-55, R. Harris 7-27, Henderson 4-10, Freeman 1-10.

PASSING—Minnesota, Cunningham 20-32-0-442. Green Bay, Favre 13-23-3-114, Pederson 10-16-0-103.

RECEIVING—Minnesota, Carter 8-119, R. Moss 5-190, Reed 4-89, R. Smith 2-38, Glover 1-6. Green Bay, Henderson 4-26, Freeman 3-53, Schroeder 3-32, T. Davis 3-23, Jervey 3-13, R. Brooks 2-29, Chmura 2-18, R. Harris 2-12, Mayes 1-11.

MISSED FIELD GOAL ATTEMPTS—None.

INTERCEPTIONS—Minnesota, Griffith 2-0, Thomas 1-27.

KICKOFF RETURNS—Minnesota, Palmer 2-55. Green Bay, Preston 8-256.

PUNT RETURNS—Green Bay, Mayes 1-9.

SACKS—Minnesota, Alexander 2.

WEEK 6

1998 REVIEW Week 6

RESULTS

ARIZONA 20, Chicago 7
Atlanta 34, N.Y. GIANTS 20
Buffalo 31, INDIANAPOLIS 24
CINCINNATI 25, Pittsburgh 20
DALLAS 27, Carolina 20
Denver 21, SEATTLE 16
NEW ENGLAND 40, Kansas City 10
OAKLAND 7, San Diego 6
PHILADELPHIA 17, Washington 12
ST. LOUIS 30, N.Y. Jets 10
San Francisco 31, NEW ORLEANS 0
Tennessee 12, BALTIMORE 8
JACKSONVILLE 28, Miami 21
  Open date: Detroit, Green Bay, Minnesota,
Tampa Bay

STANDINGS

AFC EAST	W	L	T	Pct.
New England	4	1	0	.800
Miami	3	2	0	.600
Buffalo	2	3	0	.400
N.Y. Jets	2	3	0	.400
Indianapolis	1	5	0	.167

NFC EAST	W	L	T	Pct.
Dallas	4	2	0	.667
Arizona	3	3	0	.500
N.Y. Giants	2	4	0	.333
Philadelphia	1	5	0	.167
Washington	0	6	0	.000

AFC CENTRAL	W	L	T	Pct.
Jacksonville	5	0	0	1.000
Pittsburgh	3	2	0	.600
Baltimore	2	3	0	.400
Cincinnati	2	3	0	.400
Tennessee	2	3	0	.400

NFC CENTRAL	W	L	T	Pct.
Minnesota	5	0	0	1.000
Green Bay	4	1	0	.800
Tampa Bay	2	3	0	.400
Detroit	1	4	0	.200
Chicago	1	5	0	.167

AFC WEST	W	L	T	Pct.
Denver	6	0	0	1.000
Kansas City	4	2	0	.667
Oakland	4	2	0	.667
Seattle	3	3	0	.500
San Diego	2	4	0	.333

NFC WEST	W	L	T	Pct.
Atlanta	4	1	0	.800
San Francisco	4	1	0	.800
New Orleans	3	2	0	.600
St. Louis	2	3	0	.400
Carolina	0	5	0	.000

HIGHLIGHTS

Hero of the week: Doug Flutie, who had spent the previous eight years in the CFL, replaced Rob Johnson after the Bills' starting quarterback was sacked and forced to leave the game against Indianapolis because of sore ribs. Flutie passed for two touchdowns in leading the Bills to a come-from-behind 31-24 win. Flutie finished 23-of-28 for 213 yards and no sacks or interceptions and also ran three times for 23 yards.

Goat of the week: Jets quarterbacks had a bad day. Facing a Rams team that had lost eight in a row at home, the Jets produced only 177 yards and committed five turnovers. Glenn Foley threw two interceptions and fumbled once. Vinny Testaverde took over with 3:13 left in the third quarter and didn't fare much better, going 9-of-18 for 96 yards with a fumble and three sacks.

Sub of the week: He only completed one pass in seven attempts, but Wade Wilson's 68-yard TD completion to James Jett was the decisive score in Oakland's 7-6 victory over the Chargers. Jeff George, who was injured, began the game on the sideline. Backup Donald Hollas was benched early in the fourth quarter, and Wilson, an 18-year veteran who hadn't played in a regular-season game since the previous October, took over. After six consecutive incompletions, Wilson lofted the ball to Jett, who ran untouched into the end zone.

Comeback of the week: After Norm Johnson's field goal put the Steelers ahead of the Bengals, 20-18, with 1:56 left to play, the Bengals had the ball at their 17. Three plays lost them 2 yards, but on fourth-and-12 Neil O'Donnell launched a 50-yard pass to Carl Pickens, who scrambled out of bounds. After two handoffs that got the Bengals to the 25-yard line, O'Donnell faked a spike of the ball and passed to Pickens, who again found himself open and ran into the end zone with the game-winning TD.

Blowout of the week: Handing the Chiefs their worst loss in five years, the Patriots took a 27-0 halftime lead en route to a 41-10 victory. While the Pats had 246 yards in the first half, the Chiefs crossed midfield only once.

Nail-biter of the week: Despite playing with a beat-up offensive line and secondary, a backup quarterback and a backup running back, the winless Panthers took the Cowboys to the limit in Texas Stadium. With 5:45 left in the game, the Panthers closed to within seven points after a fumble recovery led to a 43-yard drive down the field and a touchdown. Deion Sanders had an interception in the final two minutes, but Carolina still managed to put together a frantic final drive that ended when Steve Beuerlein's desperation pass fell outside the end zone. Dallas won, 27-20.

Hit of the week: After the Raiders went ahead by one with 1:28 left in the game, the Chargers got the ball back and began a drive at their 47. Facing fourth-and-six with 42 seconds left, San Diego opted against a 55-yard field-goal attempt and instead tried a screen pass to pick up the first down. Natrone Means, a 245-pound running back, caught the ball and headed for the first-down marker, but 190-pound cornerback Eric Allen threw his body at Means, throwing him off balance. Means came up about six inches short of the first down, preserving the Raiders' victory.

Oddity of the week: For only the sixth time in NFL history and the first time in the NFC East, two 0-5 teams faced each other when the Redskins played the Eagles in Philadelphia.

Top rusher: Terrell Davis rushed for 208 yards on 30 carries to help Denver beat the Seahawks, 21-16, and remain undefeated.

Top passer: Steve Young's fifth consecutive 300-yard game tied Joe Montana's NFL record as San Francisco cruised to a 31-0 win over the Saints. Young completed 21-of-40 passes for 309 yards and three TDs.

Top receiver: Carl Pickens caught a Bengals-record 13 passes for 204 yards in Cincinnati's last-minute, 25-20 victory over the Steelers.

Notes: In a mistake-filled game, Tennessee was penalized 13 times for 141 yards and scored only one touchdown. Baltimore was even worse, going 1-for-15 on third-down conversions and gaining only 36 yards on the ground. . . . The Broncos set a club record with their 11th consecutive victory.

Quote of the week: Oakland defensive coordinator Willie Shaw, on the end of the game: "I told the guys, 'Don't look at the scoreboard or the clock. Whoever flinches first loses.' It turns out, they flinched first."

GAME SUMMARIES

COWBOYS 27, PANTHERS 20

Sunday, October 11

Carolina	7	7	0	6—20
Dallas	3	7	14	3—27

First Quarter
Dal.—FG, Cunningham 27, 9:15.
Car.—Ismail 35 pass from Beuerlein (Kasay kick), 13:20.
Second Quarter
Car.—Ismail 16 pass from Beuerlein (Kasay kick), 6:06.
Dal.—E. Mills 18 pass from Garrett (Cunningham kick), 10:08.
Third Quarter
Dal.—Warren 6 pass from Garrett (Cunningham kick), 2:37.
Dal.—E. Smith 2 run (Cunningham kick), 7:46.
Fourth Quarter
Dal.—FG, Cunningham 38, 2:01.
Car.—Floyd 3 pass from Beuerlein (kick blocked), 9:15.
Attendance—64,181.

	Carolina	Dallas
First downs	16	22
Rushes-yards	22-29	36-151
Passing	273	277
Punt returns	3-30	0-0
Kickoff returns	6-128	4-78
Interception returns	0-0	1-18
Comp.-att.-int.	22-32-1	14-22-0
Sacked-yards lost	3-13	2-10
Punts	4-42	3-42
Fumbles-lost	4-2	2-2
Penalties-yards	12-83	6-77
Time of possession	28:17	31:43

INDIVIDUAL STATISTICS
RUSHING—Carolina, Johnson 16-28, Floyd 3-5, Beuerlein 3-(minus 4). Dallas, E. Smith 21-112, Warren 11-27, Garrett 2-5, B. Davis 1-4, Johnston 1-3.
PASSING—Carolina, Beuerlein 22-32-1-286. Dallas, Garrett 14-22-0-287.
RECEIVING—Carolina, Ismail 6-117, Muhammad 5-63, Walls 4-43, Johnson 3-33, Floyd 3-14, Carrier 1-16. Dallas, Irvin 6-146, E. Mills 5-110, B. Davis 1-23, Warren 1-6, Sanders 1-2.
MISSED FIELD GOAL ATTEMPTS—Dallas, Cunningham 55.
INTERCEPTIONS—Dallas, Sanders 1-18.
KICKOFF RETURNS—Carolina, Bates 6-128. Dallas, Mathis 4-78.
PUNT RETURNS—Carolina, Oliver 3-30.
SACKS—Carolina, Greene 1, Peter 1. Dallas, Lett 1, Ellis 1, Pittman 1.

BILLS 31, COLTS 24

Sunday, October 4

Buffalo	0	7	7	17—31
Indianapolis	6	6	0	12—24

First Quarter
Ind.—FG, Vanderjagt 22, 4:20.
Ind.—FG, Vanderjagt 33, 13:04.
Second Quarter
Ind.—FG, Vanderjagt 43, 6:43.
Buf.—Riemersma 7 pass from Flutie (Christie kick), 12:02.
Ind.—FG, Vanderjagt 41, 14:05.
Third Quarter
Buf.—K. Williams 6 pass from Flutie (Christie kick), 10:54.
Fourth Quarter
Buf.—A. Smith 4 run (Christie kick), 0:47.
Buf.—A. Smith 1 run (Christie kick), 3:56.
Buf.—FG, Christie 39, 9:40.
Ind.—Small 3 pass from Manning (pass failed), 12:41.
Ind.—Harrison 25 pass from Manning (pass failed), 14:54.
Attendance—52,938.

	Buffalo	Indianapolis
First downs	24	21
Rushes-yards	40-176	22-106
Passing	205	235
Punt returns	2-2	1-7
Kickoff returns	5-96	5-104
Interception returns	2-0	0-0
Comp.-att.-int.	23-28-0	20-41-2
Sacked-yards lost	1-8	0-0
Punts	4-33	3-38
Fumbles-lost	0-0	0-0
Penalties-yards	9-77	4-18
Time of possession	36:41	23:19

INDIVIDUAL STATISTICS
RUSHING—Buffalo, A. Smith 31-130, Thomas 6-23, Flutie 3-23. Indianapolis, Faulk 18-93, Heyward 3-11, Warren 1-2.
PASSING—Buffalo, Flutie 23-28-0-213. Indianapolis, Manning 20-41-2-235.
RECEIVING—Buffalo, Reed 5-76, Gash 5-45, Thomas 5-32, K. Williams 3-21, L. Johnson 2-6, Moulds 1-16, Early 1-10, Riemersma 1-7. Indianapolis, Faulk 6-80, Harrison 4-61, Small 4-48, Dilger 2-23, Pathon 2-19, Warren 2-4.
MISSED FIELD GOAL ATTEMPTS—Buffalo, Christie 53.
INTERCEPTIONS—Buffalo, Schulz 1-0, Washington 1-0.
KICKOFF RETURNS—Buffalo, K. Williams 4-87, Riemersma 1-9. Indianapolis, Warren 5-104.
PUNT RETURNS—Buffalo, K. Williams 2-2. Indianapolis, Poole 1-7.
SACKS—Indianapolis, Chester 1.

OILERS 12, RAVENS 8

Sunday, October 11

Tennessee	6	3	3	0—12
Baltimore	2	0	3	3— 8

First Quarter
Bal.—Safety, S. McNair sacked in end zone, 1:28.
Ten.—McNair 40 run (run failed), 13:45.
Second Quarter
Ten.—FG, Del Greco 26, 2:15.
Third Quarter
Ten.—FG, Del Greco 29, 8:50.
Bal.—FG, Stover 21, 12:36.
Fourth Quarter
Bal.—FG, Stover 45, 1:01.
Attendance—68,561.

	Tennessee	Baltimore
First downs	16	13
Rushes-yards	35-166	18-36
Passing	178	227
Punt returns	4-26	4-58
Kickoff returns	3-51	5-90
Interception returns	1-13	1-2
Comp.-att.-int	17-29-1	25-44-1
Sacked-yards lost	4-29	3-22
Punts	6-49	9-38
Fumbles-lost	1-0	0-0
Penalties-yards	13-141	6-50
Time of possession	34:04	25:56

INDIVIDUAL STATISTICS
RUSHING—Tennessee, E. George 30-121, McNair 3-47, Thomas 2-(minus 2). Baltimore, Holmes 14-29, Potts 3-4, J. Lewis 1-3.
PASSING—Tennessee, McNair 17-29-1-207. Baltimore, Zeier 25-44-1-249.
RECEIVING—Tennessee, Harris 4-45, Davis 3-49, Wycheck 2-43, Kent 2-26, Mason 2-23, Thigpen 2-12, E. George 2-9. Baltimore, Holmes 13-98, Kinchen 4-55, Johnson 2-42, Green 2-26, Yarborough 2-15, J. Lewis 1-9, Potts 1-4.
MISSED FIELD GOAL ATTEMPTS—Tennessee, Del Greco 42.
INTERCEPTIONS—Tennessee, Bishop 1-13. Baltimore, Woodson 1-2.
KICKOFF RETURNS—Tennessee, Archie 2-40, Roan 1-11. Baltimore, Johnson 3-54, Kinchen 1-21, Graham 1-15.
PUNT RETURNS—Tennessee, Archie 3-26, Mason 1-0. Baltimore, J. Lewis 3-20, Thompson 1-38.
SACKS—Tennessee, Bishop 1, Evans 1, Cook 1. Baltimore, McCrary 2, Boulware 1, Burnett 1.

BENGALS 25, STEELERS 20

Sunday, October 11

Pittsburgh	0	10	7	3—20
Cincinnati	0	9	3	13—25

Second Quarter

Pit.—FG, N. Johnson 40, 0:05.
Pit.—Bettis 13 run (N. Johnson kick), 6:40.
Cin.—FG, Pelfrey 44, 10:18.
Cin.—Scott 44 pass from O'Donnell (pass failed), 14:08.

Third Quarter

Pit.—Huntley 9 run (N. Johnson kick), 5:19.
Cin.—FG, Pelfrey 48, 9:21.

Fourth Quarter

Cin.—Scott 30 pass from O'Donnell (pass failed), 1:22.
Pit.—FG, N. Johnson 40, 13:04.
Cin.—Pickens 25 pass from O'Donnell (Pelfrey kick), 14:40.
Attendance—59,979.

	Pittsburgh	Cincinnati
First downs	20	17
Rushes-yards	39-257	27-108
Passing	129	281
Punt returns	3-19	1-4
Kickoff returns	5-109	5-86
Interception returns	0-0	0-0
Comp.-att.-int.	13-22-0	20-26-0
Sacked-yards lost	3-22	3-17
Punts	2-49	4-41
Fumbles-lost	1-1	0-0
Penalties-yards	11-85	5-42
Time of possession	34:34	25:26

INDIVIDUAL STATISTICS

RUSHING—Pittsburgh, Huntley 20-85, Bettis 11-55, Stewart 7-103, Hawkins 1-14. Cincinnati, Dillon 23-99, Bieniemy 3-5, O'Donnell 1-4.

PASSING—Pittsburgh, Stewart 13-22-0-151. Cincinnati, O'Donnell 20-26-0-298.

RECEIVING—Pittsburgh, Hawkins 6-75, Blackwell 3-34, C. Johnson 2-19, Witman 1-15, McAfee 1-8. Cincinnati, Pickens 13-204, Scott 3-79, Bieniemy 3-9, Gibson 1-6.

MISSED FIELD GOAL ATTEMPTS—None.

INTERCEPTIONS—None.

KICKOFF RETURNS—Pittsburgh, Arnold 3-78, McAfee 1-25, Lyons 1-6. Cincinnati, Mack 5-86.

PUNT RETURNS—Pittsburgh, Arnold 3-19. Cincinnati, Gibson 1-4.

SACKS—Pittsburgh, Gildon 1, Roye 1, Vrabel 1. Cincinnati, Bankston 1, C. Simmons 1, Wilson 0.5, Langford 0.5.

RAIDERS 7, CHARGERS 6

Sunday, October 11

San Diego	0	3	0	3—6
Oakland	0	0	0	7—7

Second Quarter

S.D.—FG, Carney 39, 4:52.

Fourth Quarter

S.D.—FG, Carney 48, 11:51.
Oak.—Jett 68 pass from Wilson (G. Davis kick), 13:32.
Attendance—42,467.

	San Diego	Oakland
First downs	9	6
Rushes-yards	43-117	18-18
Passing	78	141
Punt returns	8-105	8-76
Kickoff returns	2-41	3-60
Interception returns	1-11	4-44
Comp.-att.-int.	10-24-4	13-42-1
Sacked-yards lost	3-19	5-28
Punts	11-48	16-44
Fumbles-lost	1-0	1-0
Penalties-yards	4-25	3-25
Time of possession	36:30	23:30

INDIVIDUAL STATISTICS

RUSHING—San Diego, Means 37-101, Stephens 5-10, Leaf 1-6. Oakland, Kaufman 12-17, Hollas 2-8, Ritchie 2-(minus 1), Wilson 1-(minus 2), H. Williams 1-(minus 4).

PASSING—San Diego, Leaf 7-18-3-78, Whelihan 3-6-1-19. Oakland, Hollas 12-35-1-101, Wilson 1-7-0-68.

RECEIVING—San Diego, Means 6-66, Still 1-13, F. Jones 1-11, C. Jones 1-4, Slaughter 1-3. Oakland, T. Brown 5-51, Dudley 2-26, Ritchie 2-10, Kaufman 2-6, Jett 1-68, Mickens 1-8.

MISSED FIELD GOAL ATTEMPTS—None.

INTERCEPTIONS—San Diego, Harrison 1-11. Oakland, Allen 1-19, Wooden 1-14, Newman 1-11, Walker 1-0.

KICKOFF RETURNS—San Diego, Stephens 2-41. Oakland, Howard 3-60.

PUNT RETURNS—San Diego, Rachal 8-105. Oakland, Howard 8-76.

SACKS—San Diego, Hand 3, Dixon 1, Fuller 1. Oakland, Biekert 1, Johnstone 1, Swilling 1.

PATRIOTS 40, CHIEFS 10

Sunday, October 11

Kansas City	0	0	7	3—10
New England	7	20	10	3—40

First Quarter

N.E.—Edwards 1 run (Vinatieri kick), 10:07.

Second Quarter

N.E.—FG, Vinatieri 32, 1:25.
N.E.—Edwards 15 pass from Bledsoe (Vinatieri kick), 5:49.
N.E.—Coates 2 pass from Bledsoe (Vinatieri kick), 12:12.
N.E.—FG, Vinatieri 38, 15:00.

Third Quarter

N.E.—Coates 11 pass from Bledsoe (Vinatieri kick), 4:12.
N.E.—FG, Vinatieri 27, 11:36.
K.C.—Alexander 8 pass from Grbac (Stoyanovich kick), 14:08.

Fourth Quarter

K.C.—FG, Stoyanovich 33, 0:32.
N.E.—FG, Vinatieri 20, 8:22.
Attendance—59,749.

	Kansas City	New England
First downs	9	31
Rushes-yards	11-14	54-206
Passing	120	232
Punt returns	2-15	3-31
Kickoff returns	6-111	3-50
Interception returns	0-0	1-0
Comp.-att.-int.	14-29-1	18-28-0
Sacked-yards lost	4-24	0-0
Punts	6-46	2-43
Fumbles-lost	3-1	1-1
Penalties-yards	8-49	8-75
Time of possession	18:12	41:48

INDIVIDUAL STATISTICS

RUSHING—Kansas City, Bennett 6-6, Anders 4-8, Richardson 1-0. New England, Edwards 23-104, S. Shaw 19-68, Cullors 3-29, Bledsoe 3-8, Floyd 3-7, Tupa 2-(minus 2), Glenn 1-(minus 8).

PASSING—Kansas City, Grbac 14-29-1-144. New England, Bledsoe 17-26-0-226, Zolak 1-2-0-6.

RECEIVING—Kansas City, Shehee 4-34, Alexander 3-43, Anders 3-25, Gonzalez 2-25, Bennett 1-12, Rison 1-5. New England, Glenn 7-78, Brown 3-55, Edwards 3-32, Coates 2-13, Jefferson 1-31, Ton. Carter 1-14, Brisby 1-9.

MISSED FIELD GOAL ATTEMPTS—None.

INTERCEPTIONS—New England, Milloy 1-0.

KICKOFF RETURNS—Kansas City, Vanover 6-111. New England, Cullors 2-50, Whigham 1-0.

PUNT RETURNS—Kansas City, Vanover 2-15. New England, Brown 3-31.

SACKS—New England, Bruschi 1, Eaton 1, Slade 1, Spires 1.

49ERS 31, SAINTS 0

Sunday, October 11

San Francisco	7	14	10	0—31
New Orleans	0	0	0	0—0

First Quarter

S.F.—Clark 1 pass from S. Young (Richey kick), 4:14.

Second Quarter

S.F.—FG, Richey 42, 0:10.
S.F.—FG, Richey 37, 13:10.
S.F.—Owens 6 pass from S. Young (Hearst pass from S. Young), 14:50.

Third Quarter

S.F.—Hearst 33 pass from S. Young (Richey kick), 3:57.
S.F.—FG, Richey 43, 9:56.
Attendance—62,811.

	San Fran.	New Orleans
First downs	30	10
Rushes-yards	38-140	13-32
Passing	319	135
Punt returns	6-60	0-0
Kickoff returns	1-21	5-96
Interception returns	1-(-4)	0-0
Comp.-att.-int.	22-41-0	15-30-1
Sacked-yards lost	1-1	7-39

	San Fran.	New Orleans
Punts	3-32	8-49
Fumbles-lost	0-0	0-0
Penalties-yards	14-115	13-125
Time of possession	36:28	23:32

INDIVIDUAL STATISTICS

RUSHING—San Francisco, Hearst 22-71, Levy 8-46, Edwards 3-8, Druckenmiller 3-(minus 4), S. Young 2-19. New Orleans, L. Smith 7-18, T. Davis 3-9, Wuerffel 2-7, Zellars 1-(minus 2).

PASSING—San Francisco, S. Young 21-40-0-309, Detmer 1-1-0-11. New Orleans, Wuerffel 9-21-1-95, Tolliver 6-9-0-79.

RECEIVING—San Francisco, Owens 6-94, Rice 6-79, Stokes 3-27, Hearst 2-66, Uwaezuoke 1-25, Beasley 1-11, I. Smith 1-10, Edwards 1-7, Clark 1-1. New Orleans, Dawkins 4-56, Poole 3-38, Hastings 3-34, Cleeland 2-27, T. Davis 2-15, Zellars 1-4.

MISSED FIELD GOAL ATTEMPTS—San Francisco, Richey 45.

INTERCEPTIONS—San Francisco, Barker 1-(minus 4).

KICKOFF RETURNS—San Francisco, McQuarters 1-21. New Orleans, Ismail 4-96, Tomich 1-0.

PUNT RETURNS—San Francisco, McQuarters 6-60.

SACKS—San Francisco, Doleman 4, B. Young 1.5, McDonald 1, Bryant 0.5. New Orleans, Tomich 1.

BRONCOS 21, SEAHAWKS 16

Sunday, October 11

Denver	14	0	0	7—21
Seattle	0	7	3	6—16

First Quarter
Den.—R. Smith 50 pass from Elway (Elam kick), 7:38.
Den.—Sharpe 19 pass from Elway (Elam kick), 12:53.

Second Quarter
Sea.—Smith 23 interception return (Peterson kick), 0:52.

Third Quarter
Sea.—FG, Peterson 23, 6:36.

Fourth Quarter
Den.—Davis 2 run (Elam kick), 1:04.
Sea.—Pritchard 50 pass from Friesz (run failed), 4:26.
Attendance—66,258.

	Denver	Seattle
First downs	17	16
Rushes-yards	34-202	24-77
Passing	171	242
Punt returns	5-88	6-33
Kickoff returns	4-88	4-77
Interception returns	1-6	2-23
Comp.-att.-int.	13-27-2	21-40-1
Sacked-yards lost	3-14	3-21
Punts	7-46	9-50
Fumbles-lost	2-0	0-0
Penalties-yards	9-89	12-93
Time of possession	30:33	29:27

INDIVIDUAL STATISTICS

RUSHING—Denver, Davis 30-208, Elway 4-(minus 6). Seattle, Watters 20-76, Strong 2-2, Galloway 1-1, Moon 1-(minus 2).

PASSING—Denver, Elway 13-27-2-185. Seattle, Moon 15-32-0-154, Friesz 6-8-1-109.

RECEIVING—Denver, R. Smith 8-136, Sharpe 2-31, Griffith 2-13, McCaffrey 1-5. Seattle, Galloway 6-70, Pritchard 4-91, Fauria 4-53, Watters 3-18, Strong 2-11, McKnight 1-13, Br. Blades 1-7.

MISSED FIELD GOAL ATTEMPTS—None.

INTERCEPTIONS—Denver, Cadrez 1-6. Seattle, Smith 1-23, Springs 1-0.

KICKOFF RETURNS—Denver, Hebron 4-88. Seattle, Green 3-52, Broussard 1-25.

PUNT RETURNS—Denver, Gordon 5-88. Seattle, Galloway 5-26, Joseph 1-7.

SACKS—Denver, Tanuvasa 1, Hasselbach 1, Pryce 1. Seattle, C. Brown 1, Sinclair 1, LaBounty 1.

EAGLES 17, REDSKINS 12

Sunday, October 11

Washington	0	3	3	6—12
Philadelphia	7	3	0	7—17

First Quarter
Phi.—Peete 19 run (Boniol kick), 7:56.

Second Quarter
Was.—FG, Blanchard 46, 9:04.
Phi.—FG, Boniol 44, 13:58.

Third Quarter
Was.—FG, Blanchard 34, 12:09.

Fourth Quarter
Phi.—Sinceno 3 pass from Peete (Boniol kick), 6:28.
Was.—Mitchell 1 run (run failed), 12:14.
Attendance—66,183.

	Washington	Philadelphia
First downs	17	14
Rushes-yards	25-128	32-115
Passing	145	83
Punt returns	4-70	2-55
Kickoff returns	3-55	4-81
Interception returns	1-13	1-9
Comp.-att.-int.	19-37-1	15-28-1
Sacked-yards lost	6-43	4-38
Punts	4-46	7-44
Fumbles-lost	2-2	0-0
Penalties-yards	6-32	5-55
Time of possession	27:55	32:05

INDIVIDUAL STATISTICS

RUSHING—Washington, Allen 20-87, T. Green 2-15, Mitchell 2-6, Frerotte 1-20. Philadelphia, Garner 17-50, Staley 12-47, Peete 2-18, Turner 1-0.

PASSING—Washington, T. Green 12-21-1-115, Frerotte 7-16-0-73. Philadelphia, Peete 15-28-1-121.

RECEIVING—Washington, Westbrook 5-43, Asher 5-39, Mitchell 4-30, Connell 2-44, Shepherd 2-25, Davis 1-7. Philadelphia, Garner 4-19, Copeland 2-32, Fryar 2-29, Graham 2-17, Turner 2-6, Dunn 1-11, Staley 1-4, Sinceno 1-3.

MISSED FIELD GOAL ATTEMPTS—Washington, Blanchard 47. Philadelphia, Boniol 48.

INTERCEPTIONS—Washington, L. Evans 1-13. Philadelphia, Dawkins 1-9.

KICKOFF RETURNS—Washington, Mitchell 3-55. Philadelphia, Copeland 2-44, Staley 1-19, Hankton 1-18.

PUNT RETURNS—Washington, Mitchell 4-70. Philadelphia, Solomon 2-55.

SACKS—Washington, M. Patton 1, Stubblefield 1, Lang 1, Kalu 1. Philadelphia, H. Thomas 2, Douglas 1.5, Wallace 1.5, Darling 1.

RAMS 30, JETS 10

Sunday, October 11

N.Y. Jets	3	0	0	7—10
St. Louis	7	10	6	7—30

First Quarter
NYJ—FG, Hall 54, 7:33.
St.L.—Harris 7 pass from Banks (Wilkins kick), 14:13.

Second Quarter
St.L.—FG, Wilkins 52, 8:31.
St.L.—Lee 1 run (Wilkins kick), 14:27.

Third Quarter
St.L.—FG, Wilkins 30, 9:07.
St.L.—FG, Wilkins 34, 11:43.

Fourth Quarter
St.L.—Lee 3 run (Wilkins kick), 0:38.
NYJ—L. Johnson 17 pass from Testaverde (Hall kick), 2:39.
Attendance—55,938.

	N.Y. Jets	St. Louis
First downs	14	18
Rushes-yards	15-54	42-141
Passing	123	178
Punt returns	4-37	3-21
Kickoff returns	5-137	1-14
Interception returns	0-0	2-15
Comp.-att.-int.	14-33-2	19-25-0
Sacked-yards lost	5-49	1-0
Punts	4-42	5-45
Fumbles-lost	3-3	2-1
Penalties-yards	5-32	6-57
Time of possession	21:01	38:59

INDIVIDUAL STATISTICS

RUSHING—New York, L. Johnson 13-56, Foley 1-(minus 1), Testaverde 1-(minus 1). St. Louis, Holcombe 15-27, Lee 9-53, J. Moore 8-25, Banks 5-28, Harris 5-8.

PASSING—New York, Testaverde 9-18-0-96, Foley 5-15-2-76. St. Louis, Banks 18-24-0-171, Bono 1-1-0-7.

RECEIVING—New York, Chrebet 5-42, K. Johnson 4-79, Ward 2-29, L. Johnson 1-17, Byars 1-4, Anderson 1-1. St. Louis, Lee 6-62, Bruce 5-62, Kennison 2-15, R. Williams 2-13, Harris 2-12, Proehl 1-10, J. Moore 1-4.

MISSED FIELD GOAL ATTEMPTS—St. Louis, Wilkins 29.

INTERCEPTIONS—St. Louis, McCleon 1-15, E. Hill 1-0.

KICKOFF RETURNS—New York, Glenn 4-113, L. Johnson 1-24. St. Louis, Fletcher 1-14.

PUNT RETURNS—New York, L. Johnson 4-37. St. Louis, Kennison 3-21.

SACKS—New York, Lewis 1. St. Louis, Agnew 2, Lyght 1, Phifer 1, M. D. Jones 0.5, Little 0.5.

FALCONS 34, GIANTS 20

Sunday, October 11

Atlanta	7	7	10	10—34
N.Y. Giants	6	7	0	7—20

First Quarter
NYG—FG, Daluiso 46, 4:31.
Atl.—Martin 36 pass from Chandler (Andersen kick), 6:55.
NYG—FG, Daluiso 45, 13:34.
Second Quarter
Atl.—Edwards 2 fumble return (Andersen kick), 1:55.
NYG—Patten 39 pass from Kanell (Daluiso kick), 14:27.
Third Quarter
Atl.—FG, Andersen 26, 6:21.
Atl.—Mathis 55 pass from Chandler (Andersen kick), 11:32.
Fourth Quarter
Atl.—Chandler 1 run (Andersen kick), 5:09.
Atl.—FG, Andersen 32, 8:39.
NYG—K. Graham 5 run (Daluiso kick), 12:16.
Attendance—71,173.

	Atlanta	N.Y. Giants
First downs	20	17
Rushes-yards	34-128	25-110
Passing	253	156
Punt returns	5-46	1-6
Kickoff returns	4-89	7-116
Interception returns	0-0	0-0
Comp.-att.-int.	14-27-0	22-37-0
Sacked-yards lost	2-13	6-49
Punts	6-34	7-49
Fumbles-lost	4-2	3-3
Penalties-yards	10-75	8-76
Time of possession	34:49	25:11

INDIVIDUAL STATISTICS

RUSHING—Atlanta, J. Anderson 29-110, Chandler 4-19, Dwight 1-(minus 1). New York, Way 11-39, Brown 6-15, K. Graham 3-36, Barber 3-12, Kanell 2-8.

PASSING—Atlanta, Chandler 14-27-0-266. New York, Kanell 11-21-0-100, K. Graham 11-16-0-105.

RECEIVING—Atlanta, Martin 4-78, J. Anderson 3-40, Mathis 2-79, Santiago 2-18, Kozlowski 1-25, Dwight 1-21, Christian 1-5. New York, Barber 9-56, Toomer 4-38, Hilliard 4-35, Patten 3-59, Calloway 1-12, Cross 1-5.

MISSED FIELD GOAL ATTEMPTS—None.

INTERCEPTIONS—None.

KICKOFF RETURNS—Atlanta, Dwight 4-89. New York, Patten 5-96, Palelei 1-13, Toomer 1-7.

PUNT RETURNS—Atlanta, Dwight 5-46. New York, Toomer 1-6.

SACKS—Atlanta, C. Smith 1.5, Archambeau 1.5, Fuller 1, Edwards 1, Hall 0.5, Dronett 0.5. New York, Strahan 1, Armstead 1.

CARDINALS 20, BEARS 7

Sunday, October 11

Chicago	0	0	0	7— 7
Arizona	3	14	0	3—20

First Quarter
Ariz.—FG, Nedney 49, 8:47.
Second Quarter
Ariz.—Bates 2 run (Nedney kick), 13:07.
Ariz.—Bates 2 run (Nedney kick), 14:15.
Fourth Quarter
Ariz.—FG, Nedney 40, 3:48.
Chi.—Engram 79 pass from Kramer (Jaeger kick), 12:30.
Attendance—50,495.

	Chicago	Arizona
First downs	12	21
Rushes-yards	22-66	46-145

	Chicago	Arizona
Passing	223	150
Punt returns	1-4	4-24
Kickoff returns	5-75	2-26
Interception returns	2-26	4-35
Comp.-att.-int.	16-28-4	18-25-2
Sacked-yards lost	2-24	1-7
Punts	5-47	5-39
Fumbles-lost	4-4	5-3
Penalties-yards	5-46	7-59
Time of possession	24:00	36:00

INDIVIDUAL STATISTICS

RUSHING—Chicago, Enis 11-26, Bennett 9-29, Hallock 1-9, Kramer 1-2. Arizona, Murrell 21-67, Pittman 17-56, Plummer 4-8, Bates 3-7, Sanders 1-7.

PASSING—Chicago, Kramer 16-28-4-247. Arizona, Plummer 18-25-2-157.

RECEIVING—Chicago, Conway 6-54, Engram 5-142, Penn 3-37, Bennett 1-7, Hallock 1-7. Arizona, Centers 7-52, Sanders 4-32, R. Moore 3-24, Murrell 1-24, Metcalf 1-19, McWilliams 1-5, Gedney 1-1.

MISSED FIELD GOAL ATTEMPTS—Arizona, Nedney 46.

INTERCEPTIONS—Chicago, W. Harris 1-26, S. Harris 1-0. Arizona, McKinnon 3-20, A. Williams 1-15.

KICKOFF RETURNS—Chicago, Milburn 4-67, Wiegmann 1-8. Arizona, Metcalf 2-26.

PUNT RETURNS—Chicago, Milburn 1-4. Arizona, Metcalf 4-24.

SACKS—Chicago, Flanigan 1. Arizona, M. Smith 1, Swann 1.

JAGUARS 28, DOLPHINS 21

Monday, October 12

Miami	0	7	14	0—21
Jacksonville	7	7	0	14—28

First Quarter
Jac.—F. Taylor 77 run (Hollis kick), 0:20.
Second Quarter
Jac.—F. Taylor 2 run (Hollis kick), 0:29.
Mia.—Drayton 2 pass from Marino (Mare kick), 7:19.
Third Quarter
Mia.—Abdul-Jabbar 1 run (Mare kick), 4:31.
Mia.—Drayton 15 pass from Marino (Mare kick), 11:32.
Fourth Quarter
Jac.—McCardell 23 pass from Brunell (Hollis kick), 3:05.
Jac.—McCardell 56 pass from Brunell (Hollis kick), 12:24.
Attendance—74,051.

	Miami	Jacksonville
First downs	25	12
Rushes-yards	28-67	23-186
Passing	307	199
Punt returns	4-45	2-12
Kickoff returns	5-122	4-85
Interception returns	1-0	1-34
Comp.-att.-int.	30-49-1	12-18-1
Sacked-yards lost	2-16	2-14
Punts	6-42	7-45
Fumbles-lost	1-1	1-0
Penalties-yards	11-89	8-86
Time of possession	39:06	20:54

INDIVIDUAL STATISTICS

RUSHING—Miami, Abdul-Jabbar 21-43, Parmalee 3-15, Avery 3-4, McDuffie 1-5. Jacksonville, F. Taylor 12-89, Banks 9-75, Brunell 2-22.

PASSING—Miami, Marino 30-49-1-323. Jacksonville, Brunell 12-18-1-213.

RECEIVING—Miami, McDuffie 7-68, Drayton 6-30, Gadsden 5-91, L. Thomas 4-69, Perry 3-31, Parmalee 2-27, Pritchett 2-9, Avery 1-(minus 2). Jacksonville, Barlow 4-50, McCardell 3-86, J. Smith 1-41, Shelton 1-19, Mitchell 1-9, Banks 1-6, F. Taylor 1-2.

MISSED FIELD GOAL ATTEMPTS—Miami, Mare 54. Jacksonville, Hollis 45.

INTERCEPTIONS—Miami, Buckley 1-0. Jacksonville, Beasley 1-34.

KICKOFF RETURNS—Miami, Avery 4-96, Marion 1-26. Jacksonville, Barlow 2-50, Banks 2-35.

PUNT RETURNS—Miami, Buckley 4-45. Jacksonville, Barlow 2-12.

SACKS—Miami, Armstrong 1, Mixon 1. Jacksonville, Paup 1, Brackens 1.

WEEK 7

RESULTS

DETROIT 27, Green Bay 20
ATLANTA 31, New Orleans 23
BUFFALO 17, Jacksonville 16
CHICAGO 13, Dallas 12
MIAMI 14, St. Louis 0
MINNESOTA 41, Washington 7
N.Y. GIANTS 34, Arizona 7
PITTSBURGH 16, Baltimore 6
TAMPA BAY 16, Carolina 13
TENNESSEE 44, Cincinnati 14
SAN DIEGO 13, Philadelphia 10
SAN FRANCISCO 34, Indianapolis 31
N.Y. Jets 24, NEW ENGLAND 14
    Open date: Denver, Kansas City, Oakland, Seattle

STANDINGS

AFC EAST

	W	L	T	Pct.
New England	4	1	0	.800
Miami	4	2	0	.667
Buffalo	3	3	0	.500
N.Y. Jets	2	3	0	.400
Indianapolis	1	6	0	.143

AFC CENTRAL

	W	L	T	Pct.
Jacksonville	5	1	0	.833
Pittsburgh	4	2	0	.667
Tennessee	3	3	0	.500
Baltimore	2	4	0	.333
Cincinnati	2	4	0	.333

AFC WEST

	W	L	T	Pct.
Denver	6	0	0	1.000
Kansas City	4	2	0	.667
Oakland	4	2	0	.667
Seattle	3	3	0	.500
San Diego	3	4	0	.429

NFC EAST

	W	L	T	Pct.
Dallas	4	3	0	.571
Arizona	3	4	0	.429
N.Y. Giants	3	4	0	.429
Philadelphia	1	6	0	.143
Washington	0	7	0	.000

NFC CENTRAL

	W	L	T	Pct.
Minnesota	6	0	0	1.000
Green Bay	4	2	0	.667
Tampa Bay	3	3	0	.500
Detroit	2	4	0	.333
Chicago	2	5	0	.286

NFC WEST

	W	L	T	Pct.
Atlanta	5	1	0	.833
San Francisco	5	1	0	.833
New Orleans	3	3	0	.500
St. Louis	2	4	0	.333
Carolina	0	6	0	.000

HIGHLIGHTS

Hero of the week: Giants quarterback Danny Kanell completed 22 passes in 36 attempts and threw touchdown passes to three receivers in New York's 34-7 win over Arizona. The victory extended Kanell's record against the Cardinals to 3-0 as a starter.

Goat of the week: Bengals quarterback Neil O'Donnell completed just 6-of-11 passes in the first half, gave up a third-quarter fumble that resulted in an Oilers touchdown and was benched in the fourth quarter in favor of Jeff Blake in a 44-14 loss to Tennessee.

Sub of the week: Falcons quarterback Steve DeBerg, playing in his first NFL game in five years, replaced injured Chris Chandler and engineered a fourth-quarter, six-play, 50-yard drive that ended with an 8-yard touchdown pass to Bob Christian. The Falcons beat the Saints, 31-23.

Comeback of the week: With the Colts up 21-0 in the second quarter and holding an eight-point lead midway through the fourth quarter, it looked as if Indianapolis was going to pull the surprise of the week. But Steve Young helped the 49ers avoid defeat by hitting on 33 of 51 passes for 331 yards. He also contributed 60 yards rushing and two touchdowns. Wade Richey's 24-yard field goal with five seconds left provided the winning margin in San Francisco's 34-31 victory.

Blowout of the week: After surrendering the game's first touchdown, the Minnesota Vikings scored the next 41 points and cruised to their sixth consecutive victory, 41-7, over the Redskins. The Vikings' offense, led by Robert Smith and Cris Carter, posted 25 first downs, gave up no sacks and tallied 259 more yards than the Redskins.

Nail-biter of the week: Doug Flutie, starting his first NFL game in more than nine years, capped a 12-play, 70-yard drive with a 1-yard touchdown run, giving the Bills their first lead of the game with 13 seconds left and a 17-16 victory over Jacksonville. The previously unbeaten Jaguars could not stop Flutie on the final drive, surrendering two third-down conversions and a 38-yard pass play to Eric Moulds that

set up Flutie's game-winning touchdown.

Hit of the week: With the Eagles down by three and driving late in the fourth quarter, Chargers defensive back Charles Dimry, a former Eagle, hit Russell Copeland, jarring the ball loose. Junior Seau recovered for San Diego. The controversial play was ruled a complete pass and a fumble caused by the hit, allowing San Diego to run out the clock and preserve a 13-10 victory.

Oddity of the week: With Jaguars starting running back James Stewart out for the year and backup Fred Taylor resting a sore shoulder, the Jaguars turned to third-stringer Tavian Banks, a rookie. When Banks suffered a foot injury in the first half, the Jaguars were forced to play their No. 4 running back, Chris Howard, another rookie. Howard was able to muster only 16 yards on seven carries in a 17-16 loss to the Bills.

Top rusher: Barry Sanders rushed 25 times for 155 yards, including a 73-yard touchdown run, in the Lions' 27-20 win over the Packers.

Top passer: Steve Young completed 33-of-51 passes for 331 yards and two touchdowns in the 49ers' comeback win over the Colts.

Top receiver: Keith Poole caught three passes for 154 yards and two touchdowns in the Saints' loss to the Falcons.

Notes: Jerry Rice tied Art Monk's NFL record for consecutive games with a reception with 183. . . . Falcons quarterback Steve DeBerg's touchdown pass against the Saints was his first TD pass since 1993, when he finished the season as an injury replacement for the Dolphins' Dan Marino. . . . Vikings kicker Gary Anderson converted on two field-goal attempts to extend his streak of consecutive field goals to 18. . . . Barry Sanders' 73-yard touchdown run against Green Bay was his 15th TD run of more than 50 yards, three better than Jim Brown, the next closest on the NFL's all-time list. . . . Bills quarterback Doug Flutie made his first NFL start since October 15, 1989, when he played for the Patriots. The layoff between starts was the longest

1998 REVIEW Week 7

– 151 –

in league history.

Quote of the week: Panthers kicker John Kasay, after missing wide left on a 47-yard field goal with five seconds left, which would have sent the game into overtime: "For 4½ hours, the wind blew left to right, and for 10 seconds it didn't. I'm still scratching my head. I'm just as stumped now as I was when I was watching it."

GAME SUMMARIES

LIONS 27, PACKERS 20

Thursday, October 15

Green Bay	10	0	3	7—20
Detroit	0	10	0	17—27

First Quarter
G.B.—Freeman 67 pass from Favre (Longwell kick), 4:30.
G.B.—FG, Longwell 28, 11:52.
Second Quarter
Det.—FG, Hanson 25, 1:59.
Det.—Chryplewicz 3 pass from Batch (Hanson kick), 5:01.
Third Quarter
G.B.—FG, Longwell 40, 3:35.
Fourth Quarter
Det.—Crowell 68 pass from Batch (Hanson kick), 0:09.
Det.—Sanders 73 run (Hanson kick), 6:55.
Det.—FG, Hanson 36, 12:52.
G.B.—Freeman 14 pass from Favre (Longwell kick), 14:57.
Attendance—77,932.

	Green Bay	Detroit
First downs	23	16
Rushes-yards	21-93	32-186
Passing	275	199
Punt returns	4-26	1-(-4)
Kickoff returns	3-81	3-57
Interception returns	0-0	3-54
Comp.-att.-int.	22-43-3	16-19-0
Sacked-yards lost	2-25	3-19
Punts	5-38	5-38
Fumbles-lost	2-0	1-1
Penalties-yards	4-45	10-97
Time of possession	28:54	31:06

INDIVIDUAL STATISTICS
RUSHING—Green Bay, Jervey 19-69, Favre 1-18, R. Harris 1-6. Detroit, Sanders 25-155, Batch 3-17, Rivers 2-11, Schlesinger 1-2, Vardell 1-1.
PASSING—Green Bay, Favre 22-43-3-300. Detroit, Batch 16-19-0-218.
RECEIVING—Green Bay, Freeman 6-126, Schroeder 6-97, Henderson 4-26, Chmura 2-28, Jervey 2-1, R. Brooks 1-14, Thomason 1-8. Detroit, Morton 5-45, Crowell 3-81, Moore 3-25, Sanders 2-27, Chryplewicz 2-9, Vardell 1-31.
MISSED FIELD GOAL ATTEMPTS—None.
INTERCEPTIONS—Detroit, Carrier 2-33, Jamison 1-21.
KICKOFF RETURNS—Green Bay, Preston 3-81. Detroit, Fair 3-57.
PUNT RETURNS—Green Bay, Preston 4-26. Detroit, Abrams 1-(minus 4).
SACKS—Green Bay, White 2.5, McKenzie 0.5. Detroit, Owens 1, Fredrickson 0.5, Porcher 0.5.

BILLS 17, JAGUARS 16

Sunday, October 18

Jacksonville	7	3	6	0—16
Buffalo	0	7	3	7—17

First Quarter
Jac.—Banks 1 run (Hollis kick), 10:27.
Second Quarter
Buf.—Moulds 12 pass from Flutie (Christie kick), 2:40.
Jac.—FG, Hollis 35, 15:00.
Third Quarter
Jac.—FG, Hollis 23, 4:07.
Buf.—FG, Christie 24, 7:56.
Jac.—FG, Hollis 27, 14:40.
Fourth Quarter
Buf.—Flutie 1 run (Christie kick), 14:47.
Attendance—77,635.

	Jacksonville	Buffalo
First downs	16	22
Rushes-yards	34-134	23-110
Passing	104	227
Punt returns	1-0	3-18
Kickoff returns	3-55	3-80
Interception returns	0-0	0-0
Comp.-att.-int.	16-28-0	18-39-0
Sacked-yards lost	3-15	1-1
Punts	5-52	5-39
Fumbles-lost	1-0	1-1
Penalties-yards	8-58	6-53
Time of possession	34:02	25:58

INDIVIDUAL STATISTICS
RUSHING—Jacksonville, Shelton 13-44, Banks 8-30, Howard 7-16, Brunell 6-44. Buffalo, A. Smith 11-47, Thomas 7-30, Flutie 3-22, Gash 2-11.
PASSING—Jacksonville, Brunell 16-28-0-119. Buffalo, Flutie 18-39-0-228.
RECEIVING—Jacksonville, McCardell 6-39, J. Smith 5-42, Mitchell 2-18, Shelton 2-17, Howard 1-3. Buffalo, Reed 5-49, Moulds 4-68, Thomas 4-44, K. Williams 2-32, Riemersma 2-30, A. Smith 1-5.
MISSED FIELD GOAL ATTEMPTS—None.
INTERCEPTIONS—None.
KICKOFF RETURNS—Jacksonville, Logan 3-55. Buffalo, K. Williams 3-80.
PUNT RETURNS—Jacksonville, Barlow 1-0. Buffalo, K. Williams 3-18.
SACKS—Jacksonville, Smeenge 1. Buffalo, B. Smith 1, P. Williams 1, Rogers 0.5, Hansen 0.5.

VIKINGS 41, REDSKINS 7

Sunday, October 18

Washington	7	0	0	0— 7
Minnesota	14	7	3	17—41

First Quarter
Was.—Allen 2 run (Blanchard kick), 2:12.
Min.—Glover 11 pass from Cunningham (Anderson kick), 6:29.
Min.—Hoard 1 run (Anderson kick), 11:20.
Second Quarter
Min.—Carter 1 pass from Cunningham (Anderson kick), 14:46.
Third Quarter
Min.—FG, Anderson 49, 6:00.
Fourth Quarter
Min.—R. Smith 19 run (Anderson kick), 2:12.
Min.—FG, Anderson 46, 11:07.
Min.—Hoard 1 run (Anderson kick), 13:09.
Attendance—64,004.

	Washington	Minnesota
First downs	9	25
Rushes-yards	22-82	38-147
Passing	95	288
Punt returns	2-35	2-14
Kickoff returns	3-69	2-42
Interception returns	0-0	1-0
Comp.-att.-int.	10-26-1	22-38-0
Sacked-yards lost	5-22	0-0
Punts	8-44	5-42
Fumbles-lost	1-0	2-1
Penalties-yards	11-94	4-35
Time of possession	26:47	33:13

INDIVIDUAL STATISTICS
RUSHING—Washington, Allen 13-62, Hicks 5-4, Mitchell 2-27, Frerotte 1-1, M. Turk 1-(minus 12). Minnesota, R. Smith 24-103, Hoard 10-24, Evans 2-10, Cunningham 1-6, Palmer 1-4.
PASSING—Washington, Frerotte 10-26-1-117. Minnesota, Cunningham 20-34-0-259, Fiedler 2-4-0-29.
RECEIVING—Washington, Mitchell 3-22, Westbrook 2-35, Connell 1-22, Allen 1-15, Asher 1-9, Davis 1-8, Alexander 1-6. Minnesota, Carter 5-109, R. Moss 5-64, R. Smith 4-23, Glover 2-24, Evans 2-9, Hoard 2-7, Palmer 1-33, Reed 1-19.
MISSED FIELD GOAL ATTEMPTS—Washington, Blanchard 49.
INTERCEPTIONS—Minnesota, Fuller 1-0.
KICKOFF RETURNS—Washington, Mitchell 2-56, Asher 1-8. Minnesota, Palmer 2-42.
PUNT RETURNS—Washington, Mitchell 2-35. Minnesota, Palmer 1-14, R. Moss 1-0.
SACKS—Minnesota, Clemons 1.5, Gray 1, Alexander 1, E. McDaniel 0.5, Thomas 0.5, Wong 0.5.

GIANTS 34, CARDINALS 7

Sunday, October 18

Arizona	0	7	0	0— 7
N.Y. Giants	7	10	10	7—34

First Quarter
NYG—Way 1 pass from Kanell (Daluiso kick), 10:46.
Second Quarter
NYG—Brown 1 run (Daluiso kick), 3:43.
Ariz.—McWilliams 14 pass from Plummer (Nedney kick), 7:33.
NYG—FG, Daluiso 26, 15:00.
Third Quarter
NYG—FG, Daluiso 34, 5:33.
NYG—Calloway 19 pass from Kanell (Daluiso kick), 12:59.
Fourth Quarter
NYG—Toomer 18 pass from Kanell (Daluiso kick), 8:48.
Attendance—70,456.

	Arizona	N.Y. Giants
First downs	15	26
Rushes-yards	20-62	37-141
Passing	132	249
Punt returns	2-16	2-17
Kickoff returns	5-92	2-44
Interception returns	0-0	2-11
Comp.-att.-int.	14-26-2	22-36-0
Sacked-yards lost	8-38	1-10
Punts	5-43	3-54
Fumbles-lost	1-1	0-0
Penalties-yards	7-53	9-79
Time of possession	26:14	33:46

INDIVIDUAL STATISTICS
RUSHING—Arizona, Bates 13-45, Centers 3-7, Plummer 2-8, D. Brown 1-2, Murrell 1-0. New York, Brown 24-108, Way 9-23, Wheatley 2-9, Barber 1-2, K. Graham 1-(minus 1).
PASSING—Arizona, Plummer 12-21-2-139, D. Brown 2-5-0-31. New York, Kanell 22-36-0-259.
RECEIVING—Arizona, R. Moore 4-52, Sanders 4-42, McWilliams 2-39, Centers 2-20, Metcalf 2-17. New York, Calloway 6-97, Way 4-13, Barber 3-40, Patten 3-32, Hilliard 3-28, Cross 2-31, Toomer 1-18.
MISSED FIELD GOAL ATTEMPTS—New York, Daluiso 33.
INTERCEPTIONS—New York, Ellsworth 1-7, Armstead 1-4.
KICKOFF RETURNS—Arizona, Metcalf 3-52, Pittman 2-40. New York, Patten 2-44.
PUNT RETURNS—Arizona, Metcalf 2-16. New York, Toomer 2-17.
SACKS—Arizona, Swann 1. New York, Harris 2.5, K. Hamilton 1.5, Bratzke 1, Strahan 1, Galyon 1, Buckley 1.

OILERS 44, BENGALS 14

Sunday, October 18

Cincinnati	0	0	7	7—14
Tennessee	7	13	17	7—44

First Quarter
Ten.—Harris 18 pass from Archie (Del Greco kick), 4:50.
Second Quarter
Ten.—FG, Del Greco 35, 2:12.
Ten.—McNair 1 run (Del Greco kick), 12:42.
Ten.—FG, Del Greco 38, 14:57.
Third Quarter
Ten.—FG, Del Greco 42, 4:33.
Ten.—Bowden 12 fumble return (Del Greco kick), 4:55.
Cin.—Dillon 12 run (Pelfrey kick), 8:49.
Ten.—Dyson 45 pass from McNair (Del Greco kick), 9:09.
Fourth Quarter
Cin.—Gibson 76 pass from O'Donnell (Pelfrey kick), 2:45.
Ten.—Thomas 1 run (Del Greco kick), 10:30.
Attendance—33,288.

	Cincinnati	Tennessee
First downs	14	24
Rushes-yards	23-148	39-171
Passing	186	344
Punt returns	1-3	2-26
Kickoff returns	3-66	2-77
Interception returns	0-0	0-0
Comp.-att.-int.	13-25-0	20-25-0
Sacked-yards lost	3-16	1-8
Punts	5-43	2-49

	Cincinnati	Tennessee
Fumbles-lost	1-1	0-0
Penalties-yards	5-40	6-54
Time of possession	23:05	0:01

INDIVIDUAL STATISTICS
RUSHING—Cincinnati, Dillon 14-124, Bennett 6-14, O'Donnell 2-5, Blake 1-5. Tennessee, E. George 25-107, Thomas 11-48, McNair 3-16.
PASSING—Cincinnati, O'Donnell 11-22-0-192, Blake 2-3-0-10. Tennessee, McNair 16-21-0-277, Krieg 3-3-0-57, Archie 1-1-0-18.
RECEIVING—Cincinnati, Milne 3-16, Pickens 2-51, Scott 2-29, Bieniemy 2-18, Bennett 2-10, Gibson 1-76, Dillon 1-2. Tennessee, Byrd 5-53, Wycheck 4-84, Dyson 4-82, Sanders 3-101, Harris 1-18, Roan 1-8, Thomas 1-3, Archie 1-3.
MISSED FIELD GOAL ATTEMPTS—None.
INTERCEPTIONS—None.
KICKOFF RETURNS—Cincinnati, Mack 2-49, Bieniemy 1-17. Tennessee, Archie 2-77.
PUNT RETURNS—Cincinnati, Gibson 1-3. Tennessee, Archie 2-26.
SACKS—Cincinnati, Shade 1. Tennessee, Salave'a 1, Ford 1, D. Lewis 1.

STEELERS 16, RAVENS 6

Sunday, October 18

Baltimore	3	3	0	0— 6
Pittsburgh	3	0	7	6—16

First Quarter
Pit.—FG, N. Johnson 41, 3:34.
Bal.—FG, Stover 41, 13:34.
Second Quarter
Bal.—FG, Stover 40, 13:59.
Third Quarter
Pit.—C. Johnson 55 pass from Stewart (N. Johnson kick), 1:01.
Fourth Quarter
Pit.—FG, N. Johnson 42, 11:51.
Pit.—FG, N. Johnson 40, 12:41.
Attendance—58,620.

	Baltimore	Pittsburgh
First downs	16	13
Rushes-yards	29-96	30-79
Passing	134	162
Punt returns	3-24	2-(-1)
Kickoff returns	5-102	1-41
Interception returns	1-1	3-69
Comp.-att.-int.	17-32-3	12-27-1
Sacked-yards lost	7-39	5-34
Punts	6-48	6-43
Fumbles-lost	2-2	1-1
Penalties-yards	8-65	5-30
Time of possession	33:34	26:26

INDIVIDUAL STATISTICS
RUSHING—Baltimore, Holmes 23-76, Zeier 3-8, J. Lewis 1-6, Harbaugh 1-3, Potts 1-3. Pittsburgh, Huntley 21-52, Stewart 6-18, Fuamatu-Ma'afala 2-3, Hawkins 1-6.
PASSING—Baltimore, Zeier 17-26-1-173, Harbaugh 0-6-2-0. Pittsburgh, Stewart 12-27-1-196.
RECEIVING—Baltimore, J. Lewis 6-62, Holmes 6-42, Johnson 3-39, Yarborough 1-18, Turner 1-12. Pittsburgh, Hawkins 3-82, Blackwell 3-22, Huntley 3-18, C. Johnson 2-71, Bruener 1-3.
MISSED FIELD GOAL ATTEMPTS—None.
INTERCEPTIONS—Baltimore, Starks 1-1. Pittsburgh, Washington 1-43, Perry 1-29, Lake 1-(minus 3).
KICKOFF RETURNS—Baltimore, J. Lewis 3-57, Johnson 2-45. Pittsburgh, Dunn 1-41.
PUNT RETURNS—Baltimore, J. Lewis 3-24. Pittsburgh, Arnold 1-0, Blackwell 1-(minus 1).
SACKS—Baltimore, J. Jones 2, McCrary 1, Washington 1, C. Harris 1. Pittsburgh, Gibson 2, Emmons 1.5, Gildon 1, Vrabel 1, D. Jones 0.5, Kirkland 0.5, Roye 0.5.

CHARGERS 13, EAGLES 10

Sunday, October 18

Philadelphia	0	3	0	7—10
San Diego	3	0	7	3—13

First Quarter
S.D.—FG, Carney 23, 4:24.
Second Quarter
Phi.—FG, Boniol 35, 6:19.

Third Quarter
S.D.—Means 14 run (Carney kick), 8:44.
Fourth Quarter
Phi.—Garner 12 run (Boniol kick), 3:28.
S.D.—FG, Carney 26, 7:42.
Attendance—56,967.

	Philadelphia	San Diego
First downs	21	11
Rushes-yards	24-51	28-140
Passing	210	28
Punt returns	3-32	3-32
Kickoff returns	3-81	3-31
Interception returns	0-0	2-17
Comp.-att.-int.	22-39-2	9-19-0
Sacked-yards lost	5-22	6-55
Punts	5-41	8-48
Fumbles-lost	2-2	1-1
Penalties-yards	10-68	11-75
Time of possession	32:55	27:05

INDIVIDUAL STATISTICS
RUSHING—Philadelphia, Staley 14-41, Garner 9-8, Peete 1-2. San Diego, Means 21-112, Leaf 5-10, C. Jones 1-13, Stephens 1-5.

PASSING—Philadelphia, Peete 22-39-2-232. San Diego, Leaf 9-19-0-83.

RECEIVING—Philadelphia, Copeland 6-69, Fryar 4-44, Graham 3-42, Staley 3-35, Garner 3-18, Solomon 1-14, Dunn 1-6, Turner 1-4. San Diego, Still 3-28, Means 2-7, C. Jones 1-19, Ricks 1-11, F. Jones 1-10, Davis 1-8.

MISSED FIELD GOAL ATTEMPTS—Philadelphia, Boniol 42.

INTERCEPTIONS—San Diego, Hand 1-17, Dimry 1-0.

KICKOFF RETURNS—Philadelphia, Rossum 3-81. San Diego, Bynum 1-17, Stephens 1-14, Jacox 1-0.

PUNT RETURNS—Philadelphia, Rossum 2-24, Solomon 1-8. San Diego, Rachal 3-32.

SACKS—Philadelphia, Douglas 4.5, W. Thomas 1, H. Thomas 0.5. San Diego, Johnson 2, Hand 1, Parrella 1, Seau 0.5, Mims 0.5.

FALCONS 31, SAINTS 23
Sunday, October 18

New Orleans	0	14	2	7—23
Atlanta	3	14	0	14—31

First Quarter
Atl.—FG, Andersen 22, 7:02.
Second Quarter
N.O.—L. Smith 5 run (Brien kick), 1:25.
Atl.—J. Anderson 31 run (Andersen kick), 6:17.
Atl.—Martin 45 pass from Chandler (Andersen kick), 8:17.
N.O.—Poole 64 pass from Tolliver (Brien kick), 11:08.
Third Quarter
N.O.—Safety, DeBerg tackled by Martin, 4:28.
Fourth Quarter
Atl.—Christian 8 pass from DeBerg (Andersen kick), 3:55.
Atl.—Robinson 25 interception return (Andersen kick), 4:23.
N.O.—Poole 82 pass from Tolliver (Brien kick), 11:41.
Attendance—60,774.

	New Orleans	Atlanta
First downs	15	19
Rushes-yards	26-67	30-140
Passing	255	163
Punt returns	0-0	3-16
Kickoff returns	6-108	4-88
Interception returns	0-0	1-25
Comp.-att.-int.	14-29-1	14-21-0
Sacked-yards lost	1-6	5-26
Punts	4-44	4-42
Fumbles-lost	5-3	2-0
Penalties-yards	13-101	6-46
Time of possession	28:01	31:59

INDIVIDUAL STATISTICS
RUSHING—New Orleans, L. Smith 19-49, Zellars 4-8, Tolliver 2-9, T. Davis 1-1. Atlanta, J. Anderson 25-132, DeBerg 3-(minus 2), Christian 1-6, Dwight 1-4.

PASSING—New Orleans, Tolliver 14-29-1-261. Atlanta, DeBerg 7-10-0-60, Chandler 7-10-0-129, Dwight 0-1-0-0.

RECEIVING—New Orleans, Poole 3-154, Cleeland 3-42, Dawkins 2-25, L. Smith 2-15, Zellars 2-5, Bech 1-11, Hastings 1-9. Atlanta, Martin 7-116, Mathis 2-35, Santiago 2-26, Christian 2-5, J. Anderson 1-7.

MISSED FIELD GOAL ATTEMPTS—Atlanta, Andersen 45.

INTERCEPTIONS—Atlanta, Robinson 1-25.

KICKOFF RETURNS—New Orleans, Ismail 4-73, T. Davis 1-19, Bech 1-16. Atlanta, Dwight 4-88.

PUNT RETURNS—Atlanta, Dwight 3-16.

SACKS—New Orleans, Martin 1, Fields 1, Tomich 1, Cherry 1, Kev. Mitchell 0.5, Kei. Mitchell 0.5. Atlanta, Dronett 1.

BUCCANEERS 16, PANTHERS 13
Sunday, October 18

Carolina	0	3	10	0—13
Tampa Bay	0	3	0	13—16

Second Quarter
Car.—FG, Kasay 53, 8:32.
T.B.—FG, Husted 33, 13:45.
Third Quarter
Car.—FG, Kasay 20, 6:18.
Car.—Lane 1 run (Kasay kick), 12:29.
Fourth Quarter
T.B.—Dilfer 1 run (Husted kick), 9:55.
T.B.—Williams 29 pass from Dilfer (kick failed), 13:21.
Attendance—63,600.

	Carolina	Tampa Bay
First downs	17	21
Rushes-yards	23-67	28-136
Passing	223	213
Punt returns	2-32	1-3
Kickoff returns	4-69	4-64
Interception returns	1-18	0-0
Comp.-att.-int.	22-31-0	21-31-1
Sacked-yards lost	3-11	1-6
Punts	5-36	3-44
Fumbles-lost	2-0	1-1
Penalties-yards	6-60	6-45
Time of possession	27:27	32:33

INDIVIDUAL STATISTICS
RUSHING—Carolina, Lane 20-59, Floyd 2-4, Johnson 1-4. Tampa Bay, Dunn 17-96, Alstott 7-23, Dilfer 4-17.

PASSING—Carolina, Beuerlein 22-31-0-234. Tampa Bay, Dilfer 21-31-1-219.

RECEIVING—Carolina, Muhammad 6-56, Ismail 5-62, Johnson 4-17, Lane 3-35, Walls 2-34, Broughton 1-22, Floyd 1-8. Tampa Bay, Anthony 6-81, Alstott 6-36, Emanuel 5-66, Williams 2-38, Dunn 2-(minus 2).

MISSED FIELD GOAL ATTEMPTS—Carolina, Kasay 47.

INTERCEPTIONS—Carolina, Evans 1-18.

KICKOFF RETURNS—Carolina, Bates 4-69. Tampa Bay, Anthony 2-37, Ellison 1-19, Alstott 1-8.

PUNT RETURNS—Carolina, Oliver 2-32. Tampa Bay, Williams 1-3.

SACKS—Carolina, Greene 1. Tampa Bay, Nickerson 1, Culpepper 1, Sapp 1.

DOLPHINS 14, RAMS 0
Sunday, October 18

St. Louis	0	0	0	0— 0
Miami	0	7	0	7—14

Second Quarter
Mia.—Gadsden 1 pass from Marino (Mare kick), 14:54.
Fourth Quarter
Mia.—Avery 19 pass from Marino (Mare kick), 4:39.
Attendance—65,418.

	St. Louis	Miami
First downs	15	16
Rushes-yards	24-76	32-141
Passing	128	104
Punt returns	5-15	4-67
Kickoff returns	3-34	0-0
Interception returns	1-25	1-1
Comp.-att.-int.	14-29-1	14-26-1
Sacked-yards lost	4-15	1-10
Punts	8-47	8-42
Fumbles-lost	3-1	0-0
Penalties-yards	8-65	10-71
Time of possession	29:12	30:48

INDIVIDUAL STATISTICS
RUSHING—St. Louis, Holcombe 13-22, Lee 7-34, Banks 4-20. Miami, Abdul-Jabbar 17-59, Avery 11-85, Marino 3-(minus 3), Parmalee 1-0.

PASSING—St. Louis, Banks 14-29-1-143. Miami, Marino 14-26-1-114.

RECEIVING—St. Louis, Bruce 6-72, Lee 2-32, Conwell 2-18, Holcombe 2-9, Proehl 1-10, Flannery 1-2. Miami, Drayton 3-26, McDuffie 3-14, L. Thomas 2-20, Abdul-Jabbar 2-12, Gadsden 2-5, Avery 1-19, Parmalee 1-18.

MISSED FIELD GOAL ATTEMPTS—None.

INTERCEPTIONS—St. Louis, Jenkins 1-25. Miami, Surtain 1-1.

KICKOFF RETURNS—St. Louis, Fletcher 1-19, Horne 1-15, Clemons 1-0.

PUNT RETURNS—St. Louis, Kennison 4-15, Horne 1-0. Miami, Buckley 3-53, McDuffie 1-14.

SACKS—St. Louis, Lyle 1. Miami, Armstrong 2, Bromell 1, Rodgers 1.

BEARS 13, COWBOYS 12

Sunday, October 18

Dallas	3	3	6	0—12
Chicago	0	0	7	6—13

First Quarter
Dal.—FG, Cunningham 23, 7:12.

Second Quarter
Dal.—FG, Cunningham 23, 7:22.

Third Quarter
Chi.—Penn 13 pass from Kramer (Jaeger kick), 7:16.
Dal.—LaFleur 1 pass from Garrett (pass failed), 14:54.

Fourth Quarter
Chi.—FG, Jaeger 22, 6:36.
Chi.—FG, Jaeger 29, 14:49.
Attendance—59,201.

	Dallas	Chicago
First downs	13	18
Rushes-yards	26-108	31-79
Passing	128	220
Punt returns	2-1	0-0
Kickoff returns	3-64	4-87
Interception returns	1-18	1-(-4)
Comp.-att.-int.	14-26-1	18-30-1
Sacked-yards lost	1-8	3-13
Punts	7-45	6-40
Fumbles-lost	2-0	2-1
Penalties-yards	11-92	4-28
Time of possession	27:53	32:07

INDIVIDUAL STATISTICS

RUSHING—Dallas, E. Smith 16-78, Garrett 4-3, Warren 3-20, Johnston 2-3, E. Mills 1-4. Chicago, Enis 12-30, Bennett 12-28, Chancey 3-17, Kramer 2-0, Conway 1-3, Hallock 1-1.

PASSING—Dallas, Garrett 14-26-1-136. Chicago, Kramer 18-30-1-233.

RECEIVING—Dallas, Irvin 5-62, E. Mills 3-21, Warren 2-10, Bjornson 1-34, B. Davis 1-8, LaFleur 1-1, Johnston 1-0. Chicago, Penn 5-66, Mayes 4-57, Engram 3-49, Conway 2-29, Milburn 2-18, Chancey 1-9, Wetnight 1-5.

MISSED FIELD GOAL ATTEMPTS—None.

INTERCEPTIONS—Dallas, Coakley 1-18. Chicago, Collins 1-(minus 4).

KICKOFF RETURNS—Dallas, Mathis 3-64. Chicago, Milburn 3-69, Chancey 1-18.

PUNT RETURNS—Dallas, Sanders 2-1.

SACKS—Dallas, Coakley 1, Pittman 1, Mathis 1. Chicago, Flanigan 1.

49ERS 34, COLTS 31

Sunday, October 18

Indianapolis	14	7	10	0—31
San Francisco	0	17	0	17—34

First Quarter
Ind.—Faulk 65 run (Vanderjagt kick), 9:27.
Ind.—Harrison 4 pass from Manning (Vanderjagt kick), 12:58.

Second Quarter
Ind.—Harrison 6 pass from Manning (Vanderjagt kick), 4:04.
S.F.—FG, Richey 43, 6:43.
S.F.—Stokes 3 pass from S. Young (Richey kick), 13:06.
S.F.—Owens 10 pass from S. Young (Richey kick), 14:55.

Third Quarter
Ind.—Harrison 61 pass from Manning (Vanderjagt kick), 4:19.
Ind.—FG, Vanderjagt 38, 8:32.

Fourth Quarter
S.F.—S. Young 1 run (run failed), 5:02.
S.F.—S. Young 23 run (Rice pass from S. Young), 9:08.
S.F.—FG, Richey 24, 14:55.
Attendance—68,486.

	Indianapolis	San Francisco
First downs	15	36
Rushes-yards	20-105	25-128
Passing	231	321
Punt returns	3-59	4-33
Kickoff returns	5-66	6-118
Interception returns	0-0	0-0
Comp.-att.-int.	18-30-0	33-51-0
Sacked-yards lost	1-0	5-10
Punts	5-46	3-47
Fumbles-lost	0-0	2-2
Penalties-yards	10-83	6-55
Time of possession	24:03	33:57

INDIVIDUAL STATISTICS

RUSHING—Indianapolis, Faulk 17-103, Warren 2-3, Heyward 1-(minus 1). San Francisco, Hearst 15-66, S. Young 8-60, Edwards 1-1, Levy 1-1.

PASSING—Indianapolis, Manning 18-30-0-231. San Francisco, S. Young 33-51-0-331.

RECEIVING—Indianapolis, Harrison 6-98, Faulk 4-36, Pathon 3-44, Warren 2-20, Small 2-18, Dilger 1-15. San Francisco, Stokes 9-110, Owens 7-79, Hearst 6-33, Rice 4-36, Levy 4-32, I. Smith 2-36, Clark 1-15.

MISSED FIELD GOAL ATTEMPTS—Indianapolis, Vanderjagt 53. San Francisco, Richey 27.

INTERCEPTIONS—None.

KICKOFF RETURNS—Indianapolis, Warren 2-34, Elias 1-18, Hetherington 1-12, Morrison 1-2. San Francisco, McQuarters 4-77, Levy 2-41.

PUNT RETURNS—Indianapolis, Poole 2-6, Belser 1-53. San Francisco, McQuarters 4-33.

SACKS—Indianapolis, McCoy 2, Morrison 1, Berry 1, E. Johnson 1. San Francisco, Bryant 1.

JETS 24, PATRIOTS 14

Monday, October 19

N.Y. Jets	7	3	0	14—24
New England	7	7	0	0—14

First Quarter
NYJ—Brady 1 pass from Testaverde (Hall kick), 4:36.
N.E.—Edwards 1 run (Vinatieri kick), 11:12.

Second Quarter
N.E.—Purnell 6 pass from Bledsoe (Vinatieri kick), 6:38.
NYJ—FG, Hall 23, 15:00.

Fourth Quarter
NYJ—Brady 1 pass from Testaverde (Hall kick), 6:06.
NYJ—Ward 43 pass from Testaverde (Hall kick), 11:31.
Attendance—60,062.

	N.Y. Jets	New England
First downs	25	19
Rushes-yards	33-121	24-110
Passing	271	181
Punt returns	3-26	1-1
Kickoff returns	3-72	4-96
Interception returns	1-0	0-0
Comp.-att.-int.	22-32-0	18-30-1
Sacked-yards lost	4-23	4-25
Punts	3-39	4-41
Fumbles-lost	0-0	0-0
Penalties-yards	7-61	11-71
Time of possession	30:48	29:12

INDIVIDUAL STATISTICS

RUSHING—New York, Martin 28-107, L. Johnson 3-16, Testaverde 2-(minus 2). New England, Edwards 22-104, Bledsoe 1-5, Cullors 1-1.

PASSING—New York, Testaverde 22-32-0-294. New England, Bledsoe 18-30-1-206.

RECEIVING—New York, Chrebet 5-59, Brady 5-40, K. Johnson 4-78, Ward 2-60, L. Johnson 2-16, Van Dyke 1-15, Sowell 1-11, Martin 1-9, Byars 1-6. New England, Brown 4-41, Edwards 4-24, Jefferson 2-40, Coates 2-36, Glenn 2-34, Ton. Carter 2-21, Purnell 2-10.

MISSED FIELD GOAL ATTEMPTS—New York, Hall 38.

INTERCEPTIONS—New York, Glenn 1-0.

KICKOFF RETURNS—New York, Glenn 2-56, L. Johnson 1-16. New England, Canty 2-55, Cullors 2-41.

PUNT RETURNS—New York, L. Johnson 3-26. New England, Brown 1-1.

SACKS—New York, Lewis 2, Pleasant 1, Henderson 1. New England, Milloy 1, Eaton 1, McGinest 1, Sullivan 1.

WEEK 8

RESULTS

Buffalo 30, CAROLINA 14
Chicago 23, TENNESSEE 20
DENVER 37, Jacksonville 24
GREEN BAY 28, Baltimore 10
MIAMI 12, New England 9 (OT)
Minnesota 34, DETROIT 13
NEW ORLEANS 9, Tampa Bay 3
N.Y. JETS 28, Atlanta 3
OAKLAND 27, Cincinnati 10
San Francisco 28, ST. LOUIS 10
Seattle 27, SAN DIEGO 20
Pittsburgh 20, KANSAS CITY 13
  Open date: Arizona, Dallas, Indianapolis, N.Y.
Giants, Philadelphia, Washington

STANDINGS

AFC EAST

	W	L	T	Pct.
Miami	5	2	0	.714
New England	4	3	0	.571
Buffalo	4	3	0	.571
N.Y. Jets	4	3	0	.571
Indianapolis	1	6	0	.143

AFC CENTRAL

	W	L	T	Pct.
Jacksonville	5	2	0	.714
Pittsburgh	5	2	0	.714
Tennessee	3	4	0	.429
Baltimore	2	5	0	.286
Cincinnati	2	5	0	.286

AFC WEST

	W	L	T	Pct.
Denver	7	0	0	1.000
Oakland	5	2	0	.714
Kansas City	4	3	0	.571
Seattle	4	3	0	.571
San Diego	3	5	0	.375

NFC EAST

	W	L	T	Pct.
Dallas	4	3	0	.571
Arizona	3	4	0	.429
N.Y. Giants	3	4	0	.429
Philadelphia	1	6	0	.143
Washington	0	7	0	.000

NFC CENTRAL

	W	L	T	Pct.
Minnesota	7	0	0	1.000
Green Bay	5	2	0	.714
Tampa Bay	3	4	0	.429
Chicago	3	5	0	.375
Detroit	2	5	0	.286

NFC WEST

	W	L	T	Pct.
San Francisco	6	1	0	.857
Atlanta	5	2	0	.714
New Orleans	4	3	0	.571
St. Louis	2	5	0	.286
Carolina	0	7	0	.000

HIGHLIGHTS

Hero of the week: Jason Elam kicked a 63-yard field goal to tie the NFL record in the Broncos' 37-24 win over Jacksonville. The kick, at the end of the first half, matched Tom Dempsey's feat for New Orleans against Detroit on November 8, 1970. A delay-of-game penalty pushed the Broncos back 5 yards, and holder Tom Rouen said he lined up a little farther than normal behind the offensive line so the kick would tie the record. Elam also kicked 31- and 32-yard field goals in the game, making him 8-for-8 for the season.

Goat of the week: Tennessee's Al Del Greco didn't get on the field fast enough to attempt a game-tying field goal with 21 seconds left against Chicago. Late in the fourth quarter, Steve McNair threw to Willie Davis for a 13-yard gain that left the Oilers with fourth-and-3 at the Bears' 32. Del Greco thought the Oilers had a first down and didn't immediately go onto the field. Instead, punter Craig Hentrich, who hadn't attempted a field goal since 1995, tried the kick, which he drilled into his offensive line. Tennessee was penalized for having 12 men on the field when Del Greco ran on the field late, then tried to run off. The Oilers lost 23-20.

Sub of the week: Atlanta's Steve DeBerg, filling in for injured Chris Chandler, became the oldest quarterback to start an NFL game. The 44-year-old DeBerg, who hadn't started a game since 1993, showed his rust by throwing a pass that bounced off an official's head before being intercepted. DeBerg was replaced in the third quarter by Tony Graziani after going 9-of-20 for 117 yards.

Comeback of the week: Minnesota scored 24 points in the second half to erase a halftime deficit and beat Detroit, 34-13. Robert Smith scored on a 57-yard run in the third quarter, and Jimmy Hitchcock ran back an interception 79 yards in the fourth quarter. Detroit's Barry Sanders ran for 88 yards in the first half but only 39 in the second. The Vikings improved to 7-0.

Blowout of the week: Curtis Martin ran for more than 100 yards in his fourth straight game as the Jets pounded the Falcons, 28-3. Vinny Testaverde threw for 206 yards and two touchdowns, and Jerome Henderson returned a fumble 53 yards for a score. New York held the NFC's leading rusher, Jamal Anderson, to 46 yards.

Nail-biter of the week: Miami kicker Olindo Mare tied the game with 49 seconds left, then won it with a 43-yarder in overtime against AFC East rival New England. Mare and Patriots kicker Adam Vinatieri accounted for all the points in the Dolphins' 12-9 win. Dan Marino directed a nine-play drive that led to the tying field goal after Vinatieri gave the Patriots a 9-6 lead with 2:13 left in the fourth quarter.

Hit of the week: Oakland's Darrell Russell knocked the ball out of Bengals quarterback Neil O'Donnell's hands and Lance Johnstone returned the fumble 40 yards for a touchdown. The play, with 2:07 left in the first half, gave the Raiders a 21-7 lead. Russell had two sacks in Oakland's 27-10 win.

Oddity of the week: Chargers cornerback Terrance Shaw and Seattle receiver Joey Galloway both caught the same pass from John Friesz, so whose ball is it, anyway? Seattle's, the officials ruled. The Seahawks, who got the ball at the San Diego 2, scored two plays later to take a 27-17 lead with 8:43 left in the game. Back judge Bobby Skelton, who fell down in the end zone on the play, ruled it a simultaneous catch, giving possession to the offensive team. The Chargers claimed Shaw caught the ball first, then Galloway muscled in. Shaw received an unsportsmanlike conduct penalty and was ejected for arguing.

Top rusher: Napoleon Kaufman ran for 143 yards on 31 carries in Oakland's win over Cincinnati.

Top passer: Mark Brunell, despite being sacked seven times, was 28-for-46 for 353 yards and three touchdowns in Jacksonville's loss at Denver.

Top receiver: Eric Moulds caught five passes for 145 yards and two touchdowns in Buffalo's fourth win in a row, 30-14 over Carolina.

Notes: Terrell Davis became the third NFL player to rush for 1,000 yards in his first seven games of a season. Davis' 136-yard performance put him at 1,001 yards. O.J. Simpson (in 1973 and '75) and Jim Brown (1958) also reached the milestone in seven games. . . . Packers quarterback Brett Favre started his 100th consecutive game, a streak which began on September 27, 1992. . . . Roy Barker sacked Rams quarterback Tony Banks four times in the 49ers' 28-10 win. . . . Jerry Rice caught a pass in his 184th consecutive game to break Art Monk's NFL record. The record-breaker, a 12-yard touchdown pass from Steve Young, also tied the mark for touchdowns by a quarterback-receiver duo. Dan Marino and Mark Clayton hooked up 79 times for the Dolphins. One record run ended: Young's string of six 300-yard passing games. . . . Minnesota's Gary Anderson, the NFL all-time leader in field goals, kicked No. 400.

Quote of the Week: Del Greco, explaining the botched game-tying field-goal attempt: "I heard them yelling for Dave (Krieg) to get in there, so I started running over. I tried to run on the field, but I saw Craig (Hentrich) was on there to kick it, so I tried to run off. . . . I should have known better."

GAME SUMMARIES

VIKINGS 34, LIONS 13

Sunday, October 25

Minnesota	0	10	17	7—34
Detroit	3	10	0	0—13

First Quarter
Det.—FG, Hanson 47, 12:29.
Second Quarter
Min.—Reed 11 pass from Cunningham (Anderson kick), 3:10.
Det.—Morton 1 pass from Batch (Hanson kick), 10:45.
Min.—FG, Anderson 35, 13:44.
Det.—FG, Hanson 48, 15:00.
Third Quarter
Min.—FG, Anderson 44, 7:45.
Min.—Carter 10 pass from Cunningham (Anderson kick), 10:18.
Min —R. Smith 57 run (Anderson kick), 13:22.
Fourth Quarter
Min.—Hitchcock 79 interception return (Anderson kick), 10:52.
Attendance—77,885.

	Minnesota	Detroit
First downs	23	17
Rushes-yards	28-157	28-137
Passing	172	214
Punt returns	5-26	0-0
Kickoff returns	2-70	4-85
Interception returns	1-79	2-0
Comp.-att.-int.	17-30-2	20-37-1
Sacked-yards lost	3-18	4-17
Punts	2-49	8-45
Fumbles-lost	1-1	0-0
Penalties-yards	7-55	14-169
Time of possession	27:00	33:00

INDIVIDUAL STATISTICS
RUSHING—Minnesota, R. Smith 19-134, Hoard 6-23, Cunningham 1-4, Fiedler 1-(minus 2), Palmer 1-(minus 2). Detroit, Sanders 24-127, Batch 2-8, Rivers 1-2, Vardell 1-0.
PASSING—Minnesota, Cunningham 17-30-2-190. Detroit, Batch 20-37-1-231.
RECEIVING—Minnesota, Carter 5-73, Palmer 4-50, Reed 4-38, R. Moss 2-14, Glover 1-11, Hoard 1-4. Detroit, Morton 7-89, Sanders 6-51, Moore 4-42, Sloan 2-40, Vardell 1-9.
MISSED FIELD GOAL ATTEMPTS—None.
INTERCEPTIONS—Minnesota, Hitchcock 1-79. Detroit, Carrier 1-0, Westbrook 1-0.
KICKOFF RETURNS—Minnesota, Palmer 2-70. Detroit, Fair 4-85.
PUNT RETURNS—Minnesota, Palmer 5-26.
SACKS—Minnesota, Randle 2, Colinet 1, E. McDaniel 0.5, Fisk 0.5. Detroit, Scroggins 2, Fredrickson 1.

JETS 28, FALCONS 3

Sunday, October 25

Atlanta	0	3	0	0— 3
N.Y. Jets	7	7	14	0—28

First Quarter
NYJ—Martin 2 run (Hall kick), 12:14.
Second Quarter
NYJ—Henderson 53 fumble return (Hall kick), 0:09.
Atl.—FG, Andersen 53, 15:00.
Third Quarter
NYJ—K. Johnson 12 pass from Testaverde (Hall kick), 7:03.
NYJ—Byars 22 pass from Testaverde (Hall kick), 9:34.
Attendance—71,573.

	Atlanta	N.Y. Jets
First downs	13	21
Rushes-yards	21-55	34-119
Passing	152	192
Punt returns	2-11	1-5
Kickoff returns	2-56	1-32
Interception returns	0-0	2-11
Comp.-att.-int.	16-34-2	16-29-0
Sacked-yards lost	5-51	2-14
Punts	5-41	5-33
Fumbles-lost	1-1	1-0
Penalties-yards	8-55	5-38
Time of possession	27:56	32:04

INDIVIDUAL STATISTICS
RUSHING—Atlanta, J. Anderson 19-46, Graziani 1-12, Dwight 1-(minus 3). New York, Martin 25-101, L. Johnson 6-22, Foley 3-(minus 4).
PASSING—Atlanta, DeBerg 9-20-1-117, Graziani 7-14-1-86. New York, Testaverde 16-29-0-206.
RECEIVING—Atlanta, Mathis 4-37, Christian 3-43, Kinchen 3-35, Santiago 2-32, J. Anderson 2-26, Dwight 1-20, Martin 1-10. New York, Chrebet 4-54, Byars 3-38, Martin 3-35, L. Johnson 2-28, K. Johnson 2-20, Brady 1-26, Spence 1-5.
MISSED FIELD GOAL ATTEMPTS—None.
INTERCEPTIONS—New York, Lewis 1-11, Glenn 1-0.
KICKOFF RETURNS—Atlanta, Dwight 2-56. New York, L. Johnson 1-32.
PUNT RETURNS—Atlanta, Dwight 1-10, Kinchen 1-1. New York, L. Johnson 1-5.
SACKS—Atlanta, Archambeau 2. New York, Lewis 1, Lyle 1, Ferguson 1, Green 1, Pleasant 1.

49ERS 28, RAMS 10

Sunday, October 25

San Francisco	14	0	7	7—28
St. Louis	0	3	0	7—10

First Quarter
S.F.—Rice 12 pass from S. Young (Richey kick), 0:27.
S.F.—I. Smith 2 pass from S. Young (Richey kick), 12:54.
Second Quarter
St.L.—FG, Wilkins 46, 14:13.
Third Quarter
S.F.—Owens 27 pass from S. Young (Richey kick), 12:53.
Fourth Quarter
St.L.—Banks 6 run (Wilkins kick), 3:16.
S.F.—Owens 21 run (Richey kick), 3:35.
Attendance—58,563.

	San Fran.	St. Louis
First downs	16	15
Rushes-yards	30-93	24-79
Passing	210	89
Punt returns	4-(-7)	4-2
Kickoff returns	2-30	3-67
Interception returns	3-36	2-30
Comp.-att.-int.	13-24-2	15-35-3
Sacked-yards lost	3-17	8-32
Punts	7-41	8-43
Fumbles-lost	1-0	2-1
Penalties-yards	9-59	4-28
Time of possession	29:42	30:18

INDIVIDUAL STATISTICS

RUSHING—San Francisco, Hearst 20-58, S. Young 5-5, Levy 3-2, Owens 1-21, Edwards 1-7. St. Louis, Holcombe 12-18, Banks 6-21, Lee 4-19, J. Moore 1-18, Harris 1-3.

PASSING—San Francisco, S. Young 13-24-2-227. St. Louis, Banks 15-35-3-121.

RECEIVING—San Francisco, Owens 5-120, Rice 4-64, Uwaezuoke 1-35, Hearst 1-4, Edwards 1-2, I. Smith 1-2. St. Louis, Proehl 6-69, J. Thomas 3-18, Conwell 3-17, Henley 2-9, Holcombe 1-8.

MISSED FIELD GOAL ATTEMPTS—None.

INTERCEPTIONS—San Francisco, Walker 2-36, Pope 1-0. St. Louis, Lyght 1-17, M. A. Jones 1-13.

KICKOFF RETURNS—San Francisco, Levy 2-30. St. Louis, Horne 3-67.

PUNT RETURNS—San Francisco, McQuarters 4-(minus 7). St. Louis, Kennison 4-2.

SACKS—San Francisco, Barker 4, B. Young 1, McDonald 1, Norton 1, Bryant 1. St. Louis, Carter 1, Phifer 1, Wistrom 1.

PACKERS 28, RAVENS 10

Sunday, October 25

Baltimore	0	0	3	7—10
Green Bay	14	0	14	0—28

First Quarter
G.B.—Preston 71 punt return (Longwell kick), 1:47.
G.B.—Freeman 4 pass from Favre (Longwell kick), 14:15.

Third Quarter
G.B.—R. Brooks 28 pass from Favre (Longwell kick), 2:13.
Bal.—FG, Stover 38, 4:58.
G.B.—Favre 4 run (Longwell kick), 8:46.

Fourth Quarter
Bal.—J. Lewis 46 pass from Harbaugh (Stover kick), 8:26.
Attendance—59,860.

	Baltimore	Green Bay
First downs	11	20
Rushes-yards	17-56	33-76
Passing	177	252
Punt returns	3-14	3-75
Kickoff returns	5-120	3-56
Interception returns	2-10	2-7
Comp.-att.-int.	17-39-2	22-41-2
Sacked-yards lost	4-31	1-8
Punts	9-40	7-43
Fumbles-lost	1-0	2-0
Penalties-yards	12-98	9-70
Time of possession	26:07	33:53

INDIVIDUAL STATISTICS

RUSHING—Baltimore, Holmes 10-41, Rhett 4-13, Harbaugh 1-2, Cotton 1-1, Potts 1-(minus 1). Green Bay, Jervey 29-72, Favre 3-2, R. Brooks 1-2.

PASSING—Baltimore, Harbaugh 9-20-2-174, Zeier 8-19-0-34. Green Bay, Favre 22-41-2-260.

RECEIVING—Baltimore, J. Lewis 6-79, Holmes 4-25, Jackson 2-63, Kinchen 2-17, Potts 2-12, Turner 1-12. Green Bay, Freeman 9-103, Chmura 4-54, R. Brooks 3-54, T. Davis 3-20, R. Harris 1-12, Jervey 1-11, Schroeder 1-6.

MISSED FIELD GOAL ATTEMPTS—Baltimore, Stover 45.

INTERCEPTIONS—Baltimore, Woodson 1-10, Staten 1-0. Green Bay, Ty. Williams 1-7, Butler 1-0.

KICKOFF RETURNS—Baltimore, C. Harris 3-89, Cotton 1-18, Roe 1-13. Green Bay, Preston 3-56.

PUNT RETURNS—Baltimore, J. Lewis 3-14. Green Bay, Preston 3-75.

SACKS—Baltimore, J. Jones 0.5, Boulware 0.5. Green Bay, B. Williams 1, Booker 1, Holliday 1, S. Dotson 1.

SAINTS 9, BUCCANEERS 3

Sunday, October 25

Tampa Bay	0	0	3	0—3
New Orleans	0	3	3	3—9

Second Quarter
N.O.—FG, Brien 46, 4:38.

Third Quarter
T.B.—FG, Husted 52, 2:29.
N.O.—FG, Brien 50, 5:45.

Fourth Quarter
N.O.—FG, Brien 41, 7:45.
Attendance—52,695.

	Tampa Bay	New Orleans
First downs	11	12
Rushes-yards	18-58	27-56
Passing	180	210
Punt returns	4-91	3-1
Kickoff returns	4-110	1-27
Interception returns	0-0	2-29
Comp.-att.-int.	20-44-2	20-32-0
Sacked-yards lost	1-6	1-6
Punts	6-39	9-43
Fumbles-lost	1-1	1-1
Penalties-yards	5-55	9-65
Time of possession	27:58	32:02

INDIVIDUAL STATISTICS

RUSHING—Tampa Bay, Dunn 11-46, Alstott 7-12. New Orleans, T. Davis 18-48, Craver 4-12, Zellars 2-1, Tolliver 2-(minus 7), Hastings 1-2.

PASSING—Tampa Bay, Dilfer 20-44-2-186. New Orleans, Tolliver 20-32-0-216.

RECEIVING—Tampa Bay, Emanuel 6-86, Dunn 5-27, Moore 4-19, Anthony 3-49, Hape 1-5, Green 1-0. New Orleans, T. Davis 5-34, Craver 5-30, Cleeland 4-55, Dawkins 3-27, Poole 2-64, Hastings 1-6.

MISSED FIELD GOAL ATTEMPTS—Tampa Bay, Husted 32, 48.

INTERCEPTIONS—New Orleans, Knight 1-26, Cota 1-3.

KICKOFF RETURNS—Tampa Bay, Anthony 4-110. New Orleans, Ismail 1-27.

PUNT RETURNS—Tampa Bay, Green 3-83, Williams 1-8. New Orleans, Hastings 3-1.

SACKS—Tampa Bay, Upshaw 1. New Orleans, Kev. Mitchell 1.

BRONCOS 37, JAGUARS 24

Sunday, October 25

Jacksonville	3	7	7	7—24
Denver	3	24	0	10—37

First Quarter
Den.—FG, Elam 31, 4:21.
Jac.—FG, Hollis 45, 10:59.

Second Quarter
Den.—McCaffrey 41 pass from Elway (Elam kick), 0:08.
Den.—Davis 4 run (Elam kick), 3:52.
Jac.—F. Taylor 4 pass from Brunell (Hollis kick), 4:15.
Den.—Davis 1 run (Elam kick), 9:42.
Den.—FG, Elam 63, 15:00.

Third Quarter
Jac.—D. Jones 31 pass from Brunell (Hollis kick), 9:35.

Fourth Quarter
Den.—Davis 37 run (Elam kick), 0:46.
Jac.—Mitchell 2 pass from Brunell (Hollis kick), 4:25.
Den.—FG, Elam 32, 9:39.
Attendance—75,217.

	Jacksonville	Denver
First downs	24	24
Rushes-yards	16-66	36-170
Passing	282	295
Punt returns	2-18	1-10
Kickoff returns	7-223	5-120
Interception returns	0-0	0-0
Comp.-att.-int.	28-46-0	21-35-0
Sacked-yards lost	7-71	0-0
Punts	4-40	3-42
Fumbles-lost	2-1	0-0
Penalties-yards	9-56	8-54
Time of possession	26:13	33:47

INDIVIDUAL STATISTICS

RUSHING—Jacksonville, F. Taylor 6-27, Brunell 5-16, Shelton 3-21, G. Jones 2-2. Denver, Davis 31-136, Elway 2-16, Loville 2-10, R. Smith 1-8.

PASSING—Jacksonville, Brunell 28-46-0-353. Denver, Elway 21-35-0-295.

RECEIVING—Jacksonville, McCardell 9-113, J. Smith 8-121, F. Taylor 5-50, Mitchell 3-13, D. Jones 1-31, Barlow 1-20, Shelton 1-5. Denver, R. Smith 6-51, Davis 5-76, Sharpe 4-61, McCaffrey 3-92, Griffith 2-7, Carswell 1-8.

MISSED FIELD GOAL ATTEMPTS—Jacksonville, Hollis 51.

INTERCEPTIONS—None.

KICKOFF RETURNS—Jacksonville, Barlow 6-206, Logan 1-17. Denver, Hebron 4-110, Loville 1-10.

PUNT RETURNS—Jacksonville, Logan 1-17, Barlow 1-1. Denver, Gordon 1-10.

SACKS—Denver, Pryce 2, Romanowski 1.5, Hasselbach 1, Cadrez 1, N. Smith 1, Crockett 0.5.

BEARS 23, OILERS 20

Sunday, October 25

Chicago	7	3	10	3—23
Tennessee	0	10	0	10—20

First Quarter
Chi.—Chancey 1 run (Jaeger kick), 3:05.
Second Quarter
Ten.—FG, Del Greco 29, 0:13.
Chi.—FG, Jaeger 39, 13:05.
Ten.—Mason 13 pass from McNair (Del Greco kick), 14:36.
Third Quarter
Chi.—Hallock 6 run (Jaeger kick), 3:19.
Chi.—FG, Jaeger 26, 9:44.
Fourth Quarter
Ten.—FG, Del Greco 19, 1:28.
Ten.—Thomas 7 run (Del Greco kick), 11:16.
Chi.—FG, Jaeger 33, 13:57.
Attendance—40,089.

	Chicago	Tennessee
First downs	20	25
Rushes-yards	41-148	28-180
Passing	138	176
Punt returns	1-10	2-0
Kickoff returns	2-77	6-122
Interception returns	1-0	0-0
Comp.-att.-int.	13-24-0	18-29-1
Sacked-yards lost	1-6	4-11
Punts	3-39	2-58
Fumbles-lost	1-1	5-3
Penalties-yards	7-45	6-40
Time of possession	33:02	26:58

INDIVIDUAL STATISTICS

RUSHING—Chicago, Enis 21-85, Bennett 14-45, Kramer 3-9, Hallock 1-6, Conway 1-2, Chancey 1-1. Tennessee, E. George 21-137, McNair 4-42, Thomas 2-10, Sanders 1-(minus 9).

PASSING—Chicago, Kramer 13-24-0-144. Tennessee, McNair 18-29-1-187.

RECEIVING—Chicago, Conway 4-51, Engram 4-27, Penn 2-24, Bennett 1-18, Chancey 1-15, Hallock 1-9. Tennessee, Harris 6-53, E. George 3-22, Mason 2-28, Davis 2-21, Roan 2-7, Byrd 1-18, Wycheck 1-13, Dyson 1-5, Thomas 0-20.

MISSED FIELD GOAL ATTEMPTS—Chicago, Jaeger 34. Tennessee, Hentrich 49.

INTERCEPTIONS—Chicago, W. Harris 1-0.

KICKOFF RETURNS—Chicago, Milburn 2-77. Tennessee, Archie 6-122.

PUNT RETURNS—Chicago, Milburn 1-10. Tennessee, Archie 2-0.

SACKS—Chicago, Reeves 1, Thierry 1, Wells 1, Flanigan 1. Tennessee, Evans 1.

SEAHAWKS 27, CHARGERS 20

Sunday, October 25

Seattle	7	10	3	7—27
San Diego	0	10	7	3—20

First Quarter
Sea.—Galloway 81 pass from Friesz (Peterson kick), 6:14.
Second Quarter
S.D.—FG, Carney 21, 4:14.
Sea.—FG, Peterson 40, 6:09.
Sea.—Galloway 74 punt return (Peterson kick), 7:34.
S.D.—Ricks 5 pass from Leaf (Carney kick), 14:27.
Third Quarter
S.D.—Means 1 run (Carney kick), 9:25.
Sea.—FG, Peterson 23, 14:06.
Fourth Quarter
Sea.—Watters 1 run (Peterson kick), 6:17.
S.D.—FG, Carney 45, 10:44.
Attendance—58,512.

	Seattle	San Diego
First downs	14	27
Rushes-yards	22-40	32-111
Passing	234	280
Punt returns	4-90	1-13
Kickoff returns	5-194	5-114
Interception returns	0-0	0-0
Comp.-att.-int.	14-21-0	25-52-0
Sacked-yards lost	0-0	1-1
Punts	4-41	6-47
Fumbles-lost	1-0	0-0
Penalties-yards	8-66	10-65
Time of possession	21:54	38:06

INDIVIDUAL STATISTICS

RUSHING—Seattle, Watters 18-32, Friesz 3-7, Green 1-1. San Diego, Means 27-92, Leaf 3-18, Bynum 1-1, Stephens 1-0.

PASSING—Seattle, Friesz 14-21-0-234. San Diego, Leaf 25-52-0-281.

RECEIVING—Seattle, Watters 5-56, Galloway 4-130, Pritchard 3-34, Br. Blades 1-11, Green 1-3. San Diego, C. Jones 6-85, F. Jones 6-81, Still 6-58, Ricks 5-55, Means 2-2.

MISSED FIELD GOAL ATTEMPTS—None.

INTERCEPTIONS—None.

KICKOFF RETURNS—Seattle, Broussard 2-93, Green 2-89, R. Brown 1-12. San Diego, Bynum 3-66, Stephens 2-48.

PUNT RETURNS—Seattle, Galloway 4-90. San Diego, Rachal 1-13.

SACKS—Seattle, Sinclair 1.

BILLS 30, PANTHERS 14

Sunday, October 25

Buffalo	10	7	10	3—30
Carolina	0	7	0	7—14

First Quarter
Buf.—Moulds 20 pass from Flutie (Christie kick), 4:00.
Buf.—FG, Christie 42, 9:40.
Second Quarter
Car.—Floyd 1 run (Kasay kick), 6:08.
Buf.—Moulds 82 pass from Flutie (Christie kick), 7:59.
Third Quarter
Buf.—FG, Christie 47, 10:32.
Buf.—Thomas 17 run (Christie kick), 14:19.
Fourth Quarter
Buf.—FG, Christie 44, 9:09.
Car.—Carrier 8 pass from Beuerlein (Kasay kick), 11:22.
Attendance—64,050.

	Buffalo	Carolina
First downs	19	21
Rushes-yards	34-144	22-81
Passing	282	279
Punt returns	0-0	1-10
Kickoff returns	2-32	6-139
Interception returns	2-0	1-0
Comp.-att.-int.	18-22-1	22-40-2
Sacked-yards lost	0-0	2-7
Punts	2-46	4-41
Fumbles-lost	1-0	1-1
Penalties-yards	7-63	10-69
Time of possession	33:28	26:32

INDIVIDUAL STATISTICS

RUSHING—Buffalo, A. Smith 11-44, Linton 10-53, Thomas 7-19, Flutie 5-27, Gash 1-1. Carolina, Lane 18-74, Floyd 2-5, Beuerlein 1-1, Ismail 1-1.

PASSING—Buffalo, Flutie 18-22-1-282. Carolina, Beuerlein 22-39-2-286, Walter 0-1-0-0.

RECEIVING—Buffalo, Moulds 5-145, K. Williams 2-31, Thomas 2-26, Gash 2-22, Riemersma 2-19, Reed 2-17, L. Johnson 1-17, Early 1-9, A. Smith 1-(minus 4). Carolina, Muhammad 6-66, Carrier 5-100, Ismail 4-49, Walls 3-39, Johnson 2-22, Stone 1-7, Lane 1-3.

MISSED FIELD GOAL ATTEMPTS—None.

INTERCEPTIONS—Buffalo, Jackson 1-0, Jones 1-0. Carolina, Greene 1-0.

KICKOFF RETURNS—Buffalo, K. Williams 2-32. Carolina, Bates 5-121, Oliver 1-18.

PUNT RETURNS—Carolina, Oliver 1-10.

SACKS—Buffalo, Hansen 1, Price 1.

DOLPHINS 12, PATRIOTS 9

Sunday, October 25

New England	0	0	3	6	0— 9
Miami	0	3	0	6	3—12

Second Quarter
Mia.—FG, Mare 48, 4:34.

Third Quarter
N.E.—FG, Vinatieri 41, 8:50.

Fourth Quarter
N.E.—FG, Vinatieri 30, 5:50.
Mia.—FG, Mare 38, 9:53.
N.E.—FG, Vinatieri 36, 12:47.
Mia.—FG, Mare 25, 14:11.

Overtime
Mia.—FG, Mare 43, 4:36.
Attendance—73,973.

	New England	Miami
First downs	13	18
Rushes-yards	22-26	29-70
Passing	225	263
Punt returns	3-65	2-26
Kickoff returns	4-73	5-104
Interception returns	3-19	1-0
Comp.-att.-int.	13-33-1	23-42-3
Sacked-yards lost	2-15	3-16
Punts	7-44	6-46
Fumbles-lost	2-0	4-0
Penalties-yards	6-64	8-86
Time of possession	25:36	39:00

INDIVIDUAL STATISTICS

RUSHING—New England, Edwards 19-27, Bledsoe 2-(minus 2), S. Shaw 1-1. Miami, Abdul-Jabbar 21-56, Avery 6-17, Marino 1-(minus 1), Parmalee 1-(minus 2).

PASSING—New England, Bledsoe 13-33-1-240. Miami, Marino 23-42-3-279.

RECEIVING—New England, Jefferson 4-116, Coates 4-49, Edwards 3-26, Simmons 1-47, Purnell 1-2. Miami, McDuffie 6-77, Gadsden 4-59, Perry 3-25, Abdul-Jabbar 3-12, Parmalee 2-36, Drayton 2-35, L. Thomas 2-28, Avery 1-7.

MISSED FIELD GOAL ATTEMPTS—New England, Vinatieri 45.

INTERCEPTIONS—New England, Clay 1-19, Law 1-0, Whigham 1-0. Miami, Walker 1-0.

KICKOFF RETURNS—New England, Cullors 4-73. Miami, Avery 5-104.

PUNT RETURNS—New England, Canty 3-65. Miami, Buckley 2-26.

SACKS—New England, Mitchell 1, Eaton 1, Thomas 1. Miami, Gardener 1, Burton 1.

RAIDERS 27, BENGALS 10

Sunday, October 25

Cincinnati	0	7	3	0—10
Oakland	7	14	3	3—27

First Quarter
Oak.—T. Brown 19 pass from Hollas (G. Davis kick), 12:39.

Second Quarter
Cin.—Dillon 17 pass from O'Donnell (Pelfrey kick), 8:35.
Oak.—Jett 39 pass from Hollas (G. Davis kick), 10:42.
Oak.—Johnstone 40 fumble return (G. Davis kick), 12:53.

Third Quarter
Cin.—FG, Pelfrey 51, 5:52.
Oak.—FG, G. Davis 22, 14:24.

Fourth Quarter
Oak.—FG, G. Davis 48, 4:56.
Attendance—40,089.

	Cincinnati	Oakland
First downs	14	22
Rushes-yards	16-62	53-251
Passing	108	160
Punt returns	2-13	3-12
Kickoff returns	3-88	2-42

	Cincinnati	Oakland
Interception returns	0-0	1-22
Comp.-att.-int.	17-30-1	9-21-0
Sacked-yards lost	6-40	2-13
Punts	7-48	4-41
Fumbles-lost	2-2	0-0
Penalties-yards	7-70	11-84
Time of possession	22:51	37:09

INDIVIDUAL STATISTICS

RUSHING—Cincinnati, Dillon 13-59, Bennett 2-1, Blake 1-2. Oakland, Kaufman 31-143, H. Williams 14-63, Hollas 8-45.

PASSING—Cincinnati, O'Donnell 16-26-0-137, Blake 1-4-1-11. Oakland, Hollas 9-21-0-173.

RECEIVING—Cincinnati, McGee 3-35, Scott 3-29, Dillon 3-25, Pickens 2-22, Bieniemy 2-17, Gibson 2-14, Milne 2-6. Oakland, T. Brown 3-49, H. Williams 2-14, Jett 1-39, Mickens 1-30, Dudley 1-29, Kaufman 1-12.

MISSED FIELD GOAL ATTEMPTS—Cincinnati, Pelfrey 53. Oakland, G. Davis 28, 48.

INTERCEPTIONS—Oakland, Allen 1-22.

KICKOFF RETURNS—Cincinnati, Mack 3-88. Oakland, Howard 2-42.

PUNT RETURNS—Cincinnati, Gibson 2-13. Oakland, Howard 3-12.

SACKS—Cincinnati, C. Simmons 2. Oakland, Russell 2, Harvey 1, Maryland 1, Wooden 1, Johnstone 1.

STEELERS 20, CHIEFS 13

Monday, October 26

Pittsburgh	7	3	3	7—20
Kansas City	3	3	7	0—13

First Quarter
Pit.—McAfee recovered blocked punt in end zone (N. Johnson kick), 5:02.
K.C.—FG, Stoyanovich 20, 9:52.

Second Quarter
K.C.—FG, Stoyanovich 28, 2:24.
Pit.—FG, N. Johnson 34, 15:00.

Third Quarter
Pit.—FG, N. Johnson 22, 9:30.
K.C.—Rison 2 pass from Grbac (Stoyanovich kick), 12:32.

Fourth Quarter
Pit.—C. Johnson 5 pass from Stewart (N. Johnson kick), 4:55.
Attendance—79,431.

	Pittsburgh	Kansas City
First downs	20	16
Rushes-yards	43-182	19-72
Passing	90	218
Punt returns	1-12	4-47
Kickoff returns	3-81	4-106
Interception returns	2-34	0-0
Comp.-att.-int.	12-23-0	15-36-2
Sacked-yards lost	1-9	2-6
Punts	6-46	5-34
Fumbles-lost	1-1	1-1
Penalties-yards	4-55	10-75
Time of possession	34:32	25:28

INDIVIDUAL STATISTICS

RUSHING—Pittsburgh, Bettis 33-119, Stewart 5-14, McAfee 3-36, Hawkins 1-10, Fuamatu-Ma'afala 1-3. Kansas City, Bennett 13-47, Morris 3-11, Anders 1-6, Grbac 1-6, Richardson 1-2.

PASSING—Pittsburgh, Stewart 11-22-0-82, Ward 1-1-0-17. Kansas City, Grbac 15-36-2-224.

RECEIVING—Pittsburgh, Dunn 2-34, Hawkins 2-16, Lester 2-9, Bettis 2-4, Stewart 1-17, Blackwell 1-13, C. Johnson 1-5, Fuamatu-Ma'afala 1-1. Kansas City, Rison 7-65, Gonzalez 3-49, Lockett 2-28, Alexander 1-65, Bennett 1-14, Popson 1-3.

MISSED FIELD GOAL ATTEMPTS—None.

INTERCEPTIONS—Pittsburgh, Perry 1-40, Lake 1-(minus 6).

KICKOFF RETURNS—Pittsburgh, Blackwell 3-81. Kansas City, Vanover 3-69, Horn 1-37.

PUNT RETURNS—Pittsburgh, Hawkins 1-12. Kansas City, Vanover 4-47.

SACKS—Pittsburgh, Gildon 1, Emmons 1. Kansas City, Davis 1.

WEEK 9

RESULTS

Arizona 17, DETROIT 15
ATLANTA 37, St. Louis 15
BUFFALO 30, Miami 24
CAROLINA 31, New Orleans 17
Denver 33, CINCINNATI 26
GREEN BAY 36, San Francisco 22
Jacksonville 45, BALTIMORE 19
New England 21, INDIANAPOLIS 16
N.Y. Jets 20, KANSAS CITY 17
Oakland 31, SEATTLE 18
TAMPA BAY 27, Minnesota 24
Tennessee 41, PITTSBURGH 31
WASHINGTON 21, N.Y. Giants 14
Dallas 34, PHILADELPHIA 0
  Open date: Chicago, San Diego

STANDINGS

AFC EAST
	W	L	T	Pct.
Buffalo	5	3	0	.625
Miami	5	3	0	.625
New England	5	3	0	.625
N.Y. Jets	5	3	0	.625
Indianapolis	1	7	0	.125

AFC CENTRAL
	W	L	T	Pct.
Jacksonville	6	2	0	.750
Pittsburgh	5	3	0	.625
Tennessee	4	4	0	.500
Baltimore	2	6	0	.250
Cincinnati	2	6	0	.250

AFC WEST
	W	L	T	Pct.
Denver	8	0	0	1.000
Oakland	6	2	0	.750
Kansas City	4	4	0	.500
Seattle	4	4	0	.500
San Diego	3	5	0	.375

NFC EAST
	W	L	T	Pct.
Dallas	5	3	0	.625
Arizona	4	4	0	.500
N.Y. Giants	3	5	0	.375
Philadelphia	1	7	0	.125
Washington	1	7	0	.125

NFC CENTRAL
	W	L	T	Pct.
Minnesota	7	1	0	.875
Green Bay	6	2	0	.750
Tampa Bay	4	4	0	.500
Chicago	3	5	0	.375
Detroit	2	6	0	.250

NFC WEST
	W	L	T	Pct.
Atlanta	6	2	0	.750
San Francisco	6	2	0	.750
New Orleans	4	4	0	.500
St. Louis	2	6	0	.250
Carolina	1	7	0	.125

HIGHLIGHTS

Hero of the week: John Elway led Denver to three touchdowns in the fourth quarter as the Broncos rallied to beat Cincinnati, 33-26, and stay unbeaten. Elway threw a 25-yard touchdown pass to Ed McCaffrey to give Denver a 26-18 lead with 5:04 left. After Cincinnati tied the score at 26, Elway directed a five-play, 53-yard drive that ended with a Terrell Davis touchdown run with 58 seconds left. The drive included passes of 30 and 14 yards from Elway to McCaffrey.

Goat of the week: Colts cornerback Jeff Burris was called for pass interference three times in New England's 21-16 win at Indianapolis. The first two penalties set up New England touchdowns, and the third was declined after Tony Simmons caught the pass from Drew Bledsoe for a 63-yard touchdown. Burris, a five-year veteran, tried to break up the long pass, but Simmons held on at the Colts' 20 and scored.

Sub of the week: Less than a week after coming out of retirement, New England receiver Henry Ellard caught three passes for 52 yards. Ellard, 37, in his 16th NFL season, was signed because of injuries to Terry Glenn, Troy Brown and Vincent Brisby.

Comeback of the week: Doug Flutie lifted Buffalo from a 10-point fourth-quarter deficit to a 30-24 win over Miami. Less than two minutes after the Dolphins took a 24-14 lead, Flutie threw a 48-yard touchdown pass to Eric Moulds. Three snaps after that score, Phil Hansen recovered a Dan Marino fumble to set up Steve Christie's 22-yard field goal. Christie kicked two more field goals in the final two minutes. Marino threw a long pass to O.J. McDuffie on the final play. McDuffie caught the ball at the 4 but couldn't reach the end zone.

Blowout of the week: Dallas whipped Philadelphia 34-0 in the Monday night game to drop the Eagles to 1-7, their worst start since 1975. Troy Aikman returned after missing five games because of a broken collarbone and went 14-for-26 for 171 yards and two touchdowns. Deion Sanders returned a punt 69 yards for a touchdown, and Michael Irvin scored his first touchdown of the season. Bobby Hoying replaced Eagles starting quarterback Rodney Peete

and fumbled the handoff on his first play, setting up a Dallas touchdown two plays later.

Nail-biter of the week: John Hall kicked a 32-yard field goal as time expired to give the Jets a 20-17 win over Kansas City. New York got the ball with 1:50 left on the Kansas City 43 after Louie Aguiar's 25-yard punt, and Vinny Testaverde drove the Jets 30 yards on seven plays. The Chiefs moved the winning kick a little closer when Derrick Thomas jumped offside as Hall lined up for a 37-yard attempt.

Hit of the week: Jacksonville defenders Kevin Hardy and Donovin Darius mashed Baltimore tight end Eric Green, who fumbled at the Ravens' 25-yard line. Joel Smeenge recovered, and Jaguars scored a touchdown after a seven-play drive to take a 21-7 lead.

Oddity of the week: Both of the league's winless teams won their first games. Carolina beat New Orleans 31-17 as Steve Beuerlein threw for 132 yards and two touchdowns and cornerback Eric Davis returned an interception 56 yards for a touchdown. In Landover, Md., rookie running back Skip Hicks rushed for 65 yards and scored the winning touchdown in the third quarter as Washington beat the Giants, 21-14.

Top rusher: Jamal Anderson rushed for a career-high 172 yards on 22 carries and ran for two touchdowns and caught a TD pass as Atlanta pounded St. Louis, 37-15.

Top passer: New Orleans' Billy Joe Tolliver was 24-for-48 with 325 yards and two touchdowns in the Saints' loss to the Panthers.

Top receiver: Antonio Freeman caught seven passes for 193 yards and scored two touchdowns in the Packers' win over San Francisco.

Notes: Steve Young rushed for his 41st career touchdown, breaking Jack Kemp's NFL record. Young also threw a touchdown pass to Jerry Rice for the 80th time, breaking the record for most touchdowns by a quarterback-receiver duo. Dan Marino and Mark Clayton hooked up 79 times. The Packers sacked Young nine times, including three by Reggie White. . . . Seattle quarterback Warren Moon completed his first 17 passes against Oakland. His 18th was intercepted by Albert Lewis and returned 74 yards for a touchdown. . . . Doug Flutie improved to 3-0 in matchups with Dan Marino. . . . Jacksonville scored 42 points in the first half against Baltimore, including five touchdowns in a span of 13:43. . . . Denver's Shannon Sharpe caught his 500th pass to become the third tight end to reach that mark. Sharpe joined Ozzie Newsome (662) and Kellen Winslow (541) in the 500 club. . . . The crowd in Charlotte's Ericsson Stadium heckled former Panthers quarterback Kerry Collins throughout the game, even though Collins didn't play. Collins, Carolina's first-ever draft pick, was cut in October after saying he didn't have the heart to play. The Saints signed Collins, but coach Mike Ditka didn't use him at Carolina.

Quote of the week: Chiefs coach Marty Schottenheimer, after his team lost its third consecutive game to fall to 4-4: "We have been on the winning side and clearly, it's a lot easier to cope with winning."

GAME SUMMARIES

BILLS 30, DOLPHINS 24

Sunday, November 1

Miami	7	7	7	3—24
Buffalo	0	14	0	16—30

First Quarter
Mia.—Gadsden 12 pass from Marino (Mare kick), 10:08.
Second Quarter
Buf.—Riemersma 1 pass from Flutie (Christie kick), 2:12.
Mia.—Abdul-Jabbar 1 run (Mare kick), 8:06.
Buf.—Riemersma 16 pass from Flutie (Christie kick), 13:58.
Third Quarter
Mia.—Avery 1 run (Mare kick), 4:52.
Fourth Quarter
Mia.—FG, Mare 38, 1:21.
Buf.—Moulds 48 pass from Flutie (Christie kick), 3:14.
Buf.—FG, Christie 22, 5:06.
Buf.—FG, Christie 36, 13:02.
Buf.—FG, Christie 25, 14:37.
Attendance—79,011.

	Miami	Buffalo
First downs	15	16
Rushes-yards	33-128	30-116
Passing	168	197
Punt returns	3-11	0-0
Kickoff returns	6-180	5-92
Interception returns	1-0	0-0
Comp.-att.-int.	15-27-0	15-26-1
Sacked-yards lost	3-28	1-9
Punts	5-35	3-46
Fumbles-lost	1-1	1-1
Penalties-yards	5-35	4-27
Time of possession	31:33	28:27

INDIVIDUAL STATISTICS
RUSHING—Miami, Abdul-Jabbar 22-97, Avery 9-17, Marino 1-10, Parmalee 1-4. Buffalo, A. Smith 21-82, Thomas 6-23, Flutie 2-9, Gash 1-2.
PASSING—Miami, Marino 15-27-0-196. Buffalo, Flutie 15-26-1-206.
RECEIVING—Miami, Gadsden 3-68, McDuffie 3-57, L. Thomas 2-34, Drayton 2-13, Abdul-Jabbar 2-9, Parmalee 2-7, Perry 1-8. Buffalo, Reed 5-72, Moulds 3-61, K. Williams 2-21, Riemersma 2-17, Thomas 1-14, Gash 1-14, L. Johnson 1-7.
MISSED FIELD GOAL ATTEMPTS—Buffalo, Christie 49.
INTERCEPTIONS—Miami, Buckley 1-0.
KICKOFF RETURNS—Miami, Avery 6-180. Buffalo, K. Williams 4-77, Gash 1-15.

PUNT RETURNS—Miami, Buckley 3-11.
SACKS—Miami, Burton 1. Buffalo, Hansen 1.5, Washington 1, B. Smith 0.5.

OILERS 41, STEELERS 31

Sunday, November 1

Tennessee	3	14	10	14—41
Pittsburgh	0	7	0	24—31

First Quarter
Ten.—FG, Del Greco 43, 9:46.
Second Quarter
Ten.—Wycheck 2 pass from McNair (Del Greco kick), 5:31.
Pit.—C. Johnson 9 pass from Stewart (N. Johnson kick), 9:05.
Ten.—Dyson 6 pass from McNair (Del Greco kick), 13:55.
Third Quarter
Ten.—FG, Del Greco 32, 6:28.
Ten.—E. George 37 run (Del Greco kick), 11:28.
Fourth Quarter
Ten.—Davis 29 pass from McNair (Del Greco kick), 0:13.
Pit.—Hawkins 4 pass from Stewart (C. Johnson pass from Stewart), 2:49.
Ten.—Marts 27 interception return (Del Greco kick), 4:43.
Pit.—C. Johnson 37 pass from Tomczak (C. Johnson pass from Tomczak), 6:24.
Pit.—C. Johnson 2 pass from Tomczak (Blackwell pass from Tomczak), 12:51.
Attendance—58,222.

	Tennessee	Pittsburgh
First downs	19	26
Rushes-yards	38-169	20-54
Passing	152	347
Punt returns	0-0	1-(-4)
Kickoff returns	2-31	6-119
Interception returns	3-66	0-0
Comp.-att.-int.	13-21-0	38-49-3
Sacked-yards lost	3-15	0-0
Punts	2-51	2-54
Fumbles-lost	1-0	0-0
Penalties-yards	9-108	4-41
Time of possession	32:04	27:56

INDIVIDUAL STATISTICS
RUSHING—Tennessee, E. George 34-153, McNair 3-16, Stepnoski 1-0. Pittsburgh, Bettis 11-26, McAfee 5-20, Stewart 3-4, C. Johnson 1-4.
PASSING—Tennessee, McNair 13-21-0-167. Pittsburgh, Stewart 23-32-3-230, Tomczak 15-17-0-117.
RECEIVING—Tennessee, Davis 5-88, Wycheck 3-42, Dyson 2-16, E. George 1-14, Mason 1-4, Roan 1-3. Pittsburgh, Hawkins 14-147, C. Johnson 9-115, Dunn 5-35, McAfee 4-11, Bruener 3-19, Blackwell 2-14, Bettis 1-6.
MISSED FIELD GOAL ATTEMPTS—Pittsburgh, N. Johnson 52.
INTERCEPTIONS—Tennessee, D. Lewis 1-33, Marts 1-27, D. Walker 1-6.
KICKOFF RETURNS—Tennessee, Archie 2-31. Pittsburgh, Blackwell 3-64, Dunn 2-46, Gibson 1-9.
PUNT RETURNS—Pittsburgh, Hawkins 1-(minus 4).
SACKS—Pittsburgh, Flowers 1, Steed 1, Gildon 1.

FALCONS 37, RAMS 15

Sunday, November 1

St. Louis	0	7	0	8—15
Atlanta	17	10	7	3—37

First Quarter
Atl.—J. Anderson 9 pass from Chandler (Andersen kick), 2:33.
Atl.—FG, Andersen 23, 8:28.
Atl.—J. Anderson 12 run (Andersen kick), 12:25.
Second Quarter
St.L.—McNeil 37 interception return (Wilkins kick), 2:26.
Atl.—FG, Andersen 22, 10:14.
Atl.—Martin 18 pass from Chandler (Andersen kick), 14:08.
Third Quarter
Atl.—J. Anderson 4 run (Andersen kick), 7:34.

Fourth Quarter
St.L.—R. Williams 1 pass from Banks (Banks run), 7:09.
Atl.—FG, Andersen 43, 10:59.
  Attendance—37,996.

	St. Louis	Atlanta
First downs	16	25
Rushes-yards	13-46	38-199
Passing	201	235
Punt returns	0-0	4-22
Kickoff returns	7-175	3-44
Interception returns	1-37	0-0
Comp.-att.-int.	23-37-0	13-28-1
Sacked-yards lost	3-20	1-9
Punts	6-38	1-53
Fumbles-lost	1-1	2-0
Penalties-yards	12-95	5-35
Time of possession	23:56	36:04

INDIVIDUAL STATISTICS
RUSHING—St. Louis, Henley 9-37, Holcombe 3-5, Banks 1-4. Atlanta, J. Anderson 22-172, Green 11-26, Chandler 2-1, DeBerg 2-(minus 2), Christian 1-2.

PASSING—St. Louis, Banks 23-37-0-221. Atlanta, Chandler 12-26-1-236, DeBerg 1-2-0-8.

RECEIVING—St. Louis, Henley 6-43, Proehl 5-70, J. Moore 4-32, Hakim 3-37, R. Williams 3-16, Kennison 1-12, J. Thomas 1-11. Atlanta, Mathis 5-64, Martin 3-93, Santiago 2-39, J. Anderson 2-31, Christian 1-17.

MISSED FIELD GOAL ATTEMPTS—Atlanta, Andersen 29.

INTERCEPTIONS—St. Louis, McNeil 1-37.

KICKOFF RETURNS—St. Louis, Horne 7-175. Atlanta, Green 1-24, E. Williams 1-20, Christian 1-0.

PUNT RETURNS—Atlanta, Kinchen 3-22, Mathis 1-0.

SACKS—St. Louis, Carter, 1. Atlanta, Brooking 1, C. Smith 1, Dronett 1.

PANTHERS 31, SAINTS 17
Sunday, November 1

New Orleans	0	3	0	14—17
Carolina	7	10	7	7—31

First Quarter
Car.—Muhammad 1 pass from Beuerlein (Kasay kick), 9:38.
Second Quarter
Car.—Davis 56 interception return (Kasay kick), 2:03.
N.O.—FG, Brien 49, 4:49.
Car.—FG, Kasay 54, 8:23.
Third Quarter
Car.—Lane 5 run (Kasay kick), 2:14.
Fourth Quarter
N.O.—Cleeland 2 pass from Tolliver (Brien kick), 0:48.
Car.—Ismail 33 pass from Beuerlein (Kasay kick), 5:23.
N.O.—Bech 6 pass from Tolliver (Brien kick), 13:09.
  Attendance—62,514.

	New Orleans	Carolina
First downs	21	16
Rushes-yards	15-53	38-106
Passing	301	110
Punt returns	1-0	4-44
Kickoff returns	6-102	2-65
Interception returns	1-0	2-66
Comp.-att.-int.	24-48-2	13-17-1
Sacked-yards lost	3-24	3-22
Punts	5-44	6-41
Fumbles-lost	2-2	2-1
Penalties-yards	10-60	6-62
Time of possession	27:17	32:43

INDIVIDUAL STATISTICS
RUSHING—New Orleans, T. Davis 10-41, Craver 2-4, Perry 1-7, Zellars 1-1, Tolliver 1-0. Carolina, Lane 35-101, Floyd 2-2, Beuerlein 1-3.

PASSING—New Orleans, Tolliver 24-48-2-325. Carolina, Beuerlein 13-17-1-132.

RECEIVING—New Orleans, Dawkins 6-102, Poole 5-90, T. Davis 5-19, Cleeland 3-62, Bech 3-40, Slutzker 1-10, Craver 1-2. Carolina, Walls 4-44, Muhammad 3-23, Floyd 3-15, Ismail 2-45, Johnson 1-5.

MISSED FIELD GOAL ATTEMPTS—None.

INTERCEPTIONS—New Orleans, Knight 1-0. Carolina, Davis 1-56, Barrow 1-10.

KICKOFF RETURNS—New Orleans, Ismail 6-102. Carolina, Bates 2-65.

PUNT RETURNS—New Orleans, Hastings 1-0. Carolina, Oliver 4-44.

SACKS—New Orleans, Glover 1, Tomich 1, Wilson 1. Carolina, Greene 1, Brady 1, Lloyd 1.

BUCCANEERS 27, VIKINGS 24
Sunday, November 1

Minnesota	7	10	7	0—24
Tampa Bay	7	10	0	10—27

First Quarter
T.B.—Dunn 10 run (Husted kick), 7:15.
Min.—R. Smith 9 run (Anderson kick), 11:59.
Second Quarter
T.B.—Anthony 12 pass from Dilfer (Husted kick), 4:13.
Min.—Reed 44 pass from Cunningham (Anderson kick), 10:44.
T.B.—FG, Husted 29, 14:24.
Min.—FG, Anderson 44, 15:00.
Third Quarter
Min.—Reed 1 pass from Cunningham (Anderson kick), 5:37.
Fourth Quarter
T.B.—FG, Husted 38, 3:13.
T.B.—Alstott 6 run (Husted kick), 9:12.
  Attendance—64,979.

	Minnesota	Tampa Bay
First downs	18	22
Rushes-yards	19-70	41-246
Passing	270	132
Punt returns	0-0	2-10
Kickoff returns	5-96	2-79
Interception returns	0-0	1-25
Comp.-att.-int.	21-25-1	11-22-0
Sacked-yards lost	2-21	0-0
Punts	2-43	0-0
Fumbles-lost	0-0	0-0
Penalties-yards	7-66	4-35
Time of possession	26:25	33:35

INDIVIDUAL STATISTICS
RUSHING—Minnesota, R. Smith 13-46, Cunningham 4-15, Evans 1-7, Hoard 1-2. Tampa Bay, Alstott 19-128, Dunn 18-115, Dilfer 3-1, Anthony 1-2.

PASSING—Minnesota, Cunningham 21-25-1-291. Tampa Bay, Dilfer 11-22-0-132.

RECEIVING—Minnesota, Reed 6-117, R. Smith 5-28, Glover 2-55, R. Moss 2-52, Carter 2-13, Palmer 1-8, Goodwin 1-7, DeLong 1-6, Hoard 1-5. Tampa Bay, Anthony 5-65, Dunn 4-49, Emanuel 1-15, Neal 1-3.

MISSED FIELD GOAL ATTEMPTS—None.

INTERCEPTIONS—Tampa Bay, Brooks 1-25.

KICKOFF RETURNS—Minnesota, Palmer 5-96. Tampa Bay, Anthony 2-79.

PUNT RETURNS—Tampa Bay, Green 2-10.

SACKS—Tampa Bay, Barber 1, Culpepper 1.

PATRIOTS 21, COLTS 16
Sunday, November 1

New England	7	7	0	7—21
Indianapolis	7	3	0	6—16

First Quarter
N.E.—Coates 2 pass from Bledsoe (Vinatieri kick), 8:21.
Ind.—Warren 4 run from Manning (Vanderjagt kick), 14:08.
Second Quarter
N.E.—Edwards 1 run (Vinatieri kick), 4:06.
Ind.—FG, Vanderjagt 49, 15:00.
Fourth Quarter
N.E.—Simmons 63 pass from Bledsoe (Vinatieri kick), 0:44.
Ind.—Pollard 15 pass from Manning (run failed), 11:20.
  Attendance—58,056.

	New England	Indianapolis
First downs	20	18
Rushes-yards	27-77	14-32
Passing	293	278
Punt returns	3-21	3-34
Kickoff returns	3-58	4-91
Interception returns	2-24	1-14

	New England	Indianapolis
Comp.-att.-int.	22-35-1	30-52-2
Sacked-yards lost	1-13	0-0
Punts	7-41	7-43
Fumbles-lost	1-0	0-0
Penalties-yards	6-45	8-72
Time of possession	31:34	28:26

INDIVIDUAL STATISTICS

RUSHING—New England, Edwards 23-70, S. Shaw 2-4, Cullors 1-4, Bledsoe 1-(minus 1). Indianapolis, Faulk 11-22, Warren 3-10.

PASSING—New England, Bledsoe 22-35-1-306. Indianapolis, Manning 30-52-2-278.

RECEIVING—New England, Coates 10-109, Simmons 4-109, Ellard 3-52, Edwards 3-12, Jefferson 2-24. Indianapolis, Faulk 9-119, Pathon 7-56, Pollard 5-40, Harrison 5-34, Warren 2-2, Small 1-20, Banta 1-7.

MISSED FIELD GOAL ATTEMPTS—None.

INTERCEPTIONS—New England, Milloy 2-24. Indianapolis, Blackmon 1-14.

KICKOFF RETURNS—New England, Cullors 3-58. Indianapolis, Elias 4-91.

PUNT RETURNS—New England, Canty 3-21. Indianapolis, Poole 3-34.

SACKS—Indianapolis, Belser 1.

REDSKINS 21, GIANTS 14

Sunday, November 1

N.Y. Giants	7	0	7	0—14
Washington	7	7	7	0—21

First Quarter
Was.—T. Green 1 run (Blanchard kick), 13:05.
NYG—Patten 90 kickoff return (Daluiso kick), 13:23.

Second Quarter
Was.—Davis 12 pass from T. Green (Blanchard kick), 4:23.

Third Quarter
Was.—Hicks 4 run (Blanchard kick), 4:45.
NYG—Hilliard 11 pass from Kanell (Daluiso kick), 13:55.
Attendance—67,976.

	N.Y. Giants	Washington
First downs	10	21
Rushes-yards	22-86	38-124
Passing	143	196
Punt returns	2-8	5-57
Kickoff returns	4-146	2-47
Interception returns	0-0	0-0
Comp.-att.-int.	17-32-0	21-31-0
Sacked-yards lost	1-8	4-29
Punts	11-45	10-44
Fumbles-lost	1-0	0-0
Penalties-yards	7-49	7-45
Time of possession	22:31	37:29

INDIVIDUAL STATISTICS

RUSHING—New York, Brown 12-43, Way 4-19, Kanell 4-8, Barber 2-16. Washington, Hicks 15-65, Allen 13-46, T. Green 5-0, Mitchell 4-14, Davis 1-(minus 1).

PASSING—New York, Kanell 17-32-0-151. Washington, T. Green 21-31-0-225.

RECEIVING—New York, Calloway 7-71, Hilliard 3-63, Barber 3-14, Way 2-0, Cross 1-2, Brown 1-1. Washington, Davis 5-65, Asher 5-45, Thrash 3-40, Shepherd 3-34, Connell 3-21, Mitchell 2-20.

MISSED FIELD GOAL ATTEMPTS—None.

INTERCEPTIONS—None.

KICKOFF RETURNS—New York, Patten 4-146. Washington, Mitchell 2-47.

PUNT RETURNS—New York, Toomer 2-8. Washington, Mitchell 5-57.

SACKS—New York, Jones 3, K. Hamilton 1. Washington, M. Patton 1.

BRONCOS 33, BENGALS 26

Sunday, November 1

Denver	3	3	7	20—33
Cincinnati	3	9	0	14—26

First Quarter
Cin.—FG, Pelfrey 25, 3:56.
Den.—FG, Elam 33, 10:43.

Second Quarter
Cin.—FG, Pelfrey 23, 6:23.
Den.—FG, Elam 37, 12:48.
Cin.—Gibson 17 pass from O'Donnell (run failed), 14:03.

Third Quarter
Den.—Green 17 pass from Elway (Elam kick), 3:40.

Fourth Quarter
Cin.—Hundon 11 pass from O'Donnell (pass failed), 3:00.
Den.—Davis 2 run (run failed), 7:55.
Den.—McCaffrey 25 pass from Elway (Elam kick), 9:56.
Cin.—Battaglia 1 pass from O'Donnell (Pickens pass from O'Donnell), 12:06.
Den.—Davis 5 run (Elam kick), 14:02.
Attendance—59,974.

	Denver	Cincinnati
First downs	20	25
Rushes-yards	29-150	39-127
Passing	202	245
Punt returns	1-9	2-5
Kickoff returns	6-161	7-212
Interception returns	0-0	1-1
Comp.-att.-int.	15-26-1	20-37-0
Sacked-yards lost	2-11	2-12
Punts	3-47	3-24
Fumbles-lost	1-0	1-1
Penalties-yards	9-106	6-50
Time of possession	27:34	32:26

INDIVIDUAL STATISTICS

RUSHING—Denver, Davis 27-149, Loville 1-2, Elway 1-(minus 1). Cincinnati, Dillon 35-110, Bennett 2-6, Gibson 1-9, O'Donnell 1-2.

PASSING—Denver, Elway 15-26-1-213. Cincinnati, O'Donnell 20-37-0-257.

RECEIVING—Denver, McCaffrey 7-133, Sharpe 3-35, D. Smith 2-8, Green 1-17, R. Smith 1-17, Davis 1-3. Cincinnati, Pickens 5-65, McGee 4-73, Gibson 3-66, Hundon 2-20, Milne 2-13, Battaglia 2-4, Jackson 1-11, Dillon 1-5.

MISSED FIELD GOAL ATTEMPTS—Cincinnati, Pelfrey 52.

INTERCEPTIONS—Cincinnati, Shade 1-1.

KICKOFF RETURNS—Denver, Hebron 6-161. Cincinnati, Mack 7-212.

PUNT RETURNS—Denver, Gordon 1-9. Cincinnati, Gibson 2-5.

SACKS—Denver, Williams 1, Lodish 1. Cincinnati, Bankston 1, Purvis 1.

CARDINALS 17, LIONS 15

Sunday, November 1

Arizona	0	7	7	3—17
Detroit	0	6	3	6—15

Second Quarter
Det.—FG, Hanson 28, 3:03.
Ariz.—Sanders 16 pass from Plummer (Nedney kick), 6:15.
Det.—FG, Hanson 47, 10:58.

Third Quarter
Det.—FG, Hanson 44, 4:52.
Ariz.—R. Moore 36 pass from Plummer (Nedney kick), 6:36.

Fourth Quarter
Det.—Vardell 1 run (run failed), 5:31.
Ariz.—FG, Nedney 53, 12:14.
Attendance—66,087.

	Arizona	Detroit
First downs	11	18
Rushes-yards	25-37	29-113
Passing	172	167
Punt returns	1-9	5-44
Kickoff returns	1-24	3-59
Interception returns	3-14	1-15
Comp.-att.-int.	15-25-1	20-32-3
Sacked-yards lost	4-26	5-23
Punts	7-41	3-43
Fumbles-lost	3-1	5-3
Penalties-yards	7-69	4-20
Time of possession	27:10	32:50

INDIVIDUAL STATISTICS

RUSHING—Arizona, Bates 14-32, Plummer 5-(minus 3), Pittman 4-5, Centers 2-3. Detroit, Sanders 27-107, Batch 1-5, Vardell 1-1.

PASSING—Arizona, Plummer 15-25-1-198. Detroit, Batch 10-17-3-71, Reich 10-15-0-119.

RECEIVING—Arizona, R. Moore 5-107, Centers 3-26, Metcalf 3-11, Sanders 2-21, McWilliams 1-19, Bates 1-14. Detroit, Morton 7-115, Sanders 6-17, Moore 2-26, Crowell 1-10, Rasby 1-9, Sloan 1-7, Vardell 1-4, Schlesinger 1-2.

MISSED FIELD GOAL ATTEMPTS—Arizona, Nedney 52.

INTERCEPTIONS—Arizona, McCombs 1-14, Lassiter 1-0, McKinnon 1-0. Detroit, Westbrook 1-15.

KICKOFF RETURNS—Arizona, Metcalf 1-24. Detroit, Fair 3-59.

PUNT RETURNS—Arizona, Metcalf 1-9. Detroit, Fair 5-44.

SACKS—Arizona, Rice 2, M. Smith 1, Wilson 1, Tillman 1. Detroit, S. Boyd 1, Porcher 1, Abrams 1, Team 1.

JAGUARS 45, RAVENS 19

Sunday, November 1

Jacksonville	14	28	0	3—45
Baltimore	7	6	0	6—19

First Quarter

Jac.—J. Smith 37 pass from Brunell (Hollis kick), 7:02.

Bal.—J. Lewis 6 pass from Harbaugh (Stover kick), 13:18.

Jac.—F. Taylor 78 pass from Brunell (Hollis kick), 13:41.

Second Quarter

Jac.—F. Taylor 1 run (Hollis kick), 1:29.

Jac.—Shelton 2 run (Hollis kick), 5:27.

Jac.—Whitted 24 blocked punt return (Hollis kick), 10:57.

Jac.—Darius 83 fumble return (Hollis kick), 12:01.

Bal.—Turner 5 pass from Harbaugh (pass failed), 14:14.

Fourth Quarter

Jac.—FG, Hollis 33, 5:41.

Bal.—Johnson 3 pass from Harbaugh (pass failed), 10:30.

Attendance—68,915.

	Jacksonville	Baltimore
First downs	20	22
Rushes-yards	32-111	23-126
Passing	253	231
Punt returns	2-6	2-7
Kickoff returns	3-58	8-189
Interception returns	1-0	1-0
Comp.-att.-int.	15-22-1	27-34-1
Sacked-yards lost	2-5	2-12
Punts	3-45	4-33
Fumbles-lost	0-0	5-4
Penalties-yards	10-73	9-70
Time of possession	28:04	31:56

INDIVIDUAL STATISTICS

RUSHING—Jacksonville, F. Taylor 22-87, G. Jones 8-17, Martin 1-5, Shelton 1-2. Baltimore, Harbaugh 10-57, Potts 7-48, Holmes 3-10, Rhett 2-4, Cotton 1-7.

PASSING—Jacksonville, Brunell 13-20-1-237, Martin 2-2-0-21. Baltimore, Harbaugh 27-34-1-243.

RECEIVING—Jacksonville, J. Smith 4-75, Mitchell 4-49, McCardell 2-24, Shelton 2-11, F. Taylor 1-78, Barlow 1-12, G. Jones 1-9. Baltimore, Jackson 5-40, J. Lewis 4-57, Green 4-43, Potts 4-12, Turner 3-41, Johnson 3-26, Rhett 3-20, Holmes 1-4.

MISSED FIELD GOAL ATTEMPTS—None.

INTERCEPTIONS—Jacksonville, Figures 1-0. Baltimore, Starks 1-0.

KICKOFF RETURNS—Jacksonville, Logan 2-31, Barlow 1-27. Baltimore, C. Harris 5-105, Johnson 3-84.

PUNT RETURNS—Jacksonville, Barlow 2-6. Baltimore, J. Lewis 2-7.

SACKS—Jacksonville, Paup 1, Smeenge 1. Baltimore, McCrary 1, Boulware 1.

PACKERS 36, 49ERS 22

Sunday, November 1

San Francisco	6	7	9	0—22
Green Bay	16	3	0	17—36

First Quarter

G.B.—Freeman 80 pass from Favre (Longwell kick), 0:21.

G.B.—Safety, snap by Kirk went out of end zone, 0:29.

G.B.—R. Brooks 30 pass from Favre (Longwell kick), 5:16.

S.F.—Rice 12 pass from S. Young (kick blocked), 12:13.

Second Quarter

G.B.—FG, Longwell 26, 5:32.

S.F.—S. Young 1 run (Richey kick), 11:24.

Third Quarter

S.F.—Hearst 30 run (pass failed), 4:39.

S.F.—FG, Richey 20, 10:15.

Fourth Quarter

G.B.—FG, Longwell 45, 1:46.

G.B.—Freeman 62 pass from Favre (Longwell kick), 3:56.

G.B.—Jervey 11 run (Longwell kick), 5:30.

Attendance—59,794.

	San Fran.	Green Bay
First downs	19	15
Rushes-yards	28-134	25-98
Passing	132	274
Punt returns	3-33	4-57
Kickoff returns	7-148	6-148
Interception returns	3-35	1-9
Comp.-att.-int.	24-39-1	15-28-3
Sacked-yards lost	9-54	2-5
Punts	5-43	5-41
Fumbles-lost	3-1	0-0
Penalties-yards	3-47	6-45
Time of possession	33:05	26:55

INDIVIDUAL STATISTICS

RUSHING—San Francisco, Hearst 17-99, S. Young 6-22, Edwards 2-7, Kirby 2-6, Roby 1-0. Green Bay, Jervey 17-95, R. Harris 4-6, Favre 4-(minus 3).

PASSING—San Francisco, S. Young 24-39-1-186. Green Bay, Favre 15-28-3-279.

RECEIVING—San Francisco, Rice 7-60, Stokes 5-39, Owens 5-20, Kirby 2-29, Hearst 2-25, Edwards 2-10, Clark 1-3. Green Bay, Freeman 7-193, R. Brooks 3-48, Chmura 2-25, T. Davis 1-8, R. Harris 1-3, Jervey 1-2.

MISSED FIELD GOAL ATTEMPTS—San Francisco, Richey 47.

INTERCEPTIONS—San Francisco, Bronson 1-28, Woodall 1-4, McDonald 1-3. Green Bay, Terrell 1-9.

KICKOFF RETURNS—San Francisco, McQuarters 5-112, I. Smith 1-23, Kirby 1-13. Green Bay, Preston 5-124, Bradford 1-24.

PUNT RETURNS—San Francisco, McQuarters 3-33. Green Bay, Preston 4-57.

SACKS—San Francisco, Barker 1, Doleman 1. Green Bay, White 3, Butler 2, B. Williams 1, Holliday 1, Booker 1, McKenzie 1.

JETS 20, CHIEFS 17

Sunday, November 1

N.Y. Jets	0	10	0	10—20
Kansas City	7	0	3	7—17

First Quarter

K.C.—Richardson 2 run (Stoyanovich kick), 11:26.

Second Quarter

NYJ—FG, Hall 20, 1:19.

NYJ—Gordon 31 interception return (Hall kick), 12:26.

Third Quarter

K.C.—FG, Stoyanovich 42, 8:43.

Fourth Quarter

K.C.—Bennett 1 run (Stoyanovich kick), 1:17.

NYJ—Brady 20 pass from Testaverde (Hall kick), 2:07.

NYJ—FG, Hall 32, 15:00.

Attendance—65,104.

	N.Y. Jets	Kansas City
First downs	17	13
Rushes-yards	32-53	29-92
Passing	253	112
Punt returns	4-30	2-17
Kickoff returns	4-127	4-76
Interception returns	3-31	1-27
Comp.-att.-int.	20-34-1	13-28-3
Sacked-yards lost	1-7	1-8
Punts	6-35	6-37
Fumbles-lost	3-0	1-0
Penalties-yards	8-75	8-63
Time of possession	33:14	26:46

INDIVIDUAL STATISTICS

RUSHING—New York, Martin 30-42, Testaverde 2-11. Kansas City, Morris 13-41, Bennett 6-17, Anders 5-14, Richardson 4-13, Grbac 1-7.

PASSING—New York, Testaverde 20-34-1-260. Kansas City, Grbac 13-28-3-120. .

RECEIVING—New York, Chrebet 6-101, Brady 3-48, Byars 3-15, L. Johnson 2-25, Ward 2-25, Martin 2-14, Baxter 1-23, K. Johnson 1-9. Kansas City, Gonzalez 4-18, Alexander 3-76, Anders 2-16, Popson 2-9, Shehee 1-3, Richardson 1-(minus 2).

MISSED FIELD GOAL ATTEMPTS—New York, Hall 31, 55.

INTERCEPTIONS—New York, Gordon 1-31, Brown 1-0, P. Johnson 1-0. Kansas City, Davis 1-27.

KICKOFF RETURNS—New York, Glenn 3-107, Brady 1-20. Kansas City, Horn 3-60, Anders 1-16.

PUNT RETURNS—New York, Ward 3-25, L. Johnson 1-5. Kansas City, Lockett 2-17.

SACKS—New York, B. Cox 1. Kansas City, Thomas 1.

RAIDERS 31, SEAHAWKS 18

Sunday, November 1

Oakland	7	0	14	10—31
Seattle	3	7	8	0—18

First Quarter
Sea.—FG, Peterson 38, 4:22.
Oak.—T. Brown 28 pass from Hollas (G. Davis kick), 8:55.

Second Quarter
Sea.—Crumpler 1 pass from Moon (Peterson kick), 13:47.

Third Quarter
Oak.—Dudley 27 pass from Hollas (G. Davis kick), 2:07.
Oak.—Lewis 74 interception return (G. Davis kick), 4:45.
Sea.—Watters 1 run (Pritchard pass from Moon), 10:25.

Fourth Quarter
Oak.—FG, G. Davis 35, 0:12.
Oak.—Ashmore 1 fumble return (G. Davis kick), 4:04.
Attendance—66,246.

	Oakland	Seattle
First downs	14	22
Rushes-yards	31-73	28-80
Passing	220	253
Punt returns	1-7	2-13
Kickoff returns	4-104	6-141
Interception returns	1-74	1-8
Comp.-att.-int.	13-23-1	29-39-1
Sacked-yards lost	3-16	3-22
Punts	3-43	2-42
Fumbles-lost	3-0	6-4
Penalties-yards	9-65	4-16
Time of possession	27:11	32:49

INDIVIDUAL STATISTICS
RUSHING—Oakland, Kaufman 22-56, H. Williams 8-17, Ritchie 1-0. Seattle, Watters 18-54, Green 5-12, Moon 3-1, Galloway 2-13.

PASSING—Oakland, Hollas 12-22-1-237, Araguz 1-1-0-(minus 1). Seattle, Moon 29-39-1-275.

RECEIVING—Oakland, T. Brown 4-74, Jett 3-85, Dudley 2-35, Mickens 1-30, Ritchie 1-7, Kaufman 1-6, Folston 1-(minus 1). Seattle, Watters 9-68, Pritchard 5-60, Crumpler 5-49, Galloway 5-30, Fauria 4-56, Br. Blades 1-12.

MISSED FIELD GOAL ATTEMPTS—None.

INTERCEPTIONS—Oakland, Lewis 1-74. Seattle, W. Williams 1-8.

KICKOFF RETURNS—Oakland, Howard 3-92, Branch 1-12. Seattle, Green 5-125, Joseph 1-16.

PUNT RETURNS—Oakland, Howard 1-7. Seattle, Galloway 1-18, Harris 1-(minus 5).

SACKS—Oakland, Johnstone 1, Russell 1, Jackson 1. Seattle, Daniels 2, LaBounty 1.

COWBOYS 34, EAGLES 0

Monday, November 2

Dallas	10	7	10	7—34
Philadelphia	0	0	0	0— 0

First Quarter
Dal.—FG, Cunningham 33, 7:06.
Dal.—Irvin 10 pass from Aikman (Cunningham kick), 13:33.

Second Quarter
Dal.—Sanders 69 punt return (Cunningham kick), 13:11.

Third Quarter
Dal.—LaFleur 9 pass from Aikman (Cunningham kick), 6:18.
Dal.—FG, Cunningham 25, 13:30.

Fourth Quarter
Dal.—E. Smith 15 run (Cunningham kick), 3:10.
Attendance—67,002.

	Dallas	Philadelphia
First downs	20	15
Rushes-yards	36-121	18-96
Passing	173	104
Punt returns	3-79	3-17
Kickoff returns	1-28	6-112
Interception returns	2-22	0-0
Comp.-att.-int.	15-27-0	13-42-2
Sacked-yards lost	2-8	3-20
Punts	6-46	8-40
Fumbles-lost	0-0	2-1
Penalties-yards	10-130	11-110
Time of possession	35:40	24:20

INDIVIDUAL STATISTICS
RUSHING—Dallas, E. Smith 23-101, Warren 7-21, Quinn 2-(minus 2), B. Davis 1-2, Johnston 1-0, E. Mills 1-0, Aikman 1-(minus 1). Philadelphia, Garner 7-15, Staley 5-56, Hoying 2-5, Fryar 1-12, Peete 1-8, Turner 1-4, Hankton 1-(minus 4).

PASSING—Dallas, Aikman 14-26-0-171, Quinn 1-1-0-10. Philadelphia, Hoying 13-39-2-124, Peete 0-3-0-0.

RECEIVING—Dallas, Irvin 3-32, B. Davis 2-55, E. Mills 2-29, LaFleur 2-16, Warren 2-12, E. Smith 1-11, Sanders 1-11, Ogden 1-10, Johnston 1-5. Philadelphia, Fryar 4-22, Turner 3-31, Dunn 2-29, Staley 2-26, Solomon 2-16.

MISSED FIELD GOAL ATTEMPTS—None.

INTERCEPTIONS—Dallas, Sanders 1-21, Woodson 1-1.

KICKOFF RETURNS—Dallas, Mathis 1-28. Philadelphia, Rossum 5-104, Copeland 1-8.

PUNT RETURNS—Dallas, Sanders 2-74, Mathis 1-5. Philadelphia, Rossum 3-17.

SACKS—Dallas, Coakley 1, McCormack 1, Myers 1. Philadelphia, Vincent 1, H. Thomas 1.

WEEK 10

RESULTS

ARIZONA 29, Washington 27
Atlanta 41, NEW ENGLAND 10
BALTIMORE 13, Oakland 10
DALLAS 16, N.Y. Giants 6
DENVER 27, San Diego 10
JACKSONVILLE 24, Cincinnati 11
MIAMI 27, Indianapolis 14
MINNESOTA 31, New Orleans 24
N.Y. JETS 34, Buffalo 12
PHILADELPHIA 10, Detroit 9
St. Louis 20, CHICAGO 12
SAN FRANCISCO 25, Carolina 23
SEATTLE 24, Kansas City 3
Tennessee 31, TAMPA BAY 22
PITTSBURGH 27, Green Bay 20

STANDINGS

AFC EAST	W	L	T	Pct.
Miami	6	3	0	.667
N.Y. Jets	6	3	0	.667
Buffalo	5	4	0	.556
New England	5	4	0	.556
Indianapolis	1	8	0	.111

AFC CENTRAL	W	L	T	Pct.
Jacksonville	7	2	0	.778
Pittsburgh	6	3	0	.667
Tennessee	5	4	0	.556
Baltimore	3	6	0	.333
Cincinnati	2	7	0	.222

AFC WEST	W	L	T	Pct.
Denver	9	0	0	1.000
Oakland	6	3	0	.667
Seattle	5	4	0	.556
Kansas City	4	5	0	.444
San Diego	3	6	0	.333

NFC EAST	W	L	T	Pct.
Dallas	6	3	0	.667
Arizona	5	4	0	.556
N.Y. Giants	3	6	0	.333
Philadelphia	2	7	0	.222
Washington	1	8	0	.111

NFC CENTRAL	W	L	T	Pct.
Minnesota	8	1	0	.889
Green Bay	6	3	0	.667
Tampa Bay	4	5	0	.444
Chicago	3	6	0	.333
Detroit	2	7	0	.222

NFC WEST	W	L	T	Pct.
Atlanta	7	2	0	.778
San Francisco	7	2	0	.778
New Orleans	4	5	0	.444
St. Louis	3	6	0	.333
Carolina	1	8	0	.111

HIGHLIGHTS

Hero of the week: Brad Johnson completed 28-of-38 passes for 316 yards against the Saints despite breaking the thumb on his right (throwing) hand on the first play of the second half. Johnson, who had been recovering from an injury, replaced Randall Cunningham, who suffered a knee injury in the first quarter. Playing in his first game since the second week of the season, Johnson completed a lefthanded toss to Leroy Hoard to set up the winning touchdown.

Goat of the week: The strength of the Buccaneers was supposed to be their defense, but in a 31-22 loss to the Oilers it was the defense that did them in. The Bucs surrendered 236 yards rushing, including a 71-yard touchdown run by Steve McNair with 1:46 remaining that iced the game. After jumping to a 16-3 lead in the first half, the Bucs allowed the Oilers to go ahead with two quick scores in the third quarter, helped by 36 yards in penalties on the Bucs' secondary on the first series of the second half.

Sub of the week: Bubby Brister was a surprise starter for Denver in place of ailing John Elway. Elway entered for the Broncos' second series, but sore ribs limited him to five snaps before he departed. Brister was an efficient 20-of-33 for 229 yards and two TDs in leading the undefeated Broncos over the Chargers, 27-10.

Comeback of the week: In a Monday night matchup, Kordell Stewart led the Steelers to a 24-0 halftime advantage over the Packers. Trailing 27-3 going into the fourth quarter, the Packers got going when Keith McKenzie scooped up a fumble and returned it 88 yards for a touchdown. The Pack's furious comeback attempt included two more scores but the Steelers were able to hold them off, 27-20.

Blowout of the week: Four weeks after posting a 40-10 rout of the Chiefs, the Patriots were humiliated at home by the Falcons, 41-10. The Falcons limited New England to 18 yards rushing on 14 carries and led 28-3 with six minutes left in the first half. Jamal Anderson rushed for 104 yards and two TDs for the Falcons, who sacked Drew Bledsoe five times, causing two fumbles.

Nail-biter of the week: After holding a 17-7 halftime lead, the Redskins fell behind the Cardinals by nine points with time winding down in the fourth quarter. With less than two minutes left, the Skins pulled within two on a 35-yard touchdown pass to Leslie Shepherd. An onside kick was successful, and with 35 seconds left Cary Blanchard kicked a 54-yard field goal to give the Redskins a 27-26 lead. On the ensuing drive, however, Jake Plummer drove the Cardinals into position for Joe Nedney's 47-yard field goal as time expired. The Cardinals won 29-27.

Hit of the week: After starting the game on the bench, John Elway entered on the Broncos' second possession. He completed one pass in three attempts and was drilled by Junior Seau 9 yards deep in the backfield. Elway spent the rest of the first half getting treatment and left for home during the third quarter.

Oddity of the week: In the second quarter of the Vikings-Saints game, New Orleans' Aaron Craver fielded a kickoff (after fumbling the previous one) and stumbled to the ground after apparently being tackled by Pete Bercich at the 18. After most of the Vikings stopped, Craver popped up and kept running for the end zone, scoring on a 100-yard return after the referees ruled that Bercich did not make contact.

Top rusher: Emmitt Smith carried 29 times for 163 yards, his best game since 1995, as the Cowboys beat the Giants, 16-6. Smith rushed for 43 yards on the opening drive and broke a 32-yard run on Dallas' second drive to break Tony Dorsett's all-time team rushing record.

Top passer: Brad Johnson completed 28-of-38 passes for 316 yards in the Vikings' win over the Saints.

Top receiver: Ed McCaffrey tied personal game highs for receptions (nine) and yards (133) and scored a touchdown in the Broncos' win over the Chargers.

Notes: Miami's O.J. McDuffie, who had gone 21 games without a touchdown, caught a 61-yard TD pass in the first quarter and a 6-yarder in the second against the Colts. . . . Cris Carter's touchdown in the first quarter was his 77th as a Viking, breaking Bill Brown's team record. . . . The Chargers didn't take a snap inside Denver territory until early in the fourth quarter, and had only one first down and 34 yards in the first half. . . . Rookie running back Curtis Enis walked off the field late in the third quarter of the Bears' loss to the Rams, but later learned that he would be out for the season because of a torn ACL. . . . Barry Sanders rushed for 140 yards against the Eagles, topping 1,000 for the season early in the fourth quarter. He joined Walter Payton as the only running backs to gain 1,000 yards in 10 different seasons and became the first to do it in 10 consecutive seasons.

Quote of the week: Washington cornerback Cris Dishman, on the Redskins' last-second loss to the Cardinals: "We played 59 minutes and 25 seconds. Those last 35 seconds really hurt."

GAME SUMMARIES

COWBOYS 16, GIANTS 6

Sunday, November 8

N.Y. Giants	3	3	0	0— 6
Dallas	3	3	3	7—16

First Quarter
Dal.—FG, Cunningham 37, 6:28.
NYG—FG, Daluiso 32, 11:46.
Second Quarter
Dal.—FG, Cunningham 40, 6:45.
NYG—FG, Daluiso 23, 13:03.
Third Quarter
Dal.—FG, Cunningham 19, 12:42.
Fourth Quarter
Dal.—Bjornson 2 pass from Aikman (Cunningham kick), 6:16.
Attendance—64,316.

	N.Y. Giants	Dallas
First downs	16	16
Rushes-yards	28-159	33-162
Passing	127	165
Punt returns	1-2	3-56
Kickoff returns	5-78	3-101
Interception returns	0-0	0-0
Comp.-att.-int.	12-24-0	17-26-0
Sacked-yards lost	3-12	0-0
Punts	5-42	3-44
Fumbles-lost	1-1	0-0
Penalties-yards	7-43	8-36
Time of possession	26:34	33:26

INDIVIDUAL STATISTICS
RUSHING—New York, Brown 15-119, Way 6-19, Barber 6-17, Kanell 1-4. Dallas, E. Smith 29-163, Warren 2-1, Aikman 2-(minus 2).
PASSING—New York, Kanell 12-24-0-139. Dallas, Aikman 16-23-0-161, Garrett 1-3-0-4.
RECEIVING—New York, Way 4-17, Calloway 3-66, Patten 2-9, Jurevicius 1-17, Hilliard 1-16, Toomer 1-14. Dallas, E. Smith 5-19, E. Mills 3-69, Irvin 3-23, Sanders 2-18, B. Davis 1-21, LaFleur 1-8, Johnston 1-5, Bjornson 1-2.
MISSED FIELD GOAL ATTEMPTS—Dallas, Cunningham 38.
INTERCEPTIONS—None.
KICKOFF RETURNS—New York, Patten 4-62, Barber 1-16. Dallas, Mathis 3-101.
PUNT RETURNS—New York, Toomer 1-2. Dallas, Sanders 3-56.
SACKS—Dallas, Woodson 2, Lett 1.

RAVENS 13, RAIDERS 10

Sunday, November 8

Oakland	0	3	0	7—10
Baltimore	7	3	0	3—13

First Quarter
Bal.—Woodson 18 interception return (Stover kick), 11:52.
Second Quarter
Oak.—FG, G. Davis 23, 10:17.
Bal.—FG, Stover 30, 14:58.
Fourth Quarter
Oak.—Dudley 5 pass from Hollas (G. Davis kick), 1:01.
Bal.—FG, Stover 30, 5:46.
Attendance—69,037.

	Oakland	Baltimore
First downs	20	15
Rushes-yards	28-111	34-126
Passing	245	87
Punt returns	2-0	2-8
Kickoff returns	4-53	3-77
Interception returns	1-2	2-18
Comp.-att.-int.	18-29-2	10-17-1
Sacked-yards lost	5-39	4-15
Punts	5-36	5-46
Fumbles-lost	4-1	0-0
Penalties-yards	14-98	4-30
Time of possession	29:35	30:25

INDIVIDUAL STATISTICS
RUSHING—Oakland, Kaufman 16-79, H. Williams 8-22, Hollas 4-10. Baltimore, Holmes 27-99, Potts 4-14, J. Lewis 1-9, Harbaugh 1-2, Rhett 1-2.
PASSING—Oakland, Hollas 17-26-2-249, George 1-3-0-35. Baltimore, Harbaugh 10-17-1-102.
RECEIVING—Oakland, Dudley 6-105, Jett 5-92, T. Brown 5-68, H. Williams 1-12, Ritchie 1-7. Baltimore, Jackson 3-35, J. Lewis 2-43, Kinchen 2-12, Potts 2-1, Turner 1-11.
MISSED FIELD GOAL ATTEMPTS—Baltimore, Stover 41.
INTERCEPTIONS—Oakland, Allen 1-2. Baltimore, Woodson 1-18, Starks 1-0.
KICKOFF RETURNS—Oakland, Howard 2-37, Branch 1-13, Morton 1-3. Baltimore, C. Harris 3-77.
PUNT RETURNS—Oakland, Howard 1-0, Prior 1-0. Baltimore, Roe 1-7, J. Lewis 1-1.
SACKS—Oakland, Russell 1, Wooden 1, Johnstone 1, Jackson 1. Baltimore, McCrary 4, R. Lewis 1.

RAMS 20, BEARS 12

Sunday, November 8

St. Louis	0	14	3	3—20
Chicago	7	0	3	2—12

First Quarter
Chi.—Conway 4 pass from Stenstrom (Jaeger kick), 8:24.
Second Quarter
St.L.—Proehl 3 pass from Banks (Wilkins kick), 0:03.
St.L.—Banks 7 run (Wilkins kick), 14:02.
Third Quarter
St.L.—FG, Wilkins 24, 8:36.
Chi.—FG, Jaeger 31, 14:05.
Fourth Quarter
St.L.—FG, Wilkins 33, 3:54.
Chi.—Safety, offensive holding in the end zone on a punt attempt, 13:01.
Attendance—50,263.

	St. Louis	Chicago
First downs	20	15
Rushes-yards	29-64	24-129
Passing	202	122
Punt returns	3-28	1-2
Kickoff returns	3-71	6-106
Interception returns	1-0	0-0
Comp.-att.-int.	24-31-0	15-26-1
Sacked-yards lost	0-0	4-32
Punts	3-38	6-41
Fumbles-lost	2-1	1-0
Penalties-yards	11-82	8-99
Time of possession	30:48	29:12

INDIVIDUAL STATISTICS
RUSHING—St. Louis, Holcombe 13-25, Henley 6-8, Banks 5-10, J. Moore 3-10, Kennison 1-9, Harris 1-2. Chicago, Enis 18-76, Bennett 3-15, Stenstrom 2-24, Chancey 1-14.
PASSING—St. Louis, Banks 24-31-0-202. Chicago, Stenstrom 15-25-1-154, Conway 0-1-0-0.

RECEIVING—St. Louis, Proehl 8-99, Henley 5-32, Harris 4-22, Kennison 3-23, J. Moore 2-10, Armstrong 1-9, R. Williams 1-7. Chicago, Conway 3-27, Wetnight 3-11, Engram 2-54, Hallock 2-15, Enis 2-10, Mayes 2-10, Penn 1-27.

MISSED FIELD GOAL ATTEMPTS—None.

INTERCEPTIONS—St. Louis, Lyle 1-0.

KICKOFF RETURNS—St. Louis, Horne 2-52, Fletcher 1-19. Chicago, Milburn 6-106.

PUNT RETURNS—St. Louis, Kennison 3-28. Chicago, Milburn 1-2.

SACKS—St. Louis, M. A. Jones 1, Carter 1, Farr 1, J. Williams 1.

JAGUARS 24, BENGALS 11

Sunday, November 8

Cincinnati	0	0	3	8—11
Jacksonville	10	14	0	0—24

First Quarter

Jac.—F. Taylor 1 run (Hollis kick), 4:47.
Jac.—FG, Hollis 39, 13:23.

Second Quarter

Jac.—J. Smith 18 pass from Brunell (Hollis kick), 1:49.
Jac.—Beasley 90 fumble return (Hollis kick), 6:30.

Third Quarter

Cin.—FG, Pelfrey 50, 6:44.

Fourth Quarter

Cin.—Gibson 9 pass from Justin (Justin run), 13:05.
Attendance—67,040.

	Cincinnati	Jacksonville
First downs	19	14
Rushes-yards	27-118	32-137
Passing	200	135
Punt returns	2-6	4-50
Kickoff returns	5-128	3-77
Interception returns	0-0	1-0
Comp.-att.-int.	24-40-1	9-21-0
Sacked-yards lost	4-35	2-11
Punts	6-41	5-46
Fumbles-lost	3-1	1-1
Penalties-yards	4-40	9-58
Time of possession	35:50	24:10

INDIVIDUAL STATISTICS

RUSHING—Cincinnati, Dillon 16-76, Bennett 4-12, Bieniemy 2-11, Milne 2-11, Blair 1-4, Pickens 1-4, O'Donnell 1-0. Jacksonville, F. Taylor 27-118, Brunell 3-20, Shelton 2-(minus 1).

PASSING—Cincinnati, O'Donnell 17-30-1-128, Justin 7-10-0-107. Jacksonville, Brunell 5-12-0-111, Martin 4-9-0-35.

RECEIVING—Cincinnati, Dillon 6-27, Hundon 4-43, Pickens 3-30, Bieniemy 2-19, Gibson 2-13, Milne 2-8, Jackson 1-35, Bennett 1-24, McGee 1-24, Blair 1-7, Battaglia 1-5. Jacksonville, J. Smith 4-44, Mitchell 2-21, Whitted 1-55, F. Taylor 1-23, Shelton 1-3.

MISSED FIELD GOAL ATTEMPTS—None.

INTERCEPTIONS—Jacksonville, Davis 1-0.

KICKOFF RETURNS—Cincinnati, Mack 5-128. Jacksonville, Logan 2-77, Barlow 1-0.

PUNT RETURNS—Cincinnati, Gibson 2-6. Jacksonville, Barlow 4-50.

SACKS—Cincinnati, B. Simmons 1, Foley 1. Jacksonville, Smeenge 1, F. Smith 1, Pritchett 1, Jurkovic 0.5, White 0.5.

DOLPHINS 27, COLTS 14

Sunday, November 8

Indianapolis	0	0	0	14—14
Miami	7	13	0	7—27

First Quarter

Mia.—McDuffie 61 pass from Marino (Mare kick), 5:36.

Second Quarter

Mia.—McDuffie 6 pass from Marino (Mare kick), 1:29.
Mia.—FG, Mare 21, 6:52.
Mia.—FG, Mare 23, 15:00.

Fourth Quarter

Mia.—Avery 8 run (Mare kick), 0:49.
Ind.—Faulk 6 run (Pollard pass from Manning), 7:18.
Ind.—Dilger 9 pass from Manning (pass failed), 12:40.
Attendance—73,400.

	Indianapolis	Miami
First downs	21	20
Rushes-yards	26-114	33-153
Passing	140	207
Punt returns	3-3	3-38
Kickoff returns	4-81	2-55
Interception returns	1-22	2-16
Comp.-att.-int.	22-42-2	18-27-1
Sacked-yards lost	0-0	0-0
Punts	6-45	3-40
Fumbles-lost	1-0	1-1
Penalties-yards	4-61	9-70
Time of possession	31:07	28:53

INDIVIDUAL STATISTICS

RUSHING—Indianapolis, Faulk 21-88, Warren 4-22, Pathon 1-4. Miami, Avery 21-100, Abdul-Jabbar 9-48, McDuffie 1-4, Doxzon 1-3, Marino 1-(minus 2).

PASSING—Indianapolis, Manning 22-42-2-140. Miami, Marino 18-27-1-207.

RECEIVING—Indianapolis, Harrison 5-32, Small 4-32, Faulk 4-16, Pathon 3-23, Dilger 3-22, Warren 1-7, Green 1-6, Greene 1-2. Miami, McDuffie 9-132, Parmalee 2-28, Avery 2-19, L. Thomas 2-17, Pritchett 2-12, Abdul-Jabbar 1-(minus 1).

MISSED FIELD GOAL ATTEMPTS—None.

INTERCEPTIONS—Indianapolis, Montgomery 1-22. Miami, Buckley 1-16, Madison 1-0.

KICKOFF RETURNS—Indianapolis, Bailey 3-69, Hetherington 1-12. Miami, Avery 2-55.

PUNT RETURNS—Indianapolis, Bailey 3-3. Miami, Buckley 2-38, McDuffie 1-0.

SACKS—None.

VIKINGS 31, SAINTS 24

Sunday, November 8

New Orleans	0	7	10	7—24
Minnesota	7	10	7	7—31

First Quarter

Min.—Carter 14 pass from Johnson (Anderson kick), 12:28.

Second Quarter

Min.—FG, Anderson 28, 13:23.
Min.—Hoard 4 run (Anderson kick), 13:35.
N.O.—Craver 100 kickoff return (Brien kick), 13:49.

Third Quarter

N.O.—FG, Brien 20, 7:04.
Min.—R. Smith 61 run (Anderson kick), 7:27.
N.O.—Craver 9 pass from Tolliver (Brien kick), 11:52.

Fourth Quarter

N.O.—Knight 91 interception return (Brien kick), 4:50.
Min.—Hoard 1 run (Anderson kick), 11:17.
Attendance—63,779.

	New Orleans	Minnesota
First downs	11	23
Rushes-yards	21-52	32-162
Passing	138	303
Punt returns	2-14	1-8
Kickoff returns	3-130	5-86
Interception returns	2-98	0-0
Comp.-att.-int.	11-16-0	28-40-2
Sacked-yards lost	3-30	2-13
Punts	4-43	3-45
Fumbles-lost	1-1	0-0
Penalties-yards	9-50	6-45
Time of possession	22:51	37:09

INDIVIDUAL STATISTICS

RUSHING—New Orleans, L. Smith 11-21, Zellars 6-17, Tolliver 3-7, Craver 1-7. Minnesota, R. Smith 20-137, Hoard 4-11, Johnson 4-1, Evans 3-9, Palmer 1-4.

PASSING—New Orleans, Tolliver 11-16-0-168, Cunningham 0-2-0-0. Minnesota, Johnson 28-38-2-316.

RECEIVING—New Orleans, Dawkins 3-44, Craver 2-58, Zellars 2-23, Hastings 2-11, L. Smith 1-18, Poole 1-14. Minnesota, Glover 9-93, Carter 6-71, Reed 5-90, Palmer 3-18, Hoard 1-19, R. Smith 1-9, R. Moss 1-6, Evans 1-5, DeLong 1-5.

MISSED FIELD GOAL ATTEMPTS—None.

INTERCEPTIONS—New Orleans, Knight 2-98.

KICKOFF RETURNS—New Orleans, Craver 2-110, Bech 1-20. Minnesota, Palmer 5-86.

PUNT RETURNS—New Orleans, Hastings 2-14. Minnesota, Palmer 1-8.

SACKS—New Orleans, Fields 1, Cherry 1. Minnesota, E. McDaniel 1, Wong 1, Randle 0.5, Alexander 0.5.

FALCONS 41, PATRIOTS 10

Sunday, November 8

Atlanta	14	14	3	10—41
New England	3	0	7	0—10

First Quarter

Atl.—J. Anderson 1 run (Andersen kick), 2:50.

Atl.—Santiago 7 pass from Chandler (Andersen kick), 5:12.

N.E.—FG, Vinatieri 40, 12:31.

Second Quarter

Atl.—J. Anderson 10 run (Andersen kick), 1:55.

Atl.—C. Smith 71 fumble return (Andersen kick), 8:32.

Third Quarter

Atl.—FG, Andersen 40, 10:33.

N.E.—Coates 2 pass from Bledsoe (Vinatieri kick), 13:34.

Fourth Quarter

Atl.—Santiago 22 pass from Chandler (Andersen kick), 6:01.

Atl.—FG, Andersen 32, 13:11.

Attendance—59,790.

	Atlanta	New England
First downs	22	15
Rushes-yards	39-117	14-18
Passing	249	205
Punt returns	2-15	3-11
Kickoff returns	2-22	7-107
Interception returns	2-12	2-16
Comp.-att.-int.	16-25-2	22-44-2
Sacked-yards lost	1-2	6-57
Punts	3-44	6-43
Fumbles-lost	0-0	4-3
Penalties-yards	7-40	6-39
Time of possession	34:30	25:30

INDIVIDUAL STATISTICS

RUSHING—Atlanta, J. Anderson 32-104, Oxendine 4-4, Chandler 2-8, Green 1-1. New England, Edwards 10-11, Bledsoe 2-6, Floyd 1-1, S. Shaw 1-0.

PASSING—Atlanta, Chandler 15-22-2-240, J. Anderson 0-2-0-0, Graziani 1-1-0-11. New England, Bledsoe 19-34-1-229, Zolak 3-10-1-33.

RECEIVING—Atlanta, Mathis 8-117, Santiago 3-53, Christian 1-39, Martin 1-15, Oxendine 1-11, J. Anderson 1-8, Kozlowski 1-8. New England, Edwards 5-34, Coates 5-13, Simmons 4-95, S. Shaw 3-20, Jefferson 2-61, Ellard 2-34, Cullors 1-5.

MISSED FIELD GOAL ATTEMPTS—Atlanta, Andersen 47.

INTERCEPTIONS—Atlanta, Brooking 1-12, Robinson 1-0. New England, Law 2-16.

KICKOFF RETURNS—Atlanta, E. Williams 2-22. New England, Cullors 5-103, Bruschi 1-4, Canty 1-0.

PUNT RETURNS—Atlanta, Kinchen 2-15. New England, Canty 3-11.

SACKS—Atlanta, C. Smith 3, Archambeau 2, Hall 1. New England, Israel 1.

EAGLES 10, LIONS 9

Sunday, November 8

Detroit	0	3	3	3—9
Philadelphia	0	7	0	3—10

Second Quarter

Phi.—Garner 3 run (Boniol kick), 2:51.

Det.—FG, Hanson 41, 4:28.

Third Quarter

Det.—FG, Hanson 48, 8:06.

Fourth Quarter

Det.—FG, Hanson 35, 0:39.

Phi.—FG, Boniol 39, 4:12.

Attendance—66,785.

	Detroit	Philadelphia
First downs	9	16
Rushes-yards	22-146	35-219
Passing	111	70
Punt returns	8-43	5-40
Kickoff returns	3-98	3-74

	Detroit	Philadelphia
Interception returns	0-0	0-0
Comp.-att.-int.	14-27-0	15-21-0
Sacked-yards lost	5-35	5-27
Punts	8-47	10-43
Fumbles-lost	0-0	2-0
Penalties-yards	8-63	5-39
Time of possession	25:30	34:30

INDIVIDUAL STATISTICS

RUSHING—Detroit, Sanders 20-140, Batch 2-6. Philadelphia, Staley 17-89, Garner 16-129, Fryar 1-2, Hoying 1-(minus 1).

PASSING—Detroit, Batch 14-27-0-146. Philadelphia, Hoying 15-21-0-97.

RECEIVING—Detroit, Sanders 3-32, Moore 3-23, Sloan 2-43, Morton 2-32, Vardell 2-7, Schlesinger 1-6, Crowell 1-3. Philadelphia, Staley 7-32, Graham 3-27, Fryar 2-16, Garner 2-12, Copeland 1-10.

MISSED FIELD GOAL ATTEMPTS—Detroit, Hanson 58.

INTERCEPTIONS—None.

KICKOFF RETURNS—Detroit, Fair 3-98. Philadelphia, Rossum 3-74.

PUNT RETURNS—Detroit, Fair 8-43. Philadelphia, Rossum 4-28, Solomon 1-12.

SACKS—Detroit, Porcher 2, Owens 1, Waldroup 1, Bailey 1. Philadelphia, Douglas 2.5, Dawkins 1, Caldwell 1, Wallace 0.5.

CARDINALS 29, REDSKINS 27

Sunday, November 8

Washington	3	14	0	10—27
Arizona	0	7	7	15—29

First Quarter

Was.—FG, Blanchard 34, 13:58.

Second Quarter

Was.—Hicks 2 run (Blanchard kick), 8:30.

Ariz.—Bates 1 run (Nedney kick), 13:00.

Was.—Mitchell 6 run (Blanchard kick), 14:22.

Third Quarter

Ariz.—Centers 4 pass from Plummer (Nedney kick), 5:14.

Fourth Quarter

Ariz.—Bates 1 run (Nedney kick), 2:26.

Ariz.—Safety, M. Turk forced out of end zone, 4:12.

Ariz.—FG, Nedney 26, 11:51.

Was.—Shepherd 35 pass from T. Green (Blanchard kick), 13:21.

Was.—FG, Blanchard 54, 14:25.

Ariz.—FG, Nedney 47, 14:58.

Attendance—45,950.

	Washington	Arizona
First downs	18	23
Rushes-yards	26-89	37-187
Passing	167	164
Punt returns	4-32	3-14
Kickoff returns	6-168	4-105
Interception returns	0-0	0-0
Comp.-att.-int.	17-33-0	22-30-0
Sacked-yards lost	3-16	4-22
Punts	5-43	6-42
Fumbles-lost	3-2	2-1
Penalties-yards	3-29	4-35
Time of possession	24:34	35:26

INDIVIDUAL STATISTICS

RUSHING—Washington, Hicks 15-64, Mitchell 5-18, T. Green 3-6, Davis 2-1, M. Turk 1-0. Arizona, Murrell 23-107, Bates 10-25, Plummer 3-50, Sanders 1-5.

PASSING—Washington, T. Green 17-33-0-183. Arizona, Plummer 22-30-0-186.

RECEIVING—Washington, Mitchell 7-58, Asher 5-49, Thrash 2-44, Shepherd 1-35, Davis 1-5, T. Green 1-(minus 8). Arizona, Sanders 5-50, Gedney 4-39, Centers 4-35, McWilliams 3-24, Metcalf 3-22, R. Moore 2-11, Brock 1-5.

MISSED FIELD GOAL ATTEMPTS—None.

INTERCEPTIONS—None.

KICKOFF RETURNS—Washington, Mitchell 6-168. Arizona, Metcalf 4-105.

PUNT RETURNS—Washington, Mitchell 4-32. Arizona, Metcalf 3-14.

SACKS—Washington, M. Patton 1, L. Evans 1, Lang 1, Wilkinson 1. Arizona, Rice 2, M. Smith 1.

BRONCOS 27, CHARGERS 10

Sunday, November 8

San Diego	0	0	0	10—10
Denver	7	13	7	0—27

First Quarter

Den.—Davis 4 pass from Brister (Elam kick), 13:56.

Second Quarter

Den.—FG, Elam 31, 6:09.
Den.—Davis 24 run (Elam kick), 12:11.
Den.—FG, Elam 26, 14:56.

Third Quarter

Den.—McCaffrey 7 pass from Brister (Elam kick), 4:44.

Fourth Quarter

S.D.—F. Jones 14 pass from Whelihan (Whelihan run), 6:10.
S.D.—Safety, Brister forced out of end zone, 12:37.
    Attendance—74,925.

	San Diego	Denver
First downs	13	19
Rushes-yards	21-77	24-72
Passing	136	217
Punt returns	1-9	4-22
Kickoff returns	7-124	1-15
Interception returns	1-10	1-36
Comp.-att.-int.	17-38-1	21-36-1
Sacked-yards lost	1-3	3-24
Punts	8-32	5-46
Fumbles-lost	3-2	2-0
Penalties-yards	10-58	7-65
Time of possession	27:21	32:39

INDIVIDUAL STATISTICS

RUSHING—San Diego, Means 19-78, Whelihan 1-0, Bynum 1-(minus 1). Denver, Davis 20-69, Hebron 2-5, Brister 2-(minus 2).

PASSING—San Diego, Whelihan 13-23-0-113, Leaf 4-15-1-26. Denver, Brister 20-33-1-229, Elway 1-3-0-12.

RECEIVING—San Diego, F. Jones 5-36, Means 4-1, C. Jones 3-34, Still 2-37, Burke 1-17, Slaughter 1-12, Davis 1-2. Denver, McCaffrey 9-133, Sharpe 5-53, R. Smith 5-36, Davis 2-19.

MISSED FIELD GOAL ATTEMPTS—None.

INTERCEPTIONS—San Diego, Harrison 1-10. Denver, Gordon 1-36.

KICKOFF RETURNS—San Diego, Stephens 3-64, Bynum 2-27, Rachal 1-25, C. Jones 1-0. Denver, Hebron 1-15.

PUNT RETURNS—San Diego, Rachal 1-9. Denver, Gordon 3-22, Paul 1-0.

SACKS—San Diego, Seau 1, Johnson 1, Team 1. Denver, Tanuvasa 1.

JETS 34, BILLS 12

Sunday, November 8

Buffalo	3	6	3	0—12
N.Y. Jets	7	6	7	14—34

First Quarter

Buf.—FG, Christie 40, 10:32.
NYJ—K. Johnson 25 pass from Testaverde (Hall kick), 14:15.

Second Quarter

Buf.—FG, Christie 37, 1:55.
Buf.—FG, Christie 44, 10:09.
NYJ—FG, Hall 49, 14:33.
NYJ—FG, Hall 43, 15:00.

Third Quarter

NYJ—Ward 36 pass from Testaverde (Hall kick), 4:08.
Buf.—FG, Christie 21, 9:30.

Fourth Quarter

NYJ—Chrebet 12 pass from Testaverde (Hall kick), 1:20.
NYJ—Martin 6 run (Hall kick), 8:22.
    Attendance—75,403.

	Buffalo	N.Y. Jets
First downs	11	23
Rushes-yards	18-48	37-121
Passing	134	277
Punt returns	0-0	2-33
Kickoff returns	5-133	5-101
Interception returns	1-0	2-2
Comp.-att.-int.	12-30-2	23-32-1
Sacked-yards lost	2-20	1-8
Punts	5-37	2-34

	Buffalo	N.Y. Jets
Fumbles-lost	1-0	2-2
Penalties-yards	5-45	4-32
Time of possession	23:08	36:52

INDIVIDUAL STATISTICS

RUSHING—Buffalo, A. Smith 9-37, Thomas 6-9, Flutie 3-2. New York, Martin 21-54, Sowell 14-48, Testaverde 2-19.

PASSING—Buffalo, Flutie 12-30-2-154. New York, Testaverde 22-31-1-258, Lucas 1-1-0-27.

RECEIVING—Buffalo, Moulds 3-70, Reed 2-28, K. Williams 2-17, Thomas 2-5, Early 1-20, Gash 1-8, Riemersma 1-6. New York, K. Johnson 7-95, Martin 5-17, Chrebet 4-58, Ward 2-61, Brady 2-35, Sowell 2-14, Byars 1-5.

MISSED FIELD GOAL ATTEMPTS—None.

INTERCEPTIONS—Buffalo, Cowart 1-0. New York, Smith 1-2, Mickens 1-0.

KICKOFF RETURNS—Buffalo, K. Williams 5-133. New York, Williams 4-78, Glenn 1-23.

PUNT RETURNS—New York, Ward 2-33.

SACKS—Buffalo, B. Smith 1. New York, B. Cox 1, Lewis 1.

49ERS 25, PANTHERS 23

Sunday, November 8

Carolina	3	13	0	7—23
San Francisco	0	7	15	3—25

First Quarter

Car.—FG, Kasay 50, 7:33.

Second Quarter

Car.—FG, Kasay 42, 0:56.
Car.—Ismail 20 pass from Beuerlein (Kasay kick), 3:53.
Car.—FG, Kasay 41, 10:31.
S.F.—Owens 36 pass from Detmer (Richey kick), 11:33.

Third Quarter

S.F.—Owens 5 pass from Detmer (Richey kick), 3:33.
S.F.—Stokes 29 pass from Detmer (Owens pass from Detmer), 14:32.

Fourth Quarter

Car.—Floyd 2 run (Kasay kick), 9:17.
S.F.—FG, Richey 46, 14:27.
    Attendance—68,572.

	Carolina	San Francisco
First downs	16	22
Rushes-yards	24-50	25-105
Passing	237	261
Punt returns	3-47	1-0
Kickoff returns	4-55	6-105
Interception returns	3-57	0-0
Comp.-att.-int.	25-41-0	22-36-3
Sacked-yards lost	4-28	3-15
Punts	3-39	3-51
Fumbles-lost	6-2	4-3
Penalties-yards	5-35	5-39
Time of possession	31:34	28:26

INDIVIDUAL STATISTICS

RUSHING—Carolina, Lane 17-44, Floyd 4-8, Beuerlein 3-(minus 2). San Francisco, Hearst 22-90, Detmer 2-15, Kirby 1-0.

PASSING—Carolina, Beuerlein 25-41-0-265. San Francisco, Detmer 22-36-3-276.

RECEIVING—Carolina, Ismail 7-83, Muhammad 4-74, Carrier 3-41, Walls 3-29, Lane 3-15, Floyd 3-7, Johnson 2-16. San Francisco, Rice 6-87, Stokes 5-61, Owens 4-72, I. Smith 3-31, Edwards 2-15, Clark 1-8, Hearst 1-2.

MISSED FIELD GOAL ATTEMPTS—Carolina, Kasay 32, 51, 57.

INTERCEPTIONS—Carolina, Brady 1-26, Veland 1-24, Davis 1-7.

KICKOFF RETURNS—Carolina, Bates 2-44, Brady 1-8, Johnson 1-3. San Francisco, McQuarters 6-105.

PUNT RETURNS—Carolina, Oliver 3-47. San Francisco, McQuarters 1-0.

SACKS—Carolina, Barrow 1, Greene 1, McGill 1. San Francisco, Doleman 4.

OILERS 31, BUCCANEERS 22

Sunday, November 8

Tennessee	3	0	14	14—31
Tampa Bay	3	13	0	6—22

First Quarter

T.B.—FG, Husted 46, 6:01.
Ten.—FG, Del Greco 45, 13:04.

Second Quarter

T.B.—FG, Husted 30, 4:49.
T.B.—Emanuel 58 pass from Dilfer (Husted kick), 11:21.
T.B.—FG, Husted 24, 15:00.

Third Quarter

Ten.—E. George 14 run (Del Greco kick), 4:11.
Ten.—Archie 7 run (Del Greco kick), 8:22.

Fourth Quarter

Ten.—Bowden 1 interception return (Del Greco kick), 4:02.
T.B.—Anthony 10 pass from Dilfer (pass failed), 11:28.
Ten.—McNair 71 run (Del Greco kick), 13:14.
Attendance—65,054.

	Tennessee	Tampa Bay
First downs	20	19
Rushes-yards	36-236	26-103
Passing	117	294
Punt returns	4-28	0-0
Kickoff returns	4-66	5-115
Interception returns	1-1	0-0
Comp.-att.-int.	9-16-0	20-38-1
Sacked-yards lost	1-6	0-0
Punts	3-51	4-38
Fumbles-lost	2-1	1-0
Penalties-yards	2-10	7-66
Time of possession	28:53	31:07

INDIVIDUAL STATISTICS

RUSHING—Tennessee, E. George 27-134, McNair 8-95, Archie 1-7. Tampa Bay, Dunn 14-49, Alstott 10-32, Husted 1-20, Green 1-2.

PASSING—Tennessee, McNair 9-16-0-123. Tampa Bay, Dilfer 20-38-1-294.

RECEIVING—Tennessee, Wycheck 4-66, Dyson 2-40, Harris 1-9, Mason 1-8, E. George 1-0. Tampa Bay, Anthony 7-68, Emanuel 5-106, Moore 3-43, Dunn 2-32, Green 2-20, Alstott 1-25.

MISSED FIELD GOAL ATTEMPTS—Tennessee, Del Greco 41.

INTERCEPTIONS—Tennessee, Bowden 1-1.

KICKOFF RETURNS—Tennessee, Archie 4-66. Tampa Bay, Anthony 5-115.

PUNT RETURNS—Tennessee, Mason 4-28.

SACKS—Tampa Bay, Sapp 1.

SEAHAWKS 24, CHIEFS 12

Sunday, November 8

Kansas City	3	3	0	6—12
Seattle	14	10	0	0—24

First Quarter

K.C.—FG, Stoyanovich 53, 4:07.
Sea.—Watters 1 run (Peterson kick), 9:42.
Sea.—Watters 1 run (Peterson kick), 11:16.

Second Quarter

K.C.—FG, Stoyanovich 38, 3:10.
Sea.—FG, Peterson 38, 13:00.
Sea.—Smith 26 interception return (Peterson kick), 13:11.

Fourth Quarter

K.C.—Gannon 1 run (sack), 14:57.
Attendance—66,251.

	Kansas City	Seattle
First downs	24	16
Rushes-yards	19-97	32-108
Passing	260	94
Punt returns	2-2	1-5
Kickoff returns	4-70	3-43
Interception returns	2-5	3-59
Comp.-att.-int.	32-50-3	12-20-2
Sacked-yards lost	5-26	2-14
Punts	4-46	6-38
Fumbles-lost	4-1	0-0
Penalties-yards	17-152	13-96
Time of possession	31:12	28:48

INDIVIDUAL STATISTICS

RUSHING—Kansas City, Bennett 5-25, Anders 4-16, Gannon 3-29, Shehee 3-7, Morris 2-5, Rison 1-11, Richardson 1-4. Seattle, Watters 24-105, Moon 6-1, Green 1-2, Strong 1-0.

PASSING—Kansas City, Gannon 20-32-1-177, Grbac 12-18-2-109. Seattle, Moon 12-20-2-108.

RECEIVING—Kansas City, Anders 8-70, Alexander 7-91, Popson 4-37, Rison 3-29, Lockett 3-27, Shehee 3-18, Gonzalez 2-10, Bennett 1-2, Horn 1-2. Seattle, Broussard 3-5, Pritchard 2-22, Fauria 2-20, Watters 2-13, Galloway 1-45, Br. Blades 1-2, May 1-1.

MISSED FIELD GOAL ATTEMPTS—Kansas City, Stoyanovich 43.

INTERCEPTIONS—Kansas City, Hasty 1-5, Davis 1-0. Seattle, Smith 1-26, Springs 1-22, C. Brown 1-11.

KICKOFF RETURNS—Kansas City, Horn 4-70. Seattle, Green 3-43.

PUNT RETURNS—Kansas City, Lockett 1-2, Richardson 1-0. Seattle, Joseph 1-5.

SACKS—Kansas City, Thomas 1, R. Williams 1. Seattle, C. Brown 2, Wells 1, Sinclair 1, Team 1.

STEELERS 27, PACKERS 20

Monday, November 9

Green Bay	0	0	3	17—20
Pittsburgh	14	10	3	0—27

First Quarter

Pit.—C. Johnson 8 pass from Stewart (N. Johnson kick), 4:32.
Pit.—Stewart 1 run (N. Johnson kick), 14:39.

Second Quarter

Pit.—FG, N. Johnson 45, 8:48.
Pit.—Fuamatu-Ma'afala 5 run (N. Johnson kick), 14:32.

Third Quarter

Pit.—FG, N. Johnson 21, 7:00.
G.B.—FG, Longwell 42, 12:16.

Fourth Quarter

G.B.—McKenzie 88 fumble return (pass failed), 5:40.
G.B.—R. Harris 2 run (Freeman pass from Favre), 10:08.
G.B.—FG, Longwell 37, 12:20.
Attendance—60,507.

	Green Bay	Pittsburgh
First downs	17	19
Rushes-yards	19-39	40-144
Passing	217	216
Punt returns	1-0	2-13
Kickoff returns	6-106	2-35
Interception returns	0-0	1-0
Comp.-att.-int.	22-39-1	15-22-0
Sacked-yards lost	3-17	3-15
Punts	2-48	2-44
Fumbles-lost	0-0	1-1
Penalties-yards	4-33	4-27
Time of possession	24:44	35:16

INDIVIDUAL STATISTICS

RUSHING—Green Bay, Jervey 8-26, R. Harris 5-(minus 2), Favre 4-18, Henderson 1-7, Freeman 1-(minus 10). Pittsburgh, Bettis 34-100, Stewart 5-39, Fuamatu-Ma'afala 1-5.

PASSING—Green Bay, Favre 22-39-1-234. Pittsburgh, Stewart 15-22-0-231.

RECEIVING—Green Bay, Freeman 6-83, Schroeder 4-54, R. Brooks 3-39, R. Harris 3-19, Chmura 2-22, Henderson 2-11, Jervey 2-6. Pittsburgh, C. Johnson 5-48, Hawkins 4-82, Ward 2-56, Bettis 1-26, Fuamatu-Ma'afala 1-11, Blackwell 1-5, Lester 1-3.

MISSED FIELD GOAL ATTEMPTS—Green Bay, Longwell 51.

INTERCEPTIONS—Pittsburgh, Washington 1-0.

KICKOFF RETURNS—Green Bay, Preston 5-89, McKenzie 1-17. Pittsburgh, Huntley 1-25, Dunn 1-10.

PUNT RETURNS—Green Bay, Preston 1-0. Pittsburgh, Hawkins 2-13.

SACKS—Green Bay, White 1, Terrell 1, McKenzie 1. Pittsburgh, D. Jones 2.5, Harrison 0.5.

WEEK 11

RESULTS

ATLANTA 31, San Francisco 19
BUFFALO 13, New England 10
Dallas 35, ARIZONA 28
DETROIT 26, Chicago 3
Green Bay 37, N.Y. GIANTS 3
INDIANAPOLIS 24, N.Y. Jets 23
JACKSONVILLE 29, Tampa Bay 24
Miami 13, CAROLINA 9
MINNESOTA 24, Cincinnati 3
NEW ORLEANS 24, St. Louis 3
OAKLAND 20, Seattle 17
SAN DIEGO 14, Baltimore 13
TENNESSEE 23, Pittsburgh 14
WASHINGTON 28, Philadelphia 3
Denver 30, KANSAS CITY 7

STANDINGS

AFC EAST	W	L	T	Pct.
Miami	7	3	0	.700
Buffalo	6	4	0	.600
N.Y. Jets	6	4	0	.600
New England	5	5	0	.500
Indianapolis	2	8	0	.200

AFC CENTRAL	W	L	T	Pct.
Jacksonville	8	2	0	.800
Pittsburgh	6	4	0	.600
Tennessee	6	4	0	.600
Baltimore	3	7	0	.300
Cincinnati	2	8	0	.200

AFC WEST	W	L	T	Pct.
Denver	10	0	0	1.000
Oakland	7	3	0	.700
Seattle	5	5	0	.500
Kansas City	4	6	0	.400
San Diego	4	6	0	.400

NFC EAST	W	L	T	Pct.
Dallas	7	3	0	.700
Arizona	5	5	0	.500
N.Y. Giants	3	7	0	.300
Philadelphia	2	8	0	.200
Washington	2	8	0	.200

NFC CENTRAL	W	L	T	Pct.
Minnesota	9	1	0	.900
Green Bay	7	3	0	.700
Tampa Bay	4	6	0	.400
Chicago	3	7	0	.300
Detroit	3	7	0	.300

NFC WEST	W	L	T	Pct.
Atlanta	8	2	0	.800
San Francisco	7	3	0	.700
New Orleans	5	5	0	.500
St. Louis	3	7	0	.300
Carolina	1	9	0	.100

HIGHLIGHTS

Hero of the week: Desmond Howard of the Raiders returned six punts for 133 yards, including a 63-yard second-quarter touchdown, to help Oakland beat the Seahawks, 20-17. Howard had a 28-yard return to the Seattle 44 late in the fourth quarter that set up Greg Davis' 37-yard game-winning field goal.

Goat of the week: Trailing 13-10 with 1:25 remaining in the game and faced with fourth down at the Bills' 34, Patriots receiver Shawn Jefferson dropped a sure first-down pass at the 24-yard. The drop cost the Patriots a chance at a game-tying field goal and sent them to their fourth loss in five games.

Sub of the week: Terrell Fletcher, subbing for Natrone Means after Means suffered a broken foot early in the second quarter, helped the Chargers to a 14-13 win with a 23-carry, 47-yard performance. Fletcher scored the Chargers' go-ahead touchdown.

Comeback of the week: His team down by a touchdown with less than three minutes to go, Peyton Manning took the Colts 80 yards on the final drive, ending it with a 14-yard touchdown pass to tight end Marcus Pollard with 24 seconds remaining. Pollard initially appeared to be stopped just shy of the end zone, but a surging second effort helped him get the ball over the plane of the goal-line. The touchdown strike was the third of the game for Manning, who rallied the Colts from a 13-point deficit in the second half.

Blowout of the week: Cris Dishman picked off two Bobby Hoying passes, and rookie running back Skip Hicks scored three touchdowns as Washington whipped the Eagles, 28-3. The Philadelphia offense went 3-for-13 in short-yardage situations (third and fourth downs with 2 yards or less to go), contributing to their league-worst average of nine points per game.

Nail-biter of the week: The Cowboys looked to be in control after taking a 28-0 lead in the second quarter against the Cardinals. But Arizona climbed back with a Rob Moore touchdown catch at the end of the third quarter and a 7-yard TD catch by Adrian Murrell early in the fourth to close the gap to 35-28. With the Cowboys up by seven and time running out, Jake Plummer found Eric Metcalf for a 16-yard strike and Rob Moore on a 57-yard play, taking Arizona to the Dallas 5. Plummer's fade to Moore in the end zone with no time remaining was broken up by Kevin Smith, preserving a Cowboys victory.

Hit of the week: Punter Darren Bennett, in a last-gasp effort to stop the Ravens' Jermaine Lewis from scoring a 90-yard return, attempted to trip Lewis. Lewis lost his balance at the 45-yard line and fell down. Believing he was untouched, Lewis got up and proceeded into the end zone for an apparent touchdown, putting Baltimore ahead with about six minutes to go. After a meeting by the officials, Lewis was ruled down by contact and Bennett was assessed a tripping penalty. Lewis insisted that he was never touched. Nonetheless, the (phantom?) tackle kept the Ravens out of the end zone and preserved a 14-13 San Diego win.

Oddity of the week: With one second left in the first half, Mike Vanderjagt of the Colts lined up for a 63-yard field-goal attempt, hoping to trim the Jets' lead to three. The attempt, which fell short, was caught 4 yards deep in the end zone by Aaron Glenn, who ran the ball back an NFL record 104 yards for a touchdown that gave the Jets a 23-10 halftime lead.

Top rusher: Curtis Martin rushed for 134 yards on 28 carries in the Jets' 24-23 loss to the Colts.

Top passer: Jake Plummer of the Cardinals completed 31-of-56 passes for 465 yards and three touchdowns in a losing effort against the Cowboys.

Top receiver: Arizona's Frank Sanders caught 11 passes for 190 yards and one touchdown in the loss to Dallas.

Notes: Desmond Howard's punt return for a touchdown was his first as a Raider and his first since his MVP performance for the Packers in Super Bowl 31. . . . Chargers quarterback Craig Whelihan was 0-7 as an NFL starter prior to getting his first win against Baltimore. . . . The Bears' loss in Detroit was their fifth straight in the Silverdome. . . . Cris Dishman's two interceptions were the first by a

Washington cornerback in 1998. . . . The Panthers' 13-9 loss to Miami was Carolina's seventh loss this year by seven points or fewer. . . . Peyton Manning, with two touchdown passes against the Jets, tied the NFL rookie record of seven straight games with a touchdown pass. . . . Brett Favre completed 21-of-33 passes and two touchdowns, including the 200th of his career, in Green Bay's 37-3 win over the Giants. Favre eclipsed the 25,000-yard mark with a 6-yard pass to Antonio Freeman in the first quarter. Favre's achievements came in his 107th game. . . . Michael Irvin went without a reception in the Cowboys' win over Arizona, snapping his streak of 117 consecutive games with at least one catch.

Quote of the week: Rams coach Dick Vermeil, after his team's 24-3 loss to the Saints: "I stink. My coaching staff stinks. We all stink. We stunk up the place. A junior high coach could have done better than I did today."

GAME SUMMARIES

BILLS 13, PATRIOTS 10

Sunday, November 15

New England	0	3	0	7—10
Buffalo	3	3	7	0—13

First Quarter
Buf.—FG, Christie 31, 6:06.
Second Quarter
Buf.—FG, Christie 20, 0:40.
N.E.—FG, Vinatieri 38, 10:05.
Third Quarter
Buf.—Riemersma 10 pass from Flutie (Christie kick), 13:03.
Fourth Quarter
N.E.—Simmons 37 pass from Bledsoe (Vinatieri kick), 1:49.
Attendance—72,020.

	New England	Buffalo
First downs	11	23
Rushes-yards	16-48	46-213
Passing	158	178
Punt returns	1-3	4-38
Kickoff returns	4-80	3-36
Interception returns	2-(-4)	0-0
Comp.-att.-int.	12-31-0	14-26-2
Sacked-yards lost	3-22	0-0
Punts	5-48	2-48
Fumbles-lost	0-0	3-1
Penalties-yards	6-34	6-43
Time of possession	22:43	37:17

INDIVIDUAL STATISTICS

RUSHING—New England, Edwards 14-50, Cullors 2-(minus 2). Buffalo, A. Smith 24-88, Thomas 11-76, Flutie 11-49.

PASSING—New England, Bledsoe 12-31-0-180. Buffalo, Flutie 14-26-2-178.

RECEIVING—New England, Coates 4-70, Simmons 2-48, Jefferson 2-36, Edwards 1-10, Purnell 1-9, Brisby 1-7, S. Shaw 1-0. Buffalo, Reed 5-68, Riemersma 4-51, Moulds 3-29, Gash 1-18, L. Johnson 1-12.

MISSED FIELD GOAL ATTEMPTS—New England, Vinatieri 39, 39. Buffalo, Christie 40.

INTERCEPTIONS—New England, Clay 1-0, Milloy 1-(minus 4).

KICKOFF RETURNS—New England, Canty 2-44, Cullors 2-36. Buffalo, K. Williams 2-37, L. Johnson 1-(minus 1).

PUNT RETURNS—New England, Canty 1-3. Buffalo, K. Williams 4-38.

SACKS—Buffalo, B. Smith 2, Hansen 1.

OILERS 23, STEELERS 14

Sunday, November 15

Pittsburgh	0	14	0	0—14
Tennessee	3	10	0	10—23

First Quarter
Ten.—FG, Del Greco 46, 13:54.
Second Quarter
Pit.—Bruener 10 pass from Stewart (George kick), 2:33.
Ten.—Davis 25 pass from McNair (Del Greco kick), 8:39.
Pit.—Fuamatu-Ma'afala 26 pass from Stewart (George kick), 11:59.
Ten.—FG, Del Greco 24, 14:56.
Fourth Quarter
Ten.—FG, Del Greco 22, 14:57.
Ten.—Roan fumble recovery in end zone (Del Greco kick), 15:00.
Attendance—41,104.

	Pittsburgh	Tennessee
First downs	16	18
Rushes-yards	25-73	32-112
Passing	237	226
Punt returns	2-40	1-(-5)
Kickoff returns	3-(-10)	3-82
Interception returns	1-2	0-0
Comp.-att.-int.	22-28-0	19-31-1
Sacked-yards lost	1-2	2-8
Punts	4-38	4-55
Fumbles-lost	3-2	1-0
Penalties-yards	2-9	8-81
Time of possession	27:26	32:34

INDIVIDUAL STATISTICS

RUSHING—Pittsburgh, Bettis 14-29, Stewart 9-28, Huntley 1-10, Hawkins 1-6. Tennessee, E. George 25-79, McNair 6-34, Hentrich 1-(minus 1).

PASSING—Pittsburgh, Stewart 22-28-0-239. Tennessee, McNair 19-31-1-234.

RECEIVING—Pittsburgh, Hawkins 4-62, C. Johnson 4-47, Lester 4-26, Fuamatu-Ma'afala 2-38, Ward 2-21, Bruener 2-18, Blackwell 2-17, Bettis 2-10. Tennessee, Davis 6-90, Dyson 4-30, Mason 3-35, Wycheck 2-40, Harris 2-29, Roan 1-9, E. George 1-1.

MISSED FIELD GOAL ATTEMPTS—Pittsburgh, George 36.

INTERCEPTIONS—Pittsburgh, Flowers 1-2.

KICKOFF RETURNS—Pittsburgh, Huntley 1-22, Roye 1-0, Lyons 1-(minus 5). Tennessee, Archie 3-82.

PUNT RETURNS—Pittsburgh, Hawkins 2-40. Tennessee, Mason 1-(minus 5).

SACKS—Pittsburgh, Gildon 1, Roye 1. Tennessee, G. Walker 0.5, Ford 0.5.

COLTS 24, JETS 23

Sunday, November 15

N.Y. Jets	3	20	0	0—23
Indianapolis	10	0	7	7—24

First Quarter
Ind.—FG, Vanderjagt 31, 4:43.
NYJ—FG, Hall 37, 8:21.
Ind.—Small 4 pass from Manning (Vanderjagt kick), 11:35.
Second Quarter
NYJ—Chrebet 63 pass from Testaverde (Hall kick), 0:58.
NYJ—FG, Hall 40, 6:29.
NYJ—FG, Hall 25, 14:38.
NYJ—Glenn 104 blocked FG return (Hall kick), 15:00.
Third Quarter
Ind.—Harrison 38 pass from Manning (Vanderjagt kick), 8:32.
Fourth Quarter
Ind.—Pollard 14 pass from Manning (Vanderjagt kick), 14:36.
Attendance—55,520.

	N.Y. Jets	Indianapolis
First downs	20	24
Rushes-yards	33-157	24-90
Passing	212	253
Punt returns	2-9	2-25
Kickoff returns	5-126	3-87
Interception returns	2-(-3)	1-19
Comp.-att.-int.	12-28-1	26-44-2
Sacked-yards lost	4-37	1-23
Punts	4-47	4-41
Fumbles-lost	3-1	1-0
Penalties-yards	6-50	8-55
Time of possession	32:08	27:52

INDIVIDUAL STATISTICS

RUSHING—New York, Martin 28-134, Byars 3-21, Testaverde 2-2. Indianapolis, Faulk 20-69, Manning 4-21.

PASSING—New York, Testaverde 12-28-1-249. Indianapolis, Manning 26-44-2-276.

RECEIVING—New York, K. Johnson 5-107, Chrebet 4-112, Baxter 1-21, Anderson 1-7, Martin 1-2. Indianapolis, Harrison 9-128, Faulk 8-70, Dilger 4-22, Pathon 2-28, Small 2-14, Pollard 1-14.

MISSED FIELD GOAL ATTEMPTS—New York, Hall 47. Indianapolis, Vanderjagt 63.

INTERCEPTIONS—New York, Smith 1-0, Glenn 1-(minus 3). Indianapolis, Belser 1-19.

KICKOFF RETURNS—New York, Glenn 3-73, Williams 2-53. Indianapolis, Bailey 2-67, Hetherington 1-20.

PUNT RETURNS—New York, Ward 2-9. Indianapolis, Bailey 2-25.

SACKS—New York, Team 1. Indianapolis, McCoy 1, M. Barber 1, Berry 1, Whittington 1.

RAIDERS 20, SEAHAWKS 17

Sunday, November 15

Seattle	7	3	0	7—17
Oakland	0	7	0	13—20

First Quarter
Sea.—Galloway 56 punt return (Peterson kick), 1:04.

Second Quarter
Sea.—FG, Peterson 22, 3:28.
Oak.—Howard 63 punt return (G. Davis kick), 13:30.

Fourth Quarter
Oak.—FG, G. Davis 26, 6:43.
Oak.—H. Williams 25 run (G. Davis kick), 11:10.
Sea.—Fauria 12 pass from Moon (Peterson kick), 13:59.
Oak.—FG, G. Davis 38, 14:39.
Attendance—51,527.

	Seattle	Oakland
First downs	15	21
Rushes-yards	29-101	33-131
Passing	192	249
Punt returns	3-65	6-133
Kickoff returns	5-111	3-67
Interception returns	2-36	3-21
Comp.-att.-int.	17-33-3	20-31-2
Sacked-yards lost	5-28	3-17
Punts	10-43	6-41
Fumbles-lost	0-0	2-1
Penalties-yards	14-141	7-60
Time of possession	28:47	31:13

INDIVIDUAL STATISTICS

RUSHING—Seattle, Watters 27-85, Moon 1-9, Strong 1-7. Oakland, Kaufman 14-22, H. Williams 12-79, Hollas 5-13, Ritchie 1-4, Jett 1-3.

PASSING—Seattle, Moon 17-33-3-220. Oakland, Hollas 20-31-2-266.

RECEIVING—Seattle, Pritchard 5-79, Fauria 4-32, McKnight 3-66, Galloway 3-30, Watters 2-13. Oakland, Dudley 5-96, H. Williams 4-29, Ritchie 3-27, D. Brown 3-24, Kaufman 2-35, T. Brown 2-31, Jett 1-24.

MISSED FIELD GOAL ATTEMPTS—Oakland, G. Davis 30.

INTERCEPTIONS—Seattle, Wells 1-25, Springs 1-11. Oakland, Allen 1-16, Woodson 1-5, Lewis 1-0.

KICKOFF RETURNS—Seattle, Green 5-111. Oakland, Howard 2-40, Branch 1-27.

PUNT RETURNS—Seattle, Galloway 3-65. Oakland, Howard 6-133.

SACKS—Seattle, C. Brown 2, Kennedy 1. Oakland, Russell 2, Jackson 1, Johnstone 1, Swilling 1.

FALCONS 31, 49ERS 19

Sunday, November 15

San Francisco	0	3	3	13—19
Atlanta	0	7	3	21—31

Second Quarter
Atl.—J. Anderson 10 run (Andersen kick), 12:04.
S.F.—FG, Richey 24, 14:41.

Third Quarter
S.F.—FG, Richey 28, 4:02.
Atl.—FG, Andersen 37, 14:06.

Fourth Quarter
Atl.—J. Anderson 2 run (Andersen kick), 0:04.
Atl.—Tuggle 1 fumble return (Andersen kick), 1:00.
S.F.—Owens 54 pass from S. Young (run failed), 3:44.
S.F.—Rice 65 pass from S. Young (Richey kick), 11:51.
Atl.—Mathis 78 pass from Chandler (Andersen kick), 12:09.
Attendance—69,828.

	San Fran.	Atlanta
First downs	18	19
Rushes-yards	20-76	36-114
Passing	307	184
Punt returns	4-(-3)	0-0
Kickoff returns	2-40	0-0
Interception returns	0-0	1-34
Comp.-att.-int.	21-40-1	12-21-0
Sacked-yards lost	4-35	3-14
Punts	5-42	5-42
Fumbles-lost	1-1	1-1
Penalties-yards	6-30	5-30
Time of possession	25:30	34:30

INDIVIDUAL STATISTICS

RUSHING—San Francisco, Hearst 16-56, S. Young 3-15, Kirby 1-5. Atlanta, J. Anderson 31-100, Chandler 4-10, Oxendine 1-4.

PASSING—San Francisco, S. Young 21-40-1-342. Atlanta, Chandler 12-21-0-198.

RECEIVING—San Francisco, Rice 10-169, Owens 3-87, Edwards 2-18, Kirby 2-8, Harris 1-42, Stokes 1-10, Clark 1-9, Hearst 1-(minus 1). Atlanta, Christian 4-48, Martin 4-44, Mathis 1-78, Santiago 1-13, J. Anderson 1-8, Kozlowski 1-7.

MISSED FIELD GOAL ATTEMPTS—None.

INTERCEPTIONS—Atlanta, Buchanan 1-34.

KICKOFF RETURNS—San Francisco, Levy 2-40.

PUNT RETURNS—San Francisco, McQuarters 4-(minus 3).

SACKS—San Francisco, B. Young 1, Barker 1, Doleman 0.5, Posey 0.5. Atlanta, Dronett 1.5, Hall 1, C. Smith 1, Archambeau 0.5.

DOLPHINS 13, PANTHERS 9

Sunday, November 15

Miami	7	3	0	3—13
Carolina	3	3	0	3— 9

First Quarter
Mia.—Abdul-Jabbar 1 run (Mare kick), 5:58.
Car.—FG, Kasay 32, 11:06.

Second Quarter
Car.—FG, Kasay 27, 5:03.
Mia.—FG, Mare 22, 15:00.

Fourth Quarter
Mia.—FG, Mare 22, 0:48.
Car.—FG, Kasay 43, 6:15.
Attendance—67,887.

	Miami	Carolina
First downs	15	12
Rushes-yards	40-184	18-62
Passing	131	148
Punt returns	1-6	4-34
Kickoff returns	3-42	3-87
Interception returns	2-12	1-18
Comp.-att.-int.	14-21-1	17-30-2
Sacked-yards lost	1-9	4-12
Punts	5-45	3-38
Fumbles-lost	3-0	2-0
Penalties-yards	6-60	4-50
Time of possession	35:05	24:55

INDIVIDUAL STATISTICS

RUSHING—Miami, Abdul-Jabbar 25-127, Avery 12-53, Marino 2-(minus 3), Lusk 1-7. Carolina, Biakabutuka 8-38, Lane 6-15, Floyd 3-7, Beuerlein 1-2.

PASSING—Miami, Marino 14-21-1-140. Carolina, Beuerlein 17-30-2-160.

RECEIVING—Miami, McDuffie 7-96, Gadsden 3-21, L. Thomas 2-14, Drayton 1-7, Abdul-Jabbar 1-2. Carolina, Walls 8-84, Ismail 5-50, Muhammad 3-21, Johnson 1-5.

MISSED FIELD GOAL ATTEMPTS—None.

INTERCEPTIONS—Miami, Walker 2-12. Carolina, Greene 1-18.

KICKOFF RETURNS—Miami, Avery 3-42. Carolina, Bates 2-64, Stone 1-23.
PUNT RETURNS—Miami, Buckley 1-6. Carolina, Oliver 4-34.
SACKS—Miami, R. Jones 2, Armstrong 1, Taylor 1. Carolina, E. Jones 1.

VIKINGS 24, BENGALS 3

Sunday, November 15

Cincinnati	0	3	0	0— 3
Minnesota	7	0	7	10—24

First Quarter
Min.—Cunningham 3 run (Anderson kick), 8:29.
Second Quarter
Cin.—FG, Pelfrey 37, 8:04.
Third Quarter
Min.—Rudd 63 fumble return (Anderson kick), 11:21.
Fourth Quarter
Min.—FG, Anderson 32, 2:12.
Min.—R. Moss 61 pass from Cunningham (Anderson kick), 3:34.
   Attendance—64,232.

	Cincinnati	Minnesota
First downs	15	16
Rushes-yards	34-103	29-125
Passing	91	224
Punt returns	2-30	2-27
Kickoff returns	1-35	2-56
Interception returns	3-53	1-34
Comp.-att.-int.	16-27-1	14-22-3
Sacked-yards lost	4-22	2-12
Punts	5-40	4-56
Fumbles-lost	1-1	0-0
Penalties-yards	2-10	11-105
Time of possession	32:22	27:38

INDIVIDUAL STATISTICS
RUSHING—Cincinnati, Dillon 21-66, Bennett 7-22, Blake 2-9, Bieniemy 2-7, Pickens 1-0, O'Donnell 1-(minus 1). Minnesota, R. Smith 18-58, Hoard 7-52, Cunningham 2-13, Palmer 1-4, Fiedler 1-(minus 2).
PASSING—Cincinnati, O'Donnell 10-17-0-77, Blake 6-10-1-36. Minnesota, Cunningham 13-20-2-224, Fiedler 1-2-1-12.
RECEIVING—Cincinnati, Scott 4-31, Milne 3-29, Dillon 3-14, Bieniemy 2-16, Pickens 1-8, Battaglia 1-7, Gibson 1-5, Bennett 1-3. Minnesota, Carter 5-87, R. Moss 4-99, Reed 2-21, R. Smith 1-10, Evans 1-10, Glover 1-9.
MISSED FIELD GOAL ATTEMPTS—None.
INTERCEPTIONS—Cincinnati, Hawkins 2-21, Shade 1-32. Minnesota, Hitchcock 1-34.
KICKOFF RETURNS—Cincinnati, Mack 1-35. Minnesota, Palmer 2-56.
PUNT RETURNS—Cincinnati, Gibson 2-30. Minnesota, Palmer 2-27.
SACKS—Cincinnati, Wilson 1, Ross 1. Minnesota, Alexander 2, E. McDaniel 1, Randle 1.

SAINTS 24, RAMS 3

Sunday, November 15

St. Louis	3	0	0	0— 3
New Orleans	14	10	0	0—24

First Quarter
N.O.—Cleeland 10 pass from Collins (Brien kick), 5:59.
N.O.—Drakeford 32 interception return (Brien kick), 7:43.
St.L.—FG, Wilkins 33, 12:08.
Second Quarter
N.O.—FG, Brien 26, 12:52.
N.O.—Robbins fumble recovery in end zone (Brien kick), 13:05.
   Attendance—46,430.

	St. Louis	New Orleans
First downs	17	13
Rushes-yards	19-55	31-102
Passing	179	135
Punt returns	2-23	5-82
Kickoff returns	2-45	1-29
Interception returns	0-0	2-56
Comp.-att.-int.	24-37-2	13-26-0
Sacked-yards lost	7-67	2-15
Punts	8-52	8-40
Fumbles-lost	2-1	2-0
Penalties-yards	9-73	7-65
Time of possession	28:52	31:08

INDIVIDUAL STATISTICS
RUSHING—St. Louis, J. Moore 11-26, Lee 3-19, Henley 2-4, Banks 2-3, Harris 1-3. New Orleans, Zellars 11-23, Collins 7-38, L. Smith 7-22, Craver 6-19.
PASSING—St. Louis, Banks 24-37-2-246. New Orleans, Collins 13-26-0-150.
RECEIVING—St. Louis, Lee 7-99, Proehl 7-51, Henley 4-33, Hakim 3-28, Kennison 1-15, J. Thomas 1-12, J. Moore 1-8. New Orleans, Dawkins 3-49, Poole 3-43, Cleeland 2-19, L. Smith 2-(minus 3), Craver 1-26, Hastings 1-15, Zellars 1-1.
MISSED FIELD GOAL ATTEMPTS—St. Louis, Wilkins 53.
INTERCEPTIONS—New Orleans, Drakeford 1-32, Molden 1-24.
KICKOFF RETURNS—St. Louis, Horne 2-45. New Orleans, Craver 1-29.
PUNT RETURNS—St. Louis, Kennison 2-23. New Orleans, Hastings 5-82.
SACKS—St. Louis, Phifer 1, Lyght 1. New Orleans, Glover 3, J. Johnson 2, Tomich 2.

REDSKINS 28, EAGLES 3

Sunday, November 15

Philadelphia	0	3	0	0— 3
Washington	7	7	7	7—28

First Quarter
Was.—Hicks 1 run (Blanchard kick), 13:07.
Second Quarter
Phi.—FG, Boniol 19, 10:18.
Was.—Hicks 1 run (Blanchard kick), 14:38.
Third Quarter
Was.—Connell 56 pass from T. Green (Blanchard kick), 8:09.
Fourth Quarter
Was.—Hicks 5 run (Blanchard kick), 5:44.
   Attendance—67,704.

	Philadelphia	Washington
First downs	9	16
Rushes-yards	29-105	35-151
Passing	110	138
Punt returns	2-27	6-31
Kickoff returns	4-124	1-18
Interception returns	0-0	3-64
Comp.-att.-int.	17-36-3	14-33-0
Sacked-yards lost	5-20	4-31
Punts	7-45	8-48
Fumbles-lost	1-0	2-1
Penalties-yards	6-52	4-40
Time of possession	28:39	31:21

INDIVIDUAL STATISTICS
RUSHING—Philadelphia, Garner 13-63, Staley 12-42, Hoying 3-5, Dunn 1-(minus 5). Washington, Hicks 26-94, Mitchell 5-54, T. Green 3-(minus 1), Davis 1-4.
PASSING—Philadelphia, Hoying 16-34-2-118, Detmer 1-2-1-12. Washington, T. Green 14-33-0-169.
RECEIVING—Philadelphia, Dunn 4-32, Garner 4-24, Graham 3-32, Solomon 2-14, Sinceno 1-11, Copeland 1-9, Staley 1-4, Fryar 1-4. Washington, Mitchell 4-28, Connell 3-80, Shepherd 3-28, S. Alexander 2-21, Westbrook 2-12.
MISSED FIELD GOAL ATTEMPTS—Washington, Blanchard 32.
INTERCEPTIONS—Washington, Dishman 2-60, Wilkinson 1-4.
KICKOFF RETURNS—Philadelphia, Rossum 4-124. Washington, Mitchell 1-18.
PUNT RETURNS—Philadelphia, Solomon 1-16, Rossum 1-11. Washington, Mitchell 6-31.
SACKS—Philadelphia, Douglas 1.5, Wallace 1, H. Thomas 1, B. Johnson 0.5. Washington, Lang 2, Harvey 2, Wilkinson 1.

JAGUARS 29, BUCCANEERS 24

Sunday, November 15

Tampa Bay	3	14	0	7—24
Jacksonville	7	7	6	9—29

First Quarter
Jac.—F. Taylor 6 run (Hollis kick), 8:13.
T.B.—FG, Husted 34, 13:49.
Second Quarter
Jac.—F. Taylor 3 run (Hollis kick), 3:22.
T.B.—Anthony 47 pass from Dilfer (Husted kick), 7:18.
T.B.—Davis 1 pass from Dilfer (Husted kick), 14:36.

Third Quarter

Jac.—FG, Hollis 31, 4:35.
Jac.—FG, Hollis 27, 14:29.

Fourth Quarter

T.B.—Anthony 79 pass from Dilfer (Husted kick), 0:13.
Jac.—FG, Hollis 34, 11:33.
Jac.—F. Taylor 70 run (run failed), 12:20.
   Attendance—72,974.

	Tampa Bay	Jacksonville
First downs	13	18
Rushes-yards	33-157	28-144
Passing	186	230
Punt returns	3-41	4-19
Kickoff returns	7-143	5-95
Interception returns	0-0	2 17
Comp.-att.-int.	10-24-2	22-37-0
Sacked-yards lost	2-8	3-18
Punts	6-46	6-50
Fumbles-lost	1-1	2-0
Penalties-yards	7-52	8-57
Time of possession	28:49	31:11

INDIVIDUAL STATISTICS

RUSHING—Tampa Bay, Dunn 16-107, Alstott 16-48, Dilfer 1-2. Jacksonville, F. Taylor 20-128, Brunell 5-10, Shelton 2-7, G. Jones 1-(minus 1).

PASSING—Tampa Bay, Dilfer 9-23-2-189, Walsh 1-1-0-5. Jacksonville, Brunell 22-37-0-248.

RECEIVING—Tampa Bay, Anthony 2-126, Dunn 2-14, Williams 1-26, Green 1-8, Moore 1-7, Alstott 1-6, Emanuel 1-6, Davis 1-1. Jacksonville, J. Smith 7-72, Mitchell 6-56, F. Taylor 5-68, McCardell 2-34, Barlow 1-11, D. Jones 1-7.

MISSED FIELD GOAL ATTEMPTS—None.

INTERCEPTIONS—Jacksonville, Hardy 1-16, Beasley 1-1.

KICKOFF RETURNS—Tampa Bay, Anthony 7-143. Jacksonville, Logan 2-54, Barlow 2-34, Fordham 1-0.

PUNT RETURNS—Tampa Bay, Green 3-41. Jacksonville, C. Taylor 3-13, Barlow 1-6.

SACKS—Tampa Bay, Culpepper 1, Barber 1, Upshaw 1. Jacksonville, Paup 1, Smeenge 1.

PACKERS 37, GIANTS 3

Sunday, November 15

Green Bay	7	13	10	7—37
N.Y. Giants	0	3	0	0— 3

First Quarter

G.B.—T. Davis 2 pass from Favre (Longwell kick), 13:32.

Second Quarter

G.B.—FG, Longwell 39, 6:13.
NYG.—FG, Daluiso 24, 10:45.
G.B.—T. Davis 60 pass from Favre (Longwell kick), 12:15.
G.B.—FG, Longwell 24, 15:00.

Third Quarter

G.B.—FG, Longwell 31, 4:38.
G.B.—Henderson 7 run (Longwell kick), 10:47.

Fourth Quarter

G.B.—Holmes 2 run (Longwell kick), 7:23.
   Attendance—76,272.

	Green Bay	N.Y. Giants
First downs	24	9
Rushes-yards	46-169	19-65
Passing	264	62
Punt returns	4-36	2-(-5)
Kickoff returns	2-88	7-135
Interception returns	2-3	0-0
Comp.-att.-int.	21-34-0	10-25-2
Sacked-yards lost	1-3	5-38
Punts	3-52	8-47
Fumbles-lost	1-0	1-1
Penalties-yards	5-35	3-14
Time of possession	39:43	20:17

INDIVIDUAL STATISTICS

RUSHING—Green Bay, Holmes 27-111, R. Harris 10-33, Henderson 4-21, Favre 3-6, Pederson 2-(minus 2). New York, Brown 8-21, Wheatley 5-20, Way 5-17, K. Graham 1-7.

PASSING—Green Bay, Favre 21-33-0-267, Pederson 0-1-0-0. New York, Kanell 8-20-2-88, K. Graham 2-5-0-12.

RECEIVING—Green Bay, R. Brooks 6-60, Freeman 5-54, T. Davis 3-83, Schroeder 2-20, Holmes 2-13, Bradford 1-18, Chmura 1-11, Henderson 1-8. New York, Hilliard 3-48, Calloway 2-20, Toomer 2-16, Cross 1-12, Jurevicius 1-3, Barber 1-1.

MISSED FIELD GOAL ATTEMPTS—Green Bay, Longwell 39, 48.

INTERCEPTIONS—Green Bay, Butler 2-3.

KICKOFF RETURNS—Green Bay, Preston 2-88. New York, Barber 7-135.

PUNT RETURNS—Green Bay, Preston 4-36. New York, Toomer 2-(minus 5).

SACKS—Green Bay, Holliday 2, White 2, Waddy 1. New York, Bratzke 1.

LIONS 26, BEARS 3

Sunday, November 15

Chicago	0	3	0	0— 3
Detroit	7	10	6	3—26

First Quarter

Det.—Vardell 12 pass from Batch (Hanson kick), 10:38.

Second Quarter

Chi.—FG, Jaeger 31, 1:11.
Det.—Vardell 3 run (Hanson kick), 5:30.
Det.—FG, Hanson 24, 14:51.

Third Quarter

Det.—Vardell 1 run (kick blocked), 10:43.

Fourth Quarter

Det.—FG, Hanson 25, 12:41.
   Attendance—63,152.

	Chicago	Detroit
First downs	14	24
Rushes-yards	21-105	34-145
Passing	147	246
Punt returns	0-0	2-8
Kickoff returns	3-58	2-52
Interception returns	0-0	0-0
Comp.-att.-int.	14-27-0	16-21-0
Sacked-yards lost	5-25	1-7
Punts	3-42	2-55
Fumbles-lost	1-0	2-0
Penalties-yards	5-60	9-66
Time of possession	24:53	35:07

INDIVIDUAL STATISTICS

RUSHING—Chicago, Bennett 18-73, Conway 1-29, Chancey 1-4, Stenstrom 1-(minus 1). Detroit, Sanders 24-114, Rivers 4-22, Batch 4-5, Vardell 2-4.

PASSING—Chicago, Stenstrom 13-25-0-159, Moreno 1-2-0-13. Detroit, Batch 16-21-0-253.

RECEIVING—Chicago, Engram 4-74, Hallock 4-27, Conway 2-25, Bennett 2-14, Penn 1-18, Moreno 1-14. Detroit, Morton 5-109, Crowell 3-57, Sloan 2-28, Stablein 2-21, Rasby 1-17, Vardell 1-12, Sanders 1-6, Moore 1-3.

MISSED FIELD GOAL ATTEMPTS—Chicago, Jaeger 43.

INTERCEPTIONS—None.

KICKOFF RETURNS—Chicago, Milburn 3-58. Detroit, Fair 2-52.

PUNT RETURNS—Detroit, Fair 2-8.

SACKS—Chicago, Flanigan 1. Detroit, Porcher 2.5, Fair 1, Abrams 1, Elliss 0.5.

CHARGERS 14, RAVENS 13

Sunday, November 15

Baltimore	0	3	7	3—13
San Diego	0	7	0	7—14

Second Quarter

Bal.—FG, Stover 42, 1:33.
S.D.—C. Jones 47 pass from Whelihan (Carney kick), 11:56.

Third Quarter

Bal.—J. Lewis 58 pass from Harbaugh (Stover kick), 7:35.

Fourth Quarter

S.D.—Fletcher 3 run (Carney kick), 0:19.
Bal.—FG, Stover 42, 11:11.
   Attendance—54,388.

	Baltimore	San Diego
First downs	8	19
Rushes-yards	15-40	32-57
Passing	121	146
Punt returns	6-63	3-12
Kickoff returns	3-59	4-82

	Baltimore	San Diego
Interception returns	0-0	2-25
Comp.-att.-int.	12-34-2	15-42-0
Sacked-yards lost	6-29	2-26
Punts	8-47	10-42
Fumbles-lost	2-0	3-1
Penalties-yards	14-106	16-146
Time of possession	25:57	34:03

INDIVIDUAL STATISTICS

RUSHING—Baltimore, Holmes 6-9, Harbaugh 5-22, Rhett 3-9, Potts 1-0. San Diego, Fletcher 23-47, Means 6-5, Whelihan 3-5.

PASSING—Baltimore, Harbaugh 12-33-1-150, Holmes 0-1-1-0. San Diego, Whelihan 15-42-0-172.

RECEIVING—Baltimore, Green 4-35, Jackson 3-17, J. Lewis 2-78, Potts 2-19, Holmes 1-1. San Diego, F. Jones 5-33, Fletcher 3-18, Ricks 3-16, C. Jones 2-65, Thelwell 1-30, Slaughter 1-10.

MISSED FIELD GOAL ATTEMPTS—None.

INTERCEPTIONS—San Diego, G. Jackson 1-25, Shaw 1-0.

KICKOFF RETURNS—Baltimore, C. Harris 3-59. San Diego, Bynum 4-82.

PUNT RETURNS—Baltimore, J. Lewis 6-63. San Diego, Rachal 3-12.

SACKS—Baltimore, Boulware 1.5, Burnett 0.5. San Diego, Coleman 1.5, Hand 1, Bush 1, Mohring 1, Gouveia 0.5, Team 1.

COWBOYS 35, CARDINALS 28

Sunday, November 15

Dallas	14	14	7	0—35
Arizona	0	7	14	7—28

First Quarter
Dal.—Warren 3 run (Cunningham kick), 8:15.
Dal.—Johnston 1 pass from Aikman (Cunningham kick), 13:01.

Second Quarter
Dal.—E. Smith 1 run (Cunningham kick), 1:52.
Dal.—E. Smith 1 run (Cunningham kick), 11:31.
Ariz.—Sanders 2 pass from Plummer (Nedney kick), 14:46.

Third Quarter
Ariz.—Bates 2 run (Nedney kick), 5:13.
Dal.—E. Smith 3 run (Cunningham kick), 11:12.
Ariz.—R. Moore 4 pass from Plummer (Nedney kick), 14:56.

Fourth Quarter
Ariz.—Murrell 7 pass from Plummer (Nedney kick), 11:51.
Attendance—71,670.

	Dallas	Arizona
First downs	23	28
Rushes-yards	35-146	21-32
Passing	208	448
Punt returns	1-1	1-13
Kickoff returns	2-51	5-105
Interception returns	1-22	0-0
Comp.-att.-int.	14-18-0	31-56-1
Sacked-yards lost	0-0	3-17
Punts	5-40	2-47
Fumbles-lost	0-0	1-1
Penalties-yards	7-47	4-25
Time of possession	29:56	30:04

INDIVIDUAL STATISTICS

RUSHING—Dallas, E. Smith 26-118, Warren 7-25, E. Mills 1-5, Aikman 1-(minus 2). Arizona, Murrell 14-34, Plummer 3-6, Bates 2-1, Centers 1-4, Sanders 1-(minus 13).

PASSING—Dallas, Aikman 14-18-0-208. Arizona, Plummer 31-56-1-465.

RECEIVING—Dallas, B. Davis 3-70, LaFleur 3-33, E. Mills 2-28, E. Smith 2-16, Bjornson 1-43, Jeffers 1-11, Warren 1-6, Johnston 1-1. Arizona, Sanders 11-190, Metcalf 6-89, R. Moore 3-77, Gedney 3-67, Murrell 3-16, Centers 3-7, McWilliams 2-19.

MISSED FIELD GOAL ATTEMPTS—Arizona, Nedney 40.

INTERCEPTIONS—Dallas, Sanders 1-22.

KICKOFF RETURNS—Dallas, Ogden 1-28, Warren 1-23. Arizona, Metcalf 3-81, Pittman 2-24.

PUNT RETURNS—Dallas, Sanders 1-1. Arizona, Metcalf 1-13.

SACKS—Dallas, Godfrey 1, Myers 1, McCormack 1.

BRONCOS 30, CHIEFS 7

Monday, November 16

Denver	14	6	3	7—30
Kansas City	0	7	0	0— 7

First Quarter
Den.—Brister 38 run (Elam kick), 2:42.
Den.—Davis 41 run (Elam kick), 7:24.

Second Quarter
K.C.—Anders 3 pass from Gannon (Stoyanovich kick), 8:29.
Den.—FG, Elam 42, 11:41.
Den.—FG, Elam 46, 14:46.

Third Quarter
Den.—FG, Elam 35, 11:55.

Fourth Quarter
Den.—Loville 2 run (Elam kick), 11:49.
Attendance—78,100.

	Denver	Kansas City
First downs	26	15
Rushes-yards	34-211	19-31
Passing	168	190
Punt returns	1-0	4-17
Kickoff returns	2-45	6-94
Interception returns	1-4	0-0
Comp.-att.-int.	13-23-0	26-39-1
Sacked-yards lost	2-12	4-34
Punts	4-41	6-38
Fumbles-lost	0-0	5-0
Penalties-yards	9-99	13-137
Time of possession	28:39	31:21

INDIVIDUAL STATISTICS

RUSHING—Denver, Davis 18-111, Loville 10-40, Brister 5-53, R. Smith 1-7. Kansas City, Morris 9-20, Bennett 5-10, Anders 2-(minus 1), Rison 1-1, Shehee 1-1, Gannon 1-0.

PASSING—Denver, Brister 13-23-0-180. Kansas City, Gannon 26-39-1-224.

RECEIVING—Denver, R. Smith 5-50, Sharpe 3-56, Nash 2-36, McCaffrey 1-19, D. Smith 1-16, Green 1-3. Kansas City, Anders 10-75, Alexander 4-61, Gonzalez 4-35, Rison 3-21, Lockett 2-27, Shehee 1-13, Popson 1-0, Bennett 1-(minus 8).

MISSED FIELD GOAL ATTEMPTS—None.

INTERCEPTIONS—Denver, Romanowski 1-4.

KICKOFF RETURNS—Denver, Hebron 2-45. Kansas City, Shehee 4-72, Parten 1-22, Manusky 1-0.

PUNT RETURNS—Denver, Gordon 1-0. Kansas City, Lockett 4-17.

SACKS—Denver, Tanuvasa 2, Traylor 1, Pryce 1. Kansas City, Edwards 1, McGlockton 1.

WEEK 12

RESULTS

Arizona 45, WASHINGTON 42
ATLANTA 20, Chicago 13
Baltimore 20, CINCINNATI 13
BUFFALO 34, Indianapolis 11
Carolina 24, ST. LOUIS 20
DALLAS 30, Seattle 22
DENVER 40, Oakland 14
Detroit 28, TAMPA BAY 25
MINNESOTA 28, Green Bay 14
N.Y. GIANTS 20, Philadelphia 0
N.Y. Jets 24, TENNESSEE 3
PITTSBURGH 30, Jacksonville 15
SAN DIEGO 38, Kansas City 37
SAN FRANCISCO 31, New Orleans 20
NEW ENGLAND 26, Miami 23

STANDINGS

AFC EAST	W	L	T	Pct.
Buffalo	7	4	0	.636
Miami	7	4	0	.636
N.Y. Jets	7	4	0	.636
New England	6	5	0	.545
Indianapolis	2	9	0	.182

AFC CENTRAL	W	L	T	Pct.
Jacksonville	8	3	0	.727
Pittsburgh	7	4	0	.636
Tennessee	6	5	0	.545
Baltimore	4	7	0	.364
Cincinnati	2	9	0	.182

AFC WEST	W	L	T	Pct.
Denver	11	0	0	1.000
Oakland	7	4	0	.636
San Diego	5	6	0	.455
Seattle	5	6	0	.455
Kansas City	4	7	0	.364

NFC EAST	W	L	T	Pct.
Dallas	8	3	0	.727
Arizona	6	5	0	.545
N.Y. Giants	4	7	0	.364
Washington	3	8	0	.273
Philadelphia	2	9	0	.182

NFC CENTRAL	W	L	T	Pct.
Minnesota	10	1	0	.909
Green Bay	7	4	0	.636
Detroit	4	7	0	.364
Tampa Bay	4	7	0	.364
Chicago	3	8	0	.273

NFC WEST	W	L	T	Pct.
Atlanta	9	2	0	.818
San Francisco	8	3	0	.727
New Orleans	5	6	0	.455
St. Louis	3	8	0	.273
Carolina	2	9	0	.182

HIGHLIGHTS

Hero of the week: Drew Bledsoe engineered a 15-play, 80-yard drive that ended with a 25-yard TD strike to Shawn Jefferson, giving the Patriots a 26-23 victory over the Dolphins. Despite suffering a broken index finger on his throwing hand on the final drive, Bledsoe kept the Patriots in the game by converting on three third-down plays and two fourth-down plays.

Goat of the week: Pete Stoyanovich missed a 46-yard field-goal attempt with 57 seconds left, failing to extend the Chiefs' lead beyond six points. The decision to attempt the field goal was made by coach Marty Schottenheimer after the offense stalled at the San Diego 29 with 57 seconds left. The Chargers took possession at the 37 and drove for the winning points: a 1-yard TD pass from Craig Whelihan to Charlie Jones with nine seconds left.

Sub of the week: Detroit running back Ron Rivers, spelling Barry Sanders for one play in the second quarter, exploited his opportunity to the fullest, taking off on a 36-yard touchdown run to extend the Lions' lead to 21-7. It was Rivers' only carry of the game. His touchdown was one of the keys to Detroit's 28-25 victory over the Bucs.

Comeback of the week: The Chargers scored 21 points in the last 8:01 to steal a 38-37 victory from the Chiefs, who lost their sixth straight game. Craig Whelihan, starting in place of struggling rookie Ryan Leaf, passed for 166 yards and two touchdowns in the final quarter, including the game-winner to Charlie Jones.

Blowout of the week: Led by their defensive unit, which contributed six sacks and two interceptions (both by Phillippi Sparks), the Giants blanked Philadelphia, 20-0. It marked the third time the Eagles had been shut out this season.

Nail-biter of the week: After jumping to a 31-0 lead, the Cardinals allowed the Redskins to get back into the game behind Trent Green's 382-yard, four-touchdown performance before holding on for a 45-42 victory. Clinging to a three-point lead with four minutes left, Arizona quarterback Jake Plummer dove into the end zone from the 1-yard line. The ball came loose and was recovered by Washington. The officials signaled neither a touchdown nor a turnover. After a brief discussion, the ruling was that Plummer was down by contact, and on fourth-and-goal Plummer found his way into the end zone.

Hit of the week: Roman Phifer of the Rams looked to have an interception returned for a touchdown with 2:41 to go, but as he approached the goal line Mark Carrier stripped the ball, sending it into the end zone, where Carolina recovered for a touchback. The play preserved the Panthers' 24-20 victory, their second win of the year.

Oddity of the week: In honor of the late Weeb Ewbank, the Jets coach who led the team to its only Super Bowl victory, Jets players planned to place decals on their helmets for their game at Tennessee. However, the box of decals was stolen before the game, pushing the commemorative gesture back one week.

Top rusher: Baltimore rookie Priest Holmes carried 36 times for 227 yards and one touchdown as the Ravens beat Cincinnati, 20-13.

Top passer: Trent Green of the Redskins completed 30-of-49 passes for 382 yards and four touchdowns in Washington's 45-42 loss to the Cardinals.

Top receiver: Derrick Alexander caught five passes for 173 yards, including one touchdown, in the Chiefs' 38-37 loss at San Diego.

Notes: Priest Holmes' 227-yard rushing performance was the best game total ever by a Ravens running back. . . . With a loss to Carolina, the Rams assured themselves of a ninth straight non-winning season. . . . The Eagles' 92 points through 11 games were 73 fewer than any other team. . . . Andre Reed's 108-yard receiving game was the 36th 100-yard day of his career, most in Bills history. Reed played in his 200th regular-season game, a feat accomplished by only one other Bills player. . . . Doug Flutie's win over the Colts was his 10th in 10 home starts as an NFL quarterback. . . . With a 5-yard pass to Willie Green, the Broncos' John Elway joined Dan Marino as the only players in league history to pass for 50,000 yards. Elway's three TD passes in the 40-14 win over the Raiders gave him 290, tying him with Warren Moon and Johnny Unitas for third all-time. . . . The Broncos' victory over the Raiders marked the 10th time in league history a team began a season 11-0. . . . No visiting team has won a game in the seven games played between the Jaguars and the Steelers. . . . The Vikings' sweep of the Packers was their first over Green Bay in five years. . . . In two games against Green Bay this season, rookie Randy Moss had 13 catches for 343 yards and three touchdowns. . . . Antonio Freeman's 46 receiving yards gave him 1,003 yards for the season, making him the third receiver in Packers history to top 1,000 in consecutive years. . . . The Patriots' 26-23 win over the Dolphins was the fourth straight regular-season game between the teams decided by three points or fewer.

Quote of the week: San Francisco receiver Jerry Rice, on his diminishing role in the 49ers' offense, after a three-catch, 27-yard performance against the Saints: "Are you asking me if I'm having any fun? Hell no. Are you asking me if it's something that might make me want to retire? Hell yes."

GAME SUMMARIES

VIKINGS 28, PACKERS 14

Sunday, November 22

Green Bay	0	7	0	7—14
Minnesota	10	10	0	8—28

First Quarter
Min.—FG, Anderson 35, 3:03.
Min.—Hitchcock 58 interception return (Anderson kick), 13:37.

Second Quarter
Min.—FG, Anderson 29, 5:23.
G.B.—T. Davis 12 pass from Favre (Longwell kick), 11:22.
Min.—Carter 4 pass from Cunningham (Anderson kick), 14:36.

Fourth Quarter
G.B.—T. Davis 2 pass from Favre (Longwell kick), 7:29.
Min.—R. Moss 49 pass from Cunningham (Cunningham run), 11:43.
Attendance—64,471.

	Green Bay	Minnesota
First downs	22	15
Rushes-yards	18-53	21-92
Passing	277	248
Punt returns	2-21	0-0
Kickoff returns	1-17	2-47
Interception returns	1-15	1-58
Comp.-att.-int.	31-39-1	20-30-1
Sacked-yards lost	3-26	2-16
Punts	4-45	3-54
Fumbles-lost	3-2	0-0
Penalties-yards	9-48	7-50
Time of possession	32:11	27:49

INDIVIDUAL STATISTICS
RUSHING—Green Bay, Holmes 16-51, Favre 2-2. Minnesota, R. Smith 13-27, Cunningham 4-20, Hoard 3-39, Palmer 1-6.
PASSING—Green Bay, Favre 31-39-1-303. Minnesota, Cunningham 20-30-1-264.
RECEIVING—Green Bay, Schroeder 7-93, Holmes 5-50, Henderson 5-23, Chmura 4-37, Freeman 3-46, T. Davis 3-19, R. Brooks 2-19, Preston 1-13, Blair 1-3. Minnesota, R. Moss 8-153, Glover 3-38, Carter 3-28, Reed 3-18, R. Smith 2-10, Tate 1-17.
MISSED FIELD GOAL ATTEMPTS—None.
INTERCEPTIONS—Green Bay, Ty. Williams 1-15. Minnesota, Hitchcock 1-58.
KICKOFF RETURNS—Green Bay, Preston 1-17. Minnesota, Palmer 2-47.

PUNT RETURNS—Green Bay, Preston 2-21.
SACKS—Green Bay, Koonce 1, B. Harris 1. Minnesota, Rudd 1, Randle 1, Team 1.

FALCONS 20, BEARS 13

Sunday, November 22

Chicago	0	3	10	0—13
Atlanta	0	3	7	10—20

Second Quarter
Atl.—FG, Andersen 50, 6:26.
Chi.—FG, Jaeger 35, 13:54.

Third Quarter
Chi.—FG, Jaeger 32, 2:35.
Chi.—Lee 15 fumble return (Jaeger kick), 3:39.
Atl.—Mathis 13 pass from Chandler (Andersen kick), 13:15.

Fourth Quarter
Atl.—Kinchen 11 pass from Chandler (Andersen kick), 5:28.
Atl.—FG, Andersen 44, 13:02.
Attendance—60,804.

	Chicago	Atlanta
First downs	10	21
Rushes-yards	27-106	28-95
Passing	104	263
Punt returns	0-0	1-(-1)
Kickoff returns	2-74	4-78
Interception returns	0-0	2-0
Comp.-att.-int.	7-19-2	20-30-0
Sacked-yards lost	1-5	4-23
Punts	4-45	4-38
Fumbles-lost	1-1	4-2
Penalties-yards	10-68	8-49
Time of possession	24:15	35:45

INDIVIDUAL STATISTICS
RUSHING—Chicago, Bennett 17-69, Stenstrom 5-18, Chancey 2-12, J. Allen 2-5, Milburn 1-2. Atlanta, J. Anderson 24-72, Chandler 2-25, DeBerg 2-(minus 2).
PASSING—Chicago, Stenstrom 7-18-2-109, Bennett 0-1-0-0. Atlanta, Chandler 18-27-0-272, DeBerg 2-3-0-14.
RECEIVING—Chicago, Conway 3-64, Engram 3-42, Hallock 1-3. Atlanta, Martin 6-100, Mathis 5-76, Kinchen 4-59, Christian 2-12, Santiago 1-17, Kozlowski 1-13, J. Anderson 1-9.
MISSED FIELD GOAL ATTEMPTS—None.
INTERCEPTIONS—Atlanta, Bradford 1-0, Buchanan 1-0.
KICKOFF RETURNS—Chicago, Milburn 2-74. Atlanta, E. Williams 3-62, Harris 1-16.
PUNT RETURNS—Atlanta, Harris 1-(minus 1).
SACKS—Chicago, Wells 2, Flanigan 1, Lee 1. Atlanta, Dronett 1.

LIONS 28, BUCCANEERS 25

Sunday, November 22

Detroit	14	7	0	7—28
Tampa Bay	0	14	3	8—25

First Quarter
Det.—Crowell 53 pass from Batch (Hanson kick), 2:08.
Det.—Rasby 3 pass from Batch (Hanson kick), 8:34.

Second Quarter
T.B.—Green 44 pass from Dilfer (Husted kick), 2:08.
Det.—Rivers 36 run (Hanson kick), 11:07.
T.B.—Moore 8 pass from Dilfer (Husted kick), 14:34.

Third Quarter
T.B.—FG, Husted 33, 8:30.

Fourth Quarter
Det.—Vardell 1 run (Hanson kick), 0:03.
T.B.—Alstott 5 run (Anthony pass from Dilfer), 4:18.
Attendance—64,265.

	Detroit	Tampa Bay
First downs	19	22
Rushes-yards	27-112	35-145
Passing	188	283
Punt returns	1-5	4-31
Kickoff returns	5-99	3-66
Interception returns	2-4	0-0
Comp.-att.-int.	14-23-0	16-30-2

– 180 –

	Detroit	Tampa Bay
Sacked-yards lost	1-7	0-0
Punts	6-43	4-42
Fumbles-lost	0-0	0-0
Penalties-yards	4-30	9-59
Time of possession	26:06	33:54

INDIVIDUAL STATISTICS

RUSHING—Detroit, Sanders 21-66, Vardell 3-2, Batch 2-8, Rivers 1-36. Tampa Bay, Alstott 20-68, Dunn 14-73, Dilfer 1-4.

PASSING—Detroit, Batch 14-23-0-195. Tampa Bay, Dilfer 16-30-2-283.

RECEIVING—Detroit, Morton 5-49, Crowell 3-82, Vardell 2-28, Stablein 2-26, Sanders 1-7, Rasby 1-3. Tampa Bay, Emanuel 4-80, Anthony 4-38, Green 3-98, Dunn 3-42, Alstott 1-17, Moore 1-8.

MISSED FIELD GOAL ATTEMPTS—None.

INTERCEPTIONS—Detroit, Jordan 1-4, Rice 1-0.

KICKOFF RETURNS—Detroit, Fair 4-93, Rivers 1-6. Tampa Bay, Anthony 3-66.

PUNT RETURNS—Detroit, Fair 1-5. Tampa Bay, Green 4-31.

SACKS—Tampa Bay, Sapp 1.

BILLS 34, COLTS 11

Sunday, November 22

Indianapolis	3	0	0	8—11
Buffalo	0	24	3	7—34

First Quarter
Ind.—FG, Vanderjagt 27, 8:14.

Second Quarter
Buf.—Gash 1 pass from Flutie (Christie kick), 0:30.
Buf.—A. Smith 4 run (Christie kick), 10:55.
Buf.—Reed 67 pass from Flutie (Christie kick), 13:49.
Buf.—FG, Christie 35, 14:59.

Third Quarter
Buf.—FG, Christie 24, 8:10.

Fourth Quarter
Buf.—A. Smith 5 run (Christie kick), 6:42.
Ind.—Harrison 30 pass from Manning (Harrison pass from Manning), 10:47.
Attendance—49,032.

	Indianapolis	Buffalo
First downs	14	25
Rushes-yards	22-86	38-187
Passing	164	215
Punt returns	4-28	3-29
Kickoff returns	7-144	3-73
Interception returns	0-0	2-67
Comp.-att.-int.	14-29-2	20-30-0
Sacked-yards lost	0-0	2-15
Punts	5-48	4-43
Fumbles-lost	3-1	1-1
Penalties-yards	6-41	10-64
Time of possession	23:00	37:00

INDIVIDUAL STATISTICS

RUSHING—Indianapolis, Faulk 18-85, Warren 2-1, Manning 2-0. Buffalo, A. Smith 23-107, Linton 6-46, Thomas 5-26, Flutie 2-10, R. Johnson 1-(minus 1), K. Williams 1-(minus 1).

PASSING—Indianapolis, Manning 14-29-2-164. Buffalo, Flutie 20-28-0-230, R. Johnson 0-2-0-0.

RECEIVING—Indianapolis, Faulk 8-102, Harrison 4-49, Pathon 1-8, Small 1-5. Buffalo, Reed 6-108, Moulds 5-47, K. Williams 3-31, L. Johnson 3-24, Early 1-19, Gash 1-1, Riemersma 1-0.

MISSED FIELD GOAL ATTEMPTS—None.

INTERCEPTIONS—Buffalo, Irvin 1-43, Schulz 1-24.

KICKOFF RETURNS—Indianapolis, Bailey 4-113, Hetherington 2-27, Pollard 1-4. Buffalo, K. Williams 3-73.

PUNT RETURNS—Indianapolis, Bailey 4-28. Buffalo, K. Williams 3-29.

SACKS—Indianapolis, Whittington 1, Chorak 1.

GIANTS 20, EAGLES 0

Sunday, November 22

Philadelphia	0	0	0	0— 0
N.Y. Giants	3	0	7	10—20

First Quarter
NYG—FG, Daluiso 40, 9:59.

Third Quarter
NYG—Brown 4 run (Daluiso kick), 12:30.

Fourth Quarter
NYG—FG, Daluiso 49, 3:56.
NYG—Barber 8 pass from K. Graham (Daluiso kick), 12:51.
Attendance—65,763.

	Philadelphia	N.Y. Giants
First downs	16	15
Rushes-yards	26-117	40-123
Passing	97	138
Punt returns	3-18	4-55
Kickoff returns	3-50	1-0
Interception returns	1-30	2-10
Comp.-att.-int.	14-28-2	10-21-1
Sacked-yards lost	6-24	3-15
Punts	7-43	6-38
Fumbles-lost	1-0	2-0
Penalties-yards	11-93	9-55
Time of possession	28:04	31:56

INDIVIDUAL STATISTICS

RUSHING—Philadelphia, Staley 14-52, Garner 7-29, Hoying 4-23, Jells 1-13. New York, Brown 27-96, Way 6-15, K. Graham 5-6, Hilliard 1-4, Barber 1-2.

PASSING—Philadelphia, Hoying 14-28-2-121. New York, K. Graham 10-21-1-153.

RECEIVING—Philadelphia, Staley 4-49, Dunn 3-17, Graham 2-17, Garner 2-13, Fryar 2-9, Jells 1-16. New York, Jurevicius 2-65, Toomer 2-39, Brown 2-0, Calloway 1-22, Hilliard 1-15, Barber 1-8, Way 1-4.

MISSED FIELD GOAL ATTEMPTS—Philadelphia, Boniol 44.

INTERCEPTIONS—Philadelphia, Dawkins 1-30. New York, Sparks 2-10.

KICKOFF RETURNS—Philadelphia, Rossum 2-43, Brooks 1-7. New York, Palelei 1-0.

PUNT RETURNS—Philadelphia, Rossum 3-18. New York, Toomer 4-55.

SACKS—Philadelphia, B. Johnson 1.5, Wallace 1, Whiting 0.5. New York, Armstead 2, Wooten 2, Bratzke 1, Strahan 1.

STEELERS 30, JAGUARS 15

Sunday, November 22

Jacksonville	0	0	7	8—15
Pittsburgh	7	6	3	14—30

First Quarter
Pit.—Washington 52 interception return (N. Johnson kick), 7:12.

Second Quarter
Pit.—FG, N. Johnson 38, 6:39.
Pit.—FG, N. Johnson 29, 14:56.

Third Quarter
Jac.—F. Taylor 2 run (Hollis kick), 10:53.
Pit.—FG, N. Johnson 41, 14:45.

Fourth Quarter
Pit.—Bruener 9 pass from Stewart (N. Johnson kick), 6:01.
Jac.—J. Smith 33 pass from Brunell (McCardell pass from Brunell), 7:56.
Pit.—Washington 78 interception return (N. Johnson kick), 14:26.
Attendance—59,124.

	Jacksonville	Pittsburgh
First downs	17	18
Rushes-yards	26-97	34-121
Passing	204	208
Punt returns	2-35	3-41
Kickoff returns	7-142	3-57
Interception returns	0-0	3-132
Comp.-att.-int.	18-42-3	25-36-0
Sacked-yards lost	1-8	0-0
Punts	6-50	7-37
Fumbles-lost	1-1	0-0
Penalties-yards	5-30	3-25
Time of possession	25:16	34:44

INDIVIDUAL STATISTICS

RUSHING—Jacksonville, F. Taylor 20-67, Brunell 4-9, Whitted 1-16, Shelton 1-5. Pittsburgh, Bettis 26-77, Stewart 4-26, McAfee 3-20, Hawkins 1-(minus 2).

PASSING—Jacksonville, Brunell 18-42-3-212. Pittsburgh, Stewart 25-36-0-208.

RECEIVING—Jacksonville, J. Smith 5-71, McCardell 5-63, F. Taylor 4-21, Barlow 1-31, D. Jones 1-11, Mitchell 1-9, Whitted 1-6. Pittsburgh, Hawkins

8-80, C. Johnson 7-63, Blackwell 3-7, Ward 2-26, Bruener 2-14, Bettis 1-10, Lyons 1-5, McAfee 1-3.

MISSED FIELD GOAL ATTEMPTS—None.

INTERCEPTIONS—Pittsburgh, Washington 2-130, Emmons 1-2.

KICKOFF RETURNS—Jacksonville, Logan 3-86, Barlow 3-57, D. Jones 1-(minus 1). Pittsburgh, Huntley 1-20, Blackwell 1-19, Dunn 1-18.

PUNT RETURNS—Jacksonville, Barlow 2-35. Pittsburgh, Hawkins 3-41.

SACKS—Pittsburgh, Gildon 1.

CARDINALS 45, REDSKINS 42

Sunday, November 22

Arizona	17	14	7	7—45
Washington	0	6	21	15—42

First Quarter
Ariz.—FG, Nedney 26, 3:17.
Ariz.—McWilliams 6 pass from Plummer (Nedney kick), 6:04.
Ariz.—Plummer 1 run (Nedney kick), 10:16.
Second Quarter
Ariz.—Murrell 13 run (Nedney kick), 4:42.
Ariz.—Plummer 10 run (Nedney kick), 10:55.
Was.—Westbrook 15 pass from T. Green (kick failed), 14:07.
Third Quarter
Was.—Westbrook 12 pass from T. Green (Blanchard kick), 4:37.
Ariz.—Centers 9 pass from Plummer (Nedney kick), 10:59.
Was.—Westbrook 11 pass from T. Green (Blanchard kick), 12:59.
Was.—Shepherd 16 pass from T. Green (Blanchard kick), 14:46.
Fourth Quarter
Was.—Hicks 5 run (Shepherd pass from T. Green), 5:42.
Ariz.—Plummer 1 run (Nedney kick), 11:11.
Was.—T. Green 2 run (Blanchard kick), 13:14.
Attendance—63,435.

	Arizona	Washington
First downs	25	31
Rushes-yards	40-188	17-68
Passing	248	353
Punt returns	3-22	2-11
Kickoff returns	5-115	7-163
Interception returns	1-16	1-54
Comp.-att.-int.	17-28-1	30-49-1
Sacked-yards lost	1-3	5-29
Punts	3-40	3-43
Fumbles-lost	2-1	1-1
Penalties-yards	9-92	6-59
Time of possession	30:12	29:48

INDIVIDUAL STATISTICS

RUSHING—Arizona, Murrell 20-92, Bates 10-56, Plummer 6-10, Centers 4-30. Washington, Hicks 7-22, T. Green 5-26, Mitchell 4-15, Davis 1-5.

PASSING—Arizona, Plummer 17-28-1-251. Washington, T. Green 30-49-1-382.

RECEIVING—Arizona, R. Moore 4-71, Sanders 3-83, Murrell 3-45, Centers 3-10, McWilliams 2-14, Gedney 1-21, Metcalf 1-7. Washington, Westbrook 10-135, Shepherd 7-107, Mitchell 5-23, S. Alexander 4-72, Connell 2-34, Hicks 2-11.

MISSED FIELD GOAL ATTEMPTS—Washington, Blanchard 33, 52.

INTERCEPTIONS—Arizona, Lassiter 1-16. Washington, L. Evans 1-54.

KICKOFF RETURNS—Arizona, Metcalf 4-95, Pittman 1-20. Washington, Mitchell 6-145, Thrash 1-18.

PUNT RETURNS—Arizona, Metcalf 3-22. Washington, Mitchell 2-11.

SACKS—Arizona, M. Smith 2, Rice 2, Miller 1. Washington, Wilkinson 1.

RAVENS 20, BENGALS 13

Sunday, November 22

Baltimore	7	10	0	3—20
Cincinnati	0	3	10	0—13

First Quarter
Bal.—Potts 12 pass from Harbaugh (Stover kick), 5:26.
Second Quarter
Bal.—FG, Stover 34, 2:37.
Cin.—FG, Pelfrey 40, 8:51.
Bal.—Holmes 1 run (Stover kick), 14:52.
Third Quarter
Cin.—FG, Pelfrey 34, 4:26.
Cin.—Bennett 2 run (Pelfrey kick), 12:51.

Fourth Quarter
Bal.—FG, Stover 23, 1:47.
Attendance—52,571.

	Baltimore	Cincinnati
First downs	18	16
Rushes-yards	41-247	23-58
Passing	91	184
Punt returns	0-0	0-0
Kickoff returns	4-106	5-89
Interception returns	2-25	1-0
Comp.-att.-int.	9-18-1	19-33-2
Sacked-yards lost	1-1	2-20
Punts	3-36	4-38
Fumbles-lost	2-1	1-0
Penalties-yards	5-25	2-15
Time of possession	30:43	29:17

INDIVIDUAL STATISTICS

RUSHING—Baltimore, Holmes 36-227, Harbaugh 4-20, Potts 1-0. Cincinnati, Dillon 13-35, Bennett 6-12, Milne 3-9, Justin 1-2.

PASSING—Baltimore, Harbaugh 9-18-1-92. Cincinnati, Justin 18-32-2-202, O'Donnell 1-1-0-2.

RECEIVING—Baltimore, J. Lewis 4-48, Green 2-14, Jackson 1-18, Potts 1-12, Atkins 1-0. Cincinnati, Pickens 7-95, Milne 3-14, McGee 2-32, Hundon 2-17, Bush 1-18, Jackson 1-17, Bieniemy 1-8, Battaglia 1-6, Bennett 1-(minus 3).

MISSED FIELD GOAL ATTEMPTS—None.

INTERCEPTIONS—Baltimore, R. Lewis 2-25. Cincinnati, Randolph 1-0.

KICKOFF RETURNS—Baltimore, Johnson 2-66, C. Harris 1-28, Kinchen 1-12. Cincinnati, Mack 4-84, Battaglia 1-5.

PUNT RETURNS—None.

SACKS—Baltimore, R. Lewis 1, J. Jones 1. Cincinnati, Bankston 1.

PANTHERS 24, RAMS 20

Sunday, November 22

Carolina	7	10	0	7—24
St. Louis	0	7	7	6—20

First Quarter
Car.—Walls 1 pass from Beuerlein (Kasay kick), 13:04.
Second Quarter
Car.—Walls 13 pass from Beuerlein (Kasay kick), 0:04.
Car.—FG, Kasay 35, 8:05.
St.L.—J. Robinson 4 pass from Bono (Wilkins kick), 14:22.
Third Quarter
St.L.—J. Moore 7 run (Wilkins kick), 5:40.
Fourth Quarter
Car.—Lane 1 run (Kasay kick), 0:03.
St.L.—FG, Wilkins 39, 5:21.
St.L.—FG, Wilkins 41, 8:53.
Attendance—50,716.

	Carolina	St. Louis
First downs	17	17
Rushes-yards	30-73	19-42
Passing	184	230
Punt returns	5-68	2-28
Kickoff returns	4-102	4-123
Interception returns	0-0	1-41
Comp.-att.-int.	21-26-1	18-35-0
Sacked-yards lost	5-27	3-15
Punts	6-36	5-52
Fumbles-lost	1-0	3-2
Penalties-yards	7-44	6-45
Time of possession	35:50	24:10

INDIVIDUAL STATISTICS

RUSHING—Carolina, Lane 24-55, Biakabutuka 3-10, Johnson 1-7, Floyd 1-2, Beuerlein 1-(minus 1). St. Louis, J. Moore 15-34, Lee 2-0, Holcombe 1-8, Bono 1-0.

PASSING—Carolina, Beuerlein 21-26-1-211. St. Louis, Bono 16-33-0-221, Banks 2-2-0-24.

RECEIVING—Carolina, Ismail 6-58, Walls 6-51, Muhammad 4-36, Floyd 3-19, D. Hayes 1-35, Johnson 1-12. St. Louis, Proehl 4-75, R. Williams 2-36, J. Thomas 2-32, Armstrong 2-26, Hakim 2-25, Kennison 2-23, Lee 2-16, Henley 1-8, J. Robinson 1-4.

MISSED FIELD GOAL ATTEMPTS—None.

INTERCEPTIONS—St. Louis, Phifer 1-41.

KICKOFF RETURNS—Carolina, Stone 3-77, Oliver 1-25. St. Louis, Horne 4-123.

PUNT RETURNS—Carolina, Oliver 5-68. St. Louis, Kennison 2-28.

SACKS—Carolina, Gilbert 1, Greene 1, E. Jones 1. St. Louis, Carter 3, Jenkins 1, Farr 1.

COWBOYS 30, SEAHAWKS 22

Sunday, November 22

Seattle	0	14	0	8—	22
Dallas	10	6	0	14—	30

First Quarter
Dal.—FG, Cunningham 47, 5:57.
Dal.—E. Smith 8 pass from Aikman (Cunningham kick), 13:40.

Second Quarter
Sea.—Galloway 44 pass from Moon (Peterson kick), 3:04.
Dal.—FG, Cunningham 44, 8:32.
Sea.—Adams 25 interception return (Peterson kick), 13:08.
Dal.—FG, Cunningham 28, 15:00.

Fourth Quarter
Dal.—B. Davis 18 pass from Aikman (Cunningham kick), 1:19.
Dal.—Warren 1 run (Cunningham kick), 7:56.
Sea.—McKnight 5 pass from Moon (Watters run), 10:30.
Attendance—64,142.

	Seattle	Dallas
First downs	17	29
Rushes-yards	17-66	36-173
Passing	192	292
Punt returns	1-0	2-11
Kickoff returns	5-92	4-67
Interception returns	1-25	1-22
Comp.-att.-int.	15-28-1	28-42-1
Sacked-yards lost	2-9	1-4
Punts	4-44	3-40
Fumbles-lost	1-1	1-0
Penalties-yards	5-19	15-129
Time of possession	21:34	38:26

INDIVIDUAL STATISTICS

RUSHING—Seattle, Watters 16-66, Strong 1-0. Dallas, E. Smith 17-74, Warren 12-71, Aikman 5-14, Ogden 1-12, S. Williams 1-2.

PASSING—Seattle, Moon 15-28-1-201. Dallas, Aikman 28-42-1-296.

RECEIVING—Seattle, Pritchard 6-72, Galloway 4-71, McKnight 3-32, Mili 1-20, Watters 1-6. Dallas, Irvin 8-98, B. Davis 4-51, Ogden 4-26, LaFleur 3-39, Warren 3-20, Jeffers 2-40, E. Smith 1-8, Johnston 1-7, Bjornson 1-4, E. Mills 1-3.

MISSED FIELD GOAL ATTEMPTS—None.

INTERCEPTIONS—Seattle, Adams 1-25. Dallas, K. Smith 1-22.

KICKOFF RETURNS—Seattle, Green 4-68, Broussard 1-24. Dallas, Warren 4-67.

PUNT RETURNS—Seattle, Galloway 1-0. Dallas, Warren 2-11.

SACKS—Seattle. Dallas, Woodson 1, Pittman 1.

CHARGERS 38, CHIEFS 37

Sunday, November 22

Kansas City	7	7	13	10—	37
San Diego	7	10	0	21—	38

First Quarter
S.D.—Fletcher 4 run (Carney kick), 5:27.
K.C.—Alexander 35 pass from Gannon (Stoyanovich kick), 7:55.

Second Quarter
S.D.—Stephens 2 run (Carney kick), 1:39.
S.D.—FG, Carney 31, 5:53.
K.C.—Morris 2 run (Stoyanovich kick), 8:45.

Third Quarter
K.C.—Morris 1 run (Stoyanovich kick), 0:34.
K.C.—FG, Stoyanovich 27, 11:29.
K.C.—FG, Stoyanovich 42, 14:07.

Fourth Quarter
K.C.—Morris 3 run (Stoyanovich kick), 3:14.
S.D.—Fletcher 4 run (Carney kick), 6:59.
K.C.—FG, Stoyanovich 50, 9:32.
S.D.—F. Jones 25 pass from Whelihan (Carney kick), 10:46.
S.D.—C. Jones 1 pass from Whelihan (Carney kick), 14:51.
Attendance—59,894.

	Kansas City	San Diego
First downs	21	25
Rushes-yards	26-69	28-95
Passing	297	271
Punt returns	1-12	3-27
Kickoff returns	6-128	8-144
Interception returns	1-19	1-0
Comp.-att.-int.	21-35-1	19-37-1
Sacked-yards lost	1-8	2-8
Punts	3-45	4-47
Fumbles-lost	2-1	5-2
Penalties-yards	12-123	11-120
Time of possession	28:33	31:27

INDIVIDUAL STATISTICS

RUSHING—Kansas City, Morris 23-39, Gannon 2-26, Bennett 1-4. San Diego, Fletcher 16-52, Bynum 6-18, Stephens 4-17, Whelihan 2-8.

PASSING—Kansas City, Gannon 20-33-1-304, Grbac 1-2-0-1. San Diego, Whelihan 19-37-1-279.

RECEIVING—Kansas City, Alexander 5-173, Anders 5-23, Bennett 3-16, Rison 2-23, Morris 2-0, Gonzalez 1-32, Lockett 1-22, Hughes 1-10, Popson 1-6. San Diego, F. Jones 5-78, C. Jones 4-39, Thelwell 3-78, Ricks 3-44, Bynum 2-18, Fletcher 1-14, Davis 1-8.

MISSED FIELD GOAL ATTEMPTS—Kansas City, Stoyanovich 46.

INTERCEPTIONS—Kansas City, Woods 1-19. San Diego, Turner 1-0.

KICKOFF RETURNS—Kansas City, Vanover 5-128, Ransom 1-0. San Diego, Rachal 7-122, Bynum 1-22.

PUNT RETURNS—Kansas City, Vanover 1-12. San Diego, Rachal 3-27.

SACKS—Kansas City, Favors 1, Team 1. San Diego, Johnson 0.5, Mims 0.5.

BRONCOS 40, RAIDERS 14

Sunday, November 22

Oakland	0	7	7	0—	14
Denver	3	14	0	23—	40

First Quarter
Den.—FG, Elam 33, 6:36.

Second Quarter
Den.—Sharpe 7 pass from Elway (Elam kick), 4:07.
Den.—Davis 1 run (Elam kick), 13:47.
Oak.—Dudley 29 pass from Hollas (G. Davis kick), 14:28.

Third Quarter
Oak.—Jett 14 pass from Hollas (G. Davis kick), 9:54.

Fourth Quarter
Den.—FG, Elam 23, 1:23.
Den.—R. Smith 28 pass from Elway (pass failed), 3:10.
Den.—Griffith 3 pass from Elway (Elam kick), 10:21.
Den.—Hebron 3 run (Elam kick), 12:37.
Attendance—75,325.

	Oakland	Denver
First downs	15	28
Rushes-yards	19-49	41-196
Passing	245	201
Punt returns	1-10	2-44
Kickoff returns	5-108	3-59
Interception returns	0-0	3-74
Comp.-att.-int.	20-35-3	18-26-0
Sacked-yards lost	4-25	1-10
Punts	7-48	3-44
Fumbles-lost	0-0	1-1
Penalties-yards	9-44	6-52
Time of possession	23:56	36:04

INDIVIDUAL STATISTICS

RUSHING—Oakland, H. Williams 9-35, Kaufman 9-8, Hollas 1-6. Denver, Davis 31-162, Loville 5-29, Elway 4-2, Hebron 1-3.

PASSING—Oakland, Hollas 20-35-3-270. Denver, Elway 17-25-0-197, R. Smith 1-1-0-14.

RECEIVING—Oakland, Mickens 4-86, T. Brown 4-65, D. Brown 3-38, Kaufman 3-21, H. Williams 3-12, Dudley 1-29, Jett 1-14, Ritchie 1-5. Denver, R. Smith 6-95, Sharpe 3-41, Davis 3-26, Green 2-17, Griffith 2-8, Elway 1-14, Nash 1-10.

MISSED FIELD GOAL ATTEMPTS—None.

INTERCEPTIONS—Denver, Braxton 1-72, N. Smith 1-2, Crockett 1-0.

KICKOFF RETURNS—Oakland, Howard 5-108. Denver, Hebron 2-46, Tanuvasa 1-13.

PUNT RETURNS—Oakland, Howard 1-10. Denver, Gordon 2-44.

SACKS—Oakland, Johnstone 1. Denver, Tanuvasa 1, Pryce 1, Lodish 1, Washington 1.

JETS 24, OILERS 3

Sunday, November 22

N.Y. Jets	0	3	7	14—24
Tennessee	0	3	0	0— 3

Second Quarter
NYJ—FG, Hall 43, 0:04.
Ten.—FG, Del Greco 34, 12:24.

Third Quarter
NYJ—K. Johnson 3 pass from Testaverde (Hall kick), 10:44.

Fourth Quarter
NYJ—Byars 2 pass from Testaverde (Hall kick), 0:43.
NYJ—Martin 31 run (Hall kick), 6:00.
    Attendance—37,084.

	N.Y. Jets	Tennessee
First downs	22	12
Rushes-yards	33-130	24-94
Passing	231	129
Punt returns	4-28	1-0
Kickoff returns	2-35	2-35
Interception returns	0-0	0-0
Comp.-att.-int.	21-33-0	14-26-0
Sacked-yards lost	1-6	3-11
Punts	3-38	7-48
Fumbles-lost	0-0	5-1
Penalties-yards	3-20	6-70
Time of possession	34:02	25:58

INDIVIDUAL STATISTICS
RUSHING—New York, Martin 27-123, Sowell 2-6, L. Johnson 2-3, Testaverde 2-(minus 2). Tennessee, E. George 20-72, McNair 3-26, Archie 1-(minus 4).

PASSING—New York, Testaverde 21-33-0-237. Tennessee, McNair 13-24-0-137, Krieg 1-2-0-3.

RECEIVING—New York, K. Johnson 10-112, Chrebet 4-38, Martin 3-41, Byars 3-24, Ward 1-22. Tennessee, Wycheck 5-61, Harris 3-29, E. George 3-18, Mason 1-24, Dyson 1-5, Archie 1-3.

MISSED FIELD GOAL ATTEMPTS—New York, Hall 39.

INTERCEPTIONS—None.

KICKOFF RETURNS—New York, Glenn 1-21, L. Johnson 1-14. Tennessee, Archie 2-35.

PUNT RETURNS—New York, L. Johnson 4-28. Tennessee, Mason 1-0.

SACKS—New York, Ferguson 1.5, Cascadden 1, Logan 0.5. Tennessee, Jackson 1.

49ERS 31, SAINTS 20

Sunday, November 22

New Orleans	10	3	0	7—20
San Francisco	0	14	17	0—31

First Quarter
N.O.—FG, Brien 47, 0:50.
N.O.—Collins 1 run (Brien kick), 14:26.

Second Quarter
S.F.—Owens 8 pass from S. Young (Richey kick), 9:30.
S.F.—Owens 8 pass from S. Young (Richey kick), 13:54.
N.O.—FG, Brien 22, 15:00.

Third Quarter
S.F.—Hearst 81 pass from S. Young (Richey kick), 0:21.
S.F.—Rice 8 pass from S. Young (Richey kick), 3:06.
S.F.—FG, Richey 45, 9:26.

Fourth Quarter
N.O.—Craver 1 run (Brien kick), 13:38.
    Attendance—68,429.

	New Orleans	San Francisco
First downs	23	23
Rushes-yards	17-90	34-154
Passing	311	289
Punt returns	2-21	1-8
Kickoff returns	4-69	4-86
Interception returns	1-9	2-43

	New Orleans	San Francisco
Comp.-att.-int.	22-44-2	22-31-1
Sacked-yards lost	4-17	3-1
Punts	2-34	3-44
Fumbles-lost	4-2	2-2
Penalties-yards	4-22	11-125
Time of possession	25:12	34:48

INDIVIDUAL STATISTICS
RUSHING—New Orleans, Collins 6-30, L. Smith 4-28, Craver 4-23, Zellars 2-8, T. Davis 1-1. San Francisco, Hearst 25-90, S. Young 5-35, Edwards 2-3, Owens 1-18, Kirby 1-8.

PASSING—New Orleans, Collins 22-44-2-328. San Francisco, S. Young 22-31-1-290.

RECEIVING—New Orleans, Dawkins 8-148, Cleeland 4-50, L. Smith 3-34, Poole 2-38, Hastings 2-30, Farquhar 1-13, Bech 1-8, Craver 1-7. San Francisco, Stokes 6-72, Hearst 4-103, Owens 4-42, Rice 3-27, Kirby 2-21, Edwards 2-15, Clark 1-10.

MISSED FIELD GOAL ATTEMPTS—New Orleans, Brien 53.

INTERCEPTIONS—New Orleans, Cota 1-9. San Francisco, Hanks 1-37, Bronson 1-6.

KICKOFF RETURNS—New Orleans, Craver 3-56, Little 1-13. San Francisco, Levy 3-56, Kirby 1-30.

PUNT RETURNS—New Orleans, Hastings 2-21. San Francisco, McQuarters 1-8.

SACKS—New Orleans, Cota 1, Fields 1, Tomich 1. San Francisco, B. Young 2, McDonald 1, Doleman 1.

PATRIOTS 26, DOLPHINS 23

Monday, November 23

Miami	7	7	3	6—23
New England	7	3	6	10—26

First Quarter
Mia.—Gadsden 35 pass from Marino (Mare kick), 6:43.
N.E.—Coates 8 pass from Bledsoe (Vinatieri kick), 10:33.

Second Quarter
Mia.—Gadsden 11 pass from Marino (Mare kick), 7:55.
N.E.—FG, Vinatieri 25, 13:52.

Third Quarter
N.E.—FG, Vinatieri 44, 5:58.
Mia.—FG, Mare 21, 10:20.
N.E.—FG, Vinatieri 45, 14:29.

Fourth Quarter
N.E.—FG, Vinatieri 24, 5:59.
Mia.—Abdul-Jabbar 4 run (pass failed), 11:38.
N.E.—Jefferson 25 pass from Bledsoe (Vinatieri kick), 14:31.
    Attendance—58,729.

	Miami	New England
First downs	17	21
Rushes-yards	19-33	19-41
Passing	289	414
Punt returns	1-9	1-7
Kickoff returns	7-161	3-61
Interception returns	2-58	1-0
Comp.-att.-int.	24-38-1	28-54-2
Sacked-yards lost	0-0	1-9
Punts	5-43	2-44
Fumbles-lost	0-0	0-0
Penalties-yards	7-46	10-97
Time of possession	27:17	32:43

INDIVIDUAL STATISTICS
RUSHING—Miami, Abdul-Jabbar 10-10, Avery 8-18, Parmalee 1-5. New England, Edwards 14-24, Bledsoe 3-18, Cullors 1-0, S. Shaw 1-(minus 1).

PASSING—Miami, Marino 24-38-1-289. New England, Bledsoe 28-54-2-423.

RECEIVING—Miami, McDuffie 8-86, Drayton 4-51, Gadsden 3-49, Pritchett 3-28, Perry 2-59, Parmalee 2-4, Avery 1-8, Abdul-Jabbar 1-4. New England, Coates 9-78, Glenn 7-66, Jefferson 6-131, Simmons 4-53, Ton. Carter 1-49, Edwards 1-46.

MISSED FIELD GOAL ATTEMPTS—None.

INTERCEPTIONS—Miami, Madison 2-58. New England, Israel 1-0.

KICKOFF RETURNS—Miami, Avery 6-158, Marion 1-3. New England, Cullors 2-49, Canty 1-12.

PUNT RETURNS—Miami, Buckley 1-9. New England, Canty 1-7.

SACKS—Miami, Bromell 1.

WEEK 13

RESULTS

DETROIT 19, Pittsburgh 16 (OT)
Minnesota 46, DALLAS 36
Atlanta 21, ST. LOUIS 10
BALTIMORE 38, Indianapolis 31
Denver 31, SAN DIEGO 16
GREEN BAY 24, Philadelphia 16
Jacksonville 34, CINCINNATI 17
KANSAS CITY 34, Arizona 24
MIAMI 30, New Orleans 10
NEW ENGLAND 25, Buffalo 21
N.Y. JETS 48, Carolina 21
SEATTLE 20, Tennessee 18
Tampa Bay 31, CHICAGO 17
Washington 29, OAKLAND 19
SAN FRANCISCO 31, N.Y. Giants 7

STANDINGS

AFC EAST

	W	L	T	Pct.
Miami	8	4	0	.667
N.Y. Jets	8	4	0	.667
Buffalo	7	5	0	.583
New England	7	5	0	.583
Indianapolis	2	10	0	.167

AFC CENTRAL

	W	L	T	Pct.
Jacksonville	9	3	0	.750
Pittsburgh	7	5	0	.583
Tennessee	6	6	0	.500
Baltimore	5	7	0	.417
Cincinnati	2	10	0	.167

AFC WEST

	W	L	T	Pct.
Denver	12	0	0	1.000
Oakland	7	5	0	.583
San Diego	5	7	0	.417
Seattle	6	6	0	.500
Kansas City	5	7	0	.417

NFC EAST

	W	L	T	Pct.
Dallas	8	4	0	.667
Arizona	6	6	0	.500
N.Y. Giants	4	8	0	.333
Washington	4	8	0	.333
Philadelphia	2	10	0	.167

NFC CENTRAL

	W	L	T	Pct.
Minnesota	11	1	0	.917
Green Bay	8	4	0	.667
Detroit	5	7	0	.417
Tampa Bay	5	7	0	.417
Chicago	3	9	0	.250

NFC WEST

	W	L	T	Pct.
Atlanta	10	2	0	.833
San Francisco	9	3	0	.750
New Orleans	5	7	0	.417
St. Louis	3	9	0	.250
Carolina	2	10	0	.167

HIGHLIGHTS

Hero of the week: Drew Bledsoe threw a 1-yard touchdown pass to Ben Coates with no time left as the Patriots defeated Buffalo, 25-21, at Foxboro Stadium. The scoring pass was set up by two controversial calls, the second a pass interference ruling on Henry Jones against Terry Glenn on a pass as time expired.

Goat of the week: Chicago's Mike Horan had his punt from the end zone deflected by Tampa Bay's Jeff Gooch late in the first half. Ronde Barber picked up the ball and eluded six tacklers to score after a run of 23 yards as the Bucs beat the Bears 31-17.

Sub of the week: Steve DeBerg, the Falcons' third-string quarterback and the NFL's oldest player at 44, entered in the second half at St. Louis to lead Atlanta to a 21-10 victory . DeBerg replaced second-year quarterback Tony Graziani, who was ineffective in relief of injured Chris Chandler. DeBerg completed just five of 12 passes, but he played mistake-free in helping the Falcons clinch their first playoff berth since 1995.

Comeback of the week: The Ravens overcame a 10-point deficit in the fourth quarter and beat the Colts, 38-31, on a 36-yard run by Priest Holmes. It was the Colts' first visit to Baltimore since their infamous departure 14 years earlier.

Blowout of the week: The Jets destroyed Carolina, 48-21, by using both dominating offense and defense at the Meadowlands. Curtis Martin rushed for 110 yards, including touchdown runs of 1 and 60 yards, to put him over the 1,000-yard mark for the fourth straight year.

Nail-biter of the week: With no time left, New England rode Drew Bledsoe's arm to a 25-21 victory over the Bills and stayed within striking distance of the AFC East title. The key play was a pass interference call against Henry Jones; no one associated with either team could recall seeing pass interference called on a desperation, Hail Mary pass. Buffalo and New England came out of the game with 7-5 records, good for second place in the division behind New York and Miami.

Hit of the week: Redskins defensive tackle Marc Boutte sacked Raiders quarterback Donald Hollas at the Oakland 1-yard line late in the third quarter, forcing a fumble. Hollas fell on the ball in the end zone for a safety that gave Washington a 19-7. After the Redskins received a free kick, Trent Green marched them downfield for a touchdown. Washington won, 29-19.

Oddity of the week: After controversy over the coin flip prior to overtime in the Pittsburgh-Detroit game on Thanksgiving—a flip the Steelers lost in addition to the game when the Lions capped their first possession with a field goal—Atlanta linebacker Jessie Tuggle showed up for the coin-flip ceremony at the start of the Falcons-Rams game with a sign that said "heads" so referee Ron Winter would have no confusion.

Top rusher: Marshall Faulk of Indianapolis carried 17 times for 192 yards, ran for a touchdown and caught a TD pass against Baltimore.

Top passer: Troy Aikman of Dallas completed 34-of-57 passes for 455 yards with one touchdown and no interceptions against Minnesota.

Top receiver: Buffalo's Eric Moulds caught eight passes for 177 yards and one touchdown in the Bills' loss to New England.

Notes: Dan Marino became the first quarterback in NFL history to throw 400 touchdown passes in Miami's 30-10 victory over the Saints. He finished the game with 401 TD passes, 59 more than any other player. . . . Denver became the fourth NFL team to start a season 12-0. The last to do it was Chicago in 1985. The Broncos extended their winning streak to 18 games, dating to the 1997 season and including playoffs. . . . Tennessee defensive back Denard Walker suffered a severe concussion after a run-in with Seattle tight end Christian Fauria. . . . Doug Flutie gave the Bills their first 300-yard passing effort in 30 games, since Jim Kelly did it against Seattle on December 8, 1996. . . . Tony Horne's 102-yard kickoff return was the Rams' first for a score since Gaston Green did it in 1990. . . .

With seven receptions, Oakland's Tim Brown moved past Charley Taylor into 14th place on the NFL career list with 650 catches. Ozzie Newsome is 13th with 662 . . . The Packers welcomed halfback Dorsey Levens and wide receiver Derrick Mayes back from injuries, but lost wide receiver Antonio Freeman (broken jaw) and tight end Mark Chmura (ankle) to injuries in the second half. . . . The Chiefs snapped a six-game losing streak, the longest of coach Marty Schottenheimer's career . . . Oakland quarterback Jeff George, who hadn't played past the first quarter of a game since September because of an injured groin, was pulled at the half in favor of Donald Hollas.

Quote of the week: Eagles third-string quarterback Koy Detmer, who turned and taunted the Packers after his second touchdown pass: "I was on their home turf and acting like an idiot. And I'm sure Brett Favre got fired up about that."

GAME SUMMARIES

LIONS 19, STEELERS 16

Thursday, November 26

Pittsburgh	0	6	7	3	0—16
Detroit	0	3	3	10	3—19

Second Quarter
Pit.—FG, N. Johnson 30, 4:39.
Pit.—FG, N. Johnson 38, 10:19.
Det.—FG, Hanson 45, 13:05.

Third Quarter
Pit.—Blackwell 24 pass from Stewart (N. Johnson kick), 8:04.
Det.—FG, Hanson 51, 13:16.

Fourth Quarter
Det.—Moore 21 pass from Batch (Hanson kick), 8:24.
Det.—FG, Hanson 35, 10:27.
Pit.—FG, N. Johnson 25, 14:59.

Overtime
Det.—FG, Hanson 42, 2:52.
Attendance—78,139.

	Pittsburgh	Detroit
First downs	22	13
Rushes-yards	34-85	23-70
Passing	208	213
Punt returns	2-47	0-0
Kickoff returns	3-46	6-128
Interception returns	0-0	1-0
Comp.-att.-int.	21-36-1	17-27-0
Sacked-yards lost	5-17	4-32
Punts	5-44	4-44
Fumbles-lost	4-1	2-2
Penalties-yards	4-30	6-66
Time of possession	35:53	26:59

INDIVIDUAL STATISTICS
RUSHING—Pittsburgh, Bettis 26-67, Stewart 4-22, McAfee 3-0, Hawkins 1-(minus 4). Detroit, Sanders 20-33, Crowell 1-35, Batch 1-3, Reich 1-(minus 1).
PASSING—Pittsburgh, Stewart 21-36-1-225. Detroit, Batch 16-23-0-236, Reich 1-4-0-9.
RECEIVING—Pittsburgh, C. Johnson 5-66, Hawkins 5-41, Witman 4-35, Blackwell 3-41, Ward 2-35, McAfee 2-7. Detroit, Moore 8-148, Morton 4-53, Vardell 3-8, Sanders 1-20, Crowell 1-16.
MISSED FIELD GOAL ATTEMPTS—Pittsburgh, N. Johnson 53. Detroit, Hanson 43.
INTERCEPTIONS—Detroit, Fredrickson 1-0.
KICKOFF RETURNS—Pittsburgh, Dunn 1-20, Blackwell 1-16, Huntley 1-10. Detroit, Fair 6-128.
PUNT RETURNS—Pittsburgh, Hawkins 2-47.
SACKS—Pittsburgh, Harrison 1, Gildon 1, Holmes 0.5, Perry 0.5, Oldham 0.5, Henry 0.5. Detroit, Aldridge 2, S. Boyd 1, Elliss 1, Rice 1.

VIKINGS 46, COWBOYS 36

Thursday, November 26

Minnesota	21	3	15	7—46
Dallas	6	6	10	14—36

First Quarter
Min.—R. Moss 51 pass from Cunningham (Anderson kick), 1:57.
Dal.—FG, Cunningham 30, 5:25.
Min.—Carter 54 pass from Cunningham (Anderson kick), 7:43.
Dal.—FG, Cunningham 46, 11:56.
Min.—R. Moss 56 pass from Cunningham (Anderson kick), 12:19.

Second Quarter
Dal.—Jeffers 67 pass from Aikman (pass failed), 12:28.
Min.—FG, Anderson 45, 14:44.

Third Quarter
Dal.—E. Smith 2 run (Cunningham kick), 6:05.
Min.—Hoard 12 run (R. Moss pass from Cunningham), 8:33.
Dal.—FG, Cunningham 47, 13:40.
Min.—R. Moss 56 pass from Cunningham (Anderson kick), 14:54.

Fourth Quarter
Dal.—E. Smith 1 run (Cunningham kick), 6:12.
Min.—Hoard 50 run (Anderson kick), 7:27.
Dal.—E. Smith 4 run (Cunningham kick), 13:54.
Attendance—64,366.

	Minnesota	Dallas
First downs	21	31
Rushes-yards	19-118	24-58
Passing	353	455
Punt returns	1-0	1-11
Kickoff returns	7-149	6-140
Interception returns	0-0	1-6
Comp.-att.-int.	17-35-1	34-57-0
Sacked-yards lost	1-6	0-0
Punts	4-38	4-44
Fumbles-lost	2-0	2-0
Penalties-yards	11-78	13-152
Time of possession	21:57	38:03

INDIVIDUAL STATISTICS
RUSHING—Minnesota, R. Smith 8-46, Hoard 5-58, Cunningham 3-8, Evans 3-6. Dallas, E. Smith 18-44, S. Williams 4-8, Aikman 2-6.
PASSING—Minnesota, Cunningham 17-35-1-359. Dallas, Aikman 34-57-0-455.
RECEIVING—Minnesota, Carter 7-135, R. Moss 3-163, Evans 2-17, Hoard 2-11, DeLong 2-9, Glover 1-24. Dallas, Irvin 10-137, Johnston 5-21, B. Davis 4-70, E. Smith 4-30, Jeffers 3-92, LaFleur 3-30, S. Williams 2-43, Bjornson 2-25, Ogden 1-7.
MISSED FIELD GOAL ATTEMPTS—None.
INTERCEPTIONS—Dallas, Reese 1-6.
KICKOFF RETURNS—Minnesota, Palmer 6-142, M. Williams 1-7. Dallas, S. Williams 4-103, Ogden 2-37.
PUNT RETURNS—Minnesota, Palmer 1-0. Dallas, K. Smith 1-11.
SACKS—Dallas, C. Williams 0.5, Hennings 0.5.

JETS 48, PANTHERS 21

Sunday, November 29

Carolina	7	0	7	7—21
N.Y. Jets	10	12	19	7—48

First Quarter
NYJ—FG, Hall 30, 6:29.
Car.—Lane 1 run (Kasay kick), 11:21.
NYJ—Martin 60 run (Hall kick), 11:48.

Second Quarter
NYJ—FG, Hall 37, 5:06.
NYJ—K. Johnson 35 run (pass failed), 7:39.
NYJ—FG, Hall 26, 14:43.

Third Quarter
NYJ—Martin 1 run (Hall kick), 2:57.
NYJ—Safety, S. Beuerlein sacked by B. Cox in end zone., 3:18.
NYJ—Chrebet 36 pass from Testaverde (Hall kick), 4:49.
Car.—Walls 2 pass from Beuerlein (Kasay kick), 11:31.
NYJ—FG, Hall 38, 14:37.

Fourth Quarter
Car.—Lane 2 run (Kasay kick), 2:47.
NYJ—Chrebet 21 pass from Testaverde (Hall kick), 5:23.
Attendance—71,501.

	Carolina	N.Y. Jets
First downs	15	21
Rushes-yards	23-82	39-201
Passing	134	255
Punt returns	1-0	2-(-3)
Kickoff returns	7-176	3-79
Interception returns	0-0	1-26
Comp.-att.-int.	13-23-1	16-21-0
Sacked-yards lost	5-35	0-0
Punts	5-45	1-52
Fumbles-lost	1-0	1-0
Penalties-yards	10-75	7-51
Time of possession	25:51	34:09

INDIVIDUAL STATISTICS

RUSHING—Carolina, Lane 12-57, Johnson 3-12, Beuerlein 3-4, Biakabutuka 3-2, Floyd 2-7. New York, Martin 21-110, Sowell 10-23, L. Johnson 6-17, K. Johnson 1-35, Lucas 1-16.

PASSING—Carolina, Beuerlein 13-23-1-169. New York, Testaverde 16-21-0-255.

RECEIVING—Carolina, Walls 4-16, Muhammad 3-44, Johnson 2-29, Floyd 2-9, Ismail 1-62, Carrier 1-9. New York, Chrebet 7-107, K. Johnson 3-77, Martin 2-33, Brady 2-8, Byars 1-19, Ward 1-11.

MISSED FIELD GOAL ATTEMPTS—None.

INTERCEPTIONS—New York, Glenn 1-26.

KICKOFF RETURNS—Carolina, Bates 6-131, Stone 1-45. New York, L. Johnson 3-79.

PUNT RETURNS—Carolina, Oliver 1-0. New York, L. Johnson 2-(minus 3).

SACKS—New York, Pleasant 2, B. Cox 1, Cascadden 1, Ferguson 0.5, Lyle 0.5.

CHIEFS 34, CARDINALS 24

Sunday, November 29

Arizona	0	10	7	7—24
Kansas City	7	7	10	10—34

First Quarter

K.C.—Morris 2 run (Stoyanovich kick), 10:47.

Second Quarter

K.C.—Bennett 2 pass from Gannon (Stoyanovich kick), 4:09.

Ariz.—R. Moore 10 pass from Plummer (Nedney kick), 12:35.

Third Quarter

K.C.—Alexander 30 pass from Gannon (Stoyanovich kick), 2:55.

K.C.—FG, Stoyanovich 37, 10:58.

Ariz.—Murrell 4 run (Nedney kick), 13:10.

Fourth Quarter

K.C.—Alexander 15 pass from Gannon (Stoyanovich kick), 4:34.

Ariz.—Bates 1 run (Nedney kick), 8:53.

K.C.—FG, Stoyanovich 18, 13:03.

Attendance—69,613.

	Arizona	Kansas City
First downs	22	20
Rushes-yards	23-124	30-128
Passing	214	248
Punt returns	2-10	4-48
Kickoff returns	5-70	3-85
Interception returns	1-0	2-42
Comp.-att.-int.	20-37-2	22-29-1
Sacked-yards lost	5-36	2-8
Punts	5-47	4-42
Fumbles-lost	1-0	1-0
Penalties-yards	5-24	9-64
Time of possession	28:37	31:23

INDIVIDUAL STATISTICS

RUSHING—Arizona, Murrell 13-77, Centers 3-21, Pittman 3-17, Bates 3-1, Plummer 1-8. Kansas City, Morris 15-76, Anders 5-36, Bennett 4-10, Gannon 4-(minus 4), Shehee 2-10.

PASSING—Arizona, Plummer 20-37-2-250. Kansas City, Gannon 21-28-1-231, Hughes 1-1-0-25.

RECEIVING—Arizona, R. Moore 7-75, Sanders 6-100, Centers 4-46, Murrell 1-18, Anderson 1-8, Gedney 1-3. Kansas City, Alexander 6-116, Gonzalez 4-32, Rison 3-43, Morris 3-25, Bennett 3-14, Anders 2-9, Horn 1-17.

MISSED FIELD GOAL ATTEMPTS—Arizona, Nedney 50.

INTERCEPTIONS—Arizona, Chavous 1-0. Kansas City, Hasty 1-21, McMillian 1-21.

KICKOFF RETURNS—Arizona, Metcalf 4-65, Gedney 1-5. Kansas City, Vanover 2-85, Parten 1-0.

PUNT RETURNS—Arizona, Metcalf 2-10. Kansas City, Vanover 4-48.

SACKS—Arizona, M. Smith 1, Wadsworth 0.5, Miller 0.5. Kansas City, Edwards 2, Tongue 1, Favors 1, Davis 1.

RAVENS 38, COLTS 31

Sunday, November 29

Indianapolis	17	7	7	0—31
Baltimore	3	10	8	17—38

First Quarter

Ind.—FG, Vanderjagt 53, 4:54.

Bal.—FG, Stover 43, 6:35.

Ind.—Faulk 34 pass from Manning (Vanderjagt kick), 10:15.

Ind.—Faulk 68 run (Vanderjagt kick), 12:31.

Second Quarter

Bal.—Roe 15 pass from Harbaugh (Stover kick), 8:16.

Ind.—Small 24 pass from Manning (Vanderjagt kick), 14:19.

Bal.—FG, Stover 48, 15:00.

Third Quarter

Bal.—Holmes 2 run (Turner pass from Harbaugh), 7:04.

Ind.—Pathon 5 pass from Manning (Vanderjagt kick), 13:35.

Fourth Quarter

Bal.—Turner 22 pass from Harbaugh (Stover kick), 0:05.

Bal.—Holmes 36 run (Stover kick), 1:53.

Bal.—FG, Stover 47, 12:11.

Attendance—68,898.

	Indianapolis	Baltimore
First downs	26	18
Rushes-yards	23-196	27-116
Passing	344	198
Punt returns	1-9	2-26
Kickoff returns	7-120	5-193
Interception returns	0-0	1-11
Comp.-att.-int.	27-42-1	16-25-0
Sacked-yards lost	2-13	0-0
Punts	3-47	3-50
Fumbles-lost	0-0	1-0
Penalties-yards	8-64	1-10
Time of possession	33:44	26:16

INDIVIDUAL STATISTICS

RUSHING—Indianapolis, Faulk 17-192, Warren 4-(minus 4), Elias 1-6, Manning 1-2. Baltimore, Holmes 22-103, Harbaugh 5-13.

PASSING—Indianapolis, Manning 27-42-1-357. Baltimore, Harbaugh 16-25-0-198.

RECEIVING—Indianapolis, Small 9-153, Faulk 7-75, Warren 3-10, Harrison 2-35, Pollard 2-35, Pathon 2-21, Green 1-20, Dilger 1-8. Baltimore, Roe 4-53, Holmes 4-26, Turner 3-42, Green 2-15, Potts 2-9, J. Lewis 1-53.

MISSED FIELD GOAL ATTEMPTS—Indianapolis, Vanderjagt 52.

INTERCEPTIONS—Baltimore, Staten 1-11.

KICKOFF RETURNS—Indianapolis, Bailey 6-106, Warren 1-14. Baltimore, C. Harris 5-193.

PUNT RETURNS—Indianapolis, Bailey 1-9. Baltimore, Roe 1-15, J. Lewis 1-11.

SACKS—Baltimore, Boulware 1, McCrary 1.

FALCONS 21, RAMS 10

Sunday, November 29

Atlanta	3	0	11	7—21
St. Louis	0	0	7	3—10

First Quarter

Atl.—FG, Andersen 42, 5:59.

Third Quarter

St.L.—Horne 102 kickoff return (Wilkins kick), 0:19.

Atl.—FG, Andersen 32, 4:54.

Atl.—Mathis 27 pass from DeBerg (J. Anderson run), 11:11.

Fourth Quarter

St.L.—FG, Wilkins 39, 2:26.

Atl.—J. Anderson 27 run (Andersen kick), 11:47.

Attendance—47,971.

	Atlanta	St. Louis
First downs	20	12
Rushes-yards	35-204	20-45
Passing	170	129
Punt returns	7-75	2-22
Kickoff returns	2-40	4-206
Interception returns	0-0	1-20

	Atlanta	St. Louis
Comp.-att.-int.	13-31-1	16-34-0
Sacked-yards lost	1-7	3-20
Punts	7-42	9-46
Fumbles-lost	0-0	2-0
Penalties-yards	5-24	4-27
Time of possession	33:25	26:35

INDIVIDUAL STATISTICS

RUSHING—Atlanta, J. Anderson 31-188, Graziani 2-10, Downs 1-4, DeBerg 1-2. St. Louis, Holcombe 14-38, Banks 2-1, Lee 2-0, Bono 1-5, Harris 1-1.

PASSING—Atlanta, Graziani 8-18-1-102, DeBerg 5-12-0-75, Martin 0-1-0-0. St. Louis, Banks 10-21-0-95, Bono 6-13-0-54.

RECEIVING—Atlanta, Mathis 5-71, Martin 2-31, Santiago 2-25, J. Anderson 2-9, Kinchen 1-32, Dwight 1-9. St. Louis, Proehl 6-80, Lee 4-30, R. Williams 2-15, Armstrong 1-10, Harris 1-5, Henley 1-5, J. Thomas 1-4.

MISSED FIELD GOAL ATTEMPTS—St. Louis, Wilkins 61, 48.

INTERCEPTIONS—St. Louis, Lyle 1-20.

KICKOFF RETURNS—Atlanta, Dwight 2-40. St. Louis, Horne 4-206.

PUNT RETURNS—Atlanta, Dwight 7-75. St. Louis, Kennison 2-22.

SACKS—Atlanta, Tuggle 1, White 1, Dronett 1. St. Louis, Carter 1.

BUCCANEERS 31, BEARS 17

Sunday, November 29

Tampa Bay	7	14	10	0	31
Chicago	0	14	0	3	17

First Quarter
T.B.—Alstott 5 pass from Dilfer (Husted kick), 5:40.

Second Quarter
Chi.—Wetnight 18 pass from Horan (Jaeger kick), 0:13.
Chi.—Conway 21 pass from Moreno (Jaeger kick), 1:06.
T.B.—Barber 23 punt return (Husted kick), 11:20.
T.B.—Hunter 45 pass from Dilfer (Husted kick), 15:00.

Third Quarter
T.B.—Anthony 14 pass from Dilfer (Husted kick), 8:48.
T.B.—FG, Husted 28, 14:54.

Fourth Quarter
Chi.—FG, Jaeger 33, 4:25.
Attendance—51,938.

	Tampa Bay	Chicago
First downs	13	13
Rushes-yards	39-114	24-69
Passing	153	155
Punt returns	5-59	2-17
Kickoff returns	2-52	5-79
Interception returns	0-0	1-5
Comp.-att.-int.	13-22-1	19-42-0
Sacked-yards lost	0-0	2-16
Punts	6-43	8-35
Fumbles-lost	1-1	2-2
Penalties-yards	3-40	7-36
Time of possession	33:08	26:52

INDIVIDUAL STATISTICS

RUSHING—Tampa Bay, Dunn 22-62, Alstott 14-43, Dilfer 2-(minus 2), Emanuel 1-11. Chicago, Bennett 10-14, J. Allen 7-31, Moreno 4-9, Chancey 2-9, Conway 1-6.

PASSING—Tampa Bay, Dilfer 13-22-1-153. Chicago, Moreno 18-41-0-153, Horan 1-1-0-18.

RECEIVING—Tampa Bay, Anthony 4-47, Emanuel 3-21, Moore 2-28, Alstott 2-1, Hunter 1-45, Dunn 1-11. Chicago, Engram 4-33, Hallock 4-26, Conway 3-37, Wetnight 2-24, Mayes 2-23, Bennett 2-20, M. Robinson 1-5, J. Allen 1-3.

MISSED FIELD GOAL ATTEMPTS—None.

INTERCEPTIONS—Chicago, Collins 1-5.

KICKOFF RETURNS—Tampa Bay, Anthony 2-52. Chicago, Milburn 4-79, Wetnight 1-0.

PUNT RETURNS—Tampa Bay, Green 4-36, Barber 1-23. Chicago, Milburn 2-17.

SACKS—Tampa Bay, Quarles 1, Sapp 1.

SEAHAWKS 20, OILERS 18

Sunday, November 29

Tennessee	3	3	0	12	18
Seattle	0	3	7	10	20

First Quarter
Ten.—FG, Del Greco 26, 9:11.

Second Quarter
Ten.—FG, Del Greco 30, 9:03.
Sea.—FG, Peterson 50, 14:57.

Third Quarter
Sea.—Galloway 7 pass from Kitna (Peterson kick), 8:58.

Fourth Quarter
Ten.—FG, Del Greco 43, 3:06.
Sea.—McKnight 59 pass from Kitna (Peterson kick), 3:56.
Ten.—McNair 3 run (run failed), 10:01.
Ten.—FG, Del Greco 42, 14:27.
Sea.—FG, Peterson 48, 14:59.
Attendance—59,048.

	Tennessee	Seattle
First downs	23	20
Rushes-yards	30-164	19-82
Passing	179	296
Punt returns	1-12	3-36
Kickoff returns	5-54	5-100
Interception returns	1-0	0-0
Comp.-att.-int.	18-35-0	24-39-1
Sacked-yards lost	4-20	1-2
Punts	4-48	3-44
Fumbles-lost	3-2	2-2
Penalties-yards	8-68	8-45
Time of possession	36:00	24:00

INDIVIDUAL STATISTICS

RUSHING—Tennessee, E. George 19-76, McNair 8-64, Archie 2-20, Dyson 1-4. Seattle, Watters 14-63, Kitna 3-5, Galloway 1-14, Green 1-0.

PASSING—Tennessee, McNair 18-34-0-199, Archie 0-1-0-0. Seattle, Kitna 24-39-1-298.

RECEIVING—Tennessee, E. George 5-64, Wycheck 5-57, Davis 3-48, Archie 2-14, Harris 2-6, Mason 1-10. Seattle, Watters 7-63, McKnight 5-113, Galloway 4-36, Fauria 4-28, Pritchard 3-49, Br. Blades 1-9.

MISSED FIELD GOAL ATTEMPTS—None.

INTERCEPTIONS—Tennessee, D. Walker 1-0.

KICKOFF RETURNS—Tennessee, Archie 4-71, Harris 1-3. Seattle, Broussard 4-76, Joseph 1-24.

PUNT RETURNS—Tennessee, Mason 1-12. Seattle, Galloway 3-36.

SACKS—Tennessee, Robinson 1. Seattle, Sinclair 2, C. Brown 1, Daniels 1.

JAGUARS 34, BENGALS 17

Sunday, November 29

Jacksonville	7	10	10	7	34
Cincinnati	0	10	7	0	17

First Quarter
Jac.—J. Smith 21 pass from Brunell (Hollis kick), 11:31.

Second Quarter
Jac.—McCardell 8 pass from Brunell (Hollis kick), 2:12.
Jac.—FG, Hollis 23, 6:23.
Cin.—Milne 1 run (Pelfrey kick), 11:12.
Cin.—FG, Pelfrey 30, 15:00.

Third Quarter
Jac.—FG, Hollis 47, 3:15.
Cin.—McGee 7 pass from O'Donnell (Pelfrey kick), 4:57.
Jac.—McCardell 3 pass from Brunell (Hollis kick), 9:55.

Fourth Quarter
Jac.—D. Jones 1 pass from Brunell (Hollis kick), 4:46.
Attendance—55,432.

	Jacksonville	Cincinnati
First downs	16	20
Rushes-yards	29-79	24-131
Passing	243	224
Punt returns	3-69	5-49
Kickoff returns	2-26	7-152
Interception returns	2-26	0-0
Comp.-att.-int.	19-35-0	24-43-2
Sacked-yards lost	1-1	1-10
Punts	6-46	4-50
Fumbles-lost	0-0	3-2
Penalties-yards	7-51	3-27
Time of possession	29:25	30:35

INDIVIDUAL STATISTICS

RUSHING—Jacksonville, G. Jones 13-42, Shelton 8-17, F. Taylor 6-16, Brunell 2-4. Cincinnati, Dillon 16-107, Bennett 4-13, Milne 2-11, O'Donnell 2-0.

PASSING—Jacksonville, Brunell 19-35-0-244. Cincinnati, O'Donnell 20-36-1-203, Justin 4-7-1-31.

RECEIVING—Jacksonville, J. Smith 7-110, McCardell 7-76, Mitchell 2-39, D. Jones 2-11, Shelton 1-8. Cincinnati, Pickens 5-59, Dillon 4-44, Scott 4-33, Milne 4-8, McGee 3-35, Gibson 1-28, Hundon 1-17, Bush 1-8, Bieniemy 1-2.

MISSED FIELD GOAL ATTEMPTS—Cincinnati, Pelfrey 42.

INTERCEPTIONS—Jacksonville, Hardy 1-24, Hudson 1-2.

KICKOFF RETURNS—Jacksonville, Barlow 1-18, Logan 1-8. Cincinnati, Mack 4-86, Gibson 2-44, Bieniemy 1-22.

PUNT RETURNS—Jacksonville, Barlow 3-69. Cincinnati, Gibson 5-49.

SACKS—Jacksonville, White 1. Cincinnati, Bankston 0.5, Wilson 0.5.

DOLPHINS 30, SAINTS 10

Sunday, November 29

New Orleans	3	7	0	0—10
Miami	0	13	3	14—30

First Quarter

N.O.—FG, Brien 43, 7:57.

Second Quarter

Mia.—FG, Mare 27, 1:16.

N.O.—Kelly 79 interception return (Brien kick), 9:17.

Mia.—McDuffie 22 pass from Marino (Mare kick), 13:07.

Mia.—FG, Mare 32, 14:19.

Third Quarter

Mia.—FG, Mare 34, 6:56.

Fourth Quarter

Mia.—McDuffie 7 pass from Marino (Mare kick), 0:05.

Mia.—McDuffie 9 pass from Marino (Mare kick), 7:26.

Attendance—73,216.

	New Orleans	Miami
First downs	11	24
Rushes-yards	17-87	38-120
Passing	70	255
Punt returns	3-63	6-119
Kickoff returns	5-112	3-76
Interception returns	1-79	3-2
Comp.-att.-int.	9-24-3	22-40-1
Sacked-yards lost	6-40	0-0
Punts	7-50	6-44
Fumbles-lost	2-1	1-0
Penalties-yards	4-50	6-51
Time of possession	20:15	39:45

INDIVIDUAL STATISTICS

RUSHING—New Orleans, L. Smith 7-3, Collins 5-35, Craver 3-27, Perry 2-22. Miami, Abdul-Jabbar 18-72, Avery 14-39, Marino 3-0, Pritchett 2-6, Doxzon 1-3.

PASSING—New Orleans, Collins 9-24-3-110. Miami, Marino 22-40-1-255.

RECEIVING—New Orleans, Dawkins 2-24, Hastings 2-19, Craver 2-18, Cleeland 1-29, Bech 1-17, L. Smith 1-3. Miami, McDuffie 9-102, Gadsden 4-60, L. Thomas 4-37, Drayton 2-27, Abdul-Jabbar 2-10, Jacquet 1-19.

MISSED FIELD GOAL ATTEMPTS—None.

INTERCEPTIONS—New Orleans, Kelly 1-79. Miami, Buckley 1-2, Madison 1-0, Walker 1-0.

KICKOFF RETURNS—New Orleans, Guliford 4-93, Little 1-19. Miami, Avery 3-76.

PUNT RETURNS—New Orleans, Guliford 3-63. Miami, McDuffie 5-84, Buckley 1-35.

SACKS—Miami, Bromell 2, Z. Thomas 1, Mixon 1, Armstrong 1, Team 1.

PATRIOTS 25, BILLS 21

Sunday, November 29

Buffalo	0	6	9	6—21
New England	0	14	3	8—25

Second Quarter

N.E.—Edwards 2 pass from Bledsoe (Vinatieri kick), 5:16.

N.E.—Cullors 12 pass from Bledsoe (Vinatieri kick), 10:23.

Buf.—FG, Christie 34, 13:39.

Buf.—FG, Christie 26, 15:00.

Third Quarter

Buf.—Moulds 84 pass from Flutie (pass failed), 4:03.

N.E.—FG, Vinatieri 44, 9:54.

Buf.—FG, Christie 22, 14:10.

Fourth Quarter

Buf.—Reed 4 pass from Flutie (pass failed), 8:46.

N.E.—Coates 1 pass from Bledsoe (Vinatieri run), 15:00.

Attendance—58,304.

	Buffalo	New England
First downs	23	24
Rushes-yards	31-99	14-44
Passing	329	215
Punt returns	3-6	1-30
Kickoff returns	4-71	5-84
Interception returns	1-0	0-0
Comp.-att.-int.	21-39-0	28-43-1
Sacked-yards lost	1-10	4-31
Punts	4-32	4-47
Fumbles-lost	1-0	1-0
Penalties-yards	12-107	9-80
Time of possession	34:01	25:59

INDIVIDUAL STATISTICS

RUSHING—Buffalo, A. Smith 21-58, Flutie 5-30, Thomas 3-5, Gash 1-4, Linton 1-2. New England, Edwards 13-40, Bledsoe 1-4.

PASSING—Buffalo, Flutie 21-39-0-339. New England, Bledsoe 28-43-1-246.

RECEIVING—Buffalo, Moulds 8-177, K. Williams 4-74, Reed 4-53, Riemersma 2-17, Thomas 2-6, Early 1-12. New England, Coates 10-70, Glenn 8-104, Ton. Carter 3-24, Cullors 3-24, Jefferson 2-18, Edwards 2-6.

MISSED FIELD GOAL ATTEMPTS—Buffalo, Christie 35. New England, Vinatieri 47.

INTERCEPTIONS—Buffalo, T. Smith 1-0.

KICKOFF RETURNS—Buffalo, K. Williams 4-71. New England, Cullors 4-75, Sullivan 1-9.

PUNT RETURNS—Buffalo, K. Williams 3-6. New England, Canty 1-30.

SACKS—Buffalo, B. Smith 1, Washington 1, Simmons 1, Wiley 1. New England, Spires 1.

REDSKINS 29, RAIDERS 19

Sunday, November 29

Washington	7	10	2	10—29
Oakland	7	0	0	12—19

First Quarter

Was.—Davis 19 pass from T. Green (Blanchard kick), 0:51.

Oak.—Kaufman 23 run (G. Davis kick), 10:56.

Second Quarter

Was.—Shepherd 43 pass from T. Green (Blanchard kick), 8:58.

Was.—FG, Blanchard 28, 12:56.

Third Quarter

Was.—Safety, Hollas sacked by Boutte in end zone, 12:12.

Fourth Quarter

Was.—S. Alexander 2 pass from T. Green (Blanchard kick), 0:05.

Oak.—Mickens 12 pass from Hollas (pass failed), 5:20.

Was.—FG, Blanchard 47, 11:18.

Oak.—T. Brown 2 pass from Hollas (pass failed), 13:25.

Attendance—41,409.

	Washington	Oakland
First downs	17	23
Rushes-yards	31-94	26-187
Passing	209	189
Punt returns	3-82	2-2
Kickoff returns	4-103	4-74
Interception returns	2-36	0-0
Comp.-att.-int.	16-31-0	23-44-2
Sacked-yards lost	3-15	2-10
Punts	7-46	6-41
Fumbles-lost	1-1	3-2
Penalties-yards	7-83	3-25
Time of possession	31:05	28:55

INDIVIDUAL STATISTICS

RUSHING—Washington, Hicks 21-72, Mitchell 4-10, T. Green 3-(minus 2), Davis 2-3, Westbrook 1-11. Oakland, Kaufman 17-152, H. Williams 7-27, Hollas 2-8.

PASSING—Washington, T. Green 16-31-0-224. Oakland, Hollas 16-29-1-134, George 7-15-1-65.

RECEIVING—Washington, Davis 7-110, S. Alexander 3-24, Shepherd 2-55, Westbrook 2-28, Mitchell 1-5, Connell 1-2. Oakland, T. Brown 7-58, H. Williams 4-20, Mickens 3-40, Ritchie 3-14, Shedd 2-29, Jett 2-12, Dudley 1-19, Kaufman 1-7.

MISSED FIELD GOAL ATTEMPTS—None.

1998 REVIEW Week 13

INTERCEPTIONS—Washington, D. Green 1-36, Barber 1-0.
KICKOFF RETURNS—Washington, Mitchell 3-89, Thrash 1-14. Oakland, Howard 4-74.
PUNT RETURNS—Washington, Mitchell 3-82. Oakland, Howard 1-2, B. Brooks 1-0.
SACKS—Washington, Lang 1, Boutte 1. Oakland, Harvey 1, Biekert 1, Johnstone 1.

PACKERS 24, EAGLES 16

Sunday, November 29

Philadelphia	0	6	7	3—16
Green Bay	0	10	7	7—24

Second Quarter
G.B.—FG, Longwell 33, 6:00.
G.B.—Henderson 1 pass from Favre (Longwell kick), 11:06.
Phi.—Graham 16 pass from Detmer (kick blocked), 14:32.

Third Quarter
Phi.—Graham 4 pass from Detmer (Boniol kick), 5:04.
G.B.—Freeman 33 pass from Favre (Longwell kick), 7:51.

Fourth Quarter
Phi.—FG, Boniol 34, 6:19.
G.B.—Henderson 2 run (Longwell kick), 12:00.
Attendance—59,862.

	Philadelphia	Green Bay
First downs	15	26
Rushes-yards	19-65	39-178
Passing	167	321
Punt returns	0-0	5-21
Kickoff returns	5-120	4-91
Interception returns	2-47	0-0
Comp.-att.-int.	22-36-0	20-33-2
Sacked-yards lost	2-18	0-0
Punts	8-39	2-32
Fumbles-lost	0-0	2-1
Penalties-yards	8-42	9-74
Time of possession	26:12	33:48

INDIVIDUAL STATISTICS
RUSHING—Philadelphia, Staley 15-60, Detmer 1-6, Turner 1-2, Walker 1-1, Jells 1-(minus 4). Green Bay, Holmes 26-163, Levens 6-6, Favre 4-1, Henderson 3-8.
PASSING—Philadelphia, Detmer 22-36-0-185. Green Bay, Favre 20-33-2-321.
RECEIVING—Philadelphia, Graham 6-56, Staley 5-61, Turner 4-36, Dunn 3-16, Fryar 3-11, Solomon 1-5. Green Bay, Schroeder 5-128, Holmes 5-53, Freeman 3-67, Chmura 3-24, T. Davis 1-39, Mayes 1-10, Henderson 1-1, Bradford 1-(minus 1).
MISSED FIELD GOAL ATTEMPTS—None.
INTERCEPTIONS—Philadelphia, Vincent 1-29, McTyer 1-18.
KICKOFF RETURNS—Philadelphia, Rossum 5-120. Green Bay, Preston 3-82, Bradford 1-9.
PUNT RETURNS—Green Bay, Preston 3-16, Schroeder 2-5.
SACKS—Green Bay, McKenzie 1, White 1.

BRONCOS 31, CHARGERS 16

Sunday, November 29

Denver	14	7	10	0—31
San Diego	10	0	0	6—16

First Quarter
S.D.—FG, Carney 27, 1:48.
Den.—McCaffrey 15 pass from Elway (Elam kick), 4:22.
Den.—McCaffrey 37 pass from Elway (Elam kick), 8:17.
S.D.—Fletcher 13 run (Carney kick), 13:28.

Second Quarter
Den.—R. Smith 13 pass from Elway (Elam kick), 14:17.

Third Quarter
Den.—Sharpe 18 pass from Elway (Elam kick), 10:26.
Den.—FG, Elam 34, 15:00.

Fourth Quarter
S.D.—Still 47 pass from Whelihan (pass failed), 10:05.
Attendance—66,532.

	Denver	San Diego
First downs	18	21
Rushes-yards	30-96	17-65

	Denver	San Diego
Passing	226	302
Punt returns	4-32	2-52
Kickoff returns	3-113	6-84
Interception returns	5-86	3-38
Comp.-att.-int.	19-34-3	30-53-5
Sacked-yards lost	1-13	1-2
Punts	5-47	5-42
Fumbles-lost	1-1	3-1
Penalties-yards	8-70	10-95
Time of possession	30:01	29:59

INDIVIDUAL STATISTICS
RUSHING—Denver, Davis 24-74, Elway 4-6, R. Smith 1-12, Loville 1-4. San Diego, Fletcher 11-54, Whelihan 3-4, Bynum 2-3, C. Jones 1-4.
PASSING—Denver, Elway 19-34-3-239. San Diego, Whelihan 30-53-5-304.
RECEIVING—Denver, R. Smith 8-101, McCaffrey 5-74, Sharpe 3-31, Carswell 1-15, Green 1-14, Davis 1-4. San Diego, Fletcher 11-69, Still 5-99, C. Jones 5-59, F. Jones 5-37, Bynum 2-9, Ricks 1-20, Burke 1-11.
MISSED FIELD GOAL ATTEMPTS—None.
INTERCEPTIONS—Denver, Gordon 2-34, Johnson 1-34, Coghill 1-20, Mobley 1-(minus 2). San Diego, Dimry 2-38, G. Jackson 1-0.
KICKOFF RETURNS—Denver, Hebron 3-113. San Diego, Gaiter 6-84.
PUNT RETURNS—Denver, Gordon 4-32. San Diego, Gaiter 2-52.
SACKS—Denver, Cadrez 1. San Diego, Seau 1.

49ERS 31, GIANTS 7

Monday, November 30

N.Y. Giants	7	0	0	0—7
San Francisco	7	7	7	10—31

First Quarter
NYG—Brown 11 run (Daluiso kick), 5:39.
S.F.—Owens 79 pass from S. Young (Richey kick), 12:21.

Second Quarter
S.F.—I. Smith 1 pass from S. Young (Richey kick), 14:32.

Third Quarter
S.F.—Kirby 7 run (Richey kick), 7:59.

Fourth Quarter
S.F.—FG, Richey 39, 4:53.
S.F.—Hearst 70 run (Richey kick), 11:51.
Attendance—68,212.

	N.Y. Giants	San Francisco
First downs	18	23
Rushes-yards	25-120	34-237
Passing	224	229
Punt returns	2-3	4-48
Kickoff returns	5-85	2-26
Interception returns	0-0	1-1
Comp.-att.-int.	21-41-1	19-33-0
Sacked-yards lost	2-13	3-24
Punts	5-43	5-36
Fumbles-lost	1-1	0-0
Penalties-yards	7-59	7-65
Time of possession	28:33	31:27

INDIVIDUAL STATISTICS
RUSHING—New York, Brown 15-56, Way 6-53, Barber 2-9, K. Graham 2-2. San Francisco, Hearst 20-166, Kirby 6-14, S. Young 5-62, Detmer 3-(minus 5).
PASSING—New York, K. Graham 21-41-1-237. San Francisco, S. Young 19-33-0-253.
RECEIVING—New York, Hilliard 6-141, Calloway 5-45, Barber 4-13, Toomer 2-14, Haase 1-27, Jurevicius 1-7, Cross 1-(minus 4), Way 1-(minus 6). San Francisco, Owens 5-140, Stokes 3-38, Rice 3-25, Hearst 2-7, I. Smith 2-5, Harris 1-25, Clark 1-7, Edwards 1-4, Kirby 1-2.
MISSED FIELD GOAL ATTEMPTS—New York, Daluiso 43, 42. San Francisco, Richey 41, 43.
INTERCEPTIONS—San Francisco, McDonald 1-1.
KICKOFF RETURNS—New York, Patten 4-74, Barber 1-11. San Francisco, Kirby 1-14, I. Smith 1-12.
PUNT RETURNS—New York, Toomer 2-3. San Francisco, McQuarters 4-48.
SACKS—New York, Strahan 2, Bratzke 1. San Francisco, Peterson 1, Barker 1.

WEEK 14

RESULTS

PHILADELPHIA 17, St. Louis 14
TENNESSEE 16, Baltimore 14
Buffalo 33, CINCINNATI 20
NEW ORLEANS 22, Dallas 3
JACKSONVILLE 37, Detroit 22
ATLANTA 28, Indianapolis 21
DENVER 35, Kansas City 31
Miami 27, OAKLAND 17
New England 23, PITTSBURGH 9
N.Y. Giants 23, ARIZONA 19
WASHINGTON 24, San Diego 20
San Francisco 31, CAROLINA 28
N.Y. JETS 32, Seattle 31
MINNESOTA 48, Chicago 22
TAMPA BAY 24, Green Bay 22

STANDINGS

AFC EAST	W	L	T	Pct.
Miami	9	4	0	.692
N.Y. Jets	9	4	0	.692
Buffalo	8	5	0	.615
New England	8	5	0	.615
Indianapolis	2	11	0	.154

NFC EAST	W	L	T	Pct.
Dallas	8	5	0	.615
Arizona	6	7	0	.462
N.Y. Giants	5	8	0	.385
Washington	4	9	0	.308
Philadelphia	3	10	0	.231

AFC CENTRAL	W	L	T	Pct.
Jacksonville	10	3	0	.769
Pittsburgh	7	6	0	.538
Tennessee	7	6	0	.538
Baltimore	5	8	0	.385
Cincinnati	2	11	0	.154

NFC CENTRAL	W	L	T	Pct.
Minnesota	12	1	0	.923
Green Bay	8	5	0	.615
Tampa Bay	6	7	0	.462
Detroit	5	8	0	.385
Chicago	3	10	0	.231

AFC WEST	W	L	T	Pct.
Denver	13	0	0	1.000
Oakland	7	6	0	.538
Seattle	6	7	0	.462
Kansas City	5	8	0	.385
San Diego	5	8	0	.385

NFC WEST	W	L	T	Pct.
Atlanta	11	2	0	.846
San Francisco	10	3	0	.769
New Orleans	6	7	0	.462
St. Louis	3	10	0	.231
Carolina	2	11	0	.154

HIGHLIGHTS

Hero of the week: With 20 seconds left to play, the ball on the Seattle 5-yard line, the Jets trailing 31-26 and facing fourth down, Vinny Testaverde surprised virtually everyone with a quarterback sneak. The Jets quarterback gained 5 yards and a touchdown as New York squeaked out a 32-31 victory in East Rutherford, N.J., to retain a share of first place in the AFC East. The touchdown was tainted—video replay showed Testaverde came up short of the goal line.

Goat of the week: Oakland quarterback Donald Hollas threw six interceptions, two of which were returned for touchdowns from deep in his territory, as the Raiders fell to the Dolphins, 27-17. Zach Thomas and Robert Jones had the TD returns for Miami.

Sub of the week: Jamie Martin, a career backup in his sixth NFL season, stepped in for injured Mark Brunell and completed 15 of 23 passes for 228 yards and two touchdowns as Jacksonville defeated Detroit, 37-22. After Brunell suffered an injury to his left ankle on the second play of the game, the Jaguars turned to Martin, who had thrown 11 passes in two previous games in '98 and 45 in his career.

Comeback of the week: Denver grabbed its first lead with three minutes left when John Elway hit Shannon Sharpe on third-and-1 at the Kansas City 24 to give the Broncos a 35-31 lead they never relinquished at Mile High Stadium. Denver improved to 13-0 and remained the league's only unbeaten team.

Blowout of the week: Minnesota clinched its first NFC Central title since 1994 with a 48-22 pounding of the Bears in Minneapolis. The Vikings scored on their first four possessions despite the absence of many key players. Randy Moss caught three touchdown passes to set an NFL season record for TD receptions by a rookie, breaking a record set by Bill Howton in 1952 and tied by John Jefferson in 1978.

Nail-biter of the week: The Oilers kept their playoff hopes alive with a 16-14 victory over the Ravens in Nashville. The Oilers had to hold off a comeback bid by Jim Harbaugh, who drove the Ravens 80 yards and hit Floyd Turner with a touchdown pass with 1:46 left to play to pull Baltimore within 16-14.

The Ravens forced the Oilers to punt, and Harbaugh got the ball back with 1:18 to go. Two plays later, however, Steve Jackson intercepted Harbaugh at the Oilers' 40 to preserve the victory.

Hit of the week: Patriots tackle Chad Eaton hit Jerome Bettis at the Pittsburgh 35 early in the second half, knocking the ball out of Bettis' hands. Lawyer Milloy fell on the ball for the Patriots' third fumble recovery of the season. New England rolled to a 23-9 victory at Three Rivers Stadium.

Oddity of the week: Dallas played a turnover-free game but still couldn't avoid a 22-3 loss to New Orleans. The Cowboys gained only 8 yards rushing on 18 attempts, including a 15-carry, 6-yard performance by Emmitt Smith.

Top rusher: Jacksonville's Fred Taylor carried 32 times for 183 yards and scored two touchdowns as the Jaguars defeated Detroit.

Top passer: The Jets' Vinny Testaverde completed 42-of-63 passes for 418 yards, threw for two touchdowns and ran for another against Seattle.

Top receiver: Buffalo's Eric Moulds caught six passes for 196 yards and two touchdowns, barely topping New England's Terry Glenn, who grabbed nine passes for 193 yards and a touchdown.

Notes: Denver's Terrell Davis surpassed the 6,000-yard mark in career rushing faster than all running backs except Eric Dickerson, Earl Campbell and Jim Brown. Davis also had more touchdowns (59) than any player in his first four years. . . . The Jets' 418 passing yards against Seattle were their most since Pat Ryan and Ken O'Brien teamed for 426 against Miami in November 1988. . . . Saints kicker Doug Brien nailed two 53-yard field goals, making him 4-for-5 from 50 yards or more in 1998. . . . New England won in Pittsburgh for the first time since 1986. . . . Peyton Manning broke Rick Mirer's rookie record for passing yards, set in 1993. . . . The Eagles' 17-14 win over Dick Vermeil and the Rams improved their all-time record against their former coaches to 7-3. . . . John Elway passed for 400 or more yards for the second time in his career. His

1998 REVIEW Week 14

first such performance came 13 years earlier in a game against Seattle, the longest interval between 400-yard passing games in NFL history. . . . Oilers quarterback Steve McNair's streak of 113 passes without an interception was brought to an end by the Ravens' Rod Woodson . . . Randy Moss' 55 catches are a Vikings rookie record, breaking a mark held by Paul Flatley and Sammy White.

Quote of the week: St. Louis coach Dick Vermeil, who returned to Veterans Stadium in Philadelphia for the first time since resigning as Eagles coach in 1983, on the fans' positive reaction to his return: "These people overreact one way or another. This is probably an over-reaction, but I appreciate it. It surprised me, but I appreciate it."

GAME SUMMARIES

EAGLES 17, RAMS 14

Thursday, December 3

St. Louis	0	6	0	8—14
Philadelphia	10	0	7	0—17

First Quarter
Phi.—Solomon 7 pass from Detmer (Boniol kick), 8:55.
Phi.—FG, Boniol 50, 15:00.
Second Quarter
St.L.—FG, Wilkins 46, 4:16.
St.L.—FG, Wilkins 20, 14:43.
Third Quarter
Phi.—Fryar 61 pass from Detmer (Boniol kick), 7:42.
Fourth Quarter
St.L.—Henley 1 run (Proehl pass from Banks), 3:56.
Attendance—66,155.

	St. Louis	Philadelphia
First downs	17	16
Rushes-yards	26-82	30-130
Passing	248	169
Punt returns	2-13	1-3
Kickoff returns	4-60	3-65
Interception returns	1-0	1-4
Comp.-att.-int.	22-37-1	17-33-1
Sacked-yards lost	1-7	0-0
Punts	5-46	5-42
Fumbles-lost	1-0	0-0
Penalties-yards	6-42	4-22
Time of possession	29:19	30:41

INDIVIDUAL STATISTICS
RUSHING—St. Louis, Henley 14-53, Lee 5-23, Holcombe 5-0, Banks 2-6. Philadelphia, Staley 28-99, Fryar 1-32, Detmer 1-(minus 1).
PASSING—St. Louis, Banks 22-37-1-255. Philadelphia, Detmer 17-33-1-169.
RECEIVING—St. Louis, Lee 5-71, J. Thomas 4-79, Hakim 3-45, Henley 3-24, Proehl 3-23, Armstrong 2-9, Harris 2-9, R. Williams 1-2. Philadelphia, Staley 5-23, Solomon 4-21, Fryar 2-65, Graham 2-34, Fontenot 2-16, Turner 2-10.
MISSED FIELD GOAL ATTEMPTS—St. Louis, Wilkins 52. Philadelphia, Boniol 46.
INTERCEPTIONS—St. Louis, Agnew 1-0. Philadelphia, Zordich 1-4.
KICKOFF RETURNS—St. Louis, Horne 4-60. Philadelphia, Rossum 2-50, Turner 1-15.
PUNT RETURNS—St. Louis, Kennison 2-13. Philadelphia, Rossum 1-3.
SACKS—Philadelphia, Jefferson 1.

49ERS 31, PANTHERS 28

Sunday, December 6

San Francisco	7	14	7	0	3—31
Carolina	7	0	7	14	0—28

First Quarter
Car.—Muhammad 12 pass from Beuerlein (Kasay kick), 6:39.
S.F.—Stokes 2 pass from S. Young (Richey kick), 12:23.

Second Quarter
S.F.—Owens 28 pass from Kirby (Richey kick), 1:13.
S.F.—Stokes 33 pass from S. Young (Richey kick), 13:37.
Third Quarter
S.F.—Hearst 71 run (Richey kick), 2:16.
Car.—Johnson 38 pass from Beuerlein (Kasay kick), 14:08.
Fourth Quarter
Car.—Ismail 40 pass from Beuerlein (Kasay kick), 3:26.
Car.—Biakabutuka 10 run (Kasay kick), 8:40.
Overtime
S.F.—FG, Richey 23, 4:16.
Attendance—63,332.

	San Fran.	Carolina
First downs	22	22
Rushes-yards	35-236	34-203
Passing	238	226
Punt returns	2-2	4-50
Kickoff returns	4-104	3-69
Interception returns	1-0	1-43
Comp.-att.-int.	20-32-1	18-33-1
Sacked-yards lost	1-3	2-9
Punts	5-47	5-42
Fumbles-lost	1-1	3-2
Penalties-yards	7-50	3-20
Time of possession	33:04	31:12

INDIVIDUAL STATISTICS
RUSHING—San Francisco, Hearst 20-139, Kirby 9-68, S. Young 6-29. Carolina, Biakabutuka 22-81, Johnson 7-66, Beuerlein 3-17, Ismail 1-36, Floyd 1-3.
PASSING—San Francisco, S. Young 19-31-1-213, Kirby 1-1-0-28. Carolina, Beuerlein 18-33-1-235.
RECEIVING—San Francisco, Rice 5-36, Owens 4-53, Stokes 4-53, Kirby 2-29, Hearst 2-28, Clark 1-16, Edwards 1-16, I. Smith 1-10. Carolina, Muhammad 8-73, Walls 4-47, Ismail 2-47, Johnson 2-41, Biakabutuka 1-16, D. Hayes 1-11.
MISSED FIELD GOAL ATTEMPTS—Carolina, Kasay 47.
INTERCEPTIONS—San Francisco, Hanks 1-0. Carolina, Brady 1-43.
KICKOFF RETURNS—San Francisco, Kirby 4-104. Carolina, Stone 2-47, Floyd 1-22.
PUNT RETURNS—San Francisco, McQuarters 2-2. Carolina, Oliver 4-50.
SACKS—San Francisco, McDonald 1, Doleman 1. Carolina, Gilbert 1.

PATRIOTS 23, STEELERS 9

Sunday, December 6

New England	3	10	0	10—23
Pittsburgh	0	6	3	0— 9

First Quarter
N.E.—FG, Vinatieri 21, 9:34.
Second Quarter
N.E.—FG, Vinatieri 29, 1:22.
Pit.—FG, N. Johnson 49, 12:02.
N.E.—Glenn 86 pass from Bledsoe (Vinatieri kick), 13:04.
Pit.—FG, N. Johnson 26, 14:53.
Third Quarter
Pit.—FG, N. Johnson 43, 6:26.
Fourth Quarter
N.E.—FG, Vinatieri 35, 2:05.
N.E.—Edwards 4 run (Vinatieri kick), 5:40.
Attendance—58,632.

	New England	Pittsburgh
First downs	19	13
Rushes-yards	34-73	13-54
Passing	304	195
Punt returns	2-7	2-22
Kickoff returns	4-57	6-109
Interception returns	2-11	3-51
Comp.-att.-int.	21-34-3	21-45-2
Sacked-yards lost	2-23	3-11
Punts	3-54	5-42
Fumbles-lost	2-0	1-1
Penalties-yards	12-77	6-56
Time of possession	38:24	21:36

INDIVIDUAL STATISTICS
RUSHING—New England, Edwards 28-66, Bledsoe 5-1, Cullors 1-6. Pittsburgh, Bettis 12-48, McAfee 1-6.

PASSING—New England, Bledsoe 21-34-3-327. Pittsburgh, Stewart 21-45-2-206.

RECEIVING—New England, Glenn 9-193, Coates 6-78, Jefferson 2-29, Simmons 1-12, Edwards 1-6, Floyd 1-6, Ton. Carter 1-3. Pittsburgh, C. Johnson 5-61, Hawkins 4-30, Blackwell 3-47, Bruener 3-29, Ward 2-19, Dunn 2-18, Witman 2-2.

MISSED FIELD GOAL ATTEMPTS—None.

INTERCEPTIONS—New England, Law 1-10, Israel 1-1. Pittsburgh, Holmes 1-36, Oldham 1-14, Kirkland 1-1.

KICKOFF RETURNS—New England, Cullors 2-37, Canty 1-15, Sullivan 1-5. Pittsburgh, Dunn 3-67, Blackwell 3-42.

PUNT RETURNS—New England, Canty 2-7. Pittsburgh, Hawkins 2-22.

SACKS—New England, Eaton 3. Pittsburgh, Henry 1, Roye 1.

REDSKINS 24, CHARGERS 20

Sunday, December 6

San Diego	3	11	3	3—20
Washington	7	10	0	7—24

First Quarter

S.D.—FG, Carney 32, 8:40.
Was.—Thrash 25 pass from T. Green (Blanchard kick), 14:11.

Second Quarter

S.D.—FG, Carney 27, 4:18.
Was.—Mitchell 101 kickoff return (Blanchard kick), 4:36.
S.D.—F. Jones 23 pass from Fletcher (F. Jones pass from Whelihan), 9:59.
Was.—FG, Blanchard 35, 14:54.

Third Quarter

S.D.—FG, Carney 41, 4:39.

Fourth Quarter

S.D.—FG, Carney 25, 10:29.
Was.—Shepherd 20 pass from T. Green (Blanchard kick), 13:06.
Attendance—65,713.

	San Diego	Washington
First downs	21	17
Rushes-yards	38-127	16-66
Passing	217	212
Punt returns	1-1	3-37
Kickoff returns	5-118	5-189
Interception returns	1-0	1-10
Comp.-att.-int.	21-38-1	19-38-1
Sacked-yards lost	2-18	2-23
Punts	5-46	7-38
Fumbles-lost	2-1	2-1
Penalties-yards	2-10	5-39
Time of possession	38:31	21:29

INDIVIDUAL STATISTICS

RUSHING—San Diego, Fletcher 34-122, Whelihan 3-3, Bynum 1-2. Washington, Allen 9-28, T. Green 2-9, Hicks 2-(minus 2), Shepherd 1-25, Mitchell 1-6, Davis 1-0.

PASSING—San Diego, Whelihan 20-37-1-212, Fletcher 1-1-0-23. Washington, T. Green 18-37-1-235, Mitchell 1-1-0-0.

RECEIVING—San Diego, C. Jones 5-72, F. Jones 5-53, Ricks 4-76, Fletcher 4-10, Thelwell 2-19, Davis 1-5. Washington, Thrash 4-66, Thomas 4-62, Shepherd 3-39, S. Alexander 3-32, Westbrook 2-23, Allen 1-11, Mitchell 1-2, T. Green 1-0.

MISSED FIELD GOAL ATTEMPTS—San Diego, Carney 20.

INTERCEPTIONS—San Diego, G. Jackson 1-0. Washington, L. Evans 1-10.

KICKOFF RETURNS—San Diego, Gaiter 4-101, C. Jones 1-17. Washington, Mitchell 5-189.

PUNT RETURNS—San Diego, Gaiter 1-1. Washington, Mitchell 3-37.

SACKS—San Diego, Seau 1, Johnson 1. Washington, Duff 2.

SAINTS 22, COWBOYS 3

Sunday, December 6

Dallas	3	0	0	0— 3
New Orleans	2	17	3	0—22

First Quarter

N.O.—Safety, Aikman called for intentional grounding from end zone, 0:55.
Dal.—FG, Cunningham 33, 13:47.

Second Quarter

N.O.—Craver 4 pass from Collins (Brien kick), 7:06.
N.O.—Hastings 89 pass from Collins (Brien kick), 13:11.
N.O.—FG, Brien 53, 15:00.

Third Quarter

N.O.—FG, Brien 53, 6:19.
Attendance—65,065.

	Dallas	New Orleans
First downs	10	17
Rushes-yards	18-8	36-113
Passing	174	215
Punt returns	1-9	3-25
Kickoff returns	2-43	1-34
Interception returns	1-0	0-0
Comp.-att.-int.	16-32-0	16-28-1
Sacked-yards lost	2-18	2-24
Punts	7-46	3-51
Fumbles-lost	2-0	2-1
Penalties-yards	9-84	7-37
Time of possession	25:47	34:13

INDIVIDUAL STATISTICS

RUSHING—Dallas, E. Smith 15-6, S. Williams 2-2, Aikman 1-0. New Orleans, T. Davis 13-36, Perry 12-38, Craver 5-14, Collins 4-10, Hastings 1-16, L. Smith 1-(minus 1).

PASSING—Dallas, Aikman 16-32-0-192. New Orleans, Collins 16-28-1-239.

RECEIVING—Dallas, Irvin 5-74, Jeffers 3-40, B. Davis 3-36, S. Williams 3-26, LaFleur 1-12, Bjornson 1-4. New Orleans, Craver 5-19, Hastings 4-122, Guliford 4-62, Dawkins 2-27, T. Davis 1-9.

MISSED FIELD GOAL ATTEMPTS—None.

INTERCEPTIONS—Dallas, Mathis 1-0.

KICKOFF RETURNS—Dallas, Hughes 2-43. New Orleans, Guliford 1-34.

PUNT RETURNS—Dallas, Hughes 1-9. New Orleans, Guliford 3-25.

SACKS—Dallas, Teague 2. New Orleans, Glover 2.

FALCONS 28, COLTS 21

Sunday, December 6

Indianapolis	14	7	0	0—21
Atlanta	7	14	7	0—28

First Quarter

Ind.—Faulk 11 pass from Manning (Vanderjagt kick), 3:08.
Ind.—Small 30 pass from Manning (Vanderjagt kick), 9:24.
Atl.—Martin 40 pass from Chandler (Andersen kick), 11:50.

Second Quarter

Ind.—Faulk 3 run (Vanderjagt kick), 9:50.
Atl.—J. Anderson 1 run (Andersen kick), 13:39.
Atl.—Chandler 3 run (Andersen kick), 15:00.

Third Quarter

Atl.—Mathis 2 pass from Chandler (Andersen kick), 1:43.
Attendance—61,141.

	Indianapolis	Atlanta
First downs	17	27
Rushes-yards	21-85	35-137
Passing	159	257
Punt returns	0-0	3-29
Kickoff returns	0-0	3-88
Interception returns	1-30	2-18
Comp.-att.-int.	19-27-2	20-28-1
Sacked-yards lost	0-0	5-40
Punts	4-52	3-46
Fumbles-lost	1-1	3-1
Penalties-yards	8-57	8-65
Time of possession	24:23	35:37

INDIVIDUAL STATISTICS

RUSHING—Indianapolis, Faulk 19-76, Manning 1-7, Small 1-2. Atlanta, J. Anderson 30-122, Chandler 4-14, Christian 1-1.

PASSING—Indianapolis, Manning 19-27-2-159. Atlanta, Chandler 20-28-1-297.

RECEIVING—Indianapolis, Faulk 7-37, Dilger 5-45, Small 2-38, Pathon 2-16, Green 2-14, Pollard 1-9. Atlanta, Martin 7-140, J. Anderson 4-58, Mathis 4-51, Santiago 3-33, Christian 1-9, Kozlowski 1-6.

MISSED FIELD GOAL ATTEMPTS—Atlanta, Andersen 47.

INTERCEPTIONS—Indianapolis, Clark 1-30. Atlanta, Buchanan 1-18, Sauer 1-0.

KICKOFF RETURNS—Atlanta, Dwight 3-88.

PUNT RETURNS—Atlanta, Dwight 3-29.

SACKS—Indianapolis, Montgomery 2, E. Johnson 1, Shello 1, Tuinei 1.

JETS 32, SEAHAWKS 31

Sunday, December 6

Seattle	14	7	10	0—31
N.Y. Jets	7	6	6	13—32

First Quarter
NYJ—Byars 3 pass from Testaverde (Hall kick), 7:47.
Sea.—Galloway 70 pass from Kitna (Peterson kick), 9:22.
Sea.—Galloway 57 pass from Kitna (Peterson kick), 12:14.

Second Quarter
NYJ—FG, Hall 20, 5:10.
Sea.—Watters 39 run (Peterson kick), 13:04.
NYJ—FG, Hall 20, 15:00.

Third Quarter
Sea.—Simmons 36 interception return (Peterson kick), 1:26.
NYJ—Martin 1 run (pass failed), 7:15.
Sea.—FG, Peterson 50, 12:55.

Fourth Quarter
NYJ—K. Johnson 16 pass from Testaverde (Hall kick), 2:38.
NYJ—Testaverde 5 run (run failed), 14:40.
   Attendance—72,200.

	Seattle	N.Y. Jets
First downs	13	31
Rushes-yards	22-106	23-70
Passing	271	418
Punt returns	1-12	4-40
Kickoff returns	5-109	6-123
Interception returns	1-36	2-21
Comp.-att.-int.	17-24-2	42-63-1
Sacked-yards lost	1-7	0-0
Punts	4-48	3-45
Fumbles-lost	2-2	2-2
Penalties-yards	8-84	7-49
Time of possession	22:14	37:46

INDIVIDUAL STATISTICS
RUSHING—Seattle, Watters 18-84, Kitna 3-25, Galloway 1-(minus 3). New York, Martin 17-37, L. Johnson 3-19, Testaverde 2-14, Lucas 1-0.
PASSING—Seattle, Kitna 17-24-2-278. New York, Testaverde 42-63-1-418.
RECEIVING—Seattle, Pritchard 9-69, Fauria 3-26, Galloway 2-127, Br. Blades 1-47, Watters 1-6, Crumpler 1-3. New York, K. Johnson 9-114, Chrebet 7-74, Martin 6-47, Brady 4-47, Byars 4-33, Ward 4-27, Van Dyke 3-21, Sowell 3-20, L. Johnson 2-35.
MISSED FIELD GOAL ATTEMPTS—None.
INTERCEPTIONS—Seattle, Simmons 1-36. New York, Henderson 1-21, Glenn 1-0.
KICKOFF RETURNS—Seattle, Green 3-66, Broussard 2-43. New York, Ward 3-60, Glenn 2-44, L. Johnson 1-19.
PUNT RETURNS—Seattle, Galloway 1-12. New York, L. Johnson 4-40.
SACKS—New York, Cascadden 1.

BILLS 33, BENGALS 20

Sunday, December 6

Buffalo		10	10	6	7—33
Cincinnati		0	13	0	7—20

First Quarter
Buf.—A. Smith 1 run (Christie kick), 2:16.
Buf.—FG, Christie 20, 6:12.

Second Quarter
Cin.—Scott 8 pass from O'Donnell (run failed), 0:50.
Cin.—Pickens 3 pass from O'Donnell (Pelfrey kick), 5:47.
Buf.—Moulds 70 pass from Flutie (Christie kick), 13:19.
Buf.—FG, Christie 52, 14:56.

Third Quarter
Buf.—FG, Christie 46, 4:22.
Buf.—FG, Christie 34, 11:38.

Fourth Quarter
Buf.—Moulds 30 pass from Flutie (Christie kick), 2:48.
Cin.—Dillon 3 run (Pelfrey kick), 13:18.
   Attendance—54,359.

	Buffalo	Cincinnati
First downs	21	15
Rushes-yards	34-139	17-58
Passing	309	176
Punt returns	2-30	0-0
Kickoff returns	3-73	5-112
Interception returns	1-23	3-32
Comp.-att.-int.	18-30-3	22-36-1
Sacked-yards lost	2-10	6-38
Punts	2-44	7-46

	Buffalo	Cincinnati
Fumbles-lost	0-0	2-0
Penalties-yards	8-38	1-5
Time of possession	31:36	28:24

INDIVIDUAL STATISTICS
RUSHING—Buffalo, A. Smith 18-77, Thomas 5-22, Flutie 5-21, Linton 5-17, Gash 1-2. Cincinnati, Dillon 11-43, Bieniemy 2-9, Blake 1-5, Milne 1-2, Bennett 1-0, O'Donnell 1-(minus 1).
PASSING—Buffalo, Flutie 18-30-3-319. Cincinnati, O'Donnell 19-31-1-168, Blake 3-5-0-46.
RECEIVING—Buffalo, Reed 7-68, Moulds 6-196, Thomas 3-14, Riemersma 1-28, K. Williams 1-13. Cincinnati, Pickens 8-97, Scott 6-93, Dillon 3-2, Battaglia 2-9, Milne 2-7, Bieniemy 1-6.
MISSED FIELD GOAL ATTEMPTS—None.
INTERCEPTIONS—Buffalo, Cowart 1-23. Cincinnati, B. Simmons 1-18, Ross 1-11, Copeland 1-3.
KICKOFF RETURNS—Buffalo, K. Williams 3-73. Cincinnati, Gibson 3-72, Bennett 2-40.
PUNT RETURNS—Buffalo, K. Williams 2-30.
SACKS—Buffalo, P. Williams 3, Washington 1, Rogers 1, Wiley 1. Cincinnati, Wilson 1, B. Simmons 1.

BRONCOS 35, CHIEFS 31

Sunday, December 6

Kansas City		21	0	7	3—31
Denver		7	14	0	14—35

First Quarter
K.C.—Rison 26 pass from Gannon (Stoyanovich kick), 4:19.
K.C.—Anders 11 pass from Gannon (Stoyanovich kick), 8:31.
Den.—Davis 1 run (Elam kick), 9:54.
K.C.—Morris 1 run (Stoyanovich kick), 14:48.

Second Quarter
Den.—Davis 1 run (Elam kick), 8:29.
Den.—McCaffrey 13 pass from Elway (Elam kick), 12:00.

Third Quarter
K.C.—Horn 26 pass from Gannon (Stoyanovich kick), 11:20.

Fourth Quarter
K.C.—FG, Stoyanovich 20, 6:35.
Den.—Davis 1 run (Elam kick), 8:12.
Den.—Sharpe 24 pass from Elway (Elam kick), 11:26.
   Attendance—74,962.

	Kansas City	Denver
First downs	20	23
Rushes-yards	17-44	29-93
Passing	222	383
Punt returns	3-52	3-33
Kickoff returns	6-146	6-147
Interception returns	1-15	0-0
Comp.-att.-int.	27-43-0	22-32-1
Sacked-yards lost	4-18	2-17
Punts	5-41	3-46
Fumbles-lost	2-1	2-2
Penalties-yards	4-35	6-86
Time of possession	29:31	30:29

INDIVIDUAL STATISTICS
RUSHING—Kansas City, Morris 7-14, Gannon 4-12, Anders 3-13, Bennett 3-5. Denver, Davis 24-88, Elway 4-5, Rouen 1-0.
PASSING—Kansas City, Gannon 27-43-0-240. Denver, Elway 22-32-1-400.
RECEIVING—Kansas City, Rison 7-81, Alexander 6-68, Gonzalez 4-24, Anders 4-11, Horn 2-34, Morris 2-13, Popson 1-6, Bennett 1-3. Denver, R. Smith 8-165, McCaffrey 6-103, Davis 5-45, Green 1-50, Sharpe 1-24, Carswell 1-13.
MISSED FIELD GOAL ATTEMPTS—Denver, Elam 37.
INTERCEPTIONS—Kansas City, McMillian 1-15.
KICKOFF RETURNS—Kansas City, Vanover 6-146. Denver, Hebron 6-147.
PUNT RETURNS—Kansas City, Vanover 3-52. Denver, Gordon 3-33.
SACKS—Kansas City, Davis 1, McGlockton 1. Denver, Romanowski 1, Williams 1, N. Smith 1, Tanuvasa 1.

GIANTS 23, CARDINALS 19

Sunday, December 6

N.Y. Giants		7	3	10	3—23
Arizona		14	3	0	2—19

First Quarter
Ariz.—Murrell 20 pass from Plummer (Jacke kick), 11:10.
NYG—Barber 87 pass from K. Graham (Daluiso kick), 12:18.
Ariz.—Murrell 8 run (Jacke kick), 13:45.
Second Quarter
Ariz.—FG, Jacke 21, 3:45.
NYG—FG, Daluiso 51, 15:00.
Third Quarter
NYG—FG, Daluiso 28, 5:51.
NYG—Way 8 run (Daluiso kick), 10:52.
Fourth Quarter
NYG—FG, Daluiso 45, 3:26.
Ariz.—Safety, punter Maynard ran out of end zone, 14:43.
Attendance—46,128.

	N.Y. Giants	Arizona
First downs	15	18
Rushes-yards	42-200	26-74
Passing	144	253
Punt returns	2-13	3-27
Kickoff returns	4-48	6-136
Interception returns	2-2	2-1
Comp.-att.-int.	8-23-2	18-40-2
Sacked-yards lost	0-0	2-10
Punts	5-48	6-38
Fumbles-lost	1-0	2-1
Penalties-yards	13-100	4-43
Time of possession	29:55	30:05

INDIVIDUAL STATISTICS
RUSHING—New York, Brown 25-124, Way 13-60, K. Graham 2-19, Barber 1-2, Maynard 1-(minus 5). Arizona, Murrell 16-53, Plummer 4-17, Bates 4-4, Centers 2-0.
PASSING—New York, K. Graham 8-23-2-144. Arizona, Plummer 18-40-2-263.
RECEIVING—New York, Calloway 3-35, Barber 2-91, Cross 1-9, Haase 1-6, Hilliard 1-3. Arizona, Centers 5-68, Sanders 5-62, R. Moore 2-49, Gedney 2-34, Metcalf 2-15, Murrell 1-20, McWilliams 1-15.
MISSED FIELD GOAL ATTEMPTS—None.
INTERCEPTIONS—New York, S. Williams 1-6, Lincoln 1-(minus 4). Arizona, McCleskey 1-1, Chavous 1-0.
KICKOFF RETURNS—New York, Patten 4-48. Arizona, Metcalf 6-136.
PUNT RETURNS—New York, Toomer 2-13. Arizona, Metcalf 3-27.
SACKS—New York, Strahan 1, Jones 1.

JAGUARS 37, LIONS 22

Sunday, December 6

Detroit	3	10	3	6—22
Jacksonville	14	10	3	10—37

First Quarter
Jac.—McCardell 67 pass from Martin (Hollis kick), 4:04.
Jac.—F. Taylor 1 run (Hollis kick), 8:55.
Det.—FG, Hanson 34, 11:24.
Second Quarter
Jac.—FG, Hollis 44, 0:52.
Det.—FG, Hanson 24, 8:13.
Jac.—J. Smith 11 pass from Martin (Hollis kick), 13:06.
Det.—Crowell 27 pass from Batch (Hanson kick), 14:25.
Third Quarter
Det.—FG, Hanson 45, 4:26.
Jac.—FG, Hollis 43, 9:15.
Fourth Quarter
Jac.—F. Taylor 11 run (Hollis kick), 1:47.
Det.—Moore 20 pass from Batch (sack), 4:17.
Jac.—FG, Hollis 30, 11:38.
Attendance—70,717.

	Detroit	Jacksonville
First downs	16	24
Rushes-yards	22-120	43-205
Passing	212	221
Punt returns	2-18	2-26
Kickoff returns	6-198	5-81
Interception returns	0-0	0-0
Comp.-att.-int.	14-33-0	15-24-0
Sacked-yards lost	5-38	1-7
Punts	3-39	2-41
Fumbles-lost	0-0	0-0
Penalties-yards	9-76	7-45
Time of possession	24:21	35:39

INDIVIDUAL STATISTICS
RUSHING—Detroit, Sanders 18-102, Batch 2-17, Rivers 1-1, Vardell 1-0. Jacksonville, F. Taylor 32-183, G. Jones 7-26, Martin 3-(minus 3), Whitted 1-(minus 1).
PASSING—Detroit, Batch 14-33-0-250. Jacksonville, Martin 15-23-0-228, Brunell 0-1-0-0.
RECEIVING—Detroit, Moore 7-116, Crowell 2-72, Morton 1-31, Sloan 1-13, Rasby 1-7, Rivers 1-6, Sanders 1-5. Jacksonville, J. Smith 7-112, McCardell 3-84, F. Taylor 3-23, Mitchell 2-9.
MISSED FIELD GOAL ATTEMPTS—Detroit, Hanson 47.
INTERCEPTIONS—None.
KICKOFF RETURNS—Detroit, Fair 5-175, Vardell 1-23. Jacksonville, Logan 2-41, Barlow 2-40, D. Jones 1-0.
PUNT RETURNS—Detroit, Fair 2-18. Jacksonville, Barlow 2-26.
SACKS—Detroit, Rice 1. Jacksonville, White 1, Paup 1, Wynn 1, Brackens 1, Smeenge 0.5, Jurkovic 0.5.

DOLPHINS 27, RAIDERS 17

Sunday, December 6

Miami	17	7	0	3—27
Oakland	0	3	7	7—17

First Quarter
Mia.—FG, Mare 25, 11:24.
Mia.—Z. Thomas 1 interception return (Mare kick), 12:10.
Mia.—Gadsden 19 pass from Marino (Mare kick), 13:14.
Second Quarter
Oak.—FG, G. Davis 40, 9:33.
Mia.—R. Jones 14 interception return (Mare kick), 12:22.
Third Quarter
Oak.—T. Brown 7 pass from Hollas (G. Davis kick), 4:59.
Fourth Quarter
Mia.—FG, Mare 47, 11:46.
Oak.—T. Brown 2 pass from Wilson (G. Davis kick), 13:33.
Attendance—61,254.

	Miami	Oakland
First downs	9	20
Rushes-yards	31-90	23-107
Passing	170	207
Punt returns	4-61	3-23
Kickoff returns	2-45	4-63
Interception returns	6-63	0-0
Comp.-att.-int.	22-33-0	21-44-6
Sacked-yards lost	0-0	8-47
Punts	8-35	5-47
Fumbles-lost	2-1	2-1
Penalties-yards	4-25	6-43
Time of possession	33:44	26:16

INDIVIDUAL STATISTICS
RUSHING—Miami, Abdul-Jabbar 19-94, Avery 6-(minus 2), Marino 4-(minus 4), McDuffie 1-2, Pritchett 1-0. Oakland, Kaufman 10-26, H. Williams 6-55, Hollas 3-15, Ritchie 2-6, Wilson 2-5.
PASSING—Miami, Marino 22-33-0-170. Oakland, Hollas 12-31-6-152, Wilson 8-12-0-75, H. Williams 1-1-0-27.
RECEIVING—Miami, McDuffie 5-45, Parmalee 4-35, Perry 3-19, Pritchett 3-9, Gadsden 2-22, Abdul-Jabbar 2-21, L. Thomas 2-15, Avery 1-4. Oakland, T. Brown 9-104, H. Williams 4-28, Ritchie 4-23, Jett 2-49, Mickens 1-29, Shedd 1-21.
MISSED FIELD GOAL ATTEMPTS—Miami, Mare 46, 43. Oakland, G. Davis 48.
INTERCEPTIONS—Miami, R. Jones 2-14, Z. Thomas 2-4, Buckley 1-45, Madison 1-0.
KICKOFF RETURNS—Miami, Avery 2-45. Oakland, R. Williams 4-63.
PUNT RETURNS—Miami, McDuffie 3-23, Buckley 1-38. Oakland, T. Brown 3-23.
SACKS—Miami, Taylor 2.5, Armstrong 2, R. Jones 1.5, Madison 1, Z. Thomas 0.5, Gardener 0.5.

VIKINGS 48, BEARS 22

Sunday, December 6

Chicago	0	0	14	8—22
Minnesota	14	13	7	14—48

First Quarter
Min.—R. Moss 6 pass from Cunningham (Anderson kick), 1:46.
Min.—Hoard 24 pass from Cunningham (Anderson kick), 8:40.

Second Quarter

Min.—FG, Anderson 30, 2:39.

Min.—FG, Anderson 20, 6:25.

Min.—R. Moss 3 pass from Cunningham (Anderson kick), 14:42.

Third Quarter

Chi.—Engram 47 pass from Stenstrom (Jaeger kick), 1:27.

Min.—R. Moss 34 pass from Cunningham (Anderson kick), 2:46.

Chi.—Bennett 5 run (Jaeger kick), 9:57.

Fourth Quarter

Min.—Hoard 8 run (Anderson kick), 3:29.

Min.—Rudd 94 fumble return (Anderson kick), 9:14.

Chi.—Stenstrom 4 run (Penn pass from Stenstrom), 12:22.

Attendance—64,247.

	Chicago	Minnesota
First downs	19	23
Rushes-yards	24-67	27-109
Passing	272	349
Punt returns	1-8	5-41
Kickoff returns	4-109	3-51
Interception returns	1-2	1-0
Comp.-att.-int.	25-42-1	21-31-1
Sacked-yards lost	3-31	0-0
Punts	6-47	2-44
Fumbles-lost	1-1	0-0
Penalties-yards	5-65	10-123
Time of possession	31:17	28:43

INDIVIDUAL STATISTICS

RUSHING—Chicago, Bennett 12-21, Stenstrom 4-15, J. Allen 4-11, Hallock 3-17, Engram 1-3. Minnesota, Hoard 19-69, Evans 3-10, Palmer 2-13, Fiedler 2-(minus 2), Cunningham 1-19.

PASSING—Chicago, Stenstrom 25-42-1-303. Minnesota, Cunningham 21-31-1-349.

RECEIVING—Chicago, Engram 9-140, Conway 4-44, Bennett 3-34, Penn 3-32, Hallock 3-6, J. Allen 2-36, Mayes 1-11. Minnesota, R. Moss 8-106, Hoard 4-63, Hatchette 3-26, Glover 2-55, M. Williams 1-64, Walsh 1-25, DeLong 1-6, Palmer 1-4.

MISSED FIELD GOAL ATTEMPTS—None.

INTERCEPTIONS—Chicago, W. Harris 1-2. Minnesota, Hitchcock 1-0.

KICKOFF RETURNS—Chicago, Milburn 4-109. Minnesota, Palmer 3-51.

PUNT RETURNS—Chicago, Milburn 1-8. Minnesota, Palmer 5-41.

SACKS—Minnesota, E. McDaniel 1.5, Randle 1.5.

OILERS 16, RAVENS 14

Sunday, December 6

Baltimore	0	0	7	7—14
Tennessee	10	3	0	3—16

First Quarter

Ten.—FG, Del Greco 48, 5:34.

Ten.—E. George 2 run (Del Greco kick), 14:19.

Second Quarter

Ten.—FG, Del Greco 48, 5:24.

Third Quarter

Bal.—Turner 66 pass from Harbaugh (Stover kick), 4:04.

Fourth Quarter

Ten.—FG, Del Greco 34, 11:26.

Bal.—Turner 20 pass from Harbaugh (Stover kick), 13:14.

Attendance—31,124.

	Baltimore	Tennessee
First downs	10	19
Rushes-yards	14-58	33-78
Passing	163	213
Punt returns	4-40	6-30
Kickoff returns	1-0	1-18
Interception returns	1-2	1-0
Comp.-att.-int.	15-28-1	25-43-1
Sacked-yards lost	6-51	0-0
Punts	9-41	7-46

	Baltimore	Tennessee
Fumbles-lost	0-0	0-0
Penalties-yards	6-35	6-64
Time of possession	21:23	38:37

INDIVIDUAL STATISTICS

RUSHING—Baltimore, Holmes 11-27, Harbaugh 3-31. Tennessee, E. George 27-63, McNair 5-5, Archie 1-10.

PASSING—Baltimore, Harbaugh 15-28-1-214. Tennessee, McNair 25-43-1-213.

RECEIVING—Baltimore, Turner 4-108, Holmes 4-34, Green 4-28, Roe 2-33, Potts 1-11. Tennessee, Wycheck 7-74, Roan 4-29, E. George 4-19, Davis 3-29, Thigpen 2-31, Mason 2-19, Harris 2-7, Archie 1-5.

MISSED FIELD GOAL ATTEMPTS—None.

INTERCEPTIONS—Baltimore, Woodson 1-2. Tennessee, Jackson 1-0.

KICKOFF RETURNS—Baltimore, Johnson 1-0. Tennessee, Archie 1-18.

PUNT RETURNS—Baltimore, Roe 3-34, Johnson 1-6. Tennessee, Mason 6-30.

SACKS—Tennessee, Rolle 2, Cook 1, Evans 1, Marts 1, Holmes 0.5, Lyons 0.5.

BUCCANEERS 24, PACKERS 22

Monday, December 7

Green Bay	3	3	3	13—22
Tampa Bay	7	7	3	7—24

First Quarter

G.B.—FG, Longwell 33, 12:10.

T.B.—Green 64 pass from Dilfer (Husted kick), 13:47.

Second Quarter

T.B.—Emanuel 62 pass from Dilfer (Husted kick), 1:44.

G.B.—FG, Longwell 36, 11:03.

Third Quarter

T.B.—FG, Husted 46, 5:18.

G.B.—FG, Longwell 35, 10:27.

Fourth Quarter

G.B.—Chmura 4 pass from Favre (pass failed), 1:21.

T.B.—Dilfer 6 run (Husted kick), 8:59.

G.B.—Chmura 1 pass from Favre (Longwell kick), 12:40.

Attendance—65,497.

	Green Bay	Tampa Bay
First downs	23	12
Rushes-yards	22-105	30-105
Passing	228	178
Punt returns	1-(-10)	4-16
Kickoff returns	4-81	4-84
Interception returns	1-12	0-0
Comp.-att.-int.	29-41-0	9-23-1
Sacked-yards lost	8-34	1-3
Punts	5-44	7-42
Fumbles-lost	8-2	1-0
Penalties-yards	7-53	5-51
Time of possession	32:08	27:52

INDIVIDUAL STATISTICS

RUSHING—Green Bay, Holmes 12-46, Levens 8-43, Favre 2-16. Tampa Bay, Dunn 18-62, Alstott 10-45, Dilfer 1-6, Green 1-(minus 8).

PASSING—Green Bay, Favre 29-41-0-262. Tampa Bay, Dilfer 9-22-1-181, Alstott 0-1-0-0.

RECEIVING—Green Bay, Henderson 8-51, Chmura 6-56, Mayes 5-74, Holmes 3-24, Levens 3-10, T. Davis 1-22, Bradford 1-10, Preston 1-10, Schroeder 1-5. Tampa Bay, Emanuel 3-76, Anthony 2-22, Dunn 2-14, Green 1-64, Moore 1-5.

MISSED FIELD GOAL ATTEMPTS—Tampa Bay, Husted 38.

INTERCEPTIONS—Green Bay, Ty. Williams 1-12.

KICKOFF RETURNS—Green Bay, Preston 4-81. Tampa Bay, Anthony 3-63, Dunn 1-25.

PUNT RETURNS—Green Bay, Preston 1-(minus 10). Tampa Bay, Green 3-9, Williams 1-7.

SACKS—Green Bay, Booker 1. Tampa Bay, Upshaw 2, Culpepper 2, Barber 1, Gooch 1, Sapp 1, Jackson 1.

WEEK 15

RESULTS

Arizona 20, PHILADELPHIA 17 (OT)
Atlanta 27, NEW ORLEANS 17
BUFFALO 44, Oakland 21
GREEN BAY 26, Chicago 20
INDIANAPOLIS 39, Cincinnati 26
KANSAS CITY 20, Dallas 17
Minnesota 38, BALTIMORE 28
N.Y. GIANTS 20, Denver 16
N.Y. Jets 21, MIAMI 16
ST. LOUIS 32, New England 18
SEATTLE 38, San Diego 17
TAMPA BAY 16, Pittsburgh 3
Tennessee 16, JACKSONVILLE 13
Washington 28, CAROLINA 25
SAN FRANCISCO 35, Detroit 13

STANDINGS

AFC EAST

	W	L	T	Pct.
N.Y. Jets	10	4	0	.714
Miami	9	5	0	.643
Buffalo	9	5	0	.643
New England	8	6	0	.571
Indianapolis	3	11	0	.214

AFC CENTRAL

	W	L	T	Pct.
Jacksonville	10	4	0	.714
Tennessee	8	6	0	.571
Pittsburgh	7	7	0	.500
Baltimore	5	9	0	.357
Cincinnati	2	12	0	.143

AFC WEST

	W	L	T	Pct.
Denver	13	1	0	.929
Oakland	7	7	0	.500
Seattle	7	7	0	.500
Kansas City	6	8	0	.429
San Diego	5	9	0	.357

NFC EAST

	W	L	T	Pct.
Dallas	8	6	0	.571
Arizona	7	7	0	.500
N.Y. Giants	6	8	0	.429
Washington	5	9	0	.357
Philadelphia	3	11	0	.214

NFC CENTRAL

	W	L	T	Pct.
Minnesota	13	1	0	.929
Green Bay	9	5	0	.643
Tampa Bay	7	7	0	.500
Detroit	5	9	0	.357
Chicago	3	11	0	.214

NFC WEST

	W	L	T	Pct.
Atlanta	12	2	0	.857
San Francisco	11	3	0	.786
New Orleans	6	8	0	.429
St. Louis	4	10	0	.286
Carolina	2	12	0	.143

HIGHLIGHTS

Hero of the week: Giants quarterback Kent Graham threw a 37-yard touchdown pass to Amani Toomer with 48 seconds left, ensuring Denver's first loss of the season, 20-16. The Giants got the ball with 1:49 left, and Graham led a six-play, 86-yard drive to win the game. After a 15-yard pass to Chris Calloway, Graham scrambled for a 23-yard gain to the Denver 48. On third-and-10, he completed an 11-yard pass to Joe Jurevicius to set up the game-winning play.

Goat of the week: Philadelphia's Chris Boniol missed a 33-yard field goal with the score tied late in the fourth quarter, and the Eagles lost in overtime to Arizona, 20-17. Boniol hadn't missed from inside 35 yards in his previous 67 attempts. Cardinals kicker Chris Jacke missed a 34-yarder at the end of regulation but won the game with a 32-yarder in overtime.

Sub of the week: St. Louis' June Henley rushed for 86 yards and two touchdowns in his first start of the season in the Rams' 32-18 win over New England. Henley, who was filling in for injured Jerald Moore, spent the 1997 season on the Rams' practice squad.

Comeback of the week: Tennessee rebounded from a early 10-point deficit to beat division-leading Jacksonville, 16-13, on Al Del Greco's 41-yard field goal with four seconds left. Down 10-0 after the first quarter, Oilers quarterback Steve McNair led two scoring drives in the second. He threw a 4-yard touchdown pass to Jackie Harris, and Del Greco kicked a 28-yarder to tie the score. With the score tied at 13 in the fourth quarter, Tennessee drove 53 yards in 11 plays to set up Del Greco's winning kick.

Blowout of the week: Buffalo scored 17 points in both the second and the third quarter in a 44-21 rout of Oakland. Doug Flutie passed for two touchdowns, and the Bills' defense forced four turnovers that led to 24 points. In the second quarter, Kevin Williams returned a punt 72 yards to the Raiders' 2 to set up Flutie's second TD pass. End Phil Hansen returned a fumble 13 yards for a score in the third quarter that gave Buffalo a 37-7 lead. Linebacker Gabe Northern returned an interception 40 yards for a touchdown in the fourth.

Nail-biter of the week: Linebacker Chad Cascadden returned a fumble 23 yards for a touchdown with 1:51 left to help the Jets beat Miami, 21-16. Ernie Logan sacked Dan Marino to cause the fumble. In a wild fourth quarter, Jets quarterback Vinny Testaverde threw an end-zone interception that Terrell Buckley returned 61 yards to set up a Marino touchdown pass to O.J. McDuffie that gave the Dolphins a 14-10 lead. Miami recovered the ensuing onside kick. The Dolphins didn't score on that possession but got the ball back when Curtis Martin fumbled with 2:25 left. Two plays later, Marino fumbled, and the Jets scored. Miami scored a touchdown with three seconds left, but the Jets handled the ensuing onside kick.

Hit of the week: In a tight game at Tampa Bay, the Buccaneers' Steve White sacked Pittsburgh quarterback Mike Tomczak and forced a fumble that Warren Sapp recovered at the Steelers' 7. Mike Alstott scored two plays later to give Tampa Bay a 13-3 third-quarter lead en route to its 16-3 victory.

Oddity of the week: Baltimore returned two kick-offs for touchdowns and the Vikings returned one—all in the first quarter—to set an NFL record. Corey Harris scored on a 95-yard return, the first in Ravens' history, after Minnesota's Gary Anderson kicked the first of his six field goals. After another Anderson field goal, Patrick Johnson returned the kickoff 97 yards. The Vikings' David Palmer returned the ensuing kickoff 88 yards for a score.

Top rusher: San Francisco's Garrison Hearst ran for 198 yards on 24 carries and scored a touchdown in the 49ers' 35-13 win over Detroit. Hearst broke the 49ers' game record for rushing yards, set by Delvin Williams (194) against the Cardinals on December 31, 1976.

Top passer: Atlanta's Chris Chandler was 19-for-28 for 345 yards with two touchdowns in the Falcons' 27-17 win over New Orleans. Minnesota's Randall Cunningham passed for 345 yards and two touchdowns in the Vikings' win. Cunningham completed 32 of 55 attempts, both personal highs.

Top receiver: The Falcons' Terance Mathis caught

both of Chris Chandler's touchdown passes, a 62-yarder in the first quarter and a 63-yarder in the fourth quarter. He made six catches for 198 yards. **Notes:** Seattle's Ricky Watters became the first player in NFL history to rush for 1,000 yards in a season for three different teams. He reached the milestone for San Francisco (1992) and Philadelphia (1995, '96, '97).... Gary Anderson's six field goals extended his streak of successful attempts to 34, breaking the NFL record of 31 held by former Vikings kicker Fuad Reveiz.... Carolina's Kevin Greene was suspended for one game after grabbing linebackers coach Kevin Steele on the sideline during the Redskins-Panthers game. Steele had been yelling at the linebackers after Washington scored on its first three possessions, and Greene took exception. Coaches and players separated the two.... Indianapolis quarterback Peyton Manning broke NFL rookie season records for completions, attempts and touchdowns. Charlie Conerly's touchdown record (22) had stood for 50 years.... Randy Moss broke Terry Glenn's two-year-old NFL rookie record for receiving yards in a season.... Atlanta coach Dan Reeves underwent heart bypass surgery a day after feeling ill during the Falcons' win over the Saints. Assistant Rich Brooks assumed Reeves' duties.

Quote of the week: Toomer, on his game-winning catch which put an end to the Broncos' undefeated season: "I looked back and saw Kent (Graham) scramble a bit, and he threw it up there and it looked really big. It looked like the Hindenburg and I just caught it."

GAME SUMMARIES

COLTS 39, BENGALS 26

Sunday, December 13

Cincinnati	3	3	6	14—26
Indianapolis	10	14	7	8—39

First Quarter
Ind.—Faulk 16 run (Vanderjagt kick), 3:49.
Ind.—FG, Vanderjagt 50, 5:44.
Cin.—FG, Pelfrey 41, 13:50.

Second Quarter
Ind.—Faulk 1 run (Vanderjagt kick), 3:19.
Cin.—FG, Pelfrey 26, 12:19.
Ind.—Green 11 pass from Manning (Vanderjagt kick), 14:12.

Third Quarter
Cin.—Pickens 6 pass from Blake (pass failed), 3:59.
Ind.—Small 16 pass from Manning (Vanderjagt kick), 8:28.

Fourth Quarter
Ind.—Small 16 pass from Manning (Pollard pass from Manning), 4:15.
Cin.—Bennett 5 run (Pelfrey kick), 8:41.
Cin.—St. Williams 19 pass from Kresser (Pelfrey kick), 13:43.
Attendance—55,179.

	Cincinnati	Indianapolis
First downs	22	21
Rushes-yards	29-155	31-128
Passing	223	210
Punt returns	3-23	3-51
Kickoff returns	7-166	5-133
Interception returns	0-0	0-0
Comp.-att.-int.	19-33-0	17-26-0
Sacked-yards lost	3-19	0-0
Punts	4-52	4-53
Fumbles-lost	0-0	0-0

	Cincinnati	Indianapolis
Penalties-yards	9-85	9-66
Time of possession	32:18	27:42

INDIVIDUAL STATISTICS
RUSHING—Cincinnati, Bennett 15-87, Dillon 9-29, Blake 2-24, Bieniemy 2-10, Milne 1-5. Indianapolis, Faulk 26-115, Warren 4-14, Manning 1-(minus 1).
PASSING—Cincinnati, Blake 16-29-0-180, Kresser 3-4-0-62. Indianapolis, Manning 17-26-0-210.
RECEIVING—Cincinnati, Scott 6-70, Pickens 4-18, Jackson 3-90, St. Williams 3-49, McGee 1-8, Gibson 1-6, Milne 1-1. Indianapolis, Small 5-57, Pathon 5-48, Green 4-49, Faulk 2-39, Dilger 1-17.
MISSED FIELD GOAL ATTEMPTS—None.
INTERCEPTIONS—None.
KICKOFF RETURNS—Cincinnati, Gibson 6-145, Bennett 1-21. Indianapolis, Bailey 5-133.
PUNT RETURNS—Cincinnati, Gibson 3-23. Indianapolis, Bailey 3-51.
SACKS—Indianapolis, E. Johnson 1, Whittington 1, Chester 1.

BUCCANEERS 16, STEELERS 3

Sunday, December 13

Pittsburgh	3	0	0	0— 3
Tampa Bay	3	3	7	3—16

First Quarter
Pit.—FG, N. Johnson 27, 6:00.
T.B.—FG, Husted 39, 15:00.

Second Quarter
T.B.—FG, Husted 37, 2:57.

Third Quarter
T.B.—Alstott 3 run (Husted kick), 10:32.

Fourth Quarter
T.B.—FG, Husted 21, 13:03.
Attendance—65,335.

	Pittsburgh	Tampa Bay
First downs	10	14
Rushes-yards	27-88	45-144
Passing	80	109
Punt returns	0-0	3-73
Kickoff returns	5-124	2-38
Interception returns	0-0	4-36
Comp.-att.-int.	10-23-4	9-18-0
Sacked-yards lost	2-18	1-2
Punts	4-45	5-37
Fumbles-lost	1-1	4-1
Penalties-yards	4-50	5-45
Time of possession	24:31	35:29

INDIVIDUAL STATISTICS
RUSHING—Pittsburgh, Bettis 17-63, Stewart 5-10, Huntley 2-9, Hawkins 2-(minus 1), Fuamatu-Ma'afala 1-7. Tampa Bay, Alstott 24-78, Dunn 15-36, Dilfer 5-25, Anthony 1-5.
PASSING—Pittsburgh, Stewart 9-21-3-88, Tomczak 1-2-1-10. Tampa Bay, Dilfer 9-18-0-111.
RECEIVING—Pittsburgh, C. Johnson 4-34, Hawkins 2-27, Ward 1-18, Bettis 1-7, Bruener 1-7, Witman 1-5. Tampa Bay, Emanuel 3-58, Anthony 2-17, Moore 1-13, Dunn 1-12, Hunter 1-6, Alstott 1-5.
MISSED FIELD GOAL ATTEMPTS—Tampa Bay, Husted 33.
INTERCEPTIONS—Tampa Bay, Lynch 1-4, Kelly 1-4, Abraham 1-3.
KICKOFF RETURNS—Pittsburgh, Dunn 3-78, Blackwell 2-46. Tampa Bay, Anthony 2-38.
PUNT RETURNS—Tampa Bay, Green 3-73.
SACKS—Pittsburgh, Harrison 1. Tampa Bay, White 2.

REDSKINS 28, PANTHERS 25

Sunday, December 13

Washington	14	7	7	0—28
Carolina	3	14	0	8—25

First Quarter
Was.—Connell 16 pass from T. Green (Blanchard kick), 1:23.
Was.—Hicks 4 run (Blanchard kick), 8:19.
Car.—FG, Kasay 26, 12:51.

Second Quarter
Was.—Hicks 5 run (Blanchard kick), 3:59.
Car.—Biakabutuka 29 pass from Beuerlein (Kasay kick), 12:17.
Car.—Stone recovered blocked punt in end zone (Kasay kick), 13:18.

Third Quarter

Was.—S. Alexander 17 pass from T. Green (Blanchard kick), 8:22.

Fourth Quarter

Car.—Biakabutuka 2 run (Muhammad pass from Beuerlein), 2:22.

Attendance—46,940.

	Washington	Carolina
First downs	27	16
Rushes-yards	32-160	24-124
Passing	249	241
Punt returns	0-0	4-41
Kickoff returns	4-85	5-139
Interception returns	2-0	0-0
Comp.-att.-int.	23-42-0	16-25-2
Sacked-yards lost	1-8	3-23
Punts	6-39	4-34
Fumbles-lost	0-0	1-1
Penalties-yards	8-58	7-59
Time of possession	34:03	25:57

INDIVIDUAL STATISTICS

RUSHING—Washington, Hicks 20-55, T. Green 5-12, Mitchell 3-9, Allen 2-56, Shepherd 1-26, Davis 1-2. Carolina, Biakabutuka 17-103, Johnson 5-15, Ismail 1-5, Beuerlein 1-1.

PASSING—Washington, T. Green 23-42-0-257. Carolina, Beuerlein 16-25-2-264.

RECEIVING—Washington, Connell 8-116, S. Alexander 7-47, Davis 4-62, Thomas 2-13, Shepherd 1-14, Mitchell 1-5. Carolina, Muhammad 7-118, Walls 4-35, Biakabutuka 2-71, Broughton 1-19, Ismail 1-16, Floyd 1-5.

MISSED FIELD GOAL ATTEMPTS—None.

INTERCEPTIONS—Washington, D. Green 1-0, Richard 1-0.

KICKOFF RETURNS—Washington, Mitchell 4-85. Carolina, Bates 5-139.

PUNT RETURNS—Carolina, Oliver 4-41.

SACKS—Washington, Wilkinson 1.5, Duff 1, Kalu 0.5. Carolina, Barrow 1.

BILLS 44, RAIDERS 21

Sunday, December 13

Oakland	0	7	7	7—21
Buffalo	3	17	17	7—44

First Quarter

Buf.—FG, Christie 32, 10:02.

Second Quarter

Buf.—Riemersma 13 pass from Flutie (Christie kick), 4:22.

Buf.—L. Johnson 2 pass from Flutie (Christie kick), 6:45.

Oak.—Dudley 18 pass from Wilson (G. Davis kick), 13:06.

Buf.—FG, Christie 49, 14:44.

Third Quarter

Buf.—A. Smith 5 run (Christie kick), 4:29.

Buf.—FG, Christie 32, 6:51.

Buf.—Hansen 13 fumble return (Christie kick), 7:47.

Oak.—Howard 75 punt return (G. Davis kick), 11:05.

Fourth Quarter

Buf.—Northern 40 interception return (Christie kick), 6:39.

Oak.—T. Brown 30 pass from Wilson (G. Davis kick), 11:03.

Attendance—62,002.

	Oakland	Buffalo
First downs	13	18
Rushes-yards	22-91	39-134
Passing	87	182
Punt returns	4-112	3-95
Kickoff returns	8-149	4-64
Interception returns	0-0	2-40
Comp.-att.-int.	16-26-2	17-26-0
Sacked-yards lost	5-44	1-2
Punts	6-46	5-47
Fumbles-lost	2-2	1-0
Penalties-yards	4-41	2-25
Time of possession	25:09	34:51

INDIVIDUAL STATISTICS

RUSHING—Oakland, H. Williams 14-33, Jordan 7-53, Wilson 1-5. Buffalo, A. Smith 22-77, Linton 6-6, Thomas 5-20, Flutie 3-20, Gash 2-6, K. Williams 1-5.

PASSING—Oakland, Wilson 16-26-2-131. Buffalo, Flutie 17-26-0-184.

RECEIVING—Oakland, T. Brown 5-58, Jett 3-20, Dudley 3-12, Ritchie 2-25, Mickens 2-15, Jordan 1-1. Buffalo, Moulds 6-64, Reed 5-70, Riemersma 2-40, Linton 1-10, Gash 1-3, L. Johnson 1-2, Thomas 1-(minus 5).

MISSED FIELD GOAL ATTEMPTS—None.

INTERCEPTIONS—Buffalo, Northern 1-40, Schulz 1-0.

KICKOFF RETURNS—Oakland, Howard 6-132, Branch 1-17, Amey 1-0. Buffalo, K. Williams 3-61, L. Johnson 1-3.

PUNT RETURNS—Oakland, Howard 4-112. Buffalo, K. Williams 3-95.

SACKS—Oakland, Biekert 1. Buffalo, Smedley 2, Rogers 1, B. Smith 1, Price 1.

PACKERS 26, BEARS 20

Sunday, December 13

Chicago	7	0	6	7—20
Green Bay	3	6	7	10—26

First Quarter

Chi.—Stenstrom 1 run (Jaeger kick), 3:06.

G.B.—FG, Longwell 35, 9:06.

Second Quarter

G.B.—FG, Longwell 43, 13:31.

G.B.—FG, Longwell 40, 15:00.

Third Quarter

Chi.—W. Harris 13 interception return (run pass failed), 4:11.

G.B.—Chmura 6 pass from Favre (Longwell kick), 9:29.

Fourth Quarter

G.B.—Freeman 13 pass from Favre (Longwell kick), 0:05.

G.B.—FG, Longwell 24, 11:03.

Chi.—Milburn 94 kickoff return (Jaeger kick), 11:20.

Attendance—59,813.

	Chicago	Green Bay
First downs	12	24
Rushes-yards	20-94	27-119
Passing	98	274
Punt returns	3-10	3-25
Kickoff returns	6-202	4-71
Interception returns	2-13	0-0
Comp.-att.-int.	16-28-0	26-42-2
Sacked-yards lost	4-28	3-16
Punts	6-42	3-41
Fumbles-lost	2-0	1-0
Penalties-yards	3-35	5-35
Time of possession	25:18	49:42

INDIVIDUAL STATISTICS

RUSHING—Chicago, Bennett 15-78, Stenstrom 4-14, Hallock 1-2. Green Bay, Levens 15-105, Holmes 9-6, Favre 3-8.

PASSING—Chicago, Stenstrom 16-28-0-126. Green Bay, Favre 26-42-2-290.

RECEIVING—Chicago, Conway 3-43, Wetnight 3-31, Engram 3-17, Bennett 3-11, Mayes 2-12, Chancey 1-6, M. Robinson 1-6. Green Bay, Freeman 8-103, Mayes 5-65, Chmura 5-55, Levens 3-28, Holmes 3-28, Henderson 1-7, Thomason 1-4.

MISSED FIELD GOAL ATTEMPTS—None.

INTERCEPTIONS—Chicago, W. Harris 1-13, Cousin 1-0.

KICKOFF RETURNS—Chicago, Milburn 6-202. Green Bay, Preston 4-71.

PUNT RETURNS—Chicago, Milburn 3-10. Green Bay, Preston 3-25.

SACKS—Chicago, Lee 1, Thierry 1, Flanigan 0.5, B. Robinson 0.5. Green Bay, S. Dotson 1, White 1, Lyon 1, McKenzie 1.

RAMS 32, PATRIOTS 18

Sunday, December 13

New England	3	12	3	0—18
St. Louis	10	7	15	0—32

First Quarter

St.L.—FG, Wilkins 48, 3:07.

St.L.—Hakim 9 pass from Banks (Wilkins kick), 4:48.

N.E.—FG, Vinatieri 37, 7:31.

Second Quarter

N.E.—FG, Vinatieri 41, 7:59.

St.L.—Henley 1 run (Wilkins kick), 10:58.

N.E.—Purnell 16 pass from Bledsoe (pass failed), 13:11.

N.E.—FG, Vinatieri 55, 14:35.

Third Quarter

N.E.—FG, Vinatieri 17, 7:11.

St.L.—Hakim 34 run (Bono run), 11:00.

St.L.—Henley 1 run (Wilkins kick), 14:19.

Attendance—48,946.

	New England	St. Louis
First downs	14	18
Rushes-yards	28-200	31-116
Passing	133	176
Punt returns	2-26	3-47
Kickoff returns	2-52	6-94
Interception returns	1-12	1-13
Comp.-att.-int.	11-37-1	18-35-1
Sacked-yards lost	5-43	3-16
Punts	5-39	4-49
Fumbles-lost	1-1	2-2
Penalties-yards	8-70	3-15
Time of possession	29:36	30:24

INDIVIDUAL STATISTICS

RUSHING—New England, Edwards 24-196, S. Shaw 3-2, Cullors 1-2. St. Louis, Henley 24-86, Bono 5-(minus 4), Hakim 1-34, Harris 1-0.

PASSING—New England, Bledsoe 11-35-1-176, Zolak 0-2-0-0. St. Louis, Bono 11-22-1-122, Banks 7-12-0-70, Tuten 0-1-0-0.

RECEIVING—New England, Purnell 4-37, Jefferson 3-73, Brown 2-42, Glenn 1-14, Simmons 1-10. St. Louis, Lee 5-37, Hakim 4-50, Henley 3-14, R. Williams 2-43, J. Thomas 2-26, Proehl 2-22.

MISSED FIELD GOAL ATTEMPTS—None.

INTERCEPTIONS—New England, Israel 1-12. St. Louis, Lyght 1-13.

KICKOFF RETURNS—New England, Cullors 2-52. St. Louis, Horne 3-72, Fletcher 2-20, M. D. Jones 1-2.

PUNT RETURNS—New England, Canty 2-26. St. Louis, Kennison 3-47.

SACKS—New England, Thomas 3. St. Louis, Phifer 1.5, Jenkins 1, Agnew 1, Wistrom 1, E. Hill 0.5.

GIANTS 20, BRONCOS 16

Sunday, December 13

Denver	3	3	3	7—16
N.Y. Giants	3	7	0	10—20

First Quarter

Den.—FG, Elam 24, 7:59.
NYG—FG, Daluiso 36, 12:28.

Second Quarter

Den.—FG, Elam 38, 4:29.
NYG—Barber 21 pass from K. Graham (Daluiso kick), 14:15.

Third Quarter

Den.—FG, Elam 30, 13:12.

Fourth Quarter

NYG—FG, Daluiso 19, 7:24.
Den.—Davis 27 run (Elam kick), 10:52.
NYG—Toomer 37 pass from K. Graham (Daluiso kick), 14:12.
Attendance—72,336.

	Denver	N.Y. Giants
First downs	21	18
Rushes-yards	33-170	25-138
Passing	159	254
Punt returns	0-0	2-6
Kickoff returns	5-88	5-89
Interception returns	0-0	1-0
Comp.-att.-int.	19-36-1	21-33-0
Sacked-yards lost	3-21	1-11
Punts	3-51	3-38
Fumbles-lost	1-0	2-2
Penalties-yards	5-33	5-30
Time of possession	34:27	25:33

INDIVIDUAL STATISTICS

RUSHING—Denver, Davis 28-147, Elway 3-12, Griffith 2-11. New York, Brown 18-112, Way 4-0, K. Graham 3-26.

PASSING—Denver, Elway 19-36-1-180. New York, K. Graham 21-33-0-265.

RECEIVING—Denver, Green 6-69, R. Smith 4-51, Sharpe 4-25, McCaffrey 3-24, Griffith 2-11. New York, Calloway 5-99, Hilliard 4-41, Jurevicius 3-32, Toomer 2-42, Barber 2-29, Way 2-11, Brown 2-5, Patten 1-6.

MISSED FIELD GOAL ATTEMPTS—None.

INTERCEPTIONS—New York, S. Williams 1-0.

KICKOFF RETURNS—Denver, Hebron 3-71, Burns 2-17. New York, Patten 4-69, Barber 1-20.

PUNT RETURNS—New York, Toomer 2-6.

SACKS—Denver, Tanuvasa 0.5, Pryce 0.5. New York, C. Hamilton 1, Bratzke 1, Strahan 1.

FALCONS 27, SAINTS 17

Sunday, December 13

Atlanta	14	3	0	10—27
New Orleans	0	7	7	3—17

First Quarter

Atl.—Christian 1 run (Andersen kick), 8:03.
Atl.—Mathis 62 pass from Chandler (Andersen kick), 8:35.

Second Quarter

N.O.—Weary 63 interception return (Brien kick), 13:35.
Atl.—FG, Andersen 49, 14:57.

Third Quarter

N.O.—Fields 36 fumble return (Brien kick), 4:48.

Fourth Quarter

Atl.—FG, Andersen 33, 0:30.
N.O.—FG, Brien 36, 6:26.
Atl.—Mathis 63 pass from Chandler (Andersen kick), 8:10.
Attendance—61,678.

	Atlanta	New Orleans
First downs	25	15
Rushes-yards	37-182	18-52
Passing	322	164
Punt returns	2-5	1-1
Kickoff returns	2-57	5-98
Interception returns	3-0	2-64
Comp.-att.-int.	19-28-2	18-38-3
Sacked-yards lost	3-23	1-5
Punts	4-38	4-40
Fumbles-lost	1-1	1-1
Penalties-yards	9-87	4-30
Time of possession	35:12	24:48

INDIVIDUAL STATISTICS

RUSHING—Atlanta, J. Anderson 27-148, Chandler 5-24, Christian 4-11, Oxendine 1-(minus 1). New Orleans, Craver 5-20, Perry 5-14, L. Smith 4-5, T. Davis 3-0, Tolliver 1-13.

PASSING—Atlanta, Chandler 19-28-2-345. New Orleans, Tolliver 12-23-0-82, Collins 6-14-3-87, L. Smith 0-1-0-0.

RECEIVING—Atlanta, Martin 8-109, Mathis 6-198, Christian 2-11, Santiago 1-19, J. Anderson 1-4, Kinchen 1-4. New Orleans, Dawkins 4-56, Guliford 3-23, Poole 2-27, L. Smith 2-21, Hastings 2-21, Craver 2-7, Cleeland 2-3, Bech 1-11.

MISSED FIELD GOAL ATTEMPTS—None.

INTERCEPTIONS—Atlanta, Robinson 1-0, Buchanan 1-0, Bradford 1-0. New Orleans, Weary 2-64.

KICKOFF RETURNS—Atlanta, Dwight 2-57. New Orleans, Guliford 4-86, Craver 1-12.

PUNT RETURNS—Atlanta, Dwight 2-5. New Orleans, Guliford 1-1.

SACKS—Atlanta, Archambeau 1. New Orleans, J. Johnson 1, Kei. Mitchell 1, Hewitt 1.

CARDINALS 20, EAGLES 17

Sunday, December 13

Arizona	10	0	0	7	3—20
Philadelphia	0	10	0	7	0—17

First Quarter

Ariz.—FG, Jacke 28, 5:08.
Ariz.—Bennett 70 interception return (Jacke kick), 15:00.

Second Quarter

Phi.—Staley 30 run (Boniol kick), 3:49.
Phi.—FG, Boniol 19, 14:59.

Fourth Quarter

Phi.—Fryar 26 pass from Detmer (Boniol kick), 2:02.
Ariz.—R. Moore 9 pass from Plummer (Jacke kick), 6:46.

Overtime

Ariz.—FG, Jacke 32, 4:30.
Attendance—62,176.

	Arizona	Philadelphia
First downs	25	21
Rushes-yards	43-204	33-148
Passing	220	219
Punt returns	4-21	0-0
Kickoff returns	5-81	4-103
Interception returns	1-70	1-0
Comp.-att.-int.	18-26-1	16-28-1
Sacked-yards lost	2-14	0-0
Punts	2-33	4-44

	Arizona	Philadelphia
Fumbles-lost	2-1	0-0
Penalties-yards	3-26	5-34
Time of possession	33:41	30:49

INDIVIDUAL STATISTICS

RUSHING—Arizona, Murrell 32-174, Centers 7-19, Plummer 3-17, Bates 1-(minus 6). Philadelphia, Staley 30-141, Detmer 2-3, Turner 1-4.

PASSING—Arizona, Plummer 18-26-1-234. Philadelphia, Detmer 16-28-1-219.

RECEIVING—Arizona, R. Moore 7-109, Gedney 3-35, Centers 3-34, Sanders 2-27, Murrell 2-15, Metcalf 1-14. Philadelphia, Fontenot 4-47, Graham 3-63, Fryar 3-54, Turner 2-29, Staley 2-10, Jordan 1-8, Solomon 1-8.

MISSED FIELD GOAL ATTEMPTS—Arizona, Jacke 34. Philadelphia, Boniol 33.

INTERCEPTIONS—Arizona, Bennett 1-70. Philadelphia, Vincent 1-0.

KICKOFF RETURNS—Arizona, Metcalf 4-74, Gedney 1-7. Philadelphia, Rossum 3-75, Walker 1-28.

PUNT RETURNS—Arizona, Metcalf 4-21.

SACKS—Philadelphia, W. Thomas 1, Jefferson 1.

SEAHAWKS 38, CHARGERS 17

Sunday, December 13

San Diego	7	7	0	3—17
Seattle	14	7	7	10—38

First Quarter
Sea.—Kitna 2 run (Peterson kick), 2:29.
S.D.—J. Williams 14 interception return (Carney kick), 8:53.
Sea.—McDaniel 43 interception return (Peterson kick), 12:38.

Second Quarter
Sea.—Watters 1 run (Peterson kick), 11:18.
S.D.—Fletcher 1 run (Carney kick), 14:41.

Third Quarter
Sea.—Galloway 9 pass from Kitna (Peterson kick), 8:59.

Fourth Quarter
S.D.—FG, Carney 21, 0:07.
Sea.—Kennedy 39 fumble return (Peterson kick), 1:45.
Sea.—FG, Peterson 29, 6:44.
Attendance—62,690.

	San Diego	Seattle
First downs	16	17
Rushes-yards	25-66	34-108
Passing	211	130
Punt returns	2-16	2-2
Kickoff returns	6-110	3-104
Interception returns	3-61	7-104
Comp.-att.-int.	17-42-7	16-31-3
Sacked-yards lost	4-24	2-10
Punts	4-46	5-47
Fumbles-lost	2-1	2-0
Penalties-yards	8-105	3-18
Time of possession	30:29	29:31

INDIVIDUAL STATISTICS

RUSHING—San Diego, Fletcher 17-42, Stephens 4-16, Leaf 3-0, C. Jones 1-8. Seattle, Watters 21-69, Kitna 6-4, Green 5-33, Galloway 2-2.

PASSING—San Diego, Whelihan 8-28-5-142, Leaf 9-14-2-93. Seattle, Kitna 16-31-3-140.

RECEIVING—San Diego, C. Jones 5-78, F. Jones 5-51, Ricks 3-56, Still 3-33, Thelwell 1-17. Seattle, Galloway 7-69, Fauria 4-31, Pritchard 3-21, Br. Blades 1-13, Watters 1-6.

MISSED FIELD GOAL ATTEMPTS—None.

INTERCEPTIONS—San Diego, Hand 1-30, G. Jackson 1-17, J. Williams 1-14. Seattle, Bellamy 2-37, D. Williams 2-13, Springs 2-11, McDaniel 1-43.

KICKOFF RETURNS—San Diego, Gaiter 6-110. Seattle, Broussard 2-75, Green 1-29.

PUNT RETURNS—San Diego, Gaiter 2-16. Seattle, Galloway 2-2.

SACKS—San Diego, Coleman 1, Turner 1. Seattle, LaBounty 2, Kennedy 1, Sinclair 1.

OILERS 16, JAGUARS 13

Sunday, December 13

Tennessee	0	10	0	6—16
Jacksonville	10	0	0	3—13

First Quarter
Jac.—FG, Hollis 21, 6:44.
Jac.—F. Taylor 1 run (Hollis kick), 7:51.

Second Quarter
Ten.—Harris 4 pass from McNair (Del Greco kick), 3:06.
Ten.—FG, Del Greco 28, 13:03.

Fourth Quarter
Ten.—FG, Del Greco 30, 0:13.
Jac.—FG, Hollis 29, 8:16.
Ten.—FG, Del Greco 41, 14:56.
Attendance—65,657.

	Tennessee	Jacksonville
First downs	20	15
Rushes-yards	27-131	23-69
Passing	223	172
Punt returns	4-56	4-46
Kickoff returns	3-68	5-96
Interception returns	1-0	1-0
Comp.-att.-int.	22-39-1	18-29-1
Sacked-yards lost	2-9	2-6
Punts	4-48	6-51
Fumbles-lost	1-1	1-0
Penalties-yards	9-73	9-65
Time of possession	30:09	29:51

INDIVIDUAL STATISTICS

RUSHING—Tennessee, E. George 14-46, McNair 11-81, Thomas 2-4. Jacksonville, F. Taylor 20-42, Quinn 2-21, Martin 1-6.

PASSING—Tennessee, McNair 22-39-1-232. Jacksonville, Quinn 12-18-1-107, Martin 6-11-0-71.

RECEIVING—Tennessee, Thigpen 5-68, E. George 5-57, Wycheck 4-42, Harris 4-17, Dyson 2-23, Sanders 1-17, Thomas 1-8. Jacksonville, F. Taylor 7-32, J. Smith 6-103, Mitchell 3-17, McCardell 2-26.

MISSED FIELD GOAL ATTEMPTS—None.

INTERCEPTIONS—Tennessee, D. Lewis 1-0. Jacksonville, Beasley 1-0.

KICKOFF RETURNS—Tennessee, Archie 3-68. Jacksonville, Barlow 3-75, Logan 1-21, Sadowski 1-0.

PUNT RETURNS—Tennessee, Mason 4-56. Jacksonville, Barlow 4-46.

SACKS—Tennessee, Bowden 1, Robinson 1. Jacksonville, Brackens 1, Paup 1.

VIKINGS 38, RAVENS 28

Sunday, December 13

Minnesota	12	13	10	3—38
Baltimore	14	0	0	14—28

First Quarter
Min.—FG, Anderson 43, 4:54.
Bal.—C. Harris 95 kickoff return (Stover kick), 5:11.
Min.—FG, Anderson 31, 11:05.
Bal.—Johnson 97 kickoff return (Stover kick), 11:21.
Min.—Palmer 88 kickoff return (pass failed), 11:38.

Second Quarter
Min.—FG, Anderson 45, 2:05.
Min.—R. Moss 17 pass from Cunningham (Anderson kick), 3:24.
Min.—FG, Anderson 24, 9:43.

Third Quarter
Min.—FG, Anderson 46, 1:10.
Min.—Carter 11 pass from Cunningham (Anderson kick), 3:51.

Fourth Quarter
Bal.—Turner 42 pass from Harbaugh (run failed), 2:55.
Min.—FG, Anderson 20, 12:09.
Bal.—Holmes 2 run (Turner pass from Harbaugh), 12:54.
Attendance—69,074.

	Minnesota	Baltimore
First downs	26	16
Rushes-yards	33-88	16-55
Passing	332	212
Punt returns	0-0	0-0
Kickoff returns	4-144	10-367
Interception returns	1-10	1-0
Comp.-att.-int.	32-56-1	16-26-1
Sacked-yards lost	2-13	0-0
Punts	2-37	2-47
Fumbles-lost	0-0	5-5
Penalties-yards	6-50	4-20
Time of possession	40:34	19:26

INDIVIDUAL STATISTICS

RUSHING—Minnesota, Hoard 26-68, Evans 4-8, Cunningham 3-12. Baltimore, Holmes 8-39, Rhett 7-16, Harbaugh 1-0.

PASSING—Minnesota, Cunningham 32-55-1-345, Fiedler 0-1-0-0. Baltimore, Harbaugh 16-26-1-212.

RECEIVING—Minnesota, Carter 11-85, Hatchette 6-95, R. Moss 6-89, Palmer 4-32, Hoard 2-8, Glover 1-23, Goodwin 1-9, DeLong 1-4. Baltimore, Turner 10-147, Green 2-31, Roe 2-29, Holmes 1-5, Potts 1-0.

MISSED FIELD GOAL ATTEMPTS—None.

INTERCEPTIONS—Minnesota, Fuller 1-10. Baltimore, Starks 1-0.

KICKOFF RETURNS—Minnesota, Palmer 4-144. Baltimore, C. Harris 8-243, Johnson 1-97, Roe 1-27.

PUNT RETURNS—None.

SACKS—Baltimore, McCrary 1, Boulware 1.

CHIEFS 20, COWBOYS 17

Sunday, December 13

Dallas	0	3	0	14—17
Kansas City	3	0	14	3—20

First Quarter
K.C.—FG, Stoyanovich 24, 9:39.
Second Quarter
Dal.—FG, Cunningham 32, 10:39.
Third Quarter
K.C.—Morris 1 run (Stoyanovich kick), 10:59.
K.C.—Gannon 9 run (Stoyanovich kick), 14:23.
Fourth Quarter
Dal.—Jeffers 28 pass from Aikman (Cunningham kick), 4:35.
K.C.—FG, Stoyanovich 43, 9:04.
Dal.—E. Smith 8 pass from Aikman (Cunningham kick), 12:12.
Attendance—77,697.

	Dallas	Kansas City
First downs	14	23
Rushes-yards	16-51	38-183
Passing	196	200
Punt returns	4-66	1-1
Kickoff returns	5-109	4-82
Interception returns	0-0	1-28
Comp.-att.-int.	18-35-1	19-41-0
Sacked-yards lost	1-3	0-0
Punts	6-37	5-44
Fumbles-lost	1-1	0-0
Penalties-yards	5-31	12-75
Time of possession	22:40	37:20

INDIVIDUAL STATISTICS

RUSHING—Dallas, E. Smith 14-42, B. Davis 1-8, Irvin 1-1. Kansas City, Morris 27-137, Gannon 6-23, Anders 3-17, Bennett 2-6.

PASSING—Dallas, Aikman 18-35-1-199. Kansas City, Gannon 19-41-0-200.

RECEIVING—Dallas, Jeffers 5-74, E. Smith 4-41, Bjornson 3-16, B. Davis 2-27, Ogden 2-20, S. Williams 1-12, Irvin 1-9. Kansas City, Gonzalez 5-65, Alexander 5-53, Anders 4-39, Morris 2-18, Rison 1-11, Horn 1-9, Bennett 1-5.

MISSED FIELD GOAL ATTEMPTS—None.

INTERCEPTIONS—Kansas City, Woods 1-28.

KICKOFF RETURNS—Dallas, Hughes 3-64, Ogden 1-35, B. Davis 1-10. Kansas City, Vanover 4-82.

PUNT RETURNS—Dallas, Hughes 4-66. Kansas City, Vanover 1-1.

SACKS—Kansas City, Thomas 1.

JETS 21, DOLPHINS 16

Sunday, December 13

N.Y. Jets	7	0	7	7—21
Miami	3	0	0	13—16

First Quarter
Mia.—FG, Mare 24, 11:58.
NYJ—Chrebet 12 pass from Testaverde (Hall kick), 13:35.
Third Quarter
NYJ—Martin 9 run (Hall kick), 5:31.
Fourth Quarter
Mia.—McDuffie 3 pass from Marino (Mare kick), 8:35.
NYJ—Cascadden 23 fumble return (Hall kick), 13:09.
Mia.—Pritchett 1 run (pass failed), 14:57.
Attendance—74,369.

	N.Y. Jets	Miami
First downs	16	22
Rushes-yards	23-81	18-79

	N.Y. Jets	Miami
Passing	232	278
Punt returns	3-14	4-30
Kickoff returns	2-45	2-48
Interception returns	1-87	1-61
Comp.-att.-int.	17-29-1	30-57-1
Sacked-yards lost	0-0	5-43
Punts	5-43	7-41
Fumbles-lost	2-1	2-1
Penalties-yards	5-40	6-44
Time of possession	26:59	33:01

INDIVIDUAL STATISTICS

RUSHING—New York, Martin 19-70, Testaverde 4-11. Miami, Abdul-Jabbar 10-42, Avery 6-25, Pritchett 2-12.

PASSING—New York, Testaverde 17-29-1-232. Miami, Marino 30-57-1-321.

RECEIVING—New York, Chrebet 5-105, K. Johnson 5-44, Brady 2-42, Ward 2-31, Baxter 1-6, Van Dyke 1-4, Martin 1-0. Miami, McDuffie 11-105, Jacquet 5-68, L. Thomas 4-52, Perry 3-42, Parmalee 2-24, Gadsden 2-18, Abdul-Jabbar 1-4, Avery 1-4, Pritchett 1-4.

MISSED FIELD GOAL ATTEMPTS—New York, Hall 32.

INTERCEPTIONS—New York, Green 1-87. Miami, Buckley 1-61.

KICKOFF RETURNS—New York, Williams 2-45. Miami, Avery 2-48.

PUNT RETURNS—New York, L. Johnson 3-14. Miami, Buckley 3-18, McDuffie 1-12.

SACKS—New York, Cascadden 1.5, P. Johnson 1, B. Cox 1, Ferguson 1, Lewis 0.5.

49ERS 35, LIONS 13

Monday, December 14

Detroit	0	0	0	13—13
San Francisco	7	14	7	7—35

First Quarter
S.F.—Hearst 5 run (Richey kick), 10:19.
Second Quarter
S.F.—Kirby 1 run (Richey kick), 2:52.
S.F.—Owens 1 pass from S. Young (Richey kick), 13:54.
Third Quarter
S.F.—S. Young 9 run (Richey kick), 9:14.
Fourth Quarter
Det.—Moore 24 pass from Reich (kick blocked), 3:36.
S.F.—Kirby 1 run (Richey kick), 12:48.
Det.—Sloan 3 pass from Reich (Hanson kick), 13:58.
Attendance—68,585.

	Detroit	San Francisco
First downs	25	29
Rushes-yards	19-69	46-328
Passing	311	81
Punt returns	1-0	2-19
Kickoff returns	5-108	2-35
Interception returns	1-0	2-36
Comp.-att.-int.	21-44-2	12-18-1
Sacked-yards lost	1-5	1-1
Punts	4-34	2-36
Fumbles-lost	0-0	1-0
Penalties-yards	4-38	9-79
Time of possession	26:16	33:44

INDIVIDUAL STATISTICS

RUSHING—Detroit, Sanders 14-28, Rivers 2-14, Vardell 1-17, Reich 1-5, Schlesinger 1-5. San Francisco, Hearst 24-198, S. Young 10-66, Kirby 7-60, Edwards 2-6, Detmer 2-(minus 2), Owens 1-0.

PASSING—Detroit, Reich 18-35-2-281, Batch 3-9-0-35. San Francisco, S. Young 12-18-1-82.

RECEIVING—Detroit, Crowell 5-83, Moore 5-81, Morton 5-78, Rivers 2-52, Vardell 1-11, Stablein 1-11, Sloan 1-3, Sanders 1-(minus 3). San Francisco, Rice 4-26, Owens 3-16, Stokes 2-29, Clark 1-9, Edwards 1-5, Kirby 1-(minus 3).

MISSED FIELD GOAL ATTEMPTS—None.

INTERCEPTIONS—Detroit, Rice 1-0. San Francisco, Walker 1-36, Hanks 1-0.

KICKOFF RETURNS—Detroit, Fair 4-99, Rivers 1-9. San Francisco, Kirby 2-35.

PUNT RETURNS—Detroit, Fair 1-0. San Francisco, McQuarters 2-19.

SACKS—Detroit, Scroggins 1. San Francisco, Buckner 1.

WEEK 16

RESULTS

N.Y. Jets 17, BUFFALO 10
WASHINGTON 20, Tampa Bay 16
ARIZONA 19, New Orleans 17
Atlanta 24, DETROIT 17
CAROLINA 20, St. Louis 13
CHICAGO 24, Baltimore 3
Cincinnati 25, PITTSBURGH 24
DALLAS 13, Philadelphia 9
GREEN BAY 30, Tennessee 22
MINNESOTA 50, Jacksonville 10
NEW ENGLAND 24, San Francisco 21
N.Y. GIANTS 28, Kansas City 7
Oakland 17, SAN DIEGO 10
SEATTLE 27, Indianapolis 23
MIAMI 31, Denver 21

STANDINGS

AFC EAST

	W	L	T	Pct.
N.Y. Jets	11	4	0	.733
Miami	10	5	0	.667
Buffalo	9	6	0	.600
New England	9	6	0	.600
Indianapolis	3	12	0	.200

NFC EAST

	W	L	T	Pct.
Dallas	9	6	0	.600
Arizona	8	7	0	.533
N.Y. Giants	7	8	0	.467
Washington	6	9	0	.400
Philadelphia	3	12	0	.200

AFC CENTRAL

	W	L	T	Pct.
Jacksonville	10	5	0	.667
Tennessee	8	7	0	.533
Pittsburgh	7	8	0	.467
Baltimore	5	10	0	.333
Cincinnati	3	12	0	.200

NFC CENTRAL

	W	L	T	Pct.
Minnesota	14	1	0	.933
Green Bay	10	5	0	.667
Tampa Bay	7	8	0	.467
Detroit	5	10	0	.333
Chicago	4	11	0	.267

AFC WEST

	W	L	T	Pct.
Denver	13	2	0	.867
Oakland	8	7	0	.533
Seattle	8	7	0	.533
Kansas City	6	9	0	.400
San Diego	5	10	0	.333

NFC WEST

	W	L	T	Pct.
Atlanta	13	2	0	.867
San Francisco	11	4	0	.733
New Orleans	6	9	0	.400
St. Louis	4	11	0	.267
Carolina	3	12	0	.200

HIGHLIGHTS

Hero of the week: Adam Vinatieri kicked a 35-yard field goal with three seconds left to give the Patriots—playing without injured quarterback Drew Bledsoe—a 24-21 victory over the 49ers in Foxboro, Mass. The win boosted New England's record to 9-6 in the AFC East and clinched a playoff spot for the Patriots.

Goat of the week: Steelers quarterback Kordell Stewart was pulled from a 25-24 defeat at home to Cincinnati after a 5-for-13, 30-yard performance. It was the Steelers' fourth straight loss in a season that was rapidly deteriorating, largely because of an inept offense.

Comeback of the week: With their playoff hopes on the line, the Cardinals rode the arm and legs of Jake Plummer to a 19-17 come-from-behind win over the Saints in Tempe, Ariz. Trailing New Orleans by one point with 1:17 to play, Plummer marched the Cardinals down the field from his 9-yard line to set up a 36-yard Chris Jacke field goal for the win.

Sub of the week: With first-round draft pick Curtis Enis out for the season after knee surgery, James Allen, an undrafted rookie free agent from Oklahoma, made his first start and rushed for 163 yards as the Bears ended a six-game losing streak with a 24-3 victory over the Ravens at Soldier Field.

Blowout of the week: The Vikings pounded the Jaguars 50-10 in Minnesota to raise their record to 14-1 and clinch home-field advantage throughout the NFC playoffs.

Nail-biter of the week: Despite learning earlier in the day that they had been eliminated from the playoffs, the Seahawks rallied in the fourth quarter for a 27-23 victory over the Colts in Seattle. The winning touchdown came when Shawn Springs picked up a Marshall Faulk fumble and ran 14 yards into the end zone. Todd Peterson provided the margin of victory by hitting a 30-yard field goal with 1:57 left.

Hit of the week: Cowboys defensive back George Teague stopped Philadelphia tight end Andrew Jordan after a 1-yard gain on fourth-and-2 at the Dallas 12 with 3:10 left to play. The Cowboys held on for a 13-9 victory to maintain their one-game lead over the Cardinals in the NFC East.

Oddity of the week: In only the second meeting of their careers—an anomaly since both players were in their 16th seasons and had spent their careers in the same conference—quarterbacks Dan Marino of Miami and John Elway of Denver met on Monday night in Miami. Marino passed for 355 yards and four touchdowns in a 31-21 victory. Elway passed for just 151 yards and throwing two interceptions in the fourth quarter.

Top rusher: Ricky Watters gained 178 yards and scored a touchdown on 32 carries in Seattle's victory over Indianapolis.

Top passer: Jake Plummer was 32-of-44 for 394 yards with no touchdowns and one interception in Arizona's win over New Orleans.

Top receiver: Antonio Freeman of Green Bay caught seven passes for 186 yards and three TDs as the Packers defeated the Oilers 30-22 at Lambeau Field.

Notes: Detroit's Herman Moore reached the 600-reception mark faster than anyone else in league history. The Detroit receiver reached the milestone in his 118th game, five faster than Jerry Rice.... Atlanta snapped a five-game losing streak at the Silverdome, gaining its first win there since 1986. ... Garrison Hearst broke Roger Craig's 49ers club record for rushing yards in a season, gaining 107 against the Patriots to increase his season total to 1,549.... The Patriots made the playoffs for the third consecutive year, a first for the club.... Brett Favre became the fifth player in NFL history to have at least two 4,000 passing-yard seasons after he threw for 253 yards against Tennessee. His first 4,000-yard season came in 1995. ... Adrian Murrell of the Cardinals hit the 1,000-yard rushing mark for the third consecutive season.... The Giants' game against Kansas City was the 1,000th in club history. Only the Bears, Packers and Cardinals had played more. ... With 119 total yards, Emmitt Smith of Dallas pushed his rushing-receiving yardage total to 15,107 for his career, making him the 12th player in NFL history to reach the 15,000-yard milestone.... The Steelers lost consecutive regular-season home games for the first time since Bill Cowher became coach in 1992. . . . Seattle's Joey Galloway had five catches for 50 yards and one touchdown, giving him his third 1,000-yard receiving season in four NFL seasons. . . . After the final home game of his career, Green Bay defensive tackle Reggie White ran a lap around Lambeau Field to say goodbye to the fans. White, who joined the Packers as a free agent in 1993 after eight seasons with the Eagles and two in the USFL, retired with the most sacks (192.5) in NFL history.

Quote of the week: Jets offensive tackle Jumbo Elliott, after New York clinched the AFC East title with a 17-10 win over the Bills in Buffalo: "This is what I envisioned when I came to this franchise." Elliott, who won a Super Bowl title with the Giants in 1990, endured the 1-15 disaster of 1996 in his first season with the Jets and helped the team improve 11 games over the next two years under his former Giants coach, Bill Parcells.

GAME SUMMARIES

JETS 17, BILLS 10

Saturday, December 19

N.Y. Jets	7	0	10	0—17
Buffalo	0	7	3	0—10

First Quarter
NYJ—Chrebet 7 pass from Testaverde (Hall kick), 8:13.
Second Quarter
Buf.—Thomas 25 pass from Flutie (Christie kick), 8:21.
Third Quarter
NYJ—FG, Hall 48, 3:47.
Buf.—FG, Christie 44, 11:48.
NYJ—Ward 71 pass from Testaverde (Hall kick), 12:45.
Attendance—79,056.

	N.Y. Jets	Buffalo
First downs	14	21
Rushes-yards	27-92	36-146
Passing	177	220
Punt returns	2-1	1-8
Kickoff returns	2-38	4-79
Interception returns	1-5	0-0
Comp.-att.-int.	14-23-0	14-38-1
Sacked-yards lost	1-7	0-0
Punts	6-39	4-44
Fumbles-lost	0-0	1-1
Penalties-yards	3-20	6-43
Time of possession	27:13	32:47

INDIVIDUAL STATISTICS
RUSHING—New York, Martin 20-38, Meggett 3-17, Testaverde 3-12, K. Johnson 1-25. Buffalo, A. Smith 20-82, Thomas 8-20, Flutie 4-24, Linton 3-9, K. Williams 1-11.
PASSING—New York, Testaverde 14-23-0-184. Buffalo, Flutie 14-38-1-220.
RECEIVING—New York, K. Johnson 7-66, Chrebet 3-30, Ward 1-71, Martin 1-7, Brady 1-6, Anderson 1-4. Buffalo, Moulds 4-107, K. Williams 3-34, Reed 2-22, Thomas 1-25, L. Johnson 1-10, Gash 1-9, Early 1-8, A. Smith 1-5.
MISSED FIELD GOAL ATTEMPTS—New York, Hall 46. Buffalo, Christie 28.
INTERCEPTIONS—New York, Green 1-5.
KICKOFF RETURNS—New York, Williams 2-38. Buffalo, K. Williams 3-63, L. Johnson 1-16.
PUNT RETURNS—New York, Meggett 2-1. Buffalo, K. Williams 1-8.
SACKS—Buffalo, Washington 1.

REDSKINS 20, BUCCANEERS 16

Saturday, December 19

Tampa Bay	7	6	3	0—16
Washington	7	0	0	13—20

First Quarter
T.B.—Moore 8 pass from Dilfer (Husted kick), 6:51.
Was.—Shepherd 16 run (Blanchard kick), 11:34.
Second Quarter
T.B.—FG, Husted 20, 2:44.
T.B.—FG, Husted 42, 5:38.
Third Quarter
T.B.—FG, Husted 24, 8:59.
Fourth Quarter
Was.—FG, Blanchard 26, 1:21.
Was.—FG, Blanchard 35, 8:54.
Was.—S. Alexander 15 pass from T. Green (Blanchard kick), 9:11.
Attendance—66,309.

	Tampa Bay	Washington
First downs	17	11
Rushes-yards	37-150	20-90
Passing	87	136
Punt returns	2-25	3-46
Kickoff returns	5-136	5-91
Interception returns	1-9	2-9
Comp.-att.-int.	14-34-2	16-33-1
Sacked-yards lost	3-13	5-55
Punts	7-39	8-40
Fumbles-lost	2-1	3-1
Penalties-yards	6-50	12-92
Time of possession	33:23	26:37

INDIVIDUAL STATISTICS
RUSHING—Tampa Bay, Dunn 18-33, Alstott 13-80, Dilfer 6-37. Washington, Hicks 11-59, Mitchell 4-10, T. Green 4-5, Shepherd 1-16.
PASSING—Tampa Bay, Dilfer 14-34-2-100. Washington, T. Green 16-33-1-191.
RECEIVING—Tampa Bay, Dunn 5-27, Emanuel 3-24, Moore 3-23, Williams 2-14, Green 1-12. Washington, S. Alexander 6-62, Connell 4-86, Hicks 2-12, Mitchell 2-10, Thomas 1-12, Shepherd 1-9.
MISSED FIELD GOAL ATTEMPTS—Tampa Bay, Husted 36.
INTERCEPTIONS—Tampa Bay, Mincy 1-9. Washington, Jones 1-9, D. Green 1-0.
KICKOFF RETURNS—Tampa Bay, Green 5-136. Washington, Mitchell 4-86, Burnett 1-5.
PUNT RETURNS—Tampa Bay, Green 2-25. Washington, Mitchell 3-46.
SACKS—Tampa Bay, Lynch 2, Jackson 1, Upshaw 1, Culpepper 1. Washington, Wilkinson 1, Lang 1, Boutte 1.

PANTHERS 20, RAMS 13

Sunday, December 20

St. Louis	3	7	3	0—13
Carolina	0	7	3	10—20

First Quarter
St.L.—FG, Wilkins 43, 12:40.
Second Quarter
St.L.—Harris 1 pass from Bono (Wilkins kick), 7:31.
Car.—Muhammad 3 pass from Beuerlein (Kasay kick), 13:42.
Third Quarter
St.L.—FG, Wilkins 38, 6:09.
Car.—FG, Kasay 32, 13:17.
Fourth Quarter
Car.—Broughton 68 pass from Beuerlein (Kasay kick), 12:16.
Car.—FG, Kasay 37, 13:56.
Attendance—50,047.

	St. Louis	Carolina
First downs	16	11
Rushes-yards	26-110	27-82
Passing	151	164
Punt returns	1-0	3-39
Kickoff returns	5-88	4-94
Interception returns	0-0	2-9
Comp.-att.-int.	20-37-2	15-25-0
Sacked-yards lost	2-12	4-29
Punts	5-43	6-43
Fumbles-lost	2-2	1-1
Penalties-yards	6-39	8-72
Time of possession	30:28	29:32

INDIVIDUAL STATISTICS

RUSHING—St. Louis, Henley 17-69, Lee 5-29, Bono 2-13, Holcombe 1-3, Hakim 1-(minus 4). Carolina, Biakabutuka 23-84, Beuerlein 3-(minus 3), Johnson 1-1.

PASSING—St. Louis, Bono 20-37-2-163. Carolina, Beuerlein 15-25-0-193.

RECEIVING—St. Louis, Lee 6-61, Hakim 4-41, Henley 3-12, J. Thomas 2-19, Proehl 2-17, R. Williams 2-12, Harris 1-1. Carolina, Ismail 5-42, Biakabutuka 3-28, Broughton 2-78, Muhammad 2-22, Johnson 2-18, Mangum 1-5.

MISSED FIELD GOAL ATTEMPTS—None.

INTERCEPTIONS—Carolina, Minter 1-7, Davis 1-2.

KICKOFF RETURNS—St. Louis, Horne 5-88. Carolina, Bates 4-94.

PUNT RETURNS—St. Louis, Kennison 1-0. Carolina, Oliver 3-39.

SACKS—St. Louis, Phifer 1, Jenkins 1, M. D. Jones 1, Wistrom 1. Carolina, Gilbert 2.

BEARS 24, RAVENS 3

Sunday, December 20

Baltimore	0	0	3	0— 3
Chicago	3	21	0	0—24

First Quarter

Chi.—FG, Jaeger 20, 9:34.

Second Quarter

Chi.—J. Allen 1 run (Jaeger kick), 3:23.

Chi.—Conway 16 pass from Stenstrom (Jaeger kick), 7:37.

Chi.—Chancey 4 run (Jaeger kick), 14:55.

Third Quarter

Bal.—FG, Stover 27, 3:30.

Attendance—40,853.

	Baltimore	Chicago
First downs	12	20
Rushes-yards	16-22	34-189
Passing	154	202
Punt returns	2-20	2-7
Kickoff returns	5-117	2-57
Interception returns	0-0	1-14
Comp.-att.-int.	20-35-1	19-28-0
Sacked-yards lost	2-31	0-0
Punts	6-36	5-36
Fumbles-lost	3-0	1-0
Penalties-yards	5-35	4-44
Time of possession	25:28	34:32

INDIVIDUAL STATISTICS

RUSHING—Baltimore, Holmes 11-17, Potts 3-5, Harbaugh 2-0. Chicago, J. Allen 23-163, Chancey 6-14, Stenstrom 2-9, Milburn 2-3, Hallock 1-0.

PASSING—Baltimore, Harbaugh 20-35-1-185. Chicago, Stenstrom 19-28-0-202.

RECEIVING—Baltimore, M. Jackson 7-72, Kinchen 4-25, Turner 3-30, Johnson 2-29, Green 2-16, Rhett 1-12, Holmes 1-1. Chicago, Conway 5-83, Engram 3-34, J. Allen 3-11, Mayes 2-29, Milburn 2-19, Wetnight 2-10, Chancey 1-8, Hallock 1-8.

MISSED FIELD GOAL ATTEMPTS—Baltimore, Stover 45.

INTERCEPTIONS—Chicago, Thierry 1-14.

KICKOFF RETURNS—Baltimore, C. Harris 4-114, Potts 1-3. Chicago, Milburn 2-57.

PUNT RETURNS—Baltimore, Roe 2-20. Chicago, Milburn 2-7.

SACKS—Chicago, Parrish 1, McDonald 1.

PACKERS 30, OILERS 22

Sunday, December 20

Tennessee	0	7	7	8—22
Green Bay	14	7	3	6—30

First Quarter

G.B.—Freeman 57 pass from Favre (Longwell kick), 1:38.

G.B.—Freeman 68 pass from Favre (Longwell kick), 12:01.

Second Quarter

Ten.—Mason 25 pass from McNair (Del Greco kick), 1:18.

G.B.—Freeman 32 pass from Favre (Longwell kick), 13:49.

Third Quarter

G.B.—FG, Longwell 38, 4:55.

Ten.—Thigpen 30 pass from McNair (Del Greco kick), 13:24.

Fourth Quarter

G.B.—FG, Longwell 40, 7:33.

G.B.—FG, Longwell 40, 11:28.

Ten.—Mason 3 pass from McNair (E. George run), 14:07.

Attendance—59,888.

	Tennessee	Green Bay
First downs	22	16
Rushes-yards	23-88	32-117
Passing	253	245
Punt returns	2-15	4-41
Kickoff returns	7-134	3-78
Interception returns	0-0	1-0
Comp.-att.-int.	29-49-1	15-25-0
Sacked-yards lost	2-10	3-17
Punts	8-43	6-38
Fumbles-lost	1-0	0-0
Penalties-yards	5-40	2-25
Time of possession	29:51	30:09

INDIVIDUAL STATISTICS

RUSHING—Tennessee, E. George 15-30, McNair 8-58. Green Bay, Levens 26-70, Favre 4-49, Pederson 2-(minus 2).

PASSING—Tennessee, McNair 29-49-1-263. Green Bay, Favre 14-22-0-253, Pederson 1-3-0-9.

RECEIVING—Tennessee, Wycheck 10-71, Thigpen 8-90, Mason 4-53, Dyson 2-22, E. George 2-2, Davis 1-12, Thomas 1-9, Roan 1-4. Green Bay, Freeman 7-186, Levens 3-18, Mayes 2-15, Thomason 2-15, Henderson 1-14.

MISSED FIELD GOAL ATTEMPTS—None.

INTERCEPTIONS—Green Bay, Smith 1-0.

KICKOFF RETURNS—Tennessee, Archie 6-123, Thomas 1-11. Green Bay, Preston 3-78.

PUNT RETURNS—Tennessee, Mason 2-15. Green Bay, Preston 4-41.

SACKS—Tennessee, Bishop 1, Marts 1, Holmes 0.5, Evans 0.5 Green Bay, B. Harris 1, McKenzie 1.

PATRIOTS 24, 49ERS 21

Sunday, December 20

San Francisco	0	21	0	0—21
New England	7	7	0	10—24

First Quarter

N.E.—Edwards 19 pass from Zolak (Vinatieri kick), 12:04.

Second Quarter

S.F.—Rice 75 pass from S. Young (Richey kick), 6:37.

N.E.—Jefferson 61 pass from Zolak (Vinatieri kick), 8:19.

S.F.—Owens 7 pass from S. Young (Richey kick), 12:18.

S.F.—I. Smith 25 pass from Detmer (Richey kick), 15:00.

Fourth Quarter

N.E.—Edwards 5 run (Vinatieri kick), 7:26.

N.E.—FG, Vinatieri 35, 14:57.

Attendance—59,153.

	San Fran.	New England
First downs	21	20
Rushes-yards	34-151	31-132
Passing	259	200
Punt returns	2-5	2-24
Kickoff returns	5-84	2-44
Interception returns	2-18	2-30
Comp.-att.-int.	19-24-2	14-30-2
Sacked-yards lost	5-33	1-5
Punts	4-37	5-40
Fumbles-lost	1-1	0-0
Penalties-yards	9-64	5-38
Time of possession	32:31	27:29

INDIVIDUAL STATISTICS

RUSHING—San Francisco, Hearst 27-107, Kirby 5-37, Edwards 2-7. New England, Edwards 24-101, Floyd 2-14, Zolak 2-3, Cullors 2-(minus 1), Jefferson 1-15.

PASSING—San Francisco, S. Young 18-23-2-267, Detmer 1-1-0-25. New England, Zolak 14-30-2-205.

RECEIVING—San Francisco, Rice 5-115, Stokes 4-59, Owens 3-61, Hearst 3-17, Kirby 2-13, I. Smith 1-25, Edwards 1-2. New England, Simmons 5-56, Edwards 4-52, Coates 3-25, Jefferson 2-72.

MISSED FIELD GOAL ATTEMPTS—San Francisco, Richey 31. New England, Vinatieri 32.

INTERCEPTIONS—San Francisco, McDonald 1-18, Hanks 1-0. New England, Law 1-30, Clay 1-0.

KICKOFF RETURNS—San Francisco, Kirby 5-84. New England, Cullors 2-44.

PUNT RETURNS—San Francisco, McQuarters 2-5. New England, Brown 2-24.

SACKS—San Francisco, Doleman 1. New England, Slade 1, Israel 1, Spires 1, C. Carter 1, Sullivan 1.

GIANTS 28, CHIEFS 7

Sunday, December 20

Kansas City	0	0	7	0—7
N.Y. Giants	14	7	7	0—28

First Quarter
NYG—Ellsworth 43 interception return (Daluiso kick), 1:14.
NYG—Toomer 12 pass from K. Graham (Daluiso kick), 8:39.
Second Quarter
NYG—Brown 1 run (Daluiso kick), 11:14.
Third Quarter
NYG—K. Graham 6 run (Daluiso kick), 8:30.
K.C.—Gonzalez 4 pass from Grbac (Stoyanovich kick), 12:19.
Attendance—66,040.

	Kansas City	N.Y. Giants
First downs	15	25
Rushes-yards	18-66	36-160
Passing	213	149
Punt returns	2-21	1-(-1)
Kickoff returns	4-107	2-48
Interception returns	0-0	4-46
Comp.-att.-int.	18-36-4	16-34-0
Sacked-yards lost	4-26	2-18
Punts	4-35	5-46
Fumbles-lost	0-0	0-0
Penalties-yards	9-79	10-95
Time of possession	25:24	34:36

INDIVIDUAL STATISTICS

RUSHING—Kansas City, Morris 13-42, Anders 2-7, Gannon 2-7, Grbac 1-10. New York, Brown 25-103, Way 4-20, K. Graham 3-17, Cherry 3-(minus 3), Barber 1-23.

PASSING—Kansas City, Grbac 11-20-2-160, Gannon 7-16-2-79. New York, K. Graham 16-33-0-167, Cherry 0-1-0-0.

RECEIVING—Kansas City, Alexander 6-97, Gonzalez 6-68, Rison 3-62, Morris 1-11, Horn 1-1, Anders 1-0. New York, Toomer 4-49, Calloway 4-42, Way 2-14, Brown 2-0, Hilliard 1-32, K. Graham 1-16, Alford 1-11, Barber 1-3.

MISSED FIELD GOAL ATTEMPTS—New York, Daluiso 41, 39.

INTERCEPTIONS—New York, Ellsworth 2-43, Sparks 1-3, Armstead 1-0.

KICKOFF RETURNS—Kansas City, Vanover 4-107. New York, Barber 2-48.

PUNT RETURNS—Kansas City, Vanover 2-21. New York, Toomer 1-(minus 1).

SACKS—Kansas City, Hasty 1, Barndt 1. New York, Bratzke 2.5, Strahan 1, K. Hamilton 0.5.

BENGALS 25, STEELERS 24

Sunday, December 20

Cincinnati	3	13	6	3—25
Pittsburgh	0	7	14	3—24

First Quarter
Cin.—FG, Pelfrey 33, 10:58.
Second Quarter
Cin.—Shade 55 fumble return (Pelfrey kick), 4:52.
Cin.—FG, Pelfrey 37, 11:54.
Pit.—Lake 15 interception return (N. Johnson kick), 13:18.
Cin.—FG, Pelfrey 43, 15:00.
Third Quarter
Pit.—Oldham 54 fumble return (N. Johnson kick), 0:20.
Pit.—Bettis 4 run (N. Johnson kick), 7:55.
Cin.—Scott 61 pass from Blake (run failed), 8:14.
Fourth Quarter
Pit.—FG, N. Johnson 22, 4:43.
Cin.—FG, Pelfrey 21, 9:48.
Attendance—52,017.

	Cincinnati	Pittsburgh
First downs	23	11
Rushes-yards	33-124	23-125
Passing	359	86

	Cincinnati	Pittsburgh
Punt returns	2-5	2-24
Kickoff returns	5-78	5-168
Interception returns	1-0	1-15
Comp.-att.-int.	21-41-1	10-24-1
Sacked-yards lost	4-20	2-21
Punts	3-49	8-36
Fumbles-lost	4-1	2-1
Penalties-yards	3-15	5-32
Time of possession	35:00	25:00

INDIVIDUAL STATISTICS

RUSHING—Cincinnati, Bennett 25-63, Blake 6-49, Bieniemy 2-12. Pittsburgh, Bettis 21-104, Ward 1-13, Stewart 1-8.

PASSING—Cincinnati, Blake 20-36-1-367, Justin 1-4-0-12, Pelfrey 0-1-0-0. Pittsburgh, Stewart 5-13-0-30, Tomczak 5-11-1-77.

RECEIVING—Cincinnati, Scott 7-152, Bennett 3-119, Pickens 3-35, St. Williams 3-32, Battaglia 2-10, McGee 1-18, Milne 1-8, Bieniemy 1-5. Pittsburgh, C. Johnson 4-58, Blackwell 3-27, Ward 1-17, Lester 1-5, Fuamatu-Ma'afala 1-0.

MISSED FIELD GOAL ATTEMPTS—Cincinnati, Pelfrey 53, 46.

INTERCEPTIONS—Cincinnati, Hawkins 1-0. Pittsburgh, Lake 1-15.

KICKOFF RETURNS—Cincinnati, Bieniemy 2-32, Gibson 2-26, St. Williams 1-20. Pittsburgh, Dunn 5-168.

PUNT RETURNS—Cincinnati, Gibson 2-5. Pittsburgh, Blackwell 2-24.

SACKS—Cincinnati, Wilson 1, B. Simmons 1. Pittsburgh, Gildon 2, Emmons 1, Henry 1.

FALCONS 24, LIONS 17

Sunday, December 20

Atlanta	7	3	0	14—24
Detroit	7	7	3	0—17

First Quarter
Det.—T. Boyd 18 pass from Reich (Hanson kick), 9:47.
Atl.—J. Anderson 8 pass from Chandler (Andersen kick), 14:44.
Second Quarter
Atl.—FG, Andersen 34, 5:29.
Det.—Moore 2 pass from Reich (Hanson kick), 14:31.
Third Quarter
Det.—FG, Hanson 30, 13:17.
Fourth Quarter
Atl.—Mathis 27 pass from Chandler (Andersen kick), 0:38.
Atl.—J. Anderson 1 run (Andersen kick), 8:03.
Attendance—67,143.

	Atlanta	Detroit
First downs	20	17
Rushes-yards	35-145	30-117
Passing	123	141
Punt returns	2-11	1-3
Kickoff returns	2-67	5-113
Interception returns	2-11	0-0
Comp.-att.-int.	11-19-0	15-26-2
Sacked-yards lost	4-23	1-7
Punts	6-39	5-41
Fumbles-lost	0-0	2-1
Penalties-yards	7-56	7-49
Time of possession	31:27	28:33

INDIVIDUAL STATISTICS

RUSHING—Atlanta, J. Anderson 30-147, Chandler 5-(minus 2). Detroit, Sanders 25-95, Reich 2-2, Rivers 1-15, Vardell 1-3, Schlesinger 1-2.

PASSING—Atlanta, Chandler 11-19-0-146. Detroit, Reich 15-26-2-148.

RECEIVING—Atlanta, Martin 4-42, Mathis 2-41, Kozlowski 2-12, Green 1-28, Santiago 1-15, J. Anderson 1-8. Detroit, Rasby 4-34, Moore 3-34, T. Boyd 2-37, Stablein 2-22, Sloan 2-12, Morton 1-10, Sanders 1-(minus 1).

MISSED FIELD GOAL ATTEMPTS—None.

INTERCEPTIONS—Atlanta, Robinson 1-11, White 1-0.

KICKOFF RETURNS—Atlanta, Dwight 2-67. Detroit, T. Boyd 4-89, Fair 1-24.

PUNT RETURNS—Atlanta, Dwight 2-11. Detroit, Fair 1-3.

SACKS—Atlanta, Tuggle 1. Detroit, Porcher 3, Rice 1.

RAIDERS 17, CHARGERS 10

Sunday, December 20

Oakland	0	14	3	0—17
San Diego	3	0	7	0—10

First Quarter
S.D.—FG, Carney 28, 14:10.

Second Quarter
Oak.—Jett 45 pass from Wilson (G. Davis kick), 2:41.
Oak.—T. Brown 12 pass from Wilson (G. Davis kick), 8:50.

Third Quarter
Oak.—FG, G. Davis 25, 4:34.
S.D.—Ricks 39 pass from Whelihan (Carney kick), 14:56.
    Attendance—60,716.

	Oakland	San Diego
First downs	14	16
Rushes-yards	35-120	22-79
Passing	167	236
Punt returns	3-29	5-78
Kickoff returns	2-71	4-58
Interception returns	2-36	2-0
Comp.-att.-int.	14-25-2	19-39-2
Sacked-yards lost	0-0	3-15
Punts	7-40	5-43
Fumbles-lost	1-1	2-1
Penalties-yards	3-25	6-50
Time of possession	28:58	31:02

INDIVIDUAL STATISTICS
RUSHING—Oakland, Jordan 24-82, H. Williams 8-24, Wilson 2-14, Ritchie 1-0. San Diego, Fletcher 14-65, Stephens 8-14.
PASSING—Oakland, Wilson 14-25-2-167. San Diego, Whelihan 19-39-2-251.
RECEIVING—Oakland, T. Brown 6-48, Jett 5-106, Mickens 2-9, Dudley 1-4. San Diego, Ricks 4-72, F. Jones 4-59, C. Jones 4-50, Thelwell 4-40, Fletcher 2-13, Hartley 1-17.
MISSED FIELD GOAL ATTEMPTS—Oakland, G. Davis 52, 35. San Diego, Carney 46.
INTERCEPTIONS—Oakland, Woodson 1-30, Newman 1-6. San Diego, G. Jackson 1-0, Spencer 1-0.
KICKOFF RETURNS—Oakland, Howard 2-71. San Diego, Bynum 4-58.
PUNT RETURNS—Oakland, Howard 3-29. San Diego, Gaiter 5-78.
SACKS—Oakland, Harvey 1, Maryland 1, Russell 1.

SEAHAWKS 27, COLTS 23

Sunday, December 20

Indianapolis	7	3	10	3—23
Seattle	7	3	0	17—27

First Quarter
Ind.—Warren 4 run (Vanderjagt kick), 5:34.
Sea.—Galloway 3 pass from Kitna (Peterson kick), 12:04.

Second Quarter
Sea.—FG, Peterson 42, 7:29.
Ind.—FG, Vanderjagt 32, 15:00.

Third Quarter
Ind.—FG, Vanderjagt 48, 3:12.
Ind.—Pollard 1 pass from Manning (Vanderjagt kick), 8:42.

Fourth Quarter
Ind.—FG, Vanderjagt 20, 2:43.
Sea.—Watters 33 run (Peterson kick), 5:41.
Sea.—Springs 14 fumble return (Peterson kick), 7:24.
Sea.—FG, Peterson 30, 13:03.
    Attendance—58,703.

	Indianapolis	Seattle
First downs	18	23
Rushes-yards	18-32	41-226
Passing	330	150
Punt returns	1-17	3-10
Kickoff returns	6-113	5-118
Interception returns	0-0	1-28
Comp.-att.-int.	23-39-1	16-29-0
Sacked-yards lost	2-5	4-27
Punts	4-46	3-45
Fumbles-lost	1-1	3-0
Penalties-yards	5-45	5-62
Time of possession	25:18	34:42

INDIVIDUAL STATISTICS
RUSHING—Indianapolis, Faulk 13-19, Warren 5-13. Seattle, Watters 32-178, Kitna 5-17, Green 3-14, Pritchard 1-17.

PASSING—Indianapolis, Manning 23-39-1-335. Seattle, Kitna 16-29-0-177.
RECEIVING—Indianapolis, Pathon 6-66, Dilger 4-61, Faulk 4-16, Small 3-120, Green 3-52, Pollard 2-19, Warren 1-1. Seattle, Galloway 5-50, Watters 3-38, Br. Blades 3-30, Pritchard 2-30, McKnight 2-19, Fauria 1-10.
MISSED FIELD GOAL ATTEMPTS—Seattle, Peterson 53, 52.
INTERCEPTIONS—Seattle, D. Williams 1-28.
KICKOFF RETURNS—Indianapolis, Bailey 6-113. Seattle, Broussard 5-101.
PUNT RETURNS—Indianapolis, Bailey 1-17. Seattle, Galloway 2-1, Joseph 1-9.
SACKS—Indianapolis, McCoy 1, E. Johnson 1, Berry 1, Whittington 1. Seattle, Adams 1, Sinclair 1.

CARDINALS 19, SAINTS 17

Sunday, December 20

New Orleans	0	10	0	7—17
Arizona	3	3	7	6—19

First Quarter
Ariz.—FG, Jacke 21, 9:32.

Second Quarter
N.O.—Knight 39 interception return (Brien kick), 3:15.
Ariz.—FG, Jacke 38, 12:56.
N.O.—FG, Brien 28, 15:00.

Third Quarter
Ariz.—Murrell 21 run (Jacke kick), 6:44.

Fourth Quarter
Ariz.—FG, Jacke 46, 8:12.
N.O.—Cleeland 13 pass from Collins (Brien kick), 13:39.
Ariz.—FG, Jacke 36, 15:00.
    Attendance—51,617.

	New Orleans	Arizona
First downs	18	28
Rushes-yards	22-82	26-119
Passing	238	394
Punt returns	1-4	4-24
Kickoff returns	5-102	3-45
Interception returns	1-39	0-0
Comp.-att.-int.	25-43-0	32-44-1
Sacked-yards lost	4-27	0-0
Punts	5-50	2-32
Fumbles-lost	3-1	2-2
Penalties-yards	10-65	7-44
Time of possession	29:57	30:03

INDIVIDUAL STATISTICS
RUSHING—New Orleans, L. Smith 13-41, Craver 7-45, Collins 1-0, Perry 1-(minus 4). Arizona, Murrell 19-65, Plummer 4-38, Centers 2-15, Sanders 1-1.
PASSING—New Orleans, Collins 25-43-0-265. Arizona, Plummer 32-44-1-394.
RECEIVING—New Orleans, Dawkins 7-77, Cleeland 7-71, L. Smith 4-46, Craver 3-14, Hastings 2-24, Poole 1-20, Guliford 1-13. Arizona, Sanders 10-138, R. Moore 9-97, Centers 5-55, Metcalf 3-49, McWilliams 2-36, Murrell 2-8, Gedney 1-11.
MISSED FIELD GOAL ATTEMPTS—New Orleans, Brien 54. Arizona, Jacke 51.
INTERCEPTIONS—New Orleans, Knight 1-39.
KICKOFF RETURNS—New Orleans, Guliford 3-70, Little 2-32. Arizona, Metcalf 3-45.
PUNT RETURNS—New Orleans, Guliford 1-4. Arizona, Metcalf 4-24.
SACKS—Arizona, Maddox 1, Wadsworth 1, Sapp 1, Rice 1.

VIKINGS 50, JAGUARS 10

Sunday, December 20

Jacksonville	0	3	0	7—10
Minnesota	3	9	14	24—50

First Quarter
Min.—FG, Anderson 48, 6:29.

Second Quarter
Min.—FG, Anderson 53, 9:59.
Min.—Glover 14 pass from Cunningham (pass failed), 13:08.
Jac.—FG, Hollis 25, 15:00.

Third Quarter
Min.—R. Moss 43 pass from Cunningham (Anderson kick), 1:03.
Min.—Glover 14 pass from Cunningham (Anderson kick), 11:05.

Fourth Quarter
Min.—Carter 1 pass from Johnson (Anderson kick), 2:22.
Min.—FG, Anderson 44, 7:14.
Min.—Hitchcock 30 interception return (Anderson kick), 7:35.
Min.—Evans 1 run (Anderson kick), 8:02.
Jac.—Mitchell 1 pass from Quinn (Hollis kick), 12:04.
   Attendance—64,363.

	Jacksonville	Minnesota
First downs	15	25
Rushes-yards	28-138	33-180
Passing	59	237
Punt returns	4-36	5-21
Kickoff returns	5-144	2-41
Interception returns	0-0	2-30
Comp.-att.-int.	12-27-2	20-37-0
Sacked-yards lost	4-29	1-7
Punts	8-44	5-49
Fumbles-lost	3-2	0-0
Penalties-yards	7-56	8-108
Time of possession	26:28	33:32

INDIVIDUAL STATISTICS
RUSHING—Jacksonville, F. Taylor 23-105, Quinn 5-33. Minnesota, R. Smith 19-101, Hoard 6-38, Morrow 3-7, Johnson 2-8, Evans 2-4, Cunningham 1-22.

PASSING—Jacksonville, Quinn 12-27-2-88. Minnesota, Cunningham 16-30-0-210, Johnson 4-7-0-34.

RECEIVING—Jacksonville, F. Taylor 4-25, J. Smith 3-20, D. Jones 1-24, Moore 1-9, Barlow 1-5, Crockett 1-4, Mitchell 1-1. Minnesota, Hoard 4-30, Carter 4-27, R. Moss 3-72, Glover 3-54, Hatchette 3-41, Evans 2-16, R. Smith 1-4.

MISSED FIELD GOAL ATTEMPTS—None.

INTERCEPTIONS—Minnesota, Hitchcock 1-30, Thomas 1-0.

KICKOFF RETURNS—Jacksonville, Barlow 4-120, Logan 1-24. Minnesota, Tate 1-23, Palmer 1-18.

PUNT RETURNS—Jacksonville, Barlow 3-27, Logan 1-9. Minnesota, Palmer 5-21.

SACKS—Jacksonville, Hardy 1. Minnesota, Randle 2, Alexander 1, Fuller 1.

COWBOYS 13, EAGLES 9

Sunday, December 20

| Philadelphia | 3 | 0 | 3 | 3— 9 |
| Dallas | 7 | 0 | 6 | 0—13 |

First Quarter
Phi.—FG, Boniol 21, 4:46.
Dal.—Bjornson 7 run (Cunningham kick), 11:31.

Third Quarter
Phi.—FG, Boniol 41, 1:29.
Dal.—FG, Cunningham 42, 10:00.
Dal.—FG, Cunningham 41, 13:07.

Fourth Quarter
Phi.—FG, Boniol 39, 2:58.
   Attendance—62,722.

	Philadelphia	Dallas
First downs	15	11
Rushes-yards	26-125	34-153
Passing	231	95
Punt returns	4-2	3-4
Kickoff returns	3-62	3-70
Interception returns	1-14	1-9
Comp.-att.-int.	24-43-1	10-23-1
Sacked-yards lost	0-0	3-25
Punts	6-34	7-39
Fumbles-lost	1-0	1-1
Penalties-yards	9-60	7-64
Time of possession	30:52	29:08

INDIVIDUAL STATISTICS
RUSHING—Philadelphia, Staley 18-67, Walker 3-40, Turner 3-10, Detmer 2-8. Dallas, E. Smith 25-110, S. Williams 3-16, Aikman 3-2, Warren 2-18, Bjornson 1-7.

PASSING—Philadelphia, Detmer 24-43-1-231. Dallas, Aikman 10-23-1-120.

RECEIVING—Philadelphia, Staley 7-53, Graham 6-71, Fryar 5-61, Turner 3-18, Fontenot 2-27, Jordan 1-1. Dallas, Irvin 4-56, Jeffers 2-23, E. Smith 2-9, Clay 1-27, Warren 1-5.

MISSED FIELD GOAL ATTEMPTS—Philadelphia, Boniol 48. Dallas, Cunningham 51.

INTERCEPTIONS—Philadelphia, Zordich 1-14. Dallas, K. Smith 1-9.

KICKOFF RETURNS—Philadelphia, Rossum 2-45, Walker 1-17. Dallas, Hughes 3-70.

PUNT RETURNS—Philadelphia, Solomon 4-2. Dallas, Hughes 3-4.

SACKS—Philadelphia, Martin 2, Rossum 1.

DOLPHINS 31, BRONCOS 21

Monday, December 21

| Denver | 3 | 10 | 0 | 8—21 |
| Miami | 0 | 7 | 14 | 10—31 |

First Quarter
Den.—FG, Elam 52, 9:09.

Second Quarter
Den.—R. Smith recovered fumble in end zone (Elam kick), 7:04.
Mia.—L. Thomas 9 pass from Marino (Mare kick), 14:06.
Den.—FG, Elam 44, 15:00.

Third Quarter
Mia.—L. Thomas 56 pass from Marino (Mare kick), 4:34.
Mia.—L. Thomas 17 pass from Marino (Mare kick), 9:07.

Fourth Quarter
Mia.—Gadsden 8 pass from Marino (Mare kick), 6:45.
Den.—Hebron 95 kickoff return (McCaffrey pass from Brister), 7:03.
Mia.—FG, Mare 42, 13:50.
   Attendance—74,363.

	Denver	Miami
First downs	14	19
Rushes-yards	23-58	28-36
Passing	161	355
Punt returns	2-16	6-57
Kickoff returns	6-198	4-104
Interception returns	1-4	2-35
Comp.-att.-int.	15-40-2	23-38-1
Sacked-yards lost	2-6	0-0
Punts	7-47	6-39
Fumbles-lost	2-0	1-1
Penalties-yards	8-51	0-0
Time of possession	28:21	31:39

INDIVIDUAL STATISTICS
RUSHING—Denver, Davis 16-29, Elway 5-39, Loville 1-0, R. Smith 1-(minus 10). Miami, Abdul-Jabbar 15-5, Avery 11-32, Marino 2-(minus 1).

PASSING—Denver, Elway 13-36-2-151, Brister 2-4-0-16. Miami, Marino 23-38-1-355.

RECEIVING—Denver, Sharpe 4-36, R. Smith 3-54, McCaffrey 3-42, Davis 2-5, Griffith 1-14, Loville 1-12, Green 1-4. Miami, L. Thomas 6-136, McDuffie 6-57, Drayton 3-64, Jacquet 2-35, Gadsden 2-28, Perry 2-18, Pritchett 1-12, Abdul-Jabbar 1-5.

MISSED FIELD GOAL ATTEMPTS—Denver, Elam 43. Miami, Mare 28.

INTERCEPTIONS—Denver, Atwater 1-4. Miami, Madison 1-35, Wilson 1-0.

KICKOFF RETURNS—Denver, Hebron 4-158, Loville 1-25, D. Smith 1-15. Miami, Avery 3-85, Marion 1-19.

PUNT RETURNS—Denver, Coghill 1-8, Gordon 1-8. Miami, Buckley 5-49, McDuffie 1-8.

SACKS—Miami, Taylor 1, Bromell 1.

WEEK 17

RESULTS

Kansas City 31, OAKLAND 24
Minnesota 26, TENNESSEE 16
ARIZONA 16, San Diego 13 (OT)
ATLANTA 38, Miami 16
BALTIMORE 19, Detroit 10
Buffalo 45, NEW ORLEANS 33
Carolina 27, INDIANAPOLIS 19
DALLAS 23, Washington 7
DENVER 28, Seattle 21
Green Bay 16, CHICAGO 13
N.Y. Giants 20, PHILADELPHIA 10
N.Y. JETS 31, New England 10
SAN FRANCISCO 38, St. Louis 19
Tampa Bay 35, CINCINNATI 0
JACKSONVILLE 21, Pittsburgh 3

STANDINGS

AFC EAST	W	L	T	Pct.
N.Y. Jets	12	4	0	.750
Buffalo	10	6	0	.625
Miami	10	6	0	.625
New England	9	7	0	.563
Indianapolis	3	13	0	.188

AFC CENTRAL	W	L	T	Pct.
Jacksonville	11	5	0	.688
Tennessee	8	8	0	.500
Pittsburgh	7	9	0	.438
Baltimore	6	10	0	.375
Cincinnati	3	13	0	.188

AFC WEST	W	L	T	Pct.
Denver	14	2	0	.875
Oakland	8	8	0	.500
Seattle	8	8	0	.500
Kansas City	7	9	0	.438
San Diego	5	11	0	.313

NFC EAST	W	L	T	Pct.
Dallas	10	6	0	.625
Arizona	9	7	0	.563
N.Y. Giants	8	8	0	.500
Washington	6	10	0	.375
Philadelphia	3	13	0	.188

NFC CENTRAL	W	L	T	Pct.
Minnesota	15	1	0	.938
Green Bay	11	5	0	.688
Tampa Bay	8	8	0	.500
Detroit	5	11	0	.313
Chicago	4	12	0	.220

NFC WEST	W	L	T	Pct.
Atlanta	14	2	0	.875
San Francisco	12	4	0	.750
New Orleans	6	10	0	.375
Carolina	4	12	0	.250
St. Louis	4	12	0	.250

HIGHLIGHTS

Hero of the week: Kicker Gary Anderson finished a perfect season, and the Vikings finished close to perfect. Anderson, whose 164 points set a record for NFL kickers, became the first kicker to make all of his field goal attempts (35) and all of his point-after conversions (59) in a season. Minnesota's 26-16 win over Tennessee made it the third team to finish an NFL season with 15 victories. The Vikings also set a record with 556 points, eclipsing the 541 scored by Washington in 1983.

Goat of the week: New Orleans quarterback Kerry Collins was yanked in the first quarter after going 3-for-12 with an interception and a fumble against Buffalo. Both of the turnovers led to touchdowns in the Bills' 45-33 win. After coming to the Saints from Carolina, Collins committed 14 turnovers in his 23 quarters.

Sub of the week: Buffalo's Rob Johnson, who started at quarterback while Doug Flutie rested a sore leg for the playoffs, threw for three touchdowns and ran for one. Johnson, who had lost the starting job to Flutie after suffering an injury in the fifth game of the season, completed 12-for-18 passes for 216 yards.

Comeback of the week: Kansas City fell behind 14-0 after the first quarter but rebounded to win at Oakland, 31-24. Bam Morris scored two 1-yard touchdowns and Derrick Thomas returned a fumble 44 yards for a score. The Chiefs scored 17 points in the third quarter.

Blowout of the week: Mike Alstott ran for three touchdowns as Tampa Bay routed the Bengals 35-0 at Cincinnati. Trent Dilfer threw two touchdown passes, including a 50-yarder to Robb Thomas. The Bengals fumbled a punt and a kickoff, had a punt blocked and missed a field goal. The Buccaneers, who led 28-0 at halftime, needed a win to have any chance of making the playoffs. However, Arizona got the playoff spot when it beat San Diego later in the day.

Nail-biter of the week: Chris Jacke kicked a 52-yard field goal as time ran out to give Arizona a 16-13 win and clinch a playoff berth, the franchise's first since 1982. San Diego tied the score with 16 seconds left when Craig Whelihan threw a 30-yard touchdown pass to Ryan Thelwell on fourth and 19. Eric Metcalf returned the kickoff 46 yards, and Jake Plummer threw a 10-yard pass to Frank Sanders to set up the winning kick. Thousands of Cardinals fans rushed onto the field to celebrate the victory.

Hit of the week: LeRoy Butler sacked Chicago's Steve Stenstrom with 54 seconds left and recovered Stenstrom's fumble to seal Green Bay's 16-13 win. Chicago had moved to the Packers' 33 before Butler's big hit.

Oddity of the week: After having only two 2,000-yard rushers in its first 77 years, the NFL got its second in as many seasons when Denver's Terrell Davis rushed for 178 yards against Seattle to increase his total to 2,008. In 1997 Detroit's Barry Sanders rushed for 2,053 yards.

Top rusher: Terrell Davis, who reached the 2,000-yard milestone on his last carry of the game—a 15-yarder in the fourth quarter—joined Eric Dickerson, Sanders and O.J. Simpson in the 2,000-yard club.

Top passer: John Elway completed 26-of-36 passes for 338 yards and four touchdowns against Seattle to become the third NFL player to throw 300 touchdown passes in his career. Only Dan Marino (408) and Fran Tarkenton (342) had more.

Top receiver: Rod Smith caught nine of John Elway's passes for 158 yards and a touchdown.

Notes: Dallas' Emmitt Smith ran for two touchdowns against Washington to top Marcus Allen for the most career rushing touchdowns. Smith had 125. . . . Atlanta's Jamal Anderson had 18 carries against Miami to finish the season with 410, breaking the NFL record of 407 set by Tampa Bay's James Wilder in 1984. . . . Indianapolis' Marshall Faulk led the league in yards from scrimmage with 2,227. He fell 92 receiving yards short of becoming the second NFL player with 1,000 yards rushing and 1,000 yards receiving in the same season. San Francisco's Roger Craig accomplished the 1,000/1,000 feat in 1985. . . . After 39 seasons, the Oilers are no more. Tennessee will change its name to the Titans for 1999. . . . Priest Holmes became the Ravens' first

1,000-yard rusher, running for 132 yards in the season finale against Detroit to finish with 1,008. . . . The Jets' Vinny Testaverde threw four touchdown passes to finish the season with 29. He ended the season as the AFC's top-rated passer at 101.6, nearly 29 points higher than his pre-1998 career rating (72.8). . . . Atlanta coach Dan Reeves, recovering from bypass surgery, unexpectedly arrived at the Georgia Dome to give his team a pep talk a couple of hours before its game with Miami. Reeves then went home to watch the game on TV. The Falcons clobbered the Dolphins, 38-16, and Reeves resumed some coaching duties the next day. . . . Carolina's Michael Bates returned the second-half kickoff 99 yards for a touchdown against Indianapolis. . . . The day after the final Sunday of the season, five coaches were fired: Ted Marchibroda, Baltimore; Ray Rhodes, Philadelphia; Dave Wannstedt, Chicago; Dennis Erickson, Seattle; and Dom Capers, Carolina. All had losing records except for Erickson, whose Seahawks went 8-8 after entering the season amid high expectations. With June Jones having announced previously he was leaving San Diego to become coach at the University of Hawaii and the expansion Cleveland Browns looking for a coach, seven NFL head-coach positions were vacant at the end of the 1998 season.

Quote of the week: Plummer, after his ninth fourth-quarter win since taking over as starter, on the significance of the Cardinals' just-clinched playoff berth: "I get tired of hearing about all that, 'The last time they made it,' or 'The longest drought in NFL history.' I wasn't even born then."

GAME SUMMARIES

VIKINGS 26, OILERS 16

Saturday, December 26

Minnesota	2	6	15	3—26
Tennessee	3	10	3	0—16

First Quarter
Min.—Safety, McNair intentional grounding in end zone, 4:05.
Ten.—FG, Del Greco 36, 11:33.
Second Quarter
Min.—FG, Anderson 39, 0:07.
Ten.—FG, Del Greco 33, 4:38.
Ten.—E. George 2 run (Del Greco kick), 9:54.
Min.—FG, Anderson 23, 14:46.
Third Quarter
Min.—R. Moss 5 pass from Cunningham (R. Moss pass from Cunningham), 5:58.
Ten.—FG, Del Greco 45, 10:53.
Min.—Carter 38 pass from Cunningham (Anderson kick), 13:42.
Fourth Quarter
Min.—FG, Anderson 39, 13:57.
Attendance—41,121.

	Minnesota	Tennessee
First downs	22	20
Rushes-yards	29-103	21-90
Passing	235	264
Punt returns	0-0	3-23
Kickoff returns	6-147	6-146
Interception returns	0-0	1-0
Comp.-att.-int.	23-35-1	18-36-0
Sacked-yards lost	0-0	2-21
Punts	4-49	3-41
Fumbles-lost	1-0	0-0

	Minnesota	Tennessee
Penalties-yards	8-60	13-105
Time of possession	31:37	28:23

INDIVIDUAL STATISTICS
RUSHING—Minnesota, R. Smith 15-73, Hoard 9-26, Evans 2-8, Cunningham 2-2, Palmer 1-(minus 6). Tennessee, E. George 14-54, McNair 3-35, Thomas 3-10, Archie 1-(minus 9).
PASSING—Minnesota, Cunningham 23-35-1-235. Tennessee, McNair 16-33-0-261, S. Matthews 2-3-0-24.
RECEIVING—Minnesota, Carter 6-78, R. Moss 5-32, Hatchette 3-54, R. Smith 3-46, Palmer 2-8, Evans 2-7, Glover 1-10, Goodwin 1-0. Tennessee, Harris 4-83, Mason 3-75, Dyson 3-40, Wycheck 3-32, Thigpen 3-31, Roan 1-13, E. George 1-11.
MISSED FIELD GOAL ATTEMPTS—None.
INTERCEPTIONS—Tennessee, D. Lewis 1-0.
KICKOFF RETURNS—Minnesota, Palmer 6-147. Tennessee, Archie 5-136, Wycheck 1-10.
PUNT RETURNS—Tennessee, Mason 3-23.
SACKS—Minnesota, E. McDaniel 1, Rudd 1.

CHIEFS 31, RAIDERS 24

Saturday, December 26

Kansas City	0	7	17	7—31
Oakland	14	0	3	7—24

First Quarter
Oak.—T. Brown 13 pass from Wilson (G. Davis kick), 6:38.
Oak.—Jordan 10 run (G. Davis kick), 12:42.
Second Quarter
K.C.—Morris 1 run (Stoyanovich kick), 2:22.
Third Quarter
K.C.—Morris 1 run (Stoyanovich kick), 3:44.
Oak.—FG, G. Davis 44, 7:45.
K.C.—FG, Stoyanovich 30, 11:07.
K.C.—Thomas 44 fumble return (Stoyanovich kick), 13:45.
Fourth Quarter
Oak.—Jett 15 pass from George (G. Davis kick), 5:43.
K.C.—Gonzalez 20 pass from Grbac (Stoyanovich kick), 9:04.
Attendance—52,679.

	Kansas City	Oakland
First downs	20	25
Rushes-yards	26-119	24-40
Passing	254	281
Punt returns	3-15	4-28
Kickoff returns	5-113	6-84
Interception returns	0-0	2-15
Comp.-att.-int.	20-32-2	26-42-0
Sacked-yards lost	0-0	6-44
Punts	4-51	5-43
Fumbles-lost	1-1	6-2
Penalties-yards	12-98	10-84
Time of possession	27:16	32:44

INDIVIDUAL STATISTICS
RUSHING—Kansas City, Morris 17-96, Anders 5-23, Grbac 3-(minus 1), Richardson 1-1. Oakland, Jordan 16-24, H. Williams 5-14, Hollas 1-7, Wilson 1-2, T. Brown 1-(minus 7).
PASSING—Kansas City, Grbac 20-32-2-254. Oakland, Wilson 13-18-0-127, George 9-18-0-138, Hollas 4-6-0-60.
RECEIVING—Kansas City, Anders 8-49, Gonzalez 5-76, Alexander 3-80, Morris 2-28, Lockett 1-15, Rison 1-6. Oakland, T. Brown 10-140, Jett 6-85, Mickens 2-35, Dudley 2-26, Ritchie 2-9, Jordan 2-1, D. Brown 1-27, H. Williams 1-2.
MISSED FIELD GOAL ATTEMPTS—Kansas City, Stoyanovich 47. Oakland, G. Davis 41.
INTERCEPTIONS—Oakland, Woodson 1-13, Harvey 1-2.
KICKOFF RETURNS—Kansas City, Vanover 5-113. Oakland, Howard 6-84.
PUNT RETURNS—Kansas City, Vanover 3-15. Oakland, Howard 4-28.
SACKS—Kansas City, Thomas 2, O'Neal 2, Edwards 1, Team 1.

BUCCANEERS 35, BENGALS 0

Sunday, December 27

Tampa Bay	14	14	0	7—35
Cincinnati	0	0	0	0— 0

First Quarter
T.B.—Thomas 50 pass from Dilfer (Husted kick), 2:31.
T.B.—Alstott 1 run (Husted kick), 12:14.

Second Quarter

T.B.—Alstott 1 run (Husted kick), 0:03.

T.B.—Anthony 4 pass from Dilfer (Husted kick), 6:53.

Fourth Quarter

T.B.—Alstott 3 run (Husted kick), 5:40.

Attendance—49,826.

	Tampa Bay	Cincinnati
First downs	22	11
Rushes-yards	51-223	23-87
Passing	97	159
Punt returns	0-0	2-16
Kickoff returns	1-12	5-101
Interception returns	2-61	1-0
Comp.-att.-int.	10-16-1	11-27-2
Sacked-yards lost	2-14	2-17
Punts	4-40	4-36
Fumbles-lost	0-0	2-1
Penalties-yards	1-5	5-30
Time of possession	36:28	23:32

INDIVIDUAL STATISTICS

RUSHING—Tampa Bay, Alstott 20-69, Dunn 19-89, Ellison 6-18, Neal 4-25, Dilfer 2-22. Cincinnati, Dillon 14-70, Bennett 5-13, Milne 1-3, Scott 1-2, Costello 1-0, Kresser 1-(minus 1).

PASSING—Tampa Bay, Dilfer 10-16-1-111. Cincinnati, Kresser 7-17-2-102, Justin 4-10-0-74.

RECEIVING—Tampa Bay, Green 3-23, Williams 2-18, Alstott 2-8, Thomas 1-50, Dunn 1-8, Anthony 1-4. Cincinnati, McGee 3-68, Dillon 3-51, Scott 2-37, Pickens 2-17, Milne 1-3.

MISSED FIELD GOAL ATTEMPTS—Tampa Bay, Husted 18. Cincinnati, Pelfrey 40.

INTERCEPTIONS—Tampa Bay, Barber 1-56, Mincy 1-5. Cincinnati, Ambrose 1-0.

KICKOFF RETURNS—Tampa Bay, Green 1-12. Cincinnati, Gibson 4-85, Bieniemy 1-16.

PUNT RETURNS—Cincinnati, St. Williams 2-16.

SACKS—Tampa Bay, Upshaw 1, Culpepper 1. Cincinnati, C. Simmons 1, Bankston 1.

PANTHERS 27, COLTS 19

Sunday, December 27

Carolina	3	3	14	7—27
Indianapolis	3	13	3	0—19

First Quarter

Car.—FG, Kasay 44, 7:15.

Ind.—FG, Vanderjagt 22, 11:56.

Second Quarter

Ind.—FG, Vanderjagt 28, 0:02.

Ind.—Pollard 44 pass from Manning (Vanderjagt kick), 2:51.

Car.—FG, Kasay 27, 14:35.

Ind.—FG, Vanderjagt 47, 14:59.

Third Quarter

Car.—Bates 99 kickoff return (Kasay kick), 0:20.

Car.—Biakabutuka 5 run (Kasay kick), 6:27.

Ind.—FG, Vanderjagt 42, 13:58.

Fourth Quarter

Car.—Ismail 5 pass from Beuerlein (Kasay kick), 11:44.

Attendance—58,182.

	Carolina	Indianapolis
First downs	17	12
Rushes-yards	43-183	18-72
Passing	149	207
Punt returns	4-38	1-4
Kickoff returns	6-168	4-75
Interception returns	2-6	1-0
Comp.-att.-int.	12-21-1	17-35-2
Sacked-yards lost	5-29	5-18
Punts	5-44	7-44
Fumbles-lost	3-1	1-0
Penalties-yards	5-51	3-25
Time of possession	34:40	25:20

INDIVIDUAL STATISTICS

RUSHING—Carolina, Biakabutuka 25-109, Lane 12-72, Beuerlein 3-0, Johnson 2-2, Walter 1-0. Indianapolis, Faulk 18-72.

PASSING—Carolina, Beuerlein 12-21-1-178. Indianapolis, Manning 17-34-2-225, Small 0-1-0-0.

RECEIVING—Carolina, Ismail 7-109, Biakabutuka 2-23, Floyd 1-20, D. Hayes 1-16, Broughton 1-10. Indianapolis, Pathon 5-35, Faulk 4-30, Green 3-19, Pollard 2-65, Small 2-58, Dilger 1-18.

MISSED FIELD GOAL ATTEMPTS—None.

INTERCEPTIONS—Carolina, McGill 1-6, Davis 1-0. Indianapolis, M. Barber 1-0.

KICKOFF RETURNS—Carolina, Bates 4-152, Johnson 1-9, Stone 1-7. Indianapolis, McGuire 4-75.

PUNT RETURNS—Carolina, Oliver 4-38. Indianapolis, McGuire 1-4.

SACKS—Carolina, Terry 3, Brady 1, Greene 1. Indianapolis, E. Johnson 2, M. Barber 1, McCoy 1, M. Thomas 1.

PACKERS 16, BEARS 13

Sunday, December 27

Green Bay	7	0	6	3—16
Chicago	7	3	3	0—13

First Quarter

G.B.—McKenzie 33 interception return (Longwell kick), 7:03.

Chi.—J. Allen 14 pass from Stenstrom (Jaeger kick), 14:22.

Second Quarter

Chi.—FG, Jaeger 29, 11:06.

Third Quarter

G.B.—Freeman 8 pass from Favre (kick failed), 6:41.

Chi.—FG, Jaeger 21, 12:31.

Fourth Quarter

G.B.—FG, Longwell 18, 5:11.

Attendance—58,393.

	Green Bay	Chicago
First downs	14	17
Rushes-yards	27-70	31-98
Passing	169	183
Punt returns	2-25	1-18
Kickoff returns	4-75	4-100
Interception returns	2-39	2-36
Comp.-att.-int.	19-26-2	17-31-2
Sacked-yards lost	0-0	2-16
Punts	3-41	2-43
Fumbles-lost	1-1	2-1
Penalties-yards	4-35	3-25
Time of possession	28:36	31:24

INDIVIDUAL STATISTICS

RUSHING—Green Bay, Levens 17-52, Pederson 4-0, Favre 3-9, Holmes 3-9. Chicago, J. Allen 22-60, Bennett 5-19, Chancey 4-19.

PASSING—Green Bay, Favre 16-22-2-153, Pederson 3-4-0-16. Chicago, Stenstrom 17-30-2-199, Horan 0-1-0-0.

RECEIVING—Green Bay, Freeman 7-65, Thomason 3-27, Levens 3-22, Mayes 2-25, Copeland 2-11, Holmes 1-1, Henderson 1-8. Chicago, Engram 5-68, Conway 4-58, Bennett 3-22, J. Allen 2-27, Penn 2-21, Chancey 1-3.

MISSED FIELD GOAL ATTEMPTS—Green Bay, Longwell 39. Chicago, Jaeger 48.

INTERCEPTIONS—Green Bay, McKenzie 1-33, Ty. Williams 1-6. Chicago, Collins 1-28, Parrish 1-8.

KICKOFF RETURNS—Green Bay, Preston 4-75. Chicago, Milburn 3-81, Bownes 1-19.

PUNT RETURNS—Green Bay, Preston 2-25. Chicago, Milburn 1-18.

SACKS—Green Bay, Butler 1, Booker 1.

FALCONS 38, DOLPHINS 16

Sunday, December 27

Miami	0	6	10	0—16
Atlanta	21	3	14	0—38

First Quarter

Atl.—Santiago 62 pass from Chandler (Andersen kick), 0:24.

Atl.—Santiago 3 pass from Chandler (Andersen kick), 3:52.

Atl.—Bradford 11 interception return (Andersen kick), 8:00.

Second Quarter

Mia.—McDuffie 12 pass from Marino (kick blocked), 3:14.

Atl.—FG, Andersen 35, 10:13.

Third Quarter

Atl.—Martin 35 pass from DeBerg (Andersen kick), 0:51.

Atl.—J. Anderson 36 run (Andersen kick), 2:36.

Mia.—Marino 3 run (Mare kick), 8:56.

Mia.—FG, Mare 26, 13:05.

Attendance—69,754.

1998 REVIEW Week 17

	Miami	Atlanta
First downs	20	15
Rushes-yards	19-38	31-143
Passing	362	203
Punt returns	0-0	1-11
Kickoff returns	5-103	3-86
Interception returns	0-0	2-38
Comp.-att.-int.	25-42-2	8-13-0
Sacked-yards lost	3-22	0-0
Punts	2-41	2-43
Fumbles-lost	4-4	2-0
Penalties-yards	8-49	5-23
Time of possession	32:16	27:44

INDIVIDUAL STATISTICS

RUSHING—Miami, Avery 14-23, R. Moore 4-12, Marino 1-3. Atlanta, J. Anderson 18-103, Green 6-6, Oxendine 5-32, Chandler 1-3, Graziani 1-(minus 1).

PASSING—Miami, Marino 21-36-2-320, Huard 4-6-0-64. Atlanta, DeBerg 5-10-0-85, Chandler 3-3-0-118.

RECEIVING—Miami, Gadsden 9-153, McDuffie 5-82, L. Thomas 4-79, Drayton 4-61, Pritchett 2-8, R. Moore 1-1. Atlanta, Martin 3-105, Santiago 2-65, Harris 1-14, Mathis 1-10, Kozlowski 1-9.

MISSED FIELD GOAL ATTEMPTS—Atlanta, Andersen 19.

INTERCEPTIONS—Atlanta, Booker 1-27, Bradford 1-11.

KICKOFF RETURNS—Miami, Jacquet 4-103, Surtain 1-0. Atlanta, Dwight 3-86.

PUNT RETURNS—Atlanta, Dwight 1-11.

SACKS—Atlanta, Bennett 1, Crockett 1, C. Smith 1.

JETS 31, PATRIOTS 10

Sunday, December 27

New England	0	3	0	7—10
N.Y. Jets	3	14	7	7—31

First Quarter
NYJ—FG, Hall 36, 8:39.

Second Quarter
NYJ—Brady 4 pass from Testaverde (Hall kick), 0:40.
NYJ—Martin 8 pass from Testaverde (Hall kick), 5:55.
N.E.—FG, Vinatieri 19, 11:34.

Third Quarter
NYJ—Ward 17 pass from Testaverde (Hall kick), 4:29.

Fourth Quarter
NYJ—K. Johnson 24 pass from Testaverde (Hall kick), 0:05.
N.E.—Simmons 44 pass from Zolak (Vinatieri kick), 13:29.
Attendance—74,302.

	New England	N.Y. Jets
First downs	9	21
Rushes-yards	20-130	41-149
Passing	119	190
Punt returns	2-18	3-39
Kickoff returns	6-164	2-32
Interception returns	1-0	0-0
Comp.-att.-int.	14-31-0	18-31-1
Sacked-yards lost	1-8	0-0
Punts	6-43	4-41
Fumbles-lost	3-1	0-0
Penalties-yards	2-25	1-10
Time of possession	21:09	38:51

INDIVIDUAL STATISTICS

RUSHING—New England, Edwards 12-47, S. Shaw 6-81, Cullors 2-2. New York, Martin 29-102, Meggett 4-7, Sowell 4-4, Testaverde 2-35, Anderson 1-2, Lucas 1-(minus 1).

PASSING—New England, Zolak 14-31-0-127. New York, Testaverde 17-27-1-179, Foley 1-3-0-11, Lucas 0-1-0-0.

RECEIVING—New England, Edwards 4-8, Coates 2-25, S. Shaw 2-10, Purnell 2-8, Simmons 1-44, Cullors 1-15, Ton. Carter 1-11, Jefferson 1-6. New York, K. Johnson 6-75, Chrebet 4-44, Brady 3-16, Ward 2-28, Martin 2-12, Meggett 1-15.

MISSED FIELD GOAL ATTEMPTS—None.

INTERCEPTIONS—New England, Milloy 1-0.

KICKOFF RETURNS—New England, Cullors 5-140, Canty 1-24. New York, Meggett 1-16, Williams 1-16.

PUNT RETURNS—New England, Brown 2-18. New York, Meggett 3-39.

SACKS—New York, Pleasant 1.

RAVENS 19, LIONS 10

Sunday, December 27

Detroit	0	3	0	7—10
Baltimore	9	7	0	3—19

First Quarter
Bal.—Safety, Boyd tackled in end zone, 6:48.
Bal.—Holmes 1 run (Stover kick), 9:20.

Second Quarter
Bal.—Potts 11 pass from Harbaugh (Stover kick), 9:16.
Det.—FG, Hanson 39, 14:30.

Fourth Quarter
Det.—Schlesinger 8 pass from Reich (Hanson kick), 1:35.
Bal.—FG, Stover 30, 9:57.
Attendance—68,045.

	Detroit	Baltimore
First downs	11	19
Rushes-yards	21-44	35-153
Passing	192	142
Punt returns	4-11	5-45
Kickoff returns	4-74	3-57
Interception returns	0-0	0-0
Comp.-att.-int.	18-29-0	18-28-0
Sacked-yards lost	1-3	0-0
Punts	6-46	6-47
Fumbles-lost	1-1	4-1
Penalties-yards	12-69	6-60
Time of possession	26:43	33:17

INDIVIDUAL STATISTICS

RUSHING—Detroit, Sanders 19-41, Schlesinger 1-3, Vardell 1-0. Baltimore, Holmes 28-132, Harbaugh 3-8, Potts 2-13, Mitchell 1-0, W. Richardson 1-0.

PASSING—Detroit, Reich 18-29-0-195. Baltimore, Harbaugh 17-26-0-141, W. Richardson 1-2-0-1.

RECEIVING—Detroit, Moore 10-120, Morton 3-40, Sanders 2-15, Schlesinger 1-8, T. Boyd 1-8, Rasby 1-4. Baltimore, J. Lewis 5-40, M. Jackson 4-36, Holmes 3-12, Potts 2-29, Turner 2-19, Rhett 1-5, Kinchen 1-1.

MISSED FIELD GOAL ATTEMPTS—None.

INTERCEPTIONS—None.

KICKOFF RETURNS—Detroit, T. Boyd 4-74. Baltimore, C. Harris 3-57.

PUNT RETURNS—Detroit, T. Boyd 4-11. Baltimore, J. Lewis 3-34, Roe 2-11.

SACKS—Baltimore, Staten 1.

BILLS 45, SAINTS 33

Sunday, December 27

Buffalo	21	7	3	14—45
New Orleans	0	14	7	12—33

First Quarter
Buf.—A. Smith 1 run (Christie kick), 0:35.
Buf.—Moulds 66 pass from R. Johnson (Christie kick), 2:54.
Buf.—R. Johnson 12 run (Christie kick), 8:47.

Second Quarter
Buf.—Gash 1 pass from R. Johnson (Christie kick), 2:45.
N.O.—T. Davis 1 run (Brien kick), 8:31.
N.O.—Cleeland 5 pass from Tolliver (Brien kick), 13:04.

Third Quarter
Buf.—FG, Christie 35, 7:42.
N.O.—Bech 10 pass from Tolliver (Brien kick), 14:00.

Fourth Quarter
Buf.—L. Johnson 23 pass from R. Johnson (Christie kick), 0:05.
Buf.—Linton 8 run (Christie kick), 8:21.
N.O.—Craver 1 run (pass failed), 13:03.
N.O.—Bech 72 pass from Tolliver (pass failed), 13:18.
Attendance—39,707.

	Buffalo	New Orleans
First downs	21	26
Rushes-yards	33-130	19-75
Passing	178	291
Punt returns	3-25	2-8
Kickoff returns	2-58	6-152
Interception returns	2-24	0-0
Comp.-att.-int.	12-18-0	26-53-2
Sacked-yards lost	5-38	4-28

	Buffalo	New Orleans
Punts	3-39	4-50
Fumbles-lost	2-1	2-1
Penalties-yards	10-77	6-45
Time of possession	29:36	30:24

INDIVIDUAL STATISTICS

RUSHING—Buffalo, Linton 13-60, A. Smith 12-42, R. Johnson 4-23, Po. Williams 2-5, Gash 1-1, Van Pelt 1-(minus 1). New Orleans, Perry 9-45, Craver 5-8, T. Davis 3-1, Tolliver 2-21.

PASSING—Buffalo, R. Johnson 12-18-0-216. New Orleans, Tolliver 23-41-1-296, Collins 3-12-1-23.

RECEIVING—Buffalo, Riemersma 3-26, Moulds 2-90, Reed 2-20, K. Williams 2-19, Early 1-37, L. Johnson 1-23, Gash 1-1. New Orleans, Cleeland 10-112, Bech 4-113, Craver 3-16, Guliford 2-26, Hastings 2-17, L. Smith 2-11, Dawkins 1-12, Wilcox 1-10, Perry 1-2.

MISSED FIELD GOAL ATTEMPTS—None.

INTERCEPTIONS—Buffalo, Martin 1-23, Schulz 1-1.

KICKOFF RETURNS—Buffalo, K. Williams 1-37, Cummings 1-21. New Orleans, Guliford 6-152.

PUNT RETURNS—Buffalo, K. Williams 3-25. New Orleans, Guliford 2-8.

SACKS—Buffalo, Price 2, Wiley 1, B. Smith 1. New Orleans, Fields 2, Bordano 1, Martin 1, Kei. Mitchell 1.

BRONCOS 28, SEAHAWKS 21

Sunday, December 27

Seattle	7	0	0	14—21
Denver	0	14	7	7—28

First Quarter
Sea.—Watters 4 run (Peterson kick), 12:34.
Second Quarter
Den.—R. Smith 33 pass from Elway (Elam kick), 4:35.
Den.—Sharpe 17 pass from Elway (Elam kick), 13:59.
Third Quarter
Den.—Davis 2 pass from Elway (Elam kick), 6:34.
Fourth Quarter
Den.—Sharpe 1 pass from Elway (Elam kick), 3:15.
Sea.—Pritchard 7 pass from Kitna (Peterson kick), 9:01.
Sea.—May 1 pass from Watters (Peterson kick), 13:28.
Attendance—74,057.

	Seattle	Denver
First downs	19	31
Rushes-yards	13-24	40-195
Passing	217	316
Punt returns	2-32	2-14
Kickoff returns	5-129	3-66
Interception returns	0-0	1-5
Comp.-att.-int.	23-38-1	26-36-0
Sacked-yards lost	3-26	2-22
Punts	6-43	2-50
Fumbles-lost	1-0	2-1
Penalties-yards	5-26	8-75
Time of possession	22:08	37:52

INDIVIDUAL STATISTICS

RUSHING—Seattle, Watters 10-13, Kitna 2-5, Strong 1-6. Denver, Davis 29-178, Loville 7-9, Elway 4-8.

PASSING—Seattle, Kitna 22-37-1-242, Watters 1-1-0-1. Denver, Elway 26-36-0-338.

RECEIVING—Seattle, Pritchard 8-88, Fauria 5-67, Watters 4-29, Galloway 3-33, Br. Blades 1-16, Strong 1-9, May 1-1. Denver, R. Smith 9-158, Sharpe 6-68, McCaffrey 3-36, Davis 2-17, Green 2-16, Griffith 2-10, Loville 1-17, Chamberlain 1-16.

MISSED FIELD GOAL ATTEMPTS—Denver, Elam 42, 55.

INTERCEPTIONS—Denver, Cadrez 1-5.

KICKOFF RETURNS—Seattle, Broussard 2-91, R. Brown 2-13, Wilson 1-16. Denver, Hebron 3-66.

PUNT RETURNS—Seattle, Joseph 2-32. Denver, Coghill 2-14.

SACKS—Seattle, Daniels 1.5, Sinclair 0.5. Denver, Johnson 1, Pryce 1, Williams 1.

CARDINALS 16, CHARGERS 13

Sunday, December 27

San Diego	0	3	0	10—13
Arizona	7	3	3	3—16

First Quarter
Ariz.—Murrell 4 run (Jacke kick), 9:48.

Second Quarter
Ariz.—FG, Jacke 37, 2:28.
S.D.—FG, Carney 31, 11:45.
Third Quarter
Ariz.—FG, Jacke 36, 12:03.
Fourth Quarter
S.D.—FG, Carney 26, 5:14.
S.D.—Thelwell 30 pass from Whelihan (Carney kick), 14:44.
Ariz.—FG, Jacke 52, 15:00.
Attendance—71,670.

	San Diego	Arizona
First downs	22	16
Rushes-yards	36-174	18-25
Passing	203	245
Punt returns	3-8	1-7
Kickoff returns	4-73	4-122
Interception returns	0-0	4-36
Comp.-att.-int.	16-40-4	20-41-0
Sacked-yards lost	2-11	4-29
Punts	5-46	7-43
Fumbles-lost	1-1	0-0
Penalties-yards	6-54	2-9
Time of possession	34:53	25:07

INDIVIDUAL STATISTICS

RUSHING—San Diego, Fletcher 23-127, Stephens 10-42, Whelihan 3-5. Arizona, Murrell 18-25.

PASSING—San Diego, Whelihan 16-40-4-214. Arizona, Plummer 20-41-0-274.

RECEIVING—San Diego, Thelwell 5-84, Ricks 3-39, F. Jones 2-26, Fletcher 2-21, Stephens 2-9, C. Jones 1-24, Hartley 1-11. Arizona, Sanders 8-106, Centers 6-59, R. Moore 4-94, Murrell 1-8, Gedney 1-7.

MISSED FIELD GOAL ATTEMPTS—Arizona, Jacke 45, 42.

INTERCEPTIONS—Arizona, Lassiter 4-36.

KICKOFF RETURNS—San Diego, Bynum 4-73. Arizona, Metcalf 4-122.

PUNT RETURNS—San Diego, Gaiter 3-8. Arizona, Metcalf 1-7.

SACKS—San Diego, Harrison 1, Coleman 1, Tovar 1, Mims 1. Arizona, M. Smith 2.

GIANTS 20, EAGLES 10

Sunday, December 27

N.Y. Giants	3	3	7	7—20
Philadelphia	0	10	0	0—10

First Quarter
NYG—FG, Daluiso 43, 14:26.
Second Quarter
Phi.—Staley 64 run (Boniol kick), 0:44.
NYG—FG, Daluiso 33, 7:52.
Phi.—FG, Boniol 19, 14:25.
Third Quarter
NYG—Calloway 5 pass from K. Graham (Daluiso kick), 14:32.
Fourth Quarter
NYG—Calloway 18 pass from K. Graham (Daluiso kick), 9:18.
Attendance—66,596.

	N.Y. Giants	Philadelphia
First downs	22	11
Rushes-yards	43-209	24-123
Passing	130	141
Punt returns	1-1	4-47
Kickoff returns	3-51	5-149
Interception returns	1-13	0-0
Comp.-att.-int.	15-26-0	13-27-1
Sacked-yards lost	2-3	2-10
Punts	4-48	4-39
Fumbles-lost	1-0	1-0
Penalties-yards	6-46	0-0
Time of possession	35:39	24:21

INDIVIDUAL STATISTICS

RUSHING—New York, Brown 25-112, Way 10-62, K. Graham 6-27, Barber 2-8. Philadelphia, Staley 16-97, Walker 5-10, Turner 2-12, Detmer 1-4.

PASSING—New York, K. Graham 15-26-0-133. Philadelphia, Detmer 13-27-1-151.

RECEIVING—New York, Calloway 5-56, Barber 3-21, Brown 3-15, Toomer 2-23, Hilliard 2-18. Philadelphia, Turner 4-27, Fryar 3-36, Jells 1-37, Graham 1-25, Solomon 1-15, Miller 1-6, Staley 1-3, Walker 1-2.

MISSED FIELD GOAL ATTEMPTS—None.

INTERCEPTIONS—New York, Garnes 1-13.

KICKOFF RETURNS—New York, Barber 2-20, Toomer 1-31. Philadelphia, Rossum 3-112, Walker 2-37.

PUNT RETURNS—New York, Toomer 1-1. Philadelphia, Rossum 4-47.

SACKS—New York, Strahan 1, Armstead 1. Philadelphia, Jefferson 1, Wallace 1.

COWBOYS 23, REDSKINS 7

Sunday, December 27

Washington	7	0	0	0— 7
Dallas	3	17	0	3—23

First Quarter

Dal.—FG, Cunningham 34, 6:27.

Was.—Shepherd 6 pass from T. Green (Blanchard kick), 15:00.

Second Quarter

Dal.—E. Smith 1 run (Cunningham kick), 2:22.

Dal.—E. Smith 26 run (Cunningham kick), 7:20.

Dal.—FG, Cunningham 23, 14:35.

Fourth Quarter

Dal.—FG, Cunningham 26, 2:59.

Attendance—63,565.

	Washington	Dallas
First downs	14	22
Rushes-yards	21-80	34-156
Passing	212	222
Punt returns	0-0	2-14
Kickoff returns	6-71	2-62
Interception returns	0-0	1-0
Comp.-att.-int.	21-36-1	15-26-0
Sacked-yards lost	1-11	2-13
Punts	6-38	3-39
Fumbles-lost	1-1	0-0
Penalties-yards	7-102	5-30
Time of possession	27:34	32:26

INDIVIDUAL STATISTICS

RUSHING—Washington, Davis 17-70, Mitchell 2-4, T. Green 1-11, Shepherd 1-(minus 5). Dallas, S. Williams 23-90, E. Smith 10-67, Quinn 1-(minus 1).

PASSING—Washington, T. Green 21-35-1-223, Mitchell 0-1-0-0. Dallas, Aikman 10-15-0-184, Garrett 5-11-0-51.

RECEIVING—Washington, Shepherd 5-79, S. Alexander 4-39, Sellers 3-18, Connell 2-30, Ellard 2-29, Thomas 2-18, Mitchell 2-9, Davis 1-1. Dallas, B. Davis 4-60, Bjornson 3-55, S. Williams 3-19, Irvin 2-50, Jeffers 2-50, E. Smith 1-1.

MISSED FIELD GOAL ATTEMPTS—Dallas, Cunningham 49.

INTERCEPTIONS—Dallas, Godfrey 1-0.

KICKOFF RETURNS—Washington, Mitchell 5-57, Sellers 1-14. Dallas, Hughes 2-62.

PUNT RETURNS—Dallas, Hughes 2-14.

SACKS—Washington, Lang 1, Kalu 1. Dallas, Myers 1.

49ERS 38, RAMS 19

Sunday, December 27

St. Louis	7	0	0	12—19
San Francisco	3	7	18	10—38

First Quarter

St.L.—Proehl 5 pass from Bono (Wilkins kick), 3:16.

S.F.—FG, Richey 20, 10:41.

Second Quarter

S.F.—Rice 4 pass from S. Young (Richey kick), 1:31.

Third Quarter

S.F.—FG, Richey 26, 4:22.

S.F.—McQuarters 72 punt return (Clark pass from S. Young), 5:37.

S.F.—S. Young 16 run (Richey kick), 11:19.

Fourth Quarter

St.L.—Lee 25 pass from Bono (kick failed), 1:18.

S.F.—FG, Richey 44, 7:51.

St.L.—Proehl 17 pass from Bono (pass failed), 9:45.

S.F.—Owens 24 pass from S. Young (Richey kick), 11:22.

Attendance—68,386.

	St. Louis	San Francisco
First downs	17	22
Rushes-yards	18-57	35-120
Passing	264	277
Punt returns	1-0	5-100
Kickoff returns	7-143	3-60
Interception returns	0-0	1-6
Comp.-att.-int.	19-41-1	22-32-0
Sacked-yards lost	1-15	3-11
Punts	6-43	5-38
Fumbles-lost	1-0	0-0
Penalties-yards	3-15	6-40
Time of possession	24:17	35:43

INDIVIDUAL STATISTICS

RUSHING—St. Louis, Henley 13-51, Lee 3-3, Harris 1-4, Bono 1-(minus 1). San Francisco, Kirby 16-60, Hearst 10-21, S. Young 4-20, Edwards 3-6, Owens 1-14, Detmer 1-(minus 1).

PASSING—St. Louis, Bono 15-30-1-240, Warner 4-11-0-39. San Francisco, S. Young 22-32-0-288.

RECEIVING—St. Louis, Proehl 7-100, Henley 5-64, Lee 4-46, Kennison 2-48, Hakim 1-21. San Francisco, Owens 5-85, Rice 4-49, Kirby 4-35, Hearst 3-58, Clark 3-46, Stokes 2-11, I. Smith 1-4.

MISSED FIELD GOAL ATTEMPTS—None.

INTERCEPTIONS—San Francisco, Walker 1-6.

KICKOFF RETURNS—St. Louis, Horne 7-143. San Francisco, Kirby 3-60.

PUNT RETURNS—St. Louis, Kennison 1-0. San Francisco, McQuarters 5-100.

SACKS—St. Louis, Phifer 1, Farr 1, Carter 1. San Francisco, Bryant 1.

JAGUARS 21, STEELERS 3

Monday, December 28

Pittsburgh	0	3	0	0— 3
Jacksonville	0	14	7	0—21

Second Quarter

Pit.—FG, N. Johnson 24, 1:50.

Jac.—Quinn 15 run (Hollis kick), 6:38.

Jac.—F. Taylor 9 pass from Quinn (Hollis kick), 11:56.

Third Quarter

Jac.—F. Taylor 12 run (Hollis kick), 3:22.

Attendance—74,143.

	Pittsburgh	Jacksonville
First downs	20	16
Rushes-yards	36-205	33-129
Passing	156	168
Punt returns	2-4	2-10
Kickoff returns	4-77	2-40
Interception returns	0-0	2-0
Comp.-att.-int.	17-37-2	10-19-0
Sacked-yards lost	2-18	3-24
Punts	4-41	7-42
Fumbles-lost	1-1	1-0
Penalties-yards	7-79	7-60
Time of possession	33:47	26:13

INDIVIDUAL STATISTICS

RUSHING—Pittsburgh, Bettis 26-139, Stewart 10-66. Jacksonville, F. Taylor 21-71, G. Jones 8-35, Quinn 4-23.

PASSING—Pittsburgh, Stewart 17-37-2-174. Jacksonville, Quinn 10-19-0-192.

RECEIVING—Pittsburgh, C. Johnson 4-61, Bettis 4-24, Bruener 3-22, Blackwell 2-23, Hawkins 2-17, Ward 1-24, Lester 1-3. Jacksonville, McCardell 3-85, J. Smith 3-62, Mitchell 2-24, F. Taylor 2-21.

MISSED FIELD GOAL ATTEMPTS—Pittsburgh, N. Johnson 47.

INTERCEPTIONS—Jacksonville, Devine 1-0, Thomas 1-0.

KICKOFF RETURNS—Pittsburgh, Dunn 4-77. Jacksonville, G. Jones 1-21, Barlow 1-19.

PUNT RETURNS—Pittsburgh, Hawkins 2-4. Jacksonville, Barlow 2-10.

SACKS—Pittsburgh, Lake 1, Roye 1, Holmes 1. Jacksonville, Paup 1, Brackens 0.5, Smeenge 0.5.

WILD-CARD GAMES

MIAMI 24, BUFFALO 17

Why the Dolphins won: Their defense made a lot of big plays, recovering three fumbles and picking off a Doug Flutie pass at the Miami 1-yard line late in the first half. Defensive end Trace Armstrong contributed to the biggest play of the day when he sacked Flutie at the Miami 5 with 17 seconds to play, causing the quarterback to fumble. The Dolphins recovered to end Buffalo's final possession.

Why the Bills lost: Whenever they gained any kind of momentum, they seemed to give it right back to Miami. In addition to five turnovers, Andre Reed was called for unsportsmanlike conduct and ejected with 1:47 to play after he bumped an official. Reed thought he had scored a touchdown, but the officials ruled otherwise. The Bills were penalized 15 yards for Reed's folly and settled for a field goal.

The turning points:

1. On the first play of the game, Buffalo wide receiver Eric Moulds beat Dolphins cornerback Terrell Buckley for a 65-yard gain down the middle of the field. Moulds had a clear path to the end zone but Buckley was able to sneak up from behind and bat the ball away. Brock Marion recovered for Miami.

2. Marion intercepted a Flutie pass at the Dolphins' 1-yard line late in the second quarter, ending a Buffalo drive.

3. Reed's bump of field judge Steve Zimmer with less than two minutes to play essentially took the wind out of Buffalo's sails, with the Bills having to settle for three points instead of a seemingly guaranteed touchdown.

Notable: Moulds set an NFL playoff record with 240 yards receiving, topping Anthony Carter's mark of 227 yards against San Francisco in 1987. . . . Flutie was 21-of-36 passing for 360 yards with one interception and one touchdown. Dan Marino was 23-for-34 for 235 yards with one touchdown and one interception. . . . The game was the last for the Bills' Mark Pike, who was a starter in just one of 173 career games but retired with a club-record 273 special teams tackles.

Quotable: Armstrong, on his game-saving sack of Flutie: "I didn't know if I could make it into the locker room if I tried to walk right away. Even when I was out there before the last play, I didn't know if I could go another play." . . . Miami linebacker Zach Thomas, expressing his team's sentiments after Armstrong bowled over Bills running back Thurman Thomas to get to Flutie: "There's always anger when Thurman's around.". . . Flutie, on Reed getting tossed from the game: "Without him we were one receiver short. Everybody had to switch around and play a different position. You want your best athletes on the field." . . . Reed, on the same play: "I've never been thrown out of a game like that for a dumb reason. In a playoff game like that, it's just uncalled for."

DOLPHINS 24, BILLS 17

Saturday, January 2

Buffalo	0	7	7	3—17
Miami	3	3	8	10—24

First Quarter

Mia.—FG, Mare 31, 8:53.

Second Quarter

Mia.—FG, Mare 40, 4:24.
Buf.—Thomas 1 run (Christie kick), 6:06.

Third Quarter

Mia.—Abdul-Jabbar 3 run (Pritchett run), 12:28.
Buf.—Moulds 32 pass from Flutie (Christie kick), 14:12.

Fourth Quarter

Mia.—FG, Mare 23, 5:15.
Mia.—L. Thomas 11 pass from Marino (Mare kick), 11:18.
Buf.—FG, Christie 33, 13:27.
Attendance—72,698.

	Buffalo	Miami
First downs	23	25
Rushes-yards	18-77	34-117
Passing	339	228
Punt returns	0-0	1-20
Kickoff returns	4-54	3-65
Interception returns	1-0	1-19
Comp.-att.-int.	21-36-1	23-34-1
Sacked-yards lost	3-21	1-7
Punts	2-37	1-34
Fumbles-lost	4-4	0-0
Penalties-yards	9-93	6-75
Time of possession	22:28	37:32

INDIVIDUAL STATISTICS

RUSHING—Buffalo, Thomas 7-33, A. Smith 7-15, Flutie 4-29. Miami, Abdul-Jabbar 27-95, Parmalee 2-10, Pritchett 2-7, Avery 1-3, McDuffie 1-3, Marino 1-(minus 1).

PASSING—Buffalo, Flutie 21-36-1-360. Miami, Marino 23-34-1-235.

RECEIVING—Buffalo, Moulds 9-240, Reed 5-60, K. Williams 2-20, A. Smith 1-12, Loud 1-12, Gash 1-9, Riemersma 1-4, Thomas 1-3. Miami, McDuffie 6-53, Gadsden 5-85, L. Thomas 4-36, Drayton 3-20, Perry 2-29, Abdul-Jabbar 2-4, Ruddy 1-8.

MISSED FIELD GOAL ATTEMPTS—Miami, Mare 26.

INTERCEPTIONS—Buffalo, Jackson 1-0. Miami, Marion 1-19.

KICKOFF RETURNS—Buffalo, K. Williams 4-54. Miami, Avery 3-65.

PUNT RETURNS—Miami, McDuffie 1-20.

SACKS—Buffalo, Wiley 1. Miami, Armstrong 1, R. Jones 0.5, Gardener 0.5, Rodgers 0.5, Tanner 0.5.

JACKSONVILLE 25, NEW ENGLAND 10

Why the Jaguars won: Rookie running back Fred Taylor ran for 162 yards and a touchdown on 33 carries. Quarterback Mark Brunell returned from a four-week injury layoff to provide the offensive spark the Jaguars badly needed in the second half.

Why the Patriots lost: They couldn't compensate for injuries to many players. Quarterback Drew Bledsoe watched from the sideline because of a broken index finger on his throwing hand. Backup Scott Zolak made his third start in eight NFL seasons. The Patriots failed to convert on their first seven third-down opportunities.

The turning points:

1. Taylor's 46-yard run in the first quarter set up Mike Hollis' second field goal, giving the Jaguars a 6-0 lead.

2. Brunell marched the Jaguars 68 yards in the second quarter, ending with Taylor's 13-yard touchdown run. While the two-point conversion attempt failed, the Jaguars increased their lead to 12-0.

3. In the fourth quarter, Brunell hit Jimmy Smith for a touchdown pass just inside the back of the end zone. The touchdown broke any momentum New England thought it had and extended the Jaguars' lead to 18-10.

Notable: In addition to Bledsoe, the Patriots played without wide receiver Terry Glenn and linebacker Ted Johnson. . . . Taylor's 33 rushing attempts were a club playoff record, while his 162 yards were the third-most by a rookie running back in pro football playoff history. Washington's Timmy Smith rushed for 204 in Super Bowl 22, and Paul Lowe of the Los Angeles Chargers rushed for 165 against Houston on January 1, 1961. . . . Zolak passed for 190 yards on 21-of-44 attempts with no touchdowns and an interception. . . . Brunell passed for 161 yards on 14-for-34 accuracy with no interceptions and a touchdown. . . . New England rookie Robert Edwards rushed for 28 yards on 17 carries. The Patriots averaged just 1.8 yards per rushing attempt. Taylor, meanwhile, had runs of 46, 21 and 13 yards. . . . The playoff victory was the first for Jacksonville since a 30-27 upset win at Denver in 1996.

Quotable: Taylor, on the comparisons between himself and fellow rookie Edwards: "Coming into this game, everybody said it was 'Robert vs. Fred.' It wasn't that. I wasn't going to tackle him." . . . Brunell, on his return to the lineup after a one-month layoff: "It was a little difficult. I was able to move a little bit, and as the game went on it started feeling all right." . . . Jacksonville linebacker Kevin Hardy, on Edwards: "Robert Edwards is not the type to go down with the first hit. A lot of times it was the second or third guy who made the tackle." . . . Patriots coach Pete Carroll on Zolak: "You just have to close it out when you make those drives, and we didn't do it."

JAGUARS 25, PATRIOTS 10

Sunday, January 3

New England.........................	0	0	7	3—10
Jacksonville	6	6	0	13—25

First Quarter
Jac.—FG, Hollis 35, 6:03
Jac.—FG, Hollis 24, 12:59.

Second Quarter
Jac.—F. Taylor 13 run (run failed), 9:02.

Third Quarter
N.E.—Edwards 1 run (Vinatieri kick), 10:33.

Fourth Quarter
N.E.—FG, Vinatieri 27, 0:12.
Jac.—J. Smith 37 pass from Brunell (Hollis kick), 2:36.
Jac.—FG, Hollis 34, 9:08.
Jac.—FG, Hollis 21, 13:16.
   Attendance—71,139.

	New England	Jacksonville
First downs...........................	14	17
Rushes-yards........................	19-35	37-160
Passing.................................	171	148
Punt returns..........................	4-27	7-72
Kickoff returns......................	7-99	3-66
Interception returns	0-0	1-17
Comp.-att.-int.	21-44-1	14-34-0
Sacked-yards lost	2-19	2-13
Punts	8-47	6-45
Fumbles-lost.........................	4-2	1-0
Penalties-yards.....................	6-50	4-35
Time of possession...............	28:00	32:00

INDIVIDUAL STATISTICS

RUSHING—New England, Edwards 17-28, S. Shaw 1-4, Ton. Carter 1-3. Jacksonville, F. Taylor 33-162, Brunell 4-(minus 2).

PASSING—New England, Zolak 21-44-1-190. Jacksonville, Brunell 14-34-0-161.

RECEIVING—New England, Brown 4-46, Jefferson 4-30, Simmons 3-42, Edwards 3-33, Cullors 2-17, Coates 2-10, Ton. Carter 2-3, Purnell 1-9. Jacksonville, McCardell 6-72, J. Smith 5-56, Mitchell 1-22, D. Jones 1-8, Shelton 1-3.

MISSED FIELD GOAL ATTEMPTS—None.

INTERCEPTIONS—Jacksonville, Hudson 1-17.

KICKOFF RETURNS—New England, Cullors 6-85, S. Shaw 1-14. Jacksonville, Barlow 3-66.

PUNT RETURNS—New England, Brown 4-27. Jacksonville, Barlow 7-72.

SACKS—New England, Spires 2. Jacksonville, Brackens 1, Smeenge 1.

ARIZONA 20, DALLAS 7

Why the Cardinals won: Arizona, the much younger team, was able to use its youth and speed on offense and defense to stifle the Cowboys. Jake Plummer and the offense produced the Cardinals' two longest plays of the season, while the defense effectively shut down the Dallas receivers. Plummer was not sacked and the Cardinals did not fumble.

Why the Cowboys lost: Troy Aikman was sacked four times and threw three interceptions. The Cowboys, who beat Arizona twice during the regular season, looked sluggish and appeared to take the Cardinals lightly. Dallas had just two scoring opportunities in the first three quarters and failed to convert on either.

The turning points:

1. Plummer and wide receiver Frank Sanders connected on a 59-yard play in the first quarter, setting up Arizona's first score.

2. On fourth and 1 from the Arizona 7 in the second quarter, the Cardinals made Dallas pay for the decision not to go for a field goal, stopping Emmitt Smith for a 1-yard loss.

3. On the second play of the second half, Adrian Murrell broke a 74-yard run to the Dallas 3. Plummer then passed to Larry Centers for a touchdown and a 17-0 Arizona lead. Murrell's run was the Cardinals' longest play of the season.

Notable: The playoff victory was the first for the Cardinals since 1947, when Harry Truman was in the White House and current team owner Bill Bidwill was a team waterboy. . . . The Cowboys had beaten the Cardinals in 16 of the teams' previous 17 meetings. . . . Murrell led Arizona with 95 yards rushing on 12 carries, while Smith led Dallas with 74 yards on 16 carries . . . Deion Sanders returned to the Dallas lineup after being out for six weeks because of an injured toe . . . The loss was Dallas' worst in the postseason since dropping a 38-6 decision to Detroit in 1991. . . . The last team to beat Dallas in the postseason at Texas Stadium was the Los Angeles Rams in 1983.

Quotable: Cardinals linebacker Jamir Miller, on the Cowboys' ineptitude: "They couldn't do anything on us. Trickery, gadgets, it wasn't going to work." . . . Arizona coach Vince Tobin, on other teams' perceptions of his team: "I don't think anybody's afraid of the Cardinals. Everybody thinks it's a pretty good break in the schedule to get the Cardinals." . . . Deion Sanders, on the Cowboys' sluggishness: "This team is not getting any younger. It's time for some guys to step up or step out." . . . Aikman, on the same subject: "We didn't play well. Why didn't we? I don't have the answer for that." . . . Plummer, on other teams' perception of the Cardinals: "I'm tired of all that talk about streaks. The past is the past. We can't do anything about it. We're living in the present."

CARDINALS 20, COWBOYS 7

Saturday, January 2

Arizona	7	3	7	3—20
Dallas	0	0	0	7— 7

First Quarter
Ariz.—Murrell 12 pass from Plummer (Jacke kick), 12:13.

Second Quarter
Ariz.—FG, Jacke 37, 14:41.

Third Quarter
Ariz.—Centers 3 pass from Plummer (Jacke kick), 1:16.

Fourth Quarter
Ariz.—FG, Jacke 46, 2:05.
Dal.—B. Davis 6 pass from Aikman (Cunningham kick), 11:27.
Attendance—62,969.

	Arizona	Dallas
First downs	14	20
Rushes-yards	29-133	20-96
Passing	213	164
Punt returns	3-11	3-52
Kickoff returns	0-0	5-103
Interception returns	3-42	2-19
Comp.-att.-int.	19-36-2	22-49-3
Sacked-yards lost	0-0	4-27
Punts	8-38	6-41
Fumbles-lost	0-0	2-0
Penalties-yards	7-55	5-35
Time of possession	30:02	29:58

INDIVIDUAL STATISTICS

RUSHING—Arizona, Murrell 12-95, Bates 11-32, Centers 3-5, Plummer 3-1. Dallas, E. Smith 16-74, S. Williams 3-22, Aikman 1-0.

PASSING—Arizona, Plummer 19-36-2-213. Dallas, Aikman 22-49-3-191.

RECEIVING—Arizona, R. Moore 5-41, Sanders 3-72, Metcalf 3-48, Centers 3-16, Murrell 2-16, Gedney 2-15, McWilliams 1-5. Dallas, Jeffers 7-92, Irvin 4-32, B. Davis 4-25, Bjornson 2-12, S. Williams 2-6, E. Smith 1-10, Clay 1-9, Johnston 1-5.

MISSED FIELD GOAL ATTEMPTS—Dallas, Cunningham 36.

INTERCEPTIONS—Arizona, A. Williams 2-0, Bennett 1-42. Dallas, Woodson 1-19, Mathis 1-0.

KICKOFF RETURNS—Dallas, Hughes 5-103.

PUNT RETURNS—Arizona, Metcalf 3-11. Dallas, Sanders 2-41, Hughes 1-11.

SACKS—Arizona, Miller 2, Wadsworth 2.

SAN FRANCISCO 30, GREEN BAY 27

Why the 49ers won: They were able to run the ball more effectively than anyone could have imagined, with Garrison Hearst getting 128 of the team's 178 rushing yards. Wide receiver Terrell Owens, who had fumbled and dropped several passes, caught a 25-yard touchdown pass from Steve Young with three seconds left in the game.

Why the Packers lost: They turned over the ball four times, and their defense badly misplayed the final play. Three Packers were around Owens as the pass settled into his hands, but none touched him until it was too late.

The turning points:

1. A 40-yard field goal by Wade Richey gave the 49ers a 23-20 lead with 6:12 left.

2. Darnell Walker picked off a Brett Favre pass with 5:53 to play, but the 49ers couldn't capitalize, going three-and-out. Favre was able to march his team down the field and connect with Antonio Freeman for a 15-yard score, giving the Packers a 27-23 lead.

3. A controversial non-call on what appeared to be a fumble by wide receiver Jerry Rice with eight seconds remaining aided the 49ers.

Notable: Defensive lineman Charles Haley, who retired because of a chronic back injury in 1996, returned to the San Francisco lineup and played reasonably well, forcing Favre into a second-half interception. . . . The victory ended San Francisco's run of five straight losses to the Packers, including games in the previous three playoffs. . . . The Packers failed in their bid to become the first NFC team to reach the Super Bowl three straight years. . . . Young completed 18-of-32 passes for 182 yards, with 76 yards coming on the final drive. . . . Greg Clark caught touchdown passes of 1 and 8 yards for San Francisco. . . . Dorsey Levens rushed for 116 yards and a touchdown on 27 carries for Green Bay. . . . The game was the final one for Mike Holmgren as Packers coach. He resigned to accept a job as G.M./coach of the Seahawks.

Quotable: Owens, on his game-winning catch: "I was just hoping to have a chance to catch the ball.". . . San Francisco coach Steve Mariucci, on Owens' game-winning catch: "He was frustrated because he dropped a couple passes. I told him to keep playing and have a short memory. When he caught that TD, he became a little emotional." . . . Young, on the 49ers' five straight losses to the Packers and his 0-9 record against Green Bay: "We've been wanting to have a game with them." . . . Former Packer and current 49er Gabe Wilkins: "I knew it was going to come down to the end, but not like that." . . . Packers coach Mike Holmgren, on the game's final result: "You don't want to lose a game like that. It is the worst way that could possibly happen."

49ERS 30, PACKERS 27

Sunday, January 3

Green Bay	3	14	0	10—27
San Francisco	7	3	10	10—30

First Quarter
G.B.—FG, Longwell 23, 5:34.
S.F.—Clark 1 pass from S. Young (Richey kick), 10:50.
Second Quarter
G.B.—Freeman 2 pass from Favre (Longwell kick), 0:04.
S.F.—FG, Richey 34, 8:07.
G.B.—Levens 2 run (Longwell kick), 14:29.
Third Quarter
S.F.—Clark 8 pass from S. Young (Richey kick), 5:58.
S.F.—FG, Richey 48, 12:48.
Fourth Quarter
G.B.—FG, Longwell 37, 3:09.
S.F.—FG, Richey 40, 8:48.
G.B.—Freeman 15 pass from Favre (Longwell kick), 13:04.
S.F.—Owens 25 pass from S. Young (Richey kick), 14:57.
Attendance—66,506.

	Green Bay	San Francisco
First downs	24	20
Rushes-yards	28-121	31-178
Passing	282	169
Punt returns	1-0	2-26
Kickoff returns	7-194	6-128
Interception returns	2-0	2-20
Comp.-att.-int.	20-35-2	18-32-2
Sacked-yards lost	1-10	2-13
Punts	2-51	3-40
Fumbles-lost	3-2	1-1
Penalties-yards	4-42	6-50
Time of possession	28:57	31:03

INDIVIDUAL STATISTICS

RUSHING—Green Bay, Levens 27-116, Freeman 1-5. San Francisco, Hearst 22-128, Kirby 5-32, S. Young 3-16, Edwards 1-2.

PASSING—Green Bay, Favre 20-35-2-292. San Francisco, S. Young 18-32-2-182.

RECEIVING—Green Bay, Levens 6-37, Freeman 4-75, Henderson 3-55, Bradford 2-53, R. Brooks 2-31, Mayes 1-20, Chmura 1-12, T. Davis 1-9. San Francisco, Stokes 5-58, Owens 3-73, Hearst 3-15, Clark 3-13, Kirby 2-14, Rice 1-6, Edwards 1-3.

MISSED FIELD GOAL ATTEMPTS—Green Bay, Longwell 50.

INTERCEPTIONS—Green Bay, Koonce 1-0, Sharper 1-0. San Francisco, Woodall 1-17, Walker 1-3.

KICKOFF RETURNS—Green Bay, Preston 7-194. San Francisco, McQuarters 6-128.

PUNT RETURNS—Green Bay, Preston 1-0. San Francisco, McQuarters 2-26.

SACKS—Green Bay, B. Harris 1, Holliday 1. San Francisco, Doleman 1.

1998 REVIEW *Wild-card games*

DIVISIONAL PLAYOFFS

AFC

DENVER 38, MIAMI 3

Why the Broncos won: After gaining only 29 yards in a regular-season loss at Miami 19 days earlier, Terrell Davis rushed for 199 yards on 21 carries with two touchdowns. Davis' performance was the sixth-best in NFL playoff history and best in Broncos history.

Why the Dolphins lost: The defensive line, playing without injured Jason Taylor and Tim Bowens, surrendered huge holes to Denver's line, the lightest in the league. The Dolphins were outrushed 250-14.

The turning points:

1. The first time the Dolphins had the ball they dropped two of quarterback Dan Marino's passes.

2. Davis got off to a quick start, rushing for 34 yards on his first four carries. He ran for a 1-yard TD to cap the Broncos' 14-play, 92-yard game-opening drive.

3. John Elway threw a 33-yard pass to Ed McCaffrey, then Davis ran for a 20-yard score to give the Broncos a 14-0 lead.

Notable: Davis had 100 yards rushing by early in the second quarter and broke a 62-yard run to start the second half. . . . On the day of the game, Davis was named the league's MVP. . . . The Broncos averaged 6.6 yards per rush, the Dolphins 1.1. . . . The victory over Miami gave Elway at least one win over every NFL team in his 16-year career.

Quotable: Davis, on coach Mike Shanahan's game plan: "That formation, it opened up some wide holes for us, especially on the cutback. They saw everybody lined up on the right side. Cutting against the grain was there all day." . . . More Davis: "Any time you rush for 29 yards in a game, it's going to light a little fire underneath you. You want to go out there and do a little better. But it wasn't just me. I could sense that from everybody on our offense. The linemen wanted to go out and block better." . . . Denver end Neil Smith, on why he hesitated before running 79 yards for a touchdown on a fumble recovery: "There were so many funny calls this year, I didn't want to run that far and have it not count. I was looking at the refs to see if the whistle had blown. If it was another 5 yards, I probably would have died." . . . Smith, on the slowness of his run: "I think a piano jumped on my back after about 20 yards." . . . Miami coach Jimmy Johnson: "Not to take anything away from Denver—they played a great ball game— but our guys were pretty worn down coming out of last week (a 24-17 first-round win over Buffalo). Our tank was pretty much empty today." . . . Denver tight end Shannon Sharpe on the Dolphins, who were trying to become the first team to play in a Super Bowl held in their home city: "I did ask them, 'How does it feel to have the Super Bowl at your house and you're not invited?' " . . . More Sharpe: "The Dolphins are a sorry group. Marino looks like he needs to get his retirement papers ready."

BRONCOS 38, DOLPHINS 3

Saturday, January 9

Miami	0	3	0	0— 3
Denver	14	7	3	14—38

First Quarter
Den.—Davis 1 run (Elam kick), 9:05.
Den.—Davis 20 run (Elam kick), 13:58.

Second Quarter
Mia.—FG, Mare 22, 4:53.
Den.—Loville 11 run (Elam kick), 10:21.

Third Quarter
Den.—FG, Elam 32, 3:08.

Fourth Quarter
Den.—R. Smith 28 pass from Elway (Elam kick), 1:37.
Den.—N. Smith 79 fumble return (Elam kick), 5:11.
Attendance—75,729.

	Miami	Denver
First downs	14	24
Rushes-yards	13-14	38-250
Passing	238	174
Punt returns	1-11	2-14
Kickoff returns	5-121	1-19
Interception returns	0-0	2-48
Comp.-att.-int.	26-37-2	14-23-0
Sacked-yards lost	1-5	1-8
Punts	5-46	2-49
Fumbles-lost	1-1	0-0
Penalties-yards	10-57	5-41
Time of possession	27:36	32:24

INDIVIDUAL STATISTICS

RUSHING—Miami, Parmalee 7-14, Abdul-Jabbar 3-5, Huard 2-(minus 2), Pritchett 1-(minus 3). Denver, Davis 21-199, Loville 8-34, Brister 6-(minus 2), Elway 3-19.

PASSING—Miami, Marino 26-37-2-243. Denver, Elway 14-23-0-182.

RECEIVING—Miami, McDuffie 9-118, Parmalee 5-24, Gadsden 4-36, L. Thomas 3-31, Pritchett 3-23, Jacquet 1-6, Abdul-Jabbar 1-5. Denver, Sharpe 5-38, R. Smith 4-71, McCaffrey 3-52, Griffith 1-14, Davis 1-7.

MISSED FIELD GOAL ATTEMPTS—None.

INTERCEPTIONS—Denver, Johnson 1-48, Romanowski 1-0.

KICKOFF RETURNS—Miami, Avery 5-121. Denver, Hebron 1-19.

PUNT RETURNS—Miami, Buckley 1-11. Denver, Gordon 2-14.

SACKS—Miami, Wilson 1. Denver, Washington 1.

1998 REVIEW Divisional playoffs

N.Y. JETS 34, JACKSONVILLE 24

Why the Jets won: Keyshawn Johnson caught a touchdown pass, ran for a score and, after being inserted as an extra defensive back, intercepted a Mark Brunell pass with 9 seconds left. Johnson, who caught nine passes for 121 passes in his normal role as a wide receiver, also recovered a Jacksonville fumble.

Why the Jaguars lost: They blew the coverage on Johnson's touchdown catch, botched a lateral after a fumble return and, after picking off a pass in their end zone, ill-advisedly attempted to make a return.

The turning points:

1. Jacksonville safety Chris Hudson recovered a Curtis Martin fumble and, after returning the ball almost 50 yards, tried to lateral to teammate Dave Thomas. The ball bounced loose, and Johnson recovered. New York then scored on Johnson's 10-yard run with 33 seconds left in the first half to take a 17-0 lead.

2. Brunell threw a 52-yard pass to Jimmy Smith on the last play of the half to cut the Jets' lead to 17-7.

3. With the Jets leading 31-24 late in the game, rookie safety Donovan Darius intercepted a Vinny Testaverde pass in his end zone. But instead of downing the ball, Darius tried for a return and was tackled inside the 1-yard line. The Jaguars couldn't pick up a first down and turned over the ball on downs. New York's John Hall kicked his second field goal to finish the scoring.

Notable: Johnson became the second NFL player to run for a score, catch a touchdown pass, intercept a pass and recover a fumble in a playoff game. Jack Manders did it in the 1937 championship game for the Bears against the Redskins. . . . Johnson and Martin became the third and fourth Jets to score two touchdowns in a playoff game. Don Maynard did it in a 1968 win against the Raiders and Freeman McNeil did it in a 1985 loss to the Patriots. . . . The Jets controlled the ball for 39:16 to the Jaguars' 20:44.

Quotable: Testaverde: "There are a lot of teams with a lot more talent than us. But it's hard to measure the heart, and these guys have tremendous heart." . . . New York fullback Keith Byars, on Johnson: "He wants to go down as one of the top receivers. You can't do that after your third year. You have to do that after time. But he's shown every indication he's going to do that." . . . Jaguars' coach Tom Coughlin, on Hudson's lateral: "Just a foolish mistake. A dumb mistake, and Chris feels very badly about that." . . . Jets linebacker Mo Lewis, on Hudson: "Desperate teams do desperate things. That player, he's probably sitting on the bus now saying, 'Why did I do that?' " . . . Darius, on his attempt to return the interception: "When I caught the ball, the receiver hit me, and when I got up, my eyes were kind of blurred, so I really didn't know where I was at."

JETS 34, JAGUARS 24

Sunday, January 10

Jacksonville	0	7	7	10—24
N.Y. Jets	7	10	14	3—34

First Quarter
NYJ—K. Johnson 21 pass from Testaverde (Hall kick), 4:34.

Second Quarter
NYJ—FG, Hall 52, 4:25.
NYJ—K. Johnson 10 run (Hall kick), 14:27.
Jac.—J. Smith 52 pass from Brunell (Hollis kick), 15:00.

Third Quarter
NYJ—Martin 1 run (Hall kick), 5:47.
Jac.—McCardell 3 pass from Brunell (Hollis kick), 6:52.
NYJ—Martin 1 run (Hall kick), 12:44.

Fourth Quarter
Jac.—J. Smith 19 pass from Brunell (Hollis kick), 5:02.
Jac.—FG, Hollis 37, 8:22.
NYJ—FG, Hall 30, 14:36.
Attendance—78,817.

	Jacksonville	N.Y. Jets
First downs	14	29
Rushes-yards	22-95	39-151
Passing	156	278
Punt returns	2-(-3)	1-4
Kickoff returns	7-158	4-59
Interception returns	1-1	3-40
Comp.-att.-int.	12-31-3	24-36-1
Sacked-yards lost	0-0	2-6
Punts	3-37	2-35
Fumbles-lost	1-1	2-2
Penalties-yards	3-25	5-38
Time of possession	20:44	39:16

INDIVIDUAL STATISTICS

RUSHING—Jacksonville, F. Taylor 20-86, Brunell 2-9. New York, Martin 36-124, K. Johnson 2-28, Testaverde 1-(minus 1).

PASSING—Jacksonville, Brunell 12-31-3-156. New York, Testaverde 24-36-1-284.

RECEIVING—Jacksonville, J. Smith 5-104, McCardell 4-32, Mitchell 2-13, Banks 1-7. New York, K. Johnson 9-121, Martin 6-58, Chrebet 4-45, Byars 2-11, Ward 1-18, Brady 1-17, Meggett 1-14.

MISSED FIELD GOAL ATTEMPTS—None.

INTERCEPTIONS—Jacksonville, Darius 1-1. New York, Brown 1-40, Smith 1-0, K. Johnson 1-0.

KICKOFF RETURNS—Jacksonville, Barlow 3-118, Banks 3-40, D. Jones 1-0. New York, Meggett 4-59.

PUNT RETURNS—Jacksonville, Barlow 1-5, Devine 1-(minus 8). New York, Meggett 1-4.

SACKS—Jacksonville, Hardy 1, Curry 1.

ATLANTA 20, SAN FRANCISCO 18

Why the Falcons won: Jamal Anderson ran like he did all season, rushing for two touchdowns in the first half to give Atlanta a 14-0 lead. Anderson, the NFC's leading rusher in 1998, had 113 yards on 29 carries.

Why the 49ers lost: Garrison Hearst suffered a broken leg on the first play of the game, and sub Terry Kirby played with an injured leg. As a result, the 49ers mostly abandoned the run, and Steve Young threw three second-half interceptions.

The turning points:

1. With the 49ers trailing 14-10 in the third quarter, Young was intercepted by free safety Eugene Robinson at the Atlanta 3. Robinson returned the interception 77 yards to set up a 29-yard field goal by Morten Andersen.

2. With the Falcons trying to run out the clock, Anderson ran out of bounds on a third-down play, giving the 49ers one last chance to win the game. Atlanta punted, but rookie R.W. McQuarters lost 7 yards on the return, and the 49ers had to start from their 4 with 38 seconds left. Young's desperation pass on the last play was intercepted by safety William White.

Notable: Atlanta coach Dan Reeves returned to the sidelines a little more than three weeks after undergoing heart bypass surgery. Team doctors stood nearby. . . . The win was Atlanta's 10th in a row. . . . The playoff game was only the eighth in the Falcons' 33-year history. . . . The 49ers called 17 consecutive pass plays at one point in the first half. . . . Young's three interceptions matched his career high. . . . 49ers receiver Jerry Rice set an NFL record by catching a pass in his 23rd consecutive playoff game.

Quotable: Falcons linebacker Henri Crockett, on Reeves' return: "The guy had his chest opened up three weeks ago and he's coaching, and you just got to lay it on the line for that guy." . . . Reeves, about why he wasn't so vocal on the sidelines: "My emotions are there. Something I don't have is the lung capacity to be loud." . . . 49ers coach Steve Mariucci, on Hearst's injury: "That was an emotional thing for the first play of the game, and out comes another stretcher. That could've been a devastating thing, but we kept playing." . . . Atlanta quarterback Chris Chandler, on playoff pressure: "People say we don't have playoff experience. But look what Arizona did at Dallas. It's still a football game. You just have to be well-prepared and keep a level head." . . . Young: "I wanted to play perfectly. Especially with the running game and Garrison out, that put a big load on me." . . . Atlanta linebacker Cornelius Bennett, on the 49ers cutting the Falcons' lead to 14-10: "We let 'em back in, and we were upset at halftime. We just told ourselves, if they don't score any more, they won't win."

FALCONS 20, 49ERS 18

Saturday, January 9

San Francisco	0	10	0	8—18
Atlanta	7	7	3	3—20

First Quarter
Atl.—J. Anderson 2 run (Andersen kick), 8:35.

Second Quarter
Atl.—J. Anderson 34 run (Andersen kick), 11:48.
S.F.—Rice 17 pass from S. Young (Richey kick), 13:50.
S.F.—FG, Richey 36, 15:00.

Third Quarter
Atl.—FG, Andersen 29, 13:44.

Fourth Quarter
Atl.—FG, Andersen 32, 4:27.
S.F.—S. Young 8 run (Clark pass from Detmer), 12:03.
Attendance—70,262.

	San Fran.	Atlanta
First downs	15	16
Rushes-yards	20-46	33-136
Passing	288	153
Punt returns	1-(-7)	3-40
Kickoff returns	3-57	1-23
Interception returns	1-4	3-91
Comp.-att.-int.	23-37-3	13-19-1
Sacked-yards lost	1-1	2-16
Punts	4-47	3-41
Fumbles-lost	2-0	0-0
Penalties-yards	8-47	6-51
Time of possession	27:17	32:43

INDIVIDUAL STATISTICS

RUSHING—San Francisco, Kirby 9-22, S. Young 6-19, Edwards 3-4, Hearst 1-7, Levy 1-(minus 6). Atlanta, J. Anderson 29-113, Chandler 3-7, Downs 1-16.

PASSING—San Francisco, S. Young 23-37-3-289. Atlanta, Chandler 13-19-1-169.

RECEIVING—San Francisco, Owens 8-73, Stokes 5-76, Rice 3-63, Levy 2-58, Kirby 2-7, Edwards 2-3, Clark 1-9. Atlanta, Mathis 5-71, Martin 4-63, Kozlowski 2-3, Harris 1-22, J. Anderson 1-10.

MISSED FIELD GOAL ATTEMPTS—None.

INTERCEPTIONS—San Francisco, Bryant 1-4. Atlanta, White 2-14, Robinson 1-77.

KICKOFF RETURNS—San Francisco, McQuarters 3-57. Atlanta, Dwight 1-23.

PUNT RETURNS—San Francisco, McQuarters 1-(minus 7). Atlanta, Dwight 3-40.

SACKS—San Francisco, Doleman 1, Bonham 1. Atlanta, Tuaolo 1.

1998 REVIEW Divisional playoffs

MINNESOTA 41, ARIZONA 21

Why the Vikings won: They got off to an early lead and never were headed. Minnesota led 17-0 before Arizona gained a yard from scrimmage, and the Cardinals never got closer than 10 points. The Vikings scored on seven of their 10 possessions in a thoroughly dominating performance.

Why the Cardinals lost: Jake Plummer, rattled by the roar of the Metrodome fans, couldn't move his team until well into the second quarter. At one point, the Vikings had 203 yards of offense to the Cardinals' minus 1. Plummer threw two interceptions and no touchdown passes.

The turning points:

1. The Vikings consumed nearly half of the first quarter with a 13-play, 80-yard drive that resulted in their first score. Leroy Hoard scored the first of his three touchdowns on a 1-yard run. The Cardinals were concentrating on stopping Minnesota's big-play passing game, but Hoard and Robert Smith, who rushed for 124 yards, hurt the Cardinals on the ground.

2. Plummer threw two interceptions to safety Robert Griffith in the second quarter, and the Vikings scored 10 points off the turnovers in a 1:21 span.

3. After Arizona scored to cut Minnesota's lead to 24-14 in the third quarter, David Palmer returned the kickoff 38 yards. Randall Cunningham then threw a 45-yard pass to Cris Carter to set up a Gary Anderson field goal.

Notable: Smith's 124 yards and Hoard's three touchdowns were Vikings playoff records. . . . Arizona running back Mario Bates had an unusual game: 4 carries, 3 yards and three touchdowns, all on 1-yard runs. . . . Largely due to the noise, the Cardinals' offense was penalized four times for false starts. . . . Arizona defensive ends Simeon Rice and Andre Wadsworth, who combined for 15 sacks during the season, were held to a combined two tackles by Vikings tackles Todd Steussie and Korey Stringer.

Quotable: Carter: "The initial drive was tremendous, given that they came into the game saying we couldn't drive the ball, that we were just big plays. We drove the ball from the 20 to the end zone. That takes something out of the defense." . . . Plummer: "We have not been in a place this loud. The first interception was a case of me being young and hyped up and wanting to make a big play when I should be patient." . . . Vikings receiver Randy Moss: "It was so loud today, I was sitting beside Cris and he couldn't hear me, and I couldn't hear him." . . . Cardinals' running back Adrian Murrell: "We definitely tasted success this season, and once you've done that, you remember it. This season will go a long ways in helping us prepare for next season." . . . Cunningham, on the importance of the win considering the Vikings were to meet Atlanta in the NFC title game the following week: "Appreciate it, but don't have a party. The party is at the end."

VIKINGS 41, CARDINALS 21

Sunday, January 10

Arizona	0	7	7	7—21
Minnesota	7	17	10	7—41

First Quarter
Min.—Hoard 1 run (Anderson kick), 7:20.

Second Quarter
Min.—Glover 15 pass from Cunningham (Anderson kick), 2:15.
Min.—FG, Anderson 34, 3:36.
Ariz.—Bates 1 run (Jacke kick), 11:28.
Min.—Hoard 16 pass from Cunningham (Anderson kick), 14:36.

Third Quarter
Ariz.—Bates 1 run (Jacke kick), 7:35.
Min.—FG, Anderson 20, 11:01.
Min.—R. Moss 2 pass from Cunningham (Anderson kick), 13:29.

Fourth Quarter
Ariz.—Bates 1 run (Jacke kick), 3:15.
Min.—Hoard 6 run (Anderson kick), 10:27.
Attendance—63,760.

	Arizona	Minnesota
First downs	23	26
Rushes-yards	23-74	36-188
Passing	242	228
Punt returns	1-36	1-2
Kickoff returns	3-66	4-97
Interception returns	1-47	2-46
Comp.-att.-int.	23-41-2	17-28-1
Sacked-yards lost	0-0	1-8
Punts	2-36	1-44
Fumbles-lost	2-1	0-0
Penalties-yards	13-68	9-38
Time of possession	26:24	33:36

INDIVIDUAL STATISTICS

RUSHING—Arizona, Murrell 15-62, Plummer 4-9, Bates 4-3. Minnesota, R. Smith 19-124, Hoard 11-44, Cunningham 3-6, Palmer 2-13, Evans 1-1.

PASSING—Arizona, Plummer 23-41-2-242. Minnesota, Cunningham 17-27-1-236, Palmer 0-1-0-0.

RECEIVING—Arizona, R. Moore 6-91, Centers 6-45, Sanders 4-30, Murrell 3-52, Metcalf 2-9, Gedney 1-8, McWilliams 1-7. Minnesota, Carter 5-82, R. Moss 4-73, Glover 3-22, Palmer 2-29, R. Smith 2-14, Hoard 1-16.

MISSED FIELD GOAL ATTEMPTS—None.

INTERCEPTIONS—Arizona, A. Williams 1-47. Minnesota, Griffith 2-46.

KICKOFF RETURNS—Arizona, Metcalf 3-66. Minnesota, Palmer 4-97.

PUNT RETURNS—Arizona, Metcalf 1-36. Minnesota, Palmer 1-2.

SACKS—Arizona, McKinnon 1.

CONFERENCE CHAMPIONSHIPS

AFC

DENVER 23, N.Y. JETS 10

Why the Broncos won: Terrell Davis rushed for 167 yards and a touchdown, helping the Broncos overcome an off-day by quarterback John Elway. Davis rushed for 2,008 yards during the regular season and was selected the NFL's Most Valuable Player.

Why the Jets lost: Turnovers and mistakes. New York turned over the ball six times, three times after the team had crossed midfield. Vinny Testaverde threw two interceptions, while Curtis Martin had a fumble and gained just 14 yards on 13 carries. The Jets fumbled four times and lost them all.

The turning points:

1. After a 1-yard touchdown run by Martin in the first half gave the Jets a 10-0 lead, Elway connected with a wide-open Ed McCaffrey for a 47-yard gain. That got a quiet Mile High Stadium crowd 75,482 into the game, and those folks really had something to cheer about two plays later when fullback Howard Griffith ran into the end zone on an 11-yard reception for the Broncos' first points. After Keith Burns recovered the ensuing kickoff when the wind played havoc with the Jets' return team, Denver tied the score on a 44-yard field goal by Jason Elam.

2. Davis, who averaged 5.2 yards per rush, ran 31 yards for a touchdown with 18 seconds remaining in the third quarter, capping a string 20 consecutive points for Denver.

3. Darrien Gordon intercepted a Testaverde pass in the fourth quarter, effectively ending any chance for a New York rally and setting up Elam's third field goal.

Notable: Despite Denver having outscored opponents 158-54 in the first quarter in its first 17 games, the first quarter of this game was scoreless. . . . Elway, who had trouble on a windy day, did not complete his first pass until midway through the second quarter. . . . The Broncos won their 19th straight game at Mile High Stadium. . . . The victory improved the Broncos' record in AFC title games to 6-1 and put them in the Super Bowl against the Atlanta Falcons and former Broncos coach Dan Reeves, who fired current Broncos coach Mike Shanahan as offensive coordinator in 1992. . . . Testaverde was 31-of-52 passing for 356 yards with no touchdowns. . . . Elway completed 13-of-34 passes for 173 yards, with 140 coming in the second half. . . . Davis' sixth consecutive playoff game with 100 or more yards rushing tied an NFL record set by the Redskins' John Riggins in 1982-83.

Quotable: Broncos receiver Shannon Sharpe, on Denver's second-half surge: "We had the strength and the ability to come back. We knew that." . . . Elway, after taking a victory lap following the game: "I got a chance to see the fans and look into their eyes and I had a chance to really concentrate on them. Usually, I'm so involved in the football game, it's hard to concentrate on them. So it was nice to be

able to do that." . . . Jets coach Bill Parcells, on the reasons his team lost: "It was the combination of turning the ball over three times across midfield, which limited our scoring opportunities. Then we had special teams mistakes as well." . . . Broncos linebacker John Mobley, on Martin: "He couldn't get it going. We had guys all around him hitting him hard. He really didn't want to run that ball today." . . . Shanahan, on his relationship with Reeves when both were in Denver: "At times, we were best friends. He's done a great job with that football team."

BRONCOS 23, JETS 10

Sunday, January 17

N.Y. Jets	0	3	7	0—10
Denver	0	0	20	3—23

Second Quarter

NYJ—FG, Hall 32, 15:00.

Third Quarter

NYJ—Martin 1 run (Hall kick), 3:04.
Den.—Griffith 11 pass from Elway (Elam kick), 4:42.
Den.—FG, Elam 44, 6:37.
Den.—FG, Elam 48, 12:02.
Den.—Davis 31 run (Elam kick), 14:42.

Fourth Quarter

Den.—FG, Elam 35, 11:20.
Attendance—75,482.

	N.Y. Jets	Denver
First downs	18	14
Rushes-yards	13-14	38-178
Passing	356	153
Punt returns	3-43	5-79
Kickoff returns	5-46	1-28
Interception returns	0-0	2-48
Comp.-att.-int.	31-52-2	13-34-0
Sacked-yards lost	0-0	3-20
Punts	7-48	8-40
Fumbles-lost	4-4	2-0
Penalties-yards	6-49	6-47
Time of possession	27:00	33:00

INDIVIDUAL STATISTICS

RUSHING—New York, Martin 13-14. Denver, Davis 32-167, Elway 3-13, Loville 2-7, Rouen 1-(minus 9).

PASSING—New York, Testaverde 31-52-2-356. Denver, Elway 13-34-0-173.

RECEIVING—New York, Chrebet 8-121, K. Johnson 7-73, Ward 5-61, Martin 4-39, Byars 3-33, Brady 2-11, Van Dyke 1-16, Meggett 1-2. Denver, McCaffrey 3-66, R. Smith 3-37, Chamberlain 2-26, Sharpe 2-14, Davis 1-12, Griffith 1-11, Carswell 1-7.

MISSED FIELD GOAL ATTEMPTS—New York, Hall 42.

INTERCEPTIONS—Denver, Gordon 2-48.

KICKOFF RETURNS—New York, Meggett 3-32, Hamilton 1-14, Farrior 1-0. Denver, Hebron 1-28.

PUNT RETURNS—New York, Meggett 3-43. Denver, Gordon 5-79.

SACKS—New York, Cascadden 2, Farrior 1.

ATLANTA 30, MINNESOTA 27

Why the Falcons won: The foot of Morten Andersen, who kicked a 38-yard field goal with 3:08 left in overtime, and the gutsy play of quarterback Chris Chandler, who led the team on scoring drives of 71 and 70 yards when the Falcons needed them most.

Why the Vikings lost: The foot of Gary Anderson, who missed a 38-yard field goal with 2:07 remaining in regulation, and an offense that cooled off considerably in the second half.

The turning points:

1. With 1:17 to play in the first half and the ball on the Minnesota 18, Vikings quarterback Randall Cunningham fumbled, with Travis Hall recovering at the Minnesota 14. On the next play, Chandler connected with Terance Mathis for a touchdown to cut a 20-7 Minnesota lead to 20-14.

2. Cunningham hit Matthew Hatchette for a 5-yard touchdown pass that gave Minnesota what looked like a safe 27-17 lead late in the third quarter.

3. Anderson hadn't missed a field-goal attempt all season, but this was the first time he had kicked with the game hanging in the balance. Given another chance, Chandler drove the Falcons to the tying touchdown.

Notable: The game, at 71 minutes, 52 seconds, was the seventh-longest in NFL playoff history and the first overtime game in a conference championship game since Denver defeated Cleveland, 23-20, for the AFC title in January 1987. . . . The victory was Atlanta's 11th straight and 22nd in 26 games. . . . Minnesota wide receiver Randy Moss caught six passes for 75 yards, but had only one catch for four yards in the second half and overtime. Cunningham completed just 2-of-7 passes in OT. . . . Prior to his miss, Anderson had made an NFL record 46 consecutive field-goal attempts. . . . Chandler passed for 340 yards, including a 70-yarder to Tony Martin, who caught five passes for 129 yards. . . . Atlanta coach Dan Reeves, who had quadruple heart bypass surgery a month before the game, kept a promise to his players and danced the "Dirty Bird" jig on the sideline after the game. . . . Reeves joined Bill Parcells and Don Shula as the only coaches to lead two different teams to the Super Bowl.

Quotable: Atlanta linebacker Jessie Tuggle, a 12-year veteran, on Andersen's winning kick: "All I can remember is the ball going through the uprights. I can't remember one play I made." . . . Martin, on the Vikings' defense: "We knew going in that the Vikings safeties play very deep, so we thought we could run patterns in front of them. They never adjusted." . . . Atlanta cornerback Melvin Booker, on the league's and public's perception of the Falcons compared to the Vikings: "We deserve the same amount of respect that they did. But when we got here, we found they were already selling tickets for the Super Bowl. We came here to spoil a lot of trips. If they're coming to the Super Bowl now, they're going to have to come see the Falcons." . . . Vikings coach Dennis Green, on the expectations that accompanied his 16-1 team, which was heavily favored to win: "There's no such thing as a guarantee in football in any way, shape or form." . . . Reeves, on the unpredictability of the Falcons' win: "This is good for the league. When a team like the Atlanta Falcons can be in the Super Bowl, it gives everyone in the league hope you can turn it around in a short period of time."

FALCONS 30, VIKINGS 27

Sunday, January 17

Atlanta	7	7	3	10	3—30
Minnesota	7	13	0	7	0—27

First Quarter
Atl.—J. Anderson 5 pass from Chandler (Andersen kick), 6:39.
Min.—R. Moss 31 pass from Cunningham (Anderson kick), 9:27.

Second Quarter
Min.—FG, Anderson 29, 5:08.
Min.—Cunningham 1 run (Anderson kick), 9:07.
Min.—FG, Anderson 35, 12:15.
Atl.—Mathis 14 pass from Chandler (Andersen kick), 14:04.

Third Quarter
Atl.—FG, Andersen 27, 9:24.

Fourth Quarter
Min.—Hatchette 5 pass from Cunningham (Anderson kick), 1:19.
Atl.—FG, Andersen 24, 3:58.
Atl.—Mathis 16 pass from Chandler (Andersen kick), 14:11.

Overtime
Atl.—FG, Andersen 38, 11:52.
Attendance—64,060.

	Atlanta	Minnesota
First downs	25	26
Rushes-yards	29-110	34-102
Passing	317	254
Punt returns	2-35	0-0
Kickoff returns	4-110	3-75
Interception returns	0-0	0-0
Comp.-att.-int.	27-43-0	29-48-0
Sacked-yards lost	3-23	3-12
Punts	4-45	4-51
Fumbles-lost	2-2	3-2
Penalties-yards	4-65	6-30
Time of possession	35:04	36:48

INDIVIDUAL STATISTICS

RUSHING—Atlanta, J. Anderson 23-67, Dwight 3-28, Chandler 2-15, Oxendine 1-0. Minnesota, R. Smith 21-71, Cunningham 6-13, Hoard 6-10, Evans 1-8.

PASSING—Atlanta, Chandler 27-43-0-340. Minnesota, Cunningham 29-48-0-266.

RECEIVING—Atlanta, Mathis 6-73, J. Anderson 6-33, Martin 5-129, Santiago 3-54, Kozlowski 3-11, Green 2-9, Harris 1-29, E. Smith 1-2. Minnesota, R. Moss 6-75, Carter 6-67, Glover 4-34, Hatchette 4-34, Hoard 3-23, DeLong 2-17, Palmer 2-9, Evans 1-8, R. Smith 1-(minus 1).

MISSED FIELD GOAL ATTEMPTS—Minnesota, Anderson 38.

INTERCEPTIONS—None.

KICKOFF RETURNS—Atlanta, Dwight 4-110. Minnesota, Palmer 3-75.

PUNT RETURNS—Atlanta, Dwight 2-35.

SACKS—Atlanta, Archambeau 1, Fuller 1, C. Smith 1. Minnesota, Fisk 2, T. Williams 1.

SUPER BOWL XXXIII

DENVER 34, ATLANTA 19

Why the Broncos won: Their offense was as un-stoppable as it was the previous year in a Super Bowl victory over the Packers. This time the Broncos relied on John Elway, who shredded the Falcons' defense for 336 yards; fullback Howard Griffith, who rushed for two touchdowns; and Terrell Davis, who rushed for 102 yards. The Denver defense also was impressive, with the pass rushers harassing quarterback Chris Chandler the entire game and the defensive backs creating havoc.

Why the Falcons lost: Turnovers. In the second half, Chandler had three passes intercepted and Jamal Anderson lost a fumble that was recovered by Tyrone Braxton. The Falcons appeared shell-shocked at being in their first Super Bowl and distracted by the news that safety Eugene Robinson, one of their leaders, had been arrested the day before the game for soliciting a prostitute.

The turning points:
1. After conceding a field goal on the Falcons' opening drive, the Broncos drove downfield behind Elway's passing and scored a touchdown on Griffith's 1-yard run. It was Griffith's first touchdown of the season.
2. Trailing 7-3 and facing fourth-and-1 at the Broncos' 26 on the first play of the second quarter, the Falcons went for the first down, only to have Anderson dropped by defensive tackle Keith Traylor for a loss of 2 yards.
3. After Morten Andersen missed a 26-yard field-goal attempt in the second quarter that would have cut the Broncos' lead to 10-6, Elway broke the game open by faking a handoff to Davis, rolling to his right and finding Rod Smith behind Robinson for an 80-yard touchdown pass and a 17-3 lead.
4. The final nail in the Falcons' coffin came when cornerback Darrien Gordon picked off a Chandler pass in the third quarter on a first-down play at the Denver 21.

Notable: Atlanta coach Dan Reeves was appearing in his record ninth Super Bowl as a player, assistant or head coach. . . . Chandler was 19-of-35 for 219 yards, with one touchdown and three interceptions. . . . Broncos Pro Bowl tight end Shannon Sharpe caught two passes before leaving the game early because of a knee injury. His replacement, Byron Chamberlain, caught three passes. . . . Andersen, one of the most accurate kickers in NFL history, missed a 26-yard field goal on his first Super Bowl attempt. . . . Denver became the sixth team to win the Super Bowl in consecutive seasons and the second in the 1990s to do it. Dallas won in 1992 and 1993.

Quotable: Elway, on the Broncos' pregame strategy: "They (the Falcons) were talking all week about stopping our running game and they didn't mention anything about the passing game. I really went into the game knowing we would have an opportunity to throw the ball and that if we were to win the game, it would probably be through the air." . . . Broncos coach Mike Shanahan: "One guy doesn't do it. A head coach doesn't do it. A quarterback doesn't do it. You have a lot of people going in the same direction." . . . Anderson: "No disrespect to Denver, but I didn't feel like they were shutting us down. We just didn't execute in critical situations." . . . Reeves: "Somebody has to be the loser. If you can walk off and feel like you've given it everything you have and you come out the loser, congratulate the winner and move on. I have no problem with that."

BRONCOS 34, FALCONS 19
Sunday, January 31

Denver	7	10	0	17—34
Atlanta	3	3	0	13—19

First Quarter
Atl.—FG, Andersen 32, 5:25.
Den.—Griffith 1 run (Elam kick), 11:05.
Second Quarter
Den.—FG, Elam 26, 5:43.
Den.—R. Smith 80 pass from Elway (Elam kick), 10:06.
Atl.—FG, Andersen 28, 12:35.
Fourth Quarter
Den.—Griffith 1 run (Elam kick), 0:04.
n.—Elway 3 run (Elam kick), 3:40.
Atl.—Dwight 94 kickoff return (Andersen kick), 3:59.
Den.—FG, Elam 37, 7:52.
Atl.—Mathis 3 pass from Chandler (pass failed), 12:56.
Attendance—74,803.

	Denver	Atlanta
First downs	22	21
Rushes-yards	36-121	23-131
Passing	336	206
Punt returns	0-0	0-0
Kickoff returns	3-44	7-227
Interception returns	3-136	1-1
Comp.-att.-int.	18-29-1	19-35-3
Sacked-yards lost	0-0	2-13
Punts	1-35	1-39
Fumbles-lost	0-0	1-1
Penalties-yards	4-61	0-0
Time of possession	31:23	28:37

INDIVIDUAL STATISTICS
RUSHING—Denver, Davis 25-102, Griffith 4-9, Elway 3-2, Loville 2-8, R. Smith 1-1, Brister 1-(minus 1). Atlanta, J. Anderson 18-96, Chandler 4-30, Dwight 1-5.

PASSING—Denver, Elway 18-29-1-336. Atlanta, Chandler 19-35-3-219..

RECEIVING—Denver, R. Smith 5-152, McCaffrey 5-72, Chamberlain 3-29, Davis 2-50, Sharpe 2-26, Griffith 1-7. Atlanta, Mathis 7-85, Martin 5-79, J. Anderson 3-16, Harris 2-21, Santiago 1-13, Kozlowski 1-5.

MISSED FIELD GOAL ATTEMPTS—Denver, Elam 38, 48. Atlanta, Andersen 26.

INTERCEPTIONS—Denver, Gordon 2-108, Johnson 1-28. Atlanta, Bradford 1-1.

KICKOFF RETURNS—Denver, Hebron 2-42, Chamberlain 1-2. Atlanta, Dwight 5-210, Kozlowski 2-17.

PUNT RETURNS—None.

SACKS—Denver, Romanowski 1, Mobley 1.

1998 REVIEW *Super Bowl XXXIII*

PRO BOWL

AT ALOHA STADIUM, HONOLULU, FEBRUARY 7, 1999

AFC 23, NFC 10

Why the AFC won: New England defensive back Ty Law returned an interception 67 yards for a touchdown, made five tackles and broke up three passes. The co-MVP, Keyshawn Johnson of the Jets, made seven catches for 87 yards.

Why the NFC lost: It was unable to overcome the performances of the game's MVPs and Denver quarterback John Elway, who marched his team downfield for a touchdown the first time it had the ball, with fullback Sam Gash of Buffalo on the receiving end of a 3-yard scoring pass.

The turning points:

1. On the AFC's first possession, Elway completed four of five passes for 55 yards as the team drove 61 yards for a touchdown and the lead.

2. In the third quarter, Law grabbed an interception and returned the ball 67 yards for a touchdown.

3. In the fourth quarter, Jason Elam of the Broncos kicked his third and final field goal of the day, a 26-yarder that provided the final margin of victory.

Notable: Law's interception return for a touchdown was the longest ever in the Pro Bowl. . . . Minnesota rookie Randy Moss had 108 yards on seven catches. . . . Cowboys defensive back Deion Sanders intercepted a pass by the Jets' Vinny Testaverde just before the end of the first half and returned it for a record 87 yards before he was tackled by Denver's Ed McCaffrey at the 4-yard line. . . . Jerry Rice of the 49ers had five catches for 60 yards, giving him the Pro Bowl career mark of 439 yards, 31 more than runner-up Tim Brown.

Quotable: Gash, on his touchdown reception: "It was definitely memorable. A legend threw the ball and I was able to catch it. I'll definitely think about it later in life." . . . Elway, on San Diego linebacker Junior Seau, who lined up at tight end on the Elway-to-Gash TD: "He was lobbying hard for it in the huddle. I was going to look for him, but Junior wasn't free." . . . Elway on Law and Johnson sharing the MVP award: "They are very deserving. I'm glad they got it. Those young guys, they're fun to watch." . . . Law, who dedicated the game to Patriots teammate Robert Edwards, who underwent surgery after severely injuring a knee the previous day in a beach football game: "Robert Edwards is a big part of our team and that's the most important thing going on right now." . . . Johnson, on the $25,000 winners' share: "I had to win so I could cover all my expenses, plane tickets, hotel rooms, food."

AFC 23, NFC 10

Sunday, February 7

AFC	7	3	10	3 —23
NFC	3	0	7	0 —10

First Quarter
AFC—Gash 3 pass from Elway (Elam kick), 4:09.
NFC—FG Anderson 23, 9:11.

Second Quarter
AFC—FG Elam 23, 11:31.

Third Quarter
AFC—Law 67 interception return (Elam kick), 5:18.
NFC—Smith 2 run (G. Anderson kick), 8:29.
AFC—FG Elam 46, 12:38.

Fourth Quarter
AFC—FG Elam 26, 1:02.
Attendance—50,075.

TEAM STATISTICS

	AFC	NFC
First downs	19	17
Rushes-yards	33-108	18-57
Passing	222	223
Punt returns	3-20	3-32
Kickoff returns	3-40	5-100
Interception returns	3-70	3-102
Comp.-att.-int.	18-35-3	19-46-3
Sacked-yards lost	0-0	3-16
Punts	4-48	4-52
Fumbles-lost	1-1	2-0
Penalties-yards	10-80	5-28
Time of possession	32:08	27:52

INDIVIDUAL STATISTICS

RUSHING—AFC, George 12-33, Faulk 7-33, Martin 8-29, Gash 3-14, J. Lewis 1-1, Flutie 2-(minus 2). NFC, J. Anderson 4-21, E. Smith 8-19, M. Alstott 3-10, R. Smith 2-7, Chandler 1-0.

PASSING—AFC, Elway 4-5-0-55, Testaverde 10-16-3-87, Flutie 4-14-0-80. NFC, Young 5-12-0-35, Cunningham 5-8-2-71, Chandler 9-25-1-133, Turk 0-1-0-0.

RECEIVING—AFC, Johnson 7-87, Faulk 3-12, Gash 3-8, Moulds 1-39, Coates 1-36, George 1-23, E. McCaffrey 1-17, Martin 1-0. NFC, Moss 7-108, Rice 5-60, M. Alstott 3-31, Carter 2-16, Bates 1-18, Walls 1-6.

MISSED FIELD GOAL ATTEMPTS—None.

INTERCEPTIONS—AFC, Law 1-67, Milloy 1-3, Russell 1-0. NFC, Sanders 1-87, Armstead 1-12, Williams 1-3.

KICKOFF RETURNS—AFC, J. Lewis 3-40. NFC, Preston 4-86, Bates 1-14.

PUNT RETURNS—AFC, J. Lewis 2-9, Woodson 1-11. NFC, Preston 1-11, Sanders 1-11, Moss 1-10.

SACKS—AFC, Russell 1, McCrary 2.

AFC SQUAD

OFFENSE

WR—Ed McCaffrey, Denver*
     Jimmy Smith, Jacksonville*
     Keyshawn Johnson, New York Jets
     Eric Moulds, Buffalo
TE— Shannon Sharpe, Denver*
     Ben Coates, New England
     Frank Wycheck, Tennessee
T— Tony Boselli, Jacksonville*
     Jonathan Ogden, Baltimore*
     Tony Jones, Denver
G— Ruben Brown, Buffalo*
     Bruce Matthews, Tennessee*
     Mark Schlereth, Denver
     Will Shields, Kansas City
C— Dermontti Dawson, Pittsburgh*
     Tom Nalen, Denver
QB— John Elway, Denver*
     Vinny Testaverde, New York Jets
     Doug Flutie, Buffalo
RB— Terrell Davis, Denver*
     Marshall Faulk, Indianapolis*
     Eddie George, Tennessee
     Curtis Martin, New York Jets
FB— Sam Gash, Buffalo
NOTE: TE Sharpe replaced due to injury by Wycheck, G
     Matthews replaced due to injury by Schlereth, RB Davis
     replaced due to injury by Martin.

DEFENSE

DE— Michael McCrary, Baltimore*
     Bruce Smith, Buffalo*
     Michael Sinclair, Seattle
DT— Tim Bowens, Miami*
     Darrell Russell, Oakland*
     Cortez Kennedy, Seattle
     Ted Washington, Buffalo
OLB— Chad Brown, Seattle*
     Mo Lewis, New York Jets*
     Bill Romanowski, Denver
     Peter Boulware, Baltimore†
ILB— Junior Seau, San Diego*
     Ray Lewis, Baltimore
CB— Aaron Glenn, New York Jets*
     Ty Law, New England*
     Shawn Springs, Seattle
     Charles Woodson, Oakland
SS— Rodney Harrison, San Diego*
     Lawyer Milloy, New England
FS— Steve Atwater, Denver*
NOTE: DT Bowens replaced due to injury by Kennedy, CB Glenn
     replaced due to injury by Woodson.

SPECIALISTS

P— Craig Hentrich, Tennessee
K— Jason Elam, Denver
KR— Jermaine Lewis, Baltimore
ST— Bennie Thompson, Baltimore

NFC SQUAD

OFFENSE

WR—Antonio Freeman, Green Bay*
     Randy Moss, Minnesota*
     Cris Carter, Minnesota
     Jerry Rice, San Francisco
TE— Mark Chmura, Green Bay*
     Wesley Walls, Carolina
T— Larry Allen, Dallas*
     William Roaf, New Orleans*
     Todd Steussie, Minnesota
     Bob Whitfield, Atlanta
G— Kevin Gogan, San Francisco*
     Randall McDaniel, Minnesota*
     Nate Newton, Dallas
C— Jeff Christy, Minnesota*
     Tony Mayberry, Tampa Bay
QB— Steve Young, San Francisco*
     Chris Chandler, Atlanta
     Randall Cunningham, Minnesota
RB— Jamal Anderson, Atlanta*
     Barry Sanders, Detroit*
     Garrison Hearst, San Francisco
     Emmitt Smith, Dallas
FB— Mike Alstott, Tampa Bay
NOTE: T Roaf replaced due to injury by Whitfield, RB Hearst
     replaced due to injury by Smith.

DEFENSE

DE— Michael Strahan, New York Giants*
     Reggie White, Green Bay*
     Joe Johnson, New Orleans
DT— John Randle, Minnesota*
     Warren Sapp, Tampa Bay*
     Leon Lett, Dallas
OLB— Derrick Brooks, Tampa Bay*
     Kevin Greene, Carolina*
     Jessie Armstead, New York Giants
ILB— Jessie Tuggle, Atlanta*
     Ed McDaniel, Minnesota
     Hardy Nickerson, Tampa Bay
     Winfred Tubbs, San Francisco†
CB— Ray Buchanan, Atlanta*
     Deion Sanders, Dallas*
     Aeneas Williams, Arizona
SS— LeRoy Butler, Green Bay*
     Darren Woodson, Dallas
FS— Eugene Robinson, Atlanta*
NOTE: ILB McDaniel replaced due to injury by Nickerson.

SPECIALISTS

P— Matt Turk, Washington
K— Gary Anderson, Minnesota
KR— Roell Preston, Green Bay
ST— Michael Bates, Carolina
   *Elected starter.
   †Selected as need player.

1998 REVIEW *Pro Bowl*

PLAYER PARTICIPATION

Player, Team	GP	GS	Player, Team	GP	GS	Player, Team	GP	GS
Abdul-Jabbar, Karim, Miami	15	15	Banks, Tony, St. Louis	14	14	Blevins, Tony, S.F.-Ind.	5	0
Abraham, Donnie, Tampa Bay	13	13	Bankston, Michael, Cincinnati	16	16	Bobo, Orlando, Minnesota	4	0
Abrams, Kevin, Detroit	16	7	Banta, Brad, Indianapolis	16	0	Bock, John, Miami	16	6
Ackerman, Tom, New Orleans	15	10	Barber, Mike, Indianapolis	12	6	Bohlinger, Rob, Carolina	13	1
Adams, Flozell, Dallas	16	12	Barber, Ronde, Tampa Bay	16	9	Bolden, Juran, Atl.-G.B.-Car.	12	0
Adams, Sam, Seattle	16	11	Barber, Shawn, Washington	16	1	Bonham, Shane, San Francisco	8	0
Agnew, Ray, St. Louis	16	12	Barber, Tiki, N.Y. Giants	16	4	Boniol, Chris, Philadelphia	16	0
Aguiar, Louie, Kansas City	16	0	Barker, Bryan, Jacksonville	16	0	Bono, Steve, St. Louis	6	2
Ahanotu, Chidi, Tampa Bay	4	4	Barker, Roy, San Francisco	16	16	Booker, Michael, Atlanta	14	6
Aikman, Troy, Dallas	11	11	Barlow, Reggie, Jacksonville	16	2	Booker, Vaughn, Green Bay	16	4
Akers, David, Washington	1	0	Barndt, Tom, Kansas City	16	16	Boose, Dorian, N.Y. Jets	12	0
Albright, Ethan, Buffalo	16	0	Barnhardt, Tommy, Tampa Bay	16	0	Bordano, Chris, New Orleans	16	6
Aldridge, Allen, Detroit	16	15	Barrow, Micheal, Carolina	16	16	Boselli, Tony, Jacksonville	15	15
Aleaga, Ink, New Orleans	15	3	Bartrum, Mike, New England	16	0	Bostic, James, Philadelphia	2	0
Alexander, Brent, Carolina	16	16	Bass, Anthony, Minnesota	3	0	Bouie, Tony, Tampa Bay	16	0
Alexander, Derrick, Minnesota	16	16	Batch, Charlie, Detroit	12	12	Boulware, Peter, Baltimore	16	16
Alexander, Derrick S., K.C.	15	14	Bates, Mario, Arizona	16	1	Boutte, Marc, Washington	13	1
Alexander, Elijah, Indianapolis	13	9	Bates, Michael, Carolina	14	0	Bowden, Joe, Tennessee	16	16
Alexander, Patrise, Washington	1	0	Batiste, Michael, Washington	6	0	Bowens, Tim, Miami	16	16
Alexander, Stephen, Was.	15	5	Battaglia, Marco, Cincinnati	16	0	Bowie, Larry, Washington	5	4
Alford, Brian, N.Y. Giants	2	0	Baxter, Fred, N.Y. Jets	14	2	Bownes, Fabien, Chicago	16	0
Allen, Eric, Oakland	10	10	Bayne, Chris, Atlanta	10	0	Boyd, Stephen, Detroit	13	12
Allen, James, Chicago	6	2	Beasley, Aaron, Jacksonville	16	15	Boyd, Tommie, Detroit	9	0
Allen, Larry, Dallas	16	16	Beasley, Fred, San Francisco	16	0	Boyer, Brant, Jacksonville	11	0
Allen, Taje, St. Louis	16	0	Bech, Brett, New Orleans	16	0	Brackens, Tony, Jacksonville	12	8
Allen, Terry, Washington	10	10	Beckles, Ian, Philadelphia	16	16	Bradford, Corey, Green Bay	8	0
Allred, John, Chicago	4	0	Bell, Myron, Cincinnati	16	1	Bradford, Ronnie, Atlanta	14	10
Alstott, Mike, Tampa Bay	16	16	Bell, Ricky, Chicago	14	0	Brady, Donny, Baltimore	13	0
Ambrose, Ashley, Cincinnati	15	15	Bellamy, Jay, Seattle	16	16	Brady, Jeff, Carolina	16	16
Amey, Vincent, Oakland	4	1	Bellisari, Greg, Tampa Bay	2	0	Brady, Kyle, N.Y. Jets	16	15
Anders, Kimble, Kansas City	16	15	Belser, Jason, Indianapolis	16	16	Braham, Rich, Cincinnati	12	12
Andersen, Morten, Atlanta	16	0	Bennett, Brandon, Cincinnati	14	1	Branch, Calvin, Oakland	16	0
Anderson, Antonio, Dallas	5	0	Bennett, Cornelius, Atlanta	16	16	Brandenburg, Dan, Buffalo	16	1
Anderson, Darren, Atlanta	5	0	Bennett, Darren, San Diego	16	0	Bratzke, Chad, N.Y. Giants	16	16
Anderson, Gary, Minnesota	16	0	Bennett, Donnell, Kansas City	16	10	Braxton, Tyrone, Denver	16	6
Anderson, Jamal, Atlanta	16	16	Bennett, Edgar, Chicago	16	13	Brien, Doug, New Orleans	16	0
Anderson, Richie, N.Y. Jets	8	1	Bennett, Tommy, Arizona	16	16	Brigance, O.J., Miami	16	0
Anderson, Ronnie, Arizona	4	0	Bercich, Pete, Minnesota	15	1	Brigham, Jeremy, Oakland	2	0
Anderson, Willie, Cincinnati	16	16	Berger, Mitch, Minnesota	16	0	Brilz, Darrick, Cincinnati	16	16
Andruzzi, Joseph, Green Bay	15	1	Berry, Bert, Indianapolis	16	12	Brisby, Vincent, New England	6	1
Anthony, Reidel, Tampa Bay	15	13	Bettis, Jerome, Pittsburgh	15	15	Brister, Bubby, Denver	7	4
Araguz, Leo, Oakland	16	0	Beuerlein, Steve, Carolina	12	12	Brock, Fred, Arizona	12	0
Archambeau, Lester, Atlanta	15	15	Beverly, Eric, Detroit	16	0	Brockermeyer, Blake, Carolina	14	14
Archie, Mike, Tennessee	16	0	Biakabutuka, Tim, Carolina	10	3	Bromell, Lorenzo, Miami	14	0
Armour, Justin, Denver	8	0	Biekert, Greg, Oakland	16	16	Bronson, Zack, San Francisco	11	1
Armstead, Jessie, N.Y. Giants	16	16	Bieniemy, Eric, Cincinnati	16	0	Brooking, Keith, Atlanta	15	0
Armstrong, Bruce, N.E.	16	16	Billups, Terry, Dallas	1	0	Brooks, Barrett, Philadelphia	16	1
Armstrong, Trace, Miami	16	0	Binn, David, San Diego	15	0	Brooks, Bucky, K.C.-Oak.	12	0
Armstrong, Tyji, St. Louis	12	0	Birk, Matt, Minnesota	7	0	Brooks, Derrick, Tampa Bay	16	16
Arnold, Jahine, Pittsburgh	3	0	Bishop, Blaine, Tennessee	13	13	Brooks, Ethan, St. Louis	15	0
Asher, Jamie, Washington	9	7	Bishop, Greg, N.Y. Giants	16	16	Brooks, Robert, Green Bay	12	12
Ashmore, Darryl, Oakland	15	4	Bishop, Harold, Pittsburgh	7	1	Broughton, Luther, Carolina	16	4
Atkins, James, Baltimore	9	6	Bjornson, Eric, Dallas	16	4	Broussard, Steve, Seattle	15	0
Atwater, Steve, Denver	16	16	Blackman, Ken, Cincinnati	8	8	Brown, Anthony, Cincinnati	16	5
Austin, Billy, Indianapolis	1	0	Blackmon, Robert, Indianapolis	15	9	Brown, Chad, Seattle	16	16
Austin, Raymond, Chicago	12	0	Blackmon, Roosevelt, G.B.-Cin.	15	0	Brown, Cornell, Baltimore	16	1
Avery, John, Miami	16	0	Blackshear, Jeff, Baltimore	16	16	Brown, Corwin, N.Y. Jets	16	1
Ayanbadejo, Obafemi, Min.	1	0	Blackwell, Kory, N.Y. Giants	5	0	Brown, Cyron, Denver	4	0
Badger, Brad, Washington	16	16	Blackwell, Will, Pittsburgh	16	1	Brown, Dave, Arizona	1	0
Bailey, Aaron, Indianapolis	9	0	Blades, Brian, Seattle	16	6	Brown, Derek, Oakland	16	4
Bailey, Robert, Detroit	16	0	Blair, Michael, G.B.-Cin.	13	0	Brown, Doug, Washington	10	0
Ball, Jerry, Minnesota	16	16	Blake, Jeff, Cincinnati	8	2	Brown, Eric, Denver	11	10
Ballard, Howard, Seattle	16	16	Blanchard, Cary, Washington	13	0	Brown, Gary, N.Y. Giants	16	11
Banks, Antonio, Minnesota	4	0	Bland, Tony, Minnesota	1	0	Brown, Gilbert, Green Bay	16	16
Banks, Chris, Denver	4	0	Blanton, Scott, Washington	2	0	Brown, J.B., Arizona	15	9
Banks, Tavian, Jacksonville	6	1	Bledsoe, Drew, New England	14	14	Brown, James, Miami	16	16

Player, Team	GP	GS
Brown, Jamie, San Francisco	8	5
Brown, Jonathan, Green Bay	4	0
Brown, Lance, Pittsburgh	16	0
Brown, Larry, Dallas	4	0
Brown, Lomas, Arizona	16	16
Brown, Omar, Atlanta	2	0
Brown, Orlando, Baltimore	13	13
Brown, Ray, San Francisco	16	16
Brown, Reggie, Seattle	15	1
Brown, Ruben, Buffalo	13	13
Brown, Tim, Oakland	16	16
Brown, Troy, New England	10	0
Browning, John, Kansas City	8	8
Bruce, Aundray, Oakland	1	0
Bruce, Isaac, St. Louis	5	5
Bruener, Mark, Pittsburgh	16	16
Brunell, Mark, Jacksonville.......	13	13
Bruschi, Tedy, New England	16	7
Bryant, Junior, San Francisco....	16	16
Buchanan, Ray, Atlanta.............	16	16
Buckey, Jeff, Miami	7	0
Buckley, Curtis, S.F.-NYG	14	0
Buckley, Marcus, N.Y. Giants.....	14	12
Buckley, Terrell, Miami	16	16
Buckner, Brentson, S.F.	13	0
Burger, Todd, N.Y. Jets	16	16
Burgess, James, San Diego	16	0
Burke, John, San Diego	10	6
Burnett, Chester, Washington....	5	0
Burnett, Rob, Baltimore	16	16
Burns, Keith, Denver	16	0
Burris, Jeff, Indianapolis	14	14
Burrough, John, Atlanta	16	3
Burton, Shane, Miami	15	0
Bush, Devin, Atlanta.................	13	0
Bush, Lewis, San Diego	10	10
Bush, Steve, Cincinnati.............	12	2
Butler, Duane, Minnesota	14	0
Butler, Hillary, Seattle	7	0
Butler, LeRoy, Green Bay..........	16	16
Byars, Keith, N.Y. Jets	13	8
Bynum, Kenny, San Diego	10	0
Byrd, Isaac, Tennessee.............	4	3
Cadrez, Glenn, Denver	16	15
Caldwell, Mike, Philadelphia	16	8
Calloway, Chris, N.Y. Giants	16	16
Campbell, Jesse, Washington ...	3	3
Campbell, Lamar, Detroit...........	12	0
Campbell, Matt, Carolina	10	10
Cannida, James, Tampa Bay......	10	0
Canty, Chris, New England	16	9
Carney, John, San Diego	16	0
Carpenter, Ron, St. Louis	6	0
Carrier, Mark, Carolina (WR)	16	1
Carrier, Mark, Detroit (S)	13	13
Carruth, Rae, Carolina	2	1
Carswell, Dwayne, Denver	16	1
Carter, Chris, New England.......	16	0
Carter, Cris, Minnesota.............	16	16
Carter, Dale, Kansas City	11	9
Carter, Kevin, St. Louis	16	16
Carter, Ki-Jana, Cincinnati	1	0
Carter, Marty, Chicago	16	16
Carter, Perry, Oakland..............	6	0
Carter, Tom, Chicago	4	4
Carter, Tony, New England	11	7
Cascadden, Chad, N.Y. Jets	13	4
Cavil, Ben, Baltimore	16	6
Centers, Larry, Arizona.............	16	12
Chalenski, Mike, Detroit	8	0
Chamberlain, Byron, Denver......	16	0
Chancey, Robert, Chicago	16	1
Chandler, Chris, Atlanta.............	14	14
Chavous, Corey, Arizona...........	16	5
Cherry, Je'Rod, New Orleans.....	14	0
Cherry, Mike, N.Y. Giants	1	0
Chester, Larry, Indianapolis.......	14	2
Chmura, Mark, Green Bay	15	14
Chorak, Jason, Indianapolis	8	0
Chrebet, Wayne, N.Y. Jets	16	15
Christian, Bob, Atlanta..............	14	11
Christie, Steve, Buffalo	16	0
Christy, Jeff, Minnesota............	16	16
Chryplewicz, Pete, Detroit	16	2
Clark, Greg, San Francisco	13	9
Clark, Jon, Arizona	6	0
Clark, Rico, Indianapolis............	16	0
Clark, Willie, San Diego	5	0
Clay, Hayward, Dallas...............	3	2
Clay, Willie, New England	16	16
Cleeland, Cameron, N.O.	16	16
Clement, Anthony, Arizona	1	0
Clemons, Charlie, St. Louis.......	16	0
Clemons, Duane, Minnesota......	16	4
Coakley, Dexter, Dallas	16	16
Coates, Ben, New England	14	14
Coghill, George, Denver	9	0
Coleman, Andre, Pittsburgh	4	0
Coleman, Ben, Jacksonville.......	16	16
Coleman, Marco, San Diego	16	16
Coleman, Marcus, N.Y. Jets	14	0
Colinet, Stalin, Minnesota.........	11	3
Collins, Andre, Chicago	16	2
Collins, Calvin, Atlanta..............	16	16
Collins, Kerry, Car.-N.O.	11	11
Collins, Mark, Seattle	9	0
Collins, Mo, Oakland	16	11
Collins, Todd, New England	12	10
Collons, Ferric, New England	14	13
Colman, Doug, N.Y. Giants	16	0
Comella, Greg, N.Y. Giants	16	0
Compton, Mike, Detroit	16	16
Conaty, Bill, Buffalo	15	1
Conley, Steven, Ind.-Pit.	3	1
Connell, Albert, Washington......	14	5
Conrad, Chris, Pittsburgh..........	6	1
Conway, Brett, Washington	6	0
Conway, Curtis, Chicago	15	15
Conwell, Ernie, St. Louis	7	7
Cook, Anthony, Tennessee	13	3
Cooks, Kerry, Green Bay	9	0
Cooper, Richard, Philadelphia ...	15	15
Copeland, Horace, Miami	2	0
Copeland, John, Cincinnati........	5	0
Copeland, Russell, Phi.-G.B.	14	1
Costello, Brad, Cincinnati	3	0
Cota, Chad, New Orleans	16	16
Cotton, Kenyon, Baltimore	12	0
Cottrell, Dana, New England	2	0
Cousin, Terry, Chicago	16	12
Cowart, Sam, Buffalo	16	11
Cox, Bryan, N.Y. Jets................	16	10
Crafts, Jerry, Philadelphia	1	0
Craver, Aaron, New Orleans	16	10
Crawford, Keith, Kansas City.....	8	0
Crawford, Vernon, N.E.	16	1
Criswell, Jeff, Kansas City	14	14
Crockett, Henri, Atlanta	10	10
Crockett, Ray, Denver	16	16
Crockett, Zack, Ind.-Jac.	12	2
Croel, Mike, Seattle	12	0
Cross, Howard, N.Y. Giants	16	16
Crowell, Germane, Detroit	14	2
Crumpler, Carlester, Seattle.......	11	1
Crutchfield, Buddy, Washington..	2	0
Cullors, Derrick, New England...	16	0
Culpepper, Brad, Tampa Bay	16	16
Cummings, Joe, Buffalo	9	2
Cunningham, Randall, Min.	15	14
Cunningham, Richie, Dallas	16	0
Cunningham, Rick, Oakland	12	0
Curry, Eric, Jacksonville	11	0
Curtis, Canute, Cincinnati	5	0
Dalman, Chris, San Francisco ...	15	15
Dalton, Lional, Baltimore	2	0
Daluiso, Brad, N.Y. Giants	16	0
Daniels, Jerome, Arizona...........	8	5
Daniels, Phillip, Seattle	16	15
Dar Dar, Kirby, Miami	2	0
Darius, Donovin, Jacksonville	14	14
Darling, James, Philadelphia	12	8
Davidds-Garrido, Norbert, Car. .	16	16
Davis, Anthony, Kansas City......	16	16
Davis, Billy, Dallas	16	11
Davis, Don, N.O.-T.B.	9	0
Davis, Eric, Carolina	16	16
Davis, Greg, Oakland	16	0
Davis, John, Tampa Bay	16	0
Davis, Rob, Green Bay	16	0
Davis, Stephen, Washington	16	12
Davis, Terrell, Denver	16	16
Davis, Travis, Jacksonville.........	16	5
Davis, Troy, New Orleans	14	2
Davis, Tyrone, Green Bay	13	1
Davis, Wendell, San Diego	11	7
Davis, Willie, Tennessee	13	10
Dawkins, Brian, Philadelphia	14	14
Dawkins, Sean, New Orleans.....	15	15
Dawson, Dermontti, Pittsburgh .	16	16
DeBerg, Steve, Atlanta..............	8	1
Deese, Derrick, San Francisco...	16	16
DeGraffenreid, Allen, Arizona ...	5	0
Del Greco, Al, Tennessee	16	0
Dellenbach, Jeff, Green Bay	16	3
DeLong, Greg, Minnesota	15	5
DeMarco, Brian, Jacksonville	16	9
Denson, Damon, New England..	11	4
Denton, Tim, Washington..........	16	0
Detmer, Koy, Philadelphia	8	5
Detmer, Ty, San Francisco	16	1
Devine, Kevin, Jacksonville	5	0
Devlin, Mike, Arizona................	15	3
Dexter, James, Arizona	16	16
Diaz, Jorge, Tampa Bay	12	12
Diaz-Infante, David, Denver.......	10	0
Dilfer, Trent, Tampa Bay	16	16
Dilger, Ken, Indianapolis...........	16	16
Dillon, Corey, Cincinnati	15	15
Dimry, Charles, San Diego	16	15
Dishman, Chris, Arizona	12	11
Dishman, Cris, Washington.......	16	16
Dixon, David, Minnesota	16	16
Dixon, Ernest, Oak.-K.C.	4	0
Dixon, Gerald, San Diego	16	6
Dixon, Mark, Miami	11	10
Dixon, Ronnie, Kansas City	4	0
Dodge, Dedrick, San Diego	8	0
Dogins, Kevin, Tampa Bay........	6	4
Doleman, Chris, San Francisco ..	16	16
Donnalley, Kevin, Miami	14	14
Dorsett, Anthony, Tennessee ...	16	0
Dotson, Earl, Green Bay	16	16
Dotson, Santana, Green Bay.....	16	16
Douglas, Hugh, Philadelphia	15	13
Downs, Gary, Atlanta.................	16	1
Doxzon, Todd, Miami	9	0

Player, Team	GP	GS	Player, Team	GP	GS	Player, Team	GP	GS
Draft, Chris, Chicago	1	0	Fletcher, London, St. Louis	16	1	Gonzalez, Tony, Kansas City	16	16
Drake, Jerry, Arizona	1	1	Fletcher, Terrell, San Diego	12	5	Gooch, Jeff, Tampa Bay	16	16
Drake, Troy, Washington	11	2	Flowers, Lethon, Pittsburgh	16	16	Goodwin, Hunter, Minnesota	15	0
Drakeford, Tyronne, N.O.	16	15	Floyd, Chris, New England	16	2	Gordon, Darrien, Denver	16	16
Drayton, Troy, Miami	15	15	Floyd, William, Carolina	16	13	Gordon, Dwayne, N.Y. Jets	16	4
Dronett, Shane, Atlanta	16	16	Flutie, Doug, Buffalo	13	10	Gordon, Steve, San Francisco	13	1
Druckenmiller, Jim, S.F.	2	0	Flynn, Mike, Baltimore	3	0	Gouveia, Kurt, San Diego	14	12
Dudley, Rickey, Oakland	16	15	Folau, Spencer, Baltimore	3	3	Gowin, Toby, Dallas	16	0
Duff, Jamal, Washington	13	3	Foley, Glenn, N.Y. Jets	5	3	Gragg, Scott, N.Y. Giants	16	16
Duffy, Roger, Pittsburgh	16	4	Foley, Steve, Cincinnati	10	1	Graham, Aaron, Arizona	14	13
Dulaney, Mike, Carolina	8	0	Folston, James, Oakland	16	5	Graham, Derrick, Oakland	12	12
Dumas, Mike, San Diego	3	3	Fontenot, Al, Indianapolis	7	5	Graham, Jay, Baltimore	5	1
Duncan, Jamie, Tampa Bay	14	6	Fontenot, Chris, Philadelphia	5	3	Graham, Jeff, Philadelphia	15	15
Dunn, David, Cin.-Pit.	11	0	Fontenot, Jerry, New Orleans	4	4	Graham, Kent, N.Y. Giants	11	6
Dunn, Jason, Philadelphia	10	10	Footman, Dan, Indianapolis	3	3	Granville, Billy, Cincinnati	16	0
Dunn, Warrick, Tampa Bay	16	14	Forbes, Marlon, Chicago	16	2	Grasmanis, Paul, Chicago	15	0
Dwight, Tim, Atlanta	12	0	Ford, Cole, Buffalo	1	0	Gray, Carlton, N.Y. Giants	14	3
Dyson, Kevin, Tennessee	13	9	Ford, Henry, Tennessee	13	5	Gray, Chris, Seattle	15	8
Early, Quinn, Buffalo	16	2	Fordham, Todd, Jacksonville	11	1	Gray, Derwin, Carolina	3	0
Eaton, Chad, New England	15	14	Fortin, Roman, San Diego	16	16	Gray, Torrian, Minnesota	9	1
Edwards, Antonio, Atlanta	15	0	Fox, Mike, Carolina	16	7	Graziani, Tony, Atlanta	3	1
Edwards, Dixon, Minnesota	15	14	Francis, James, Cincinnati	14	14	Grbac, Elvis, Kansas City	8	6
Edwards, Donnie, Kansas City	15	15	Frase, Paul, Baltimore	11	0	Green, Ahman, Seattle	16	0
Edwards, Marc, San Francisco	16	10	Frederick, Mike, Baltimore	10	0	Green, Darrell, Washington	16	16
Edwards, Robert, New England	16	15	Fredrickson, Rob, Detroit	16	16	Green, E.G., Indianapolis	11	0
Elam, Jason, Denver	16	0	Freeman, Antonio, Green Bay	15	15	Green, Eric, Baltimore	12	12
Elias, Keith, Indianapolis	13	0	Frerotte, Gus, Washington	3	2	Green, Harold, Atlanta	6	0
Ellard, Henry, N.E.-Was.	7	0	Friesz, John, Seattle	6	1	Green, Jacquez, Tampa Bay	12	1
Elliott, Jumbo, N.Y. Jets	16	16	Frost, Scott, N.Y. Jets	13	0	Green, Trent, Washington	15	14
Ellis, Ed, New England	7	0	Fryar, Irving, Philadelphia	16	16	Green, Victor, N.Y. Jets	16	16
Ellis, Greg, Dallas	16	16	Fuamatu-Ma'afala, Chris, Pit.	12	0	Green, Willie, Denver	15	1
Ellison, Jerry, Tampa Bay	16	0	Fuller, Corey, Minnesota	16	16	Greene, Andrew, Seattle	4	0
Elliss, Luther, Detroit	16	16	Fuller, Randy, Atlanta	13	0	Greene, Kevin, Carolina	15	15
Ellsworth, Percy, N.Y. Giants	16	9	Fuller, William, San Diego	13	13	Greene, Scott, Indianapolis	5	0
Eloms, Joey, Seattle	1	0	Gadsden, Oronde, Miami	16	12	Greer, Donovan, Buffalo	11	2
Elway, John, Denver	13	12	Gaiter, Tony, San Diego	5	0	Griese, Brian, Denver	1	0
Emanuel, Bert, Tampa Bay	11	11	Galbraith, Scott, Green Bay	1	0	Griffith, Howard, Denver	14	13
Emmons, Carlos, Pittsburgh	15	14	Gallery, Nick, N.Y. Jets	1	0	Griffith, Rich, Jacksonville	7	0
Engler, Derek, N.Y. Giants	11	0	Galloway, Joey, Seattle	16	16	Griffith, Robert, Minnesota	16	16
Engram, Bobby, Chicago	16	16	Galyon, Scott, N.Y. Giants	10	1	Gruber, Paul, Tampa Bay	16	16
Enis, Curtis, Chicago	9	1	Gammon, Kendall, New Orleans	16	0	Grunhard, Tim, Kansas City	16	16
Evans, Chuck, Minnesota	16	8	Gandy, Wayne, St. Louis	16	16	Gruttadauria, Mike, St. Louis	11	2
Evans, Doug, Carolina	9	7	Gannon, Rich, Kansas City	12	10	Guliford, Eric, New Orleans	5	1
Evans, Greg, Washington	13	0	Garcia, Frank, Carolina	14	14	Gutierrez, Brock, Cincinnati	1	0
Evans, Josh, Tennessee	14	11	Gardener, Daryl, Miami	16	16	Haase, Andy, N.Y. Giants	7	1
Evans, Leomont, Washington	16	13	Gardocki, Chris, Indianapolis	16	0	Habib, Brian, Seattle	16	16
Everitt, Steve, Philadelphia	13	13	Garner, Charlie, Philadelphia	10	3	Hakim, Az-Zahir, St. Louis	9	4
Fabini, Jason, N.Y. Jets	16	16	Garnes, Sam, N.Y. Giants	11	11	Hall, John, N.Y. Jets	16	0
Fair, Terry, Detroit	14	10	Garrett, Jason, Dallas	8	5	Hall, Lemanski, Chicago	15	0
Faneca, Alan, Pittsburgh	16	12	Gash, Sam, Buffalo	16	13	Hall, Rhett, Philadelphia	2	0
Fann, Chad, San Francisco	12	0	Gedney, Chris, Arizona	16	3	Hall, Travis, Atlanta	14	13
Farmer, Ray, Philadelphia	2	0	George, Eddie, Tennessee	16	16	Hallen, Bob, Atlanta	12	0
Farquhar, John, New Orleans	5	0	George, Jeff, Oakland	8	7	Hallock, Ty, Chicago	16	10
Farr, D'Marco, St. Louis	16	16	George, Matt, Pittsburgh	1	0	Hambrick, Darren, Dallas	14	0
Farrior, James, N.Y. Jets	12	2	George, Ron, Kansas City	16	0	Hamilton, Bobby, N.Y. Jets	16	1
Faulk, Marshall, Indianapolis	16	15	George, Spencer, Tennessee	5	0	Hamilton, Conrad, N.Y. Giants	16	15
Fauria, Christian, Seattle	15	15	German, Jammi, Atlanta	6	0	Hamilton, James, Jacksonville	7	0
Favors, Greg, Kansas City	16	4	Gibson, Damon, Cincinnati	16	0	Hamilton, Keith, N.Y. Giants	16	16
Favre, Brett, Green Bay	16	16	Gibson, Oliver, Pittsburgh	16	0	Hamilton, Malcolm, Was.	2	0
Feagles, Jeff, Seattle	16	0	Gilbert, Sean, Carolina	16	16	Hamilton, Michael, San Diego	13	0
Ferguson, Jason, N.Y. Jets	16	16	Gildon, Jason, Pittsburgh	16	16	Hamilton, Ruffin, Atlanta	16	0
Fiala, John, Pittsburgh	16	0	Gisler, Mike, N.Y. Jets	16	0	Hand, Norman, San Diego	16	16
Fiedler, Jay, Minnesota	5	0	Givens, Reggie, San Francisco	16	0	Hanks, Merton, San Francisco	16	16
Fields, Mark, New Orleans	15	15	Glenn, Aaron, N.Y. Jets	13	13	Hankton, Karl, Philadelphia	10	0
Figures, Deon, Jacksonville	16	5	Glenn, Tarik, Indianapolis	16	16	Hansen, Brian, N.Y. Jets	7	0
Fina, John, Buffalo	14	14	Glenn, Terry, New England	10	9	Hansen, Carl, N.Y. Jets	5	0
Fiore, Dave, San Francisco	9	3	Glover, Andrew, Minnesota	16	12	Hansen, Phil, Buffalo	15	15
Fischer, Mark, Washington	6	0	Glover, Kevin, Seattle	8	8	Hanshaw, Tim, San Francisco	16	0
Fisk, Jason, Minnesota	16	0	Glover, La'Roi, New Orleans	16	15	Hanson, Jason, Detroit	16	0
Flanagan, Mike, Green Bay	2	0	Godfrey, Randall, Dallas	16	16	Hape, Patrick, Tampa Bay	16	2
Flanigan, Jim, Chicago	16	16	Goff, Mike, Cincinnati	10	5	Harbaugh, Jim, Baltimore	14	12
Flannery, John, St. Louis	16	16	Gogan, Kevin, San Francisco	16	16	Hardy, Kevin, Jacksonville	16	16

– 230 –

Player, Team	GP	GS	Player, Team	GP	GS	Player, Team	GP	GS
Hardy, Terry, Arizona	9	0	Hollas, Donald, Oakland	12	6	Jervey, Travis, Green Bay	8	5
Harlow, Pat, Oakland	5	5	Holliday, Vonnie, Green Bay	12	12	Jett, James, Oakland	16	16
Harper, Dwayne, San Diego	1	1	Hollier, Dwight, Miami	16	0	Jett, John, Detroit	14	0
Harris, Al, Philadelphia	16	7	Hollinquest, Lamont, Green Bay	14	2	Johnson, Alonzo, New Orleans	1	0
Harris, Anthony, Miami	5	0	Hollis, Mike, Jacksonville	16	0	Johnson, Andre, Detroit	3	0
Harris, Bernardo, Green Bay	16	16	Holmberg, Rob, Ind.-NYJ	12	4	Johnson, Anthony, Carolina	16	2
Harris, Corey, Baltimore	16	6	Holmes, Darick, Buf.-G.B.	14	0	Johnson, Bill, Philadelphia	13	13
Harris, Derrick, St. Louis	16	14	Holmes, Earl, Pittsburgh	14	14	Johnson, Brad, Minnesota	4	2
Harris, Jackie, Tennessee	16	16	Holmes, Kenny, Tennessee	14	11	Johnson, Charles, Pittsburgh	16	16
Harris, James, Oakland	16	16	Holmes, Lester, Oakland	16	16	Johnson, Darrius, Denver	16	2
Harris, Jon, Philadelphia	16	4	Holmes, Priest, Baltimore	16	13	Johnson, Ellis, Indianapolis	16	16
Harris, Mark, San Francisco	10	0	Holsey, Bernard, N.Y. Giants	16	0	Johnson, Jason, Indianapolis	14	0
Harris, Raymont, Green Bay	8	3	Hopkins, Brad, Tennessee	13	13	Johnson, Jimmie, Philadelphia	3	3
Harris, Robert, N.Y. Giants	10	10	Horan, Mike, Chicago	13	0	Johnson, Joe, New Orleans	16	16
Harris, Ronnie, Sea.-Atl.	8	0	Horn, Joe, Kansas City	16	1	Johnson, Keyshawn, N.Y. Jets	16	16
Harris, Sean, Chicago	16	14	Horne, Tony, St. Louis	16	0	Johnson, Lee, Cincinnati	13	0
Harris, Walt, Chicago	14	14	Houston, Bobby, Minnesota	8	1	Johnson, Leon, N.Y. Jets	12	2
Harrison, Marvin, Indianapolis	12	12	Howard, Chris, Jacksonville	8	0	Johnson, Lonnie, Buffalo	16	16
Harrison, Nolan, Pittsburgh	9	7	Howard, Desmond, Oakland	15	1	Johnson, Melvin, Kansas City	7	1
Harrison, Rodney, San Diego	16	16	Howard, Eddie, San Francisco	2	0	Johnson, Norm, Pittsburgh	15	0
Hartings, Jeff, Detroit	13	13	Howard, Ty, Arizona	9	0	Johnson, Pat, Baltimore	13	0
Hartley, Frank, San Diego	16	3	Hoying, Bobby, Philadelphia	8	7	Johnson, Pepper, N.Y. Jets	16	16
Harvey, Ken, Washington	11	9	Huard, Damon, Miami	2	0	Johnson, Raylee, San Diego	16	3
Harvey, Richard, Oakland	16	16	Hudson, Chris, Jacksonville	13	13	Johnson, Rob, Buffalo	8	6
Haskins, Jon, San Diego	2	0	Hudson, John, N.Y. Jets	16	0	Johnson, Ted, New England	13	13
Hasselbach, Harald, Denver	16	3	Hughes, Danan, Kansas City	16	0	Johnson, Tony, New Orleans	11	0
Hastings, Andre, New Orleans	16	12	Hughes, Tyrone, Dallas	4	0	Johnson, Tre', Washington	10	10
Hasty, James, Kansas City	16	14	Hundon, James, Cincinnati	9	3	Johnston, Daryl, Dallas	16	13
Hatchette, Matthew, Minnesota	5	0	Hunter, Brice, Tampa Bay	10	0	Johnstone, Lance, Oakland	16	15
Hauck, Tim, Indianapolis	16	7	Huntington, Greg, Chicago	2	0	Jones, Brian, New Orleans	1	0
Hawkins, Artrell, Cincinnati	16	16	Huntley, Richard, Pittsburgh	16	1	Jones, Cedric, N.Y. Giants	16	1
Hawkins, Courtney, Pittsburgh	15	14	Husted, Michael, Tampa Bay	16	0	Jones, Charlie, San Diego	16	11
Hayden, Aaron, Philadelphia	1	0	Hutson, Tony, Dallas	10	1	Jones, Clarence, New Orleans	14	14
Hayes, Chris, N.Y. Jets	15	0	Hutton, Tom, Philadelphia	16	0	Jones, Damon, Jacksonville	16	7
Hayes, Donald, Carolina	7	0	Irvin, Ken, Buffalo	16	16	Jones, Donta, Pittsburgh	16	3
Hayes, Jarius, Arizona	16	0	Irvin, Michael, Dallas	16	15	Jones, Ernest, Den.-Car.	8	0
Hearst, Garrison, San Francisco	16	16	Irving, Terry, Arizona	6	1	Jones, Freddie, San Diego	16	16
Hebron, Vaughn, Denver	15	0	Irwin, Heath, New England	13	3	Jones, George, Jacksonville	12	0
Heck, Andy, Chicago	14	14	Ismail, Qadry, New Orleans	10	1	Jones, Greg, Washington	16	5
Hegamin, George, Philadelphia	16	6	Ismail, Raghib, Carolina	16	15	Jones, Henry, Buffalo	16	16
Hellestrae, Dale, Dallas	16	0	Israel, Steve, New England	11	7	Jones, James, Baltimore	16	16
Hemsley, Nate, Dallas	3	0	Izzo, Larry, Miami	13	0	Jones, Lenoy, Tennessee	9	0
Henderson, Jerome, N.Y. Jets	13	8	Jacke, Chris, Arizona	4	0	Jones, Marcus, Tampa Bay	15	0
Henderson, William, Green Bay	16	10	Jackson, Calvin, Miami	16	15	Jones, Mike A., St. Louis	16	16
Henley, June, St. Louis	11	3	Jackson, Grady, Oakland	15	1	Jones, Mike D., St. Louis	16	15
Hennings, Chad, Dallas	16	16	Jackson, Greg, San Diego	16	13	Jones, Robert, Miami	16	16
Henry, Kevin, Pittsburgh	16	16	Jackson, John, San Diego	16	16	Jones, Rod, Cincinnati	6	2
Hentrich, Craig, Tennessee	16	0	Jackson, Michael, Baltimore	13	12	Jones, Tebucky, New England	16	0
Herndon, Jimmy, Chicago	9	2	Jackson, Raymond, Buffalo	14	0	Jones, Tony, Denver	16	16
Herring, Kim, Baltimore	7	7	Jackson, Steve, Tennessee	14	4	Jones, Walter, Seattle	16	16
Herrod, Jeff, Indianapolis	10	7	Jackson, Tyoka, Tampa Bay	16	12	Jordan, Andrew, Philadelphia	3	0
Hesse, Jon, St. Louis	5	0	Jackson, Waverly, Indianapolis	6	2	Jordan, Charles, Miami	3	0
Hetherington, Chris, Ind.	14	1	Jackson, Willie, Cincinnati	8	0	Jordan, Randy, Oakland	16	0
Hewitt, Chris, New Orleans	16	2	Jacoby, Mitch, St. Louis	5	0	Jordan, Richard, Detroit	16	4
Heyward, Craig, Indianapolis	4	3	Jacox, Kendyl, San Diego	16	6	Jordon, Antony, Indianapolis	15	3
Hickman, Kevin, Detroit	3	0	Jacquet, Nate, Miami	15	0	Joseph, Kerry, Seattle	16	0
Hicks, Eric, Kansas City	3	0	Jaeger, Jeff, Chicago	16	0	Joyce, Matt, Arizona	11	0
Hicks, Robert, Buffalo	9	2	James, Tory, Denver	16	0	Joyner, Seth, Denver	16	1
Hicks, Skip, Washington	9	5	Jamison, George, Detroit	14	0	Junkin, Trey, Arizona	16	0
Hill, Eric, St. Louis	15	13	Janus, Paul, Carolina	5	1	Jurevicius, Joe, N.Y. Giants	14	1
Hill, Greg, St. Louis	2	2	Jasper, Edward, Philadelphia	7	0	Jurkovic, John, Jacksonville	16	16
Hill, Ray, Buf.-Mia.	6	0	Jeffers, Patrick, Dallas	8	1	Justin, Paul, Cincinnati	5	3
Hilliard, Ike, N.Y. Giants	16	16	Jefferson, Greg, Philadelphia	15	14	Kaiser, Jason, Kansas City	1	0
Hilliard, Randy, Chicago	9	2	Jefferson, Shawn, New England	16	16	Kalu, Ndukwe, Washington	13	1
Hills, Keno, New Orleans	12	1	Jeffries, Greg, Detroit	15	3	Kanell, Danny, N.Y. Giants	10	10
Hitchcock, Jimmy, Minnesota	16	16	Jells, Dietrich, Philadelphia	9	0	Kasay, John, Carolina	16	0
Hoard, Leroy, Minnesota	16	1	Jenkins, Billy, St. Louis	16	13	Kaufman, Napoleon, Oakland	13	13
Hobert, Billy Joe, New Orleans	1	1	Jenkins, DeRon, Baltimore	16	7	Kelly, Brian, Tampa Bay	16	3
Hoelscher, David, Washington	1	0	Jenkins, James, Washington	16	4	Kelly, Rob, New Orleans	16	3
Holcombe, Robert, St. Louis	13	6	Jenkins, John, Pittsburgh	1	0	Kendall, Pete, Seattle	16	16
Holecek, John, Buffalo	13	13	Jenkins, Kerry, N.Y. Jets	16	0	Kennedy, Cortez, Seattle	15	15
Holland, Darius, K.C.-Det.	16	4	Jensen, Jerry, Carolina	10	0	Kennedy, Lincoln, Oakland	16	16

Player, Team	GP	GS
Kennison, Eddie, St. Louis	16	13
Kent, Joey, Tennessee	10	0
Kerner, Marlon, Buffalo	1	0
Kidd, John, Det.-NYJ	10	0
Killens, Terry, Tennessee	16	1
Kinchen, Brian, Baltimore	16	5
Kinchen, Todd, Atlanta	11	0
King, Carlos, Pittsburgh	1	0
Kinney, Kelvin, Washington	14	12
Kirby, Terry, San Francisco	9	0
Kirk, Randy, San Francisco	16	0
Kirkland, Levon, Pittsburgh	16	16
Kiselak, Mike, Dallas	15	7
Kitna, Jon, Seattle	6	5
Kitts, Jim, Was.-G.B.	5	0
Knight, Sammy, New Orleans	14	13
Knight, Tom, Arizona	8	5
Koonce, George, Green Bay	14	14
Kopp, Jeff, Jac.-Bal.	13	0
Kowalkowski, Scott, Detroit	15	0
Kozlowski, Brian, Atlanta	16	4
Kramer, Erik, Chicago	8	8
Kresser, Eric, Cincinnati	2	0
Kreutz, Olin, Chicago	9	1
Krieg, Dave, Tennessee	5	0
Kuberski, Bob, Green Bay	16	0
Kyle, Jason, Seattle	16	0
LaBounty, Matt, Seattle	16	1
Lacina, Corbin, Carolina	10	10
Ladd, Anthony, New England	3	0
LaFleur, David, Dallas	13	13
Lageman, Jeff, Jacksonville	1	1
Lake, Carnell, Pittsburgh	16	16
Landeta, Sean, Green Bay	16	0
Lane, Fred, Carolina	14	11
Lane, Max, New England	16	11
Lang, Kenard, Washington	16	16
Langford, Jevon, Cincinnati	14	1
Langham, Antonio, S.F.	11	6
Lassiter, Kwamie, Arizona	16	6
Lathon, Lamar, Carolina	2	2
Law, Ty, New England	16	16
Layman, Jason, Tennessee	16	15
Leaf, Ryan, San Diego	10	9
LeBel, Harper, Baltimore	5	0
Lee, Amp, St. Louis	14	2
Lee, Lloyd, San Diego	8	0
Lee, Shawn, Chicago	15	14
Leeuwenburg, Jay, Indianapolis	16	16
Legette, Tyrone, San Francisco	7	0
Lepsis, Matt, Denver	16	0
Lester, Tim, Pittsburgh	9	7
Lett, Leon, Dallas	16	15
Levens, Dorsey, Green Bay	7	4
Levy, Chuck, San Francisco	12	0
Lewis, Albert, Oakland	15	12
Lewis, Chad, Philadelphia	2	0
Lewis, Darryll, Tennessee	16	15
Lewis, Jermaine, Baltimore	13	13
Lewis, Mo, N.Y. Jets	16	16
Lewis, Ray, Baltimore	14	14
Lincoln, Jeremy, N.Y. Giants	16	1
Lindsay, Everett, Minnesota	16	3
Linton, Jonathan, Buffalo	14	0
Little, Earl, New Orleans	16	0
Little, Leonard, St. Louis	6	0
Liwienski, Chris, Minnesota	1	0
Lloyd, Greg, Carolina	16	14
Lockett, Kevin, Kansas City	13	3
Lodish, Mike, Denver	15	1
Lofton, Steve, N.E.-Car.	16	7
Logan, Ernie, N.Y. Jets	16	12

Player, Team	GP	GS
Logan, James, Seattle	4	1
Logan, Mike, Jacksonville	15	0
London, Antonio, Green Bay	1	0
Long, Kevin, Tennessee	16	2
Longwell, Ryan, Green Bay	16	0
Loud, Kamil, Buffalo	5	0
Love, Clarence, Philadelphia	6	0
Loville, Derek, Denver	16	0
Lowe, Reggie, Jacksonville	4	0
Lucas, Ray, N.Y. Jets	15	0
Lusk, Henry, Miami	3	1
Lyght, Todd, St. Louis	16	16
Lyle, Keith, St. Louis	16	16
Lyle, Rick, N.Y. Jets	16	16
Lynch, John, Tampa Bay	15	15
Lynn, Anthony, Denver	16	0
Lyon, Billy, Green Bay	4	0
Lyons, Mitch, Pittsburgh	15	0
Lyons, Pratt, Tennessee	16	12
Mack, Tremain, Cincinnati	12	0
Maddox, Mark, Arizona	14	3
Madison, Sam, Miami	16	16
Mandarich, Tony, Indianapolis	10	10
Mangum, John, Chicago	3	0
Mangum, Kris, Carolina	6	0
Maniecki, Jason, Tampa Bay	3	0
Mannelly, Patrick, Chicago	16	0
Manning, Brian, Green Bay	3	0
Manning, Peyton, Indianapolis	16	16
Manuel, Rod, Pittsburgh	2	0
Manusky, Greg, Kansas City	16	1
Mare, Olindo, Miami	16	0
Marino, Dan, Miami	16	16
Marion, Brock, Miami	16	16
Marshall, Anthony, Philadelphia	16	0
Martin, Curtis, N.Y. Jets	15	15
Martin, Emanuel, Buffalo	14	4
Martin, Jamie, Jacksonville	4	1
Martin, Steve, Ind.-Phi.	13	3
Martin, Tony, Atlanta	16	16
Martin, Wayne, New Orleans	16	16
Marts, Lonnie, Tennessee	16	15
Maryland, Russell, Oakland	15	15
Mason, Derrick, Tennessee	16	0
Mason, Eddie, Jacksonville	4	0
Maston, Le'Shai, Washington	1	0
Mathews, Jason, Tennessee	3	0
Mathias, Ric, Cincinnati	3	0
Mathis, Kevin, Dallas	13	4
Mathis, Terance, Atlanta	16	16
Matthews, Bruce, Tennessee	16	16
Matthews, Steve, Tennessee	1	0
Mawae, Kevin, N.Y. Jets	16	16
May, Deems, Seattle	16	1
Mayberry, Jermane, Phi.	15	10
Mayberry, Tony, Tampa Bay	16	16
Mayes, Alonzo, Chicago	16	16
Mayes, Derrick, Green Bay	10	6
Maynard, Brad, N.Y. Giants	16	0
Mays, Kivuusama, Minnesota	16	0
McAfee, Fred, Pittsburgh	14	0
McBurrows, Gerald, St. Louis	10	0
McCaffrey, Ed, Denver	15	15
McCardell, Keenan, Jacksonville	15	15
McCleon, Dexter, St. Louis	15	6
McCleskey, J.J., Arizona	12	0
McCloud, Tyrus, Baltimore	7	2
McCollum, Andy, New Orleans	16	5
McCombs, Tony, Arizona	14	13
McCormack, Hurvin, Dallas	16	1
McCoy, Tony, Indianapolis	14	13
McCrary, Michael, Baltimore	16	16

Player, Team	GP	GS
McCullough, George, Ten.	7	0
McDaniel, Ed, Minnesota	16	16
McDaniel, Randall, Minnesota	16	16
McDaniel, Terry, Seattle	9	0
McDaniels, Pellom, K.C.	11	2
McDonald, Ramos, Minnesota	15	0
McDonald, Ricardo, Chicago	15	14
McDonald, Tim, San Francisco	16	16
McDuffie, O.J., Miami	16	16
McElmurry, Blaine, Jacksonville	2	0
McElroy, Ray, Indianapolis	16	0
McEndoo, Jason, Seattle	1	0
McGarrahan, Scott, Green Bay	15	0
McGee, Dell, Arizona	3	0
McGee, Tony, Cincinnati	16	16
McGill, Lenny, Carolina	10	0
McGinest, Willie, New England	9	8
McGlockton, Chester, K.C.	10	9
McGuire, Kaipo, Indianapolis	1	0
McIver, Everett, Dallas	6	6
McKenzie, Keith, Green Bay	16	0
McKenzie, Raleigh, San Diego	16	16
McKinney, Steve, Indianapolis	16	16
McKinnon, Ronald, Arizona	13	13
McKnight, James, Seattle	14	3
McManus, Tom, Jacksonville	16	4
McMillian, Mark, Kansas City	16	10
McNair, Steve, Tennessee	16	16
McNeil, Ryan, St. Louis	16	12
McPhail, Jerris, Detroit	3	0
McQuarters, R.W., S.F.	16	7
McTyer, Tim, Philadelphia	16	1
McWilliams, Johnny, Arizona	16	15
Meadows, Adam, Indianapolis	14	14
Means, Natrone, San Diego	10	10
Meggett, Dave, N.Y. Jets	2	0
Metcalf, Eric, Arizona	16	3
Mickens, Ray, N.Y. Jets	16	4
Mickens, Terry, Oakland	16	2
Middleton, Frank, Tampa Bay	16	16
Milburn, Glyn, Chicago	16	1
Mili, Itula, Seattle	7	0
Miller, Bubba, Philadelphia	15	4
Miller, Fred, St. Louis	15	15
Miller, Jamir, Arizona	16	16
Miller, Josh, Pittsburgh	16	0
Miller, Les, Carolina	14	3
Milloy, Lawyer, New England	16	16
Mills, Ernie, Dallas	11	1
Mills, John Henry, Oakland	5	0
Milne, Brian, Cincinnati	14	14
Milstead, Rod, Washington	14	11
Mims, Chris, San Diego	6	0
Mincy, Charles, Tampa Bay	16	16
Minter, Barry, Chicago	16	16
Minter, Mike, Carolina	6	4
Mitchell, Brandon, N.E.	7	1
Mitchell, Brian, Washington	16	0
Mitchell, Jeff, Baltimore	11	10
Mitchell, Keith, New Orleans	16	15
Mitchell, Kevin, New Orleans	8	8
Mitchell, Pete, Jacksonville	16	16
Mitchell, Scott, Detroit	2	2
Mixon, Kenny, Miami	16	16
Mobley, John, Denver	16	15
Mobley, Singor, Dallas	16	0
Mohr, Chris, Buffalo	16	0
Mohring, Mike, San Diego	10	0
Molden, Alex, New Orleans	16	15
Montgomery, Monty, Ind.	16	5
Monty, Pete, N.Y. Giants	11	0
Moon, Warren, Seattle	10	10

Player, Team	GP	GS	Player, Team	GP	GS	Player, Team	GP	GS
Moore, Dave, Tampa Bay	16	16	Panos, Joe, Buffalo	16	16	Purvis, Andre, Cincinnati	9	0
Moore, Herman, Detroit	15	15	Parker, Anthony, Tampa Bay	11	7	Pyne, Jim, Detroit	16	16
Moore, Jerald, St. Louis	11	4	Parker, Glenn, Kansas City	15	15	Quarles, Shelton, Tampa Bay	16	0
Moore, Kelvin, Cincinnati	4	0	Parker, Riddick, Seattle	8	0	Quinn, Jonathan, Jacksonville	4	2
Moore, Larry, Indianapolis	6	5	Parker, Vaughn, San Diego	6	6	Quinn, Mike, Dallas	3	0
Moore, Marty, New England	14	2	Parmalee, Bernie, Miami	15	0	Raab, Marc, San Diego	1	0
Moore, Rob, Arizona	16	16	Parrella, John, San Diego	16	16	Rachal, Latario, San Diego	11	0
Moore, Ronald, Miami	1	1	Parrish, Tony, Chicago	16	16	Ramirez, Tony, Detroit	16	7
Moore, Stevon, Baltimore	16	16	Parten, Ty, Kansas City	16	6	Randle, John, Minnesota	16	16
Moore, Will, Jacksonville	16	0	Pathon, Jerome, Indianapolis	16	15	Randolph, Thomas, Cincinnati	16	1
Morabito, Tim, Carolina	8	8	Patten, David, N.Y. Giants	12	0	Ransom, Derrick, Kansas City	7	0
Moran, Sean, Buffalo	9	2	Patton, Joe, Washington	11	10	Rasby, Walter, Detroit	16	16
Moreno, Moses, Chicago	2	1	Patton, Marvcus, Washington	16	16	Raymer, Cory, Washington	16	16
Morris, Bam, Chi.-K.C.	12	5	Paul, Tito, Denver	16	0	Redmon, Anthony, Carolina	10	4
Morris, Mike, Minnesota	16	0	Paup, Bryce, Jacksonville	16	16	Reece, Travis, Detroit	3	0
Morrison, Steve, Indianapolis	16	12	Payne, Rod, Cincinnati	6	0	Reed, Andre, Buffalo	15	13
Morrow, Harold, Minnesota	11	0	Payne, Seth, Jacksonville	6	1	Reed, Jake, Minnesota	11	11
Morton, Johnnie, Detroit	16	16	Pederson, Doug, Green Bay	12	0	Reed, Mike, Philadelphia	4	0
Morton, Mike, Oakland	16	0	Peete, Rodney, Philadelphia	5	4	Reese, Ike, Philadelphia	16	0
Moss, Randy, Minnesota	16	11	Pelfrey, Doug, Cincinnati	16	0	Reese, Izell, Dallas	16	0
Moss, Zefross, New England	14	14	Penn, Chris, Chicago	14	1	Reeves, Carl, Chicago	11	0
Moten, Mike, Arizona	1	0	Perry, Darren, Pittsburgh	14	14	Rehberg, Scott, New England	2	0
Moulds, Eric, Buffalo	16	15	Perry, Ed, Miami	14	5	Reich, Frank, Detroit	6	2
Muhammad, Muhsin, Carolina	16	16	Perry, Marlo, Buffalo	16	1	Reid, Spencer, Carolina	16	0
Murrell, Adrian, Arizona	15	14	Perry, Todd, Chicago	16	16	Reynolds, Jerry, N.Y. Giants	12	2
Myers, Greg, Cincinnati	16	16	Perry, Wilmont, New Orleans	6	2	Rheams, Leonta, New England	6	0
Myers, Michael, Dallas	16	1	Peter, Christian, N.Y. Giants	16	6	Rhett, Errict, Baltimore	13	2
Myles, DeShone, Seattle	12	7	Peter, Jason, Carolina	14	11	Rice, Jerry, San Francisco	16	16
Myslinski, Tom, Indianapolis	4	1	Peters, Tyrell, Baltimore	10	0	Rice, Ron, Detroit	16	16
Naeole, Chris, New Orleans	16	16	Peterson, Todd, Seattle	16	0	Rice, Simeon, Arizona	16	16
Nails, Jamie, Buffalo	15	3	Peterson, Tony, San Francisco	16	1	Richard, Stanley, Washington	15	15
Nalen, Tom, Denver	16	16	Phenix, Perry, Tennessee	15	3	Richardson, Damien, Carolina	14	7
Nash, Marcus, Denver	8	0	Phifer, Roman, St. Louis	13	13	Richardson, Kyle, Baltimore	16	0
Neal, Lorenzo, Tampa Bay	16	1	Phillips, Anthony, Minnesota	2	0	Richardson, Tony, Kansas City	14	1
Neal, Randy, San Francisco	1	0	Phillips, Joe, St. Louis	13	4	Richardson, Wally, Baltimore	1	0
Nedney, Joe, Arizona	12	0	Phillips, Ryan, N.Y. Giants	16	3	Richey, Wade, San Francisco	16	0
Neil, Dan, Denver	16	16	Pickens, Carl, Cincinnati	16	16	Richie, David, San Francisco	8	0
Neujahr, Quentin, Jacksonville	16	16	Pierson, Pete, Tampa Bay	16	0	Ricks, Mikhael, San Diego	16	9
Newman, Anthony, Oakland	11	11	Pike, Mark, Buffalo	13	0	Riddick, Louis, Oakland	15	3
Newsome, Craig, Green Bay	13	13	Pilgrim, Evan, Tennessee	3	0	Riemersma, Jay, Buffalo	16	3
Newton, Nate, Dallas	16	16	Pittman, Julian, New Orleans	2	0	Riley, Victor, Kansas City	16	15
Nickerson, Hardy, Tampa Bay	10	10	Pittman, Kavika, Dallas	15	15	Rison, Andre, Kansas City	14	13
Norgard, Erik, Tennessee	1	1	Pittman, Michael, Arizona	15	0	Ritchie, Jon, Oakland	15	10
Northern, Gabe, Buffalo	16	16	Player, Scott, Arizona	16	0	Rivera, Marco, Green Bay	15	15
Norton, Ken, San Francisco	16	16	Pleasant, Anthony, N.Y. Jets	16	15	Rivers, Ron, Detroit	15	0
Novak, Jeff, Jacksonville	4	0	Plummer, Jake, Arizona	16	16	Roaf, Willie, New Orleans	15	15
Nutten, Tom, St. Louis	5	2	Pollard, Marcus, Indianapolis	16	11	Roan, Michael, Tennessee	16	1
O'Donnell, Neil, Cincinnati	13	11	Ponds, Antwaune, Washington	3	0	Robbins, Austin, New Orleans	16	1
O'Dwyer, Matt, N.Y. Jets	16	16	Poole, Keith, New Orleans	15	4	Robbins, Barret, Oakland	16	16
O'Neal, Leslie, Kansas City	16	13	Poole, Tyrone, Indianapolis	15	15	Roberson, James, Tennessee	10	5
O'Neill, Kevin, Detroit	11	0	Pope, Marquez, San Francisco	6	3	Roberts, Ray, Detroit	16	16
Oben, Roman, N.Y. Giants	16	16	Popson, Ted, Kansas City	12	1	Robertson, Marcus, Tennessee	12	12
Odom, Jason, Tampa Bay	15	15	Porcher, Robert, Detroit	16	16	Robinson, Bryan, Chicago	11	5
Ofodile, A.J., Baltimore	5	0	Porter, Daryl, Buffalo	2	0	Robinson, Damien, Tampa Bay	7	0
Ogbogu, Eric, N.Y. Jets	12	0	Portilla, Jose, Atlanta	16	0	Robinson, Eddie, Tennessee	16	16
Ogden, Jeff, Dallas	16	0	Posey, Jeff, San Francisco	16	0	Robinson, Eugene, Atlanta	16	16
Ogden, Jonathan, Baltimore	13	13	Potts, Roosevelt, Baltimore	16	15	Robinson, Jeff, St. Louis	16	0
Oldham, Chris, Pittsburgh	16	1	Pounds, Darryl, Washington	16	3	Robinson, Marcus, Chicago	3	0
Oliver, Winslow, Carolina	16	0	Pourdanesh, Shar, Washington	16	15	Roby, Reggie, San Francisco	14	0
Olivo, Brock, Detroit	1	0	Powell, Craig, N.Y. Jets	2	0	Roche, Brian, Kansas City	4	1
Olsavsky, Jerry, Baltimore	9	0	Preston, Roell, Green Bay	16	0	Rodenhauser, Mark, Pittsburgh	16	0
Olson, Benji, Tennessee	13	1	Price, Marcus, San Diego	10	0	Rodgers, Derrick, Miami	16	16
Orlando, Bo, Pittsburgh	11	1	Price, Shawn, Buffalo	14	2	Roe, James, Baltimore	10	3
Osborne, Chuck, Oakland	6	0	Prior, Anthony, Oakland	4	0	Rogers, Sam, Buffalo	15	15
Ostroski, Jerry, Buffalo	16	16	Prior, Mike, Green Bay	16	1	Rolle, Samari, Tennessee	15	1
Owens, Dan, Detroit	11	11	Pritchard, Mike, Seattle	16	16	Romanowski, Bill, Denver	16	16
Owens, Terrell, San Francisco	16	10	Pritchett, Kelvin, Jacksonville	15	9	Ross, Adrian, Cincinnati	14	1
Oxendine, Ken, Atlanta	9	0	Pritchett, Stanley, Miami	16	12	Ross, Oliver, Dallas	2	0
Pace, Orlando, St. Louis	16	16	Proehl, Ricky, St. Louis	16	11	Rossum, Allen, Philadelphia	15	2
Palelei, Lonnie, N.Y. Giants	9	0	Pryce, Trevor, Denver	16	15	Rouen, Tom, Denver	16	0
Palmer, David, Minnesota	16	0	Pupunu, Alfred, N.Y. Giants	9	0	Roundtree, Raleigh, San Diego	15	5
Palmer, Mitch, Tampa Bay	16	0	Purnell, Lovett, New England	16	5	Royal, Andre, Indianapolis	13	9

– 233 –

Player, Team	GP	GS
Royals, Mark, New Orleans	16	0
Roye, Orpheus, Pittsburgh	16	9
Rucci, Todd, New England	16	16
Rudd, Dwayne, Minnesota	15	15
Ruddy, Tim, Miami	16	16
Ruhman, Chris, San Francisco	6	0
Runyan, Jon, Tennessee	16	16
Russ, Bernard, New England	1	0
Russell, Darrell, Oakland	16	16
Russell, Twan, Washington	3	0
Rutledge, Rod, New England	16	4
Sadowski, Troy, Jacksonville	5	0
Salaam, Ephraim, Atlanta	16	16
Salave'a, Joe, Tennessee	13	0
Saleaumua, Dan, Seattle	11	6
Saleh, Tarek, Carolina	11	1
Sanders, Barry, Detroit	16	16
Sanders, Brandon, N.Y. Giants	13	0
Sanders, Chris, Tennessee	14	1
Sanders, Deion, Dallas	11	11
Sanders, Frank, Arizona	16	16
Sanderson, Scott, Tennessee	16	3
Santiago, O.J., Atlanta	16	16
Sapp, Patrick, Arizona	16	1
Sapp, Warren, Tampa Bay	16	16
Sargent, Kevin, Cincinnati	16	16
Sasa, Don, Car.-Det.	4	0
Sauer, Craig, Atlanta	16	6
Sauerbrun, Todd, Chicago	3	0
Sawyer, Corey, Cincinnati	3	0
Schlereth, Mark, Denver	16	16
Schlesinger, Cory, Detroit	15	2
Schreiber, Adam, Atlanta	16	0
Schroeder, Bill, Green Bay	13	3
Schulters, Lance, S.F.	15	0
Schulz, Kurt, Buffalo	12	12
Schwantz, Jim, Chicago	16	0
Schwartz, Bryan, Jacksonville	13	12
Scifres, Steve, Carolina	1	0
Scott, Darnay, Cincinnati	13	13
Scott, Freddie, Indianapolis	1	0
Scott, Lance, N.Y. Giants	16	16
Scrafford, Kirk, San Francisco	9	8
Scroggins, Tracy, Detroit	11	3
Scurlock, Mike, St. Louis	16	0
Sears, Corey, St. Louis	4	0
Seau, Junior, San Diego	16	16
Sellers, Mike, Washington	14	1
Semple, Tony, Detroit	16	3
Settles, Tawambi, Jacksonville	7	0
Shade, Sam, Cincinnati	16	15
Sharpe, Shannon, Denver	16	16
Sharper, Darren, Green Bay	16	16
Sharper, Jamie, Baltimore	16	16
Shaw, Harold, New England	11	0
Shaw, Scott, Cincinnati	2	0
Shaw, Sedrick, New England	13	1
Shaw, Terrance, San Diego	13	13
Shedd, Kenny, Oakland	15	0
Shehee, Rashaan, Kansas City	16	0
Sheldon, Mike, Miami	9	2
Shello, Kendel, Indianapolis	6	1
Shelton, Daimon, Jacksonville	14	8
Shepherd, Leslie, Washington	16	16
Shields, Will, Kansas City	16	16
Shiver, Clay, Dallas	14	9
Sidney, Dainon, Tennessee	16	1
Sienkiewicz, Troy, San Diego	7	0
Siglar, Ricky, Car.-N.O.-K.C.	6	0
Simmons, Anthony, Seattle	12	4
Simmons, Brian, Cincinnati	14	12

Player, Team	GP	GS
Simmons, Clyde, Cincinnati	16	16
Simmons, Jason, Pittsburgh	6	0
Simmons, Tony, New England	11	6
Simmons, Wayne, K.C.-Buf.	16	10
Simpson, Carl, Arizona	13	1
Sims, Keith, Washington	4	0
Sinceno, Kaseem, Philadelphia	10	0
Sinclair, Michael, Seattle	16	16
Singleton, Alshermond, T.B.	15	0
Siragusa, Tony, Baltimore	15	15
Slade, Chris, New England	15	15
Slaughter, Webster, San Diego	10	0
Slay, Henry, Philadelphia	3	0
Sloan, David, Detroit	10	2
Slutzker, Scott, New Orleans	3	0
Small, Torrance, Indianapolis	16	4
Smedley, Eric, Buffalo	16	0
Smeenge, Joel, Jacksonville	16	14
Smith, Antowain, Buffalo	16	14
Smith, Artie, Dallas	16	0
Smith, Brady, New Orleans	14	5
Smith, Brent, Miami	8	7
Smith, Bruce, Buffalo	15	15
Smith, Chuck, Atlanta	16	16
Smith, Darrin, Seattle	13	12
Smith, Derek, Washington	16	15
Smith, Detron, Denver	15	2
Smith, Ed, Atlanta	15	0
Smith, Emmitt, Dallas	16	16
Smith, Fernando, Jacksonville	15	0
Smith, Frankie, Chicago	15	0
Smith, Irv, San Francisco	16	8
Smith, Jeff, Kansas City	11	3
Smith, Jimmy, Jacksonville	16	15
Smith, Kevin, Dallas	14	14
Smith, Lamar, New Orleans	14	9
Smith, Mark, Arizona	14	13
Smith, Neil, Denver	14	14
Smith, Otis, N.Y. Jets	16	16
Smith, Robert, Minnesota	14	14
Smith, Rod, Denver	16	16
Smith, Rod M., Car.-G.B.	14	2
Smith, Shevin, Tampa Bay	3	0
Smith, Thomas, Buffalo	14	14
Smith, Travian, Oakland	2	0
Smith, Vinson, New Orleans	15	0
Solomon, Freddie, Philadelphia	16	1
Sowell, Jerald, N.Y. Jets	16	2
Sparks, Phillippi, N.Y. Giants	13	13
Spears, Marcus, Kansas City	12	0
Spence, Blake, N.Y. Jets	5	0
Spencer, Jimmy, San Diego	15	4
Spikes, Takeo, Cincinnati	16	16
Spindler, Marc, Detroit	15	1
Spires, Greg, New England	15	1
Spriggs, Marcus, Buffalo	1	0
Springs, Shawn, Seattle	16	16
Sprotte, Jimmy, Cincinnati	5	0
Staat, Jeremy, Pittsburgh	6	0
Stablein, Brian, Detroit	10	0
Stai, Brenden, Pittsburgh	16	16
Staley, Duce, Philadelphia	16	13
Stallings, Dennis, Tennessee	15	0
Starks, Duane, Baltimore	16	8
Staten, Ralph, Baltimore	15	3
Steed, Joel, Pittsburgh	16	16
Steele, Glen, Cincinnati	10	0
Stenstrom, Steve, Chicago	7	7
Stephens, Jamain, Pittsburgh	11	10
Stephens, Tremayne, San Diego	13	1
Stepnoski, Mark, Tennessee	13	13
Steussie, Todd, Minnesota	15	15

Player, Team	GP	GS
Stevens, Matt, Phi.-Was.	10	1
Stewart, James, Jacksonville	3	3
Stewart, Kordell, Pittsburgh	16	16
Stewart, Rayna, Miami	14	0
Stewart, Ryan, Detroit	16	0
Still, Bryan, San Diego	14	9
Stokes, Barry, Miami	3	0
Stokes, Eric, Seattle	4	0
Stokes, J.J., San Francisco	16	11
Stoltenberg, Bryan, Carolina	14	10
Stone, Dwight, Carolina	16	0
Stone, Ron, N.Y. Giants	14	14
Storz, Erik, Jacksonville	1	0
Stoutmire, Omar, Dallas	16	12
Stover, Matt, Baltimore	16	0
Stoyanovich, Pete, Kansas City	16	0
Strahan, Michael, N.Y. Giants	16	15
Strickland, Fred, Dallas	16	15
Stringer, Korey, Minnesota	14	14
Strong, Mack, Seattle	16	5
Stryzinski, Dan, Atlanta	16	0
Strzelczyk, Justin, Pittsburgh	7	7
Stubblefield, Dana, Washington	7	7
Stubbs, Danny, Miami	5	1
Stuckey, Shawn, New England	6	0
Styles, Lorenzo, St. Louis	7	3
Sualua, Nicky, Dallas	16	0
Sullivan, Chris, New England	15	10
Supernaw, Kywin, Detroit	2	0
Surtain, Patrick, Miami	16	0
Sutter, Ryan, Carolina	1	0
Sutton, Mike, Tennessee	1	0
Swann, Eric, Arizona	7	5
Swayda, Shawn, Atlanta	5	0
Swayne, Harry, Denver	16	16
Sweeney, Jim, Pittsburgh	8	1
Swilling, Pat, Oakland	16	0
Swinger, Rashod, Arizona	16	11
Szott, David, Kansas City	1	1
Talley, Ben, Atlanta	8	0
Tamm, Ralph, Kansas City	16	0
Tanner, Barron, Miami	13	0
Tanuvasa, Maa, Denver	16	16
Tate, Robert, Minnesota	15	1
Tate, Willy, Kansas City	1	0
Tatum, Kinnon, Carolina	15	0
Taylor, Aaron, San Diego	15	15
Taylor, Bobby, Philadelphia	11	10
Taylor, Cordell, Jacksonville	11	0
Taylor, Fred, Jacksonville	15	12
Taylor, Henry, Detroit	1	0
Taylor, Jason, Miami	16	15
Teague, George, Dallas	16	5
Terrell, Pat, Green Bay	16	3
Terry, Rick, Carolina	7	3
Testaverde, Vinny, N.Y. Jets	14	13
Tharpe, Larry, Detroit	16	9
Thelwell, Ryan, San Diego	6	3
Thierry, John, Chicago	16	9
Thigpen, Yancey, Tennessee	9	8
Thomas, Chris, Washington	14	0
Thomas, Corey, Detroit	1	0
Thomas, Dave, Jacksonville	14	12
Thomas, Derrick, Kansas City	15	10
Thomas, Fred, Seattle	15	2
Thomas, Henry, New England	16	15
Thomas, Hollis, Philadelphia	12	12
Thomas, J.T., St. Louis	16	0
Thomas, Lamar, Miami	16	2
Thomas, Mark, Chi.-Ind.	14	5
Thomas, Marvin, Detroit	4	0
Thomas, Orlando, Minnesota	16	16

Player, Team	GP	GS	Player, Team	GP	GS	Player, Team	GP	GS
Thomas, Ratcliff, Indianapolis...	5	0	Walker, Darnell, San Francisco..	16	16	Williams, Gene, Atlanta	16	16
Thomas, Robb, Tampa Bay	7	0	Walker, Denard, Tennessee........	16	16	Williams, George, N.Y. Giants....	2	0
Thomas, Robert, Dallas	16	0	Walker, Gary, Tennessee...........	16	16	Williams, Gerome, San Diego....	16	0
Thomas, Rodney, Tennessee	11	0	Walker, Marquis, Oakland	16	7	Williams, Grant, Seattle	16	0
Thomas, Thurman, Buffalo........	14	3	Wallace, Aaron, Oakland...........	4	0	Williams, Harvey, Oakland	16	3
Thomas, Tra, Philadelphia	16	16	Wallace, Al, Philadelphia	15	0	Williams, Jamal, San Diego.......	9	0
Thomas, William, Philadelphia ..	16	16	Walls, Wesley, Carolina	14	14	Williams, Jamel, Washington	16	0
Thomas, Zach, Miami	16	16	Walsh, Chris, Minnesota	15	0	Williams, James E., S.F.	15	0
Thomason, Jeff, Green Bay	16	2	Walsh, Steve, Tampa Bay	5	0	Williams, James O., Chicago.....	16	16
Thompson, Bennie, Baltimore ...	16	0	Walter, Ken, Carolina	16	0	Williams, Jay, St. Louis	16	1
Thompson, David, St. Louis......	1	0	Walz, Zack, Arizona	16	0	Williams, Jermaine, Oakland.....	10	0
Thompson, Mike, Cincinnati	10	0	Ward, Dedric, N.Y. Jets	16	4	Williams, John, Baltimore	16	0
Thrash, James, Washington	10	1	Ward, Hines, Pittsburgh	16	0	Williams, Karl, Tampa Bay........	13	6
Threats, Jabbar, Jacksonville	2	0	Ward, Phillip, St. Louis.............	2	0	Williams, Kevin, N.Y. Jets	15	6
Tillman, Pat, Arizona	16	10	Warfield, Eric, Kansas City	12	0	Williams, Kevin R., Buffalo	16	0
Timmerman, Adam, Green Bay .	16	16	Warner, Kurt, St. Louis.............	1	0	Williams, Lamanzer, Jac.	2	0
Tobeck, Robbie, Atlanta............	16	16	Warner, Ron, New Orleans	1	0	Williams, Moe, Minnesota	12	1
Tolliver, Billy Joe, New Orleans .	7	4	Warren, Chris, Dallas	9	0	Williams, Pat, Buffalo	13	0
Tomczak, Mike, Pittsburgh	16	0	Warren, Lamont, Indianapolis ...	12	2	Williams, Robert, Kansas City ...	16	1
Tomich, Jared, New Orleans......	16	11	Washington, Dewayne, Pit.	16	16	Williams, Rodney, Oakland........	1	0
Tongue, Reggie, Kansas City	15	15	Washington, Keith, Baltimore ...	16	0	Williams, Roland, St. Louis	13	9
Toomer, Amani, N.Y. Giants.......	16	0	Washington, Marvin, Denver.....	16	0	Williams, Shaun, N.Y. Giants	13	0
Tovar, Steve, San Diego	16	2	Washington, Ted, Buffalo	16	16	Williams, Sherman, Dallas	16	2
Townsend, Deshea, Pittsburgh..	12	0	Washington, Todd, Tampa Bay ..	4	0	Williams, Stepfret, Cincinnati ...	5	0
Trapp, James, Oakland	16	0	Watters, Ricky, Seattle	16	16	Williams, Tony, Minnesota	14	9
Traylor, Keith, Denver	15	14	Way, Charles, N.Y. Giants	16	15	Williams, Tyrone, Green Bay	16	16
Treu, Adam, Oakland	16	0	Wayne, Nate, Denver	1	0	Williams, Wally, Baltimore.........	13	13
Trotter, Jeremiah, Philadelphia ..	8	0	Weary, Fred, New Orleans	14	1	Williams, Willie, Seattle	14	14
Truitt, Greg, Cincinnati	11	0	Webb, Richmond, Miami...........	9	9	Willig, Matt, Green Bay.............	16	0
Tuaolo, Esera, Atlanta.............	13	1	Webster, Larry, Baltimore	15	1	Willis, James, Philadelphia.......	16	16
Tubbs, Winfred, San Francisco..	16	15	Weiner, Todd, Seattle...............	6	0	Wilmsmeyer, Klaus, Miami	16	0
Tucker, Ryan, St. Louis	5	0	Wells, Dean, Seattle	9	8	Wilson, Bernard, Arizona	16	3
Tuggle, Jessie, Atlanta............	16	16	Wells, Mike, Chicago	16	16	Wilson, Jerry, Miami	16	0
Tuinei, Van, Indianapolis	12	0	Westbrook, Bryant, Detroit.......	16	16	Wilson, Reinard, Cincinnati	16	15
Tumulty, Tom, Cincinnati	4	4	Westbrook, Michael, Was.	11	10	Wilson, Robert, Seattle.............	16	0
Tupa, Tom, New England	16	0	Wetnight, Ryan, Chicago..........	15	4	Wilson, Troy, New Orleans	15	0
Turk, Dan, Washington	16	0	Wheatley, Tyrone, N.Y. Giants....	5	0	Wilson, Wade, Oakland	5	3
Turk, Matt, Washington	16	0	Wheaton, Kenny, Dallas............	15	1	Winters, Frank, Green Bay........	13	13
Turley, Kyle, New Orleans.........	15	15	Wheeler, Leonard, Carolina	16	0	Wisniewski, Steve, Oakland......	16	16
Turner, Eric, Oakland	6	6	Wheeler, Mark, New England	10	2	Wistrom, Grant, St. Louis	13	0
Turner, Floyd, Baltimore	16	3	Whelihan, Craig, San Diego	10	7	Witman, Jon, Pittsburgh...........	16	9
Turner, Kevin, Philadelphia	16	15	Whigham, Larry, New England..	16	0	Wohlabaugh, Dave, N.E.	16	16
Turner, Scott, San Diego	16	1	White, Jose, Jacksonville	15	0	Wolford, Will, Pittsburgh	13	13
Tuten, Rick, St. Louis..............	16	0	White, Reggie, Green Bay.........	16	16	Wong, Kailee, Minnesota	15	0
Tylski, Rich, Jacksonville..........	12	8	White, Steve, Tampa Bay	16	0	Woodall, Lee, San Francisco	15	15
Unutoa, Morris, Philadelphia.....	16	0	White, William, Atlanta.............	16	16	Wooden, Shawn, Miami	2	1
Upshaw, Regan, Tampa Bay	16	16	Whitfield, Bob, Atlanta.............	16	16	Wooden, Terry, Oakland	16	10
Uwaezuoke, Iheanyi, S.F.-Mia. ..	11	0	Whiting, Brandon, Philadelphia .	16	5	Woods, Jerome, Kansas City	16	16
Van Dyke, Alex, N.Y. Jets	16	0	Whitted, Alvis, Jacksonville	16	0	Woodson, Charles, Oakland	16	16
Van Pelt, Alex, Buffalo	1	0	Whittington, Bernard, Ind.	15	11	Woodson, Darren, Dallas	16	15
Vance, Eric, Tampa Bay	3	1	Whittle, Jason, N.Y. Giants	1	0	Woodson, Rod, Baltimore	16	16
Vanderjagt, Mike, Indianapolis ..	14	0	Widell, Dave, Atlanta	1	0	Wooten, Tito, N.Y. Giants	14	13
Vanover, Tamarick, Kansas City.	12	0	Widmer, Corey, N.Y. Giants	16	15	Wortham, Barron, Tennessee	13	0
Vardell, Tommy, Detroit...........	14	9	Wiegert, Zach, St. Louis...........	13	13	Wright, Toby, St. Louis.............	3	3
Veland, Tony, Carolina	15	5	Wiegmann, Casey, Chicago	16	15	Wuerffel, Danny, New Orleans...	5	4
Verba, Ross, Green Bay	16	16	Wiggins, Paul, Washington	1	0	Wunsch, Jerry, Tampa Bay	16	1
Villa, Danny, Carolina	7	0	Wilcox, Josh, New Orleans........	3	1	Wycheck, Frank, Tennessee	16	16
Villarrial, Chris, Chicago...........	16	16	Wiley, Marcellus, Buffalo	16	3	Wynn, Renaldo, Jacksonville	15	15
Vinatieri, Adam, New England ...	16	0	Wilkins, Gabe, San Francisco....	8	4	Yarborough, Ryan, Baltimore	6	1
Vincent, Troy, Philadelphia	13	13	Wilkins, Jeff, St. Louis	16	0	Young, Bryant, San Francisco ...	12	12
von Oelhoffen, Kimo, Cincinnati..	16	16	Wilkinson, Dan, Washington	16	16	Young, Duane, Buffalo..............	4	0
Vrabel, Mike, Pittsburgh...........	11	0	Willard, Jerrott, Kansas City......	1	0	Young, Floyd, Tampa Bay	11	0
Waddy, Jude, Green Bay	13	0	Williams, Aeneas, Arizona	16	16	Young, Rodney, N.Y. Giants	2	0
Wade, John, Jacksonville	5	0	Williams, Alfred, Denver............	10	0	Young, Steve, San Francisco	15	15
Wadsworth, Andre, Arizona.......	16	15	Williams, Ben, Minnesota	1	0	Zeier, Eric, Baltimore	10	4
Wahle, Mike, Green Bay	1	0	Williams, Brian, Green Bay	16	15	Zeigler, Dusty, Buffalo	16	16
Wainright, Frank, Miami	16	1	Williams, Charlie, Dallas	15	3	Zellars, Ray, New Orleans.........	11	7
Waldroup, Kerwin, Detroit........	13	13	Williams, Clarence, Buffalo........	3	0	Zgonina, Jeff, Indianapolis	2	0
Walker, Bracey, Kansas City	8	0	Williams, Darryl, Seattle	16	16	Zolak, Scott, New England	6	2
Walker, Brian, Miami	16	0	Williams, Elijah, Atlanta	15	0	Zordich, Mike, Philadelphia	16	16
Walker, Corey, Philadelphia	14	0	Williams, Erik, Dallas................	15	15			

PLAYERS WITH TWO OR MORE CLUBS

Player, Team	GP	GS	Player, Team	GP	GS	Player, Team	GP	GS
Blackmon, Roosevelt, G.B.	3	0	Dixon, Ernest, Oakland	3	0	Kopp, Jeff, Baltimore	7	0
Blackmon, Roosevelt, Cin.	12	0	Dixon, Ernest, Kansas City	1	0	Lofton, Steve, New England	6	0
Blair, Michael, Green Bay	11	0	Dunn, David, Cincinnati	1	0	Lofton, Steve, Carolina	10	7
Blair, Michael, Cincinnati	2	0	Dunn, David, Pittsburgh	10	0	Martin, Steve, Indianapolis	4	0
Blevins, Tony, San Francisco	2	0	Ellard, Henry, New England	5	0	Martin, Steve, Philadelphia	9	3
Blevins, Tony, Indianapolis	3	0	Ellard, Henry, Washington	2	0	Morris, Bam, Chicago	2	0
Bolden, Juran, Atlanta	3	0	Harris, Ronnie, Seattle	2	0	Morris, Bam, Kansas City	10	5
Bolden, Juran, Green Bay	3	0	Harris, Ronnie, Atlanta	6	0	Sasa, Don, Carolina	2	0
Bolden, Juran, Carolina	6	0	Hill, Ray, Buffalo	4	0	Sasa, Don, Detroit	2	0
Brooks, Bucky, Kansas City	6	0	Hill, Ray, Miami	2	0	Siglar, Ricky, Carolina	1	0
Brooks, Bucky, Oakland	6	0	Holland, Darius, Kansas City	6	0	Siglar, Ricky, New Orleans	1	0
Buckley, Curtis, San Francisco	8	0	Holland, Darius, Detroit	10	4	Siglar, Ricky, Kansas City	4	0
Buckley, Curtis, N.Y. Giants	6	0	Holmberg, Rob, Indianapolis	3	0	Simmons, Wayne, Kansas City	10	10
Collins, Kerry, Carolina	4	4	Holmberg, Rob, N.Y. Jets	9	0	Simmons, Wayne, Buffalo	6	0
Collins, Kerry, New Orleans	7	7	Holmes, Darick, Buffalo	3	0	Smith, Rod M., Carolina	6	2
Conley, Steven, Indianapolis	1	0	Holmes, Darick, Green Bay	11	4	Smith, Rod M., Green Bay	8	0
Conley, Steven, Pittsburgh	2	1	Jones, Ernest, Denver	1	0	Stevens, Matt, Philadelphia	7	1
Copeland, Russell, Philadelphia	11	0	Jones, Ernest, Carolina	7	0	Stevens, Matt, Washington	3	0
Copeland, Russell, Green Bay	3	1	Kidd, John, Detroit	2	0	Thomas, Mark, Chicago	10	4
Crockett, Zack, Indianapolis	2	0	Kidd, John, N.Y. Jets	8	0	Thomas, Mark, Indianapolis	4	1
Crockett, Zack, Jacksonville	10	1	Kitts, Jim, Washington	3	0	Uwaezuoke, Iheanyi, S.F.	7	0
Davis, Don, New Orleans	4	0	Kitts, Jim, Green Bay	2	0	Uwaezuoke, Iheanyi, Miami	4	0
Davis, Don, Tampa Bay	5	0	Kopp, Jeff, Jacksonville	6	0			

ATTENDANCE

REGULAR SEASON

Team	Home Attendance	Average	NFL Rank	Road Attendance	Average	NFL Rank
Arizona	430,552	53,819	27	508,879	63,610	13
Atlanta	457,477	57,185	22	506,753	63,344	14
Baltimore	549,531	68,691	10	434,548	54,319	30
Buffalo	560,570	70,071	8	481,895	60,237	22
Carolina	489,622	61,203	17	479,391	59,924	23
Chicago	429,607	53,701	28	462,012	57,752	27
Cincinnati	444,335	55,542	23	446,353	55,794	29
Dallas	510,438	63,805	15	565,971	70,746	1
Denver	597,462	74,683	1	546,021	68,253	3
Detroit	571,416	71,427	6	517,168	64,646	9
Green Bay	479,292	59,912	18	529,141	66,143	5
Indianapolis	440,930	55,116	24	519,197	64,900	8
Jacksonville	561,472	70,184	7	490,956	61,370	19
Kansas City	589,038	73,630	3	516,071	64,509	11
Miami	581,784	72,723	4	546,530	68,316	2
Minnesota	510,741	63,843	14	491,291	61,411	17
New England	475,828	59,479	20	516,846	64,606	10
New Orleans	436,473	54,559	25	485,752	60,719	20
N.Y. Giants	576,708	72,089	5	474,434	59,304	24
N.Y. Jets	589,768	73,721	2	491,552	61,444	16
Oakland	386,548	48,319	29	529,055	66,132	6
Philadelphia	527,990	65,999	12	472,474	59,059	25
Pittsburgh	464,619	58,077	21	540,926	67,616	4
San Diego	476,718	59,590	19	484,272	60,534	21
San Francisco	537,385	67,173	11	526,894	65,862	7
Seattle	500,210	62,526	16	511,687	63,961	12
St. Louis	431,143	53,893	26	449,894	56,237	28
Tampa Bay	518,047	64,756	13	491,128	61,391	18
Tennessee	299,555	37,444	30	492,251	61,531	15
Washington	552,099	69,012	9	468,016	58,502	26
NFL total	14,977,358	62,406		14,977,358	62,406	

Note: Attendance figures are unofficial and are based on box scores of games.

HISTORICAL

TOP REGULAR-SEASON HOME CROWDS

Team	Attendance	Date	Site	Opponent
Arizona	73,400	October 30, 1994	Sun Devil Stadium	Pittsburgh
Atlanta	71,253	November 21, 1993	Georgia Dome	Dallas
Baltimore	69,074	December 13, 1998	Ravens Stadium	Minnesota
Buffalo	80,368	October 4, 1992	Rich Stadium	Miami
Carolina	76,136	December 10, 1995	Clemson Memorial Stadium	San Francisco
Chicago	66,900	September 5, 1993	Soldier Field	N.Y. Giants
Cincinnati	60,284	October 17, 1971	Riverfront Stadium	Cleveland
Dallas	80,259	November 24, 1966	Cotton Bowl	Cleveland
Denver	76,089	October 26,1986	Mile High Stadium	Seattle
Detroit	80,444	December 20, 1981	Pontiac Silverdome	Tampa Bay
Green Bay	60,766	September 1, 1997	Lambeau Field	Chicago
Indianapolis	61,282	December 14, 1997	RCA Dome	Miami
Jacksonville	74,143	December 28, 1998	ALLTEL Stadium	Pittsburgh
Kansas City	82,094	November 5, 1972	Arrowhead Stadium	Oakland
Miami	78,914	November 19, 1972	Orange Bowl	N.Y. Jets
Minnesota	64,471	November 22, 1998	Metrodome	Green Bay
New England	61,457	December 5, 1971	Schaefer Stadium*	Miami
New Orleans	83,437	November 12, 1967	Tulane Stadium	Dallas
		November 26, 1967	Tulane Stadium	Atlanta
New York Giants	78,039	September 21, 1998	Giants Stadium	Dallas
New York Jets	79,469	September 20, 1998	Giants Stadium	Indianapolis
Oakland	74,121	September 23, 1973	Memorial Stadium; Berkeley, Cal.	Miami
Philadelphia	72,111	November 1, 1981	Veterans Stadium	Dallas
Pittsburgh	60,808	December 18, 1994	Three Rivers Stadium	Cleveland
St. Louis	66,030	December 14, 1997	Trans World Dome	Chicago

Team	Attendance	Date	Site	Opponent
San Diego	66,532	November 29, 1998	Qualcomm Stadium	Denver
San Francisco	69,014	November 13, 1994	Candlestick Park	Dallas
Seattle	66,264	October 26, 1997	Kingdome	Oakland
Tampa Bay	73,523	December 12, 1997	Houlihan's Stadium	Green Bay
Tennessee	50,677	December 21, 1997	Liberty Bowl Memorial Stadium	Pittsburgh
Washington	78,270	September 14, 1997	Jack Kent Cooke Stadium	Arizona

*Now known as Foxboro Stadium.

NATIONAL FOOTBALL LEAGUE

Year	Regular season*		Average	Postseason†	
1934	492,684	(60)	8,211	35,059	(1)
1935	638,178	(53)	12,041	15,000	(1)
1936	816,007	(54)	15,111	29,545	(1)
1937	963,039	(55)	17,510	15,878	(1)
1938	937,197	(55)	17,040	48,120	(1)
1939	1,071,200	(55)	19,476	32,279	(1)
1940	1,063,025	(55)	19,328	36,034	(1)
1941	1,108,615	(55)	20,157	55,870	(2)
1942	887,920	(55)	16,144	36,006	(1)
1943	969,128	(50)	19,383	71,315	(2)
1944	1,019,649	(50)	20,393	46,016	(1)
1945	1,270,401	(50)	25,408	32,178	(1)
1946	1,732,135	(55)	31,493	58,346	(1)
1947	1,837,437	(60)	30,624	66,268	(2)
1948	1,525,243	(60)	25,421	36,309	(1)
1949	1,391,735	(60)	23,196	27,980	(1)
1950	1,977,753	(78)	25,356	136,647	(3)
1951	1,913,019	(72)	26,570	57,522	(1)
1952	2,052,126	(72)	28,502	97,507	(2)
1953	2,164,585	(72)	30,064	54,577	(1)
1954	2,190,571	(72)	30,425	43,827	(1)
1955	2,521,836	(72)	35,026	85,693	(1)
1956	2,551,263	(72)	35,434	56,836	(1)
1957	2,836,318	(72)	39,393	119,579	(2)
1958	3,006,124	(72)	41,752	123,659	(2)
1959	3,140,000	(72)	43,617	57,545	(1)
1960	3,128,296	(78)	40,106	67,325	(1)
1961	3,986,159	(98)	40,675	39,029	(1)
1962	4,003,421	(98)	40,851	64,892	(1)
1963	4,163,643	(98)	42,486	45,801	(1)
1964	4,563,049	(98)	46,562	79,544	(1)
1965	4,634,021	(98)	47,296	100,304	(2)
1966	5,337,044	(105)	50,829	135,098	(2)
1967	5,938,924	(112)	53,026	241,754	(4)
1968	5,882,313	(112)	52,521	291,279	(4)
1969	6,096,127	(112)	54,430	242,841	(4)
1970	9,533,333	(182)	52,381	410,371	(7)
1971	10,076,035	(182)	55,363	430,244	(7)
1972	10,445,827	(182)	57,395	435,466	(7)
1973	10,730,933	(182)	58,961	458,515	(7)
1974	10,236,322	(182)	56,224	412,180	(7)
1975	10,213,193	(182)	56,116	443,811	(7)
1976	11,070,543	(196)	56,482	428,733	(7)
1977	11,018,632	(196)	56,218	483,588	(7)
1978	12,771,800	(224)	57,017	578,107	(9)
1979	13,182,039	(224)	58,848	582,266	(9)
1980	13,392,230	(224)	59,787	577,186	(9)
1981	13,606,990	(224)	60,745	587,361	(9)
1982§	7,367,438	(126)	58,472	985,952	(15)
1983	13,277,222	(224)	59,273	625,068	(9)
1984	13,398,112	(224)	59,813	614,809	(9)
1985	13,345,047	(224)	59,567	660,667	(9)
1986	13,588,551	(224)	60,663	683,901	(9)
1987∞	10,032,493	(168)	59,717	606,864	(9)
1988	13,539,848	(224)	60,446	608,204	(9)
1989	13,625,662	(224)	60,829	635,326	(9)
1990	14,266,240	(224)	63,689	797,198	(11)
1991	13,187,478	(224)	58,873	758,186	(11)
1992	13,159,387	(224)	58,747	756,005	(11)
1993	13,328,760	(224)	59,503	755,625	(11)
1994	13,479,680	(224)	60,177	719,143	(11)
1995	14,196,205	(240)	59,151	733,729	(11)
1996	13,695,748	(240)	57,066	711,601	(11)
1997	14,691,416	(240)	61,214	751,884	(11)
1998	14,977,358	(240)	62,406	776,225	(11)

*Number of tickets sold, including no-shows; number of regular-season games in parentheses.

†Includes conference, league championship and Super Bowl games, but not Pro Bowl; number of postseason games in parentheses.

‡A 57-day players strike reduced 224-game schedule to 126 games.

§A 24-day players strike reduced 224-game schedule to 168 non-strike games.

AMERICAN FOOTBALL LEAGUE

Year	Regular season*	Average	AFL Champ. Game
1960	926,156 (56)	16,538	32,183
1961	1,002,657 (56)	17,904	29,556
1962	1,147,302 (56)	20,487	37,981
1963	1,241,741 (56)	22,174	30,127
1964	1,447,875 (56)	25,855	40,242
1965	1,782,384 (56)	31,828	30,361
1966	2,160,369 (63)	34,291	42,080
1967	2,295,697 (63)	36,439	53,330
1968	2,635,004 (70)	37,643	62,627
1969	2,843,373 (70)	40,620	53,564

*Number of regular-season games in parentheses.

TRADES

(Covering June 1998 through May 1999)

JUNE 5

San Diego traded WR Tony Martin to Atlanta for a 1999 second-round draft choice. San Diego selected RB Jermaine Fazande (Oklahoma).

JUNE 8

San Diego traded DT Shawn Lee to Chicago for a 1999 fifth-round draft choice. San Diego selected DE Adrian Dingle (Clemson).

JULY 22

Carolina traded CB Tyrone Poole to Indianapolis for a 1999 second-round draft choice. Carolina selected T Chris Terry (Georgia).

AUGUST 17

N.Y. Jets traded P Brian Hansen to Green Bay for undisclosed terms.

AUGUST 20

Denver traded TE Kendall Watkins to Dallas for a 1999 fifth-round draft choice. Denver selected DE David Bowens (Western Illinois).

AUGUST 21

Green Bay traded K Brett Conway to N.Y. Jets for an undisclosed draft choice.

AUGUST 24

Pittsburgh traded NT Angel Rubio to San Francisco for past considerations.

AUGUST 25

Pittsburgh traded CB J.B. Brown to Arizona for a 1999 conditional draft choice. Pittsburgh selected K Kris Brown (Nebraska) in the seventh round.

Denver traded C Steve Gordon and DT David Richie to San Francisco for past considerations.

AUGUST 29

Green Bay traded KR Glyn Milburn to Chicago for a 1999 seventh-round draft choice. Green Bay selected WR Donald Driver (Alcorn State).

New England traded DE Mike Jones to St. Louis for a 2000 fifth-round draft choice.

New Orleans traded LB Andre Royal to Indianapolis for TE Scott Slutzker.

Pittsburgh traded LB Steve Conley to Indianapolis for a 1999 fifth-round draft choice. Pittsburgh selected TE Jerame Tuman (Michigan).

SEPTEMBER 1

Tennessee traded LB Lemanski Hall to Chicago for an undisclosed draft choice.

SEPTEMBER 29

Buffalo traded RB Darick Holmes to Green Bay for a 1999 fourth-round draft choice. Buffalo selected TE Bobby Collins (North Alabama).

FEBRUARY 12

San Francisco traded DE Roy Barker and TE Irv Smith to Cleveland for past considerations.

N.Y. Giants traded RB Tyrone Wheatley to Miami for a 1999 seventh-round draft choice. The Giants selected LB O.J. Childress (Clemson).

FEBRUARY 15

Minnesota traded QB Brad Johnson to Washington for 1999 first- and third-round draft choices and a 2000 second-round draft choice. Minnesota selected QB Daunte Culpepper (Central Florida) in the first round and traded its third-round pick to Pittsburgh.

FEBRUARY 16

Buffalo traded LB Chris Spielman to Cleveland for past considerations.

FEBRUARY 18

St. Louis traded WR Eddie Kennison to New Orleans for a 1999 second-round draft choice. St. Louis selected DB Dre' Bly (North Carolina).

FEBRUARY 23

San Francisco traded QB Ty Detmer and a 1999 fourth-round draft choice to Cleveland for 1999 fourth- and fifth-round draft choices. San Francisco later traded its fourth-round pick to Indianapolis and its fifth-round pick to Miami. Cleveland selected LB Wali Rainer (Virginia) in the fourth round.

MARCH 1

Denver traded QB Jeff Lewis to Carolina for a 1999 third-round draft choice and a 2000 undisclosed draft choice. Denver selected DB Chris Watson (Eastern Illinois).

San Francisco traded G Kevin Gogan to Miami for a 1999 fifth-round draft choice. San Francisco selected RB Terry Jackson (Florida).

MARCH 19

N.Y. Jets traded QB Glenn Foley to Seattle for a 1999 seventh-round draft choice. The Jets selected T Ryan Young (Kansas State) in the seventh round.

MARCH 25

N.Y. Jets traded WR Alex Van Dyke to Pittsburgh for a 1999 sixth-round draft choice. The Jets selected LB Marc Megna (Richmond).

MARCH 31

New England traded TE Lovett Purnell to Baltimore in exchange for a 1999 sixth-round draft choice. New England selected DB Marcus Washington (Colorado).

APRIL 5

Pittsburgh traded WR Jahine Arnold to Green Bay for past considerations.

APRIL 15

Indianapolis traded RB Marshall Faulk to St. Louis for 1999 second- and fifth-round draft choices. Indianapolis selected LB Mike Peterson (Florida) in the second round and DE Brad Scioli (Penn State) in the fifth round.

APRIL 17

Baltimore traded QB Eric Zeier to Tampa Bay for a 1999 sixth-round draft choice. Baltimore traded the sixth-round pick to Minnesota.

1998 REVIEW Trades

St. Louis traded QB Tony Banks to Baltimore for a 1999 fifth-round draft choice and a 2000 seventh-round draft choice. St. Louis selected G Cameron Spikes (Texas A&M).

San Francisco traded FB Marc Edwards to Cleveland for a 1999 fourth-round draft choice. San Francisco selected DB Pierson Prioleau (Virginia Tech).

APRIL 18

Minnesota traded T Everett Lindsay to Baltimore for a 1999 sixth-round draft choice. Minnesota selected DE Talance Sawyer (UNLV).

APRIL 22

New England traded RB Sedrick Shaw to Cleveland for past considerations.

APRIL 28

Philadelphia traded QB Rodney Peete to Washington for a 2000 sixth-round draft choice.

Basketball

NBA preseason

Eastern Conference
Atlantic Division

	W	L	Pct	GB

Kelly Hiller, Glen Ulin, N.D	72
Greg Hiller, Glen Ulin, N.D	72
Larry Barber, Sherman	73
Brad Martin, Los Altos, Cal.	73
Chad Magee, Tyler	73
Clint Frost, Mexia	73
John Richman, Leawood, Kan.	73
Jeff Klein, Mitchell, Neb.	73
Chad Campbell, Andrews	73
Andre Van Staden, South Africa	73
Jason Follen, Anaheim Hills, Cal	73
Craig Hainline, Houston, Tex.	73
D.Rohrbaugh, Carbondale, Col.	73
Vince Anderson, Houston	74
Albert Ochoa, Mission	74
Sushi Ishigaki, Japan	74
Andy Dillard, Edmond, Okla	74
Anthony Aguilar, Arvada, Col.	74
Brett Bingham, Burbank, Cal.	74
Carl Cooper, Kingwood	74
Jody Bellflower, Milledgeville, Ga	74
Derrick Pursley, El Paso	74
Marty Schiene, Naperville, Ill	74
Bobby Lucio, Brownsville	74
Jason Bryant, Conroe	74
Chris Parra, Irving	75
Bryan Novoa, Laredo	75
Chris Rieve, Beaumont	75
Stuart Hendley, Canada	75
Michael Brennan, Houston	75
Bill Heim, Austin	75
Kevin Marsh, Goleta, Cal.	75
Warrick Druian, Houston	75
Brandt Kieschnick, Hunstville	75

4. Gustavo Kuerten
5. Pete Sampras
6. Tommy Haas
7. Patrick Rafter
8. Richard Krajicek
9. Marcelo Rios
10. Thomas Enqvist
11. Tim Henman
12. Todd Martin
13. Nicolas Kiefer
14. Nicolas Lapentti
15. Mark Philippoussis
16. Andrei Medvedev
17. Carlos Moya
18. Jonas Bjorkman
19. Thomas Johansson
20. Dominik Hrbaty
21. Karol Kucera
22. Cedric Pioline
23. Leander Paes
24. Felix Mantilla
25. Albert Costa
26. Fabrice Santoro
27. Vincent Spadea
28. Sandon Stolle
29. Magnus Norman
30. Fernando Meligeni
31. Alex Corretja
32. Jiri Novak
33. Mahesh Bhupathi
34. Daniel Vacek
35. Byron Black
36. Sebastien Grosjean
37. Sebastien Lareau

Through six games, Texas A&M quarterback Randy McCown (15) has completed 92 of 172 passes for 1,528 yards and nine touchdowns, an average of 254.7 yards per game. If he continues on that pace, he will finish the 11-game season 169-of-315 for 2,801 yards and 17 touchdowns. The top five seasons in Aggies history in those categories:

PASSING YARDAGE

Player	Year	Yds.
Kevin Murray	1986	2,463
Edd Hargett	1968	2,321
Corey Pullig	1995	2,105
Corey Pullig	1994	2,056
Kevin Murray	1985	1,965

YARDS PER GAME

Player	Year	Yds
Edd Hargett	1968	232.1
Kevin Murray	1986	223.9
Corey Pullig	1995	191.4
Corey Pullig	1994	186.9
Kevin Murray	1985	178.6

COMPLETIONS

Player	Year	Com.
Kevin Murray	1987	212
Gary Kubiak	1982	181
Edd Hargett	1968	169
Corey Pullig	1995	165
Corey Pullig	1994	161

ATTEMPTS

Player	Year	Att.
Kevin Murray	1986	349
Edd Hargett	1968	348
Gary Kubiak	1982	324
Corey Pullig	1995	307
Brandon Stewart	1996	299

TD PASSES

Player	Year	TDs
Gary Kubiak	1982	19
Corey Pullig	1993	17
Kevin Murray	1986	17
Edd Hargett	1968	16
Corey Pullig	1995	14
Kevin Murray	1983	14

1998 STATISTICS

Rushing
Passing
Receiving
Scoring
Interceptions
Sacks
Fumbles
Field goals
Punting
Punt returns
Kickoff returns
Miscellaneous

RUSHING

TEAM

AFC

Team	Att.	Yds.	Avg.	Long	TD
Denver	525	2468	4.7	70	26
Buffalo	531	2161	4.1	32	13
Jacksonville	487	2102	4.3	t77	19
Pittsburgh	490	2034	4.2	56	8
Tennessee	462	1970	4.3	t71	12
N.Y. Jets	500	1879	3.8	t60	12
San Diego	460	1728	3.8	t72	11
Oakland	449	1727	3.8	t80	6
Cincinnati	405	1639	4.0	66	7
Baltimore	408	1629	4.0	56	7
Seattle	426	1626	3.8	64	11
Kansas City	433	1548	3.6	38	19
Miami	458	1535	3.4	45	10
Indianapolis	384	1486	3.9	t68	7
New England	403	1480	3.7	71	9
AFC total	6821	27012	4.0	t80	177
AFC average	454.7	1800.8	4.0	...	11.8

t—touchdown.

NFC

Team	Att.	Yds.	Avg.	Long	TD
San Francisco	491	2544	5.2	t96	19
Tampa Bay	523	2148	4.1	50	12
Atlanta	516	2101	4.1	48	18
Dallas	499	2014	4.0	49	21
Detroit	441	1955	4.4	t73	12
Minnesota	450	1936	4.3	t74	17
N.Y. Giants	474	1889	4.0	45	10
Philadelphia	427	1775	4.2	t64	10
Chicago	454	1713	3.8	57	9
Washington	401	1685	4.2	45	15
Arizona	450	1627	3.6	32	18
Green Bay	447	1526	3.4	50	7
Carolina	405	1458	3.6	41	11
St. Louis	395	1385	3.5	46	17
New Orleans	374	1325	3.5	33	6
NFC total	6747	27081	4.0	t96	202
NFC average	449.8	1805.4	4.0	...	13.5
NFL total	13568	54093	...	t96	379
NFL average	452.3	1803.1	4.0	...	12.6

INDIVIDUAL

BESTS OF THE SEASON

Yards, season
AFC: 2008—Terrell Davis, Denver.
NFC: 1846—Jamal Anderson, Atlanta.

Yards, game
AFC: 227—Priest Holmes, Baltimore at Cincinnati, Nov. 22 (36 attempts, 1 TD).
NFC: 198—Garrison Hearst, San Francisco vs. Detroit, Dec. 14 (24 attempts, 1 TD).

Longest gain
NFC: 96—Garrison Hearst, San Francisco vs. N.Y. Jets, Sept. 6 (TD).
AFC: 80—Napoleon Kaufman, Oakland vs. N.Y. Giants, Sept. 13 (TD).

Attempts, season
NFC: 410—Jamal Anderson, Atlanta.
AFC: 392—Terrell Davis, Denver.

Attempts, game
AFC: 37—Natrone Means, San Diego at Oakland, Oct. 11 (101 yards).
NFC: 35—Fred Lane, Carolina vs. New Orleans, Nov. 1 (101 yards, 1 TD).

Yards per attempt, season
AFC: 5.2—Terrell Davis, Denver.
NFC: 5.1—Garrison Hearst, San Francisco.

Touchdowns, season
AFC: 21—Terrell Davis, Denver.
NFC: 14—Jamal Anderson, Atlanta.

Team leaders, yards
AFC:

Team	Yds.	Player
Baltimore	1008	Priest Holmes
Buffalo	1124	Antowain Smith
Cincinnati	1130	Corey Dillon
Denver	2008	Terrell Davis
Indianapolis	1319	Marshall Faulk
Jacksonville	1223	Fred Taylor
Kansas City	527	Donnell Bennett
Miami	960	Karim Abdul-Jabbar

AFC:

Team	Yds.	Player
New England	1115	Robert Edwards
N.Y. Jets	1287	Curtis Martin
Oakland	921	Napoleon Kaufman
Pittsburgh	1185	Jerome Bettis
San Diego	883	Natrone Means
Seattle	1239	Ricky Watters
Tennessee	1294	Eddie George

NFC:

Team	Yds.	Player
Arizona	1042	Adrian Murrell
Atlanta	1846	Jamal Anderson
Carolina	717	Fred Lane
Chicago	611	Edgar Bennett
Dallas	1332	Emmitt Smith
Detroit	1491	Barry Sanders
Green Bay	386	Darick Holmes
Minnesota	1187	Robert Smith
New Orleans	457	Lamar Smith
N.Y. Giants	1063	Gary Brown
Philadelphia	1065	Duce Staley
St. Louis	313	June Henley
San Francisco	1570	Garrison Hearst
Tampa Bay	1026	Warrick Dunn
Washington	700	Terry Allen

NFL LEADERS

Player, Team	Att.	Yds.	Avg.	Long	TD
Davis, Terrell, Denver*	392	2008	5.1	70	21
Anderson, Jamal, Atlanta	410	1846	4.5	48	14
Hearst, Garrison, San Francisco	310	1570	5.1	t96	7
Sanders, Barry, Detroit	343	1491	4.3	t73	4
Smith, Emmitt, Dallas	319	1332	4.2	32	13
Faulk, Marshall, Indianapolis*	324	1319	4.1	t68	6
George, Eddie, Tennessee*	348	1294	3.7	t37	5
Martin, Curtis, N.Y. Jets*	369	1287	3.5	t60	8
Watters, Ricky, Seattle*	319	1239	3.9	t39	9
Taylor, Fred, Jacksonville*	264	1223	4.6	t77	14
Smith, Robert, Minnesota	249	1187	4.8	t74	6
Bettis, Jerome, Pittsburgh*	316	1185	3.8	42	3
Dillon, Corey, Cincinnati*	262	1130	4.3	66	4
Smith, Antowain, Buffalo*	300	1124	3.7	30	8

Player, Team	Att.	Yds.	Avg.	Long	TD
Edwards, Robert, New England* ...	291	1115	3.8	53	9
Staley, Duce, Philadelphia	258	1065	4.1	t64	5
Brown, Gary, N.Y. Giants	247	1063	4.3	45	5
Murrell, Adrian, Arizona	274	1042	3.8	32	8
Dunn, Warrick, Tampa Bay	245	1026	4.2	50	2
Holmes, Priest, Baltimore*	233	1008	4.3	56	7
Abdul-Jabbar, Karim, Miami*	270	960	3.6	45	6
Kaufman, Napoleon, Oakland*	217	921	4.2	t80	2
Means, Natrone, San Diego*	212	883	4.2	t72	5
Alstott, Mike, Tampa Bay	215	846	3.9	37	8
Lane, Fred, Carolina	205	717	3.5	31	5
Allen, Terry, Washington	148	700	4.7	45	2
Bennett, Edgar, Chicago	173	611	3.5	43	2
McNair, Steve, Tennessee*	77	559	7.3	t71	4
Fletcher, Terrell, San Diego*	153	543	3.5	21	5
Bennett, Donnell, Kansas City*	148	527	3.6	26	5

*AFC.

t—touchdown.

Leader based on yards gained.

AFC

Player, Team	Att.	Yds.	Avg.	Long	TD
Abdul-Jabbar, Karim, Miami	270	960	3.6	45	6
Anders, Kimble, Kansas City	58	230	4.0	20	1
Anderson, Richie, N.Y. Jets	1	2	2.0	2	0
Araguz, Leo, Oakland	1	-12	-12.0	-12	0
Archie, Mike, Tennessee	6	24	4.0	20	1
Avery, John, Miami	143	503	3.5	44	2
Banks, Tavian, Jacksonville	26	140	5.4	51	1
Bennett, Brandon, Cincinnati	77	243	3.2	17	2
Bennett, Donnell, Kansas City	148	527	3.6	26	5
Bettis, Jerome, Pittsburgh	316	1185	3.8	42	3
Bieniemy, Eric, Cincinnati	17	56	3.3	9	0
Blake, Jeff, Cincinnati	15	103	6.9	18	0
Bledsoe, Drew, New England	28	44	1.6	10	0
Brister, Bubby, Denver	19	102	5.4	t38	1
Broussard, Steve, Seattle	5	4	0.8	3	0
Brown, Reggie, Seattle	1	2	2.0	2	0
Brown, Tim, Oakland	1	-7	-7.0	-7	0
Brunell, Mark, Jacksonville	49	192	3.9	18	0
Byars, Keith, N.Y. Jets	4	34	8.5	13	0
Bynum, Kenny, San Diego	11	23	2.1	14	0
Carter, Ki-Jana, Cincinnati	2	4	2.0	4	0
Carter, Tony, New England	2	3	1.5	3	0
Costello, Brad, Cincinnati	1	0	0.0	0	0
Cotton, Kenyon, Baltimore	2	8	4.0	7	0
Crockett, Zack, Indianapolis	2	5	2.5	5	0
Cullors, Derrick, New England	18	48	2.7	15	0
Davis, Terrell, Denver	392	2008	5.1	70	21
Dillon, Corey, Cincinnati	262	1130	4.3	66	4
Doxzon, Todd, Miami	2	6	3.0	3	0
Dudley, Rickey, Oakland	1	-2	-2.0	-2	0
Dyson, Kevin, Tennessee	1	4	4.0	4	0
Edwards, Robert, New England	291	1115	3.8	53	9
Elias, Keith, Indianapolis	8	24	3.0	8	0
Elway, John, Denver	37	94	2.5	16	1
Faulk, Marshall, Indianapolis	324	1319	4.1	t68	6
Fletcher, Terrell, San Diego	153	543	3.5	21	5
Floyd, Chris, New England	6	22	3.7	10	0
Flutie, Doug, Buffalo	48	248	5.2	23	1
Foley, Glenn, N.Y. Jets	5	-11	-2.2	-1	0
Friesz, John, Seattle	5	5	1.0	8	0
Fuamatu-Ma'afala, Chris, Pit.	7	30	4.3	t10	2
Galloway, Joey, Seattle	9	26	2.9	14	0
Gannon, Rich, Kansas City	44	168	3.8	21	3
Gash, Sam, Buffalo	11	32	2.9	11	0
George, Eddie, Tennessee	348	1294	3.7	t37	5
George, Jeff, Oakland	8	2	0.3	8	0
Gibson, Damon, Cincinnati	1	9	9.0	9	0
Glenn, Terry, New England	2	-1	-0.5	7	0
Graham, Jay, Baltimore	35	109	3.1	12	0
Grbac, Elvis, Kansas City	7	27	3.9	10	0

Player, Team	Att.	Yds.	Avg.	Long	TD
Green, Ahman, Seattle	35	209	6.0	64	1
Griese, Brian, Denver	4	-4	-1.0	0	0
Griffith, Howard, Denver	4	13	3.3	16	0
Harbaugh, Jim, Baltimore	40	172	4.3	15	0
Hawkins, Courtney, Pittsburgh	10	41	4.1	14	0
Hebron, Vaughn, Denver	9	31	3.4	8	1
Hentrich, Craig, Tennessee	1	-1	-1.0	-1	0
Heyward, Craig, Indianapolis	6	15	2.5	8	0
Hollas, Donald, Oakland	29	120	4.1	14	1
Holmes, Priest, Baltimore	233	1008	4.3	56	7
Horn, Joe, Kansas City	1	0	0.0	0	0
Howard, Chris, Jacksonville	7	16	2.3	5	0
Huntley, Richard, Pittsburgh	55	242	4.4	48	1
Jefferson, Shawn, New England	1	15	15.0	15	0
Jett, James, Oakland	1	3	3.0	3	0
Johnson, Charles, Pittsburgh	1	4	4.0	4	0
Johnson, Keyshawn, N.Y. Jets	2	60	30.0	t35	1
Johnson, Leon, N.Y. Jets	41	185	4.5	40	2
Johnson, Rob, Buffalo	24	123	5.1	32	1
Jones, Charlie, San Diego	4	39	9.8	14	0
Jones, George, Jacksonville	39	121	3.1	21	0
Jordan, Randy, Oakland	47	159	3.4	23	1
Justin, Paul, Cincinnati	1	2	2.0	2	0
Kaufman, Napoleon, Oakland	217	921	4.2	t80	2
Kitna, Jon, Seattle	20	67	3.4	21	1
Kresser, Eric, Cincinnati	1	-1	-1.0	-1	0
Krieg, Dave, Tennessee	3	-1	-0.3	0	0
Leaf, Ryan, San Diego	27	80	3.0	20	0
Lewis, Jermaine, Baltimore	5	20	4.0	9	0
Linton, Jonathan, Buffalo	45	195	4.3	20	1
Loville, Derek, Denver	53	161	3.0	12	2
Lucas, Ray, N.Y. Jets	5	23	4.6	16	0
Lusk, Henry, Miami	1	7	7.0	7	0
Manning, Peyton, Indianapolis	15	62	4.1	15	0
Marino, Dan, Miami	21	-3	-0.1	10	1
Martin, Curtis, N.Y. Jets	369	1287	3.5	t60	8
Martin, Jamie, Jacksonville	5	8	1.6	9	0
McAfee, Fred, Pittsburgh	18	111	6.2	14	0
McDuffie, O.J., Miami	3	11	3.7	5	0
McNair, Steve, Tennessee	77	559	7.3	t71	4
Means, Natrone, San Diego	212	883	4.2	t72	5
Meggett, David, N.Y. Jets	7	24	3.4	18	0
Milne, Brian, Cincinnati	10	41	4.1	10	1
Moon, Warren, Seattle	16	10	0.6	9	0
Moore, Ronald, Miami	4	12	3.0	4	0
Morris, Bam, Chi.-K.C.*	132	489	3.7	38	8
O'Donnell, Neil, Cincinnati	13	34	2.6	10	0
Parmalee, Bernie, Miami	8	20	2.5	10	0
Pathon, Jerome, Indianapolis	3	-2	-0.7	4	0
Pickens, Carl, Cincinnati	2	4	2.0	4	0
Potts, Roosevelt, Baltimore	36	115	3.2	33	0
Pritchard, Mike, Seattle	1	17	17.0	17	0
Pritchett, Stanley, Miami	6	19	3.2	11	1
Quinn, Jonathan, Jacksonville	11	77	7.0	17	1
Rhett, Errict, Baltimore	44	180	4.1	46	0
Richardson, Kyle, Baltimore	1	0	0.0	0	0
Richardson, Tony, Kansas City	20	45	2.3	6	2
Richardson, Wally, Baltimore	1	0	0.0	0	0
Rison, Andre, Kansas City	2	12	6.0	11	0
Ritchie, Jon, Oakland	9	23	2.6	14	0
Rouen, Tom, Denver	1	0	0.0	0	0
Sanders, Chris, Tennessee	1	-9	-9.0	-9	0
Scott, Darnay, Cincinnati	2	10	5.0	8	0
Shaw, Sedrick, New England	48	236	4.9	71	0
Shehee, Rashaan, Kansas City	22	57	2.6	10	0
Shelton, Daimon, Jacksonville	30	95	3.2	16	1
Small, Torrance, Indianapolis	1	2	2.0	2	0
Smith, Antowain, Buffalo	300	1124	3.7	30	8
Smith, Rod, Denver	6	63	10.5	37	0
Sowell, Jerald, N.Y. Jets	40	164	4.1	33	0
Stephens, Tremayne, San Diego	35	122	3.5	12	1
Stepnoski, Mark, Tennessee	1	0	0.0	0	0

Player, Team	Att.	Yds.	Avg.	Long	TD
Stewart, James, Jacksonville.........	53	217	4.1	30	2
Stewart, Kordell, Pittsburgh	81	406	5.0	56	2
Strong, Mack, Seattle	15	47	3.1	9	0
Taylor, Fred, Jacksonville...............	264	1223	4.6	t77	14
Testaverde, Vinny, N.Y. Jets...........	24	104	4.3	25	1
Thomas, Rodney, Tennessee	24	100	4.2	21	2
Thomas, Thurman, Buffalo.............	93	381	4.1	t17	2
Tupa, Tom, New England	2	-2	-1.0	-1	0
Van Pelt, Alex, Buffalo	1	-1	-1.0	-1	0
Vanover, Tamarick, Kansas City.....	2	1	0.5	2	0
Ward, Dedric, N.Y. Jets..................	2	7	3.5	4	0
Ward, Hines, Pittsburgh	1	13	13.0	13	0
Warren, Lamont, Indianapolis	25	61	2.4	14	1
Watters, Ricky, Seattle...................	319	1239	3.9	t39	9
Whelihan, Craig, San Diego...........	18	38	2.1	13	0
Whitted, Alvis, Jacksonville	3	13	4.3	16	0
Williams, Harvey, Oakland	128	496	3.9	t25	2
Williams, Kevin, Buffalo	5	46	9.2	28	0
Williams, Pooh Bear, Buffalo	2	5	2.5	3	0
Wilson, Wade, Oakland..................	7	24	3.4	12	0
Witman, Jon, Pittsburgh	1	2	2.0	2	0
Zeier, Eric, Baltimore	11	17	1.5	7	0
Zolak, Scott, New England	5	0	0.0	4	0

*Includes both NFC and AFC statistics.
t—touchdown.

NFC

Player, Team	Att.	Yds.	Avg.	Long	TD
Aikman, Troy, Dallas	22	69	3.1	23	2
Allen, James, Chicago	58	270	4.7	57	1
Allen, Terry, Washington................	148	700	4.7	45	2
Alstott, Mike, Tampa Bay	215	846	3.9	37	8
Anderson, Jamal, Atlanta...............	410	1846	4.5	48	14
Anthony, Reidel, Tampa Bay	4	43	10.8	32	0
Banks, Tony, St. Louis	40	156	3.9	19	3
Barber, Tiki, N.Y. Giants	52	166	3.2	23	0
Batch, Charlie, Detroit	41	229	5.6	17	1
Bates, Mario, Arizona	60	165	2.8	15	6
Bennett, Edgar, Chicago	173	611	3.5	43	2
Beuerlein, Steve, Carolina.............	22	26	1.2	13	0
Biakabutuka, Tim, Carolina	101	427	4.2	41	3
Bjornson, Eric, Dallas	1	7	7.0	t7	1
Blair, Michael, G.B.-Cin.-G.B.*	3	7	2.3	4	0
Bono, Steve, St. Louis	10	13	1.3	7	0
Bowie, Larry, Washington	4	8	2.0	4	0
Brooks, Robert, Green Bay	1	2	2.0	2	0
Brown, Dave, Arizona	1	2	2.0	2	0
Brown, Gary, N.Y. Giants	247	1063	4.3	45	5
Bruce, Isaac, St. Louis	1	30	30.0	30	0
Carter, Cris, Minnesota..................	1	-1	-1.0	-1	0
Centers, Larry, Arizona	31	110	3.5	14	0
Chancey, Robert, Chicago	29	122	4.2	14	2
Chandler, Chris, Atlanta.................	36	121	3.4	19	2
Cherry, Mike, N.Y. Giants	3	-3	-1.0	-1	0
Christian, Bob, Atlanta...................	8	21	2.6	6	2
Collins, Kerry, Car.-N.O.	30	153	5.1	20	1
Comella, Greg, N.Y. Giants	1	6	6.0	6	0
Conway, Curtis, Chicago................	5	48	9.6	29	0
Craver, Aaron, New Orleans...........	45	180	4.0	25	2
Crowell, Germane, Detroit	1	35	35.0	35	0
Cunningham, Randall, Minnesota..	32	132	4.1	22	1
Davis, Billy, Dallas	4	15	3.8	8	0
Davis, Stephen, Washington..........	34	109	3.2	12	0
Davis, Troy, New Orleans..............	55	143	2.6	14	1
DeBerg, Steve, Atlanta...................	8	-10	-1.2	2	0
Detmer, Koy, Philadelphia.............	7	20	2.9	8	0
Detmer, Ty, San Francisco	8	7	0.9	10	0
Dilfer, Trent, Tampa Bay................	40	141	3.5	17	2
Downs, Gary, Atlanta	1	4	4.0	4	0
Druckenmiller, Jim, San Francisco..	3	-4	-1.3	-1	0
Dunn, Jason, Philadelphia.............	1	-5	-5.0	-5	0

Player, Team	Att.	Yds.	Avg.	Long	TD
Dunn, Warrick, Tampa Bay	245	1026	4.2	50	2
Dwight, Tim, Atlanta.......................	8	19	2.4	7	0
Edwards, Marc, San Francisco	22	94	4.3	32	1
Ellison, Jerry, Tampa Bay..............	9	24	2.7	10	0
Emanuel, Bert, Tampa Bay............	1	11	11.0	11	0
Engram, Bobby, Chicago	1	3	3.0	3	0
Enis, Curtis, Chicago	133	497	3.7	29	0
Evans, Charles, Minnesota	23	67	2.9	12	1
Favre, Brett, Green Bay..................	40	133	3.3	35	1
Fiedler, Jay, Minnesota	4	-6	-1.5	-1	0
Floyd, William, Carolina.................	28	71	2.5	7	3
Freeman, Antonio, Green Bay........	3	5	1.7	10	0
Frerotte, Gus, Washington.............	3	20	6.7	20	0
Fryar, Irving, Philadelphia..............	3	46	15.3	32	0
Garner, Charlie, Philadelphia.........	96	381	4.0	40	4
Garrett, Jason, Dallas....................	11	14	1.3	5	0
Gowin, Toby, Dallas	1	33	33.0	33	0
Graham, Kent, N.Y. Giants............	27	138	5.1	23	2
Graziani, Tony, Atlanta...................	4	21	5.3	12	0
Green, Harold, Atlanta	20	37	1.9	6	0
Green, Jacquez, Tampa Bay	3	12	4.0	18	0
Green, Trent, Washington	42	117	2.8	13	2
Hakim, Az-Zahir, St. Louis	2	30	15.0	t34	1
Hallock, Ty, Chicago	13	41	3.2	14	1
Hankton, Karl, Philadelphia	1	-4	-4.0	-4	0
Harris, Derrick, St. Louis	14	38	2.7	15	0
Harris, Raymont, Green Bay	79	228	2.9	14	1
Hastings, Andre, New Orleans.......	3	32	10.7	16	0
Hearst, Garrison, San Francisco	310	1570	5.1	t96	7
Henderson, William, Green Bay.....	23	70	3.0	9	2
Henley, June, St. Louis	88	313	3.6	22	3
Hicks, Skip, Washington................	122	433	3.5	28	8
Hill, Greg, St. Louis	40	240	6.0	46	4
Hilliard, Ike, N.Y. Giants	1	4	4.0	4	0
Hoard, Leroy, Minnesota	115	479	4.2	t50	9
Hobert, Billy Joe, New Orleans	2	13	6.5	14	0
Holcombe, Robert, St. Louis..........	98	230	2.3	12	2
Holmes, Darick, Buf.-G.B.*	95	394	4.1	13	1
Hoying, Bobby, Philadelphia..........	22	84	3.8	11	0
Husted, Michael, Tampa Bay	1	20	20.0	20	0
Irvin, Michael, Dallas	1	1	1.0	1	0
Ismail, Raghib, Carolina	3	42	14.0	36	0
Jells, Dietrich, Philadelphia	2	9	4.5	13	0
Jervey, Travis, Green Bay	83	325	3.9	16	1
Johnson, Anthony, Carolina...........	36	135	3.8	21	0
Johnson, Brad, Minnesota.............	12	15	1.3	6	0
Johnston, Daryl, Dallas	8	17	2.1	6	0
Kanell, Danny, N.Y. Giants	15	36	2.4	10	0
Kennison, Eddie, St. Louis	2	9	4.5	9	0
Kirby, Terry, San Francisco	48	258	5.4	t31	3
Kramer, Erik, Chicago	13	17	1.3	8	1
Lane, Fred, Carolina.......................	205	717	3.5	31	5
Lee, Amp, St. Louis	44	175	4.0	38	2
Levens, Dorsey, Green Bay...........	115	378	3.3	50	1
Levy, Chuck, San Francisco	25	112	4.5	t21	1
Mathis, Terance, Atlanta	1	-6	-6.0	-6	0
Maynard, Brad, N.Y. Giants	1	-5	-5.0	-5	0
Milburn, Glyn, Chicago..................	4	8	2.0	3	0
Mills, Ernie, Dallas	3	9	3.0	5	0
Mitchell, Brian, Washington	39	208	5.3	22	2
Mitchell, Scott, Detroit....................	7	30	4.3	17	0
Moore, Jerald, St. Louis.................	55	137	2.5	18	2
Moreno, Moses, Chicago...............	4	9	2.3	9	0
Morrow, Harold, Minnesota	3	7	2.3	8	0
Morton, Johnnie, Detroit	1	11	11.0	11	0
Moss, Randy, Minnesota	1	4	4.0	4	0
Murrell, Adrian, Arizona.................	274	1042	3.8	32	8
Neal, Lorenzo, Tampa Bay	5	25	5.0	12	0
Ogden, Jeff, Dallas........................	1	12	12.0	12	0
Owens, Terrell, San Francisco	4	53	13.3	t21	0
Oxendine, Ken, Atlanta	18	50	2.8	21	0
Palmer, David, Minnesota..............	10	52	5.2	15	0

Player, Team	Att.	Yds.	Avg.	Long	TD
Pederson, Doug, Green Bay	8	-4	-0.5	1	0
Peete, Rodney, Philadelphia	5	30	6.0	t19	1
Perry, Wilmont, New Orleans	30	122	4.1	19	0
Pittman, Michael, Arizona	29	91	3.1	11	0
Plummer, Jake, Arizona	51	217	4.3	27	4
Proehl, Ricky, St. Louis	1	14	14.0	14	0
Quinn, Mike, Dallas	5	-6	-1.2	-1	0
Reich, Frank, Detroit	6	3	0.5	5	0
Rivers, Ron, Detroit	19	102	5.4	t36	1
Roby, Reggie, San Francisco	1	0	0.0	0	0
Sanders, Barry, Detroit	343	1491	4.3	t73	4
Sanders, Frank, Arizona	4	0	0.0	7	0
Schlesinger, Cory, Detroit	5	17	3.4	5	0
Shepherd, Leslie, Washington	6	91	15.2	29	1
Smith, Emmitt, Dallas	319	1332	4.2	32	13
Smith, Lamar, Dallas	138	457	3.3	33	1
Smith, Robert, Minnesota	249	1187	4.8	t74	6
Staley, Duce, Philadelphia	258	1065	4.1	t64	5
Stenstrom, Steve, Chicago	18	79	4.4	14	2
Tolliver, Billy Joe, New Orleans	11	43	3.9	16	0
Turk, Matt, Washington	2	-12	-6.0	0	0
Turner, Kevin, Philadelphia	20	94	4.7	19	0
Vardell, Tommy, Detroit	18	37	2.1	17	6
Walker, Corey, Philadelphia	12	55	4.6	20	0
Walter, Ken, Carolina	3	0	0.0	0	0
Warren, Chris, Dallas	59	291	4.9	49	4
Way, Charles, N.Y. Giants	113	432	3.8	21	3
Westbrook, Michael, Washington	1	11	11.0	11	0
Wheatley, Tyrone, N.Y. Giants	14	52	3.7	15	0
Williams, Elijah, Atlanta	2	-2	-1.0	2	0
Williams, Sherman, Dallas	64	220	3.4	24	1
Wuerffel, Danny, New Orleans	11	60	5.5	18	0
Young, Steve, San Francisco	70	454	6.5	24	6
Zellars, Ray, New Orleans	56	162	2.9	t15	1

*Includes both NFC and AFC statistics.
t—touchdown.

PLAYERS WITH TWO CLUBS

Player, Team	Att.	Yds.	Avg.	Long	TD
Blair, Michael, Green Bay	2	3	1.5	2	0
Blair, Michael, Cincinnati	1	4	4.0	4	0
Collins, Kerry, Carolina	7	40	5.7	16	0
Collins, Kerry, New Orleans	23	113	4.9	20	1
Holmes, Darick, Buffalo	2	8	4.0	5	0
Holmes, Darick, Green Bay	93	386	4.2	13	1
Morris, Bam, Chicago	3	8	2.7	6	0
Morris, Bam, Kansas City	129	481	3.7	38	8

PASSING

AFC

Team	Att.	Comp.	Pct. Comp.	Gross Yds.	Sack	Yds. Lost	Net Yds.	Yds./ Att.	Yds./ Comp.	TD	Pct. TD	Long	Had Int.	Pct. Int.
N.Y. Jets	532	318	59.8	4032	25	196	3836	7.58	12.68	33	6.20	t82	13	2.4
New England	556	295	53.1	4004	40	344	3660	7.20	13.57	23	4.14	t86	17	3.1
Denver	491	290	59.1	3808	25	184	3624	7.76	13.13	32	6.52	58	14	2.9
Indianapolis	576	326	56.6	3739	22	109	3630	6.49	11.47	26	4.51	t78	28	4.9
Buffalo	461	269	58.4	3621	41	241	3380	7.85	13.46	28	6.07	t84	14	3.0
Miami	546	316	57.9	3582	24	187	3395	6.56	11.34	23	4.21	t61	16	2.9
Cincinnati	521	307	58.9	3545	53	360	3185	6.80	11.55	20	3.84	t76	12	2.3
Oakland	519	282	54.3	3534	67	446	3088	6.81	12.53	21	4.05	t75	25	4.8
Tennessee	519	305	58.8	3482	35	191	3291	6.71	11.42	16	3.08	55	10	1.9
Kansas City	543	305	56.2	3472	36	212	3260	6.39	11.38	15	2.76	t80	18	3.3
Jacksonville	463	269	58.1	3343	39	231	3112	7.22	12.43	24	5.18	t78	12	2.6
Seattle	480	273	56.9	3219	34	219	3000	6.71	11.79	21	4.38	t81	18	3.8
Baltimore	477	272	57.0	3152	41	283	2869	6.61	11.59	16	3.35	t73	15	3.1
San Diego	566	261	46.1	3115	37	251	2864	5.50	11.93	11	1.94	67	34	6.0
Pittsburgh	489	274	56.0	2781	35	229	2552	5.69	10.15	13	2.66	t55	20	4.1
AFC total	7739	4362	...	52429	554	3683	48746	...	...	322	...	t86	266	...
AFC average	515.9	290.8	56.4	3495.3	36.9	245.5	3249.7	6.77	12.02	21.5	4.2	...	17.7	3.4

t—touchdown.

NFC

Team	Att.	Comp.	Pct. Comp.	Gross Yds.	Sack	Yds. Lost	Net Yds.	Yds./ Att.	Yds./ Comp.	TD	Pct. TD	Long	Had Int.	Pct. Int.
San Francisco	556	347	62.4	4510	53	254	4256	8.11	13.00	41	7.37	t81	15	2.7
Minnesota	533	327	61.4	4492	25	164	4328	8.43	13.74	41	7.69	t67	16	3.0
Green Bay	575	361	62.8	4340	39	230	4110	7.55	12.02	33	5.74	t84	23	4.0
Arizona	552	326	59.1	3768	50	286	3482	6.83	11.56	17	3.08	57	20	3.6
Atlanta	424	237	55.9	3744	53	358	3386	8.83	15.80	28	6.60	t78	15	3.5
Washington	565	304	53.8	3724	61	399	3325	6.59	12.25	24	4.25	t75	14	2.5
Carolina	507	292	57.6	3624	54	302	3322	7.15	12.41	25	4.93	t72	18	3.6
Dallas	474	279	58.9	3546	19	110	3436	7.48	12.71	17	3.59	t80	8	1.7
New Orleans	535	278	52.0	3514	57	376	3138	6.57	12.64	19	3.55	t89	19	3.6
Detroit	489	274	56.0	3398	45	268	3130	6.95	12.40	17	3.48	t98	13	2.7
St. Louis	556	314	56.5	3381	47	294	3087	6.08	10.77	12	2.16	t80	18	3.2
Chicago	494	284	57.5	3277	31	224	3053	6.63	11.54	16	3.24	t79	13	2.6
N.Y. Giants	507	265	52.3	2822	35	256	2566	5.57	10.65	18	3.55	t87	15	3.0
Tampa Bay	449	234	52.1	2787	28	181	2606	6.21	11.91	21	4.68	t79	18	4.0
Philadelphia	534	282	52.8	2730	56	317	2413	5.11	9.68	7	1.31	t61	18	3.4
NFC total	7750	4404	...	53657	653	4019	49638	...	...	336	...	t98	243	...
NFC average	516.7	293.6	56.8	3577.1	43.5	267.9	3309.2	6.92	12.18	22.4	4.3	...	16.2	3.1
NFL total	15489	8766	...	106086	1207	7702	98384	...	...	658	...	t98	509	...
NFL average	516.3	292.2	56.6	3536.2	40.2	256.7	3279.5	6.85	12.10	21.9	4.2	...	17.0	3.3

INDIVIDUAL

BESTS OF THE SEASON

Highest rating, season
NFC: 106.0—Randall Cunningham, Minnesota.
AFC: 101.6—Vinny Testaverde, N.Y. Jets.

Completion percentage, season
NFC: 63.0—Brett Favre, Green Bay.
AFC: 61.8—Neil O'Donnell, Cincinnati.

Attempts, season
AFC: 575—Peyton Manning, Indianapolis.
NFC: 551—Brett Favre, Green Bay.

Completions, season
NFC: 347—Brett Favre, Green Bay.
AFC: 326—Peyton Manning, Indianapolis.

Yards, season
NFC: 4212—Brett Favre, Green Bay.
AFC: 3739—Peyton Manning, Indianapolis.

Yards, game
NFC: 465—Jake Plummer, Arizona vs. Dallas, Nov. 15 (31-56, 3 TDs).
AFC: 423—Drew Bledsoe, New England vs. Miami, Nov. 23 (28-54, 2 TDs).

Longest gain
NFC: 98—Charlie Batch (to Johnnie Morton), Detroit at Chicago, Oct. 4 (TD).
AFC: 86—Drew Bledsoe (to Terry Glenn), New England at Pittsburgh, Dec. 6 (TD).

Yards per attempt, season
NFC: 9.65—Chris Chandler, Atlanta.
AFC: 7.88—John Elway, Denver.

Touchdown passes, season
NFC: 36—Steve Young, San Francisco.
AFC: 29—Vinny Testaverde, N.Y. Jets.

NFC: 5—Brett Favre, Green Bay at Carolina, Sept. 27 (27-45, 388 yards).

AFC: 4—Vinny Testaverde, N.Y.Jets vs. Indianapolis, Sept. 20 (12-21, 203 yards); Bubby Brister, Denver vs. Philadelphia, Oct. 4 (16-29, 203 yards); Mark Brunell, Jacksonville at Cincinnati, Nov. 29 (19-35, 244 yards); John Elway, Denver at San Diego, Nov. 29 (19-34, 239 yards); Dan Marino, Miami vs. Denver, Dec. 21 (23-38, 355 yards); Vinny Testaverde, N.Y.Jets vs. New England, Dec. 27 (17-27, 179 yards); John Elway, Denver vs. Seattle, Dec. 27 (26-36, 338 yards).

Lowest interception percentage, season
AFC: 1.2—Neil O'Donnell, Cincinnati.
NFC: 1.6—Troy Aikman, Dallas.

NFL LEADERS

Player, Team	Att.	Comp.	Pct. Comp.	Yds.	Avg. Gain	TD	Pct. TD	Long	Int.	Pct. Int.	Sack	Yds. Lost	Rat. Pts.
Cunningham, Randall, Minnesota	425	259	60.9	3704	8.72	34	8.0	t67	10	2.4	20	132	106.0
Testaverde, Vinny, N.Y. Jets*	421	259	61.5	3256	7.73	29	6.9	t82	7	1.7	19	140	101.6
Young, Steve, San Francisco	517	322	62.3	4170	8.07	36	7.0	t81	12	2.3	48	234	101.1
Chandler, Chris, Atlanta	327	190	58.1	3154	9.65	25	7.6	t78	12	3.7	45	283	100.9
Elway, John, Denver*	356	210	59.0	2806	7.88	22	6.2	58	10	2.8	18	135	93.0
O'Donnell, Neil, Cincinnati*	343	212	61.8	2216	6.46	15	4.4	t76	4	1.2	30	217	90.2
Brunell, Mark, Jacksonville*	354	208	58.8	2601	7.35	20	5.6	t78	9	2.5	28	172	89.9
Aikman, Troy, Dallas	315	187	59.4	2330	7.40	12	3.8	t67	5	1.6	9	58	88.5
Beuerlein, Steve, Carolina	343	216	63.0	2613	7.62	17	5.0	t68	12	3.5	44	251	88.2
Favre, Brett, Green Bay	551	347	63.0	4212	7.64	31	5.6	t84	23	4.2	38	223	87.8
Flutie, Doug, Buffalo*	354	202	57.1	2711	7.66	20	5.6	t84	11	3.1	12	78	87.4
Batch, Charlie, Detroit..........................	303	173	57.1	2178	7.19	11	3.6	t98	6	2.0	37	222	83.5
Kramer, Erik, Chicago	250	151	60.4	1823	7.29	9	3.6	t79	7	2.8	10	71	83.1
Green, Trent, Washington	509	278	54.6	3441	6.76	23	4.5	t75	11	2.2	49	338	81.8
Bledsoe, Drew, New England*	481	263	54.7	3633	7.55	20	4.2	t86	14	2.9	36	295	80.9
McNair, Steve, Tennessee*	492	289	58.7	3228	6.56	15	3.0	47	10	2.0	33	176	80.1
Gannon, Rich, Kansas City*	354	206	58.2	2305	6.51	10	2.8	t80	6	1.7	25	155	80.1
Marino, Dan, Miami*	537	310	57.7	3497	6.51	23	4.3	t61	15	2.8	23	178	80.0
Moon, Warren, Seattle*	258	145	56.2	1632	6.33	11	4.3	45	8	3.1	22	140	76.6
Plummer, Jake, Arizona	547	324	59.2	3737	6.83	17	3.1	57	20	3.7	49	280	75.0
Dilfer, Trent, Tampa Bay	429	225	52.4	2729	6.36	21	4.9	t79	15	3.5	27	172	74.0
Harbaugh, Jim, Baltimore*	293	164	56.0	1839	6.28	12	4.1	t66	11	3.8	23	145	72.9
Manning, Peyton, Indianapolis*	575	326	56.7	3739	6.50	26	4.5	t78	28	4.9	22	109	71.2
Banks, Tony, St. Louis	408	241	59.1	2535	6.21	7	1.7	t80	14	3.4	41	237	68.6
Kanell, Danny, N.Y. Giants..................	299	160	53.5	1603	5.36	11	3.7	46	10	3.3	22	172	67.3
Stewart, Kordell, Pittsburgh*	458	252	55.0	2560	5.59	11	2.4	t55	18	3.9	33	211	62.9
Collins, Kerry, Car.-N.O.	353	170	48.2	2213	6.27	12	3.4	t89	15	4.2	31	191	62.0
Hollas, Donald, Oakland*	260	135	51.9	1754	6.75	10	3.8	47	16	6.2	36	207	60.6
Whelihan, Craig, San Diego*	320	149	46.6	1803	5.63	8	2.5	55	19	5.9	15	111	48.0
Hoying, Bobby, Philadelphia	224	114	50.9	961	4.29	0	0.0	38	9	4.0	35	185	45.6

*AFC.

t—touchdown.

Leader based on rating points, minimum 224 attempts.

AFC

Player, Team	Att.	Comp.	Pct. Comp.	Yds.	Avg. Gain	TD	Pct. TD	Long	Int.	Pct. Int.	Sack	Yds. Lost	Rat. Pts.
Araguz, Leo, Oakland	1	1	100.0	-1	-1.00	0	0.0	-1	0	0.0	0	0	79.2
Archie, Mike, Tennessee	2	1	50.0	18	9.00	1	50.0	t18	0	0.0	0	0	120.8
Blake, Jeff, Cincinnati...........................	93	51	54.8	739	7.95	3	3.2	t67	3	3.2	15	79	78.2
Bledsoe, Drew, New England	481	263	54.7	3633	7.55	20	4.2	t86	14	2.9	36	295	80.9
Brister, Bubby, Denver	131	78	59.5	986	7.53	10	7.6	48	3	2.3	7	49	99.0
Brunell, Mark, Jacksonville	354	208	58.8	2601	7.35	20	5.6	t78	9	2.5	28	172	89.9
Dillon, Corey, Cincinnati......................	0	0	...	0	...	0	...	...	0	...	1	4	...
Elway, John, Denver	356	210	59.0	2806	7.88	22	6.2	58	10	2.8	18	135	93.0
Fletcher, Terrell, San Diego	1	1	100.0	23	23.00	1	100.0	t23	0	0.0	0	0	158.3
Flutie, Doug, Buffalo	354	202	57.1	2711	7.66	20	5.6	t84	11	3.1	12	78	87.4
Foley, Glenn, N.Y. Jets	108	58	53.7	749	6.94	4	3.7	48	6	5.6	5	49	64.9
Friesz, John, Seattle...........................	49	29	59.2	409	8.35	2	4.1	t81	2	4.1	1	7	82.8
Gannon, Rich, Kansas City..................	354	206	58.2	2305	6.51	10	2.8	t80	6	1.7	25	155	80.1
George, Jeff, Oakland	169	93	55.0	1186	7.02	4	2.4	t75	5	3.0	22	162	72.7
Grbac, Elvis, Kansas City	188	98	52.1	1142	6.07	5	2.7	65	12	6.4	11	57	53.1
Griese, Brian, Denver	3	1	33.3	2	0.67	0	0.0	2	1	33.3	0	0	2.8
Harbaugh, Jim, Baltimore	293	164	56.0	1839	6.28	12	4.1	t66	11	3.8	23	145	72.9
Hentrich, Craig, Tennessee	1	1	100.0	13	13.00	0	0.0	13	0	0.0	0	0	118.8
Hollas, Donald, Oakland......................	260	135	51.9	1754	6.75	10	3.8	47	16	6.2	36	207	60.6
Holmes, Priest, Baltimore	1	0	0.0	0	0.00	0	0.0	0	1	100.0	0	0	0.0
Huard, Damon, Miami..........................	9	6	66.7	85	9.44	0	0.0	24	1	11.1	1	9	57.4
Hughes, Danan, Kansas City	1	1	100.0	25	25.00	0	0.0	25	0	0.0	0	0	118.8

Player, Team	Att.	Comp.	Pct. Comp.	Yds.	Avg. Gain	TD	Pct. TD	Long	Int.	Pct. Int.	Sack	Yds. Lost	Rat. Pts.
Johnson, Leon, N.Y. Jets	0	0	...	0	...	0	...	...	0	...	1	7	...
Johnson, Rob, Buffalo	107	67	62.6	910	8.50	8	7.5	t66	3	2.8	29	163	102.9
Justin, Paul, Cincinnati	63	34	54.0	426	6.76	1	1.6	41	3	4.8	7	60	60.7
Kitna, Jon, Seattle	172	98	57.0	1177	6.84	7	4.1	t70	8	4.7	11	72	72.3
Kresser, Eric, Cincinnati	21	10	47.6	164	7.81	1	4.8	37	2	9.5	0	0	50.6
Krieg, Dave, Tennessee	21	12	57.1	199	9.48	0	0.0	55	0	0.0	2	15	89.2
Leaf, Ryan, San Diego	245	111	45.3	1289	5.26	2	0.8	67	15	6.1	22	140	39.0
Lucas, Ray, N.Y. Jets	3	1	33.3	27	9.00	0	0.0	27	0	0.0	0	0	67.4
Manning, Peyton, Indianapolis	575	326	56.7	3739	6.50	26	4.5	t78	28	4.9	22	109	71.2
Marino, Dan, Miami	537	310	57.7	3497	6.51	23	4.3	t61	15	2.8	23	178	80.0
Martin, Jamie, Jacksonville	45	27	60.0	355	7.89	2	4.4	t67	0	0.0	2	10	99.8
Matthews, Steve, Tennessee	3	2	66.7	24	8.00	0	0.0	13	0	0.0	0	0	91.0
McNair, Steve, Tennessee	492	289	58.7	3228	6.56	15	3.0	47	10	2.0	33	176	80.1
Moon, Warren, Seattle	258	145	56.2	1632	6.33	11	4.3	45	8	3.1	22	140	76.6
O'Donnell, Neil, Cincinnati	343	212	61.8	2216	6.46	15	4.4	t76	4	1.2	30	217	90.2
Pelfrey, Doug, Cincinnati	1	0	0.0	0	0.00	0	0.0	0	0	0.0	0	0	39.6
Quinn, Jonathan, Jacksonville	64	34	53.1	387	6.05	2	3.1	64	3	4.7	9	49	62.4
Richardson, Wally, Baltimore	2	1	50.0	1	0.50	0	0.0	1	0	0.0	0	0	56.3
Small, Torrance, Indianapolis	1	0	0.0	0	0.00	0	0.0	0	0	0.0	0	0	39.6
Smith, Rod, Denver	1	1	100.0	14	14.00	0	0.0	14	0	0.0	0	0	118.8
Stewart, Kordell, Pittsburgh	458	252	55.0	2560	5.59	11	2.4	t55	18	3.9	33	211	62.9
Testaverde, Vinny, N.Y. Jets	421	259	61.5	3256	7.73	29	6.9	t82	7	1.7	19	140	101.6
Tomczak, Mike, Pittsburgh	30	21	70.0	204	6.80	2	6.7	42	2	6.7	2	18	83.2
Ward, Hines, Pittsburgh	1	1	100.0	17	17.00	0	0.0	17	0	0.0	0	0	118.8
Watters, Ricky, Seattle	1	1	100.0	1	1.00	1	100.0	t1	0	0.0	0	0	118.8
Whelihan, Craig, San Diego	320	149	46.6	1803	5.63	8	2.5	55	19	5.9	15	111	48.0
Williams, Harvey, Oakland	1	1	100.0	27	27.00	0	0.0	27	0	0.0	0	0	118.8
Wilson, Wade, Oakland	88	52	59.1	568	6.45	7	8.0	t68	4	4.5	9	77	85.8
Zeier, Eric, Baltimore	181	107	59.1	1312	7.25	4	2.2	t73	3	1.7	18	138	82.0
Zolak, Scott, New England	75	32	42.7	371	4.95	3	4.0	t61	4	4.0	4	49	54.9

t—touchdown.

NFC

Player, Team	Att.	Comp.	Pct. Comp.	Yds.	Avg. Gain	TD	Pct. TD	Long	Int.	Pct. Int.	Sack	Yds. Lost	Rat. Pts.
Aikman, Troy, Dallas	315	187	59.4	2330	7.40	12	3.8	t67	5	1.6	9	58	88.5
Alstott, Mike, Tampa Bay	1	0	0.0	0	0.00	0	0.0	0	0	0.0	0	0	39.6
Anderson, Jamal, Atlanta	2	0	0.0	0	0.00	0	0.0	0	0	0.0	0	0	39.6
Banks, Tony, St. Louis	408	241	59.1	2535	6.21	7	1.7	t80	14	3.4	41	237	68.6
Batch, Charlie, Detroit	303	173	57.1	2178	7.19	11	3.6	t98	6	2.0	37	222	83.5
Bennett, Edgar, Chicago	2	1	50.0	18	9.00	1	50.0	t18	0	0.0	0	0	120.8
Beuerlein, Steve, Carolina	343	216	63.0	2613	7.62	17	5.0	t68	12	3.5	44	251	88.2
Bono, Steve, St. Louis	136	69	50.7	807	5.93	5	3.7	47	4	2.9	6	57	69.1
Brown, Dave, Arizona	5	2	40.0	31	6.20	0	0.0	19	0	0.0	1	6	61.3
Chandler, Chris, Atlanta	327	190	58.1	3154	9.65	25	7.6	t78	12	3.7	45	283	100.9
Cherry, Mike, N.Y. Giants	1	0	0.0	0	0.00	0	0.0	0	0	0.0	1	9	39.6
Collins, Kerry, Car.-N.O.	353	170	48.2	2213	6.27	12	3.4	t89	15	4.2	31	191	62.0
Conway, Curtis, Chicago	1	0	0.0	0	0.00	0	0.0	0	0	0.0	0	0	39.6
Craver, Aaron, New Orleans	1	0	0.0	0	0.00	0	0.0	0	0	0.0	0	0	39.6
Cunningham, Randall, Minnesota	425	259	60.9	3704	8.72	34	8.0	t67	10	2.4	20	132	106.0
DeBerg, Steve, Atlanta	59	30	50.8	369	6.25	3	5.1	t35	1	1.7	6	60	80.4
Detmer, Koy, Philadelphia	181	97	53.6	1011	5.59	5	2.8	t61	5	2.8	5	29	67.7
Detmer, Ty, San Francisco	38	24	63.2	312	8.21	4	10.5	t36	3	7.9	5	20	91.1
Dilfer, Trent, Tampa Bay	429	225	52.4	2729	6.36	21	4.9	t79	15	3.5	27	172	74.0
Dwight, Tim, Atlanta	2	1	50.0	22	11.00	0	0.0	22	0	0.0	0	0	89.6
Favre, Brett, Green Bay	551	347	63.0	4212	7.64	31	5.6	t84	23	4.2	38	223	87.8
Fiedler, Jay, Minnesota	7	3	42.9	41	5.86	0	0.0	19	1	14.3	0	0	22.6
Floyd, William, Carolina	1	0	0.0	0	0.00	0	0.0	0	1	100.0	0	0	0.0
Frerotte, Gus, Washington	54	25	46.3	283	5.24	1	1.9	22	3	5.6	12	61	45.5
Garrett, Jason, Dallas	158	91	57.6	1206	7.63	5	3.2	t80	5	1.9	10	52	84.5
Graham, Kent, N.Y. Giants	205	105	51.2	1219	5.95	7	3.4	t87	5	2.4	12	75	70.8
Graziani, Tony, Atlanta	33	16	48.5	199	6.03	0	0.0	32	2	6.1	2	15	42.4
Green, Trent, Washington	509	278	54.6	3441	6.76	23	4.5	t75	11	2.2	49	338	81.8
Hobert, Billy Joe, New Orleans	23	11	47.8	170	7.39	1	4.3	t35	0	0.0	2	17	87.2
Horan, Mike, Chicago	2	1	50.0	18	9.00	1	50.0	t18	0	0.0	0	0	120.8
Hoying, Bobby, Philadelphia	224	114	50.9	961	4.29	0	0.0	38	9	4.0	35	185	45.6
Jett, John, Detroit	1	0	0.0	0	0.00	0	0.0	0	0	0.0	0	0	39.6
Johnson, Brad, Minnesota	101	65	64.4	747	7.40	7	6.9	t48	5	5.0	4	30	89.0
Kanell, Danny, N.Y. Giants	299	160	53.5	1603	5.36	11	3.7	46	10	3.3	22	172	67.3
Kirby, Terry, San Francisco	1	1	100.0	28	28.00	1	100.0	t28	0	0.0	0	0	158.3

Player, Team	Att.	Comp.	Pct. Comp.	Yds.	Avg. Gain	TD	Pct. TD	Long	Int.	Pct. Int.	Sack	Yds. Lost	Rat. Pts.
Kramer, Erik, Chicago	250	151	60.4	1823	7.29	9	3.6	t79	7	2.8	10	71	83.1
Martin, Tony, Atlanta..............................	1	0	0.0	0	0.00	0	0.0	0	0	0.0	0	0	39.6
Maynard, Brad, N.Y. Giants......................	1	0	0.0	0	0.00	0	0.0	0	0	0.0	0	0	39.6
Mitchell, Brian, Washington....................	2	1	50.0	0	0.00	0	0.0	0	0	0.0	0	0	56.3
Mitchell, Scott, Detroit...........................	75	38	50.7	452	6.03	1	1.3	44	3	4.0	4	28	57.2
Moreno, Moses, Chicago	43	19	44.2	166	3.86	1	2.3	t21	0	0.0	2	16	62.7
Palmer, David, Minnesota	0	0	...	0	...	0	...	0	0	...	1	2	...
Pederson, Doug, Green Bay....................	24	14	58.3	128	5.33	2	8.3	29	0	0.0	1	7	100.7
Peete, Rodney, Philadelphia....................	129	71	55.0	758	5.88	2	1.6	25	4	3.1	16	103	64.7
Plummer, Jake, Arizona	547	324	59.2	3737	6.83	17	3.1	57	20	3.7	49	280	75.0
Quinn, Mike, Dallas................................	1	1	100.0	10	10.00	0	0.0	10	0	0.0	0	0	108.3
Reich, Frank, Detroit	110	63	57.3	768	6.98	5	4.5	41	4	3.6	4	18	78.9
Smith, Lamar, New Orleans	2	1	50.0	20	10.00	1	50.0	t20	0	0.0	0	0	125.0
Stenstrom, Steve, Chicago	196	112	57.1	1252	6.39	4	2.0	48	6	3.1	19	137	70.4
Tolliver, Billy Joe, New Orleans	199	110	55.3	1427	7.17	8	4.0	t82	4	2.0	11	88	83.1
Toomer, Amani, N.Y. Giants	1	0	0.0	0	0.00	0	0.0	0	0	0.0	0	0	39.6
Tuten, Rick, St. Louis.............................	1	0	0.0	0	0.00	0	0.0	0	0	0.0	0	0	39.6
Walsh, Steve, Tampa Bay........................	19	9	47.4	58	3.05	0	0.0	12	3	15.8	1	9	14.7
Walter, Ken, Carolina..............................	1	0	0.0	0	0.00	0	0.0	0	0	0.0	0	0	39.6
Warner, Kurt, St. Louis	11	4	36.4	39	3.55	0	0.0	21	0	0.0	0	0	47.2
Wuerffel, Danny, New Orleans	119	62	52.1	695	5.84	5	4.2	t64	5	4.2	23	131	66.3
Young, Steve, San Francisco	517	322	62.3	4170	8.07	36	7.0	t81	12	2.3	48	234	101.1

t—touchdown.

PLAYERS WITH TWO CLUBS

Player, Team	Att.	Comp.	Pct. Comp.	Yds.	Avg. Gain	TD	Pct. TD	Long	Int.	Pct. Int.	Sack	Yds. Lost	Rat. Pts.
Collins, Kerry, Carolina	162	76	46.9	1011	6.24	8	4.9	t72	5	3.1	10	51	70.8
Collins, Kerry, New Orleans	191	94	49.2	1202	6.29	4	2.1	t89	10	5.2	21	140	54.5

RECEIVING

BESTS OF THE SEASON

Receptions, season
AFC: 90—O.J. McDuffie, Miami.
NFC: 89—Frank Sanders, Arizona.

Receptions, game
AFC: 14—Courtney Hawkins, Pittsburgh vs. Tennessee, Nov. 1 (147 yards, 1 TD).
NFC: 11—Isaac Bruce, St. Louis vs. Minnesota, Sept. 13 (192 yards, 1 TD); Frank Sanders, Arizona vs. Dallas, Nov. 15 (190 yards, 1 TD); Cris Carter, Minnesota at Baltimore, Dec. 13 (85 yards, 1 TD); .

Yards, season
NFC: 1424—Antonio Freeman, Green Bay.
AFC: 1368—Eric Moulds, Buffalo.

Yards, game
AFC: 204—Carl Pickens, Cincinnati vs. Pittsburgh, Oct. 11 (13 receptions, 1 TD).
NFC: 198—Terance Mathis, Atlanta at New Orleans, Dec. 13 (6 receptions, 2 TDs).

Longest gain
NFC: 98—Johnnie Morton (from Charlie Batch), Detroit at Chicago, Oct. 4 (TD).
AFC: 86—Terry Glenn (from Drew Bledsoe), New England at Pittsburgh, Dec. 6 (TD).

Yards per reception, season
AFC: 22.7—Shawn Jefferson, New England.
NFC: 19.0—Randy Moss, Minnesota.

Touchdowns, season
NFC: 17—Randy Moss, Minnesota.
AFC: 10—Shannon Sharpe, Denver; Ed McCaffrey, Denver; Joey Galloway, Seattle; Keyshawn Johnson, N.Y.Jets.

Team leaders, receptions
AFC:

Baltimore	43	Priest Holmes
Buffalo	67	Eric Moulds
Cincinnati	82	Carl Pickens
Denver	86	Rod Smith
Indianapolis	86	Marshall Faulk
Jacksonville	78	Jimmy Smith
Kansas City	64	Kimble Anders
Miami	90	O.J. McDuffie
New England	67	Ben Coates
N.Y. Jets	83	Keyshawn Johnson
Oakland	81	Tim Brown
Pittsburgh	66	Courtney Hawkins
San Diego	57	Freddie Jones
Seattle	65	Joey Galloway
Tennessee	70	Frank Wycheck

NFC:

Arizona	89	Frank Sanders
Atlanta	66	Tony Martin
Carolina	69	Raghib Ismail
Chicago	64	Bobby Engram
Dallas	74	Michael Irvin
Detroit	82	Herman Moore
Green Bay	84	Antonio Freeman
Minnesota	78	Cris Carter
New Orleans	54	Cameron Cleeland
N.Y. Giants	62	Chris Calloway
Philadelphia	57	Duce Staley
St. Louis	64	Amp Lee
San Francisco	82	Jerry Rice
Tampa Bay	51	Reidel Anthony
Washington	44	Brian Mitchell
		Michael Westbrook

NFL LEADERS

Player, Team	No.	Yds.	Avg.	Long	TD
McDuffie, O.J., Miami*	90	1050	11.7	t61	7
Sanders, Frank, Arizona	89	1145	12.9	42	3
Smith, Rod, Denver*	86	1222	14.2	58	6
Faulk, Marshall, Indianapolis*	86	908	10.6	t78	4
Freeman, Antonio, Green Bay	84	1424	17.0	t84	14
Johnson, Keyshawn, N.Y. Jets*	83	1131	13.6	t41	10
Rice, Jerry, San Francisco	82	1157	14.1	t75	9
Pickens, Carl, Cincinnati*	82	1023	12.5	t67	5
Moore, Herman, Detroit	82	983	12.0	36	5
Brown, Tim, Oakland*	81	1012	12.5	49	9
Smith, Jimmy, Jacksonville*	78	1182	15.2	t72	8
Carter, Cris, Minnesota	78	1011	13.0	t54	12
Chrebet, Wayne, N.Y. Jets*	75	1083	14.4	t63	8
Irvin, Michael, Dallas	74	1057	14.3	51	1
Wycheck, Frank, Tennessee*	70	768	11.0	38	2
Moss, Randy, Minnesota	69	1313	19.0	t61	17
Morton, Johnnie, Detroit	69	1028	14.9	t98	2
Ismail, Raghib, Carolina	69	1024	14.8	62	8
Centers, Larry, Arizona	69	559	8.1	54	2
Muhammad, Muhsin, Carolina	68	941	13.8	t72	6
Moulds, Eric, Buffalo*	67	1368	20.4	t84	9
Owens, Terrell, San Francisco	67	1097	16.4	t79	14
Moore, Rob, Arizona	67	982	14.7	57	5
Coates, Ben, New England*	67	668	10.0	33	6
Martin, Tony, Atlanta	66	1181	17.9	62	6
Hawkins, Courtney, Pittsburgh*	66	751	11.4	53	1
Galloway, Joey, Seattle*	65	1047	16.1	t81	10
Johnson, Charles, Pittsburgh*	65	815	12.5	t55	7
Mathis, Terance, Atlanta	64	1136	17.8	t78	11
McCaffrey, Ed, Denver*	64	1053	16.5	48	10

*AFC.
t—touchdown.
Leader based on most passes caught.

AFC

Player, Team	No.	Yds.	Avg.	Long	TD
Abdul-Jabbar, Karim, Miami	21	102	4.9	18	0
Alexander, Derrick, Kansas City	54	992	18.4	65	4
Anders, Kimble, Kansas City	64	462	7.2	29	2
Anderson, Richie, N.Y. Jets	3	12	4.0	7	0
Archie, Mike, Tennessee	5	25	5.0	7	0
Armour, Justin, Denver	1	23	23.0	23	0
Atkins, James, Baltimore	1	0	0.0	0	0
Avery, John, Miami	10	67	6.7	t19	1
Banks, Tavian, Jacksonville	4	20	5.0	10	0
Banta, Bradford, Indianapolis	1	7	7.0	7	0
Barlow, Reggie, Jacksonville	11	168	15.3	31	0
Battaglia, Marco, Cincinnati	10	47	4.7	16	1
Baxter, Fred, N.Y. Jets	3	50	16.7	23	0
Bennett, Brandon, Cincinnati	8	153	19.1	55	0
Bennett, Donnell, Kansas City	16	91	5.7	14	1
Bettis, Jerome, Pittsburgh	16	90	5.6	26	0
Bieniemy, Eric, Cincinnati	27	153	5.7	15	0
Bishop, Harold, Pittsburgh	1	4	4.0	4	0
Blackwell, Will, Pittsburgh	32	297	9.3	t24	1
Blades, Brian, Seattle	15	184	12.3	47	0
Blair, Michael, G.B.-Cin.*	3	20	6.7	10	0
Brady, Kyle, N.Y. Jets	30	315	10.5	35	5
Brisby, Vincent, New England	7	96	13.7	27	2
Broussard, Steve, Seattle	4	21	5.3	16	0
Brown, Derek, Oakland	7	89	12.7	27	0
Brown, Tim, Oakland	81	1012	12.5	49	9
Brown, Troy, New England	23	346	15.0	52	1
Bruener, Mark, Pittsburgh	19	157	8.3	20	2

– 250 –

Player, Team	No.	Yds.	Avg.	Long	TD
Burke, John, San Diego	3	32	10.7	17	0
Bush, Steve, Cincinnati	4	39	9.8	18	0
Byars, Keith, N.Y. Jets	26	258	9.9	29	3
Bynum, Kenny, San Diego	4	27	6.8	12	0
Byrd, Isaac, Tennessee	6	71	11.8	18	0
Carswell, Dwayne, Denver	4	51	12.8	15	0
Carter, Ki-Jana, Cincinnati	6	25	4.2	8	0
Carter, Tony, New England	18	166	9.2	49	0
Chamberlain, Byron, Denver	3	35	11.7	16	0
Chrebet, Wayne, N.Y. Jets	75	1083	14.4	t63	8
Coates, Ben, New England	67	668	10.0	33	6
Coleman, Andre, Pittsburgh	4	49	12.3	t13	1
Crockett, Zack, Ind.-Jac.	2	5	2.5	4	0
Crumpler, Carlester, Seattle	6	52	8.7	16	1
Cullors, Derrick, New England	14	146	10.4	43	1
Davis, Terrell, Denver	25	217	8.7	35	2
Davis, Wendell, San Diego	4	23	5.8	8	0
Davis, Willie, Tennessee	32	461	14.4	38	3
Dilger, Ken, Indianapolis	31	303	9.8	27	1
Dillon, Corey, Cincinnati	28	178	6.4	41	1
Drayton, Troy, Miami	30	334	11.1	35	3
Dudley, Rickey, Oakland	36	549	15.3	32	5
Dunn, David, Pittsburgh	9	87	9.7	24	0
Dyson, Kevin, Tennessee	21	263	12.5	t45	2
Early, Quinn, Buffalo	19	217	11.4	37	1
Edwards, Robert, New England	35	331	9.5	46	3
Elias, Keith, Indianapolis	1	11	11.0	11	0
Elway, John, Denver	1	14	14.0	14	0
Faulk, Marshall, Indianapolis	86	908	10.6	t78	4
Fauria, Christian, Seattle	37	377	10.2	25	2
Fletcher, Terrell, San Diego	30	188	6.3	22	0
Floyd, Chris, New England	1	6	6.0	6	0
Folston, James, Oakland	1	-1	-1.0	-1	0
Fuamatu-Ma'afala, Chris, Pit.	9	84	9.3	t26	1
Gadsden, Oronde, Miami	48	713	14.9	50	7
Galloway, Joey, Seattle	65	1047	16.1	t81	10
Gash, Sam, Buffalo	19	165	8.7	20	3
George, Eddie, Tennessee	37	310	8.4	29	1
Gibson, Damon, Cincinnati	19	258	13.6	t76	3
Glenn, Terry, New England	50	792	15.8	t86	3
Gonzalez, Tony, Kansas City	59	621	10.5	32	2
Graham, Jay, Baltimore	5	41	8.2	14	0
Green, Ahman, Seattle	3	2	0.7	3	0
Green, E.G., Indianapolis	15	177	11.8	25	1
Green, Eric, Baltimore	34	422	12.4	56	1
Green, Willie, Denver	16	194	12.1	50	1
Greene, Scott, Indianapolis	1	2	2.0	2	0
Griffith, Howard, Denver	15	97	6.5	15	3
Harris, Jackie, Tennessee	43	412	9.6	32	2
Harrison, Marvin, Indianapolis	59	776	13.2	t61	7
Hartley, Frank, San Diego	2	28	14.0	17	0
Hawkins, Courtney, Pittsburgh	66	751	11.4	53	1
Hebron, Vaughn, Denver	2	5	2.5	3	0
Heyward, Craig, Indianapolis	1	9	9.0	9	0
Holmes, Priest, Baltimore	43	260	6.0	25	0
Horn, Joe, Kansas City	14	198	14.1	57	1
Howard, Chris, Jacksonville	1	3	3.0	3	0
Howard, Desmond, Oakland	2	16	8.0	10	0
Hughes, Danan, Kansas City	1	10	10.0	10	0
Hundon, James, Cincinnati	10	112	11.2	17	1
Huntley, Richard, Pittsburgh	3	18	6.0	7	0
Jackson, Michael, Baltimore	38	477	12.6	53	0
Jackson, Willie, Cincinnati	7	165	23.6	47	0
Jacquet, Nate, Miami	8	122	15.3	29	0
Jefferson, Shawn, New England	34	771	22.7	t61	2
Jett, James, Oakland	45	882	19.6	t75	6
Johnson, Charles, Pittsburgh	65	815	12.5	t55	7
Johnson, Keyshawn, N.Y. Jets	83	1131	13.6	t41	10
Johnson, Leon, N.Y. Jets	13	222	17.1	t82	2
Johnson, Lonnie, Buffalo	14	146	10.4	27	2
Johnson, Pat, Baltimore	12	159	13.3	35	1
Jones, Charlie, San Diego	46	699	15.2	56	3
Jones, Damon, Jacksonville	8	90	11.3	t31	4
Jones, Freddie, San Diego	57	602	10.6	28	3
Jones, George, Jacksonville	1	9	9.0	9	0
Jordan, Charles, Miami	2	17	8.5	9	0
Jordan, Randy, Oakland	3	2	0.7	2	0
Kaufman, Napoleon, Oakland	25	191	7.6	39	0
Kent, Joey, Tennessee	4	62	15.5	23	0
Kinchen, Brian, Baltimore	13	110	8.5	24	0
Lester, Tim, Pittsburgh	9	46	5.1	9	0
Lewis, Jermaine, Baltimore	41	784	19.1	t73	6
Linton, Jonathan, Buffalo	1	10	10.0	10	0
Lockett, Kevin, Kansas City	19	281	14.8	38	0
Loville, Derek, Denver	2	29	14.5	17	0
Lyons, Mitch, Pittsburgh	3	19	6.3	11	0
Martin, Curtis, N.Y. Jets	43	365	8.5	23	1
Mason, Derrick, Tennessee	25	333	13.3	47	3
May, Deems, Seattle	3	7	2.3	5	1
McAfee, Fred, Pittsburgh	9	27	3.0	11	0
McCaffrey, Ed, Denver	64	1053	16.5	48	10
McCardell, Keenan, Jacksonville	64	892	13.9	t67	6
McDuffie, O.J., Miami	90	1050	11.7	t61	7
McGee, Tony, Cincinnati	22	363	16.5	40	1
McKnight, James, Seattle	21	346	16.5	t59	2
Means, Natrone, San Diego	16	91	5.7	22	0
Meggett, David, N.Y. Jets	1	15	15.0	15	0
Mickens, Terry, Oakland	24	346	14.4	32	1
Mili, Itula, Seattle	1	20	20.0	20	0
Milne, Brian, Cincinnati	26	124	4.8	18	0
Mitchell, Pete, Jacksonville	38	363	9.6	38	2
Moore, Ronald, Miami	1	1	1.0	1	0
Moore, Will, Jacksonville	1	9	9.0	9	0
Morris, Bam, Kansas City	12	95	7.9	29	0
Moulds, Eric, Buffalo	67	1368	20.4	t84	9
Nash, Marcus, Denver	4	76	19.0	31	0
Parmalee, Bernie, Miami	21	221	10.5	23	0
Pathon, Jerome, Indianapolis	50	511	10.2	45	1
Perry, Ed, Miami	25	255	10.2	46	0
Pickens, Carl, Cincinnati	82	1023	12.5	t67	5
Pollard, Marcus, Indianapolis	24	309	12.9	t44	4
Popson, Ted, Kansas City	13	90	6.9	17	0
Potts, Roosevelt, Baltimore	30	168	5.6	18	2
Pritchard, Mike, Seattle	58	742	12.8	t50	3
Pritchett, Stanley, Miami	17	97	5.7	24	0
Purnell, Lovett, New England	12	92	7.7	22	2
Reed, Andre, Buffalo	63	795	12.6	t67	5
Rhett, Errict, Baltimore	11	65	5.9	16	0
Richardson, Tony, Kansas City	2	13	6.5	15	0
Ricks, Mikhael, San Diego	30	450	15.0	t39	2
Riemersma, Jay, Buffalo	25	288	11.5	28	6
Rison, Andre, Kansas City	40	542	13.6	t80	5
Ritchie, Jon, Oakland	29	225	7.8	31	0
Roan, Michael, Tennessee	13	93	7.2	16	0
Roe, James, Baltimore	8	115	14.4	27	1
Sanders, Chris, Tennessee	5	136	27.2	46	0
Scott, Darnay, Cincinnati	51	817	16.0	t70	7
Sharpe, Shannon, Denver	64	768	12.0	t38	10
Shaw, Sedrick, New England	6	30	5.0	11	0
Shedd, Kenny, Oakland	3	50	16.7	21	0
Shehee, Rashaan, Kansas City	10	73	7.3	14	0
Shelton, Daimon, Jacksonville	10	79	7.9	19	0
Shields, Will, Kansas City	1	4	4.0	4	0
Simmons, Tony, New England	23	474	20.6	t63	3
Slaughter, Webster, San Diego	8	93	11.6	31	0
Small, Torrance, Indianapolis	45	681	15.1	53	7
Smith, Antowain, Buffalo	5	11	2.2	9	0
Smith, Detron, Denver	3	24	8.0	16	0
Smith, Jimmy, Jacksonville	78	1182	15.2	t72	8
Smith, Rod, Denver	86	1222	14.2	58	6
Sowell, Jerald, N.Y. Jets	10	59	5.9	13	0
Spence, Blake, N.Y. Jets	1	5	5.0	5	0
Stephens, Tremayne, San Diego	2	9	4.5	5	0
Stewart, James, Jacksonville	6	42	7.0	19	1

Player, Team	No.	Yds.	Avg.	Long	TD
Stewart, Kordell, Pittsburgh	1	17	17.0	17	0
Still, Bryan, San Diego.................	43	605	14.1	67	2
Strong, Mack, Seattle..................	8	48	6.0	t11	2
Taylor, Fred, Jacksonville..............	44	421	9.6	t78	3
Thelwell, Ryan, San Diego.............	16	268	16.8	55	1
Thigpen, Yancey, Tennessee..........	38	493	13.0	55	3
Thomas, Lamar, Miami.................	43	603	14.0	t56	5
Thomas, Rodney, Tennessee..........	6	55	9.2	20	0
Thomas, Thurman, Buffalo............	26	220	8.5	26	1
Turner, Floyd, Baltimore..............	32	512	16.0	t66	5
Van Dyke, Alex, N.Y. Jets.............	5	40	8.0	15	0
Ward, Dedric, N.Y. Jets...............	25	477	19.1	t71	4
Ward, Hines, Pittsburgh	15	246	16.4	45	0
Warren, Lamont, Indianapolis	11	44	4.0	12	1
Watters, Ricky, Seattle................	52	373	7.2	24	0
Whitted, Alvis, Jacksonville	2	61	30.5	55	0
Williams, Harvey, Oakland	26	173	6.7	15	0
Williams, Kevin, Buffalo...............	29	392	13.5	55	1
Williams, Stepfret, Cincinnati	6	81	13.5	t19	1
Witman, Jon, Pittsburgh	13	74	5.7	15	0
Wycheck, Frank, Tennessee..........	70	768	11.0	38	2
Yarborough, Ryan, Baltimore	4	39	9.8	18	0

*Includes both NFC and AFC statistics.
t—touchdown.

NFC

Player, Team	No.	Yds.	Avg.	Long	TD
Alexander, Stephen, Washington ...	37	383	10.4	33	4
Alford, Brian, N.Y. Giants.............	1	11	11.0	11	0
Allen, James, Chicago	8	77	9.6	33	1
Allen, Terry, Washington..............	17	128	7.5	17	0
Alstott, Mike, Tampa Bay.............	22	152	6.9	26	1
Anderson, Jamal, Atlanta.............	27	319	11.8	27	2
Anderson, Ronnie, Arizona	1	8	8.0	8	0
Anthony, Reidel, Tampa Bay..........	51	708	13.9	t79	7
Armstrong, Tyji, St. Louis..............	6	54	9.0	20	0
Asher, Jamie, Washington	28	294	10.5	28	0
Barber, Tiki, N.Y. Giants	42	348	8.3	t87	3
Bates, Mario, Arizona	1	14	14.0	14	0
Beasley, Fred, San Francisco	1	11	11.0	11	0
Bech, Brett, New Orleans.............	14	264	18.9	t72	3
Bennett, Edgar, Chicago..............	28	209	7.5	31	0
Biakabutuka, Tim, Carolina...........	8	138	17.3	42	1
Bjornson, Eric, Dallas.................	15	218	14.5	43	1
Bowie, Larry, Washington	7	53	7.6	17	1
Bownes, Fabien, Chicago.............	5	69	13.8	44	1
Boyd, Tommie, Detroit.................	4	52	13.0	19	1
Bradford, Corey, Green Bay	3	27	9.0	18	0
Brock, Fred, Arizona	2	12	6.0	7	0
Brooks, Robert, Green Bay	31	420	13.5	t30	3
Broughton, Luther, Carolina	6	142	23.7	t68	1
Brown, Gary, N.Y. Giants	13	36	2.8	12	0
Bruce, Isaac, St. Louis	32	457	14.3	t80	1
Calloway, Chris, N.Y. Giants.........	62	812	13.1	36	6
Carrier, Mark, Carolina................	19	301	15.8	42	2
Carruth, Rae, Carolina	4	59	14.8	47	0
Carter, Cris, Minnesota	78	1011	13.0	t54	12
Centers, Larry, Arizona	69	559	8.1	54	2
Chancey, Robert, Chicago	11	102	9.3	15	0
Chandler, Chris, Atlanta..............	1	22	22.0	22	0
Chmura, Mark, Green Bay	47	554	11.8	t25	4
Christian, Bob, Atlanta................	19	214	11.3	39	1
Chryplewicz, Pete, Detroit	4	20	5.0	8	2
Clark, Greg J., San Francisco	12	124	10.3	23	1
Clay, Hayward, Dallas.................	1	27	27.0	27	0
Cleeland, Cameron, New Orleans ..	54	684	12.7	53	6
Collins, Kerry, Carolina................	1	-11	-11.0	-11	0
Comella, Greg, N.Y. Giants	1	3	3.0	3	0
Connell, Albert, Washington	28	451	16.1	61	2
Conway, Curtis, Chicago..............	54	733	13.6	47	3
Conwell, Ernie, St. Louis	15	105	7.0	13	0

Player, Team	No.	Yds.	Avg.	Long	TD
Copeland, Russell, Phi.-G.B.	20	232	11.6	20	0
Craver, Aaron, New Orleans...........	33	214	6.5	49	2
Cross, Howard, N.Y. Giants	13	90	6.9	22	0
Crowell, Germane, Detroit	25	464	18.6	t68	3
Cunningham, Randall, Minnesota..	1	-3	-3.0	-3	0
Davis, Billy, Dallas	39	691	17.7	t80	3
Davis, John, Tampa Bay	2	12	6.0	11	1
Davis, Stephen, Washington..........	21	263	12.5	30	2
Davis, Troy, New Orleans..............	16	99	6.2	19	0
Davis, Tyrone, Green Bay	18	250	13.9	t60	7
Dawkins, Sean, New Orleans.........	53	823	15.5	t64	1
DeLong, Greg, Minnesota.............	8	58	7.3	17	0
Downs, Gary, Atlanta..................	4	31	7.8	11	0
Dunn, Jason, Philadelphia	18	132	7.3	21	0
Dunn, Warrick, Tampa Bay	44	344	7.8	31	0
Dwight, Tim, Atlanta...................	4	94	23.5	t44	1
Edwards, Marc, San Francisco	22	218	9.9	t47	2
Ellard, Henry, N.E.-Was.*	7	115	16.4	19	0
Emanuel, Bert, Tampa Bay...........	41	636	15.5	t62	2
Engram, Bobby, Chicago..............	64	987	15.4	t79	5
Enis, Curtis, Chicago..................	6	20	3.3	7	0
Evans, Charles, Minnesota	12	84	7.0	14	0
Farquhar, John, New Orleans	1	13	13.0	13	0
Flannery, John, St. Louis.............	1	2	2.0	2	0
Floyd, William, Carolina	24	123	5.1	20	1
Fontenot, Chris, Philadelphia........	8	90	11.3	19	0
Freeman, Antonio, Green Bay	84	1424	17.0	t84	14
Fryar, Irving, Philadelphia............	48	556	11.6	t61	2
Garner, Charlie, Philadelphia........	19	110	5.8	21	0
Gedney, Chris, Arizona	22	271	12.3	32	1
Glover, Andrew, Minnesota...........	35	522	14.9	36	5
Goodwin, Hunter, Minnesota.........	3	16	5.3	9	0
Graham, Jeff, Philadelphia	47	600	12.8	45	2
Graham, Kent, N.Y. Giants	1	16	16.0	16	0
Green, Harold, Atlanta.................	2	34	17.0	28	0
Green, Jacquez, Tampa Bay	14	251	17.9	t64	2
Green, Trent, Washington.............	2	-8	-4.0	0	0
Guliford, Eric, New Orleans	10	124	12.4	24	0
Haase, Andy, N.Y. Giants	2	33	16.5	27	0
Hakim, Az-zahir, St. Louis	20	247	12.4	22	1
Hallock, Ty, Chicago...................	25	166	6.6	16	0
Hape, Patrick, Tampa Bay............	4	27	6.8	11	0
Harris, Derrick, St. Louis.............	12	57	4.8	8	2
Harris, Mark, San Francisco	2	67	33.5	42	0
Harris, Raymont, Green Bay..........	10	68	6.8	12	0
Harris, Ronnie, Atlanta................	1	14	14.0	14	0
Hastings, Andre, New Orleans.......	35	455	13.0	t89	3
Hatchette, Matthew, Minnesota.....	15	216	14.4	25	0
Hayes, Donald, Carolina..............	3	62	20.7	35	0
Hearst, Garrison, San Francisco	39	535	13.7	t81	2
Henderson, William, Green Bay.....	37	241	6.5	15	1
Henley, June, St. Louis................	35	252	7.2	43	0
Hicks, Skip, Washington..............	4	23	5.8	9	0
Hill, Greg, St. Louis	1	6	6.0	6	0
Hilliard, Ike, N.Y. Giants..............	51	715	14.0	50	2
Hoard, Leroy, Minnesota..............	22	198	9.0	t24	1
Holcombe, Robert, St. Louis.........	6	34	5.7	14	0
Holmes, Darick, Buf.-G.B.*	20	188	9.4	24	0
Hunter, Brice, Tampa Bay............	4	73	18.3	t45	1
Irvin, Michael, Dallas..................	74	1057	14.3	51	1
Ismail, Raghib, Carolina..............	69	1024	14.8	62	8
Jeffers, Patrick, Dallas................	18	330	18.3	t67	2
Jells, Dietrich, Philadelphia	2	53	26.5	37	0
Jervey, Travis, Green Bay	9	33	3.7	11	0
Johnson, Anthony, Carolina..........	27	242	9.0	t38	1
Johnson, Jimmie, Philadelphia......	2	14	7.0	9	0
Johnson, Tony, New Orleans	1	8	8.0	8	0
Johnston, Daryl, Dallas...............	18	60	3.3	9	1
Jordan, Andrew, Philadelphia	2	9	4.5	8	0
Jurevicius, Joe, N.Y. Giants	9	146	16.2	59	0
Kennison, Eddie, St. Louis	17	234	13.8	45	1
Kinchen, Todd, Atlanta................	11	157	14.3	32	1

Player, Team	No.	Yds.	Avg.	Long	TD
Kirby, Terry, San Francisco	16	134	8.4	25	0
Kozlowski, Brian, Atlanta	10	103	10.3	25	1
LaFleur, David, Dallas	20	176	8.8	24	2
Lane, Fred, Carolina	12	85	7.1	16	0
Lee, Amp, St. Louis	64	667	10.4	44	2
Levens, Dorsey, Green Bay	27	162	6.0	17	0
Levy, Chuck, San Francisco	15	64	4.3	13	0
Mangum, Kris, Carolina	1	5	5.0	5	0
Martin, Tony, Atlanta	66	1181	17.9	62	6
Mathis, Terance, Atlanta	64	1136	17.8	t78	11
Mayes, Alonzo, Chicago	21	217	10.3	22	0
Mayes, Derrick, Green Bay	30	394	13.1	t33	3
McWilliams, Johnny, Arizona	26	284	10.9	26	4
Metcalf, Eric, Arizona	31	324	10.5	29	0
Milburn, Glyn, Chicago	4	37	9.3	13	0
Miller, Bubba, Philadelphia	1	11	11.0	11	0
Mills, Ernie, Dallas	28	479	17.1	t43	4
Mitchell, Brian, Washington	44	306	7.0	24	0
Moore, Dave, Tampa Bay	24	255	10.6	t44	4
Moore, Herman, Detroit	82	983	12.0	36	5
Moore, Jerald, St. Louis	9	60	6.7	14	0
Moore, Rob, Arizona	67	982	14.7	57	5
Morton, Johnnie, Detroit	69	1028	14.9	t98	2
Moss, Randy, Minnesota	69	1313	19.0	t61	17
Muhammad, Muhsin, Carolina	68	941	13.8	t72	6
Murrell, Adrian, Arizona	18	169	9.4	30	2
Neal, Lorenzo, Tampa Bay	5	14	2.8	5	1
Ogden, Jeff, Dallas	8	63	7.9	12	0
Owens, Terrell, San Francisco	67	1097	16.4	t79	14
Oxendine, Ken, Atlanta	1	11	11.0	11	0
Palmer, David, Minnesota	18	185	10.3	33	0
Patten, David, N.Y. Giants	11	119	10.8	t39	1
Penn, Chris, Chicago	31	448	14.5	37	3
Perry, Wilmont, New Orleans	1	2	2.0	2	0
Poole, Keith, New Orleans	24	509	21.2	t82	2
Preston, Roell, Green Bay	2	23	11.5	13	0
Proehl, Ricky, St. Louis	60	771	12.9	47	3
Pupunu, Alfred, N.Y. Giants	1	2	2.0	2	0
Rasby, Walter, Detroit	15	119	7.9	17	1
Reed, Jake, Minnesota	34	474	13.9	t56	4
Rice, Jerry, San Francisco	82	1157	14.1	t75	9
Rivers, Ron, Detroit	3	58	19.3	38	0
Robinson, Jeff, St. Louis	1	4	4.0	t4	1
Robinson, Marcus, Chicago	4	44	11.0	t20	1
Sanders, Barry, Detroit	37	289	7.8	44	0
Sanders, Deion, Dallas	7	100	14.3	55	0
Sanders, Frank, Arizona	89	1145	12.9	42	3
Santiago, O.J., Atlanta	27	428	15.9	t62	5
Schlesinger, Cory, Detroit	3	16	5.3	t8	1
Schroeder, Bill, Green Bay	31	452	14.6	46	1
Sellers, Mike, Washington	3	18	6.0	8	0
Shepherd, Leslie, Washington	43	712	16.6	t43	8
Sinceno, Kaseem, Philadelphia	3	42	14.0	28	1
Sloan, David, Detroit	11	146	13.3	33	1
Slutzker, Scott, New Orleans	1	10	10.0	10	0
Smith, Emmitt, Dallas	27	175	6.5	24	2
Smith, Irv, San Francisco	25	266	10.6	t25	5
Smith, Lamar, New Orleans	24	249	10.4	t35	2
Smith, Robert, Minnesota	28	291	10.4	t67	2
Solomon, Freddie, Philadelphia	21	193	9.2	20	1
Stablein, Brian, Detroit	7	80	11.4	15	0
Staley, Duce, Philadelphia	57	432	7.6	33	1
Stokes, J.J., San Francisco	63	770	12.2	t33	8
Stone, Dwight, Carolina	1	7	7.0	7	0
Tate, Robert, Minnesota	1	17	17.0	17	0
Thomas, Chris, Washington	14	173	12.4	25	0
Thomas, J.T., St. Louis	20	287	14.4	42	0
Thomas, Robb, Tampa Bay	2	63	31.5	t50	1
Thomason, Jeff, Green Bay	9	89	9.9	22	0
Thrash, James, Washington	10	163	16.3	28	1
Toomer, Amani, N.Y. Giants	27	360	13.3	t37	5
Turner, Kevin, Philadelphia	34	232	6.8	18	0
Uwaezuoke, Iheanyi, San Francisco	3	67	22.3	35	0
Vardell, Tommy, Detroit	14	143	10.2	31	1
Walker, Corey, Philadelphia	2	35	17.5	33	0
Walls, Wesley, Carolina	49	506	10.3	30	5
Walsh, Chris, Minnesota	2	46	23.0	25	0
Warren, Chris, Dallas	13	66	5.1	15	1
Way, Charles, N.Y. Giants	31	131	4.2	16	1
Westbrook, Michael, Washington	44	736	16.7	t75	6
Wetnight, Ryan, Chicago	23	168	7.3	30	2
Wilcox, Josh, New Orleans	1	10	10.0	10	0
Williams, Karl, Tampa Bay	21	252	12.0	t29	1
Williams, Moe, Minnesota	1	64	64.0	64	0
Williams, Roland, St. Louis	15	144	9.6	33	1
Williams, Sherman, Dallas	11	104	9.5	30	0
Zellars, Ray, New Orleans	10	50	5.0	14	0

*Includes both NFC and AFC statistics.
t—touchdown.

PLAYERS WITH TWO CLUBS

Player, Team	No.	Yds.	Avg.	Long	TD
Blair, Michael, Green Bay	2	13	6.5	10	0
Blair, Michael, Cincinnati	1	7	7.0	7	0
Copeland, Russell, Philadelphia	18	221	12.3	20	0
Copeland, Russell, Green Bay	2	11	5.5	12	0
Crockett, Zack, Indianapolis	1	1	1.0	1	0
Crockett, Zack, Jacksonville	1	4	4.0	4	0
Ellard, Henry, New England	5	86	17.2	19	0
Ellard, Henry, Washington	2	29	14.5	19	0
Holmes, Darick, Buffalo	1	9	9.0	9	0
Holmes, Darick, Green Bay	19	179	9.4	24	0

SCORING

TEAM

AFC

Team	Total TD	TD Rush	TD Pass	TD Misc.	XP	2Pt.	XPA	FG	FGA	Safeties	Total Pts.
Denver	62	26	32	4	58	1	59	23	27	0	501
N.Y. Jets	49	12	33	4	45	0	46	25	35	1	416
Buffalo	43	13	28	2	41	0	41	33	41	1	400
Jacksonville	47	19	24	4	45	1	45	21	26	0	392
Seattle	45	11	21	13	41	2	41	19	24	0	372
New England	35	9	23	3	32	1	32	31	39	0	337
Tennessee	32	12	16	4	28	1	28	36	40	0	330
Kansas City	35	19	15	1	34	0	34	27	32	1	327
Miami	37	10	23	4	33	0	34	22	27	0	321
Indianapolis	33	7	26	0	23	4	23	27	31	0	310
Oakland	34	6	21	7	31	1	31	17	27	0	288
Baltimore	29	7	16	6	24	2	24	21	28	2	269
Cincinnati	31	7	20	4	21	2	21	19	27	0	268
Pittsburgh	26	8	13	5	23	3	23	26	32	0	263
San Diego	23	11	11	1	19	2	19	26	30	1	241
AFC total	561	177	322	62	498	20	501	373	466	6	5035
AFC average	37.4	11.8	21.5	4.1	33.2	1.3	33.4	24.9	31.1	0.4	335.7

NFC

Team	Total TD	TD Rush	TD Pass	TD Misc.	XP	2Pt.	XPA	FG	FGA	Safeties	Total Pts.
Minnesota	64	17	41	6	59	3	59	35	35	1	556
San Francisco	61	19	41	1	49	5	51	18	27	0	479
Atlanta	53	18	28	7	51	1	52	23	28	1	442
Green Bay	46	7	33	6	41	1	43	29	33	1	408
Dallas	42	21	17	4	40	0	40	29	35	1	381
Carolina	40	11	25	4	35	2	37	19	26	0	336
Arizona	36	18	17	1	36	0	36	23	33	2	325
Washington	40	15	24	1	36	1	37	13	23	1	319
Tampa Bay	36	12	21	3	29	3	30	21	28	0	314
Detroit	32	12	17	3	27	0	29	29	33	0	306
New Orleans	35	6	19	10	31	0	31	20	22	2	305
N.Y. Giants	32	10	18	4	32	0	32	21	27	0	287
St. Louis	32	17	12	3	25	4	26	20	26	0	285
Chicago	30	9	16	5	27	1	28	21	26	2	276
Philadelphia	17	10	7	0	15	0	17	14	21	1	161
NFC total	596	202	336	58	533	21	548	335	423	12	5180
NFC average	39.7	13.5	22.4	3.9	35.5	1.4	36.5	22.3	28.2	0.8	345.3
NFL total	1157	379	658	120	1031	41	1049	708	889	18	10215
NFL average	38.6	12.6	21.9	4.0	34.4	1.4	35.0	23.6	29.6	0.6	340.5

INDIVIDUAL

BESTS OF THE SEASON

Points, season
NFC: 164—Gary Anderson, Minnesota.
AFC: 140—Steve Christie, Buffalo.

Touchdowns, season
AFC: 23—Terrell Davis, Denver.
NFC: 17—Randy Moss, Minnesota.

Extra points, season
NFC: 59—Gary Anderson, Minnesota.
AFC: 58—Jason Elam, Denver.

Field goals, season
AFC: 36—Al Del Greco, Tennessee.
NFC: 35—Gary Anderson, Minnesota.

Field goal attempts, season
AFC: 41—Steve Christie, Buffalo.
NFC: 35—Gary Anderson, Minnesota; Richie Cunningham, Dallas.

Longest field goal
AFC: 63—Jason Elam, Jacksonville vs. Denver, Oct. 25.
NFC: 57—Jeff Wilkins, St. Louis vs. Arizona, Sept. 27.

Most points, game
AFC: 22—Charles Johnson, Pittsburgh vs. Tennessee, Nov. 1 (3 TD, 2-2pt.).
NFC: 20—Randy Moss, Minnesota at Dallas, Nov. 26 (3 TD, 1-2pt.); Gary Anderson, Minnesota at Baltimore, Dec. 13 (6 FG, 2 XP).

Team leaders, points
AFC:

Team		
Baltimore	87	Matt Stover
Buffalo	140	Steve Christie
Cincinnati	78	Doug Pelfrey
Denver	138	Terrell Davis
Indianapolis	104	Mike Vanderjagt
Jacksonville	108	Mike Hollis
Kansas City	115	Pete Stoyanovich
Miami	99	Olindo Mare

AFC:

New England	127	Adam Vinatieri
N.Y. Jets	120	John Hall
Oakland	82	Greg Davis
Pittsburgh	99	Norm Johnson
San Diego	97	John Carney
Seattle	98	Todd Peterson
Tennessee	136	Al Del Greco

NFC:

Arizona	69	Joe Nedney
Atlanta	120	Morten Andersen
Carolina	92	John Kasay
Chicago	90	Jeff Jaeger
Dallas	127	Richie Cunningham
Detroit	114	Jason Hanson
Green Bay	128	Ryan Longwell
Minnesota	164	Gary Anderson
New Orleans	91	Doug Brien
N.Y. Giants	95	Brad Daluiso
Philadelphia	57	Chris Boniol
St. Louis	85	Jeff Wilkins
San Francisco	103	Wade Richey
Tampa Bay	92	Michael Husted
Washington	63	Cary Blanchard

NFL LEADERS

KICKERS

Player, Team	XPM	XPA	FGM	FGA	Tot. Pts.
Anderson, Gary, Minnesota	59	59	35	35	164
Christie, Steve, Buffalo*	41	41	33	41	140
Del Greco, Al, Tennessee*	28	28	36	39	136
Longwell, Ryan, Green Bay	41	43	29	33	128
Elam, Jason, Denver*	58	58	23	27	127
Cunningham, Richie, Dallas	40	40	29	35	127
Vinatieri, Adam, New England*	32	32	31	39	†127
Andersen, Morten, Atlanta	51	52	23	28	120
Hall, John, N.Y. Jets*	45	46	25	35	120
Stoyanovich, Pete, Kansas City*	34	34	27	32	115
Hanson, Jason, Detroit	27	29	29	33	114
Hollis, Mike, Jacksonville*	45	45	21	26	108
Vanderjagt, Mike, Indianapolis*	23	23	27	31	104
Richey, Wade, San Francisco	49	51	18	27	103
Johnson, Norm, Pittsburgh*	21	21	26	31	99
Mare, Olindo, Miami*	33	34	22	27	99
Peterson, Todd, Seattle*	41	41	19	24	98
Carney, John, San Diego*	19	19	26	30	97
Daluiso, Brad, N.Y. Giants	32	32	21	27	95
Kasay, John, Carolina	35	37	19	26	92

*AFC.
†Includes 2-pt. conversion run.

NON-KICKERS

Player, Team	TD	RTD	PTD	MTD	2Pt.	Tot. Pts.
Davis, Terrell, Denver*	23	21	2	0	0	138
Moss, Randy, Minnesota	17	0	17	0	2	106
Taylor, Fred, Jacksonville*	17	14	3	0	0	102
Anderson, Jamal, Atlanta	16	14	2	0	1	98
Owens, Terrell, San Francisco	15	1	14	0	1	92
Smith, Emmitt, Dallas	15	13	2	0	0	90
Freeman, Antonio, Green Bay	14	0	14	0	1	86
Carter, Cris, Minnesota	12	0	12	0	0	72
Galloway, Joey, Seattle*	12	0	10	2	0	72
Edwards, Robert, N.E.*	12	9	3	0	0	72
Mathis, Terance, Atlanta	11	0	11	0	0	66
Johnson, Keyshawn, NYJ*	11	1	10	0	0	66
McCaffrey, Ed, Denver*	10	0	10	0	1	62
Hoard, Leroy, Minnesota	10	9	1	0	0	60
Sharpe, Shannon, Denver*	10	0	10	0	0	60
Murrell, Adrian, Arizona	10	8	2	0	0	60

Player, Team	TD	RTD	PTD	MTD	2Pt.	Tot. Pts.
Faulk, Marshall, Indianapolis*	10	6	4	0	0	60
Rice, Jerry, San Francisco	9	0	9	0	2	58
Watters, Ricky, Seattle*	9	9	0	0	1	56
Hearst, Garrison, S.F.	9	7	2	0	1	56
Shepherd, Leslie, Washington	9	1	8	0	1	56
Brown, Tim, Oakland*	9	0	9	0	0	54
Martin, Curtis, N.Y. Jets*	9	8	1	0	0	54
Alstott, Mike, Tampa Bay	9	8	1	0	0	54
Moulds, Eric, Buffalo*	9	0	9	0	0	54
Smith, Jimmy, Jacksonville*	8	0	8	0	0	48
Smith, Robert, Minnesota	8	6	2	0	0	48
Ismail, Raghib, Carolina	8	0	8	0	0	48
Morris, Bam, Kansas City*	8	8	0	0	0	48
Stokes, J.J., San Francisco	8	0	8	0	0	48

*AFC.

AFC

KICKERS

Player, Team	XPM	XPA	FGM	FGA	Tot. Pts.
Carney, John, San Diego	19	19	26	30	97
Christie, Steve, Buffalo	41	41	33	41	140
Davis, Greg, Oakland	31	31	17	27	82
Del Greco, Al, Tennessee	28	28	36	39	136
Elam, Jason, Denver	58	58	23	27	127
George, Matt, Pittsburgh	2	2	0	1	2
Hall, John, N.Y. Jets	45	46	25	35	120
Hentrich, Craig, Tennessee	0	0	0	1	0
Hollis, Mike, Jacksonville	45	45	21	26	108
Johnson, Norm, Pittsburgh	21	21	26	31	99
Mare, Olindo, Miami	33	34	22	27	99
Pelfrey, Doug, Cincinnati	21	21	19	27	78
Peterson, Todd, Seattle	41	41	19	24	98
Rouen, Tom, Denver	0	1	0	0	0
Stover, Matt, Baltimore	24	24	21	28	87
Stoyanovich, Pete, Kansas City	34	34	27	32	115
Vanderjagt, Mike, Indianapolis	23	23	27	31	104
Vinatieri, Adam, New England	32	32	31	39	†127

†Includes 2-pt. conversion run.

NON-KICKERS

Player, Team	TD	RTD	PTD	MTD	2Pt.	Tot. Pts.
Abdul-Jabbar, Karim, Miami	6	6	0	0	0	36
Adams, Sam, Seattle	1	0	0	1	0	6
Alexander, Derrick, K.C.	4	0	4	0	0	24
Anders, Kimble, Kansas City	3	1	2	0	0	18
Archie, Mike, Tennessee	1	1	0	0	0	6
Ashmore, Darryl, Oakland	1	0	0	1	0	6
Avery, John, Miami	3	2	1	0	0	18
Banks, Tavian, Jacksonville	1	1	0	0	0	6
Barlow, Reggie, Jacksonville	1	0	0	1	0	6
Battaglia, Marco, Cincinnati	1	0	1	0	0	6
Beasley, Aaron, Jacksonville	1	0	0	1	0	6
Bennett, Brandon, Cincinnati	2	2	0	0	0	12
Bennett, Donnell, Kansas City	6	5	1	0	0	36
Bettis, Jerome, Pittsburgh	3	3	0	0	0	18
Blackwell, Will, Pittsburgh	1	0	1	0	1	8
Bowden, Joe, Tennessee	2	0	0	2	0	12
Brady, Kyle, N.Y. Jets	5	0	5	0	0	30
Brisby, Vincent, New England	2	0	2	0	0	12
Brister, Bubby, Denver	1	1	0	0	0	6
Broussard, Steve, Seattle	1	0	0	1	0	6
Brown, Tim, Oakland	9	0	9	0	0	54
Brown, Troy, New England	1	0	1	0	0	6
Bruener, Mark, Pittsburgh	2	0	2	0	0	12
Buckley, Terrell, Miami	1	0	0	1	0	6
Burnett, Rob, Baltimore	0	0	0	0	0	*2
Byars, Keith, N.Y. Jets	3	0	3	0	0	18

1998 STATISTICS Scoring

Player, Team	Tot. TD	RTD	PTD	MTD	2Pt.	Tot. Pts.
Cascadden, Chad, N.Y. Jets	1	0	0	1	0	6
Chrebet, Wayne, N.Y. Jets	8	0	8	0	0	48
Coates, Ben, New England......	6	0	6	0	0	36
Coleman, Andre, Pittsburgh....	1	0	1	0	0	6
Cox, Bryan, N.Y. Jets	0	0	0	0	0	*2
Crockett, Ray, Denver	1	0	0	1	0	6
Crumpler, Carlester, Seattle	1	0	1	0	0	6
Cullors, Derrick, New England..	1	0	1	0	0	6
Darius, Donovin, Jacksonville..	1	0	0	1	0	6
Davis, Terrell, Denver	23	21	2	0	0	138
Davis, Willie, Tennessee	3	0	3	0	0	18
Dilger, Ken, Indianapolis	1	0	1	0	1	8
Dillon, Corey, Cincinnati..........	5	4	1	0	0	30
Drayton, Troy, Miami	3	0	3	0	0	18
Dudley, Rickey, Oakland..........	5	0	5	0	1	32
Dyson, Kevin, Tennessee	2	0	2	0	0	12
Early, Quinn, Buffalo	1	0	1	0	0	6
Edwards, Robert, N.E.	12	9	3	0	0	72
Elway, John, Denver	1	1	0	0	0	6
Faulk, Marshall, Indianapolis ..	10	6	4	0	0	60
Fauria, Christian, Seattle........	2	0	2	0	0	12
Fletcher, Terrell, San Diego	5	5	0	0	0	30
Flutie, Doug, Buffalo	1	1	0	0	0	6
Fuamatu-Ma'afala, Chris, Pit. .	3	2	1	0	0	18
Gadsden, Oronde, Miami	7	0	7	0	0	42
Galloway, Joey, Seattle	12	0	10	2	0	72
Gannon, Rich, Kansas City	3	3	0	0	0	18
Gash, Sam, Buffalo	3	0	3	0	0	18
George, Eddie, Tennessee.......	6	5	1	0	1	38
Gibson, Damon, Cincinnati	4	0	3	1	0	24
Glenn, Aaron, N.Y. Jets	1	0	0	1	0	6
Glenn, Terry, New England......	3	0	3	0	0	18
Gonzalez, Tony, Kansas City ...	2	0	2	0	0	12
Gordon, Darrien, Denver	1	0	0	1	0	6
Gordon, Dwayne, N.Y. Jets	1	0	0	1	0	6
Green, Ahman, Seattle	1	1	0	0	0	6
Green, E.G., Indianapolis	1	0	1	0	0	6
Green, Eric, Baltimore.............	1	0	1	0	0	6
Green, Willie, Denver	1	0	1	0	0	6
Griffith, Howard, Denver..........	3	0	3	0	0	18
Hansen, Phil, Buffalo	1	0	0	1	0	6
Harris, Corey, Baltimore..........	1	0	0	1	0	6
Harris, Jackie, Tennessee	2	0	2	0	0	12
Harrison, Marvin, Indianapolis.	7	0	7	0	1	44
Hawkins, Courtney, Pittsburgh.	1	0	1	0	0	6
Hebron, Vaughn, Denver	2	1	0	1	0	12
Henderson, Jerome, N.Y. Jets.	1	0	0	1	0	6
Hollas, Donald, Oakland..........	1	1	0	0	0	6
Holmes, Priest, Baltimore.......	7	7	0	0	0	42
Horn, Joe, Kansas City	1	0	1	0	0	6
Howard, Desmond, Oakland ...	2	0	0	2	0	12
Hundon, James, Cincinnati.....	1	0	1	0	0	6
Huntley, Richard, Pittsburgh...	1	1	0	0	0	6
Jefferson, Shawn, N.E.	2	0	2	0	0	12
Jett, James, Oakland..............	6	0	6	0	0	36
Johnson, Charles, Pittsburgh .	7	0	7	0	2	46
Johnson, Keyshawn, N.Y. Jets .	11	1	10	0	0	66
Johnson, Leon, N.Y. Jets	4	2	2	0	0	24
Johnson, Lonnie, Buffalo.........	2	0	2	0	0	12
Johnson, Pat, Baltimore..........	2	0	1	1	0	12
Johnson, Rob, Buffalo	1	1	0	0	0	6
Johnstone, Lance, Oakland.....	1	0	0	1	0	6
Jones, Charlie, San Diego	3	0	3	0	0	18
Jones, Damon, Jacksonville ...	4	0	4	0	0	24
Jones, Freddie, San Diego	3	0	3	0	1	20
Jones, Robert, Miami	1	0	0	1	0	6
Jordan, Randy, Oakland..........	1	1	0	0	0	6
Justin, Paul, Cincinnati	0	0	0	0	1	2
Kaufman, Napoleon, Oakland..	2	2	0	0	0	12
Kennedy, Cortez, Seattle	1	0	0	1	0	6
Kitna, Jon, Seattle..................	1	1	0	0	0	6

Player, Team	Tot. TD	RTD	PTD	MTD	2Pt.	Tot. Pts.
Lake, Carnell, Pittsburgh	1	0	0	1	0	6
Law, Ty, New England.............	1	0	0	1	0	6
Lewis, Albert, Oakland	1	0	0	1	0	6
Lewis, Jermaine, Baltimore.....	8	0	6	2	0	48
Linton, Jonathan, Buffalo........	1	1	0	0	0	6
Loville, Derek, Denver.............	2	2	0	0	0	12
Mack, Tremain, Cincinnati.......	1	0	0	1	0	6
Marino, Dan, Miami	1	1	0	0	0	6
Martin, Curtis, N.Y. Jets	9	8	1	0	0	54
Marts, Lonnie, Tennessee	1	0	0	1	0	6
Mason, Derrick, Tennessee.....	3	0	3	0	0	18
May, Deems, Seattle	1	0	1	0	0	6
McAfee, Fred, Pittsburgh	1	0	0	1	0	6
McCaffrey, Ed, Denver	10	0	10	0	1	62
McCardell, Keenan, Jac.	6	0	6	0	1	38
McDaniel, Terry, Seattle	1	0	0	1	0	6
McDuffie, O.J., Miami	7	0	7	0	0	42
McGee, Tony, Cincinnati	1	0	1	0	0	6
McKnight, James, Seattle	2	0	2	0	0	12
McNair, Steve, Tennessee	4	4	0	0	0	24
Means, Natrone, San Diego	5	5	0	0	0	30
Mickens, Terry, Oakland..........	1	0	1	0	0	6
Milloy, Lawyer, New England ..	1	0	0	1	0	6
Milne, Brian, Cincinnati..........	1	1	0	0	0	6
Mitchell, Pete, Jacksonville.....	2	0	2	0	0	12
Morris, Bam, Kansas City	8	8	0	0	0	48
Moulds, Eric, Buffalo	9	0	9	0	0	54
Northern, Gabe, Buffalo	1	0	0	1	0	6
Oldham, Chris, Pittsburgh	1	0	0	1	0	6
Pathon, Jerome, Indianapolis .	1	0	1	0	0	6
Pickens, Carl, Cincinnati	5	0	5	0	1	32
Pollard, Marcus, Indianapolis .	4	0	4	0	2	28
Potts, Roosevelt, Baltimore	2	0	2	0	0	12
Pritchard, Mike, Seattle..........	3	0	3	0	1	20
Pritchett, Stanley, Miami.........	1	1	0	0	0	6
Purnell, Lovett, New England..	2	0	2	0	0	12
Quinn, Jonathan, Jacksonville..	1	1	0	0	0	6
Reed, Andre, Buffalo	5	0	5	0	0	30
Richardson, Tony, Kansas City.	2	2	0	0	0	12
Ricks, Mikhael, San Diego	2	0	2	0	0	12
Riemersma, Jay, Buffalo	6	0	6	0	0	36
Rison, Andre, Kansas City	5	0	5	0	0	30
Roan, Michael, Tennessee	1	0	0	1	0	6
Roe, James, Baltimore............	1	0	1	0	0	6
Sawyer, Corey, Cincinnati	1	0	0	1	0	6
Scott, Darnay, Cincinnati	7	0	7	0	0	42
Shade, Sam, Cincinnati..........	1	0	0	1	0	6
Sharpe, Shannon, Denver.......	10	0	10	0	0	60
Shelton, Daimon, Jacksonville.	1	1	0	0	0	6
Simmons, Anthony, Seattle	1	0	0	1	0	6
Simmons, Tony, New England..	3	0	3	0	0	18
Small, Torrance, Indianapolis .	7	0	7	0	0	42
Smith, Antowain, Buffalo	8	8	0	0	0	48
Smith, Darrin, Seattle	2	0	0	2	0	12
Smith, Jimmy, Jacksonville	8	0	8	0	0	48
Smith, Rod, Denver	7	0	6	1	0	42
Springs, Shawn, Seattle..........	3	0	0	3	0	18
Stephens, Tremayne, S.D.	1	1	0	0	0	6
Stewart, James, Jacksonville ..	3	2	1	0	0	18
Stewart, Kordell, Pittsburgh....	2	2	0	0	0	12
Still, Bryan, San Diego............	2	0	2	0	0	12
Strong, Mack, Seattle	2	0	2	0	0	12
Taylor, Fred, Jacksonville	17	14	3	0	0	102
Testaverde, Vinny, N.Y. Jets ...	1	1	0	0	0	6
Thelwell, Ryan, San Diego	1	0	1	0	0	6
Thigpen, Yancey, Tennessee ...	3	0	3	0	0	18
Thomas, Derrick, Kansas City.	1	0	0	1	0	*8
Thomas, Henry, New England..	1	0	0	1	0	6
Thomas, Lamar, Miami...........	5	0	5	0	0	30
Thomas, Rodney, Tennessee ..	2	2	0	0	0	12
Thomas, Thurman, Buffalo	3	2	1	0	0	18

Player, Team	Tot. TD	RTD	PTD	MTD	2Pt.	Tot. Pts.
Thomas, Zach, Miami	2	0	0	2	0	12
Turner, Eric, Oakland	1	0	0	1	0	6
Turner, Floyd, Baltimore	5	0	5	0	2	34
Ward, Dedric, N.Y. Jets	4	0	4	0	0	24
Warren, Lamont, Indianapolis.	2	1	1	0	0	12
Washington, Dewayne, Pit.	2	0	0	2	0	12
Washington, Ted, Buffalo	0	0	0	0	0	*2
Watters, Ricky, Seattle	9	9	0	0	1	56
Whelihan, Craig, San Diego	0	0	0	0	1	2
Whitted, Alvis, Jacksonville	1	0	0	1	0	6
Williams, Harvey, Oakland	2	2	0	0	0	12
Williams, Jamal, San Diego	1	0	0	1	0	6
Williams, Kevin, Buffalo	1	0	1	0	0	6
Williams, Stepfret, Cincinnati..	1	0	1	0	0	6
Williams, Willie, Seattle	1	0	0	1	0	6
Woodson, Charles, Oakland	1	0	0	1	0	6
Woodson, Rod, Baltimore	2	0	0	2	0	12
Wycheck, Frank, Tennessee	2	0	2	0	0	12

*Includes safety.

NOTE: One team safety apiece credited to Baltimore and San Diego.

NFC

KICKERS

Player, Team	XPM	XPA	FGM	FGA	Tot. Pts.
Akers, David, Washington	2	2	0	2	2
Andersen, Morten, Atlanta	51	52	23	28	120
Anderson, Gary, Minnesota	59	59	35	35	164
Blanchard, Cary, Washington	30	31	11	17	63
Blanton, Scott, Washington	4	4	2	4	10
Boniol, Chris, Philadelphia	15	17	14	21	57
Brien, Doug, New Orleans	31	31	20	22	91
Cunningham, Richie, Dallas	40	40	29	35	127
Daluiso, Brad, N.Y. Giants	32	32	21	27	95
Hanson, Jason, Detroit	27	29	29	33	114
Husted, Michael, Tampa Bay	29	30	21	28	92
Jacke, Chris, Arizona	6	6	10	14	36
Jaeger, Jeff, Chicago	27	28	21	26	90
Kasay, John, Carolina	35	37	19	26	92
Longwell, Ryan, Green Bay	41	43	29	33	128
Nedney, Joe, Arizona	30	30	13	19	69
Richey, Wade, San Francisco	49	51	18	27	103
Wilkins, Jeff, St. Louis	25	26	20	26	85

NON-KICKERS

Player, Team	Tot. TD	RTD	PTD	MTD	2Pt.	Tot. Pts.
Aikman, Troy, Dallas	2	2	0	0	0	12
Alexander, Stephen, Was.	4	0	4	0	0	24
Allen, James, Chicago	2	1	1	0	0	12
Allen, Terry, Washington	2	2	0	0	0	12
Alstott, Mike, Tampa Bay	9	8	1	0	0	54
Anderson, Jamal, Atlanta	16	14	2	0	1	98
Anthony, Reidel, Tampa Bay	7	0	7	0	1	44
Banks, Tony, St. Louis	3	3	0	0	1	20
Barber, Ronde, Tampa Bay	1	0	0	1	0	6
Barber, Tiki, N.Y. Giants	3	0	3	0	0	18
Batch, Charlie, Detroit	1	1	0	0	0	6
Bates, Mario, Arizona	6	6	0	0	2	36
Bates, Michael, Carolina	1	0	0	1	0	6
Bech, Brett, New Orleans	3	0	3	0	0	18
Bennett, Edgar, Chicago	2	2	0	0	0	12
Bennett, Tommy, Arizona	1	0	0	1	0	6
Biakabutuka, Tim, Carolina	4	3	1	0	0	24
Bjornson, Eric, Dallas	2	1	1	0	0	12
Bono, Steve, St. Louis	0	0	0	0	1	2
Boutte, Marc, Washington	0	0	0	0	0	*2
Bowie, Larry, Washington	1	0	1	0	0	6

Player, Team	Tot. TD	RTD	PTD	MTD	2Pt.	Tot. Pts.
Bownes, Fabien, Chicago	1	0	1	0	0	6
Boyd, Tommie, Detroit	1	0	1	0	0	6
Bradford, Ronnie, Atlanta	1	0	0	1	0	*8
Brooks, Robert, Green Bay	3	0	3	0	0	18
Broughton, Luther, Carolina	1	0	1	0	0	6
Brown, Gary, N.Y. Giants	5	5	0	0	0	30
Bruce, Isaac, St. Louis	1	0	1	0	0	6
Butler, LeRoy, Green Bay	1	0	0	1	0	6
Calloway, Chris, N.Y. Giants	6	0	6	0	0	36
Carrier, Mark, Carolina	2	0	2	0	0	12
Carter, Cris, Minnesota	12	0	12	0	0	72
Centers, Larry, Arizona	2	0	2	0	0	12
Chancey, Robert, Chicago	2	2	0	0	0	12
Chandler, Chris, Atlanta	2	2	0	0	0	12
Chmura, Mark, Green Bay	4	0	4	0	0	24
Christian, Bob, Atlanta	3	2	1	0	0	18
Chryplewicz, Pete, Detroit	2	0	2	0	0	12
Clark, Greg J., San Francisco..	1	0	1	0	1	8
Cleeland, Cameron, N.O.	6	0	6	0	0	36
Collins, Kerry, Car.-N.O.	1	1	0	0	1	8
Connell, Albert, Washington	2	0	2	0	0	12
Conway, Curtis, Chicago	3	0	3	0	0	18
Craver, Aaron, New Orleans	5	2	2	1	0	30
Crowell, Germane, Detroit	3	0	3	0	0	18
Cunningham, Randall, Min.	1	1	0	0	1	8
Davis, Billy, Dallas	3	0	3	0	0	18
Davis, Eric, Carolina	2	0	0	2	0	12
Davis, John, Tampa Bay	1	0	1	0	0	6
Davis, Stephen, Washington	2	0	2	0	0	12
Davis, Troy, New Orleans	1	1	0	0	0	6
Davis, Tyrone, Green Bay	7	0	7	0	0	42
Dawkins, Sean, New Orleans ..	1	0	1	0	0	6
Dilfer, Trent, Tampa Bay	2	2	0	0	0	12
Drakeford, Tyronne, N.O.	1	0	0	1	0	6
Dunn, Warrick, Tampa Bay	2	2	0	0	0	12
Dwight, Tim, Atlanta	2	0	1	1	0	12
Edwards, Antonio, Atlanta	1	0	0	1	0	6
Edwards, Marc, San Francisco .	3	1	2	0	0	18
Ellsworth, Percy, N.Y. Giants...	2	0	0	2	0	12
Emanuel, Bert, Tampa Bay	2	0	2	0	0	12
Engram, Bobby, Chicago	5	0	5	0	0	30
Evans, Charles, Minnesota	1	1	0	0	0	6
Fair, Terry, Detroit	2	0	0	2	0	12
Favre, Brett, Green Bay	1	1	0	0	0	6
Fields, Mark, New Orleans	1	0	0	1	0	6
Floyd, William, Carolina	4	3	1	0	0	24
Freeman, Antonio, Green Bay .	14	0	14	0	1	86
Fryar, Irving, Philadelphia	2	0	2	0	0	12
Garner, Charlie, Philadelphia...	4	4	0	0	0	24
Gedney, Chris, Arizona	1	0	1	0	0	6
Glover, Andrew, Minnesota	5	0	5	0	0	30
Graham, Jeff, Philadelphia	2	0	2	0	0	12
Graham, Kent, N.Y. Giants	2	2	0	0	0	12
Green, Jacquez, Tampa Bay	3	0	2	1	0	18
Green, Trent, Washington	2	2	0	0	0	12
Hakim, Az-zahir, St. Louis	2	1	1	0	0	12
Hallock, Ty, Chicago	1	1	0	0	0	6
Hape, Patrick, Tampa Bay	0	0	0	0	1	2
Harris, Derrick, St. Louis	2	0	2	0	0	12
Harris, Raymont, Green Bay ...	1	1	0	0	0	6
Harris, Walt, Chicago	1	0	0	1	0	6
Hastings, Andre, N.O.	3	0	3	0	0	18
Hearst, Garrison, S.F.	9	7	2	0	1	56
Henderson, William, G.B.	3	2	1	0	0	18
Henley, June, St. Louis	3	3	0	0	0	18
Hicks, Skip, Washington	8	8	0	0	0	48
Hill, Greg, St. Louis	4	4	0	0	0	24
Hilliard, Ike, N.Y. Giants	2	0	2	0	0	12
Hitchcock, Jimmy, Minnesota.	3	0	0	3	0	18
Hoard, Leroy, Minnesota	10	9	1	0	0	60
Holcombe, Robert, St. Louis ..	2	2	0	0	0	12

1998 STATISTICS *Scoring*

Player, Team	Tot. TD	RTD	PTD	MTD	2Pt.	Tot. Pts.
Holmes, Darick, Green Bay	1	1	0	0	0	6
Horne, Tony, St. Louis	1	0	0	1	0	6
Hunter, Brice, Tampa Bay	1	0	1	0	1	8
Irvin, Michael, Dallas	1	0	1	0	0	6
Ismail, Raghib, Carolina	8	0	8	0	0	48
Jeffers, Patrick, Dallas	2	0	2	0	0	12
Jervey, Travis, Green Bay	1	1	0	0	0	6
Johnson, Anthony, Carolina	1	0	1	0	0	6
Johnson, Joe, New Orleans	1	0	0	1	0	6
Johnston, Daryl, Dallas	1	0	1	0	0	6
Kelly, Rob, New Orleans	1	0	0	1	0	6
Kennison, Eddie, St. Louis	2	0	1	1	0	12
Kinchen, Todd, Atlanta	1	0	1	0	0	6
Kirby, Terry, San Francisco	3	3	0	0	0	18
Knight, Sammy, New Orleans	2	0	0	2	0	12
Kozlowski, Brian, Atlanta	1	0	1	0	0	6
Kramer, Erik, Chicago	1	1	0	0	0	6
LaFleur, David, Dallas	2	0	2	0	0	12
Lane, Fred, Carolina	5	5	0	0	0	30
Lee, Amp, St. Louis	4	2	2	0	1	26
Lee, Shawn, Chicago	1	0	0	1	0	6
Levens, Dorsey, Green Bay	1	1	0	0	0	6
Levy, Chuck, San Francisco	1	1	0	0	0	6
Martin, Tony, Atlanta	6	0	6	0	0	36
Martin, Wayne, New Orleans	0	0	0	0	0	*2
Mathis, Terance, Atlanta	11	0	11	0	0	66
Mayes, Derrick, Green Bay	3	0	3	0	0	18
McKenzie, Keith, Green Bay	2	0	0	2	0	12
McNeil, Ryan, St. Louis	1	0	0	1	0	6
McQuarters, R.W., S.F.	1	0	0	1	0	6
McWilliams, Johnny, Arizona	4	0	4	0	0	24
Milburn, Glyn, Chicago	3	0	0	3	0	18
Mills, Ernie, Dallas	4	0	4	0	0	24
Mincy, Charles, Tampa Bay	1	0	0	1	0	6
Mitchell, Brian, Washington	3	2	0	1	0	18
Mitchell, Keith, New Orleans	1	0	0	1	0	6
Moore, Dave, Tampa Bay	4	0	4	0	0	24
Moore, Herman, Detroit	5	0	5	0	0	30
Moore, Jerald, St. Louis	2	2	0	0	0	12
Moore, Rob, Arizona	5	0	5	0	0	30
Morton, Johnnie, Detroit	2	0	2	0	0	12
Moss, Randy, Minnesota	17	0	17	0	2	106
Muhammad, Muhsin, Carolina	6	0	6	0	1	38
Murrell, Adrian, Arizona	10	8	2	0	0	60
Neal, Lorenzo, Tampa Bay	1	0	1	0	0	6
Owens, Terrell, S.F.	15	1	14	0	1	92
Palmer, David, Minnesota	1	0	0	1	0	6
Patten, David, N.Y. Giants	2	0	1	1	0	12
Peete, Rodney, Philadelphia	1	1	0	0	0	6
Penn, Chris, Chicago	3	0	3	0	1	20
Plummer, Jake, Arizona	4	4	0	0	0	24
Poole, Keith, New Orleans	2	0	2	0	0	12
Preston, Roell, Green Bay	3	0	0	3	0	18
Proehl, Ricky, St. Louis	3	0	3	0	1	20
Rasby, Walter, Detroit	1	0	1	0	0	6
Reed, Jake, Minnesota	4	0	4	0	0	24
Rice, Jerry, San Francisco	9	0	9	0	2	58
Rivers, Ron, Detroit	1	1	0	0	0	6
Robbins, Austin, New Orleans	1	0	0	1	0	6
Robinson, Eugene, Atlanta	1	0	0	1	0	6
Robinson, Jeff, St. Louis	1	0	1	0	0	6
Robinson, Marcus, Chicago	1	0	1	0	0	6
Rudd, Dwayne, Minnesota	2	0	0	2	0	12
Sanders, Barry, Detroit	4	4	0	0	0	24
Sanders, Deion, Dallas	3	0	0	3	0	18
Sanders, Frank, Arizona	3	0	3	0	0	18
Santiago, O.J., Atlanta	5	0	5	0	0	30
Schlesinger, Cory, Detroit	1	0	1	0	0	6
Schroeder, Bill, Green Bay	1	0	1	0	0	6
Shepherd, Leslie, Washington	9	1	8	0	1	56
Sinceno, Kaseem, Phi.	1	0	1	0	0	6
Sloan, David, Detroit	1	0	1	0	0	6
Smith, Chuck, Atlanta	1	0	0	1	0	6
Smith, Emmitt, Dallas	15	13	2	0	0	90
Smith, Irv, San Francisco	5	0	5	0	0	30
Smith, Lamar, New Orleans	3	1	2	0	0	18
Smith, Robert, Minnesota	8	6	2	0	0	48
Solomon, Freddie, Philadelphia	1	0	1	0	0	6
Staley, Duce, Philadelphia	6	5	1	0	0	36
Stenstrom, Steve, Chicago	2	2	0	0	0	12
Stokes, J.J., San Francisco	8	0	8	0	0	48
Stone, Dwight, Carolina	1	0	0	1	0	6
Strahan, Michael, N.Y. Giants	1	0	0	1	0	6
Thierry, John, Chicago	0	0	0	0	0	*2
Thomas, Robb, Tampa Bay	1	0	1	0	0	6
Thomas, William, Philadelphia	0	0	0	0	0	*2
Thrash, James, Washington	1	0	1	0	0	6
Toomer, Amani, N.Y. Giants	5	0	5	0	0	30
Tuggle, Jessie, Atlanta	1	0	0	1	0	6
Vardell, Tommy, Detroit	7	6	1	0	0	42
Walls, Wesley, Carolina	5	0	5	0	0	30
Warren, Chris, Dallas	5	4	1	0	0	30
Way, Charles, N.Y. Giants	4	3	1	0	0	24
Weary, Fred, New Orleans	1	0	0	1	0	6
Westbrook, Bryant, Detroit	1	0	0	1	0	6
Westbrook, Michael, Was.	6	0	6	0	0	36
Wetnight, Ryan, Chicago	2	0	2	0	0	12
Wheaton, Kenny, Dallas	1	0	0	1	0	*8
White, William, Atlanta	1	0	0	1	0	6
Williams, Karl, Tampa Bay	1	0	1	0	0	6
Williams, Roland, St. Louis	1	0	1	0	0	6
Williams, Sherman, Dallas	1	1	0	0	0	6
Young, Steve, San Francisco	6	6	0	0	0	36
Zellars, Ray, New Orleans	1	1	0	0	0	6

*Includes safety.

NOTE: Two team safeties credited to Arizona, one team safety apiece credited to Chicago, Green Bay, Minnesota, New Orleans and Philadelphia.

INTERCEPTIONS

TEAM

AFC

Team	No.	Yds.	Avg.	Long	TD
Miami	29	318	11.0	61	4
Seattle	24	455	19.0	t56	8
New England	24	255	10.6	t59	3
Oakland	21	420	20.0	t94	3
N.Y. Jets	21	263	12.5	87	1
San Diego	20	203	10.2	30	1
Denver	19	439	23.1	t80	2
Buffalo	18	204	11.3	43	1
Baltimore	17	161	9.5	t60	2
Pittsburgh	16	335	20.9	t78	3
Kansas City	13	187	14.4	28	0
Cincinnati	13	144	11.1	t58	1
Jacksonville	13	119	9.2	34	0
Tennessee	12	98	8.2	33	2
Indianapolis	8	97	12.1	30	0
AFC total	268	3698	13.8	t94	31
AFC average	17.9	246.5	13.8	...	2.1

t—touchdown.

NFC

Team	No.	Yds.	Avg.	Long	TD
New Orleans	21	466	22.2	t91	5
San Francisco	21	178	8.5	37	0
Arizona	20	235	11.8	t70	1
Minnesota	19	341	17.9	t79	3
Carolina	19	295	15.5	t56	2
Atlanta	19	224	11.8	36	2
N.Y. Giants	19	217	11.4	t43	3
St. Louis	16	201	12.6	41	1
Dallas	14	250	17.9	t71	1
Chicago	14	129	9.2	28	1
Washington	13	190	14.6	54	0
Green Bay	13	111	8.5	t33	1
Tampa Bay	12	212	17.7	56	1
Detroit	12	132	11.0	t34	1
Philadelphia	9	158	17.6	33	0
NFC total	241	3339	13.9	t91	22
NFC average	16.1	222.6	13.9	...	1.5
NFL total	509	7037	...	t94	53
NFL average	17.0	234.6	13.8	...	1.8

INDIVIDUAL

BESTS OF THE SEASON

Interceptions, season
AFC: 9—Ty Law, New England.
NFC: 8—Kwamie Lassiter, Arizona.

Interceptions, game
NFC: 4—Kwamie Lassiter, Arizona vs. San Diego, Dec. 27.
AFC: 2—Held by many players.

Yards, season
NFC: 242—Jimmy Hitchcock, Minnesota.
AFC: 178—Dewayne Washington, Pittsburgh.

Longest
AFC: 94—Eric Turner, Oakland vs. Denver, Sept. 20 (TD).
NFC: 91—Sammy Knight, New Orleans at Minnesota, Nov. 8 (TD).

Touchdowns, season
NFC: 3—Jimmy Hitchcock, Minnesota.
AFC: 2—Darrin Smith, Seattle; Shawn Springs, Seattle; Zach Thomas, Miami; Dewayne Washington, Pittsburgh; Rod Woodson, Baltimore.

Team leaders, interceptions
AFC:

Team		Player
Baltimore	6	Rod Woodson
Buffalo	6	Kurt Schulz
Cincinnati	3	Sam Shade
		Artrell Hawkins
Denver	4	Darrien Gordon
Indianapolis	1	Rico Clark
		Monty Montgomery
		Jason Belser
		Robert Blackmon
		Elijah Alexander
		Jeff Burris
		Tyrone Poole
		Michael Barber
Jacksonville	3	Aaron Beasley
		Chris Hudson
Kansas City	4	James Hasty
Miami	8	Terrell Buckley
		Sam Madison

Team		Player
New England	9	Ty Law
N.Y. Jets	6	Aaron Glenn
Oakland	5	Charles Woodson
		Eric Allen
Pittsburgh	5	Dewayne Washington
San Diego	6	Greg Jackson
Seattle	7	Shawn Springs
Tennessee	4	Darryll Lewis

NFC:

Team		Player
Arizona	8	Kwamie Lassiter
Atlanta	7	Ray Buchanan
Carolina	5	Eric Davis
Chicago	4	Walt Harris
Dallas	5	Deion Sanders
Detroit	3	Bryant Westbrook
		Mark Carrier
		Ron Rice
Green Bay	5	Tyrone Williams
Minnesota	7	Jimmy Hitchcock
New Orleans	6	Sammy Knight
N.Y. Giants	5	Percy Ellsworth
Philadelphia	2	Brian Dawkins
		Troy Vincent
		Michael Zordich
St. Louis	3	Todd Lyght
		Keith Lyle
San Francisco	4	Darnell Walker
		Merton Hanks
		Zack Bronson
		Tim McDonald
Tampa Bay	4	Charles Mincy
Washington	3	Leomont Evans
		Darrell Green

NFL LEADERS

Player, Team	No.	Yds.	Avg.	Long	TD
Law, Ty, New England*	9	133	14.8	t59	1
Buckley, Terrell, Miami*	8	157	19.6	61	1
Madison, Sam, Miami*	8	114	14.3	35	0
Lassiter, Kwamie, Arizona	8	80	10.0	29	0

Player, Team	No.	Yds.	Avg.	Long	TD
Hitchcock, Jimmy, Minnesota	7	242	34.6	t79	3
Springs, Shawn, Seattle*	7	142	20.3	t56	2
Buchanan, Ray, Atlanta..............	7	102	14.6	34	0
Knight, Sammy, New Orleans	6	171	28.5	t91	2
Woodson, Rod, Baltimore*	6	108	18.0	t60	2
Milloy, Lawyer, New England*	6	54	9.0	t30	1
Jackson, Greg, San Diego	6	50	8.3	25	0
Schulz, Kurt, Buffalo*................	6	48	8.0	24	0
Glenn, Aaron, N.Y.Jets*	6	23	3.8	26	0

*AFC.
t—touchdown.
Leader based on most interceptions.

AFC

Player, Team	No.	Yds.	Avg.	Long	TD
Adams, Sam, Seattle	1	25	25.0	t25	1
Alexander, Elijah, Indianapolis	1	12	12.0	12	0
Allen, Eric, Oakland	5	59	11.8	22	0
Ambrose, Ashley, Cincinnati..........	2	0	0.0	0	0
Atwater, Steve, Denver	1	4	4.0	4	0
Barber, Michael, Indianapolis	1	0	0.0	0	0
Beasley, Aaron, Jacksonville..........	3	35	11.7	34	0
Bellamy, Jay, Seattle..................	3	40	13.3	24	0
Belser, Jason, Indianapolis	1	19	19.0	19	0
Bishop, Blaine, Tennessee	1	13	13.0	13	0
Blackmon, Robert, Indianapolis.....	1	14	14.0	14	0
Bowden, Joe, Tennessee	1	1	1.0	t1	1
Braxton, Tyrone, Denver	1	72	72.0	72	0
Brown, Chad, Seattle	1	11	11.0	11	0
Brown, Corwin, N.Y. Jets	1	0	0.0	0	0
Buckley, Terrell, Miami	8	157	19.6	61	1
Burris, Jeff, Indianapolis	1	0	0.0	0	0
Cadrez, Glenn, Denver	2	11	5.5	6	0
Canty, Chris, New England	1	12	12.0	12	0
Carter, Dale, Kansas City	2	23	11.5	23	0
Clark, Rico, Indianapolis.............	1	30	30.0	30	0
Clay, Willie, New England	3	19	6.3	19	0
Coghill, George, Denver...............	1	20	20.0	20	0
Collins, Mark, Seattle..................	1	0	0.0	0	0
Copeland, John, Cincinnati...........	1	3	3.0	3	0
Cowart, Sam, Buffalo.................	2	23	11.5	23	0
Crockett, Ray, Denver.................	3	105	35.0	t80	1
Davis, Anthony, Kansas City	2	27	13.5	27	0
Davis, Travis, Jacksonville...........	2	34	17.0	34	0
Devine, Kevin, Jacksonville	1	0	0.0	0	0
Dimry, Charles, San Diego	3	38	12.7	30	0
Emmons, Carlos, Pittsburgh	1	2	2.0	2	0
Figures, Deon, Jacksonville..........	1	0	0.0	0	0
Flowers, Lethon, Pittsburgh	1	2	2.0	2	0
Gardener, Daryl, Miami...............	1	-1	-1.0	-1	0
Glenn, Aaron, N.Y. Jets................	6	23	3.8	26	0
Gordon, Darrien, Denver	4	125	31.3	t55	1
Gordon, Dwayne, N.Y. Jets	1	31	31.0	t31	1
Green, Victor, N.Y. Jets	4	99	24.8	87	0
Hand, Norman, San Diego	2	47	23.5	30	0
Hardy, Kevin, Jacksonville	2	40	20.0	24	0
Harper, Dwayne, San Diego..........	1	12	12.0	12	0
Harrison, Rodney, San Diego	3	42	14.0	21	0
Harvey, Richard, Oakland	1	2	2.0	2	0
Hasty, James, Kansas City	4	42	10.5	21	0
Hawkins, Artrell, Cincinnati	3	21	7.0	12	0
Henderson, Jerome, N.Y. Jets	1	21	21.0	21	0
Holmes, Earl, Pittsburgh	1	36	36.0	36	0
Hudson, Chris, Jacksonville	3	10	3.3	8	0
Irvin, Ken, Buffalo	1	43	43.0	43	0
Israel, Steve, New England	3	13	4.3	12	0
Jackson, Greg, San Diego	6	50	8.3	25	0
Jackson, Ray, Buffalo	2	27	13.5	27	0
Jackson, Steve, Tennessee	1	0	0.0	0	0
Jenkins, DeRon, Baltimore	1	0	0.0	0	0
Johnson, Darrius, Denver..............	2	79	39.5	45	0
Johnson, Pepper, N.Y. Jets	1	0	0.0	0	0

Player, Team	No.	Yds.	Avg.	Long	TD
Jones, Henry, Buffalo	3	0	0.0	0	0
Jones, Robert, Miami	2	14	7.0	t14	1
Kirkland, Levon, Pittsburgh	1	1	1.0	1	0
Lake, Carnell, Pittsburgh	4	33	8.3	27	1
Law, Ty, New England.................	9	133	14.8	t59	1
Lewis, Albert, Oakland	2	74	37.0	t74	1
Lewis, Darryll, Tennessee.............	4	40	10.0	33	0
Lewis, Mo, N.Y. Jets	1	11	11.0	11	0
Lewis, Ray, Baltimore.................	2	25	12.5	26	0
Madison, Sam, Miami	8	114	14.3	35	0
Martin, Emanuel, Buffalo	1	23	23.0	23	0
Marts, Lonnie, Tennessee	1	27	27.0	t27	1
McDaniel, Terry, Seattle...............	1	43	43.0	t43	1
McMillian, Mark, Kansas City	3	48	16.0	21	0
Mickens, Ray, N.Y. Jets	3	10	3.3	10	0
Milloy, Lawyer, New England	6	54	9.0	t30	1
Mobley, John, Denver..................	1	-2	-2.0	-2	0
Montgomery, Delmonico, Ind.	1	22	22.0	22	0
Newman, Anthony, Oakland..........	2	17	8.5	11	0
Northern, Gabe, Buffalo	1	40	40.0	t40	1
Oldham, Chris, Pittsburgh	1	14	14.0	14	0
Perry, Darren, Pittsburgh..............	2	69	34.5	40	0
Poole, Tyrone, Indianapolis	1	0	0.0	0	0
Pryce, Trevor, Denver	1	1	1.0	1	0
Randolph, Thomas, Cincinnati.......	1	0	0.0	0	0
Robertson, Marcus, Tennessee	1	0	0.0	0	0
Robinson, Eddie, Tennessee..........	1	11	11.0	11	0
Romanowski, Bill, Denver	2	22	11.0	18	0
Ross, Adrian, Cincinnati	1	11	11.0	11	0
Sawyer, Corey, Cincinnati............	1	58	58.0	t58	1
Schulz, Kurt, Buffalo..................	6	48	8.0	24	0
Shade, Sam, Cincinnati	3	33	11.0	32	0
Shaw, Terrance, San Diego...........	2	0	0.0	0	0
Simmons, Anthony, Seattle	1	36	36.0	t36	1
Simmons, Brian, Cincinnati..........	1	18	18.0	18	0
Smith, Darrin, Seattle	3	56	18.7	t26	2
Smith, Neil, Denver	1	2	2.0	2	0
Smith, Otis, N.Y. Jets..................	2	34	17.0	32	0
Smith, Thomas, Buffalo	1	0	0.0	0	0
Spencer, Jimmy, San Diego	1	0	0.0	0	0
Springs, Shawn, Seattle	7	142	20.3	t56	2
Starks, Duane, Baltimore.............	5	3	0.6	2	0
Staten, Ralph, Baltimore	3	25	8.3	14	0
Surtain, Patrick, Miami................	2	1	0.5	1	0
Thomas, Dave, Jacksonville	1	0	0.0	0	0
Thomas, Henry, New England	1	24	24.0	t24	1
Thomas, Zach, Miami	3	21	7.0	t17	2
Turner, Eric, Oakland	3	108	36.0	t94	1
Turner, Scott, San Diego..............	1	0	0.0	0	0
Walker, Brian, Miami	4	12	3.0	7	0
Walker, Denard, Tennessee...........	2	6	3.0	6	0
Walker, Marquis, Oakland	2	28	14.0	28	0
Washington, Dewayne, Pittsburgh ..	5	178	35.6	t78	2
Washington, Ted, Buffalo	1	0	0.0	0	0
Wells, Dean, Seattle....................	1	25	25.0	25	0
Whigham, Larry, New England	1	0	0.0	0	0
Williams, Darryl, Seattle	3	41	13.7	28	0
Williams, Jamal, San Diego	1	14	14.0	t14	1
Williams, Kevin, N.Y. Jets	1	34	34.0	34	0
Williams, Willie, Seattle	2	36	18.0	t28	1
Wilson, Jerry, Miami	1	0	0.0	0	0
Wooden, Terry, Oakland	1	14	14.0	14	0
Woods, Jerome, Kansas City.........	2	47	23.5	28	0
Woodson, Charles, Oakland	5	118	23.6	t46	1
Woodson, Rod, Baltimore	6	108	18.0	t60	2

t—touchdown.

NFC

Player, Team	No.	Yds.	Avg.	Long	TD
Abraham, Donnie, Tampa Bay	1	3	3.0	3	0
Agnew, Ray, St. Louis	1	0	0.0	0	0
Armstead, Jessie, N.Y. Giants........	2	4	2.0	4	0

Player, Team	No.	Yds.	Avg.	Long	TD
Barber, Ronde, Tampa Bay	2	67	33.5	56	0
Barber, Shawn, Washington	1	0	0.0	0	0
Barker, Roy, San Francisco	1	-4	-4.0	-4	0
Barrow, Micheal, Carolina	1	10	10.0	10	0
Bennett, Tommy, Arizona	2	100	50.0	t70	1
Booker, Michael, Atlanta	1	27	27.0	27	0
Bradford, Ronnie, Atlanta	3	11	3.7	t11	1
Brady, Jeff, Carolina	4	85	21.3	43	0
Bronson, Zack, San Francisco	4	34	8.5	28	0
Brooking, Keith, Atlanta	1	12	12.0	12	0
Brooks, Derrick, Tampa Bay	1	25	25.0	25	0
Buchanan, Ray, Atlanta	7	102	14.6	34	0
Buckley, Marcus, N.Y. Giants	1	0	0.0	0	0
Butler, LeRoy, Green Bay	3	3	1.0	3	0
Caldwell, Mike, Philadelphia	1	33	33.0	33	0
Campbell, Jesse, Washington	1	4	4.0	4	0
Carrier, Mark, Detroit	3	33	11.0	33	0
Carter, Tom, Chicago	2	20	10.0	19	0
Chavous, Corey, Arizona	2	0	0.0	0	0
Coakley, Dexter, Dallas	1	18	18.0	18	0
Collins, Andre, Chicago	3	29	9.7	28	0
Cota, Chad, New Orleans	4	16	4.0	9	0
Cousin, Terry, Chicago	1	0	0.0	0	0
Davis, Eric, Carolina	5	81	16.2	t56	2
Dawkins, Brian, Philadelphia	2	39	19.5	30	0
Dishman, Cris, Washington	2	60	30.0	49	0
Drakeford, Tyronne, New Orleans	4	76	19.0	t32	1
Ellsworth, Percy, N.Y. Giants	5	92	18.4	t43	2
Evans, Doug, Carolina	2	18	9.0	18	0
Evans, Leomont, Washington	3	77	25.7	54	0
Fredrickson, Rob, Detroit	1	0	0.0	0	0
Fuller, Corey, Minnesota	4	36	9.0	26	0
Garnes, Sam, N.Y. Giants	1	13	13.0	13	0
Glover, La'Roi, New Orleans	1	0	0.0	0	0
Godfrey, Randall, Dallas	1	0	0.0	0	0
Gray, Carlton, N.Y. Giants	1	36	36.0	36	0
Gray, Torrian, Minnesota	1	11	11.0	11	0
Green, Darrell, Washington	3	36	12.0	36	0
Greene, Kevin, Carolina	2	18	9.0	18	0
Griffith, Robert, Minnesota	5	25	5.0	17	0
Hamilton, Conrad, N.Y. Giants	1	17	17.0	17	0
Hanks, Merton, San Francisco	4	37	9.3	37	0
Harris, Sean, Chicago	1	0	0.0	0	0
Harris, Walt, Chicago	4	41	10.3	26	1
Hill, Eric, St. Louis	1	0	0.0	0	0
Hitchcock, Jimmy, Minnesota	7	242	34.6	t79	3
Jamison, George, Detroit	1	21	21.0	21	0
Jenkins, Billy, St. Louis	2	31	15.5	25	0
Jones, Greg, Washington	1	9	9.0	9	0
Jones, Mike A., St. Louis	2	13	6.5	13	0
Jordan, Richard, Detroit	1	4	4.0	4	0
Kelly, Brian, Tampa Bay	1	4	4.0	4	0
Kelly, Rob, New Orleans	2	104	52.0	t79	1
Knight, Sammy, New Orleans	6	171	28.5	t91	2
Langham, Antonio, San Francisco	1	0	0.0	0	0
Lassiter, Kwamie, Arizona	8	80	10.0	29	0
Lincoln, Jeremy, N.Y. Giants	1	0	0.0	0	0
Lloyd, Greg, Carolina	1	3	3.0	3	0
Lyght, Todd, St. Louis	3	30	10.0	17	0
Lyle, Keith, St. Louis	3	20	6.7	20	0
Lynch, John, Tampa Bay	2	29	14.5	17	0
Mathis, Kevin, Dallas	2	0	0.0	0	0
McCleon, Dexter, St. Louis	2	29	14.5	15	0
McCleskey, J.J., Arizona	1	1	1.0	1	0
McCombs, Tony, Arizona	1	14	14.0	14	0
McDonald, Tim, San Francisco	4	22	5.5	18	0
McGill, Lenny, Carolina	1	6	6.0	6	0
McKenzie, Keith, Green Bay	1	33	33.0	t33	1
McKinnon, Ronald, Arizona	5	25	5.0	17	0
McNeil, Ryan, St. Louis	1	37	37.0	t37	1
McTyer, Tim, Philadelphia	1	18	18.0	18	0
Mincy, Charles, Tampa Bay	4	58	14.5	t22	1
Minter, Barry, Chicago	1	17	17.0	17	0
Minter, Mike, Carolina	1	7	7.0	7	0
Molden, Alex, New Orleans	2	35	17.5	24	0
Newsome, Craig, Green Bay	1	26	26.0	26	0
Parrish, Tony, Chicago	1	8	8.0	8	0
Phifer, Roman, St. Louis	1	41	41.0	41	0
Pope, Marquez, San Francisco	1	0	0.0	0	0
Prior, Mike, Green Bay	1	0	0.0	0	0
Reese, Izell, Dallas	1	6	6.0	6	0
Rice, Ron, Detroit	3	25	8.3	25	0
Richard, Stanley, Washington	1	0	0.0	0	0
Robinson, Eugene, Atlanta	4	36	9.0	t25	1
Sanders, Deion, Dallas	5	153	30.6	t71	1
Sauer, Craig, Atlanta	1	0	0.0	0	0
Smith, Kevin, Dallas	2	31	15.5	22	0
Smith, Rod, Car.-G.B.	2	43	21.5	43	0
Sparks, Phillippi, N.Y. Giants	4	25	6.3	12	0
Strahan, Michael, N.Y. Giants	1	24	24.0	t24	1
Terrell, Pat, Green Bay	1	9	9.0	9	0
Thierry, John, Chicago	1	14	14.0	14	0
Thomas, Orlando, Minnesota	2	27	13.5	27	0
Thomas, William, Philadelphia	1	21	21.0	21	0
Tubbs, Winfred, San Francisco	1	7	7.0	7	0
Upshaw, Regan, Tampa Bay	1	26	26.0	26	0
Veland, Tony, Carolina	1	24	24.0	24	0
Vincent, Troy, Philadelphia	2	29	14.5	29	0
Walker, Darnell, San Francisco	4	78	19.5	36	0
Weary, Fred, New Orleans	2	64	32.0	t63	1
Westbrook, Bryant, Detroit	3	49	16.3	t34	1
Wheaton, Kenny, Dallas	1	41	41.0	41	0
White, William, Atlanta	2	36	18.0	36	0
Wilkinson, Dan, Washington	1	4	4.0	4	0
Williams, Aeneas, Arizona	1	15	15.0	15	0
Williams, Shaun, N.Y. Giants	2	6	3.0	6	0
Williams, Tyrone, Green Bay	5	40	8.0	15	0
Woodall, Lee, San Francisco	1	4	4.0	4	0
Woodson, Darren, Dallas	1	1	1.0	1	0
Zordich, Michael, Philadelphia	2	18	9.0	14	0

t—touchdown.

PLAYERS WITH TWO CLUBS

Player, Team	No.	Yds.	Avg.	Long	TD
Smith, Rod, Carolina	1	43	43.0	43	0
Smith, Rod, Green Bay	1	0	0.0	0	0

SACKS

AFC

Team	Sacks	Yards
Seattle	53	282
Denver	47	335
Miami	45	270
Buffalo	43	276
Oakland	41	258
Pittsburgh	41	238
Kansas City	40	268
Baltimore	39	286
San Diego	39	246
Indianapolis	38	231
N.Y. Jets	36	259
New England	36	222
Jacksonville	30	209
Tennessee	30	172
Cincinnati	28	199
AFC total	**586**	**3751**
AFC average	**39.1**	**250.1**

NFC

Team	Sacks	Yards
N.Y. Giants	54	336
San Francisco	51	259
St. Louis	50	349
Green Bay	50	336
New Orleans	47	288
Detroit	43	261
Philadelphia	42	281
Arizona	39	250
Atlanta	38	275
Minnesota	38	247
Tampa Bay	37	252
Carolina	37	228
Dallas	34	222
Washington	33	194
Chicago	28	173
NFC total	**621**	**3951**
NFC average	**41.4**	**263.4**
NFL total	**1207**	**7702**
NFL average	**40.2**	**256.7**

INDIVIDUAL

BESTS OF THE SEASON

Sacks, season
AFC: 16.5—Michael Sinclair, Seattle.
NFC: 16.0—Reggie White, Green Bay.

Sacks, game
AFC: 6.0—Derrick Thomas, Kansas City vs. Oakland, Sept. 6.
NFC: 4.5—Hugh Douglas, Philadelphia at San Diego, Oct. 18.

NFL LEADERS

Player, Team	No.
Sinclair, Michael, Seattle*	16.5
White, Reggie, Green Bay	16.0
Greene, Kevin, Carolina	15.0
Strahan, Michael, N.Y. Giants	15.0
Doleman, Chris, San Francisco	15.0
McCrary, Michael, Baltimore*	14.5
Douglas, Hugh, Philadelphia	12.5
Thomas, Derrick, Kansas City*	12.0
Carter, Kevin, St. Louis	12.0
Barker, Roy, San Francisco	12.0
Porcher, Robert, Detroit	11.5
Bratzke, Chad, N.Y. Giants	11.0
Johnstone, Lance, Oakland*	11.0
Gildon, Jason, Pittsburgh*	11.0
Randle, John, Minnesota	10.5
Armstrong, Trace, Miami*	10.5
Glover, La'Roi, New Orleans	10.0
Smith, Bruce, Buffalo*	10.0
Archambeau, Lester, Atlanta	10.0
Russell, Darrell, Oakland*	10.0
Rice, Simeon, Arizona	10.0
Young, Bryant, San Francisco	9.5

*AFC.

AFC

Player, Team	No.
Adams, Sam, Seattle	2.0
Armstrong, Trace, Miami	10.5

Player, Team	No.
Bankston, Michael, Cincinnati	4.5
Barber, Mike, Indianapolis	2.0
Barndt, Tom, Kansas City	3.5
Bell, Myron, Cincinnati	1.0
Bellamy, Jay, Seattle	1.0
Belser, Jason, Indianapolis	1.0
Berry, Bert, Indianapolis	4.0
Biekert, Greg, Oakland	3.0
Bishop, Blaine, Tennessee	3.0
Blackmon, Robert, Indianapolis	1.0
Boulware, Peter, Baltimore	8.5
Bowden, Joe, Tennessee	1.5
Boyer, Brant, Jacksonville	1.0
Brackens, Tony, Jacksonville	3.5
Brady, Donny, Baltimore	1.0
Bromell, Lorenzo, Miami	8.0
Brown, Chad, Seattle	7.5
Bruschi, Tedy, New England	2.0
Burnett, Rob, Baltimore	2.5
Burton, Shane, Miami	2.0
Bush, Lewis, San Diego	1.0
Cadrez, Glenn, Denver	4.0
Canty, Chris, New England	1.0
Carter, Chris, New England	1.0
Cascadden, Chad, N.Y. Jets	5.0
Chester, Larry, Indianapolis	3.0
Chorak, Jason, Indianapolis	1.0
Coleman, Marco, San Diego	3.5
Collins, Mark, Seattle	1.5
Cook, Anthony, Tennessee	2.0
Cox, Bryan, N.Y. Jets	6.0
Crockett, Ray, Denver	0.5
Daniels, Phillip, Seattle	6.5
Davis, Anthony, Kansas City	4.5
Davis, Travis, Jacksonville	0.5
Dixon, Gerald, San Diego	2.5
Dumas, Mike, San Diego	1.0
Eaton, Chad, New England	6.0
Edwards, Donnie, Kansas City	6.0
Emmons, Carlos, Pittsburgh	3.5

Player, Team	No.	Player, Team	No.
Evans, Josh, Tennessee	3.5	Morrison, Steve, Indianapolis	1.0
Favors, Greg, Kansas City	2.0	Northern, Gabe, Buffalo	2.0
Ferguson, Jason, N.Y. Jets	4.0	Oldham, Chris, Buffalo	0.5
Flowers, Lethon, Pittsburgh	1.0	O'Neal, Leslie, Kansas City	4.5
Foley, Steve, Cincinnati	2.0	Parker, Riddick, Seattle	1.0
Folston, James, Oakland	1.0	Parrella, John, San Diego	1.5
Fontenot, Al, Indianapolis	1.0	Paup, Bryce, Jacksonville	6.5
Ford, Henry, Tennessee	1.5	Perry, Darren, Pittsburgh	0.5
Fuller, William, San Diego	3.0	Pleasant, Anthony, N.Y. Jets	6.0
Gardener, Daryl, Miami	1.0	Price, Shawn, Buffalo	5.0
Gibson, Oliver, Pittsburgh	2.0	Pritchett, Kelvin, Jacksonville	3.0
Gildon, Jason, Pittsburgh	11.0	Pryce, Trevor, Denver	8.5
Gouveia, Kurt, San Diego	0.5	Purvis, Andre, Cincinnati	1.0
Green, Victor, N.Y. Jets	1.0	Robinson, Eddie, Tennessee	3.5
Hand, Norman, San Diego	6.0	Rodgers, Derrick, Miami	2.5
Hansen, Phil, Buffalo	7.5	Rogers, Sam, Buffalo	4.5
Hardy, Kevin, Jacksonville	1.5	Rolle, Samari, Tennessee	2.0
Harris, Corey, Baltimore	1.0	Romanowski, Bill, Denver	7.5
Harris, James, Oakland	1.0	Roye, Orpheus, Pittsburgh	3.5
Harrison, Nolan, Pittsburgh	3.5	Russell, Darrell, Oakland	10.0
Harrison, Rodney, San Diego	4.0	Salave'a, Joe, Tennessee	1.0
Harvey, Richard, Oakland	4.0	Seau, Junior, San Diego	3.5
Hasselbach, Harald, Denver	3.0	Shade, Sam, Cincinnati	1.0
Hasty, James, Kansas City	1.0	Sharper, Jamie, Baltimore	1.0
Hawkins, Artrell, Cincinnati	1.0	Shello, Kendel, Indianapolis	1.0
Henderson, Jerome, N.Y. Jets	1.0	Simmons, Brian, Cincinnati	3.0
Henry, Kevin, Pittsburgh	4.0	Simmons, Clyde, Cincinnati	5.0
Holmes, Earl, Pittsburgh	1.5	Simmons, Wayne, Buffalo	0.5
Holmes, Kenny, Tennessee	2.5	Sinclair, Michael, Seattle	16.5
Israel, Steve, New England	2.0	Slade, Chris, New England	4.0
Jackson, Calvin, Miami	1.0	Smedley, Eric, Buffalo	2.0
Jackson, Grady, Oakland	3.0	Smeenge, Joel, Jacksonville	7.5
Jackson, Steve, Tennessee	1.5	Smith, Bruce, Buffalo	10.0
Johnson, Darrius, Denver	1.0	Smith, Darrin, Seattle	5.0
Johnson, Ellis, Indianapolis	8.0	Smith, Fernando, Jacksonville	2.0
Johnson, Melvin, Kansas City	1.0	Smith, Neil, Denver	4.0
Johnson, Pepper, N.Y. Jets	1.0	Spikes, Takeo, Cincinnati	2.0
Johnson, Raylee, San Diego	5.5	Spires, Greg, New England	3.0
Johnson, Ted, New England	2.0	Staten, Ralph, Baltimore	1.0
Johnstone, Lance, Oakland	11.0	Steed, Joel, Pittsburgh	1.0
Jones, Donta, Pittsburgh	3.0	Sullivan, Chris, New England	2.0
Jones, James, Baltimore	5.5	Swilling, Pat, Oakland	2.0
Jones, Robert, Miami	5.0	Tanuvasa, Maa, Denver	8.5
Jurkovic, John, Jacksonville	0.5	Taylor, Jason, Miami	9.0
Kennedy, Cortez, Seattle	2.0	Thomas, Derrick, Kansas City	12.0
Kirkland, Levon, Pittsburgh	2.5	Thomas, Henry, New England	6.5
LaBounty, Matt, Seattle	6.0	Thomas, Mark, Chi.-Ind.*	5.5
Lake, Carnell, Pittsburgh	1.0	Thomas, Zach, Miami	2.0
Langford, Jevon, Cincinnati	0.5	Thompson, Mike, Cincinnati	0.5
Lewis, Albert, Oakland	1.0	Tongue, Reggie, Kansas City	2.0
Lewis, Darryll, Tennessee	1.0	Tovar, Steve, San Diego	1.0
Lewis, Mo, N.Y. Jets	7.0	Traylor, Keith, Denver	2.0
Lewis, Ray, Baltimore	3.0	Tuinei, Van, Indianapolis	2.0
Lodish, Mike, Denver	2.0	Tumulty, Tom, Cincinnati	0.5
Logan, Ernie, N.Y. Jets	2.5	Turner, Eric, Oakland	1.0
Logan, James, Seattle	1.0	Turner, Scott, San Diego	1.0
Lyle, Rick, N.Y. Jets	1.5	Vrabel, Mike, Pittsburgh	2.5
Lyons, Pratt, Tennessee	2.0	Walker, Gary, Tennessee	1.0
Madison, Sam, Miami	1.0	Washington, Keith, Baltimore	1.0
Marts, Lonnie, Tennessee	4.0	Washington, Marvin, Denver	2.0
Maryland, Russell, Oakland	2.0	Washington, Ted, Buffalo	4.5
McCoy, Tony, Indianapolis	6.0	White, Jose, Jacksonville	3.0
McCrary, Michael, Baltimore	14.5	Whittington, Bernard, Indianapolis	4.0
McGinest, Willie, New England	3.5	Wiley, Marcellus, Buffalo	3.5
McGlockton, Chester, Kansas City	1.0	Williams, Alfred, Denver	3.0
Milloy, Lawyer, New England	1.0	Williams, Pat, Buffalo	3.5
Mims, Chris, San Diego	2.0	Williams, Robert, Kansas City	0.5
Mitchell, Brandon, New England	2.0	Wilson, Reinard, Cincinnati	6.0
Mixon, Kenny, Miami	2.0	Wooden, Terry, Oakland	2.0
Mobley, John, Denver	1.0	Wynn, Renaldo, Jacksonville	1.0
Mohring, Mike, San Diego	1.0	*Includes both NFC and AFC statistics.	
Montgomery, Monty, Indianapolis	2.0		

1998 STATISTICS *Sacks*

NFC

Player, Team	No.
Abrams, Kevin, Detroit	3.0
Agnew, Ray, St. Louis	5.0
Aldridge, Allen, Detroit	3.0
Aleaga, Ink, New Orleans	1.0
Alexander, Derrick, Minnesota	7.5
Archambeau, Lester, Atlanta	10.0
Armstead, Jessie, N.Y. Giants	5.0
Barber, Ronde, Tampa Bay	3.0
Barker, Roy, San Francisco	12.0
Barrow, Micheal, Carolina	4.0
Bennett, Cornelius, Atlanta	1.0
Booker, Vaughn, Green Bay	3.0
Bordano, Chris, New Orleans	1.0
Boutte, Marc, Washington	2.0
Boyd, Stephen, Detroit	4.0
Brady, Jeff, Carolina	4.0
Bratzke, Chad, N.Y. Giants	11.0
Bryant, Junior, San Francisco	5.0
Buckley, Marcus, N.Y. Giants	1.5
Buckner, Brentson, San Francisco	0.5
Burrough, John, Atlanta	0.5
Butler, LeRoy, Green Bay	4.0
Caldwell, Mike, Philadelphia	1.0
Carter, Kevin, St. Louis	12.0
Cherry, Je'Rod, New Orleans	2.0
Clemons, Charlie, St. Louis	2.0
Clemons, Duane, Minnesota	2.5
Coakley, Dexter, Dallas	2.0
Colinet, Stalin, Minnesota	1.0
Cota, Chad, New Orleans	2.0
Crockett, Henri, Atlanta	1.0
Culpepper, Brad, Tampa Bay	9.0
Darling, James, Philadelphia	2.0
Davis, Eric, Carolina	1.0
Dawkins, Brian, Philadelphia	1.0
Doleman, Chris, San Francisco	15.0
Dotson, Santana, Green Bay	3.0
Douglas, Hugh, Philadelphia	12.5
Dronett, Shane, Atlanta	6.5
Duff, Jamal, Washington	3.0
Edwards, Antonio, Atlanta	1.0
Ellis, Greg, Dallas	3.0
Elliss, Luther, Detroit	3.0
Evans, Leomont, Washington	1.0
Fair, Terry, Detroit	1.0
Farr, D'Marco, St. Louis	7.0
Fields, Mark, New Orleans	6.0
Fisk, Jason, Minnesota	1.5
Flanigan, Jim, Chicago	8.5
Fox, Mike, Carolina	1.0
Fredrickson, Rob, Detroit	2.5
Fuller, Corey, Minnesota	1.0
Fuller, Randy, Atlanta	2.0
Galyon, Scott, N.Y. Giants	1.0
Gilbert, Sean, Carolina	6.0
Glover, La'Roi, New Orleans	10.0
Godfrey, Randall, Dallas	3.0
Gooch, Jeff, Tampa Bay	1.0
Grasmanis, Paul, Chicago	1.0
Gray, Carlton, N.Y. Giants	1.0
Gray, Torrian, Minnesota	1.0
Greene, Kevin, Carolina	15.0
Hall, Travis, Atlanta	4.5
Hamilton, Conrad, N.Y. Giants	1.0
Hamilton, Keith, N.Y. Giants	7.0
Hanks, Merton, San Francisco	0.5
Harris, Bernardo, Green Bay	2.0
Harris, Jon, Philadelphia	1.0
Harris, Robert, N.Y. Giants	3.5
Harris, Sean, Chicago	1.0

Player, Team	No.
Harvey, Ken, Washington	2.0
Hennings, Chad, Dallas	1.0
Hewitt, Chris, New Orleans	2.0
Hill, Eric, St. Louis	1.0
Holliday, Vonnie, Green Bay	8.0
Jackson, Tyoka, Tampa Bay	3.0
Jefferson, Greg, Philadelphia	4.0
Jenkins, Billy, St. Louis	3.0
Johnson, Bill, Philadelphia	2.5
Johnson, Joe, New Orleans	7.0
Jones, Cedric, N.Y. Giants	4.0
Jones, Ernest, Carolina	1.0
Jones, Greg, Washington	1.0
Jones, Mike A., St. Louis	3.0
Jones, Mike D., St. Louis	2.5
Kalu, Ndukwe, Washington	3.0
Kinney, Kelvin, Washington	1.0
Knight, Tom, Arizona	1.0
Koonce, George, Green Bay	1.0
Lang, Kenard, Washington	7.0
Lee, Shawn, Chicago	2.0
Lett, Leon, Dallas	4.0
Little, Leonard, St. Louis	0.5
Lloyd, Greg, Carolina	1.0
Lyght, Todd, St. Louis	1.5
Lyle, Keith, St. Louis	1.0
Lynch, John, Tampa Bay	2.0
Lyon, Billy, Green Bay	1.0
Maddox, Mark, Arizona	1.0
Martin, Steve, Philadelphia	1.0
Martin, Wayne, New Orleans	3.0
Mathis, Kevin, Dallas	1.0
McCormack, Hurvin, Dallas	5.0
McDaniel, Ed, Minnesota	7.0
McDonald, Ricardo, Chicago	1.0
McDonald, Tim, San Francisco	4.0
McGill, Lenny, Carolina	1.0
McKenzie, Keith, Green Bay	8.0
McKinnon, Ronald, Arizona	2.0
McTyer, Tim, Philadelphia	0.5
Miller, Jamir, Arizona	3.0
Minter, Barry, Chicago	1.0
Mitchell, Keith, New Orleans	2.5
Mitchell, Kevin, New Orleans	2.5
Myers, Michael, Dallas	3.0
Nickerson, Hardy, Tampa Bay	1.0
Norton, Ken, San Francisco	2.0
Owens, Dan, Detroit	2.5
Parker, Anthony, Tampa Bay	1.0
Parrish, Tony, Chicago	1.0
Patton, Marvcus, Washington	3.0
Peter, Christian, N.Y. Giants	1.0
Peter, Jason, Carolina	1.0
Peterson, Tony, San Francisco	1.0
Phifer, Roman, St. Louis	6.5
Pittman, Kavika, Dallas	6.0
Porcher, Robert, Detroit	11.5
Posey, Jeff, San Francisco	0.5
Pounds, Darryl, Washington	0.5
Quarles, Shelton, Tampa Bay	1.0
Randle, John, Minnesota	10.5
Reeves, Carl, Chicago	1.0
Rice, Ron, Detroit	3.5
Rice, Simeon, Arizona	10.0
Robbins, Austin, New Orleans	1.0
Robinson, Bryan, Chicago	0.5
Rossum, Allen, Philadelphia	1.0
Rudd, Dwayne, Minnesota	2.0
Sapp, Patrick, Arizona	1.0
Sapp, Warren, Tampa Bay	7.0
Scroggins, Tracy, Detroit	6.5
Smith, Chuck, Atlanta	8.5

Player, Team	No.	Player, Team	No.
Smith, Derek, Washington	0.5	Wells, Mike, Chicago	3.0
Smith, Mark, Arizona	9.0	White, Reggie, Green Bay	16.0
Stoutmire, Omar, Dallas	1.0	White, Steve, Tampa Bay	2.0
Strahan, Michael, N.Y. Giants	15.0	Whiting, Brandon, Philadelphia	1.5
Stubblefield, Dana, Washington	1.5	Wilkinson, Dan, Washington	7.5
Swann, Eric, Arizona	4.0	Williams, Aeneas, Arizona	1.0
Teague, George, Dallas	2.0	Williams, Brian, Green Bay	2.0
Terrell, Pat, Green Bay	1.0	Williams, Jay, St. Louis	1.0
Terry, Rick, Carolina	2.0	Williams, Tony, Minnesota	1.0
Thierry, John, Chicago	3.5	Wilson, Bernard, Arizona	1.0
Thomas, Hollis, Philadelphia	5.0	Wilson, Troy, New Orleans	1.0
Thomas, Orlando, Minnesota	0.5	Wistrom, Grant, St. Louis	3.0
Thomas, William, Philadelphia	2.0	Wong, Kailee, Minnesota	1.5
Tillman, Pat, Arizona	1.0	Woodson, Darren, Dallas	3.0
Tomich, Jared, New Orleans	6.0	Wooten, Tito, N.Y. Giants	3.0
Tubbs, Winfred, San Francisco	1.0	Wright, Toby, St. Louis	1.0
Tuggle, Jessie, Atlanta	3.0	Young, Bryant, San Francisco	9.5
Upshaw, Regan, Tampa Bay	7.0		
Vincent, Troy, Philadelphia	1.0		
Waddy, Jude, Green Bay	1.0		
Wadsworth, Andre, Arizona	5.0		
Waldroup, Kerwin, Detroit	1.5		
Wallace, Al, Philadelphia	6.0		

PLAYERS WITH TWO CLUBS

Player, Team	No.
Thomas, Mark, Chicago	4.5
Thomas, Mark, Indianapolis	1.0

FUMBLES

TEAM

AFC

Team	Fum.	Own Fum. Rec.	Own Fum. *O.B.	Own Fum. Lost	TD	Opp Fum. Rec.	TD	†Yards	Total Rec.
Indianapolis	10	4	1	5	0	11	0	27	15
Buffalo	17	10	1	6	0	13	1	40	23
Denver	17	9	2	6	1	11	0	-25	20
Jacksonville	18	10	0	8	0	17	2	212	27
Pittsburgh	18	6	1	11	1	13	0	53	19
New England	20	12	1	7	0	7	0	5	19
Cincinnati	21	10	1	10	0	7	1	93	17
N.Y. Jets	23	11	1	11	0	9	2	86	20
Miami	25	12	1	12	0	7	0	-8	19
Tennessee	25	15	1	9	0	7	2	20	22
Seattle	30	14	0	16	0	18	2	40	32
Baltimore	31	14	2	15	0	5	0	-48	19
San Diego	33	16	0	17	0	7	0	-18	23
Kansas City	35	18	3	14	0	20	1	69	38
Oakland	38	18	2	18	1	14	1	79	32
AFC total	361	179	17	165	3	166	12	625	345
AFC average	24.1	11.9	1.1	11.0	0.2	11.1	0.8	41.7	23.0

*Fumbled out of bounds.

†Includes all fumble yardage (aborted plays and recoveries of own and opponents' fumbles).

NFC

Team	Fum.	Own Fum. Rec.	Own Fum. *O.B.	Own Fum. Lost	TD	Opp Fum. Rec.	TD	†Yards	Total Rec.
Minnesota	10	5	1	4	0	15	2	197	20
Detroit	17	4	1	12	0	9	0	-1	13
N.Y. Giants	17	7	1	9	0	7	0	0	14
Dallas	18	9	2	7	0	12	1	-7	21
Philadelphia	20	11	1	8	0	8	0	22	19
San Francisco	22	6	1	15	0	12	0	7	18
Tampa Bay	23	7	3	13	0	14	0	10	21
Atlanta	24	13	2	9	0	25	4	120	38
Green Bay	27	10	6	11	0	10	2	127	20
Washington	27	10	2	15	0	7	0	-8	17
New Orleans	28	11	3	14	0	11	4	93	22
Chicago	29	7	1	21	0	14	1	13	21
Arizona	30	13	1	16	0	19	0	56	32
St. Louis	32	16	1	15	0	7	0	26	23
Carolina	39	21	2	16	0	14	0	5	35
NFC total	363	150	28	185	0	184	14	660	334
NFC average	24.2	10.0	1.9	12.3	0.0	12.3	0.9	44.0	22.3
NFL total	724	329	45	350	3	350	26	1285	679
NFL average	24.1	11.0	1.5	11.7	0.1	11.7	0.9	42.8	22.6

INDIVIDUAL

BESTS OF THE SEASON

Fumbles, season
NFC: 14—Trent Green, Washington.
AFC: 10—Donald Hollas, Oakland.

Fumbles, game
NFC: 6—Brett Favre, Green Bay at Tampa Bay, Dec. 7.
AFC: 4—Jeff George, Oakland at Kansas City, Sept. 6; Ryan Leaf, San Diego at Kansas City, Sept. 20.

Own fumbles recovered, season
NFC: 8—Tony Banks, St. Louis.
AFC: 4—Held by six players.

Own fumbles recovered, game
AFC: 2—Held by 10 players.
NFC: 2—Held by five players.

Opponents' fumbles recovered, season
AFC: 4—Chris Oldham, Pittsburgh; Bryan Schwartz, Jacksonville.
NFC: 4—Travis Hall, Atlanta; Simeon Rice, Arizona.

Opponents' fumbles recovered, game
AFC: 3—Darryl Williams, Seattle at Kansas City, Oct. 4.
NFC: 3—Stephen Boyd, Detroit at Chicago, Oct. 4.

Yards returning fumbles, season
NFC: 157—Dwayne Rudd, Minnesota.
AFC: 120—Aaron Beasley, Jacksonville.

Longest fumble return
NFC: 94—Dwayne Rudd, Minnesota vs. Chicago, Dec. 6 (TD).
AFC: 90—Aaron Beasley, Jacksonville vs. Cincinnati, Nov. 8 (TD).

AFC

Player, Team	Fum.	Own Rec.	Opp. Rec.	Yds.	Tot. Rec.	TD
Abdul-Jabbar, Karim, Miami ...	2	1	0	0	1	0
Adams, Sam, Seattle	0	0	1	0	1	0
Aguiar, Louie, Kansas City	0	0	1	0	1	0
Albright, Ethan, Buffalo	0	0	1	0	1	0
Alexander, Elijah, Indianapolis	0	0	2	0	2	0
Anders, Kimble, Kansas City	6	1	0	0	1	0
Anderson, Willie, Cincinnati	0	1	0	0	1	0
Archie, Mike, Tennessee	3	0	0	0	0	0
Armstrong, Bruce, N.E.	0	3	0	0	3	0
Armstrong, Trace, Miami	0	0	1	2	1	0
Ashmore, Darryl, Oakland	0	1	0	1	1	1
Avery, John, Miami	5	2	0	0	2	0
Bailey, Aaron, Indianapolis	2	1	0	0	1	0
Ballard, Howard, Seattle	0	1	1	0	2	0
Banks, Tavian, Jacksonville	2	1	0	0	1	0
Bankston, Michael, Cincinnati	0	0	1	5	1	0
Banta, Bradford, Indianapolis	0	0	1	0	1	0
Barlow, Reggie, Jacksonville	1	1	0	0	1	0
Barndt, Tom, Kansas City	0	0	2	0	2	0
Battaglia, Marco, Cincinnati	1	3	0	0	3	0
Baxter, Fred, N.Y. Jets	0	1	0	0	1	0
Beasley, Aaron, Jacksonville	0	0	1	120	1	1
Bellamy, Jay, Seattle	0	0	2	0	2	0
Belser, Jason, Indianapolis	0	0	1	0	1	0
Bennett, Brandon, Cincinnati	1	1	0	0	1	0
Bennett, Darren, San Diego	1	1	0	0	1	0
Bennett, Donnell, Kansas City	4	0	0	0	0	0
Bettis, Jerome, Pittsburgh	2	0	0	0	0	0
Biekert, Greg, Oakland	0	0	1	0	1	0
Bieniemy, Eric, Cincinnati	1	0	0	0	0	0
Bishop, Blaine, Tennessee	0	0	1	0	1	0
Blackwell, Will, Pittsburgh	1	0	0	0	0	0
Blades, Brian, Seattle	1	0	0	0	0	0
Blair, Michael, Cincinnati	1	1	0	0	1	0
Blake, Jeff, Cincinnati	1	0	0	0	0	0
Bledsoe, Drew, New England	9	4	0	-10	4	0
Boselli, Tony, Jacksonville	0	1	0	2	1	0
Boulware, Peter, Baltimore	0	0	1	0	1	0
Bowden, Joe, Tennessee	0	0	2	17	2	1
Brackens, Tony, Jacksonville	0	0	3	8	3	0
Brady, Kyle, N.Y. Jets	1	0	0	0	0	0
Branch, Calvin, Oakland	1	1	0	0	1	0
Brister, Bubby, Denver	2	1	0	-1	1	0
Bromell, Lorenzo, Miami	0	0	1	0	1	0
Brooks, Bucky, Oakland	1	0	0	0	0	0
Broussard, Steve, Seattle	1	1	0	0	1	0
Brown, Chad, Seattle	0	0	1	0	1	0
Brown, Corwin, N.Y. Jets	0	0	1	16	1	0
Brown, Derek, Oakland	0	1	0	0	1	0
Brown, Eric, Denver	0	0	1	0	1	0
Brown, Lance, Pittsburgh	0	0	2	1	2	0
Brown, Tim, Oakland	3	2	0	0	2	0
Brunell, Mark, Jacksonville	3	2	0	-1	2	0
Buckley, Terrell, Miami	1	1	1	0	2	0
Burger, Todd, N.Y. Jets	0	2	0	0	2	0
Burnett, Rob, Baltimore	0	0	1	0	1	0
Burns, Keith, Denver	1	1	0	0	1	0
Burton, Shane, Miami	0	0	1	0	1	0
Bynum, Kenny, San Diego	3	2	0	0	2	0
Byrd, Isaac, Tennessee	0	1	0	0	1	0
Canty, Chris, New England	2	0	0	0	0	0
Cascadden, Chad, N.Y. Jets	0	0	2	23	2	1
Clay, Willie, New England	0	0	1	3	1	0
Coleman, Andre, Pittsburgh	1	0	0	0	0	0
Coleman, Marco, San Diego	0	0	2	0	2	0
Crockett, Zack, Indianapolis	1	0	0	0	0	0
Cullors, Derrick, New England	1	0	0	0	0	0
Daniels, Phillip, Seattle	0	0	2	0	2	0
Darius, Donovin, Jacksonville	0	0	1	83	1	1
Davis, Terrell, Denver	2	1	0	0	1	0
Davis, Travis, Jacksonville	0	0	1	0	1	0
Davis, Wendell, San Diego	0	1	0	0	1	0
Dawson, Dermontti, Pit.	1	0	0	-25	0	0
Dillon, Corey, Cincinnati	2	0	0	0	0	0
Dixon, Mark, Miami	0	2	0	0	2	0
Donnalley, Kevin, Miami	0	1	0	0	1	0
Dudley, Rickey, Oakland	1	0	0	0	0	0
Dunn, David, Pittsburgh	1	0	0	0	0	0
Eaton, Chad, New England	0	0	1	2	1	0
Edwards, Donnie, Kansas City	0	0	1	0	1	0
Edwards, Robert, New England	5	2	0	0	2	0
Elway, John, Denver	7	2	0	-18	2	0
Emmons, Carlos, Pittsburgh	0	0	1	0	1	0
Farrior, James, N.Y. Jets	0	0	1	0	1	0
Faulk, Marshall, Indianapolis	3	2	0	13	2	0
Fauria, Christian, Seattle	1	1	0	0	1	0
Favors, Gregory, Kansas City	0	1	0	41	1	0
Fletcher, Terrell, San Diego	1	2	0	21	2	0
Flowers, Lethon, Pittsburgh	0	0	2	0	2	0
Flutie, Doug, Buffalo	3	4	0	-13	4	0
Foley, Glenn, N.Y. Jets	1	0	0	0	0	0
Fontenot, Al, Indianapolis	0	0	1	0	1	0
Ford, Henry, Tennessee	0	0	1	0	1	0
Fordham, Todd, Jacksonville	0	1	0	0	1	0
Frost, Scott, N.Y. Jets	1	0	0	0	0	0
Gadsden, Oronde, Miami	2	0	0	0	0	0
Gaiter, Tony, San Diego	1	0	0	0	0	0
Galloway, Joey, Seattle	1	0	0	0	0	0
Gannon, Rich, Kansas City	9	4	0	-15	4	0
George, Eddie, Tennessee	7	4	1	0	5	0
George, Jeff, Oakland	7	1	0	-6	1	0
George, Ron, Kansas City	0	0	1	0	1	0
Gibson, Damon, Cincinnati	3	1	0	0	1	0
Gildon, Jason, Pittsburgh	0	0	1	0	1	0
Glenn, Aaron, N.Y. Jets	1	0	0	0	1	0
Gonzalez, Tony, Kansas City	3	0	0	0	0	0
Gordon, Darrien, Denver	1	0	0	0	1	0
Granville, Billy, Cincinnati	0	0	1	0	1	0
Grbac, Elvis, Kansas City	1	0	1	0	1	0
Green, Ahman, Seattle	1	1	0	0	1	0
Green, Eric, Baltimore	4	0	0	0	0	0
Green, Victor, N.Y. Jets	0	0	1	0	1	0
Greer, Donovan, Buffalo	0	0	1	18	1	0
Griese, Brian, Denver	1	0	0	-1	0	0
Habib, Brian, Seattle	0	2	0	0	2	0
Hamilton, Michael, San Diego	0	0	1	0	1	0
Hansen, Phil, Buffalo	0	0	3	13	3	1
Harbaugh, Jim, Baltimore	7	3	0	-7	3	0
Hardy, Kevin, Jacksonville	0	0	1	0	1	0
Harlow, Pat, Oakland	0	2	0	0	2	0
Harris, Corey, Baltimore	2	1	0	0	1	0
Harris, James, Oakland	0	0	1	1	1	0
Hasty, James, Kansas City	0	0	1	0	1	0
Hawkins, Artrell, Cincinnati	0	0	1	25	1	0
Hawkins, Courtney, Pittsburgh	1	1	0	0	1	0
Hebron, Vaughn, Denver	0	1	0	0	1	0
Henderson, Jerome, N.Y. Jets	1	0	1	53	1	1
Hetherington, Chris, Ind.	1	0	0	0	0	0
Hicks, Eric, Kansas City	0	1	0	0	1	0
Hollas, Donald, Oakland	10	4	0	0	4	0
Hollier, Dwight, Miami	0	0	1	0	1	0
Holmes, Priest, Baltimore	3	1	0	1	1	0
Horn, Joe, Kansas City	2	2	1	-8	3	0
Howard, Desmond, Oakland ...	4	0	0	0	0	0
Hudson, Chris, Jacksonville	0	0	1	0	1	0
Hughes, Danan, Kansas City	0	1	1	0	2	0
Huntley, Richard, Pittsburgh	5	0	0	0	0	0
Jackson, Grady, Oakland	0	0	1	2	1	0

Player, Team	Fum.	Own Rec.	Opp. Rec.	Yds.	Tot. Rec.	TD
Jackson, Greg, San Diego	0	1	0	0	1	0
Jackson, Michael, Baltimore	1	0	0	0	0	0
James, Tory, Denver	0	0	1	0	1	0
Jefferson, Shawn, N.E.	0	1	0	0	1	0
Jenkins, DeRon, Baltimore	0	1	0	0	1	0
Jett, James, Oakland	0	1	0	4	1	0
Johnson, Leon, N.Y. Jets	3	3	0	0	3	0
Johnson, Lonnie, Buffalo	1	0	0	0	0	0
Johnson, Pat, Baltimore	1	0	0	0	0	0
Johnson, Pepper, N.Y. Jets	0	0	1	0	1	0
Johnson, Rob, Buffalo	2	1	0	-1	1	0
Johnstone, Lance, Oakland	0	0	1	40	1	1
Jones, Charlie, San Diego	1	0	0	0	0	0
Jones, Damon, Jacksonville	1	0	0	0	0	0
Jones, Freddie, San Diego	1	0	0	0	0	0
Jones, James, Baltimore	0	0	1	0	1	0
Jones, Tebucky, New England	0	1	0	0	1	0
Jordan, Charles, Miami	2	1	0	0	1	0
Jordan, Randy, Oakland	1	0	0	0	0	0
Joseph, Kerry, Seattle	1	0	0	0	0	0
Kaufman, Napoleon, Oakland	2	1	0	0	1	0
Kennedy, Cortez, Seattle	0	0	1	39	1	1
Kennedy, Lincoln, Oakland	0	1	0	27	1	0
Kitna, Jon, Seattle	6	4	0	-10	4	0
Krieg, Dave, Tennessee	3	1	0	-2	1	0
LaBounty, Matt, Seattle	1	0	1	13	1	0
Lake, Carnell, Pittsburgh	0	0	1	-2	1	0
Law, Ty, New England	0	0	1	17	1	0
Layman, Jason, Tennessee	0	1	0	0	1	0
Leaf, Ryan, San Diego	8	2	0	-18	2	0
Le Bel, Harper, Baltimore	1	0	0	-31	0	0
Leeuwenburg, Jay, Ind.	0	1	0	0	1	0
Lewis, Jermaine, Baltimore	3	3	0	0	3	0
Lewis, Mo, N.Y. Jets	1	0	1	0	1	0
Linton, Jonathan, Buffalo	0	1	0	0	1	0
Lockett, Kevin, Kansas City	2	2	0	0	2	0
Logan, Mike, Jacksonville	1	0	1	2	1	0
Loud, Kamil, Buffalo	0	0	1	0	1	0
Mack, Tremain, Cincinnati	2	1	0	0	1	0
Manning, Peyton, Indianapolis	3	0	0	0	0	0
Manusky, Greg, Kansas City	0	0	2	7	2	0
Marino, Dan, Miami	9	2	0	-9	2	0
Marion, Brock, Miami	0	0	1	2	1	0
Martin, Curtis, N.Y. Jets	5	1	0	0	1	0
Martin, Emanuel, Buffalo	0	0	1	0	1	0
Mason, Derrick, Tennessee	1	1	0	0	1	0
Matthews, Bruce, Tennessee	0	1	0	0	1	0
McCaffrey, Ed, Denver	1	0	0	0	0	0
McEndoo, Jason, Seattle	1	0	0	-4	0	0
McGlockton, Chester, K.C.	0	0	1	0	1	0
McNair, Steve, Tennessee	5	3	0	-7	3	0
Means, Natrone, San Diego	2	1	0	0	1	0
Mickens, Ray, N.Y. Jets	0	0	1	0	1	0
Mickens, Terry, Oakland	0	1	1	3	2	0
Milloy, Lawyer, New England	0	0	1	0	1	0
Milne, Brian, Cincinnati	0	1	0	0	1	0
Mitchell, Jeff, Baltimore	1	0	0	-11	0	0
Mitchell, Pete, Jacksonville	0	1	0	0	1	0
Mobley, John, Denver	0	0	1	0	1	0
Montgomery, Monty, Ind.	0	0	2	14	2	0
Moon, Warren, Seattle	8	1	0	-12	1	0
Moore, Marty, New England	0	0	1	0	1	0
Moore, Ronald, Miami	1	0	0	0	0	0
Morris, Bam, Kansas City	3	1	0	0	1	0
Morton, Mike, Oakland	0	0	2	0	2	0
Myers, Greg, Cincinnati	0	0	1	0	1	0
Myles, Deshone, Seattle	0	0	1	0	1	0
O'Donnell, Neil, Cincinnati	6	1	0	-2	1	0
Oldham, Chris, Pittsburgh	0	1	4	79	5	1
O'Neal, Leslie, Kansas City	0	0	2	0	2	0
Parker, Glenn, Kansas City	0	1	0	0	1	0
Parmalee, Bernie, Miami	2	1	1	0	2	0
Parrella, John, San Diego	0	0	1	0	1	0
Parten, Ty, Kansas City	0	0	1	0	1	0
Paul, Tito, Denver	1	0	1	0	1	0
Perry, Darren, Pittsburgh	1	0	1	0	1	0
Phenix, Perry, Tennessee	0	0	1	18	1	0
Pickens, Carl, Cincinnati	2	0	0	0	0	0
Potts, Roosevelt, Baltimore	4	2	0	0	2	0
Prior, Anthony, Oakland	1	0	0	0	0	0
Pritchard, Mike, Seattle	1	0	0	0	0	0
Pritchett, Stanley, Miami	0	1	0	0	1	0
Quinn, Jonathan, Jacksonville	3	0	0	0	0	0
Rachal, Latorio, San Diego	4	1	0	0	1	0
Richardson, Kyle, Baltimore	0	1	0	0	1	0
Richardson, Tony, Kansas City	0	1	0	0	1	0
Richardson, Wally, Baltimore	1	0	0	0	0	0
Ricks, Mikhael, San Diego	1	0	0	0	0	0
Riddick, Louis, Oakland	0	0	1	0	1	0
Riemersma, Jay, Buffalo	0	0	1	0	1	0
Riley, Victor, Kansas City	0	1	0	0	1	0
Rison, Andre, Kansas City	1	1	0	0	1	0
Ritchie, Jon, Oakland	2	0	0	0	0	0
Roan, Michael, Tennessee	1	0	1	0	1	1
Romanowski, Bill, Denver	0	0	3	0	3	0
Rouen, Tom, Denver	1	0	0	-15	0	0
Roundtree, Raleigh, S.D.	0	1	0	0	1	0
Ruddy, Tim, Miami	1	0	0	-3	0	0
Russell, Darrell, Oakland	0	0	1	0	1	0
Sanders, Chris, Tennessee	1	0	0	0	0	0
Schulz, Kurt, Buffalo	0	0	1	9	1	0
Schwartz, Bryan, Jacksonville	0	0	4	4	4	0
Seau, Junior, San Diego	0	0	2	0	2	0
Shade, Sam, Cincinnati	0	0	2	55	2	1
Shaw, Sedrick, New England	2	1	0	-7	1	0
Shedd, Kenny, Oakland	0	0	2	4	2	0
Shehee, Rashaan, Kansas City	2	0	0	0	0	0
Shello, Kendel, Indianapolis	0	0	1	0	1	0
Shields, Will, Kansas City	0	1	0	0	1	0
Simmons, Brian, Cincinnati	0	0	1	22	1	0
Simmons, Wayne, Kansas City	0	0	2	17	2	0
Siragusa, Tony, Baltimore	0	0	1	0	1	0
Smeenge, Joel, Jacksonville	0	0	1	0	1	0
Smith, Antowain, Buffalo	5	2	0	0	2	0
Smith, Bruce, Buffalo	0	0	2	18	2	0
Smith, Darrin, Seattle	0	0	2	0	2	0
Smith, Fernando, Jacksonville	0	0	1	0	1	0
Smith, Jimmy, Jacksonville	2	2	0	0	2	0
Smith, Rod, Denver	0	2	0	11	2	1
Smith, Thomas, Buffalo	0	0	1	0	1	0
Sowell, Jerald, N.Y. Jets	2	0	0	0	0	0
Springs, Shawn, Seattle	0	1	1	14	2	1
Staten, Ralph, Baltimore	1	0	0	0	0	0
Stephens, Tremayne, S.D.	1	0	0	0	0	0
Stepnoski, Mark, Tennessee	2	1	0	-6	1	0
Stewart, James, Jacksonville	2	0	0	-11	0	0
Stewart, Kordell, Pittsburgh	3	2	0	0	2	0
Strong, Mack, Seattle	2	1	0	0	1	0
Stuckey, Shawn, New England	0	0	1	0	1	0
Swayne, Harry, Denver	0	1	0	0	1	0
Swilling, Pat, Oakland	0	0	1	0	1	0
Tanuvasa, Maa, Denver	0	0	2	-1	2	0
Taylor, Aaron, San Diego	0	1	0	0	1	0
Taylor, Fred, Jacksonville	3	1	0	9	1	0
Testaverde, Vinny, N.Y. Jets	7	3	0	-6	3	0
Thomas, Dave, Jacksonville	0	0	1	0	1	0
Thomas, Derrick, Kansas City	0	0	2	27	2	1
Thomas, Fred, Seattle	0	0	1	0	1	0
Thomas, Henry, New England	0	0	1	0	1	0
Tomczak, Mike, Pittsburgh	2	0	0	0	0	0
Tongue, Reggie, Kansas City	0	0	1	0	1	0
Traylor, Keith, Denver	0	0	1	0	1	0

Player, Team	Fum.	Own Rec.	Opp. Rec.	Yds.	Tot. Rec.	TD
Truitt, Greg, Cincinnati	1	0	0	-12	0	0
Tuinei, Van, Indianapolis	0	0	1	0	1	0
Vanover, Tamarick, K.C.	2	0	0	0	0	0
Walker, Marquis, Oakland	0	0	1	3	1	0
Wallace, Aaron, Oakland	0	0	1	0	1	0
Washington, Dewayne, Pit.	0	1	1	0	2	0
Watters, Ricky, Seattle	4	1	0	0	1	0
Whelihan, Craig, San Diego	9	3	0	-21	3	0
Whittington, Bernard, Ind.	0	0	2	0	2	0
Wiley, Marcellus, Buffalo	0	0	1	15	1	0
Williams, Darryl, Seattle	0	0	3	0	3	0
Williams, Gerome, San Diego	0	0	1	0	1	0
Williams, Harvey, Oakland	3	1	0	0	1	0
Williams, John, Baltimore	0	0	1	0	1	0
Williams, Kevin, Buffalo	3	2	0	0	2	0
Williams, Rodney, Oakland	1	0	0	0	0	0
Williams, Wally, Baltimore	0	1	0	0	1	0
Williams, Willie, Seattle	0	0	1	0	1	0
Wilson, Wade, Oakland	1	0	0	0	0	0
Wolford, Will, Pittsburgh	0	1	0	0	1	0
Wooden, Terry, Oakland	0	1	0	0	1	0
Wycheck, Frank, Tennessee	2	2	0	0	2	0
Wynn, Renaldo, Jacksonville	0	0	1	0	1	0
Zeier, Eric, Baltimore	2	1	0	0	1	0
Zeigler, Dusty, Buffalo	3	0	0	-19	0	0
Zolak, Scott, New England	1	0	0	0	0	0

NFC

Player, Team	Fum.	Own Rec.	Opp. Rec.	Yds.	Tot. Rec.	TD
Abraham, Donnie, Tampa Bay	0	0	2	0	2	0
Abrams, Kevin, Detroit	0	0	1	7	1	0
Adams, Flozell, Dallas	0	1	0	0	1	0
Agnew, Ray, St. Louis	0	0	1	0	1	0
Aikman, Troy, Dallas	3	0	0	-20	0	0
Aldridge, Allen, Detroit	0	0	1	0	1	0
Alexander, Brent, Carolina	0	1	0	12	1	0
Alexander, Stephen, Was.	2	0	0	0	0	0
Allen, James, Chicago	1	2	0	0	2	0
Allen, Terry, Washington	4	1	0	0	1	0
Alstott, Mike, Tampa Bay	5	0	0	0	0	0
Anderson, Jamal, Atlanta	5	1	0	0	1	0
Anderson, Ronnie, Arizona	0	1	0	0	1	0
Andruzzi, Joe, Green Bay	0	1	0	0	1	0
Anthony, Reidel, Tampa Bay	0	1	0	0	1	0
Archambeau, Lester, Atlanta	0	0	2	0	2	0
Asher, Jamie, Washington	0	1	0	0	1	0
Ball, Jerry, Minnesota	0	0	1	0	1	0
Banks, Tony, St. Louis	10	8	0	-23	8	0
Barber, Tiki, N.Y. Giants	1	0	0	0	0	0
Barrow, Micheal, Carolina	0	0	2	0	2	0
Batch, Charlie, Detroit	2	0	0	0	0	0
Bates, Michael, Carolina	1	0	0	0	0	0
Beckles, Ian, Philadelphia	0	2	0	0	2	0
Bell, Ricky, Chicago	0	0	1	0	1	0
Bellisari, Greg, Tampa Bay	0	0	1	0	1	0
Bennett, Cornelius, Atlanta	0	0	2	10	2	0
Bennett, Edgar, Chicago	2	1	0	0	1	0
Beuerlein, Steve, Carolina	13	5	0	-19	5	0
Biakabutuka, Tim, Carolina	1	0	0	0	0	0
Bohlinger, Rob, Carolina	0	1	0	0	1	0
Bolden, Juran, Carolina	0	0	1	0	1	0
Bono, Steve, St. Louis	4	0	0	-11	0	0
Booker, Michael, Atlanta	1	0	1	5	1	0
Bouie, Tony, Tampa Bay	0	0	1	0	1	0
Boyd, Stephen, Detroit	0	1	3	1	4	0
Bradford, Corey, Green Bay	1	0	0	0	0	0
Bradford, Ronnie, Atlanta	0	0	1	0	1	0
Brady, Jeff, Carolina	1	1	0	0	1	0
Bratzke, Chad, N.Y. Giants	0	0	1	0	1	0

Player, Team	Fum.	Own Rec.	Opp. Rec.	Yds.	Tot. Rec.	TD
Brock, Fred, Arizona	0	0	1	19	1	0
Brockermeyer, Blake, Carolina	0	2	0	0	2	0
Broughton, Luther, Carolina	1	1	0	0	1	0
Brown, Gary, N.Y. Giants	1	1	0	0	1	0
Brown, J.B., Arizona	0	0	1	0	1	0
Buckley, Marcus, N.Y. Giants	0	0	1	0	1	0
Buckner, Brentson, S.F.	0	0	1	0	1	0
Burrough, John, Atlanta	0	0	1	0	1	0
Butler, LeRoy, Green Bay	0	0	2	32	2	1
Calloway, Chris, N.Y. Giants	1	0	0	0	0	0
Campbell, Jesse, Washington	1	0	0	0	0	0
Carrier, Mark, Detroit	1	0	0	0	0	0
Carter, Marty, Chicago	0	0	2	0	2	0
Centers, Larry, Arizona	1	0	0	0	0	0
Chancey, Robert, Chicago	2	0	0	0	0	0
Chandler, Chris, Atlanta	6	1	0	-4	1	0
Chmura, Mark, Green Bay	1	0	0	0	0	0
Christian, Bob, Atlanta	1	0	2	0	2	0
Chryplewicz, Pete, Detroit	1	0	0	0	0	0
Cleeland, Cameron, N.O.	1	2	0	7	2	0
Coakley, Dexter, Dallas	0	0	1	0	1	0
Collins, Calvin, Atlanta	0	1	0	0	1	0
Collins, Kerry, Car.-N.O.	13	2	0	-9	2	0
Comella, Greg, N.Y. Giants	0	1	0	0	1	0
Conway, Curtis, Chicago	1	0	1	0	1	0
Cooks, Kerry, Green Bay	0	1	0	0	1	0
Copeland, Russell, Phi.	1	0	0	0	0	0
Cota, Chad, New Orleans	0	0	1	0	1	0
Cousin, Terry, Chicago	0	0	2	0	2	0
Craver, Aaron, New Orleans	2	1	0	0	1	0
Cross, Howard, N.Y. Giants	2	0	0	0	0	0
Crowell, Germane, Detroit	1	0	0	0	0	0
Culpepper, Brad, Tampa Bay	0	0	1	0	1	0
Cunningham, Randall, Min.	2	0	0	0	0	0
Davidds-Garrido, Norberto, Car.	0	1	0	0	1	0
Davis, Billy, Dallas	1	1	0	0	1	0
Davis, Eric, Carolina	0	0	1	0	1	0
Davis, Troy, New Orleans	1	0	0	0	0	0
Davis, Tyrone, Green Bay	1	0	0	0	0	0
Dawkins, Brian, Philadelphia	0	0	1	0	1	0
Dawkins, Sean, New Orleans	2	0	0	0	0	0
DeBerg, Steve, Atlanta	2	1	0	0	1	0
Deese, Derrick, San Francisco	0	1	0	0	1	0
Dellenbach, Jeff, Green Bay	0	2	0	0	2	0
Detmer, Koy, Philadelphia	1	0	0	0	0	0
Detmer, Ty, San Francisco	1	0	0	0	0	0
Devlin, Mike, Arizona	0	1	0	0	1	0
Dexter, James, Arizona	0	2	0	0	2	0
Dilfer, Trent, Tampa Bay	9	2	0	-5	2	0
Dishman, Chris, Arizona	0	1	0	0	1	0
Dixon, David, Minnesota	0	1	0	0	1	0
Doleman, Chris, S.F.	0	0	2	0	2	0
Dotson, Santana, Green Bay	0	0	1	0	1	0
Dronett, Shane, Atlanta	1	1	0	0	1	0
Dunn, Jason, Philadelphia	1	0	0	0	1	0
Dunn, Warrick, Tampa Bay	1	1	0	0	1	0
Dwight, Tim, Atlanta	3	0	0	0	0	0
Edwards, Antonio, Atlanta	0	0	1	2	1	1
Edwards, Dixon, Minnesota	0	0	1	0	1	0
Ellis, Greg, Dallas	0	0	1	2	1	0
Ellison, Jerry, Tampa Bay	0	0	2	0	2	0
Elliss, Luther, Detroit	0	0	1	0	1	0
Engram, Bobby, Chicago	1	0	0	0	0	0
Enis, Curtis, Chicago	1	0	0	0	0	0
Evans, Greg, Washington	0	1	0	0	1	0
Fair, Terry, Detroit	5	1	0	0	1	0
Farr, D'Marco, St. Louis	0	0	1	18	1	0
Favre, Brett, Green Bay	8	3	0	-1	3	0
Fields, Mark, New Orleans	0	0	1	36	1	1
Fisk, Jason, Minnesota	0	0	1	0	1	0
Flanigan, Jim, Chicago	0	0	1	0	1	0

Player, Team	Fum.	Own Rec.	Opp. Rec.	Yds.	Tot. Rec.	TD
Flannery, John, St. Louis	2	0	0	-5	0	0
Fletcher, London, St. Louis	1	0	0	0	0	0
Floyd, William, Carolina	1	1	0	0	1	0
Fuller, Randy, Atlanta	0	0	2	0	2	0
Galyon, Scott, N.Y. Giants	0	0	1	0	1	0
Garcia, Frank, Carolina	0	1	1	2	2	0
Garner, Charlie, Philadelphia	1	0	0	0	0	0
Garrett, Jason, Dallas	4	0	0	-17	0	0
Gedney, Chris, Arizona	1	0	0	0	0	0
Godfrey, Randall, Dallas	0	0	1	0	1	0
Gooch, Jeff, Tampa Bay	0	0	1	0	1	0
Goodwin, Hunter, Minnesota	0	1	0	0	1	0
Gragg, Scott, N.Y. Giants	0	1	0	0	1	0
Graham, Kent, N.Y. Giants	2	0	0	-3	0	0
Gray, Torrian, Minnesota	0	0	1	14	1	0
Green, Harold, Atlanta	1	0	0	0	0	0
Green, Jacquez, Tampa Bay	5	2	0	0	2	0
Green, Trent, Washington	14	4	0	0	4	0
Greene, Kevin, Carolina	0	0	1	2	1	0
Guliford, Eric, New Orleans	1	1	0	0	1	0
Hakim, Az-zahir, St. Louis	1	0	0	0	0	0
Hall, Lemanski, Chicago	0	0	1	5	1	0
Hall, Travis, Atlanta	0	0	4	0	4	0
Hallock, Ty, Chicago	3	0	1	0	1	0
Hamilton, Conrad, N.Y. Giants	0	0	1	0	1	0
Hamilton, Keith, N.Y. Giants	0	0	1	0	1	0
Hanks, Merton, San Francisco	0	0	1	0	1	0
Hape, Patrick, Tampa Bay	1	0	0	0	0	0
Harris, Al, Philadelphia	1	0	0	0	0	0
Harris, Derrick, St. Louis	1	2	0	0	2	0
Harris, Jon, Philadelphia	0	0	1	0	1	0
Harris, Raymont, Green Bay	3	0	0	0	0	0
Harris, Ronnie, Sea.-Atl.*	2	1	0	0	1	0
Harris, Walt, Chicago	0	0	1	0	1	0
Harvey, Ken, Washington	0	0	1	0	1	0
Hastings, Andre, New Orleans	0	1	0	0	1	0
Hearst, Garrison, S.F.	4	1	0	0	1	0
Henderson, William, G.B.	1	0	0	0	0	0
Henley, June, St. Louis	1	1	0	0	1	0
Hennings, Chad, Dallas	0	0	1	0	1	0
Hilliard, Ike, N.Y. Giants	2	0	0	0	0	0
Hitchcock, Jimmy, Min.	0	0	1	1	1	0
Hoard, Leroy, Minnesota	1	1	0	0	1	0
Holliday, Vonnie, Green Bay	0	0	2	0	2	0
Holmes, Darick, Green Bay	1	1	0	0	1	0
Horne, Tony, St. Louis	1	0	0	0	0	0
Houston, Bobby, Minnesota	0	0	1	14	1	0
Hoying, Bobby, Philadelphia	6	2	0	-2	2	0
Hughes, Tyrone, Dallas	1	0	0	0	0	0
Irvin, Michael, Dallas	1	0	0	0	0	0
Ismail, Qadry, New Orleans	2	0	0	0	0	0
Ismail, Raghib, Carolina	2	1	0	0	1	0
Jeffries, Greg, Detroit	0	0	1	0	1	0
Jenkins, James, Washington	0	1	0	0	1	0
Jensen, Jerry, Carolina	1	0	0	-20	0	0
Johnson, Anthony, Carolina	3	1	0	0	1	0
Johnson, Brad, Minnesota	1	0	0	0	0	0
Johnson, Joe, New Orleans	0	0	1	5	1	1
Jones, Cedric, N.Y. Giants	0	0	1	0	1	0
Jones, Clarence, New Orleans	0	1	0	0	1	0
Jones, Marcus, Tampa Bay	0	0	1	0	1	0
Jones, Mike D., St. Louis	0	0	2	43	2	0
Kanell, Danny, N.Y. Giants	6	1	0	0	1	0
Kelly, Brian, Tampa Bay	1	0	1	15	1	0
Kennison, Eddie, St. Louis	4	1	0	0	1	0
Kinchen, Todd, Atlanta	2	0	0	0	0	0
Kirk, Randy, San Francisco	1	0	0	-18	0	0
Kiselak, Mike, Dallas	0	1	0	0	1	0
Knight, Sammy, New Orleans	0	0	2	3	2	0
Koonce, George, Green Bay	0	0	1	4	1	0
Kowalkowski, Scott, Detroit	0	0	1	0	1	0
Kramer, Erik, Chicago	3	0	0	0	0	0
Lacina, Corbin, Carolina	0	1	0	0	1	0
LaFleur, David, Dallas	1	0	0	0	0	0
Lane, Fred, Carolina	4	0	0	0	0	0
Lassiter, Kwamie, Arizona	0	0	1	0	1	0
Lee, Amp, St. Louis	3	0	0	0	0	0
Lee, Shawn, Chicago	0	0	1	15	1	1
Lloyd, Greg, Carolina	0	0	1	6	1	0
Lynch, John, Tampa Bay	0	0	1	0	1	0
Maddox, Mark, Arizona	0	0	1	0	1	0
Marshall, Anthony, Phi.	0	0	1	0	1	0
Martin, Wayne, New Orleans	0	0	1	0	1	0
Mathis, Kevin, Dallas	2	2	2	6	4	0
Mathis, Terance, Atlanta	0	2	0	0	2	0
Mayes, Alonzo, Chicago	2	0	0	0	0	0
Mayes, Derrick, Green Bay	1	0	0	0	0	0
Mays, Kivuusama, Minnesota	0	0	1	0	1	0
McBurrows, Gerald, St. Louis	0	1	0	0	1	0
McCollum, Andy, N.O.	0	1	0	0	1	0
McCombs, Tony, Arizona	0	0	1	0	1	0
McCormack, Hurvin, Dallas	0	0	1	0	1	0
McDaniel, Ed, Minnesota	0	0	2	5	2	0
McDonald, Tim, S.F.	0	0	2	0	2	0
McKenzie, Keith, Green Bay	0	0	3	88	3	1
McKinnon, Ronald, Arizona	1	0	2	0	2	0
McNeil, Ryan, St. Louis	0	0	1	0	1	0
McQuarters, R.W., S.F.	4	2	0	0	2	0
McTyer, Tim, Philadelphia	0	1	0	0	1	0
Metcalf, Eric, Arizona	5	2	0	0	2	0
Milburn, Glyn, Chicago	1	0	0	0	0	0
Miller, Jamir, Arizona	0	0	2	0	2	0
Miller, Les, Carolina	1	0	3	8	3	0
Minter, Barry, Chicago	0	0	1	11	1	0
Mitchell, Brian, Washington	3	0	0	0	0	0
Mitchell, Keith, New Orleans	0	0	3	63	3	1
Mitchell, Scott, Detroit	1	0	0	-9	0	0
Mobley, Singor, Dallas	0	1	0	0	1	0
Moore, Dave, Tampa Bay	1	0	0	0	0	0
Moore, Jerald, St. Louis	3	2	0	0	2	0
Moreno, Moses, Chicago	2	0	0	-4	0	0
Morrow, Harold, Minnesota	0	0	1	0	1	0
Moss, Randy, Minnesota	2	0	0	0	0	0
Muhammad, Muhsin, Carolina	2	1	0	0	1	0
Murrell, Adrian, Arizona	6	1	0	0	1	0
Naeole, Chris, New Orleans	0	1	0	0	1	0
Nickerson, Hardy, Tampa Bay	0	0	1	0	1	0
Norton, Ken, San Francisco	0	0	3	12	3	0
Ogden, Jeff, Dallas	1	0	0	0	0	0
Oliver, Winslow, Carolina	1	0	0	0	0	0
Owens, Terrell, San Francisco	1	0	1	13	1	0
Oxendine, Ken, Atlanta	1	0	0	0	0	0
Pace, Orlando, St. Louis	0	0	1	0	1	0
Palelei, Lonnie, N.Y. Giants	1	0	0	0	0	0
Palmer, David, Minnesota	2	1	0	0	1	0
Parrish, Tony, Chicago	1	0	2	-2	2	0
Pederson, Doug, Green Bay	1	0	0	-2	0	0
Peete, Rodney, Philadelphia	1	0	0	0	0	0
Penn, Chris, Chicago	1	0	0	0	0	0
Perry, Wilmont, New Orleans	1	0	0	0	0	0
Peter, Jason, Carolina	0	0	1	0	1	0
Phifer, Roman, St. Louis	1	0	0	0	0	0
Pittman, Kavika, Dallas	0	0	2	7	2	0
Pittman, Michael, Arizona	1	0	1	0	1	0
Plummer, Jake, Arizona	12	3	0	-2	3	0
Portilla, Jose, Atlanta	0	1	0	0	1	0
Pounds, Darryl, Washington	0	0	1	0	1	0
Pourdanesh, Shar, Was.	1	1	0	-4	1	0
Preston, Roell, Green Bay	7	1	0	0	1	0
Prior, Mike, Green Bay	1	0	0	0	0	0
Randle, John, Minnesota	0	0	1	0	1	0
Raymer, Cory, Washington	0	1	0	0	1	0

Player, Team	Fum.	Own Rec.	Opp. Rec.	Yds.	Tot. Rec.	TD
Reich, Frank, Detroit	2	1	0	0	1	0
Rice, Jerry, San Francisco	2	0	0	0	0	0
Rice, Simeon, Arizona	0	0	4	39	4	0
Richard, Stanley, Washington	0	0	1	0	1	0
Richardson, Damien, Carolina	0	0	1	0	1	0
Robbins, Austin, New Orleans	0	0	1	0	1	1
Robinson, Eugene, Atlanta	0	0	2	16	2	0
Rossum, Allen, Philadelphia	4	2	1	0	3	0
Rudd, Dwayne, Minnesota	0	0	3	157	3	2
Ruhman, Chris, San Francisco	0	1	0	0	1	0
Sanders, Barry, Detroit	3	1	0	0	1	0
Sanders, Deion, Dallas	1	1	0	0	1	0
Sanders, Frank, Arizona	3	2	0	0	2	0
Santiago, O.J., Atlanta	1	1	0	0	1	0
Sapp, Warren, Tampa Bay	0	0	1	0	1	0
Schroeder, Bill, Green Bay	1	0	0	0	0	0
Schwantz, Jim, Chicago	0	1	0	0	1	0
Scott, Lance, N.Y. Giants	1	1	0	-1	1	0
Sellers, Mike, Washington	0	0	1	0	1	0
Sinceno, Kaseem, Phi.	1	0	0	0	0	0
Smith, Chuck, Atlanta	0	1	3	71	4	1
Smith, Derek, Washington	0	0	1	0	1	0
Smith, Emmitt, Dallas	3	1	0	0	1	0
Smith, Lamar, New Orleans	4	0	0	0	0	0
Smith, Mark, Arizona	0	0	1	0	1	0
Smith, Robert, Minnesota	1	0	0	0	0	0
Smith, Rod, Carolina	0	0	1	35	1	0
Staley, Duce, Philadelphia	2	2	0	0	2	0
Stenstrom, Steve, Chicago	6	1	0	-9	1	0
Stoutmire, Omar, Dallas	0	0	1	0	1	0
Talley, Ben, Atlanta	0	1	0	0	1	0
Tatum, Kinnon, Carolina	0	1	0	0	1	0
Terrell, Pat, Green Bay	0	0	1	6	1	0
Thomas, Chris, Washington	0	0	1	0	1	0
Thomas, Hollis, Philadelphia	0	1	0	0	1	0
Thomas, Tra, Philadelphia	0	1	0	0	1	0
Tobeck, Robbie, Atlanta	0	1	0	1	1	0
Tolliver, Billy Joe, N.O.	3	0	0	-13	0	0
Tomich, Jared, New Orleans	0	0	1	0	1	0
Tuaolo, Esera, Atlanta	0	0	1	0	1	0
Tubbs, Winfred, S.F.	0	0	1	0	1	0
Tuggle, Jessie, Atlanta	0	0	1	1	1	1
Turk, Dan, Washington	1	0	0	-4	0	0
Turk, Matt, Washington	1	0	0	0	0	0
Turner, Kevin, Philadelphia	1	0	0	0	0	0
Vardell, Tommy, Detroit	1	0	0	0	0	0
Villarrial, Chris, Chicago	0	1	0	0	1	0
Wadsworth, Andre, Arizona	0	0	3	0	3	0
Waldroup, Kerwin, Detroit	0	0	1	0	1	0
Walter, Ken, Carolina	2	2	0	-20	2	0
Walz, Zack, Arizona	0	0	1	0	1	0
Warren, Chris, Dallas	0	1	0	0	1	0
Way, Charles, N.Y. Giants	0	2	0	0	2	0
Wetnight, Ryan, Chicago	1	0	0	0	0	0
Wheaton, Kenny, Dallas	0	0	2	15	2	1
Wheeler, Leonard, Carolina	0	0	1	0	1	0
White, Steve, Tampa Bay	0	0	1	0	1	0
White, William, Atlanta	0	0	1	18	1	1
Whiting, Brandon, Phi.	0	0	1	24	1	0
Widmer, Corey, N.Y. Giants	0	0	1	4	1	0
Wiegert, Zach, St. Louis	0	1	0	0	1	0
Wiegmann, Casey, Chicago	1	1	0	-3	1	0
Wilkinson, Dan, Washington	0	0	1	0	1	0
Williams, Gene, Atlanta	0	1	0	0	1	0
Williams, Moe, Minnesota	1	1	0	0	1	0
Williams, Tony, Minnesota	0	0	1	6	1	0
Willig, Matt, Green Bay	0	1	0	0	1	0
Willis, James, Philadelphia	0	0	1	0	1	0
Wistrom, Grant, St. Louis	0	0	1	4	1	0
Wuerffel, Danny, New Orleans	1	1	0	0	1	0
Young, Bryant, San Francisco	0	0	1	0	1	0
Young, Floyd, Tampa Bay	0	1	0	0	1	0
Young, Steve, San Francisco	9	1	0	0	1	0
Zellars, Ray, New Orleans	2	0	0	0	0	0
Zordich, Michael, Philadelphia	0	0	1	0	1	0

*Includes both NFC and AFC statistics.

PLAYERS WITH TWO CLUBS

Player, Team	Fum.	Own Rec.	Opp. Rec.	Yds.	Tot. Rec.	TD
Collins, Kerry, Carolina	5	0	0	-1	0	0
Collins, Kerry, New Orleans	8	2	0	-8	2	0
Harris, Ronnie, Seattle	1	0	0	0	0	0
Harris, Ronnie, Atlanta	1	1	0	0	1	0

FIELD GOALS

TEAM

AFC

Team	Made	Att.	Pct.	Long
Tennessee	36	40	.900	48
Indianapolis	27	31	.871	53
San Diego	26	30	.867	54
Denver	23	27	.852	63
Kansas City	27	32	.844	53
Miami	22	27	.815	48
Pittsburgh	26	32	.813	49
Jacksonville	21	26	.808	47
Buffalo	33	41	.805	52
New England	31	39	.795	55
Seattle	19	24	.792	51
Baltimore	21	28	.750	48
N.Y. Jets	25	35	.714	54
Cincinnati	19	27	.704	51
Oakland	17	27	.630	51
AFC total	373	466	...	63
AFC average	24.9	31.1	.800	...

NFC

Team	Made	Att.	Pct.	Long
Minnesota	35	35	1.000	53
New Orleans	20	22	.909	56
Detroit	29	33	.879	51
Green Bay	29	33	.879	45
Dallas	29	35	.829	54
Atlanta	23	28	.821	53
Chicago	21	26	.808	52
N.Y. Giants	21	27	.778	51
St. Louis	20	26	.769	57
Tampa Bay	21	28	.750	52
Carolina	19	26	.731	56
Arizona	23	33	.697	53
Philadelphia	14	21	.667	50
San Francisco	18	27	.667	46
Washington	13	23	.565	54
NFC total	335	423	...	57
NFC average	22.3	28.2	.792	...
NFL total	708	889	...	63
NFL average	23.6	29.6	.796	...

INDIVIDUAL

BESTS OF THE SEASON

Field goal percentage, season
NFC: 1.000—Gary Anderson, Minnesota.
AFC: .923—Al Del Greco, Tennessee.

Field goals, season
AFC: 36—Al Del Greco, Tennessee.
NFC: 35—Gary Anderson, Minnesota.

Field goal attempts, season
AFC: 41—Steve Christie, Buffalo.
NFC: 35—Gary Anderson, Minnesota; Richie Cunningham, Dallas.

Longest field goal
AFC: 63—Jason Elam, Denver vs. Jacksonville, Oct. 25.
NFC: 57—Jeff Wilkins, St. Louis vs. Arizona, Sept. 27.

Average yards made, season
NFC: 38.5—John Kasay, Carolina.
AFC: 37.2—Jason Elam, Denver.

NFL LEADERS

Team	Made	Att.	Pct.	Long
Anderson, Gary, Minnesota	35	35	1.000	53
Del Greco, Al, Tennessee*	36	39	.923	48
Brien, Doug, New Orleans	20	22	.909	56
Hanson, Jason, Detroit	29	33	.879	51
Longwell, Ryan, Green Bay	29	33	.879	45
Vanderjagt, Mike, Indianapolis*	27	31	.871	53
Carney, John, San Diego*	26	30	.867	54
Elam, Jason, Denver*	23	27	.852	63
Stoyanovich, Pete, Kansas City*	27	32	.844	53
Johnson, Norm, Pittsburgh*	26	31	.839	49

*AFC.

Leader based on percentage, minimum 16 attempts.

AFC

Player, Team	1-19	20-29	30-39	40-49	Over	Totals	Avg. Yds. Att.	Avg. Yds. Made	Avg. Yds. Miss	Long
Carney, John	0-0	11-12	5-5	8-10	2-3	26-30	35.7	34.9	41.0	54
San Diego	...	.917	1.000	.800	.667	.867				
Christie, Steve	1-1	10-12	12-14	9-11	1-3	33-41	35.0	33.9	39.5	52
Buffalo	1.000	.833	.857	.818	.333	.805				
Davis, Greg	0-0	5-6	5-8	6-11	1-2	17-27	37.3	35.6	40.2	51
Oakland	...	.833	.625	.545	.500	.630				
Del Greco, Al	1-1	8-8	15-15	12-15	0-0	36-39	35.8	35.2	43.3	48
Tennessee	1.000	1.000	1.000	.800	...	.923				
Elam, Jason	0-0	3-3	13-14	4-6	3-4	23-27	38.3	37.2	44.3	63
Denver	...	1.000	.929	.667	.750	.852				
George, Matt	0-0	0-0	0-1	0-0	0-0	0-1	36.0	-	36.0	0
Pittsburgh	...	...	.000	...	...	.000				
Hall, John	0-0	9-9	9-13	6-10	1-3	25-35	36.4	33.4	43.7	54
N.Y. Jets	...	1.000	.692	.600	.333	.714				
Hentrich, Craig	0-0	0-0	0-0	0-1	0-0	0-1	49.0	-	49.0	0
Tennessee	...	...	...	.000	...	.000				

Player, Team	1-19	20-29	30-39	40-49	Over	Totals	Avg. Yds. Att.	Avg. Yds. Made	Avg. Yds. Miss	Long
Hollis, Mike	1-1	8-10	8-9	4-5	0-1	21-26	32.5	31.8	35.8	47
Jacksonville	1.000	.800	.889	.800	.000	.808				
Johnson, Norm	0-0	10-10	5-5	11-14	0-2	26-31	36.8	34.6	48.2	49
Pittsburgh	...	1.000	1.000	.786	.000	.839				
Mare, Olindo	0-0	12-13	5-5	5-7	0-2	22-27	33.6	31.2	44.4	48
Miami	...	.923	1.000	.714	.000	.815				
Pelfrey, Doug	1-1	4-4	6-7	6-10	2-5	19-27	39.1	36.2	46.1	51
Cincinnati	1.000	1.000	.857	.600	.400	.704				
Peterson, Todd	0-0	7-7	4-5	5-5	3-7	19-24	38.5	35.6	49.4	51
Seattle	...	1.000	.800	1.000	.429	.792				
Stover, Matt	0-0	6-6	5-5	10-17	0-0	21-28	37.5	35.6	43.4	48
Baltimore	...	1.000	1.000	.588	...	.750				
Stoyanovich, Pete	2-2	9-9	9-9	5-10	2-2	27-32	34.6	32.7	44.6	53
Kansas City	1.000	1.000	1.000	.500	1.000	.844				
Vanderjagt, Mike	1-1	8-8	4-4	8-9	6-9	27-31	39.0	37.1	52.0	53
Indianapolis	1.000	1.000	1.000	.889	.667	.871				
Vinatieri, Adam	3-3	8-8	9-14	9-12	2-2	31-39	35.4	34.2	40.0	55
New England	1.000	1.000	.643	.750	1.000	.795				

NFC

Player, Team	1-19	20-29	30-39	40-49	Over	Totals	Avg. Yds. Att.	Avg. Yds. Made	Avg. Yds. Miss	Long
Akers, David	0-0	0-0	0-0	0-2	0-0	0-2	48.5	...	48.5	0
Washington	...	...	...	.000	...	.000				
Andersen, Morten	0-1	8-9	7-7	6-9	2-2	23-28	34.9	34.4	37.4	53
Atlanta	.000	.889	1.000	.667	1.000	.821				
Anderson, Gary	1-1	11-11	9-9	12-12	2-2	35-35	35.6	35.6	...	53
Minnesota	1.000	1.000	1.000	1.000	1.000	1.000				
Blanchard, Cary	0-0	2-2	6-8	2-5	1-2	11-17	39.1	37.0	42.8	54
Washington	...	1.000	.750	.400	.500	.647				
Blanton, Scott	0-0	0-0	1-2	1-2	0-0	2-4	41.0	41.5	40.5	46
Washington	...	...	.500	.500	...	.500				
Boniol, Chris	3-3	3-3	4-5	3-9	1-1	14-21	36.2	32.5	43.7	50
Philadelphia	1.000	1.000	.800	.333	1.000	.667				
Brien, Doug	0-0	7-7	3-3	6-6	4-6	20-22	39.0	37.6	53.5	56
New Orleans	...	1.000	1.000	1.000	.667	.909				
Cunningham, Richie	1-1	9-9	8-11	10-11	1-3	29-35	36.1	34.3	44.7	54
Dallas	1.000	1.000	.727	.909	.333	.829				
Daluiso, Brad	2-2	5-5	6-8	7-11	1-1	21-27	35.7	34.5	39.7	51
N.Y. Giants	1.000	1.000	.750	.636	1.000	.778				
Hanson, Jason	0-0	8-8	7-7	13-15	1-3	29-33	39.2	37.7	50.3	51
Detroit	...	1.000	1.000	.867	.333	.879				
Husted, Michael	0-1	7-7	8-12	5-7	1-1	21-28	34.8	34.6	35.1	52
Tampa Bay	.000	1.000	.667	.714	1.000	.750				
Jacke, Chris	0-0	3-3	5-6	1-3	1-2	10-14	37.1	34.7	43.0	52
Arizona	...	1.000	.833	.333	.500	.714				
Jaeger, Jeff	2-2	8-9	9-10	1-4	1-1	21-26	32.0	30.3	39.2	52
Chicago	1.000	.889	.900	.250	1.000	.808				
Kasay, John	0-0	5-5	4-5	6-9	4-7	19-26	40.9	38.5	47.6	56
Carolina	...	1.000	.800	.667	.571	.731				
Longwell, Ryan	1-1	6-6	13-15	9-10	0-1	29-33	35.4	34.1	44.3	45
Green Bay	1.000	1.000	.867	.900	.000	.879				
Nedney, Joe	0-0	6-6	1-1	5-8	1-4	13-19	39.8	36.0	48.0	53
Arizona	...	1.000	1.000	.625	.250	.684				
Richey, Wade	0-0	9-10	3-4	6-13	0-0	18-27	35.2	32.2	41.3	46
San Francisco	...	.900	.750	.462	...	.667				
Wilkins, Jeff	0-0	4-5	8-8	5-7	3-6	20-26	40.4	38.1	48.0	57
St. Louis	...	.800	1.000	.714	.500	.769				

1998 STATISTICS Field goals

PUNTING

AFC

Team	Total Punts	Yards	Long	Avg.	TB	Blocked	Opp. Ret.	Ret. Yards	Inside 20	Net Avg.
Tennessee	69	3258	71	47.2	11	0	34	332	18	39.2
Denver	67	3097	76	46.2	10	1	43	381	14	37.6
Indianapolis	79	3583	62	45.4	10	0	42	451	23	37.1
Jacksonville	85	3824	65	45.0	11	0	40	332	28	38.5
New England	74	3294	64	44.5	9	0	43	493	13	35.4
Cincinnati	81	3578	73	44.2	11	2	36	503	14	35.2
Seattle	81	3568	59	44.0	12	0	33	369	27	36.5
San Diego	95	4174	65	43.9	8	0	49	515	27	36.8
Pittsburgh	82	3565	73	43.5	12	0	30	310	35	36.8
Oakland	98	4256	64	43.4	10	0	53	787	29	33.4
Baltimore	92	3948	67	42.9	7	2	40	284	25	38.3
Kansas City	77	3255	59	42.3	5	1	41	513	21	34.3
Miami	97	4064	57	41.9	14	1	43	339	24	35.5
Buffalo	69	2882	57	41.8	11	0	32	374	18	33.2
N.Y. Jets	65	2637	62	40.6	4	0	30	309	16	34.6
AFC total	1211	52983	76	...	145	7	589	6292	332	...
AFC average	80.7	3532.2	...	43.8	9.7	0.5	39.3	419.5	22.1	36.2

Leader based on average.

NFC

Team	Total Punts	Yards	Long	Avg.	TB	Blocked	Opp. Ret.	Ret. Yards	Inside 20	Net Avg.
New Orleans	90	4089	64	45.4	11	0	53	649	26	35.8
N.Y. Giants	101	4566	63	45.2	8	0	53	587	33	37.8
Minnesota	55	2458	67	44.7	5	0	27	325	17	37.0
St. Louis	95	4202	64	44.2	10	0	58	652	16	35.3
Washington	97	4216	69	43.5	9	1	32	261	34	38.9
Green Bay	65	2788	72	42.9	7	0	27	237	30	37.1
Dallas	78	3342	65	42.8	14	1	34	210	31	36.6
Detroit	82	3506	60	42.8	6	0	47	471	19	35.5
Chicago	80	3411	71	42.6	7	0	38	349	18	36.5
Philadelphia	104	4339	61	41.7	10	0	61	511	21	34.9
Tampa Bay	81	3340	55	41.2	9	0	38	302	19	35.3
Arizona	82	3378	67	41.2	6	1	38	313	12	35.9
San Francisco	69	2835	66	41.1	7	0	36	341	16	34.1
Carolina	77	3131	59	40.7	5	0	20	94	20	38.1
Atlanta	74	2963	55	40.0	7	0	20	112	25	36.6
NFC total	1230	52564	72	...	121	3	582	5414	337	...
NFC average	82.0	3504.3	...	42.7	8.1	0.2	38.7	360.9	22.5	36.4
NFL total	2441	105547	76	...	266	10	1171	11706	669	...
NFL average	81.4	3518.2	...	43.2	8.9	0.3	39.0	390.2	22.3	36.3

INDIVIDUAL

BESTS OF THE SEASON

Average yards per punt, season
AFC: 47.2—Craig Hentrich, Tennessee.
NFC: 45.6—Mark Royals, New Orleans.

Net average yards per punt, season
AFC: 39.2—Craig Hentrich, Tennessee.
NFC: 39.0—Matt Turk, Washington.

Longest
AFC: 76—Tom Rouen, Denver at Oakland, Sept. 20.
NFC: 72—Sean Landeta, Green Bay at Cincinnati, Sept. 20.

Punts, season
NFC: 104—Tom Hutton, Philadelphia.
AFC: 98—Leo Araguz, Oakland.

Punts, game
AFC: 16—Leo Araguz, Oakland vs. San Diego, Oct. 11.
NFC: 11—Brad Maynard, N.Y. Giants at Washington, Nov. 1.

NFL LEADERS

Player, Team	Net Punts	Yards	Long	Avg.	Total Punts	TB	Blk.	Opp. Ret.	Ret. Yds.	In 20	Net Avg.
Hentrich, Craig, Tennessee*	69	3258	71	47.2	69	11	0	34	332	18	39.2
Rouen, Tom, Denver*	66	3097	76	46.9	67	10	1	43	381	14	37.6
Royals, Mark, New Orleans	88	4017	64	45.6	88	10	0	52	649	26	36.0
Gardocki, Chris, Indianapolis*	79	3583	62	45.4	79	10	0	42	451	23	37.1

Player, Team	Net Punts	Yards	Long	Avg.	Total Punts	TB	Blk.	Opp. Ret.	Ret. Yds.	In 20	Net Avg.
Maynard, Brad, N.Y. Giants................	101	4566	63	45.2	101	8	0	53	587	33	37.8
Barker, Bryan, Jacksonville*..............	85	3824	65	45.0	85	11	0	40	332	28	38.5
Berger, Mitch, Minnesota.................	55	2458	67	44.7	55	5	0	27	325	17	37.0
Johnson, Lee, Cincinnati*.................	69	3083	69	44.7	70	8	1	31	428	14	35.6
Tupa, Tom, New England*.................	74	3294	64	44.5	74	9	0	43	493	13	35.4
Tuten, Rick, St. Louis	95	4202	64	44.2	95	10	0	58	652	16	35.3
Turk, Matt, Washington	93	4103	69	44.1	94	9	1	31	260	33	39.0
Feagles, Jeff, Seattle*.....................	81	3568	59	44.0	81	12	0	33	369	27	36.5
Bennett, Darren, San Diego*..............	95	4174	65	43.9	95	8	0	49	515	27	36.8
Richardson, Kyle, Baltimore*............	90	3948	67	43.9	92	7	2	40	284	25	38.3
Jett, John, Detroit............................	66	2892	60	43.8	66	6	0	38	398	17	36.0

*AFC.

Leader based on average, minimum 40 punts.

Player, Team	Net Punts	Yards	Long	Avg.	Total Punts	TB	Blk.	Opp. Ret.	Ret. Yds.	In 20	Net Avg.
Aguiar, Louie, Kansas City	75	3226	59	43.0	76	5	1	41	513	20	34.4
Araguz, Leo, Oakland........................	98	4256	64	43.4	98	10	0	53	787	29	33.4
Barker, Bryan, Jacksonville................	85	3824	65	45.0	85	11	0	40	332	28	38.5
Bennett, Darren, San Diego	95	4174	65	43.9	95	8	0	49	515	27	36.8
Costello, Brad, Cincinnati..................	10	495	73	49.5	11	3	1	5	75	0	32.7
Feagles, Jeff, Seattle.......................	81	3568	59	44.0	81	12	0	33	369	27	36.5
Gallery, Nick, N.Y. Jets....................	6	238	49	39.7	6	0	0	3	38	2	33.3
Gardocki, Chris, Indianapolis	79	3583	62	45.4	79	10	0	42	451	23	37.1
Hansen, Brian, N.Y. Jets	31	1233	62	39.8	31	2	0	15	178	6	32.7
Hentrich, Craig, Tennessee	69	3258	71	47.2	69	11	0	34	332	18	39.2
Johnson, Lee, Cincinnati	69	3083	69	44.7	70	8	1	31	428	14	35.6
Kidd, John, Det.-NYJ*	41	1686	57	41.1	41	2	0	20	159	9	36.3
Mare, Olindo, Miami	3	115	43	38.3	3	1	0	0	0	1	31.7
Miller, Josh, Pittsburgh	81	3530	73	43.6	81	12	0	30	310	34	36.8
Mohr, Chris, Buffalo.........................	69	2882	57	41.8	69	11	0	32	374	18	33.2
Richardson, Kyle, Baltimore	90	3948	67	43.9	92	7	2	40	284	25	38.3
Rouen, Tom, Denver..........................	66	3097	76	46.9	67	10	1	43	381	14	37.6
Stewart, Kordell, Pittsburgh..............	1	35	35	35.0	1	0	0	0	0	1	35.0
Stoyanovich, Pete, Kansas City	1	29	29	29.0	1	0	0	0	0	1	29.0
Tupa, Tom, New England	74	3294	64	44.5	74	9	0	43	493	13	35.4
Wilmsmeyer, Klaus, Miami	93	3949	57	42.5	94	13	1	43	339	23	35.6

*Includes both NFC and AFC statistics.

Player, Team	Net Punts	Yards	Long	Avg.	Total Punts	TB	Blk.	Opp. Ret.	Ret. Yds.	In 20	Net Avg.
Barnhardt, Tommy, Tampa Bay..........	81	3340	55	41.2	81	9	0	38	302	19	35.3
Berger, Mitch, Minnesota..................	55	2458	67	44.7	55	5	0	27	325	17	37.0
Blanchard, Cary, Washington..............	3	113	43	37.7	3	0	0	1	1	1	37.3
Brien, Doug, New Orleans	2	72	37	36.0	2	1	0	1	0	0	26.0
Gowin, Toby, Dallas	77	3342	65	43.4	78	14	1	34	210	31	36.6
Hanson, Jason, Detroit......................	3	94	36	31.3	3	0	0	1	7	1	29.0
Horan, Mike, Chicago	64	2643	57	41.3	64	4	0	33	299	12	35.4
Howard, Eddie, San Francisco	9	324	45	36.0	9	1	0	2	9	2	32.8
Hutton, Tom, Philadelphia	104	4339	61	41.7	104	10	0	61	511	21	34.9
Jaeger, Jeff, Chicago	1	27	27	27.0	1	0	0	0	0	0	27.0
Jett, John, Detroit............................	66	2892	60	43.8	66	6	0	38	398	17	36.0
Landeta, Sean, Green Bay.................	65	2788	72	42.9	65	7	0	27	237	30	37.1
Maynard, Brad, N.Y. Giants...............	101	4566	63	45.2	101	8	0	53	587	33	37.8
Player, Scott, Arizona.......................	81	3378	67	41.7	82	6	1	38	313	12	35.9
Roby, Reggie, San Francisco	60	2511	66	41.9	60	6	0	34	332	14	34.3
Royals, Mark, New Orleans	88	4017	64	45.6	88	10	0	52	649	26	36.0
Sauerbrun, Todd, Chicago	15	741	71	49.4	15	3	0	5	50	6	42.1
Stryzinski, Dan, Atlanta....................	74	2963	55	40.0	74	7	0	20	112	25	36.6
Turk, Matt, Washington	93	4103	69	44.1	94	9	1	31	260	33	39.0
Tuten, Rick, St. Louis	95	4202	64	44.2	95	10	0	58	652	16	35.3
Walter, Ken, Carolina	77	3131	59	40.7	77	5	0	20	94	20	38.1

PLAYERS WITH TWO CLUBS

Player, Team	Net Punts	Yards	Long	Avg.	Total Punts	TB	Blk.	Opp. Ret.	Ret. Yds.	In 20	Net Avg.
Kidd, John, Detroit............................	13	520	54	40.0	13	0	0	8	66	1	34.9
Kidd, John, N.Y. Jets	28	1166	57	41.6	28	2	0	12	93	8	36.9

1998 STATISTICS Punting

PUNT RETURNS

TEAM

AFC

Team	No.	FC	Yds.	Avg.	Long	TD
Jacksonville......	45	14	581	12.9	t85	1
Baltimore.........	43	12	541	12.6	t87	2
San Diego........	45	14	542	12.0	56	0
New England.....	33	17	395	12.0	39	0
Miami..............	46	15	542	11.8	39	0
Oakland............	50	14	564	11.3	t75	2
Denver.............	38	8	399	10.5	44	0
Seattle.............	41	10	428	10.4	t74	2
Indianapolis......	34	11	340	10.0	53	0
Buffalo.............	37	11	369	10.0	73	0
Kansas City......	38	12	316	8.3	37	0
Pittsburgh........	33	16	269	8.2	47	0
Cincinnati........	29	22	234	8.1	t65	1
Tennessee........	38	17	280	7.4	25	0
N.Y. Jets	43	15	315	7.3	23	0
AFC total	593	208	6115	10.3	t87	8
AFC average .	39.5	13.9	407.7	10.3	...	0.5

t—touchdown.

NFC

Team	No.	FC	Yds.	Avg.	Long	TD
Tampa Bay........	41	15	559	13.6	t95	2
New Orleans	32	24	408	12.8	76	0
Dallas..............	39	13	493	12.6	t69	2
Chicago............	25	15	291	11.6	t93	1
Washington	44	18	506	11.5	47	0
Carolina	44	11	464	10.5	35	0
St. Louis	41	25	415	10.1	t71	1
Minnesota........	29	20	289	10.0	53	0
San Francisco ...	47	10	406	8.6	t72	1
Green Bay	48	21	412	8.6	t71	1
Philadelphia	34	19	285	8.4	40	0
Atlanta	40	24	304	7.6	23	0
N.Y. Giants.......	35	22	252	7.2	39	0
Arizona	43	7	295	6.9	24	0
Detroit.............	36	19	212	5.9	23	0
NFC total	578	263	5591	9.7	t95	8
NFC average .	38.5	17.5	372.7	9.7	...	0.5
NFL total	1171	471	11706	...	t95	16
NFL average .	39.0	15.7	390.2	10.0	...	0.5

INDIVIDUAL

BESTS OF THE SEASON

Yards per attempt, season
NFC: 15.6—Deion Sanders, Dallas.
AFC: 12.9—Reggie Barlow, Jacksonville.

Yards, season
AFC: 555—Reggie Barlow, Jacksonville.
NFC: 506—Brian Mitchell, Washington.

Yards, game
AFC: 134—Reggie Barlow, Jacksonville vs. Kansas City, Sept. 13 (3 returns, 1 TD).
NFC: 106—Glyn Milburn, Chicago at Tampa Bay, Sept. 20 (2 returns, 1 TD).

Longest
NFC: 95—Jacquez Green, Tampa Bay at Green Bay, Sept. 13 (TD).
AFC: 87—Jermaine Lewis, Baltimore vs. Cincinnati, Sept. 27 (TD).

Returns, season
NFC: 47—R.W. McQuarters, San Francisco.
AFC: 45—Desmond Howard, Oakland.

Returns, game
AFC: 8—Latorio Rachal, San Diego at Oakland, Oct. 11 (105 yards); Desmond Howard, Oakland vs. San Diego, Oct. 11 (76 yards).
NFC: 8—Terry Fair, Detroit at Philadelphia, Nov. 8 (43 yards).

Fair catches, season
NFC: 25—Eddie Kennison, St. Louis.
AFC: 19—Damon Gibson, Cincinnati.

Touchdowns, season
AFC: 2—Joey Galloway, Seattle; Jermaine Lewis, Baltimore; Desmond Howard, Oakland.
NFC: 2—Deion Sanders, Dallas.

NFL LEADERS

Player, Team	No.	FC	Yds.	Avg.	Long	TD
Sanders, Deion, Dallas............	24	8	375	15.6	t69	2
Green, Jacquez, Tampa Bay	30	9	453	15.1	t95	1
Hastings, Andre, New Orleans .	22	17	307	14.0	76	0
Barlow, Reggie, Jacksonville*..	43	14	555	12.9	t85	1

Player, Team	No.	FC	Yds.	Avg.	Long	TD
Lewis, Jermaine, Baltimore*....	32	10	405	12.7	t87	2
Buckley, Terrell, Miami*..........	29	3	354	12.2	35	0
Rachal, Latorio, San Diego*	32	8	387	12.1	56	0
Howard, Desmond, Oakland* ..	45	13	541	12.0	t75	2
Milburn, Glyn, Chicago	25	15	291	11.6	t93	1
Mitchell, Brian, Washington.....	44	18	506	11.5	47	0
Gordon, Darrien, Denver*........	34	6	379	11.1	44	0
Oliver, Winslow, Carolina	44	11	464	10.5	35	0
Kennison, Eddie, St. Louis	40	25	415	10.4	t71	0
Palmer, David, Minnesota	28	18	289	10.3	53	0
Galloway, Joey, Seattle*..........	25	5	251	10.0	t74	2

*AFC.
t—touchdown.
Leader based on average return, minimum 20.

AFC

Player, Team	No.	FC	Yds.	Avg.	Long	TD
Archie, Mike, Tennessee..........	7	6	52	7.4	22	0
Arnold, Jahine, Pittsburgh	4	1	19	4.8	8	0
Bailey, Aaron, Indianapolis	19	4	176	9.3	33	0
Barlow, Reggie, Jacksonville	43	14	555	12.9	t85	1
Belser, Jason, Indianapolis	1	0	53	53.0	53	0
Blackwell, Will, Pittsburgh	4	4	22	5.5	13	0
Brooks, Bucky, Oakland	1	0	0	0.0	0	0
Brown, Tim, Oakland................	3	1	23	7.7	8	0
Brown, Troy, New England.......	17	8	225	13.2	39	0
Buckley, Terrell, Miami............	29	3	354	12.2	35	0
Canty, Chris, New England.......	16	7	170	10.6	36	0
Clay, Willie, New England........	0	2	...	...	...	0
Coghill, George, Denver	3	2	20	6.7	8	0
Coleman, Andre, Pittsburgh.....	10	3	53	5.3	12	0
Frost, Scott, N.Y. Jets	1	0	0	0.0	0	0
Gaiter, Tony, San Diego	13	6	155	11.9	49	0
Galloway, Joey, Seattle...........	25	5	251	10.0	t74	2
Gibson, Damon, Cincinnati	27	19	218	8.1	t65	1
Gordon, Darrien, Denver	34	6	379	11.1	44	0
Hawkins, Courtney, Pittsburgh.	15	8	175	11.7	47	0
Horn, Joe, Kansas City............	1	0	6	6.0	6	0
Howard, Desmond, Oakland	45	13	541	12.0	t75	2
Hughes, Danan, Kansas City	2	0	10	5.0	11	0

Player, Team	No.	FC	Yds.	Avg.	Long	TD
Johnson, Leon, N.Y. Jets	29	12	203	7.0	23	0
Johnson, Pat, Baltimore	1	0	6	6.0	6	0
Jordan, Charles, Miami	5	4	47	9.4	24	0
Joseph, Kerry, Seattle	15	5	182	12.1	66	0
Lewis, Jermaine, Baltimore	32	10	405	12.7	t87	2
Lockett, Kevin, Kansas City	7	1	36	5.1	16	0
Logan, Mike, Jacksonville	2	0	26	13.0	17	0
Mason, Derrick, Tennessee	31	11	228	7.4	25	0
McDuffie, O.J., Miami	12	8	141	11.8	39	0
McGuire, Kaipo, Indianapolis	2	1	4	2.0	4	0
Meggett, David, N.Y. Jets	5	0	40	8.0	18	0
Paul, Tito, Denver	1	0	0	0.0	0	0
Poole, Tyrone, Indianapolis	12	6	107	8.9	16	0
Prior, Anthony, Oakland	1	0	0	0.0	0	0
Rachal, Latorio, San Diego	32	8	387	12.1	56	0
Richardson, Tony, Kansas City	1	0	0	0.0	0	0
Roe, James, Baltimore	9	2	87	9.7	19	0
Thompson, Bennie, Baltimore	1	0	43	43.0	43	0
Vanover, Tamarick, K.C.	27	11	264	9.8	37	0
Ward, Dedric, N.Y. Jets	8	3	72	9.0	20	0
Williams, Kevin, Buffalo	37	11	369	10.0	73	0
Williams, Stepfret, Cincinnati	2	3	16	8.0	10	0

t—touchdown.

NFC

Player, Team	No.	FC	Yds.	Avg.	Long	TD
Abrams, Kevin, Detroit	2	1	12	6.0	16	0
Barber, Ronde, Tampa Bay	1	0	23	23.0	t23	1
Boyd, Tommie, Detroit	4	0	11	2.8	3	0
Buchanan, Ray, Atlanta	1	0	4	4.0	4	0
Dwight, Tim, Atlanta	31	13	263	8.5	23	0
Fair, Terry, Detroit	30	15	189	6.3	23	0
Green, Jacquez, Tampa Bay	30	9	453	15.1	t95	1
Guliford, Eric, New Orleans	10	7	101	10.1	40	0
Harris, Al, Philadelphia	1	0	-2	-2.0	-2	0
Harris, Ronnie, Sea.-Atl.*	2	6	-6	-3.0	-1	0
Hastings, Andre, New Orleans	22	17	307	14.0	76	0
Horne, Tony, St. Louis	1	0	0	0.0	0	0
Hughes, Tyrone, Dallas	10	3	93	9.3	35	0
Kennison, Eddie, St. Louis	40	25	415	10.4	t71	1
Kinchen, Todd, Atlanta	6	5	38	6.3	9	0
Mathis, Kevin, Dallas	2	1	3	1.5	5	0
Mathis, Terance, Atlanta	1	0	0	0.0	0	0
Mayes, Derrick, Green Bay	1	0	9	9.0	9	0
McQuarters, R.W., S.F.	47	10	406	8.6	t72	1
Metcalf, Eric, Arizona	43	7	295	6.9	24	0
Milburn, Glyn, Chicago	25	15	291	11.6	t93	1
Mitchell, Brian, Washington	44	18	506	11.5	47	0
Moss, Randy, Minnesota	1	2	0	0.0	0	0
Oliver, Winslow, Carolina	44	11	464	10.5	35	0
Palmer, David, Minnesota	28	18	289	10.3	53	0
Preston, Roell, Green Bay	44	17	398	9.0	t71	1
Prior, Mike, Green Bay	1	4	0	0.0	0	0
Rossum, Allen, Philadelphia	22	7	187	8.5	25	0
Sanders, Deion, Dallas	24	8	375	15.6	t69	2
Schroeder, Bill, Green Bay	2	0	5	2.5	3	0
Smith, Kevin, Dallas	1	0	11	11.0	11	0
Solomon, Freddie, Philadelphia	11	12	100	9.1	40	0
Stablein, Brian, Detroit		3	0	...	...	0
Toomer, Amani, N.Y. Giants	35	22	252	7.2	39	0
Warren, Chris, Dallas	2	1	11	5.5	6	0
Williams, Karl, Tampa Bay	10	6	83	8.3	18	0

t—touchdown.
*Includes both AFC and NFC statistics.

PLAYERS WITH TWO CLUBS

Player, Team	No.	FC	Yds.	Avg.	Long	TD
Harris, Ronnie, Seattle	1	0	-5	-5.0	-5	0
Harris, Ronnie, Atlanta	1	6	-1	-1.0	-1	0

1998 STATISTICS Punt returns

KICKOFF RETURNS

AFC

Team	No.	Yds.	Avg.	Long	TD
Baltimore	69	1700	24.6	t97	2
Miami	53	1297	24.5	55	0
Denver	58	1402	24.2	t95	1
Cincinnati	72	1710	23.8	t97	1
Seattle	64	1510	23.6	t90	1
N.Y. Jets	57	1285	22.5	62	0
Jacksonville	61	1366	22.4	91	0
New England	62	1330	21.5	68	0
Kansas City	63	1319	20.9	62	0
Buffalo	56	1168	20.9	46	0
Tennessee	56	1148	20.5	50	0
Pittsburgh	55	1112	20.2	44	0
Indianapolis	71	1432	20.2	44	0
Oakland	62	1208	19.5	42	0
San Diego	70	1293	18.5	36	0
AFC total	929	20280	21.8	t97	5
AFC average	61.9	1352.0	21.8	...	0.3

t—touchdown.

NFC

Team	No.	Yds.	Avg.	Long	TD
Green Bay	60	1547	25.8	t101	2
Atlanta	46	1157	25.2	t93	1
Detroit	68	1700	25.0	t105	2
Chicago	66	1595	24.2	t94	2
Carolina	76	1834	24.1	t99	1
Tampa Bay	59	1399	23.7	60	0
Dallas	51	1191	23.4	42	0
Minnesota	54	1238	22.9	t88	1
Philadelphia	60	1363	22.7	54	0
New Orleans	62	1354	21.8	t100	1
St. Louis	68	1472	21.6	t102	1
Washington	70	1512	21.6	t101	1
Arizona	63	1314	20.9	59	0
N.Y. Giants	66	1286	19.5	t90	1
San Francisco	59	1108	18.8	45	0
NFC total	928	21070	22.7	t105	13
NFC average	61.9	1404.7	22.7	...	0.9
NFL total	1857	41350	...	t105	18
NFL average	61.9	1378.3	22.3	...	0.6

INDIVIDUAL

BESTS OF THE SEASON

Yards per attempt, season
NFC: 28.0—Terry Fair, Detroit.
AFC: 27.6—Corey Harris, Baltimore.

Yards, season
NFC: 1550—Glyn Milburn, Chicago.
AFC: 1216—Vaughn Hebron, Denver.

Yards, game
NFC: 256—Roell Preston, Green Bay vs. Minnesota, Oct. 5 (8 returns, 1 TD).
AFC: 243—Corey Harris, Baltimore vs. Minnesota, Dec. 13 (8 returns, 1 TD).

Longest
NFC: 105—Terry Fair, Detroit vs. Tampa Bay, Sept. 28 (TD).
AFC: 97—Tremain Mack, Cincinnati at Baltimore, Sept. 27 (TD). Pat Johnson, Baltimore vs. Minnesota, Dec. 13 (TD).

Returns, season
NFC: 62—Glyn Milburn, Chicago.
AFC: 49—Desmond Howard, Oakland.

Returns, game
NFC: 9—Michael Bates, Carolina at Atlanta, Oct. 4 (200 yards).
AFC: 8—Corey Harris, Baltimore vs. Minnesota, Dec. 13 (243 yards, 1 TD).

Touchdowns, season
NFC: 2—Terry Fair, Detroit; Roell Preston, Green Bay; Glyn Milburn, Chicago.
AFC: 1—Held by five players.

NFL LEADERS

Player, Team	No.	Yds.	Avg.	Long	TD
Fair, Terry, Detroit	51	1428	28.0	t105	2
Harris, Corey, Baltimore*	35	965	27.6	t95	1
Dwight, Tim, Atlanta	36	973	27.0	t93	1
Broussard, Steve, Seattle*	29	781	26.9	t90	1
Hebron, Vaughn, Denver*	46	1216	26.4	t95	1
Preston, Roell, Green Bay	57	1497	26.3	t101	2
Mack, Tremain, Cincinnati*	45	1165	25.9	t97	1

Player, Team	No.	Yds.	Avg.	Long	TD
Avery, John, Miami*	43	1085	25.2	55	0
Bates, Michael, Carolina	59	1480	25.1	t99	1
Milburn, Glyn, Chicago	62	1550	25.0	t94	2
Dunn, David, Pittsburgh*	21	525	25.0	44	0
Barlow, Reggie, Jacksonville*	30	747	24.9	91	0
Mathis, Kevin, Dallas	25	621	24.8	42	0
Rossum, Allen, Philadelphia	44	1080	24.5	54	0
Glenn, Aaron, N.Y. Jets*	24	585	24.4	62	0

*AFC.
t—touchdown.
Leader based on average return, minimum 20.

AFC

Player, Team	No.	Yds.	Avg.	Long	TD
Amey, Vince, Oakland	1	0	0.0	0	0
Anders, Kimble, Kansas City	1	16	16.0	16	0
Archie, Mike, Tennessee	42	913	21.7	50	0
Arnold, Jahine, Pittsburgh	3	78	26.0	31	0
Avery, John, Miami	43	1085	25.2	55	0
Bailey, Aaron, Indianapolis	34	759	22.3	44	0
Banks, Tavian, Jacksonville	5	133	26.6	65	0
Barlow, Reggie, Jacksonville	30	747	24.9	91	0
Battaglia, Marco, Cincinnati	1	5	5.0	5	0
Baxter, Fred, N.Y. Jets	1	8	8.0	8	0
Bennett, Brandon, Cincinnati	3	61	20.3	21	0
Bieniemy, Eric, Cincinnati	5	87	17.4	22	0
Blackwell, Will, Pittsburgh	20	382	19.1	43	0
Brady, Kyle, N.Y. Jets	1	20	20.0	20	0
Branch, Calvin, Oakland	5	70	14.0	27	0
Broussard, Steve, Seattle	29	781	26.9	t90	1
Brown, Reggie, Seattle	4	44	11.0	19	0
Bruener, Mark, Pittsburgh	0	-7	...	-7	0
Bruschi, Tedy, New England	1	4	4.0	4	0
Burke, John, San Diego	1	5	5.0	5	0
Burns, Keith, Denver	2	17	8.5	17	0
Bynum, Kenny, San Diego	19	345	18.2	30	0
Canty, Chris, New England	11	198	18.0	29	0
Clark, Rico, Indianapolis	3	38	12.7	15	0
Cotton, Kenyon, Baltimore	2	33	16.5	18	0
Cullors, Derrick, New England	45	1085	24.1	68	0

Player, Team	No.	Yds.	Avg.	Long	TD
Cummings, Joe, Buffalo	1	21	21.0	21	0
Dilger, Ken, Indianapolis	1	14	14.0	14	0
Dunn, David, Pittsburgh	21	525	25.0	44	0
Eaton, Chad, New England	1	13	13.0	13	0
Elias, Keith, Indianapolis	14	317	22.6	29	0
Fauria, Christian, Seattle	1	0	0.0	0	0
Fletcher, Terrell, San Diego	3	71	23.7	36	0
Fordham, Todd, Jacksonville	1	0	0.0	0	0
Gaiter, Tony, San Diego	16	295	18.4	33	0
Gash, Sam, Buffalo	3	41	13.7	17	0
Gibson, Damon, Cincinnati	17	372	21.9	30	0
Gibson, Oliver, Pittsburgh	1	9	9.0	9	0
Glenn, Aaron, N.Y. Jets	24	585	24.4	62	0
Graham, Jay, Baltimore	3	52	17.3	22	0
Green, Ahman, Seattle	27	620	23.0	57	0
Harris, Corey, Baltimore	35	965	27.6	t95	1
Harris, Jackie, Tennessee	1	3	3.0	3	0
Hartley, Frank, San Diego	1	11	11.0	11	0
Hebron, Vaughn, Denver	46	1216	26.4	t95	1
Hetherington, Chris, Indianapolis	5	71	14.2	20	0
Holmes, Darick, Buffalo	1	20	20.0	20	0
Holmes, Priest, Baltimore	2	30	15.0	19	0
Horn, Joe, Kansas City	f11	233	21.2	37	0
Howard, Desmond, Oakland	49	1040	21.2	42	0
Huntley, Richard, Pittsburgh	6	119	19.8	26	0
Jacox, Kendyl, San Diego	1	0	0.0	0	0
Jacquet, Nate, Miami	4	103	25.8	37	0
Johnson, Leon, N.Y. Jets	16	366	22.9	37	0
Johnson, Lonnie, Buffalo	3	18	6.0	16	0
Johnson, Pat, Baltimore	16	399	24.9	t97	1
Jones, Charlie, San Diego	2	25	12.5	17	0
Jones, Damon, Jacksonville	2	-1	-0.5	0	0
Jones, George, Jacksonville	1	21	21.0	21	0
Joseph, Kerry, Seattle	2	49	24.5	24	0
Kinchen, Brian, Baltimore	2	33	16.5	21	0
Lewis, Jermaine, Baltimore	6	145	24.2	37	0
Logan, Mike, Jacksonville	18	414	23.0	53	0
Loville, Derek, Denver	6	105	17.5	25	0
Lyons, Mitch, Pittsburgh	2	-4	-2.0	6	0
Mack, Tremain, Cincinnati	45	1165	25.9	t97	1
Manusky, Greg, Kansas City	3	20	6.7	12	0
Marion, Brock, Miami	6	109	18.2	28	0
Mason, Derrick, Tennessee	8	154	19.3	26	0
McAfee, Fred, Pittsburgh	1	10	10.0	25	0
McCardell, Keenan, Jacksonville	1	15	15.0	15	0
McGuire, Kaipo, Indianapolis	4	75	18.8	28	0
Meggett, David, N.Y. Jets	1	16	16.0	16	0
Mitchell, Pete, Jacksonville	2	27	13.5	14	0
Moore, Will, Jacksonville	0	10	...	10	0
Morrison, Steve, Indianapolis	1	2	2.0	2	0
Morton, Mike, Oakland	1	3	3.0	3	0
Parten, Ty, Kansas City	2	22	11.0	22	0
Pollard, Marcus, Indianapolis	1	4	4.0	4	0
Potts, Roosevelt, Baltimore	1	3	3.0	3	0
Rachal, Latorio, San Diego	11	192	17.5	25	0
Ransom, Derrick, Kansas City	f1	0	0.0	0	0
Riemersma, Jay, Buffalo	1	9	9.0	9	0
Roan, Michael, Tennessee	1	4	4.0	11	0
Roe, James, Baltimore	2	40	20.0	27	0
Roye, Orpheus, Pittsburgh	1	0	0.0	0	0
Sadowski, Troy, Jacksonville	1	0	0.0	0	0
Shaw, Sedrick, New England	1	16	16.0	16	0
Shedd, Kenny, Oakland	2	32	16.0	21	0
Shehee, Rashaan, Kansas City	4	72	18.0	20	0
Smith, Detron, Denver	3	51	17.0	21	0
Stephens, Tremayne, San Diego	16	349	21.8	36	0
Sullivan, Chris, New England	2	14	7.0	9	0
Tanuvasa, Maa, Denver	1	13	13.0	13	0
Thomas, Rodney, Tennessee	3	64	21.3	39	0
Vanover, Tamarick, Kansas City	41	956	23.3	62	0
Ward, Dedric, N.Y. Jets	3	60	20.0	23	0
Warren, Lamont, Indianapolis	8	152	19.0	26	0
Whigham, Larry, New England	1	0	0.0	0	0
Williams, Kevin, Buffalo	47	1059	22.5	46	0
Williams, Kevin, N.Y. Jets	11	230	20.9	31	0
Williams, Rodney, Oakland	4	63	15.8	21	0
Williams, Stepfret, Cincinnati	1	20	20.0	20	0
Wilson, Robert, Seattle	1	16	16.0	16	0
Wycheck, Frank, Tennessee	1	10	10.0	10	0

t—touchdown.
f—includes at least one fair catch.

NFC

Player, Team	No.	Yds.	Avg.	Long	TD
Alstott, Mike, Tampa Bay	1	8	8.0	8	0
Anthony, Reidel, Tampa Bay	46	1118	24.3	60	0
Asher, Jamie, Washington	1	8	8.0	8	0
Barber, Tiki, N.Y. Giants	14	250	17.9	32	0
Bates, Michael, Carolina	59	1480	25.1	t99	1
Bech, Brett, New Orleans	1	20	20.0	20	0
Bownes, Fabien, Chicago	1	19	19.0	19	0
Boyd, Tommie, Detroit	8	163	20.4	26	0
Bradford, Corey, Green Bay	2	33	16.5	24	0
Brady, Jeff, Carolina	1	8	8.0	8	0
Brooks, Barrett, Philadelphia	1	7	7.0	7	0
Burnett, Chester, Washington	1	5	5.0	5	0
Chancey, Robert, Chicago	2	18	9.0	18	0
Clemons, Charlie, St. Louis	1	0	0.0	0	0
Comella, Greg, N.Y. Giants	1	12	12.0	12	0
Copeland, Russell, Philadelphia	3	52	17.3	23	0
Craver, Aaron, New Orleans	7	212	30.3	t100	1
Davis, Billy, Dallas	1	10	10.0	10	0
Davis, Troy, New Orleans	2	21	10.5	19	0
Dunn, Warrick, Tampa Bay	1	25	25.0	25	0
Dwight, Tim, Atlanta	f36	973	27.0	t93	1
Ellison, Jerry, Tampa Bay	1	19	19.0	19	0
Fair, Terry, Detroit	51	1428	28.0	t105	2
Fletcher, London, St. Louis	5	72	14.4	20	0
Floyd, William, Carolina	1	22	22.0	22	0
Gedney, Chris, Arizona	2	12	6.0	7	0
Green, Harold, Atlanta	1	24	24.0	24	0
Green, Jacquez, Tampa Bay	10	229	22.9	44	0
Guliford, Eric, New Orleans	18	431	23.9	34	0
Hankton, Karl, Philadelphia	1	18	18.0	18	0
Harris, Ronnie, Atlanta	1	16	16.0	16	0
Hastings, Andre, New Orleans	1	16	16.0	16	0
Hayden, Aaron, Philadelphia	1	22	22.0	22	0
Henley, June, St. Louis	1	13	13.0	13	0
Horne, Tony, St. Louis	56	1306	23.3	t102	1
Hughes, Tyrone, Dallas	11	274	24.9	36	0
Ismail, Qadry, New Orleans	28	590	21.1	39	0
Jenkins, James, Washington	1	0	0.0	0	0
Jensen, Jerry, Carolina	1	9	9.0	9	0
Johnson, Anthony, Carolina	2	12	6.0	9	0
Jones, Mike D., St. Louis	1	2	2.0	2	0
Kirby, Terry, San Francisco	17	340	20.0	33	0
Kozlowski, Brian, Atlanta	1	12	12.0	12	0
LaFleur, David, Dallas	1	12	12.0	12	0
Levy, Chuck, San Francisco	22	383	17.4	30	0
Little, Earl, New Orleans	4	64	16.0	20	0
Mathis, Kevin, Dallas	25	621	24.8	42	0
McKenzie, Keith, Green Bay	1	17	17.0	17	0
McPhail, Jerris, Detroit	6	71	11.8	20	0
McQuarters, R.W., San Francisco	17	339	19.9	45	0
Metcalf, Eric, Arizona	57	1218	21.4	59	0
Milburn, Glyn, Chicago	62	1550	25.0	t94	2
Mitchell, Brian, Washington	59	1337	22.7	t101	1
Ogden, Jeff, Dallas	3	65	21.7	28	0
Oliver, Winslow, Carolina	2	43	21.5	25	0
Palelei, Lonnie, N.Y. Giants	3	14	4.7	13	0
Palmer, David, Minnesota	50	1176	23.5	t88	1
Patten, David, N.Y. Giants	43	928	21.6	t90	1
Pittman, Michael, Arizona	4	84	21.0	22	0

1998 STATISTICS Kickoff returns

Player, Team	No.	Yds.	Avg.	Long	TD
Preston, Roell, Green Bay	57	1497	26.3	t101	2
Richie, David, San Francisco	f1	11	11.0	11	0
Rivers, Ron, Detroit......................	2	15	7.5	9	0
Rossum, Allen, Philadelphia	44	1080	24.5	54	0
Saleh, Tarek, Carolina...................	1	8	8.0	8	0
Sanders, Deion, Dallas	1	16	16.0	16	0
Sellers, Mike, Washington.............	2	33	16.5	14	0
Smith, Irv, San Francisco	2	35	17.5	23	0
Staley, Duce, Philadelphia	1	19	19.0	19	0
Stone, Dwight, Carolina.................	9	252	28.0	45	0
Tate, Robert, Minnesota	2	43	21.5	23	0
Thomas, J.T., St. Louis.................	4	79	19.8	24	0
Thrash, James, Washington	6	129	21.5	39	0

Player, Team	No.	Yds.	Avg.	Long	TD
Tomich, Jared, New Orleans..........	1	0	0.0	0	0
Toomer, Amani, N.Y. Giants..........	4	66	16.5	31	0
Turner, Kevin, Philadelphia	1	15	15.0	15	0
Vardell, Tommy, Detroit................	1	23	23.0	23	0
Walker, Corey, Philadelphia	8	150	18.8	28	0
Warren, Chris, Dallas....................	5	90	18.0	23	0
Wheatley, Tyrone, N.Y. Giants.......	1	16	16.0	16	0
Wiegmann, Casey, Chicago	1	8	8.0	8	0
Williams, Elijah, Atlanta................	7	132	18.9	28	0
Williams, Moe, Minnesota.............	2	19	9.5	12	0
Williams, Sherman, Dallas.............	4	103	25.8	40	0

t—touchdown.
f—includes at least one fair catch.

1998 STATISTICS *Kickoff returns*

MISCELLANEOUS

CLUB RANKINGS BY YARDS

Team	OFFENSE			DEFENSE		
	Total	Rush	Pass	Total	Rush	Pass
Arizona.............	13	21	8	21	20	17
Atlanta..............	7	6	11	8	2	21
Baltimore..........	26	20	25	22	17	24
Buffalo..............	6	3	12	6	5	14
Carolina............	20	28	14	30	26	28
Chicago............	21	17	23	14	19	15
Cincinnati.........	17	19	17	28	30	12
Dallas...............	8	8	9	18	12	22
Denver..............	3	2	7	11	3	26
Detroit..............	14	10	19	15	25	8
Green Bay	5	25	3	4	4	10
Indianapolis......	12	26	6	29	29	16
Jacksonville......	10	5	20	25	22	23
Kansas City	19	23	16	9	18	7
Miami...............	16	24	10	3	6	6
Minnesota	2	11	*1	13	11	19
New England	11	27	5	20	7	25
New Orleans......	28	30	18	26	16	30
N.Y. Giants	29	12	28	19	23	13
N.Y. Jets	4	13	4	7	14	9
Oakland	18	16	21	5	15	4
Philadelphia......	30	14	30	17	27	*1
Pittsburgh	25	7	29	12	13	18
St. Louis...........	27	29	22	10	24	3
San Diego	24	15	26	*1	*1	11
San Francisco ...	*1	*1	2	23	T9	29
Seattle	23	22	24	27	21	27
Tampa Bay	22	4	27	2	8	2
Tennessee........	9	9	15	16	T9	20
Washington.......	15	18	13	24	28	5

*NFL leader.

TAKEAWAYS / GIVEAWAYS

	TAKEAWAYS			GIVEAWAYS			
	Int.	Fum.	Tot.	Int.	Fum.	Tot.	Net Diff.
New Orleans	21	11	32	19	14	33	-1
Carolina	19	14	33	18	17	35	-2
Detroit	12	9	21	13	12	25	-4
Tampa Bay.........	12	14	26	18	13	31	-5
Chicago	14	14	28	13	21	34	-6
Washington	13	8	21	14	15	29	-8
Philadelphia.......	9	8	17	18	8	26	-9
St. Louis............	16	7	23	18	15	33	-10
Green Bay..........	13	10	23	23	11	34	-11

CLUB LEADERS

	Offense	Defense
First downs	S.F. 381	T.B. 244
Rushing................................	Den. 135	Atl. 65
Passing................................	S.F. 223	Phi. 133
Penalty................................	Ari. 38	G.B. 13
Rushes	Buf. 531	Den. 356
Net yards gained	S.D. 2544	S.D. 1140
Average gain........................	S.F. 5.2	S.D. 2.7
Passes attempted	Ind. 576	Cin. 406
Completed	G.B. 361	Cin. 233
Percent completed..................	G.B. 62.8	Mia. 50.0
Total yards gained	S.F. 4510	Phi. 3001
Times sacked........................	Dal. 19	NYG 54
Yards lost	Ind. 109	St.L. 349
Net yards gained	Min. 4328	Phi. 2720
Net yards per pass play..............	Min. 7.76	G.B. 5.19
Yards gained per completion.......	Atl. 15.80	Oak. 10.77
Combined net yards gained	S.F. 6800	S.D. 4208
Percent total yards rushing	T.B. 45.2	Atl. 25.4
Percent total yards passing........	G.B. 72.9	Phi. 53.0
Ball-control plays....................	S.F. 1100	T.B. 925
Average yards per play	Min. 6.21	S.D. 4.25
Avg. time of possession	Atl. 33:10	—
Third-down efficiency	Min. 51.4	Oak. 26.3
Interceptions	—	Mia. 29
Yards returned.....................	—	N.O. 466
Returned for TD	—	Sea. 8
Punts	Phi. 104	—
Yards punted	NYG 4566	—
Average yards per punt	Ten. 47.2	—
Punt returns	Oak. 50	Atl., Car. 20
Yards returned.....................	Jac. 581	Car. 94
Average yds. per return.............	T.B. 13.6	Car. 4.7
Returned for TD	5 tied with 2	—
Kickoff returns	Car. 76	Phi. 40
Yards returned.....................	Car. 1834	Phi. 764
Average yards per return.........	G.B. 25.8	Dal. 18.5
Returned for TD	4 tied with 2	—
Total points scored	Min. 556	Mia. 265
Total TDs	Min. 64	Mia. 28
TDs rushing.........................	Den. 26	Mia. 6
TDs passing.........................	Min., S.F. 41	T.B. 15
TDs on ret. and recov.	Sea. 13	4 tied with 1
Extra point kicks....................	Min. 59	Pit. 23
2-Pt. conversions	S.F. 5	6 tied with 0
Safeties..............................	4 tied with 2	—
Field goals made	Ten. 36	Den. 14
Field goals attempted	Buf. 41	Dal., Min. 19
Percent successful	Min. 100.0	S.F. 59.4
Extra points	Min. 62	Pit. 25

TAKEAWAYS/GIVEAWAYS

AFC

	TAKEAWAYS			GIVEAWAYS			
	Int.	Fum.	Tot.	Int.	Fum.	Tot.	Net Diff.
Buffalo	18	13	31	14	6	20	11
Denver...............	19	11	30	14	6	20	10
Jacksonville.......	13	17	30	12	8	20	10
Miami	29	7	36	16	12	28	8
Seattle	24	18	42	18	16	34	8
New England	24	7	31	17	7	24	7
N.Y. Jets	21	9	30	13	11	24	6
Kansas City........	13	20	33	18	14	32	1
Tennessee.........	12	7	19	10	9	19	0
Cincinnati	13	7	20	12	10	22	-2
Pittsburgh	16	13	29	20	12	32	-3
Baltimore...........	17	6	23	15	15	30	-7
Oakland	21	14	35	25	18	43	-8
Indianapolis........	8	11	19	28	5	33	-14
San Diego..........	20	7	27	34	17	51	-24

NFC

	TAKEAWAYS			GIVEAWAYS			
	Int.	Fum.	Tot.	Int.	Fum.	Tot.	Net Diff.
Atlanta	19	25	44	15	9	24	20
Minnesota	19	15	34	16	4	20	14
Dallas	14	12	26	8	7	15	11
Arizona	20	19	39	20	16	36	3
San Francisco.....	21	12	33	15	15	30	3
N.Y. Giants.........	19	7	26	15	9	24	2

1998 STATISTICS Miscellaneous

OFFENSE

	Bal.	Buf.	Cin.	Den.	Ind.	Jac.	K.C.	Mia.	N.E.	NYJ	Oak.	Pit.	S.D.	Sea.	Ten.
First downs	243	319	271	347	298	287	289	269	281	338	273	268	272	267	308
Rushing	86	115	92	135	77	111	103	73	68	99	89	106	95	92	118
Passing	140	176	148	186	190	153	153	176	184	207	156	135	146	144	171
Penalty	17	28	31	26	31	23	33	20	29	32	28	27	31	31	19
Rushes	408	531	405	525	384	487	433	458	403	500	449	490	460	426	462
Net yards gained	1629	2161	1639	2468	1486	2102	1548	1535	1480	1879	1727	2034	1728	1626	1970
Average gain	4.0	4.1	4.0	4.7	3.9	4.3	3.6	3.4	3.7	3.8	3.8	4.2	3.8	3.8	4.3
Average yards per game	101.8	135.1	102.4	154.3	92.9	131.4	96.8	95.9	92.5	117.4	107.9	127.1	108.0	101.6	123.1
Passes attempted	477	461	521	491	576	463	543	546	556	532	519	489	566	480	519
Completed	272	269	307	290	326	269	305	316	295	318	282	274	261	273	305
Percent completed	57.0	58.4	58.9	59.1	56.6	58.1	56.2	57.9	53.1	59.8	54.3	56.0	46.1	56.9	58.8
Total yards gained	3152	3621	3545	3808	3739	3343	3472	3582	4004	4032	3534	2781	3115	3219	3482
Times sacked	41	41	53	25	22	39	36	24	40	25	67	35	37	34	35
Yards lost	283	241	360	184	109	231	212	187	344	196	446	229	251	219	191
Net yards gained	2869	3380	3185	3624	3630	3112	3260	3395	3660	3836	3088	2552	2864	3000	3291
Average yards per game	179.3	211.3	199.1	226.5	226.9	194.5	203.8	212.2	228.8	239.8	193.0	159.5	179.0	187.5	205.7
Net yards per pass play	5.54	6.73	5.55	7.02	6.07	6.20	5.63	5.96	6.14	6.89	5.27	4.87	4.75	5.84	5.94
Yards gained per completion	11.59	13.46	11.55	13.13	11.47	12.43	11.38	11.34	13.57	12.68	12.53	10.15	11.93	11.79	11.42
Combined net yards gained	4498	5541	4824	6092	5116	5214	4808	4930	5140	5715	4815	4586	4592	4626	5261
Percent total yards rushing	36.2	39.0	34.0	40.5	29.0	40.3	32.2	31.1	28.8	32.9	35.9	44.4	37.6	35.1	37.4
Percent total yards passing	63.8	61.0	66.0	59.5	71.0	59.7	67.8	68.9	71.2	67.1	64.1	55.6	62.4	64.9	62.6
Average yards per game	281.1	346.3	301.5	380.8	319.8	325.9	300.5	308.1	321.3	357.2	300.9	286.6	287.0	289.1	328.8
Ball-control plays	926	1033	979	1041	982	989	1012	1028	999	1057	1035	1014	1063	940	1016
Average yards per play	4.9	5.4	4.9	5.9	5.2	5.3	4.8	4.8	5.1	5.4	4.7	4.5	4.3	4.9	5.2
Average time of possession	28:04	32:26	28:31	32:08	27:47	28:59	29:53	32:10	28:34	32:17	28:51	30:20	31:17	27:05	31:41
Third-down efficiency	30.9	44.3	33.9	43.5	35.1	42.7	31.8	35.8	38.0	46.0	31.6	38.8	32.9	27.7	40.0
Had intercepted	15	14	12	14	28	12	18	16	17	13	25	20	34	18	10
Yards opponents returned	148	65	206	270	353	216	189	365	197	234	435	169	512	220	88
Returned by opponents for TD	0	0	1	2	2	3	3	2	0	2	5	2	2	2	1
Punts	92	69	81	67	79	85	77	97	74	65	98	82	95	81	69
Yards punted	3948	2882	3578	3097	3583	3824	3255	4064	3294	2637	4256	3565	4174	3568	3258
Average yards per punt	42.9	41.8	44.2	46.2	45.4	45.0	42.3	41.9	44.5	40.6	43.4	43.5	43.9	44.0	47.2
Punt returns	43	37	29	38	34	45	38	46	33	43	50	33	45	41	38
Yards returned	541	369	234	399	340	581	316	542	395	315	564	269	542	428	280
Average yards per return	12.6	10.0	8.1	10.5	10.0	12.9	8.3	11.8	12.0	7.3	11.3	8.2	12.0	10.4	7.4
Returned for TD	2	0	1	0	0	1	0	0	0	0	2	0	0	2	0
Kickoff returns	69	56	72	58	71	61	63	53	62	57	62	55	70	64	56
Yards returned	1700	1168	1710	1402	1432	1366	1319	1297	1330	1285	1208	1112	1293	1510	1148
Average yards per return	24.6	20.9	23.8	24.2	20.2	22.4	20.9	24.5	21.5	22.5	19.5	20.2	18.5	23.6	20.5
Returned for TD	2	0	1	1	0	0	0	0	0	0	0	0	0	1	0
Fumbles	31	17	21	17	10	18	35	25	20	23	38	18	33	30	25
Lost	15	6	10	6	5	8	14	12	7	11	18	12	17	16	9
Out of bounds	2	1	1	2	1	0	3	1	1	1	2	1	0	0	1
Recovered for TD	0	0	0	1	0	0	0	0	0	0	1	1	0	0	0
Penalties	113	123	69	115	106	121	158	106	108	85	127	79	137	117	126
Yards penalized	909	993	620	1023	853	898	1304	864	853	651	986	691	1229	914	1135
Total points scored	269	400	268	501	310	392	327	321	337	416	288	263	241	372	330
Total TDs	29	43	31	62	33	47	35	37	35	49	34	26	23	45	32
TDs rushing	7	13	7	26	7	19	19	10	9	12	6	8	11	11	12
TDs passing	16	28	20	32	26	24	15	23	23	33	21	13	11	21	16
TDs on returns and recoveries	6	2	4	4	0	4	1	4	3	4	7	5	1	13	4
Extra points	24	41	21	58	23	45	34	33	32	45	31	23	19	41	28
Extra point kick att.	24	41	21	59	23	45	34	33	32	46	31	23	19	41	28
2-Pt. conversions	2	0	2	1	4	1	0	0	1	0	1	3	2	2	1
2-Pt. conversions att.	5	2	9	3	10	2	3	3	3	3	3	3	4	4	4
Safeties	2	1	0	0	0	0	1	0	0	1	0	0	1	0	0
Field goals made	21	33	19	23	27	21	27	22	31	25	17	26	26	19	36
Field goals attempted	28	41	27	27	31	26	32	27	39	35	27	32	30	24	40
Percent successful	75.0	80.5	70.4	85.2	87.1	80.8	84.4	81.5	79.5	71.4	63.0	81.3	86.7	79.2	90.0

DEFENSE

	Bal.	Buf.	Cin.	Den.	Ind.	Jac.	K.C.	Mia.	N.E.	NYJ	Oak.	Pit.	S.D.	Sea.	Ten.
First downs	298	283	310	283	341	309	321	257	305	263	273	266	256	337	279
Rushing	90	79	142	80	131	108	119	75	76	87	95	88	72	111	81
Passing	180	168	152	183	181	178	146	148	208	150	150	155	149	197	170
Penalty	28	36	16	20	29	23	56	34	21	26	28	23	35	29	28
Rushes	472	375	558	356	544	450	491	395	447	400	482	479	422	487	414
Net yards gained	1705	1493	2612	1287	2570	2000	1869	1511	1547	1659	1674	1642	1140	1999	1610
Average gain	3.6	4.0	4.7	3.6	4.7	4.4	3.8	3.8	3.5	4.1	3.5	3.4	2.7	4.1	3.9
Average yards per game	106.6	93.3	163.3	80.4	160.6	125.0	116.8	94.4	96.7	103.7	104.6	102.6	71.3	124.9	100.6
Passes attempted	539	532	406	596	461	577	479	504	570	544	497	482	530	597	511
Completed	316	294	233	345	275	325	259	252	336	285	291	268	271	343	319
Percent completed	58.6	55.3	57.4	57.9	59.7	56.3	54.1	50.0	58.9	52.4	58.6	55.6	51.1	57.5	62.4
Total yards gained	3878	3474	3350	3983	3497	3768	3253	3194	3857	3299	3134	3559	3314	3972	3683
Times sacked	39	43	28	47	38	30	40	45	36	36	41	41	39	53	30
Yards lost	286	276	199	335	231	209	268	270	222	259	258	238	246	282	172
Net yards gained	3592	3198	3151	3648	3266	3559	2985	2924	3635	3040	2876	3321	3068	3690	3511
Average yards per game	224.5	199.9	196.9	228.0	204.1	222.4	186.6	182.8	227.2	190.0	179.8	207.6	191.8	230.6	219.4
Net yards per pass play	6.21	5.56	7.26	5.67	6.55	5.86	5.75	5.33	6.00	5.24	5.35	6.35	5.39	5.68	6.49
Yards gained per completion	12.27	11.82	14.38	11.54	12.72	11.59	12.56	12.67	11.48	11.58	10.77	13.28	12.23	11.58	11.55
Combined net yards gained	5297	4691	5763	4935	5836	5559	4854	4435	5182	4699	4550	4963	4208	5689	5121
Percent total yards rushing	32.2	31.8	45.3	26.1	44.0	36.0	38.5	34.1	29.9	35.3	36.8	33.1	27.1	35.1	31.4
Percent total yards passing	67.8	68.2	54.7	73.9	56.0	64.0	61.5	65.9	70.1	64.7	63.2	66.9	72.9	64.9	68.6
Average yards per game	331.1	293.2	360.2	308.4	364.8	347.4	303.4	277.2	323.9	293.7	284.4	310.2	263.0	355.6	320.1
Ball-control plays	1050	950	992	999	1043	1057	1010	944	1053	980	1020	1002	991	1137	955
Average yards per play	5.0	4.9	5.8	4.9	5.6	5.3	4.8	4.7	4.9	4.8	4.5	5.0	4.2	5.0	5.4
Average time of possession	31:56	27:34	31:29	27:52	32:13	31:01	30:07	27:50	31:26	27:43	31:09	29:40	28:44	32:55	29:20
Third-down efficiency	39.2	38.6	44.5	39.1	42.8	36.5	33.8	32.9	42.6	35.6	26.3	37.7	30.0	39.0	37.8
Intercepted by	17	18	13	19	8	13	13	29	24	21	21	16	20	24	12
Yards returned by	161	204	144	439	97	119	187	318	255	263	420	335	203	455	98
Returned for TD	2	1	1	2	0	0	0	4	3	1	3	3	1	8	2
Punts	86	77	64	88	68	78	77	88	73	85	96	76	103	78	74
Yards punted	3653	3459	2850	3733	3032	3395	3248	3986	3100	3587	4300	3482	4546	3397	3190
Average yards per punt	42.5	44.9	44.5	42.4	44.6	43.5	42.2	45.3	42.5	42.2	44.8	45.8	44.1	43.6	43.1
Punt returns	40	32	36	43	42	40	41	43	43	30	53	30	49	33	34
Yards returned	284	374	503	381	451	332	513	339	493	309	787	310	515	369	332
Average yards per return	7.1	11.7	14.0	8.9	10.7	8.3	12.5	7.9	11.5	10.3	14.8	10.3	10.5	11.2	9.8
Returned for TD	1	1	1	0	0	0	1	0	0	1	1	0	1	1	0
Kickoff returns	57	77	46	89	65	76	69	56	71	60	60	64	54	68	55
Yards returned	1168	1638	1199	2006	1688	1858	1374	1227	1335	1370	1388	1212	1484	1311	1114
Average yards per return	20.5	21.3	26.1	22.5	26.0	24.4	19.9	21.9	18.8	22.8	23.1	18.9	27.5	19.3	20.3
Returned for TD	2	0	0	0	1	1	0	1	0	0	0	0	1	0	0
Fumbles	17	21	12	28	29	25	36	25	16	25	26	28	21	34	11
Recovered by	6	13	7	11	11	17	20	7	7	9	14	13	7	18	7
Out of bounds	3	2	0	0	0	1	3	0	1	1	2	2	2	0	1
Recovered for TD	0	0	1	0	0	0	0	1	0	0	0	0	0	1	0
Penalties	122	104	127	113	108	109	138	97	104	109	115	106	120	130	93
Yards penalized	1013	836	1012	865	917	953	1292	875	787	967	921	854	1005	1157	704
Total points scored	335	333	452	309	444	338	363	265	329	266	356	303	342	310	320
Total TDs	37	39	53	38	52	36	44	28	36	30	38	30	38	35	34
TDs rushing	12	11	23	8	20	9	22	6	8	11	8	8	12	13	9
TDs passing	20	27	23	28	27	23	17	17	26	16	22	17	21	18	24
TDs on returns and recoveries	5	1	7	2	5	4	5	5	2	3	8	5	5	4	1
Extra point kicks	35	28	51	31	44	30	43	24	30	26	36	23	37	31	29
Extra point kick att.	35	28	51	31	45	30	43	24	30	27	36	24	37	31	29
2-Pt. conversions	0	4	1	2	2	1	1	2	1	0	1	2	1	0	4
2-Pt. conversions att.	2	11	2	7	6	6	1	4	6	2	2	6	1	4	5
Safeties	0	0	0	2	0	0	0	0	0	0	3	0	0	0	2
Field goals made	26	21	27	14	28	30	18	23	27	20	28	32	25	23	25
Field goals attempted	30	26	31	20	37	35	30	32	32	25	37	41	34	30	30
Percent successful	86.7	80.8	87.1	70.0	75.7	85.7	60.0	71.9	84.4	80.0	75.7	78.0	73.5	76.7	83.3

OFFENSE

	Ari.	Atl.	Car.	Chi.	Dal.	Det.	G.B.	Min.	N.O.	NYG	Phi.	St.L.	S.F.	T.B.	Was.
First downs	315	319	261	264	308	278	329	335	258	263	259	281	381	262	295
Rushing	98	111	68	89	125	94	93	98	67	104	86	81	129	111	84
Passing	179	175	171	154	154	160	210	210	165	129	141	164	223	139	186
Penalty	38	33	22	21	29	24	26	27	26	30	32	36	29	12	25
Rushes	450	516	405	454	499	441	447	450	374	474	427	395	491	523	401
Net yards gained	1627	2101	1458	1713	2014	1955	1526	1936	1325	1889	1775	1385	2544	2148	1685
Average gain	3.6	4.1	3.6	3.8	4.0	4.4	3.4	4.3	3.5	4.0	4.2	3.5	5.2	4.1	4.2
Average yards per game	101.7	131.3	91.1	107.1	125.9	122.2	95.4	121.0	82.8	118.1	110.9	86.6	159.0	134.3	105.3
Passes attempted	552	424	507	494	474	489	575	533	535	507	534	556	556	449	565
Completed	326	237	292	284	279	274	361	327	278	265	282	314	347	234	304
Percent completed	59.1	55.9	57.6	57.5	58.9	56.0	62.8	61.4	52.0	52.3	52.8	56.5	62.4	52.1	53.8
Total yards gained	3768	3744	3624	3277	3546	3398	4340	4492	3514	2822	2730	3381	4510	2787	3724
Times sacked	50	53	31	19	45	39	25	57	35	56	47	53	28	61
Yards lost	286	358	302	224	110	268	230	164	376	256	317	294	254	181	399
Net yards gained	3482	3386	3322	3053	3436	3130	4110	4328	3138	2566	2413	3087	4256	2606	3325
Average yards per game	217.6	211.6	207.6	190.8	214.8	195.6	256.9	270.5	196.1	160.4	150.8	192.9	266.0	162.9	207.8
Net yards per pass play	5.78	7.10	5.92	5.82	6.97	5.86	6.69	7.76	5.30	4.73	4.09	5.12	6.99	5.46	5.31
Yards gained per completion	11.56	15.80	12.41	11.54	12.71	12.40	12.02	13.74	12.64	10.65	9.68	10.77	14.36	11.91	12.25
Combined net yards gained	5109	5487	4780	4766	5450	5085	5636	6264	4463	4455	4188	4472	6800	4754	5010
Percent total yards rushing	31.8	38.3	30.5	35.9	37.0	38.4	27.1	30.9	29.7	42.4	42.4	31.0	37.4	45.2	33.6
Percent total yards passing	68.2	61.7	69.5	64.1	63.0	61.6	72.9	69.1	70.3	57.6	57.6	69.0	62.6	54.8	66.4
Average yards per game	319.3	342.9	298.8	297.9	340.6	317.8	352.3	391.5	278.9	278.4	261.8	279.5	425.0	297.1	313.1
Ball-control plays	1052	993	966	979	992	975	1061	1008	966	1016	1017	998	1100	1000	1027
Average yards per play	4.9	5.5	4.9	4.9	5.5	5.2	5.3	6.2	4.6	4.4	4.1	4.5	6.2	4.8	4.9
Average time of possession	29:15	33:10	28:10	29:26	31:50	29:22	31:37	29:58	28:03	28:21	29:24	28:59	31:52	31:58	28:34
Third-down efficiency	34.9	41.7	37.0	34.9	36.9	34.1	45.4	51.4	35.8	30.6	33.3	34.7	45.5	40.4	31.6
Had intercepted	20	15	18	13	8	13	23	16	19	15	18	18	15	18	14
Yards opponents returned	373	224	179	146	121	198	312	221	186	232	319	194	304	192	169
Returned by opponents for TD	4	2	0	1	1	2	3	1	3	2	2	1	0	2	2
Punts	82	74	77	80	78	82	65	55	90	101	104	95	69	81	97
Yards punted	3378	2963	3131	3411	3342	3506	2788	2458	4089	4566	4339	4202	2835	3340	4216
Average yards per punt	41.2	40.0	40.7	42.6	42.8	42.8	42.9	44.7	45.4	45.2	41.7	44.2	41.1	41.2	43.5
Punt returns	43	40	44	25	39	36	48	29	32	35	34	41	47	41	44
Yards returned	295	304	464	291	493	212	412	289	408	252	285	415	406	559	506
Average yards per return	6.9	7.6	10.5	11.6	12.6	5.9	8.6	10.0	12.8	7.2	8.4	10.1	8.6	13.6	11.5
Returned for TD	0	0	0	1	2	0	1	0	0	0	0	1	1	2	0
Kickoff returns	63	46	76	66	51	68	60	54	62	66	60	68	59	59	70
Yards returned	1314	1157	1834	1595	1191	1700	1547	1238	1354	1286	1363	1472	1108	1399	1512
Average yards per return	20.9	25.2	24.1	24.2	23.4	25.0	25.8	22.9	21.8	19.5	22.7	21.6	18.8	23.7	21.6
Returned for TD	0	1	1	2	0	2	2	1	1	1	0	1	0	0	1
Fumbles	30	24	39	29	18	17	27	10	28	17	20	32	22	23	27
Lost	16	9	17	21	7	12	11	4	14	9	8	15	15	13	15
Out of bounds	1	2	2	1	2	1	6	1	3	1	1	1	1	3	2
Recovered for TD	0	0	0	0	0	0	0	0	0	0	0	0	0	0	0
Penalties	88	116	113	86	128	121	88	116	121	124	102	111	133	99	112
Yards penalized	758	841	931	714	1106	1019	681	1045	928	946	852	945	1156	840	975
Total points scored	325	442	336	276	381	306	408	556	305	287	161	285	479	314	319
Total TDs	36	53	40	30	42	32	46	64	35	32	17	32	61	36	40
TDs rushing	18	18	11	9	21	12	7	17	6	10	10	17	19	12	15
TDs passing	17	28	25	16	17	17	33	41	19	18	7	12	41	21	24
TDs on returns and recoveries	1	7	4	5	4	3	6	6	10	4	0	3	1	3	1
Extra point kicks	36	51	35	27	40	27	41	59	31	32	15	25	49	29	36
Extra point kick att	36	52	37	28	40	29	43	59	31	32	17	26	51	30	37
2-Pt. conversions	0	1	2	1	0	0	1	3	0	0	0	4	5	3	1
2-Pt. conversions att	0	1	3	2	2	3	3	5	3	0	0	6	9	6	3
Safeties	2	1	0	2	1	0	1	1	2	0	1	0	0	0	1
Field goals made	23	23	19	21	29	29	29	35	20	21	14	20	18	21	13
Field goals attempted	33	28	26	26	35	33	33	35	22	27	21	26	27	28	23
Percent successful	69.7	82.1	73.1	80.8	82.9	87.9	87.9	100.0	90.9	77.8	66.7	76.9	66.7	75.0	56.5

DEFENSE

	Ari.	Atl.	Car.	Chi.	Dal.	Det.	G.B.	Min.	N.O.	NYG	Phi.	St.L.	S.F.	T.B.	Was.
First downs	321	267	315	300	276	308	246	300	326	286	286	282	297	244	303
Rushing	117	65	95	121	84	113	67	102	86	103	125	92	91	75	127
Passing	177	172	197	155	162	167	166	171	208	163	133	161	178	148	152
Penalty	27	30	23	24	30	28	13	27	32	20	28	29	28	21	24
Rushes	492	361	491	479	401	487	390	404	467	476	528	479	395	415	531
Net yards gained	1989	1203	2133	1875	1619	2102	1442	1614	1700	2004	2416	2049	1610	1583	2436
Average gain	4.0	3.3	4.3	3.9	4.0	4.3	3.7	4.0	3.6	4.2	4.6	4.3	4.1	3.8	4.6
Average yards per game	124.3	75.2	133.3	117.2	101.2	131.4	90.1	100.9	106.3	125.3	151.0	128.1	100.6	98.9	152.3
Passes attempted	518	551	501	456	553	474	540	555	539	521	449	475	566	473	493
Completed	299	311	298	292	290	284	296	320	328	282	249	256	294	274	281
Percent completed	57.7	56.4	59.5	64.0	52.4	59.9	54.8	57.7	60.9	54.1	55.5	53.9	51.9	57.9	57.0
Total yards gained	3526	3806	3937	3401	3767	3276	3401	3699	4256	3503	3001	3180	3992	3014	3112
Times sacked	39	38	37	28	34	43	50	38	47	54	42	50	51	37	33
Yards lost	250	275	228	173	222	261	336	247	288	336	281	349	259	252	194
Net yards gained	3276	3531	3709	3228	3545	3015	3065	3452	3968	3167	2720	2831	3733	2762	2918
Average yards per game	204.8	220.7	231.8	201.8	221.6	188.4	191.6	215.8	248.0	197.9	170.0	176.9	233.3	172.6	182.4
Net yards per pass play	5.88	5.99	6.89	6.67	6.04	5.83	5.19	5.82	6.77	5.51	5.54	5.39	6.05	5.42	5.55
Yards gained per completion	11.79	12.24	13.21	11.65	12.99	11.54	11.49	11.56	12.98	12.42	12.05	12.42	13.58	11.00	11.07
Combined net yards gained	5265	4734	5842	5103	5164	5117	4507	5066	5668	5171	5136	4880	5343	4345	5354
Percent total yards rushing	37.8	25.4	36.5	36.7	31.4	41.1	32.0	31.9	30.0	38.8	47.0	42.0	30.1	36.4	45.5
Percent total yards passing	62.2	74.6	63.5	63.3	68.6	58.9	68.0	68.1	70.0	61.2	53.0	58.0	69.9	63.6	54.5
Average yards per game	329.1	295.9	365.1	318.9	322.8	319.8	281.7	316.6	354.3	323.2	321.0	305.0	333.9	271.6	334.6
Ball-control plays	1049	950	1029	963	988	1004	980	997	1053	1051	1019	1004	1012	925	1057
Average yards per play	5.0	5.0	5.7	5.3	5.2	5.1	4.6	5.1	5.4	4.9	5.0	4.9	5.3	4.7	5.1
Average time of possession	30:45	26:50	31:50	30:34	28:10	30:38	28:23	30:02	31:57	31:39	30:36	31:01	28:08	28:02	31:26
Third-down efficiency	37.1	35.8	41.7	40.8	33.8	41.0	39.5	34.0	43.8	37.6	37.0	37.6	34.3	31.7	38.1
Intercepted by	20	19	19	14	14	12	13	19	21	19	9	16	21	12	13
Yards returned by	235	224	295	129	250	132	111	341	466	217	158	201	178	212	190
Returned for TD	1	2	2	1	1	1	1	3	5	3	0	1	0	1	0
Punts	75	80	71	72	85	81	90	74	75	88	85	92	83	87	92
Yards punted	3296	3427	3125	3084	3604	3460	3920	3155	3263	3701	3616	3825	3492	3655	3966
Average yards per punt	43.9	42.8	44.0	42.8	42.4	42.7	43.6	42.6	43.5	42.1	42.5	41.6	42.1	42.0	43.1
Punt returns	38	20	20	38	34	47	27	27	53	53	61	58	36	38	32
Yards returned	313	112	94	349	210	471	237	325	649	587	511	652	341	302	261
Average yards per return	8.2	5.6	4.7	9.2	6.2	10.0	8.8	12.0	12.2	11.1	8.4	11.2	9.5	7.9	8.2
Returned for TD	0	0	0	1	0	1	1	1	0	1	1	1	0	1	0
Kickoff returns	56	69	65	55	69	49	74	73	52	51	40	47	67	62	61
Yards returned	1200	1613	1439	1097	1274	1196	1807	2008	1128	1234	764	1020	1296	1333	1569
Average yards per return	21.4	23.4	22.1	19.9	18.5	24.4	24.4	27.5	21.7	24.2	19.1	21.7	19.3	21.5	25.7
Returned for TD	0	1	1	0	0	1	2	4	0	0	0	0	0	1	2
Fumbles	31	37	24	33	23	27	20	21	24	25	20	16	24	28	17
Recovered	19	25	14	14	12	9	10	15	11	7	8	7	12	14	8
Out of bounds	3	2	0	4	3	3	2	0	3	2	2	1	1	0	1
Recovered for TD	0	0	0	0	0	0	0	0	0	0	0	0	0	0	0
Penalties	114	118	110	102	120	98	94	132	132	124	113	112	101	88	95
Yards penalized	954	858	892	852	917	791	828	1167	1164	967	904	915	800	669	824
Total points scored	378	289	413	368	275	378	319	296	359	309	344	378	328	295	421
Total TDs	44	35	46	42	32	43	36	35	40	34	39	43	39	31	50
TDs rushing	18	7	14	12	10	15	7	12	13	13	18	11	13	12	24
TDs passing	21	22	30	27	21	23	23	17	24	17	18	28	25	15	21
TDs on returns and recoveries	5	6	2	3	1	5	6	6	3	4	3	4	1	4	5
Extra point kicks	40	28	41	36	29	41	28	31	39	34	36	40	35	29	46
Extra point kick att	41	31	43	38	30	41	30	31	39	34	37	40	38	29	46
2-Pt. conversions	1	2	1	1	2	1	3	2	1	0	1	2	0	0	2
2-Pt. conversions att	3	4	3	4	2	1	6	4	1	0	2	3	1	2	4
Safeties	0	1	2	0	1	1	0	0	0	1	0	2	1	1	1
Field goals made	24	15	30	26	16	25	23	17	26	23	24	24	19	26	23
Field goals attempted	30	20	31	31	19	30	27	19	33	30	32	27	32	30	28
Percent successful	80.0	75.0	96.8	83.9	84.2	83.3	85.2	89.5	78.8	76.7	75.0	88.9	59.4	86.7	82.1

	AFC Offense Total	AFC Offense Average	AFC Defense Total	AFC Defense Average	NFC Offense Total	NFC Offense Average	NFC Defense Total	NFC Defense Average	NFL Total	NFL Average
First downs	4330	288.7	4381	292.1	4408	293.9	4357	290.5	8738	291.3
Rushing	1459	97.3	1434	95.6	1438	95.9	1463	97.5	2897	96.6
Passing	2465	164.3	2515	167.7	2560	170.7	2510	167.3	5025	167.5
Penalty	406	27.1	432	28.8	410	27.3	384	25.6	816	27.2
Rushes	6821	454.7	6772	451.5	6747	449.8	6796	453.1	13568	452.3
Net yards gained	27012	1800.8	26318	1754.5	27081	1805.4	27775	1851.7	54093	1803.1
Average gain	....	4.0	....	3.9	....	4.0	....	4.1	....	4.0
Average yards per game	....	112.6	....	109.7	....	112.8	....	115.7	....	112.7
Passes attempted	7739	515.9	7825	521.7	7750	516.7	7664	510.9	15489	516.3
Completed	4362	290.8	4412	294.1	4404	293.6	4354	290.3	8766	292.2
Percent completed	....	56.4	....	56.4	....	56.8	....	56.8	....	56.6
Total yards gained	52429	3495.3	53215	3547.7	53657	3577.1	52871	3524.7	106086	3536.2
Times sacked	554	36.9	586	39.1	653	43.5	621	41.4	1207	40.2
Yards lost	3683	245.5	3751	250.1	4019	267.9	3951	263.4	7702	256.7
Net yards gained	48746	3249.7	49464	3297.6	49638	3309.2	48920	3261.3	98384	3279.5
Average yards per game	....	203.1	....	206.1	....	206.8	....	203.8	....	205.0
Net yards per pass play	....	5.88	....	5.88	....	5.91	....	5.90	....	5.89
Yards gained per completion	....	12.02	....	12.06	....	12.18	....	12.14	....	12.10
Combined net yards gained	75758	5050.5	75782	5052.1	76719	5114.6	76695	5113.0	152477	5082.6
Percent total yards rushing	....	35.7	....	34.7	....	35.3	....	36.2	....	35.5
Percent total yards passing	....	64.3	....	65.3	....	64.7	....	63.8	....	64.5
Average yards per game	....	315.7	....	315.8	....	319.7	....	319.6	....	317.7
Ball-control plays	15114	1007.6	15183	1012.2	15150	1010.0	15081	1005.4	30264	1008.8
Average yards per play	....	5.0	....	5.0	....	5.1	....	5.1	....	5.0
Third-down efficiency	....	36.9	....	37.1	....	37.8	....	37.6	....	37.4
Interceptions	266	17.7	268	17.9	243	16.2	241	16.1	509	17.0
Yards returned	3667	244.5	3698	246.5	3370	224.7	3339	222.6	7037	234.6
Returned for TD	27	1.8	31	2.1	26	1.7	22	1.5	53	1.8
Punts	1211	80.7	1211	80.7	1230	82.0	1230	82.0	2441	81.4
Yards punted	52983	3532.2	52958	3530.5	52564	3504.3	52589	3505.9	105547	3518.2
Average yards per punt	....	43.8	....	43.7	....	42.7	....	42.8	....	43.2
Punt returns	593	39.5	589	39.3	578	38.5	582	38.8	1171	39.0
Yards returned	6115	407.7	6292	419.5	5591	372.7	5414	360.9	11706	390.2
Average yards per return	....	10.3	....	10.7	....	9.7	....	9.3	....	10.0
Returned for TD	8	0.5	8	0.5	8	0.5	8	0.5	16	0.5
Kickoff returns	929	61.9	967	64.5	928	61.9	890	59.3	1857	61.9
Yards returned	20280	1352.0	21372	1424.8	21070	1404.7	19978	1331.9	41350	1378.3
Average yards per return	....	21.8	....	22.1	....	22.7	....	22.4	....	22.3
Returned for TD	5	0.3	6	0.4	13	0.9	12	0.8	18	0.6
Fumbles	361	24.1	354	23.6	363	24.2	370	24.7	724	24.1
Lost	166	11.1	167	11.1	186	12.4	185	12.3	352	11.7
Out of bounds	17	1.1	18	1.2	28	1.9	27	1.8	45	1.5
Own recovered for TD	3	0.2	3	0.2	0	0.0	0	0.0	3	0.1
Opponents recovered by	166	11.1	165	11.0	184	12.3	185	12.3	350	11.7
Opponents recovered for TD	12	0.8	15	1.0	14	0.9	11	0.7	26	0.9
Penalties	1690	112.7	1695	113.0	1658	110.5	1653	110.2	3348	111.6
Yards penalized	13923	928.2	14158	943.9	13737	915.8	13502	900.1	27660	922.0
Total points scored	5035	335.7	5065	337.7	5180	345.3	5150	343.3	10215	340.5
Total TDs	561	37.4	568	37.9	596	39.7	589	39.3	1157	38.6
TDs rushing	177	11.8	180	12.0	202	13.5	199	13.3	379	12.6
TDs passing	322	21.5	326	21.7	336	22.4	332	22.1	658	21.9
TDs on returns and recoveries	62	4.1	62	4.1	58	3.9	58	3.9	120	4.0
Extra point kicks	498	33.2	498	33.2	533	35.5	533	35.5	1031	34.4
Extra point kick att.	501	33.4	501	33.4	548	36.5	548	36.5	1049	35.0
2-Pt. conversions	20	1.3	22	1.5	21	1.4	19	1.3	41	1.4
2-Pt. conversion att.	59	3.9	65	4.3	46	3.1	40	2.7	105	3.5
Safeties	6	0.4	7	0.5	12	0.8	11	0.7	18	0.6
Field goals made	373	24.9	367	24.5	335	22.3	341	22.7	708	23.6
Field goals attempted	466	31.1	470	31.3	423	28.2	419	27.9	889	29.6
Percent successful	....	80.0	....	78.1	....	79.2	....	81.4	....	79.6

1998 STATISTICS *Miscellaneous*

RUSHING

Player, Team	Opponent	Date	Att.	Yds.	TD
Priest Holmes, Baltimore	at Cincinnati	November 22	36	227	1
Terrell Davis, Denver	at Seattle	October 11	30	208	1
Garrison Hearst, San Francisco	vs. Detroit	December 14	24	198	1
Robert Edwards, New England	at St. Louis	December 13	24	196	0
Marshall Faulk, Indianapolis	at Baltimore	November 29	17	192	1
Terrell Davis, Denver	vs. Dallas	September 13	23	191	3
Jamal Anderson, Atlanta	at St. Louis	November 29	31	188	1
Garrison Hearst, San Francisco	vs. N.Y. Jets	September 6*	20	187	2
Barry Sanders, Detroit	vs. Cincinnati	September 13*	26	185	3
Fred Taylor, Jacksonville	vs. Detroit	December 6	32	183	2
Robert Smith, Minnesota	at St. Louis	September 13	23	179	2
Ricky Watters, Seattle	vs. Indianapolis	December 20	32	178	1
Terrell Davis, Denver	vs. Seattle	December 27	29	178	0
Adrian Murrell, Arizona	at Philadelphia	December 13*	32	174	0
Priest Holmes, Baltimore	vs. Cincinnati	September 27	27	173	2
Jamal Anderson, Atlanta	vs. St. Louis	November 1	22	172	2
Terrell Davis, Denver	vs. Philadelphia	October 4	20	168	2
Garrison Hearst, San Francisco	vs. N.Y. Giants	November 30	20	166	1
Natrone Means, San Diego	at Kansas City	September 20	22	165	1
Emmitt Smith, Dallas	vs. N.Y. Giants	November 8	29	163	0
Darick Holmes, Green Bay	vs. Philadelphia	November 29	26	163	0
James Allen, Chicago	vs. Baltimore	December 20	23	163	1
Terrell Davis, Denver	vs. Oakland	November 22	31	162	1
Greg Hill, St. Louis	at Buffalo	September 20	19	158	2
Lamar Smith, New Orleans	at Indianapolis	September 27*	24	157	0
Barry Sanders, Detroit	vs. Green Bay	October 15	25	155	1
Eddie George, Tennessee	at Pittsburgh	November 1	34	153	1
Napoleon Kaufman, Oakland	vs. Washington	November 29	17	152	1
Terrell Davis, Denver	at Cincinnati	November 1	27	149	2
Jamal Anderson, Atlanta	at New Orleans	December 13	27	148	0
Terrell Davis, Denver	at N.Y. Giants	December 13	28	147	1
Jamal Anderson, Atlanta	at Detroit	December 20	30	147	1
Adrian Murrell, Arizona	vs. Philadelphia	September 20	22	145	1
Curtis Martin, N.Y. Jets	vs. Indianapolis	September 20	23	144	0
Napoleon Kaufman, Oakland	vs. Cincinnati	October 25	31	143	0
Duce Staley, Philadelphia	vs. Arizona	December 13*	30	141	1
Barry Sanders, Detroit	at Philadelphia	November 8	20	140	0
Napoleon Kaufman, Oakland	vs. N.Y. Giants	September 13	20	139	1
Garrison Hearst, San Francisco	at Carolina	December 6*	20	139	1
Jerome Bettis, Pittsburgh	at Jacksonville	December 28	26	139	0
Garrison Hearst, San Francisco	at Washington	September 14	22	138	0
Jerome Bettis, Pittsburgh	vs. Seattle	September 27	28	138	0
Eddie George, Tennessee	vs. Chicago	October 25	21	137	0
Robert Smith, Minnesota	vs. New Orleans	November 8	20	137	1
Bam Morris, Kansas City	vs. Dallas	December 13	27	137	1
Ricky Watters, Seattle	vs. Washington	September 20	24	136	1
Terrell Davis, Denver	vs. Jacksonville	October 25	31	136	3
Robert Smith, Minnesota	at Detroit	October 25	19	134	1
Eddie George, Tennessee	at Tampa Bay	November 8	27	134	1
Curtis Martin, N.Y. Jets	at Indianapolis	November 15	28	134	0
Jamal Anderson, Atlanta	vs. New Orleans	October 18	25	132	1
Priest Holmes, Baltimore	vs. Detroit	December 27	28	132	1
Jerome Bettis, Pittsburgh	vs. Chicago	September 13	21	131	1
Barry Sanders, Detroit	vs. Tampa Bay	September 28	27	131	0
Natrone Means, San Diego	at Indianapolis	October 4	31	130	1
Antowain Smith, Buffalo	at Indianapolis	October 11	31	130	2
Charlie Garner, Philadelphia	vs. Detroit	November 8	16	129	1
Fred Taylor, Jacksonville	vs. Baltimore	September 20	23	128	1
Mike Alstott, Tampa Bay	vs. Minnesota	November 1	19	128	1
Fred Taylor, Jacksonville	vs. Tampa Bay	November 15	20	128	3
Marshall Faulk, Indianapolis	at New England	September 13	29	127	0
Barry Sanders, Detroit	vs. Minnesota	October 25	24	127	0
Karim Abdul-Jabbar, Miami	at Carolina	November 15	25	127	1
Terrell Fletcher, San Diego	at Arizona	December 27	23	127	0
Emmitt Smith, Dallas	vs. Arizona	September 6	29	124	0
Corey Dillon, Cincinnati	at Tennessee	October 18	14	124	1
Gary Brown, N.Y. Giants	at Arizona	December 6	25	124	0
Jamal Anderson, Atlanta	at San Francisco	September 27	13	123	1
Curtis Martin, N.Y. Jets	at Tennessee	November 22	27	123	1
Terrell Fletcher, San Diego	at Washington	December 6	34	122	0

Player, Team	Opponent	Date	Att.	Yds.	TD
Jamal Anderson, Atlanta	vs. Indianapolis	December 6	30	122	1
Eddie George, Tennessee	at Baltimore	October 11	30	121	0
Emmitt Smith, Dallas	at Washington	October 4	28	120	1
Terrell Davis, Denver	at Washington	September 27	21	119	1
Jerome Bettis, Pittsburgh	at Kansas City	October 26	33	119	0
Gary Brown, N.Y. Giants	at Dallas	November 8	15	119	0
Antowain Smith, Buffalo	vs. St. Louis	September 20	22	118	0
Fred Taylor, Jacksonville	vs. Cincinnati	November 8	27	118	1
Emmitt Smith, Dallas	at Arizona	November 15	26	118	3
Jamal Anderson, Atlanta	vs. Carolina	October 4	31	117	1
Napoleon Kaufman, Oakland	at Dallas	September 27	24	116	0
Fred Taylor, Jacksonville	at Tennessee	September 27	25	116	1
Corey Dillon, Cincinnati	at Baltimore	September 27	25	116	0
James Stewart, Jacksonville	at Chicago	September 6	26	115	1
Donnell Bennett, Kansas City	vs. Oakland	September 6	24	115	1
Warrick Dunn, Tampa Bay	vs. Minnesota	November 1	18	115	1
Marshall Faulk, Indianapolis	vs. Cincinnati	December 13	26	115	2
Barry Sanders, Detroit	vs. Chicago	November 15	24	114	0
Emmitt Smith, Dallas	vs. Carolina	October 11	21	112	1
Natrone Means, San Diego	vs. Philadelphia	October 18	21	112	1
Gary Brown, N.Y. Giants	vs. Denver	December 13	18	112	0
Gary Brown, N.Y. Giants	at Philadelphia	December 27	25	112	0
Darick Holmes, Green Bay	at N.Y. Giants	November 15	27	111	1
Terrell Davis, Denver	at Kansas City	November 16	18	111	1
Jamal Anderson, Atlanta	at N.Y. Giants	October 11	29	110	0
Corey Dillon, Cincinnati	vs. Denver	November 1	35	110	0
Curtis Martin, N.Y. Jets	vs. Carolina	November 29	21	110	2
Emmitt Smith, Dallas	vs. Philadelphia	December 20	25	110	0
Tim Biakabutuka, Carolina	at Indianapolis	December 27	25	109	1
Karim Abdul-Jabbar, Miami	at Indianapolis	September 6	23	108	1
Karim Abdul-Jabbar, Miami	vs. Pittsburgh	September 20	33	108	1
Curtis Martin, N.Y. Jets	vs. Miami	October 4	36	108	1
Gary Brown, N.Y. Giants	vs. Arizona	October 18	24	108	1
Eddie George, Tennessee	vs. Cincinnati	October 18	25	107	0
Curtis Martin, N.Y. Jets	at New England	October 19	28	107	0
Barry Sanders, Detroit	vs. Arizona	November 1	27	107	0
Adrian Murrell, Arizona	vs. Washington	November 8	23	107	0
Warrick Dunn, Tampa Bay	at Jacksonville	November 15	16	107	0
Antowain Smith, Buffalo	vs. Indianapolis	November 22	23	107	2
Garrison Hearst, San Francisco	at New England	December 20	27	107	0
Corey Dillon, Cincinnati	vs. Jacksonville	November 29	16	107	0
Ricky Watters, Seattle	vs. Arizona	September 13	22	105	0
Ricky Watters, Seattle	vs. Kansas City	November 8	24	105	2
Dorsey Levens, Green Bay	vs. Chicago	December 13	15	105	0
Fred Taylor, Jacksonville	at Minnesota	December 20	23	105	0
Terrell Davis, Denver	at Oakland	September 20	28	104	0
Chris Warren, Dallas	at Washington	October 4	14	104	2
Robert Edwards, New England	vs. Kansas City	October 11	23	104	1
Robert Edwards, New England	vs. N.Y. Jets	October 19	22	104	1
Jamal Anderson, Atlanta	at New England	November 8	32	104	2
Jerome Bettis, Pittsburgh	vs. Cincinnati	December 20	21	104	1
James Stewart, Jacksonville	vs. Kansas City	September 13	26	103	1
Mike Alstott, Tampa Bay	vs. Chicago	September 20	20	103	1
Kordell Stewart, Pittsburgh	at Cincinnati	October 11	7	103	0
Marshall Faulk, Indianapolis	at San Francisco	October 18	17	103	1
Robert Smith, Minnesota	vs. Washington	October 18	24	103	1
Priest Holmes, Baltimore	vs. Indianapolis	November 29	22	103	2
Tim Biakabutuka, Carolina	vs. Washington	December 13	17	103	1
Gary Brown, N.Y. Giants	vs. Kansas City	December 20	25	103	1
Jamal Anderson, Atlanta	vs. Miami	December 27	18	103	1
Barry Sanders, Detroit	at Jacksonville	December 6	18	102	0
Curtis Martin, N.Y. Jets	vs. New England	December 27	29	102	1
Natrone Means, San Diego	at Oakland	October 11	37	101	0
Curtis Martin, N.Y. Jets	vs. Atlanta	October 25	25	101	1
Fred Lane, Carolina	vs. New Orleans	November 1	35	101	1
Emmitt Smith, Dallas	at Philadelphia	November 2	23	101	1
Robert Smith, Minnesota	vs. Jacksonville	December 20	19	101	0
Robert Edwards, New England	vs. San Francisco	December 20	24	101	1
Ahman Green, Seattle	at Philadelphia	September 6	6	100	0
Fred Lane, Carolina	at New Orleans	September 13	18	100	0
Eddie George, Tennessee	at New England	September 20	23	100	0
Jerome Bettis, Pittsburgh	vs. Green Bay	November 9	34	100	0
Jamal Anderson, Atlanta	vs. San Francisco	November 15	31	100	2

*Overtime game.

PASSING

Player, Team	Opponent	Date	Att.	Comp.	Yds.	TD	Int.
Jake Plummer, Arizona	vs. Dallas	November 15	56	31	465	3	1
Troy Aikman, Dallas	vs. Minnesota	November 26	57	34	455	1	0
Randall Cunningham, Minnesota	at Green Bay	October 5	32	20	442	4	0
Drew Bledsoe, New England	vs. Miami	November 23	54	28	423	2	2
Vinny Testaverde, N.Y. Jets	vs. Seattle	December 6	63	42	418	2	1
Glenn Foley, N.Y. Jets	at San Francisco	September 6*	58	30	415	3	1
John Elway, Denver	vs. Kansas City	December 6	32	22	400	2	1
Jake Plummer, Arizona	vs. New Orleans	December 20	44	32	394	0	1
Brett Favre, Green Bay	at Carolina	September 27	45	27	388	5	3
Steve Young, San Francisco	vs. Atlanta	September 27	39	28	387	3	1
Trent Green, Washington	at Seattle	September 20	54	27	383	2	2
Trent Green, Washington	vs. Arizona	November 22	49	30	382	4	1
Mark Brunell, Jacksonville	vs. Baltimore	September 20	34	25	376	2	0
Erik Kramer, Chicago	vs. Minnesota	September 27	39	25	372	4	1
Jeff Blake, Cincinnati	at Pittsburgh	December 20	36	20	367	1	1
Steve Young, San Francisco	vs. N.Y. Jets	September 6*	46	26	363	3	1
Randall Cunningham, Minnesota	at Dallas	November 26	35	17	359	4	1
Peyton Manning, Indianapolis	at Baltimore	November 29	42	27	357	3	1
Dan Marino, Miami	vs. Denver	December 21	38	23	355	4	1
Mark Brunell, Jacksonville	at Denver	October 25	46	28	353	3	0
Randall Cunningham, Minnesota	vs. Chicago	December 6	31	21	349	4	1
Chris Chandler, Atlanta	at New Orleans	December 13	28	19	345	2	2
Randall Cunningham, Minnesota	at Baltimore	December 13	55	32	345	2	1
Steve Young, San Francisco	at Atlanta	November 15	40	21	342	2	1
Doug Flutie, Buffalo	at New England	November 29	39	21	339	2	0
John Elway, Denver	vs. Seattle	December 27	36	26	338	4	0
Peyton Manning, Indianapolis	at Seattle	December 20	39	23	335	1	1
Steve Young, San Francisco	vs. Indianapolis	October 18	51	33	331	2	0
Steve Young, San Francisco	at Buffalo	October 4	38	23	329	3	1
Kerry Collins, New Orleans	at San Francisco	November 22	44	22	328	0	2
Drew Bledsoe, New England	at Pittsburgh	December 6	34	21	327	1	3
Billy Joe Tolliver, New Orleans	at Carolina	November 1	48	24	325	2	2
Dan Marino, Miami	at Jacksonville	October 12	49	30	323	2	1
Brett Favre, Green Bay	vs. Philadelphia	November 29	33	20	321	2	2
Dan Marino, Miami	vs. N.Y. Jets	December 13	57	30	321	1	1
Dan Marino, Miami	at Atlanta	December 27	36	21	320	1	2
Doug Flutie, Buffalo	at Cincinnati	December 6	30	18	319	2	3
Drew Bledsoe, New England	at New Orleans	October 4	35	21	317	1	3
Brad Johnson, Minnesota	vs. New Orleans	November 8	38	28	316	1	2
Peyton Manning, Indianapolis	vs. New Orleans	September 27*	32	19	309	1	3
Steve Young, San Francisco	at New Orleans	October 11	40	21	309	3	0
Drew Bledsoe, New England	at Indianapolis	November 1	35	22	306	2	1
Rich Gannon, Kansas City	at San Diego	November 22	33	20	304	1	1
Craig Whelihan, San Diego	vs. Denver	November 29	53	30	304	1	5
Neil O'Donnell, Cincinnati	at Detroit	September 13*	36	25	303	2	0
Jeff George, Oakland	vs. N.Y. Giants	September 13	44	25	303	1	0
Steve Young, San Francisco	at Washington	September 14	32	21	303	3	0
Brett Favre, Green Bay	at Minnesota	November 22	39	31	303	2	1
Steve Stenstrom, Chicago	at Minnesota	December 6	42	25	303	1	1
Peyton Manning, Indianapolis	vs. Miami	September 6	37	21	302	1	3
Kerry Collins, Carolina	at Atlanta	October 4	38	20	302	3	2
Brett Favre, Green Bay	at Detroit	October 15	43	22	300	2	3

*Overtime game.

RECEIVING

Player, Team	Opponent	Date	Rec.	Yds.	TD
Carl Pickens, Cincinnati	vs. Pittsburgh	October 11	13	204	1
Terance Mathis, Atlanta	at New Orleans	December 13	6	198	2
Eric Moulds, Buffalo	at Cincinnati	December 6	6	196	2
Antonio Freeman, Green Bay	vs. San Francisco	November 1	7	193	2
Terry Glenn, New England	at Pittsburgh	December 6	9	193	1
Muhsin Muhammad, Carolina	at New Orleans	September 13	9	192	1
Isaac Bruce, St. Louis	vs. Minnesota	September 13	11	192	1
Randy Moss, Minnesota	at Green Bay	October 5	5	190	2
Frank Sanders, Arizona	vs. Dallas	November 15	11	190	1
Antonio Freeman, Green Bay	vs. Tennessee	December 20	7	186	3
Eric Moulds, Buffalo	at New England	November 29	8	177	1
Derrick Alexander, Kansas City	at San Diego	November 22	5	173	1
Jerry Rice, San Francisco	at Atlanta	November 15	10	169	1
Rod Smith, Denver	vs. Kansas City	December 6	8	165	0
Randy Moss, Minnesota	at Dallas	November 26	3	163	3

Player, Team	Opponent	Date	Rec.	Yds.	TD
Jerry Rice, San Francisco	vs. Atlanta	September 27	8	162	2
Rod Smith, Denver	vs. Seattle	December 27	9	158	1
Keith Poole, New Orleans	at Atlanta	October 18	3	154	2
Randy Moss, Minnesota	vs. Green Bay	November 22	8	153	1
Torrance Small, Indianapolis	at Baltimore	November 29	9	153	1
Oronde Gadsden, Miami	at Atlanta	December 27	9	153	0
Darnay Scott, Cincinnati	at Pittsburgh	December 20	7	152	1
Sean Dawkins, New Orleans	at San Francisco	November 22	8	148	0
Herman Moore, Detroit	vs. Pittsburgh	November 26*	8	148	1
Courtney Hawkins, Pittsburgh	vs. Tennessee	November 1	14	147	1
Floyd Turner, Baltimore	vs. Minnesota	December 13	10	147	1
Michael Irvin, Dallas	vs. Carolina	October 11	6	146	0
Eric Moulds, Buffalo	at Carolina	October 25	5	145	2
Joey Galloway, Seattle	at Philadelphia	September 6	6	142	2
Bobby Engram, Chicago	at Arizona	October 11	5	142	1
Ike Hilliard, N.Y. Giants	at San Francisco	November 30	6	141	0
Terrell Owens, San Francisco	vs. N.Y. Giants	November 30	5	140	1
Tony Martin, Atlanta	vs. Indianapolis	December 6	7	140	1
Bobby Engram, Chicago	at Minnesota	December 6	9	140	1
Tim Brown, Oakland	vs. Kansas City	December 26	10	140	1
Joey Galloway, Seattle	at Pittsburgh	September 27	7	139	0
Johnnie Morton, Detroit	at Chicago	October 4	2	138	1
Frank Sanders, Arizona	vs. New Orleans	December 20	10	138	0
Michael Irvin, Dallas	vs. Minnesota	November 26	10	137	0
Rod Smith, Denver	at Seattle	October 11	8	136	1
Lamar Thomas, Miami	vs. Denver	December 21	6	136	3
Michael Westbrook, Washington	vs. Arizona	November 22	10	135	3
Cris Carter, Minnesota	at Dallas	November 26	7	135	1
Ed McCaffrey, Denver	at Cincinnati	November 1	7	133	1
Ed McCaffrey, Denver	vs. San Diego	November 8	9	133	1
Michael Westbrook, Washington	at Seattle	September 20	7	132	2
O.J. McDuffie, Miami	vs. Indianapolis	November 8	9	132	2
Isaac Bruce, St. Louis	vs. New Orleans	September 6	10	131	0
Shawn Jefferson, New England	vs. Miami	November 23	6	131	1
Darnay Scott, Cincinnati	at Detroit	September 13*	5	130	2
Terance Mathis, Atlanta	at San Francisco	September 27	7	130	2
Joey Galloway, Seattle	at San Diego	October 25	4	130	1
Bryan Still, San Diego	vs. Buffalo	September 6	6	128	1
Marshall Faulk, Indianapolis	vs. New Orleans	September 27*	6	128	1
Marvin Harrison, Indianapolis	vs. N.Y. Jets	November 15	9	128	1
Bill Schroeder, Green Bay	vs. Philadelphia	November 29	5	128	0
Tim Brown, Oakland	vs. N.Y. Giants	September 13	6	127	1
Joey Galloway, Seattle	at N.Y. Jets	December 6	2	127	2
Keyshawn Johnson, N.Y. Jets	at San Francisco	September 6*	9	126	2
Antonio Freeman, Green Bay	at Detroit	October 15	6	126	2
Reidel Anthony, Tampa Bay	at Jacksonville	November 15	2	126	2
Wayne Chrebet, N.Y. Jets	at San Francisco	September 6*	6	125	1
Bobby Engram, Chicago	vs. Minnesota	September 27	6	123	2
Jermaine Lewis, Baltimore	vs. Cincinnati	September 27	4	122	1
Andre Hastings, New Orleans	vs. Dallas	December 6	4	122	1
Jimmy Smith, Jacksonville	at Denver	October 25	8	121	0
Carl Pickens, Cincinnati	at Baltimore	September 27	7	120	2
Terrell Owens, San Francisco	at St. Louis	October 25	5	120	1
Torrance Small, Indianapolis	at Seattle	December 20	3	120	0
Herman Moore, Detroit	at Baltimore	December 27	10	120	0
Raghib Ismail, Carolina	vs. Atlanta	September 6	6	119	1
Michael Irvin, Dallas	vs. Arizona	September 6	9	119	0
Cris Carter, Minnesota	at Green Bay	October 5	8	119	0
Marshall Faulk, Indianapolis	vs. New England	November 1	9	119	0
Brandon Bennett, Cincinnati	at Pittsburgh	December 20	3	119	0
Frank Sanders, Arizona	vs. Oakland	October 4	10	118	0
Muhsin Muhammad, Carolina	vs. Washington	December 13	7	118	0
Ed McCaffrey, Denver	vs. Dallas	September 13	5	117	0
Jermaine Lewis, Baltimore	at Jacksonville	September 20	4	117	1
Raghib Ismail, Carolina	at Dallas	October 11	6	117	0
Jake Reed, Minnesota	at Tampa Bay	November 1	6	117	2
Terance Mathis, Atlanta	at New England	November 8	8	117	1
Jimmy Smith, Jacksonville	vs. Baltimore	September 20	2	116	1
James Jett, Oakland	vs. Denver	September 20	5	116	0
Tony Martin, Atlanta	vs. New Orleans	October 18	7	116	1
Shawn Jefferson, New England	at Miami	October 25*	4	116	0
Derrick Alexander, Kansas City	vs. Arizona	November 29	6	116	2
Herman Moore, Detroit	at Jacksonville	December 6	7	116	1
Albert Connell, Washington	at Carolina	December 13	8	116	1

Player, Team	Opponent	Date	Rec.	Yds.	TD
Johnnie Morton, Detroit	vs. Arizona	November 1	7	115	0
Charles Johnson, Pittsburgh	vs. Tennessee	November 1	9	115	3
Jerry Rice, San Francisco	at New England	December 20	5	115	1
Keyshawn Johnson, N.Y. Jets	vs. Seattle	December 6	9	114	1
Keenan McCardell, Jacksonville	at Denver	October 25	9	113	0
James McKnight, Seattle	vs. Tennessee	November 29	5	113	1
Brett Bech, New Orleans	vs. Buffalo	December 27	4	113	2
Wayne Chrebet, N.Y. Jets	at Indianapolis	November 15	4	112	1
Keyshawn Johnson, N.Y. Jets	at Tennessee	November 22	10	112	1
Jimmy Smith, Jacksonville	vs. Detroit	December 6	7	112	1
Cameron Cleeland, New Orleans	vs. Buffalo	December 27	10	112	1
J.J. Stokes, San Francisco	vs. N.Y. Jets	September 6*	7	111	2
Antonio Freeman, Green Bay	vs. Detroit	September 6	4	110	2
Sean Dawkins, New Orleans	vs. Carolina	September 13	5	110	1
Ernie Mills, Dallas	vs. Carolina	October 11	5	110	1
J.J. Stokes, San Francisco	vs. Indianapolis	October 18	9	110	1
Stephen Davis, Washington	at Oakland	November 29	7	110	1
Jimmy Smith, Jacksonville	at Cincinnati	November 29	7	110	1
Michael Westbrook, Washington	vs. San Francisco	September 14	5	109	0
Cris Carter, Minnesota	vs. Washington	October 18	5	109	1
Ben Coates, New England	at Indianapolis	November 1	10	109	1
Tony Simmons, New England	at Indianapolis	November 1	4	109	1
Johnnie Morton, Detroit	vs. Chicago	November 15	5	109	0
Rob Moore, Arizona	at Philadelphia	December 13*	7	109	1
Tony Martin, Atlanta	at New Orleans	December 13	8	109	0
Raghib Ismail, Carolina	at Indianapolis	December 27	7	109	1
Keenan McCardell, Jacksonville	vs. Baltimore	September 20	8	108	0
Andre Reed, Buffalo	vs. Indianapolis	November 22	6	108	1
Floyd Turner, Baltimore	at Tennessee	December 6	4	108	2
Rob Moore, Arizona	at Detroit	November 1	5	107	1
Keyshawn Johnson, N.Y. Jets	at Indianapolis	November 15	5	107	0
Leslie Shepherd, Washington	vs. Arizona	November 22	7	107	1
Wayne Chrebet, N.Y. Jets	vs. Carolina	November 29	7	107	2
Eric Moulds, Buffalo	vs. N.Y. Jets	December 19	4	107	0
Chris Penn, Chicago	vs. Detroit	October 4	6	106	1
Bert Emanuel, Tampa Bay	vs. Tennessee	November 8	5	106	1
Randy Moss, Minnesota	vs. Chicago	December 6	8	106	3
James Jett, Oakland	at San Diego	December 20	5	106	1
Frank Sanders, Arizona	vs. San Diego	December 27	8	106	0
Garrison Hearst, San Francisco	vs. Atlanta	September 27	4	105	0
Terry Glenn, New England	at New Orleans	October 4	4	105	0
Rickey Dudley, Oakland	at Baltimore	November 8	6	105	1
Wayne Chrebet, N.Y. Jets	at Miami	December 13	5	105	1
O.J. McDuffie, Miami	vs. N.Y. Jets	December 13	11	105	1
Tony Martin, Atlanta	vs. Miami	December 27	3	105	1
Michael Westbrook, Washington	vs. Denver	September 27	3	104	1
Bryan Still, San Diego	vs. N.Y. Giants	September 27	8	104	0
Muhsin Muhammad, Carolina	at Atlanta	October 4	4	104	1
Terry Glenn, New England	vs. Buffalo	November 29	8	104	0
Tim Brown, Oakland	vs. Miami	December 6	9	104	2
Antonio Freeman, Green Bay	vs. Baltimore	October 25	9	103	1
Garrison Hearst, San Francisco	vs. New Orleans	November 22	4	103	1
Ed McCaffrey, Denver	vs. Kansas City	December 6	6	103	1
Jimmy Smith, Jacksonville	vs. Tennessee	December 13	6	103	0
Antonio Freeman, Green Bay	vs. Chicago	December 13	8	103	1
Marvin Harrison, Indianapolis	vs. Miami	September 6	5	102	1
Terry Glenn, New England	vs. Tennessee	September 20	4	102	1
Yancey Thigpen, Tennessee	vs. Jacksonville	September 27	6	102	2
Sean Dawkins, New Orleans	at Carolina	November 1	6	102	0
Marshall Faulk, Indianapolis	at Buffalo	November 22	8	102	0
O.J. McDuffie, Miami	vs. New Orleans	November 29	9	102	3
Chris Sanders, Tennessee	vs. Cincinnati	October 18	3	101	0
Wayne Chrebet, N.Y. Jets	at Kansas City	November 1	6	101	0
Rod Smith, Denver	at San Diego	November 29	8	101	1
Herman Moore, Detroit	at Green Bay	September 6	9	100	1
Mark Carrier, Carolina	vs. Buffalo	October 25	5	100	1
Tony Martin, Atlanta	vs. Chicago	November 22	6	100	0
Frank Sanders, Arizona	at Kansas City	November 29	6	100	0
Ricky Proehl, St. Louis	at San Francisco	December 27	7	100	2

*Overtime game.

OFFENSE

TOTAL SCORES

Team	Series	TD Rush	TD Pass	Total TDs	TD Efficiency Pct.	FGM	Total Scores	Scoring Efficiency Pct.
Denver	63	18	22	40	63.49	16	56	88.89
Minnesota	56	12	21	33	58.93	20	53	94.64
Buffalo	57	13	16	29	50.88	21	50	87.72
N.Y. Jets	58	9	21	30	51.72	20	50	86.21
Dallas	55	20	11	31	56.36	18	49	89.09
Jacksonville	55	16	15	31	56.36	18	49	89.09
Kansas City	51	19	7	26	50.98	20	46	90.20
Miami	49	10	18	28	57.14	17	45	91.84
Arizona	59	16	15	31	52.54	14	45	76.27
San Francisco	51	11	22	33	64.71	11	44	86.27
Green Bay	47	7	17	24	51.06	19	43	91.49
New England	55	9	15	24	43.64	19	43	78.18
Tennessee	42	9	10	19	45.24	23	42	100.00
Atlanta	46	15	12	27	58.70	14	41	89.13
Chicago	50	9	10	19	38.00	19	38	76.00
Washington	47	15	15	30	63.83	8	38	80.85
Tampa Bay	51	11	11	22	43.14	14	36	70.59
N.Y. Giants	39	10	10	20	51.28	15	35	89.74
Carolina	49	11	15	26	53.06	9	35	71.43
Indianapolis	41	5	17	22	53.66	12	34	82.93
St. Louis	40	16	9	25	62.50	9	34	85.00
Detroit	40	9	9	18	45.00	15	33	82.50
San Diego	37	10	4	14	37.84	17	31	83.78
Seattle	38	9	12	21	55.26	10	31	81.58
Pittsburgh	37	8	8	16	43.24	14	30	81.08
New Orleans	36	6	11	17	47.22	11	28	77.78
Cincinnati	36	7	11	18	50.00	9	27	75.00
Oakland	37	4	12	16	43.24	11	27	72.97
Baltimore	32	6	6	12	37.50	11	23	71.88
Philadelphia	32	8	5	13	40.63	9	22	68.75
Totals	1386	328	387	715	51.59	443	1158	83.55
Average	46.2	10.9	12.9	23.8	51.59	14.8	38.6	83.55

SCORING EFFICIENCY

Team	Series	TD Rush	TD Pass	Total TDs	TD Efficiency Pct.	FGM	Total Scores	Scoring Efficiency Pct.
Tennessee	42	9	10	19	45.24	23	42	100.00
Minnesota	56	12	21	33	58.93	20	53	94.64
Miami	49	10	18	28	57.14	17	45	91.84
Green Bay	47	7	17	24	51.06	19	43	91.49
Kansas City	51	19	7	26	50.98	20	46	90.20
N.Y. Giants	39	10	10	20	51.28	15	35	89.74
Atlanta	46	15	12	27	58.70	14	41	89.13
Dallas	55	20	11	31	56.36	18	49	89.09
Jacksonville	55	16	15	31	56.36	18	49	89.09
Denver	63	18	22	40	63.49	16	56	88.89
Buffalo	57	13	16	29	50.88	21	50	87.72
San Francisco	51	11	22	33	64.71	11	44	86.27
N.Y. Jets	58	9	21	30	51.72	20	50	86.21
St. Louis	40	16	9	25	62.50	9	34	85.00
San Diego	37	10	4	14	37.84	17	31	83.78
Indianapolis	41	5	17	22	53.66	12	34	82.93
Detroit	40	9	9	18	45.00	15	33	82.50
Seattle	38	9	12	21	55.26	10	31	81.58
Pittsburgh	37	8	8	16	43.24	14	30	81.08
Washington	47	15	15	30	63.83	8	38	80.85
New England	55	9	15	24	43.64	19	43	78.18
New Orleans	36	6	11	17	47.22	11	28	77.78
Arizona	59	16	15	31	52.54	14	45	76.27
Chicago	50	9	10	19	38.00	19	38	76.00
Cincinnati	36	7	11	18	50.00	9	27	75.00
Oakland	37	4	12	16	43.24	11	27	72.97
Baltimore	32	6	6	12	37.50	11	23	71.88
Carolina	49	11	15	26	53.06	9	35	71.43
Tampa Bay	51	11	11	22	43.14	14	36	70.59
Philadelphia	32	8	5	13	40.63	9	22	68.75
Totals	1386	328	387	715	51.59	443	1158	83.55
Average	46.2	10.9	12.9	23.8	51.59	14.8	38.6	83.55

TOTAL SCORES

Team	Series	TD Rush	TD Pass	Total TDs	TD Efficiency Pct.	FGM	Total Scores	Scoring Efficiency Pct.
Dallas	31	7	9	16	51.61	11	27	87.10
Atlanta	35	7	10	17	48.57	11	28	80.00
N.Y. Jets	39	9	9	18	46.15	11	29	74.36
Green Bay	36	5	11	16	44.44	14	30	83.33
Miami	36	5	10	15	41.67	15	30	83.33
San Francisco	46	12	11	23	50.00	8	31	67.39
Minnesota	42	12	11	23	54.76	9	32	76.19
N.Y. Giants	41	9	9	18	43.90	15	33	80.49
Pittsburgh	37	7	7	14	37.84	19	33	89.19
Baltimore	39	9	10	19	48.72	14	33	84.62
Tennessee	43	8	11	19	44.19	15	34	79.07
Denver	44	8	16	24	54.55	12	36	81.82
Tampa Bay	40	9	9	18	45.00	18	36	90.00
Buffalo	44	11	16	27	61.36	11	38	86.36
San Diego	46	11	10	21	45.65	17	38	82.61
Carolina	43	11	12	23	53.49	15	38	88.37
Seattle	48	13	11	24	50.00	15	39	81.25
New Orleans	55	10	14	24	43.64	16	40	72.73
Detroit	50	13	14	27	54.00	15	42	84.00
Oakland	51	8	16	24	47.06	19	43	84.31
New England	52	7	19	26	50.00	17	43	82.69
Philadelphia	52	16	13	29	55.77	14	43	82.69
Jacksonville	50	8	15	23	46.00	20	43	86.00
St. Louis	52	7	21	28	53.85	17	45	86.54
Arizona	53	17	14	31	58.49	14	45	84.91
Kansas City	56	19	13	32	57.14	14	46	82.14
Chicago	50	11	19	30	60.00	17	47	94.00
Washington	58	20	15	35	60.34	16	51	87.93
Cincinnati	59	22	14	36	61.02	16	52	88.14
Indianapolis	58	17	18	35	60.34	18	53	91.38
Totals	1386	328	387	715	51.59	443	1158	83.55
Average	46.2	10.9	12.9	23.8	51.59	14.8	38.6	83.55

SCORING EFFICIENCY

Team	Series	TD Rush	TD Pass	Total TDs	TD Efficiency Pct.	FGM	Total Scores	Scoring Efficiency Pct.
San Francisco	46	12	11	23	50.00	8	31	67.39
New Orleans	55	10	14	24	43.64	16	40	72.73
N.Y. Jets	39	9	9	18	46.15	11	29	74.36
Minnesota	42	12	11	23	54.76	9	32	76.19
Tennessee	43	8	11	19	44.19	15	34	79.07
Atlanta	35	7	10	17	48.57	11	28	80.00
N.Y. Giants	41	9	9	18	43.90	15	33	80.49
Seattle	48	13	11	24	50.00	15	39	81.25
Denver	44	8	16	24	54.55	12	36	81.82
Kansas City	56	19	13	32	57.14	14	46	82.14
San Diego	46	11	10	21	45.65	17	38	82.61
New England	52	7	19	26	50.00	17	43	82.69
Philadelphia	52	16	13	29	55.77	14	43	82.69
Green Bay	36	5	11	16	44.44	14	30	83.33
Miami	36	5	10	15	41.67	15	30	83.33
Detroit	50	13	14	27	54.00	15	42	84.00
Oakland	51	8	16	24	47.06	19	43	84.31
Baltimore	39	9	10	19	48.72	14	33	84.62
Arizona	53	17	14	31	58.49	14	45	84.91
Jacksonville	50	8	15	23	46.00	20	43	86.00
Buffalo	44	11	16	27	61.36	11	38	86.36
St. Louis	52	7	21	28	53.85	17	45	86.54
Dallas	31	7	9	16	51.61	11	27	87.10
Washington	58	20	15	35	60.34	16	51	87.93
Cincinnati	59	22	14	36	61.02	16	52	88.14
Carolina	43	11	12	23	53.49	15	38	88.37
Pittsburgh	37	7	7	14	37.84	19	33	89.19
Tampa Bay	40	9	9	18	45.00	18	36	90.00
Indianapolis	58	17	18	35	60.34	18	53	91.38
Chicago	50	11	19	30	60.00	17	47	94.00
Totals	1386	328	387	715	51.59	443	1158	83.55
Average	46.2	10.9	12.9	23.8	51.59	14.8	38.6	83.55

1998 STATISTICS *Miscellaneous*

HISTORY

Championship games
Year-by-year standings
Super Bowls
Pro Bowls
Records
Statistical leaders
Coaching records
Hall of Fame
The Sporting News awards
Team by team

CHAMPIONSHIP GAMES

NFL (1933-1969); NFC (1970-1998)

RESULTS

Sea.	Date	Winner (Share)	Loser (Share)	Score	Site	Attendance
1933	Dec. 17	Chicago Bears ($210.34)	N.Y. Giants ($140.22)	23-21	Chicago	26,000
1934	Dec. 9	N.Y. Giants ($621)	Chicago Bears ($414.02)	30-13	N.Y. Giants	35,059
1935	Dec. 15	Detroit ($313.35)	N.Y. Giants ($200.20)	26-7	Detroit	15,000
1936	Dec. 13	Green Bay ($250)	Boston Redskins ($180)	21-6	N.Y. Giants	29,545
1937	Dec. 12	Washington ($225.90)	Chicago Bears ($127.78)	28-21	Chicago	15,870
1938	Dec. 11	N.Y. Giants ($504.45)	Green Bay ($368.81)	23-17	N.Y. Giants	48,120
1939	Dec. 10	Green Bay ($703.97)	N.Y. Giants ($455.57)	27-0	Milwaukee	32,279
1940	Dec. 8	Chicago Bears ($873)	Washington ($606)	73-0	Washington	36,034
1941	Dec. 21	Chicago Bears ($430)	N.Y. Giants ($288)	37-9	Chicago	13,341
1942	Dec. 13	Washington ($965)	Chicago Bears ($637)	14-6	Washington	36,006
1943	Dec. 26	Chicago Bears ($1,146)	Washington ($765)	41-21	Chicago	34,320
1944	Dec. 17	Green Bay ($1,449)	N.Y. Giants ($814)	14-7	N.Y. Giants	46,016
1945	Dec. 16	Cleveland Rams ($1,469)	Washington ($902)	15-14	Cleveland	32,178
1946	Dec. 15	Chicago Bears ($1,975)	N.Y. Giants ($1,295)	24-14	N.Y. Giants	58,346
1947	Dec. 28	Chi. Cardinals ($1,132)	Philadelphia ($754)	28-21	Chicago	30,759
1948	Dec. 19	Philadelphia ($1,540)	Chi. Cardinals ($874)	7-0	Philadelphia	36,309
1949	Dec. 18	Philadelphia ($1,094)	L.A. Rams ($739)	14-0	L.A. Rams	27,980
1950	Dec. 24	Cleveland Browns ($1,113)	L.A. Rams ($686)	30-28	Cleveland	29,751
1951	Dec. 23	L. A. Rams ($2,108)	Cleve. Browns ($1,483)	24-17	L.A. Rams	57,522
1952	Dec. 28	Detroit ($2,274)	Cleveland Browns ($1,712)	17-7	Cleveland	50,934
1953	Dec. 27	Detroit ($2,424)	Cleveland Browns ($1,654)	17-16	Detroit	54,577
1954	Dec. 26	Cleveland Browns ($2,478)	Detroit ($1,585)	56-10	Cleveland	43,827
1955	Dec. 26	Cleveland Browns ($3,508)	L.A. Rams ($2,316)	38-14	L.A. Rams	85,693
1956	Dec. 30	N.Y. Giants ($3,779)	Chicago Bears ($2,485)	47-7	N.Y. Giants	56,836
1957	Dec. 29	Detroit ($4,295)	Cleveland Browns ($2,750)	59-14	Detroit	55,263
1958	Dec. 28	Baltimore ($4,718)	N.Y. Giants ($3,111)	23-17*	N.Y. Giants	64,185
1959	Dec. 27	Baltimore ($4,674)	N.Y. Giants ($3,083)	31-16	Baltimore	57,545
1960	Dec. 26	Philadelphia ($5,116)	Green Bay ($3,105)	17-13	Philadelphia	67,325
1961	Dec. 31	Green Bay ($5,195)	N.Y. Giants ($3,339)	37-0	Green Bay	39,029
1962	Dec. 30	Green Bay ($5,888)	N.Y. Giants ($4,166)	16-7	N.Y. Giants	64,892
1963	Dec. 29	Chicago Bears ($5,899)	N.Y. Giants ($4,218)	14-10	Chicago	45,801
1964	Dec. 27	Cleveland Browns ($8,052)	Baltimore ($5,571)	27-0	Cleveland	79,544
1965	Jan. 2	Green Bay ($7,819)	Cleveland Browns ($5,288)	23-12	Green Bay	50,777
1966	Jan. 1	Green Bay ($9,813)	Dallas ($6,527)	34-27	Dallas	74,152
1967	Dec. 31	Green Bay ($7,950)	Dallas ($5,299)	21-17	Green Bay	50,861
1968	Dec. 29	Baltimore ($9,306)	Cleveland Browns ($5,963)	34-0	Cleveland	78,410
1969	Jan. 4	Minnesota ($7,930)	Cleveland Browns ($5,118)	27-7	Minnesota	46,503
1970	Jan. 3	Dallas ($8,500)	San Francisco ($5,500)	17-10	San Francisco	59,364
1971	Jan. 2	Dallas ($8,500)	San Francisco ($5,500)	14-3	Dallas	63,409
1972	Dec. 31	Washington ($8,500)	Dallas ($5,500)	26-3	Washington	53,129
1973	Dec. 30	Minnesota ($8,500)	Dallas ($5,500)	27-10	Dallas	64,422
1974	Dec. 29	Minnesota ($8,500)	L.A. Rams ($5,500)	14-10	Minnesota	48,444
1975	Jan. 4	Dallas ($8,500)	L.A. Rams ($5,500)	37-7	L.A. Rams	88,919
1976	Dec. 26	Minnesota ($8,500)	L.A. Rams ($5,500)	24-13	Minnesota	48,379
1977	Jan. 1	Dallas ($9,000)	Minnesota ($9,000)	23-6	Dallas	64,293
1978	Jan. 7	Dallas ($9,000)	L.A. Rams ($9,000)	28-0	L.A. Rams	71,086
1979	Jan. 6	L.A. Rams ($9,000)	Tampa Bay ($9,000)	9-0	Tampa Bay	72,033
1980	Jan. 11	Philadelphia ($9,000)	Dallas ($9,000)	20-7	Philadelphia	70,696
1981	Jan. 10	San Francisco ($9,000)	Dallas ($9,000)	28-27	San Francisco	60,525
1982	Jan. 22	Washington ($18,000)	Dallas ($18,000)	31-17	Washington	55,045
1983	Jan. 8	Washington ($18,000)	San Francisco ($18,000)	24-21	Washington	55,363
1984	Jan. 6	San Francisco ($18,000)	Chicago Bears ($18,000)	23-0	San Francisco	61,040
1985	Jan. 12	Chicago Bears ($18,000)	L.A. Rams ($18,000)	24-0	Chicago	63,522
1986	Jan. 11	N. Y. Giants ($18,000)	Washington ($18,000)	17-0	N.Y. Giants	76,633
1987	Jan. 17	Washington ($18,000)	Minnesota ($18,000)	17-10	Washington	55,212
1988	Jan. 8	San Francisco ($18,000)	Chicago Bears ($18,000)	28-3	Chicago	64,830
1989	Jan. 14	San Francisco ($18,000)	L.A. Rams ($18,000)	30-3	San Francisco	64,769
1990	Jan. 20	N. Y. Giants ($18,000)	San Francisco ($18,000)	15-13	San Francisco	65,750
1991	Jan. 12	Washington ($18,000)	Detroit ($18,000)	41-10	Washington	55,585
1992	Jan. 17	Dallas ($18,000)	San Francisco ($18,000)	30-20	San Francisco	64,920
1993	Jan. 23	Dallas ($23,500)	San Francisco ($23,500)	38-21	Dallas	64,902
1994	Jan. 15	San Francisco ($26,000)	Dallas ($26,000)	38-28	San Francisco	69,125
1995	Jan. 14	Dallas ($27,000)	Green Bay ($27,000)	38-27	Dallas	65,135
1996	Jan. 12	Green Bay ($29,000)	Carolina ($29,000)	30-13	Green Bay	60,216
1997	Jan. 11	Green Bay ($30,000)	San Francisco ($30,000)	23-10	San Francisco	68,987
1998	Jan. 17	Atlanta ($32,500)	Minnesota ($32,500)	30-27*	Minnesota	64,060

*Overtime.

COMPOSITE STANDINGS

	W	L	Pct.	PF	PA		W	L	Pct.	PF	PA
Atlanta Falcons	1	0	1.000	30	27	Dallas Cowboys	8	8	.500	361	319
Philadelphia Eagles	4	1	.800	79	48	Phoenix Cardinals*	1	1	.500	28	28
Green Bay Packers	10	3	.769	303	177	San Francisco 49ers	5	7	.417	245	222
Baltimore Colts	3	1	.750	88	60	Cleveland Browns	4	7	.364	224	253
Detroit Lions	4	2	.667	139	141	New York Giants	5	11	.313	240	322
Washington Redskins†	7	5	.583	222	255	Los Angeles Rams‡	3	9	.250	123	270
Minnesota Vikings	4	3	.571	135	110	Carolina Panthers	0	1	.000	13	30
Chicago Bears	7	6	.538	286	245	Tampa Bay Buccaneers	0	1	.000	0	9

*Both games played when franchise was in Chicago; won 28-21, lost 7-0.
†One game played when franchise was in Boston; lost 21-6.
‡One game played when franchise was in Cleveland; won 15-14.

AFL (1960-1969); AFC (1970-1998)
RESULTS

Sea.	Date	Winner (Share)	Loser (Share)	Score	Site	Attendance
1960	Jan. 1	Houston ($1,025)	L.A. Chargers ($718)	24-16	Houston	32,183
1961	Dec. 24	Houston ($1,792)	San Diego ($1,111)	10-3	San Diego	29,556
1962	Dec. 23	Dallas Texans ($2,206)	Houston ($1,471)	20-17*	Houston	37,981
1963	Jan. 5	San Diego ($2,498)	Boston Patriots ($1,596)	51-10	San Diego	30,127
1964	Dec. 26	Buffalo ($2,668)	San Diego ($1,738)	20-7	Buffalo	40,242
1965	Dec. 26	Buffalo ($5,189)	San Diego ($3,447)	23-0	San Diego	30,361
1966	Jan. 1	Kansas City ($5,309)	Buffalo ($3,799)	31-7	Buffalo	42,080
1967	Dec. 31	Oakland ($6,321)	Houston ($4,996)	40-7	Oakland	53,330
1968	Dec. 29	N.Y. Jets ($7,007)	Oakland ($5,349)	27-23	New York	62,627
1969	Jan. 4	Kansas City ($7,755)	Oakland ($6,252)	17-7	Oakland	53,564
1970	Jan. 3	Baltimore ($8,500)	Oakland ($5,500)	27-17	Baltimore	54,799
1971	Jan. 2	Miami ($8,500)	Baltimore ($5,500)	21-0	Miami	76,622
1972	Dec. 31	Miami ($8,500)	Pittsburgh ($5,500)	21-17	Pittsburgh	50,845
1973	Dec. 30	Miami ($8,500)	Oakland ($5,500)	27-10	Miami	79,325
1974	Dec. 29	Pittsburgh ($8,500)	Oakland ($5,500)	24-13	Oakland	53,800
1975	Jan. 4	Pittsburgh ($8,500)	Oakland ($5,500)	16-10	Pittsburgh	50,609
1976	Dec. 28	Oakland ($8,500)	Pittsburgh ($5,500)	24-7	Oakland	53,821
1977	Jan. 1	Denver ($9,000)	Oakland ($9,000)	20-17	Denver	75,044
1978	Jan. 7	Pittsburgh ($9,000)	Houston ($9,000)	34-5	Pittsburgh	50,725
1979	Jan. 6	Pittsburgh ($9,000)	Houston ($9,000)	27-13	Pittsburgh	50,475
1980	Jan. 11	Oakland ($9,000)	San Diego ($9,000)	34-27	San Diego	52,428
1981	Jan. 10	Cincinnati ($9,000)	San Diego ($9,000)	27-7	Cincinnati	46,302
1982	Jan. 23	Miami ($18,000)	N.Y. Jets ($18,000)	14-0	Miami	67,396
1983	Jan. 8	L.A. Raiders ($18,000)	Seattle ($18,000)	30-14	Los Angeles	88,734
1984	Jan. 6	Miami ($18,000)	Pittsburgh ($18,000)	45-28	Miami	76,029
1985	Jan. 12	New England ($18,000)	Miami ($18,000)	31-14	Miami	74,978
1986	Jan. 11	Denver ($18,000)	Cleveland ($18,000)	23-20*	Cleveland	79,915
1987	Jan. 17	Denver ($18,000)	Cleveland ($18,000)	38-33	Denver	75,993
1988	Jan. 8	Cincinnati ($18,000)	Buffalo ($18,000)	21-10	Cincinnati	59,747
1989	Jan. 14	Denver ($18,000)	Cleveland ($18,000)	37-21	Denver	76,046
1990	Jan. 20	Buffalo ($18,000)	L.A. Raiders ($18,000)	51-3	Buffalo	80,234
1991	Jan. 12	Buffalo ($18,000)	Denver ($18,000)	10-7	Buffalo	80,272
1992	Jan. 17	Buffalo ($18,000)	Miami ($18,000)	29-10	Miami	72,703
1993	Jan. 23	Buffalo ($23,500)	Kansas City ($23,500)	30-13	Buffalo	76,642
1994	Jan. 15	San Diego ($26,000)	Pittsburgh ($26,000)	17-13	Pittsburgh	61,545
1995	Jan. 14	Pittsburgh ($27,000)	Indianapolis ($27,000)	20-16	Pittsburgh	61,062
1996	Jan. 12	New England ($29,000)	Jacksonville ($29,000)	20-6	New England	60,190
1997	Jan. 11	Denver ($30,000)	Pittsburgh ($30,000)	24-21	Pittsburgh	61,382
1998	Jan. 17	Denver ($32,500)	N.Y. Jets ($32,500)	23-10	Denver	75,482

*Overtime.

COMPOSITE STANDINGS

	W	L	Pct.	PF	PA		W	L	Pct.	PF	PA
Cincinnati Bengals	2	0	1.000	48	17	Houston Oilers	2	4	.333	76	140
Denver Broncos	6	1	.857	172	132	Indianapolis Colts∞	1	2	.333	43	58
Buffalo Bills	6	2	.750	180	92	Oakland Raiders§	4	8	.333	228	264
Kansas City Chiefs†	3	1	.750	81	61	San Diego Chargers*	2	6	.250	128	161
Miami Dolphins	5	2	.714	152	115	Seattle Seahawks	0	1	.000	14	30
New England Patriots‡	2	1	.667	61	71	Jacksonville Jaguars	0	1	.000	6	20
Pittsburgh Steelers	5	5	.500	207	188	Cleveland Browns	0	3	.000	74	98
New York Jets	1	2	.333	37	60						

*One game played when franchise was in Los Angeles; lost 24-16.
†One game played when franchise was in Dallas (Texans); won 20-17.
‡One game played when franchise was in Boston; lost 51-10.
§Two games played when franchise was in Los Angeles; record of 1-1.
∞Two games played when franchise was in Baltimore; record of 1-1.

POSTSEASON GAME COMPOSITE STANDINGS

	W	L	Pct.	PF	PA		W	L	Pct.	PF	PA
Green Bay Packers	22	10	.688	772	558	Detroit Lions	7	9	.438	352	377
San Francisco 49ers	24	15	.615	984	759	Seattle Seahawks	3	4	.429	128	139
Dallas Cowboys	32	20	.615	1261	952	New York Giants	14	19	.424	551	616
Washington Redskins‡	21	14	.600	738	625	Kansas City Chiefs*	8	11	.421	301	384
Denver Broncos	16	11	.593	613	636	Minnesota Vikings	15	21	.417	681	797
Pittsburgh Steelers	21	15	.583	801	707	Cincinnati Bengals	5	7	.417	246	257
Oakland Raiders◆	21	15	.583	855	659	New England Patriots§	7	10	.412	320	357
Miami Dolphins	18	16	.529	727	705	Tennessee Oilers▼	9	13	.409	371	533
Buffalo Bills	14	14	.500	665	636	Atlanta Falcons	4	6	.400	208	260
Chicago Bears	14	14	.500	579	552	St. Louis Rams†@	13	20	.394	501	697
Indianapolis Colts■	10	10	.500	360	389	San Diego Chargers▲	7	11	.389	332	428
Jacksonville Jaguars	3	3	.500	132	160	Cleveland Browns	11	19	.367	596	702
Carolina Panthers	1	1	.500	39	47	Tampa Bay Buccaneers	2	4	.333	68	125
New York Jets	6	7	.462	260	247	Arizona Cardinals∞	2	5	.286	122	182
Philadelphia Eagles	9	11	.450	356	369	New Orleans Saints	0	4	.000	56	123

*One game played when franchise was in Dallas (Texans); won 20-17.
†One game played when franchise was in Cleveland; won 15-14.
‡One game played when franchise was in Boston; lost 21-6.
§Two games played when franchise was in Boston; won 26-8, lost 51-10.
∞Two games played when franchise was in Chicago; won 28-21, lost 7-0. Three games played when franchise was in St. Louis; lost 35-23, lost 30-14, lost 41-16.
▲One game played when franchise was in Los Angeles; lost 24-16.
◆12 games played when franchise was in Los Angeles; record of 6-6.
■15 games played when franchise was in Baltimore; record of 8-7.
▼All 22 games played when franchise was in Houston; record of 9-13.
@32 games played when franchise was in Los Angeles; record of 12-20.

CHAMPIONS OF DEFUNCT PRO FOOTBALL LEAGUES

ALL-AMERICAN FOOTBALL CONFERENCE

Year	Winner	Coach	Loser	Coach	Score, Site
1946	Cleveland Browns	Paul Brown	N.Y. Yankees	Ray Flaherty	14-9, Cleveland
1947	Cleveland Browns	Paul Brown	N.Y. Yankees	Ray Flaherty	14-3, New York
1948	Cleveland Browns	Paul Brown	Buffalo Bills	Red Dawson	49-7, Cleveland
1949	Cleveland Browns	Paul Brown	S.F. 49ers	Buck Shaw	21-7, Cleveland

NOTE: Cleveland Browns and San Francisco 49ers joined the NFL after the AAFC folded in 1949.

WORLD FOOTBALL LEAGUE

Year	Winner	Coach	Loser	Coach	Score, Site
1974	Birmingham Americans	Jack Gotta	Florida Blazers	Jack Pardee	22-21, Birmingham
1975	League folded October 22				

UNITED STATES FOOTBALL LEAGUE

Year	Winner	Coach	Loser	Coach	Score, Site
1983	Michigan Panthers	Jim Stanley	Philadelphia Stars	Jim Mora	24-22, Denver
1984	Philadelphia Stars	Jim Mora	Arizona Wranglers	George Allen	23-3, Tampa
1985	Baltimore Stars	Jim Mora	Oakland Invaders	Charlie Sumner	28-24, E. Rutherford, N.J.

YEAR-BY-YEAR STANDINGS

1920

Team	W	L	T	Pct.
Akron Pros*	8	0	3	1.000
Decatur Staleys	10	1	2	.909
Buffalo All-Americans	9	1	1	.900
Chicago Cardinals	6	2	2	.750
Rock Island Independents	6	2	2	.750
Dayton Triangles	5	2	2	.714
Rochester Jeffersons	6	3	2	.667
Canton Bulldogs	7	4	2	.636
Detroit Heralds	2	3	3	.400
Cleveland Tigers	2	4	2	.333
Chicago Tigers	2	5	1	.286
Hammond Pros	2	5	0	.286
Columbus Panhandles	2	6	2	.250
Muncie Flyers	0	1	0	.000

*No official standings were maintained for the 1920 season, and the championship was awarded to the Akron Pros in a League meeting on April 30, 1921. Clubs played schedules which included games against non-league opponents. Records of clubs against all opponents are listed above.

1921

Team	W	L	T	Pct.
Chicago Staleys	9	1	1	.900
Buffalo All-Americans	9	1	2	.900
Akron Pros	8	3	1	.727
Canton Bulldogs	5	2	3	.714
Rock Island Independents	4	2	1	.667
Evansville Crimson Giants	3	2	0	.600
Green Bay Packers	3	2	1	.600
Dayton Triangles	4	4	1	.500
Chicago Cardinals	3	3	2	.500
Rochester Jeffersons	2	3	0	.400
Cleveland Indians	3	5	0	.375
Washington Senators	1	2	0	.333
Cincinnati Celts	1	3	0	.250
Hammond Pros	1	3	1	.250
Minneapolis Marines	1	3	1	.250
Detroit Heralds	1	5	1	.167
Columbus Panhandles	1	8	0	.111
Tonawanda Kardex	0	1	0	.000
Muncie Flyers	0	2	0	.000
Louisville Brecks	0	2	0	.000
New York Giants	0	2	0	.000

1922

Team	W	L	T	Pct.
Canton Bulldogs	10	0	2	1.000
Chicago Bears	9	3	0	.750
Chicago Cardinals	8	3	0	.727
Toledo Maroons	5	2	2	.714
Rock Island Independents	4	2	1	.667
Racine Legion	6	4	1	.600
Dayton Triangles	4	3	1	.571
Green Bay Packers	4	3	3	.571
Buffalo All-Americans	5	4	1	.556
Akron Pros	3	5	2	.375
Milwaukee Badgers	2	4	3	.333
Oorang Indians	2	6	0	.250
Minneapolis Marines	1	3	0	.250
Louisville Brecks	1	3	0	.250
Evansville Crimson Giants	0	3	0	.000
Rochester Jeffersons	0	4	1	.000
Hammond Pros	0	5	1	.000
Columbus Panhandles	0	7	0	.000

1923

Team	W	L	T	Pct.
Canton Bulldogs	11	0	1	1.000
Chicago Bears	9	2	1	.818
Green Bay Packers	7	2	1	.778
Milwaukee Badgers	7	2	3	.778
Cleveland Indians	3	1	3	.750
Chicago Cardinals	8	4	0	.667
Duluth Kelleys	4	3	0	.571
Columbus Tigers	5	4	1	.556
Buffalo All-Americans	4	4	3	.500
Racine Legion	4	4	2	.500
Toledo Maroons	2	3	2	.400
Rock Island Independents	2	3	3	.400
Minneapolis Marines	2	5	2	.286
St. Louis All-Stars	1	4	2	.200
Hammond Pros	1	5	1	.167
Dayton Triangles	1	6	1	.143
Akron Indians	1	6	0	.143
Oorang Indians	1	10	0	.091
Rochester Jeffersons	0	2	0	.000
Louisville Brecks	0	3	0	.000

1924

Team	W	L	T	Pct.
Cleveland Bulldogs	7	1	1	.875
Chicago Bears	6	1	4	.857
Frankford Yellow Jackets	11	2	1	.846
Duluth Kelleys	5	1	0	.833
Rock Island Independents	6	2	2	.750
Green Bay Packers	7	4	0	.636
Racine Legion	4	3	3	.571
Chicago Cardinals	5	4	1	.556
Buffalo Bisons	6	5	0	.545
Columbus Tigers	4	4	0	.500
Hammond Pros	2	2	1	.500
Milwaukee Badgers	5	8	0	.385
Akron Indians	2	6	0	.250
Dayton Triangles	2	6	0	.250
Kansas City Blues	2	7	0	.222
Kenosha Maroons	0	5	1	.000
Minneapolis Marines	0	6	0	.000
Rochester Jeffersons	0	7	0	.000

1925

Team	W	L	T	Pct.
Chicago Cardinals	11	2	1	.846
Pottsville Maroons	10	2	0	.833
Detroit Panthers	8	2	2	.800
New York Giants	8	4	0	.667
Akron Indians	4	2	2	.667
Frankford Yellow Jackets	13	7	0	.650
Chicago Bears	9	5	3	.643
Rock Island Independents	5	3	3	.625
Green Bay Packers	8	5	0	.615
Providence Steam Roller	6	5	1	.545
Canton Bulldogs	4	4	0	.500
Cleveland Bulldogs	5	8	1	.385
Kansas City Cowboys	2	5	1	.286
Hammond Pros	1	4	0	.200
Buffalo Bisons	1	6	2	.143
Duluth Kelleys	0	3	0	.000
Rochester Jeffersons	0	6	1	.000
Milwaukee Badgers	0	6	0	.000
Dayton Triangles	0	7	1	.000
Columbus Tigers	0	9	0	.000

1926

Team	W	L	T	Pct.
Frankford Yellow Jackets	14	1	1	.933
Chicago Bears	12	1	3	.923
Pottsville Maroons	10	2	1	.833
Kansas City Cowboys	8	3	0	.727
Green Bay Packers	7	3	3	.700
Los Angeles Buccaneers	6	3	1	.667
New York Giants	8	4	1	.667
Duluth Eskimos	6	5	3	.545
Buffalo Rangers	4	4	2	.500
Chicago Cardinals	5	6	1	.455
Providence Steam Roller	5	7	1	.417
Detroit Panthers	4	6	2	.400
Hartford Blues	3	7	0	.300
Brooklyn Lions	3	8	0	.273
Milwaukee Badgers	2	7	0	.222
Akron Pros	1	4	3	.200
Dayton Triangles	1	4	1	.200
Racine Tornadoes	1	4	0	.200
Columbus Tigers	1	6	0	.143
Canton Bulldogs	1	9	3	.100
Hammond Pros	0	4	0	.000
Louisville Colonels	0	4	0	.000

1927

Team	W	L	T	Pct.
New York Giants	11	1	1	.917
Green Bay Packers	7	2	1	.778
Chicago Bears	9	3	2	.750
Cleveland Bulldogs	8	4	1	.667
Providence Steam Roller	8	5	1	.615
New York Yankees	7	8	1	.467
Frankford Yellow Jackets	6	9	3	.400
Pottsville Maroons	5	8	0	.385
Chicago Cardinals	3	7	1	.300
Dayton Triangles	1	6	1	.143
Duluth Eskimos	1	8	0	.111
Buffalo Bisons	0	5	0	.000

1928

Team	W	L	T	Pct.
Providence Steam Roller	8	1	2	.889
Frankford Yellow Jackets	11	3	2	.786
Detroit Wolverines	7	2	1	.778
Green Bay Packers	6	4	3	.600
Chicago Bears	7	5	1	.583
New York Giants	4	7	2	.364
New York Yankees	4	8	1	.333
Pottsville Maroons	2	8	0	.200
Chicago Cardinals	1	5	0	.167
Dayton Triangles	0	7	0	.000

1929

Team	W	L	T	Pct.
Green Bay Packers	12	0	1	1.000
New York Giants	13	1	1	.929
Frankford Yellow Jackets	9	4	5	.692
Chicago Cardinals	6	6	1	.500
Boston Bulldogs	4	4	0	.500
Orange Tornadoes	3	4	4	.429
Staten Island Stapletons	3	4	3	.429
Providence Steam Roller	4	6	2	.400
Chicago Bears	4	9	2	.308
Buffalo Bisons	1	7	1	.125
Minneapolis Red Jackets	1	9	0	.100
Dayton Triangles	0	6	0	.000

1930

Team	W	L	T	Pct.
Green Bay Packers	10	3	1	.769
New York Giants	13	4	0	.765
Chicago Bears	9	4	1	.692
Brooklyn Dodgers	7	4	1	.636
Providence Steam Roller	6	4	1	.600
Staten Island Stapletons	5	5	2	.500
Chicago Cardinals	5	6	2	.455
Portsmouth Spartans	5	6	3	.455
Frankford Yellow Jackets	4	13	1	.222
Minneapolis Red Jackets	1	7	1	.125
Newark Tornadoes	1	10	1	.091

1931

Team	W	L	T	Pct.
Green Bay Packers	12	2	0	.857
Portsmouth Spartans	11	3	0	.786
Chicago Bears	8	5	0	.615
Chicago Cardinals	5	4	0	.556
New York Giants	7	6	1	.538
Providence Steam Roller	4	4	3	.500
Staten Island Stapletons	4	6	1	.400
Cleveland Indians	2	8	0	.200
Brooklyn Dodgers	2	12	0	.143
Frankford Yellow Jackets	1	6	1	.143

1932

Team	W	L	T	Pct.
Chicago Bears	7	1	6	.875
Green Bay Packers	10	3	1	.769
Portsmouth Spartans	6	2	4	.750
Boston Braves	4	4	2	.500
New York Giants	4	6	2	.400
Brooklyn Dodgers	3	9	0	.250
Chicago Cardinals	2	6	2	.250
Staten Island Stapletons	2	7	3	.222

NOTE: Chicago Bears and Portsmouth finished regularly scheduled games tied for first place. Bears won playoff game, which counted in standings, 9-0.

1933

EASTERN DIVISION

Team	W	L	T	Pct.	PF	PA
N.Y. Giants	11	3	0	.786	244	101
Brooklyn	5	4	1	.556	93	54
Boston	5	5	2	.500	103	97
Philadelphia	3	5	1	.375	77	158
Pittsburgh	3	6	2	.333	67	208

WESTERN DIVISION

Team	W	L	T	Pct.	PF	PA
Chicago Bears	10	2	1	.833	133	82
Portsmouth	6	5	0	.545	128	87
Green Bay	5	7	1	.417	170	107
Cincinnati	3	6	1	.333	38	110
Chi. Cardinals	1	9	1	.100	52	101

PLAYOFFS

NFL championship

Chicago Bears 23 vs. N.Y. Giants 21

1934

EASTERN DIVISION

Team	W	L	T	Pct.	PF	PA
N.Y. Giants	8	5	0	.615	147	107
Boston	6	6	0	.500	107	94
Brooklyn	4	7	0	.364	61	153
Philadelphia	4	7	0	.364	127	85
Pittsburgh	2	10	0	.167	51	206

WESTERN DIVISION

Team	W	L	T	Pct.	PF	PA
Chicago Bears	13	0	0	1.000	286	86
Detroit	10	3	0	.769	238	59
Green Bay	7	6	0	.538	156	112
Chi. Cardinals	5	6	0	.455	80	84
St. Louis	1	2	0	.333	27	61
Cincinnati	0	8	0	.000	10	243

PLAYOFFS

NFL championship
N.Y. Giants 30 vs. Chicago Bears 13

1935

EASTERN DIVISION

Team	W	L	T	Pct.	PF	PA
N.Y. Giants	9	3	0	.750	180	96
Brooklyn	5	6	1	.455	90	141
Pittsburgh	4	8	0	.333	100	209
Boston	2	8	1	.200	65	123
Philadelphia	2	9	0	.182	60	179

NOTE: One game between Boston and Philadelphia was cancelled.

WESTERN DIVISION

Team	W	L	T	Pct.	PF	PA
Detroit	7	3	2	.700	191	111
Green Bay	8	4	0	.667	181	96
Chicago Bears	6	4	2	.600	192	106
Chi. Cardinals	6	4	2	.600	99	97

PLAYOFFS

NFL championship
Detroit 26 vs. N.Y. Giants 7

1936

EASTERN DIVISION

Team	W	L	T	Pct.	PF	PA
Boston	7	5	0	.583	149	110
Pittsburgh	6	6	0	.500	98	187
N.Y. Giants	5	6	1	.455	115	163
Brooklyn	3	8	1	.273	92	161
Philadelphia	1	11	0	.083	51	206

WESTERN DIVISION

Team	W	L	T	Pct.	PF	PA
Green Bay	10	1	1	.909	248	118
Chicago Bears	9	3	0	.750	222	94
Detroit	8	4	0	.667	235	102
Chi. Cardinals	3	8	1	.273	74	143

PLAYOFFS

NFL championship
Green Bay 21, Boston 6, at New York.

1937

EASTERN DIVISION

Team	W	L	T	Pct.	PF	PA
Washington	8	3	0	.727	195	120
N.Y. Giants	6	3	2	.667	128	109
Pittsburgh	4	7	0	.364	122	145
Brooklyn	3	7	1	.300	82	174
Philadelphia	2	8	1	.200	86	177

WESTERN DIVISION

Team	W	L	T	Pct.	PF	PA
Chicago Bears	9	1	1	.900	201	100
Green Bay	7	4	0	.636	220	122
Detroit	7	4	0	.636	180	105
Chi. Cardinals	5	5	1	.500	135	165
Cleveland	1	10	0	.091	75	207

PLAYOFFS

NFL championship
Washington 28 at Chicago Bears 21

1938

EASTERN DIVISION

Team	W	L	T	Pct.	PF	PA
N.Y. Giants	8	2	1	.800	194	79
Washington	6	3	2	.667	148	154
Brooklyn	4	4	3	.500	131	161
Philadelphia	5	6	0	.455	154	164
Pittsburgh	2	9	0	.182	79	169

WESTERN DIVISION

Team	W	L	T	Pct.	PF	PA
Green Bay	8	3	0	.727	223	118
Detroit	7	4	0	.636	119	108
Chicago Bears	6	5	0	.545	194	148
Cleveland	4	7	0	.364	131	215
Chi. Cardinals	2	9	0	.182	111	168

PLAYOFFS

NFL championship
N.Y. Giants 23 vs. Green Bay 17

1939

EASTERN DIVISION

Team	W	L	T	Pct.	PF	PA
N.Y. Giants	9	1	1	.900	168	85
Washington	8	2	1	.800	242	94
Brooklyn	4	6	1	.400	108	219
Philadelphia	1	9	1	.100	105	200
Pittsburgh	1	9	1	.100	114	216

WESTERN DIVISION

Team	W	L	T	Pct.	PF	PA
Green Bay	9	2	0	.818	233	153
Chicago Bears	8	3	0	.727	298	157
Detroit	6	5	0	.545	145	150
Cleveland	5	5	1	.500	195	164
Chi. Cardinals	1	10	0	.091	84	254

PLAYOFFS

NFL championship
Green Bay 27 vs. N.Y. Giants 0

1940

EASTERN DIVISION

Team	W	L	T	Pct.	PF	PA
Washington	9	2	0	.818	245	142
Brooklyn	8	3	0	.727	186	120
N.Y. Giants	6	4	1	.600	131	133
Pittsburgh	2	7	2	.222	60	178
Philadelphia	1	10	0	.091	111	211

WESTERN DIVISION

Team	W	L	T	Pct.	PF	PA
Chicago Bears	8	3	0	.727	238	152
Green Bay	6	4	1	.600	238	155
Detroit	5	5	1	.500	138	153
Cleveland	4	6	1	.400	171	191
Chi. Cardinals	2	7	2	.222	139	222

PLAYOFFS

NFL championship
Chicago Bears 73 at Washington 0

1941

EASTERN DIVISION

Team	W	L	T	Pct.	PF	PA
N.Y. Giants	8	3	0	.727	238	114
Brooklyn	7	4	0	.636	158	127
Washington	6	5	0	.545	176	174
Philadelphia	2	8	1	.200	119	218
Pittsburgh	1	9	1	.100	103	276

WESTERN DIVISION

Team	W	L	T	Pct.	PF	PA
Chicago Bears	10	1	0	.909	396	147
Green Bay	10	1	0	.909	258	120
Detroit	4	6	1	.400	121	195
Chi. Cardinals	3	7	1	.300	127	197
Cleveland	2	9	0	.182	116	244

PLAYOFFS

Western Division playoff
Chicago Bears 33 vs. Green Bay 14

NFL championship
Chicago Bears 37 vs. N.Y. Giants 9

1942

EASTERN DIVISION

Team	W	L	T	Pct.	PF	PA
Washington	10	1	0	.909	227	102
Pittsburgh	7	4	0	.636	167	119
N.Y. Giants	5	5	1	.500	155	139
Brooklyn	3	8	0	.273	100	168
Philadelphia	2	9	0	.182	134	239

WESTERN DIVISION

Team	W	L	T	Pct.	PF	PA
Chicago Bears	11	0	0	1.000	376	84
Green Bay	8	2	1	.800	300	215
Cleveland	5	6	0	.455	150	207
Chi. Cardinals	3	8	0	.273	98	209
Detroit	0	11	0	.000	38	263

PLAYOFFS

NFL championship
Washington 14 vs. Chicago Bears 6

1943

EASTERN DIVISION

Team	W	L	T	Pct.	PF	PA
Washington	6	3	1	.667	229	137
N.Y. Giants	6	3	1	.667	197	170
Phil.-Pitt.	5	4	1	.556	225	230
Brooklyn	2	8	0	.200	65	234

NOTE: Cleveland Rams did not play in 1943.

WESTERN DIVISION

Team	W	L	T	Pct.	PF	PA
Chicago Bears	8	1	1	.889	303	157
Green Bay	7	2	1	.778	264	172
Detroit	3	6	1	.333	178	218
Chi. Cardinals	0	10	0	.000	95	238

PLAYOFFS

Eastern Division playoff
Washington 28 at N.Y. Giants 0

NFL championship
Chicago Bears 41 vs. Washington 21

1944

EASTERN DIVISION

Team	W	L	T	Pct.	PF	PA
N.Y. Giants	8	1	1	.889	206	75
Philadelphia	7	1	2	.875	267	131
Washington	6	3	1	.667	169	180
Boston	2	8	0	.200	82	233
Brooklyn	0	10	0	.000	69	166

WESTERN DIVISION

Team	W	L	T	Pct.	PF	PA
Green Bay	8	2	0	.800	238	141
Chicago Bears	6	3	1	.667	258	172
Detroit	6	3	1	.667	216	151
Cleveland	4	6	0	.400	188	224
Card-Pitt	0	10	0	.000	108	328

PLAYOFFS

NFL championship
Green Bay 14 at N.Y. Giants 7

1945

EASTERN DIVISION

Team	W	L	T	Pct.	PF	PA
Washington	8	2	0	.800	209	121
Philadelphia	7	3	0	.700	272	133
N.Y. Giants	3	6	1	.333	179	198
Boston	3	6	1	.333	123	211
Pittsburgh	2	8	0	.200	79	220

WESTERN DIVISION

Team	W	L	T	Pct.	PF	PA
Cleveland	9	1	0	.900	244	136
Detroit	7	3	0	.700	195	194
Green Bay	6	4	0	.600	258	173
Chicago Bears	3	7	0	.300	192	235
Chi. Cardinals	1	9	0	.100	98	228

PLAYOFFS

NFL championship
Cleveland 15 vs. Washington 14

1946

AAFC

EASTERN DIVISION

Team	W	L	T	Pct.	PF	PA
New York	10	3	1	.769	270	192
Brooklyn	3	10	1	.231	226	339
Buffalo	3	10	1	.231	249	370
Miami	3	11	0	.154	167	378

WESTERN DIVISION

Team	W	L	T	Pct.	PF	PA
Cleveland	12	2	0	.857	423	137
San Francisco	9	5	0	.643	307	189
Los Angeles	7	5	2	.583	305	290
Chicago	5	6	3	.455	263	315

PLAYOFFS

AAFC championship
Cleveland 14 vs. New York 9

NFL

EASTERN DIVISION

Team	W	L	T	Pct.	PF	PA
N.Y. Giants	7	3	1	.700	236	162
Philadelphia	6	5	0	.545	231	220
Washington	5	5	1	.500	171	191
Pittsburgh	5	5	1	.500	136	117
Boston	2	8	1	.200	189	273

WESTERN DIVISION

Team	W	L	T	Pct.	PF	PA
Chicago Bears	8	2	1	.800	289	193
Los Angeles	6	4	1	.600	277	257
Green Bay	6	5	0	.545	148	158
Chi. Cardinals	6	5	0	.545	260	198
Detroit	1	10	0	.091	142	310

PLAYOFFS

NFL championship
Chicago Bears 24 at N.Y. Giants 14

1947

AAFC

EASTERN DIVISION

Team	W	L	T	Pct.	PF	PA
New York	11	2	1	.846	378	239
Buffalo	8	4	2	.667	320	288
Brooklyn	3	10	1	.231	181	340
Baltimore	2	11	1	.154	167	377

WESTERN DIVISION

Team	W	L	T	Pct.	PF	PA
Cleveland	12	1	1	.923	410	185
San Francisco	8	4	2	.667	327	264
Los Angeles	7	7	0	.500	328	256
Chicago	1	13	0	.071	263	425

PLAYOFFS

AAFC championship
Cleveland 14 at New York 3

NFL

EASTERN DIVISION

Team	W	L	T	Pct.	PF	PA
Philadelphia	8	4	0	.667	308	242
Pittsburgh	8	4	0	.667	240	259
Boston	4	7	1	.364	168	256
Washington	4	8	0	.333	295	367
N.Y. Giants	2	8	2	.200	190	309

WESTERN DIVISION

Team	W	L	T	Pct.	PF	PA
Chi. Cardinals	9	3	0	.750	306	231
Chicago Bears	8	4	0	.667	363	241
Green Bay	6	5	1	.545	274	210
Los Angeles	6	6	0	.500	259	214
Detroit	3	9	0	.250	231	305

PLAYOFFS

Eastern Division playoff
Philadelphia 21 at Pittsburgh 0

NFL championship
Chicago Cardinals 28 vs. Philadelphia 21

1948

AAFC

EASTERN DIVISION

Team	W	L	T	Pct.	PF	PA
Buffalo	7	7	0	.500	360	358
Baltimore	7	7	0	.500	333	327
New York	6	8	0	.429	265	301
Brooklyn	2	12	0	.143	253	387

WESTERN DIVISION

Team	W	L	T	Pct.	PF	PA
Cleveland	14	0	0	1.000	389	190
San Francisco	12	2	0	.857	495	248
Los Angeles	7	7	0	.500	258	305
Chicago	1	13	0	.071	202	439

PLAYOFFS

Eastern Division playoff
Buffalo 28 vs. Baltimore 17

AAFC championship
Cleveland 49 vs. Buffalo 7

NFL

EASTERN DIVISION

Team	W	L	T	Pct.	PF	PA
Philadelphia	9	2	1	.818	376	156
Washington	7	5	0	.583	291	287
N.Y. Giants	4	8	0	.333	297	388
Pittsburgh	4	8	0	.333	200	243
Boston	3	9	0	.250	174	372

WESTERN DIVISION

Team	W	L	T	Pct.	PF	PA
Chi. Cardinals	11	1	0	.917	395	226
Chicago Bears	10	2	0	.833	375	151
Los Angeles	6	5	1	.545	327	269
Green Bay	3	9	0	.250	154	290
Detroit	2	10	0	.167	200	407

PLAYOFFS

NFL championship
Philadelphia 7 vs. Chicago Cardinals 0

1949

AAFC

Team	W	L	T	Pct.	PF	PA
Cleveland	9	1	2	.900	339	171
San Francisco	9	3	0	.750	416	227
Brooklyn-N.Y.	8	4	0	.667	196	206
Buffalo	5	5	2	.500	236	256
Chicago	4	8	0	.333	179	268
Los Angeles	4	8	0	.333	253	322
Baltimore	1	11	0	.083	172	341

PLAYOFFS

AAFC Semifinals
Cleveland 31 vs. Buffalo 21
San Francisco 17 vs. Brooklyn-N.Y. 7

AAFC championship
Cleveland 21 vs. San Francisco 7

NFL

EASTERN DIVISION

Team	W	L	T	Pct.	PF	PA
Philadelphia	11	1	0	.917	364	134
Pittsburgh	6	5	1	.545	224	214
N.Y. Giants	6	6	0	.500	287	298
Washington	4	7	1	.364	268	339
N.Y. Bulldogs	1	10	1	.091	153	365

WESTERN DIVISION

Team	W	L	T	Pct.	PF	PA
Los Angeles	8	2	2	.800	360	239
Chicago Bears	9	3	0	.750	332	218
Chi. Cardinals	6	5	1	.545	360	301
Detroit	4	8	0	.333	237	259
Green Bay	2	10	0	.167	114	329

PLAYOFFS

NFL championship
Philadelphia 14 at Los Angeles 0

1950

AMERICAN CONFERENCE

Team	W	L	T	Pct.	PF	PA
Cleveland	10	2	0	.833	310	144
N.Y. Giants	10	2	0	.833	268	150
Philadelphia	6	6	0	.500	254	141
Pittsburgh	6	6	0	.500	180	195
Chi. Cardinals	5	7	0	.417	233	287
Washington	3	9	0	.250	232	326

NATIONAL CONFERENCE

Team	W	L	T	Pct.	PF	PA
Los Angeles	9	3	0	.750	466	309
Chicago Bears	9	3	0	.750	279	207
N.Y. Yanks	7	5	0	.583	366	367
Detroit	6	6	0	.500	321	285
Green Bay	3	9	0	.250	244	406
San Francisco	3	9	0	.250	213	300
Baltimore	1	11	0	.083	213	462

PLAYOFFS

American Conference playoff
Cleveland 8 vs. N.Y. Giants 3

National Conference playoff
Los Angeles 24 vs. Chicago Bears 14

NFL championship
Cleveland 30 vs. Los Angeles 28

1951

AMERICAN CONFERENCE

Team	W	L	T	Pct.	PF	PA
Cleveland	11	1	0	.917	331	152
N.Y. Giants	9	2	1	.818	254	161
Washington	5	7	0	.417	183	296
Pittsburgh	4	7	1	.364	183	235
Philadelphia	4	8	0	.333	234	264
Chi. Cardinals	3	9	0	.250	210	287

NATIONAL CONFERENCE

Team	W	L	T	Pct.	PF	PA
Los Angeles	8	4	0	.667	392	261
Detroit	7	4	1	.636	336	259
San Francisco	7	4	1	.636	255	205
Chicago Bears	7	5	0	.583	286	282
Green Bay	3	9	0	.250	254	375
N.Y. Yanks	1	9	2	.100	241	382

PLAYOFFS

NFL championship
Los Angeles 24 vs. Cleveland 17

1952

AMERICAN CONFERENCE

Team	W	L	T	Pct.	PF	PA
Cleveland	8	4	0	.667	310	213
N.Y. Giants	7	5	0	.583	234	231
Philadelphia	7	5	0	.583	252	271
Pittsburgh	5	7	0	.417	300	273
Chi. Cardinals	4	8	0	.333	172	221
Washington	4	8	0	.333	240	287

NATIONAL CONFERENCE

Team	W	L	T	Pct.	PF	PA
Detroit	9	3	0	.750	344	192
Los Angeles	9	3	0	.750	349	234
San Francisco	7	5	0	.583	285	221
Green Bay	6	6	0	.500	295	312
Chicago Bears	5	7	0	.417	245	326
Dallas Texans	1	11	0	.083	182	427

PLAYOFFS

National Conference playoff
Detroit 31 vs. Los Angeles 21

NFL championship
Detroit 17 at Cleveland 7

1953

EASTERN CONFERENCE

Team	W	L	T	Pct.	PF	PA
Cleveland	11	1	0	.917	348	162
Philadelphia	7	4	1	.636	352	215
Washington	6	5	1	.545	208	215
Pittsburgh	6	6	0	.500	211	263
N.Y. Giants	3	9	0	.250	179	277
Chi. Cardinals	1	10	1	.091	190	337

WESTERN CONFERENCE

Team	W	L	T	Pct.	PF	PA
Detroit	10	2	0	.833	271	205
San Francisco	9	3	0	.750	372	237
Los Angeles	8	3	1	.727	366	236
Chicago Bears	3	8	1	.273	218	262
Baltimore	3	9	0	.250	182	350
Green Bay	2	9	1	.182	200	338

PLAYOFFS

NFL championship
Detroit 17 vs. Cleveland 16

1954

EASTERN CONFERENCE

Team	W	L	T	Pct.	PF	PA
Cleveland	9	3	0	.750	336	162
Philadelphia	7	4	1	.636	284	230
N.Y. Giants	7	5	0	.583	293	184
Pittsburgh	5	7	0	.417	219	263
Washington	3	9	0	.250	207	432
Chi. Cardinals	2	10	0	.167	183	347

WESTERN CONFERENCE

Team	W	L	T	Pct.	PF	PA
Detroit	9	2	1	.818	337	189
Chicago Bears	8	4	0	.667	301	279
San Francisco	7	4	1	.636	313	251
Los Angeles	6	5	1	.545	314	285
Green Bay	4	8	0	.333	234	251
Baltimore	3	9	0	.250	131	279

PLAYOFFS

NFL championship
Cleveland 56 vs. Detroit 10

1955

EASTERN CONFERENCE

Team	W	L	T	Pct.	PF	PA
Cleveland	9	2	1	.818	349	218
Washington	8	4	0	.667	246	222
N.Y. Giants	6	5	1	.545	267	223
Chi. Cardinals	4	7	1	.364	224	252
Philadelphia	4	7	1	.364	248	231
Pittsburgh	4	8	0	.333	195	285

WESTERN CONFERENCE

Team	W	L	T	Pct.	PF	PA
Los Angeles	8	3	1	.727	260	231
Chicago Bears	8	4	0	.667	294	251
Green Bay	6	6	0	.500	258	276
Baltimore	5	6	1	.455	214	239
San Francisco	4	8	0	.333	216	298
Detroit	3	9	0	.250	230	275

PLAYOFFS

NFL championship
Cleveland 38 at Los Angeles 14

1956

EASTERN CONFERENCE

Team	W	L	T	Pct.	PF	PA
N.Y. Giants	8	3	1	.727	264	197
Chi. Cardinals	7	5	0	.583	240	182
Washington	6	6	0	.500	183	225
Cleveland	5	7	0	.417	167	177
Pittsburgh	5	7	0	.417	217	250
Philadelphia	3	8	1	.273	143	215

WESTERN CONFERENCE

Team	W	L	T	Pct.	PF	PA
Chicago Bears	9	2	1	.818	363	246
Detroit	9	3	0	.750	300	188
San Francisco	5	6	1	.455	233	284
Baltimore	5	7	0	.417	270	322
Green Bay	4	8	0	.333	264	342
Los Angeles	4	8	0	.333	291	307

PLAYOFFS

NFL championship
N.Y. Giants 47 vs. Chicago Bears 7

1957

EASTERN CONFERENCE

Team	W	L	T	Pct.	PF	PA
Cleveland	9	2	1	.818	269	172
N.Y. Giants	7	5	0	.583	254	211
Pittsburgh	6	6	0	.500	161	178
Washington	5	6	1	.455	251	230
Philadelphia	4	8	0	.333	173	230
Chi. Cardinals	3	9	0	.250	200	299

WESTERN CONFERENCE

Team	W	L	T	Pct.	PF	PA
Detroit	8	4	0	.667	251	231
San Francisco	8	4	0	.667	260	264
Baltimore	7	5	0	.583	303	235
Los Angeles	6	6	0	.500	307	278
Chicago Bears	5	7	0	.417	203	211
Green Bay	3	9	0	.250	218	311

PLAYOFFS

Western Conference playoff
Detroit 31 at San Francisco 27

NFL championship
Detroit 59 vs. Cleveland 14

1958

EASTERN CONFERENCE

Team	W	L	T	Pct.	PF	PA
N.Y. Giants	9	3	0	.750	246	183
Cleveland	9	3	0	.750	302	217
Pittsburgh	7	4	1	.636	261	230
Washington	4	7	1	.364	214	268
Chi. Cardinals	2	9	1	.182	261	356
Philadelphia	2	9	1	.182	235	306

WESTERN CONFERENCE

Team	W	L	T	Pct.	PF	PA
Baltimore	9	3	0	.750	381	203
Chicago Bears	8	4	0	.667	298	230
Los Angeles	8	4	0	.667	344	278
San Francisco	6	6	0	.500	257	324
Detroit	4	7	1	.364	261	276
Green Bay	1	10	1	.091	193	382

PLAYOFFS

Eastern Conference playoff
N.Y. Giants 10 vs. Cleveland 0

NFL championship
Baltimore 23 at N.Y. Giants 17 (OT)

1959

EASTERN CONFERENCE

Team	W	L	T	Pct.	PF	PA
N.Y. Giants	10	2	0	.833	284	170
Cleveland	7	5	0	.583	270	214
Philadelphia	7	5	0	.583	268	278
Pittsburgh	6	5	1	.545	257	216
Washington	3	9	0	.250	185	350
Chi. Cardinals	2	10	0	.167	234	324

WESTERN CONFERENCE

Team	W	L	T	Pct.	PF	PA
Baltimore	9	3	0	.750	374	251
Chicago Bears	8	4	0	.667	252	196
Green Bay	7	5	0	.583	248	246
San Francisco	7	5	0	.583	255	237
Detroit	3	8	1	.273	203	275
Los Angeles	2	10	0	.167	242	315

PLAYOFFS

NFL championship
Baltimore 31 vs. N.Y. Giants 16

1960

AFL

EASTERN DIVISION

Team	W	L	T	Pct.	PF	PA
Houston	10	4	0	.714	379	285
N.Y. Titans	7	7	0	.500	382	399
Buffalo	5	8	1	.385	296	303
Boston Patriots	5	9	0	.357	286	349

WESTERN DIVISION

Team	W	L	T	Pct.	PF	PA
L.A. Chargers	10	4	0	.714	373	336
Dallas Texans	8	6	0	.571	362	253
Oakland	6	8	0	.429	319	388
Denver	4	9	1	.308	309	393

PLAYOFFS

AFL championship
Houston 24 vs. L.A. Chargers 16

NFL

EASTERN CONFERENCE

Team	W	L	T	Pct.	PF	PA
Philadelphia	10	2	0	.833	321	246
Cleveland	8	3	1	.727	362	217
N.Y. Giants	6	4	2	.600	271	261
St. Louis	6	5	1	.545	288	230
Pittsburgh	5	6	1	.455	240	275
Washington	1	9	2	.100	178	309

WESTERN CONFERENCE

Team	W	L	T	Pct.	PF	PA
Green Bay	8	4	0	.667	332	209
Detroit	7	5	0	.583	239	212
San Francisco	7	5	0	.583	208	205
Baltimore	6	6	0	.500	288	234
Chicago	5	6	1	.455	194	299
L.A. Rams	4	7	1	.364	265	297
Dallas Cowboys	0	11	1	.000	177	369

PLAYOFFS

NFL championship
Philadelphia 17 vs. Green Bay 13

1961

AFL

EASTERN DIVISION

Team	W	L	T	Pct.	PF	PA
Houston	10	3	1	.769	513	242
Boston Patriots	9	4	1	.692	413	313
N.Y. Titans	7	7	0	.500	301	390
Buffalo	6	8	0	.429	294	342

WESTERN DIVISION

Team	W	L	T	Pct.	PF	PA
San Diego	12	2	0	.857	396	219
Dallas Texans	6	8	0	.429	334	343
Denver	3	11	0	.214	251	432
Oakland	2	12	0	.143	237	458

PLAYOFFS

AFL championship
Houston 10 at San Diego 3

– 305 –

NFL

EASTERN CONFERENCE

Team	W	L	T	Pct.	PF	PA
N.Y. Giants	10	3	1	.769	368	220
Philadelphia	10	4	0	.714	361	297
Cleveland	8	5	1	.615	319	270
St. Louis	7	7	0	.500	279	267
Pittsburgh	6	8	0	.429	295	287
Dallas Cowboys	4	9	1	.308	236	380
Washington	1	12	1	.077	174	392

WESTERN CONFERENCE

Team	W	L	T	Pct.	PF	PA
Green Bay	11	3	0	.786	391	223
Detroit	8	5	1	.615	270	258
Baltimore	8	6	0	.571	302	307
Chicago	8	6	0	.571	326	302
San Francisco	7	6	1	.538	346	272
Los Angeles	4	10	0	.286	263	333
Minnesota	3	11	0	.214	285	407

PLAYOFFS

NFL championship
Green Bay 37 vs. N.Y. Giants 0

1962

AFL

EASTERN DIVISION

Team	W	L	T	Pct.	PF	PA
Houston	11	3	0	.786	387	270
Boston Patriots	9	4	1	.692	346	295
Buffalo	7	6	1	.538	309	272
N.Y. Titans	5	9	0	.357	278	423

WESTERN DIVISION

Team	W	L	T	Pct.	PF	PA
Dallas Texans	11	3	0	.786	389	233
Denver	7	7	0	.500	353	334
San Diego	4	10	0	.286	314	392
Oakland	1	13	0	.071	213	370

PLAYOFFS

AFL championship
Dallas Texans 20 at Houston 17 (OT)

NFL

EASTERN CONFERENCE

Team	W	L	T	Pct.	PF	PA
N.Y. Giants	12	2	0	.857	398	283
Pittsburgh	9	5	0	.643	312	363
Cleveland	7	6	1	.538	291	257
Washington	5	7	2	.417	305	376
Dallas Cowboys	5	8	1	.385	398	402
St. Louis	4	9	1	.308	287	361
Philadelphia	3	10	1	.231	282	356

WESTERN CONFERENCE

Team	W	L	T	Pct.	PF	PA
Green Bay	13	1	0	.929	415	148
Detroit	11	3	0	.786	315	177
Chicago	9	5	0	.643	321	287
Baltimore	7	7	0	.500	293	288
San Francisco	6	8	0	.429	282	331
Minnesota	2	11	1	.154	254	410
Los Angeles	1	12	1	.077	220	334

PLAYOFFS

NFL championship
Green Bay 16 at N.Y. Giants 7

1963

AFL

EASTERN DIVISION

Team	W	L	T	Pct.	PF	PA
Boston Patriots	7	6	1	.538	327	257
Buffalo	7	6	1	.538	304	291
Houston	6	8	0	.429	302	372
N.Y. Jets	5	8	1	.385	249	399

WESTERN DIVISION

Team	W	L	T	Pct.	PF	PA
San Diego	11	3	0	.786	399	256
Oakland	10	4	0	.714	363	288
Kansas City	5	7	2	.417	347	263
Denver	2	11	1	.154	301	473

PLAYOFFS

Eastern Division playoff
Boston 26 at Buffalo 8

AFL championship
San Diego 51 vs. Boston 10

NFL

EASTERN CONFERENCE

Team	W	L	T	Pct.	PF	PA
N.Y. Giants	11	3	0	.786	448	280
Cleveland	10	4	0	.714	343	262
St. Louis	9	5	0	.643	341	283
Pittsburgh	7	4	3	.636	321	295
Dallas	4	10	0	.286	305	378
Washington	3	11	0	.214	279	398
Philadelphia	2	10	2	.167	242	381

WESTERN CONFERENCE

Team	W	L	T	Pct.	PF	PA
Chicago	11	1	2	.917	301	144
Green Bay	11	2	1	.846	369	206
Baltimore	8	6	0	.571	316	285
Detroit	5	8	1	.385	326	265
Minnesota	5	8	1	.385	309	390
Los Angeles	5	9	0	.357	210	350
San Francisco	2	12	0	.143	198	391

PLAYOFFS

NFL championship
Chicago 14 vs. N.Y. Giants 10

1964

AFL

EASTERN DIVISION

Team	W	L	T	Pct.	PF	PA
Buffalo	12	2	0	.857	400	242
Boston Patriots	10	3	1	.769	365	297
N.Y. Jets	5	8	1	.385	278	315
Houston	4	10	0	.286	310	355

WESTERN DIVISION

Team	W	L	T	Pct.	PF	PA
San Diego	8	5	1	.615	341	300
Kansas City	7	7	0	.500	366	306
Oakland	5	7	2	.417	303	350
Denver	2	11	1	.154	240	438

PLAYOFFS

AFL championship
Buffalo 20 vs. San Diego 7

NFL

EASTERN CONFERENCE

Team	W	L	T	Pct.	PF	PA
Cleveland	10	3	1	.769	415	293
St. Louis	9	3	2	.750	357	331
Philadelphia	6	8	0	.429	312	313
Washington	6	8	0	.429	307	305
Dallas	5	8	1	.385	250	289
Pittsburgh	5	9	0	.357	253	315
N.Y. Giants	2	10	2	.167	241	399

WESTERN CONFERENCE

Team	W	L	T	Pct.	PF	PA
Baltimore	12	2	0	.857	428	225
Green Bay	8	5	1	.615	342	245
Minnesota	8	5	1	.615	355	296
Detroit	7	5	2	.583	280	260
Los Angeles	5	7	2	.417	283	339
Chicago	5	9	0	.357	260	379
San Francisco	4	10	0	.286	236	330

PLAYOFFS

NFL championship
Cleveland 27 vs. Baltimore 0

1965

AFL

EASTERN DIVISION

Team	W	L	T	Pct.	PF	PA
Buffalo	10	3	1	.769	313	226
N.Y. Jets	5	8	1	.385	285	303
Boston Patriots	4	8	2	.333	244	302
Houston	4	10	0	.286	298	429

WESTERN DIVISION

Team	W	L	T	Pct.	PF	PA
San Diego	9	2	3	.818	340	227
Oakland	8	5	1	.615	298	239
Kansas City	7	5	2	.583	322	285
Denver	4	10	0	.286	303	392

PLAYOFFS

AFL championship
Buffalo 23 at San Diego 0

NFL

EASTERN CONFERENCE

Team	W	L	T	Pct.	PF	PA
Cleveland	11	3	0	.786	363	325
Dallas	7	7	0	.500	325	280
N.Y. Giants	7	7	0	.500	270	338
Washington	6	8	0	.429	257	301
Philadelphia	5	9	0	.357	363	359
St. Louis	5	9	0	.357	296	309
Pittsburgh	2	12	0	.143	202	397

WESTERN CONFERENCE

Team	W	L	T	Pct.	PF	PA
Green Bay	10	3	1	.769	316	224
Baltimore	10	3	1	.769	389	284
Chicago	9	5	0	.643	409	275
San Francisco	7	6	1	.538	421	402
Minnesota	7	7	0	.500	383	403
Detroit	6	7	1	.462	257	295
Los Angeles	4	10	0	.286	269	328

PLAYOFFS

Western Conference playoff
Green Bay 13 vs. Baltimore 10 (OT)
NFL championship
Green Bay 23 vs. Cleveland 12

1966

AFL

EASTERN DIVISION

Team	W	L	T	Pct.	PF	PA
Buffalo	9	4	1	.692	358	255
Boston Patriots	8	4	2	.667	315	283
N.Y. Jets	6	6	2	.500	322	312
Houston	3	11	0	.214	335	396
Miami	3	11	0	.214	213	362

WESTERN DIVISION

Team	W	L	T	Pct.	PF	PA
Kansas City	11	2	1	.846	448	276
Oakland	8	5	1	.615	315	288
San Diego	7	6	1	.538	335	284
Denver	4	10	0	.286	196	381

PLAYOFFS

AFL championship
Kansas City 31 at Buffalo 7

NFL

EASTERN CONFERENCE

Team	W	L	T	Pct.	PF	PA
Dallas	10	3	1	.769	445	239
Cleveland	9	5	0	.643	403	259
Philadelphia	9	5	0	.643	326	340
St. Louis	8	5	1	.615	264	265
Washington	7	7	0	.500	351	355
Pittsburgh	5	8	1	.385	316	347
Atlanta	3	11	0	.214	204	437
N.Y. Giants	1	12	1	.077	263	501

WESTERN CONFERENCE

Team	W	L	T	Pct.	PF	PA
Green Bay	12	2	0	.857	335	163
Baltimore	9	5	0	.643	314	226
Los Angeles	8	6	0	.571	289	212
San Francisco	6	6	2	.500	320	325
Chicago	5	7	2	.417	234	272
Detroit	4	9	1	.308	206	317
Minnesota	4	9	1	.308	292	304

PLAYOFFS

NFL championship
Green Bay 34 at Dallas 27
Super Bowl I
Green Bay 35, Kansas City 10, at Los Angeles.

1967

AFL

EASTERN DIVISION

Team	W	L	T	Pct.	PF	PA
Houston	9	4	1	.692	258	199
N.Y. Jets	8	5	1	.615	371	329
Buffalo	4	10	0	.286	237	285
Miami	4	10	0	.286	219	407
Boston Patriots	3	10	1	.231	280	389

WESTERN DIVISION

Team	W	L	T	Pct.	PF	PA
Oakland	13	1	0	.929	468	233
Kansas City	9	5	0	.643	408	254
San Diego	8	5	1	.615	360	352
Denver	3	11	0	.214	256	409

PLAYOFFS

AFL championship
Oakland 40 vs. Houston 7

NFL

EASTERN CONFERENCE

CAPITOL DIVISION

Team	W	L	T	Pct.	PF	PA
Dallas	9	5	0	.643	342	268
Philadelphia	6	7	1	.462	351	409
Washington	5	6	3	.455	347	353
New Orleans	3	11	0	.214	233	379

CENTURY DIVISION

Team	W	L	T	Pct.	PF	PA
Cleveland	9	5	0	.643	334	297
N.Y. Giants	7	7	0	.500	369	379
St. Louis	6	7	1	.462	333	356
Pittsburgh	4	9	1	.308	281	320

WESTERN CONFERENCE

COASTAL DIVISION

Team	W	L	T	Pct.	PF	PA
Los Angeles	11	1	2	.917	398	196
Baltimore	11	1	2	.917	394	198
San Francisco	7	7	0	.500	273	337
Atlanta	1	12	1	.077	175	422

CENTRAL DIVISION

Team	W	L	T	Pct.	PF	PA
Green Bay	9	4	1	.692	332	209
Chicago	7	6	1	.538	239	218
Detroit	5	7	2	.417	260	259
Minnesota	3	8	3	.273	233	294

PLAYOFFS

Conference championships
Dallas 52 vs. Cleveland 14
Green Bay 28 vs. Los Angeles 7

NFL championship
Green Bay 21 vs. Dallas 17

Super Bowl II
Green Bay 33, Oakland 14, at Miami.

1968

AFL

EASTERN DIVISION

Team	W	L	T	Pct.	PF	PA
N.Y. Jets	11	3	0	.786	419	280
Houston	7	7	0	.500	303	248
Miami	5	8	1	.385	276	355
Boston Patriots	4	10	0	.286	229	406
Buffalo	1	12	1	.077	199	367

WESTERN DIVISION

Team	W	L	T	Pct.	PF	PA
Oakland	12	2	0	.857	453	233
Kansas City	12	2	0	.857	371	170
San Diego	9	5	0	.643	382	310
Denver	5	9	0	.357	255	404
Cincinnati	3	11	0	.214	215	329

PLAYOFFS

Western Division playoff
Oakland 41 vs. Kansas City 6

AFL championship
N.Y. Jets 27 vs. Oakland 23

NFL

EASTERN CONFERENCE

CAPITOL DIVISION

Team	W	L	T	Pct.	PF	PA
Dallas	12	2	0	.857	431	186
N.Y. Giants	7	7	0	.500	294	325
Washington	5	9	0	.357	249	358
Philadelphia	2	12	0	.143	202	351

CENTURY DIVISION

Team	W	L	T	Pct.	PF	PA
Cleveland	10	4	0	.714	394	273
St. Louis	9	4	1	.692	325	289
New Orleans	4	9	1	.308	246	327
Pittsburgh	2	11	1	.154	244	397

WESTERN CONFERENCE

COASTAL DIVISION

Team	W	L	T	Pct.	PF	PA
Baltimore	13	1	0	.929	402	144
Los Angeles	10	3	1	.769	312	200
San Francisco	7	6	1	.538	303	310
Atlanta	2	12	0	.143	170	389

CENTRAL DIVISION

Team	W	L	T	Pct.	PF	PA
Minnesota	8	6	0	.571	282	242
Chicago	7	7	0	.500	250	333
Green Bay	6	7	1	.462	281	227
Detroit	4	8	2	.333	207	241

PLAYOFFS

Conference championships
Cleveland 31 vs. Dallas 20
Baltimore 24 vs. Minnesota 14

NFL championship
Baltimore 34 at Cleveland 0

Super Bowl III
N.Y. Jets 16, Baltimore 7, at Miami.

1969

AFL

EASTERN DIVISION

Team	W	L	T	Pct.	PF	PA
N.Y. Jets	10	4	0	.714	353	269
Houston	6	6	2	.500	278	279
Boston Patriots	4	10	0	.286	266	316
Buffalo	4	10	0	.286	230	359
Miami	3	10	1	.231	233	332

WESTERN DIVISION

Team	W	L	T	Pct.	PF	PA
Oakland	12	1	1	.923	377	242
Kansas City	11	3	0	.786	359	177
San Diego	8	6	0	.571	288	276
Denver	5	8	1	.385	297	344
Cincinnati	4	9	1	.308	280	367

PLAYOFFS

Divisional games
Kansas City 13 at N.Y. Jets 6
Oakland 56 vs. Houston 7

AFL championship
Kansas City 17 at Oakland 7

NFL

EASTERN CONFERENCE

CAPITOL DIVISION

Team	W	L	T	Pct.	PF	PA
Dallas	11	2	1	.846	369	223
Washington	7	5	2	.583	307	319
New Orleans	5	9	0	.357	311	393
Philadelphia	4	9	1	.308	279	377

CENTURY DIVISION

Team	W	L	T	Pct.	PF	PA
Cleveland	10	3	1	.769	351	300
N.Y. Giants	6	8	0	.429	264	298
St. Louis	4	9	1	.308	314	389
Pittsburgh	1	13	0	.071	218	404

WESTERN CONFERENCE

COASTAL DIVISION

Team	W	L	T	Pct.	PF	PA
Los Angeles	11	3	0	.786	320	243
Baltimore	8	5	1	.615	279	268
Atlanta	6	8	0	.429	276	268
San Francisco	4	8	2	.333	277	319

CENTRAL DIVISION

Team	W	L	T	Pct.	PF	PA
Minnesota	12	2	0	.857	379	133
Detroit	9	4	1	.692	259	188
Green Bay	8	6	0	.571	269	221
Chicago	1	13	0	.071	210	339

PLAYOFFS

Conference championships
Cleveland 38 at Dallas 14
Minnesota 23 vs. Los Angeles 20

NFL championship
Minnesota 27 vs. Cleveland 7

Super Bowl IV
Kansas City 23, Minnesota 7, at New Orleans.

AMERICAN CONFERENCE

EASTERN DIVISION

Team	W	L	T	Pct.	PF	PA
Baltimore*	11	2	1	.846	321	234
Miami†	10	4	0	.714	297	228
N.Y. Jets	4	10	0	.286	255	286
Buffalo	3	10	1	.231	204	337
Boston Patriots	2	12	0	.143	149	361

CENTRAL DIVISION

Team	W	L	T	Pct.	PF	PA
Cincinnati*	8	6	0	.571	312	255
Cleveland	7	7	0	.500	286	265
Pittsburgh	5	9	0	.357	210	272
Houston	3	10	1	.231	217	352

WESTERN DIVISION

Team	W	L	T	Pct.	PF	PA
Oakland*	8	4	2	.667	300	293
Kansas City	7	5	2	.583	272	244
San Diego	5	6	3	.455	282	278
Denver	5	8	1	.385	253	264

*Division champion.
†Wild-card team.

NATIONAL CONFERENCE

EASTERN DIVISION

Team	W	L	T	Pct.	PF	PA
Dallas*	10	4	0	.714	299	221
N.Y. Giants	9	5	0	.643	301	270
St. Louis	8	5	1	.615	325	228
Washington	6	8	0	.429	297	314
Philadelphia	3	10	1	.231	241	332

CENTRAL DIVISION

Team	W	L	T	Pct.	PF	PA
Minnesota*	12	2	0	.857	335	143
Detroit†	10	4	0	.714	347	202
Chicago	6	8	0	.429	256	261
Green Bay	6	8	0	.429	196	293

WESTERN DIVISION

Team	W	L	T	Pct.	PF	PA
San Francisco*	10	3	1	.769	352	267
Los Angeles	9	4	1	.692	325	202
Atlanta	4	8	2	.333	206	261
New Orleans	2	11	1	.154	172	347

PLAYOFFS

AFC divisional games
Baltimore 17 vs. Cincinnati 0
Oakland 21 vs. Miami 14

AFC championship
Baltimore 27 vs. Oakland 17

NFC divisional games
Dallas 5 vs. Detroit 0
San Francisco 17 at Minnesota 14

NFC championship
Dallas 17 at San Francisco 10

Super Bowl V
Baltimore 16, Dallas 13, at Miami.

AMERICAN CONFERENCE

EASTERN DIVISION

Team	W	L	T	Pct.	PF	PA
Miami*	10	3	1	.769	315	174
Baltimore†	10	4	0	.714	313	140
New England	6	8	0	.429	238	325
N.Y. Jets	6	8	0	.429	212	299
Buffalo	1	13	0	.071	184	394

CENTRAL DIVISION

Team	W	L	T	Pct.	PF	PA
Cleveland*	9	5	0	.643	285	273
Pittsburgh	6	8	0	.429	246	292
Houston	4	9	1	.308	251	330
Cincinnati	4	10	0	.286	284	265

WESTERN DIVISION

Team	W	L	T	Pct.	PF	PA
Kansas City*	10	3	1	.769	302	208
Oakland	8	4	2	.667	344	278
San Diego	6	8	0	.429	311	341
Denver	4	9	1	.308	203	275

*Division champion.
†Wild-card team.

NATIONAL CONFERENCE

EASTERN DIVISION

Team	W	L	T	Pct.	PF	PA
Dallas*	11	3	0	.786	406	222
Washington†	9	4	1	.692	276	190
Philadelphia	6	7	1	.462	221	302
St. Louis	4	9	1	.308	231	279
N.Y. Giants	4	10	0	.286	228	362

CENTRAL DIVISION

Team	W	L	T	Pct.	PF	PA
Minnesota*	11	3	0	.786	245	139
Detroit	7	6	1	.538	341	286
Chicago	6	8	0	.429	185	276
Green Bay	4	8	2	.333	274	298

WESTERN DIVISION

Team	W	L	T	Pct.	PF	PA
San Francisco*	9	5	0	.643	300	216
Los Angeles	8	5	1	.615	313	260
Atlanta	7	6	1	.538	274	277
New Orleans	4	8	2	.333	266	347

PLAYOFFS

AFC divisional games
Miami 27 at Kansas City 24 (OT)
Baltimore 20 at Cleveland 3

AFC championship
Miami 21 vs. Baltimore 0

NFC divisional games
Dallas 20 at Minnesota 12
San Francisco 24 vs. Washington 20

NFC championship
Dallas 14 vs. San Francisco 3

Super Bowl VI
Dallas 24, Miami 3, at New Orleans.

THE LONGEST DAY

In the longest game in NFL history, the Miami Dolphins defeated the Kansas City Chiefs, 27-24, on Christmas Day 1971 in the first round of the AFC playoffs. Garo Yepremian's 37-yard field goal won it for Miami in the second overtime—after 82 minutes and 40 seconds of play—after Chiefs counterpart Jan Stenerud missed a 31-yard attempt with 35 seconds left in regulation time. Kickers aside, the hero of the game was Chiefs running back Ed Podolak, who gained 350 yards on rushes, receptions and returns. It was the last game played at Kansas City's Municipal Stadium.

1972

AMERICAN CONFERENCE

EASTERN DIVISION

Team	W	L	T	Pct.	PF	PA
Miami*	14	0	0	1.000	385	171
N.Y. Jets	7	7	0	.500	367	324
Baltimore	5	9	0	.357	235	252
Buffalo	4	9	1	.321	257	377
New England	3	11	0	.214	192	446

CENTRAL DIVISION

Team	W	L	T	Pct.	PF	PA
Pittsburgh*	11	3	0	.786	343	175
Cleveland†	10	4	0	.714	268	249
Cincinnati	8	6	0	.571	299	229
Houston	1	13	0	.071	164	380

WESTERN DIVISION

Team	W	L	T	Pct.	PF	PA
Oakland*	10	3	1	.750	365	248
Kansas City	8	6	0	.571	287	254
Denver	5	9	0	.357	325	350
San Diego	4	9	1	.321	264	344

*Division champion.
†Wild-card team.

NATIONAL CONFERENCE

EASTERN DIVISION

Team	W	L	T	Pct.	PF	PA
Washington*	11	3	0	.786	336	218
Dallas†	10	4	0	.714	319	240
N.Y. Giants	8	6	0	.571	331	247
St. Louis	4	9	1	.321	193	303
Philadelphia	2	11	1	.179	145	352

CENTRAL DIVISION

Team	W	L	T	Pct.	PF	PA
Green Bay*	10	4	0	.714	304	226
Detroit	8	5	1	.607	339	290
Minnesota	7	7	0	.500	301	252
Chicago	4	9	1	.321	225	275

WESTERN DIVISION

Team	W	L	T	Pct.	PF	PA
San Francisco*	8	5	1	.607	353	249
Atlanta	7	7	0	.500	269	274
Los Angeles	6	7	1	.464	291	286
New Orleans	2	11	1	.179	215	361

PLAYOFFS

AFC divisional games
Pittsburgh 13 vs. Oakland 7
Miami 20 vs. Cleveland 14

AFC championship
Miami 21 at Pittsburgh 17

NFC divisional games
Dallas 30 at San Francisco 28
Washington 16 vs. Green Bay 3

NFC championship
Washington 26 vs. Dallas 3

Super Bowl VII
Miami 14, Washington 7, at Los Angeles.

1973

AMERICAN CONFERENCE

EASTERN DIVISION

Team	W	L	T	Pct.	PF	PA
Miami*	12	2	0	.857	343	150
Buffalo	9	5	0	.643	259	230
New England	5	9	0	.357	258	300
Baltimore	4	10	0	.286	226	341
N.Y. Jets	4	10	0	.286	240	306

CENTRAL DIVISION

Team	W	L	T	Pct.	PF	PA
Cincinnati*	10	4	0	.714	286	231
Pittsburgh†	10	4	0	.714	347	210
Cleveland	7	5	2	.571	234	255
Houston	1	13	0	.071	199	447

WESTERN DIVISION

Team	W	L	T	Pct.	PF	PA
Oakland*	9	4	1	.679	292	175
Denver	7	5	2	.571	354	296
Kansas City	7	5	2	.571	231	192
San Diego	2	11	1	.179	188	386

*Division champion.
†Wild-card team.

NATIONAL CONFERENCE

EASTERN DIVISION

Team	W	L	T	Pct.	PF	PA
Dallas*	10	4	0	.714	382	203
Washington†	10	4	0	.714	325	198
Philadelphia	5	8	1	.393	310	393
St. Louis	4	9	1	.321	286	365
N.Y. Giants	2	11	1	.179	226	362

CENTRAL DIVISION

Team	W	L	T	Pct.	PF	PA
Minnesota*	12	2	0	.857	296	168
Detroit	6	7	1	.464	271	247
Green Bay	5	7	2	.429	202	259
Chicago	3	11	0	.214	195	334

WESTERN DIVISION

Team	W	L	T	Pct.	PF	PA
Los Angeles*	12	2	0	.857	388	178
Atlanta	9	5	0	.643	318	224
New Orleans	5	9	0	.357	163	312
San Francisco	5	9	0	.357	262	319

PLAYOFFS

AFC divisional games
Oakland 33 vs. Pittsburgh 14
Miami 34 vs. Cincinnati 16

AFC championship
Miami 27 vs. Oakland 10

NFC divisional games
Minnesota 27 vs. Washington 20
Dallas 27 vs. Los Angeles 16

NFC championship
Minnesota 27 at Dallas 10

Super Bowl VIII
Miami 24, Minnesota 7, at Houston.

1974

AMERICAN CONFERENCE

EASTERN DIVISION

Team	W	L	T	Pct.	PF	PA
Miami*	11	3	0	.786	327	216
Buffalo†	9	5	0	.643	264	244
New England	7	7	0	.500	348	289
N.Y. Jets	7	7	0	.500	279	300
Baltimore	2	12	0	.143	190	329

CENTRAL DIVISION

Team	W	L	T	Pct.	PF	PA
Pittsburgh*	10	3	1	.750	305	189
Cincinnati	7	7	0	.500	283	259
Houston	7	7	0	.500	236	282
Cleveland	4	10	0	.286	251	344

WESTERN DIVISION

Team	W	L	T	Pct.	PF	PA
Oakland*	12	2	0	.857	355	228
Denver	7	6	1	.536	302	294
Kansas City	5	9	0	.357	233	293
San Diego	5	9	0	.357	212	285

*Division champion.
†Wild-card team.

NATIONAL CONFERENCE

EASTERN DIVISION

Team	W	L	T	Pct.	PF	PA
St. Louis*	10	4	0	.714	285	218
Washington†	10	4	0	.714	320	196
Dallas	8	6	0	.571	297	235
Philadelphia	7	7	0	.500	242	217
N.Y. Giants	2	12	0	.143	195	299

CENTRAL DIVISION

Team	W	L	T	Pct.	PF	PA
Minnesota*	10	4	0	.714	310	195
Detroit	7	7	0	.500	256	270
Green Bay	6	8	0	.429	210	206
Chicago	4	10	0	.286	152	279

WESTERN DIVISION

Team	W	L	T	Pct.	PF	PA
Los Angeles*	10	4	0	.714	263	181
San Francisco	6	8	0	.429	226	236
New Orleans	5	9	0	.357	166	263
Atlanta	3	11	0	.214	111	271

PLAYOFFS

AFC divisional games
Oakland 28 vs. Miami 26
Pittsburgh 32 vs. Buffalo 14

AFC championship
Pittsburgh 24 at Oakland 13

NFC divisional games
Minnesota 30 vs. St. Louis 14
Los Angeles 19 vs. Washington 10

NFC championship
Minnesota 14 vs. Los Angeles 10

Super Bowl IX
Pittsburgh 16, Minnesota 6, at New Orleans.

1975

AMERICAN CONFERENCE

EASTERN DIVISION

Team	W	L	T	Pct.	PF	PA
Baltimore*	10	4	0	.714	395	269
Miami	10	4	0	.714	357	222
Buffalo	8	6	0	.571	420	355
New England	3	11	0	.214	258	358
N.Y. Jets	3	11	0	.214	258	433

CENTRAL DIVISION

Team	W	L	T	Pct.	PF	PA
Pittsburgh*	12	2	0	.857	373	162
Cincinnati†	11	3	0	.786	340	246
Houston	10	4	0	.714	293	226
Cleveland	3	11	0	.214	218	372

WESTERN DIVISION

Team	W	L	T	Pct.	PF	PA
Oakland*	11	3	0	.786	375	255
Denver	6	8	0	.429	254	307
Kansas City	5	9	0	.357	282	341
San Diego	2	12	0	.143	189	345

*Division champion.
†Wild-card team.

NATIONAL CONFERENCE

EASTERN DIVISION

Team	W	L	T	Pct.	PF	PA
St. Louis*	11	3	0	.786	356	276
Dallas†	10	4	0	.714	350	268
Washington	8	6	0	.571	325	276
N.Y. Giants	5	9	0	.357	216	306
Philadelphia	4	10	0	.286	225	302

CENTRAL DIVISION

Team	W	L	T	Pct.	PF	PA
Minnesota*	12	2	0	.857	377	180
Detroit	7	7	0	.500	245	262
Chicago	4	10	0	.286	191	379
Green Bay	4	10	0	.286	226	285

WESTERN DIVISION

Team	W	L	T	Pct.	PF	PA
Los Angeles*	12	2	0	.857	312	135
San Francisco	5	9	0	.357	255	286
Atlanta	4	10	0	.286	240	289
New Orleans	2	12	0	.143	165	360

PLAYOFFS

AFC divisional games
Pittsburgh 28 vs. Baltimore 10
Oakland 31 vs. Cincinnati 28

AFC championship
Pittsburgh 16 vs. Oakland 10

NFC divisional games
Los Angeles 35 vs. St. Louis 23
Dallas 17 at Minnesota 14

NFC championship
Dallas 37 at Los Angeles 7

Super Bowl X
Pittsburgh 21, Dallas 17, at Miami.

1976

AMERICAN CONFERENCE

EASTERN DIVISION

Team	W	L	T	Pct.	PF	PA
Baltimore*	11	3	0	.786	417	246
New England†	11	3	0	.786	376	236
Miami	6	8	0	.429	263	264
N.Y. Jets	3	11	0	.214	169	383
Buffalo	2	12	0	.143	245	363

CENTRAL DIVISION

Team	W	L	T	Pct.	PF	PA
Pittsburgh*	10	4	0	.714	342	138
Cincinnati	10	4	0	.714	335	210
Cleveland	9	5	0	.643	267	287
Houston	5	9	0	.357	222	273

WESTERN DIVISION

Team	W	L	T	Pct.	PF	PA
Oakland*	13	1	0	.929	350	237
Denver	9	5	0	.643	315	206
San Diego	6	8	0	.429	248	285
Kansas City	5	9	0	.357	290	376
Tampa Bay	0	14	0	.000	125	412

*Division champion.
†Wild-card team.

NATIONAL CONFERENCE

EASTERN DIVISION

Team	W	L	T	Pct.	PF	PA
Dallas*	11	3	0	.786	296	194
Washington†	10	4	0	.714	291	217
St. Louis	10	4	0	.714	309	267
Philadelphia	4	10	0	.286	165	286
N.Y. Giants	3	11	0	.214	170	250

CENTRAL DIVISION

Team	W	L	T	Pct.	PF	PA
Minnesota*	11	2	1	.821	305	176
Chicago	7	7	0	.500	253	216
Detroit	6	8	0	.429	262	220
Green Bay	5	9	0	.357	218	299

WESTERN DIVISION

Team	W	L	T	Pct.	PF	PA
Los Angeles*	10	3	1	.750	351	190
San Francisco	8	6	0	.571	270	190
Atlanta	4	10	0	.286	172	312
New Orleans	4	10	0	.286	253	346
Seattle	2	12	0	.143	229	429

PLAYOFFS

AFC divisional games
Oakland 24 vs. New England 21
Pittsburgh 40 at Baltimore 14

AFC championship
Oakland 24 vs. Pittsburgh 7

NFC divisional games
Minnesota 35 vs. Washington 20
Los Angeles 14 at Dallas 12

NFC championship
Minnesota 24 vs. Los Angeles 13

Super Bowl XI
Oakland 32, Minnesota 14, at Pasadena, Calif.

JUICE WAS HOT

On December 16, 1973, O.J. Simpson of the Buffalo Bills rushed for 200 yards against the New York Jets, becoming the first player to rush for 2,000 in an NFL season. The feat has since been accomplished three more times—by Eric Dickerson in 1984, Barry Sanders in 1997 and Terrell Davis in 1998—but all of them needed 16 games to reach the milestone. Simpson did it in 14. The 200-yard game was Simpson's third that season, and he still holds the league record with six career 200-yard games. The 1973 Bills became the first NFL team to rush for 3,000 yards in a season.

1977

AMERICAN CONFERENCE

EASTERN DIVISION

Team	W	L	T	Pct.	PF	PA
Baltimore*	10	4	0	.714	295	221
Miami	10	4	0	.714	313	197
New England	9	5	0	.643	278	217
N.Y. Jets	3	11	0	.214	191	300
Buffalo	3	11	0	.214	160	313

CENTRAL DIVISION

Team	W	L	T	Pct.	PF	PA
Pittsburgh*	9	5	0	.643	283	243
Houston	8	6	0	.571	299	230
Cincinnati	8	6	0	.571	238	235
Cleveland	6	8	0	.429	269	267

WESTERN DIVISION

Team	W	L	T	Pct.	PF	PA
Denver*	12	2	0	.857	274	148
Oakland†	11	3	0	.786	351	230
San Diego	7	7	0	.500	222	205
Seattle	5	9	0	.357	282	373
Kansas City	2	12	0	.143	225	349

*Division champion.
†Wild-card team.

NATIONAL CONFERENCE

EASTERN DIVISION

Team	W	L	T	Pct.	PF	PA
Dallas*	12	2	0	.857	345	212
Washington	9	5	0	.643	196	189
St. Louis	7	7	0	.500	272	287
Philadelphia	5	9	0	.357	220	207
N.Y. Giants	5	9	0	.357	181	265

CENTRAL DIVISION

Team	W	L	T	Pct.	PF	PA
Minnesota*	9	5	0	.643	231	227
Chicago†	9	5	0	.643	255	253
Detroit	6	8	0	.429	183	252
Green Bay	4	10	0	.286	134	219
Tampa Bay	2	12	0	.143	103	223

WESTERN DIVISION

Team	W	L	T	Pct.	PF	PA
Los Angeles*	10	4	0	.714	302	146
Atlanta	7	7	0	.500	179	129
San Francisco	5	9	0	.357	220	260
New Orleans	3	11	0	.214	232	336

PLAYOFFS

AFC divisional games
Denver 34 vs. Pittsburgh 21
Oakland 37 at Baltimore 31 (OT)

AFC championship
Denver 20 vs. Oakland 17

NFC divisional games
Dallas 37 vs. Chicago 7
Minnesota 14 at Los Angeles 7

NFC championship
Dallas 23 vs. Minnesota 6

Super Bowl XII
Dallas 27, Denver 10, at New Orleans.

1978

AMERICAN CONFERENCE

EASTERN DIVISION

Team	W	L	T	Pct.	PF	PA
New England*	11	5	0	.688	358	286
Miami†	11	5	0	.688	372	254
N.Y. Jets	8	8	0	.500	359	364
Buffalo	5	11	0	.313	302	354
Baltimore	5	11	0	.313	239	421

CENTRAL DIVISION

Team	W	L	T	Pct.	PF	PA
Pittsburgh*	14	2	0	.875	356	195
Houston†	10	6	0	.625	283	298
Cleveland	8	8	0	.500	334	356
Cincinnati	4	12	0	.250	252	284

WESTERN DIVISION

Team	W	L	T	Pct.	PF	PA
Denver*	10	6	0	.625	282	198
Oakland	9	7	0	.563	311	283
Seattle	9	7	0	.563	345	358
San Diego	9	7	0	.563	355	309
Kansas City	4	12	0	.250	243	327

*Division champion.
†Wild-card team.

NATIONAL CONFERENCE

EASTERN DIVISION

Team	W	L	T	Pct.	PF	PA
Dallas*	12	4	0	.750	384	208
Philadelphia†	9	7	0	.563	270	250
Washington	8	8	0	.500	273	283
St. Louis	6	10	0	.375	248	296
N.Y. Giants	6	10	0	.375	264	298

CENTRAL DIVISION

Team	W	L	T	Pct.	PF	PA
Minnesota*	8	7	1	.531	294	306
Green Bay	8	7	1	.531	249	269
Detroit	7	9	0	.438	290	300
Chicago	7	9	0	.438	253	274
Tampa Bay	5	11	0	.313	241	259

WESTERN DIVISION

Team	W	L	T	Pct.	PF	PA
Los Angeles*	12	4	0	.750	316	245
Atlanta†	9	7	0	.563	240	290
New Orleans	7	9	0	.438	281	298
San Francisco	2	14	0	.125	219	350

PLAYOFFS

AFC wild-card game
Houston 17 at Miami 9

AFC divisional games
Houston 31 at New England 14
Pittsburgh 33 vs. Denver 10

AFC championship
Pittsburgh 34 vs. Houston 5

NFC wild-card game
Atlanta 14 vs. Philadelphia 13

NFC divisional games
Dallas 27 vs. Atlanta 20
Los Angeles 34 vs. Minnesota 10

NFC championship
Dallas 28 at Los Angeles 0

Super Bowl XIII
Pittsburgh 35, Dallas 31, at Miami.

NO HEISMAN JINX FOR T.D.

In a case of the rich getting richer, the Dallas Cowboys—on the heels of a division-winning, 11-win season in 1976—used the second pick in the 1977 draft to select Heisman Trophy-winning running back Tony Dorsett of Pittsburgh. (The Cowboys had acquired the No. 2 pick in a trade with the Seattle Seahawks.) And Dorsett didn't disappoint, rushing for 1,007 yards and scoring 12 touchdown as a rookie and helping Dallas win its second Super Bowl. He was a consensus choice for NFL Rookie of the Year.

1979

AMERICAN CONFERENCE

EASTERN DIVISION

Team	W	L	T	Pct.	PF	PA
Miami*	10	6	0	.625	341	257
New England	9	7	0	.563	411	326
N.Y. Jets	8	8	0	.500	337	383
Buffalo	7	9	0	.438	268	279
Baltimore	5	11	0	.313	271	351

CENTRAL DIVISION

Team	W	L	T	Pct.	PF	PA
Pittsburgh*	12	4	0	.750	416	262
Houston†	11	5	0	.688	362	331
Cleveland	9	7	0	.563	359	352
Cincinnati	4	12	0	.250	337	421

WESTERN DIVISION

Team	W	L	T	Pct.	PF	PA
San Diego*	12	4	0	.750	411	246
Denver†	10	6	0	.625	289	262
Seattle	9	7	0	.563	378	372
Oakland	9	7	0	.563	365	337
Kansas City	7	9	0	.438	238	262

*Division champion.
†Wild-card team.

NATIONAL CONFERENCE

EASTERN DIVISION

Team	W	L	T	Pct.	PF	PA
Dallas*	11	5	0	.688	371	313
Philadelphia†	11	5	0	.688	339	282
Washington	10	6	0	.625	348	295
N.Y. Giants	6	10	0	.375	237	323
St. Louis	5	11	0	.313	307	358

CENTRAL DIVISION

Team	W	L	T	Pct.	PF	PA
Tampa Bay*	10	6	0	.625	273	237
Chicago†	10	6	0	.625	306	249
Minnesota	7	9	0	.438	259	337
Green Bay	5	11	0	.313	246	316
Detroit	2	14	0	.125	219	365

WESTERN DIVISION

Team	W	L	T	Pct.	PF	PA
Los Angeles*	9	7	0	.563	323	309
New Orleans	8	8	0	.500	370	360
Atlanta	6	10	0	.375	300	388
San Francisco	2	14	0	.125	308	416

PLAYOFFS

AFC wild-card game
Houston 13 vs. Denver 7

AFC divisional games
Houston 17 at San Diego 14
Pittsburgh 34 vs. Miami 14

AFC championship
Pittsburgh 27 vs. Houston 13

NFC wild-card game
Philadelphia 27 vs. Chicago 17

NFC divisional games
Tampa Bay 24 vs. Philadelphia 17
Los Angeles 21 at Dallas 19

NFC championship
Los Angeles 9 at Tampa Bay 0

Super Bowl XIV
Pittsburgh 31, Los Angeles 19, at Pasadena, Calif.

1980

AMERICAN CONFERENCE

EASTERN DIVISION

Team	W	L	T	Pct.	PF	PA
Buffalo*	11	5	0	.688	320	260
New England	10	6	0	.625	441	325
Miami	8	8	0	.500	266	305
Baltimore	7	9	0	.438	355	387
N.Y. Jets	4	12	0	.250	302	395

CENTRAL DIVISION

Team	W	L	T	Pct.	PF	PA
Cleveland*	11	5	0	.688	357	310
Houston†	11	5	0	.688	295	251
Pittsburgh	9	7	0	.563	352	313
Cincinnati	6	10	0	.375	244	312

WESTERN DIVISION

Team	W	L	T	Pct.	PF	PA
San Diego*	11	5	0	.688	418	327
Oakland†	11	5	0	.688	364	306
Kansas City	8	8	0	.500	319	336
Denver	8	8	0	.500	310	323
Seattle	4	12	0	.250	291	408

*Division champion.
†Wild-card team.

NATIONAL CONFERENCE

EASTERN DIVISION

Team	W	L	T	Pct.	PF	PA
Philadelphia*	12	4	0	.750	384	222
Dallas†	12	4	0	.750	454	311
Washington	6	10	0	.375	261	293
St. Louis	5	11	0	.313	299	350
N.Y. Giants	4	12	0	.250	249	425

CENTRAL DIVISION

Team	W	L	T	Pct.	PF	PA
Minnesota*	9	7	0	.563	317	308
Detroit	9	7	0	.563	334	272
Chicago	7	9	0	.438	304	264
Tampa Bay	5	10	1	.344	271	341
Green Bay	5	10	1	.344	231	371

WESTERN DIVISION

Team	W	L	T	Pct.	PF	PA
Atlanta*	12	4	0	.750	405	272
Los Angeles†	11	5	0	.688	424	289
San Francisco	6	10	0	.375	320	415
New Orleans	1	15	0	.063	291	487

PLAYOFFS

AFC wild-card game
Oakland 27 vs. Houston 7

AFC divisional games
San Diego 20 vs. Buffalo 14
Oakland 14 at Cleveland 12

AFC championship
Oakland 34 at San Diego 27

NFC wild-card game
Dallas 34 vs. Los Angeles 13

NFC divisional games
Philadelphia 31 vs. Minnesota 16
Dallas 30 at Atlanta 27

NFC championship
Philadelphia 20 vs. Dallas 7

Super Bowl XV
Oakland 27, Philadelphia 10, at New Orleans.

THE BIGGEST COMEBACK

The San Francisco 49ers rallied from a 35-7 deficit to beat New Orleans, 38-35, on December 7, 1980. An otherwise meaningless late-season game became the biggest comeback in NFL history as the 49ers tied the game with a touchdown with 1:50 left and won it on Ray Wersching's 36-yard field goal at 7:40 of overtime. Second-year quarterback Joe Montana threw two touchdown passes for San Francisco to offset the three TD passes Archie Manning tossed for the Saints, who finished the season with the league's worst record (1-15).

1981

AMERICAN CONFERENCE

EASTERN DIVISION

Team	W	L	T	Pct.	PF	PA
Miami*	11	4	1	.719	345	275
N.Y. Jets†	10	5	1	.656	355	287
Buffalo†	10	6	0	.625	311	276
Baltimore	2	14	0	.125	259	533
New England	2	14	0	.125	322	370

CENTRAL DIVISION

Team	W	L	T	Pct.	PF	PA
Cincinnati*	12	4	0	.750	421	304
Pittsburgh	8	8	0	.500	356	297
Houston	7	9	0	.438	281	355
Cleveland	5	11	0	.313	276	375

WESTERN DIVISION

Team	W	L	T	Pct.	PF	PA
San Diego*	10	6	0	.625	478	390
Denver	10	6	0	.625	321	289
Kansas City	9	7	0	.563	343	290
Oakland	7	9	0	.438	273	343
Seattle	6	10	0	.375	322	388

*Division champion.
†Wild-card team.

NATIONAL CONFERENCE

EASTERN DIVISION

Team	W	L	T	Pct.	PF	PA
Dallas*	12	4	0	.750	367	277
Philadelphia†	10	6	0	.625	368	221
N.Y. Giants†	9	7	0	.563	295	257
Washington	8	8	0	.500	347	349
St. Louis	7	9	0	.438	315	408

CENTRAL DIVISION

Team	W	L	T	Pct.	PF	PA
Tampa Bay*	9	7	0	.563	315	268
Detroit	8	8	0	.500	397	322
Green Bay	8	8	0	.500	324	361
Minnesota	7	9	0	.438	325	369
Chicago	6	10	0	.375	253	324

WESTERN DIVISION

Team	W	L	T	Pct.	PF	PA
San Francisco*	13	3	0	.813	357	250
Atlanta	7	9	0	.438	426	355
Los Angeles	6	10	0	.375	303	351
New Orleans	4	12	0	.250	207	378

PLAYOFFS

AFC wild-card game
Buffalo 31 at New York Jets 27

AFC divisional games
San Diego 41 at Miami 38 (OT)
Cincinnati 28 vs. Buffalo 21

AFC championship
Cincinnati 27 vs. San Diego 7

NFC wild-card game
N.Y. Giants 27 at Philadelphia 21

NFC divisional games
Dallas 38 vs. Tampa Bay 0
San Francisco 38 vs. N.Y. Giants 24

NFC championship
San Francisco 28 vs. Dallas 27

Super Bowl XVI
San Francisco 26, Cincinnati 21, at Pontiac, Mich.

1982

AMERICAN CONFERENCE

Team	W	L	T	Pct.	PF	PA
L.A. Raiders	8	1	0	.889	260	200
Miami	7	2	0	.778	198	131
Cincinnati	7	2	0	.778	232	177
Pittsburgh	6	3	0	.667	204	146
San Diego	6	3	0	.667	288	221
N.Y. Jets	6	3	0	.667	245	166
New England	5	4	0	.556	143	157
Cleveland	4	5	0	.444	140	182
Buffalo	4	5	0	.444	150	154
Seattle	4	5	0	.444	127	147
Kansas City	3	6	0	.333	176	184
Denver	2	7	0	.222	148	226
Houston	1	8	0	.111	136	245
Baltimore	0	8	1	.056	113	236

NATIONAL CONFERENCE

Team	W	L	T	Pct.	PF	PA
Washington	8	1	0	.889	190	128
Dallas	6	3	0	.667	226	145
Green Bay	5	3	1	.611	226	169
Minnesota	5	4	0	.556	187	198
Atlanta	5	4	0	.556	183	199
St. Louis	5	4	0	.556	135	170
Tampa Bay	5	4	0	.556	158	178
Detroit	4	5	0	.444	181	176
New Orleans	4	5	0	.444	129	160
N.Y. Giants	4	5	0	.444	164	160
San Francisco	3	6	0	.333	209	206
Chicago	3	6	0	.333	141	174
Philadelphia	3	6	0	.333	191	195
L.A. Rams	2	7	0	.222	200	250

As a result of a 57-day players' strike, the 1982 NFL regular season schedule was reduced from 16 weeks to 9. At the conclusion of the regular season, a 16-team Super Bowl Tournament was held. Eight teams from each conference were seeded 1 through 8 based on their records during regular season play.

Miami finished ahead of Cincinnati based on a better conference record. Pittsburgh won common games tiebreaker with San Diego after New York Jets were eliminated from three-way tie based on conference record. Cleveland finished ahead of Buffalo and Seattle based on better conference record. Minnesota, Atlanta, St. Louis and Tampa Bay seeds were determined by best won-lost record in conference games. Detroit finished ahead of New Orleans and the New York Giants based on a better conference record.

PLAYOFFS

AFC first round
Miami 28 vs. New England 13
L.A. Raiders 27 vs. Cleveland 10
New York Jets 44 at Cincinnati 17
San Diego 31 at Pittsburgh 28

AFC second round
N.Y. Jets 17 at L.A. Raiders 14
Miami 34 vs. San Diego 13

AFC championship
Miami 14 vs. New York Jets 0

NFC first round
Washington 31 vs. Detroit 7
Green Bay 41 vs. St. Louis 16
Minnesota 30 vs. Atlanta 24
Dallas 30 vs. Tampa Bay 17

NFC second round
Washington 21 vs. Minnesota 7
Dallas 37 vs. Green Bay 26

NFC championship
Washington 31 vs. Dallas 17

Super Bowl XVII
Washington 27, Miami 17, at Pasadena, Calif.

A GAME FOR THE AGES

In a game voted the NFL's "Game of the '80s" by the Pro Football Hall of Fame, the San Diego Chargers beat the Miami Dolphins, 41-38, in an AFC divisional playoff game on January 2, 1982. The two teams combined to set 11 NFL playoff records, including most points (79) and most total yards (1,036). Five players caught passes for at least 100 yards, including Chargers tight end Kellen Winslow, who caught 13 passes for 166 yards. Winslow also blocked a 43-yard field goal attempt by the Dolphins' Uwe von Schamann on the final play of regulation time, enabling Rolf Benirschke to win it for San Diego with a 29-yard field goal at 13:52 of overtime.

AMERICAN CONFERENCE

EASTERN DIVISION

Team	W	L	T	Pct.	PF	PA
Miami*	12	4	0	.750	389	250
New England	8	8	0	.500	274	289
Buffalo	8	8	0	.500	283	351
Baltimore	7	9	0	.438	264	354
N.Y. Jets	7	9	0	.438	313	331

CENTRAL DIVISION

Team	W	L	T	Pct.	PF	PA
Pittsburgh*	10	6	0	.625	355	303
Cleveland	9	7	0	.563	356	342
Cincinnati	7	9	0	.438	346	302
Houston	2	14	0	.125	288	460

WESTERN DIVISION

Team	W	L	T	Pct.	PF	PA
L.A. Raiders*	12	4	0	.750	442	338
Seattle†	9	7	0	.563	403	397
Denver†	9	7	0	.563	302	327
San Diego	6	10	0	.375	358	462
Kansas City	6	10	0	.375	386	367

*Division champion.
†Wild-card team.

NATIONAL CONFERENCE

EASTERN DIVISION

Team	W	L	T	Pct.	PF	PA
Washington*	14	2	0	.875	541	332
Dallas†	12	4	0	.750	479	360
St. Louis	8	7	1	.531	374	428
Philadelphia	5	11	0	.313	233	322
N.Y. Giants	3	12	1	.219	267	347

CENTRAL DIVISION

Team	W	L	T	Pct.	PF	PA
Detroit*	9	7	0	.563	347	286
Green Bay	8	8	0	.500	429	439
Chicago	8	8	0	.500	311	301
Minnesota	8	8	0	.500	316	348
Tampa Bay	2	14	0	.125	241	380

WESTERN DIVISION

Team	W	L	T	Pct.	PF	PA
San Francisco*	10	6	0	.625	432	293
L.A. Rams†	9	7	0	.563	361	344
New Orleans	8	8	0	.500	319	337
Atlanta	7	9	0	.438	370	389

PLAYOFFS

AFC wild-card game
Seattle 31 vs. Denver 7

AFC divisional games
Seattle 27 at Miami 20
L.A. Raiders 38 vs. Pittsburgh 10

AFC championship game
L.A. Raiders 30 vs. Seattle 14

NFC wild-card game
Los Angeles Rams 24 at Dallas 17

NFC divisional games
San Francisco 24 vs. Detroit 23
Washington 51 vs. L.A. Rams 7

NFC championship
Washington 24 vs. San Francisco 21

Super Bowl XVIII
L.A. Raiders 38, Washington 9, at Tampa, Fla.

AMERICAN CONFERENCE

EASTERN DIVISION

Team	W	L	T	Pct.	PF	PA
Miami*	14	2	0	.875	513	298
New England	9	7	0	.563	362	352
N.Y. Jets	7	9	0	.438	332	364
Indianapolis	4	12	0	.250	239	414
Buffalo	2	14	0	.125	250	454

CENTRAL DIVISION

Team	W	L	T	Pct.	PF	PA
Pittsburgh*	9	7	0	.563	387	310
Cincinnati	8	8	0	.500	339	339
Cleveland	5	11	0	.313	250	297
Houston	3	13	0	.188	240	437

WESTERN DIVISION

Team	W	L	T	Pct.	PF	PA
Denver*	13	3	0	.813	353	241
Seattle†	12	4	0	.750	418	282
L.A. Raiders†	11	5	0	.688	368	278
Kansas City	8	8	0	.500	314	324
San Diego	7	9	0	.438	394	413

*Division champion.
†Wild-card team.

NATIONAL CONFERENCE

EASTERN DIVISION

Team	W	L	T	Pct.	PF	PA
Washington*	11	5	0	.688	426	310
N.Y. Giants†	9	7	0	.563	299	301
St. Louis	9	7	0	.563	423	345
Dallas	9	7	0	.563	308	308
Philadelphia	6	9	1	.406	278	320

CENTRAL DIVISION

Team	W	L	T	Pct.	PF	PA
Chicago*	10	6	0	.625	325	248
Green Bay	8	8	0	.500	390	309
Tampa Bay	6	10	0	.375	335	380
Detroit	4	11	1	.281	283	408
Minnesota	3	13	0	.188	276	484

WESTERN DIVISION

Team	W	L	T	Pct.	PF	PA
San Francisco*	15	1	0	.938	475	227
L.A. Rams†	10	6	0	.625	346	316
New Orleans	7	9	0	.438	298	361
Atlanta	4	12	0	.250	281	382

PLAYOFFS

AFC wild-card game
Seattle 13 vs. Los Angeles Raiders 7

AFC divisional games
Miami 31 vs. Seattle 10
Pittsburgh 24 at Denver 17

AFC championship
Miami 45 vs. Pittsburgh 28

NFC wild-card game
N.Y. Giants 16 at L.A. Rams 13

NFC divisional games
San Francisco 21 vs. N.Y. Giants 10
Chicago 23 at Washington 19

NFC championship
San Francisco 23 vs. Chicago 0

Super Bowl XIX
San Francisco 38, Miami 16, at Palo Alto, Calif.

DAN'S THE MAN

In 1984, Dan Marino of the Miami Dolphins had perhaps the greatest season of any quarterback in NFL history. In only his second year Marino led the league in attempts (564), completions (362), yards (5,084), average gain per pass attempt (9.0), percentage of TDs per attempt (8.5), touchdowns (48) and QB rating (108.9). His yards, TDs and completion totals set NFL records. It took Marino just eight games to break Bob Griese's team record for touchdown passes in a season and nine games to break Griese's yardage mark. At 23, Marino also became the youngest quarterback to take his team to the Super Bowl, where the Dolphins lost to the 49ers.

1985

AMERICAN CONFERENCE

EASTERN DIVISION

Team	W	L	T	Pct.	PF	PA
Miami*	12	4	0	.750	428	320
N.Y. Jets†	11	5	0	.688	393	264
New England†	11	5	0	.688	362	290
Indianapolis	5	11	0	.313	320	386
Buffalo	2	14	0	.125	200	381

CENTRAL DIVISION

Team	W	L	T	Pct.	PF	PA
Cleveland*	8	8	0	.500	287	294
Cincinnati	7	9	0	.438	441	437
Pittsburgh	7	9	0	.438	379	355
Houston	5	11	0	.313	284	412

WESTERN DIVISION

Team	W	L	T	Pct.	PF	PA
L.A. Raiders*	12	4	0	.750	354	308
Denver	11	5	0	.688	380	329
Seattle	8	8	0	.500	349	303
San Diego	8	8	0	.500	467	435
Kansas City	6	10	0	.375	317	360

*Division champion.
†Wild-card team.

NATIONAL CONFERENCE

EASTERN DIVISION

Team	W	L	T	Pct.	PF	PA
Dallas*	10	6	0	.625	357	333
N.Y. Giants†	10	6	0	.625	399	283
Washington	10	6	0	.625	297	312
Philadelphia	7	9	0	.438	286	310
St. Louis	5	11	0	.313	278	414

CENTRAL DIVISION

Team	W	L	T	Pct.	PF	PA
Chicago*	15	1	0	.938	456	198
Green Bay	8	8	0	.500	337	355
Minnesota	7	9	0	.438	346	359
Detroit	7	9	0	.438	307	366
Tampa Bay	2	14	0	.125	294	448

WESTERN DIVISION

Team	W	L	T	Pct.	PF	PA
L.A. Rams*	11	5	0	.688	340	277
San Francisco†	10	6	0	.625	411	263
New Orleans	5	11	0	.313	294	401
Atlanta	4	12	0	.250	282	452

PLAYOFFS

AFC wild-card game
New England 26 at N.Y. Jets 14

AFC divisional games
Miami 24 vs. Cleveland 21
New England 27 at L.A. Raiders 20

AFC championship
New England 31 at Miami 14

NFC wild-card game
N.Y. Giants 17 vs. San Francisco 3

NFC divisional games
Los Angeles Rams 20 vs. Dallas 0
Chicago 21 vs. New York Giants 0

NFC championship
Chicago 24 vs. Los Angeles Rams 0

Super Bowl XX
Chicago 46, New England 10, at New Orleans.

1986

AMERICAN CONFERENCE

EASTERN DIVISION

Team	W	L	T	Pct.	PF	PA
New England*	11	5	0	.688	412	307
N.Y. Jets†	10	6	0	.625	364	386
Miami	8	8	0	.500	430	405
Buffalo	4	12	0	.250	287	348
Indianapolis	3	13	0	.188	229	400

CENTRAL DIVISION

Team	W	L	T	Pct.	PF	PA
Cleveland*	12	4	0	.750	391	310
Cincinnati	10	6	0	.625	409	394
Pittsburgh	6	10	0	.375	307	336
Houston	5	11	0	.313	274	329

WESTERN DIVISION

Team	W	L	T	Pct.	PF	PA
Denver*	11	5	0	.688	378	327
Kansas City†	10	6	0	.625	358	326
Seattle	10	6	0	.625	366	293
L.A. Raiders	8	8	0	.500	323	346
San Diego	4	12	0	.250	335	396

*Division champion.
†Wild-card team.

NATIONAL CONFERENCE

EASTERN DIVISION

Team	W	L	T	Pct.	PF	PA
N.Y. Giants*	14	2	0	.875	371	236
Washington†	12	4	0	.750	368	296
Dallas	7	9	0	.438	346	337
Philadelphia	5	10	1	.344	256	312
St. Louis	4	11	1	.281	218	351

CENTRAL DIVISION

Team	W	L	T	Pct.	PF	PA
Chicago*	14	2	0	.875	352	187
Minnesota	9	7	0	.563	398	273
Detroit	5	11	0	.313	277	326
Green Bay	4	12	0	.250	254	418
Tampa Bay	2	14	0	.125	239	473

WESTERN DIVISION

Team	W	L	T	Pct.	PF	PA
San Francisco*	10	5	1	.656	374	247
L.A. Rams†	10	6	0	.625	309	267
Atlanta	7	8	1	.469	280	280
New Orleans	7	9	0	.438	288	287

PLAYOFFS

AFC wild-card game
N.Y. Jets 35 vs. Kansas City 15

AFC divisional games
Cleveland 23 vs. N.Y. Jets 20 (OT)
Denver 22 vs. New England 17

AFC championship
Denver 23 at Cleveland 20 (OT)

NFC wild-card game
Washington 19 vs. L.A. Rams 7

NFC divisional games
Washington 27 at Chicago 13
N.Y. Giants 49 vs. San Francisco 3

NFC championship
N.Y. Giants 17 vs. Washington 0

Super Bowl XXI
New York Giants 39, Denver 20, at Pasadena, Calif.

DOUBLE GRAND

In 1985, Roger Craig of the San Francisco 49ers did something no NFL player had done before or has done since—rush for more than 1,000 yards and catch passes for more than 1,000 in the same season. Craig's final numbers were 1,050 yards rushing on 214 attempts and 1,016 yards receiving on a NFL-high 92 receptions. Despite Craig's heroics, the 49ers had (for them) one of their most disappointing seasons of the 1980s. Although they won 10 games, the defending Super Bowl champions finished second to the Rams in the NFC West and lost in the first round of the playoffs.

1987

AMERICAN CONFERENCE

EASTERN DIVISION

Team	W	L	T	Pct.	PF	PA
Indianapolis*	9	6	0	.600	300	238
New England	8	7	0	.533	320	293
Miami	8	7	0	.533	362	335
Buffalo	7	8	0	.467	270	305
N.Y. Jets	6	9	0	.400	334	360

CENTRAL DIVISION

Team	W	L	T	Pct.	PF	PA
Cleveland*	10	5	0	.667	390	239
Houston†	9	6	0	.600	345	349
Pittsburgh	8	7	0	.533	285	299
Cincinnati	4	11	0	.267	285	370

WESTERN DIVISION

Team	W	L	T	Pct.	PF	PA
Denver*	10	4	1	.700	379	288
Seattle†	9	6	0	.600	371	314
San Diego	8	7	0	.533	253	317
L.A. Raiders	5	10	0	.333	301	289
Kansas City	4	11	0	.267	273	388

*Division champion.
†Wild-card team.

NOTE: The 1987 NFL regular season was reduced from 224 games to 210 (16 to 15 for each team) due to players' strike.

NATIONAL CONFERENCE

EASTERN DIVISION

Team	W	L	T	Pct.	PF	PA
Washington*	11	4	0	.733	379	285
Dallas	7	8	0	.467	340	348
St. Louis	7	8	0	.467	362	368
Philadelphia	7	8	0	.467	337	380
N.Y. Giants	6	9	0	.400	280	312

CENTRAL DIVISION

Team	W	L	T	Pct.	PF	PA
Chicago*	11	4	0	.733	356	282
Minnesota†	8	7	0	.533	336	335
Green Bay	5	9	1	.367	255	300
Tampa Bay	4	11	0	.267	286	360
Detroit	4	11	0	.267	269	384

WESTERN DIVISION

Team	W	L	T	Pct.	PF	PA
San Francisco*	13	2	0	.867	459	253
New Orleans†	12	3	0	.800	422	283
L.A. Rams	6	9	0	.400	317	361
Atlanta	3	12	0	.200	205	436

PLAYOFFS

AFC wild-card game
Houston 23 vs. Seattle 20 (OT)

AFC divisional games
Cleveland 38 vs. Indianapolis 21
Denver 34 vs. Houston 10

AFC championship
Denver 38 vs. Cleveland 33

NFC wild-card game
Minnesota 44 at New Orleans 10

NFC divisional games
Minnesota 36 at San Francisco 24
Washington 21 at Chicago 17

NFC championship
Washington 17 vs. Minnesota 10

Super Bowl XXII
Washington 42, Denver 10, at San Diego.

1988

AMERICAN CONFERENCE

EASTERN DIVISION

Team	W	L	T	Pct.	PF	PA
Buffalo*	12	4	0	.750	329	237
Indianapolis	9	7	0	.563	354	315
New England	9	7	0	.563	250	284
N.Y. Jets	8	7	1	.531	372	354
Miami	6	10	0	.375	319	380

CENTRAL DIVISION

Team	W	L	T	Pct.	PF	PA
Cincinnati*	12	4	0	.750	448	329
Cleveland†	10	6	0	.625	304	288
Houston†	10	6	0	.625	424	365
Pittsburgh	5	11	0	.313	336	421

WESTERN DIVISION

Team	W	L	T	Pct.	PF	PA
Seattle*	9	7	0	.563	339	329
Denver	8	8	0	.500	327	352
L.A. Raiders	7	9	0	.438	325	369
San Diego	6	10	0	.375	231	332
Kansas City	4	11	1	.281	254	320

*Division champion.
†Wild-card team.

NATIONAL CONFERENCE

EASTERN DIVISION

Team	W	L	T	Pct.	PF	PA
Philadelphia*	10	6	0	.625	379	319
N.Y. Giants	10	6	0	.625	359	304
Washington	7	9	0	.438	345	387
Phoenix	7	9	0	.438	344	398
Dallas	3	13	0	.188	265	381

CENTRAL DIVISION

Team	W	L	T	Pct.	PF	PA
Chicago*	12	4	0	.750	312	215
Minnesota†	11	5	0	.688	406	233
Tampa Bay	5	11	0	.313	261	350
Detroit	4	12	0	.250	220	313
Green Bay	4	12	0	.250	240	315

WESTERN DIVISION

Team	W	L	T	Pct.	PF	PA
San Francisco*	10	6	0	.625	369	294
L.A. Rams†	10	6	0	.625	407	293
New Orleans	10	6	0	.625	312	283
Atlanta	5	11	0	.313	244	315

PLAYOFFS

AFC wild-card game
Houston 24 at Cleveland 23

AFC divisional games
Cincinnati 21 vs. Seattle 13
Buffalo 17 vs. Houston 10

AFC championship
Cincinnati 21 vs. Buffalo 10

NFC wild-card game
Minnesota 28 vs. L.A. Rams 17

NFC divisional games
Chicago 20 vs. Philadelphia 12
San Francisco 34 vs. Minnesota 9

NFC championship
San Francisco 28 at Chicago 3

Super Bowl XXIII
San Francisco 20, Cincinnati 16, at Miami.

BENGALS HAD BITE

In one of the most improbable turnarounds in NFL history, the Cincinnati Bengals went from being a sack-sad, 4-11 team in 1987 to within 34 seconds of winning the Super Bowl a year later. Many players stepped up their level of play in 1988, as nine Cincinnati players were selected to the Pro Bowl. But it was someone who wasn't Pro Bowl-bound—rookie running back Ickey Woods—who sparked the turnaround. Woods, a second-round draft choice from UNLV, rushed for 1,066 yards that season and performed what came to be known as the "Ickey Shuffle" after every touchdown he scored. He performed it 15 times that year.

1989

AMERICAN CONFERENCE

EASTERN DIVISION

Team	W	L	T	Pct.	PF	PA
Buffalo*	9	7	0	.563	409	317
Indianapolis	8	8	0	.500	298	301
Miami	8	8	0	.500	331	379
New England	5	11	0	.313	297	391
N.Y. Jets	4	12	0	.250	253	411

CENTRAL DIVISION

Team	W	L	T	Pct.	PF	PA
Cleveland*	9	6	1	.594	334	254
Houston†	9	7	0	.563	365	412
Pittsburgh†	9	7	0	.563	265	326
Cincinnati	8	8	0	.500	404	285

WESTERN DIVISION

Team	W	L	T	Pct.	PF	PA
Denver*	11	5	0	.688	362	226
Kansas City	8	7	1	.531	318	286
L.A. Raiders	8	8	0	.500	315	297
Seattle	7	9	0	.438	241	327
San Diego	6	10	0	.375	266	290

*Division champion.
†Wild-card team.

NATIONAL CONFERENCE

EASTERN DIVISION

Team	W	L	T	Pct.	PF	PA
N.Y. Giants*	12	4	0	.750	348	252
Philadelphia†	11	5	0	.688	342	274
Washington	10	6	0	.625	386	308
Phoenix	5	11	0	.313	258	377
Dallas	1	15	0	.063	204	393

CENTRAL DIVISION

Team	W	L	T	Pct.	PF	PA
Minnesota*	10	6	0	.625	351	275
Green Bay	10	6	0	.625	362	356
Detroit	7	9	0	.438	312	364
Chicago	6	10	0	.375	358	377
Tampa Bay	5	11	0	.313	320	419

WESTERN DIVISION

Team	W	L	T	Pct.	PF	PA
San Francisco*	14	2	0	.875	442	253
L.A. Rams†	11	5	0	.688	426	344
New Orleans	9	7	0	.563	386	301
Atlanta	3	13	0	.188	279	437

PLAYOFFS

AFC wild-card game
Pittsburgh 26 at Houston 23 (OT)

AFC divisional games
Cleveland 34 vs. Buffalo 30
Denver 24 vs. Pittsburgh 23

AFC championship
Denver 37 vs. Cleveland 21

NFC wild-card game
L.A. Rams 21 at Philadelphia 7

NFC divisional games
L.A. Rams 19 at N.Y. Giants 13 (OT)
San Francisco 41 vs. Minnesota 13

NFC championship
San Francisco 30 vs. L.A. Rams 3

Super Bowl XXIV
San Francisco 55, Denver 10, at New Orleans.

1990

AMERICAN CONFERENCE

EASTERN DIVISION

Team	W	L	T	Pct.	PF	PA
Buffalo*	13	3	0	.813	428	263
Miami†	12	4	0	.750	336	242
Indianapolis	7	9	0	.438	281	353
N.Y. Jets	6	10	0	.375	295	345
New England	1	15	0	.063	181	446

CENTRAL DIVISION

Team	W	L	T	Pct.	PF	PA
Cincinnati*	9	7	0	.563	360	352
Houston†	9	7	0	.563	405	307
Pittsburgh	9	7	0	.563	292	240
Cleveland	3	13	0	.188	228	462

WESTERN DIVISION

Team	W	L	T	Pct.	PF	PA
L.A. Raiders*	12	4	0	.750	337	268
Kansas City†	11	5	0	.688	369	257
Seattle	9	7	0	.563	306	286
San Diego	6	10	0	.375	315	281
Denver	5	11	0	.313	331	374

*Division champion.
†Wild-card team.

NATIONAL CONFERENCE

EASTERN DIVISION

Team	W	L	T	Pct.	PF	PA
N.Y. Giants*	13	3	0	.813	335	211
Philadelphia†	10	6	0	.625	396	299
Washington†	10	6	0	.625	381	301
Dallas	7	9	0	.438	244	308
Phoenix	5	11	0	.313	268	396

CENTRAL DIVISION

Team	W	L	T	Pct.	PF	PA
Chicago*	11	5	0	.688	348	280
Tampa Bay	6	10	0	.375	264	367
Detroit	6	10	0	.375	373	413
Green Bay	6	10	0	.375	271	347
Minnesota	6	10	0	.375	351	326

WESTERN DIVISION

Team	W	L	T	Pct.	PF	PA
San Francisco*	14	2	0	.875	353	239
New Orleans†	8	8	0	.500	274	275
L.A. Rams	5	11	0	.313	345	412
Atlanta	5	11	0	.313	348	365

PLAYOFFS

AFC wild-card playoffs
Miami 17 vs. Kansas City 16
Cincinnati 41 vs. Houston 14

AFC divisional playoffs
Buffalo 44 vs. Miami 34
L.A. Raiders 20 vs. Cincinnati 10

AFC championship
Buffalo 51 vs. L.A. Raiders 3

NFC wild-card playoffs
Washington 20 at Philadelphia 6
Chicago 16 vs. New Orleans 6

NFC divisional playoffs
San Francisco 28 vs. Washington 10
N.Y. Giants 31 vs. Chicago 3

NFC championship
N.Y. Giants 15 at San Francisco 13

Super Bowl XXV
N.Y. Giants 20 vs. Buffalo 19, at Tampa, Fla.

A STACKED CUPBOARD

Some first-time NFL head coaches inherit terrible teams. In 1989, George Seifert inherited a great one. After succeeding Bill Walsh in San Francisco, Seifert did what his predecessor had done the year before: win a Super Bowl. The 49ers simply dominated the NFL in 1989, winning a league-high 14 games (10 of them by at least 10 points) and losing just twice (by a combined five points). They won their three playoff games by a combined score of 126-26, including 55-10 over Denver in the most lopsided Super Bowl ever.

AMERICAN CONFERENCE

EASTERN DIVISION

Team	W	L	T	Pct.	PF	PA
Buffalo*	13	3	0	.813	458	318
N.Y. Jets†	8	8	0	.500	314	293
Miami	8	8	0	.500	343	349
New England	6	10	0	.375	211	305
Indianapolis	1	15	0	.063	143	381

CENTRAL DIVISION

Team	W	L	T	Pct.	PF	PA
Houston*	11	5	0	.688	386	251
Pittsburgh	7	9	0	.438	292	344
Cleveland	6	10	0	.375	293	298
Cincinnati	3	13	0	.188	263	435

WESTERN DIVISION

Team	W	L	T	Pct.	PF	PA
Denver*	12	4	0	.750	304	235
Kansas City†	10	6	0	.625	322	252
L.A. Raiders†	9	7	0	.563	298	297
Seattle	7	9	0	.438	276	261
San Diego	4	12	0	.250	274	342

*Division champion.
†Wild-card team.

NATIONAL CONFERENCE

EASTERN DIVISION

Team	W	L	T	Pct.	PF	PA
Washington*	14	2	0	.875	485	224
Dallas†	11	5	0	.688	342	310
Philadelphia	10	6	0	.625	285	244
N.Y. Giants	8	8	0	.500	281	297
Phoenix	4	12	0	.250	196	344

CENTRAL DIVISION

Team	W	L	T	Pct.	PF	PA
Detroit*	12	4	0	.750	339	295
Chicago†	11	5	0	.688	299	269
Minnesota	8	8	0	.500	301	306
Green Bay	4	12	0	.250	273	313
Tampa Bay	3	13	0	.188	199	365

WESTERN DIVISION

Team	W	L	T	Pct.	PF	PA
New Orleans*	11	5	0	.688	341	211
Atlanta†	10	6	0	.625	361	338
San Francisco	10	6	0	.625	393	239
L.A. Rams	3	13	0	.188	234	390

PLAYOFFS

AFC wild-card playoffs
Kansas City 10 vs. L.A. Raiders 6
Houston 17 vs. N.Y. Jets 10

AFC divisional playoffs
Denver 26 vs. Houston 24
Buffalo 37 vs. Kansas City 14

AFC championship
Buffalo 10 vs. Denver 7

NFC wild-card playoffs
Atlanta 27 at New Orleans 20
Dallas 17 at Chicago 13

NFC divisional playoffs
Washington 24 vs. Atlanta 7
Detroit 38 vs. Dallas 6

NFC championship
Washington 41 vs. Detroit 10

Super Bowl XXVI
Washington 37 vs. Buffalo 24, at Minneapolis.

AMERICAN CONFERENCE

EASTERN DIVISION

Team	W	L	T	Pct.	PF	PA
Miami*	11	5	0	.688	340	281
Buffalo†	11	5	0	.688	381	283
Indianapolis	9	7	0	.563	216	302
N.Y. Jets	4	12	0	.250	220	315
New England	2	14	0	.125	205	363

CENTRAL DIVISION

Team	W	L	T	Pct.	PF	PA
Pittsburgh*	11	5	0	.688	299	225
Houston†	10	6	0	.625	352	258
Cleveland	7	9	0	.438	272	275
Cincinnati	5	11	0	.313	274	364

WESTERN DIVISION

Team	W	L	T	Pct.	PF	PA
San Diego*	11	5	0	.688	335	241
Kansas City†	10	6	0	.625	348	282
Denver	8	8	0	.500	262	329
L.A. Raiders	7	9	0	.438	249	281
Seattle	2	14	0	.125	140	312

*Division champion.
†Wild-card team.

NATIONAL CONFERENCE

EASTERN DIVISION

Team	W	L	T	Pct.	PF	PA
Dallas*	13	3	0	.813	409	243
Philadelphia†	11	5	0	.688	354	245
Washington†	9	7	0	.563	300	255
N.Y. Giants	6	10	0	.375	306	367
Phoenix	4	12	0	.250	243	332

CENTRAL DIVISION

Team	W	L	T	Pct.	PF	PA
Minnesota*	11	5	0	.688	374	249
Green Bay	9	7	0	.563	276	296
Tampa Bay	5	11	0	.313	267	365
Chicago	5	11	0	.313	295	361
Detroit	5	11	0	.313	273	332

WESTERN DIVISION

Team	W	L	T	Pct.	PF	PA
San Francisco*	14	2	0	.875	431	236
New Orleans†	12	4	0	.750	330	202
Atlanta	6	10	0	.375	327	414
L.A. Rams	6	10	0	.375	313	383

PLAYOFFS

AFC wild-card playoffs
San Diego 17 vs. Kansas City 0
Buffalo 41 vs. Houston 38 (OT)

AFC divisional playoffs
Buffalo 24 at Pittsburgh 3
Miami 31 vs. San Diego 0

AFC championship
Buffalo 29 at Miami 10

NFC wild-card playoffs
Washington 24 at Minnesota 7
Philadelphia 36 at New Orleans 20

NFC divisional playoffs
San Francisco 20 vs. Washington 13
Dallas 34 vs. Philadelphia 10

NFC championship
Dallas 30 at San Francisco 20

Super Bowl XXVII
Dallas 52 vs. Buffalo 17, at Pasadena, Calif.

QB III

In the final hurrah of his Hall of Fame coaching career, Joe Gibbs led the Washington Redskins to their third Super Bowl title in 10 years in January 1992. Chuck Noll and Bill Walsh also had coached as many Super Bowl winners, but Gibbs outdid both of them in one respect: he had different quarterbacks in every one. Whereas Noll won four Super Bowls with Terry Bradshaw calling the signals and Walsh won three with Joe Montana, Gibbs won his with Joe Theismann, Doug Williams and Mark Rypien.

1993

AMERICAN CONFERENCE

EASTERN DIVISION

Team	W	L	T	Pct.	PF	PA
Buffalo*	12	4	0	.750	329	242
Miami	9	7	0	.563	349	351
N.Y. Jets	8	8	0	.500	270	247
New England	5	11	0	.313	238	286
Indianapolis	4	12	0	.250	189	378

CENTRAL DIVISION

Team	W	L	T	Pct.	PF	PA
Houston*	12	4	0	.750	368	238
Pittsburgh†	9	7	0	.563	308	281
Cleveland	7	9	0	.438	304	307
Cincinnati	3	13	0	.188	187	319

WESTERN DIVISION

Team	W	L	T	Pct.	PF	PA
Kansas City*	11	5	0	.688	328	291
L.A. Raiders†	10	6	0	.625	306	326
Denver†	9	7	0	.563	373	284
San Diego	8	8	0	.500	322	290
Seattle	6	10	0	.375	280	314

*Division champion.
†Wild-card team.

NATIONAL CONFERENCE

EASTERN DIVISION

Team	W	L	T	Pct.	PF	PA
Dallas*	12	4	0	.750	376	229
N.Y. Giants†	11	5	0	.688	288	205
Philadelphia	8	8	0	.500	293	315
Phoenix	7	9	0	.438	326	269
Washington	4	12	0	.250	230	345

CENTRAL DIVISION

Team	W	L	T	Pct.	PF	PA
Detroit*	10	6	0	.625	298	292
Minnesota†	9	7	0	.563	277	290
Green Bay†	9	7	0	.563	340	282
Chicago	7	9	0	.438	234	230
Tampa Bay	5	11	0	.313	237	376

WESTERN DIVISION

Team	W	L	T	Pct.	PF	PA
San Francisco*	10	6	0	.625	473	295
New Orleans	8	8	0	.500	317	343
Atlanta	6	10	0	.375	316	385
L.A. Rams	5	11	0	.313	221	367

PLAYOFFS

AFC wild-card playoffs
Kansas City 27 vs. Pittsburgh 24 (OT)
L.A. Raiders 42 vs. Denver 24

AFC divisional playoffs
Buffalo 29 vs. L.A. Raiders 23
Kansas City 28 at Houston 20

AFC championship
Buffalo 30 vs. Kansas City 13

NFC wild-card playoffs
Green Bay 28 at Detroit 24
N.Y. Giants 17 vs. Minnesota 10

NFC divisional playoffs
San Francisco 44 vs. N.Y. Giants 3
Dallas 27 vs. Green Bay 17

NFC championship
Dallas 38 vs. San Francisco 21

Super Bowl XXVIII
Dallas 30 vs. Buffalo 13, at Atlanta.

1994

AMERICAN CONFERENCE

EASTERN DIVISION

Team	W	L	T	Pct.	PF	PA
Miami*	10	6	0	.625	389	327
New England†	10	6	0	.625	351	312
Indianapolis	8	8	0	.500	307	320
Buffalo	7	9	0	.438	340	356
N.Y. Jets	6	10	0	.375	264	320

CENTRAL DIVISION

Team	W	L	T	Pct.	PF	PA
Pittsburgh*	12	4	0	.750	316	234
Cleveland†	11	5	0	.688	340	204
Cincinnati	3	13	0	.188	276	406
Houston	2	14	0	.125	226	352

WESTERN DIVISION

Team	W	L	T	Pct.	PF	PA
San Diego*	11	5	0	.688	381	306
Kansas City†	9	7	0	.563	319	298
L.A. Raiders	9	7	0	.563	303	327
Denver	7	9	0	.438	347	396
Seattle	6	10	0	.375	287	323

*Division champion.
†Wild-card team.

NATIONAL CONFERENCE

EASTERN DIVISION

Team	W	L	T	Pct.	PF	PA
Dallas*	12	4	0	.750	414	248
N.Y. Giants	9	7	0	.563	279	305
Arizona	8	8	0	.500	235	267
Philadelphia	7	9	0	.438	308	308
Washington	3	13	0	.188	320	412

CENTRAL DIVISION

Team	W	L	T	Pct.	PF	PA
Minnesota*	10	6	0	.625	356	314
Detroit†	9	7	0	.563	357	342
Green Bay†	9	7	0	.563	382	287
Chicago†	9	7	0	.563	271	307
Tampa Bay	6	10	0	.375	251	351

WESTERN DIVISION

Team	W	L	T	Pct.	PF	PA
San Francisco*	13	3	0	.813	505	296
New Orleans	7	9	0	.438	348	407
Atlanta	7	9	0	.438	313	389
L.A. Rams	4	12	0	.250	286	365

PLAYOFFS

AFC wild-card playoffs
Miami 27 vs. Kansas City 17
Cleveland 20 vs. New England 13

AFC divisional playoffs
Pittsburgh 29 vs. Cleveland 9
San Diego 22 vs. Miami 21

AFC championship
San Diego 17 at Pittsburgh 13

NFC wild-card playoffs
Green Bay 16 vs. Detroit 12
Chicago 35 at Minnesota 18

NFC divisional playoffs
San Francisco 44 vs. Chicago 15
Dallas 35 vs. Green Bay 9

NFC championship
San Francisco 38 vs. Dallas 28

Super Bowl XXIX
San Francisco 49 vs. San Diego 26 at Miami.

FOUR IN A ROW

In 1993, the Buffalo Bills accomplished something unprecendented in NFL history: they played in the Super Bowl for a fourth successive year. Although they lost all four—joining the Minnesota Vikings and Denver Broncos as the only four-time Super Bowl losers—their achievement should not be minimized. Fifteen different Bills played in the Pro Bowl over the four-year span (1990 through '93), including perennials Cornelius Bennett, Jim Kelly, Andre Reed, Bruce Smith and Thurman Thomas.

AMERICAN CONFERENCE

EASTERN DIVISION

	W	L	T	Pct.	Pts.	Opp.
Buffalo*	10	6	0	.625	350	335
Indianapolis†	9	7	0	.563	331	316
Miami†	9	7	0	.563	398	332
New England	6	10	0	.375	294	377
N.Y. Jets	3	13	0	.188	233	384

CENTRAL DIVISION

	W	L	T	Pct.	Pts.	Opp.
Pittsburgh*	11	5	0	.689	407	327
Cincinnati	7	9	0	.438	349	374
Houston	7	9	0	.438	348	324
Cleveland	5	11	0	.313	289	356
Jacksonville	4	12	0	.250	275	404

WESTERN DIVISION

	W	L	T	Pct.	Pts.	Opp.
Kansas City*	13	3	0	.813	358	241
San Diego†	9	7	0	.563	321	323
Seattle	8	8	0	.500	363	366
Denver	8	8	0	.500	388	345
Oakland	8	8	0	.500	348	332

*Division champion.
†Wild-card team.

NATIONAL CONFERENCE

EASTERN DIVISION

	W	L	T	Pct.	Pts.	Opp.
Dallas*	12	4	0	.750	435	291
Philadelphia†	10	6	0	.625	318	338
Washington	6	10	0	.375	326	359
N.Y. Giants	5	11	0	.313	290	340
Arizona	4	12	0	.250	275	422

CENTRAL DIVISION

	W	L	T	Pct.	Pts.	Opp.
Green Bay*	11	5	0	.689	404	314
Detroit†	10	6	0	.625	436	336
Chicago	9	7	0	.563	392	360
Minnesota	8	8	0	.500	412	385
Tampa Bay	7	9	0	.438	238	335

WESTERN DIVISION

	W	L	T	Pct.	Pts.	Opp.
San Francisco*	11	5	0	.688	457	258
Atlanta†	9	7	0	.563	362	349
St. Louis	7	9	0	.438	309	418
Carolina	7	9	0	.438	289	325
New Orleans	7	9	0	.438	319	348

PLAYOFFS

AFC wild-card playoffs
Buffalo 37 vs. Miami 22
Indianapolis 35 at San Diego 20
AFC divisional playoffs
Pittsburgh 40 vs. Buffalo 21
Indianapolis 10 at Kansas City 7
AFC championship
Pittsburgh 20 vs. Indianapolis 16
NFC wild-card playoffs
Philadelphia 58 vs. Detroit 37
Green Bay 37 vs. Atlanta 20
NFC divisional playoffs
Green Bay 27 at San Francisco 17
Dallas 30 vs. Philadelphia 11
NFC championship
Dallas 38 vs. Green Bay 27
Super Bowl XXX
Dallas 27 vs Pittsburgh 17, at Tempe, Ariz.

AMERICAN CONFERENCE

EASTERN DIVISION

	W	L	T	Pct.	Pts.	Opp.
New England*	11	5	0	.687	418	313
Buffalo†	10	6	0	.625	319	266
Indianapolis†	9	7	0	.563	317	334
Miami	8	8	0	.500	339	325
N.Y. Jets	1	15	0	.063	279	454

CENTRAL DIVISION

	W	L	T	Pct.	Pts.	Opp.
Pittsburgh*	10	6	0	.625	344	257
Jacksonville†	9	7	0	.563	325	335
Cincinnati	8	8	0	.500	372	369
Houston	8	8	0	.500	345	319
Baltimore	4	12	0	.250	371	441

WESTERN DIVISION

	W	L	T	Pct.	Pts.	Opp.
Denver*	13	3	0	.813	391	275
Kansas City	9	7	0	.563	297	300
San Diego	8	8	0	.500	310	376
Oakland	7	9	0	.438	340	293
Seattle	7	9	0	.438	317	376

*Division champion.
†Wild-card team.

NATIONAL CONFERENCE

EASTERN DIVISION

	W	L	T	Pct.	Pts.	Opp.
Dallas*	10	6	0	.625	286	250
Philadelphia†	10	6	0	.625	363	341
Washington	9	7	0	.563	364	312
Arizona	7	9	0	.438	300	397
N.Y. Giants	6	10	0	.375	242	297

CENTRAL DIVISION

	W	L	T	Pct.	Pts.	Opp.
Green Bay*	13	3	0	.813	456	210
Minnesota†	9	7	0	.563	298	315
Chicago	7	9	0	.438	283	305
Tampa Bay	6	10	0	.375	221	293
Detroit	5	11	0	.313	302	368

WESTERN DIVISION

	W	L	T	Pct.	Pts.	Opp.
Carolina*	12	4	0	.750	367	218
San Francisco†	12	4	0	.750	398	257
St. Louis	6	10	0	.375	303	409
Atlanta	3	13	0	.188	309	465
New Orleans	3	13	0	.188	229	339

PLAYOFFS

AFC wild-card playoffs
Jacksonville 30, Buffalo 27
Pittsburgh 42, Indianapolis 14
AFC divisional playoffs
Jacksonville 30, Denver 27
New England 28, Pittsburgh 3
AFC championship
New England 20, Jacksonville 16
NFC wild-card playoffs
Dallas 40, Minnesota 15
San Francisco 14, Philadelphia 0
NFC divisional playoffs
Green Bay 35, San Francisco 14
Carolina 26, Dallas 17
NFC championship
Green Bay 30, Carolina 13
Super Bowl XXXI
Green Bay 35, New England 21, at New Orleans.

TWO FOR THE SHOW

The 1995 season marked the debut of two new teams for the first time in 19 seasons: the Carolina Panthers and the Jacksonville Jaguars. Although neither team was a serious contender (that would take a year), neither was an embarrassment, either. The Panthers went 7-9 in the NFC West and the Jaguars went 4-12 in the AFC Central. It was a far cry from 1976, when the expansion Seattle Seahawks and Tampa Bay Buccaneers—who were afforded few of the first-year perks given the Panthers and Jaguars—combined to go 2-26.

AMERICAN CONFERENCE

EASTERN DIVISION

	W	L	T	Pct.	Pts.	Opp.
New England*	10	6	0	.625	369	289
Miami†	9	7	0	.563	339	327
N.Y. Jets	9	7	0	.563	348	287
Buffalo	6	10	0	.375	255	367
Indianapolis	3	13	0	.188	313	401

CENTRAL DIVISION

	W	L	T	Pct.	Pts.	Opp.
Pittsburgh*	11	5	0	.688	372	307
Jacksonville†	11	5	0	.688	394	318
Tennessee	8	8	0	.500	333	310
Cincinnati	7	9	0	.438	355	405
Baltimore	6	9	1	.406	326	345

WESTERN DIVISION

	W	L	T	Pct.	Pts.	Opp.
Kansas City*	13	3	0	.813	375	232
Denver†	12	4	0	.750	472	287
Seattle	8	8	0	.500	365	362
Oakland	4	12	0	.250	324	419
San Diego	4	12	0	.250	266	425

*Division champion.
†Wild-card team.

NATIONAL CONFERENCE

EASTERN DIVISION

	W	L	T	Pct.	Pts.	Opp.
N.Y. Giants*	10	5	1	.656	307	265
Washington	8	7	1	.531	327	289
Philadelphia	6	9	1	.406	317	372
Dallas	6	10	0	.375	304	314
Arizona	4	12	0	.250	283	379

CENTRAL DIVISION

	W	L	T	Pct.	Pts.	Opp.
Green Bay*	13	3	0	.813	422	282
Tampa Bay†	10	6	0	.625	299	263
Detroit†	9	7	0	.563	379	306
Minnesota†	9	7	0	.563	354	359
Chicago	4	12	0	.250	263	421

WESTERN DIVISION

	W	L	T	Pct.	Pts.	Opp.
San Francisco*	13	3	0	.813	375	265
Carolina	7	9	0	.438	265	314
Atlanta	7	9	0	.438	320	361
New Orleans	6	10	0	.375	237	327
St. Louis	5	11	0	.313	299	359

PLAYOFFS

AFC wild-card playoffs
Denver 42, Jacksonville 17
New England 17, Miami 3
AFC divisional playoffs
Pittsburgh 7, New England 6
Denver 14, Kansas City 10
AFC championship
Denver 24, Pittsburgh 21
NFC wild-card playoffs
Minnesota 23, N.Y. Giants 22
Tampa Bay 20, Detroit 10
NFC divisional playoffs
San Francisco 38, Minnesota 22
Green Bay 21, Tampa Bay 7
NFC championship
Green Bay 23, San Francisco 10
Super Bowl XXXII
Denver 31, Green Bay 24, at San Diego.

SUPER BOWLS

SUPER BOWL I
JANUARY 15, 1967, AT LOS ANGELES

Kansas City (AFL)	0	10	0	0 — 10
Green Bay (NFL)	7	7	14	7 — 35

Winning coach—Vince Lombardi.
Most Valuable Player—Bart Starr.
Attendance—61,946.

SUPER BOWL II
JANUARY 14, 1968, AT MIAMI

Green Bay (NFL)	3	13	10	7 — 33
Oakland (AFL)	0	7	0	7 — 14

Winning coach—Vince Lombardi.
Most Valuable Player—Bart Starr.
Attendance—75,546.

SUPER BOWL III
JANUARY 12, 1969, AT MIAMI

New York (AFL)	0	7	6	3 — 16
Baltimore (NFL)	0	0	0	7 — 7

Winning coach—Weeb Ewbank.
Most Valuable Player—Joe Namath.
Attendance—75,389.

SUPER BOWL IV
JANUARY 11, 1970, AT NEW ORLEANS

Minnesota (NFL)	0	0	7	0 — 7
Kansas City (AFL)	3	13	7	0 — 23

Winning coach—Hank Stram.
Most Valuable Player—Len Dawson.
Attendance—80,562.

SUPER BOWL V
JANUARY 17, 1971, AT MIAMI

Baltimore (AFC)	0	6	0	10 — 16
Dallas (NFC)	3	10	0	0 — 13

Winning coach—Don McCafferty.
Most Valuable Player—Chuck Howley.
Attendance—79,204.

SUPER BOWL VI
JANUARY 16, 1972, AT NEW ORLEANS

Dallas (NFC)	3	7	7	7 — 24
Miami (AFC)	0	3	0	0 — 3

Winning coach—Tom Landry.
Most Valuable Player—Roger Staubach.
Attendance—81,023.

SUPER BOWL VII
JANUARY 14, 1973, AT LOS ANGELES

Miami (AFC)	7	7	0	0 — 14
Washington (NFC)	0	0	0	7 — 7

Winning coach—Don Shula.
Most Valuable Player—Jake Scott.
Attendance—90,182.

SUPER BOWL VIII
JANUARY 13, 1974, AT HOUSTON

Minnesota (NFC)	0	0	0	7 — 7
Miami (AFC)	14	3	7	0 — 24

Winning coach—Don Shula.
Most Valuable Player—Larry Csonka.
Attendance—71,882.

SUPER BOWL IX
JANUARY 12, 1975, AT NEW ORLEANS

Pittsburgh (AFC)	0	2	7	7 — 16
Minnesota (NFC)	0	0	0	6 — 6

Winning coach—Chuck Noll.
Most Valuable Player—Franco Harris.
Attendance—80,997.

SUPER BOWL X
JANUARY 18, 1976, AT MIAMI

Dallas (NFC)	7	3	0	7 — 17
Pittsburgh (AFC)	7	0	0	14 — 21

Winning coach—Chuck Noll.
Most Valuable Player—Lynn Swann.
Attendance—80,187.

SUPER BOWL XI
JANUARY 9, 1977, AT PASADENA, CALIF.

Oakland (AFC)	0	16	3	13 — 32
Minnesota (NFC)	0	0	7	7 — 14

Winning coach—John Madden.
Most Valuable Player—Fred Biletnikoff.
Attendance—103,428.

SUPER BOWL XII
JANUARY 15, 1978, AT NEW ORLEANS

Dallas (NFC)	10	3	7	7 — 27
Denver (AFC)	0	0	10	0 — 10

Winning coach—Tom Landry.
Most Valuable Players—Harvey Martin and Randy White.
Attendance—75,804.

SUPER BOWL XIII
JANUARY 21, 1979, AT MIAMI

Pittsburgh (AFC)	7	14	0	14 — 35
Dallas (NFC)	7	7	3	14 — 31

Winning coach—Chuck Noll.
Most Valuable Player—Terry Bradshaw.
Attendance—78,656.

SUPER BOWL XIV
JANUARY 20, 1980, PASADENA, CALIF.

Los Angeles (NFC)	7	6	6	0 — 19
Pittsburgh (AFC)	3	7	7	14 — 31

Winning coach—Chuck Noll.
Most Valuable Player—Terry Bradshaw.
Attendance—103,985.

SUPER BOWL XV
JANUARY 25, 1981, AT NEW ORLEANS

Oakland (AFC)	14	0	10	3 — 27
Philadelphia (NFC)	0	3	0	7 — 10

Winning coach—Tom Flores.
Most Valuable Player—Jim Plunkett.
Attendance—75,500.

SUPER BOWL XVI
JANUARY 24, 1982, AT PONTIAC, MICH.

San Francisco (NFC)	7	13	0	6 — 26
Cincinnati (AFC)	0	0	7	14 — 21

Winning coach—Bill Walsh.
Most Valuable Player—Joe Montana.
Attendance—81,270.

SUPER BOWL XVII
JANUARY 30, 1983, AT PASADENA, CALIF.

Miami (AFC)	7	10	0	0 — 17
Washington (NFC)	0	10	3	14 — 27

Winning coach—Joe Gibbs.
Most Valuable Player—John Riggins.
Attendance—103,667.

SUPER BOWL XVIII
JANUARY 22, 1984, AT TAMPA

Washington (NFC)	0	3	6	0 — 9
Los Angeles (AFC)	7	14	14	3 — 38

Winning coach—Tom Flores.
Most Valuable Player—Marcus Allen.
Attendance—72,920.

SUPER BOWL XIX
JANUARY 20, 1985, AT PALO ALTO, CALIF.

Miami (AFC)	10	6	0	0 — 16
San Francisco (NFC)	7	21	10	0 — 38

Winning coach—Bill Walsh.
Most Valuable Player—Joe Montana.
Attendance—84,059.

SUPER BOWL XX
JANUARY 26, 1986, AT NEW ORLEANS

Chicago (NFC)	13	10	21	2 — 46
New England (AFC)	3	0	0	7 — 10

Winning coach—MIke Ditka.
Most Valuable Player—Richard Dent.
Attendance—73,818.

SUPER BOWL XXI
JANUARY 25, 1987, AT PASADENA, CALIF.

Denver (AFC)	10	0	0	10 — 20
N.Y. Giants (NFC)	7	2	17	13 — 39

Winning coach—Bill Parcells.
Most Valuable Player—Phil Simms.
Attendance—101,063.

SUPER BOWL XXII
JANUARY 31, 1988, AT SAN DIEGO

Washington (NFC)	0	35	0	7 — 42
Denver (AFC)	10	0	0	0 — 10

Winning coach—Joe Gibbs.
Most Valuable Player—Doug Williams.
Attendance—73,302.

SUPER BOWL XXIII
JANUARY 22, 1989, AT MIAMI

Cincinnati (AFC)	0	3	10	3 — 16
San Francisco (NFC)	3	0	3	14 — 20

Winning coach—Bill Walsh.
Most Valuable Player—Jerry Rice.
Attendance—75,179.

SUPER BOWL XXIV
JANUARY 28, 1990, AT NEW ORLEANS

San Francisco (NFC)	13	14	14	14 — 55
Denver (AFC)	3	0	7	0 — 10

Winning coach—George Seifert.
Most Valuable Player—Joe Montana.
Attendance—72,919.

SUPER BOWL XXV
JANUARY 27, 1991, AT TAMPA

Buffalo (AFC)	3	9	0	7 — 19
New York (NFC)	3	7	7	3 — 20

Winning coach—Bill Parcells.
Most Valuable Player—Ottis Anderson.
Attendance—73,813.

SUPER BOWL XXVI
JANUARY 26, 1992, AT MINNEAPOLIS

Washington (NFC)	0	17	14	6 — 37
Buffalo (AFC)	0	0	10	14 — 24

Winning coach—Joe Gibbs.
Most Valuable Player—Mark Rypien.
Attendance—63,130.

SUPER BOWL XXVII
JANUARY 31, 1993, AT PASADENA, CALIF.

Buffalo (AFC)	7	3	7	0 — 17
Dallas (NFC)	14	14	3	21 — 52

Winning coach—Jimmy Johnson.
Most Valuable Player—Troy Aikman.
Attendance—98,374.

SUPER BOWL XXVIII
JANUARY 30, 1994, AT ATLANTA, GA.

Dallas (NFC)	6	0	14	10 — 30
Buffalo (AFC)	3	10	0	0 — 13

Winning coach—Jimmy Johnson.
Most Valuable Player—Emmitt Smith.
Attendance—72,817.

SUPER BOWL XXIX
JANUARY 29, 1995, AT MIAMI, FLA.

San Diego (AFC)	7	3	8	8 — 26
San Francisco (NFC)	14	14	14	7 — 49

Winning coach—George Seifert.
Most Valuable Player—Steve Young.
Attendance—74,107.

SUPER BOWL XXX
JANUARY 28, 1996, AT TEMPE, ARIZ.

Dallas (NFC)	10	3	7	7 — 27
Pittsburgh (AFC)	0	7	0	10 — 17

Winning coach—Barry Switzer.
Most Valuable Player—Larry Brown.
Attendance—76,347.

SUPER BOWL XXXI
JANUARY 26, 1997, AT NEW ORLEANS

New England (AFC)	14	0	7	0 — 21
Green Bay (NFC)	10	17	8	0 — 35

Winning coach—Mike Holmgren.
Most Valuable Player—Desmond Howard.
Attendance—72,301.

SUPER BOWL XXXII
JANUARY 25, 1998, AT SAN DIEGO

Green Bay (NFC)	7	7	3	7 — 24
Denver (AFC)	7	10	7	7 — 31

Winning coach—Mike Shanahan.
Most Valuable Player—Terrell Davis.
Attendance—68,912.

SUPER BOWL XXXIII
JANUARY 31, 1999, AT MIAMI

Denver (AFC)	7	10	0	17 — 34
Atlanta (NFC)	3	3	0	13 — 19

Winning coach—Mike Shanahan.
Most Valuable Player—John Elway.
Attendance—74,803.

PRO BOWLS

RESULTS

Date	Site	Winning team, score	Losing team, score	Att.
1-15-39	Wrigley Field, Los Angeles	New York Giants, 13	Pro All-Stars, 10	†20,000
1-14-40	Gilmore Stadium, Los Angeles	Green Bay Packers, 16	NFL All-Stars, 7	†18,000
12-29-40	Gilmore Stadium, Los Angeles	Chicago Bears, 28	NFL All-Stars, 14	21,624
1-4-42	Polo Grounds, New York	Chicago Bears, 35	NFL All-Stars, 24	17,725
12-27-42	Shibe Park, Philadelphia	NFL All-Stars, 17	Washington Redskins, 14	18,671
1943-50	No game was played.			
1-14-51	Los Angeles Memorial Coliseum	American Conference, 28	National Conference, 27	53,676
1-12-52	Los Angeles Memorial Coliseum	National Conference, 30	American Conference, 13	19,400
1-10-53	Los Angeles Memorial Coliseum	National Conference, 27	American Conference, 7	34,208
1-17-54	Los Angeles Memorial Coliseum	East, 20	West, 9	44,214
1-16-55	Los Angeles Memorial Coliseum	West, 26	East, 19	43,972
1-15-56	Los Angeles Memorial Coliseum	East, 31	West, 30	37,867
1-13-57	Los Angeles Memorial Coliseum	West, 19	East, 10	44,177
1-12-58	Los Angeles Memorial Coliseum	West, 26	East, 7	66,634
1-11-59	Los Angeles Memorial Coliseum	East, 28	West, 21	72,250
1-17-60	Los Angeles Memorial Coliseum	West, 38	East, 21	56,876
1-15-61	Los Angeles Memorial Coliseum	West, 35	East, 31	62,971
1-7-62*	Balboa Stadium, San Diego	West, 47	East, 27	20,973
1-14-62	Los Angeles Memorial Coliseum	West, 31	East, 30	57,409
1-13-63*	Balboa Stadium, San Diego	West, 21	East, 14	27,641
1-13-63	Los Angeles Memorial Coliseum	East, 30	West, 20	61,374
1-12-64	Los Angeles Memorial Coliseum	West, 31	East, 17	67,242
1-19-64*	Balboa Stadium, San Diego	West, 27	East, 24	20,016
1-10-65	Los Angeles Memorial Coliseum	West, 34	East, 14	60,598
1-16-65*	Jeppesen Stadium, Houston	West, 38	East, 14	15,446
1-15-66*	Rice Stadium, Houston	AFL All-Stars, 30	Buffalo Bills, 19	35,572
1-15-66	Los Angeles Memorial Coliseum	East, 36	West, 7	60,124
1-21-67*	Oakland-Alameda County Coliseum	East, 30	West, 23	18,876
1-22-67	Los Angeles Memorial Coliseum	East, 20	West, 10	15,062
1-21-68*	Gator Bowl, Jacksonville, Fla.	East, 25	West, 24	40,103
1-21-68	Los Angeles Memorial Coliseum	West, 38	East, 20	53,289
1-19-69*	Gator Bowl, Jacksonville, Fla.	West, 38	East, 25	41,058
1-19-69	Los Angeles Memorial Coliseum	West, 10	East, 7	32,050
1-17-70*	Astrodome, Houston	West, 26	East, 3	30,170
1-18-70	Los Angeles Memorial Coliseum	West, 16	East, 13	57,786
1-24-71	Los Angeles Memorial Coliseum	NFC, 27	AFC, 6	48,222
1-23-72	Los Angeles Memorial Coliseum	AFC, 26	NFC, 13	53,647
1-21-73	Texas Stadium, Irving	AFC, 33	NFC, 28	37,091
1-20-74	Arrowhead Stadium, Kansas City	AFC, 15	NFC, 13	66,918
1-20-75	Orange Bowl, Miami	NFC, 17	AFC, 10	26,484
1-26-76	Louisiana Superdome, New Orleans	NFC, 23	AFC, 20	30,546
1-17-77	Kingdome, Seattle	AFC, 24	NFC, 14	64,752
1-23-78	Tampa Stadium	NFC, 14	AFC, 13	51,337
1-29-79	Los Angeles Memorial Coliseum	NFC, 13	AFC, 7	46,281
1-27-80	Aloha Stadium, Honolulu	NFC, 37	AFC, 27	49,800
2-1-81	Aloha Stadium, Honolulu	NFC, 21	AFC, 7	50,360
1-31-82	Aloha Stadium, Honolulu	AFC, 16	NFC, 13	50,402
2-6-83	Aloha Stadium, Honolulu	NFC, 20	AFC, 19	49,883
1-29-84	Aloha Stadium, Honolulu	NFC, 45	AFC, 3	50,445
1-27-85	Aloha Stadium, Honolulu	AFC, 22	NFC, 14	50,385
2-2-86	Aloha Stadium, Honolulu	NFC, 28	AFC, 24	50,101
2-1-87	Aloha Stadium, Honolulu	AFC, 10	NFC, 6	50,101
2-7-88	Aloha Stadium, Honolulu	AFC, 15	NFC, 6	50,113
1-29-89	Aloha Stadium, Honolulu	NFC, 34	AFC, 3	50,113
2-4-90	Aloha Stadium, Honolulu	NFC, 27	AFC, 21	50,445
2-3-91	Aloha Stadium, Honolulu	AFC, 23	NFC, 21	50,345
2-2-92	Aloha Stadium, Honolulu	NFC, 21	AFC, 15	50,209
2-7-93	Aloha Stadium, Honolulu	AFC, 23 (OT)	NFC, 20	50,007
2-6-94	Aloha Stadium, Honolulu	NFC, 17	AFC, 3	50,026
2-5-95	Aloha Stadium, Honolulu	AFC, 41	NFC, 13	49,121
2-4-96	Aloha Stadium, Honolulu	NFC, 20	AFC, 13	50,034
2-2-97	Aloha Stadium, Honolulu	AFC, 26 (OT)	NFC, 23	50,031
2-1-98	Aloha Stadium, Honolulu	AFC, 29	NFC, 24	49,995
2-7-99	Aloha Stadium, Honolulu	AFC, 23	NFC, 10	50,075

*AFL game.
†Estimated figure.

HISTORY *Pro Bowls*

Year—Name, team
1951— Otto Graham, Cleveland Browns
1952— Dan Towler, Los Angeles Rams
1953— Dan Doll, Detroit Lions
1954— Chuck Bednarik, Philadelphia Eagles
1955— Billy Wilson, San Francisco 49ers
1956— Ollie Matson, Chicago Cardinals
1957— Bert Rechichar, Baltimore Colts (back)
       Ernie Stautner, Pittsburgh Steelers (lineman)
1958— Hugh McElhenny, San Francisco 49ers (back)
       Gene Brito, Washington Redskins (lineman)
1959— Frank Gifford, New York Giants (back)
       Doug Atkins, Chicago Bears (lineman)
1960— Johnny Unitas, Baltimore Colts (back)
       Gene Lipscomb, Baltimore Colts (lineman)
1961— Johnny Unitas, Baltimore Colts (back)
       Sam Huff, New York Giants (lineman)
1962— Cotton Davidson, Dallas Texans*
       Jim Brown, Cleveland Browns (back)
       Henry Jordan, Green Bay Packers (lineman)
1963— Curtis McClinton, Dallas Texans* (offense)
       Earl Faison, San Diego Chargers* (defense)
       Jim Brown, Cleveland Browns (back)
       Gene Lipscomb, Pittsburgh Steelers (lineman)
1964— Keith Lincoln, San Diego Chargers* (offense)
       Archie Matsos, Oakland Raiders* (defense)
       Johnny Unitas, Baltimore Colts (back)
       Gino Marchetti, Baltimore Colts (lineman)
1965— Keith Lincoln, San Diego Chargers* (offense)
       Willie Brown, Denver Broncos* (defense)
       Fran Tarkenton, Minnesota Vikings (back)
       Terry Barr, Detroit Lions (lineman)
1966— Joe Namath, New York Jets* (offense)
       Frank Buncom, San Diego Chargers* (defense)
       Jim Brown, Cleveland Browns (back)
       Dale Meinert, St. Louis Cardinals (lineman)
1967— Babe Parilli, Boston Patriots* (offense)
       Verlon Biggs, New York Jets* (defense)
       Gale Sayers, Chicago Bears (back)
       Floyd Peters, Philadelphia Eagles (lineman)
1968— Joe Namath, New York Jets* (offense)
       Don Maynard, New York Jets* (offense)
       Speedy Duncan, San Diego Chargers (defense)
       Gale Sayers, Chicago Bears (back)
       Dave Robinson, Green Bay Packers (lineman)

Year—Name, team
1969— Len Dawson, Kansas City Chiefs* (offense)
       George Webster, Houston* (defense)
       Roman Gabriel, Los Angeles Rams (back)
       Merlin Olsen, Los Angeles Rams (lineman)
1970— John Hadl, San Diego Chargers*
       Gale Sayers, Chicago Bears (back)
       George Andrie, Dallas Cowboys (lineman)
1971— Mel Renfro, Dallas Cowboys (back)
       Fred Carr, Green Bay Packers (lineman)
1972— Jan Stenerud, Kansas City Chiefs (offense)
       Willie Lanier, Kansas City Chiefs (defense)
1973— O.J. Simpson, Buffalo Bills
1974— Garo Yepremian, Miami Dolphins
1975— James Harris, Los Angeles Rams
1976— Billy Johnson, Houston Oilers
1977— Mel Blount, Pittsburgh Steelers
1978— Walter Payton, Chicago Bears
1979— Ahmad Rashad, Minnesota Vikings
1980— Chuck Muncie, New Orleans Saints
1981— Eddie Murray, Detroit Lions
1982— Kellen Winslow, San Diego Chargers
       Lee Roy Selmon, Tampa Bay Buccaneers
1983— Dan Fouts, San Diego Chargers
       John Jefferson, Green Bay Packers
1984— Joe Theismann, Washington Redskins
1985— Mark Gastineau, New York Jets
1986— Phil Simms, New York Giants
1987— Reggie White, Philadelphia Eagles
1988— Bruce Smith, Buffalo Bills
1989— Randall Cunningham, Philadelphia Eagles
1990— Jerry Gray, Los Angeles Rams
1991— Jim Kelly, Buffalo Bills
1992— Michael Irvin, Dallas Cowboys
1993— Steve Tasker, Buffalo Bills
1994— Andre Rison, Atlanta Falcons
1995— Marshall Faulk, Indianapolis Colts
1996— Jerry Rice, San Francisco 49ers
1997— Mark Brunell, Jacksonville Jaguars
1998— Warren Moon, Seattle Seahawks
1999— Ty Law, New England Patriots
       Keyshawn Johnson, New York Jets
   *AFL game.

RECORDS

INDIVIDUAL SERVICE
PLAYERS

Most years played
26—George Blanda, Chicago Bears, Baltimore, Houston, Oakland, 1949 through 1975, except 1959.

Most years with one club
20—Jackie Slater, L.A. Rams, St. Louis Rams, 1976 through 1995.

Most games played, career
340—George Blanda, Chicago Bears, Baltimore, Houston, Oakland, 1949 through 1975, except 1959.

Most consecutive games played, career
282—Jim Marshall, Cleveland, Minnesota, September 25, 1960 through December 16, 1979.

COACHES

Most years as head coach
40—George Halas, Chicago Bears, 1920 through 1929, 1933 through 1942, 1946 through 1955 and 1958 through 1967.

Most games won as head coach
328—Don Shula, Baltimore, 1963 through 1969; Miami, 1970 through 1995.

Most games lost as head coach
162—Tom Landry, Dallas, 1960 through 1988.

INDIVIDUAL OFFENSE
RUSHING
YARDS

Most yards, career
16,726—Walter Payton, Chicago, 1975 through 1987.

Most yards, season
2,105—Eric Dickerson, Los Angeles Rams, 1984.

Most years leading league in yards
8—Jim Brown, Cleveland, 1957 through 1965, except 1962.

Most consecutive years leading league in yards
5—Jim Brown, Cleveland, 1957 through 1961.

Most years with 1,000 or more yards
10—Walter Payton, Chicago, 1976 through 1986, except 1982.
Barry Sanders, Detroit, 1989 through 1998.

Most consecutive years with 1,000 or more yards
10—Barry Sanders, Detroit, 1989 through 1998.

Most yards, game
275—Walter Payton, Chicago vs. Minnesota, November 20, 1977.

Most games with 200 or more yards, career
6—O.J. Simpson, Buffalo, San Francisco, 1969 through 1979.

Most games with 200 or more yards, season
4—Earl Campbell, Houston, 1980.

Most consecutive games with 200 or more yards, season
2—O.J. Simpson, Buffalo, December 9 through 16, 1973.
O.J. Simpson, Buffalo, November 25 through December 5, 1976.
Earl Campbell, Houston, October 19 through 26, 1980.

Most games with 100 or more yards, career
77—Walter Payton, Chicago, 1975 through 1987.

Most games with 100 or more yards, season
14—Barry Sanders, Detroit, 1997.

Most consecutive games with 100 or more yards, career
14—Barry Sanders, Detroit, September 14 through December 21, 1997.

Most consecutive games with 100 or more yards, season
14—Barry Sanders, Detroit, September 14 through December 21, 1997.

Longest run from scrimmage
99 yards—Tony Dorsett, Dallas at Minnesota, January 3, 1983 (touchdown).

ATTEMPTS

Most attempts, career
3,838—Walter Payton, Chicago, 1975 through 1987.

Most attempts, season
410—Jamal Anderson, Atlanta, 1998.

Most attempts, game
45—Jamie Morris, Washington at Cincinnati, December 17, 1988, overtime.
43—Butch Woolfolk, New York Giants at Philadelphia, November 20, 1983.
James Wilder, Tampa Bay vs. Green Bay, September 30, 1984, overtime.

Most years leading league in attempts
6—Jim Brown, Cleveland, 1958 through 1965, except 1960 and 1962.

Most consecutive years leading league in attempts
4—Steve Van Buren, Philadelphia, 1947 through 1950.
Walter Payton, Chicago, 1976 through 1979.

TOUCHDOWNS

Most touchdowns, career
125—Emmitt Smith, Dallas, 1990 through 1998.

Most touchdowns, season
25—Emmitt Smith, Dallas, 1995.

Most years leading league in touchdowns
5—Jim Brown, Cleveland, 1957 through 1959, 1963, 1965.

Most consecutive years leading league in touchdowns
3—Steve Van Buren, Philadelphia, 1947 through 1949.
Jim Brown, Cleveland, 1957 through 1959.
Abner Haynes, Dallas Texans, 1960 through 1962.
Cookie Gilchrist, Buffalo, 1962 through 1964.
Leroy Kelly, Cleveland, 1966 through 1968.

Most touchdowns, game
6—Ernie Nevers, Chicago Cardinals vs. Chicago Bears, November 28, 1929.

Most consecutive games with one or more touchdowns, career
13—John Riggins, Washington, December 26, 1982 through November 27, 1983.
George Rogers, Washington, November 24, 1985 through November 2, 1986.

Most consecutive games with one or more touchdowns, season
12—John Riggins, Washington, September 5 through November 27, 1983.

PASSING
PASSER RATING

Highest rating, career (1,500 or more attempts)
97.6—Steve Young, Tampa Bay, San Francisco, 1985 through 1998.

Highest rating, season (qualifiers)
112.8—Steve Young, San Francisco, 1994.

ATTEMPTS

Most attempts, career
7,989—Dan Marino, Miami, 1983 through 1998.

Most attempts, season
691—Drew Bledsoe, New England, 1994.

Most years leading league in attempts
5—Dan Marino, Miami, 1984, 1986, 1988, 1992, 1997.

Most consecutive years leading league in attempts
3—Johnny Unitas, Baltimore, 1959 through 1961.
George Blanda, Houston, 1963 through 1965.

Most attempts, game
70—Drew Bledsoe, New England vs. Minnesota, November 13, 1994 (overtime).
68—George Blanda, Houston vs. Buffalo, November 1, 1964.

COMPLETIONS

Most completions, career
4,763—Dan Marino, Miami, 1983 through 1998.

Most completions, season
404—Warren Moon, Houston, 1991.

Most years leading league in completions
6—Dan Marino, Miami, 1984, 1985, 1986, 1988, 1992, 1997.

Most consecutive years leading league in completions
3—George Blanda, Houston, 1963 through 1965.
Dan Marino, Miami, 1984 through 1986.

Most completions, game
45—Drew Bledsoe, New England vs. Minnesota, November 13, 1994 (overtime).
42—Richard Todd, New York Jets vs. San Francisco, September 21, 1980.

YARDS

Most yards, career
58,913—Dan Marino, Miami, 1983 through 1998.

Most yards, season
5,084—Dan Marino, Miami, 1984.

Most years leading league in yards
5—Sonny Jurgensen, Philadelphia, Washington, 1961, 1962, 1966, 1967, 1969.
Dan Marino, Miami, 1984 through 1986, 1988, 1992.

Most consecutive years leading league in yards
4—Dan Fouts, San Diego, 1979 through 1982.

Most years with 3,000 or more yards
13—Dan Marino, Miami, 1984 through 1998, except 1993 and 1996.

Most yards, game
554—Norm Van Brocklin, Los Angeles at New York Yanks, September 28, 1951.

Most games with 400 or more yards, career
13—Dan Marino, Miami, 1983 through 1996.

Most games with 400 or more yards, season
4—Dan Marino, Miami, 1984.

Most consecutive games with 400 or more yards, season
2—Dan Fouts, San Diego, December 11 through 20, 1982.
Dan Marino, Miami, December 2 through 9, 1984.
Phil Simms, New York Giants, October 6 through 13, 1985.

Most games with 300 or more yards, career
60—Dan Marino, Miami, 1983 through 1998.

Most games with 300 or more yards, season
9—Dan Marino, Miami, 1984.
Warren Moon, Houston, 1990.

Most consecutive games with 300 or more yards, season
6—Steve Young, San Francisco, September 6 through October 18, 1998.

Longest pass completion
99 yards—Frank Filchock, Washington vs. Pittsburgh, October 15, 1939 (touchdown).

George Izo, Washington at Cleveland, September 15, 1963 (touchdown).
Karl Sweetan, Detroit at Baltimore, October 16, 1966 (touchdown).
Sonny Jurgensen, Washington at Chicago, September 15, 1968 (touchdown).
Jim Plunkett, Los Angeles Raiders vs. Washington, October 2, 1983 (touchdown).
Ron Jaworski, Philadelphia vs. Atlanta, November 10, 1985 (touchdown).
Stan Humphries, San Diego at Seattle, September 18, 1994 (touchdown).
Brett Favre, Green Bay at Chicago, September 11, 1995 (touchdown).

YARDS PER ATTEMPT

Most yards per attempt, career (1,500 or more attempts)
8.63—Otto Graham, Cleveland, 1950 through 1955 (13,499 yards, 1,565 attempts).

Most yards per attempt, season (qualifiers)
11.17—Tommy O'Connell, Cleveland, 1957 (1,229 yards, 110 attempts).

Most years leading league in yards per attempt
7—Sid Luckman, Chicago Bears, 1939 through 1943, 1946, 1947.

Most consecutive years leading league in yards per attempt
5—Sid Luckman, Chicago Bears, 1939 through 1943.

Most yards per attempt, game (20 or more attempts)
18.58—Sammy Baugh, Washington vs. Boston, October 31, 1948 (446 yards, 24 attempts).

TOUCHDOWNS

Most touchdowns, career
408—Dan Marino, Miami, 1983 through 1998.

Most touchdowns, season
48—Dan Marino, Miami, 1984.

Most years leading league in touchdowns
4—Johnny Unitas, Baltimore, 1957 through 1960.
Len Dawson, Dallas Texans, Kansas City, 1962 through 1966, except 1964.
Steve Young, San Francisco, 1992 through 1994, 1998.

Most consecutive years leading league in touchdowns
4—Johnny Unitas, Baltimore, 1957 through 1960.

Most touchdowns, game
7—Sid Luckman, Chicago Bears at New York Giants, November 14, 1943.
Adrian Burk, Philadelphia at Washington, October 17, 1954.
George Blanda, Houston vs. New York Titans, November 19, 1961.
Y.A. Tittle, New York Giants vs. Washington, October 28, 1962.
Joe Kapp, Minnesota vs. Baltimore, September 28, 1969.

INTERCEPTIONS

Most interceptions, career
277—George Blanda, Chicago Bears, Baltimore, Houston, Oakland, 1949 through 1975, except 1959.

Most interceptions, season
42—George Blanda, Houston, 1962.

Most interceptions, game
8—Jim Hardy, Chicago Cardinals vs. Philadelphia, September 24, 1950.

Most attempts with no interceptions, game
70—Drew Bledsoe, New England vs. Minnesota, November 13, 1994 (overtime).
63—Rich Gannon, Minnesota at New England, October 20, 1991 (overtime).
60—Davey O'Brien, Philadelphia at Washington, December 1, 1940.

INTERCEPTION PERCENTAGE

Lowest interception percentage, career (1,500 or more attempts)
1.99—Neil O'Donnell, Pittsburgh, N.Y. Jets, Cincinnati, 1991 through 1998 (2,862 attempts, 57 interceptions).

Lowest interception percentage, season (qualifiers)
0.66—Joe Ferguson, Buffalo, 1976 (151 attempts, one interception).

Most years leading league in lowest interception percentage
5—Sammy Baugh, Washington, 1940, 1942, 1944, 1945, 1947.

SACKS (SINCE 1963)

Most times sacked, career
516—John Elway, Denver, 1983 through 1998.

Most times sacked, season
72—Randall Cunningham, Philadelphia, 1986.

Most times sacked, game
12—Bert Jones, Baltimore vs. St. Louis, October 26, 1980.
Warren Moon, Houston vs. Dallas, September 29, 1985.

RECEIVING

RECEPTIONS

Most receptions, career
1,139—Jerry Rice, San Francisco, 1985 through 1998.

Most receptions, season
123—Herman Moore, Detroit, 1995.

Most years leading league in receptions
8—Don Hutson, Green Bay, 1936 through 1945, except 1938 and 1940.

Most consecutive years leading league in receptions
5—Don Hutson, Green Bay, 1941 through 1945.

Most receptions, game
18—Tom Fears, Los Angeles vs. Green Bay, December 3, 1950.

Most consecutive games with one or more receptions
193—Jerry Rice, San Francisco, December 9, 1985 through December 27, 1998.

YARDS

Most yards, career
17,612—Jerry Rice, San Francisco, 1985 through 1998.

Most yards, season
1,848—Jerry Rice, San Francisco, 1995.

Most years leading league in yards
7—Don Hutson, Green Bay, 1936 through 1944, except 1937 and 1940.

Most consecutive years leading league in yards
4—Don Hutson, Green Bay, 1941 through 1944.

Most years with 1,000 or more yards
12—Jerry Rice, San Francisco, 1986 through 1998, except 1997.

Most yards, game
336—Willie Anderson, Los Angeles Rams at New Orleans, November 26, 1989 (overtime).
309—Stephone Paige, Kansas City vs. San Diego, December 22, 1985.

Most games with 200 or more yards, career
5—Lance Alworth, San Diego, Dallas, 1962 through 1972.

Most games with 200 or more yards, season
3—Charley Hennigan, Houston, 1961.

Most games with 100 or more yards, career
64—Jerry Rice, San Francisco, 1985 through 1998.

Most games with 100 or more yards, season
11—Michael Irvin, Dallas, 1995.

Most consecutive games with 100 or more yards, season
7—Charley Hennigan, Houston, 1961.
Bill Groman, Houston, 1961.
Michael Irvin, Dallas, 1995.

Longest reception
99 yards—Andy Farkas, Washington vs. Pittsburgh, October 15, 1939 (touchdown).
Bobby Mitchell, Washington at Cleveland, September 15, 1963 (touchdown).
Pat Studstill, Detroit at Baltimore, October 16, 1966 (touchdown).
Gerry Allen, Washington at Chicago, September 15, 1968 (touchdown).
Cliff Branch, Los Angeles Raiders vs. Washington, October 2, 1983 (touchdown).
Mike Quick, Philadelphia vs. Atlanta, November 10, 1985 (touchdown).
Tony Martin, San Diego at Seattle, September 18, 1994 (touchdown).
Robert Brooks, Green Bay at Chicago, September 11, 1995 (touchdown).

TOUCHDOWNS

Most touchdowns, career
164—Jerry Rice, San Francisco, 1985 through 1998.

Most touchdowns, season
22—Jerry Rice, San Francisco, 1987.

Most years leading league in touchdowns
9—Don Hutson, Green Bay, 1935 through 1944, except 1939.

Most consecutive years leading league in touchdowns
5—Don Hutson, Green Bay, 1940 through 1944.

Most touchdowns, game
5—Bob Shaw, Chicago Cardinals vs. Baltimore, October 2, 1950.
Kellen Winslow, San Diego at Oakland, November 22, 1981.
Jerry Rice, San Francisco at Atlanta, October 14, 1990.

Most consecutive games with one or more touchdowns
13—Jerry Rice, San Francisco, December 19, 1986 through December 27, 1987.

COMBINED NET YARDS

(Rushing, receiving, interception returns, punt returns, kickoff returns and fumble returns)

ATTEMPTS

Most attempts, career
4,368—Walter Payton, Chicago, 1975 through 1987.

Most attempts, season
496—James Wilder, Tampa Bay, 1984.

Most attempts, game
48—James Wilder, Tampa Bay at Pittsburgh, October 30, 1983.

YARDS

Most yards, career
21,803—Walter Payton, Chicago, 1975 through 1987.

Most yards, season
2,535—Lionel James, San Diego, 1985.

Most years leading league in yards
5—Jim Brown, Cleveland, 1958 through 1961, 1964.

Most consecutive years leading league in yards
4—Jim Brown, Cleveland, 1958 through 1961.

Most yards, game
404—Glyn Milburn, Denver vs. Seattle, December 10, 1995.

SCORING

POINTS

Most points, career
2,002—George Blanda, Chicago Bears, Baltimore, Houston, Oakland, 1949 through 1975, except 1959.

Most points, season
176—Paul Hornung, Green Bay, 1960.

Most years leading league in points
5—Don Hutson, Green Bay, 1940 through 1944.
Gino Cappelletti, Boston, 1961 through 1966, except 1962.

Most consecutive years leading league in points
5—Don Hutson, Green Bay, 1940 through 1944.

Most years with 100 or more points
12—Morten Andersen, New Orleans, Atlanta, 1985 through 1998, except 1990 and 1996.

Most points, game
40—Ernie Nevers, Chicago Cardinals vs. Chicago Bears, November 28, 1929.

Most consecutive games with one or more points
238—Morten Andersen, New Orleans, Atlanta, December 11, 1983 through December 27, 1998.

TOUCHDOWNS

Most touchdowns, career
175—Jerry Rice, San Francisco, 1985 through 1998.

Most touchdowns, season
25—Emmitt Smith, Dallas, 1995.

Most years leading league in touchdowns
8—Don Hutson, Green Bay, 1935 through 1938 and 1941 through 1944.

Most consecutive years leading league in touchdowns
4—Don Hutson, Green Bay, 1935 through 1938 and 1941 through 1944.

Most touchdowns, game
6—Ernie Nevers, Chicago Cardinals vs. Chicago Bears, November 28, 1929.
Dub Jones, Cleveland vs. Chicago Bears, November 25, 1951.
Gale Sayers, Chicago vs. San Francisco, December 12, 1965.

Most consecutive games with one or more touchdowns
18—Lenny Moore, Baltimore, October 27, 1963 through September 19, 1965.

EXTRA POINTS

Most extra points attempted, career
959—George Blanda, Chicago Bears, Baltimore, Houston, Oakland, 1949 through 1975, except 1959.

Most extra points made, career
943—George Blanda, Chicago Bears, Baltimore, Houston, Oakland, 1949 through 1975, except 1959.

Most extra points attempted, season
70—Uwe von Schamann, Miami, 1984.

Most extra points made, season
66—Uwe von Schamann, Miami, 1984.

Most extra points attempted, game
10—Charlie Gogolak, Washington vs. New York Giants, November 27, 1966.

Most extra points made, game
9—Pat Harder, Chicago Cardinals at New York Giants, October 17, 1948.
Bob Waterfield, Los Angeles vs. Baltimore, October 22, 1950.
Charlie Gogolak, Washington vs. New York Giants, November 27, 1966.

FIELD GOALS AND FIELD-GOAL PERCENTAGE

Most field goals attempted, career
637—George Blanda, Chicago Bears, Baltimore, Houston, Oakland, 1949 through 1975, except 1959.

Most field goals made, career
420—Gary Anderson, Pittsburgh, Philadelphia, San Francisco, Minnesota, 1982 through 1998.

Most field goals attempted, season
49—Bruce Gossett, Los Angeles, 1966.
Curt Knight, Washington, 1971.

Most field goals made, season
37—John Kasay, Carolina, 1996.

Most field goals attempted, game
9—Jim Bakken, St. Louis at Pittsburgh, September 24, 1967.

Most field goals made, game
7—Jim Bakken, St. Louis at Pittsburgh, September 24, 1967.
Rich Karlis, Minnesota vs. Los Angeles Rams, November 5, 1989 (overtime).
Chris Boniol, Dallas vs. Green Bay, November 18, 1996.

Most field goals made, one quarter
4—Garo Yepremian, Detroit vs. Minnesota, November 13, 1966, second quarter.
Curt Knight, Washington at New York Giants, November 15, 1970, second quarter.
Roger Ruzek, Dallas vs. New York Giants, November 2, 1987, fourth quarter.

Most consecutive games with one or more field goals made, career
31—Fred Cox, Minnesota, November 17, 1968 through December 5, 1970.

Most consecutive field goals made, career
40—Gary Anderson, San Francisco, Minnesota, December 15, 1997 through December 26, 1998.

Most field goals of 50 or more yards, career
35—Morten Andersen, New Orleans, Atlanta, 1982 through 1998.

Most field goals of 50 or more yards, season
8—Morten Andersen, Atlanta, 1995.

Most field goals of 50 or more yards, game
3—Morten Andersen, Atlanta vs. New Orleans, December 10, 1995.

Longest field goal made
63 yards—Tom Dempsey, New Orleans vs. Detroit, November 8, 1970.
Jason Elam, Denver vs. Jacksonville, October 25, 1998.

Highest field-goal percentage, career (100 or more made)
81.06—John Carney, Tampa Bay, L.A. Rams, San Diego, 1988 through 1998 (264 attempted, 214 made).

Highest field-goal percentage, season (qualifiers)
100.00—Tony Zendejas, Los Angeles Rams, 1991 (17 made).
Gary Anderson, Minnesota, 1998 (35 made).

SAFETIES

Most safeties, career
4—Ted Hendricks, Baltimore, Green Bay, Oakland, Los Angeles Raiders, 1969 through 1983.
Doug English, Detroit, 1975 through 1985, except 1980.

Most safeties, season
2—Held by many players.

Most safeties, game
2—Fred Dryer, Los Angeles vs. Green Bay, October 21, 1973.

PUNTING

Most punts, career
1,154—Dave Jennings, New York Giants, New York Jets, 1974 through 1987.

Most punts, season
114—Bob Parsons, Chicago, 1981.

Most seasons leading league in punting
4—Sammy Baugh, Washington, 1940 through 1943.
   Jerrel Wilson, Kansas City, 1965, 1968, 1972, 1973.

Most consecutive seasons leading league in punting
4—Sammy Baugh, Washington, 1940 through 1943.

Most punts, game
16— Leo Araguz, Oakland vs. San Diego, October 11, 1998.

Longest punt
98 yards—Steve O'Neal, New York Jets at Denver, September
   21, 1969.

FUMBLES

Most fumbles, career
160—Warren Moon, Houston, Minnesota, Seattle, 1984 through
   1998.

Most fumbles, season
21—Tony Banks, St. Louis, 1996.

Most fumbles, game
7—Len Dawson, Kansas City vs. San Diego, November 15, 1964.

PUNT RETURNS

Most punt returns, career
349—Dave Meggett, N.Y. Giants, New England, N.Y. Jets, 1989
   through 1998.

Most punt returns, season
70—Danny Reece, Tampa Bay, 1979.

Most years leading league in punt returns
3—Les "Speedy" Duncan, San Diego, Washington, 1965, 1966,
   1971.
   Rick Upchurch, Denver, 1976, 1978, 1982.

Most punt returns, game
11—Eddie Brown, Washington at Tampa Bay, October 9, 1977.

YARDS

Most yards, career
3,708—Dave Meggett, N.Y. Giants, New England, N.Y. Jets, 1989
   through 1998.

Most yards, season
875—Desmond Howard, Green Bay, 1996.

Most yards, game
207—LeRoy Irvin, Los Angeles at Atlanta, October 11, 1981.

Longest punt return
103 yards—Robert Bailey, Los Angeles Rams at New Orleans,
   October 23, 1994 (touchdown).

FAIR CATCHES

Most fair catches, career
114—Dave Meggett, N.Y. Giants, New England, N.Y. Jets, 1989
   through 1998.

Most fair catches, season
27—Leo Lewis, Minnesota, 1989.

Most fair catches, game
7—Lem Barney, Detroit vs. Chicago, November 21, 1976.
   Bobby Morse, Philadelphia vs. Buffalo, December 27, 1987.

TOUCHDOWNS

Most touchdowns, career
9—Eric Metcalf, Cleveland, Atlanta, San Diego, Arizona, 1989
   through 1998.

Most touchdowns, season
4—Jack Christiansen, Detroit, 1951.
   Rick Upchurch, Denver, 1976.

Most touchdowns, game
2—Jack Christiansen, Detroit vs. Los Angeles, October 14, 1951.
   Jack Christiansen, Detroit vs. Green Bay, November 22, 1951.
   Dick Christy, New York Titans vs. Denver, September 24, 1961.
   Rick Upchurch, Denver vs. Cleveland, September 26, 1976.
   LeRoy Irvin, Los Angeles at Atlanta, October 11, 1981.
   Vai Sikahema, St. Louis vs. Tampa Bay, December 21, 1986.
   Todd Kinchen, Los Angeles Rams vs. Atlanta, December 27,
      1992.
   Eric Metcalf, San Diego at Cincinnati, November 2, 1997.
   Darrien Gordon, Denver vs. Carolina, November 9, 1997.
   Jermaine Lewis, Baltimore vs. Seattle, December 7, 1997.

KICKOFF RETURNS

Most kickoff returns, career
421—Mel Gray, New Orleans, Detroit, Houston, Tennessee,
   Philadelphia, 1986 through 1997.

Most kickoff returns, season
70—Tyrone Hughes, New Orleans, 1996.

Most years leading league in kickoff returns
3—Abe Woodson, San Francisco, 1959, 1962, 1963.
   Tyrone Hughes, New Orleans, 1994 through 1996.

Most kickoff returns, game
10—Desmond Howard, Oakland at Seattle, October 26, 1997.

YARDS

Most yards, career
10,250—Mel Gray, New Orleans, Detroit, Houston, Tennessee,
   Philadelphia, 1986 through 1997.

Most yards, season
1,791—Tyrone Hughes, New Orleans, 1996.

Most years leading league in yards
3—Bruce Harper, New York Jets, 1977 through 1979.
   Tyrone Hughes, New Orleans, 1994 through 1996.

Most yards, game
304—Tyrone Hughes, New Orleans vs. Los Angeles Rams, October
   23, 1994.

Longest kickoff return
106 yards—Al Carmichael, Green Bay vs. Chicago Bears,
   October 7, 1956 (touchdown).
   Noland Smith, Kansas City at Denver, December 17, 1967.
   Roy Green, St. Louis at Dallas, October 21, 1979.

TOUCHDOWNS

Most touchdowns, career
6—Ollie Matson, Chicago Cardinals, Los Angeles Rams, Detroit,
   Philadelphia, 1952 through 1964, except 1953.
   Gale Sayers, Chicago, 1965 through 1971.
   Travis Williams, Green Bay, Los Angeles, 1967 through 1971.
   Mel Gray, New Orleans, Detroit, Houston, Tennessee, Phila-
      delphia, 1986 through 1997.

Most touchdowns, season
4—Travis Williams, Green Bay, 1967.
   Cecil Turner, Chicago, 1970.

Most touchdowns, game
2—Timmy Brown, Philadelphia vs. Dallas, November 6, 1966.
   Travis Williams, Green Bay vs. Cleveland, November 12, 1967.
   Ron Brown, Los Angeles Rams vs. Green Bay, November
      24, 1985.
   Tyrone Hughes, New Orleans vs. Los Angeles Rams,
      October 23, 1994.

COMBINED KICK RETURNS

(KICKOFFS AND PUNTS)

Most kick returns, career
664—Mel Gray, New Orleans, Detroit, Houston, Tennessee, Philadelphia, 1986 through 1997.

Most kick returns, season
102—Glyn Milburn, Detroit, 1997.

Most kick returns, game
13—Stump Mitchell, St. Louis at Atlanta, October 18, 1981.
Ron Harris, New England at Pittsburgh, December 5, 1993.

YARDS

Most yards, career
12,810—Mel Gray, New Orleans, Detroit, Houston, Tennessee, Philadelphia, 1986 through 1997.

Most yards, season
1,943—Tyrone Hughes, New Orleans, 1996.

Most yards, game
347—Tyrone Hughes, New Orleans vs. Los Angeles Rams, October 23, 1994.

TOUCHDOWNS

Most touchdowns, career
9—Ollie Matson, Chicago Cardinals, Los Angeles Rams, Detroit, Philadelphia, 1952 through 1966, except 1953.
Mel Gray, New Orleans, Detroit, Houston, 1986 through 1997.

Most touchdowns, season
4—Jack Christiansen, Detroit, 1951.
Emlen Tunnell, New York Giants, 1951.
Gale Sayers, Chicago, 1967.
Travis Williams, Green Bay, 1967.
Cecil Turner, Chicago, 1970.
Billy "White Shoes" Johnson, Houston, 1975.
Rick Upchurch, Denver, 1976.

Most touchdowns, game
2—Held by many players.

INDIVIDUAL DEFENSE
INTERCEPTIONS

Most interceptions, career
81—Paul Krause, Washington, Minnesota, 1964 through 1979.

Most interceptions, season
14—Dick "Night Train" Lane, Los Angeles, 1952.

Most interceptions, game
4—Held by many players.

Most consecutive games with one or more interceptions
8—Tom Morrow, Oakland, 1962 through 1963.

Most yards on interceptions, career
1,282—Emlen Tunnell, New York Giants, Green Bay, 1948 through 1961.

Most yards on interceptions, season
349—Charlie McNeil, San Diego, 1961.

Most yards on interceptions, game
177—Charlie McNeil, San Diego vs. Houston, September 24, 1961.

Longest interception return
103—Vencie Glenn, San Diego vs. Denver, November 29, 1987.
Louis Oliver, Miami vs. Buffalo, October 4, 1992.
(Note: James Willis, 14 yards, and Troy Vincent, 90 yards, combined for a 104-yard interception return for Philadelphia vs. Dallas, November 3, 1996.)

TOUCHDOWNS

Most touchdowns, career
9—Ken Houston, Houston, Washington, 1967 through 1980.

Most touchdowns, season
4—Ken Houston, Houston, 1971.
Jim Kearney, Kansas City, 1972.
Eric Allen, Philadelphia, 1993.

Most touchdowns, game
2—Held by many players.

FUMBLES RECOVERED

Most fumbles recovered (own and opponents'), career
55—Warren Moon, Houston, Minnesota, Seattle, 1984 through 1998.

Most fumbles recovered (own), career
55—Warren Moon, Houston, Minnesota, Seattle, 1984 through 1998.

Most opponents' fumbles recovered, career
29—Jim Marshall, Cleveland, Minnesota, 1960 through 1979.

Most fumbles recovered (own and opponents'), season
9—Don Hultz, Minnesota, 1963.
Dave Krieg, Seattle, 1989.

Most fumbles recovered (own), season
9—Dave Krieg, Seattle, 1989.

Most opponents' fumbles recovered, season
9—Don Hultz, Minnesota, 1963.

Most fumbles recovered (own and opponents'), game
4—Otto Graham, Cleveland at New York Giants, October 25, 1953.
Sam Etcheverry, St. Louis at New York Giants, September 17, 1961.
Roman Gabriel, Los Angeles at San Francisco, October 12, 1969.
Joe Ferguson, Buffalo vs. Miami, September 18, 1977.
Randall Cunningham, Philadelphia at Los Angeles Raiders, November 30, 1986 (overtime).

Most fumbles recovered (own), game
4—Otto Graham, Cleveland at New York Giants, October 25, 1953.
Sam Etcheverry, St. Louis at New York Giants, September 17, 1961.
Roman Gabriel, Los Angeles at San Francisco, October 12, 1969.
Joe Ferguson, Buffalo vs. Miami, September 18, 1977.
Randall Cunningham, Philadelphia at Los Angeles Raiders, November 30, 1986 (overtime).

Most opponents' fumbles recovered, game
3—Held by many players.

Longest fumble return
104 yards—Jack Tatum, Oakland at Green Bay, September 24, 1972 (touchdown).

TOUCHDOWNS

Most touchdowns (own and opponents' recovered), career
5—Jessie Tuggle, Atlanta, 1987 through 1998.

Most touchdowns (own recovered), career
2—Held by many players.

Most touchdowns (opponents' recovered), career
4—Jessie Tuggle, Atlanta, 1987 through 1992.

Most touchdowns, season
2—Held by many players.

Most touchdowns, game
2—Fred "Dippy" Evans, Chicago Bears vs. Washington, November 28, 1948.

SACKS (SINCE 1982)

Most sacks, career
192.5—Reggie White, Philadelphia, Green Bay, 1985 through 1998.

Most sacks, season
22—Mark Gastineau, New York Jets, 1984.

Most sacks, game
7—Derrick Thomas, Kansas City vs. Seattle, November 11, 1990.

TEAM MISCELLANEOUS
CHAMPIONSHIPS

Most league championships won
12—Green Bay, 1929, 1930, 1931, 1936, 1939, 1944, 1961, 1962, 1965, 1966, 1967, 1996.

Most consecutive league championships won
3—Green Bay, 1929 through 1931.
   Green Bay, 1965 through 1967.

Most first-place finishes during regular season (since 1933)
18—Cleveland Browns, 1950 through 1955, 1957, 1964, 1965, 1967, 1968, 1969, 1971, 1980, 1985, 1986, 1987, 1989.

Most consecutive first-place finishes during regular season (since 1933)
7—Los Angeles, 1973 through 1979.

GAMES WON

Most games won, season
15—San Francisco, 1984.
   Chicago, 1985.
   Minnesota, 1998.

Most consecutive games won, season
14—Miami, September 17 through December 16, 1972.

Most consecutive games won from start of season
14—Miami, September 17 through December 16, 1972 (entire season).

Most consecutive games won at end of season
14—Miami, September 17 through December 16, 1972 (entire season).

Most consecutive undefeated games, season
14—Miami, September 17 through December 16, 1972 (entire season).

Most consecutive games won
17—Chicago Bears, November 26, 1933 through December 2, 1934.

Most consecutive undefeated games
25—Canton, 1921 through 1923 (won 22, tied three).

Most consecutive home games won
27—Miami, October 17, 1971 through December 15, 1974.

Most consecutive undefeated home games
30—Green Bay, 1928 through 1933 (won 27, tied three).

Most consecutive road games won
18—San Francisco, November 27, 1988 through December 30, 1990.

Most consecutive undefeated road games
18—San Francisco, November 27, 1988 through December 30, 1990 (won 18).

GAMES LOST

Most games lost, season
15—New Orleans, 1980.
   Dallas, 1989.
   New England, 1990.
   Indianapolis, 1991.
   New York Jets, 1996.

Most consecutive games lost
26—Tampa Bay, September 12, 1976 through December 4, 1977.

Most consecutive winless games
26—Tampa Bay, September 12, 1976 through December 4, 1977 (lost 26).

Most consecutive games lost, season
14—Tampa Bay, September 12 through December 12, 1976.
   New Orleans, September 7 through December 7, 1980.
   Baltimore, September 13 through December 13, 1981.
   New England, September 23 through December 30, 1990.

Most consecutive games lost from start of season
14—Tampa Bay, September 12 through December 12, 1976 (entire season).
   New Orleans, September 7 through December 7, 1980.

Most consecutive games lost at end of season
14—Tampa Bay, September 12 through December 12, 1976 (entire season).
   New England, September 23 through December 30, 1990.

Most consecutive winless games, season
14—Tampa Bay, September 12 through December 12, 1976 (lost 14; entire season).
   New Orleans, September 7 through December 7, 1980 (lost 14).
   Baltimore, September 13 through December 13, 1981 (lost 14).
   New England, September 23 through December 30, 1990 (lost 14).

Most consecutive home games lost
14—Dallas, October 9, 1988 through December 24, 1989.

Most consecutive winless home games
14—Dallas, October 9, 1988 through December 24, 1989 (lost 14).

Most consecutive road games lost
23—Houston, September 27, 1981 through November 4, 1984.

Most consecutive winless road games
23—Houston, September 27, 1981 through November 4, 1984 (lost 23).

TIE GAMES

Most tie games, season
6—Chicago Bears, 1932.

Most consecutive tie games
3—Chicago Bears, September 25 through October 9, 1932.

TEAM OFFENSE
RUSHING

Most years leading league in rushing
16—Chicago Bears, 1932, 1934, 1935, 1939, 1940, 1941, 1942, 1951, 1955, 1956, 1968, 1977, 1983, 1984, 1985, 1986.

Most consecutive years leading league in rushing
4—Chicago Bears, 1939 through 1942.
   Chicago Bears, 1983 through 1986.

ATTEMPTS

Most attempts, season
681—Oakland, 1977.

Most attempts, game
72—Chicago Bears vs. Brooklyn, October 20, 1935.

Most attempts by both teams, game
108—Chicago Cardinals 70, Green Bay 38, December 5, 1948.

Fewest attempts, game
6—Chicago Cardinals at Boston, October 29, 1933.

Fewest attempts by both teams, game
35—New Orleans 20, Seattle 15, September 1, 1991.

YARDS

Most yards, season
3,165—New England, 1978.

Fewest yards, season
298—Philadelphia, 1940.

Most yards, game
426—Detroit vs. Pittsburgh, November 4, 1934.

Most yards by both teams, game
595—Los Angeles 371, New York Yanks 224, November 18, 1951.

Fewest yards, game
-53—Detroit at Chicago Cardinals, October 17, 1943.

Fewest yards by both teams, game
-15—Detroit -53, Chicago Cardinals 38, October 17, 1943.

TOUCHDOWNS

Most touchdowns, season
36—Green Bay, 1962.

Fewest touchdowns, season
1—Brooklyn, 1934.

Most touchdowns, game
7—Los Angeles vs. Atlanta, December 4, 1976.

Most touchdowns by both teams, game
8—Los Angeles 6, New York Yanks 2, November 18, 1951.
Chicago Bears 5, Green Bay 3, November 6, 1955.
Cleveland 6, Los Angeles 2, November 24, 1957.

PASSING

ATTEMPTS

Most attempts, season
709—Minnesota, 1981.

Fewest attempts, season
102—Cincinnati, 1933.

Most attempts, game
70—New England vs. Minnesota, November 13, 1994 (overtime).
68—Houston at Buffalo, November 1, 1964.

Most attempts by both teams, game
112—New England 70, Minnesota 42, November 13, 1994 (overtime).
104—Miami 55, New York Jets 49, October 18, 1987 (overtime).
102—San Francisco 57, Atlanta 45, October 6, 1985.

Fewest attempts, game
0—Green Bay vs. Portsmouth, October 8, 1933.
Detroit at Cleveland, September 10, 1937.
Pittsburgh vs. Brooklyn, November 16, 1941.
Pittsburgh vs. Los Angeles, November 13, 1949.
Cleveland vs. Philadelphia, December 3, 1950.

Fewest attempts by both teams, game
4—Detroit 3, Chicago Cardinals 1, November 3, 1935.
Cleveland 4, Detroit 0, September 10, 1937.

COMPLETIONS

Most completions, season
432—San Francisco, 1995.

Fewest completions, season
25—Cincinnati, 1933.

Most completions, game
45—New England vs. Minnesota, November 13, 1994 (overtime).
42—New York Jets vs. San Francisco, September 21, 1980.

Most completions by both teams, game
71—New England 45, Minnesota 26, November 13, 1994 (overtime).
68—San Francisco 37, Atlanta 31, October 6, 1985.

Fewest completions, game
0—Held by many teams. Last team: Buffalo vs. New York Jets, September 29, 1974.

Fewest completions by both teams, game
1—Philadelphia 1, Chicago Cardinals 0, November 8, 1936.
Cleveland 1, Detroit 0, September 10, 1937.
Detroit 1, Chicago Cardinals 0, September 15, 1940.
Pittsburgh 1, Brooklyn 0, November 29, 1942.

YARDS

Most yards, season
5,018—Miami, 1984.

Most years leading league in yards
10—San Diego, 1965, 1968, 1971, 1978 through 1983, 1985.

Most consecutive years leading league in yards
6—San Diego, 1978 through 1983.

Fewest yards, season
302—Chicago Cardinals, 1934.

Most yards, game
554—Los Angeles at New York Yanks, September 28, 1951.

Most yards by both teams, game
884—New York Jets 449, Miami 435, September 21, 1986 (overtime).
883—San Diego 486, Cincinnati 397, December 20, 1982.

Fewest yards, game
-53—Denver at Oakland, September 10, 1967.

Fewest yards by both teams, game
-11—Green Bay -10, Dallas -1, October 24, 1965.

TOUCHDOWNS

Most touchdowns, season
49—Miami, 1984.

Fewest touchdowns, season
0—Cincinnati, 1933.
Pittsburgh, 1945.

Most touchdowns, game
7—Chicago Bears at New York Giants, November 14, 1943.
Philadelphia at Washington, October 17, 1954.
Houston vs. New York Titans, November 19, 1961.
Houston vs. New York Titans, October 14, 1962.
New York Giants vs. Washington, October 28, 1962.
Minnesota vs. Baltimore, September 28, 1969.
San Diego at Oakland, November 22, 1981.

Most touchdowns by both teams, game
12—New Orleans 6, St. Louis 6, November 2, 1969.

INTERCEPTIONS

Most interceptions, season
48—Houston, 1962.

Fewest interceptions, season
5—Cleveland, 1960.
Green Bay, 1966.
Kansas City, 1990.
New York Giants, 1990.

Most interceptions, game
9—Detroit vs. Green Bay, October 24, 1943.
Pittsburgh vs. Philadelphia, December 12, 1965.

Most interceptions by both teams, game
13—Denver 8, Houston 5, December 2, 1962.

SACKS

Most sacks allowed, season
104—Philadelphia, 1986.

Most years leading league in fewest sacks allowed
10—Miami, 1973 and 1982 through 1990.

Most consecutive years leading league in fewest sacks allowed
9—Miami, 1982 through 1990.

Fewest sacks allowed, season
7—Miami, 1988.

Most sacks allowed, game
12—Pittsburgh at Dallas, November 20, 1966.
Baltimore vs. St. Louis, October 26, 1980.
Detroit vs. Chicago, December 16, 1984.
Houston vs. Dallas, September 29, 1985.

Most sacks allowed by both teams, game
18—Green Bay 10, San Diego 8, September 24, 1978.

SCORING

POINTS

Most points, season
556—Minnesota, 1998.

Most points, game
72—Washington vs. New York Giants, November 27, 1966.

Most points by both teams, game
113—Washington 72, New York Giants 41, November 27, 1966.

Fewest points by both teams, game
0—Occurred many times. Last time: New York Giants 0, Detroit 0, November 7, 1943.

Most points in a shutout victory
64—Philadelphia vs. Cincinnati, November 6, 1934.

Fewest points in a shutout victory
2—Green Bay at Chicago Bears, October 16, 1932.
Chicago Bears at Green Bay, September 18, 1938.

Most points in first half of game
49—Green Bay vs. Tampa Bay, October 2, 1983.

Most points in first half of game by both teams
70—Houston 35, Oakland 35, December 22, 1963.

Most points in second half of game
49—Chicago Bears at Philadelphia, November 30, 1941.

Most points in second half of game by both teams
65—Washington 38, New York Giants 27, November 27, 1966.

Most points in one quarter
41—Green Bay vs. Detroit, October 7, 1945, second quarter.
Los Angeles vs. Detroit, October 29, 1950, third quarter.

Most points in one quarter by both teams
49—Oakland 28, Houston 21, December 22, 1963, second quarter.

Most points in first quarter
35—Green Bay vs. Cleveland, November 12, 1967.

Most points in first quarter by both teams
42—Green Bay 35, Cleveland 7, November 12, 1967.

Most points in second quarter
41—Green Bay vs. Detroit, October 7, 1945.

Most points in second quarter by both teams
49—Oakland 28, Houston 21, December 22, 1963.

Most points in third quarter
41—Los Angeles vs. Detroit, October 29, 1950.

Most points in third quarter by both teams
48—Los Angeles 41, Detroit 7, October 29, 1950.

Most points in fourth quarter
31—Oakland vs. Denver, December 17, 1960.
Oakland vs. San Diego, December 8, 1963.
Atlanta at Green Bay, September 13, 1981.

Most points in fourth quarter by both teams
42—Chicago Cardinals 28, Philadelphia 14, December 7, 1947.
Green Bay 28, Chicago Bears 14, November 6, 1955.
New York Jets 28, Boston 14, October 27, 1968.
Pittsburgh 21, Cleveland 21, October 18, 1969.

Most consecutive games without being shut out
338—San Francisco, October 16, 1977 through December 27, 1998.

TIMES SHUT OUT

Most times shut out, season
8—Frankford, 1927 (lost six, tied two).
Brooklyn, 1931 (lost eight).

Most consecutive times shut out
8—Rochester, 1922 through 1924 (lost eight).

TOUCHDOWNS

Most touchdowns, season
70—Miami, 1984.

Most years leading league in touchdowns
13—Chicago Bears, 1932, 1934, 1935, 1939, 1941, 1942, 1943, 1944, 1946, 1947, 1948, 1956, 1965.

Most consecutive years leading league in touchdowns
4—Chicago Bears, 1941 through 1944.
Los Angeles, 1949 through 1952.

Most touchdowns, game
10—Philadelphia vs. Cincinnati, November 6, 1934.
Los Angeles vs. Baltimore, October 22, 1950.
Washington vs. New York Giants, November 27, 1966.

Most touchdowns by both teams, game
16—Washington 10, New York Giants 6, November 27, 1966.

Most consecutive games with one or more touchdowns
166—Cleveland, 1957 through 1969.

EXTRA POINTS

Most extra points, season
66—Miami, 1984.

Fewest extra points, season
2—Chicago Cardinals, 1933.

Most extra points, game
10—Los Angeles vs. Baltimore, October 22, 1950.

Most extra points by both teams, game
14—Chicago Cardinals 9, New York Giants 5, October 17, 1948.
Houston 7, Oakland 7, December 22, 1963.
Washington 9, New York Giants 5, November 27, 1966.

FIELD GOALS

Most field goals attempted, season
49—Los Angeles, 1966.
Washington, 1971.

Most field goals made, season
37—Carolina, 1996.

Most field goals attempted, game
9—St. Louis at Pittsburgh, September 24, 1967.

Most field goals made, game
7—St. Louis at Pittsburgh, September 24, 1967.
Minnesota vs. Los Angeles Rams, November 5, 1989 (overtime).

Most field goals attempted by both teams, game
11—St. Louis 6, Pittsburgh 5, November 13, 1966.
Washington 6, Chicago 5, November 14, 1971.
Green Bay 6, Detroit 5, September 29, 1974.
Washington 6, New York Giants 5, November 14, 1976.

Most field goals made by both teams, game
8—Cleveland 4, St. Louis 4, September 20, 1964.
Chicago 5, Philadelphia 3, October 20, 1968.
Washington 5, Chicago 3, November 14, 1971.
Kansas City 5, Buffalo 3, December 19, 1971.
Detroit 4, Green Bay 4, September 29, 1974.
Cleveland 5, Denver 3, October 19, 1975.

New England 4, San Diego 4, November 9, 1975.
San Francisco 6, New Orleans 2, October 16, 1983.
Seattle 5, Los Angeles Raiders 3, December 18, 1988.

Most consecutive games with one or more field goals made
31—Minnesota, November 17, 1968 through December 5, 1970.

SAFETIES

Most safeties, season
4—Cleveland, 1927.
Detroit, 1962.
Seattle, 1993.

Most safeties, game
3—Los Angeles Rams vs. New York Giants, September 30, 1984.

Most safeties by both teams, game
3—Los Angeles Rams 3, New York Giants 0, September 30, 1984.

FIRST DOWNS

Most first downs, season
387—Miami, 1984.

Most first downs, game
39—New York Jets vs. Miami, November 27, 1988.
Washington at Detroit, November 4, 1990 (overtime).

Most first downs by both teams, game
62—San Diego 32, Seattle 30, September 15, 1985.

PUNTING

Most punts, season
114—Chicago, 1981.

Fewest punts, season
23—San Diego, 1982.

Most punts, game
17—Chicago Bears vs. Green Bay, October 22, 1933.
Cincinnati vs. Pittsburgh, October 22, 1933.

Most punts by both teams, game
31—Chicago Bears 17, Green Bay 14, October 22, 1933.
Cincinnati 17, Pittsburgh 14, October 22, 1933.

Fewest punts, game
0—Held by many teams.

Fewest punts by both teams, game
0—Buffalo 0, San Francisco 0, September 13, 1992.

FUMBLES

Most fumbles, season
56—Chicago Bears, 1938.
San Francisco, 1978.

Fewest fumbles, season
8—Cleveland, 1959.

Most fumbles, game
10—Philadelphia/Pittsburgh vs. New York, October 9, 1943.
Detroit at Minnesota, November 12, 1967.
Kansas City vs. Houston, October 12, 1969.
San Francisco at Detroit, December 17, 1978.

Most fumbles by both teams, game
14—Washington 8, Pittsburgh 6, November 14, 1937.
Chicago Bears 7, Cleveland 7, November 24, 1940.
St. Louis 8, New York Giants 6, September 17, 1961.
Kansas City 10, Houston 4, October 12, 1969.

LOST

Most fumbles lost, season
36—Chicago Cardinals, 1959.

Fewest fumbles lost, season
3—Philadelphia, 1938.
Minnesota, 1980.

Most fumbles lost, game
8—St. Louis at Washington, October 25, 1976.
Cleveland at Pittsburgh, December 23, 1990.

RECOVERED

Most fumbles recovered (own and opponents'), season
58—Minnesota, 1963.

Fewest fumbles recovered (own and opponents'), season
9—San Francisco, 1982.

Most fumbles recovered (own and opponents'), game
10—Denver vs. Buffalo, December 13, 1964.
Pittsburgh vs. Houston, December 9, 1973.
Washington vs. St. Louis, October 25, 1976.

Most fumbles recovered (own), season
37—Chicago Bears, 1938.

Fewest fumbles recovered (own), season
2—Washington, 1958.

TOUCHDOWNS

Most touchdowns on fumbles recovered (own and opponents'), season
5—Chicago Bears, 1942.
Los Angeles, 1952.
San Francisco, 1965.
Oakland, 1978.

Most touchdowns on own fumbles recovered, season
2—Held by many teams. Last team: Miami, 1996.

Most touchdowns on fumbles recovered (own and opponents'), game
2—Held by many teams.

Most touchdowns on fumbles recovered (own and opponents'), game
3—Detroit 2, Minnesota 1, December 9, 1962.
Green Bay 2, Dallas 1, November 29, 1964.
Oakland 2, Buffalo 1, December 24, 1967.

Most touchdowns on own fumbles recovered, game
1—Held by many teams.

Most touchdowns on opponents' fumbles recovered by both teams, game
3—Green Bay 2, Dallas 1, November 29, 1964.
Oakland 2, Buffalo 1, December 24, 1967.

TURNOVERS

Most turnovers, season
63—San Francisco, 1978.

Fewest turnovers, season
12—Kansas City, 1982.

Most turnovers, game
12—Detroit vs. Chicago Bears, November 22, 1942.
Chicago Cardinals vs. Philadelphia, September 24, 1950.
Pittsburgh vs. Philadelphia, December 12, 1965.

Most turnovers by both teams, game
17—Detroit 12, Chicago Bears 5, November 22, 1942.
Boston 9, Philadelphia 8, December 8, 1946.

PUNT RETURNS

Most punt returns, season
71—Pittsburgh, 1976.
Tampa Bay, 1979.
Los Angeles Raiders, 1985.

Fewest punt returns, season
12—Baltimore, 1981.
San Diego, 1982.

Most punt returns, game
12—Philadelphia at Cleveland, December 3, 1950.

Most punt returns by both teams, game
17—Philadelphia 12, Cleveland 5, December 3, 1950.

YARDS

Most yards, season
785—Los Angeles Raiders, 1985.

Fewest yards, season
27—St. Louis, 1965.

Most yards, game
231—Detroit vs. San Francisco, October 6, 1963.

Most yards by both teams, game
282—Los Angeles 219, Atlanta 63, October 11, 1981.

TOUCHDOWNS

Most touchdowns, season
5—Chicago Cardinals, 1959.

Most touchdowns, game
2—Held by many teams. Last team: Cleveland vs. Pittsburgh, October 24, 1993.

Most touchdowns by both teams, game
2—Occurred many times. Last time: Cleveland 2, Pittsburgh 0, October 24, 1993.

KICKOFF RETURNS

Most kickoff returns, season
88—New Orleans, 1980.

Fewest kickoff returns, season
17—New York Giants, 1944.

Most kickoff returns, game
12—New York Giants at Washington, November 27, 1966.

Most kickoff returns by both teams, game
19—New York Giants 12, Washington 7, November 27, 1966.

YARDS

Most yards, season
1,973—New Orleans, 1980.

Fewest yards, season
282—New York Giants, 1940.

Most yards, game
362—Detroit at Los Angeles, October 29, 1950.

Most yards by both teams, game
560—Detroit 362, Los Angeles 198, October 29, 1950.

TOUCHDOWNS

Most touchdowns, season
4—Green Bay, 1967.
    Chicago, 1970.
    Detroit, 1994.

Most touchdowns, game
2—Chicago Bears at Green Bay, September 22, 1940.
    Chicago Bears vs. Green Bay, November 9, 1952.
    Philadelphia vs. Dallas, November 6, 1966.
    Green Bay vs. Cleveland, November 12, 1967.
    Los Angeles Rams vs. Green Bay, November 24, 1985.
    New Orleans vs. Los Angeles Rams, October 23, 1994.

Most touchdowns by both teams, game (each team scoring)
2—Occurred many times. Last time: Houston 1, Pittsburgh 1, December 4, 1988.

PENALTIES

Most penalties, season
158—Kansas City, 1998.

Fewest penalties, season
19—Detroit, 1937.

Most penalties, game
22—Brooklyn at Green Bay, September 17, 1944.
    Chicago Bears at Philadelphia, November 26, 1944.
    San Francisco at Buffalo, October 4, 1998.

Most penalties by both teams, game
37—Cleveland 21, Chicago Bears 16, November 25, 1951.

Fewest penalties, game
0—Held by many teams. Last team: San Francisco vs. Philadelphia, November 29, 1992.

Fewest penalties by both teams, game
0—Brooklyn 0, Pittsburgh 0, October 28, 1934.
    Brooklyn 0, Boston 0, September 28, 1936.
    Cleveland 0, Chicago Bears 0, October 9, 1938.
    Pittsburgh 0, Philadelphia 0, November 10, 1940.

YARDS PENALIZED

Most yards penalized, season
1,304—Kansas City, 1998.

Fewest yards penalized, season
139—Detroit, 1937.

Most yards penalized, game
209—Cleveland vs. Chicago Bears, November 25, 1951.

Most yards penalized by both teams, game
374—Cleveland 209, Chicago Bears 165, November 25, 1951.

Fewest yards penalized, game
0—Held by many teams. Last team: San Francisco vs. Philadelphia, November 29, 1992.

Fewest yards penalized by both teams, game
0—Brooklyn 0, Pittsburgh 0, October 28, 1934.
    Brooklyn 0, Boston 0, September 28, 1936.
    Cleveland 0, Chicago Bears 0, October 9, 1938.
    Pittsburgh 0, Philadelphia 0, November 10, 1940.

TEAM DEFENSE
RUSHING

YARDS ALLOWED

Most yards allowed, season
3,228—Buffalo, 1978.

Fewest yards allowed, season
519—Chicago Bears, 1942.

TOUCHDOWNS ALLOWED

Most touchdowns allowed, season
36—Oakland, 1961.

Fewest touchdowns allowed, season
2—Detroit, 1934.
    Dallas, 1968.
    Minnesota, 1971.

PASSING

YARDS ALLOWED

Most yards allowed, season
4,751—Atlanta, 1995.

Fewest yards allowed, season
545—Philadelphia, 1934.

TOUCHDOWNS ALLOWED

Most touchdowns allowed, season
40—Denver, 1963.

Fewest touchdowns allowed, season
1—Portsmouth, 1932.
    Philadelphia, 1934.

YARDS ALLOWED

(RUSHING AND PASSING)

Most yards allowed rushing and passing, season
6,793—Baltimore, 1981.

Fewest yards allowed rushing and passing, season
1,539—Chicago Cardinals, 1934.

SCORING

POINTS ALLOWED

Most points allowed, season
533—Baltimore, 1981.

Fewest points allowed, season (since 1932)
44—Chicago Bears, 1932.

SHUTOUTS

Most shutouts, season
10—Pottsville, 1926 (won nine, tied one).
New York Giants, 1927 (won nine, tied one).

Most consecutive shutouts
13—Akron, 1920 through 1921 (won 10, tied three).

TOUCHDOWNS ALLOWED

Most touchdowns allowed, season
68—Baltimore, 1981.

Fewest touchdowns allowed, season (since 1932)
6—Chicago Bears, 1932.
Brooklyn, 1933.

FIRST DOWNS ALLOWED

Most first downs allowed, season
406—Baltimore, 1981.

Fewest first downs allowed, season
77—Detroit, 1935.

Most first downs allowed by rushing, season
179—Detroit, 1985.

Fewest first downs allowed by rushing, season
35—Chicago Bears, 1942.

Most first downs allowed by passing, season
230—Atlanta, 1995.

Fewest first downs allowed by passing, season
33—Chicago Bears, 1943.

Most first downs allowed by penalties, season
56—Kansas City, 1998.

Fewest first downs allowed by penalties, season
1—Boston, 1944.

INTERCEPTIONS

Most interceptions, season
49—San Diego, 1961.

Fewest interceptions, season
3—Houston, 1982.

Most interceptions, game
9—Green Bay at Detroit, October 24, 1943.
Philadelphia at Pittsburgh, December 12, 1965.

Most yards returning interceptions, season
929—San Diego, 1961.

Fewest yards returning interceptions, season
5—Los Angeles, 1959.

Most yards returning interceptions, game
325—Seattle vs. Kansas City, November 4, 1984.

Most touchdowns returning interceptions, season
9—San Diego, 1961.

Most touchdowns returning interceptions, game
4—Seattle vs. Kansas City, November 4, 1984.

Most touchdowns returning interceptions by both teams, game
4—Philadelphia 3, Pittsburgh 1, December 12, 1965.
Seattle 4, Kansas City 0, November 4, 1984.

FUMBLES

Most opponents' fumbles forced, season
50—Minnesota, 1963.
San Francisco, 1978.

Fewest opponents' fumbles forced, season
11—Cleveland, 1956.
Baltimore, 1982.
Tennessee, 1998.

RECOVERED

Most opponents' fumbles recovered, season
31—Minnesota, 1963.

Fewest opponents' fumbles recovered, season
3—Los Angeles, 1974.

Most opponents' fumbles recovered, game
8—Washington vs. St. Louis, October 25, 1976.
Pittsburgh vs. Cleveland, December 23, 1990.

TOUCHDOWNS

Most touchdowns on opponents' fumbles recovered, season
4—Held by many teams. Last team: Cincinnati, 1998.

Most touchdowns on opponents' fumbles recovered, game
2—Held by many teams. Last team: Cincinnati at Pittsburgh, December 20, 1998.

TURNOVERS

Most opponents' turnovers, season
66—San Diego, 1961.

Fewest opponents' turnovers, season
11—Baltimore, 1982.

Most opponents' turnovers, game
12—Chicago Bears at Detroit, November 22, 1942.
Philadelphia at Chicago Cardinals, September 24, 1950.
Philadelphia at Pittsburgh, December 12, 1965.

SACKS

Most sacks, season
72—Chicago, 1984.

Fewest sacks, season
11—Baltimore, 1982.

Most sacks, game
12—Dallas at Pittsburgh, November 20, 1966.
St. Louis at Baltimore, October 26, 1980.
Chicago at Detroit, December 16, 1984.
Dallas at Houston, September 29, 1985.

PUNTS RETURNED

Most punts returned by opponents, season
71—Tampa Bay, 1976.
Tampa Bay, 1977.

Fewest punts returned by opponents, season
7—Washington, 1962.
San Diego, 1982.

Most yards allowed on punts returned by opponents, season
932—Green Bay, 1949.

Fewest yards allowed on punts returned by opponents, season
22—Green Bay, 1967.

Most touchdowns allowed on punts returned by opponents, season
4—New York, 1959.
　Atlanta, 1992.

KICKOFFS RETURNED

Most kickoffs returned by opponents, season
91—Washington, 1983.

Fewest kickoffs returned by opponents, season
10—Brooklyn, 1943.

Most yards allowed on kickoffs returned by opponents, season
2,045—Kansas City, 1966.

Fewest yards allowed on kickoffs returned by opponents, season
225—Brooklyn, 1943.

Most touchdowns allowed on kickoffs returned by opponents, season
4—Minnesota, 1998.

STATISTICAL LEADERS

CAREER MILESTONES

TOP 20 RUSHERS

Player	League	Years	Att.	Yds.	Avg.	Long	TD
Walter Payton	NFL	13	3838	16726	4.4	76	110
Barry Sanders*	NFL	10	3062	15269	5.0	85	99
Eric Dickerson	NFL	11	2996	13259	4.4	85	90
Tony Dorsett	NFL	12	2936	12739	4.3	99	77
Emmitt Smith*	NFL	9	2914	12566	4.3	75	125
Jim Brown	NFL	9	2359	12312	5.2	80	106
Marcus Allen	NFL	16	3022	12243	4.1	61	123
Franco Harris	NFL	13	2949	12120	4.1	75	91
Thurman Thomas*	NFL	11	2813	11786	4.2	80	65
John Riggins	NFL	14	2916	11352	3.9	66	104
O.J. Simpson	AFL-NFL	11	2404	11236	4.7	94	61
Ottis Anderson	NFL	14	2562	10273	4.0	76	81
Joe Perry	AAFC-NFL	16	1929	9723	5.0	78	71
Earl Campbell	NFL	8	2187	9407	4.3	81	74
Jim Taylor	NFL	10	1941	8597	4.4	84	83
Earnest Byner	NFL	14	2095	8261	3.9	54	56
Herschel Walker	NFL	12	1954	8225	4.2	91	61
Roger Craig	NFL	11	1991	8189	4.1	71	56
Gerald Riggs	NFL	10	1989	8188	4.1	58	69
Larry Csonka	AFL-NFL	11	1891	8081	4.3	54	64

*Active through 1998 season.

TOP 20 PASSERS

Player	League	Years	Att.	Comp.	Yds.	TD	Int.	Rating Pts.
Steve Young*	NFL	14	4065	2622	32678	229	103	97.6
Joe Montana	NFL	15	5391	3409	40551	273	139	92.3
Brett Favre*	NFL	8	3757	2318	26803	213	118	89.0
Dan Marino*	NFL	16	7989	4763	58913	408	235	87.3
Otto Graham	AAFC-NFL	10	2626	1464	23584	174	135	86.6
Mark Brunell*	NFL	6	1719	1038	12512	72	43	86.3
Jim Kelly	NFL	11	4779	2874	35467	237	175	84.4
Roger Staubach	NFL	11	2958	1685	22700	153	109	83.4
Troy Aikman*	NFL	10	4011	2479	28346	141	115	82.8
Neil Lomax	NFL	8	3153	1817	22771	136	90	82.7
Sonny Jurgensen	NFL	18	4262	2433	32224	255	189	82.625
Len Dawson	NFL-AFL	19	3741	2136	28711	239	183	82.555
Ken Anderson	NFL	16	4475	2654	32838	197	160	81.9
Bernie Kosar	NFL	12	3365	1994	23301	124	87	81.8
Danny White	NFL	13	2950	1761	21959	155	132	81.7
Neil O'Donnell*	NFL	9	2862	1650	19026	104	57	81.64
Randall Cunningham*	NFL	13	3875	2177	27082	190	119	81.57
Dave Krieg*	NFL	19	5311	3105	38147	261	199	81.5
Boomer Esiason	NFL	14	5205	2969	37920	247	184	81.1
Warren Moon*	NFL	15	6786	3972	49097	290	232	81.0

*Active through 1998 season.

TOP 20 RECEIVERS

Player	League	Years	No.	Yds.	Avg.	Long	TD
Jerry Rice*	NFL	14	1139	17612	15.5	96	164
Art Monk	NFL	16	940	12721	13.5	79	68
Andre Reed*	NFL	14	889	12559	14.1	83	85
Cris Carter*	NFL	12	834	10447	12.5	80	101
Steve Largent	NFL	14	819	13089	16.0	74	100
Henry Ellard*	NFL	16	814	13777	16.9	81	65
Irving Fryar*	NFL	15	784	11983	15.3	80	77
James Lofton	NFL	16	764	14004	18.3	80	75
Charlie Joiner	AFL-NFL	18	750	12146	16.2	87	65
Michael Irvin*	NFL	11	740	11737	15.9	87	62
Gary Clark	NFL	11	699	10856	15.5	84	65
Andre Rison*	NFL	10	681	9381	13.8	80	78
Tim Brown*	NFL	11	680	9600	14.1	80	69
Ozzie Newsome	NFL	13	662	7980	12.1	74	47
Charley Taylor	NFL	13	649	9110	14.0	88	79

Player	League	Years	No.	Yds.	Avg.	Long	TD
Drew Hill	NFL	15	634	9831	15.5	81	60
Don Maynard	NFL-AFL	15	633	11834	18.7	87	88
Raymond Berry	NFL	13	631	9275	14.7	70	68
Keith Byars*	NFL	13	610	5661	9.3	60	31
Herman Moore*	NFL	8	610	8467	13.9	93	57

*Active through 1998 season.

TOP 20 SCORERS

Player	League	Years	TD	XP Made	FG Made	Total
George Blanda	NFL-AFL	26	9	943	335	2002
Gary Anderson*	NFL	17	0	585	420	1845
Morten Andersen*	NFL	17	0	558	401	1761
Nick Lowery	NFL	18	0	562	383	1711
Jan Stenerud	AFL-NFL	19	0	580	373	1699
Norm Johnson*	NFL	17	0	613	348	1657
Lou Groza	AAFC-NFL	21	1	810	264	1608
Eddie Murray	NFL	17	0	521	337	1532
Pat Leahy	NFL	18	0	558	304	1470
Jim Turner	AFL-NFL	16	1	521	304	1439
Matt Bahr	NFL	17	0	522	300	1422
Mark Moseley	NFL	16	0	482	300	1382
Jim Bakken	NFL	17	0	534	282	1380
Fred Cox	NFL	15	0	519	282	1365
Al Del Greco*	NFL	15	0	463	299	1360
Jim Breech	NFL	14	0	517	243	1246
Chris Bahr	NFL	14	0	490	241	1213
Kevin Butler	NFL	13	0	413	265	1208
Gino Cappelletti	AFL-NFL	11	42	350	†176	†1130
Ray Wersching	NFL	15	0	456	222	1122

*Active through 1998 season.
†Includes four two-point conversions.

YEAR BY YEAR

AFC

RUSHING
(Based on most net yards)

	Net Yds.	Att.	TD
1960—Abner Haynes, Dallas	875	156	9
1961—Billy Cannon, Houston	948	200	6
1962—Cookie Gilchrist, Buffalo	1096	214	13
1963—Clem Daniels, Oakland	1099	215	3
1964—Cookie Gilchrist, Buffalo	981	230	6
1965—Paul Lowe, San Diego	1121	222	7
1966—Jim Nance, Boston	1458	299	11
1967—Jim Nance, Boston	1216	269	7
1968—Paul Robinson, Cincinnati	1023	238	8
1969—Dick Post, San Diego	873	182	6
1970—Floyd Little, Denver	901	209	3
1971—Floyd Little, Denver	1133	284	6
1972—O.J. Simpson, Buffalo	1251	292	6
1973—O.J. Simpson, Buffalo	2003	332	12
1974—Otis Armstrong, Denver	1407	263	9
1975—O.J. Simpson, Buffalo	1817	329	16
1976—O.J. Simpson, Buffalo	1503	290	8
1977—Mark van Eeghen, Oakland	1273	324	7
1978—Earl Campbell, Houston	1450	302	13
1979—Earl Campbell, Houston	1697	368	19
1980—Earl Campbell, Houston	1934	373	13
1981—Earl Campbell, Houston	1376	361	10
1982—Freeman McNeil, N.Y. Jets	786	151	6
1983—Curt Warner, Seattle	1449	335	13
1984—Earnest Jackson, San Diego	1179	296	8
1985—Marcus Allen, L.A. Raiders	1759	380	11
1986—Curt Warner, Seattle	1481	319	13
1987—Eric Dickerson, Indianapolis	1288	283	6
1988—Eric Dickerson, Indianapolis	1659	388	14

	Net Yds.	Att.	TD
1989—Christian Okoye, Kansas City	1480	370	12
1990—Thurman Thomas, Buffalo	1297	271	11
1991—Thurman Thomas, Buffalo	1407	288	7
1992—Barry Foster, Pittsburgh	1690	390	11
1993—Thurman Thomas, Buffalo	1315	355	6
1994—Chris Warren, Seattle	1545	333	9
1995—Curtis Martin, New England	1487	368	14
1996—Terrell Davis, Denver	1538	345	13
1997—Terrell Davis, Denver	1750	369	15
1998—Terrell Davis, Denver	2008	392	21

PASSING
(Based on highest passer rating among qualifiers*)

	Att.	Com.	Yds.	TD	Int.	Rat.
1960— Jack Kemp, Chargers	406	211	3018	20	25	67.1
1961— George Blanda, Hou.	362	187	3330	36	22	91.3
1962— Len Dawson, Dal.	310	189	2759	29	17	98.3
1963— Tobin Rote, S.D.	286	170	2510	20	17	86.7
1964— Len Dawson, K.C.	354	199	2879	30	18	89.9
1965— John Hadl, S.D.	348	174	2798	20	21	71.3
1966— Len Dawson, K.C.	284	159	2527	26	10	101.7
1967— Daryle Lamonica, Oak.	425	220	3228	30	20	80.8
1968— Len Dawson, K.C.	224	131	2109	17	9	98.6
1969— Greg Cook, Cin.	197	106	1854	15	11	88.3
1970— Daryle Lamonica, Oak.	356	179	2516	22	15	76.5
1971— Bob Griese, Mia.	263	145	2089	19	9	90.9
1972— Earl Morrall, Mia.	150	83	1360	11	7	91.0
1973— Ken Stabler, Oak.	260	163	1997	14	10	88.5
1974— Ken Anderson, Cin.	328	213	2667	18	10	95.9
1975— Ken Anderson, Cin.	377	228	3169	21	11	94.1
1976— Ken Stabler, Oak.	291	194	2737	27	17	103.7
1977— Bob Griese, Mia.	307	180	2252	22	13	88.0
1978— Terry Bradshaw, Pit.	368	207	2915	28	20	84.8
1979— Dan Fouts, S.D.	530	332	4082	24	24	82.6

	Att.	Com.	Yds.	TD	Int.	Rat.
1980— Brian Sipe, Cle.	554	337	4132	30	14	91.4
1981— Ken Anderson, Cin.	479	300	3754	29	10	98.5
1982— Ken Anderson, Cin.	309	218	2495	12	9	95.5
1983— Dan Marino, Mia.	296	173	2210	20	6	96.0
1984— Dan Marino, Mia.	564	362	5084	48	17	108.9
1985— Ken O'Brien, NYJ	488	297	3888	25	8	96.2
1986— Dan Marino, Mia.	623	378	4746	44	23	92.5
1987— Bernie Kosar, Cle.	389	241	3033	22	9	95.4
1988— Boomer Esiason, Cin.	388	223	3572	28	14	97.4
1989— Boomer Esiason, Cin.	455	258	3525	28	11	92.1
1990— Jim Kelly, Buf.	346	219	2829	24	9	101.2
1991— Jim Kelly, Buf.	474	304	3844	33	17	97.6
1992— Warren Moon, Hou.	346	224	2521	18	12	89.3
1993— John Elway, Den.	551	348	4030	25	10	92.8
1994— Dan Marino, Mia.	615	385	4453	30	17	89.2
1995— Jim Harbaugh, Ind.	314	200	2575	17	5	100.7
1996— John Elway, Den.	466	287	3328	26	14	89.2
1997— Mark Brunell, Jac.	435	264	3281	18	7	†91.17
1998— Vinny Testaverde, NYJ	421	259	3256	29	7	101.6

*This chart includes passer rating points for all leaders, although the same rating system was not used for determining leading quarterbacks prior to 1973. The old system was less equitable, yet similar to the new in that the rating was based on percentage of completions, touchdown passes, percentage of interceptions and average gain in yards.

†Brunell and Jeff George of Oakland (521, 290, 3917, 29, 9), tied with 91.2 rating points, but rounded to another decimal place, Brunell's rating is higher, 91.17 to 91.15.

RECEIVING

(Based on most receptions)

	No.	Yds.	TD
1960—Lionel Taylor, Denver	92	1235	12
1961—Lionel Taylor, Denver	100	1176	4
1962—Lionel Taylor, Denver	77	908	4
1963—Lionel Taylor, Denver	78	1101	10
1964—Charley Hennigan, Houston	101	1546	8
1965—Lionel Taylor, Denver	85	1131	6
1966—Lance Alworth, San Diego	73	1383	13
1967—George Sauer, N.Y. Jets	75	1189	6
1968—Lance Alworth, San Diego	68	1312	10
1969—Lance Alworth, San Diego	64	1003	4
1970—Marlin Briscoe, Buffalo	57	1036	8
1971—Fred Biletnikoff, Oakland	61	929	9
1972—Fred Biletnikoff, Oakland	58	802	7
1973—Fred Willis, Houston	57	371	1
1974—Lydell Mitchell, Baltimore	72	544	2
1975—Reggie Rucker, Cleveland	60	770	3
Lydell Mitchell, Baltimore	60	544	4
1976—MacArthur Lane, Kansas City	66	686	1
1977—Lydell Mitchell, Baltimore	71	620	4
1978—Steve Largent, Seattle	71	1168	8
1979—Joe Washington, Baltimore	82	750	3
1980—Kellen Winslow, San Diego	89	1290	9
1981—Kellen Winslow, San Diego	88	1075	10
1982—Kellen Winslow, San Diego	54	721	6
1983—Todd Christensen, L.A. Raiders	92	1247	12
1984—Ozzie Newsome, Cleveland	89	1001	5
1985—Lionel James, San Diego	86	1027	6
1986—Todd Christensen, L.A. Raiders	95	1153	8
1987—Al Toon, N.Y. Jets	68	976	5
1988—Al Toon, N.Y. Jets	93	1067	5
1989—Andre Reed, Buffalo	88	1312	9
1990—Haywood Jeffires, Houston	74	1048	8
Drew Hill, Houston	74	1019	5
1991—Haywood Jeffires, Houston	100	1181	7
1992—Haywood Jeffires, Houston	90	913	9
1993—Reggie Langhorne, Indianapolis	85	1038	3
1994—Ben Coates, New England	96	1174	7
1995—Carl Pickens, Cincinnati	99	1234	17
1996—Carl Pickens, Cincinnati	100	1180	12
1997—Tim Brown, Oakland	104	1408	5
1998—O.J. McDuffie, Miami	90	1050	7

SCORING

(Based on most total points)

	TD	PAT	FG	Tot.
1960— Gene Mingo, Denver	6	33	18	123
1961— Gino Cappelletti, Boston	8	48	17	147
1962— Gene Mingo, Denver	4	32	27	137
1963— Gino Cappelletti, Boston	2	35	22	113
1964— Gino Cappelletti, Boston	7	36	25	155
1965— Gino Cappelletti, Boston	9	27	17	132
1966— Gino Cappelletti, Boston	6	35	16	119
1967— George Blanda, Oakland	0	56	20	116
1968— Jim Turner, N.Y. Jets	0	43	34	145
1969— Jim Turner, N.Y. Jets	0	33	32	129
1970— Jan Stenerud, Kansas City	0	26	30	116
1971— Garo Yepremian, Miami	0	33	28	117
1972— Bobby Howfield, N.Y. Jets	0	40	27	121
1973— Roy Gerela, Pittsburgh	0	36	29	123
1974— Roy Gerela, Pittsburgh	0	33	20	93
1975— O.J. Simpson, Buffalo	23	0	0	138
1976— Toni Linhart, Baltimore	0	49	20	109
1977— Errol Mann, Oakland	0	39	20	99
1978— Pat Leahy, N.Y. Jets	0	41	22	107
1979— John Smith, New England	0	46	23	115
1980— John Smith, New England	0	51	26	129
1981— Jim Breech, Cincinnati	0	49	22	115
Nick Lowery, Kansas City	0	37	26	115
1982— Marcus Allen, L.A. Raiders	14	0	0	84
1983— Gary Anderson, Pittsburgh	0	38	27	119
1984— Gary Anderson, Pittsburgh	0	45	24	117
1985— Gary Anderson, Pittsburgh	0	40	33	139
1986— Tony Franklin, New England	0	44	32	140
1987— Jim Breech, Cincinnati	0	25	24	97
1988— Scott Norwood, Buffalo	0	33	32	129
1989— David Treadwell, Denver	0	39	27	120
1990— Nick Lowery, Kansas City	0	37	34	139
1991— Pete Stoyanovich, Miami	0	28	31	121
1992— Pete Stoyanovich, Miami	0	34	30	124
1993— Jeff Jaeger, L.A. Raiders	0	27	35	132
1994— John Carney, San Diego	0	33	34	135
1995— Norm Johnson, Pittsburgh	0	39	34	141
1996— Cary Blanchard, Indianapolis	0	27	36	135
1997— Mike Hollis, Jacksonville	0	41	31	134
1998— Steve Christie, Buffalo	0	41	33	140

FIELD GOALS

	No.
1960— Gene Mingo, Denver	18
1961— Gino Cappelletti, Boston	17
1962— Gene Mingo, Denver	27
1963— Gino Cappelletti, Boston	22
1964— Gino Cappelletti, Boston	25
1965— Pete Gogolak, Buffalo	28
1966— Mike Mercer, Oakland-Kansas City	21
1967— Jan Stenerud, Kansas City	21
1968— Jim Turner, N.Y. Jets	34
1969— Jim Turner, N.Y. Jets	32
1970— Jan Stenerud, Kansas City	30
1971— Garo Yepremian, Miami	28
1972— Roy Gerela, Pittsburgh	28
1973— Roy Gerela, Pittsburgh	29
1974— Roy Gerela, Pittsburgh	20
1975— Jan Stenerud, Kansas City	22
1976— Jan Stenerud, Kansas City	21
1977— Errol Mann, Oakland	20
1978— Pat Leahy, N.Y. Jets	22
1979— John Smith, New England	23
1980— John Smith, New England	26
Fred Steinfort, Denver	26
1981— Nick Lowery, Kansas City	26
1982— Nick Lowery, Kansas City	19
1983— Raul Allegre, Baltimore	30
1984— Gary Anderson, Pittsburgh	24
Matt Bahr, Cleveland	24

	No.
1985— Gary Anderson, Pittsburgh	33
1986— Tony Franklin, New England	32
1987— Dean Biasucci, Indianapolis	24
Jim Breech, Cincinnati	24
1988— Scott Norwood, Buffalo	32
1989— David Treadwell, Denver	27
1990— Nick Lowery, Kansas City	34
1991— Pete Stoyanovich, Miami	31
1992— Pete Stoyanovich, Miami	30
1993— Jeff Jaeger, L.A. Raiders	35
1994— John Carney, San Diego	34
1995— Norm Johnson, Pittsburgh	34
1996— Cary Blanchard, Indianapolis	36
1997— Cary Blanchard, Indianapolis	32
1998— Al Del Greco, Tennessee	36

INTERCEPTIONS

	No.	Yds.
1960— Austin Gonsoulin, Denver	11	98
1961— Bill Atkins, Buffalo	10	158
1962— Lee Riley, N.Y. Jets	11	122
1963— Fred Glick, Houston	12	180
1964— Dainard Paulson, N.Y. Jets	12	157
1965— W.K. Hicks, Houston	9	156
1966— Johnny Robinson, Kansas City	10	136
Bobby Hunt, Kansas City	10	113
1967— Miller Farr, Houston	10	264
Tom Janik, Buffalo	10	222
Dick Westmoreland, Miami	10	127
1968— Dave Grayson, Oakland	10	195
1969— Emmitt Thomas, Kansas City	9	146
1970— Johnny Robinson, Kansas City	10	155
1971— Ken Houston, Houston	9	220
1972— Mike Sensibaugh, Kansas City	8	65
1973— Dick Anderson, Miami	8	136
Mike Wagner, Pittsburgh	8	134
1974— Emmitt Thomas, Kansas City	12	214
1975— Mel Blount, Pittsburgh	11	121
1976— Ken Riley, Cincinnati	9	141
1977— Lyle Blackwood, Baltimore	10	163
1978— Thom Darden, Cleveland	10	200
1979— Mike Reinfeldt, Houston	12	205
1980— Lester Hayes, Oakland	13	273
1981— John Harris, Seattle	10	155
1982— Ken Riley, Cincinnati	5	88
Bobby Jackson, N.Y. Jets	5	84
Dwayne Woodruff, Pittsburgh	5	53
Donnie Shell, Pittsburgh	5	27
1983— Ken Riley, Cincinnati	8	89
Vann McElroy, Los Angeles	8	68
1984— Kenny Easley, Seattle	10	126
1985— Eugene Daniel, Indianapolis	8	53
Albert Lewis, Kansas City	8	59
1986— Deron Cherry, Kansas City	9	150
1987— Mike Prior, Indianapolis	6	57
Mark Kelso, Buffalo	6	25
Keith Bostic, Houston	6	-14
1988— Erik McMillan, N.Y. Jets	8	168
1989— Felix Wright, Cleveland	9	91
1990— Richard Johnson, Houston	8	100
1991— Ronnie Lott, L.A. Raiders	8	52
1992— Henry Jones, Buffalo	8	263
1993— Nate Odomes, Buffalo	9	65
Eugene Robinson, Seattle	9	80
1994— Eric Turner, Cleveland	9	199
1995— Willie Williams, Pittsburgh	7	122
1996— Tyrone Braxton, Denver	9	128
1997— Mark McMillian, Kansas City	8	274
Darryl Williams, Seattle	8	172
1998— Ty Law, New England	9	133

PUNTING

(Based on highest average yardage per punt by qualifiers)

	No.	Avg.
1960— Paul Maguire, L.A. Chargers	43	40.5
1961— Bill Atkins, Buffalo	85	44.5
1962— Jim Fraser, Denver	55	43.6
1963— Jim Fraser, Denver	81	44.4
1964— Jim Fraser, Denver	73	44.2
1965— Jerrel Wilson, Kansas City	69	45.4
1966— Bob Scarpitto, Denver	76	45.8
1967— Bob Scarpitto, Denver	105	44.9
1968— Jerrel Wilson, Kansas City	63	45.1
1969— Dennis Partee, San Diego	71	44.6
1970— Dave Lewis, Cincinnati	79	46.2
1971— Dave Lewis, Cincinnati	72	44.8
1972— Jerrel Wilson, Kansas City	66	44.8
1973— Jerrel Wilson, Kansas City	80	45.5
1974— Ray Guy, Oakland	74	42.2
1975— Ray Guy, Oakland	68	43.8
1976— Marv Bateman, Buffalo	86	42.8
1977— Ray Guy, Oakland	59	43.4
1978— Pat McInally, Cincinnati	91	43.1
1979— Bob Grupp, Kansas City	89	43.6
1980— Luke Prestridge, Denver	70	43.9
1981— Pat McInally, Cincinnati	72	45.4
1982— Luke Prestridge, Denver	45	45.0
1983— Rohn Stark, Baltimore	91	45.3
1984— Jim Arnold, Kansas City	98	44.9
1985— Rohn Stark, Indianapolis	78	45.9
1986— Rohn Stark, Indianapolis	76	45.2
1987— Ralf Mojsiejenko, San Diego	67	42.9
1988— Harry Newsome, Pittsburgh	65	45.4
1989— Greg Montgomery, Houston	56	43.3
1990— Mike Horan, Denver	58	44.4
1991— Reggie Roby, Miami	54	45.7
1992— Greg Montgomery, Houston	53	46.9
1993— Greg Montgomery, Houston	54	45.6
1994— Jeff Gossett, L.A. Raiders	77	43.9
1995— Rick Tuten, Seattle	83	45.0
1996— John Kidd, Miami	78	46.3
1997— Tom Tupa, New England	71	45.7
1998— Craig Hentrich, Tennessee	69	47.2

PUNT RETURNS

(Based on most total yards)

	No.	Yds.	Avg.
1960— Abner Haynes, Dallas	14	215	15.4
1961— Dick Christy, N.Y. Jets	18	383	21.3
1962— Dick Christy, N.Y. Jets	15	250	16.7
1963— Claude Gibson, Oakland	26	307	11.8
1964— Bobby Jancik, Houston	12	220	18.3
1965— Leslie Duncan, San Diego	30	464	15.5
1966— Leslie Duncan, San Diego	18	238	13.2
1967— Floyd Little, Denver	16	270	16.9
1968— Noland Smith, Kansas City	18	270	15.0
1969— Bill Thompson, Denver	25	288	11.5
1970— Ed Podolak, Kansas City	23	311	13.5
1971— Leroy Kelly, Cleveland	30	292	9.7
1972— Chris Farasopolous, N.Y. Jets	17	179	10.5
1973— Ron Smith, San Diego	27	352	15.0
1974— Lemar Parrish, Cincinnati	18	338	18.8
1975— Billy Johnson, Houston	40	612	18.8
1976— Rick Upchurch, Denver	39	536	13.7
1977— Billy Johnson, Houston	30	539	15.4
1978— Rick Upchurch, Denver	36	493	13.7
1979— Tony Nathan, Miami	28	306	10.9
1980— J.T. Smith, Kansas City	40	581	14.5
1981— James Brooks, San Diego	22	290	13.2
1982— Rick Upchurch, Denver	15	242	16.1
1983— Kirk Springs, N.Y. Jets	23	287	12.5
1984— Mike Martin, Cincinnati	24	376	15.7
1985— Irving Fryar, New England	37	520	14.1

	No.	Yds.	Avg.
1986—Bobby Joe Edmonds, Seattle	34	419	12.3
1987—Bobby Joe Edmonds, Seattle	20	251	12.6
1988—Jojo Townsell, N.Y. Jets	35	409	11.7
1989—Clarence Verdin, Indianapolis	23	296	12.9
1990—Clarence Verdin, Indianapolis	31	396	12.8
1991—Rod Woodson, Pittsburgh	28	320	11.4
1992—Rod Woodson, Pittsburgh	32	364	11.4
1993—Tim Brown, L.A. Raiders	40	465	11.6
1994—Tim Brown, L.A. Raiders	40	487	12.2
1995—Tamarick Vanover, Kansas City	51	540	10.6
1996—David Meggett, New England	52	588	11.3
1997—Leon Johnson, N.Y. Jets	51	619	12.1
1998—Reggie Barlow, Jacksonville	43	555	12.9

KICKOFF RETURNS

(Based on most total yards)

	No.	Yds.	Avg.
1960—Ken Hall, Houston	19	594	31.3
1961—Dave Grayson, Dallas	16	453	28.3
1962—Bobby Jancik, Houston	24	726	30.3
1963—Bobby Jancik, Houston	45	1317	29.3
1964—Bo Roberson, Oakland	36	975	27.1
1965—Abner Haynes, Denver	34	901	26.5
1966—Goldie Sellers, Denver	19	541	28.5
1967—Zeke Moore, Houston	14	405	28.9
1968—George Atkinson, Oakland	32	802	25.1
1969—Bill Thompson, Denver	19	594	31.3
1970—Jim Duncan, Baltimore	20	707	35.4
1971—Mercury Morris, Miami	15	423	28.2
1972—Bruce Laird, Baltimore	29	843	29.1
1973—Wallace Francis, Buffalo	23	687	29.9
1974—Greg Pruitt, Cleveland	22	606	27.5
1975—Harold Hart, Oakland	17	518	30.5
1976—Duriel Harris, Miami	17	559	32.9
1977—Raymond Clayborn, New England	20	869	31.0
1978—Keith Wright, Cleveland	30	789	26.3
1979—Larry Brunson, Oakland	17	441	25.9
1980—Horace Ivory, New England	36	992	27.6
1981—Carl Roaches, Houston	28	769	27.5

	No.	Yds.	Avg.
1982—Mike Mosley, Buffalo	18	487	27.1
1983—Fulton Walker, Miami	36	962	26.7
1984—Bobby Humphrey, N.Y. Jets	22	675	30.7
1985—Glen Young, Cleveland	35	898	25.7
1986—Lupe Sanchez, Pittsburgh	25	591	23.6
1987—Paul Palmer, Kansas City	38	923	24.3
1988—Tim Brown, L.A. Raiders	41	1098	26.8
1989—Rod Woodson, Pittsburgh	36	982	27.3
1990—Kevin Clark, Denver	20	505	25.3
1991—Nate Lewis, San Diego	23	578	25.1
1992—Jon Vaughn, New England	20	564	28.2
1993—Clarence Verdin, Indianapolis	50	1050	21.0
1994—Andre Coleman, San Diego	49	1293	26.4
1995—Andre Coleman, San Diego	62	1411	22.8
1996—Mel Gray, Houston	50	1224	24.5
1997—Kevin Williams, Arizona	59	1459	24.7
1998—Vaughn Hebron, Denver	46	1216	26.4

SACKS

	No.
1982— Jesse Baker, Houston	7.5
1983— Mark Gastineau, N.Y. Jets	19.0
1984— Mark Gastineau, N.Y. Jets	22.0
1985— Andre Tippett, New England	16.5
1986— Sean Jones, L.A. Raiders	15.5
1987— Andre Tippett, New England	12.5
1988— Greg Townsend, L.A. Raiders	11.5
1989— Lee Williams, San Diego	14.0
1990— Derrick Thomas, Kansas City	20.0
1991— William Fuller, Houston	15.0
1992— Leslie O'Neal, San Diego	17.0
1993— Neil Smith, Kansas City	15.0
1994— Kevin Greene, Pittsburgh	14.0
1995— Bryce Paup, Buffalo	17.5
1996— Michael McCrary, Seattle	13.5
Bruce Smith, Buffalo	13.5
1997— Bruce Smith, Buffalo	15.0
1998— Michael Sinclair, Seattle	16.5

NFC

RUSHING

(Based on most net yards)

	Net Yds.	Att.	TD
1960—Jim Brown, Cleveland	1257	215	9
1961—Jim Brown, Cleveland	1408	305	8
1962—Jim Taylor, Green Bay	1474	272	19
1963—Jim Brown, Cleveland	1863	291	12
1964—Jim Brown, Cleveland	1446	280	7
1965—Jim Brown, Cleveland	1544	289	17
1966—Gale Sayers, Chicago	1231	229	8
1967—Leroy Kelly, Cleveland	1205	235	11
1968—Leroy Kelly, Cleveland	1239	248	16
1969—Gale Sayers, Chicago	1032	236	8
1970—Larry Brown, Washington	1125	237	5
1971—John Brockington, Green Bay	1105	216	4
1972—Larry Brown, Washington	1216	285	8
1973—John Brockington, Green Bay	1144	265	3
1974—Lawrence McCutcheon, L.A. Rams	1109	236	3
1975—Jim Otis, St. Louis	1076	269	5
1976—Walter Payton, Chicago	1390	311	13
1977—Walter Payton, Chicago	1852	339	14
1978—Walter Payton, Chicago	1395	333	11
1979—Walter Payton, Chicago	1610	369	14
1980—Walter Payton, Chicago	1460	317	6
1981—George Rogers, New Orleans	1674	378	13
1982—Tony Dorsett, Dallas	745	177	5
1983—Eric Dickerson, L.A. Rams	1808	390	18
1984—Eric Dickerson, L.A. Rams	2105	379	14

	Net Yds.	Att.	TD
1985—Gerald Riggs, Atlanta	1719	397	10
1986—Eric Dickerson, L.A. Rams	1821	404	11
1987—Charles White, L.A. Rams	1374	324	11
1988—Herschel Walker, Dallas	1514	361	5
1989—Barry Sanders, Detroit	1470	280	14
1990—Barry Sanders, Detroit	1304	255	13
1991—Emmitt Smith, Dallas	1563	365	12
1992—Emmitt Smith, Dallas	1713	373	18
1993—Emmitt Smith, Dallas	1486	283	9
1994—Barry Sanders, Detroit	1883	331	7
1995—Emmitt Smith, Dallas	1773	377	25
1996—Barry Sanders, Detroit	1553	307	11
1997—Barry Sanders, Detroit	2053	335	11
1998—Jamal Anderson, Atlanta	1846	410	14

PASSING

(Based on highest passer rating among qualifiers*)

	Att.	Com.	Yds.	TD	Int.	Rat.
1960— Milt Plum, Cle.	250	151	2297	21	5	110.4
1961— Milt Plum, Cle.	302	177	2416	18	10	90.3
1962— Bart Starr, G.B.	285	178	2438	12	9	90.7
1963— Y.A. Tittle, NYG	367	221	3145	36	14	104.8
1964— Bart Starr, G.B.	272	163	2144	15	4	97.1
1965— Rudy Bukich, Chi.	312	176	2641	20	9	93.7
1966— Bart Starr, G.B.	251	156	2257	14	3	105.0
1967— Sonny Jurgensen, Was.	508	288	3747	31	16	87.3
1968— Earl Morrall, Bal.	317	182	2909	26	17	93.2
1969— Sonny Jurgensen, Was.	442	274	3102	22	15	85.4

	Att.	Com.	Yds.	TD	Int.	Rat.
1970— John Brodie, S.F.	378	223	2941	24	10	93.8
1971— Roger Staubach, Dal.	211	126	1882	15	4	104.8
1972— Norm Snead, NYG	325	196	2307	17	12	84.0
1973— Roger Staubach, Dal.	286	179	2428	23	15	94.6
1974— Sonny Jurgensen, Was.	167	107	1185	11	5	94.6
1975— Fran Tarkenton, Min.	425	273	2994	25	13	91.7
1976— James Harris, L.A.	158	91	1460	8	6	89.8
1977— Roger Staubach, Dal.	361	210	2620	18	9	87.1
1978— Roger Staubach, Dal.	413	231	3190	25	16	84.9
1979— Roger Staubach, Dal.	461	267	3586	27	11	92.4
1980— Ron Jaworski, Phi.	451	257	3529	27	12	90.0
1981— Joe Montana, S.F.	488	311	3565	19	12	88.4
1982— Joe Theismann, Was.	252	161	2033	13	9	91.3
1983— Steve Bartkowski, Atl.	432	274	3167	22	5	97.6
1984— Joe Montana, S.F.	432	279	3630	28	10	102.9
1985— Joe Montana, S.F.	494	303	3653	27	13	91.3
1986— Tommy Kramer, Min.	372	208	3000	24	10	92.6
1987— Joe Montana, S.F.	398	266	3054	31	13	102.1
1988— Wade Wilson, Min.	332	204	2746	15	9	91.5
1989— Joe Montana, S.F.	386	271	3521	26	8	112.4
1990— Phil Simms, NYG	311	184	2284	15	4	92.7
1991— Steve Young, S.F.	279	180	2517	17	8	101.8
1992— Steve Young, S.F.	402	268	3465	25	7	107.0
1993— Steve Young, S.F.	462	314	4023	29	16	101.5
1994— Steve Young, S.F.	461	324	3969	35	10	112.8
1995— Brett Favre, G.B.	570	359	4413	38	13	99.5
1996— Steve Young, S.F.	316	214	2410	14	6	97.2
1997— Steve Young, S.F.	356	241	3029	19	6	104.7
1998— Ran. Cunningham, Min.	425	259	3704	34	10	106.0

*This chart includes passer rating points for all leaders, although the same rating system was not used for determining leading quarterbacks prior to 1973. The old system was less equitable, yet similar to the new in that the rating was based on percentage of completions, touchdown passes, percentage of interceptions and average gain in yards.

RECEIVING
(Based on most receptions)

	No.	Yds.	TD
1960—Raymond Berry, Baltimore	74	1298	10
1961—Jim Phillips, L.A. Rams	78	1092	5
1962—Bobby Mitchell, Washington	72	1384	11
1963—Bobby Joe Conrad, St. Louis	73	967	10
1964—Johnny Morris, Chicago	93	1200	10
1965—Dave Parks, San Francisco	80	1344	12
1966—Charley Taylor, Washington	72	1119	12
1967—Charley Taylor, Washington	70	990	9
1968—Clifton McNeil, San Francisco	71	994	7
1969—Dan Abramowicz, New Orleans	73	1015	7
1970—Dick Gordon, Chicago	71	1026	13
1971—Bob Tucker, N.Y. Giants	59	791	4
1972—Harold Jackson, Philadelphia	62	1048	4
1973—Harold Carmichael, Philadelphia	67	1116	9
1974—Charles Young, Philadelphia	63	696	3
1975—Chuck Foreman, Minnesota	73	691	9
1976—Drew Pearson, Dallas	58	806	6
1977—Ahmad Rashad, Minnesota	51	681	2
1978—Rickey Young, Minnesota	88	704	5
1979—Ahmad Rashad, Minnesota	80	1156	9
1980—Earl Cooper, San Francisco	83	567	4
1981—Dwight Clark, San Francisco	85	1105	4
1982—Dwight Clark, San Francisco	60	913	5
1983—Roy Green, St. Louis	78	1227	14
Charlie Brown, Washington	78	1225	8
Earnest Gray, N.Y. Giants	78	1139	5
1984—Art Monk, Washington	106	1372	7
1985—Roger Craig, San Francisco	92	1016	6
1986—Jerry Rice, San Francisco	86	1570	15
1987—J.T. Smith, St. Louis	91	1117	8
1988—Henry Ellard, L.A. Rams	86	1414	10
1989—Sterling Sharpe, Green Bay	90	1423	12
1990—Jerry Rice, San Francisco	100	1502	13

	No.	Yds.	TD
1991—Michael Irvin, Dallas	93	1523	8
1992—Sterling Sharpe, Green Bay	108	1461	13
1993—Sterling Sharpe, Green Bay	112	1274	11
1994—Cris Carter, Minnesota	122	1256	7
1995—Herman Moore, Detroit	123	1686	14
1996—Jerry Rice, San Francisco	108	1254	8
1997—Herman Moore, Detroit	104	1293	8
1998—Frank Sanders, Arizona	89	1145	3

SCORING
(Based on most total points)

	TD	PAT	FG	Tot.
1960— Paul Hornung, Green Bay	15	41	15	176
1961— Paul Hornung, Green Bay	10	41	15	146
1962— Jim Taylor, Green Bay	19	0	0	114
1963— Don Chandler, N.Y. Giants	0	52	18	106
1964— Lenny Moore, Baltimore	20	0	0	120
1965— Gale Sayers, Chicago	22	0	0	132
1966— Bruce Gossett, L.A. Rams	0	29	28	113
1967— Jim Bakken, St. Louis	0	36	27	117
1968— Leroy Kelly, Cleveland	20	0	0	120
1969— Fred Cox, Minnesota	0	43	26	121
1970— Fred Cox, Minnesota	0	35	30	125
1971— Curt Knight, Washington	0	27	29	114
1972— Chester Marcol, Green Bay	0	29	33	128
1973— David Ray, L.A. Rams	0	40	30	130
1974— Chester Marcol, Green Bay	0	19	25	94
1975— Chuck Foreman, Minnesota	22	0	0	132
1976— Mark Moseley, Washington	0	31	22	97
1977— Walter Payton, Chicago	16	0	0	96
1978— Frank Corral, L.A. Rams	0	31	29	118
1979— Mark Moseley, Washington	0	39	25	114
1980— Ed Murray, Detroit	0	35	27	116
1981— Ed Murray, Detroit	0	46	25	121
Rafael Septien, Dallas	0	40	27	121
1982— Wendell Tyler, L.A. Rams	13	0	0	78
1983— Mark Moseley, Washington	0	62	33	161
1984— Ray Wersching, S.F.	0	56	25	131
1985— Kevin Butler, Chicago	0	51	31	144
1986— Kevin Butler, Chicago	0	36	28	120
1987— Jerry Rice, San Francisco	23	0	0	138
1988— Mike Cofer, San Francisco	0	40	27	121
1989— Mike Cofer, San Francisco	0	49	29	136
1990— Chip Lohmiller, Washington	0	41	30	131
1991— Chip Lohmiller, Washington	0	56	31	149
1992— Morten Andersen, New Orleans	0	33	29	120
Chip Lohmiller, Washington	0	30	30	120
1993— Jason Hanson, Detroit	0	28	34	130
1994— Fuad Reveiz, Minnesota	0	30	34	132
1995— Emmitt Smith, Dallas	25	0	0	150
1996— John Kasay, Carolina	0	34	37	145
1997— Richie Cunningham, Dallas	0	24	34.	126
1998— Gary Anderson, Minnesota	0	59	35	164

FIELD GOALS

	No.
1960— Tommy Davis, San Francisco	19
1961— Steve Myhra, Baltimore	21
1962— Lou Michaels, Pittsburgh	26
1963— Jim Martin, Baltimore	24
1964— Jim Bakken, St. Louis	25
1965— Fred Cox, Minnesota	23
1966— Bruce Gossett, L.A. Rams	28
1967— Jim Bakken, St. Louis	27
1968— Mac Percival, Chicago	25
1969— Fred Cox, Minnesota	26
1970— Fred Cox, Minnesota	30
1971— Curt Knight, Washington	29
1972— Chester Marcol, Green Bay	33
1973— David Ray, L.A. Rams	30
1974— Chester Marcol, Green Bay	25

HISTORY *Statistical leaders*

– 345 –

	No.
1975— Toni Fritsch, Dallas	22
1976— Mark Moseley, Washington	22
1977— Mark Moseley, Washington	21
1978— Frank Corral, L.A. Rams	29
1979— Mark Moseley, Washington	25
1980— Eddie Murray, Detroit	27
1981— Rafael Septien, Dallas	27
1982— Mark Moseley, Washington	20
1983— Ali Haji-Sheikh, N.Y. Giants	35
1984— Paul McFadden, Philadelphia	30
1985— Morten Andersen, New Orleans	31
Kevin Butler, Chicago	31
1986— Kevin Butler, Chicago	28
1987— Morten Andersen, New Orleans	28
1988— Mike Cofer, San Francisco	27
1989— Rich Karlis, Minnesota	31
1990— Chip Lohmiller, Washington	30
1991— Chip Lohmiller, Washington	31
1992— Chip Lohmiller, Washington	30
1993— Jason Hanson, Detroit	34
1994— Fuad Reveiz, Minnesota	34
1995— Morten Andersen, Atlanta	31
1996— John Kasay, Carolina	37
1997— Richie Cunningham, Dallas	34
1998— Gary Anderson, Minnesota	35

INTERCEPTIONS

	No.	Yds.
1960— Dave Baker, San Francisco	10	96
Jerry Norton, St. Louis	10	96
1961— Dick Lynch, N.Y. Giants	9	60
1962— Willie Wood, Green Bay	9	132
1963— Dick Lynch, N.Y. Giants	9	251
Rosie Taylor, Chicago	9	172
1964— Paul Krause, Washington	12	140
1965— Bobby Boyd, Baltimore	9	78
1966— Larry Wilson, St. Louis	10	180
1967— Lem Barney, Detroit	10	232
Dave Whitsell, New Orleans	10	178
1968— Willie Williams, N.Y. Giants	10	103
1969— Mel Renfro, Dallas	10	118
1970— Dick Le Beau, Detroit	9	96
1971— Bill Bradley, Philadelphia	11	248
1972— Bill Bradley, Philadelphia	9	73
1973— Bob Bryant, Minnesota	7	105
1974— Ray Brown, Atlanta	8	164
1975— Paul Krause, Minnesota	10	201
1976— Monte Jackson, L.A. Rams	10	173
1977— Rolland Lawrence, Atlanta	7	138
1978— Ken Stone, St. Louis	9	139
Willie Buchanon, Green Bay	9	93
1979— Lemar Parrish, Washington	9	65
1980— Nolan Cromwell, L.A. Rams	8	140
1981— Everson Walls, Dallas	11	133
1982— Everson Walls, Dallas	7	61
1983— Mark Murphy, Washington	9	127
1984— Tom Flynn, Green Bay	9	106
1985— Everson Walls, Dallas	9	31
1986— Ronnie Lott, San Francisco	10	134
1987— Barry Wilburn, Washington	9	135
1988— Scott Case, Atlanta	10	47
1989— Eric Allen, Philadelphia	8	38
1990— Mark Carrier, Chicago	10	39
1991— Ray Crockett, Detroit	6	141
Tim McKyer, Atlanta	6	24
Deion Sanders, Atlanta	6	119
Aeneas Williams, Phoenix	6	60
1992— Aubray McMillian, Minnesota	8	157
1993— Deion Sanders, Atlanta	7	91
1994— Aeneas Williams, Arizona	9	89
1995— Orlando Thomas, Minnesota	9	108

	No.	Yds.
1996— Keith Lyle, St. Louis	9	152
1997— Ryan McNeil, St. Louis	9	127
1998— Kwamie Lassiter, Arizona	8	80

PUNTING

(Based on highest average yardage per punt by qualifiers)

	No.	Avg.
1960— Jerry Norton, St. Louis	39	45.6
1961— Yale Lary, Detroit	52	48.4
1962— Tommy Davis, San Francisco	48	45.8
1963— Yale Lary, Detroit	35	48.9
1964— Bobby Walden, Minnesota	72	46.4
1965— Gary Collins, Cleveland	65	46.7
1966— David Lee, Baltimore	49	45.6
1967— Billy Lothridge, Atlanta	87	43.7
1968— Billy Lothridge, Atlanta	75	44.3
1969— David Lee, Baltimore	50	45.3
1970— Julian Fagan, New Orleans	77	42.5
1971— Tom McNeill, Philadelphia	73	42.0
1972— Dave Chapple, L.A. Rams	53	44.2
1973— Tom Wittum, San Francisco	79	43.7
1974— Tom Blanchard, New Orleans	88	42.1
1975— Herman Weaver, Detroit	80	42.0
1976— John James, Atlanta	101	42.1
1977— Tom Blanchard, New Orleans	82	42.4
1978— Tom Skladany, Detroit	86	42.5
1979— Dave Jennings, N.Y. Giants	104	42.7
1980— Dave Jennings, N.Y. Giants	94	44.8
1981— Tom Skladany, Detroit	64	43.5
1982— Carl Birdsong, St. Louis	54	43.8
1983— Frank Garcia, Tampa Bay	95	42.2
1984— Brian Hansen, New Orleans	69	43.8
1985— Rick Donnelly, Atlanta	59	43.6
1986— Sean Landeta, N.Y. Giants	79	44.8
1987— Rick Donnelly, Atlanta	61	44.0
1988— Jim Arnold, Detroit	97	42.4
1989— Rich Camarillo, Phoenix	76	43.4
1990— Sean Landeta, N.Y. Giants	75	44.1
1991— Harry Newsome, Minnesota	68	45.5
1992— Harry Newsome, Minnesota	72	45.0
1993— Jim Arnold, Detroit	72	44.5
1994— Sean Landeta, L.A. Rams	78	44.8
1995— Sean Landeta, St. Louis	83	44.3
1996— Matt Turk, Washington	75	45.1
1997— Mark Royals, New Orleans	88	45.9
1998— Mark Royals, New Orleans	88	45.6

PUNT RETURNS

(Based on most total yards)

	No.	Yds.	Avg.
1960— Abe Woodson, San Francisco	13	174	13.4
1961— Willie Wood, Green Bay	14	225	16.1
1962— Pat Studstill, Detroit	29	457	15.8
1963— Dick James, Washington	16	214	13.4
1964— Tommy Watkins, Detroit	16	238	14.9
1965— Leroy Kelly, Cleveland	17	265	15.6
1966— Johnny Roland, St. Louis	20	221	11.1
1967— Ben Davis, Cleveland	18	229	12.7
1968— Bob Hayes, Dallas	15	312	20.8
1969— Alvin Haymond, L.A. Rams	33	435	13.2
1970— Bruce Taylor, San Francisco	43	516	12.0
1971— Les Duncan, Washington	22	233	10.6
1972— Ken Ellis, Green Bay	14	215	15.4
1973— Bruce Taylor, San Francisco	15	207	13.8
1974— Dick Jauron, Detroit	17	286	16.8
1975— Terry Metcalf, St. Louis	23	285	12.4
1976— Eddie Brown, Washington	48	646	13.5
1977— Larry Marshall, Philadelphia	46	489	10.6
1978— Jackie Wallace, L.A. Rams	52	618	11.9
1979— John Sciarra, Philadelphia	16	182	11.4
1980— Kenny Johnson, Atlanta	23	281	12.2

	No.	Yds.	Avg.
1981— LeRoy Irvin, L.A. Rams	46	615	13.4
1982— Billy Johnson, Atlanta	24	273	11.4
1983— Henry Ellard, L.A. Rams	16	217	13.6
1984— Henry Ellard, L.A. Rams	30	403	13.4
1985— Henry Ellard, L.A. Rams	37	501	13.5
1986— Vai Sikahema, St. Louis	43	522	12.1
1987— Mel Gray, New Orleans	24	352	14.7
1988— John Taylor, San Francisco	44	556	12.6
1989— Walter Stanley, Detroit	36	496	13.8
1990— Johnny Bailey, Chicago	36	399	11.1
1991— Mel Gray, Detroit	25	385	15.4
1992— Johnny Bailey, Phoenix	20	263	13.2
1993— Tyrone Hughes, New Orleans	37	503	13.6
1994— Brian Mitchell, Washington	32	452	14.1
1995— Eric Guliford, Carolina	43	475	11.0
1996— Desmond Howard, Green Bay	58	875	15.1
1997— Karl Williams, Tampa Bay	46	597	13.0
1998— Brian Mitchell, Washington	44	506	11.5

KICKOFF RETURNS

(Based on most total yards)

	No.	Yds.	Avg.
1960— Tom Moore, Green Bay	12	397	33.1
1961— Dick Bass, L.A. Rams	23	698	30.3
1962— Abe Woodson, San Francisco	37	1157	31.3
1963— Abe Woodson, San Francisco	29	935	32.3
1964— Clarence Childs, N.Y. Giants	34	987	29.0
1965— Tommy Watkins, Detroit	17	584	34.4
1966— Gale Sayers, Chicago	23	718	31.2
1967— Travis Williams, Green Bay	18	739	41.1
1968— Preston Pearson, Baltimore	15	527	35.1
1969— Bobby Williams, Detroit	17	563	33.1
1970— Cecil Turner, Chicago	23	752	32.7
1971— Travis Williams, L.A. Rams	25	743	29.7
1972— Ron Smith, Chicago	30	924	30.8
1973— Carl Garrett, Chicago	16	486	30.4
1974— Terry Metcalf, St. Louis	20	623	31.2
1975— Walter Payton, Chicago	14	444	31.7
1976— Cullen Bryant, L.A. Rams	16	459	28.7
1977— Wilbert Montgomery, Phila.	23	619	26.9
1978— Steve Odom, Green Bay	25	677	27.1
1979— Jimmy Edwards, Minnesota	44	1103	25.1

	No.	Yds.	Avg.
1980— Rich Mauti, New Orleans	31	798	27.6
1981— Mike Nelms, Washington	37	1099	29.7
1982— Alvin Hall, Detroit	16	426	26.6
1983— Darrin Nelson, Minnesota	18	445	24.7
1984— Barry Redden, L.A. Rams	23	530	23.0
1985— Ron Brown, L.A. Rams	28	918	32.8
1986— Dennis Gentry, Chicago	20	576	28.8
1987— Sylvester Stamps, Atlanta	24	660	27.5
1988— Donnie Elder, Tampa Bay	34	772	22.7
1989— Mel Gray, Detroit	24	640	26.7
1990— Dave Meggett, N.Y. Giants	21	492	23.4
1991— Mel Gray, Detroit	36	929	25.8
1992— Deion Sanders, Atlanta	40	1067	26.7
1993— Tony Smith, Atlanta	38	948	24.9
1994— Tyrone Hughes, New Orleans	63	1556	24.7
1995— Tyrone Hughes, New Orleans	66	1617	24.5
1996— Tyrone Hughes, New Orleans	70	1791	25.6
1997— Glyn Milburn, Detroit	55	1315	23.9
1998— Glyn Milburn, Chicago	62	1550	25.0

SACKS

	No.
1982— Doug Martin, Minnesota	11.5
1983— Fred Dean, San Francisco	17.5
1984— Richard Dent, Chicago	17.5
1985— Richard Dent, Chicago	17.0
1986— Lawrence Taylor, N.Y. Giants	20.5
1987— Reggie White, Philadelphia	21.0
1988— Reggie White, Philadelphia	18.0
1989— Chris Doleman, Minnesota	21.0
1990— Charles Haley, San Francisco	16.0
1991— Pat Swilling, New Orleans	17.0
1992— Clyde Simmons, Philadelphia	19.0
1993— Renaldo Turnbull, New Orleans	13.0
Reggie White, Green Bay	13.0
1994— Ken Harvey, Washington	13.5
John Randle, Minnesota	13.5
1995— William Fuller, Philadelphia	13.0
Wayne Martin, New Orleans	13.0
1996— Kevin Greene, Carolina	14.5
1997— John Randle, Minnesota	15.5
1998— Reggie White, Green Bay	16.0

COACHING RECORDS

(Ranked according to career wins)

	Yrs.	REGULAR SEASON				POSTSEASON			CAREER			
		Won	Lost	Tied	Pct.	Won	Lost	Pct.	Won	Lost	Tied	Pct.
Don Shula	33	328	156	6	.676	19	17	.528	347	173	6	.665
George Halas	40	318	148	31	.671	6	3	.667	324	151	31	.671
Tom Landry	29	250	162	6	.605	20	16	.556	270	178	6	.601
Curly Lambeau	33	226	132	22	.624	3	2	.600	229	134	22	.623
Chuck Noll	23	193	148	1	.566	16	8	.667	209	156	1	.572
Chuck Knox	22	186	147	1	.558	7	11	.389	193	158	1	.550
*Dan Reeves	18	162	117	1	.580	10	8	.556	172	125	1	.579
Paul Brown	21	166	100	6	.621	4	9	.308	170	109	6	.607
Bud Grant	18	158	96	5	.620	10	12	.455	168	108	5	.607
Steve Owen	23	153	100	17	.598	2	8	.200	155	108	17	.584
Marv Levy	17	143	112	0	.561	11	8	.579	154	120	0	.562
*Marty Schottenheimer	15	145	85	1	.630	5	11	.313	150	96	1	.609
*Bill Parcells	14	130	92	1	.585	11	6	.647	141	98	1	.590
Joe Gibbs	12	124	60	0	.674	16	5	.762	140	65	0	.683
Hank Stram	17	131	97	10	.571	5	3	.625	136	100	10	.573
Weeb Ewbank	20	130	129	7	.502	4	1	.800	134	130	7	.507
*Mike Ditka	13	118	82	0	.590	6	6	.500	124	88	0	.585
Sid Gillman	18	122	99	7	.550	1	5	.167	123	104	7	.541
George Allen	12	116	47	5	.705	4	7	.364	120	54	5	.684
Don Coryell	14	111	83	1	.572	3	6	.333	114	89	1	.561
John Madden	10	103	32	7	.750	9	7	.563	112	39	7	.731
George Seifert	8	98	30	0	.766	10	5	.667	108	35	0	.755
Buddy Parker	15	104	75	9	.577	3	2	.600	107	77	9	.578
Vince Lombardi	10	96	34	6	.728	9	1	.900	105	35	6	.740
Bill Walsh	10	92	59	1	.609	10	4	.714	102	63	1	.617

*Active NFL coaches in 1998.

(Ranked according to career NFL percentages)

	Yrs.	REGULAR SEASON				POSTSEASON			CAREER			
		Won	Lost	Tied	Pct.	Won	Lost	Pct.	Won	Lost	Tied	Pct.
George Seifert	8	98	30	0	.766	10	5	.667	108	35	0	.755
Steve Mariucci	2	25	7	0	.781	2	2	.500	27	9	0	.750
Mike Shanahan	6	55	29	0	.655	7	1	.875	62	30	0	.674
Mike Holmgren	7	75	37	0	.670	9	5	.643	84	42	0	.667
Bill Cowher	7	71	41	0	.634	5	6	.455	76	47	0	.618
Dennis Green	7	71	41	0	.634	2	6	.250	73	47	0	.608
Bill Parcells	14	130	92	1	.585	11	6	.647	141	98	1	.590
Chan Gailey	1	10	6	0	.625	0	1	.000	10	7	0	.588
Mike Ditka	13	118	82	0	.590	6	6	.500	124	88	0	.585
Dan Reeves	18	162	117	1	.580	10	8	.556	172	125	1	.579
Jimmy Johnson	8	71	57	0	.555	8	3	.727	79	60	0	.568
Jim Fassel	2	18	13	1	.578	0	1	.000	18	14	1	.561
Tom Coughlin	4	35	29	0	.547	3	3	.500	38	32	0	.543
Bobby Ross	7	61	51	0	.545	3	4	.429	64	55	0	.538
Jim Mora	12	96	87	0	.525	0	4	.000	96	91	0	.513
USFL Totals	3	41	12	1	.769	7	1	.875	48	13	1	.782
Pete Carroll	3	25	23	0	.521	1	2	.333	26	25	0	.510
Wade Phillips	4	27	25	0	.519	0	2	.000	27	27	0	.500
Tony Dungy	3	24	24	0	.500	1	1	.500	25	25	0	.500
Jon Gruden	1	8	8	0	.500	0	0	.000	8	8	0	.500
Dick Vermeil	9	63	70	0	.474	3	4	.429	66	74	0	.471
Jeff Fisher	5	32	38	0	.457	0	0	.000	32	38	0	.457
Ray Rhodes	4	29	34	1	.461	1	2	.333	30	36	1	.455
Vince Tobin	3	20	28	0	.417	1	1	.500	21	29	0	.420
Bruce Coslet	7	43	62	0	.410	0	1	.000	43	63	0	.406
Norv Turner	5	32	47	1	.406	0	0	.000	32	47	1	.406
Brian Billick	0	0	0	0	.000	0	0	.000	0	0	0	.000
Dick Jauron	0	0	0	0	.000	0	0	.000	0	0	0	.000
Chris Palmer	0	0	0	0	.000	0	0	.000	0	0	0	.000
Gunther Cunningham	0	0	0	0	.000	0	0	.000	0	0	0	.000
Andy Reid	0	0	0	0	.000	0	0	.000	0	0	0	.000
Mike Riley	0	0	0	0	.000	0	0	.000	0	0	0	.000

HALL OF FAME

ROSTER OF MEMBERS
FIVE NEW INDUCTEES IN 1999

Eric Dickerson, Tom Mack, Ozzie Newsome, Billy Shaw and Lawrence Taylor were inducted into Pro Football's Hall of Fame in 1999, expanding the list of former stars honored at Canton, Ohio, to 199.

Name	Elec. year	College	Pos.	NFL teams
Adderley, Herb	1980	Michigan State	CB	Green Bay Packers, 1961-69; Dallas Cowboys, 1970-72
Alworth, Lance†	1978	Arkansas	WR	San Diego Chargers, 1962-70; Dallas Cowboys, 1971-72.
Atkins, Doug	1982	Tennessee	DE	Cleveland Browns, 1953-54; Chicago Bears, 1955-66; New Orleans Saints, 1967-69
Badgro, Morris (Red)	1981	Southern California	E	New York Yankees, 1926; New York Giants, 1930-35
Barney, Lem	1992	Jackson State	CB	Detroit Lions, 1967-77
Battles, Cliff	1968	W. Virginia Wesleyan	HB/QB	Boston Braves, Boston Redskins, Washington Redskins, 1932-37; coach, Brooklyn Dodgers, 1946-47
Baugh, Sammy	1963	Texas Christian	QB	Washington Redskins, 1937-52; coach, New York Titans, 1960-61; Houston Oilers, 1964
Bednarik, Chuck	1967	Pennsylvania	C/LB	Philadelphia Eagles, 1949-62
Bell, Bert	1963	Pennsylvania	*	NFL Commissioner, 1946-59
Bell, Bobby	1983	Minnesota	LB	Kansas City Chiefs, 1963-74
Berry, Raymond†	1973	Southern Methodist	E	Baltimore Colts, 1955-67; coach, New England Patriots, 1984-89
Bidwill, Charles W.	1967	Loyola	*	Owner, Chicago Cardinals, 1933-47
Biletnikoff, Fred	1988	Florida State	WR	Oakland Raiders, 1965-78
Blanda, George†	1981	Kentucky	QB/PK	Chicago Bears, 1949-58; Baltimore Colts, 1950; Houston Oilers, 1960-66; Oakland Raiders, 1967-73
Blount, Mel†	1989	Southern	CB	Pittsburgh Steelers, 1970-83
Bradshaw, Terry†	1989	Louisiana Tech	QB	Pittsburgh Steelers, 1970-83
Brown, Jim†	1971	Syracuse	FB	Cleveland Browns, 1957-65
Brown, Paul	1967	Miami of Ohio	*	Coach, Cleveland Browns, 1946-62; Cincinnati Bengals, 1968-75
Brown, Roosevelt	1975	Morgan State	T	New York Giants, 1953-66
Brown, Willie†	1984	Grambling	DB	Denver Broncos, 1963-66; Oakland Raiders, 1967-78
Buchanan, Buck	1990	Grambling	DT	Kansas City Chiefs, 1963-75
Butkus, Dick†	1979	Illinois	LB	Chicago Bears, 1965-73
Campbell, Earl†	1991	Texas	RB	Houston Oilers, 1978-84; New Orleans Saints, 1984-85
Canadeo, Tony	1974	Gonzaga	HB	Green Bay Packers, 1941-44, 46-52
Carr, Joe	1963			NFL President, 1921-39
Chamberlin, Guy	1965	Nebraska	E/WB*	Player/coach, Canton Bulldogs, Cleveland, Frankford Yellowjackets, Chicago Bears, Chicago Cardinals, 1919-28
Christiansen, Jack	1970	Colorado A&M	DB	Detroit Lions, 1951-58; coach, San Francisco 49ers, 1963-67
Clark, Dutch	1963	Colorado College	QB	Portsmouth Spartans, Detroit Lions, 1931-38
Connor, George	1975	Notre Dame	T/LB	Chicago Bears, 1948-55
Conzelman, Jimmy	1964	Washington (Mo.)	HB*	Coach/executive, Decatur, Rock Island, Milwaukee, Detroit, Providence, Chicago Cardinals, 1920-48
Creekmur, Lou	1996	William & Mary	T/G	Detroit Lions, 1950-59
Csonka, Larry	1987	Syracuse	RB	Miami Dolphins, 1968-74, 79; New York Giants, 1976-78
Davis, Al	1992	Syracuse	*	Coach/general manager/president, Oakland-Los Angeles Raiders, 1963-present
Davis, Willie	1981	Grambling	DE	Cleveland Browns, 1958-59; Green Bay Packers, 1960-69
Dawson, Len	1987	Purdue	QB	Pittsburgh Steelers, 1957-58; Cleveland Browns, 1960-61; Dallas Texans, 1962; Kansas City Chiefs, 1963-75
Dickerson, Eric†	1999	Southern Methodist	RB	Los Angeles Rams, 1983-87; Indianapolis Colts, 1987-91; Los Angeles Raiders, 1992; Atlanta Falcons, 1993
Dierdorf, Dan	1996	Michigan	T/C	St. Louis Cardinals, 1971-83
Ditka, Mike	1988	Pittsburgh	TE	Chicago Bears, 1961-66; Philadelphia Eagles, 1967-68; Dallas Cowboys, 1969-72; coach, Chicago Bears, 1982-92; New Orleans Saints, 1997-present
Donovan, Art	1968	Boston College	DT	Baltimore Colts, New York Yanks, Dallas Texans, 1950-61
Dorsett, Tony	1994	Pittsburgh	RB	Dallas Cowboys, 1977-87; Denver Broncos, 1988
Driscoll, Paddy	1965	Northwestern	TB/HB/QB	Player/coach, Chicago Cardinals, Chicago Bears, 1919-31, 41-68
Dudley, Bill	1966	Virginia	HB	Pittsburgh Steelers, Detroit Lions, Washington Redskins, 1942-53
Edwards, Turk	1969	Washington State	T	Boston Braves, Boston Redskins, Washington Redskins, 1932-40
Ewbank, Weeb	1978	Miami of Ohio	*	Coach, Baltimore Colts, 1954-62; New York Jets, 1963-73
Fears, Tom	1970	Santa Clara	E	Los Angeles Rams, 1948-56; coach, New Orleans Saints, 1967-70
Finks, Jim	1995	Tulsa	QB*	Pittsburgh Steelers, 1949-55; administrator, Minnesota Vikings, 1964-73; Chicago Bears, 1974-86; New Orleans Saints, 1987-93

Name	Elec. year	College	Pos.	NFL teams
Flaherty, Ray	1976	Gonzaga	E*	Player/coach, Los Angeles Wildcats, New York Yankees, AFL; New York Giants, Boston Redskins, Washington Redskins, New York Yankees, AAFC; Chicago Hornets, 1926-49
Ford, Len	1976	Michigan	E	Los Angeles Dons, Cleveland Browns, 1948-58
Fortmann, Danny	1965	Colgate	G	Chicago Bears, 1936-43
Fouts, Dan†	1993	Oregon	QB	San Diego Chargers, 1973-87
Gatski, Frank	1985	Marshall	C	Cleveland Browns, 1946-56; Detroit Lions, 1957
George, Bill	1974	Wake Forest	LB	Chicago Bears, Los Angeles Rams, 1952-66
Gibbs, Joe	1996	San Diego State	*	Washington Redskins, 1981-92
Gifford, Frank	1977	Southern California	HB/E	New York Giants, 1952-60, 62-64
Gillman, Sid	1983	Ohio State	E*	Cleveland Rams, 1936; coach, Los Angeles Rams, 1955-59; Los Angeles Chargers, 1960; San Diego Chargers, 1961-69, 71; Houston Oilers, 1973-74
Graham, Otto	1965	Northwestern	QB	Cleveland Browns, 1946-55; coach, Washington Redskins, 1966-68
Grange, Red	1963	Illinois	HB	Chicago Bears, 1925, 29-34; New York Yankees, 1926-27
Grant, Bud	1994	Minnesota	WR*	Philadelphia Eagles, 1951-52; coach, Minnesota Vikings, 1967-83, 1985
Greene, Joe†	1987	North Texas State	DT	Pittsburgh Steelers, 1969-81
Gregg, Forrest†	1977	Southern Methodist	T	Green Bay Packers, Dallas Cowboys, 1956, 58-71; coach, Cleveland Browns, 1975-77; Cincinnati Bengals, 1980-83; Green Bay Packers, 1984-87
Griese, Bob	1990	Purdue	QB	Miami Dolphins, 1967-80
Groza, Lou	1974	Ohio State	T/PK	Cleveland Browns, 1946-59, 61-67
Guyon, Joe	1966	Carlisle, Georgia Tech	HB	Canton Bulldogs, Cleveland Indians, Oorang Indians, Rock Island Independents, Kansas City Cowboys, New York Giants, 1918-27
Halas, George	1963	Illinois	E*	Player/coach/ founder, Chicago Bears, 1920-83
Ham, Jack†	1988	Penn State	LB	Pittsburgh Steelers, 1971-82
Hannah, John†	1991	Alabama	G	New England Patriots, 1973-85
Harris, Franco†	1990	Penn State	RB	Pittsburgh Steelers, 1972-83; Seattle Seahawks, 1984
Haynes, Mike	1997	Arizona State	CB	New England Patriots, 1976-82; Los Angeles Raiders, 1983-89
Healey, Ed	1964	Dartmouth	T	Rock Island, Chicago Bears, 1920-27
Hein, Mel	1963	Washington State	C	New York Giants, 1931-45
Hendricks, Ted	1990	Miami, Fla.	LB	Baltimore Colts, 1969-73; Green Bay Packers, 1974; Oakland/Los Angeles Raiders, 1975-83
Henry, Wilbur	1963	Wash'ton & Jefferson	T	Canton Bulldogs, Akron Indians, New York Giants, Pottsville Maroons, Pittsburgh Steelers, 1920-30
Herber, Arnie	1966	Regis	HB	Green Bay Packers, New York Giants, 1930-45
Hewitt, Bill	1971	Michigan	E	Chicago Bears, 1932-36; Philadelphia Eagles, 1937-39; Philadelphia/Pittsburgh, 1943
Hinkle, Clarke	1964	Bucknell	FB	Green Bay Packers, 1932-41
Hirsch, Elroy (Crazylegs)	1968	Wisconsin	E/HB	Chicago Rockets, Los Angeles Rams, 1946-57
Hornung, Paul	1986	Notre Dame	RB	Green Bay Packers, 1957-62, 64-66
Houston, Ken†	1986	Prairie View	DB	Houston Oilers, 1967-72; Washington Redskins, 1973-80
Hubbard, Cal	1963	Centenary, Geneva	T/E	New York Giants, Green Bay Packers, Pittsburgh Steelers, 1927-36
Huff, Sam	1982	West Virginia	LB	New York Giants, 1956-63; Washington Redskins, 1964-67, 69
Hunt, Lamar	1972	Southern Methodist	*	Founder, American Football League, 1959; president, Dallas Texans, 1960-62; Kansas City Chiefs, 1963-present
Hutson, Don	1963	Alabama	E	Green Bay Packers, 1935-45
Johnson, Jimmy	1994	UCLA	DB	San Francisco 49ers, 1961-76
Johnson, John Henry	1987	Arizona State	FB	San Francisco 49ers, 1954-56; Detroit Lions, 1957-59; Pittsburgh Steelers, 1960-65; Houston Oilers, 1966
Joiner, Charlie	1996	Grambling	WR	Houston Oilers, 1969-72; Cincinnati Bengals, 1972-75; San Diego Chargers, 1976-86
Jones, Deacon†	1980	South Carolina State	DE	Los Angeles Rams, 1961-71; San Diego Chargers, 1972-73; Washington Redskins, 1974
Jones, Stan	1991	Maryland	G/DT	Chicago Bears, 1954-65; Washington Redskins, 1966
Jordan, Henry	1995	Virginia	DT	Cleveland Browns, 1957-58; Green Bay Packers, 1959-69
Jurgensen, Sonny	1983	Duke	QB	Philadelphia Eagles, 1957-63; Washington Redskins, 1964-74
Kelly, Leroy	1994	Morgan State	RB	Cleveland Browns, 1964-73
Kiesling, Walter	1966	St. Thomas	G/T*	Player/coach, Duluth Eskimos, Pottsville Maroons, Boston Braves, Chicago Cardinals, Chicago Bears, Green Bay Packers, Pittsburgh Steelers, 1926-56
Kinard, Frank (Bruiser)	1971	Mississippi	T	Brooklyn Dodgers, 1938-45; New York Yankees, 1946-47
Krause, Paul	1998	Iowa	S	Washington Redskins, 1964-67; Minnesota Vikings, 1968-79
Lambeau, Curly	1963	Notre Dame	TB/FB/E*	Founder/player/coach, Green Bay Packers, 1919-49
Lambert, Jack†	1990	Kent State	LB	Pittsburgh Steelers, 1974-84
Landry, Tom†	1990	Texas	*	Coach, Dallas Cowboys, 1960-88
Lane, Dick (Night Train)	1974	Scottsbluff J.C.	DB	Los Angeles Rams, Chicago Cardinals, Detroit Lions, 1952-65
Langer, Jim†	1987	South Dakota State	C	Miami Dolphins, 1970-79; Minnesota Vikings, 1980-81

Name	Elec. year	College	Pos.	NFL teams
Lanier, Willie	1986	Morgan State	LB	Kansas City Chiefs, 1967-77
Largent, Steve†	1995	Tulsa	WR	Seattle Seahawks, 1976-89
Lary, Yale	1979	Texas A&M	DB	Detroit Lions, 1952-53, 56-64
Lavelli, Dante	1975	Ohio State	E	Cleveland Browns, 1946-56
Layne, Bobby	1967	Texas	QB	Chicago Bears, New York Bulldogs, Detroit Lions, Pittsburgh Steelers, 1948-62
Leemans, Tuffy	1978	George Washington	FB	New York Giants, 1936-43
Lilly, Bob†	1980	Texas Christian	DT	Dallas Cowboys, 1961-74
Little, Larry	1993	Bethune Cookman	G	San Diego Chargers, 1967-68; Miami Dolphins, 1969-80
Lombardi, Vince	1971	Fordham	*	Coach, Green Bay Packers, 1959-67; Washington Redskins, 1969
Luckman, Sid	1965	Columbia	QB	Chicago Bears, 1939-50
Lyman, Roy (Link)	1964		T	Canton Bulldogs, Cleveland, Chicago Bears, 1922-34
Mack, Tom	1999	Michigan	G	Los Angeles Rams, 1966-78
Mackey, John	1992	Syracuse	TE	Baltimore Colts, 1963-71; San Diego Chargers, 1972
Mara, Tim	1963		*	Founder, New York Giants, 1925-65
Mara, Wellington	1997	Fordham	*	President, New York Giants, 1965-present
Marchetti, Gino†	1972	San Francisco	DE	Dallas Texans, 1952; Baltimore Colts, 1953-66
Marshall, George Preston	1963		*	Founder, Washington Redskins, 1932-65
Matson, Ollie†	1972	San Francisco	HB	Chicago Cardinals, 1952, 54-58; Los Angeles Rams, 1959-62; Detroit Lions, 1963; Philadelphia Eagles, 1964-66
Maynard, Don	1987	Texas Western College	WR	New York Giants, 1958; New York Jets, 1960-72; St. Louis Cardinals, 1973
McAfee, George	1966	Duke	HB	Chicago Bears, 1940-41, 45-50
McCormack, Mike	1984	Kansas	T	New York Yanks, 1951; Cleveland Browns, 1954-62
McDonald, Tommy	1998	Oklahoma	WR	Philadelphia Eagles,1957-63; Dallas Cowboys, 1964; Los Angeles Rams, 1965-66; Atlanta Falcons, 1967; Cleveland Browns,1968
McElhenny, Hugh†	1970	Washington	HB	San Francisco 49ers, Minnesota Vikings, New York Giants, Detroit Lions, 1952-64
McNally, Johnny Blood	1963	St. John's	HB	Milwaukee Badgers, Duluth Eskimos, Pottsville Maroons, Green Bay Packers, Pittsburgh Steelers, 1925-39
Michalske, August (Mike)	1964	Penn State	G	New York Yankees, Green Bay Packers, 1927-37
Millner, Wayne	1968	Notre Dame	E	Boston Redskins, Washington Redskins, 1936-41, 45
Mitchell, Bobby	1983	Illinois	RB/FL/WR	Cleveland Browns, 1958-61; Washington Redskins, 1962-68
Mix, Ron	1979	Southern California	T	Los Angeles Chargers, 1960; San Diego Chargers, 1961-69; Oakland Raiders, 1971
Moore, Lenny	1975	Penn State	HB	Baltimore Colts, 1956-67
Motley, Marion	1968	Nevada	FB/LB	Cleveland Browns, Pittsburgh Steelers, 1946-55
Munoz, Anthony†	1998	Southern California	OT	Cincinnati Bengals, 1980-92
Musso, George	1982	Milliken	G/DT	Chicago Bears, 1933-44
Nagurski, Bronko	1963	Minnesota	FB/T	Chicago Bears, 1930-37, 43
Namath, Joe	1985	Alabama	QB	New York Jets, 1965-76; Los Angeles Rams, 1977
Neale, Earle (Greasy)	1969	W. Virginia Wesleyan	*	Coach, Philadelphia Eagles, 1941-50
Nevers, Ernie	1963	Stanford	FB	Duluth Eskimos, Chicago Cardinals, 1926-37
Newsome, Ozzie	1999	Alabama	TE	Cleveland Browns, 1978-90
Nitschke, Ray†	1978	Illinois	LB	Green Bay Packers, 1958-72
Noll, Chuck†	1993	Dayton	*	Coach, Pittsburgh Steelers, 1969-91
Nomellini, Leo†	1969	Minnesota	DT	San Francisco 49ers, 1953-63
Olsen, Merlin†	1982	Utah State	DT	Los Angeles Rams, 1962-76
Otto, Jim†	1980	Miami, Fla.	C	Oakkland Raiders, 1960-74
Owen, Steve	1966	Phillips	T/G	Player/coach, Kansas City Cowboys, New York Giants, 1924-53
Page, Alan	1988	Notre Dame	DT	Minnesota Vikings, 1967-78; Chicago Bears, 1978-81
Parker, Clarence (Ace)	1972	Duke	HB	Brooklyn Dodgers, 1937-41; Boston Yanks, 1945; New York Yankees, 1946
Parker, Jim†	1973	Ohio State	G	Baltimore Colts, 1957-67
Payton, Walter†	1993	Jackson State	RB	Chicago Bears, 1975-87
Perry, Joe†	1969	Compton J.C.	FB	San Francisco 49ers, Baltimore Colts, 1948-63
Pihos, Pete	1970	Indiana	E	Philadelphia Eagles, 1947-55
Ray, Hugh (Shorty)	1966	Illinois	*	NFL technical adviser and supervisor of officials, 1938-56
Reeves, Daniel F.	1967	Georgetown	*	Founder, Los Angeles Rams, 1941-71
Renfro, Mel	1996	Oregon	DB	Dallas Cowboys, 1964-77
Riggins, John	1992	Kansas	FB	New York Jets, 1971-75; Washington Redskins, 1976-85
Ringo, Jim	1981	Syracuse	C	Green Bay Packers, 1953-63; Philadelphia Eagles, 1964-67
Robustelli, Andy	1971	Arnold	DE	Los Angeles Rams, 1951-55; New York Giants, 1956-64
Rooney, Arthur J.	1964	Georgetown	*	Founder, Pittsburgh Steelers, 1933-82
Rozelle, Pete	1985	San Francisco	*	NFL Commissioner, 1960-89
St. Clair, Bob	1990	Tulsa	T	San Francisco 49ers, 1953-63
Sayers, Gale†	1977	Kansas	RB	Chicago Bears, 1965-71
Schmidt, Joe	1973	Pittsburgh	LB	Detroit Lions, 1953-65; coach, Detroit Lions, 1967-72
Schramm, Tex	1991	Texas	*	President/general manager, Dallas Cowboys, 1960-88
Selmon, Lee Roy	1995	Oklahoma	DE	Tampa Bay Buccaneers, 1976-84

Name	Elec. year	College	Pos.	NFL teams
Shaw, Billy	1999	Georgia Tech	G	Buffalo Bills, 1961-69
Shell, Art	1989	Md.-Eastern Shore	T	Oakland-Los Angeles Raiders, 1968-82; coach, Los Angeles Raiders, 1989-94
Shula, Don†	1997	John Carroll	DB	Cleveland Browns, 1951-52; Baltimore Colts, 1953-56; Washington Redskins, 1957; coach, Baltimore Colts, 1963-69, Miami Dolphins, 1970-95
Simpson, O.J.†	1985	Southern California	RB	Buffalo Bills, 1969-77; San Francisco 49ers, 1978
Singletary, Mike†	1998	Baylor	LB	Chicago Bears, 1981-92
Smith, Jackie	1994	N'western Louisiana	TE	St. Louis Cardinals, 1963-77; Dallas Cowboys, 1978
Starr, Bart†	1977	Alabama	QB	Green Bay Packers, 1956-71; coach, Green Bay Packers, 1975-83
Staubach, Roger†	1985	Navy	QB	Dallas Cowboys, 1969-79
Stautner, Ernie†	1969	West Virginia	DT	Pittsburgh Steelers, 1950-63
Stenerud, Jan†	1991	Montana State	PK	Kansas City Chiefs, 1967-79; Green Bay Packers, 1980-83; Minnesota Vikings, 1984-85
Stephenson, Dwight	1998	Alabama	C	Miami Dolphins, 1980-87
Strong, Ken	1967	New York U.	HB/PK	Staten Island Stapletons, New York Yankees, New York Giants, 1929-39, 44-47
Stydahar, Joe	1967	West Virginia	T	Chicago Bears, 1936-42, 45-46
Tarkenton, Fran	1986	Georgia	QB	Minnesota Vikings, 1961-66, 72-78; New York Giants, 1967-71
Taylor, Charley	1984	Arizona State	WR	Washington Redskins, 1964-75, 77
Taylor, Lawrence†	1999	North Carolina	LB	New York Giants, 1981-93
Taylor, Jim	1976	Louisiana State	FB	Green Bay Packers, 1958-66; New Orleans Saints, 1967
Thorpe, Jim	1963	Carlisle	HB	Canton Bulldogs, Oorang Indians, Cleveland Indians, Toledo Maroons, Rock Island Independents, New York Giants, 1915-26, 29
Tittle, Y.A.	1971	Louisiana State	QB	Baltimore Colts, 1948-50; San Francisco 49ers, 1951-60; New York Giants, 1961-64
Trafton, George	1964	Notre Dame	C	Chicago Bears, 1920-32
Trippi, Charlie	1968	Georgia	HB	Chicago Cardinals, 1947-55
Tunnell, Emlen	1967	Iowa	DB	New York Giants, Green Bay Packers, 1948-61
Turner, Clyde (Bulldog)	1966	Hardin-Simmons	C/LB	Chicago Bears, 1940-52; coach, New York Titans, 1962
Unitas, John†	1979	Louisville	QB	Baltimore Colts, 1956-72; San Diego Chargers, 1973
Upshaw, Gene†	1987	Texas A&I	G	Oakland Raiders, 1967-81
Van Brocklin, Norm	1971	Oregon	QB	Los Angeles Rams, 1949-57; Philadelphia Eagles, 1958-60; coach, Minnesota Vikings, 1961-66; Atlanta Falcons, 1968-74
Van Buren, Steve	1965	Louisiana State	HB	Philadelphia Eagles, 1944-51
Walker, Doak	1986	Southern Methodist	RB	Detroit Lions, 1950-55
Walsh, Bill	1993	San Jose State	*	Coach, San Francisco 49ers, 1979-88
Warfield, Paul†	1983	Ohio State	WR	Cleveland Browns, 1964-69, 76-77; Miami Dolphins, 1970-74
Waterfield, Bob	1965	UCLA	QB	Cleveland Rams, Los Angeles Rams, 1945-52; coach, Los Angeles Rams, 1960-62
Webster, Mike	1997	Wisconsin	C-G	Pittsburgh Steelers, 1974-88; Kansas City Chiefs, 1989-90
Weinmeister, Arnie	1984	Washington	T	New York Yankees, 1948-49; New York Giants, 1950-53
White, Randy	1994	Maryland	DT	Dallas Cowboys, 1975-88
Willis, Bill	1977	Ohio State	G	Cleveland Browns, 1946-53
Wilson, Larry†	1978	Utah	DB	St. Louis Cardinals, 1960-72
Winslow, Kellen	1995	Missouri	TE	San Diego Chargers, 1979-87
Wojciechowicz, Alex	1968	Fordham	C/LB	Detroit Lions, Philadelphia Eagles, 1938-50
Wood, Willie	1989	Southern California	S	Green Bay Packers, 1960-71

*Hall of Fame member was selected for contributions other than as a player.
†Elected his first year of eligibility.
Abbreviations of positions: C—Center, CB—Cornerback, DB—Defensive back, DE—Defensive end, DT—Defensive tackle, E—End, FB—Fullback, FL—Flanker, G—Guard, HB—Halfback, LB—Linebacker, PK—Placekicker, QB—Quarterback, RB—Running back, S—Safety, T—Tackle, TB—Tailback, TE—Tight end.

THE SPORTING NEWS AWARDS

PLAYER OF THE YEAR

1954—Lou Groza, OT/K, Cleveland
1955—Otto Graham, QB, Cleveland
1956—Frank Gifford, HB, N.Y. Giants
1957—Jim Brown, RB, Cleveland
1958—Jim Brown, RB, Cleveland
1959—Johnny Unitas, QB, Baltimore
1960—Norm Van Brocklin, QB, Philadelphia
1961—Paul Hornung, HB, Green Bay
1962—Y.A. Tittle, QB, N.Y. Giants
1963—Y.A. Tittle, QB, N.Y. Giants
1964—Johnny Unitas, QB, Baltimore
1965—Jim Brown, RB, Cleveland
1966—Bart Starr, QB, Green Bay
1967—Johnny Unitas, QB, Baltimore
1968—Earl Morrall, QB, Baltimore
1969—Roman Gabriel, QB, L.A. Rams
1970—NFC: John Brodie, QB, San Francisco
      AFC: George Blanda, QB/PK, Oakland
1971—NFC: Roger Staubach, QB, Dallas
      AFC: Bob Griese, QB, Miami
1972—NFC: Larry Brown, RB, Washington
      AFC: Earl Morrall, QB, Miami
1973—NFC: John Hadl, QB, L.A. Rams
      AFC: O.J. Simpson, RB, Buffalo
1974—NFC: Chuck Foreman, RB, Minnesota
      AFC: Ken Stabler, QB, Oakland
1975—NFC: Fran Tarkenton, QB, Minnesota
      AFC: O.J. Simpson, RB, Buffalo
1976—NFC: Walter Payton, RB, Chicago
      AFC: Ken Stabler, QB, Oakland

1977—NFC: Walter Payton, RB, Chicago
      AFC: Craig Morton, QB, Denver
1978—NFC: Archie Manning, QB, New Orleans
      AFC: Earl Campbell, RB, Houston
1979—NFC: Ottis Anderson, RB, St. Louis
      AFC: Dan Fouts, QB, San Diego
1980—Brian Sipe, QB, Cleveland
1981—Ken Anderson, QB, Cincinnati
1982—Mark Moseley, PK, Washington
1983—Eric Dickerson, RB, L.A. Rams
1984—Dan Marino, QB, Miami
1985—Marcus Allen, RB, L.A. Raiders
1986—Lawrence Taylor, LB, N.Y. Giants
1987—Jerry Rice, WR, San Francisco
1988—Boomer Esiason, QB, Cincinnati
1989—Joe Montana, QB, San Francisco
1990—Jerry Rice, WR, San Francisco
1991—Thurman Thomas, RB, Buffalo
1992—Steve Young, QB, San Francisco
1993—Emmitt Smith, RB, Dallas
1994—Steve Young, QB, San Francisco
1995—Brett Favre, QB, Green Bay
1996—Brett Favre, QB, Green Bay
1997—Barry Sanders, RB, Detroit
1998—Terrell Davis, RB, Denver
    NOTE: From 1970-79, a player was selected as Player of the Year for both the NFC and AFC. In 1980 The Sporting News reinstated the selection of one player as Player of the Year for the entire NFL.

ROOKIE OF THE YEAR

1955—Alan Ameche, FB, Baltimore
1956—J.C. Caroline, HB, Chicago
1957—Jim Brown, FB, Cleveland
1958—Bobby Mitchell, HB, Cleveland
1959—Nick Pietrosante, FB, Detroit
1960—Gail Cogdill, E, Detroit
1961—Mike Ditka, E, Chicago
1962—Ronnie Bull, HB, Chicago
1963—Paul Flatley, WR, Minnesota
1964—Charley Taylor, HB, Washington
1965—Gale Sayers, RB, Chicago
1966—Tommy Nobis, LB, Atlanta
1967—Mel Farr, RB, Detroit
1968—Earl McCullouch, WR, Detroit
1969—Calvin Hill, RB, Dallas
1970—NFC: Bruce Taylor, CB, San Francisco
      AFC: Dennis Shaw, QB, Buffalo
1971—NFC: John Brockington, RB, Green Bay
      AFC: Jim Plunkett, QB, New England
1972—NFC: Chester Marcol, PK, Green Bay
      AFC: Franco Harris, RB, Pittsburgh
1973—NFC: Chuck Foreman, RB, Minnesota
      AFC: Boobie Clark, RB, Cincinnati
1974—NFC: Wilbur Jackson, RB, San Francisco
      AFC: Don Woods, RB, San Diego
1975—NFC: Steve Bartkowski, QB, Atlanta
      AFC: Robert Brazile, LB, Houston
1976—NFC: Sammy White, WR, Minnesota
      AFC: Mike Haynes, CB, New England

1977—NFC: Tony Dorsett, RB, Dallas
      AFC: A.J. Duhe, DT, Miami
1978—NFC: Al Baker, DE, Detroit
      AFC: Earl Campbell, RB, Houston
1979—NFC: Ottis Anderson, RB, St. Louis
      AFC: Jerry Butler, WR, Buffalo
1980—Billy Sims, RB, Detroit
1981—George Rogers, RB, New Orleans
1982—Marcus Allen, RB, L.A. Raiders
1983—Dan Marino, QB, Miami
1984—Louis Lipps, WR, Pittsburgh
1985—Eddie Brown, WR, Cincinnati
1986—Rueben Mayes, RB, New Orleans
1987—Robert Awalt, TE, St. Louis
1988—Keith Jackson, TE, Philadelphia
1989—Barry Sanders, RB, Detroit
1990—Richmond Webb, T, Miami
1991—Mike Croel, LB, Denver
1992—Santana Dotson, DL, Tampa Bay
1993—Jerome Bettis, RB, L.A. Rams
1994—Marshall Faulk, RB, Indianapolis
1995—Curtis Martin, RB, New England
1996—Eddie George, RB, Houston
1997—Warrick Dunn, RB, Tampa Bay
1998—Randy Moss, WR, Minnesota
    NOTE: In 1980, The Sporting News began selecting one rookie as Rookie of the Year for the entire NFL.

NFL COACH OF THE YEAR

1947—Jimmy Conzelman, Chi. Cardinals
1948—Earle (Greasy) Neale, Philadelphia
1949—Paul Brown, Cleveland (AAFC)
1950—Steve Owen, N.Y. Giants

1951—Paul Brown, Cleveland
1952—J. Hampton Pool, L.A. Rams
1953—Paul Brown, Cleveland
1954—None

1955—Joe Kuharich, Washington
1956—Jim Lee Howell, N.Y. Giants
1957—None
1958—None
1959—None
1960—None
1961—Vince Lombardi, Green Bay
1962—None
1963—George Halas, Chicago
1964—Don Shula, Baltimore
1965—George Halas, Chicago
1966—Tom Landry, Dallas
1967—George Allen, L.A. Rams
1968—Don Shula, Baltimore
1969—Bud Grant, Minnesota
1970—Don Shula, Miami
1971—George Allen, Washington
1972—Don Shula, Miami
1973—Chuck Knox, L.A. Rams
1974—Don Coryell, St. Louis
1975—Ted Marchibroda, Baltimore
1976—Chuck Fairbanks, New England

1977—Red Miller, Denver
1978—Jack Patera, Seattle
1979—Dick Vermeil, Philadelphia
1980—Chuck Knox, Buffalo
1981—Bill Walsh, San Francisco
1982—Joe Gibbs, Washington
1983—Joe Gibbs, Washington
1984—Chuck Knox, Seattle
1985—Mike Ditka, Chicago
1986—Bill Parcells, N.Y. Giants
1987—Jim Mora, New Orleans
1988—Marv Levy, Buffalo
1989—Lindy Infante, Green Bay
1990—George Seifert, San Francisco
1991—Joe Gibbs, Washington
1992—Bill Cowher, Pittsburgh
1993—Dan Reeves, N.Y. Giants
1994—George Seifert, San Francisco
1995—Ray Rhodes, Philadelphia
1996—Dom Capers, Carolina
1997—Jim Fassel, N.Y. Giants
1998—Dan Reeves, Atlanta

NFL EXECUTIVE OF THE YEAR

1955—Dan Reeves, L.A. Rams
1956—George Halas, Chicago
1972—Dan Rooney, Pittsburgh
1973—Jim Finks, Minnesota
1974—Art Rooney, Pittsburgh
1975—Joe Thomas, Baltimore
1976—Al Davis, Oakland
1977—Tex Schramm, Dallas
1978—John Thompson, Seattle
1979—John Sanders, San Diego
1980—Eddie LeBaron, Atlanta
1981—Paul Brown, Cincinnati
1982—Bobby Beathard, Washington
1983—Bobby Beathard, Washington
1984—George Young, N.Y. Giants
1985—Mike McCaskey, Chicago

1986—George Young, N.Y. Giants
1987—Jim Finks, New Orleans
1988—Bill Polian, Buffalo
1989—John McVay, San Francisco
1990—George Young, N.Y. Giants
1991—Bill Polian, Buffalo
1992—Ron Wolf, Green Bay
1993—George Young, N.Y. Giants
1994—Carmen Policy, San Francisco
1995—Bill Polian, Carolina
1996—Bill Polian, Carolina
1997—George Young, N.Y. Giants
1998—Jeff Diamond, Minnesota
NOTE: The Executive of the Year Award was not given from 1957-71.

1998 NFL ALL-PRO TEAM

OFFENSE

WR—Antonio Freeman, Green Bay
    Randy Moss, Minnesota
TE—Shannon Sharpe, Denver
T—Larry Allen, Dallas
    Tony Boselli, Jacksonville
C—Dermontti Dawson, Pittsburgh
G—Bruce Matthews, Tennessee
    Randall McDaniel, Minnesota
QB—Steve Young, San Francisco
RB—Jamal Anderson, Atlanta
    Terrell Davis, Denver

DEFENSE

DE—Michael McCrary, Baltimore
    Reggie White, Green Bay
DT—John Randle, Minnesota
    Bryant Young, San Francisco
LB—Chad Brown, Seattle
    Ray Lewis, Baltimore
    Junior Seau, San Diego
CB—Ty Law, New England
    Deion Sanders, Dallas
S—LeRoy Butler, Green Bay
    Robert Griffith, Minnesota
    Rodney Harrison, San Diego
    Darren Woodson, Dallas

SPECIALISTS

PR—Jermaine Lewis, Baltimore
KR—Terry Fair, Detroit
K—Gary Anderson, Minnesota
P—Craig Hentrich, Tennessee

TEAM BY TEAM

ARIZONA CARDINALS
YEAR-BY-YEAR RECORDS

HISTORY *Team by team*

	REGULAR SEASON							PLAYOFFS			
Year	W	L	T	Pct.	PF	PA	Finish	W	L	Highest round	Coach
1920*	6	2	2	.750	...	...	T4th				Paddy Driscoll
1921*	3	3	2	.500	...	...	T8th				Paddy Driscoll
1922*	8	3	0	.727	...	...	3rd				Paddy Driscoll
1923*	8	4	0	.667	...	...	6th				Arnold Horween
1924*	5	4	1	.556	...	...	8th				Arnold Horween
1925*	11	2	1	.846	...	...	1st				Norman Barry
1926*	5	6	1	.455	...	...	10th				Norman Barry
1927*	3	7	1	.300	...	...	9th				Guy Chamberlin
1928*	1	5	0	.167	...	...	9th				Fred Gillies
1929*	6	6	1	.500	...	...	T4th				Dewey Scanlon
1930*	5	6	2	.455	...	...	T7th				Ernie Nevers
1931*	5	4	0	.556	...	...	4th				LeRoy Andrews, E. Nevers
1932*	2	6	2	.250	...	...	7th				Jack Chevigny
1933*	1	9	1	.100	52	101	5th/Western Div.	—	—		Paul Schissler
1934*	5	6	0	.455	80	84	4th/Western Div.	—	—		Paul Schissler
1935*	6	4	2	.600	99	97	T3rd/Western Div.	—	—		Milan Creighton
1936*	3	8	1	.273	74	143	4th/Western Div.	—	—		Milan Creighton
1937*	5	5	1	.500	135	165	4th/Western Div.	—	—		Milan Creighton
1938*	2	9	0	.182	111	168	5th/Western Div.	—	—		Milan Creighton
1939*	1	10	0	.091	84	254	5th/Western Div.	—	—		Ernie Nevers
1940*	2	7	2	.222	139	222	5th/Western Div.	—	—		Jimmy Conzelman
1941*	3	7	1	.300	127	197	4th/Western Div.	—	—		Jimmy Conzelman
1942*	3	8	0	.273	98	209	4th/Western Div.	—	—		Jimmy Conzelman
1943*	0	10	0	.000	95	238	4th/Western Div.	—	—		Phil Handler
1944†	0	10	0	.000	108	328	5th/Western Div.	—	—		P. Handler-Walt Kiesling
1945*	1	9	0	.100	98	228	5th/Western Div.	—	—		Phil Handler
1946*	6	5	0	.545	260	198	T3rd/Western Div.	—	—		Jimmy Conzelman
1947*	9	3	0	.750	306	231	1st/Western Div.	1	0	NFL champ	Jimmy Conzelman
1948*	11	1	0	.917	395	226	1st/Western Div.	0	1	NFL championship game	Jimmy Conzelman
1949*	6	5	1	.545	360	301	3rd/Western Div.	—	—		P. Handler-Buddy Parker
1950*	5	7	0	.417	233	287	5th/American Conf.	—	—		Curly Lambeau
1951*	3	9	0	.250	210	287	6th/American Conf.	—	—		Curly Lambeau, P. Handler-Cecil Isbell
1952*	4	8	0	.333	172	221	T5th/American Conf.	—	—		Joe Kuharich
1953*	1	10	1	.091	190	337	6th/Eastern Conf.	—	—		Joe Stydahar
1954*	2	10	0	.167	183	347	6th/Eastern Conf.	—	—		Joe Stydahar
1955*	4	7	1	.364	224	252	T4th/Eastern Conf.	—	—		Ray Richards
1956*	7	5	0	.583	240	182	2nd/Eastern Conf.	—	—		Ray Richards
1957*	3	9	0	.250	200	299	6th/Eastern Conf.	—	—		Ray Richards
1958*	2	9	1	.182	261	356	T5th/Eastern Conf.	—	—		Pop Ivy
1959*	2	10	0	.167	234	324	6th/Eastern Conf.	—	—		Pop Ivy
1960‡	6	5	1	.545	288	230	4th/Eastern Conf.	—	—		Pop Ivy
1961‡	7	7	0	.500	279	267	4th/Eastern Conf.	—	—		Pop Ivy
1962‡	4	9	1	.308	287	361	6th/Eastern Conf.	—	—		Wally Lemm
1963‡	9	5	0	.643	341	283	3rd/Eastern Conf.	—	—		Wally Lemm
1964‡	9	3	2	.750	357	331	2nd/Eastern Conf.	—	—		Wally Lemm
1965‡	5	9	0	.357	296	309	T5th/Eastern Conf.	—	—		Wally Lemm
1966‡	8	5	1	.615	264	265	4th/Eastern Conf.	—	—		Charley Winner
1967‡	6	7	1	.462	333	356	3rd/Century Div.	—	—		Charley Winner
1968‡	9	4	1	.692	325	289	2nd/Century Div.	—	—		Charley Winner
1969‡	4	9	1	.308	314	389	3rd/Century Div.	—	—		Charley Winner
1970‡	8	5	1	.615	325	228	3rd/NFC Eastern Div.	—	—		Charley Winner
1971‡	4	9	1	.308	231	279	4th/NFC Eastern Div.	—	—		Bob Hollway
1972‡	4	9	1	.308	193	303	4th/NFC Eastern Div.	—	—		Bob Hollway
1973‡	4	9	1	.308	286	365	4th/NFC Eastern Div.	—	—		Don Coryell
1974‡	10	4	0	.714	285	218	1st/NFC Eastern Div.	0	1	NFC div. playoff game	Don Coryell
1975‡	11	3	0	.786	356	276	1st/NFC Eastern Div.	0	1	NFC div. playoff game	Don Coryell
1976‡	10	4	0	.714	309	267	3rd/NFC Eastern Div.	—	—		Don Coryell
1977‡	7	7	0	.500	272	287	3rd/NFC Eastern Div.	—	—		Don Coryell
1978‡	6	10	0	.375	248	296	T4th/NFC Eastern Div.	—	—		Bud Wilkinson
1979‡	5	11	0	.313	307	358	5th/NFC Eastern Div.	—	—		B. Wilkinson, Larry Wilson
1980‡	5	11	0	.313	299	350	4th/NFC Eastern Div.	—	—		Jim Hanifan
1981‡	7	9	0	.438	315	408	5th/NFC Eastern Div.	—	—		Jim Hanifan
1982‡	5	4	0	.556	135	170	T4th/NFC	0	1	NFC first-round pl. game	Jim Hanifan

				REGULAR SEASON					PLAYOFFS		
Year	W	L	T	Pct.	PF	PA	Finish	W	L	Highest round	Coach
1983‡	8	7	1	.531	374	428	3rd/NFC Eastern Div.	—	—		Jim Hanifan
1984‡	9	7	0	.563	423	345	T3rd/NFC Eastern Div.	—	—		Jim Hanifan
1985‡	5	11	0	.313	278	414	5th/NFC Eastern Div.	—	—		Jim Hanifan
1986‡	4	11	1	.281	218	351	5th/NFC Eastern Div.	—	—		Gene Stallings
1987‡	7	8	0	.467	362	368	T2nd/NFC Eastern Div.	—	—		Gene Stallings
1988§	7	9	0	.438	344	398	T3rd/NFC Eastern Div.	—	—		Gene Stallings
1989§	5	11	0	.313	258	377	4th/NFC Eastern Div.	—	—		G. Stallings, Hank Kuhlmann
1990§	5	11	0	.313	268	396	5th/NFC Eastern Div.	—	—		Joe Bugel
1991§	4	12	0	.250	196	344	5th/NFC Eastern Div.	—	—		Joe Bugel
1992§	4	12	0	.250	243	332	5th/NFC Eastern Div.	—	—		Joe Bugel
1993§	7	9	0	.438	326	269	4th/NFC Eastern Div.	—	—		Joe Bugel
1994	8	8	0	.500	235	267	3rd/NFC Eastern Div.	—	—		Buddy Ryan
1995	4	12	0	.250	275	422	5th/NFC Eastern Div.	—	—		Buddy Ryan
1996	7	9	0	.438	300	397	4th/NFC Eastern Div.	—	—		Vince Tobin
1997	4	12	0	.250	283	379	5th/NFC Eastern Div.	—	—		Vince Tobin
1998	9	7	0	.563	325	378	2nd/NFC Eastern Div.	1	1	NFC div. playoff game	Vince Tobin

*Chicago Cardinals.
†Card-Pitt, a combined squad of Chicago Cardinals and Pittsburgh Steelers.
‡St. Louis Cardinals.
§Phoenix Cardinals.

FIRST-ROUND DRAFT PICKS

1936—Jim Lawrence, B, Texas Christian
1937—Ray Buivid, B, Marquette
1938—Jack Robbins, B, Arkansas
1939—Charles Aldrich, C, Texas Christian*
1940—George Cafego, B, Tennessee*
1941—John Kimbrough, B, Texas A&M
1942—Steve Lach, B, Duke
1943—Glenn Dobbs, B, Tulsa
1944—Pat Harder, B, Wisconsin*
1945—Charley Trippi, B, Georgia*
1946—Dub Jones, B, Louisiana State
1947—DeWitt (Tex) Coulter, T, Army
1948—Jim Spavital, B, Oklahoma A&M
1949—Bill Fischer, G, Notre Dame
1950—None
1951—Jerry Groom, C, Notre Dame
1952—Ollie Matson, B, San Francisco
1953—Johnny Olszewski, QB, California
1954—Lamar McHan, B, Arkansas
1955—Max Boydston, E, Oklahoma
1956—Joe Childress, B, Auburn
1957—Jerry Tubbs, C, Oklahoma
1958—King Hill, B, Rice*
1959—Billy Stacy, B, Mississippi State
1960—George Izo, QB, Notre Dame
1961—Ken Rice, T, Auburn
1962—Fate Echols, DT, Northwestern
       Irv Goode, C, Kentucky
1963—Jerry Stovall, DB, Louisiana State
       Don Brumm, E, Purdue
1964—Ken Kortas, DT, Louisville
1965—Joe Namath, QB, Alabama
1966—Carl McAdams, LB, Oklahoma
1967—Dave Williams, WR, Washington
1968—MacArthur Lane, RB, Utah State
1969—Roger Wehrli, DB, Missouri

1970—Larry Stegent, RB, Texas A&M
1971—Norm Thompson, DB, Utah
1972—Bobby Moore, RB, Oregon
1973—Dave Butz, DT, Purdue
1974—J.V. Cain, TE, Colorado
1975—Tim Gray, DB, Texas A&M
1976—Mike Dawson, DT, Arizona
1977—Steve Pisarkiewicz, QB, Missouri
1978—Steve Little, K, Arkansas
       Ken Greene, DB, Washington St.
1979—Ottis Anderson, RB, Miami (Fla.)
1980—Curtis Greer, DE, Michigan
1981—E.J. Junior, LB, Alabama
1982—Luis Sharpe, T, UCLA
1983—Leonard Smith, DB, McNeese State
1984—Clyde Duncan, WR, Tennessee
1985—Freddie Joe Nunn, LB, Mississippi
1986—Anthony Bell, LB, Michigan St.
1987—Kelly Stouffer, QB, Colorado St.
1988—Ken Harvey, LB, California
1989—Eric Hill, LB, Louisiana State
       Joe Wolf, G, Boston College
1990—None
1991—Eric Swann, DL, None
1992—None
1993—Garrison Hearst, RB, Georgia
       Ernest Dye, T, South Carolina
1994—Jamir Miller, LB, UCLA
1995—None
1996—Simeon Rice, DE, Illinois
1997—Tom Knight, DB, Iowa
1998—Andre Wadsworth, DE, Florida State
1999—David Boston, WR, Ohio State
       L.J. Shelton, T, Eastern Michigan
*First player chosen in draft.

FRANCHISE RECORDS

Most rushing yards, career
7,999—Ottis Anderson
Most rushing yards, season
1,605—Ottis Anderson, 1979
Most rushing yards, game
214—LeShon Johnson at N.O., Sept. 22, 1996

Most rushing touchdowns, season
14—John David Crow, 1962
Most passing attempts, season
560—Neil Lomax, 1984
Most passing attempts, game
61—Neil Lomax at S.D., Sept. 20, 1987
Most passes completed, season
345—Neil Lomax, 1984

Most passes completed, game
37—Neil Lomax at Was., Dec. 16, 1984
       Kent Graham vs. St.L., Sept. 29, 1996 (OT)
Most passing yards, career
34,639—Jim Hart
Most passing yards, season
4,614—Neil Lomax, 1984

Most passing yards, game
522—Boomer Esiason at Was., Nov. 10, 1996 (OT)
468—Neil Lomax at Was., Dec. 16, 1984
Most touchdown passes, season
28—Charley Johnson, 1963
Neil Lomax, 1984
Most pass receptions, career
522—Roy Green
Most pass receptions, season
101—Larry Centers, 1995

Most pass receptions, game
16—Sonny Randle at NYG, Nov. 4, 1962
Most receiving yards, career
8,497—Roy Green
Most receiving yards, season
1,555—Roy Green, 1984
Most receiving yards, game
256—Sonny Randle vs. NYG, Nov. 4, 1962
Most receiving touchdowns, season
16—Sonny Randle, 1960
Most touchdowns, career
66—Roy Green

Most field goals, season
30—Greg Davis, 1995
Longest field goal
55 yards—Greg Davis at Sea., Dec. 19, 1993
Greg Davis at Det., Sept. 17, 1995
Most interceptions, career
52—Larry Wilson
Most interceptions, season
12—Bob Nussbaumer, 1949

SERIES RECORDS

Arizona vs.: Atlanta 13-6; Baltimore, 1-0; Buffalo 3-3; Carolina 0-1; Chicago 26-54-6; Cincinnati 2-4; Dallas 23-49-1; Denver 0-4-1; Detroit 16-28-3; Green Bay 21-41-4; Indianapolis 6-6; Jacksonville 0-0; Kansas City 1-5-1; Miami 0-7; Minnesota 8-7; New England 6-3; New Orleans 12-10; N.Y. Giants 37-74-2; N.Y. Jets 2-2; Oakland 1-3; Philadelphia 49-49-5; Pittsburgh 21-30-3; St. Louis 14-16-2; San Diego 2-6; San Francisco 9-10; Seattle 5-1; Tampa Bay 7-7; Tennessee 4-3; Washington 41-61-1.
NOTE: Includes records for entire franchise, from 1920 to present.

COACHING RECORDS

LeRoy Andrews, 0-1-0; Norman Barry, 16-8-2; Joe Bugel, 20-44-0; Guy Chamberlain, 3-7-1; Jack Chevigny, 2-6-2; Jimmy Conzelman, 34-31-3 (1-1); Don Coryell, 42-27-1 (0-2); Milan Creighton, 16-26-4; Paddy Driscoll, 17-8-4; Chuck Drulis-Ray Prochaska-Ray Willsey*, 2-0-0; Fred Gillies, 1-5-0; Phil Handler, 1-29-0; Phil Handler-Cecil Isbell*, 1-1-0; Phil Handler-Buddy Parker*, 2-4-0; Jim Hanifan, 39-49-1 (0-1); Bob Hollway, 8-18-2; Arnold Horween, 13-8-1; Frank Ivy, 17-29-2; Joe Kuharich, 4-8-0; Hank Kuhlmann, 0-5-0; Curly Lambeau, 7-15-0; Wally Lemm, 27-26-3; Ernie Nevers, 11-19-2; Buddy Parker, 4-1-1; Ray Richards, 14-21-1; Buddy Ryan, 12-20-0; Dewey Scanlon, 6-6-1; Paul Schissler, 6-15-1; Gene Stallings, 23-34-1; Joe Stydahar, 3-20-1; Vince Tobin, 20-28-0 (1-1); Bud Wilkinson, 9-20-0; Larry Wilson, 2-1-0; Charley Winner, 35-30-5.
NOTE: Playoff games in parentheses.
*Co-coaches.

RETIRED UNIFORM NUMBERS

No.	Player
8	Larry Wilson
77	Stan Mauldin
88	J.V. Cain
99	Marshall Goldberg

ATLANTA FALCONS
YEAR-BY-YEAR RECORDS

			REGULAR SEASON				PLAYOFFS			
Year	W	L	T	Pct.	PF	PA	Finish	W	L	Highest round	Coach
1966	3	11	0	.214	204	437	7th/Eastern Conf.	—	—		Norb Hecker
1967	1	12	1	.077	175	422	4th/Coastal Div.	—	—		Norb Hecker
1968	2	12	0	.143	170	389	4th/Coastal Div.	—	—		N. Hecker, N. Van Brocklin
1969	6	8	0	.429	276	268	3rd/Coastal Div.	—	—		Norm Van Brocklin
1970	4	8	2	.333	206	261	3rd/NFC Western Div.	—	—		Norm Van Brocklin
1971	7	6	1	.538	274	277	3rd/NFC Western Div.	—	—		Norm Van Brocklin
1972	7	7	0	.500	269	274	2nd/NFC Western Div.	—	—		Norm Van Brocklin
1973	9	5	0	.643	318	224	2nd/NFC Western Div.	—	—		Norm Van Brocklin
1974	3	11	0	.214	111	271	4th/NFC Western Div.	—	—		N. Van Brocklin, M. Campbell
1975	4	10	0	.286	240	289	3rd/NFC Western Div.	—	—		Marion Campbell
1976	4	10	0	.286	172	312	T3rd/NFC Western Div.	—	—		M. Campbell, Pat Peppler
1977	7	7	0	.500	179	129	2nd/NFC Western Div.	—	—		Leeman Bennett
1978	9	7	0	.563	240	290	2nd/NFC Western Div.	1	1	NFC div. playoff game	Leeman Bennett
1979	6	10	0	.375	300	388	3rd/NFC Western Div.	—	—		Leeman Bennett
1980	12	4	0	.750	405	272	1st/NFC Western Div.	0	1	NFC div. playoff game	Leeman Bennett
1981	7	9	0	.438	426	355	2nd/NFC Western Div.	—	—		Leeman Bennett
1982	5	4	0	.556	183	199	T4th/NFC	0	1	NFC first-round pl. game	Leeman Bennett
1983	7	9	0	.438	370	389	4th/NFC Western Div.	—	—		Dan Henning
1984	4	12	0	.250	281	382	4th/NFC Western Div.	—	—		Dan Henning
1985	4	12	0	.250	282	452	4th/NFC Western Div.	—	—		Dan Henning
1986	7	8	1	.469	280	280	3rd/NFC Western Div.	—	—		Dan Henning
1987	3	12	0	.200	205	436	4th/NFC Western Div.	—	—		Marion Campbell
1988	5	11	0	.313	244	315	4th/NFC Western Div.	—	—		Marion Campbell
1989	3	13	0	.188	279	437	4th/NFC Western Div.	—	—		M. Campbell, Jim Hanifan
1990	5	11	0	.313	348	365	T3rd/NFC Western Div.	—	—		Jerry Glanville
1991	10	6	0	.625	361	338	2nd/NFC Western Div.	1	1	NFC div. playoff game	Jerry Glanville
1992	6	10	0	.375	327	414	T3rd/NFC Western Div.	—	—		Jerry Glanville
1993	6	10	0	.375	316	385	3rd/NFC Western Div.	—	—		Jerry Glanville
1994	7	9	0	.438	313	389	T2nd/NFC Western Div.	—	—		June Jones

			REGULAR SEASON					PLAYOFFS		
Year	W	L	T	Pct.	PF	PA	Finish	W	L	Highest round	Coach
1995	9	7	0	.563	362	349	2nd/NFC Western Div.	0	1	NFC wild-card game	June Jones
1996	3	13	0	.188	309	465	T4th/NFC Western Div.	—	—		June Jones
1997	7	9	0	.438	320	361	T2nd/NFC Western Div.	—	—		Dan Reeves
1998	14	2	0	.875	442	289	1st/NFC Western Div.	2	1	Super Bowl	Dan Reeves

FIRST-ROUND DRAFT PICKS

1966—Tommy Nobis, LB, Texas*
    Randy Johnson, QB, Texas A&I
1967—None
1968—Claude Humphrey, DE, Tennessee State
1969—George Kunz, T, Notre Dame
1970—John Small, LB, Citadel
1971—Joe Profit, RB, Northeast Louisiana State
1972—Clarence Ellis, DB, Notre Dame
1973—None
1974—None
1975—Steve Bartkowski, QB, California*
1976—Bubba Bean, RB, Texas A&M
1977—Warren Bryant, T, Kentucky
    Wilson Faumuina, DT, San Jose State
1978—Mike Kenn, T, Michigan
1979—Don Smith, DE, Miami (Fla.)
1980—Junior Miller, TE, Nebraska
1981—Bobby Butler, DB, Florida State
1982—Gerald Riggs, RB, Arizona State
1983—Mike Pitts, DE, Alabama
1984—Rick Bryan, DT, Oklahoma

1985—Bill Fralic, T, Pittsburgh
1986—Tony Casillas, DT, Oklahoma
    Tim Green, LB, Syracuse
1987—Chris Miller, QB, Oregon
1988—Aundray Bruce, LB, Auburn*
1989—Deion Sanders, DB, Florida State
    Shawn Collins, WR, Northern Arizona
1990—Steve Broussard, RB, Washington State
1991—Bruce Pickens, CB, Nebraska
    Mike Pritchard, WR, Colorado
1992—Bob Whitfield, T, Stanford
    Tony Smith, RB, Southern Mississippi
1993—Lincoln Kennedy, T, Washington
1994—None
1995—Devin Bush, DB, Florida State
1996—None
1997—Michael Booker, DB, Nebraska
1998—Keith Brooking, LB, Georgia Tech
1999—Patrick Kerney, DE, Virginia
    *First player chosen in draft.

FRANCHISE RECORDS

Most rushing yards, career
6,631—Gerald Riggs
Most rushing yards, season
1,846—Jamal Anderson, 1998
Most rushing yards, game
202—Gerald Riggs at N.O., Sept. 2, 1984
Most rushing touchdowns, season
14—Jamal Anderson, 1998
Most passing attempts, season
557—Jeff George, 1995
Most passing attempts, game
66—Chris Miller vs. Det., Dec. 24, 1989
Most passes completed, season
336—Jeff George, 1995
Most passes completed, game
37—Chris Miller vs. Det., Dec. 24, 1989
Most passing yards, career
23,468—Steve Bartkowski
Most passing yards, season
4,143—Jeff George, 1995

Most passing yards, game
416—Steve Bartkowski vs. Pit., Nov. 15, 1981
Most touchdown passes, season
31—Steve Bartkowski, 1980
Most pass receptions, career
423—Andre Rison
Most pass receptions, season
111—Terance Mathis, 1994
Most pass receptions, game
15—William Andrews vs. Pit., Nov. 15, 1981
Most receiving yards, career
6,257—Alfred Jenkins
Most receiving yards, season
1,358—Alfred Jenkins, 1981
Most receiving yards, game
198—Terance Mathis at N.O., Dec. 13, 1998

Most receiving touchdowns, season
15—Andre Rison, 1993
Most touchdowns, career
56—Andre Rison
Most field goals, season
31—Morten Andersen, 1995
Longest field goal
59 yards—Morten Andersen vs. S.F., Dec. 24, 1995
Most interceptions, career
39—Rolland Lawrence
Most interceptions, season
10—Scott Case, 1988
Most sacks, career
62.5—Claude Humphrey
Most sacks, season
16—Joel Williams, 1980

SERIES RECORDS

Atlanta vs.: Arizona 6-13; Buffalo 3-4; Carolina 4-4; Chicago 10-9; Cincinnati 2-7; Dallas 6-11; Denver 3-6; Detroit 7-20; Green Bay 9-10; Indianapolis 1-10; Jacksonville 0-1; Kansas City 0-4; Miami 2-6; Minnesota 6-13; New England 6-3; New Orleans 35-24; N.Y. Giants 7-6; N.Y. Jets 4-4; Oakland 3-6; Philadelphia 9-9-1; Pittsburgh 1-10; St. Louis 23-39-2; San Diego 5-1; San Francisco 23-40-1; Seattle 2-4; Tampa Bay 8-7; Tennessee 5-4; Washington 4-13-1.

COACHING RECORDS

Leeman Bennett, 46-41-0 (1-3); Marion Campbell, 17-51-0; Jerry Glanville, 27-37-0 (1-1); Jim Hanifan, 0-4-0; Norb Hecker, 4-26-1; Dan Henning, 22-41-1; June Jones, 19-29-0 (0-1); Pat Peppler, 3-6-0; Dan Reeves, 21-11-0 (2-1); Norm Van Brocklin, 37-49-3. NOTE: Playoff games in parentheses.

RETIRED UNIFORM NUMBERS

No.	Player
10	Steve Bartkowski
31	William Andrews
57	Jeff Van Note
60	Tommy Nobis

BALTIMORE RAVENS
YEAR-BY-YEAR RECORDS

	REGULAR SEASON						PLAYOFFS			
Year	W	L	T	Pct.	PF	PA	Finish	W	L	Highest round	Coach
1996	4	12	0	.250	371	441	5th/AFC Central Div.	—	—		Ted Marchibroda
1997	6	9	1	.406	326	345	5th/AFC Central Div.	—	—		Ted Marchibroda
1998	6	10	0	.375	269	335	4th/AFC Central Div.	—	—		Ted Marchibroda

FIRST-ROUND DRAFT PICKS

1996—Jonathan Ogden, T, UCLA
Ray Lewis, LB, Miami (Fla.)

1997—Peter Boulware, DE, Florida State
1998—Duane Starks, DB, Miami (Fla.)

1999—Chris McAlister, DB, Arizona
*First player chosen in draft.

FRANCHISE RECORDS

Most rushing yards, career
1,511—Bam Morris
Most rushing yards, season
1,008—Priest Holmes, 1998
Most rushing yards, game
227—Priest Holmes at Cin., Nov. 22, 1998
Most rushing touchdowns, season
7—Priest Holmes, 1998
Most passing attempts, season
549—Vinny Testaverde, 1996
Most passing attempts, game
51—Vinny Testaverde vs. St.L., Oct. 27, 1996 (OT)
50—Vinny Testaverde vs. Jac., Nov. 24, 1996 (OT)
47—Vinny Testaverde vs. Pit., Oct. 5, 1997
Vinny Testaverde at Mia., Oct. 19, 1997
Most passes completed, season
325—Vinny Testaverde, 1996
Most passes completed, game
32—Vinny Testaverde vs. Mia., Oct. 19, 1997

Most passing yards, career
7,148—Vinny Testaverde
Most passing yards, season
4,177—Vinny Testaverde, 1996
Most passing yards, game
429—Vinny Testaverde vs. St.L., Oct. 27, 1996 (OT)
366—Vinny Testaverde vs. Jac., Nov. 24, 1996 (OT)
353—Vinny Testaverde vs. N.E., Oct. 6, 1996
Most touchdown passes, season
33—Vinny Testaverde, 1996
Most pass receptions, career
183—Michael Jackson
Most pass receptions, season
76—Michael Jackson, 1996
Most pass receptions, game
13—Priest Holmes vs. Ten., Oct. 11, 1998
Most receiving yards, career
2,596—Michael Jackson
Most receiving yards, season
1,201—Michael Jackson, 1996

Most receiving yards, game
198—Derrick Alexander vs. Pit., Dec. 1, 1996
Most receiving touchdowns, season
14—Michael Jackson, 1996
Most touchdowns, career
18—Derrick Alexander
Michael Jackson
Most field goals, season
26—Matt Stover, 1997
Longest field goal
50 yards—Matt Stover vs. St.L., Oct. 27, 1996
Most interceptions, career
8—Antonio Langham
Most interceptions, season
6—Rod Woodson, 1998
Most sacks, career
23.5—Michael McCrary
Most sacks, season
14.5—Michael McCrary, 1998

SERIES RECORDS

Baltimore vs.: Arizona, 0-1; Carolina 0-1; Chicago 0-1; Cincinnati 3-3; Denver 0-1; Detroit 1-0; Green Bay 0-1; Indianapolis 1-1; Jacksonville 0-6; Miami, 0-1; Minnesota 0-1; New England 0-1; New Orleans 1-0; N.Y. Giants, 1-0; N.Y. Jets, 1-1; Oakland 2-0; Philadelphia, 0-0-1; Pittsburgh 1-5; St. Louis 1-0; San Diego, 0-2; San Francisco 0-1; Seattle, 1-0; Tennessee 2-4; Washington, 1-0.

COACHING RECORDS

Ted Marchibroda, 16-31-1.

RETIRED UNIFORM NUMBERS

No.	Player
	None

BUFFALO BILLS
YEAR-BY-YEAR RECORDS

	REGULAR SEASON						PLAYOFFS			
Year	W	L	T	Pct.	PF	PA	Finish	W	L	Highest round	Coach
1960*	5	8	1	.385	296	303	3rd/Eastern Div.	—	—		Buster Ramsey
1961*	6	8	0	.429	294	342	4th/Eastern Div.	—	—		Buster Ramsey
1962*	7	6	1	.538	309	272	3rd/Eastern Div.	—	—		Lou Saban
1963*	7	6	1	.538	304	291	2nd/Eastern Div.	0	1	E. Div. championship game	Lou Saban
1964*	12	2	0	.857	400	242	1st/Eastern Div.	1	0	AFL champ	Lou Saban
1965*	10	3	1	.769	313	226	1st/Eastern Div.	1	0	AFL champ	Lou Saban
1966*	9	4	1	.692	358	255	1st/Eastern Div.	0	1	AFL championship game	Joe Collier
1967*	4	10	0	.286	237	285	T3rd/Eastern Div.	—	—		Joe Collier
1968*	1	12	1	.077	199	367	5th/Eastern Div.	—	—		J. Collier, H. Johnson
1969*	4	10	0	.286	230	359	T3rd/Eastern Div.	—	—		John Rauch

				REGULAR SEASON				PLAYOFFS			
Year	W	L	T	Pct.	PF	PA	Finish	W	L	Highest round	Coach
1970	3	10	1	.231	204	337	4th/AFC Eastern Div.	—	—		John Rauch
1971	1	13	0	.071	184	394	5th/AFC Eastern Div.	—	—		Harvey Johnson
1972	4	9	1	.321	257	377	4th/AFC Eastern Div.	—	—		Lou Saban
1973	9	5	0	.643	259	230	2nd/AFC Eastern Div.	—	—		Lou Saban
1974	9	5	0	.643	264	244	2nd/AFC Eastern Div.	0	1	AFC div. playoff game	Lou Saban
1975	8	6	0	.571	420	355	3rd/AFC Eastern Div.	—	—		Lou Saban
1976	2	12	0	.143	245	363	5th/AFC Eastern Div.	—	—		Lou Saban, Jim Ringo
1977	3	11	0	.214	160	313	T4th/AFC Eastern Div.	—	—		Jim Ringo
1978	5	11	0	.313	302	354	T4th/AFC Eastern Div.	—	—		Chuck Knox
1979	7	9	0	.438	268	279	4th/AFC Eastern Div.	—	—		Chuck Knox
1980	11	5	0	.688	320	260	1st/AFC Eastern Div.	0	1	AFC div. playoff game	Chuck Knox
1981	10	6	0	.625	311	276	3rd/AFC Eastern Div.	1	1	AFC div. playoff game	Chuck Knox
1982	4	5	0	.444	150	154	T8th/AFC	—	—		Chuck Knox
1983	8	8	0	.500	283	351	T2nd/AFC Eastern Div.	—	—		Kay Stephenson
1984	2	14	0	.125	250	454	5th/AFC Eastern Div.	—	—		Kay Stephenson
1985	2	14	0	.125	200	381	5th/AFC Eastern Div.	—	—		Hank Bullough
1986	4	12	0	.250	287	348	4th/AFC Eastern Div.	—	—		H. Bullough, M. Levy
1987	7	8	0	.467	270	305	4th/AFC Eastern Div.	—	—		Marv Levy
1988	12	4	0	.750	329	237	1st/AFC Eastern Div.	1	1	AFC championship game	Marv Levy
1989	9	7	0	.563	409	317	1st/AFC Eastern Div.	0	1	AFC div. playoff game	Marv Levy
1990	13	3	0	.813	428	263	1st/AFC Eastern Div.	2	1	Super Bowl	Marv Levy
1991	13	3	0	.813	458	318	1st/AFC Eastern Div.	2	1	Super Bowl	Marv Levy
1992	11	5	0	.688	381	283	2nd/AFC Eastern Div.	3	1	Super Bowl	Marv Levy
1993	12	4	0	.750	329	242	1st/AFC Eastern Div.	2	1	Super Bowl	Marv Levy
1994	7	9	0	.438	340	356	4th/AFC Eastern Div.	—	—		Marv Levy
1995	10	6	0	.625	350	335	1st/AFC Eastern Div.	1	1	AFC div. playoff game	Marv Levy
1996	10	6	0	.625	319	266	2nd/AFC Eastern Div.	0	1	AFC wild-card game	Marv Levy
1997	6	10	0	.375	255	367	4th/AFC Eastern Div.	—	—		Marv Levy
1998	10	6	0	.625	400	333	T2nd/AFC Eastern Div.	0	1	AFC wild-card game	Wade Phillips

*American Football League.

FIRST-ROUND DRAFT PICKS

1960—Richie Lucas, QB, Penn State
1961—Ken Rice, T, Auburn* (AFL)
1962—Ernie Davis, RB, Syracuse
1963—Dave Behrman, C, Michigan State
1964—Carl Eller, DE, Minnesota
1965—Jim Davidson, T, Ohio State
1966—Mike Dennis, RB, Mississippi
1967—John Pitts, DB, Arizona State
1968—Haven Moses, WR, San Diego St.
1969—O.J. Simpson, RB, Southern California*
1970—Al Cowlings, DE, Southern California
1971—J.D. Hill, WR, Arizona State
1972—Walt Patulski, DE, Notre Dame*
1973—Paul Seymour, T, Michigan
       Joe DeLamielleure, G, Michigan State
1974—Reuben Gant, TE, Oklahoma State
1975—Tom Ruud, LB, Nebraska
1976—Mario Clark, DB, Oregon
1977—Phil Dokes, DT, Oklahoma State
1978—Terry Miller, RB, Oklahoma State
1979—Tom Cousineau, LB, Ohio State*
       Jerry Butler, WR, Clemson
1980—Jim Ritcher, C, North Carolina State

1981—Booker Moore, RB, Penn State
1982—Perry Tuttle, WR, Clemson
1983—Tony Hunter, TE, Notre Dame
       Jim Kelly, QB, Miami (Fla.)
1984—Greg Bell, RB, Notre Dame
1985—Bruce Smith, DT, Virginia Tech*
       Derrick Burroughs, DB, Memphis State
1986—Ronnie Harmon, RB, Iowa
       Will Wolford, T, Vanderbilt
1987—Shane Conlan, LB, Penn State
1988—None
1989—None
1990—James Williams, DB, Fresno State
1991—Henry Jones, S, Illinois
1992—John Fina, T, Arizona
1993—Thomas Smith, DB, North Carolina
1994—Jeff Burris, DB, Notre Dame
1995—Ruben Brown, G, Pittsburgh
1996—Eric Moulds, WR, Mississippi State
1997—Antowain Smith, RB, Houston
1998—None
1999—Antoine Winfield, DB, Ohio State
*First player chosen in draft.

FRANCHISE RECORDS

Most rushing yards, career
11,786—Thurman Thomas
Most rushing yards, season
2,003—O.J. Simpson, 1973
Most rushing yards, game
273—O.J. Simpson at Det., Nov. 25, 1976
Most rushing touchdowns, season
16—O.J. Simpson, 1975

Most passing attempts, season
508—Joe Ferguson, 1983
Most passing attempts, game
55—Joe Ferguson at Mia., Oct. 9, 1983
Most passes completed, season
304—Jim Kelly, 1991
Most passes completed, game
38—Joe Ferguson at Mia., Oct. 9, 1983
Most passing yards, career
35,467—Jim Kelly

Most passing yards, season
3,844—Jim Kelly, 1991
Most passing yards, game
419—Joe Ferguson at Mia., Oct. 9, 1983
Most touchdown passes, season
33—Jim Kelly, 1991
Most pass receptions, career
889—Andre Reed
Most pass receptions, season
90—Andre Reed, 1994

Most pass receptions, game
15—Andre Reed vs. G.B., Nov. 20, 1994
Most receiving yards, career
12,559—Andre Reed
Most receiving yards, season
1,368—Eric Moulds, 1998
Most receiving yards, game
255—Jerry Butler vs. NYJ, Sept. 23, 1979

Most receiving touchdowns, season
11—Bill Brooks, 1995
Most touchdowns, career
86—Thurman Thomas
Most field goals, season
33—Steve Christie, 1998
Longest field goal
59 yards—Steve Christie vs. Mia., Sept. 26, 1993

Most interceptions, career
40—George Byrd
Most interceptions, season
10—Billy Atkins, 1961
Tom Janik, 1967
Most sacks, career
164—Bruce Smith
Most sacks, season
19—Bruce Smith, 1990

SERIES RECORDS

Buffalo vs.: Arizona 3-3; Atlanta 4-3; Carolina 2-0; Chicago 2-5; Cincinnati 9-10; Dallas 3-3; Denver 17-12-1; Detroit 2-3-1; Green Bay 5-2; Indianapolis 33-23-1; Jacksonville 1-1; Kansas City 17-14-1; Miami 23-42-1; Minnesota 2-6; New England 36-41-1; New Orleans 4-2; N.Y. Giants 5-2; N.Y. Jets 44-33; Oakland 15-15; Philadelphia 4-4; Pittsburgh 7-8; St. Louis 4-4; San Diego 7-17-2; San Francisco 4-3; Seattle 2-4; Tampa Bay 2-4; Tennessee 13-22; Washington 4-4.

COACHING RECORDS

Hank Bullough, 4-17-0; Joe Collier, 13-16-1 (0-1); Harvey Johnson, 2-23-1; Chuck Knox, 37-36-0 (1-2); Marv Levy, 112-70-0 (11-8); Wade Phillips, 10-6 (0-1); Buster Ramsey, 11-16-1; John Rauch, 7-20-1; Jim Ringo, 3-20-0; Lou Saban, 68-45-4 (2-2); Kay Stephenson, 10-26-0.
NOTE: Playoff games in parentheses.

RETIRED UNIFORM NUMBERS

No.	Player
	None

CAROLINA PANTHERS
YEAR-BY-YEAR RECORDS

	REGULAR SEASON							PLAYOFFS			
Year	W	L	T	Pct.	PF	PA	Finish	W	L	Highest round	Coach
1995	7	9	0	.438	289	325	T3rd/NFC Western Div.	—	—		Dom Capers
1996	12	4	0	.750	367	218	1st/NFC Western Div.	1	1	NFC championship game	Dom Capers
1997	7	9	0	.438	265	314	T2nd/NFC Western Div.	—	—		Dom Capers
1998	4	12	0	.250	336	413	T4th/NFC Western Div.	—	—		Dom Capers

FIRST-ROUND DRAFT PICKS

1995—Kerry Collins, QB, Penn State
Tyrone Poole, DB, Fort Valley (Ga.) St.
Blake Brockermeyer, T, Texas
1996—Tim Biakabutuka, RB, Michigan

1997—Rae Carruth, WR, Colorado
1998—Jason Peter, DT, Nebraska
1999—None

FRANCHISE RECORDS

Most rushing yards, career
1,724—Anthony Johnson
Most rushing yards, season
1,120—Anthony Johnson, 1996
Most rushing yards, game
147—Fred Lane vs. Oak., Nov. 2, 1997
Most rushing touchdowns, season
7—Fred Lane, 1997
Most passing attempts, season
433—Kerry Collins, 1995
Most passing attempts, game
53—Kerry Collins vs. G.B., Sept. 27, 1998
Most passes completed, season
216—Steve Beuerlein, 1998
Most passes completed, game
26—Kerry Collins vs. Bal., Dec. 15, 1996
Most passing yards, career
8,306—Kerry Collins
Most passing yards, season
2,717—Kerry Collins, 1995

Most passing yards, game
335—Kerry Collins at N.O., Nov. 26, 1995
Most touchdown passes, season
17—Steve Beuerlein, 1998
Most pass receptions, career
176—Mark Carrier
Most pass receptions, season
69—Rocket Ismail, 1998
Most pass receptions, game
9—Willie Green at Atl., Nov. 3, 1996
Muhsin Muhammad at N.O., Sept. 13, 1998
Most receiving yards, career
2,547—Mark Carrier
Most receiving yards, season
1,024—Rocket Ismail, 1998
Most receiving yards, game
192—Muhsin Muhammad at N.O., Sept. 13, 1998

Most receiving touchdowns, season
10—Wesley Walls, 1996
Most touchdowns, career
21—Wesley Walls
Most field goals, season
37—John Kasay, 1996
Longest field goal
56 yards—John Kasay vs. G.B., Sept. 27, 1998
Most interceptions, career
15—Eric Davis
Most interceptions, season
6—Brett Maxie, 1995
Most sacks, career
29.5—Kevin Greene
Most sacks, season
15—Kevin Greene, 1998

SERIES RECORDS

Carolina vs.: Arizona 1-0; Atlanta 4-4; Buffalo 0-2; Baltimore 1-0; Chicago 0-1; Cincinnati 0-0; Dallas 1-1; Denver 0-1; Detroit 0-0; Green Bay 0-2; Indianapolis 2-0; Jacksonville 0-1; Kansas City 0-1; Miami 0-1; Minnesota 0-2; New England 1-0; New Orleans 5-3; N.Y. Giants 1-0; N.Y. Jets 1-1; Oakland 1-0; Philadelphia 0-1; Pittsburgh 1-0; St. Louis 5-3; San Diego 1-0; San Francisco 3-5; Seattle 0-0; Tampa Bay 1-2; Tennessee 1-0; Washington 0-3.

COACHING RECORDS

Dom Capers, 30-34-0 (1-1).
NOTE: Playoff games in parentheses.

RETIRED UNIFORM NUMBERS

No.	Player
None	

CHICAGO BEARS
YEAR-BY-YEAR RECORDS

	REGULAR SEASON							PLAYOFFS			
Year	W	L	T	Pct.	PF	PA	Finish	W	L	Highest round	Coach
1920*	10	1	2	.909	...	...	2nd				George Halas
1921†	9	1	1	.900	...	...	1st				George Halas
1922	9	3	0	.750	...	...	2nd				George Halas
1923	9	2	1	.818	...	...	2nd				George Halas
1924	6	1	4	.857	...	...	2nd				George Halas
1925	9	5	3	.643	...	...	7th				George Halas
1926	12	1	3	.923	...	...	2nd				George Halas
1927	9	3	2	.750	...	...	3rd				George Halas
1928	7	5	1	.583	...	...	5th				George Halas
1929	4	9	2	.308	...	...	9th				George Halas
1930	9	4	1	.692	...	...	3rd				Ralph Jones
1931	8	5	0	.615	...	...	3rd				Ralph Jones
1932	7	1	6	.875	...	...	1st				Ralph Jones
1933	10	2	1	.833	133	82	1st/Western Div.	1	0	NFL champ	George Halas
1934	13	0	0	1.000	286	86	1st/Western Div.	0	1	NFL championship game	George Halas
1935	6	4	2	.600	192	106	T3rd/Western Div.	—	—		George Halas
1936	9	3	0	.750	222	94	2nd/Western Div.	—	—		George Halas
1937	9	1	1	.900	201	100	1st/Western Div.	0	1	NFL championship game	George Halas
1938	6	5	0	.545	194	148	3rd/Western Div.	—	—		George Halas
1939	8	3	0	.727	298	157	2nd/Western Div.	—	—		George Halas
1940	8	3	0	.727	238	152	1st/Western Div.	1	0	NFL champ	George Halas
1941	10	1	0	.909	396	147	1st/Western Div.	2	0	NFL champ	George Halas
1942	11	0	0	1.000	376	84	1st/Western Div.	0	1	NFL championship game	George Halas, Hunk Anderson-Luke Johnsos
1943	8	1	1	.889	303	157	1st/Western Div.	1	0	NFL champ	H. Anderson-L. Johnsos
1944	6	3	1	.667	258	172	T2nd/Western Div.	—	—		H. Anderson-L. Johnsos
1945	3	7	0	.300	192	235	4th/Western Div.	—	—		H. Anderson-L. Johnsos
1946	8	2	1	.800	289	193	1st/Western Div.	1	0	NFL champ	George Halas
1947	8	4	0	.667	363	241	2nd/Western Div.	—	—		George Halas
1948	10	2	0	.833	375	151	2nd/Western Div.	—	—		George Halas
1949	9	3	0	.750	332	218	2nd/Western Div.	—	—		George Halas
1950	9	3	0	.750	279	207	2nd/National Conf.	0	1	Nat. Conf. champ. game	George Halas
1951	7	5	0	.583	286	282	4th/National Conf.	—	—		George Halas
1952	5	7	0	.417	245	326	5th/National Conf.	—	—		George Halas
1953	3	8	1	.273	218	262	T4th/Western Conf.	—	—		George Halas
1954	8	4	0	.667	301	279	2nd/Western Conf.	—	—		George Halas
1955	8	4	0	.667	294	251	2nd/Western Conf.	—	—		George Halas
1956	9	2	1	.818	363	246	1st/Western Conf.	0	1	NFL championship game	Paddy Driscoll
1957	5	7	0	.417	203	211	5th/Western Conf.	—	—		Paddy Driscoll
1958	8	4	0	.667	298	230	T2nd/Western Conf.	—	—		George Halas
1959	8	4	0	.667	252	196	2nd/Western Conf.	—	—		George Halas
1960	5	6	1	.455	194	299	5th/Western Conf.	—	—		George Halas
1961	8	6	0	.571	326	302	T3rd/Western Conf.	—	—		George Halas
1962	9	5	0	.643	321	287	3rd/Western Conf.	—	—		George Halas
1963	11	1	2	.917	301	144	1st/Western Conf.	1	0	NFL champ	George Halas
1964	5	9	0	.357	260	379	6th/Western Conf.	—	—		George Halas
1965	9	5	0	.643	409	275	3rd/Western Conf.	—	—		George Halas
1966	5	7	2	.417	234	272	5th/Western Conf.	—	—		George Halas
1967	7	6	1	.538	239	218	2nd/Central Div.	—	—		George Halas
1968	7	7	0	.500	250	333	2nd/Central Div.	—	—		Jim Dooley
1969	1	13	0	.071	210	339	4th/Central Div.	—	—		Jim Dooley
1970	6	8	0	.429	256	261	T3rd/NFC Central Div.	—	—		Jim Dooley
1971	6	8	0	.429	185	276	3rd/NFC Central Div.	—	—		Jim Dooley
1972	4	9	1	.321	225	275	4th/NFC Central Div.	—	—		Abe Gibron

Year	W	L	T	Pct.	PF	PA	Finish	W	L	Highest round	Coach
				REGULAR SEASON						**PLAYOFFS**	
1973	3	11	0	.214	195	334	4th/NFC Central Div.	—	—		Abe Gibron
1974	4	10	0	.286	152	279	4th/NFC Central Div.	—	—		Abe Gibron
1975	4	10	0	.286	191	379	T3rd/NFC Central Div.	—	—		Jack Pardee
1976	7	7	0	.500	253	216	2nd/NFC Central Div.	—	—		Jack Pardee
1977	9	5	0	.643	255	253	2nd/NFC Central Div.	0	1	NFC div. playoff game	Jack Pardee
1978	7	9	0	.438	253	274	T3rd/NFC Central Div.	—	—		Neill Armstrong
1979	10	6	0	.625	306	249	2nd/NFC Central Div.	0	1	AFC wild-card game	Neill Armstrong
1980	7	9	0	.438	304	264	3rd/NFC Central Div.	—	—		Neill Armstrong
1981	6	10	0	.375	253	324	5th/NFC Central Div.	—	—		Neill Armstrong
1982	3	6	0	.333	141	174	T11th/NFC	—	—		Mike Ditka
1983	8	8	0	.500	311	301	T2nd/NFC Central Div.	—	—		Mike Ditka
1984	10	6	0	.625	325	248	1st/NFC Central Div.	1	1	NFC championship game	Mike Ditka
1985	15	1	0	.938	456	198	1st/NFC Central Div.	3	0	Super Bowl champ	Mike Ditka
1986	14	2	0	.875	352	187	1st/NFC Central Div.	0	1	NFC div. playoff game	Mike Ditka
1987	11	4	0	.733	356	282	1st/NFC Central Div.	0	1	NFC div. playoff game	Mike Ditka
1988	12	4	0	.750	312	215	1st/NFC Central Div.	1	1	NFC championship game	Mike Ditka
1989	6	10	0	.375	358	377	4th/NFC Central Div.	—	—		Mike Ditka
1990	11	5	0	.688	348	280	1st/NFC Central Div.	1	1	NFC div. playoff game	Mike Ditka
1991	11	5	0	.688	299	269	2nd/NFC Central Div.	0	1	NFC wild-card game	Mike Ditka
1992	5	11	0	.313	295	361	T3rd/NFC Central Div.	—	—		Mike Ditka
1993	7	9	0	.438	234	230	4th/NFC Central Div.	—	—		Dave Wannstedt
1994	9	7	0	.563	271	307	T2nd/NFC Central Div.	1	1	NFC div. playoff game	Dave Wannstedt
1995	9	7	0	.563	392	360	3rd/NFC Central Div.	—	—		Dave Wannstedt
1996	7	9	0	.438	283	305	3rd/NFC Central Div.	—	—		Dave Wannstedt
1997	4	12	0	.250	263	421	5th/NFC Central Div.	—	—		Dave Wannstedt
1998	4	12	0	.250	276	368	5th/NFC Central Div.	—	—		Dave Wannstedt

*Decatur Staleys.
†Chicago Staleys.

FIRST-ROUND DRAFT PICKS

1936—Joe Stydahar, T, West Virginia
1937—Les McDonald, E, Nebraska
1938—Joe Gray, B, Oregon State
1939—Sid Luckman, B, Columbia
    Bill Osmanski, B, Holy Cross
1940—C. Turner, C, Hardin-Simmons
1941—Tom Harmon, B, Michigan*
    Norm Standlee, B, Stanford
    Don Scott, B, Ohio State
1942—Frankie Albert, B, Stanford
1943—Bob Steuber, B, Missouri
1944—Ray Evans, B, Kansas
1945—Don Lund, B, Michigan
1946—Johnny Lujack, QB, Notre Dame
1947—Bob Fenimore, B, Oklahoma A&M*
1948—Bobby Layne, QB, Texas
    Max Baumgardner, E, Texas
1949—Dick Harris, C, Texas
1950—Chuck Hunsinger, B, Florida
1951—Bob Williams, B, Notre Dame
    Billy Stone, B, Bradley
    Gene Schroeder, E, Virginia
1952—Jim Dooley, B, Miami
1953—Billy Anderson, B, Compton (Ca.) J.C.
1954—Stan Wallace, B, Illinois
1955—Ron Drzewiecki, B, Marquette
1956—Menan (Tex) Schriewer, E, Texas
1957—Earl Leggett, DT, Louisiana State
1958—Chuck Howley, LB, West Virginia
1959—Don Clark, B, Ohio State
1960—Roger Davis, G, Syracuse
1961—Mike Ditka, E, Pittsburgh
1962—Ron Bull, RB, Baylor
1963—Dave Behrman, C, Michigan State
1964—Dick Evey, DT, Tennessee
1965—Dick Butkus, LB, Illinois
1965—Gale Sayers, RB, Kansas
    Steve DeLong, DE, Tennessee
1966—George Rice, DT, Louisiana State
1967—Loyd Phillips, DE, Arkansas

1968—Mike Hull, RB, Southern California
1969—Rufus Mayes, T, Ohio State
1970—None
1971—Joe Moore, RB, Missouri
1972—Lionel Antoine, T, Southern Illinois
    Craig Clemons, DB, Iowa
1973—Wally Chambers, DE, Eastern Kentucky
1974—Waymond Bryant, LB, Tennessee State
    Dave Gallagher, DE, Michigan
1975—Walter Payton, RB, Jackson State
1976—Dennis Lick, T, Wisconsin
1977—Ted Albrecht, T, California
1978—None
1979—Dan Hampton, DT, Arkansas
    Al Harris, DE, Arizona State
1980—Otis Wilson, LB, Louisville
1981—Keith Van Horne, T, Southern California
1982—Jim McMahon, QB, Brigham Young
1983—Jimbo Covert, T, Pittsburgh
    Willie Gault, WR, Tennessee
1984—Wilber Marshall, LB, Florida
1985—William Perry, DT, Clemson
1986—Neal Anderson, RB, Florida
1987—Jim Harbaugh, QB, Michigan
1988—Brad Muster, RB, Stanford
    Wendell Davis, WR, Louisiana State
1989—Donnell Woolford, DB, Clemson
    Trace Armstrong, DE, Florida
1990—Mark Carrier, DB, Southern California
1991—Stan Thomas, T, Texas
1992—Alonzo Spellman, DE, Ohio State
1993—Curtis Conway, WR, Southern California
1994—John Thierry, LB, Alcorn State
1995—Rashaan Salaam, RB, Colorado
1996—Walt Harris, DB, Mississippi State
1997—None
1998—Curtis Enis, RB, Penn State
1999—Cade McNown, QB, UCLA
    *First player chosen in draft.

FRANCHISE RECORDS

Most rushing yards, career
16,726—Walter Payton
Most rushing yards, season
1,852—Walter Payton, 1977
Most rushing yards, game
275—Walter Payton vs. Min., Nov. 20, 1977
Most rushing touchdowns, season
14—Gale Sayers, 1965
Walter Payton, 1977
Walter Payton, 1979
Most passing attempts, season
522—Erik Kramer, 1995
Most passing attempts, game
60—Erik Kramer vs. NYJ, Nov. 16, 1997
Most passes completed, season
315—Erik Kramer, 1995
Most passes completed, game
33—Bill Wade at Was., Oct. 25, 1964
Most passing yards, career
14,686—Sid Luckman

Most passing yards, season
3,838—Erik Kramer, 1995
Most passing yards, game
468—Johnny Lujack vs. Chi. Cards, Dec. 11, 1949
Most touchdown passes, season
29—Erik Kramer, 1995
Most pass receptions, career
492—Walter Payton
Most pass receptions, season
93—Johnny Morris, 1964
Most pass receptions, game
14—Jim Keane at NYG, Oct. 23, 1949
Most receiving yards, career
5,059—Johnny Morris
Most receiving yards, season
1,301—Jeff Graham, 1995
Most receiving yards, game
214—Harlon Hill at S.F., Oct. 31, 1954
Most receiving touchdowns, season
13—Ken Kavanaugh, 1947
Dick Gordon, 1970

Most touchdowns, career
125—Walter Payton
Most field goals, season
31—Kevin Butler, 1985
Longest field goal
55 yards—Bob Thomas at L.A. Rams, Nov. 23, 1975
Kevin Butler vs. Min., Oct. 25, 1993
Kevin Butler at T.B., Dec. 12, 1993
Most interceptions, career
38—Gary Fencik
Most interceptions, season
10—Mark Carrier, 1990
Most sacks, career
124.5—Richard Dent
Most sacks, season
17.5—Richard Dent, 1984

SERIES RECORDS

Chicago vs.: Arizona 54-26-6; Atlanta 9-10; Baltimore 1-0; Buffalo 5-2; Carolina 1-0; Cincinnati 2-4; Dallas 8-9; Denver 5-6; Detroit 72-54-3; Green Bay 82-69-6; Indianapolis 16-21; Jacksonville 1-1; Kansas City 4-3; Miami 3-5; Minnesota 32-41-2; New England 2-5; New Orleans 10-7; N.Y. Giants 25-16-2; N.Y. Jets 4-2; Oakland 4-5; Philadelphia 25-4-1; Pittsburgh 19-6-1; St. Louis 36-26-3; San Diego 3-4; San Francisco 25-25-1; Seattle 2-4; Tampa Bay 30-12; Tennessee 4-4; Washington 14-13.
NOTE: Includes records as Decatur Staleys in 1920 and Chicago Staleys in 1921.

COACHING RECORDS

Hunk Anderson-Luke Johnsos*, 23-11-2 (1-1); Neill Armstrong, 30-34-0 (0-1); Mike Ditka, 106-62-0 (6-6); Jim Dooley, 20-36-0; Paddy Driscoll, 14-9-1 (0-1); Abe Gibron, 11-30-1; George Halas, 318-148-31 (6-3); Ralph Jones, 24-10-7; Jack Pardee, 20-22-0 (0-1); Dave Wannstedt, 40-56-0 (1-1).
NOTE: Playoff games in parentheses.
*Co-coaches.

RETIRED UNIFORM NUMBERS

No.	Player
3	Bronko Nagurski
5	George McAfee
7	George Halas
28	Willie Galimore
34	Walter Payton
40	Gale Sayers
41	Brian Piccolo
42	Sid Luckman
51	Dick Butkus
56	Bill Hewitt
61	Bill George
66	Bulldog Turner
77	Red Grange

CINCINNATI BENGALS
YEAR-BY-YEAR RECORDS

Year	REGULAR SEASON							PLAYOFFS			Coach
	W	L	T	Pct.	PF	PA	Finish	W	L	Highest round	
1968*	3	11	0	.214	215	329	5th/Western Div.	—	—		Paul Brown
1969*	4	9	1	.308	280	367	5th/Western Div.	—	—		Paul Brown
1970	8	6	0	.571	312	255	1st/AFC Central Div.	0	1	AFC div. playoff game	Paul Brown
1971	4	10	0	.286	284	265	4th/AFC Central Div.	—	—		Paul Brown
1972	8	6	0	.571	299	229	3rd/AFC Central Div.	—	—		Paul Brown
1973	10	4	0	.714	286	231	1st/AFC Central Div.	0	1	AFC div. playoff game	Paul Brown
1974	7	7	0	.500	283	259	T2nd/AFC Central Div.	—	—		Paul Brown
1975	11	3	0	.786	340	246	2nd/AFC Central Div.	0	1	AFC div. playoff game	Paul Brown
1976	10	4	0	.714	335	210	2nd/AFC Central Div.	—	—		Bill Johnson
1977	8	6	0	.571	238	235	T2nd/AFC Central Div.	—	—		Bill Johnson
1978	4	12	0	.250	252	284	4th/AFC Central Div.	—	—		B. Johnson, H. Rice
1979	4	12	0	.250	337	421	4th/AFC Central Div.	—	—		Homer Rice
1980	6	10	0	.375	244	312	4th/AFC Central Div.	—	—		Forrest Gregg
1981	12	4	0	.750	421	304	1st/AFC Central Div.	2	1	Super Bowl	Forrest Gregg

						REGULAR SEASON			PLAYOFFS		
Year	W	L	T	Pct.	PF	PA	Finish	W	L	Highest round	Coach
1982	7	2	0	.778	232	177	T2nd/AFC	0	1	AFC first-round pl. game	Forrest Gregg
1983	7	9	0	.438	346	302	3rd/AFC Central Div.	—	—		Forrest Gregg
1984	8	8	0	.500	339	339	2nd/AFC Central Div.	—	—		Sam Wyche
1985	7	9	0	.438	441	437	T2nd/AFC Central Div.	—	—		Sam Wyche
1986	10	6	0	.625	409	394	2nd/AFC Central Div.	—	—		Sam Wyche
1987	4	11	0	.267	285	370	4th/AFC Central Div.	—	—		Sam Wyche
1988	12	4	0	.750	448	329	1st/AFC Central Div.	2	1	Super Bowl	Sam Wyche
1989	8	8	0	.500	404	285	4th/AFC Central Div.	—	—		Sam Wyche
1990	9	7	0	.563	360	352	1st/AFC Central Div.	1	1	AFC div. playoff game	Sam Wyche
1991	3	13	0	.188	263	435	4th/AFC Central Div.	—	—		Sam Wyche
1992	5	11	0	.313	274	364	4th/AFC Central Div.	—	—		David Shula
1993	3	13	0	.188	187	319	4th/AFC Central Div.	—	—		David Shula
1994	3	13	0	.188	276	406	3rd/AFC Central Div.	—	—		David Shula
1995	7	9	0	.438	349	374	T2nd/AFC Central Div.	—	—		David Shula
1996	8	8	0	.500	372	369	T3rd/AFC Central Div.	—	—		D. Shula, B. Coslet
1997	7	9	0	.438	355	405	4th/AFC Central Div.	—	—		Bruce Coslet
1998	3	13	0	.188	268	452	5th/AFC Central Div.	—	—		Bruce Coslet

*American Football League.

FIRST-ROUND DRAFT PICKS

1968—Bob Johnson, C, Tennessee
1969—Greg Cook, QB, Cincinnati
1970—Mike Reid, DT, Penn State
1971—Vernon Holland, T, Tennessee State
1972—Sherman White, DE, California
1973—Issac Curtis, WR, San Diego State
1974—Bill Kollar, DT, Montana State
1975—Glenn Cameron, LB, Florida
1976—Billy Brooks, WR, Oklahoma
    Archie Griffin, RB, Ohio State
1977—Eddie Edwards, DT, Miami (Fla.)
    Wilson Whitley, DT, Houston
    Mike Cobb, TE, Michigan State
1978—Ross Browner, DE, Notre Dame
    Blair Bush, C, Washington
1979—Jack Thompson, QB, Washington State
    Charles Alexander, RB, Louisiana State
1980—Anthony Munoz, T, Southern California
1981—David Verser, WR, Kansas
1982—Glen Collins, DE, Mississippi State
1983—Dave Rimington, C, Nebraska
1984—Ricky Hunley, LB, Arizona
    Pete Koch, DE, Maryland

    Brian Blados, T, North Carolina
1985—Eddie Brown, WR, Miami (Fla.)
    Emanuel King, LB, Alabama
1986—Joe Kelly, LB, Washington
    Tim McGee, WR, Tennessee
1987—Jason Buck, DT, Brigham Young
1988—Rickey Dixon, S, Oklahoma
1989—None
1990—James Francis, LB, Baylor
1991—Alfred Williams, LB, Colorado
1992—David Klingler, QB, Houston
    Darryl Williams, DB, Miami (Fla.)
1993—John Copeland, DE, Alabama
1994—Dan Wilkinson, DT, Ohio State*
1995—Ki-Jana Carter, RB, Penn State*
1996—Willie Anderson, T, Auburn
1997—Reinard Wilson, LB, Florida State
1998—Takeo Spikes, LB, Auburn
    Brian Simmons, LB, North Carolina
1999—Akili Smith, QB, Oregon
    *First player chosen in draft.

FRANCHISE RECORDS

Most rushing yards, career
6,447—James Brooks

Most rushing yards, season
1,239—James Brooks, 1989

Most rushing yards, game
246—Corey Dillon vs. Ten., Dec. 4, 1997

Most rushing touchdowns, season
15—Ickey Woods, 1988

Most passing attempts, season
567—Jeff Blake, 1995

Most passing attempts, game
56—Ken Anderson at S.D., Dec. 20, 1982

Most passes completed, season
326—Jeff Blake, 1995

Most passes completed, game
40—Ken Anderson at S.D., Dec. 20, 1982

Most passing yards, career
32,838—Ken Anderson

Most passing yards, season
3,959—Boomer Esiason, 1986

Most passing yards, game
490—Boomer Esiason at L.A. Rams, Oct. 7, 1990

Most touchdown passes, season
29—Ken Anderson, 1981

Most pass receptions, career
473—Carl Pickens

Most pass receptions, season
100—Carl Pickens, 1996

Most pass receptions, game
13—Carl Pickens vs. Pit., Oct. 11, 1998

Most receiving yards, career
7,101—Isaac Curtis

Most receiving yards, season
1,273—Eddie Brown, 1988

Most receiving yards, game
216—Eddie Brown vs. Pit., Nov. 16, 1988

Most receiving touchdowns, season
17—Carl Pickens, 1995

Most touchdowns, career
70—Pete Johnson

Most field goals, season
29—Doug Pelfrey, 1995

Longest field goal
55 yards—Chris Bahr vs. Hou., Sept. 23, 1979

Most interceptions, career
65—Ken Riley

Most interceptions, season
9—Ken Riley, 1976

Most sacks, career
84.5—Eddie Edwards

Most sacks, season
21.5—Coy Bacon, 1976

SERIES RECORDS

Cincinnati vs.: Arizona 4-2; Atlanta 7-2; Baltimore 3-3; Buffalo 10-9; Carolina 0-0; Chicago 4-2; Dallas 3-4; Denver 6-14; Detroit 4-3; Green Bay 4-5; Indianapolis 8-11; Jacksonville 4-4; Kansas City 9-11; Miami 3-12; Minnesota 4-5; New England 7-9; New Orleans 4-5; N.Y. Giants 4-2; N.Y. Jets 6-10; Oakland 7-16; Philadelphia 6-2; Pittsburgh 25-32; St. Louis 5-3; San Diego 9-14; San Francisco 1-7; Seattle 7-7; Tampa Bay 3-3; Tennessee 28-31-1; Washington 2-4.

COACHING RECORDS

Paul Brown, 55-56-1 (0-3); Bruce Coslet, 17-24-0; Forrest Gregg, 32-25-0 (2-2); Bill Johnson, 18-15-0; Homer Rice, 8-19-0; Dave Shula, 19-52-0; Sam Wyche, 61-66-0 (3-2). NOTE: Playoff games in parentheses.

RETIRED UNIFORM NUMBERS

No.	Player
54	Bob Johnson

CLEVELAND BROWNS
YEAR-BY-YEAR RECORDS

	REGULAR SEASON							PLAYOFFS			
Year	W	L	T	Pct.	PF	PA	Finish	W	L	Highest round	Coach
1946*	12	2	0	.857	423	137	1st/Western Div.	—	—		Paul Brown
1947*	12	1	1	.923	410	185	1st/Western Div.	—	—		Paul Brown
1948*	14	0	0	1.000	389	190	1st/Western Div.	—	—		Paul Brown
1949*	9	1	2	.900	339	171	1st	—	—		Paul Brown
1950	10	2	0	.833	310	144	1st/American Conf.	2	0	NFL champ	Paul Brown
1951	11	1	0	.917	331	152	1st/American Conf.	0	1	NFL championship game	Paul Brown
1952	8	4	0	.667	310	213	1st/American Conf.	0	1	NFL championship game	Paul Brown
1953	11	1	0	.917	348	162	1st/Eastern Conf.	0	1	NFL championship game	Paul Brown
1954	9	3	0	.750	336	162	1st/Eastern Conf.	1	0	NFL champ	Paul Brown
1955	9	2	1	.818	349	218	1st/Eastern Conf.	1	0	NFL champ	Paul Brown
1956	5	7	0	.417	167	177	4th/Eastern Conf.	—	—		Paul Brown
1957	9	2	1	.818	269	172	1st/Eastern Conf.	0	1	NFL championship game	Paul Brown
1958	9	3	0	.750	302	217	2nd/Eastern Conf.	0	1	E. Conf. championship game	Paul Brown
1959	7	5	0	.583	270	214	T2nd/Eastern Conf.	—	—		Paul Brown
1960	8	3	1	.727	362	217	2nd/Eastern Conf.	—	—		Paul Brown
1961	8	5	1	.615	319	270	3rd/Eastern Conf.	—	—		Paul Brown
1962	7	6	1	.538	291	257	3rd/Eastern Conf.	—	—		Paul Brown
1963	10	4	0	.714	343	262	2nd/Eastern Conf.	—	—		Blanton Collier
1964	10	3	1	.769	415	293	1st/Eastern Conf.	1	0	NFL champ	Blanton Collier
1965	11	3	0	.786	363	325	1st/Eastern Conf.	0	1	NFL championship game	Blanton Collier
1966	9	5	0	.643	403	259	T2nd/Eastern Conf.	—	—		Blanton Collier
1967	9	5	0	.643	334	297	1st/Century Div.	0	1	E. Conf. championship game	Blanton Collier
1968	10	4	0	.714	394	273	1st/Century Div.	1	1	NFL championship game	Blanton Collier
1969	10	3	1	.769	351	300	1st/Century Div.	1	1	NFL championship game	Blanton Collier
1970	7	7	0	.500	286	265	2nd/AFC Central Div.	—	—		Blanton Collier
1971	9	5	0	.643	285	273	1st/AFC Central Div.	0	1	AFC div. playoff game	Nick Skorich
1972	10	4	0	.714	268	249	2nd/AFC Central Div.	0	1	AFC div. playoff game	Nick Skorich
1973	7	5	2	.571	234	255	3rd/AFC Central Div.	—	—		Nick Skorich
1974	4	10	0	.286	251	344	4th/AFC Central Div.	—	—		Nick Skorich
1975	3	11	0	.214	218	372	4th/AFC Central Div.	—	—		Forrest Gregg
1976	9	5	0	.643	267	287	3rd/AFC Central Div.	—	—		Forrest Gregg
1977	6	8	0	.429	269	267	4th/AFC Central Div.	—	—		F. Gregg, Dick Modzelewski
1978	8	8	0	.500	334	356	3rd/AFC Central Div.	—	—		Sam Rutigliano
1979	9	7	0	.563	359	352	3rd/AFC Central Div.	—	—		Sam Rutigliano
1980	11	5	0	.688	357	310	1st/AFC Central Div.	0	1	AFC div. playoff game	Sam Rutigliano
1981	5	11	0	.313	276	375	4th/AFC Central Div.	—	—		Sam Rutigliano
1982	4	5	0	.444	140	182	T8th/AFC	0	1	AFC first-round pl. game	Sam Rutigliano
1983	9	7	0	.563	356	342	2nd/AFC Central Div.	—	—		Sam Rutigliano
1984	5	11	0	.313	250	297	3rd/AFC Central Div.	—	—		Rutigliano, Schottenheimer
1985	8	8	0	.500	287	294	1st/AFC Central Div.	0	1	AFC div. playoff game	Marty Schottenheimer
1986	12	4	0	.750	391	310	1st/AFC Central Div.	1	1	AFC championship game	Marty Schottenheimer
1987	10	5	0	.667	390	239	1st/AFC Central Div.	1	1	AFC championship game	Marty Schottenheimer
1988	10	6	0	.625	304	288	T2nd/AFC Central Div.	0	1	AFC wild-card game	Marty Schottenheimer
1989	9	6	1	.594	334	254	1st/AFC Central Div.	1	1	AFC championship game	Bud Carson
1990	3	13	0	.188	228	462	4th/AFC Central Div.	—	—		Bud Carson, Jim Shofner
1991	6	10	0	.375	293	298	3rd/AFC Central Div.	—	—		Bill Belichick
1992	7	9	0	.438	272	275	3rd/AFC Central Div.	—	—		Bill Belichick
1993	7	9	0	.438	304	307	3rd/AFC Central Div.	—	—		Bill Belichick
1994	11	5	0	.688	340	204	2nd/AFC Central Div.	1	1	AFC div. playoff game	Bill Belichick
1995	5	11	0	.313	289	356	4th/AFC Central Div.	—	—		Bill Belichick

*All-America Football Conference.

FIRST-ROUND DRAFT PICKS

1950—Ken Carpenter, B, Oregon State
1951—Ken Konz, B, Louisiana State
1952—Bert Rechichar, DB, Tennessee
    Harry Agganis, QB, Boston University
1953—Doug Atkins, DT, Tennessee
1954—Bobby Garrett, QB, Stanford*
    John Bauer, G, Illinois
1955—Kent Burris, C, Oklahoma
1956—Preston Carpenter, B, Arkansas
1957—Jim Brown, B, Syracuse
1958—Jim Shofner, DB, Texas Christian
1959—Rich Kreitling, DE, Illinois
1960—Jim Houston, DE, Ohio State
1961—None
1962—Gary Collins, WR, Maryland
    Leroy Jackson, B, Western Illinois
1963—Tom Hutchinson, TE, Kentucky
1964—Paul Warfield, WR, Ohio State
1965—None
1966—Milt Morin, TE, Massachusetts
1967—Bob Matheson, LB, Duke
1968—M. Upshaw, DE, Trinity (Tex.)
1969—Ron Johnson, RB, Michigan
1970—Mike Phipps, QB, Purdue
    Bob McKay, T, Texas
1971—Clarence Scott, DB, Kansas State
1972—Thom Darden, DB, Michigan
1973—Steve Holden, WR, Arizona State
    Pete Adams, G, Southern California

1974—None
1975—Mack Mitchell, DE, Houston
1976—Mike Pruitt, RB, Purdue
1977—Robert Jackson, LB, Texas A&M
1978—Clay Matthews, LB, Southern California
    Ozzie Newsome, WR, Alabama
1979—Willis Adams, WR, Houston
1980—Charles White, RB, Southern California
1981—Hanford Dixon, CB, Southern Mississippi
1982—Chip Banks, LB, Southern California
1983—None
1984—Don Rogers, DB, UCLA
1985—None
1986—None
1987—Mike Junkin, LB, Duke
1988—Clifford Charlton, LB, Florida
1989—Eric Metcalf, RB, Texas
1990—None
1991—Eric Turner, S, UCLA
1992—Tommy Vardell, FB, Stanford
1993—Steve Everitt, C, Michigan
1994—Antonio Langham, DB, Alabama
    Derrick Alexander, WR, Michigan
1995—Craig Powell, LB, Ohio State
1999—Tim Couch, QB, Kentucky*
    *First player chosen in draft.

HISTORY Team by team

FRANCHISE RECORDS

Most rushing yards, career
12,312—Jim Brown
Most rushing yards, season
1,863—Jim Brown, 1963
Most rushing yards, game
237—Jim Brown vs. L.A., Nov. 24, 1957
    Jim Brown vs. Phi., Nov. 19, 1961
Most rushing touchdowns, season
17— Jim Brown, 1958
    Jim Brown, 1965
Most passing attempts, season
567—Brian Sipe, 1981
Most passing attempts, game
57—Brian Sipe vs. S.D., Sept. 7, 1981
Most passes completed, season
337—Brian Sipe, 1980
Most passes completed, game
33—Brian Sipe vs. S.D., Dec. 5, 1982
Most passing yards, career
23,713—Brian Sipe

Most passing yards, season
4,132—Brian Sipe, 1980
Most passing yards, game
444—Brian Sipe vs. Bal., Oct. 25, 1981
Most touchdown passes, season
30—Brian Sipe, 1980
Most pass receptions, career
662—Ozzie Newsome
Most pass receptions, season
89—Ozzie Newsome, 1983
    Ozzie Newsome, 1984
Most pass receptions, game
14—Ozzie Newsome vs. NYJ, Oct. 14, 1984
Most receiving yards, career
7,980—Ozzie Newsome
Most receiving yards, season
1,236—Webster Slaughter, 1989
Most receiving yards, game
191—Ozzie Newsome vs. NYJ, Oct. 14, 1984

Most receiving touchdowns, season
13—Gary Collins, 1963
Most touchdowns, career
126—Jim Brown
Most field goals, season
29—Matt Stover, 1995
Longest field goal
60 yards—Steve Cox at Cin., Oct. 21, 1984
Most interceptions, career
45—Thom Darden
Most interceptions, season
10—Thom Darden, 1978
Most sacks, career
63.5—Clay Matthews
Most sacks, season
14.5—Bill Glass, 1965

SERIES RECORDS

Cleveland vs.: Arizona 32-10-3; Atlanta 8-2; Buffalo 7-4; Carolina 0-0; Chicago 8-3; Cincinnati 27-24; Dallas 15-9; Denver 5-13; Detroit 3-12; Green Bay 6-8; Houston 30-21; Indianapolis 13-7; Jacksonville 0-2; Kansas City 8-7-2; Miami 4-6; Minnesota 3-8; New England 10-4; New Orleans 9-3; N.Y. Giants 25-17-2; N.Y. Jets 9-6; Oakland 3-9; Philadelphia 31-12-1; Pittsburgh 52-40; St. Louis 8-7; San Diego 6-9-1; San Francisco 9-6; Seattle 4-9; Tampa Bay 5-0; Washington 32-9-1.

COACHING RECORDS

Bill Belichick, 36-55 (1-1); Paul Brown, 158-48-8 (4-5); Bud Carson, 11-12-1 (1-1); Blanton Collier, 76-34-2 (3-4); Forrest Gregg (18-23); Dick Modzelewski, 0-1; Sam Rutigliano, 47-50 (0-2); Marty Schottenheimer, 44-27 (2-4); Jim Shofner, 1-7; Nick Skorich, 30-24-2 (0-2).
NOTE: Playoff games in parentheses.

RETIRED UNIFORM NUMBERS

No.	Player
14	Otto Graham
32	Jim Brown
45	Ernie Davis
46	Don Fleming
76	Lou Groza

DALLAS COWBOYS
YEAR-BY-YEAR RECORDS

	REGULAR SEASON							PLAYOFFS			
Year	W	L	T	Pct.	PF	PA	Finish	W	L	Highest round	Coach
1960	0	11	1	.000	177	369	7th/Western Conf.	—	—		Tom Landry
1961	4	9	1	.308	236	380	6th/Eastern Conf.	—	—		Tom Landry
1962	5	8	1	.385	398	402	5th/Eastern Conf.	—	—		Tom Landry
1963	4	10	0	.286	305	378	5th/Eastern Conf.	—	—		Tom Landry
1964	5	8	1	.385	250	289	5th/Eastern Conf.	—	—		Tom Landry
1965	7	7	0	.500	325	280	T2nd/Eastern Conf.	—	—		Tom Landry
1966	10	3	1	.769	445	239	1st/Eastern Conf.	0	1	NFL championship game	Tom Landry
1967	9	5	0	.643	342	268	1st/Capitol Div.	1	1	NFL championship game	Tom Landry
1968	12	2	0	.857	431	186	1st/Capitol Div.	0	1	E. Conf. championship game	Tom Landry
1969	11	2	1	.846	369	223	1st/Capitol Div.	0	1	E. Conf. championship game	Tom Landry
1970	10	4	0	.714	299	221	1st/NFC Eastern Div.	2	1	Super Bowl	Tom Landry
1971	11	3	0	.786	406	222	1st/NFC Eastern Div.	3	0	Super Bowl champ	Tom Landry
1972	10	4	0	.714	319	240	2nd/NFC Eastern Div.	1	1	NFC championship game	Tom Landry
1973	10	4	0	.714	382	203	1st/NFC Eastern Div.	1	1	NFC championship game	Tom Landry
1974	8	6	0	.571	297	235	3rd/NFC Eastern Div.	—	—		Tom Landry
1975	10	4	0	.714	350	268	2nd/NFC Eastern Div.	2	1	Super Bowl	Tom Landry
1976	11	3	0	.786	296	194	1st/NFC Eastern Div.	0	1	NFC div. playoff game	Tom Landry
1977	12	2	0	.857	345	212	1st/NFC Eastern Div.	3	0	Super Bowl champ	Tom Landry
1978	12	4	0	.750	384	208	1st/NFC Eastern Div.	2	1	Super Bowl	Tom Landry
1979	11	5	0	.688	371	313	1st/NFC Eastern Div.	0	1	NFC div. playoff game	Tom Landry
1980	12	4	0	.750	454	311	2nd/NFC Eastern Div.	2	1	NFC championship game	Tom Landry
1981	12	4	0	.750	367	277	1st/NFC Eastern Div.	1	1	NFC championship game	Tom Landry
1982	6	3	0	.667	226	145	2nd/NFC	2	1	NFC championship game	Tom Landry
1983	12	4	0	.750	479	360	2nd/NFC Eastern Div.	0	1	NFC wild-card game	Tom Landry
1984	9	7	0	.563	308	308	T3rd/NFC Eastern Div.	—	—		Tom Landry
1985	10	6	0	.625	357	333	1st/NFC Eastern Div.	0	1	NFC div. playoff game	Tom Landry
1986	7	9	0	.438	346	337	3rd/NFC Eastern Div.	—	—		Tom Landry
1987	7	8	0	.467	340	348	T2nd/NFC Eastern Div.	—	—		Tom Landry
1988	3	13	0	.188	265	381	5th/NFC Eastern Div.	—	—		Tom Landry
1989	1	15	0	.063	204	393	5th/NFC Eastern Div.	—	—		Jimmy Johnson
1990	7	9	0	.438	244	308	4th/NFC Eastern Div.	—	—		Jimmy Johnson
1991	11	5	0	.688	342	310	2nd/NFC Eastern Div.	1	1	NFC div. playoff game	Jimmy Johnson
1992	13	3	0	.813	409	243	1st/NFC Eastern Div.	3	0	Super Bowl champ	Jimmy Johnson
1993	12	4	0	.750	376	229	1st/NFC Eastern Div.	3	0	Super Bowl champ	Jimmy Johnson
1994	12	4	0	.750	414	248	1st/NFC Eastern Div.	1	1	NFC championship game	Barry Switzer
1995	12	4	0	.750	435	291	1st/NFC Eastern Div.	3	0	Super Bowl champ	Barry Switzer
1996	10	6	0	.625	286	250	1st/NFC Eastern Div.	1	1	NFC div. playoff game	Barry Switzer
1997	6	10	0	.375	304	314	4th/NFC Eastern Div.	—	—		Barry Switzer
1998	10	6	0	.625	381	275	1st/NFC Eastern Div.	0	1	NFC wild-card game	Chan Gailey

FIRST-ROUND DRAFT PICKS

1961—Bob Lilly, DT, Texas Christian
1962—None
1963—Lee Roy Jordan, LB, Alabama
1964—Scott Appleton, DT, Texas
1965—Craig Morton, QB, California
1966—John Niland, G, Iowa
1967—None
1968—Dennis Homan, WR, Alabama
1969—Calvin Hill, RB, Yale
1970—Duane Thomas, RB, West Texas State
1971—Tody Smith, DE, Southern California
1972—Bill Thomas, RB, Boston College
1973—Billy Joe DuPree, TE, Michigan State
1974—Ed Jones, DE, Tennessee State*
    Charles Young, RB, North Carolina State
1975—Randy White, LB, Maryland
    Thomas Henderson, LB, Langston
1976—Aaron Kyle, DB, Wyoming
1977—Tony Dorsett, RB, Pittsburgh
1978—Larry Bethea, DE, Michigan State
1979—Robert Shaw, C, Tennessee
1980—None
1981—Howard Richards, T, Missouri

1982—Rod Hill, DB, Kentucky State
1983—Jim Jeffcoat, DE, Arizona State
1984—Billy Cannon Jr., LB, Texas A&M
1985—Kevin Brooks, DE, Michigan
1986—Mike Sherrard, WR, UCLA
1987—Danny Noonan, DT, Nebraska
1988—Michael Irvin, WR, Miami (Fla.)
1989—Troy Aikman, QB, UCLA*
1990—Emmitt Smith, RB, Florida
1991—Russell Maryland, DL, Miami (Fla.)*
    Alvin Harper, WR, Tennessee
    Kelvin Pritchett, DT, Mississippi
1992—Kevin Smith, DB, Texas A&M
    Robert Jones, LB, East Carolina
1993—None
1994—Shante Carver, DE, Arizona State
1995—None
1996—None
1997—David LaFleur, TE, Louisiana State
1998—Greg Ellis, DE, North Carolina
1999—Ebenezer Ekuban, DE, North Carolina
  *First player chosen in draft.

FRANCHISE RECORDS

Most rushing yards, career
12,566—Emmitt Smith
Most rushing yards, season
1,773—Emmitt Smith, 1995
Most rushing yards, game
237—Emmitt Smith at Phi., Oct. 31, 1993
Most rushing touchdowns, season
25—Emmitt Smith, 1995
Most passing attempts, season
533—Danny White, 1983
Most passing attempts, game
57—Troy Aikman vs. Min., Nov. 26, 1998
Most passes completed, season
334—Danny White, 1983
Most passes completed, game
34—Troy Aikman at NYG, Oct. 5, 1997
Troy Aikman vs. Min., Nov. 26, 1998
Most passing yards, career
28,346—Troy Aikman

Most passing yards, season
3,980—Danny White, 1983
Most passing yards, game
460—Don Meredith at S.F., Nov. 10, 1963
Most touchdown passes, season
29—Danny White, 1983
Most pass receptions, career
740—Michael Irvin
Most pass receptions, season
111—Michael Irvin, 1995
Most pass receptions, game
13—Lance Rentzel vs. Was., Nov. 19, 1967
Most receiving yards, career
11,737—Michael Irvin
Most receiving yards, season
1,603—Michael Irvin, 1995
Most receiving yards, game
246—Bob Hayes at Was., Nov. 13, 1966
Most receiving touchdowns, season
14—Frank Clarke, 1962

Most touchdowns, career
134—Emmitt Smith
Most field goals, season
34—Richie Cunningham, 1997
Longest field goal
54 yards—Toni Fritsch at NYG,
  Sept. 24, 1972
  Ken Willis at Cle., Sept. 1, 1991
  Richie Cunningham at Den., Sept.
  13, 1998
Most interceptions, career
52—Mel Renfro
Most interceptions, season
11—Everson Walls, 1981
Most sacks, career
113—Harvey Martin
Most sacks, season
20—Harvey Martin, 1977

SERIES RECORDS

Dallas vs.: Arizona 49-23-1; Atlanta 11-6; Buffalo 3-3; Carolina 1-1; Chicago 9-8; Cincinnati 4-3; Denver 4-3; Detroit 7-6; Green Bay 8-10; Indianapolis 7-3; Jacksonville 1-0; Kansas City 4-3; Miami 2-6; Minnesota 9-7; New England 7-0; New Orleans 14-4; N.Y. Giants 46-25-2; N.Y. Jets 5-1; Oakland 3-4; Philadelphia 47-29; Pittsburgh 14-11; St. Louis 8-9; San Diego 5-1; San Francisco 7-12-1; Seattle 5-1; Tampa Bay 6-0; Tennessee 5-4; Washington 43-31-2.

COACHING RECORDS

Chan Gailey, 10-6-0; Jimmy Johnson, 44-36-0 (7-1); Tom Landry, 250-162-6 (20-16); Barry Switzer, 40-24-0 (5-2).
NOTE: Playoff games in parentheses.

RETIRED UNIFORM NUMBERS

No.	Player
	None

DENVER BRONCOS
YEAR-BY-YEAR RECORDS

			REGULAR SEASON						PLAYOFFS		
Year	W	L	T	Pct.	PF	PA	Finish	W	L	Highest round	Coach
1960*	4	9	1	.308	309	393	4th/Western Div.	—	—		Frank Filchock
1961*	3	11	0	.214	251	432	3rd/Western Div.	—	—		Frank Filchock
1962*	7	7	0	.500	353	334	2nd/Western Div.	—	—		Jack Faulkner
1963*	2	11	1	.154	301	473	4th/Western Div.	—	—		Jack Faulkner
1964*	2	11	1	.154	240	438	4th/Western Div.	—	—		J. Faulkner, M. Speedie
1965*	4	10	0	.286	303	392	4th/Western Div.	—	—		Mac Speedie
1966*	4	10	0	.286	196	381	4th/Western Div.	—	—		M. Speedie, Ray Malavasi
1967*	3	11	0	.214	256	409	4th/Western Div.	—	—		Lou Saban
1968*	5	9	0	.357	255	404	4th/Western Div.	—	—		Lou Saban
1969*	5	8	1	.385	297	344	4th/Western Div.	—	—		Lou Saban
1970	5	8	1	.385	253	264	4th/AFC Western Div.	—	—		Lou Saban
1971	4	9	1	.308	203	275	4th/AFC Western Div.	—	—		Lou Saban, Jerry Smith
1972	5	9	0	.357	325	350	3rd/AFC Western Div.	—	—		John Ralston
1973	7	5	2	.571	354	296	T2nd/AFC Western Div.	—	—		John Ralston
1974	7	6	1	.536	302	294	2nd/AFC Western Div.	—	—		John Ralston
1975	6	8	0	.429	254	307	2nd/AFC Western Div.	—	—		John Ralston
1976	9	5	0	.643	315	206	2nd/AFC Western Div.	—	—		John Ralston
1977	12	2	0	.857	274	148	1st/AFC Western Div.	2	1	Super Bowl	Red Miller
1978	10	6	0	.625	282	198	1st/AFC Western Div.	0	1	AFC div. playoff game	Red Miller
1979	10	6	0	.625	289	262	2nd/AFC Western Div.	0	1	AFC wild-card game	Red Miller
1980	8	8	0	.500	310	323	T3rd/AFC Western Div.	—	—		Red Miller
1981	10	6	0	.625	321	289	2nd/AFC Western Div.	—	—		Dan Reeves
1982	2	7	0	.222	148	226	12th/AFC	—	—		Dan Reeves
1983	9	7	0	.563	302	327	T2nd/AFC Western Div.	0	1	AFC wild-card game	Dan Reeves
1984	13	3	0	.813	353	241	1st/AFC Western Div.	0	1	AFC div. playoff game	Dan Reeves
1985	11	5	0	.688	380	329	2nd/AFC Western Div.	—	—		Dan Reeves

	REGULAR SEASON							PLAYOFFS			
Year	W	L	T	Pct.	PF	PA	Finish	W	L	Highest round	Coach
1986	11	5	0	.688	378	327	1st/AFC Western Div.	2	1	Super Bowl	Dan Reeves
1987	10	4	1	.700	379	288	1st/AFC Western Div.	2	1	Super Bowl	Dan Reeves
1988	8	8	0	.500	327	352	2nd/AFC Western Div.	—	—		Dan Reeves
1989	11	5	0	.688	362	226	1st/AFC Western Div.	2	1	Super Bowl	Dan Reeves
1990	5	11	0	.313	331	374	5th/AFC Western Div.	—	—		Dan Reeves
1991	12	4	0	.750	304	235	1st/AFC Western Div.	1	1	AFC championship game	Dan Reeves
1992	8	8	0	.500	262	329	3rd/AFC Western Div.	—	—		Dan Reeves
1993	9	7	0	.563	373	284	3rd/AFC Western Div.	0	1	AFC wild-card game	Wade Phillips
1994	7	9	0	.438	347	396	4th/AFC Western Div.	—	—		Wade Phillips
1995	8	8	0	.500	388	345	T3rd/AFC Western Div.	—	—		Mike Shanahan
1996	13	3	0	.813	391	275	1st/AFC Western Div.	0	1	AFC div. playoff game	Mike Shanahan
1997	12	4	0	.750	472	287	2nd/AFC Western Div.	4	0	Super Bowl champ	Mike Shanahan
1998	14	2	0	.875	501	309	1st/AFC Western Div.	3	0	Super Bowl champ	Mike Shanahan

*American Football League.

FIRST-ROUND DRAFT PICKS

1960—Roger Leclerc, C, Trinity (Conn.)
1961—Bob Gaiters, RB, New Mexico State
1962—Merlin Olsen, DT, Utah State
1963—Kermit Alexander, DB, UCLA
1964—Bob Brown, T, Nebraska
1965—None
1966—Jerry Shay, DT, Purdue
1967—Floyd Little, RB, Syracuse
1968—None
1969—None
1970—Bob Anderson, RB, Colorado
1971—Marv Montgomery, T, Southern California
1972—Riley Odoms, TE, Houston
1973—Otis Armstrong, RB, Purdue
1974—Randy Gradishar, LB, Ohio State
1975—Louis Wright, DB, San Jose State
1976—Tom Glassic, G, Virginia
1977—Steve Schindler, G, Boston College
1978—Don Latimer, DT, Miami (Fla.)
1979—Kevin Clark, T, Nebraska
1980—None
1981—Dennis Smith, DB, Southern California
1982—Gerald Willhite, RB, San Jose State
1983—Chris Hinton, G, Northwestern
1984—None
1985—Steve Sewell, RB, Oklahoma
1986—None
1987—Ricky Nattiel, WR, Florida
1988—Ted Gregory, DT, Syracuse
1989—Steve Atwater, DB, Arkansas
1990—None
1991—Mike Croel, LB, Nebraska
1992—Tommy Maddox, QB, UCLA
1993—Dan Williams, DE, Toledo
1994—None
1995—None
1996—John Mobley, LB, Kutztown (Pa.)
1997—Trevor Pryce, DT, Clemson
1998—Marcus Nash, WR, Tennessee
1999—Al Wilson, LB, Tennessee

FRANCHISE RECORDS

Most rushing yards, career
6,413—Terrell Davis
Most rushing yards, season
2,008—Terrell Davis, 1998
Most rushing yards, game
215—Terrell Davis vs. Cin., Sept. 21, 1997
Most rushing touchdowns, season
21—Terrell Davis, 1998
Most passing attempts, season
605—John Elway, 1985
Most passing attempts, game
59—John Elway at G.B., Oct. 10, 1993
Most passes completed, season
348—John Elway, 1993
Most passes completed, game
36—John Elway vs. S.D., Sept. 4, 1994
Most passing yards, career
51,475—John Elway
Most passing yards, season
4,030—John Elway, 1993
Most passing yards, game
447—Frank Tripucka at Buf., Sept. 15, 1962
Most touchdown passes, season
27—John Elway, 1997
Most pass receptions, career
543—Lionel Taylor
Most pass receptions, season
100—Lionel Taylor, 1961
Most pass receptions, game
13—Lionel Taylor vs. Oak., Nov. 29, 1964
Robert Anderson vs. Chi., Sept. 30, 1973
Shannon Sharpe vs. S.D., Oct. 6, 1996
Most receiving yards, career
6,872—Lionel Taylor
Most receiving yards, season
1,244—Steve Watson, 1981
Most receiving yards, game
199—Lionel Taylor vs. Buf., Nov. 27, 1960
Most receiving touchdowns, season
13—Steve Watson, 1981
Most touchdowns, career
61—Terrell Davis
Most field goals, season
31—Jason Elam, 1995
Longest field goal
63 yards—Jason Elam vs. Jac., Oct. 25, 1998
Most interceptions, career
44—Steve Foley
Most interceptions, season
11—Goose Gonsoulin, 1960
Most sacks, career
97.5—Simon Fletcher
Most sacks, season
16—Simon Fletcher, 1992

SERIES RECORDS

Denver vs.: Arizona 4-0-1; Atlanta 6-3; Baltimore 1-0; Buffalo 12-17-1; Carolina 1-0; Chicago 6-5; Cincinnati 14-6; Dallas 3-4; Detroit 4-3; Green Bay 4-3-1; Indianapolis 9-2; Jacksonville 2-0; Kansas City 34-43; Miami 2-6-1; Minnesota 4-5; New England 20-12; New Orleans 4-2; N.Y. Giants 3-4; N.Y. Jets 13-12-1; Oakland 26-49-2; Philadelphia 3-6; Pittsburgh 10-6-1; San Diego 42-35-1; St. Louis 4-4; San Francisco 4-4; Seattle 28-15; Tampa Bay 3-1; Tennessee 11-20-1; Washington 5-3.

COACHING RECORDS

Jack Faulkner, 9-22-1; Frank Filchock, 7-20-1; Ray Malavasi, 4-8-0; Red Miller, 40-22 (2-3); Wade Phillips, 16-16-0 (0-1); John Ralston, 34-33-3; Dan Reeves, 110-73-1 (7-6); Lou Saban, 20-42-3; Mike Shanahan, 47-17-0 (7-1); Jerry Smith, 2-3; Mac Speedie, 6-19-1.

NOTE: Playoff games in parentheses.

RETIRED UNIFORM NUMBERS

No.	Player
18	Frank Tripucka
44	Floyd Little

DETROIT LIONS
YEAR-BY-YEAR RECORDS

		REGULAR SEASON							PLAYOFFS			
Year	W	L	T	Pct.	PF	PA	Finish	W	L	Highest round	Coach
1930*	5	6	3	.455	...	...	T7th				Tubby Griffen
1931*	11	3	0	.786	...	...	2nd				Potsy Clark
1932*	6	2	4	.750	...	...	3rd				Potsy Clark
1933*	6	5	0	.545	128	87	2nd/Western Div.	—	—		Potsy Clark
1934	10	3	0	.769	238	59	2nd/Western Div.	—	—		Potsy Clark
1935	7	3	2	.700	191	111	1st/Western Div.	1	0	NFL champ	Potsy Clark
1936	8	4	0	.667	235	102	3rd/Western Div.	—	—		Potsy Clark
1937	7	4	0	.636	180	105	T2nd/Western Div.	—	—		Dutch Clark
1938	7	4	0	.636	119	108	2nd/Western Div.	—	—		Dutch Clark
1939	6	5	0	.545	145	150	3rd/Western Div.	—	—		Gus Henderson
1940	5	5	1	.500	138	153	3rd/Western Div.	—	—		Potsy Clark
1941	4	6	1	.400	121	195	3rd/Western Div.	—	—		Bill Edwards
1942	0	11	0	.000	38	263	5th/Western Div.	—	—		B. Edwards, John Karcis
1943	3	6	1	.333	178	218	3rd/Western Div.	—	—		Gus Dorais
1944	6	3	1	.667	216	151	T2nd/Western Div.	—	—		Gus Dorais
1945	7	3	0	.700	195	194	2nd/Western Div.	—	—		Gus Dorais
1946	1	10	0	.091	142	310	2nd/Western Div.	—	—		Gus Dorais
1947	3	9	0	.250	231	305	5th/Western Div.	—	—		Gus Dorais
1948	2	10	0	.167	200	407	5th/Western Div.	—	—		Bo McMillin
1949	4	8	0	.333	237	259	4th/Western Div.	—	—		Bo McMillin
1950	6	6	0	.500	321	285	4th/National Conf.	—	—		Bo McMillin
1951	7	4	1	.636	336	259	T2nd/National Conf.	—	—		Buddy Parker
1952	9	3	0	.750	344	192	1st/National Conf.	2	0	NFL champ	Buddy Parker
1953	10	2	0	.833	271	205	1st/Western Conf.	1	0	NFL champ	Buddy Parker
1954	9	2	1	.818	337	189	1st/Western Conf.	0	1	NFL championship game	Buddy Parker
1955	3	9	0	.250	230	275	6th/Western Conf.	—	—		Buddy Parker
1956	9	3	0	.750	300	188	2nd/Western Conf.	—	—		Buddy Parker
1957	8	4	0	.667	251	231	1st/Western Conf.	2	0	NFL champ	George Wilson
1958	4	7	1	.364	261	276	5th/Western Conf.	—	—		George Wilson
1959	3	8	1	.273	203	275	5th/Western Conf.	—	—		George Wilson
1960	7	5	0	.583	239	212	T2nd/Western Conf.	—	—		George Wilson
1961	8	5	1	.615	270	258	2nd/Western Conf.	—	—		George Wilson
1962	11	3	0	.786	315	177	2nd/Western Conf.	—	—		George Wilson
1963	5	8	1	.385	326	265	T4th/Western Conf.	—	—		George Wilson
1964	7	5	2	.583	280	260	4th/Western Conf.	—	—		George Wilson
1965	6	7	1	.462	257	295	6th/Western Conf.	—	—		Harry Gilmer
1966	4	9	1	.308	206	317	T6th/Western Conf.	—	—		Harry Gilmer
1967	5	7	2	.417	260	259	3rd/Central Div.	—	—		Joe Schmidt
1968	4	8	2	.333	207	241	4th/Central Div.	—	—		Joe Schmidt
1969	9	4	1	.692	259	188	2nd/Central Div.	—	—		Joe Schmidt
1970	10	4	0	.714	347	202	2nd/NFC Central Div.	0	1	NFC div. playoff game	Joe Schmidt
1971	7	6	1	.538	341	286	2nd/NFC Central Div.	—	—		Joe Schmidt
1972	8	5	1	.607	339	290	2nd/NFC Central Div.	—	—		Joe Schmidt
1973	6	7	1	.464	271	247	2nd/NFC Central Div.	—	—		Don McCafferty
1974	7	7	0	.500	256	270	2nd/NFC Central Div.	—	—		Rick Forzano
1975	7	7	0	.500	245	262	2nd/NFC Central Div.	—	—		Rick Forzano
1976	6	8	0	.429	262	220	3rd/NFC Central Div.	—	—		R. Forzano, T. Hudspeth
1977	6	8	0	.429	183	252	3rd/NFC Central Div.	—	—		Tommy Hudspeth
1978	7	9	0	.438	290	300	T3rd/NFC Central Div.	—	—		Monte Clark
1979	2	14	0	.125	219	365	5th/NFC Central Div.	—	—		Monte Clark
1980	9	7	0	.563	334	272	2nd/NFC Central Div.	—	—		Monte Clark
1981	8	8	0	.500	397	322	2nd/NFC Central Div.	—	—		Monte Clark
1982	4	5	0	.444	181	176	T8th/NFC	0	1	NFC first-round pl. game	Monte Clark
1983	9	7	0	.563	347	286	1st/NFC Central Div.	0	1	NFC div. playoff game	Monte Clark
1984	4	11	1	.281	283	408	4th/NFC Central Div.	—	—		Monte Clark
1985	7	9	0	.438	307	366	T3rd/NFC Central Div.	—	—		Darryl Rogers
1986	5	11	0	.313	277	326	3rd/NFC Central Div.	—	—		Darryl Rogers
1987	4	11	0	.267	269	384	T4th/NFC Central Div.	—	—		Darryl Rogers

Year	W	L	T	Pct.	PF	PA	Finish	W	L	Highest round	Coach
				REGULAR SEASON						**PLAYOFFS**	
1988	4	12	0	.250	220	313	T4th/NFC Central Div.	—	—		Darryl Rogers
1989	7	9	0	.438	312	364	3rd/NFC Central Div.	—	—		Wayne Fontes
1990	6	10	0	.375	373	413	T2nd/NFC Central Div.	—	—		Wayne Fontes
1991	12	4	0	.750	339	295	1st/NFC Central Div.	1	1	NFC championship game	Wayne Fontes
1992	5	11	0	.313	273	332	T3rd/NFC Central Div.	—	—		Wayne Fontes
1993	10	6	0	.625	298	292	1st/NFC Central Div.	0	1	NFC wild-card game	Wayne Fontes
1994	9	7	0	.563	357	342	T2nd/NFC Central Div.	0	1	NFC wild-card game	Wayne Fontes
1995	10	6	0	.625	436	336	2nd/NFC Central Div.	0	1	NFC wild-card game	Wayne Fontes
1996	5	11	0	.313	302	368	5th/NFC Central Div.	—	—		Wayne Fontes
1997	9	7	0	.563	379	306	T3rd/NFC Central Div.	0	1	NFC wild-card game	Bobby Ross
1998	5	11	0	.313	306	378	4th/NFC Central Div.	—	—		Bobby Ross

*Portsmouth Spartans.

FIRST-ROUND DRAFT PICKS

1936—Sid Wagner, G, Michigan State
1937—Lloyd Cardwell, B, Nebraska
1938—Alex Wojciechowicz, C, Fordham
1939—John Pingel, B, Michigan State
1940—Doyle Nave, B, Southern California
1941—Jim Thomason, B, Texas A&M
1942—Bob Westfall, B, Michigan
1943—Frank Sinkwich, B, Georgia*
1944—Otto Graham, B, Northwestern
1945—Frank Szymanski, B, Notre Dame
1946—Bill Dellastatious, B, Missouri
1947—Glenn Davis, B, Army
1948—Y.A. Tittle, B, Louisiana State
1949—John Rauch, B, Georgia
1950—Leon Hart, E, Notre Dame*
    Joe Watson, C, Rice
1951—None
1952—None
1953—Harley Sewell, G, Texas
1954—Dick Chapman, T, Rice
1955—Dave Middleton, B, Auburn
1956—Howard Cassidy, B, Ohio State
1957—Bill Glass, G, Baylor
1958—Alex Karras, DT, Iowa
1959—Nick Pietrosante, B, Notre Dame
1960—John Robinson, DB, Louisiana State
1961—None
1962—John Hadl, QB, Kansas
1963—Daryl Sanders, T, Ohio State
1964—Pete Beathard, QB, Southern California
1965—Tom Nowatzke, RB, Indiana
1966—None
1967—Mel Farr, RB, UCLA
1968—Greg Landry, QB, Massachusetts
    Earl McCullouch, E, Southern California

1969—None
1970—Steve Owens, RB, Oklahoma
1971—Bob Bell, DT, Cincinnati
1972—Herb Orvis, DE, Colorado
1973—Ernie Price, DE, Texas A&I
1974—Ed O'Neil, LB, Penn State
1975—Lynn Boden, G, South Dakota State
1976—James Hunter, DB, Grambling State
    Lawrence Gaines, FB, Wyoming
1977—None
1978—Luther Bradley, DB, Notre Dame
1979—Keith Dorney, T, Penn State
1980—Billy Sims, RB, Oklahoma*
1981—Mark Nichols, WR, San Jose State
1982—Jimmy Williams, LB, Nebraska
1983—James Jones, RB, Florida
1984—David Lewis, TE, California
1985—Lomas Brown, T, Florida
1986—Chuck Long, QB, Iowa
1987—Reggie Rogers, DE, Washington
1988—Bennie Blades, S, Miami (Fla.)
1989—Barry Sanders, RB, Oklahoma State
1990—Andre Ware, QB, Houston
1991—Herman Moore, WR, Virginia
1992—Robert Porcher, DE, South Carolina State
1993—None
1994—Johnnie Morton, WR, Southern California
1995—Luther Elliss, DT, Utah
1996—Reggie Brown, LB, Texas A&M
    Jeff Hartings, G, Penn State
1997—Bryant Westbrook, DB, Texas
1998—Terry Fair, DB, Tennessee
1999—Chris Claiborne, LB, Southern California
    Aaron Gibson, T, Wisconsin
*First player chosen in draft.

FRANCHISE RECORDS

Most rushing yards, career
15,269—Barry Sanders
Most rushing yards, season
2,053—Barry Sanders, 1997
Most rushing yards, game
237—Barry Sanders vs. T.B., Nov. 13, 1994
Most rushing touchdowns, season
16—Barry Sanders, 1991
Most passing attempts, season
583—Scott Mitchell, 1995
Most passing attempts, game
50—Eric Hipple at L.A. Rams, Oct. 19, 1986
    Scott Mitchell at Was., Oct. 22, 1995
    Scott Mitchell at Atl., Nov. 5, 1995
    Scott Mitchell at Oak., Oct. 13, 1996
    Scott Mitchell vs. T.B., Sept. 7, 1997

Most passes completed, season
346—Scott Mitchell, 1995
Most passes completed, game
33—Eric Hipple at Cle., Sept. 28, 1986
    Chuck Long vs. G.B., Oct. 25, 1987
Most passing yards, career
15,710—Bobby Layne
Most passing yards, season
4,338—Scott Mitchell, 1995
Most passing yards, game
410—Scott Mitchell vs. Min., Nov. 23, 1995
Most touchdown passes, season
32—Scott Mitchell, 1995
Most pass receptions, career
610—Herman Moore

Most pass receptions, season
123—Herman Moore, 1995
Most pass receptions, game
14—Herman Moore vs. Chi., Dec. 5, 1995
Most receiving yards, career
8,467—Herman Moore
Most receiving yards, season
1,686—Herman Moore, 1995
Most receiving yards, game
302—Cloyce Box vs. Bal., Dec. 3, 1950
Most receiving touchdowns, season
15—Cloyce Box, 1952
Most touchdowns, career
109—Barry Sanders

Most field goals, season
34—Jason Hanson, 1993
Longest field goal
56 yards—Jason Hanson vs. Cle., Oct. 8,
    1995

Most interceptions, career
62—Dick LeBeau
Most interceptions, season
12—Don Doll, 1950
    Jack Christiansen, 1953

Most sacks, season
23—Al Baker, 1978

SERIES RECORDS

Detroit vs.: Arizona 28-16-3; Atlanta 20-7; Baltimore 0-1; Buffalo 3-2-1; Carolina 0-0; Chicago 54-72-3; Cincinnati 3-4; Dallas 6-7; Denver 3-4; Green Bay 58-67-6; Indianapolis 19-17-2; Jacksonville 1-1; Kansas City 3-5; Miami 2-4; Minnesota 27-46-2; New England 3-3; New Orleans 6-8-1; N.Y. Giants 14-14-1; N.Y. Jets 5-3; Oakland 2-6; Philadelphia 11-11-2; Pittsburgh 14-12-1; St. Louis 27-32-1; San Diego 3-3; San Francisco 26-29-1; Seattle 3-4; Tampa Bay 24-18; Tennessee 3-4; Washington 3-24.
NOTE: Includes records only from 1934 to present.

COACHING RECORDS

Dutch Clark, 14-8-0; Monte Clark, 43-61-1 (0-2); Potsy Clark, 53-25-7 (1-0); Gus Dorais, 20-31-2; Bill Edwards, 4-9-1; Wayne Fontes, 66-67-0 (1-4); Rick Forzano, 15-17-0; Harry Gilmer, 10-16-2; Hal Griffen, 5-6-3; Elmer Henderson, 6-5-0; Tommy Hudspeth, 11-13-0; John Karcis, 0-8-0; Don McCafferty, 6-7-1; Alvin McMillin, 12-24-0; Buddy Parker, 47-23-2 (3-1); Darryl Rogers, 18-40-0; Bobby Ross, 14-18-0 (0-1); Joe Schmidt, 43-34-7 (0-1); George Wilson, 53-45-6 (2-0).
NOTE: Playoff games in parentheses.

RETIRED UNIFORM NUMBERS

No.	Player
7	Dutch Clark
22	Bobby Layne
37	Doak Walker
56	Joe Schmidt
85	Chuck Hughes
88	Charlie Sanders

GREEN BAY PACKERS
YEAR-BY-YEAR RECORDS

		REGULAR SEASON							PLAYOFFS		
Year	W	L	T	Pct.	PF	PA	Finish	W	L	Highest round	Coach
1921	3	2	1	.600	...	...	T6th				Curly Lambeau
1922	4	3	3	.571	...	...	T7th				Curly Lambeau
1923	7	2	1	.778	...	...	3rd				Curly Lambeau
1924	7	4	0	.636	...	...	6th				Curly Lambeau
1925	8	5	0	.615	...	...	9th				Curly Lambeau
1926	7	3	3	.700	...	...	5th				Curly Lambeau
1927	7	2	1	.778	...	...	2nd				Curly Lambeau
1928	6	4	3	.600	...	...	4th				Curly Lambeau
1929	12	0	1	1.000	...	...	1st				Curly Lambeau
1930	10	3	1	.769	...	...	1st				Curly Lambeau
1931	12	2	0	.857	...	...	1st				Curly Lambeau
1932	10	3	1	.769	...	...	2nd				Curly Lambeau
1933	5	7	1	.417	170	107	3rd/Western Div.	—	—		Curly Lambeau
1934	7	6	0	.538	156	112	3rd/Western Div.	—	—		Curly Lambeau
1935	8	4	0	.667	181	96	2nd/Western Div.	—	—		Curly Lambeau
1936	10	1	1	.909	248	118	1st/Western Div.	1	0	NFL champ	Curly Lambeau
1937	7	4	0	.636	220	122	T2nd/Western Div.				Curly Lambeau
1938	8	3	0	.727	223	118	1st/Western Div.	0	1	NFL championship game	Curly Lambeau
1939	9	2	0	.818	233	153	1st/Western Div.	1	0	NFL champ	Curly Lambeau
1940	6	4	1	.600	238	155	2nd/Western Div.	—	—		Curly Lambeau
1941	10	1	0	.909	258	120	2nd/Western Div.	0	1	W. Div. championship game	Curly Lambeau
1942	8	2	1	.800	300	215	2nd/Western Div.	—	—		Curly Lambeau
1943	7	2	1	.778	264	172	2nd/Western Div.	—	—		Curly Lambeau
1944	8	2	0	.800	238	141	1st/Western Div.	1	0	NFL champ	Curly Lambeau
1945	6	4	0	.600	258	173	3rd/Western Div.	—	—		Curly Lambeau
1946	6	5	0	.545	148	158	T3rd/Western Div.	—	—		Curly Lambeau
1947	6	5	1	.545	274	210	3rd/Western Div.	—	—		Curly Lambeau
1948	3	9	0	.250	154	290	4th/Western Div.	—	—		Curly Lambeau
1949	2	10	0	.167	114	329	5th/Western Div.	—	—		Curly Lambeau
1950	3	9	0	.250	244	406	T5th/National Conf.	—	—		Gene Ronzani
1951	3	9	0	.250	254	375	5th/National Conf.	—	—		Gene Ronzani
1952	6	6	0	.500	295	312	4th/National Conf.	—	—		Gene Ronzani
1953	2	9	1	.182	200	338	6th/Western Conf.	—	—		Gene Ronzani, Hugh Devore-S. McLean
1954	4	8	0	.333	234	251	5th/Western Conf.	—	—		Lisle Blackbourn
1955	6	6	0	.500	258	276	3rd/Western Conf.	—	—		Lisle Blackbourn
1956	4	8	0	.333	264	342	5th/Western Conf.	—	—		Lisle Blackbourn
1957	3	9	0	.250	218	311	6th/Western Conf.	—	—		Lisle Blackbourn
1958	1	10	1	.091	193	382	6th/Western Conf.	—	—		Scooter McLean
1959	7	5	0	.583	248	246	T3rd/Western Conf.	—	—		Vince Lombardi
1960	8	4	0	.667	332	209	1st/Western Conf.	0	1	NFL championship game	Vince Lombardi

			REGULAR SEASON				PLAYOFFS			
Year	W	L	T	Pct.	PF	PA	Finish	W	L	Highest round	Coach
1961	11	3	0	.786	391	223	1st/Western Conf.	1	0	NFL champ	Vince Lombardi
1962	13	1	0	.929	415	148	1st/Western Conf.	1	0	NFL champ	Vince Lombardi
1963	11	2	1	.846	369	206	2nd/Western Conf.	—	—		Vince Lombardi
1964	8	5	1	.615	342	245	T2nd/Western Conf.	—	—		Vince Lombardi
1965	10	3	1	.769	316	224	1st/Western Conf.	2	0	NFL champ	Vince Lombardi
1966	12	2	0	.857	335	163	1st/Western Conf.	2	0	Super Bowl champ	Vince Lombardi
1967	9	4	1	.692	332	209	1st/Central Div.	3	0	Super Bowl champ	Vince Lombardi
1968	6	7	1	.462	281	227	3rd/Central Div.	—	—		Phil Bengtson
1969	8	6	0	.571	269	221	3rd/Central Div.	—	—		Phil Bengtson
1970	6	8	0	.429	196	293	T3rd/NFC Central Div.	—	—		Phil Bengtson
1971	4	8	2	.333	274	298	4th/NFC Central Div.	—	—		Dan Devine
1972	10	4	0	.714	304	226	1st/NFC Central Div.	0	1	NFC div. playoff game	Dan Devine
1973	5	7	2	.429	202	259	3rd/NFC Central Div.	—	—		Dan Devine
1974	6	8	0	.429	210	206	3rd/NFC Central Div.	—	—		Dan Devine
1975	4	10	0	.286	226	285	T3rd/NFC Central Div.	—	—		Bart Starr
1976	5	9	0	.357	218	299	4th/NFC Central Div.	—	—		Bart Starr
1977	4	10	0	.286	134	219	4th/NFC Central Div.	—	—		Bart Starr
1978	8	7	1	.531	249	269	2nd/NFC Central Div.	—	—		Bart Starr
1979	5	11	0	.313	246	316	4th/NFC Central Div.	—	—		Bart Starr
1980	5	10	1	.344	231	371	T4th/NFC Central Div.	—	—		Bart Starr
1981	8	8	0	.500	324	361	2nd/NFC Central Div.	—	—		Bart Starr
1982	5	3	1	.611	226	169	3rd/NFC	1	1	NFC second-round pl. game	Bart Starr
1983	8	8	0	.500	429	439	T2nd/NFC Central Div.	—	—		Bart Starr
1984	8	8	0	.500	390	309	2nd/NFC Central Div.	—	—		Forrest Gregg
1985	8	8	0	.500	337	355	2nd/NFC Central Div.	—	—		Forrest Gregg
1986	4	12	0	.250	254	418	4th/NFC Central Div.	—	—		Forrest Gregg
1987	5	9	1	.367	255	300	3rd/NFC Central Div.	—	—		Forrest Gregg
1988	4	12	0	.250	240	315	T4th/NFC Central Div.	—	—		Lindy Infante
1989	10	6	0	.625	362	356	2nd/NFC Central Div.	—	—		Lindy Infante
1990	6	10	0	.375	271	347	T2nd/NFC Central Div.	—	—		Lindy Infante
1991	4	12	0	.250	273	313	4th/NFC Central Div.	—	—		Lindy Infante
1992	9	7	0	.563	276	296	2nd/NFC Central Div.	—	—		Mike Holmgren
1993	9	7	0	.563	340	282	T2nd/NFC Central Div.	1	1	NFC div. playoff game	Mike Holmgren
1994	9	7	0	.563	382	287	T2nd/NFC Central Div.	1	1	NFC div. playoff game	Mike Holmgren
1995	11	5	0	.689	404	314	1st/NFC Central Div.	2	1	NFC championship game	Mike Holmgren
1996	13	3	0	.813	456	210	1st/NFC Central Div.	3	0	Super Bowl champ	Mike Holmgren
1997	13	3	0	.813	422	282	1st/NFC Central Div.	2	1	Super Bowl	Mike Holmgren
1998	11	5	0	.688	408	319	2nd/NFC Central Div.	0	1	NFC wild-card game	Mike Holmgren

FIRST-ROUND DRAFT PICKS

1936—Russ Letlow, G, San Francisco
1937—Ed Jankowski, B, Wisconsin
1938—Cecil Isbell, B, Purdue
1939—Larry Buhler, B, Minnesota
1940—Hal Van Every, B, Marquette
1941—George Paskvan, B, Wisconsin
1942—Urban Odson, T, Minnesota
1943—Dick Wildung, T, Minnesota
1944—Merv Pregulman, G, Michigan
1945—Walt Schlinkman, G, Texas Tech
1946—Johnny Strzykalski, B, Marquette
1947—Ernie Case, B, UCLA
1948—Earl Girard, B, Wisconsin
1949—Stan Heath, B, Nevada
1950—Clayton Tonnemaker, G, Minnesota
1951—Bob Gain, T, Kentucky
1952—Babe Parilli, QB, Kentucky
1953—Al Carmichael, B, Southern California
1954—Art Hunter, T, Notre Dame
    Veryl Switzer, B, Kansas State
1955—Tom Bettis, G, Purdue
1956—Jack Losch, B, Miami
1957—Paul Hornung, B, Notre Dame*
    Ron Kramer, E, Michigan
1958—Dan Currie, C, Michigan State
1959—Randy Duncan, B, Iowa*
1960—Tom Moore, RB, Vanderbilt
1961—Herb Adderley, DB, Michigan State

1962—Earl Gros, RB, Louisiana State
1963—Dave Robinson, LB, Penn State
1964—Lloyd Voss, DT, Nebraska
1965—Donny Anderson, RB, Texas Tech
    Larry Elkins, E, Baylor
1966—Jim Grabowski, RB, Illinois
    Gale Gillingham, G, Minnesota
1967—Bob Hyland, C, Boston College
    Don Horn, QB, San Diego State
1968—Fred Carr, LB, Texas-El Paso
    Bill Lueck, G, Arizona
1969—Rich Moore, DT, Villanova
1970—Mike McCoy, DT, Notre Dame
    Rich McGeorge, TE, Elon
1971—John Brockington, RB, Ohio State
1972—Willie Buchanon, DB, San Diego State
    Jerry Tagge, QB, Nebraska
1973—Barry Smith, WR, Florida State
1974—Barty Smith, RB, Richmond
1975—None
1976—Mark Koncar, T, Colorado
1977—Mike Butler, DE, Kansas
    Ezra Johnson, DE, Morris Brown
1978—James Lofton, WR, Stanford
    John Anderson, LB, Michigan
1979—Eddie Lee Ivery, RB, Georgia Tech
1980—Bruce Clark, DT, Penn State
    George Cumby, LB, Oklahoma

1981—Rich Campbell, QB, California
1982—Ron Hallstrom, G, Iowa
1983—Tim Lewis, DB, Pittsburgh
1984—Alphonso Carreker, DT, Florida State
1985—Ken Ruettgers, T, Southern California
1986—None
1987—Brent Fullwood, RB, Auburn
1988—Sterling Sharpe, WR, South Carolina
1989—Tony Mandarich, T, Michigan State
1990—Tony Bennett, LB, Mississippi
     Darrell Thompson, RB, Minnesota

1991—Vincent Clark, DB, Ohio State
1992—Terrell Buckley, DB, Florida State
1993—Wayne Simmons, LB, Clemson
     George Teague, DB, Alabama
1994—Aaron Taylor, T, Notre Dame
1995—Craig Newsome, DB, Arizona State
1996—John Michaels, T, Southern California
1997—Ross Verba, T, Iowa
1998—Vonnie Holliday, DT, North Carolina
1999—Antuan Edwards, DB, Clemson
    *First player chosen in draft.

FRANCHISE RECORDS

Most rushing yards, career
8,207—Jim Taylor
Most rushing yards, season
1,474—Jim Taylor, 1962
Most rushing yards, game
190—Dorsey Levens vs. Dal., Nov. 23, 1997
Most rushing touchdowns, season
19—Jim Taylor, 1962
Most passing attempts, season
599—Don Majkowski, 1989
Most passing attempts, game
61—Brett Favre vs. S.F., Oct. 14, 1996 (OT)
59—Don Majkowski at Det., Nov. 12, 1989
Most passes completed, season
363—Brett Favre, 1994
Most passes completed, game
36—Brett Favre at Chi., Dec. 5, 1993
Most passing yards, career
26,803—Brett Favre

Most passing yards, season
4,458—Lynn Dickey, 1983
Most passing yards, game
418—Lynn Dickey at T.B., Oct. 12, 1980
Most touchdown passes, season
39—Brett Favre, 1996
Most pass receptions, career
595—Sterling Sharpe
Most pass receptions, season
112—Sterling Sharpe, 1993
Most pass receptions, game
14—Don Hutson at NYG, Nov. 22, 1942
Most receiving yards, career
9,656—James Lofton
Most receiving yards, season
1,497—Robert Brooks, 1995
Most receiving yards, game
257—Bill Howton vs. L.A. Rams, Oct.
    21, 1956

Most receiving touchdowns, season
18—Sterling Sharpe, 1994
Most touchdowns, career
105—Don Hutson
Most field goals, season
33—Chester Marcol, 1972
Longest field goal
54 yards—Chris Jacke at Det., Jan. 2, 1994
Most interceptions, career
52—Bobby Dillon
Most interceptions, season
10—Irv Comp, 1943
Most sacks, career
84—Ezra Johnson
Most sacks, season
20.5—Ezra Johnson, 1978

SERIES RECORDS

Green Bay vs.: Arizona 41-21-4; Atlanta 10-9; Baltimore 1-0; Buffalo 2-5; Carolina 2-0; Chicago 69-82-6; Cincinnati 5-4; Dallas 10-8; Denver 3-4-1; Detroit 67-58-6; Indianapolis 18-19-1; Jacksonville 1-0; Kansas City 1-5-1; Miami 1-8; Minnesota 36-38-1; New England 3-3; New Orleans 13-4; N.Y. Giants 23-20-2; N.Y. Jets 2-5; Oakland 2-5; Philadelphia 21-9; Pittsburgh 21-12; St. Louis 27-40-1; San Diego 5-1; San Francisco 23-25-1; Seattle 4-3; Tampa Bay 25-14-1; Tennessee 4-3; Washington 9-11.

COACHING RECORDS

Phil Bengtson, 20-21-1; Lisle Blackbourn, 17-31-0; Dan Devine, 25-27-4 (0-1); Hugh Devore-Ray (Scooter) McLean, 0-2-0; Forrest Gregg, 25-37-1; Mike Holmgren, 75-37-0 (9-5); Lindy Infante, 24-40-0; Curly Lambeau, 209-104-21 (3-2); Vince Lombardi, 89-29-4 (9-1); Ray (Scooter) McLean, 1-10-1; Gene Ronzani, 14-31-1; Bart Starr, 52-76-3 (1-1).
NOTE: Playoff games in parentheses.

RETIRED UNIFORM NUMBERS

No.	Player
3	Tony Canadeo
14	Don Hutson
15	Bart Starr
66	Ray Nitschke

INDIANAPOLIS COLTS
YEAR-BY-YEAR RECORDS

			REGULAR SEASON						PLAYOFFS		
Year	W	L	T	Pct.	PF	PA	Finish	W	L	Highest round	Coach
1953*	3	9	0	.250	182	350	5th/Western Conf.	—	—		Keith Molesworth
1954*	3	9	0	.250	131	279	6th/Western Conf.	—	—		Weeb Ewbank
1955*	5	6	1	.455	214	239	4th/Western Conf.	—	—		Weeb Ewbank
1956*	5	7	0	.417	270	322	4th/Western Conf.	—	—		Weeb Ewbank
1957*	7	5	0	.583	303	235	3rd/Western Conf.	—	—		Weeb Ewbank
1958*	9	3	0	.750	381	203	1st/Western Conf.	1	0	NFL champ	Weeb Ewbank
1959*	9	3	0	.750	374	251	1st/Western Conf.	1	0	NFL champ	Weeb Ewbank
1960*	6	6	0	.500	288	234	4th/Western Conf.	—	—		Weeb Ewbank
1961*	8	6	0	.571	302	307	T3rd/Western Conf.	—	—		Weeb Ewbank
1962*	7	7	0	.500	293	288	4th/Western Conf.	—	—		Weeb Ewbank
1963*	8	6	0	.571	316	285	3rd/Western Conf.	—	—		Don Shula
1964*	12	2	0	.857	428	225	1st/Western Conf.	0	1	NFL championship game	Don Shula
1965*	10	3	1	.769	389	284	2nd/Western Conf.	0	1	W. Conf. champ. game	Don Shula

Year	W	L	T	Pct.	PF	PA	Finish	W	L	Highest round	Coach
1966*	9	5	0	.643	314	226	2nd/Western Conf.	—	—		Don Shula
1967*	11	1	2	.917	394	198	2nd/Coastal Div.	—	—		Don Shula
1968*	13	1	0	.929	402	144	1st/Coastal Div.	2	1	Super Bowl	Don Shula
1969*	8	5	1	.615	279	268	2nd/Coastal Div.	—	—		Don Shula
1970*	11	2	1	.846	321	234	1st/AFC Eastern Div.	3	0	Super Bowl champ	Don McCafferty
1971*	10	4	0	.714	313	140	2nd/AFC Eastern Div.	1	1	AFC championship game	Don McCafferty
1972*	5	9	0	.357	235	252	3rd/AFC Eastern Div.	—	—		McCafferty, John Sandusky
1973*	4	10	0	.286	226	341	T4th/AFC Eastern Div.	—	—		Howard Schnellenberger
1974*	2	12	0	.143	190	329	5th/AFC Eastern Div.	—	—		H. Schnellenberger, Joe Thomas
1975*	10	4	0	.714	395	269	1st/AFC Eastern Div.	0	1	AFC div. playoff game	Ted Marchibroda
1976*	11	3	0	.786	417	246	1st/AFC Eastern Div.	0	1	AFC div. playoff game	Ted Marchibroda
1977*	10	4	0	.714	295	221	1st/AFC Eastern Div.	0	1	AFC div. playoff game	Ted Marchibroda
1978*	5	11	0	.313	239	421	T4th/AFC Eastern Div.	—	—		Ted Marchibroda
1979*	5	11	0	.313	271	351	5th/AFC Eastern Div.	—	—		Ted Marchibroda
1980*	7	9	0	.438	355	387	4th/AFC Eastern Div.	—	—		Mike McCormack
1981*	2	14	0	.125	259	533	T4th/AFC Eastern Div.	—	—		Mike McCormack
1982*	0	8	1	.056	113	236	14th/AFC	—	—		Frank Kush
1983*	7	9	0	.438	264	354	T4th/AFC Eastern Div.	—	—		Frank Kush
1984	4	12	0	.250	239	414	4th/AFC Eastern Div.	—	—		Frank Kush, Hal Hunter
1985	5	11	0	.313	320	386	4th/AFC Eastern Div.	—	—		Rod Dowhower
1986	3	13	0	.188	229	400	5th/AFC Eastern Div.	—	—		Rod Dowhower, Ron Meyer
1987	9	6	0	.600	300	238	1st/AFC Eastern Div.	0	1	AFC div. playoff game	Ron Meyer
1988	9	7	0	.563	354	315	T2nd/AFC Eastern Div.	—	—		Ron Meyer
1989	8	8	0	.500	298	301	T2nd/AFC Eastern Div.	—	—		Ron Meyer
1990	7	9	0	.438	281	353	3rd/AFC Eastern Div.	—	—		Ron Meyer
1991	1	15	0	.063	143	381	5th/AFC Eastern Div.	—	—		Ron Meyer, Rick Venturi
1992	9	7	0	.563	216	302	3rd/AFC Eastern Div.	—	—		Ted Marchibroda
1993	4	12	0	.250	189	378	5th/AFC Eastern Div.	—	—		Ted Marchibroda
1994	8	8	0	.500	307	320	3rd/AFC Eastern Div.	—	—		Ted Marchibroda
1995	9	7	0	.563	331	316	T2nd/AFC Eastern Div.	2	1	AFC championship game	Ted Marchibroda
1996	9	7	0	.563	317	334	3rd/AFC Eastern Div.	0	1	AFC wild-card game	Lindy Infante
1997	3	13	0	.188	313	401	5th/AFC Eastern Div.	—	—		Lindy Infante
1998	3	13	0	.188	310	444	5th/AFC Eastern Div.	—	—		Jim Mora

REGULAR SEASON — PLAYOFFS

*Baltimore Colts.

FIRST-ROUND DRAFT PICKS

1953—Billy Vessels, B, Oklahoma
1954—Cotton Davidson, B, Baylor
1955—George Shaw, B, Oregon*
    Alan Ameche, B, Wisconsin
1956—Lenny Moore, B, Penn State
1957—Jim Parker, T, Ohio State
1958—Lenny Lyles, B, Louisville
1959—Jackie Burkett, C, Auburn
1960—Ron Mix, T, Southern California
1961—Tom Matte, RB, Ohio State
1962—Wendell Harris, DB, Louisiana State
1963—Bob Vogel, T, Ohio State
1964—Marv Woodson, DB, Indiana
1965—Mike Curtis, LB, Duke
1966—Sam Ball, T, Kentucky
1967—Bubba Smith, DT, Michigan State*
    Jim Detwiler, RB, Michigan
1968—John Williams, G, Minnesota
1969—Eddie Hinton, WR, Oklahoma
1970—Norm Bulaich, RB, Texas Christian
1971—Don McCauley, RB, North Carolina
    Leonard Dunlap, DB, North Texas State
1972—Tom Drougas, T, Oregon
1973—Bert Jones, QB, Louisiana State
    Joe Ehrmann, DT, Syracuse
1974—John Dutton, DE, Nebraska
    Roger Carr, WR, Louisiana Tech
1975—Ken Huff, G, North Carolina
1976—Ken Novak, DT, Purdue
1977—Randy Burke, WR, Kentucky

1978—Reese McCall, TE, Auburn
1979—Barry Krauss, LB, Alabama
1980—Curtis Dickey, RB, Texas A&M
    Derrick Hatchett, DB, Texas
1981—Randy McMillan, RB, Pittsburgh
    Donnell Thompson, DT, North Carolina
1982—Johnie Cooks, LB, Mississippi State
    Art Schlichter, QB, Ohio State
1983—John Elway, QB, Stanford*
1984—L. Coleman, DB, Vanderbilt
    Ron Solt, G, Maryland
1985—Duane Bickett, LB, Southern California
1986—Jon Hand, DT, Alabama
1987—Cornelius Bennett, LB, Alabama
1988—None
1989—Andre Rison, WR, Michigan State
1990—Jeff George, QB, Illinois*
1991—None
1992—Steve Emtman, DE, Washington*
    Quentin Coryatt, LB, Texas A&M
1993—Sean Dawkins, WR, California
1994—Marshall Faulk, RB, San Diego State
    Trev Alberts, LB, Nebraska
1995—Ellis Johnson, DT, Florida
1996—Marvin Harrison, WR, Syracuse
1997—Tarik Glenn, T, California
1998—Peyton Manning, QB, Tennessee*
1999—Edgerrin James, RB, Miami (Fla.)
    *First player chosen in draft.

FRANCHISE RECORDS

Most rushing yards, career
5,487—Lydell Mitchell
Most rushing yards, season
1,659—Eric Dickerson, 1988
Most rushing yards, game
198—Norm Bulaich vs. NYJ, Sept. 19, 1971
Most rushing touchdowns, season
16—Lenny Moore, 1964
Most passing attempts, season
575—Peyton Manning, 1998
Most passing attempts, game
59—Jeff George at Was., Nov. 7, 1993
Most passes completed, season
326—Peyton Manning, 1998
Most passes completed, game
37—Jeff George at Was., Nov. 7, 1993
Most passing yards, career
39,768—Johnny Unitas
Most passing yards, season
3,739—Peyton Manning, 1998

Most passing yards, game
401—Johnny Unitas vs. Atl., Sept. 17, 1967
Most touchdown passes, season
32—Johnny Unitas, 1959
Most pass receptions, career
631—Raymond Berry
Most pass receptions, season
86—Marshall Faulk, 1998
Most pass receptions, game
13—Lydell Mitchell vs. NYJ, Dec. 15, 1974
   Joe Washington at K.C., Sept. 2, 1979
Most receiving yards, career
9,275—Raymond Berry
Most receiving yards, season
1,298—Raymond Berry, 1960
Most receiving yards, game
224—Raymond Berry at Was., Nov. 10, 1957
Most receiving touchdowns, season
14—Raymond Berry, 1959

Most touchdowns, career
113—Lenny Moore
Most field goals, season
36—Cary Blanchard, 1996
Longest field goal
58 yards—Dan Miller at S.D., Dec. 26, 1982
Most interceptions, career
57—Bob Boyd
Most interceptions, season
11—Tom Keane, 1953
Most sacks, career
56.5—Fred Cook
Most sacks, season
17—John Dutton, 1975

SERIES RECORDS

Indianapolis vs.: Arizona 6-6; Atlanta 10-1; Baltimore 0-1; Buffalo 23-33-1; Carolina 0-2; Chicago 21-16; Cincinnati 11-8; Dallas 3-7; Denver 2-9; Detroit 17-19-2; Green Bay 19-18-1; Jacksonville 1-0; Kansas City 5-6; Miami 19-39; Minnesota 11-7-1; New England 22-35; New Orleans 3-4; N.Y. Giants 5-5; N.Y. Jets 34-23; Oakland 2-5; Philadelphia 7-6; Pittsburgh 4-13; St. Louis 21-17-2; San Diego 7-11; San Francisco 22-17; Seattle 4-3; Tampa Bay 5-4; Tennessee 7-7; Washington 16-9.
NOTE: Includes records as Baltimore Colts from 1953 through 1983.

COACHING RECORDS

Rod Dowhower, 5-24-0; Weeb Ewbank, 59-52-1 (2-0); Hal Hunter, 0-1-0; Lindy Infante, 12-19-0 (0-1); Frank Kush, 11-28-1; Ted Marchibroda, 71-67-0 (2-4); Don McCafferty, 22-10-1 (4-1); Mike McCormack, 9-23-0; Ron Meyer, 36-35-0 (0-1); Keith Molesworth, 3-9-0; Jim Mora, 3-13-0; John Sandusky, 4-5-0; Howard Schnellenberger, 4-13-0; Don Shula, 71-23-4 (2-3); Joe Thomas, 2-9-0; Rick Venturi, 1-10.
NOTE: Playoff games in parentheses.

RETIRED UNIFORM NUMBERS

No.	Player
19	Johnny Unitas
22	Buddy Young
24	Lenny Moore
70	Art Donovan
77	Jim Parker
82	Raymond Berry
89	Gino Marchetti

JACKSONVILLE JAGUARS
YEAR-BY-YEAR RECORDS

	REGULAR SEASON							PLAYOFFS			
Year	W	L	T	Pct.	PF	PA	Finish	W	L	Highest round	Coach
1995	4	12	0	.250	275	404	5th/AFC Central Div.	—	—		Tom Coughlin
1996	9	7	0	.563	325	335	2nd/AFC Central Div.	2	1	AFC championship game	Tom Coughlin
1997	11	5	0	.688	394	318	2nd/AFC Central Div.	0	1	AFC wild-card game	Tom Coughlin
1998	11	5	0	.688	392	338	1st/AFC Central Div.	1	1	AFC div. playoff game	Tom Coughlin

FIRST-ROUND DRAFT PICKS

1995—Tony Boselli, T, Southern California
   James Stewart, RB, Tennessee
1996—Kevin Hardy, LB, Illinois
1997—Renaldo Wynn, DT, Notre Dame

1998—Fred Taylor, RB, Florida
   Donovin Darius, DB, Syracuse
1999—Fernando Bryant, DB, Alabama

FRANCHISE RECORDS

Most rushing yards, career
2,020—James Stewart
Most rushing yards, season
1,223—Fred Taylor, 1998

Most rushing yards, game
183—Fred Taylor vs. Det., Dec. 6, 1998
Most rushing touchdowns, season
14—Fred Taylor, 1998

Most passing attempts, season
557—Mark Brunell, 1996
Most passing attempts, game
52—Mark Brunell at St.L., Oct. 20, 1996

Most passes completed, season
353—Mark Brunell, 1996
Most passes completed, game
37—Mark Brunell at St.L., Oct. 20, 1996
Most passing yards, career
12,417—Mark Brunell
Most passing yards, season
4,367—Mark Brunell, 1996
Most passing yards, game
432—Mark Brunell at N.E., Sept. 22, 1996
Most touchdown passes, season
20—Mark Brunell, 1998
Most pass receptions, career
265—Jimmy Smith
Most pass receptions, season
85—Keenan McCardell, 1996, 1997

Most pass receptions, game
16—Keenan McCardell at St.L., Oct. 20, 1996
Most receiving yards, career
4,038—Jimmy Smith
Most receiving yards, season
1,244—Jimmy Smith, 1996
Most receiving yards, game
232—Keenan McCardell at St.L., Oct. 20, 1996
Most receiving touchdowns, season
8—Jimmy Smith, 1998
Most touchdowns, career
25—James Stewart
Most field goals, season
31—Mike Hollis, 1997

Longest field goal
53 yards—Mike Hollis vs. Pit., Oct. 8, 1995
Mike Hollis vs. Car., Sept. 29, 1996
Most interceptions, career
8—Chris Hudson
Most interceptions, season
5—Deon Figures, 1997
Most sacks, career
23—Joel Smeenge
Most sacks, season
8.5—Clyde Simmons, 1997

SERIES RECORDS

Jacksonville vs.: Arizona 0-0; Atlanta 1-0; Baltimore 6-0; Buffalo 1-1; Carolina 1-0; Chicago 1-1; Cincinnati 4-4; Dallas 0-1; Denver 0-2; Detroit 1-1; Green Bay 0-1; Indianapolis 0-1; Kansas City 2-0; Miami 1-0; Minnesota 0-1; New England 0-2; New Orleans 0-1; N.Y. Giants 1-0; N.Y. Jets 1-1; Oakland 1-1; Philadelphia 1-0; Pittsburgh 4-4; St. Louis 0-1; San Diego 0-0; San Francisco 0-0; Seattle 1-1; Tampa Bay 1-1; Tennessee 4-4; Washington 0-1.

COACHING RECORDS

Tom Coughlin, 35-29-0 (3-3).
NOTE: Playoff games in parentheses.

RETIRED UNIFORM NUMBERS

No.   **Player**
None

KANSAS CITY CHIEFS
YEAR-BY-YEAR RECORDS

		REGULAR SEASON						PLAYOFFS			
Year	W	L	T	Pct.	PF	PA	Finish	W	L	Highest round	Coach
1960*†	8	6	0	.571	362	253	2nd/Western Div.	—	—		Hank Stram
1961*†	6	8	0	.429	334	343	2nd/Western Div.	—	—		Hank Stram
1962*†	11	3	0	.786	389	233	1st/Western Div.	1	0	AFL champ	Hank Stram
1963*	5	7	2	.417	347	263	3rd/Western Div.	—	—		Hank Stram
1964*	7	7	0	.500	366	306	2nd/Western Div.	—	—		Hank Stram
1965*	7	5	2	.583	322	285	3rd/Western Div.	—	—		Hank Stram
1966*	11	2	1	.846	448	276	1st/Western Div.	1	1	Super Bowl	Hank Stram
1967*	9	5	0	.643	408	254	2nd/Western Div.	—	—		Hank Stram
1968*	12	2	0	.857	371	170	2nd/Western Div.	0	1	W. Div. champ. game	Hank Stram
1969*	11	3	0	.786	359	177	2nd/Western Div.	3	0	Super Bowl champ	Hank Stram
1970	7	5	2	.583	272	244	2nd/AFC Western Div.	—	—		Hank Stram
1971	10	3	1	.769	302	208	1st/AFC Western Div.	0	1	AFC div. playoff game	Hank Stram
1972	8	6	0	.571	287	254	2nd/AFC Western Div.	—	—		Hank Stram
1973	7	5	2	.571	231	192	T2nd/AFC Western Div.	—	—		Hank Stram
1974	5	9	0	.357	233	293	T3rd/AFC Western Div.	—	—		Hank Stram
1975	5	9	0	.357	282	341	3rd/AFC Western Div.	—	—		Paul Wiggin
1976	5	9	0	.357	290	376	4th/AFC Western Div.	—	—		Paul Wiggin
1977	2	12	0	.143	225	349	5th/AFC Western Div.	—	—		Paul Wiggin, Tom Bettis
1978	4	12	0	.250	243	327	5th/AFC Western Div.	—	—		Marv Levy
1979	7	9	0	.438	238	262	5th/AFC Western Div.	—	—		Marv Levy
1980	8	8	0	.500	319	336	T3rd/AFC Western Div.	—	—		Marv Levy
1981	9	7	0	.563	343	290	3rd/AFC Western Div.	—	—		Marv Levy
1982	3	6	0	.333	176	184	11th/AFC	—	—		Marv Levy
1983	6	10	0	.375	386	367	T4th/AFC Western Div.	—	—		John Mackovic
1984	8	8	0	.500	314	324	4th/AFC Western Div.	—	—		John Mackovic
1985	6	10	0	.375	317	360	4th/AFC Western Div.	—	—		John Mackovic
1986	10	6	0	.625	358	326	2nd/AFC Western Div.	0	1	AFC wild-card game	John Mackovic
1987	4	11	0	.267	273	388	5th/AFC Western Div.	—	—		Frank Gansz
1988	4	11	1	.281	254	320	5th/AFC Western Div.	—	—		Frank Gansz
1989	8	7	1	.531	318	286	2nd/AFC Western Div.	—	—		Marty Schottenheimer
1990	11	5	0	.688	369	257	2nd/AFC Western Div.	0	1	AFC wild-card game	Marty Schottenheimer
1991	10	6	0	.625	322	252	2nd/AFC Western Div.	1	1	AFC div. playoff game	Marty Schottenheimer
1992	10	6	0	.625	348	282	2nd/AFC Western Div.	0	1	AFC wild-card game	Marty Schottenheimer
1993	11	5	0	.688	328	291	1st/AFC Western Div.	2	1	AFC championship game	Marty Schottenheimer

				REGULAR SEASON					PLAYOFFS			
Year	W	L	T	Pct.	PF	PA	Finish	W	L	Highest round	Coach
1994	9	7	0	.563	319	298	2nd/AFC Western Div.	0	1	AFC wild-card game	Marty Schottenheimer
1995	13	3	0	.813	358	241	1st/AFC Western Div.	0	1	AFC div. playoff game	Marty Schottenheimer
1996	9	7	0	.563	297	300	2nd/AFC Western Div.	—	—		Marty Schottenheimer
1997	13	3	0	.813	375	232	1st/AFC Western Div.	0	1	AFC div. playoff game	Marty Schottenheimer
1998	7	9	0	.438	327	363	4th/AFC Western Div.	—	—		Marty Schottenheimer

*American Football League.
†Dallas Texans.

FIRST-ROUND DRAFT PICKS

1960—Don Meredith, QB, Southern Methodist
1961—E.J. Holub, C, Texas Tech
1962—Ronnie Bull, RB, Baylor
1963—Buck Buchanan, DT, Grambling* (AFL)
      Ed Budde, G, Michigan State
1964—Pete Beathard, QB, Southern California
1965—Gale Sayers, RB, Kansas
1966—Aaron Brown, DE, Minnesota
1967—Gene Trosch, DE, Miami
1968—Mo Moorman, G, Texas A&M
      George Daney, G, Texas-El Paso
1969—Jim Marsalis, DB, Tennessee State
1970—Sid Smith, T, Southern California
1971—Elmo Wright, WR, Houston
1972—Jeff Kinney, RB, Nebraska
1973—None
1974—Woody Green, RB, Arizona State
1975—None
1976—Rod Walters, G, Iowa
1977—Gary Green, DB, Baylor
1978—Art Still, DE, Kentucky
1979—Mike Bell, DE, Colorado State
      Steve Fuller, QB, Clemson

1980—Brad Budde, G, Southern California
1981—Willie Scott, TE, South Carolina
1982—Anthony Hancock, WR, Tennessee
1983—Todd Blackledge, QB, Penn State
1984—Bill Maas, DT, Pittsburgh
      John Alt, T, Iowa
1985—Ethan Horton, RB, North Carolina
1986—Brian Jozwiak, T, West Virginia
1987—Paul Palmer, RB, Temple
1988—Neil Smith, DE, Nebraska
1989—Derrick Thomas, LB, Alabama
1990—Percy Snow, LB, Michigan State
1991—Harvey Williams, RB, Louisiana State
1992—Dale Carter, DB, Tennessee
1993—None
1994—Greg Hill, RB, Texas A&M
1995—Trezelle Jenkins, T, Michigan
1996—Jerome Woods, DB, Memphis
1997—Tony Gonzalez, TE, California
1998—Victor Riley, T, Auburn
1999—John Tait, T, Brigham Young
      *First player chosen in draft.

FRANCHISE RECORDS

Most rushing yards, career
4,897—Christian Okoye
Most rushing yards, season
1,480—Christian Okoye, 1989
Most rushing yards, game
200—Barry Word vs. Det., Oct. 14, 1990
Most rushing touchdowns, season
13—Abner Haynes, 1962
Most passing attempts, season
603—Bill Kenney, 1983
Most passing attempts, game
55—Joe Montana at S.D., Oct. 9, 1994
    Steve Bono at Mia., Dec. 12, 1994
Most passes completed, season
346—Bill Kenney, 1983
Most passes completed, game
37—Joe Montana at S.D., Oct. 9, 1994
Most passing yards, career
28,507—Len Dawson
Most passing yards, season
4,348—Bill Kenney, 1983

Most passing yards, game
435—Len Dawson vs. Den., Nov. 1, 1964
Most touchdown passes, season
30—Len Dawson, 1964
Most pass receptions, career
416—Henry Marshall
Most pass receptions, season
80—Carlos Carson, 1983
Most pass receptions, game
12—Ed Podolak vs. Den., Oct. 7, 1973
Most receiving yards, career
7,306—Otis Taylor
Most receiving yards, season
1,351—Carlos Carson, 1983
Most receiving yards, game
309—Stephone Paige vs. S.D., Dec. 22, 1985
Most receiving touchdowns, season
12—Chris Burford, 1962
Most touchdowns, career
60—Otis Taylor

Most field goals, season
34—Nick Lowery, 1990
Longest field goals
58 yards—Nick Lowery at Was., Sept. 18, 1983
    Nick Lowery vs. L.A. Raiders, Sept. 12, 1985
Most interceptions, career
58—Emmitt Thomas
Most interceptions, season
12—Emmitt Thomas, 1974
Most sacks, career
119.5—Derrick Thomas
Most sacks, season
20—Derrick Thomas, 1990

SERIES RECORDS

Kansas City vs.: Arizona 5-1-1; Atlanta 4-0; Buffalo 14-17-1; Carolina 1-0; Chicago 3-4; Cincinnati 11-9; Dallas 3-4; Denver 43-34; Detroit 5-3; Green Bay 5-1-1; Indianapolis 6-5; Jacksonville 0-2; Miami 10-10; Minnesota 3-3; New England 14-8-3; New Orleans 4-3; N.Y. Giants 3-7; N.Y. Jets 14-13-1; Oakland 39-36-2; Philadelphia 2-1; Pittsburgh 6-15; St. Louis 2-4; San Diego 40-36-1; San Francisco 3-4; Seattle 27-13; Tampa Bay 5-2; Tennessee 24-17; Washington 4-1.
NOTE: Includes records as Dallas Texans from 1960 through 1962.

COACHING RECORDS

Tom Bettis, 1-6-0; Frank Gansz, 8-22-1; Marv Levy, 31-42-0; John Mackovic, 30-34-0 (0-1); Marty Schottenheimer, 101-58-1 (3-7); Hank Stram, 124-76-10 (5-3); Paul Wiggin, 11-24-0.
NOTE: Playoff games in parentheses.

RETIRED UNIFORM NUMBERS

No.	Player
3	Jan Stenerud
16	Len Dawson
28	Abner Haynes
33	Stone Johnson
36	Mack Lee Hill
63	Willie Lanier
78	Bobby Bell
86	Buck Buchanan

MIAMI DOLPHINS
YEAR-BY-YEAR RECORDS

	REGULAR SEASON							PLAYOFFS			
Year	W	L	T	Pct.	PF	PA	Finish	W	L	Highest round	Coach
1966*	3	11	0	.214	213	362	T4th/Eastern Div.	—	—		George Wilson
1967*	4	10	0	.286	219	407	T3rd/Eastern Div.	—	—		George Wilson
1968*	5	8	1	.385	276	355	3rd/Eastern Div.	—	—		George Wilson
1969*	3	10	1	.231	233	332	5th/Eastern Div.	—	—		George Wilson
1970	10	4	0	.714	297	228	2nd/AFC Eastern Div.	0	1	AFC div. playoff game	Don Shula
1971	10	3	1	.769	315	174	1st/AFC Eastern Div.	2	1	Super Bowl	Don Shula
1972	14	0	0	1.000	385	171	1st/AFC Eastern Div.	3	0	Super Bowl champ	Don Shula
1973	12	2	0	.857	343	150	1st/AFC Eastern Div.	3	0	Super Bowl champ	Don Shula
1974	11	3	0	.786	327	216	1st/AFC Eastern Div.	0	1	AFC div. playoff game	Don Shula
1975	10	4	0	.714	357	222	2nd/AFC Eastern Div.	—	—		Don Shula
1976	6	8	0	.429	263	264	3rd/AFC Eastern Div.	—	—		Don Shula
1977	10	4	0	.714	313	197	2nd/AFC Eastern Div.	—	—		Don Shula
1978	11	5	0	.688	372	254	2nd/AFC Eastern Div.	0	1	AFC wild-card game	Don Shula
1979	10	6	0	.625	341	257	1st/AFC Eastern Div.	0	1	AFC div. playoff game	Don Shula
1980	8	8	0	.500	266	305	3rd/AFC Eastern Div.	—	—		Don Shula
1981	11	4	1	.719	345	275	1st/AFC Eastern Div.	0	1	AFC div. playoff game	Don Shula
1982	7	2	0	.778	198	131	T2nd/AFC	3	1	Super Bowl	Don Shula
1983	12	4	0	.750	389	250	1st/AFC Eastern Div.	0	1	AFC div. playoff game	Don Shula
1984	14	2	0	.875	513	298	1st/AFC Eastern Div.	2	1	Super Bowl	Don Shula
1985	12	4	0	.750	428	320	1st/AFC Eastern Div.	1	1	AFC championship game	Don Shula
1986	8	8	0	.500	430	405	3rd/AFC Eastern Div.	—	—		Don Shula
1987	8	7	0	.533	362	335	T2nd/AFC Eastern Div.	—	—		Don Shula
1988	6	10	0	.375	319	380	5th/AFC Eastern Div.	—	—		Don Shula
1989	8	8	0	.500	331	379	T2nd/AFC Eastern Div.	—	—		Don Shula
1990	12	4	0	.750	336	242	2nd/AFC Eastern Div.	1	1	AFC div. playoff game	Don Shula
1991	8	8	0	.500	343	349	3rd/AFC Eastern Div.	—	—		Don Shula
1992	11	5	0	.688	340	281	1st/AFC Eastern Div.	1	1	AFC championship game	Don Shula
1993	9	7	0	.563	349	351	2nd/AFC Eastern Div.	—	—		Don Shula
1994	10	6	0	.625	389	327	1st/AFC Eastern Div.	1	1	AFC div. playoff game	Don Shula
1995	9	7	0	.563	398	332	T2nd/AFC Eastern Div.	0	1	AFC wild-card game	Don Shula
1996	8	8	0	.500	279	454	4th/AFC Eastern Div.	—	—		Jimmy Johnson
1997	9	7	0	.563	339	327	T2nd/AFC Eastern Div.	0	1	AFC wild-card game	Jimmy Johnson
1998	10	6	0	.625	321	265	T2nd/AFC Eastern Div.	1	1	AFC div. playoff game	Jimmy Johnson

*American Football League.

FIRST-ROUND DRAFT PICKS

1966—Jim Grabowski, RB, Illinois*
    Rick Norton, QB, Kentucky
1967—Bob Griese, QB, Purdue
1968—Larry Csonka, RB, Syracuse
    Doug Crusan, T, Indiana
1969—Bill Stanfill, DE, Georgia
1970—None
1971—None
1972—Mike Kadish, DT, Notre Dame
1973—None
1974—Don Reese, DE, Jackson State
1975—Darryl Carlton, T, Tampa
1976—Larry Gordon, LB, Arizona State
    Kim Bokamper, LB, San Jose State
1977—A.J. Duhe, DE, Louisiana State
1978—None
1979—Jon Giesler, T, Michigan

1980—Don McNeal, DB, Alabama
1981—David Overstreet, RB, Oklahoma
1982—Roy Foster, G, Southern California
1983—Dan Marino, QB, Pittsburgh
1984—Jackie Shipp, LB, Oklahoma
1985—Lorenzo Hampton, RB, Florida
1986—None
1987—John Bosa, DE, Boston College
1988—Eric Kumerow, DE, Ohio State
1989—Sammie Smith, RB, Florida State
    Louis Oliver, DB, Florida
1990—Richmond Webb, T, Texas A&M
1991—Randal Hill, WR, Miami (Fla.)
1992—Troy Vincent, DB, Wisconsin
    Marco Coleman, LB, Georgia Tech
1993—O.J. McDuffie, WR, Penn State
1994—Tim Bowens, DT, Mississippi

1995—Billy Milner, T, Houston
1996—Daryl Gardener, DT, Baylor
1997—Yatil Green, WR, Miami (Fla.)

1998—John Avery, RB, Mississippi
1999—None
*First player chosen in draft.

FRANCHISE RECORDS

Most rushing yards, career
6,737—Larry Csonka
Most rushing yards, season
1,258—Delvin Williams, 1978
Most rushing yards, game
197—Mercury Morris vs. N.E., Sept. 30, 1973
Most rushing touchdowns, season
15—Karim Abdul-Jabbar, 1997
Most passing attempts, season
623—Dan Marino, 1986
Most passing attempts, game
60—Dan Marino vs. NYJ, Oct. 23, 1988
    Dan Marino at N.E., Nov. 23, 1997
Most passes completed, season
385—Dan Marino, 1994
Most passes completed, game
39—Dan Marino at Buf., Nov. 16, 1986
Most passing yards, career
58,913—Dan Marino

Most passing yards, season
5,084—Dan Marino, 1984
Most passing yards, game
521—Dan Marino vs. NYJ, Oct. 23, 1988
Most touchdown passes, season
48—Dan Marino, 1984
Most pass receptions, career
550—Mark Clayton
Most pass receptions, season
90—O.J. McDuffie, 1998
Most pass receptions, game
12—Jim Jensen at N.E., Nov. 6, 1988
Most receiving yards, career
8,869—Mark Duper
Most receiving yards, season
1,389—Mark Clayton, 1984
Most receiving yards, game
217—Mark Duper vs. NYJ, Nov. 10, 1985
Most receiving touchdowns, season
18—Mark Clayton, 1984

Most touchdowns, career
82—Mark Clayton
Most field goals, season
31—Pete Stoyanovich, 1991
Longest field goal
59 yards—Pete Stoyanovich at NYJ, Nov. 12, 1989
Most interceptions, career
35—Jake Scott
Most interceptions, season
10—Dick Westmoreland, 1967
Most sacks, career
67.5—Bill Stanfill
Most sacks, season
18.5—Bill Stanfill, 1973

SERIES RECORDS

Miami vs.: Arizona 7-0; Atlanta 6-2; Baltimore, 1-0; Buffalo 42-23-1; Carolina 1-0; Chicago 5-3; Cincinnati 12-3; Dallas 6-2; Denver 6-2-1; Detroit 4-2, Green Bay 8-1; Indianapolis 39-19; Jacksonville 0-1; Kansas City 10-10; Minnesota 4-2; New England 38-27; New Orleans 6-4; N.Y. Giants 1-3; N.Y. Jets 33-30-1; Oakland 7-15-1; Philadelphia 6-3; Pittsburgh 9-7; St. Louis 7-1; San Diego 6-10; San Francisco 4-3; Seattle 4-2; Tampa Bay 4-2; Tennessee 13-11; Washington 5-2.

COACHING RECORDS

Jimmy Johnson, 27-21-0 (1-2); Don Shula, 257-133-2 (17-14); George Wilson, 15-39-2.

RETIRED UNIFORM NUMBERS

No.	Player
12	Bob Griese

MINNESOTA VIKINGS
YEAR-BY-YEAR RECORDS

		REGULAR SEASON						PLAYOFFS			
Year	W	L	T	Pct.	PF	PA	Finish	W	L	Highest round	Coach
1961	3	11	0	.214	285	407	7th/Western Conf.	—	—		Norm Van Brocklin
1962	2	11	1	.154	254	410	6th/Western Conf.	—	—		Norm Van Brocklin
1963	5	8	1	.385	309	390	T4th/Western Conf.	—	—		Norm Van Brocklin
1964	8	5	1	.615	355	296	T2nd/Western Conf.	—	—		Norm Van Brocklin
1965	7	7	0	.500	383	403	5th/Western Conf.	—	—		Norm Van Brocklin
1966	4	9	1	.308	292	304	T6th/Western Conf.	—	—		Norm Van Brocklin
1967	3	8	3	.273	233	294	4th/Central Div.	—	—		Bud Grant
1968	8	6	0	.571	282	242	1st/Central Div.	0	1	W. Conf. champ. game	Bud Grant
1969	12	2	0	.857	379	133	1st/Central Div.	2	1	Super Bowl	Bud Grant
1970	12	2	0	.857	335	143	1st/NFC Central Div.	0	1	NFC div. playoff game	Bud Grant
1971	11	3	0	.786	245	139	1st/NFC Central Div.	0	1	NFC div. playoff game	Bud Grant
1972	7	7	0	.500	301	252	3rd/NFC Central Div.	—	—		Bud Grant
1973	12	2	0	.857	296	168	1st/NFC Central Div.	2	1	Super Bowl	Bud Grant
1974	10	4	0	.714	310	195	1st/NFC Central Div.	2	1	Super Bowl	Bud Grant
1975	12	2	0	.857	377	180	1st/NFC Central Div.	0	1	NFC div. playoff game	Bud Grant
1976	11	2	1	.821	305	176	1st/NFC Central Div.	2	1	Super Bowl	Bud Grant
1977	9	5	0	.643	231	227	1st/NFC Central Div.	1	1	NFC championship game	Bud Grant
1978	8	7	1	.531	294	306	1st/NFC Central Div.	0	1	NFC div. playoff game	Bud Grant
1979	7	9	0	.438	259	337	3rd/NFC Central Div.	—	—		Bud Grant
1980	9	7	0	.563	317	308	1st/NFC Central Div.	0	1	NFC div. playoff game	Bud Grant
1981	7	9	0	.438	325	369	4th/NFC Central Div.	—	—		Bud Grant
1982	5	4	0	.556	187	198	T4th/NFC	1	1	NFC second-round pl. game	Bud Grant
1983	8	8	0	.500	316	348	T2nd/NFC Central Div.	—	—		Bud Grant
1984	3	13	0	.188	276	484	5th/NFC Central Div.	—	—		Les Steckel

Year	\multicolumn{7}{c}{REGULAR SEASON}							\multicolumn{3}{c}{PLAYOFFS}			
Year	W	L	T	Pct.	PF	PA	Finish	W	L	Highest round	Coach
1985	7	9	0	.438	346	359	T3rd/NFC Central Div.	—	—		Bud Grant
1986	9	7	0	.563	398	273	2nd/NFC Central Div.	—	—		Jerry Burns
1987	8	7	0	.533	336	335	2nd/NFC Central Div.	2	1	NFC championship game	Jerry Burns
1988	11	5	0	.688	406	233	2nd/NFC Central Div.	1	1	NFC div. playoff game	Jerry Burns
1989	10	6	0	.625	351	275	1st/NFC Central Div.	0	1	NFC div. playoff game	Jerry Burns
1990	6	10	0	.375	351	326	T2nd/NFC Central Div.	—	—		Jerry Burns
1991	8	8	0	.500	301	306	3rd/NFC Central Div.	—	—		Jerry Burns
1992	11	5	0	.688	374	249	1st/NFC Central Div.	0	1	NFC wild-card game	Dennis Green
1993	9	7	0	.563	277	290	T2nd/NFC Central Div.	0	1	NFC wild-card game	Dennis Green
1994	10	6	0	.625	356	314	1st/NFC Central Div.	0	1	NFC wild-card game	Dennis Green
1995	8	8	0	.500	412	385	4th/NFC Central Div.	—	—		Dennis Green
1996	9	7	0	.563	298	315	2nd/NFC Central Div.	0	1	NFC wild-card game	Dennis Green
1997	9	7	0	.563	354	359	T3rd/NFC Central Div.	1	1	NFC div. playoff game	Dennis Green
1998	15	1	0	.938	556	296	1st/NFC Central Div.	1	1	NFC championship game	Dennis Green

FIRST-ROUND DRAFT PICKS

1961—Tommy Mason, RB, Tulane*
1962—None
1963—Jim Dunaway, T, Mississippi
1964—Carl Eller, DE, Minnesota
1965—Jack Snow, WR, Notre Dame
1966—Jerry Shay, DT, Purdue
1967—Clint Jones, RB, Michigan State
    Gene Washington, WR, Michigan State
    Alan Page, DT, Notre Dame
1968—Ron Yary, T, Southern California*
1969—None
1970—John Ward, DT, Oklahoma State
1971—Leo Hayden, RB, Ohio State
1972—Jeff Siemon, LB, Stanford
1973—Chuck Foreman, RB, Miami (Fla.)
1974—Fred McNeill, LB, UCLA
    Steve Riley, T, Southern California
1975—Mark Mullaney, DE, Colorado State
1976—James White, DT, Oklahoma State
1977—Tommy Kramer, QB, Rice
1978—Randy Holloway, DE, Pittsburgh
1979—Ted Brown, RB, North Carolina State
1980—Doug Martin, DT, Washington

1981—None
1982—Darrin Nelson, RB, Stanford
1983—Joey Browner, DB, Southern California
1984—Keith Millard, DE, Washington State
1985—Chris Doleman, LB, Pittsburgh
1986—Gerald Robinson, DE, Auburn
1987—D.J. Dozier, RB, Penn State
1988—Randall McDaniel, G, Arizona State
1989—None
1990—None
1991—None
1992—None
1993—Robert Smith, RB, Ohio State
1994—DeWayne Washington, CB, North Carolina State
    Todd Steussie, T, California
1995—Derrick Alexander, DE, Florida State
    Korey Stringer, T, Ohio State
1996—Duane Clemons, DE, California
1997—Dwayne Rudd, LB, Alabama
1998—Randy Moss, WR, Marshall
1999—Daunte Culpepper, QB, Central Florida
    Dimitrius Underwood, DE, Michigan State
*First player chosen in draft.

FRANCHISE RECORDS

Most rushing yards, career
5,879—Chuck Foreman
Most rushing yards, season
1,266—Terry Allen, 1997
Most rushing yards, game
200—Chuck Foreman at Phi., Oct. 24, 1976
Most rushing touchdowns, season
13—Chuck Foreman, 1975
    Chuck Foreman, 1976
    Terry Allen, 1992
Most passing attempts, season
606—Warren Moon, 1995
Most passing attempts, game
63—Rich Gannon at N.E., Oct. 20, 1991
Most passes completed, season
377—Warren Moon, 1995
Most passes completed, game
38—Tommy Kramer vs. Cle., Dec. 14, 1980
    Tommy Kramer vs. G.B., Nov. 29, 1981
Most passing yards, career
33,098—Fran Tarkenton

Most passing yards, season
4,264—Warren Moon, 1994
Most passing yards, game
490—Tommy Kramer at Was., Nov. 2, 1986
Most touchdown passes, season
34—Randall Cunningham, 1998
Most pass receptions, career
745—Cris Carter
Most pass receptions, season
122—Cris Carter, 1994, 1995
Most pass receptions, game
15—Rickey Young at N.E., Dec. 16, 1979
Most receiving yards, career
8,997—Cris Carter
Most receiving yards, season
1,371—Cris Carter, 1995
Most receiving yards, game
210—Sammy White vs. Det., Nov. 7, 1976
Most receiving touchdowns, season
17—Cris Carter, 1995
    Randy Moss, 1998

Most touchdowns, career
82—Cris Carter
Most field goals, season
46—Fred Cox, 1970
Longest field goal
54 yards—Jan Stenerud vs. Atl., Sept. 16, 1984
Most interceptions, career
53—Paul Krause
Most interceptions, season
10—Paul Krause, 1975
Most sacks, career
130—Carl Eller
Most sacks, season
21—Chris Doleman, 1989

SERIES RECORDS

Minnesota vs.: Arizona 7-8; Atlanta 13-6; Baltimore 1-0; Buffalo 6-2; Carolina 2-0; Chicago 41-32-2; Cincinnati 5-4; Dallas 7-9; Denver 5-4; Detroit 46-27-2; Green Bay 38-36-1; Indianapolis 7-11-1; Jacksonville 1-0; Kansas City 3-3; Miami 2-4; New England 3-4; New Orleans 14-6; N.Y. Giants 7-5; N.Y. Jets 1-5; Oakland 3-6; Philadelphia 11-6; Pittsburgh 8-4; St. Louis 16-11-2; San Diego 3-4; San Francisco 16-17-1; Seattle 2-4; Tampa Bay 28-14; Tennessee 5-3; Washington 5-6.

COACHING RECORDS

Jerry Burns, 52-43-0 (3-3); Bud Grant, 158-96-5 (10-12); Dennis Green, 71-41-0 (1-5); Les Steckel, 3-13-0; Norm Van Brocklin, 29-51-4.
NOTE: Playoff games in parentheses.

RETIRED UNIFORM NUMBERS

No.	Player
10	Fran Tarkenton
88	Alan Page

NEW ENGLAND PATRIOTS
YEAR-BY-YEAR RECORDS

		REGULAR SEASON						PLAYOFFS			
Year	W	L	T	Pct.	PF	PA	Finish	W	L	Highest round	Coach
1960*†	5	9	0	.357	286	349	4th/Eastern Div.	—	—		Lou Saban
1961*†	9	4	1	.692	413	313	2nd/Eastern Div.	—	—		Lou Saban, Mike Holovak
1962*†	9	4	1	.692	346	295	2nd/Eastern Div.	—	—		Mike Holovak
1963*†	7	6	1	.538	327	257	1st/Eastern Div.	1	1	AFL championship game	Mike Holovak
1964*†	10	3	1	.769	365	297	2nd/Eastern Div.	—	—		Mike Holovak
1965*†	4	8	2	.333	244	302	3rd/Eastern Div.	—	—		Mike Holovak
1966*†	8	4	2	.667	315	283	2nd/Eastern Div.	—	—		Mike Holovak
1967*†	3	10	1	.231	280	389	5th/Eastern Div.	—	—		Mike Holovak
1968*†	4	10	0	.286	229	406	4th/Eastern Div.	—	—		Mike Holovak
1969*†	4	10	0	.286	266	316	T3rd/Eastern Div.	—	—		Clive Rush
1970†	2	12	0	.143	149	361	5th/AFC Eastern Div.	—	—		Clive Rush, John Mazur
1971	6	8	0	.429	238	325	T3rd/AFC Eastern Div.	—	—		John Mazur
1972	3	11	0	.214	192	446	5th/AFC Eastern Div.	—	—		J. Mazur, Phil Bengtson
1973	5	9	0	.357	258	300	3rd/AFC Eastern Div.	—	—		Chuck Fairbanks
1974	7	7	0	.500	348	289	T3rd/AFC Eastern Div.	—	—		Chuck Fairbanks
1975	3	11	0	.214	258	358	T4th/AFC Eastern Div.	—	—		Chuck Fairbanks
1976	11	3	0	.786	376	236	2nd/Eastern Div.	0	1	AFC div. playoff game	Chuck Fairbanks
1977	9	5	0	.643	278	217	3rd/AFC Eastern Div.	—	—		Chuck Fairbanks
1978	11	5	0	.688	358	286	1st/AFC Eastern Div.	0	1	AFC div. playoff game	Chuck Fairbanks, Hank Bullough-R. Erhardt
1979	9	7	0	.563	411	326	2nd/AFC Eastern Div.	—	—		Ron Erhardt
1980	10	6	0	.625	441	325	2nd/AFC Eastern Div.	—	—		Ron Erhardt
1981	2	14	0	.125	322	370	T4th/AFC Eastern Div.	—	—		Ron Erhardt
1982	5	4	0	.556	143	157	7th/AFC	0	1	AFC first-round pl. game	Ron Meyer
1983	8	8	0	.500	274	289	T2nd/AFC Eastern Div.	—	—		Ron Meyer
1984	9	7	0	.563	362	352	2nd/AFC Eastern Div.	—	—		R. Meyer, R. Berry
1985	11	5	0	.688	362	290	T2nd/AFC Eastern Div.	3	1	Super Bowl	Raymond Berry
1986	11	5	0	.688	412	307	1st/AFC Eastern Div.	0	1	AFC div. playoff game	Raymond Berry
1987	8	7	0	.533	320	293	T2nd/AFC Eastern Div.	—	—		Raymond Berry
1988	9	7	0	.563	250	284	T2nd/AFC Eastern Div.	—	—		Raymond Berry
1989	5	11	0	.313	297	391	4th/AFC Eastern Div.	—	—		Raymond Berry
1990	1	15	0	.063	181	446	5th/AFC Eastern Div.	—	—		Rod Rust
1991	6	10	0	.375	211	305	4th/AFC Eastern Div.	—	—		Dick MacPherson
1992	2	14	0	.125	205	363	5th/AFC Eastern Div.	—	—		Dick MacPherson
1993	5	11	0	.313	238	286	4th/AFC Eastern Div.	—	—		Bill Parcells
1994	10	6	0	.625	351	312	2nd/AFC Eastern Div.	0	1	AFC wild-card game	Bill Parcells
1995	6	10	0	.375	294	377	4th/AFC Eastern Div.	—	—		Bill Parcells
1996	11	5	0	.687	418	313	1st/AFC Eastern Div.	2	1	Super Bowl	Bill Parcells
1997	10	6	0	.625	369	289	1st/AFC Eastern Div.	1	1	AFC div. playoff game	Pete Carroll
1998	9	7	0	.563	337	329	4th/AFC Eastern Div.	0	1	AFC wild-card game	Pete Carroll

*American Football League.
†Boston Patriots.

FIRST-ROUND DRAFT PICKS

1960—Ron Burton, RB, Northwestern
1961—Tommy Mason, RB, Tulane
1962—Gary Collins, WR, Maryland
1963—Art Graham, E, Boston College
1964—Jack Concannon, QB, Boston College* (AFL)
1965—Jerry Rush, DE, Michigan State
     Dave McCormick, T, Louisiana State

1966—Karl Singer, T, Purdue
     Willie Townes, T, Tulsa
1967—John Charles, DB, Purdue
1968—Dennis Byrd, DE, North Carolina State
1969—Ron Sellers, WR, Florida State
1970—Phil Olsen, DT, Utah State
1971—Jim Plunkett, QB, Stanford*

1972—None
1973—John Hannah, G, Alabama
Sam Cunningham, RB, Southern California
Darryl Stingley, WR, Purdue
1974—None
1975—Russ Francis, TE, Oregon
1976—Mike Haynes, DB, Arizona State
Pete Brock, C, Colorado
Tim Fox, DB, Ohio State
1977—Raymond Clayborn, DB, Texas
Stanley Morgan, WR, Tennessee
1978—Bob Cryder, G, Alabama
1979—Rick Sanford, DB, South Carolina
1980—Roland James, DB, Tennessee
Vagas Ferguson, RB, Notre Dame
1981—Brian Holloway, T, Stanford
1982—Kenneth Sims, DT, Texas*
Lester Williams, DT, Nebraska
1983—Tony Eason, QB, Illinois
1984—Irving Fryar, WR, Nebraska*

1985—Trevor Matich, C, Brigham Young
1986—Reggie Dupard, RB, Southern Methodist
1987—Bruce Armstrong, G, Louisville
1988—J. Stephens, RB, Northwestern Louisiana State
1989—Hart Lee Dykes, WR, Oklahoma State
1990—Chris Singleton, LB, Arizona
Ray Agnew, DL, North Carolina State
1991—Pat Harlow, T, Southern California
Leonard Russell, RB, Arizona State
1992—Eugene Chung, T, Virginia Tech
1993—Drew Bledsoe, QB, Washington State*
1994—Willie McGinest, DE, Southern California
1995—Ty Law, DB, Michigan
1996—Terry Glenn, WR, Ohio State
1997—Chris Canty, DB, Kansas State
1998—Robert Edwards, RB, Georgia
Tebucky Jones, DB, Syracuse
1999—Damien Woody, C, Boston College
Andy Katzenmoyer, LB, Ohio State
*First player chosen in draft.

FRANCHISE RECORDS

Most rushing yards, career
5,453—Sam Cunningham
Most rushing yards, season
1,487—Curtis Martin, 1995
Most rushing yards, game
212—Tony Collins vs. NYJ, Sept. 18, 1983
Most rushing touchdowns, season
14—Curtis Martin, 1995, 1996
Most passing attempts, season
691—Drew Bledsoe, 1994
Most passing attempts, game
70—Drew Bledsoe vs. Min., Nov. 13, 1994 (OT)
60—Drew Bledsoe at Pit., Dec. 16, 1995
Most passes completed, season
400—Drew Bledsoe, 1994
Most passes completed, game
45—Drew Bledsoe vs. Min., Nov. 13, 1994 (OT)
39—Drew Bledsoe at Pit., Dec. 16, 1995
Most passing yards, career
26,886—Steve Grogan

Most passing yards, season
4,555—Drew Bledsoe, 1994
Most passing yards, game
426—Drew Bledsoe vs. Min., Nov. 13, 1994 (OT)
423—Drew Bledsoe vs. Mia., Nov. 23, 1998
Most touchdown passes, season
31—Babe Parilli, 1964
Most pass receptions, career
534—Stanley Morgan
Most pass receptions, season
96—Ben Coates, 1994
Most pass receptions, game
12—Ben Coates at Ind., Nov. 27, 1994
Most receiving yards, career
10,352—Stanley Morgan
Most receiving yards, season
1,491—Stanley Morgan, 1986
Most receiving yards, game
193—Terry Glenn at Pittsburgh, Dec. 6, 1998

Most receiving touchdowns, season
12—Stanley Morgan, 1979
Most touchdowns, career
68—Stanley Morgan
Most field goals, season
32—Tony Franklin, 1986
Longest field goal
55 yards—Matt Bahr at Mia., Nov. 12, 1995
Adam Vinatieri at St.L., Dec. 13, 1998
Most interceptions, career
36—Raymond Clayborn
Most interceptions, season
11—Ron Hall, 1964
Most sacks, career
100—Andre Tippett
Most sacks, season
18.5—Andre Tippett, 1984

SERIES RECORDS

New England vs.: Arizona 3-6; Atlanta 3-6; Baltimore 1-0; Buffalo 41-36-1; Carolina 0-1; Chicago 5-2; Cincinnati 9-7; Dallas 0-7; Denver 12-20; Detroit 3-3; Green Bay 3-3; Indianapolis 35-22; Jacksonville 2-0; Kansas City 8-14-3; Miami 26-38; Minnesota 4-3; New Orleans 6-3; N.Y. Giants 2-3; N.Y. Jets 34-42-1; Oakland 12-13-1; Philadelphia 2-5; Pittsburgh 4-11; St. Louis 3-4; San Diego 16-11-2; San Francisco 2-7; Seattle 6-7; Tampa Bay 3-1; Tennessee 18-14-1; Washington 1-5.
NOTE: Includes records as Boston Patriots from 1960 through 1970.

COACHING RECORDS

Phil Bengtson, 1-4-0; Raymond Berry, 48-39-0 (3-2); Hank Bullough, 0-1-0; Pete Carroll, 19-13-0 (1-2); Ron Erhardt, 21-27-0; Chuck Fairbanks, 46-39-0 (0-2); Mike Holovak, 52-46-9 (1-1); Dick MacPherson, 8-24-0; John Mazur, 9-21-0; Ron Meyer, 18-15-0 (0-1); Bill Parcells, 32-32-0 (2-2); Clive Rush, 5-16-0; Rod Rust, 1-15-0; Lou Saban, 7-12-0.
NOTE: Playoff games in parentheses.

RETIRED UNIFORM NUMBERS

No.	Player
14	Steve Grogan
20	Gino Cappelletti
57	Steve Nelson
73	John Hannah
79	Jim Hunt
89	Bob Dee

NEW ORLEANS SAINTS
YEAR-BY-YEAR RECORDS

	REGULAR SEASON						PLAYOFFS			
Year	W	L	T	Pct.	PF	PA	Finish	W	L	Highest round	Coach
1967	3	11	0	.214	233	379	4th/Capitol Div.	—	—		Tom Fears
1968	4	9	1	.308	246	327	3rd/Century Div.	—	—		Tom Fears
1969	5	9	0	.357	311	393	3rd/Capitol Div.	—	—		Tom Fears
1970	2	11	1	.154	172	347	4th/NFC Western Div.	—	—		Tom Fears, J.D. Roberts
1971	4	8	2	.333	266	347	4th/NFC Western Div.	—	—		J.D. Roberts
1972	2	11	1	.179	215	361	4th/NFC Western Div.	—	—		J.D. Roberts
1973	5	9	0	.357	163	312	T3rd/NFC Western Div.	—	—		John North
1974	5	9	0	.357	166	263	3rd/NFC Western Div.	—	—		John North
1975	2	12	0	.143	165	360	4th/NFC Western Div.	—	—		J. North, Ernie Hefferle
1976	4	10	0	.286	253	346	T3rd/NFC Western Div.	—	—		Hank Stram
1977	3	11	0	.214	232	336	4th/NFC Western Div.	—	—		Hank Stram
1978	7	9	0	.438	281	298	3rd/NFC Western Div.	—	—		Dick Nolan
1979	8	8	0	.500	370	360	2nd/NFC Western Div.	—	—		Dick Nolan
1980	1	15	0	.063	291	487	4th/NFC Western Div.	—	—		Dick Nolan, Dick Stanfel
1981	4	12	0	.250	207	378	4th/NFC Western Div.	—	—		Bum Phillips
1982	4	5	0	.444	129	160	T8th/NFC	—	—		Bum Phillips
1983	8	8	0	.500	319	337	3rd/NFC Western Div.	—	—		Bum Phillips
1984	7	9	0	.438	298	361	3rd/NFC Western Div.	—	—		Bum Phillips
1985	5	11	0	.313	294	401	3rd/NFC Western Div.	—	—		B. Phillips, Wade Phillips
1986	7	9	0	.438	288	287	4th/NFC Western Div.	—	—		Jim Mora
1987	12	3	0	.800	422	283	2nd/NFC Western Div.	0	1	NFC wild-card game	Jim Mora
1988	10	6	0	.625	312	283	3rd/NFC Western Div.	—	—		Jim Mora
1989	9	7	0	.563	386	301	3rd/NFC Western Div.	—	—		Jim Mora
1990	8	8	0	.500	274	275	2nd/NFC Western Div.	0	1	NFC wild-card game	Jim Mora
1991	11	5	0	.688	341	211	1st/NFC Western Div.	0	1	NFC wild-card game	Jim Mora
1992	12	4	0	.750	330	202	2nd/NFC Western Div.	0	1	NFC wild-card game	Jim Mora
1993	8	8	0	.500	317	343	2nd/NFC Western Div.	—	—		Jim Mora
1994	7	9	0	.438	348	407	T2nd/NFC Western Div.	—	—		Jim Mora
1995	7	9	0	.438	319	348	T3rd/NFC Western Div.	—	—		Jim Mora
1996	3	13	0	.188	229	339	T4th/NFC Western Div.	—	—		Jim Mora, Rick Venturi
1997	6	10	0	.375	237	327	4th/NFC Western Div.	—	—		Mike Ditka
1998	6	10	0	.375	305	359	3rd/NFC Western Div.	—	—		Mike Ditka

FIRST-ROUND DRAFT PICKS

1967—Les Kelley, RB, Alabama
1968—Kevin Hardy, DE, Notre Dame
1969—John Shinners, G, Xavier (Ohio)
1970—Ken Burrough, WR, Texas Southern
1971—Archie Manning, QB, Mississippi
1972—Royce Smith, G, Georgia
1973—None
1974—Rick Middleton, LB, Ohio State
1975—Larry Burton, WR, Purdue
      Kurt Schumacher, G, Ohio State
1976—Chuck Muncie, RB, California
1977—Joe Campbell, DE, Maryland
1978—Wes Chandler, WR, Florida
1979—Russell Erxleben, P, Texas
1980—Stan Brock, T, Colorado
1981—George Rogers, RB, South Carolina*
1982—Lindsay Scott, WR, Georgia
1983—None

1984—None
1985—Alvin Toles, LB, Tennessee
1986—Jim Dombrowski, T, Virginia
1987—Shawn Knight, DE, Brigham Young
1988—Craig Heyward, RB, Pittsburgh
1989—Wayne Martin, DE, Arkansas
1990—Renaldo Turnbull, DE, West Virginia
1991—None
1992—Vaughn Dunbar, RB, Indiana
1993—Willie Roaf, T, Louisiana Tech
      Irv Smith, TE, Notre Dame
1994—Joe Johnson, DE, Louisville
1995—Mark Fields, LB, Washington State
1996—Alex Molden, DB, Oregon
1997—Chris Naeole, G, Colorado
1998—Kyle Turley, T, San Diego State
1999—Ricky Williams, RB, Texas
    *First player chosen in draft.

FRANCHISE RECORDS

Most rushing yards, career
4,267—George Rogers
Most rushing yards, season
1,674—George Rogers, 1981
Most rushing yards, game
206—George Rogers vs. St.L., Sept. 4, 1983

Most rushing touchdowns, season
13—George Rogers, 1981
    Dalton Hilliard, 1989
Most passing attempts, season
567—Jim Everett, 1995
Most passing attempts, game
55—Jim Everett at S.F., Sept. 25, 1994

Most passes completed, season
346—Jim Everett, 1994
Most passes completed, game
33—Archie Manning at G.B., Sept. 10, 1978
Most passing yards, career
21,734—Archie Manning

Most passing yards, season
3,970—Jim Everett, 1995
Most passing yards, game
377—Archie Manning at S.F., Dec. 7, 1980
Most touchdown passes, season
26—Jim Everett, 1995
Most pass receptions, career
532—Eric Martin
Most pass receptions, season
85—Eric Martin, 1988
Most pass receptions, game
14—Tony Galbreath at G.B., Sept. 10, 1978

Most receiving yards, career
7,854—Eric Martin
Most receiving yards, season
1,090—Eric Martin, 1989
Most receiving yards, game
205—Wes Chandler vs. Atl., Sept. 2, 1979
Most receiving touchdowns, season
9—Henry Childs, 1977
Most touchdowns, career
53—Dalton Hilliard
Most field goals, season
31—Morten Andersen, 1985

Longest field goal
63 yards—Tom Dempsey vs. Det., Nov. 8, 1970
Most interceptions, career
37—Dave Waymer
Most interceptions, season
10—Dave Whitsell, 1967
Most sacks, career
115—Rickey Jackson
Most sacks, season
17—Pat Swilling, 1991

SERIES RECORDS

New Orleans vs.: Arizona 10-12; Atlanta 24-35; Baltimore 0-1; Buffalo 2-4; Carolina 3-5; Chicago 7-10; Cincinnati 5-4; Dallas 4-14; Denver 2-4; Detroit 8-6-1; Green Bay 4-13; Indianapolis 4-3; Jacksonville 1-0; Kansas City 3-4; Miami 4-6; Minnesota 6-14; New England 3-6; N.Y. Giants 8-11; N.Y. Jets 4-4; Philadelphia 8-12; Oakland 3-4-1; Pittsburgh 5-6; St. Louis 25-31; San Diego 1-6; San Francisco 15-42-2; Seattle 4-2; Tampa Bay 13-5; Tennessee 4-4-1; Washington 5-12.

COACHING RECORDS

Mike Ditka, 12-20-0; Tom Fears, 13-34-2; Ernie Hefferle, 1-7-0; Jim Mora, 93-74-0 (0-4); Dick Nolan, 15-29-0; John North, 11-23-0; Bum Phillips, 27-42-0; Wade Phillips, 1-3-0; J.D. Roberts, 7-25-3; Dick Stanfel, 1-3-0; Hank Stram, 7-21-0; Rick Venturi, 1-7-0. NOTE: Playoff games in parentheses.

RETIRED UNIFORM NUMBERS

No.	Player
31	Jim Taylor
81	Doug Atkins

NEW YORK GIANTS
YEAR-BY-YEAR RECORDS

Year	W	L	T	Pct.	PF	PA	Finish	W	L	Highest round	Coach
1925	8	4	0	.667	122	67	T4th				Bob Folwell
1926	8	4	1	.667	147	51	T6th				Joe Alexander
1927	11	1	1	.917	197	20	1st				Earl Potteiger
1928	4	7	2	.364	79	136	6th				Earl Potteiger
1929	13	1	1	.929	312	86	2nd				LeRoy Andrews
1930	13	4	0	.765	308	98	2nd				L. Andrews, Benny Friedman-Steve Owen
1931	7	6	1	.538	154	100	5th				Steve Owen
1932	4	6	2	.400	93	113	5th				Steve Owen
1933	11	3	0	.786	244	101	1st/Eastern Div.	0	1	NFL championship game	Steve Owen
1934	8	5	0	.615	147	107	1st/Eastern Div.	1	0	NFL champ	Steve Owen
1935	9	3	0	.750	180	96	1st/Eastern Div.	0	1	NFL championship game	Steve Owen
1936	5	6	1	.455	115	163	3rd/Eastern Div.	—	—		Steve Owen
1937	6	3	2	.667	128	109	2nd/Eastern Div.	—	—		Steve Owen
1938	8	2	1	.800	194	79	1st/Eastern Div.	1	0	NFL champ	Steve Owen
1939	9	1	1	.900	168	85	1st/Eastern Div.	0	1	NFL championship game	Steve Owen
1940	6	4	1	.600	131	133	3rd/Eastern Div.	—	—		Steve Owen
1941	8	3	0	.727	238	114	1st/Eastern Div.	0	1	NFL championship game	Steve Owen
1942	5	5	1	.500	155	139	3rd/Eastern Div.	—	—		Steve Owen
1943	6	3	1	.667	197	170	2nd/Eastern Div.	0	1	E. Div. champ. game	Steve Owen
1944	8	1	1	.889	206	75	1st/Eastern Div.	0	1	NFL championship game	Steve Owen
1945	3	6	1	.333	179	198	T3rd/Eastern Div.	—	—		Steve Owen
1946	7	3	1	.700	236	162	1st/Eastern Div.	0	1	NFL championship game	Steve Owen
1947	2	8	2	.200	190	309	5th/Eastern Div.	—	—		Steve Owen
1948	4	8	0	.333	297	388	T3rd/Eastern Div.	—	—		Steve Owen
1949	6	6	0	.500	287	298	3rd/Eastern Div.	—	—		Steve Owen
1950	10	2	0	.833	268	150	2nd/American Conf.	0	1	Am. Conf. champ. game	Steve Owen
1951	9	2	1	.818	254	161	2nd/American Conf.	—	—		Steve Owen
1952	7	5	0	.583	234	231	T2nd/American Conf.	—	—		Steve Owen
1953	3	9	0	.250	179	277	5th/Eastern Conf.	—	—		Steve Owen
1954	7	5	0	.583	293	184	3rd/Eastern Conf.	—	—		Jim Lee Howell
1955	6	5	1	.545	267	223	3rd/Eastern Conf.	—	—		Jim Lee Howell
1956	8	3	1	.727	264	197	1st/Eastern Conf.	1	0	NFL champ	Jim Lee Howell
1957	7	5	0	.583	254	211	2nd/Eastern Conf.	—	—		Jim Lee Howell
1958	9	3	0	.750	246	183	1st/Eastern Conf.	1	1	NFL championship game	Jim Lee Howell
1959	10	2	0	.833	284	170	1st/Eastern Conf.	0	1	NFL championship game	Jim Lee Howell
1960	6	4	2	.600	271	261	3rd/Eastern Conf.	—	—		Jim Lee Howell

	REGULAR SEASON							PLAYOFFS			
Year	W	L	T	Pct.	PF	PA	Finish	W	L	Highest round	Coach
1961	10	3	1	.769	368	220	1st/Eastern Conf.	0	1	NFL championship game	Allie Sherman
1962	12	2	0	.857	398	283	1st/Eastern Conf.	0	1	NFL championship game	Allie Sherman
1963	11	3	0	.786	448	280	1st/Eastern Conf.	0	1	NFL championship game	Allie Sherman
1964	2	10	2	.167	241	399	7th/Eastern Conf.	—	—		Allie Sherman
1965	7	7	0	.500	270	338	T2nd/Eastern Conf.	—	—		Allie Sherman
1966	1	12	1	.077	263	501	8th/Eastern Conf.	—	—		Allie Sherman
1967	7	7	0	.500	369	379	2nd/Century Div.	—	—		Allie Sherman
1968	7	7	0	.500	294	325	2nd/Capitol Div.	—	—		Allie Sherman
1969	6	8	0	.429	264	298	2nd/Century Div.	—	—		Alex Webster
1970	9	5	0	.643	301	270	2nd/NFC Eastern Div.	—	—		Alex Webster
1971	4	10	0	.286	228	362	5th/NFC Eastern Div.	—	—		Alex Webster
1972	8	6	0	.571	331	247	3rd/NFC Eastern Div.	—	—		Alex Webster
1973	2	11	1	.179	226	362	5th/NFC Eastern Div.	—	—		Alex Webster
1974	2	12	0	.143	195	299	5th/NFC Eastern Div.	—	—		Bill Arnsparger
1975	5	9	0	.357	216	306	4th/NFC Eastern Div.	—	—		Bill Arnsparger
1976	3	11	0	.214	170	250	5th/NFC Eastern Div.	—	—		B. Arnsparger, J. McVay
1977	5	9	0	.357	181	265	T4th/NFC Eastern Div.	—	—		John McVay
1978	6	10	0	.375	264	298	T4th/NFC Eastern Div.	—	—		John McVay
1979	6	10	0	.375	237	323	4th/NFC Eastern Div.	—	—		Ray Perkins
1980	4	12	0	.250	249	425	5th/NFC Eastern Div.	—	—		Ray Perkins
1981	9	7	0	.563	295	257	3rd/NFC Eastern Div.	1	1	NFC div. playoff game	Ray Perkins
1982	4	5	0	.444	164	160	T8th/NFC	—	—		Ray Perkins
1983	3	12	1	.219	267	347	5th/NFC Eastern Div.	—	—		Bill Parcells
1984	9	7	0	.563	299	301	2nd/NFC Eastern Div.	1	1	NFC div. playoff game	Bill Parcells
1985	10	6	0	.625	399	283	2nd/NFC Eastern Div.	1	1	NFC div. playoff game	Bill Parcells
1986	14	2	0	.875	371	236	1st/NFC Eastern Div.	3	0	Super Bowl champ	Bill Parcells
1987	6	9	0	.400	280	312	5th/NFC Eastern Div.	—	—		Bill Parcells
1988	10	6	0	.625	359	304	2nd/NFC Eastern Div.	—	—		Bill Parcells
1989	12	4	0	.750	348	252	1st/NFC Eastern Div.	0	1	NFC div. playoff game	Bill Parcells
1990	13	3	0	.813	335	211	1st/NFC Eastern Div.	3	0	Super Bowl champ	Bill Parcells
1991	8	8	0	.500	281	297	4th/NFC Eastern Div.	—	—		Ray Handley
1992	6	10	0	.375	306	367	4th/NFC Eastern Div.	—	—		Ray Handley
1993	11	5	0	.688	288	205	2nd/NFC Eastern Div.	1	1	NFC div. playoff game	Dan Reeves
1994	9	7	0	.563	279	305	2nd/NFC Eastern Div.	—	—		Dan Reeves
1995	5	11	0	.313	290	340	4th/NFC Eastern Div.	—	—		Dan Reeves
1996	6	10	0	.375	242	297	5th/NFC Eastern Div.	—	—		Dan Reeves
1997	10	5	1	.656	307	265	1st/NFC Eastern Div.	0	1	NFC wild-card game	Jim Fassel
1998	8	8	0	.500	287	309	3rd/NFC Eastern Div.	—	—		Jim Fassel

FIRST-ROUND DRAFT PICKS

1936—Art Lewis, T, Ohio
1937—Ed Widseth, T, Minnesota
1938—George Karamatic, B, Gonzaga
1939—Walt Nielson, B, Arizona
1940—Grenville Lansdell, B, Southern California
1941—George Franck, B, Minnesota
1942—Merle Hapes, B, Mississippi
1943—Steve Filipowicz, B, Fordham
1944—Billy Hillenbrand, B, Indiana
1945—Elmer Barbour, B, Wake Forest
1946—George Connor, T, Notre Dame
1947—Vic Schwall, B, Northwestern
1948—Tony Minisi, B, Pennsylvania
1949—Paul Page, B, Southern Methodist
1950—Travis Tidwell, B, Auburn
1951—Kyle Rote, B, Southern Methodist*
    Kim Spavital, B, Oklahoma A&M
1952—Frank Gifford, B, Southern California
1953—Bobby Marlow, B, Alabama
1954—None
1955—Joe Heap, B, Notre Dame
1956—Henry Moore, B, Arkansas
1957—None
1958—Phil King, B, Vanderbilt
1959—Lee Grosscup, B, Utah
1960—Lou Cordileone, G, Clemson
1961—None
1962—Jerry Hillebrand, LB, Colorado
1963—None

1964—Joe Don Looney, RB, Oklahoma
1965—T. Frederickson, RB, Auburn*
1966—Francis Peay, T, Missouri
1967—None
1968—None
1969—Fred Dryer, DE, San Diego State
1970—Jim Files, LB, Oklahoma
1971—Rocky Thompson, RB, West Texas State
1972—Eldridge Small, DB, Texas A&I
    Larry Jacobson, DT, Nebraska
1973—None
1974—John Hicks, G, Ohio State
1975—None
1976—Troy Archer, DE, Colorado
1977—Gary Jeter, DT, Southern Cal
1978—Gordon King, T, Stanford
1979—Phil Simms, QB, Morehead State
1980—Mark Haynes, DB, Colorado
1981—Lawrence Taylor, LB, North Carolina
1982—Butch Woolfolk, RB, Michigan
1983—Terry Kinard, DB, Clemson
1984—Carl Banks, LB, Michigan State
    Bill Roberts, T, Ohio State
1985—George Adams, RB, Kentucky
1986—Eric Dorsey, DT, Notre Dame
1987—Mark Ingram, WR, Michigan State
1988—Eric Moore, T, Indiana
1989—Brian Williams, G, Minnesota
1990—Rodney Hampton, RB, Georgia

1991—Jarrod Bunch, FB, Michigan
1992—Derek Brown, TE, Notre Dame
1993—None
1994—Thomas Lewis, WR, Indiana
1995—Tyrone Wheatley, RB, Michigan

1996—Cedric Jones, DE, Oklahoma
1997—Ike Hilliard, WR, Florida
1998—Shaun Williams, DB, UCLA
1999—Luke Petitgout, T, Notre Dame
*First player chosen in draft.

FRANCHISE RECORDS

Most rushing yards, career
6,897—Rodney Hampton
Most rushing yards, season
1,516—Joe Morris, 1986
Most rushing yards, game
218—Gene Roberts vs. Chi. Cardinals,
   Nov. 12, 1950
Most rushing touchdowns, season
21—Joe Morris, 1985
Most passing attempts, season
533—Phil Simms, 1984
Most passing attempts, game
62—Phil Simms at Cin., Oct. 13, 1985
Most passes completed, season
286—Phil Simms, 1984
Most passes completed, game
40—Phil Simms at Cin., Oct. 13, 1985
Most passing yards, career
33,462—Phil Simms

Most passing yards, season
4,044—Phil Simms, 1984
Most passing yards, game
513—Phil Simms at Cin., Oct. 13, 1985
Most touchdown passes, season
36—Y.A. Tittle, 1963
Most pass receptions, career
395—Joe Morrison
Most pass receptions, season
78—Earnest Gray, 1983
Most pass receptions, game
12—Mark Bavaro at Cin., Oct. 13, 1985
Most receiving yards, career
5,434—Frank Gifford
Most receiving yards, season
1,209—Homer Jones
Most receiving yards, game
269—Del Shofner vs. Was., Oct. 28, 1962

Most receiving touchdowns, season
13—Homer Jones, 1967
Most touchdowns, career
50—Rodney Hampton
Most field goals, season
35—Ali Haji-Sheikh, 1983
Longest field goal
56 yards—Ali Haji-Sheikh at Det.,
   Nov. 7, 1983
Most interceptions, career
74—Emlen Tunnell
Most interceptions, season
11—Otto Schellbacher, 1951
   Jimmy Patton, 1958
Most sacks, career
132.5—Lawrence Taylor
Most sacks, season
20.5—Lawrence Taylor, 1986

SERIES RECORDS

N.Y. Giants vs.: Arizona 74-37-2; Atlanta 6-7; Baltimore, 0-1; Buffalo 2-5; Carolina 0-1; Chicago 16-25-2; Cincinnati 2-4; Dallas 25-46-2; Denver 4-3; Detroit 14-14-1; Green Bay 20-23-2; Indianapolis 5-5; Jacksonville 0-1; Kansas City 7-3; Miami 3-1; Minnesota 5-7; New England 3-2; New Orleans 11-8; N.Y. Jets 4-4; Oakland 2-6; Philadelphia 67-59-2; Pittsburgh 44-28-3; St. Louis 7-20; San Diego 5-3; San Francisco 11-12; Seattle 5-3; Tampa Bay 8-5; Tennessee 5-1; Washington 68-51-3.

COACHING RECORDS

Joe Alexander, 8-4-1; LeRoy Andrews, 24-5-1; Bill Arnsparger, 7-28-0; Jim Fassel, 18-13-1 (0-1); Bob Folwell, 8-4-0; Benny Friedman, 2-0-0; Ray Handley, 14-18-0; Jim Lee Howell, 53-27-4 (2-2); John McVay, 14-23-0; Steve Owen, 153-100-17 (2-8); Bill Parcells, 77-49-1 (8-3); Ray Perkins, 23-34-0 (1-1); Earl Potteiger, 15-8-3; Dan Reeves, 31-33-0 (1-1); Allie Sherman, 57-51-4 (0-3); Alex Webster, 29-40-1.
NOTE: Playoff games in parentheses.

RETIRED UNIFORM NUMBERS

No.	Player
1	Ray Flaherty
7	Mel Hein
11	Phil Simms
14	Y.A. Tittle
32	Al Blozis
40	Joe Morrison
42	Charlie Conerly
50	Ken Strong
56	Lawrence Taylor

NEW YORK JETS
YEAR-BY-YEAR RECORDS

Year	W	L	T	Pct.	PF	PA	Finish	W	L	Highest round	Coach
					REGULAR SEASON				PLAYOFFS		
1960*†	7	7	0	.500	382	399	2nd/Eastern Div.	—	—		Sammy Baugh
1961*†	7	7	0	.500	301	390	3rd/Eastern Div.	—	—		Sammy Baugh
1962*†	5	9	0	.357	278	423	4th/Eastern Div.	—	—		Bulldog Turner
1963*	5	8	1	.385	249	399	4th/Eastern Div.	—	—		Weeb Ewbank
1964*	5	8	1	.385	278	315	3rd/Eastern Div.	—	—		Weeb Ewbank
1965*	5	8	1	.385	285	303	2nd/Eastern Div.	—	—		Weeb Ewbank
1966*	6	6	2	.500	322	312	3rd/Eastern Div.	—	—		Weeb Ewbank
1967*	8	5	1	.615	371	329	2nd/Eastern Div.	—	—		Weeb Ewbank
1968*	11	3	0	.786	419	280	1st/Eastern Div.	2	0	Super Bowl champ	Weeb Ewbank
1969*	10	4	0	.714	353	269	1st/Eastern Div.	0	1	Div. playoff game	Weeb Ewbank
1970	4	10	0	.286	255	286	3rd/AFC Eastern Div.	—	—		Weeb Ewbank
1971	6	8	0	.429	212	299	T3rd/AFC Eastern Div.	—	—		Weeb Ewbank
1972	7	7	0	.500	367	324	2nd/AFC Eastern Div.	—	—		Weeb Ewbank
1973	4	10	0	.286	240	306	T4th/AFC Eastern Div.	—	—		Weeb Ewbank
1974	7	7	0	.500	279	300	T3rd/AFC Eastern Div.	—	—		Charley Winner
1975	3	11	0	.214	258	433	T4th/AFC Eastern Div.	—	—		C. Winner, Ken Shipp
1976	3	11	0	.214	169	383	4th/AFC Eastern Div.	—	—		Lou Holtz, Mike Holovak

Year	REGULAR SEASON W	L	T	Pct.	PF	PA	Finish	PLAYOFFS W	L	Highest round	Coach
1977	3	11	0	.214	191	300	T4th/AFC Eastern Div.	—	—		Walt Michaels
1978	8	8	0	.500	359	364	3rd/AFC Eastern Div.	—	—		Walt Michaels
1979	8	8	0	.500	337	383	3rd/AFC Eastern Div.	—	—		Walt Michaels
1980	4	12	0	.250	302	395	5th/AFC Eastern Div.	—	—		Walt Michaels
1981	10	5	1	.656	355	287	2nd/AFC Eastern Div.	0	1	AFC wild-card game	Walt Michaels
1982	6	3	0	.667	245	166	T4th/AFC	2	1	AFC championship game	Walt Michaels
1983	7	9	0	.438	313	331	T4th/AFC Eastern Div.	—	—		Joe Walton
1984	7	9	0	.438	332	364	3rd/AFC Eastern Div.	—	—		Joe Walton
1985	11	5	0	.688	393	264	T2nd/AFC Eastern Div.	0	1	AFC wild-card game	Joe Walton
1986	10	6	0	.625	364	386	2nd/AFC Eastern Div.	1	1	AFC div. playoff game	Joe Walton
1987	6	9	0	.400	334	360	5th/AFC Eastern Div.	—	—		Joe Walton
1988	8	7	1	.531	372	354	4th/AFC Eastern Div.	—	—		Joe Walton
1989	4	12	0	.250	253	411	5th/AFC Eastern Div.	—	—		Bruce Coslet
1990	6	10	0	.375	295	345	4th/AFC Eastern Div.	—	—		Bruce Coslet
1991	8	8	0	.500	314	293	2nd/AFC Eastern Div.	0	1	AFC wild-card game	Bruce Coslet
1992	4	12	0	.250	220	315	4th/AFC Eastern Div.	—	—		Bruce Coslet
1993	8	8	0	.500	270	247	3rd/AFC Eastern Div.	—	—		Pete Carroll
1994	6	10	0	.375	264	320	5th/AFC Eastern Div.	—	—		Rich Kotite
1995	3	13	0	.188	233	384	5th/AFC Eastern Div.	—	—		Rich Kotite
1996	1	15	0	.063	279	454	5th/AFC Eastern Div.	—	—		Bill Parcells
1997	9	7	0	.563	348	287	T2nd/AFC Eastern Div.	—	—		Bill Parcells
1998	12	4	0	.750	416	266	1st/AFC Eastern Div.	1	1	AFC championship game	Bill Parcells

*American Football League.
†New York Titans.

FIRST-ROUND DRAFT PICKS

1960—George Izo, QB, Notre Dame
1961—Tom Brown, G, Minnesota
1962—Sandy Stephens, QB, Minnesota
1963—Jerry Stovall, RB, Louisiana State
1964—Matt Snell, RB, Ohio State
1965—Joe Namath, QB, Alabama
    Tom Nowatzke, RB, Indiana
1966—Bill Yearby, DT, Michigan
1967—Paul Seiler, G, Notre Dame
1968—Lee White, RB, Weber State
1969—Dave Foley, T, Ohio State
1970—Steve Tannen, DB, Florida
1971—John Riggins, RB, Kansas
1972—Jerome Barkum, WR, Jackson State
1972—Mike Taylor, LB, Michigan
1973—Burgess Owens, DB, Miami
1974—Carl Barzilauskas, DT, Indiana
1975—None
1976—Richard Todd, QB, Alabama
1977—Marvin Powell, T, Southern California
1978—Chris Ward, T, Ohio State
1979—Marty Lyons, DT, Alabama
1980—Lam Jones, WR, Texas

1981—Freeman McNeil, RB, UCLA
1982—Bob Crable, LB, Notre Dame
1983—Ken O'Brien, QB, California-Davis
1984—Russell Carter, DB, Southern Methodist
    Ron Faurot, DE, Arkansas
1985—Al Toon, WR, Wisconsin
1986—Mike Haight, T, Iowa
1987—Roger Vick, FB, Texas A&M
1988—Dave Cadigan, T, Southern California
1989—Jeff Lageman, LB, Virginia
1990—Blair Thomas, RB, Penn State
1991—None
1992—Johnny Mitchell, TE, Nebraska
1993—Marvin Jones, LB, Florida State
1994—Aaron Glenn, DB, Texas A&M
1995—Kyle Brady, TE, Penn State
    Hugh Douglas, DE, Central State (O.)
1996—Keyshawn Johnson, WR, Southern California*
1997—James Farrior, LB, Virginia
1998—None
1999—None
    *First player chosen in draft.

FRANCHISE RECORDS

Most rushing yards, career
8,074—Freeman McNeil
Most rushing yards, season
1,331—Freeman McNeil, 1985
Most rushing yards, game
199—Adrian Murrell at Ariz., Oct. 27, 1996
Most rushing touchdowns, season
11—Emerson Boozer, 1972
    Johnny Hector, 1987
    Brad Baxter, 1991
Most passing attempts, season
518—Richard Todd, 1983
Most passing attempts, game
62—Joe Namath vs. Bal., Oct. 18, 1970

Most passes completed, season
308—Richard Todd, 1983
Most passes completed, game
42—Richard Todd vs. S.F., Sept. 21, 1980
Most passing yards, career
27,057—Joe Namath
Most passing yards, season
4,007—Joe Namath, 1967
Most passing yards, game
496—Joe Namath at Bal., Sept. 24, 1972
Most touchdown passes, season
29—Vinny Testaverde, 1998
Most pass receptions, career
627—Don Maynard

Most pass receptions, season
93—Al Toon, 1988
Most pass receptions, game
17—Clark Gaines vs. S.F., Sept. 21, 1980
Most receiving yards, career
11,732—Don Maynard
Most receiving yards, season
1,434—Don Maynard, 1967
Most receiving yards, game
228—Don Maynard at Oak., Nov. 17, 1968
Most receiving touchdowns, season
14—Art Powell, 1960
    Don Maynard, 1965

HISTORY *Team by team*

Most touchdowns, career
88—Don Maynard
Most field goals, season
34—Jim Turner, 1968
Longest field goal
55 yards—Pat Leahy vs. Chi., Dec. 14, 1985

John Hall at Sea., Aug. 31, 1997
Most interceptions, career
34—Bill Baird
Most interceptions, season
12—Dainard Paulson, 1964

Most sacks, career
107.5—Mark Gastineau
Most sacks, season
22—Mark Gastineau, 1984

SERIES RECORDS

N.Y. Jets vs.: Arizona 2-2; Atlanta 4-4; Baltimore, 1-1; Buffalo 33-44; Carolina 1-1; Chicago 2-4; Cincinnati 10-6; Dallas 1-5; Denver 12-13-1; Detroit 3-5; Green Bay 5-2; Indianapolis 23-34; Jacksonville 1-1; Kansas City 13-14-1; Miami 30-33-1; Minnesota 5-1; New England 42-34-1; New Orleans 4-4; N.Y. Giants 4-4; Oakland 10-16-2; Philadelphia 0-6; Pittsburgh 1-12; St. Louis 2-7; San Diego 9-17-1; San Francisco 1-7; Seattle 6-8; Tampa Bay 6-1; Tennessee 13-20-1; Washington 1-5.
NOTE: Includes records as New York Titans from 1960 through 1962.

COACHING RECORDS

Sammy Baugh, 14-14-0; Pete Carroll, 6-10-0; Bruce Coslet, 26-38-0 (0-1); Weeb Ewbank, 71-77-6 (2-1); Mike Holovak, 0-1-0; Lou Holtz, 3-10-0; Rich Kotite, 4-28-0; Walt Michaels, 39-47-1 (2-2); Bill Parcells, 21-11-0 (1-1); Ken Shipp, 1-4-0; Clyde Turner, 5-9-0; Joe Walton, 53-57-1 (1-2); Charley Winner, 9-14-0.
NOTE: Playoff games in parentheses.

RETIRED UNIFORM NUMBERS

No.	Player
12	Joe Namath
13	Don Maynard

OAKLAND RAIDERS
YEAR-BY-YEAR RECORDS

Year	W	L	T	Pct.	PF	PA	Finish	W	L	Highest round	Coach
1960*	6	8	0	.429	319	388	3rd/Western Div.	—	—		Eddie Erdelatz
1961*	2	12	0	.143	237	458	4th/Western Div.	—	—		E. Erdelatz, Marty Feldman
1962*	1	13	0	.071	213	370	4th/Western Div.	—	—		M. Feldman, Red Conkright
1963*	10	4	0	.714	363	288	2nd/Western Div.	—	—		Al Davis
1964*	5	7	2	.417	303	350	3rd/Western Div.	—	—		Al Davis
1965*	8	5	1	.615	298	239	2nd/Western Div.	—	—		Al Davis
1966*	8	5	1	.615	315	288	2nd/Western Div.	—	—		John Rauch
1967*	13	1	0	.929	468	233	1st/Western Div.	1	1	Super Bowl	John Rauch
1968*	12	2	0	.857	453	233	1st/Western Div.	1	1	AFL championship game	John Rauch
1969*	12	1	1	.923	377	242	1st/Western Div.	1	1	AFL championship game	John Madden
1970	8	4	2	.667	300	293	1st/AFC Western Div.	1	1	AFC championship game	John Madden
1971	8	4	2	.667	344	278	2nd/AFC Western Div.	—	—		John Madden
1972	10	3	1	.750	365	248	1st/AFC Western Div.	0	1	AFC div. playoff game	John Madden
1973	9	4	1	.679	292	175	1st/AFC Western Div.	1	1	AFC championship game	John Madden
1974	12	2	0	.857	355	228	1st/AFC Western Div.	1	1	AFC championship game	John Madden
1975	11	3	0	.786	375	255	1st/AFC Western Div.	1	1	AFC championship game	John Madden
1976	13	1	0	.929	350	237	1st/AFC Western Div.	3	0	Super Bowl champ	John Madden
1977	11	3	0	.786	351	230	2nd/AFC Western Div.	1	1	AFC championship game	John Madden
1978	9	7	0	.563	311	283	T2nd/AFC Western Div.	—	—		John Madden
1979	9	7	0	.563	365	337	T3rd/AFC Western Div.	—	—		Tom Flores
1980	11	5	0	.688	364	306	2nd/AFC Western Div.	4	0	Super Bowl champ	Tom Flores
1981	7	9	0	.438	273	343	4th/AFC Western Div.	—	—		Tom Flores
1982†	8	1	0	.889	260	200	1st/AFC	1	1	AFC second-round pl. game	Tom Flores
1983†	12	4	0	.750	442	338	1st/AFC Western Div.	3	0	Super Bowl champ	Tom Flores
1984†	11	5	0	.688	368	278	3rd/AFC Western Div.	0	1	AFC wild-card game	Tom Flores
1985†	12	4	0	.750	354	308	1st/AFC Western Div.	0	1	AFC div. playoff game	Tom Flores
1986†	8	8	0	.500	323	346	4th/AFC Western Div.	—	—		Tom Flores
1987†	5	10	0	.333	301	289	4th/AFC Western Div.	—	—		Tom Flores
1988†	7	9	0	.438	325	369	3rd/AFC Western Div.	—	—		Mike Shanahan
1989†	8	8	0	.500	315	297	3rd/AFC Western Div.	—	—		Mike Shanahan, Art Shell
1990†	12	4	0	.750	337	268	1st/AFC Western Div.	1	1	AFC championship game	Art Shell
1991†	9	7	0	.563	298	297	3rd/AFC Western Div.	0	1	AFC wild-card game	Art Shell
1992†	7	9	0	.438	249	281	4th/AFC Western Div.	—	—		Art Shell
1993†	10	6	0	.625	306	326	2nd/AFC Western Div.	1	1	AFC div. playoff game	Art Shell
1994†	9	7	0	.563	303	327	3rd/AFC Western Div.	—	—		Art Shell
1995	8	8	0	.500	348	332	T3rd/AFC Western Div.	—	—		Mike White
1996	7	9	0	.438	340	293	T4th/AFC Western Div.	—	—		Mike White
1997	4	12	0	.250	324	419	T4th/AFC Western Div.	—	—		Joe Bugel
1998	8	8	0	.500	288	356	2nd/AFC Western Div.	—	—		Jon Gruden

*American Football League.
†Los Angeles Raiders.

FIRST-ROUND DRAFT PICKS

1960—Dale Hackbart, DB, Wisconsin
1961—Joe Rutgens, DT, Illinois
1962—Roman Gabriel, QB, North Carolina State* (AFL)
1963—None
1964—Tony Lorick, RB, Arizona State
1965—Harry Schuh, T, Memphis State
1966—Rodger Bird, DB, Kentucky
1967—Gene Upshaw, G, Texas A&I
1968—Eldridge Dickey, QB, Tenn. State
1969—Art Thoms, DT, Syracuse
1970—Raymond Chester, TE, Morgan State
1971—Jack Tatum, DB, Ohio State
1972—Mike Siani, WR, Villanova
1973—Ray Guy, P, So. Mississippi
1974—Henry Lawrence, T, Florida A&M
1975—Neal Colzie, DB, Ohio State
1976—None
1977—None
1978—None
1979—None
1980—Marc Wilson, QB, Brigham Young
1981—Ted Watts, DB, Texas Tech
    Curt Marsh, G, Washington

1982—Marcus Allen, RB, Southern California
1983—Don Mosebar, T, Southern California
1984—None
1985—Jessie Hester, WR, Florida State
1986—Bob Buczkowski, DT, Pittsburgh
1987—John Clay, T, Missouri
1988—Tim Brown, WR, Notre Dame
    Terry McDaniel, CB, Tennessee
    Scott Davis, DE, Illinois
1989—None
1990—Anthony Smith, DE, Arizona
1991—Todd Marinovich, QB, Southern California
1992—Chester McGlockton, DT, Clemson
1993—Patrick Bates, DB, Texas A&M
1994—Rob Fredrickson, LB, Michigan State
1995—Napoleon Kaufman, RB, Washington
1996—Rickey Dudley, TE, Ohio State
1997—Darrell Russell, DT, Southern California
1998—Charles Woodson, DB, Michigan
    Mo Collins, T, Florida
1999—Matt Stinchcomb, T, Georgia
    *First player chosen in draft.

FRANCHISE RECORDS

Most rushing yards, career
8,545—Marcus Allen
Most rushing yards, season
1,759—Marcus Allen, 1985
Most rushing yards, game
221—Bo Jackson at Sea., Nov. 30, 1987
Most rushing touchdowns, season
16—Pete Banaszak, 1975
Most passing attempts, season
521—Jeff George, 1997
Most passing attempts, game
59—Todd Marinovich vs. Cle., Sept. 20, 1992
Most passes completed, season
304—Ken Stabler, 1979
Most passes completed, game
34—Jim Plunkett at K.C., Sept. 12, 1985
Most passing yards, career
19,078—Ken Stabler

Most passing yards, season
3,917—Jeff George, 1997
Most passing yards, game
424—Jeff Hostetler vs. S.D., Oct. 18, 1993
Most touchdown passes, season
34—Daryle Lamonica, 1969
Most pass receptions, career
680—Tim Brown
Most pass receptions, season
104—Tim Brown, 1997
Most pass receptions, game
14—Tim Brown vs. Jac., Dec. 21, 1997
Most receiving yards, career
9,600—Tim Brown
Most receiving yards, season
1,408—Tim Brown, 1997
Most receiving yards, game
247—Art Powell vs. Hou., Dec. 22, 1963

Most receiving touchdowns, season
16—Art Powell, 1964
Most touchdowns, career
95—Marcus Allen
Most field goals, season
35—Jeff Jaeger, 1993
Longest field goal
54 yards—George Fleming vs. Den., Oct. 2, 1961
Most interceptions, career
39—Willie Brown
    Lester Hayes
Most interceptions, season
13—Lester Hayes, 1980
Most sacks, career
107.5—Greg Townsend
Most sacks, season
17.5—Tony Cline, 1970

SERIES RECORDS

Oakland vs.: Arizona 3-1; Atlanta 6-3; Baltimore 0-2; Buffalo 15-15; Carolina 0-1; Chicago 5-4; Cincinnati 16-7; Dallas 4-3; Denver 49-26-2; Detroit 6-2; Green Bay 5-2; Indianapolis 5-2; Jacksonville 1-1; Kansas City 36-39-2; Miami 15-7-1; Minnesota 6-3; New England 13-12-1; New Orleans 4-3-1; N.Y. Giants 6-2; N.Y. Jets 16-10-2; Philadelphia 3-4; Pittsburgh 7-5; St. Louis 7-2; San Diego 47-29-2; San Francisco 5-3; Seattle 23-19; Tampa Bay 3-1; Tennessee 20-14; Washington 6-3.
NOTE: Includes records as Los Angeles Raiders from 1982 through 1994.

COACHING RECORDS

Joe Bugel, 4-12-0; Red Conkright, 1-8-0; Al Davis, 23-16-3; Eddie Erdelatz, 6-10-0; Marty Feldman, 2-15-0; Tom Flores, 83-53-0 (8-3); Jon Gruden, 8-8-0; John Madden, 103-32-7 (9-7); John Rauch, 33-8-1 (2-2); Mike Shanahan, 8-12-0; Art Shell, 54-38-0 (2-3); Mike White, 15-17-0.
NOTE: Playoff games in parentheses.

RETIRED UNIFORM NUMBERS

No.	Player
	None

HISTORY *Team by team*

	REGULAR SEASON							PLAYOFFS			
Year	W	L	T	Pct.	PF	PA	Finish	W	L	Highest round	Coach
1933	3	5	1	.375	77	158	4th/Eastern Div.	—	—		Lud Wray
1934	4	7	0	.364	127	85	T3rd/Eastern Div.	—	—		Lud Wray
1935	2	9	0	.182	60	179	5th/Eastern Div.	—	—		Lud Wray
1936	1	11	0	.083	51	206	5th/Eastern Div.	—	—		Bert Bell
1937	2	8	1	.200	86	177	5th/Eastern Div.	—	—		Bert Bell
1938	5	6	0	.455	154	164	4th/Eastern Div.	—	—		Bert Bell
1939	1	9	1	.100	105	200	T4th/Eastern Div.	—	—		Bert Bell
1940	1	10	0	.091	111	211	5th/Eastern Div.	—	—		Bert Bell
1941	2	8	1	.200	119	218	4th/Eastern Div.	—	—		Greasy Neale
1942	2	9	0	.182	134	239	5th/Eastern Div.	—	—		Greasy Neale
1943*	5	4	1	.556	225	230	3rd/Eastern Div.	—	—		G. Neale-Walt Kiesling
1944	7	1	2	.875	267	131	2nd/Eastern Div.	—	—		Greasy Neale
1945	7	3	0	.700	272	133	2nd/Eastern Div.	—	—		Greasy Neale
1946	6	5	0	.545	231	220	2nd/Eastern Div.	—	—		Greasy Neale
1947	8	4	0	.667	308	242	1st/Eastern Div.	1	1	NFL championship game	Greasy Neale
1948	9	2	1	.818	376	156	1st/Eastern Div.	1	0	NFL champ	Greasy Neale
1949	11	1	0	.917	364	134	1st/Eastern Div.	1	0	NFL champ	Greasy Neale
1950	6	6	0	.500	254	141	T3rd/American Conf.	—	—		Greasy Neale
1951	4	8	0	.333	234	264	5th/American Conf.	—	—		Bo McMillin, Wayne Millner
1952	7	5	0	.583	252	271	T2nd/American Conf.	—	—		Jim Trimble
1953	7	4	1	.636	352	215	2nd/Eastern Conf.	—	—		Jim Trimble
1954	7	4	1	.636	284	230	2nd/Eastern Conf.	—	—		Jim Trimble
1955	4	7	1	.364	248	231	T4th/Eastern Conf.	—	—		Jim Trimble
1956	3	8	1	.273	143	215	6th/Eastern Conf.	—	—		Hugh Devore
1957	4	8	0	.333	173	230	5th/Eastern Conf.	—	—		Hugh Devore
1958	2	9	1	.182	235	306	T5th/Eastern Conf.	—	—		Buck Shaw
1959	7	5	0	.583	268	278	T2nd/Eastern Conf.	—	—		Buck Shaw
1960	10	2	0	.833	321	246	1st/Eastern Conf.	1	0	NFL champ	Buck Shaw
1961	10	4	0	.714	361	297	2nd/Eastern Conf.	—	—		Nick Skorich
1962	3	10	1	.231	282	356	7th/Eastern Conf.	—	—		Nick Skorich
1963	2	10	2	.167	242	381	7th/Western Conf.	—	—		Nick Skorich
1964	6	8	0	.429	312	313	T3rd/Eastern Conf.	—	—		Joe Kuharich
1965	5	9	0	.357	363	359	T5th/Eastern Conf.	—	—		Joe Kuharich
1966	9	5	0	.643	326	340	T2nd/Eastern Conf.	—	—		Joe Kuharich
1967	6	7	1	.462	351	409	2nd/Capitol Div.	—	—		Joe Kuharich
1968	2	12	0	.143	202	351	4th/Capitol Div.	—	—		Joe Kuharich
1969	4	9	1	.308	279	377	4th/Capitol Div.	—	—		Jerry Williams
1970	3	10	1	.231	241	332	5th/NFC Eastern Div.	—	—		Jerry Williams
1971	6	7	1	.462	221	302	3rd/NFC Eastern Div.	—	—		J. Williams, Ed Khayat
1972	2	11	1	.179	145	352	5th/NFC Eastern Div.	—	—		Ed Khayat
1973	5	8	1	.393	310	393	3rd/NFC Eastern Div.	—	—		Mike McCormack
1974	7	7	0	.500	242	217	4th/NFC Eastern Div.	—	—		Mike McCormack
1975	4	10	0	.286	225	302	5th/NFC Eastern Div.	—	—		Mike McCormack
1976	4	10	0	.286	165	286	4th/NFC Eastern Div.	—	—		Dick Vermeil
1977	5	9	0	.357	220	207	T4th/NFC Eastern Div.	—	—		Dick Vermeil
1978	9	7	0	.563	270	250	2nd/NFC Eastern Div.	0	1	NFC wild-card game	Dick Vermeil
1979	11	5	0	.688	339	282	2nd/NFC Eastern Div.	1	1	NFC div. playoff game	Dick Vermeil
1980	12	4	0	.750	384	222	1st/NFC Eastern Div.	2	1	Super Bowl	Dick Vermeil
1981	10	6	0	.625	368	221	2nd/NFC Eastern Div.	0	1	NFC wild-card game	Dick Vermeil
1982	3	6	0	.333	191	195	T11th/NFC	—	—		Dick Vermeil
1983	5	11	0	.313	233	322	4th/NFC Eastern Div.	—	—		Marion Campbell
1984	6	9	1	.406	278	320	5th/NFC Eastern Div.	—	—		Marion Campbell
1985	7	9	0	.438	286	310	4th/NFC Eastern Div.	—	—		M. Campbell, Fred Bruney
1986	5	10	1	.344	256	312	4th/NFC Eastern Div.	—	—		Buddy Ryan
1987	7	8	0	.467	337	380	T2nd/NFC Eastern Div.	—	—		Buddy Ryan
1988	10	6	0	.625	379	319	1st/NFC Eastern Div.	0	1	NFC div. playoff game	Buddy Ryan
1989	11	5	0	.688	342	274	2nd/NFC Eastern Div.	0	1	NFC wild-card game	Buddy Ryan
1990	10	6	0	.625	396	299	T2nd/NFC Eastern Div.	0	1	NFC wild-card game	Buddy Ryan
1991	10	6	0	.625	285	244	3rd/NFC Eastern Div.	—	—		Rich Kotite
1992	11	5	0	.688	354	245	2nd/NFC Eastern Div.	1	1	NFC div. playoff game	Rich Kotite
1993	8	8	0	.500	293	315	3rd/NFC Eastern Div.	—	—		Rich Kotite
1994	7	9	0	.438	308	308	4th/NFC Eastern Div.	—	—		Rich Kotite
1995	10	6	0	.625	318	338	2nd/NFC Eastern Div.	1	1	NFC div. playoff game	Ray Rhodes
1996	10	6	0	.625	363	341	2nd/NFC Eastern Div.	0	1	NFC wild-card game	Ray Rhodes
1997	6	9	1	.406	317	372	3rd/NFC Eastern Div.	—	—		Ray Rhodes
1998	3	13	0	.188	161	344	5th/NFC Eastern Div.	—	—		Ray Rhodes

*Phil-Pitt "Steagles," a combined squad of Philadelphia Eagles and Pittsburgh Steelers.

FIRST-ROUND DRAFT PICKS

1936—Jay Berwanger, B, Chicago*
1937—Sam Francis, B, Nebraska*
1938—John McDonald, B, Nebraska
1939—Davey O'Brien, QB, Texas Christian
1940—Wes McAfee, B, Duke
1941—None
1942—Pete Kmetovic, B, Stanford
1943—Joe Muha, B, Virginia Military
1944—Steve Van Buren, B, Louisiana State
1945—John Yonaker, E, Notre Dame
1946—Leo Riggs, B, Southern California
1947—Neil Armstrong, E, Oklahoma A&M
1948—Clyde Scott, B, Arkansas
1949—Chuck Bednarik, C, Pennsylvania*
    Frank Tripucka, QB, Notre Dame
1950—Bud Grant, E, Minnesota
1951—Ebert Van Buren, B, Louisiana State
    Chet Mutryn, B, Xavier
1952—John Bright, B, Drake
1953—None
1954—Neil Worden, B, Notre Dame
1955—Dick Bielski, B, Maryland
1956—Bob Pellegrini, C, Maryland
1957—Clarence Peaks, B, Michigan State
1958—Walter Kowalczyk, B, Michigan State
1959—None
1960—Ron Burton, B, Northwestern
1961—Art Baker, B, Syracuse
1962—None
1963—Ed Budde, T, Michigan State
1964—Bob Brown, T, Nebraska
1965—None
1966—Randy Beisler, T, Indiana
1967—Harry Jones, RB, Arkansas
1968—Tim Rossovich, DE, Southern California

1969—Leroy Keyes, RB, Purdue
1970—Steve Zabel, E, Oklahoma
1971—Richard Harris, DE, Grambling State
1972—John Reaves, QB, Florida
1973—Jerry Sisemore, T, Texas
    Charle Young, TE, Southern California
1974—None
1975—None
1976—None
1977—None
1978—None
1979—Jerry Robinson, LB, UCLA
1980—Roynell Young, DB, Alcorn State
1981—Leonard Mitchell, DE, Houston
1982—Mike Quick, WR, North Carolina State
1983—Michael Haddix, RB, Mississippi State
1984—Kenny Jackson, WR, Penn State
1985—Kevin Allen, T, Indiana
1986—Keith Byars, RB, Ohio State
1987—Jerome Brown, DT, Miami (Fla.)
1988—Keith Jackson, TE, Oklahoma
1989—None
1990—Ben Smith, DB, Georgia
1991—Antone Davis, T, Tennessee
1992—None
1993—Lester Holmes, T, Jackson State
    Leonard Renfro, DT, Colorado
1994—Bernard Williams, T, Georgia
1995—Mike Mamula, DE, Boston College
1996—Jermane Mayberry, T, Texas A&M-Kingsville
1997—Jon Harris, DE, Virginia
1998—Tra Thomas, T, Florida State
1999—Donovan McNabb, QB, Syracuse
    *First player chosen in draft.

FRANCHISE RECORDS

Most rushing yards, career
6,538—Wilbert Montgomery
Most rushing yards, season
1,512—Wilbert Montgomery, 1979
Most rushing yards, game
205—Steve Van Buren vs. Pit., Nov. 27, 1949
Most rushing touchdowns, season
15—Steve Van Buren, 1945
Most passing attempts, season
560—Randall Cunningham, 1988
Most passing attempts, game
62—Randall Cunningham at Chi., Oct. 2, 1989
Most passes completed, season
301—Randall Cunningham, 1988
Most passes completed, game
34—Randall Cunningham at Was., Sept. 17, 1989
Most passing yards, career
26,963—Ron Jaworski

Most passing yards, season
3,808—Randall Cunningham, 1988
Most passing yards, game
447—Randall Cunningham at Was., Sept. 17, 1989
Most touchdown passes, season
32—Sonny Jurgensen, 1961
Most pass receptions, career
589—Harold Carmichael
Most pass receptions, season
88—Irving Fryar, 1996
Most pass receptions, game
14—Don Looney at Was., Dec. 1, 1940
Most receiving yards, career
8,978—Harold Carmichael
Most receiving yards, season
1,409—Mike Quick, 1983
Most receiving yards, game
237—Tommy McDonald vs. NYG, Dec. 10, 1961

Most receiving touchdowns, season
13—Tommy McDonald, 1960
    Tommy McDonald, 1961
    Mike Quick, 1983
Most touchdowns, career
79—Harold Carmichael
Most field goals, season
30—Paul McFadden, 1984
Longest field goal
59 yards—Tony Franklin at Dal., Nov. 12, 1979
Most interceptions, career
34—Bill Bradley
Most interceptions, season
11—Bill Bradley, 1971
Most sacks, career
124—Reggie White
Most sacks, season
21—Reggie White, 1987

SERIES RECORDS

Philadelphia vs.: Arizona 49-49-5; Atlanta 9-9-1; Baltimore, 0-0-1; Buffalo 4-4; Carolina 1-0; Chicago 4-25-1; Cincinnati 2-6; Dallas 29-47; Denver 6-3; Detroit 11-11-2; Green Bay 9-21; Indianapolis 6-7; Jacksonville 0-1; Kansas City 1-2; Miami 3-6; Minnesota 6-11; New England 5-2; New Orleans 12-8; N.Y. Giants 59-67-2; N.Y. Jets 6-0; Oakland 4-3; Pittsburgh 44-26-3; St. Louis 13-14-1; San Diego 2-5; San Francisco 6-14-1; Seattle 4-3; Tampa Bay 3-2; Tennessee 6-0; Washington 55-65-6.
NOTE: Includes records when team combined with Pittsburgh squad and was known as Phil-Pitt in 1943.

COACHING RECORDS

Bert Bell, 10-44-2; Fred Bruney, 1-0-0; Marion Campbell, 17-29-1; Hugh Devore, 7-16-1; Ed Khayat, 8-15-2; Rich Kotite, 36-28-0 (1-1); Joe Kuharich, 28-41-1; Mike McCormack, 16-25-1; Alvin McMillin, 2-0-0; Wayne Millner, 2-8-0; Earle (Greasy) Neale, 63-43-5 (3-1); Ray Rhodes, 29-34-1 (1-2); Buddy Ryan, 43-35-1 (0-3); Buck Shaw, 19-16-1 (1-0); Nick Skorich, 15-24-3; Jim Trimble, 25-20-3; Dick Vermeil, 54-47-0 (3-4); Jerry Williams, 7-22-2; Lud Wray, 9-21-1.

RETIRED UNIFORM NUMBERS

No.	Player
15	Steve Van Buren
40	Tom Brookshier
44	Pete Retzlaff
60	Chuck Bednarik
70	Al Wistert
99	Jerome Brown

PITTSBURGH STEELERS
YEAR-BY-YEAR RECORDS

Year	W	L	T	Pct.	PF	PA	Finish	W	L	Highest round	Coach
				REGULAR SEASON				PLAYOFFS			
1933*	3	6	2	.333	67	208	5th/Eastern Div.	—	—		Jap Douds
1934*	2	10	0	.167	51	206	5th/Eastern Div.	—	—		Luby DiMello
1935*	4	8	0	.333	100	209	3rd/Eastern Div.	—	—		Joe Bach
1936*	6	6	0	.500	98	187	2nd/Eastern Div.	—	—		Joe Bach
1937*	4	7	0	.364	122	145	3rd/Eastern Div.	—	—		Johnny Blood
1938*	2	9	0	.182	79	169	5th/Eastern Div.	—	—		Johnny Blood
1939*	1	9	1	.100	114	216	T4th/Eastern Div.	—	—		J. Blood-W. Kiesling
1940*	2	7	2	.222	60	178	4th/Eastern Div.	—	—		Walt Kiesling
1941	1	9	1	.100	103	276	5th/Eastern Div.	—	—		Bert Bell-Buff Donelli-Walt Kiesling
1942	7	4	0	.636	167	119	2nd/Eastern Div.	—	—		Walt Kiesling
1943†	5	4	1	.556	225	230	3rd/Eastern Div.	—	—		W. Kiesling-Greasy Neale
1944‡	0	10	0	.000	108	328	5th/Western Div.	—	—		W. Kiesling-Phil Handler
1945	2	8	0	.200	79	220	5th/Eastern Div.	—	—		Jim Leonard
1946	5	5	1	.500	136	117	T3rd/Eastern Div.	—	—		Jock Sutherland
1947	8	4	0	.667	240	259	2nd/Eastern Div.	0	1	E. Div. champ. game	Jock Sutherland
1948	4	8	0	.333	200	243	T3rd/Eastern Div.	—	—		John Michelosen
1949	6	5	1	.545	224	214	2nd/Eastern Div.	—	—		John Michelosen
1950	6	6	0	.500	180	195	T3rd/American Conf.	—	—		John Michelosen
1951	4	7	1	.364	183	235	4th/American Conf.	—	—		John Michelosen
1952	5	7	0	.417	300	273	3rd/American Conf.	—	—		Joe Bach
1953	6	6	0	.500	211	263	4th/Eastern Conf.	—	—		Joe Bach
1954	5	7	0	.417	219	263	4th/Eastern Conf.	—	—		Walt Kiesling
1955	4	8	0	.333	195	285	6th/Eastern Conf.	—	—		Walt Kiesling
1956	5	7	0	.417	217	250	5th/Eastern Conf.	—	—		Walt Kiesling
1957	6	6	0	.500	161	178	3rd/Eastern Conf.	—	—		Buddy Parker
1958	7	4	1	.636	261	230	3rd/Eastern Conf.	—	—		Buddy Parker
1959	6	5	1	.545	257	216	4th/Eastern Conf.	—	—		Buddy Parker
1960	5	6	1	.455	240	275	5th/Eastern Conf.	—	—		Buddy Parker
1961	6	8	0	.429	295	287	5th/Eastern Conf.	—	—		Buddy Parker
1962	9	5	0	.643	312	363	2nd/Eastern Conf.	—	—		Buddy Parker
1963	7	4	3	.636	321	295	4th/Eastern Conf.	—	—		Buddy Parker
1964	5	9	0	.357	253	315	6th/Eastern Conf.	—	—		Buddy Parker
1965	2	12	0	.143	202	397	7th/Eastern Conf.	—	—		Mike Nixon
1966	5	8	1	.385	316	347	6th/Eastern Conf.	—	—		Bill Austin
1967	4	9	1	.308	281	320	4th/Century Div.	—	—		Bill Austin
1968	2	11	1	.154	244	397	4th/Century Div.	—	—		Bill Austin
1969	1	13	0	.071	218	404	4th/Century Div.	—	—		Chuck Noll
1970	5	9	0	.357	210	272	3rd/AFC Central Div.	—	—		Chuck Noll
1971	6	8	0	.429	246	292	2nd/AFC Central Div.	—	—		Chuck Noll
1972	11	3	0	.786	343	175	1st/AFC Central Div.	1	1	AFC championship game	Chuck Noll
1973	10	4	0	.714	347	210	2nd/AFC Central Div.	0	1	AFC div. playoff game	Chuck Noll
1974	10	3	1	.750	305	189	1st/AFC Central Div.	3	0	Super Bowl champ	Chuck Noll
1975	12	2	0	.857	373	162	1st/AFC Central Div.	3	0	Super Bowl champ	Chuck Noll
1976	10	4	0	.714	342	138	1st/AFC Central Div.	1	1	AFC championship game	Chuck Noll
1977	9	5	0	.643	283	243	1st/AFC Central Div.	0	1	AFC div. playoff game	Chuck Noll
1978	14	2	0	.875	356	195	1st/AFC Central Div.	3	0	Super Bowl champ	Chuck Noll
1979	12	4	0	.750	416	262	1st/AFC Central Div.	3	0	Super Bowl champ	Chuck Noll
1980	9	7	0	.563	352	313	3rd/AFC Central Div.	—	—		Chuck Noll
1981	8	8	0	.500	356	297	2nd/AFC Central Div.	—	—		Chuck Noll
1982	6	3	0	.667	204	146	T4th/AFC	0	1	AFC first-round pl. game	Chuck Noll
1983	10	6	0	.625	355	303	1st/AFC Central Div.	0	1	AFC div. playoff game	Chuck Noll
1984	9	7	0	.563	387	310	1st/AFC Central Div.	1	1	AFC championship game	Chuck Noll
1985	7	9	0	.438	379	355	T2nd/AFC Central Div.	—	—		Chuck Noll
1986	6	10	0	.375	307	336	3rd/AFC Central Div.	—	—		Chuck Noll
1987	8	7	0	.533	285	299	3rd/AFC Central Div.	—	—		Chuck Noll

			REGULAR SEASON							PLAYOFFS		
Year	W	L	T	Pct.	PF	PA	Finish	W	L	Highest round	Coach
1988	5	11	0	.313	336	421	4th/AFC Central Div.	—	—		Chuck Noll
1989	9	7	0	.563	265	326	T2nd/AFC Central Div.	1	1	AFC div. playoff game	Chuck Noll
1990	9	7	0	.563	292	240	3rd/AFC Central Div.	—	—		Chuck Noll
1991	7	9	0	.438	292	344	2nd/AFC Central Div.	—	—		Chuck Noll
1992	11	5	0	.688	299	225	1st/AFC Central Div.	0	1	AFC div. playoff game	Bill Cowher
1993	9	7	0	.563	308	281	2nd/AFC Central Div.	0	1	AFC wild-card game	Bill Cowher
1994	12	4	0	.750	316	234	1st/AFC Central Div.	1	1	AFC championship game	Bill Cowher
1995	11	5	0	.689	407	327	1st/AFC Central Div.	2	1	Super Bowl	Bill Cowher
1996	10	6	0	.625	344	257	1st/AFC Central Div.	1	1	AFC div. playoff game	Bill Cowher
1997	11	5	0	.688	372	307	1st/AFC Central Div.	1	1	AFC championship game	Bill Cowher
1998	7	9	0	.438	263	303	3rd/AFC Central Div.	—	—		Bill Cowher

*Pittsburgh Pirates.
†Phil-Pitt "Steagles," a combined squad of Philadelphia Eagles and Pittsburgh Steelers.
‡Card-Pitt, a combined squad of Chicago Cardinals and Pittsburgh Steelers.

FIRST-ROUND DRAFT PICKS

1936—Bill Shakespeare, B, Notre Dame
1937—Mike Basrak, C, Duquesne
1938—Byron White, B, Colorado
      Frank Filchock, B, Indiana
1939—None
1940—Kay Eakin, B, Arkansas
1941—Chet Gladchuk, C, Boston College
1942—Bill Dudley, B, Virginia*
1943—Bill Daley, B, Minnesota
1944—Johnny Podesto, B, St. Mary's (Calif.)
1945—Paul Duhart, B, Florida
1946—Doc Blanchard, B, Army
1947—Hub Bechtol, E, Texas
1948—Dan Edwards, E, Georgia
1949—Bobby Gage, B, Clemson
1950—Lynn Chandnois, B, Michigan State
1951—Clarence Avinger, B, Alabama
1952—Ed Modzelewski, B, Maryland
1953—Ted Marchibroda, QB, St. Bonaventure
1954—John Lattner, B, Notre Dame
1955—Frank Varrichione, T, Notre Dame
1956—Gary Glick, B, Colorado State*
      Art Davis, B, Mississippi State
1957—Len Dawson, QB, Purdue
1958—None
1959—None
1960—Jack Spikes, B, Texas Christian
1961—None
1962—Bob Ferguson, RB, Ohio State
1963—None
1964—Paul Martha, RB, Pittsburgh
1965—None
1966—Dick Leftridge, RB, West Virginia
1967—None

1968—Mike Taylor, T, Southern California
1969—Joe Greene, DT, North Texas State
1970—Terry Bradshaw, QB, Louisiana Tech*
1971—Frank Lewis, WR, Grambling State
1972—Franco Harris, RB, Penn State
1973—James Thomas, DB, Florida State
1974—Lynn Swann, WR, Southern California
1975—Dave Brown, DB, Michigan
1976—Bennie Cunningham, TE, Clemson
1977—Robin Cole, LB, New Mexico
1978—Ron Johnson, DB, Eastern Michigan
1979—Greg Hawthorne, RB, Baylor
1980—Mark Malone, QB, Arizona State
1981—Keith Gary, DE, Oklahoma
1982—Walter Abercrombie, RB, Baylor
1983—Gabriel Rivera, DT, Texas Tech
1984—Louis Lipps, WR, Southern Mississippi
1985—Darryl Sims, DT, Wisconsin
1986—John Rienstra, G, Temple
1987—Rod Woodson, DB, Purdue
1988—Aaron Jones, DE, Eastern Kentucky
1989—Tim Worley, RB, Georgia
      Tom Ricketts, T, Pittsburgh
1990—Eric Green, TE, Liberty (Va.)
1991—Huey Richardson, LB, Florida
1992—Leon Searcy, T, Miami (Fla.)
1993—Deon Figures, DB, Colorado
1994—Charles Johnson, WR, Colorado
1995—Mark Bruener, TE, Washington
1996—Jermain Stephens, T, North Carolina A&T
1997—Chad Scott, DB, Maryland
1998—Alan Faneca, G, Louisiana State
1999—Troy Edwards, WR, Louisiana Tech
    *First player chosen in draft.

FRANCHISE RECORDS

Most rushing yards, career
11,950—Franco Harris
Most rushing yards, season
1,690—Barry Foster, 1992
Most rushing yards, game
218—John Fuqua at Phi., Dec. 20, 1970
Most rushing touchdowns, season
14—Franco Harris, 1976
Most passing attempts, season
486—Neil O'Donnell, 1993
Most passing attempts, game
55—Neil O'Donnell vs. G.B., Dec. 24, 1995
Most passes completed, season
270—Neil O'Donnell, 1993

Most passes completed, game
34—Neil O'Donnell at Chi., Nov. 5, 1995
    (OT)
31—Joe Gilliam at Den., Sept. 22, 1974
    (OT)
30—Terry Bradshaw vs. Cle., Nov. 25,
    1979 (OT)
29—Terry Bradshaw vs. Cin., Sept. 19,
    1982 (OT)
28—Kent Nix vs. Dal., Oct. 22, 1967
Most passing yards, career
27,989—Terry Bradshaw
Most passing yards, season
3,724—Terry Bradshaw, 1979

Most passing yards, game
409—Bobby Layne vs. Chi. Cardinals,
    Dec. 13, 1958
Most touchdown passes, season
28—Terry Bradshaw, 1978
Most pass receptions, career
537—John Stallworth
Most pass receptions, season
85—Yancey Thigpen, 1995
Most pass receptions, game
14—Courtney Hawkins vs. Ten., Nov. 1,
    1998
Most receiving yards, career
8,723—John Stallworth

Most receiving yards, season
1,398—Yancey Thigpen, 1997
Most receiving yards, game
235—Buddy Dial vs. Cle., Oct. 22, 1961
Most receiving touchdowns, season
12—Buddy Dial, 1961
Louis Lipps, 1985
Most touchdowns, career
100—Franco Harris

Most field goals, season
34—Norm Johnson, 1995
Longest field goal
55 yards—Gary Anderson vs. S.D.,
Nov. 25, 1984
Most interceptions, career
57—Mel Blount
Most interceptions, season
11—Mel Blount, 1975

Most sacks, career
73.5—L.C. Greenwood
Most sacks, season
15—Mike Merriweather, 1984

SERIES RECORDS

Pittsburgh vs.: Arizona 30-21-3; Atlanta 10-1; Baltimore 5-1; Buffalo 8-7; Carolina 0-1; Chicago 6-19-1; Cincinnati 32-25; Dallas 11-14; Denver 6-10-1; Detroit 12-14-1; Green Bay 12-21; Indianapolis 13-4; Jacksonville 4-4; Kansas City 15-6; Miami 6-9; Minnesota 4-8; New England 11-4; New Orleans 6-5; N.Y. Giants 28-44-3; N.Y. Jets 13-1; Oakland 5-7; Philadelphia 26-44-3; St. Louis 6-17-2; San Diego 16-5; San Francisco 7-9; Seattle 6-6; Tampa Bay 4-1; Tennessee 35-22; Washington 25-39-4.
NOTE: Includes records as Pittsburgh Pirates from 1933 through 1940; also includes records when team combined with Philadelphia squad and was known as Phil-Pitt in 1943 and when team combined with Chicago Cardinals squad and was known as Card-Pitt in 1944.

COACHING RECORDS

Bill Austin, 11-28-3; Joe Bach, 21-27-0; Bert Bell, 0-2-0; Bill Cowher, 71-41-0 (5-6); Luby DiMelio, 2-10-0; Aldo Donelli, 0-5-0; Forrest Douds, 3-6-2; Walt Kiesling, 30-55-5; Jim Leonard, 2-8-0; Johnny (Blood) McNally, 6-19-0; Johnny Michelosen, 20-26-2; Mike Nixon, 2-12-0; Chuck Noll, 193-148-1 (16-8); Buddy Parker, 51-47-6 (0-1); Jock Sutherland, 13-9-1 (0-1).

RETIRED UNIFORM NUMBERS

No.	Player
	None

ST. LOUIS RAMS
YEAR-BY-YEAR RECORDS

	REGULAR SEASON							PLAYOFFS			
Year	W	L	T	Pct.	PF	PA	Finish	W	L	Highest round	Coach
1937*	1	10	0	.091	75	207	5th/Western Div.	—	—		Hugo Bezdek
1938*	4	7	0	.364	131	215	4th/Western Div.	—	—		Hugo Bezdek, Art Lewis
1939*	5	5	1	.500	195	164	4th/Western Div.	—	—		Dutch Clark
1940*	4	6	1	.400	171	191	4th/Western Div.	—	—		Dutch Clark
1941*	2	9	0	.182	116	244	5th/Western Div.	—	—		Dutch Clark
1942*	5	6	0	.455	150	207	3rd/Western Div.	—	—		Dutch Clark
1943*				Rams did not play in 1943.							
1944*	4	6	0	.400	188	224	4th/Western Div.	—	—		Buff Donelli
1945*	9	1	0	.900	244	136	1st/Western Div.	1	0	NFL champ	Adam Walsh
1946†	6	4	1	.600	277	257	2nd/Western Div.	—	—		Adam Walsh
1947†	6	6	0	.500	259	214	4th/Western Div.	—	—		Bob Snyder
1948†	6	5	1	.545	327	269	3rd/Western Div.	—	—		Clark Shaughnessy
1949†	8	2	2	.800	360	239	1st/Western Div.	0	1	NFL championship game	Clark Shaughnessy
1950†	9	3	0	.750	466	309	1st/National Conf.	1	1	NFL championship game	Joe Stydahar
1951†	8	4	0	.667	392	261	1st/National Conf.	1	0	NFL champ	Joe Stydahar
1952†	9	3	0	.750	349	234	2nd/National Conf.	0	1	Nat. Conf. champ. game	J. Stydahar, Hamp Pool
1953†	8	3	1	.727	366	236	3rd/Western Conf.	—	—		Hamp Pool
1954†	6	5	1	.545	314	285	4th/Western Conf.	—	—		Hamp Pool
1955†	8	3	1	.727	260	231	1st/Western Conf.	0	1	NFL championship game	Sid Gillman
1956†	4	8	0	.333	291	307	6th/Western Conf.	—	—		Sid Gillman
1957†	6	6	0	.500	307	278	4th/Western Conf.	—	—		Sid Gillman
1958†	8	4	0	.667	344	278	T2nd/Western Conf.	—	—		Sid Gillman
1959†	2	10	0	.167	242	315	6th/Western Conf.	—	—		Sid Gillman
1960†	4	7	1	.364	265	297	6th/Western Conf.	—	—		Bob Waterfield
1961†	4	10	0	.286	263	333	6th/Western Conf.	—	—		Bob Waterfield
1962†	1	12	1	.077	220	334	7th/Western Conf.	—	—		B. Waterfield, H. Svare
1963†	5	9	0	.357	210	350	6th/Western Conf.	—	—		Harland Svare
1964†	5	7	2	.417	283	339	5th/Western Conf.	—	—		Harland Svare
1965†	4	10	0	.286	269	328	7th/Western Conf.	—	—		Harland Svare
1966†	8	6	0	.571	289	212	3rd/Western Conf.	—	—		George Allen
1967†	11	1	2	.917	398	196	1st/Coastal Div.	0	1	W. Conf. champ. game	George Allen
1968†	10	3	1	.769	312	200	2nd/Coastal Div.	—	—		George Allen
1969†	11	3	0	.786	320	243	1st/Coastal Div.	0	1	W. Conf. champ. game	George Allen
1970†	9	4	1	.692	325	202	2nd/NFC Western Div.	—	—		George Allen
1971†	8	5	1	.615	313	260	2nd/NFC Western Div.	—	—		Tommy Prothro
1972†	6	7	1	.464	291	286	3rd/NFC Western Div.	—	—		Tommy Prothro
1973†	12	2	0	.857	388	178	1st/NFC Western Div.	0	1	NFC div. playoff game	Chuck Knox
1974†	10	4	0	.714	263	181	1st/NFC Western Div.	1	1	NFC championship game	Chuck Knox

			REGULAR SEASON							PLAYOFFS		
Year	W	L	T	Pct.	PF	PA	Finish	W	L	Highest round	Coach
1975†	12	2	0	.857	312	135	1st/NFC Western Div.	1	1	NFC championship game	Chuck Knox
1976†	10	3	1	.750	351	190	1st/NFC Western Div.	1	1	NFC championship game	Chuck Knox
1977†	10	4	0	.714	302	146	1st/NFC Western Div.	0	1	NFC div. playoff game	Chuck Knox
1978†	12	4	0	.750	316	245	1st/NFC Western Div.	1	1	NFC championship game	Ray Malavasi
1979†	9	7	0	.563	323	309	1st/NFC Western Div.	2	1	Super Bowl	Ray Malavasi
1980†	11	5	0	.688	424	289	2nd/NFC Western Div.	0	1	NFC wild-card game	Ray Malavasi
1981†	6	10	0	.375	303	351	3rd/NFC Western Div.	—	—		Ray Malavasi
1982†	2	7	0	.222	200	250	14th/NFC	—	—		Ray Malavasi
1983†	9	7	0	.563	361	344	2nd/NFC Western Div.	1	1	NFC div. playoff game	John Robinson
1984†	10	6	0	.625	346	316	2nd/NFC Western Div.	0	1	NFC wild-card game	John Robinson
1985†	11	5	0	.688	340	277	1st/NFC Western Div.	1	1	NFC championship game	John Robinson
1986†	10	6	0	.625	309	267	2nd/NFC Western Div.	0	1	NFC wild-card game	John Robinson
1987†	6	9	0	.400	317	361	3rd/NFC Western Div.	—	—		John Robinson
1988†	10	6	0	.625	407	293	2nd/NFC Western Div.	0	1	NFC wild-card game	John Robinson
1989†	11	5	0	.688	426	344	2nd/NFC Western Div.	2	1	NFC championship game	John Robinson
1990†	5	11	0	.313	345	412	T3rd/NFC Western Div.	—	—		John Robinson
1991†	3	13	0	.188	234	390	4th/NFC Western Div.	—	—		John Robinson
1992†	6	10	0	.375	313	383	T3rd/NFC Western Div.	—	—		Chuck Knox
1993†	5	11	0	.313	221	367	4th/NFC Western Div.	—	—		Chuck Knox
1994†	4	12	0	.250	286	365	4th/NFC Western Div.	—	—		Chuck Knox
1995	7	9	0	.438	309	418	T3rd/NFC Western Div.	—	—		Rich Brooks
1996	6	10	0	.375	303	409	3rd/NFC Western Div.	—	—		Rich Brooks
1997	5	11	0	.313	299	359	5th/NFC Western Div.	—	—		Dick Vermeil
1998	4	12	0	.250	285	378	5th/NFC Western Div.	—	—		Dick Vermeil

*Cleveland Rams.
†Los Angeles Rams.

FIRST-ROUND DRAFT PICKS

1937—Johnny Drake, B, Purdue
1938—Corbett Davis, B, Indiana*
1939—Parker Hall, B, Mississippi
1940—Ollie Cordill, B, Rice
1941—Rudy Mucha, C, Washington
1942—Jack Wilson, B, Baylor
1943—Mike Holovak, B, Boston College
1944—Tony Butkovich, B, Illinois
1945—Elroy Hirsch, B, Wisconsin
1946—Emil Sitko, B, Notre Dame
1947—Herman Wedemeyer, B, St. Mary's (Cal.)
1948—None
1949—Bobby Thomason, B, Virginia Military
1950—Ralph Pasquariello, B, Villanova
        Stan West, G, Oklahoma
1951—Bud McFadin, G, Texas
1952—Bill Wade, B, Vanderbilt*
        Bob Carey, E, Michigan State
1953—Donn Moomaw, C, UCLA
        Ed Barker, E, Washington State
1954—Ed Beatty, C, Cincinnati
1955—Larry Morris, C, Georgia Tech
1956—Joe Marconi, B, West Virginia
        Charlie Horton, B, Vanderbilt
1957—Jon Arnett, B, Southern California
        Del Shofner, B, Baylor
1958—Lou Michaels, T, Kentucky
        Jim Phillips, E, Auburn
1959—Dick Bass, B, Pacific
        Paul Dickson, G, Baylor
1960—Billy Cannon, RB, Louisiana State*
1961—Marlin McKeever, LB, Southern California
1962—Roman Gabriel, QB, North Carolina State
        Merlin Olsen, DT, Utah State
1963—Terry Baker, QB, Oregon State*
        Rufus Guthrie, G, Georgia Tech
1964—Bill Munson, QB, Utah State
1965—Clancy Williams, DB, Washington State
1966—Tom Mack, G, Michigan
1967—None
1968—None

1969—Larry Smith, RB, Florida
        Jim Seymour, E, Notre Dame
        Bob Klein, TE, Southern California
1970—Jack Reynolds, LB, Tennessee
1971—Isiah Robertson, LB, Southern
        Jack Youngblood, DE, Florida
1972—None
1973—None
1974—John Cappelletti, RB, Penn State
1975—Mike Fanning, DT, Notre Dame
        Dennis Harrah, G, Miami (Fla.)
        Doug France, T, Ohio State
1976—Kevin McLain, LB, Colorado State
1977—Bob Brudzinski, LB, Ohio State
1978—Elvis Peacock, RB, Oklahoma
1979—George Andrews, LB, Nebraska
        Kent Hill, G, Georgia Tech
1980—Johnnie Johnson, DB, Texas
1981—Mel Owens, LB, Michigan
1982—Barry Redden, RB, Richmond
1983—Eric Dickerson, RB, Southern Methodist
1984—None
1985—Jerry Gray, DB, Texas
1986—Mike Schad, T, Queens College (Ont.)
1987—None
1988—Gaston Green, RB, UCLA
        Aaron Cox, WR, Arizona State
1989—Bill Hawkins, DE, Miami (Fla.)
        Cleveland Gary, RB, Miami (Fla.)
1990—Bern Brostek, C, Washington
1991—Todd Lyght, CB, Notre Dame
1992—Sean Gilbert, DE, Pittsburgh
1993—Jerome Bettis, RB, Notre Dame
1994—Wayne Gandy, T, Auburn
1995—Kevin Carter, DE, Florida
1996—Lawrence Phillips, RB, Nebraska
        Eddie Kennison, WR, Louisiana State
1997—Orlando Pace, T, Ohio State*
1998—Grant Wistrom, DE, Nebraska
1999—Torry Holt, WR, North Carolina State
        *First player chosen in draft.

FRANCHISE RECORDS

Most rushing yards, career
7,245—Eric Dickerson
Most rushing yards, season
2,105—Eric Dickerson, 1984
Most rushing yards, game
247—Willie Ellison vs. N.O., Dec. 5, 1971
Most rushing touchdowns, season
18—Eric Dickerson, 1983
Most passing attempts, season
554—Jim Everett, 1990
Most passing attempts, game
55—Mark Rypien vs. Buf., Dec. 10, 1995
Most passes completed, season
308—Jim Everett, 1988
Most passes completed, game
35—Dieter Brock vs. S.F., Oct. 27, 1985
Most passing yards, career
23,758—Jim Everett
Most passing yards, season
4,310—Jim Everett, 1989

Most passing yards, game
554—Norm Van Brocklin at N.Y. Yanks,
Sept. 28, 1951
Most touchdown passes, season
31—Jim Everett, 1988
Most pass receptions, career
593—Henry Ellard
Most pass receptions, season
119—Isaac Bruce, 1995
Most pass receptions, game
18—Tom Fears vs. G.B., Dec. 3, 1950
Most receiving yards, career
9,761—Henry Ellard
Most receiving yards, season
1,781—Isaac Bruce, 1995
Most receiving yards, game
336—Willie Anderson at N.O., Nov. 26,
1989
Most receiving touchdowns, season
17—Elroy Hirsch, 1951

Most touchdowns, career
58—Eric Dickerson
Most field goals, season
30—David Ray, 1973
Longest field goal
57 yards—Jeff Wilkins vs. Ari., Sept. 27,
1998
Most interceptions, career
46—Ed Meador
Most interceptions, season
14—Night Train Lane, 1952
Most sacks, career
151.5—Deacon Jones
Most sacks, season
22—Deacon Jones, 1964
Deacon Jones, 1968

SERIES RECORDS

St. Louis vs.: Arizona 16-14-2; Atlanta 39-23-2; Baltimore 0-1; Buffalo 4-4; Carolina 3-5; Chicago 26-36-3; Cincinnati 3-5; Dallas 9-8; Denver 4-4; Detroit 32-27-1; Green Bay 40-27-1; Indianapolis 17-21-2; Jacksonville 1-0; Kansas City 4-2; Miami 1-7; Minnesota 11-16-2; New England 4-3; New Orleans 31-25; N.Y. Giants 20-7; N.Y. Jets 7-2; Oakland 2-7; Philadelphia 14-13-1; Pittsburgh 17-6-2; San Diego 3-3; San Francisco 47-47-2; Seattle 4-2; Tampa Bay 8-3; Tennessee 5-2; Washington 7-16-1.
NOTE: Includes records as Los Angeles Rams from 1946 through 1994.

COACHING RECORDS

George Allen, 47-17-4 (2-2); Hugo Bezdek, 1-13-0; Rich Brooks, 13-19-0; Dutch Clark, 16-26-2; Aldo Donelli, 4-6-0; Sid Gillman, 28-31-1 (0-1); Chuck Knox, 69-48-1 (3-5); Art Lewis, 4-4-0; Ray Malavasi, 40-33-0 (3-3); Hamp Pool, 23-10-2 (0-1); Tommy Prothro, 14-12-2; John Robinson, 75-68-0 (4-6); Clark Shaughnessy, 14-7-3 (0-1); Bob Snyder, 6-6-0; Joe Stydahar, 17-8-0 (2-1); Harland Svare, 14-31-3; Dick Vermeil, 9-23-0; Adam Walsh, 15-5-1 (1-0); Bob Waterfield, 9-24-1.

RETIRED UNIFORM NUMBERS

No.	Player
7	Bob Waterfield
74	Merlin Olsen

SAN DIEGO CHARGERS
YEAR-BY-YEAR RECORDS

		REGULAR SEASON							PLAYOFFS		
Year	W	L	T	Pct.	PF	PA	Finish	W	L	Highest round	Coach
1960*†	10	4	0	.714	373	336	1st/Western Div.	0	1	AFL championship game	Sid Gillman
1961*	12	2	0	.857	396	219	1st/Western Div.	0	1	AFL championship game	Sid Gillman
1962*	4	10	0	.286	314	392	3rd/Western Div.	—	—		Sid Gillman
1963*	11	3	0	.786	399	256	1st/Western Div.	1	0	AFL champ	Sid Gillman
1964*	8	5	1	.615	341	300	1st/Western Div.	0	1	AFL championship game	Sid Gillman
1965*	9	2	3	.818	340	227	1st/Western Div.	0	1	AFL championship game	Sid Gillman
1966*	7	6	1	.538	335	284	3rd/Western Div.	—	—		Sid Gillman
1967*	8	5	1	.615	360	352	3rd/Western Div.	—	—		Sid Gillman
1968*	9	5	0	.643	382	310	3rd/Western Div.	—	—		Sid Gillman
1969*	8	6	0	.571	288	276	3rd/Western Div.	—	—		S. Gillman, C. Waller
1970	5	6	3	.455	282	278	3rd/AFC Western Div.	—	—		Charlie Waller
1971	6	8	0	.429	311	341	3rd/AFC Western Div.	—	—		Harland Svare
1972	4	9	1	.308	264	344	4th/AFC Western Div.	—	—		Harland Svare
1973	2	11	1	.179	188	386	4th/AFC Western Div.	—	—		H. Svare, Ron Waller
1974	5	9	0	.357	212	285	T3rd/AFC Western Div.	—	—		Tommy Prothro
1975	2	12	0	.143	189	345	4th/AFC Western Div.	—	—		Tommy Prothro
1976	6	8	0	.429	248	285	3rd/AFC Western Div.	—	—		Tommy Prothro
1977	7	7	0	.500	222	205	3rd/AFC Western Div.	—	—		Tommy Prothro
1978	9	7	0	.563	355	309	T2nd/AFC Western Div.	—	—		T. Prothro, Don Coryell
1979	12	4	0	.750	411	246	1st/AFC Western Div.	0	1	AFC div. playoff game	Don Coryell
1980	11	5	0	.688	418	327	1st/AFC Western Div.	1	1	AFC championship game	Don Coryell
1981	10	6	0	.625	478	390	1st/AFC Western Div.	1	1	AFC championship game	Don Coryell
1982	6	3	0	.667	288	221	T4th/AFC	1	1	AFC second-round pl. game	Don Coryell
1983	6	10	0	.375	358	462	T4th/AFC Western Div.	—	—		Don Coryell

		REGULAR SEASON						**PLAYOFFS**		
Year	W	L	T	Pct.	PF	PA	Finish	W	L	Highest round	Coach
1984	7	9	0	.438	394	413	5th/AFC Western Div.	—	—		Don Coryell
1985	8	8	0	.500	467	435	T3rd/AFC Western Div.	—	—		Don Coryell
1986	4	12	0	.250	335	396	5th/AFC Western Div.	—	—		D. Coryell, Al Saunders
1987	8	7	0	.533	253	317	3rd/AFC Western Div.	—	—		Al Saunders
1988	6	10	0	.375	231	332	4th/AFC Western Div.	—	—		Al Saunders
1989	6	10	0	.375	266	290	5th/AFC Western Div.	—	—		Dan Henning
1990	6	10	0	.375	315	281	4th/AFC Western Div.	—	—		Dan Henning
1991	4	12	0	.250	274	342	5th/AFC Western Div.	—	—		Dan Henning
1992	11	5	0	.688	335	241	1st/AFC Western Div.	1	1	AFC div. playoff game	Bobby Ross
1993	8	8	0	.500	322	290	4th/AFC Western Div.	—	—		Bobby Ross
1994	11	5	0	.688	381	306	1st/AFC Western Div.	2	1	Super Bowl	Bobby Ross
1995	9	7	0	.563	321	323	2nd/AFC Western Div.	0	1	AFC wild-card game	Bobby Ross
1996	8	8	0	.500	310	376	3rd/AFC Western Div.	—	—		Bobby Ross
1997	4	12	0	.250	266	425	T4th/AFC Western Div.	—	—		Kevin Gilbride
1998	5	11	0	.313	241	342	5th/AFC Western Div.	—	—		K. Gilbride, June Jones

*American Football League.
†Los Angeles Chargers.

FIRST-ROUND DRAFT PICKS

1960—Monty Stickles, E, Notre Dame
1961—Earl Faison, E, Indiana
1962—Bob Ferguson, RB, Ohio State
1963—Walt Sweeney, E, Syracuse
1964—Ted Davis, E, Georgia Tech
1965—Steve DeLong, DE, Tennessee
1966—Don Davis, T, Los Angeles State
1967—Ron Billingsley, DT, Wyoming
1968—Russ Washington, T, Missouri
    Jim Hill, DB, Texas A&I
1969—Marty Domres, QB, Columbia
    Bob Babich, LB, Miami of Ohio
1970—Walker Gillette, WR, Richmond
1971—Leon Burns, RB, Long Beach State
1972—None
1973—Johnny Rodgers, WR, Nebraska
1974—Bo Matthews, RB, Colorado
    Don Goode, LB, Kansas
1975—Gary Johnson, DT, Grambling State
    Mike Williams, DB, Louisiana State
1976—Joe Washington, RB, Oklahoma
1977—Bob Rush, C, Memphis State
1978—John Jefferson, WR, Arizona State
1979—Kellen Winslow, TE, Missouri

1980—None
1981—James Brooks, RB, Auburn
1982—None
1983—Billy Ray Smith, LB, Arkansas
    Gary Anderson, WR, Arkansas
    Gill Byrd, DB, San Jose State
1984—Mossy Cade, DB, Texas
1985—Jim Lachey, G, Ohio State
1986—Leslie O'Neal, DE, Oklahoma State
    Jim FitzPatrick, T, Southern California
1987—Rod Bernstine, TE, Texas A&M
1988—Anthony Miller, WR, Tennessee
1989—Burt Grossman, DE, Pittsburgh
1990—Junior Seau, LB, Southern California
1991—Stanley Richard, CB, Texas
1992—Chris Mims, DT, Tennessee
1993—Darrien Gordon, DB, Stanford
1994—None
1995—None
1996—None
1997—None
1998—Ryan Leaf, QB, Washington State
1999—None

FRANCHISE RECORDS

Most rushing yards, career
4,963—Paul Lowe

Most rushing yards, season
1,350—Natrone Means, 1994

Most rushing yards, game
217—Gary Anderson vs. K.C., Dec. 18, 1988

Most rushing touchdowns, season
19—Chuck Muncie, 1981

Most passing attempts, season
609—Dan Fouts, 1981

Most passing attempts, game
58—Mark Herrmann at K.C., Dec. 22, 1985

Most passes completed, season
360—Dan Fouts, 1981

Most passes completed, game
37—Dan Fouts vs. Mia., Nov. 18, 1984
    (OT)
    Mark Herrmann at K.C., Dec. 22, 1985

Most passing yards, career
43,040—Dan Fouts

Most passing yards, season
4,802—Dan Fouts, 1981

Most passing yards, game
444—Dan Fouts vs. NYG, Oct. 19, 1980
    Dan Fouts at S.F., Dec. 11, 1982

Most touchdown passes, season
33—Dan Fouts, 1981

Most pass receptions, career
586—Charlie Joiner

Most pass receptions, season
90—Tony Martin, 1995

Most pass receptions, game
15—Kellen Winslow at G.B., Oct. 7, 1984

Most receiving yards, career
9,585—Lance Alworth

Most receiving yards, season
1,602—Lance Alworth, 1965

Most receiving yards, game
260—Wes Chandler vs. Cin., Dec. 20, 1982

Most receiving touchdowns, season
14—Lance Alworth, 1965
    Tony Martin, 1996

Most touchdowns, career
83—Lance Alworth

Most field goals, season
34—John Carney, 1994

Longest field goal
54 yards—John Carney vs. Sea., Nov. 10, 1991
    John Carney vs. Buf., Sept. 6, 1998

Most interceptions, career
42—Gill Byrd

Most interceptions, season
9—Charlie McNeil, 1961

Most sacks, career
105.5—Leslie O'Neal

Most sacks, season
17.5—Gary Johnson, 1980

SERIES RECORDS

San Diego vs.: Arizona 6-2; Atlanta 1-5; Baltimore, 2-0; Buffalo 17-7-2; Carolina 0-1; Chicago 4-3; Cincinnati 14-9; Dallas 1-5; Denver 35-42-1; Detroit 3-3; Green Bay 1-5; Indianapolis 11-7; Jacksonville 0-0; Kansas City 36-40-1; Miami 10-6; Minnesota 4-3; New England 11-16-2; New Orleans 6-1; N.Y. Giants 3-5; N.Y. Jets 17-9-1; Oakland 29-47-2; Philadelphia 5-2; Pittsburgh 5-16; St. Louis 3-3; San Francisco 3-5; Seattle 20-20; Tampa Bay 6-1; Tennessee 19-13-1; Washington 0-6.
NOTE: Includes records as Los Angeles Chargers in 1960.

COACHING RECORDS

Don Coryell, 69-56-0 (3-4); Kevin Gilbride, 6-16-0; Sid Gillman, 86-53-6 (1-4); Dan Henning, 16-32-0; June Jones, 3-7-0; Tommy Prothro, 21-39-0; Bobby Ross, 47-33-0 (3-3); Al Saunders, 17-22-0; Harland Svare, 7-17-2; Charlie Waller, 9-7-3; Ron Waller, 1-5-0.

RETIRED UNIFORM NUMBERS

No.	Player
14	Dan Fouts

SAN FRANCISCO 49ERS
YEAR-BY-YEAR RECORDS

Year	W	L	T	Pct.	PF	PA	Finish	W	L	Highest round	Coach
1946*	9	5	0	.643	307	189	2nd/Western Div.	—	—		Buck Shaw
1947*	8	4	2	.667	327	264	2nd/Western Div.	—	—		Buck Shaw
1948*	12	2	0	.857	495	248	2nd/Western Div.	—	—		Buck Shaw
1949*	9	3	0	.750	416	227	2nd	—	—		Buck Shaw
1950	3	9	0	.250	213	300	T5th/National Conf.	—	—		Buck Shaw
1951	7	4	1	.636	255	205	T2nd/National Conf.	—	—		Buck Shaw
1952	7	5	0	.583	285	221	3rd/National Conf.	—	—		Buck Shaw
1953	9	3	0	.750	372	237	2nd/Western Conf.	—	—		Buck Shaw
1954	7	4	1	.636	313	251	3rd/Western Conf.	—	—		Buck Shaw
1955	4	8	0	.333	216	298	5th/Western Conf.	—	—		Red Strader
1956	5	6	1	.455	233	284	3rd/Western Conf.	—	—		Frankie Albert
1957	8	4	0	.667	260	264	2nd/Western Conf.	0	1	W. Conf. champ. game	Frankie Albert
1958	6	6	0	.500	257	324	4th/Western Conf.	—	—		Frankie Albert
1959	7	5	0	.583	255	237	T3rd/Western Conf.	—	—		Red Hickey
1960	7	5	0	.583	208	205	T2nd/Western Conf.	—	—		Red Hickey
1961	7	6	1	.538	346	272	5th/Western Conf.	—	—		Red Hickey
1962	6	8	0	.429	282	331	5th/Western Conf.	—	—		Red Hickey
1963	2	12	0	.143	198	391	7th/Western Conf.	—	—		R. Hickey, J. Christiansen
1964	4	10	0	.286	236	330	7th/Western Conf.	—	—		Jack Christiansen
1965	7	6	1	.538	421	402	4th/Western Conf.	—	—		Jack Christiansen
1966	6	6	2	.500	320	325	4th/Western Conf.	—	—		Jack Christiansen
1967	7	7	0	.500	273	337	3rd/Coastal Div.	—	—		Jack Christiansen
1968	7	6	1	.538	303	310	3rd/Coastal Div.	—	—		Dick Nolan
1969	4	8	2	.333	277	319	4th/Coastal Div.	—	—		Dick Nolan
1970	10	3	1	.769	352	267	1st/NFC Western Div.	1	1	NFC championship game	Dick Nolan
1971	9	5	0	.643	300	216	1st/NFC Western Div.	1	1	NFC championship game	Dick Nolan
1972	8	5	1	.607	353	249	1st/NFC Western Div.	0	1	NFC div. playoff game	Dick Nolan
1973	5	9	0	.357	262	319	T3rd/NFC Western Div.	—	—		Dick Nolan
1974	6	8	0	.429	226	236	2nd/NFC Western Div.	—	—		Dick Nolan
1975	5	9	0	.357	255	286	2nd/NFC Western Div.	—	—		Dick Nolan
1976	8	6	0	.571	270	190	2nd/NFC Western Div.	—	—		Monte Clark
1977	5	9	0	.357	220	260	3rd/NFC Western Div.	—	—		Ken Meyer
1978	2	14	0	.125	219	350	4th/NFC Western Div.	—	—		Pete McCulley, Fred O'Connor
1979	2	14	0	.125	308	416	4th/NFC Western Div.	—	—		Bill Walsh
1980	6	10	0	.375	320	415	3rd/NFC Western Div.	—	—		Bill Walsh
1981	13	3	0	.813	357	250	1st/NFC Western Div.	3	0	Super Bowl champ	Bill Walsh
1982	3	6	0	.333	209	206	T11th/NFC	—	—		Bill Walsh
1983	10	6	0	.625	432	293	1st/NFC Western Div.	1	1	NFC championship game	Bill Walsh
1984	15	1	0	.938	475	227	1st/NFC Western Div.	3	0	Super Bowl champ	Bill Walsh
1985	10	6	0	.625	411	263	2nd/NFC Western Div.	0	1	NFC wild-card game	Bill Walsh
1986	10	5	1	.656	374	247	1st/NFC Western Div.	0	1	NFC div. playoff game	Bill Walsh
1987	13	2	0	.867	459	253	1st/NFC Western Div.	0	1	NFC div. playoff game	Bill Walsh
1988	10	6	0	.625	369	294	1st/NFC Western Div.	3	0	Super Bowl champ	Bill Walsh
1989	14	2	0	.875	442	253	1st/NFC Western Div.	3	0	Super Bowl champ	George Seifert
1990	14	2	0	.875	353	239	1st/NFC Western Div.	1	1	NFC championship game	George Seifert
1991	10	6	0	.625	393	239	3rd/NFC Western Div.	—	—		George Seifert
1992	14	2	0	.875	431	236	1st/NFC Western Div.	1	1	NFC championship game	George Seifert
1993	10	6	0	.625	473	295	1st/NFC Western Div.	1	1	NFC championship game	George Seifert
1994	13	3	0	.813	505	296	1st/NFC Western Div.	3	0	Super Bowl champ	George Seifert
1995	11	5	0	.688	457	258	1st/NFC Western Div.	0	1	NFC div. playoff game	George Seifert

Year	W	L	T	Pct.	PF	PA	Finish	W	L	Highest round	Coach
				REGULAR SEASON						PLAYOFFS	
1996	12	4	0	.750	398	257	2nd/NFC Western Div.	1	1	NFC div. playoff game	George Seifert
1997	13	3	0	.813	375	265	1st/NFC Western Div.	1	1	NFC championship game	Steve Mariucci
1998	12	4	0	.750	479	328	2nd/NFC Western Div.	1	1	NFC div. playoff game	Steve Mariucci

*All-America Football Conference.

FIRST-ROUND DRAFT PICKS

1950—Leo Nomellini, T, Minnesota
1951—Y.A. Tittle, QB, Louisiana State
1952—Hugh McElhenny, RB, Washington
1953—Harry Babcock, E, Georgia*
    Tom Stolhandske, E, Texas
1954—Bernie Faloney, QB, Maryland
1955—Dick Moegel, HB, Rice
1956—Earl Morrall QB, Michigan State
1957—John Brodie, QB, Stanford
1958—Jim Pace, RB, Michigan
    Charles Krueger, T, Texas A&M
1959—Dave Baker, RB, Oklahoma
    Dan James, C, Ohio State
1960—Monty Stickles, E, Notre Dame
1961—Jim Johnson, RB, UCLA
    Bernie Casey, RB, Bowling Green State
    Billy Kilmer, QB, UCLA
1962—Lance Alworth, RB, Arkansas
1963—Kermit Alexander, RB, UCLA
1964—Dave Parks, E, Texas Tech*
1965—Ken Willard, RB, North Carolina
    George Donnelly, DB, Illinois
1966—Stan Hindman, DE, Mississippi
1967—Steve Spurrier, QB, Florida
    Cas Banaszek, LB, Northwestern
1968—Forrest Blue, C, Auburn
1969—Ted Kwalick, TE, Penn State
    Gene Washington, WR, Stanford
1970—Cedrick Hardman, DE, North Texas State
    Bruce Taylor, DB, Boston University
1971—Tim Anderson, DD, Ohio State
1972—Terry Beasley, WR, Auburn
1973—Mike Holmes, DB, Tex. Southern

1974—Wilbur Jackson, RB, Alabama
    Bill Sandifer, DT, UCLA
1975—Jimmy Webb, DT, Mississippi State
1976—None
1977—None
1978—Ken McAfee, TE, Notre Dame
    Dan Bunz, LB, Long Beach State
1979—None
1980—Earl Cooper, RB, Rice
    Jim Stuckey, DE, Clemson
1981—Ronnie Lott, DB, Southern California
1982—None
1983—None
1984—Todd Shell, LB, Brigham Young
1985—Jerry Rice, WR, Mississippi Valley State
1986—None
1987—Harris Barton, T, North Carolina
    Terrence Flager, RB, Clemson
1988—None
1989—Keith DeLong, LB, Tennessee
1990—Dexter Carter, RB, Florida State
1991—Ted Washington, DL, Louisville
1992—Dana Hall, DB, Washington
1993—Dana Stubblefield, DT, Kansas
    Todd Kelly, DE, Tennessee
1994—Bryant Young, DT, Notre Dame
    William Floyd, RB, Florida State
1995—J.J. Stokes, WR, UCLA
1996—None
1997—Jim Druckenmiller, QB, Virginia Tech
1998—R.W. McQuarters, DB, Oklahoma State
1999—Reggie McGrew, DT, Florida
    *First player chosen in draft.

FRANCHISE RECORDS

Most rushing yards, career
7,344—Joe Perry

Most rushing yards, season
1,570—Garrison Hearst, 1998

Most rushing yards, game
198—Garrison Hearst vs. Det., Dec. 14, 1998

Most rushing touchdowns, season
10—Joe Perry, 1953
    J.D. Smith, 1959
    Billy Kilmer, 1961
    Ricky Watters, 1993
    Derek Loville, 1995

Most passing attempts, season
578—Steve DeBerg, 1979

Most passing attempts, game
60—Joe Montana at Was., Nov. 17, 1986

Most passes completed, season
347—Steve DeBerg, 1979

Most passes completed, game
37—Joe Montana at Atl., Nov. 6, 1985

Most passing yards, career
35,142—Joe Montana

Most passing yards, season
4,170—Steve Young, 1998

Most passing yards, game
476—Joe Montana at Atl., Oct. 14, 1990

Most touchdown passes, season
36—Steve Young, 1998

Most pass receptions, career
1,139—Jerry Rice

Most pass receptions, season
122—Jerry Rice, 1995

Most pass receptions, game
16—Jerry Rice at L.A. Rams, Nov. 20, 1994

Most receiving yards, career
17,612—Jerry Rice

Most receiving yards, season
1,848—Jerry Rice, 1995

Most receiving yards, game
289—Jerry Rice vs. Min., Dec. 18, 1995

Most receiving touchdowns, season
22—Jerry Rice, 1987

Most touchdowns, career
175—Jerry Rice

Most field goals, season
30—Jeff Wilkins, 1996

Longest field goal
56 yards—Mike Cofer at Atl., Oct. 14, 1990

Most interceptions, career
51—Ronnie Lott

Most interceptions, season
10—Dave Baker, 1960
    Ronnie Lott, 1986

Most sacks, career
111.5—Cedrick Hardman

Most sacks, season
18—Cedrick Hardman

SERIES RECORDS

San Francisco vs.: Arizona 10-9; Atlanta 40-23-1; Baltimore 1-0; Buffalo 3-4; Carolina 5-3; Chicago 25-25-1; Cincinnati 7-1; Dallas 12-7-1; Denver 4-4; Detroit 29-26-1; Green Bay 25-23-1; Indianapolis 17-22; Jacksonville 0-0; Kansas City 4-3; Miami 3-4; Minnesota 17-16-1; New England 7-2; New Orleans 42-15-2; N.Y. Giants 12-11; N.Y. Jets 7-1; Oakland 3-5; Philadelphia 14-6-1; Pittsburgh 9-7; St. Louis 47-47-2; San Diego 5-3; Seattle 4-2; Tampa Bay 12-2; Tennessee 6-3; Washington 12-6-1.
NOTE: Includes records only from 1950 to present.

COACHING RECORDS

Frankie Albert, 19-16-1 (0-1); Jack Christiansen, 26-38-3; Monte Clark, 8-6-0; Red Hickey, 27-27-1; Steve Mariucci, 25-7-0 (2-2); Pete McCulley, 1-8-0; Ken Meyer, 5-9-0; Dick Nolan, 54-53-5 (2-3); Fred O'Connor, 1-6-0; George Seifert, 98-30-0 (10-5); Buck Shaw, 33-25-2; Red Strader, 4-8-0; Bill Walsh, 92-59-1 (10-4).

RETIRED UNIFORM NUMBERS

No.	Player
12	John Brodie
16	Joe Montana
34	Joe Perry
37	Jimmy Johnson
39	Hugh McElhenny
70	Charlie Krueger
73	Leo Nomellini
87	Dwight Clark

SEATTLE SEAHAWKS
YEAR-BY-YEAR RECORDS

		REGULAR SEASON						PLAYOFFS		
Year	W	L	T	Pct.	PF	PA	Finish	W	L	Highest round	Coach
1976	2	12	0	.143	229	429	5th/NFC Western Div.	—	—		Jack Patera
1977	5	9	0	.357	282	373	4th/AFC Western Div.	—	—		Jack Patera
1978	9	7	0	.563	345	358	T2nd/AFC Western Div.	—	—		Jack Patera
1979	9	7	0	.563	378	372	T3rd	—	—		Jack Patera
1980	4	12	0	.250	291	408	5th/AFC Western Div.	—	—		Jack Patera
1981	6	10	0	.375	322	388	5th/AFC Western Div.	—	—		Jack Patera
1982	4	5	0	.444	127	147	T8th/AFC	—	—		J. Patera, Mike McCormack
1983	9	7	0	.562	403	397	T2nd/AFC Western Div.	2	1	AFC championship game	Chuck Knox
1984	12	4	0	.750	418	282	2nd/AFC Western Div.	1	1	AFC div. playoff game	Chuck Knox
1985	8	8	0	.500	349	303	T3rd/AFC Western Div.	—	—		Chuck Knox
1986	10	6	0	.625	366	293	T2nd/AFC Western Div.	—	—		Chuck Knox
1987	9	6	0	.600	371	314	2nd/AFC Western Div.	0	1	AFC wild-card game	Chuck Knox
1988	9	7	0	.563	339	329	1st/AFC Western Div.	0	1	AFC div. playoff game	Chuck Knox
1989	7	9	0	.438	241	327	4th/AFC Western Div.	—	—		Chuck Knox
1990	9	7	0	.563	306	286	3rd/AFC Western Div.	—	—		Chuck Knox
1991	7	9	0	.438	276	261	4th/AFC Western Div.	—	—		Chuck Knox
1992	2	14	0	.125	140	312	5th/AFC Western Div.	—	—		Tom Flores
1993	6	10	0	.375	280	314	5th/AFC Western Div.	—	—		Tom Flores
1994	6	10	0	.375	287	323	5th/AFC Western Div.	—	—		Tom Flores
1995	8	8	0	.500	363	366	T3rd/AFC Western Div.	—	—		Dennis Erickson
1996	7	9	0	.438	317	376	T4th/AFC Western Div.	—	—		Dennis Erickson
1997	8	8	0	.500	365	362	3rd/AFC Western Div.	—	—		Dennis Erickson
1998	8	8	0	.500	372	310	3rd/AFC Western Div.	—	—		Dennis Erickson

FIRST-ROUND DRAFT PICKS

1976—Steve Niehaus, DT, Notre Dame
1977—Steve August, G, Tulsa
1978—Keith Simpson, DB, Memphis State
1979—Manu Tuiasosopo, DT, UCLA
1980—Jacob Green, DE, Texas A&M
1981—Kenny Easley, DB, UCLA
1982—Jeff Bryant, DE, Clemson
1983—Curt Warner, RB, Penn State
1984—Terry Taylor, DB, Southern Illinois
1985—None
1986—John L. Williams, RB, Florida
1987—Tony Woods, LB, Pittsburgh
1988—None

1989—Andy Heck, T, Notre Dame
1990—Cortez Kennedy, DT, Miami (Fla.)
1991—Dan McGwire, QB, San Diego State
1992—Ray Roberts, T, Virginia
1993—Rick Mirer, QB, Notre Dame
1994—Sam Adams, DE, Texas A&M
1995—Joey Galloway, WR, Ohio State
1996—Pete Kendall, T, Boston College
1997—Shawn Springs, CB, Ohio State
    Walter Jones, T, Florida State
1998—Anthony Simmons, LB, Clemson
1999—Lamar King, DE, Saginaw Valley State

FRANCHISE RECORDS

Most rushing yards, career
6,706—Chris Warren
Most rushing yards, season
1,545—Chris Warren, 1994

Most rushing yards, game
207—Curt Warner vs. K.C., Nov. 27, 1983
    (OT)
192—Curt Warner vs. Den., Dec. 20, 1986

Most rushing touchdowns, season
15—Chris Warren, 1995
Most passing attempts, season
532—Dave Krieg, 1985

Most passing attempts, game
51—Dave Krieg vs. Atl., Oct. 13, 1985
Most passes completed, season
313—Warren Moon, 1997
Most passes completed, game
33—Dave Krieg vs. Atl., Oct. 13, 1985
Most passing yards, career
26,132—Dave Krieg
Most passing yards, season
3,678—Warren Moon, 1997
Most passing yards, game
418—Dave Krieg vs. Den., Nov. 20, 1983
Most touchdown passes, season
32—Dave Krieg, 1984
Most pass receptions, career
819—Steve Largent

Most pass receptions, season
81—Brian Blades, 1994
Most pass receptions, game
15—Steve Largent vs. Det., Oct. 18, 1987
Most receiving yards, career
13,089—Steve Largent
Most receiving yards, season
1,287—Steve Largent, 1985
Most receiving yards, game
261—Steve Largent vs. Det., Oct. 18, 1987
Most receiving touchdowns, season
13—Daryl Turner, 1985
Most touchdowns, career
101—Steve Largent
Most field goals, season
28—Todd Peterson, 1996

Longest field goal
55 yards—John Kasay vs. K.C., Jan. 2, 1994
Most interceptions, career
50—Dave Brown
Most interceptions, season
10—John Harris, 1981
    Kenny Easley, 1984
Most sacks, career
116.0—Jacob Green
Most sacks, season
16.5—Michael Sinclair, 1998

SERIES RECORDS

Seattle vs.: Arizona 1-5; Atlanta 4-2; Baltimore, 0-1; Buffalo 4-2; Carolina 0-0; Chicago 4-2; Cincinnati 7-7; Dallas 1-5; Denver 15-28; Detroit 4-3; Green Bay 3-4; Indianapolis 3-4; Jacksonville 1-1; Kansas City 13-27; Miami 2-4; Minnesota 4-2; New England 7-6; New Orleans 2-4; N.Y. Giants 3-5; N.Y. Jets 8-6; Oakland 19-23; Philadelphia 3-4; Pittsburgh 6-6; St. Louis 2-4; San Diego 20-20; San Francisco 2-4; Tampa Bay 4-0; Tennessee 7-4; Washington 4-5.

COACHING RECORDS

Dennis Erickson, 31-33-0; Tom Flores, 14-34-0; Chuck Knox, 80-63-0 (3-4); Mike McCormack, 4-3-0; Jack Patera, 35-59-0.

RETIRED UNIFORM NUMBERS

No.	Player
80	Steve Largent

TAMPA BAY BUCCANEERS
YEAR-BY-YEAR RECORDS

Year	W	L	T	Pct.	PF	PA	Finish	W	L	Highest round	Coach
				REGULAR SEASON						**PLAYOFFS**	
1976	0	14	0	.000	125	412	5th/AFC Western Div.	—	—		John McKay
1977	2	12	0	.143	103	223	5th/NFC Central Div.	—	—		John McKay
1978	5	11	0	.313	241	259	5th/NFC Central Div.	—	—		John McKay
1979	10	6	0	.625	273	237	1st/NFC Central Div.	1	1	NFC championship game	John McKay
1980	5	10	1	.344	271	341	T4th/NFC Central Div.	—	—		John McKay
1981	9	7	0	.563	315	268	1st/NFC Central Div.	0	1	NFC div. playoff game	John McKay
1982	5	4	0	.556	158	178	T4th/NFC	0	1	NFC first-round pl. game	John McKay
1983	2	14	0	.125	241	380	5th/NFC Central Div.	—	—		John McKay
1984	6	10	0	.375	335	380	3rd/NFC Central Div.	—	—		John McKay
1985	2	14	0	.125	294	448	5th/NFC Central Div.	—	—		Leeman Bennett
1986	2	14	0	.125	239	473	5th/NFC Central Div.	—	—		Leeman Bennett
1987	4	11	0	.267	286	360	T4th/NFC Central Div.	—	—		Ray Perkins
1988	5	11	0	.313	261	350	3rd/NFC Central Div.	—	—		Ray Perkins
1989	5	11	0	.313	320	419	5th/NFC Central Div.	—	—		Ray Perkins
1990	6	10	0	.375	264	367	T2nd/NFC Central Div.	—	—		R. Perkins, R. Williamson
1991	3	13	0	.188	199	365	5th/NFC Central Div.	—	—		Richard Williamson
1992	5	11	0	.313	267	365	T3rd/NFC Central Div.	—	—		Sam Wyche
1993	5	11	0	.313	237	376	5th/NFC Central Div.	—	—		Sam Wyche
1994	6	10	0	.375	251	351	5th/NFC Central Div.	—	—		Sam Wyche
1995	7	9	0	.438	238	335	5th/NFC Central Div.	—	—		Sam Wyche
1996	6	10	0	.375	221	293	4th/NFC Central Div.	—	—		Tony Dungy
1997	10	6	0	.625	299	263	3rd/AFC Western Div.	1	1	NFC div. playoff game	Tony Dungy
1998	8	8	0	.500	314	295	3rd/AFC Western Div.	—	—		Tony Dungy

FIRST-ROUND DRAFT PICKS

1976—Lee Roy Selmon, DE, Oklahoma*
1977—Ricky Bell, RB, Southern California*
1978—Doug Williams, QB, Grambling State
1979—None
1980—Ray Snell, T, Wisconsin
1981—Hugh Green, LB, Pittsburgh
1982—Sean Farrell, G, Penn State
1983—None
1984—None

1985—Ron Holmes, DE, Washington
1986—Bo Jackson, RB, Auburn*
    Rod Jones, DB, Southern Methodist
1987—Vinny Testaverde, QB, Miami (Fla.)*
1988—Paul Gruber, T, Wisconsin
1989—Broderick Thomas, LB, Nebraska
1990—Keith McCants, LB, Alabama
1991—Charles McRae, T, Tennessee
1992—None

1993—Eric Curry, DE, Alabama
1994—Trent Dilfer, QB, Fresno State
1995—Warren Sapp, DT, Miami (Fla.)
  Derrick Brooks, LB, Florida State
1996—Regan Upshaw, DE, California
  Marcus Jones, DT, North Carolina

1997—Warrick Dunn, RB, Florida State
  Reidel Anthony, WR, Florida
1998—None
1999—Anthony McFarland, DT, Louisiana State
  *First player chosen in draft.

FRANCHISE RECORDS

Most rushing yards, career
5,957—James Wilder
Most rushing yards, season
1,544—James Wilder, 1984
Most rushing yards, game
219—James Wilder at Min., Nov. 6, 1983
Most rushing touchdowns, season
13—James Wilder, 1984
Most passing attempts, season
521—Doug Williams, 1980
Most passing attempts, game
56—Doug Williams vs. Cle., Sept. 28, 1980
Most passes completed, season
308—Steve DeBerg, 1984
Most passes completed, game
31—Vinny Testaverde at Hou., Dec. 10, 1989
Most passing yards, career
14,820—Vinny Testaverde

Most passing yards, season
3,563—Doug Williams, 1981
Most passing yards, game
486—Doug Williams at Min., Nov. 16, 1980
Most touchdown passes, season
21—Trent Dilfer, 1997, 1998
Most pass receptions, career
430—James Wilder
Most pass receptions, season
86—Mark Carrier, 1989
Most pass receptions, game
13—James Wilder vs. Min., Sept. 15, 1985
Most receiving yards, career
5,018—Mark Carrier
Most receiving yards, season
1,422—Mark Carrier, 1989
Most receiving yards, game
212—Mark Carrier at N.O., Dec. 6, 1987

Most receiving touchdowns, season
9—Kevin House, 1981
  Bruce Hill, 1988
  Mark Carrier, 1989
Most touchdowns, career
46—James Wilder
Most field goals, season
25—Michael Husted, 1996
Longest field goal
57 yards—Michael Husted at L.A. Raiders, Dec. 19, 1993
Most interceptions, career
29—Cedric Brown
Most interceptions, season
9—Cedric Brown, 1981
Most sacks, career
78.5—Lee Roy Selmon
Most sacks, season
13—Lee Roy Selmon, 1977

SERIES RECORDS

Tampa Bay vs.: Arizona 7-7; Atlanta 7-8; Buffalo 4-2; Carolina 2-1; Chicago 12-30; Cincinnati 3-3; Dallas 0-6; Denver 1-3; Detroit 18-24; Green Bay 14-25-1; Indianapolis 4-5; Jacksonville 1-1; Kansas City 2-5; Miami 2-4; Minnesota 14-28; New England 1-3; New Orleans 5-13; N.Y. Giants 5-8; N.Y. Jets 1-6; Oakland 1-3; Philadelphia 2-3; Pittsburgh 1-4; St. Louis 3-8; San Diego 1-6; San Francisco 2-12; Seattle 0-4; Tennessee 1-5; Washington 4-5.

COACHING RECORDS

Leeman Bennett, 4-28-0; Tony Dungy, 24-24-0 (1-1); John McKay, 44-88-1 (1-3); Ray Perkins, 19-41-0; Richard Williamson, 4-15-0; Sam Wyche, 23-41-0.

RETIRED UNIFORM NUMBERS

No.	Player
63	Lee Roy Selmon

TENNESSEE TITANS
YEAR-BY-YEAR RECORDS

Year	W	L	T	Pct.	PF	PA	Finish	W	L	Highest round	Coach
							REGULAR SEASON			**PLAYOFFS**	
1960*†	10	4	0	.714	379	285	1st/Eastern Div.	1	0	AFL champ	Lou Rymkus
1961*†	10	3	1	.769	513	242	1st/Eastern Div.	1	0	AFL champ	L. Rymkus, Wally Lemm
1962*†	11	3	0	.786	387	270	1st/Eastern Div.	0	1	AFL championship game	Pop Ivy
1963*†	6	8	0	.429	302	372	3rd/Eastern Div.	—	—		Pop Ivy
1964*†	4	10	0	.286	310	355	4th/Eastern Div.	—	—		Sammy Baugh
1965*†	4	10	0	.286	298	429	4th/Eastern Div.	—	—		Hugh Taylor
1966*†	3	11	0	.214	335	396	T4th/Eastern Div.	—	—		Wally Lemm
1967*†	9	4	1	.692	258	199	1st/Eastern Div.	0	1	AFL championship game	Wally Lemm
1968*†	7	7	0	.500	303	248	2nd/Eastern Div.	—	—		Wally Lemm
1969*†	6	6	2	.500	278	279	2nd/Eastern Div.	0	1	Div. playoff game	Wally Lemm
1970†	3	10	1	.231	217	352	4th/AFC Central Div.	—	—		Wally Lemm
1971†	4	9	1	.308	251	330	3rd/AFC Central Div.	—	—		Ed Hughes
1972†	1	13	0	.071	164	380	4th/AFC Central Div.	—	—		Bill Peterson
1973†	1	13	0	.071	199	447	4th/AFC Central Div.	—	—		B. Peterson, S. Gillman
1974†	7	7	0	.500	236	282	T2nd/AFC Central Div.	—	—		Sid Gillman
1975†	10	4	0	.714	293	226	3rd/AFC Central Div.	—	—		Bum Phillips
1976†	5	9	0	.357	222	273	4th/AFC Central Div.	—	—		Bum Phillips
1977†	8	6	0	.571	299	230	T2nd/AFC Central Div.	—	—		Bum Phillips
1978†	10	6	0	.625	283	298	2nd/AFC Central Div.	2	1	AFC championship game	Bum Phillips
1979†	11	5	0	.688	362	331	2nd/AFC Central Div.	2	1	AFC championship game	Bum Phillips
1980†	11	5	0	.688	295	251	2nd/AFC Central Div.	0	1	AFC wild-card game	Bum Phillips
1981†	7	9	0	.438	281	355	3rd/AFC Central Div.	—	—		Ed Biles

	REGULAR SEASON							PLAYOFFS			
Year	W	L	T	Pct.	PF	PA	Finish	W	L	Highest round	Coach
1982†	1	8	0	.111	136	245	13th/AFC	—	—		Ed Biles
1983†	2	14	0	.125	288	460	4th/AFC Central Div.	—	—		Ed Biles, Chuck Studley
1984†	3	13	0	.188	240	437	4th/AFC Central Div.	—	—		Hugh Campbell
1985†	5	11	0	.313	284	412	4th/AFC Central Div.	—	—		H. Campbell, J. Glanville
1986†	5	11	0	.313	274	329	4th/AFC Central Div.	—	—		Jerry Glanville
1987†	9	6	0	.600	345	349	2nd/AFC Central Div.	1	1	AFC div. playoff game	Jerry Glanville
1988†	10	6	0	.625	424	365	T2nd/AFC Central Div.	1	1	AFC div. playoff game	Jerry Glanville
1989†	9	7	0	.563	365	412	T2nd/AFC Central Div.	0	1	AFC wild-card game	Jerry Glanville
1990†	9	7	0	.563	405	307	2nd/AFC Central Div.	0	1	AFC wild-card game	Jack Pardee
1991†	11	5	0	.688	386	251	1st/AFC Central Div.	1	1	AFC div. playoff game	Jack Pardee
1992†	10	6	0	.625	352	258	2nd/AFC Central Div.	0	1	AFC wild-card game	Jack Pardee
1993†	12	4	0	.750	368	238	1st/AFC Central Div.	0	1	AFC div. playoff game	Jack Pardee
1994†	2	14	0	.125	226	352	4th/AFC Central Div.	—	—		Jack Pardee, Jeff Fisher
1995†	7	9	0	.438	348	324	T2nd/AFC Central Div.	—	—		Jeff Fisher
1996†	8	8	0	.500	345	319	T3rd/AFC Central Div.	—	—		Jeff Fisher
1997‡	8	8	0	.500	333	310	3rd/AFC Central Div.	—	—		Jeff Fisher
1998‡	8	8	0	.500	330	320	2nd/AFC Central Div.	—	—		Jeff Fisher

*American Football League.
†Houston Oilers.
‡Tennessee Oilers.

FIRST-ROUND DRAFT PICKS

1960—Billy Cannon, RB, Louisiana State
1961—Mike Ditka, E, Pittsburgh
1962—Ray Jacobs, DT, Howard Payne
1963—Danny Brabham, LB, Arkansas
1964—Scott Appleton, DT, Texas
1965—Lawrence Elkins, WR, Baylor* (AFL)
1966—Tommy Nobis, LB, Texas
1967—George Webster, LB, Michigan State
    Tom Regner, G, Notre Dame
1968—None
1969—Ron Pritchard, LB, Arizona State
1970—Doug Wilkerson, G, North Carolina Central
1971—Dan Pastorini, QB, Santa Clara
1972—Greg Sampson, DE, Stanford
1973—John Matuszak, DE, Tampa*
    George Amundson, RB, Iowa State
1974—None
1975—Robert Brazile, LB, Jackson State
    Don Hardeman, RB, Texas A&I
1976—None
1977—Morris Towns, T, Missouri
1978—Earl Campbell, RB, Texas*
1979—None

1980—None
1981—None
1982—Mike Munchak, G, Penn State
1983—Bruce Matthews, G, Southern California
1984—Dean Steinkuhler, G, Nebraska
1985—Ray Childress, DE, Texas A&M
    Richard Johnson, DB, Wisconsin
1986—Jim Everett, QB, Purdue
1987—Alonzo Highsmith, FB, Miami (Fla.)
    Haywood Jeffires, WR, North Carolina State
1988—Lorenzo White, RB, Michigan State
1989—David Williams, T, Florida
1990—Lamar Lathon, LB, Houston
1991—None
1992—None
1993—Brad Hopkins, G, Illinois
1994—Henry Ford, DE, Arkansas
1995—Steve McNair, QB, Alcorn State
1996—Eddie George, RB, Ohio State
1997—Kenny Holmes, DE, Miami (Fla.)
1998—Kevin Dyson, WR, Utah
1999—Jevon Kearse, LB, Florida
    *First player chosen in draft.

FRANCHISE RECORDS

Most rushing yards, career
8,574—Earl Campbell
Most rushing yards, season
1,934—Earl Campbell, 1980
Most rushing yards, game
216—Billy Cannon at N.Y. Titans, Dec. 10, 1961
    Eddie George vs. Oak., Aug. 31, 1997 (OT)
Most rushing touchdowns, season
19—Earl Campbell, 1979
Most passing attempts, season
655—Warren Moon, 1991
Most passing attempts, game
68—George Blanda at Buf., Nov. 1, 1964
Most passes completed, season
404—Warren Moon, 1991
Most passes completed, game
41—Warren Moon vs. Dal., Nov. 10, 1991

Most passing yards, career
33,685—Warren Moon
Most passing yards, season
4,690—Warren Moon, 1991
Most passing yards, game
527—Warren Moon at K.C., Dec. 16, 1990
Most touchdown passes, season
36—George Blanda, 1961
Most pass receptions, career
542—Ernest Givins
Most pass receptions, season
101—Charlie Hennigan, 1964
Most pass receptions, game
13—Charlie Hennigan at Boston, Oct. 13, 1961
    Haywood Jeffires at NYJ, Oct. 13, 1991
Most receiving yards, career
7,935—Ernest Givins
Most receiving yards, season
1,746—Charlie Hennigan, 1961

Most receiving yards, game
272—Charlie Hennigan at Boston, Oct. 13, 1961
Most receiving touchdowns, season
17—Bill Groman, 1961
Most touchdowns, career
73—Earl Campbell
Most field goals, season
36—Al Del Greco, 1998
Longest field goal
56 yards—Al Del Greco vs. S.F., Oct. 27, 1996
Most interceptions, career
45—Jim Norton
Most interceptions, season
12—Freddy Glick, 1963
    Mike Reinfeldt, 1979
Most sacks, season
15.5—Jesse Baker, 1979

SERIES RECORDS

Tennessee vs.: Arizona 3-4; Atlanta 4-5; Baltimore 4-2; Buffalo 22-13; Carolina 0-1; Chicago 4-4; Cincinnati 31-28-1; Dallas 4-5; Denver 20-11-1; Detroit 4-3; Green Bay 3-4; Indianapolis 7-7; Jacksonville 4-4; Kansas City 17-24; Miami 11-13; Minnesota 3-5; New England 14-18-1; New Orleans 4-4-1; N.Y. Giants 1-5; N.Y. Jets 20-13-1; Oakland 14-20; Philadelphia 0-6; Pittsburgh 22-35; St. Louis 2-5; San Diego 13-19-1; San Francisco 3-6; Seattle 4-7; Tampa Bay 5-1; Washington 4-3.
NOTE: Includes records as Houston Oilers from 1960 through 1996.

COACHING RECORDS

Sammy Baugh, 4-10-0; Ed Biles, 8-23-0; Hugh Campbell, 8-22-0; Jeff Fisher, 32-38-0; Sid Gillman, 8-15-0; Jerry Glanville, 33-32-0 (2-3); Ed Hughes, 4-9-1; Frank Ivy, 17-11-0 (0-1); Wally Lemm, 37-38-4 (1-2); Jack Pardee, 43-31-0 (1-4); Bill Peterson, 1-18-0; Bum Phillips, 55-35-0 (4-3); Lou Rymkus, 11-7-1 (1-0); Chuck Studley, 2-8-0; Hugh Taylor, 4-10-0.

RETIRED UNIFORM NUMBERS

No.	Player
34	Earl Campbell
43	Jim Norton
63	Mike Munchak
65	Elvin Bethea

WASHINGTON REDSKINS
YEAR-BY-YEAR RECORDS

| | REGULAR SEASON | | | | | | | PLAYOFFS | | | |
Year	W	L	T	Pct.	PF	PA	Finish	W	L	Highest round	Coach
1932*	4	4	2	.500	55	79	4th				Lud Wray
1933†	5	5	2	.500	103	97	3rd/Eastern Div.	—	—		Lone Star Dietz
1934†	6	6	0	.500	107	94	2nd/Eastern Div.	—	—		Lone Star Dietz
1935†	2	8	1	.200	65	123	4th/Eastern Div.	—	—		Eddie Casey
1936†	7	5	0	.583	149	110	1st/Eastern Div.	0	1	NFL championship game	Ray Flaherty
1937	8	3	0	.727	195	120	1st/Eastern Div.	1	0	NFL champ	Ray Flaherty
1938	6	3	2	.667	148	154	2nd/Eastern Div.	—	—		Ray Flaherty
1939	8	2	1	.800	242	94	2nd/Eastern Div.	—	—		Ray Flaherty
1940	9	2	0	.818	245	142	1st/Eastern Div.	0	1	NFL championship game	Ray Flaherty
1941	6	5	0	.545	176	174	3rd/Eastern Div.	—	—		Ray Flaherty
1942	10	1	0	.909	227	102	1st/Eastern Div.	1	0	NFL champ	Ray Flaherty
1943	6	3	1	.667	229	137	1st/Eastern Div.	1	1	NFL championship game	Dutch Bergman
1944	6	3	1	.667	169	180	3rd/Eastern Div.	—	—		Dudley DeGroot
1945	8	2	0	.800	209	121	1st/Eastern Div.	0	1	NFL championship game	Dudley DeGroot
1946	5	5	1	.500	171	191	T3rd/Eastern Div.	—	—		Turk Edwards
1947	4	8	0	.333	295	367	4th/Eastern Div.	—	—		Turk Edwards
1948	7	5	0	.583	291	287	2nd/Eastern Div.	—	—		Turk Edwards
1949	4	7	1	.364	268	339	4th/Eastern Div.	—	—		John Whelchel, H. Ball
1950	3	9	0	.250	232	326	6th/American Conf.	—	—		Herman Ball
1951	5	7	0	.417	183	296	3rd/American Conf.	—	—		Herman Ball, Dick Todd
1952	4	8	0	.333	240	287	T5th/American Conf.	—	—		Curly Lambeau
1953	6	5	1	.545	208	215	3rd/Eastern Conf.	—	—		Curly Lambeau
1954	3	9	0	.250	207	432	5th/Eastern Conf.	—	—		Joe Kuharich
1955	8	4	0	.667	246	222	2nd/Eastern Conf.	—	—		Joe Kuharich
1956	6	6	0	.500	183	225	3rd/Eastern Conf.	—	—		Joe Kuharich
1957	5	6	1	.455	251	230	4th/Eastern Conf.	—	—		Joe Kuharich
1958	4	7	1	.364	214	268	4th/Eastern Conf.	—	—		Joe Kuharich
1959	3	9	0	.250	185	350	5th/Eastern Conf.	—	—		Mike Nixon
1960	1	9	2	.100	178	309	6th/Eastern Conf.	—	—		Mike Nixon
1961	1	12	1	.077	174	392	7th/Eastern Conf.	—	—		Bill McPeak
1962	5	7	2	.417	305	376	4th/Eastern Conf.	—	—		Bill McPeak
1963	3	11	0	.214	279	398	6th/Eastern Conf.	—	—		Bill McPeak
1964	6	8	0	.429	307	305	T3rd/Eastern Conf.	—	—		Bill McPeak
1965	6	8	0	.429	257	301	4th/Eastern Conf.	—	—		Bill McPeak
1966	7	7	0	.500	351	355	5th/Eastern Conf.	—	—		Otto Graham
1967	5	6	3	.455	347	353	3rd/Capitol Div.	—	—		Otto Graham
1968	5	9	0	.357	249	358	3rd/Capitol Div.	—	—		Otto Graham
1969	7	5	2	.583	307	319	2nd/Capitol Div.	—	—		Vince Lombardi
1970	6	8	0	.429	297	314	4th/NFC Eastern Div.	—	—		Bill Austin
1971	9	4	1	.692	276	190	2nd/NFC Eastern Div.	0	1	NFC div. playoff game	George Allen
1972	11	3	0	.786	336	218	1st/NFC Eastern Div.	2	1	Super Bowl	George Allen
1973	10	4	0	.714	325	198	2nd/NFC Eastern Div.	0	1	NFC div. playoff game	George Allen
1974	10	4	0	.714	320	196	2nd/NFC Eastern Div.	0	1	NFC div. playoff game	George Allen
1975	8	6	0	.571	325	276	3rd/NFC Eastern Div.	—	—		George Allen
1976	10	4	0	.714	291	217	2nd/NFC Eastern Div.	0	1	NFC div. playoff game	George Allen
1977	9	5	0	.643	196	189	2nd/NFC Eastern Div.	—	—		George Allen
1978	8	8	0	.500	273	283	3rd/NFC Eastern Div.	—	—		Jack Pardee
1979	10	6	0	.625	348	295	3rd/NFC Eastern Div.	—	—		Jack Pardee
1980	6	10	0	.375	261	293	3rd/NFC Eastern Div.	—	—		Jack Pardee

			REGULAR SEASON					PLAYOFFS		
Year	W	L	T	Pct.	PF	PA	Finish	W	L	Highest round	Coach
1981	8	8	0	.500	347	349	4th/NFC Eastern Div.	—	—		Joe Gibbs
1982	8	1	0	.889	190	128	1st/NFC	4	0	Super Bowl champ	Joe Gibbs
1983	14	2	0	.875	541	332	1st/NFC Eastern Div.	2	1	Super Bowl	Joe Gibbs
1984	11	5	0	.688	426	310	1st/NFC Eastern Div.	0	1	NFC div. playoff game	Joe Gibbs
1985	10	6	0	.625	297	312	3rd/NFC Eastern Div.	—	—		Joe Gibbs
1986	12	4	0	.750	368	296	2nd/NFC Eastern Div.	2	1	NFC championship game	Joe Gibbs
1987	11	4	0	.733	379	285	1st/NFC Eastern Div.	3	0	Super Bowl champ	Joe Gibbs
1988	7	9	0	.438	345	387	T3rd/NFC Eastern Div.	—	—		Joe Gibbs
1989	10	6	0	.625	386	308	3rd/NFC Eastern Div.	—	—		Joe Gibbs
1990	10	6	0	.625	381	301	T2nd/NFC Eastern Div.	1	1	NFC div. playoff game	Joe Gibbs
1991	14	2	0	.875	485	224	1st/NFC Eastern Div.	3	0	Super Bowl champ	Joe Gibbs
1992	9	7	0	.563	300	255	3rd/NFC Eastern Div.	1	1	NFC div. playoff game	Joe Gibbs
1993	4	12	0	.250	230	345	5th/NFC Eastern Div.	—	—		Richie Petitbon
1994	3	13	0	.188	320	412	5th/NFC Eastern Div.	—	—		Norv Turner
1995	6	10	0	.375	326	359	3rd/NFC Eastern Div.	—	—		Norv Turner
1996	9	7	0	.563	364	312	3rd/NFC Eastern Div.	—	—		Norv Turner
1997	8	7	1	.533	327	289	2nd/NFC Eastern Div.	—	—		Norv Turner
1998	6	10	0	.375	319	421	4th/NFC Eastern Div.	—	—		Norv Turner

*Boston Braves.
†Boston Redskins.

FIRST-ROUND DRAFT PICKS

1936—Riley Smith, QB, Alabama
1937—Sammy Baugh, QB, Texas Christian
1938—Andy Farkas, B, Detroit
1939—I.B. Hale, T, Texas Christian
1940—Ed Boell, B, New York University
1941—Forrest Evashevski, B, Michigan
1942—Orban Sanders, B, Texas
1943—Jack Jenkins, B, Missouri
1944—Mike Micka, B, Colgate
1945—Jim Hardy, B, Southern California
1946—Cal Rossi, B, UCLA
1947—Cal Rossi, B, UCLA
1948—Harry Gilmer, QB, Alabama*
1949—Rob Goode, RB, Texas A&M
1950—George Thomas, RB, Oklahoma
1951—Leon Heath, RB, Oklahoma
1952—Larry Isbell, QB, Baylor
1953—Jack Scarbath, QB, Maryland
1954—Steve Meilinger, TE, Kentucky
1955—Ralph Guglielmi, QB, Notre Dame
1956—Ed Vereb, RB, Maryland
1957—Don Bosseler, RB, Miami (Fla.)
1958—None
1959—Don Allard, QB, Boston College
1960—Richie Lucas, QB, Penn State
1961—Joe Rutgens, T, Illinois
      Norm Snead, QB, Wake Forest
1962—Ernie Davis, RB, Syracuse*
      Leroy Jackson, RB, Illinois Central
1963—Pat Richter, TE, Wisconsin
1964—Charley Taylor, RB, Arizona State
1965—None
1966—Charlie Gogolak, K, Princeton
1967—Ray McDonald, RB, Idaho

1968—Jim Smith, DB, Oregon
1969—None
1970—None
1971—None
1972—None
1973—None
1974—None
1975—None
1976—None
1977—None
1978—None
1979—None
1980—Art Monk, WR, Syracuse
1981—Mark May, T, Pittsburgh
1982—None
1983—Darrell Green, DB, Texas A&I
1984—None
1985—None
1986—None
1987—None
1988—None
1989—None
1990—None
1991—Bobby Wilson, DT, Michigan State
1992—Desmond Howard, WR, Michigan
1993—Tom Carter, DB, Notre Dame
1994—Heath Shuler, QB, Tennessee
1995—Michael Westbrook, WR, Colorado
1996—Andre Johnson, T, Penn State
1997—Kenard Lang, DE, Miami (Fla.)
1998—None
1999—Champ Bailey, DB, Georgia
      *First player chosen in draft.

FRANCHISE RECORDS

Most rushing yards, career
7,472—John Riggins

Most rushing yards, season
1,353—Terry Allen, 1996

Most rushing yards, game
221—Gerald Riggs vs. Phi., Sept. 17, 1989

Most rushing touchdowns, season
24—John Riggins, 1983

Most passing attempts, season
541—Jay Schroeder, 1986

Most passing attempts, game
58—Jay Schroeder vs. S.F., Dec. 1, 1985

Most passes completed, season
293—Joe Theismann, 1981

Most passes completed, game
32—Sonny Jurgensen at Cle., Nov. 26, 1967
    John Friesz at NYG, Sept. 18, 1994

Most passing yards, career
25,206—Joe Theismann
Most passing yards, season
4,109—Jay Schroeder, 1986
Most passing yards, game
446—Sammy Baugh vs. N.Y. Yanks, Oct. 31, 1948
Most touchdown passes, season
31—Sonny Jurgensen, 1967
Most pass receptions, career
888—Art Monk
Most pass receptions, season
106—Art Monk, 1984
Most pass receptions, game
13—Art Monk vs. Cin., Dec. 15, 1985
   Kelvin Bryant vs. NYG, Dec. 7, 1986
   Art Monk at Det., Nov. 4, 1990

Most receiving yards, career
13,026—Art Monk
Most receiving yards, season
1,436—Bobby Mitchell, 1963
Most receiving yards, game
255—Anthony Allen vs. St.L., Oct. 4, 1987
Most receiving touchdowns, season
12—Hugh Taylor, 1952
   Charley Taylor, 1966
   Jerry Smith, 1967
   Ricky Sanders, 1988
Most touchdowns, career
90—Charley Taylor
Most field goals, season
33—Mark Moseley, 1983

Longest field goal
57 yards—Steve Cox vs. Sea., Sept. 28, 1986
Most interceptions, career
47—Darrell Green
Most interceptions, season
13—Dan Sandifer, 1948
Most sacks, career
97.5—Dexter Manley
Most sacks, season
18.0—Dexter Manley, 1986

SERIES RECORDS

Washington vs.: Arizona 61-41-1; Atlanta 13-4-1; Baltimore, 0-1; Buffalo 4-4; Carolina 3-0; Chicago 13-14; Cincinnati 4-2; Dallas 31-43-2; Denver 3-5; Detroit 24-3; Green Bay 11-9; Indianapolis 9-16; Jacksonville 1-0; Kansas City 1-4; Miami 2-5; Minnesota 6-5; New England 5-1; New Orleans 12-5; N.Y. Giants 51-68-3; N.Y. Jets 5-1; Oakland 3-6; Philadelphia 65-55-6; Pittsburgh 39-25-4; St. Louis 16-7-1; San Diego 6-0; San Francisco 6-12-1; Seattle 5-4; Tampa Bay 5-4; Tennessee 3-4.
NOTE: Includes records only from 1937 to present.

COACHING RECORDS

George Allen, 67-30-1 (2-5); Bill Austin, 6-8-0; Herman Bell, 4-16-0; Dutch Bergman, 6-3-1 (1-1); Eddie Casey, 2-8-1; Dudley DeGroot, 14-5-1 (0-1); William Dietz, 11-11-2; Turk Edwards, 16-18-1; Ray Flaherty, 54-21-3 (2-2); Joe Gibbs, 124-60-0 (16-5); Otto Graham, 17-22-3; Joe Kuharich, 26-32-2; Curly Lambeau, 10-13-1; Vince Lombardi, 7-5-2; Bill McPeak, 21-46-3; Mike Nixon, 4-18-2; Jack Pardee, 24-24-0; Richie Petitbon, 4-12-0; Dick Todd, 5-4-0; Norv Turner, 32-47-1; John Whelchel, 3-3-1; Lud Wray, 4-4-2.

RETIRED UNIFORM NUMBERS

No.	Player
33	Sammy Baugh